C++
An Introduction to Computing

C++
An Introduction to Computing

Joel Adams
Sanford Leestma
Larry Nyhoff

Calvin College
Grand Rapids, Michigan

 Prentice Hall, Englewood Cliffs, New Jersey 07632

Library of Congress Cataloging-in-Publication Data
Adams, Joel
    C++ : an introduction to computing / Joel Adams, Sanford Leestma,
Larry Nyhoff.
        p.   cm.
    Includes index.
    ISBN 0-02-369402-5
    1. C++ (Computer program language)   2. Computer science.
I. Leestma, Sanford.   II. Nyhoff, Larry R.   III. Title.
QA76.73.C153A33   1995
005.13'3—dc20   93-42130
                                                                                    CIP

About the Cover: The rose window on the cover is the Rose de France (c. 1233) in the north transept of the Chartres cathedral. Like many of the other beautiful rose windows in French cathedrals, it is an early example of object-oriented design, in which objects of various shapes, sizes, colors, and meanings are fitted together according to certain basic principles. An interesting property of this window is how its components— the outer semicircles containing the last twelve Old Testament prophets; the quatrefoils containing the three-petaled fleur-de-lis, symbols of the Annunciation and of royalty; the twelve squares containing the kings of the Virgin Mary's ancestry as recorded by St. Matthew; the twelve circles containing doves, angels and other celestial beings; and the twelve-petaled central rosette containing the Virgin Mary—are arranged into spiral-shaped patterns based on the golden section and the Fibonacci sequence.

Publisher: Alan Apt
Production Supervisor: Spectrum Publisher Services
Production Manager: Aliza Greenblatt
Cover Design: Robert Freese
Cover Art: Giraudon/Art Resource LAC 58289. Rose Window, North Transept, Chartres Cathedral (13th C.).
Illustrations: York Graphic Services, Inc.

The author and publisher of this book have used their best efforts in preparing this book. These efforts include the development, research, and testing of the theories and programs to determine their effectiveness. The author and publisher shall not be liable in any event for incidental or consequential damages in connection with, or arising out of, the furnishing, performance, or use of these programs.

Printed in the United States of America

10 9 8 7 6 5 4 3 2 1

ISBN   0-02-369402-5

PRENTICE-HALL INTERNATIONAL (UK) LIMITED, *London*
PRENTICE-HALL OF AUSTRALIA PTY. LIMITED, *Sydney*
PRENTICE-HALL CANADA, INC., *Toronto*
PRENTICE-HALL HISPANOAMERICANA, S.A., *Mexico*
PRENTICE-HALL OF INDIA PRIVATE LIMITED, *New Delhi*
PRENTICE-HALL OF JAPAN, INC., *Tokyo*
SIMON & SCHUSTER ASIA PTE., LTD., *Singapore*
EDITORA PRENTICE-HALL DO BRAZIL, LTDA., *Rio de Janeiro*

PREFACE

In order to properly introduce students to computing, we believe that the first computer course for students should accomplish two goals:

1. The student should be introduced to the discipline, methodologies, and techniques of computer programming using a modern programming language.
2. The student should be introduced to the breadth of the discipline of computing, so that he or she comes to understand the role of programming in the broader context of computing.

The aim of this textbook is to accomplish both of these goals.

The Programming Goal

In order to accomplish our first goal, we have chosen the language C++, whose features (we believe) make it the language of choice in the immediate future. A few of the reasons for this choice are as follows:

1. C++ provides *a strong type-checking system.*
2. C++ provides *reference parameters* for its functions.
3. C++ provides a *library* mechanism, whereby a programmer can store generally useful functions in a library, so that they can be reused by any program that needs them.
4. C++ provides function name and operator *overloading,* allowing a programmer to use the same name to define subprograms that perform similar operations on different data types.
5. C++ provides *the class,* whereby both an object's data members and its operations can be encapsulated within a single, protected structure.
6. C++ provides *derived classes,* a mechanism whereby one class can *inherit* the data members and operations from another class, allowing a *class hierarchy* to be built.

These latter features of C++ allow it to be characterized as an *object-oriented programming* (OOP) language. From windowing systems to graphic user interfaces to object-oriented databases, more and more of today's best computing applications are being developed in C++ using the OOP approach, making it today's language of choice.

C++ Is Not C. Many people erroneously believe that C++ is simply its parent language C with a few additional features and that C++ is therefore inappropriate as a first programming language. In fact, most of the design flaws of C have been corrected in C++, making it a suitable language for a first course in computing.

The Importance of Modeling. Another popular misconception is that because many C programs are cryptically written, C++ programs probably suffer the same drawback. We believe that cryptic programs are caused by *people,* not by a *language,* and an undisciplined programmer will write cryptic programs in any language, not just C. This is because:

1. Most people learn C from the examples they see in a book; and
2. Most C books are not introductory programming texts, but rather *language references* intended for professional programmers.

One of the aims of this text is to teach a disciplined programming style (to those with no programming experience) that results in well-documented, easy-to-read programs.

We believe that *what students learn depends on the models that they see.* That is, if they are presented with examples that are well-written, well-documented, and maintainable, then the programs they write will exhibit these same characteristics, regardless of the language used. To that end, this text contains a large number of examples that illustrate good programming style.

Standard C++. At the time of this writing, the American National Standards Institute (ANSI) Committee X3J16 had not completed a C++ standard. In the absence of such a standard, we have used the *Annotated C++ Reference Manual*[1] as our primary reference in preparing this text.

As much as possible, we have designed our examples to be independent of any particular implementation of C++ by compiling most of them in several popular environments. Almost all our examples compiled and linked correctly in the following environments:

Computing Environment	C++ Compiler
UNIX (Sun, Apollo, etc.)	GNU g++ (v. 2.4.5)[2]
DOS, Windows, OS-2 (IBM PC)	Turbo C++ (v. 3.0)[3]
MacOS (Apple Macintosh)	Symantec C++ For Macintosh (v. 6.01)[4]

---

[1] Margaret Ellis and Bjarne Stroustrup, *The Annotated C++ Reference Manual.* (Addison-Wesley, 1992).

[2] GNU g++ is a copylefted product of the Free Software Foundation, Inc., 675 Mass Ave., Cambridge, MA 02139; and is available for free via anonymous ftp from `prep.ai.mit.edu:/pub/gnu`.

[3] Turbo C++ is a copyrighted product of Borland International Inc., 1800 Green Hills Rd., P.O. Box 660001, Scotts Valley, CA 95067; and is available from most software vendors for the IBM PC.

[4] Symantec C++ for Macintosh is a copyrighted product of Symantec Corporation, 10201 Torre Ave., Cupertino, CA 95014; and is available from most software vendors for the Apple Macintosh.

The Breadth of Computing

In 1991, a new set of curriculum recommendations was published in *Computing Curricula 1991: Report of the ACM/IEEE-CS Joint Curriculum Task Force*. One theme of this report is that an introductory course in computing should introduce the various knowledge areas of the discipline:

- Architecture
- Artificial intelligence and robotics
- Database and information retrieval
- Human-computer communication
- Numerical and symbolic computation
- Operating systems
- Programming languages
- Software methodology and engineering
- Social, ethical, and professional context

In this text, we include a number of sections that illustrate these areas, trying to capture the spirit of these curriculum guidelines in a natural, unobtrusive way. These sections have been carefully selected in accordance with the *Computing Curricula 1991* report to provide an overview of computer science and to provide a foundation for further study in theoretical and/or applied computer science. They have been highlighted in special PART OF THE PICTURE sections, which are marked with an icon in the shape of a puzzle piece. These sections include:

- What Is Computer Science?
- The History of Computing
- Computer Organization
- Social, Professional, and Ethical Issues
- Syntax and Semantics
- Computer Architecture
- Computability Theory
- Introduction to Numeric Computation
- Introduction to Algorithm Analysis
- Simulation
- Artificial Intelligence
- Databases
- Data Encryption
- The Type Hierarchy
- Analysis of Algorithms
- Automata and Language Translation
- Numeric Computation
- Computer Graphics
- Expert Systems

A solid base is thus established for later courses in theoretical and/or applied computer science.

About the Text

Organization. We have organized the text material into four parts:

- The text begins with an *Introduction* consisting of two chapters that present an overview of computing and programming.
- The second part of the text, *Computing with Simple Objects,* consists of five chapters that introduce the student to the basic ideas of computing, including types, variables, constants, functions, I/O, libraries, selective control, repetitive control, parameter passing mechanisms, and so on. Each of these topics is covered in the context of simple data types: the integer, real, character, and boolean types.
- The third part, *Computing with Class Objects,* consists of seven chapters that extend the ideas from the second part to problems involving more sophisticated data types, including files, character strings, enumerations, arrays, and sets. Where applicable, C++ class libraries are used to implement objects that can be easily reused and maintained.
- The final part, *Computing with Advanced Objects,* consists of three chapters that introduce advanced topics, including indirection, run-time allocation/deallocation, and linked structures, such as linked lists, stacks, queues, and trees, each implemented using C++ classes.

We think that most of the first three parts can be covered in a typical semester course. Some or all of the fourth part can be covered in accelerated courses or in a second course or can be used as enrichment material or for honors work.

Features. This first edition text breaks new ground in many ways, by providing a gentle introduction to new topics such as designing for reusability; the use, design, and implementation of class libraries; the overloading of operators and function names; and the OOP approach to program design. A few of the features of the text are:

- Each chapter begins with an example problem, whose solution is used to introduce the ideas of that chapter. Following this example, the concepts and theory behind these ideas are explored, and other examples are presented to reinforce the ideas. In this approach, students see the *practice* of a new topic before the *abstract* definitions and theory behind that topic, providing them with a framework in which those abstract aspects can be organized and understood.
- A wealth of examples illustrate each topic, allowing students to distinguish what is essential from what is optional. In the spirit of *Computing Curricula 1991,* these examples are chosen from a wide range of applications and have been written to model good structure and style. Those marked in the text with a disk icon are included on the data disk that accompanies this text.
- Optional sections (marked with asterisks) delve into the more advanced topics, without requiring that they be covered in a normal introductory course.
- Each chapter ends with *Programming Pointers* that highlight important points, especially proper techniques of design, style, as well as common programming pitfalls.

- Each chapter ends with *Programming Pointers* that highlight important points, especially proper techniques of design, style, as well as common programming pitfalls.
- Color is used to emphasize and highlight important features.
- Exercise sets include short written exercises as well as a large number of programming exercises and projects drawn from a wide range of application areas.

Supplementary Materials

A number of supplementary materials are available from the publisher. These include the following:

- An instructor's manual.
- A solutions manual that contains solutions to the exercises in the text, including many of the programming exercises.
- A lab manual and diskette prepared by Professor Joel Adams.
- Disks containing solutions to many of the programming exercises.
- Disks containing all the sample programs and data files used in the text.
- Disks containing all text exercises.
- A test bank, both in printed form and on disk.

Suggestions

The authors welcome feedback, both positive and negative. Comments about features of the text that work especially well, as well as about features of the text that need improvement, will aid us in the preparation of subsequent editions. We would also appreciate being notified of errors. Such comments can be directed to any of the authors at the following U.S. mail address:

> Department of Mathematics and Computer Science
> Calvin College
> Grand Rapids, Michigan 49546
> USA

or to **adams@calvin.edu**, **lees@calvin.edu**, or **nyhl@calvin.edu** via the Internet.

Acknowledgments

The comments and suggestions made by the following reviewers were valuable, and their work is much appreciated: Jose Cisnaros, Metropolitan College of Denver; Ann Ford, University of Michigan; Mike Holland, Northern Virginia Community College; John Lowther, Michigan Technological University; Dick Reed,

Michigan State University; and Peter Spoerri, Fairfield University. We must also thank our wives, Barbara, Marjory, and Shar, for not complaining about the times that their needs and wants were slighted by our busyness. Above all, we give thanks to God for giving us the opportunity, ability, and stamina to prepare this text.

L.R.N.
S.C.L.
J.C.A.

CONTENTS

INTRODUCTION TO COMPUTING

1

In Chapters 1 and 2, we lay the foundation for the study of computing. Chapter 1 introduces the discipline of computing, *providing a brief history and examining basic topics such as how computer hardware is organized and how data is represented in a computer's memory. Chapter 2 introduces* software engineering, *discussing and illustrating the stages of software development. Together, these two chapters form the foundation for the chapters that follow.*

THE SCIENCE OF COMPUTING

1

Is computer science a science? An engineering discipline? Or merely a technology, an inventor and purveyor of computing commodities? What is the intellectual substance of the discipline? Is it lasting, or will it fade within a generation?
From the 1989 report of the Task Force on the Core of Computer Science

I wish these calculations had been executed by steam.
CHARLES BABBAGE

One machine can do the work of fifty ordinary men. No machine can do the work of one extraordinary man.
ELBERT HUBBARD

For, contrary to the unreasoned opinion of the ignorant, the choice of a system of numeration is a mere matter of convention.
BLAISE PASCAL

CHAPTER CONTENTS

The term "computer science" has been the source of much confusion. Although there are sciences called physics and biology, there are not disciplines called "telescope science" or "microscope science." How can there be a "computer science" if a computer is simply another scientific tool or instrument?

1.1   PART OF THE PICTURE: What Is Computer Science?

Let us begin with what computer science is not. Computer science is not simply writing computer programs. Although problem solving and programming are indeed the primary focus of this text, the discipline of computing consists of much more. The breadth of the discipline is evidenced by the following list of the main areas of computer science from *Computing Curricula 1991: Report of the ACM/IEEE-CS Joint Curriculum Task Force.*[1]

- **Algorithms and Data Structures.** This area deals with specific classes of problems and their efficient solutions. The performance characteristics of algorithms and the organization of data relative to different access requirements are major components.
- **Architecture.** Methods of organizing efficient, reliable computing systems are the central focus of this area. This area includes implementation of processors, memory, communications, and software interfaces, as well as the design and control of large, reliable computational systems.
- **Artificial Intelligence and Robotics.** The basic models of behavior and the building of (virtual or actual) machines to simulate animal and human behavior are included here. Inference, deduction, pattern recognition, and knowledge representation are major components of this area of computer science.
- **Database and Information Retrieval.** This area is concerned with organizing information and designing algorithms for the efficient access and update of stored information. The modeling of data relationships, security and protection of information in a shared environment, and the characteristics of external storage devices are included.
- **Human–Computer Communication.** The efficient transfer of information between humans and machines is the central focus of this area. Graphics, human factors that affect efficient interaction, and the organization and display of information for effective utilization by humans are included.
- **Numerical and Symbolic Computation.** General methods for efficiently and accurately using computers to solve equations from mathematical models are central to this area. The effectiveness and efficiency of various approaches to the solution of equations, and the development of high-quality mathematical software packages are important components.
- **Operating Systems.** This area deals with control mechanisms that allow multiple resources to be efficiently coordinated during the execution of

---

[1] Allen B. Tucker, ed., *Computing Curricula 1991: Report of the ACM/IEEE-CS Joint Curriculum Task Force* (ACM Press and IEEE Computer Society Press, 1991).

programs. Included are appropriate service of user requests, effective strategies for resource control, and effective organization to support distributed computation.

- **Programming Languages.** The fundamental questions addressed in this area involve notations for defining virtual machines that execute algorithms, the efficient translation from high-level languages to machine codes, and the various extension mechanisms that can be provided in programming languages.
- **Software Methodology and Engineering.** The major focus of this area is the specification, design, and production of large software systems. Principles of programming and software development, verification, and validation of software, and the specification and production of software systems that are safe, secure, reliable, and dependable are of special interest.
- **Social and Professional Context.** This area is concerned with the cultural, social, legal, and ethical issues related to computing.

Because to some people the term computer science seems inadequate to describe such a broad range of areas, the *Computing Curricula 1991 Report* suggested that "computing" is a more appropriate term than is "computer science." However, we use the two terms interchangeably throughout this text.

To help students develop an accurate and balanced picture of computer science as a discipline, a first course in computing should touch on many of these areas. This is especially important to students majoring in computer science, for whom this introduction to the discipline will be fleshed out in later courses, as well as to those majoring in other disciplines, for whom the portrayal of computing should be a realistic one. Thus, although most of this text is devoted to developing problem-solving and programming skills, we attempt to paint a more complete picture of computer science by including special "PART OF THE PICTURE" sections throughout the text that introduce topics from several of these areas.

1.2 PART OF THE PICTURE: The History of Computing

The modern electronic computer is one of the most important inventions of the twentieth century. It is an essential tool in many areas, including business, industry, government, science, and education; indeed, it has touched nearly every aspect of our lives. The impact of this twentieth-century information revolution brought about by the development of high-speed computing systems has been nearly as widespread as the impact of the nineteenth-century Industrial Revolution. As part of the picture of computing, it is necessary to be aware of some of the events that led to modern-day computing.

Two important concepts in the history of computation are the **mechanization of arithmetic** and the concept of a **stored program** for the automatic control of computations. We focus on some of the devices that have implemented these concepts.

The Mechanization of Arithmetic

A variety of mechanical devices were used in ancient civilizations to assist in computation. One of the earliest is the **abacus** (Figure 1.1), which has movable beads strung on rods and is used to count and to do calculations. Although its exact origin is unknown, the abacus was used by the Chinese perhaps three thousand to four thousand years ago and is still used today throughout Asia. The ancient British stone monument **Stonehenge** (Figure 1.2), located in southern England, was built between 1900 and 1600 B.C. and, evidently, was an astronomical calculator used to predict the changes of the seasons. Five hundred years ago, the Inca Indians of South America used a system of knotted cords called **quipus** (Figure 1.3) to count and record divisions of land among the various tribal groups. In Western Europe, **Napier's bones** (Figure 1.4) and tables of **logarithms** were designed by the Scottish mathematician John Napier (1550–1617) to simplify calculations. These led to the subsequent invention of the **slide rule** (Figure 1.5).

In 1642, the young French mathematician **Blaise Pascal** (1623–1662) invented one of the first mechanical adding machines (Figure 1.6), a device that used a system of gears and wheels similar to that found in odometers and other modern

FIGURE 1.1   Abacus.

FIGURE 1.2 Stonehenge.

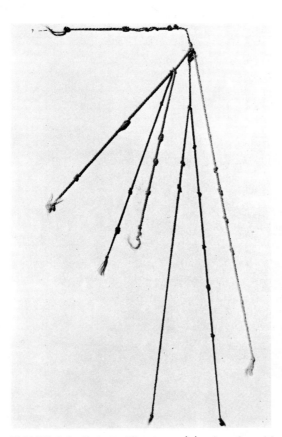

FIGURE 1.3 Quipus. (Courtesy of the American Museum of Natural History)

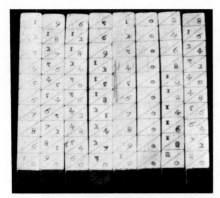

FIGURE 1.4   Napier's bones. (Courtesy of the Smithsonian Institution)

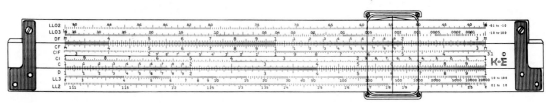

FIGURE 1.5   Slide rule.

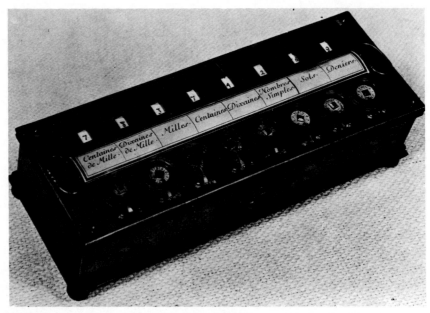

FIGURE 1.6   Pascal's adder. (Courtesy of IBM)

FIGURE 1.7 Leibniz's calculator. (Courtesy of IBM)

counting devices. **Pascal's adder** could add and subtract and was invented to calculate taxes. Pascal's announcement of his invention reveals the motivation for its development:

> Dear reader, this notice will serve to inform you that I submit to the public a small machine of my invention, by means of which you alone may, without any effort, perform all the operations of arithmetic, and may be relieved of the work which has often times fatigued your spirit, when you have worked with the counters or with the pen. As for simplicity of movement of the operations, I have so devised it that, although the operations of arithmetic are in a way opposed the one to the other—as addition to subtraction, and multiplication to division—nevertheless they are all performed on this machine by a single movement. The facility of this movement of operation is very evident since it is just as easy to move one thousand or ten thousand dials, all at one time, if one desires to make a single dial move, although all accomplish the movement perfectly. The most ignorant find as many advantages as the most experienced. The instrument makes up for ignorance and for lack of practice, and even without any effort of the operator, it makes possible shortcuts by itself, whenever the numbers are set down.

Although Pascal built more than fifty of his adding machines, his commercial venture failed because the devices could not be built with sufficient precision for practical use.

In the 1670s, the German mathematician **Gottfried Wilhelm von Leibniz** (1646–1716) produced a machine that was similar to Pascal's but somewhat more reliable and accurate (Figure 1.7). Leibniz's calculator could perform all four of the basic arithmetic operations of addition, subtraction, multiplication, and division.

A number of other mechanical calculators followed that further refined Pascal's and Leibniz's designs. By the end of the nineteenth century, these calculators had become important tools in science, business, and commerce.

The Stored Program Concept

As noted earlier, the second fundamental idea to emerge in the history of computing was the concept of a stored program to control the calculations. One early

FIGURE 1.8 Jacquard loom. (Courtesy of IBM)

example of an automatically controlled device is the weaving loom (Figure 1.8) invented by the Frenchman **Joseph-Marie Jacquard** (1752–1834). This automatic loom, introduced at a Paris exhibition in 1801, used metal cards punched with holes to position threads for the weaving process. A collection of these cards made up a program that directed the loom. Within a decade, eleven thousand of these machines were being used in French textile plants, resulting in what may have been the first incidence of unemployment caused by automation. Indeed, unemployed workers rioted and destroyed several of the new looms and cards. According to Jacquard, "The iron was sold for iron, the wood for wood, and I its inventor delivered up to public ignominy." The **Jacquard loom** is still used today, although modern versions are controlled by programs stored on magnetic tape rather than punched cards.

Mechanical Computers

The two fundamental concepts, mechanized calculation and stored program control, were combined by the English mathematician **Charles Babbage** (1792–1871), who began work in 1822 on a machine that he called the **Difference Engine**

FIGURE 1.9 Babbage's Difference Engine.

(Figure 1.9). This machine was designed to compute polynomials for the preparation of mathematical tables. Babbage continued his work until 1833 with support from the British government, which was interested in possible military applications of the Difference Engine. However, Babbage later abandoned this project because, according to Doran Swade, curator of the London Science Museum, the cantankerous Babbage argued with his engineer, ran out of money, and was beset by personal rivalry. Babbage went on to design a more sophisticated machine that he called his **Analytical Engine** (Figure 1.10). This machine had several special-purpose components that were intended to work together. The ''mill'' was designed to carry out the arithmetic computations; the ''store'' was the machine's memory for storing data and intermediate results; and other components were designed for the input and output of information and for the transfer of information between components. The operation of this machine was to be fully automatic, controlled by programs stored on punched cards, an idea based on Jacquard's earlier work. In fact, as Babbage himself observed: ''The analogy of the Analytical Engine with this well-known process is nearly perfect.'' **Ada Augusta,** Lord

FIGURE 1.10   Babbage's Analytical Engine. (Courtesy of IBM)

George Byron's daughter, the countess of Lovelace, and lifelong friend of Babbage, understood how the device was to operate and supported Babbage in his work. Considered by some to be the first programmer, Lady Lovelace described the similarity of Jacquard's and Babbage's inventions: "The Analytical Engine weaves algebraic patterns just as the Jacquard loom weaves flowers and leaves." Although Babbage's machine was not built during his lifetime, it is nevertheless an important part of the history of computing because many of the concepts of its design are used in modern computers.

A related development in the United States was the census bureau's use of punched-card systems to help compile the 1890 census (Figure 1.11). These systems, designed by **Herman Hollerith,** a young mathematician employed by the bureau, used electrical sensors to interpret the information stored on the punched cards. In 1896, Hollerith left the census bureau and formed his own tabulating company, which in 1924 became the International Business Machines (IBM) Corporation.

The development of computing devices continued at a rapid pace in the United States. Some of the pioneers in this effort were Howard Aiken, John Atanasoff, J. P. Eckert, J. W. Mauchly, and John von Neumann. Repeating much of the work of Babbage, Aiken designed a system consisting of several mechanical calculators working together. This work, which was supported by IBM, led to the invention in 1944 of the electromechanical **Mark I** computer (Figure 1.12). This machine is the best-known computer built before 1945 and may be regarded as the first realization of Babbage's Analytical Engine.

FIGURE 1.11   Hollerith equipment. (Courtesy of IBM)

FIGURE 1.12   Mark I. (Courtesy of IBM)

Early Electronic Computers

The first fully electronic computer was developed by **John Atanasoff** at Iowa State University. With the help of his assistant, **Clifford Berry,** he built a prototype in 1939 and completed the first working model in 1942 (Figure 1.13). The best known of the early electronic computers was the **ENIAC** (Electronic Numerical Integrator and Computer), constructed in 1946 by J. P. Eckert and J. W. Mauchly at the Moore School of Electrical Engineering of the University of Pennsylvania (Figure 1.14). This extremely large machine contained more than 18,000 vacuum tubes and 1500 relays, and it nearly filled a room 20 feet by 40 feet in size. It could multiply numbers approximately one thousand times faster than the Mark I could, but it was quite limited in its applications and was used primarily by the Army Ordnance Department to calculate firing tables and trajectories for various types of shells. Eckert and Mauchly later left the University of Pennsylvania to form the Eckert–Mauchly Computer Corporation, which built the **UNIVAC** (Universal Automatic Computer), the first commercially available computer designed for both scientific and business applications. The first UNIVAC was sold to the census bureau in 1951.

The instructions, or program, that controlled the ENIAC's operation were entered into the machine by rewiring some of the computer's circuits. This complicated process was very time-consuming, sometimes taking several people several days, and during this time, the computer was idle. In other early computers, the instructions were stored outside the machine on punched cards or some other medium and were transferred into the machine one at a time for interpretation and execution. A new scheme, developed by Princeton mathematician John von Neumann and others, used internally stored commands. The advantages of this stored program concept are that internally stored instructions can be processed more

FIGURE 1.13   Atanasoff–Berry computer. (Courtesy of Iowa State University)

FIGURE 1.14   ENIAC. (Courtesy of Sperry Corporation)

rapidly and, more important, that they can be modified by the computer itself while computations are taking place. The stored program concept made possible the general-purpose computers so commonplace today.

Modern Computers

The actual physical components that make up a computer system are its **hardware.** Several generations of computers can be identified by the type of hardware used. The ENIAC and UNIVAC are examples of **first-generation** computers, which are characterized by their extensive use of vacuum tubes. Advances in electronics brought changes in computing systems, and in 1958, IBM introduced the first of the **second-generation** computers, the IBM 7090. These computers were built between 1959 and 1965 and used transistors in place of vacuum tubes. Consequently, these computers were smaller, required less power, generated far less heat, and were more reliable than their predecessors. They were also less expensive. The first **minicomputer,** the PDP-8, which was introduced in 1963, sold for $18,000, in contrast with earlier computers whose six-digit price tags limited their sales to large companies. The **third-generation** computers that followed used integrated circuits and introduced new techniques for better system utilization, such as multi-programming and time-sharing. The IBM System/360 introduced in 1964 is commonly accepted as the first of this generation of computers. Computers of the 1980s and 1990s, called **fourth-generation** computers, use very large-scale integrated circuits (VLSI) on silicon chips and other microelectronic advances to shrink their size and cost still more while enlarging their capability. A typical chip is equivalent to many thousands of transistors, is smaller than a baby's fingernail, weighs a small fraction of an ounce, requires only a trickle of power, and costs but a few dollars. One of the pioneers in the development of transistors was Robert Noyce, one of the cofounders of the Intel Corporation, which introduced the 4004 microprocessor in 1971. Noyce contrasted microcomputers with the ENIAC as follows:

> An individual integrated circuit on a chip perhaps a quarter of an inch square now can embrace more electronic elements than the most complex piece of electronic equipment that could be built in 1950. Today's microcomputer, at a cost of perhaps $300, has more computing capacity than the first electronic computer, ENIAC. It is twenty times faster, has a larger memory, consumes the power of a light bulb rather than that of a locomotive, occupies 1/30,000 the volume and costs 1/10,000 as much. It is available by mail order or at your local hobby shop.

Microprocessors such as the Intel 4004 made possible the development of the personal computers (PCs) that are so common today. One of the most popular personal computers was the **Apple II,** first constructed in a garage and introduced in 1977 by **Steven Jobs** and **Steve Wozniak,** then 21 and 26 years old, respectively. They founded the Apple Computer Company, one of the major manufacturers of microcomputers today. This was followed in 1981 by the first of **IBM's PCs,** which have become the microcomputer standard in business and industry (Figure 1.15).

FIGURE 1.15 A modern personal computer. (Courtesy of IBM)

Continued advances in technology have produced a wide array of computer systems, ranging from portable **laptop** and **notebook** computers to powerful desktop machines known as **workstations,** to **supercomputers** capable of performing billions of operations each second, and to **massively parallel computers,** which use a large number of microprocessors working together in parallel to solve large problems. Someone once noted that if progress in the automotive industry had been as rapid as in computer technology since 1960, today's automobile would have an engine that is less than 0.1 inch in length, would get 120,000 miles to a gallon of gas, have a top speed of 240,000 miles per hour, and would cost $4.

Computer Software

The stored program concept, introduced by John Von Neumann, was a significant improvement over manual programming methods, but early computers still were difficult to use because of the complex coding schemes used to represent programs and data. Consequently, in addition to improved hardware, computer manufacturers began to develop collections of programs known as **system software,** which make computers easier to use. One of the more important advances in this area was the development of **operating systems,** which allocate memory for programs and data and carry out many other supervisory functions. In particular, an operating system acts as an interface between the user and the machine. It interprets commands given by the user and then directs the appropriate system software and hardware to carry them out. One of the most popular operating systems is UNIX, begun in 1971 but still undergoing development today. It is the only operating system that has been implemented on computers ranging from microcomputers to supercomputers. The most popular operating system for personal computers has for many years been MS-DOS, the first version of which was developed by the Microsoft Corporation in 1981. In more recent years, **graphical user interfaces (GUI),** such as that of the Apple Macintosh and Microsoft's Windows, have been devised to provide a simpler and more intuitive interface between humans and computers.

Another important advance in system software was the development of **high-level languages,** which allow users to write programs in a language similar to natural language. A program written in a high-level language is known as a **source program.** For most high-level languages, the instructions that make up a source program must be translated into **machine language**—the language used directly by a particular computer for all its calculations and processing. This machine language program is called an **object program.** The programs that translate source programs into object programs are called **compilers.**

One of the primary advantages of high-level languages is portability. Programs written in low-level languages (machine or **assembly** languages) will run only on the type of computer for which they were written. This is the reason that an application written for a Macintosh computer will not run on an IBM PC. In contrast, a program written in a high-level language can be written and compiled on one computer and subsequently transferred to and compiled on an entirely different computer, so long as a compiler for the high-level language is available on the second computer. For this reason, programs written in high-level languages are **portable,** whereas programs written in low-level languages are not.

One of the first high-level languages to gain widespread acceptance was **FORTRAN** (**FOR**mula **TRAN**slation), which was developed for the IBM 704 computer by **John Backus** and a team of 13 other programmers at IBM during a 3-year period (1954–1957). Since that time many other high-level languages have become popular, including ALGOL, BASIC, COBOL, Pascal, C, Ada, and Modula-2. In this text, we use the C++ programming language.

A Brief History of C++

In 1969, Ken Thompson was beginning the design and implementation of the UNIX operating system at AT&T's Bell Laboratories. His first implementation of UNIX was written in the assembly language of a spare Digital Equipment Corporation PDP-7. It was not long before it became necessary to implement UNIX on a more powerful machine, a DEC PDP-11. However, because UNIX had been written in PDP-7 assembly language, it was not portable to the PDP-11. The prospect of rewriting the thousands of lines of UNIX in a different assembly language was distinctly unpleasant, particularly because it was obvious that this problem would recur each time Thompson wanted to implement UNIX on a new machine. To simplify the task of transferring UNIX to other computers, Thompson began to search for a high-level language in which to rewrite UNIX.

None of the high-level languages in existence at the time were appropriate; therefore, in 1970, Thompson began designing a new language called **B** that was based on the existing language **BCPL**. By 1972, it had become apparent that B was not adequate for implementing UNIX. At that time, Dennis Ritchie, also at Bell Labs, designed a successor language to B that he called **C**, and approximately 90% of UNIX was rewritten in C. This new language quickly became very popular in colleges and universities across the country and eventually spread to the business world as well. With the availability of inexpensive C compilers for microcomputers, C has become the language in which most microcomputer applications are written.

Although C is a very powerful language, it has two characteristics that make it inappropriate for a modern introduction to programming. First, C requires a level of sophistication in its users beyond that of the typical beginning programmer. Second, C was designed in the early 1970s, and the nature of programming has changed significantly since that time.

In the late 1970s, a new approach to programming called **object-oriented programming** (**OOP**) was becoming increasingly popular. In response to the growing popularity of this new method of programming, Bjarne Stroustrup, another researcher at Bell Labs, undertook the project of adding object-oriented features to C. Stroustrup also added new capabilities that eliminated many of the difficulties C posed for beginning programmers. The resulting language was first called **C with Classes,** but by 1983, more improvements had been added and the language was renamed **C++** (for reasons that will become clear in Chapter 3).

Summary

The history of computation and computational aids began several thousand years ago, and in some cases, the theory underlying such devices progressed much more rapidly than did the technical skills required to produce working models. Although the modern electronic computer, with its mechanized calculation and automatic program control, has its roots in the mid-nineteenth-century work of Charles Babbage, the electronic computer is a fairly recent development. The rapid changes that have marked its progression since its inception in 1945 can be expected to continue into the future.

1.3   PART OF THE PICTURE: Computer Organization

In our discussion of the history of computing, we noted that Babbage designed his Analytical Engine as a system of several separate components, each with its own particular function. This general scheme was incorporated in many later computers and is, in fact, a common feature of most modern computers. In this section we briefly describe the major components of a modern computing system and how program instructions and data are stored and processed.

Computing Systems

The heart of any computing system is its **central processing unit (CPU).** The CPU controls the operation of the entire system, performs the arithmetic and logic operations, and stores and retrieves instructions and data. The instructions and data are stored in a high-speed **memory unit**, and the **control unit** fetches these instructions from memory, decodes them, and directs the system to execute the operations indicated by the instructions. Those operations that are arithmetical or logical in nature are carried out using the circuits of the **arithmetic-logic unit (ALU)** of the CPU.

The memory unit usually consists of several components. One of these components is used to store the instructions and data of the programs being executed and has many names, including **internal, main, primary,** and **random access memory (RAM).** A second component is a set of special high-speed memory locations within the CPU called **registers.** Values that are stored in registers can typically be accessed thousands of times faster than values that are stored in RAM.

One problem with both RAM and registers is that if the power to the computing system is shut off (either intentionally or accidentally), values that are stored in these memory components are lost. To provide long-term storage of programs and data, most computing systems also have memory components that are called **external, auxiliary,** or **secondary memory.** Common forms of this type of memory include magnetic disks (such as hard disks and floppy disks) and magnetic tapes. These **peripheral devices** provide long-term storage for large collections of data, even if power is lost. However, the time required to access data that is stored on such devices can be thousands of times greater than the access time for data stored in RAM.

Other peripherals are used to transmit instructions, data, and computed results between the user and the CPU. These are the **input/output devices,** which have a variety of forms, such as terminals, scanners, voice input devices, printers, and plotters. Their function is to convert information from an external form understandable to the user to a form that can be processed by the computer system, and vice versa.

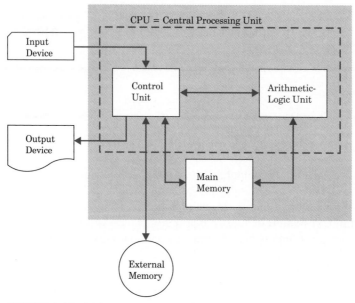

FIGURE 1.16   Major components of a computing system.

Figure 1.16 shows the relationship between these components in a computer system. The arrows indicate how information flows through the system.

Memory Organization

The devices comprising the memory unit of a computer are two-state devices. If one of the states is interpreted as 0 and the other as 1, then it is natural to use a **binary scheme,** using only the two binary digits (**bits**) 0 and 1 to represent information in a computer. These two-state devices are organized into groups called **bytes.** Usually a byte consists of eight bits. Memory is commonly measured in bytes, and a block of $2^{10} = 1024$ bytes is called **1K** of memory. Thus, a 512K memory usually refers to a memory that consists of $512 \times 2^{10} = 2^9 \times 2^{10} = 2^{19} = 524,288$ bytes, or, equivalently, $2^{19} \times 2^3 = 2^{22} = 4,194,304$ bits (1 byte = 8 bits).

Bytes are typically grouped together into **words.** The number of bits in a word is equal to the number of bits in a CPU register. The word size thus varies with different computers, but common word sizes are 16 bits (= 2 bytes) and 32 bits (= 4 bytes). Associated with each word or byte is an **address** that can be used to directly access that word or byte. This makes it possible to store information in a specific memory location and then to retrieve it later. To understand how this is done, we must first examine the binary number system.

Number Systems

The number system that we are accustomed to using is a **decimal** or **base-10** number system, which uses the digits 0, 1, 2, 3, 4, 5, 6, 7, 8, and 9. The significance of these digits in a numeral depends on the positions that they occupy in that numeral. For example, in the numeral

$$485$$

the digit 4 is interpreted as

$$4 \text{ hundreds}$$

and the digit 8 as

$$8 \text{ tens}$$

and the digit 5 as

$$5 \text{ ones}$$

Thus, the numeral 485 represents the number four hundred eighty-five and can be written in **expanded form** as

$$(4 \times 100) + (8 \times 10) + (5 \times 1)$$

or

$$(4 \times 10^2) + (8 \times 10^1) + (5 \times 10^0)$$

The digits that appear in the various positions of a decimal (base-10) numeral thus are coefficients of powers of 10.

Similar positional number systems can be devised using numbers other than 10 as a base. The **binary** number system uses 2 as the base and has only two digits, 0 and 1. As in a decimal system, the significance of the bits in a binary numeral is determined by their positions in that numeral. For example, the binary numeral

$$101$$

can be written in expanded form (using decimal notation) as

$$(1 \times 2^2) + (0 \times 2^1) + (1 \times 2^0)$$

that is, the binary numeral 101 has the decimal value

$$4 + 0 + 1 = 5$$

Similarly, the binary numeral 111010 has the decimal value

$$(1 \times 2^5) + (1 \times 2^4) + (1 \times 2^3) + (0 \times 2^2) + (1 \times 2^1) + (0 \times 2^0)$$
$$= 32 + 16 + 8 + 0 + 2 + 0$$
$$= 58$$

When necessary, to avoid confusion about which base is being used, it is customary to write the base as a subscript for nondecimal numerals. Using this convention, we could indicate that 5 and 58 have the binary representations just given by writing

$$5 = 101_2$$

and

$$58 = 111010_2$$

Two other nondecimal numeration systems are important in the consideration of computer systems: **octal** and **hexadecimal.** The octal system is a base-8 system and uses the eight digits 0, 1, 2, 3, 4, 5, 6, and 7. In an octal numeral such as

$$1703_8$$

the digits are coefficients of powers of 8; this numeral is therefore an abbreviation for the expanded form

$$(1 \times 8^3) + (7 \times 8^2) + (0 \times 8^1) + (3 \times 8^0)$$

and thus has the decimal value

$$512 + 448 + 0 + 3 = 963$$

A hexadecimal system uses a base of 16 and the digits 0, 1, 2, 3, 4, 5, 6, 7, 8, 9, A (10), B (11), C (12), D (13), E (14), and F (15). The hexadecimal numeral

$$5E4_{16}$$

has the expanded form

$$(5 \times 16^2) + (14 \times 16^1) + (4 \times 16^0)$$

which has the decimal value

$$1280 + 224 + 4 = 1508$$

Table 1.1 shows the decimal, binary, octal, and hexadecimal representations for the first 31 nonnegative integers.

Data Storage

Integers. When an integer value such as 5 or 58 must be stored in the computer's memory, the binary representation of that value is typically stored in one word of memory. To illustrate, consider a computer whose word size is sixteen, and suppose that the integer value 58 is to be stored. A memory word is selected, and a sequence of sixteen bits formed from the binary representation 111010 of 58 is stored there:

Memory

0	0	0	0	0	0	0	0	0	0	1	1	1	0	1	0

Negative integers must also be stored in a binary form in which the sign of the integer is part of the representation. There are several ways that this can be done, but one of the most common is the **two's complement** representation. In this scheme, positive integers are represented in binary form as just described, with the leftmost bit set to 0 to indicate that the value is positive. The representation of a negative integer $-n$ is obtained by first finding the binary representation of n,

TABLE 1.1   Numeric representations

Decimal	Binary	Octal	Hexadecimal
0	0	0	0
1	1	1	1
2	10	2	2
3	11	3	3
4	100	4	4
5	101	5	5
6	110	6	6
7	111	7	7
8	1000	10	8
9	1001	11	9
10	1010	12	A
11	1011	13	B
12	1100	14	C
13	1101	15	D
14	1110	16	E
15	1111	17	F
16	10000	20	10
17	10001	21	11
18	10010	22	12
19	10011	23	13
20	10100	24	14
21	10101	25	15
22	10110	26	16
23	10111	27	17
24	11000	30	18
25	11001	31	19
26	11010	32	1A
27	11011	33	1B
28	11100	34	1C
29	11101	35	1D
30	11110	36	1E
31	11111	37	1F

complementing it—that is, changing each 0 to 1 and each 1 to 0 and then adding 1 to the result. For example, the two's complement representation of −58 using sixteen bits is obtained as follows:

1. Represent 58 by a 16-bit binary numeral:

    0000000000111010

2. Complement this bit string:

    1111111111000101

3. Add 1:

    1111111111000110

Note that the leftmost bit in the two's complement representation of a negative integer is always 1, indicating that the number is negative.

Since integers are stored in a single word of memory, the word size of a computer determines the range of the integers that can be stored internally. For example, the largest positive integer that can be stored in a 16-bit word is

$$0111111111111111_2 = 2^{15} - 1 = 32767$$

and the smallest negative integer is

$$1000000000000000_2 = -2^{15} = -32768$$

The range of integers that can be represented using a 32-bit word is

$$10000000000000000000000000000000_2 = -2^{31} = -2147483648$$

through

$$01111111111111111111111111111111_2 = 2^{31} - 1 = 2147483647$$

Representation of an integer outside the allowed range would require more bits than can be stored in a single word, a phenomenon known as **overflow.** This limitation may be partially overcome by using more than one word to store an integer. Although this enlarges the range of integers that can be stored exactly, it does not solve the overflow problem; the range of representable integers is still finite.

Real Numbers.   Numbers that contain decimal points are called **real numbers** or **floating-point numbers.** Each digit in the decimal representation of such numbers is the coefficient of some power of 10. Digits to the left of the decimal point are coefficients of nonnegative powers of 10, and those to the right are coefficients of negative powers of 10. For example, the decimal numeral 56.317 can be written in expanded form as

$$(5 \times 10^1) + (6 \times 10^0) + (3 \times 10^{-1}) + (1 \times 10^{-2}) + (7 \times 10^{-3})$$

or, equivalently, as

$$(5 \times 10) + (6 \times 1) + \left(3 \times \frac{1}{10}\right) + \left(1 \times \frac{1}{100}\right) + \left(7 \times \frac{1}{1000}\right)$$

Digits in the binary representation of a real number are coefficients of powers of two. Those to the left of the **binary point** are coefficients of nonnegative powers of two, and those to the right are coefficients of negative powers of two. For example, the expanded form of 110.101 is

$$(1 \times 2^2) + (1 \times 2^1) + (0 \times 2^0) + (1 \times 2^{-1}) + (0 \times 2^{-2}) + (1 \times 2^{-3})$$

and thus has the decimal value

$$4 + 2 + 0 + \frac{1}{2} + 0 + \frac{1}{8} = 6.625$$

There is some variation in the schemes used for storing real numbers in computer memory, but one common method is the following. The binary representation

$$110.101_2$$

of the real number 6.625 can also be written as

$$0.110101_2 \times 2^3$$

Typically, one part of a memory word (or words) is used to store a fixed number of bits of the **mantissa** or **fractional part,** 0.110101_2, and another part to store the **exponent,** $3 = 11_2$. For example, if the leftmost eleven bits in a 16-bit word are used for the mantissa and the remaining five bits for the exponent, 6.625 can be stored as

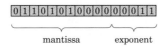

where the first bit in each part is reserved for the sign.

Because the binary representation of the exponent may require more than the available number of bits, the overflow problem discussed in connection with integer representation may also occur when storing a real number. Also, there obviously are some real numbers whose mantissas have more than the allotted number of bits; consequently, some bits will be lost when such numbers are stored. In fact, most real numbers do not have finite binary representations and thus cannot be stored exactly in any computer. For example, the binary representation of the real number 0.7 is

$$(0.10110011001100110 \ldots)_2$$

where the block 0110 is repeated indefinitely. If only the first eleven bits are stored and all remaining bits are truncated, the stored representation of 0.7 will be

$$0.10110011002$$

which has the decimal value 0.69921875. If the binary representation is rounded to eleven bits, the stored representation for 0.7 will be

$$0.10110011012$$

which has the decimal value 0.700195312. In either case, the stored value is not exactly 0.7. This error, called **roundoff error,** can be reduced, but not eliminated, by using a larger number of bits to store the binary representation of real numbers.

Boolean and Character Values. Computers store and process not only numeric data but also boolean or logical data (false or true), character data, and other types of nonnumeric information. The schemes used to store such values depend on the number of values that must be represented. For example, consider the logical values false and true. Since there are only two logical values, the logical value false can be represented as the integer 0, and the logical value true can be represented as the integer 1.

Character values are represented in a similar fashion. Each character is represented by a unique numeric code. Several standard coding schemes have been developed, such as **ASCII** (American Standard Code for Information Interchange) and **EBCDIC** (Extended Binary Coded Decimal Interchange Code). Table 1.2 shows these codes for capital letters. A complete table of ASCII and EBCDIC codes for all characters is given in Appendix A.

These binary codes are used to represent characters internally. A byte (eight bits) can store the binary representation of one character, so that a 16-bit word (two

TABLE 1.2   Character codes

Character	ASCII		EBCDIC	
	Decimal	Binary	Decimal	Binary
A	65	01000001	193	11000001
B	66	01000010	194	11000010
C	67	01000011	195	11000011
D	68	01000100	196	11000100
E	69	01000101	197	11000101
F	70	01000110	198	11000110
G	71	01000111	199	11000111
H	72	01001000	200	11001000
I	73	01001001	201	11001001
J	74	01001010	209	11010001
K	75	01001011	210	11010010
L	76	01001100	211	11010011
M	77	01001101	212	11010100
N	78	01001110	213	11010101
O	79	01001111	214	11010110
P	80	01010000	215	11010111
Q	81	01010001	216	11011000
R	82	01010010	217	11011001
S	83	01010011	226	11100010
T	84	01010100	227	11100011
U	85	01010101	228	11100100
V	86	01010110	229	11100101
W	87	01010111	230	11100110
X	88	01011000	231	11100111
Y	89	01011001	232	11101000
Z	90	01011010	233	11101001

bytes) can store two characters. For example, the character string HI can be stored in a single 16-bit word with the code for H in the left byte and the code for I in the right byte; using the ASCII code, these values are stored as follows:

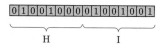

Memory words of size 32 (bits) are usually divided into four bytes and thus can store four characters. Character strings whose length exceeds the number of bytes in a word are usually stored in adjacent words of memory.

Instruction Processing

We have now seen how various types of data can be stored in a computer's memory. Program instructions for processing data must also be stored in memory. As an example, suppose that three values, $8 = 1000_2$, $24 = 11000_2$, and $58 = 111010_2$, have been stored in memory locations with addresses 4, 5, and 6 and that we want to multiply the first two values, add the third, and store the result in memory word 7.

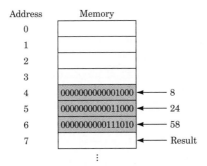

To perform this computation, the following instructions must be executed:

1. Fetch the contents of memory word 4 and load it into the accumulator register of the ALU.
2. Fetch the contents of memory word 5 and compute the product of this value and the value in the accumulator register.
3. Fetch the contents of memory word 6 and add this value to the value in the accumulator register.
4. Store the contents of the accumulator register in memory word 7.

In order to store these instructions in computer memory, they must be represented in binary form. The addresses of the data value present no problem, because they can easily be converted to binary addresses:

$$4 = 100_2$$
$$5 = 101_2$$
$$6 = 110_2$$
$$7 = 111_2$$

The operations load, multiply, add, store, and other basic machine instructions are represented by numeric codes, called **opcodes;** for example,

$$LOAD = 16 = 00010000_2$$
$$STORE = 17 = 00010001_2$$
$$ADD = 35 = 00100011_2$$
$$MULTIPLY = 36 = 00100100_2$$

Using part of a word to store the opcode and another part for the address of the **operand,** we can represent our sequence of instructions in **machine language** as

1. 0001000000000100   LOAD the value in memory word 4 into the accumulator
2. 0010010000000101   MULTIPLY the accumulator by memory word 5
3. 0010001100000110   ADD memory word 6 to the accumulator
4. 0001000100000111   STORE the value in the accumulator into memory word 7

Opcode Operand

These instructions can be stored in four (consecutive) memory words. When the program is executed, the control unit will fetch each of these instructions, decode it to determine the operation and the address of the operand, fetch the operand, and then perform the required operation, using the ALU if necessary.

Programs for early computers had to be written in machine language. Later it became possible to write programs in **assembly language,** which uses mnemonics (names) in place of numeric opcodes and variable names in place of numeric addresses. For example, the preceding sequence of instructions might be written in assembly language as

1. LOAD A
2. MULT B
3. ADD C
4. STORE X

An **assembler,** which is part of the system software, translates assembly language instructions into machine language.

Today, most programs are written in a high-level language such as C++, and a **compiler** translates each statement in this program into a sequence of machine (or assembly) language instructions.

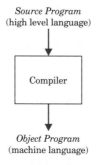

Source Program
(high level language)

Compiler

Object Program
(machine language)

For example, for the preceding problem, the programmer could write the C++ statement

$$X \; = \; A \; * \; B \; + \; C;$$

which instructs the computer to multiply the values of **A** and **B**, add the value of **C**, and assign the value to **X**. The compiler would translate this statement into a sequence of four machine (or assembly) language instructions like those given earlier.

As the preceding diagram indicates, a compiler translates the entire source program into an equivalent object program consisting of machine language instructions. After this translation is complete, this object program is executed by the computer. Some languages are processed using an **interpreter** rather than a compiler. An interpreter also examines a source program statement by statement. However, after each statement is translated, the resulting machine language instructions are executed before the next statement is examined; no object program is actually produced. Still another approach is to compile the source program into simple machine-independent language called **intermediate code.** The resulting program may be either interpreted or compiled. In any case, the original source program in a high-level language must be translated into strings of 0s and 1s that represent machine instructions.

1.4   PART OF THE PICTURE: Social, Professional, and Ethical Issues

The impact of the computer revolution on modern society is as great as was the impact of the nineteenth century Industrial Revolution and, in the introduction to this chapter, we gave a number of examples to illustrate the wide range of computer applications. As the diversity of computing applications continues to grow, computing will affect more and more individuals, groups, and institutions. As a result, the influence exerted by computer professionals, either wittingly or unwittingly, will continue to increase, as will the importance of responsible and ethical conduct. Like all technology, computer technology is neither inherently good nor evil. It is the responsibility of computer professionals to ensure that it is used for the benefit, and not to the detriment, of society.

The following are some of the ethical concerns that are raised by the growth of computer technology:

- *Privacy.* Computing technology has made possible the construction of large databases of information about individuals and institutions. Although the purpose for which this information was collected may be legitimate (credit ratings, crime networks, medical records, and government records), there is always the potential for the misuse of sensitive information by unauthorized individuals.[2] Indeed, such misuse has become so prevalent in recent years that state and federal governments have enacted statutes such as the Electronic Communication Privacy Act of 1986 to combat such invasions of privacy. Computer professionals and computer scientists perhaps more than others have the knowledge and ability to access private information. Therefore, they have a special responsibility to respect the rights of others by not accessing these databases without authorization and, in applications that require access to these databases, using this information only for the purpose for which it was intended. Those who design these databases and/or software to process them also have a responsibility to maintain the integrity and security of that information. In particular, this most assuredly means that they have no right to develop programs like computer viruses that damage, destroy, or interfere in any way with other people's computer systems or the data stored in these systems. The infamous worm program injected into the Internet in November 1988 and the more recent Michelan-

---

[2] See the quotation in Section 8.5, "PART OF THE PICTURE: Databases."

gelo virus are but two of many examples of malicious programs that attacked computers around the world, shutting down thousands of them and/or destroying data files. Such irresponsible behavior obviously is not appropriate to those who call themselves, or who aspire to be, computer professionals.

■ *Intellectual Property.* Computer hardware and software are the property of the individuals or companies that developed them. Those who wish to use these products should obtain them through legal channels and abide by the conditions that govern their use. It has been estimated, however, that 60% to 80% of all software used today has been pirated and that the resulting loss to the software industry exceeds several billion dollars per year. It is important that all computer professionals respect their fellow professionals and do not create, use, or disseminate illegal copies of software. This applies not only to copyrighted software but also to shareware that is distributed with the understanding that those who use it will register their copy with the developer and pay the nominal fee for its use.

■ *Truth in Software.* Computer professionals are responsible for ensuring that the software or hardware they are developing functions in the manner claimed. This means that these products should be thoroughly tested and made as error-free as possible before they are delivered to the customer. It also means that potential users should be made fully aware of the hardware and software needed to use the product and that errors found and difficulties encountered after the product is released are remedied promptly.

The major societies for computer professionals such as ACM (Association for Computing Machinery), BCS (British Computer Society), DPMA (Data Processing Management Association), and IEEE (Institute of Electrical and Electronics Engineers) recognize the importance of the ethical issues that arise in computing and have published codes of conduct for computer professionals. These codes describe the computer professional's obligations to: (1) society, (2) employers, (3) clients, and (4) coprofessionals and professional societies. In a recent article, C. Dianne Martin and David H. Martin identify seven common themes in these codes:[3]

1. Dignity and worth of other people
2. Personal integrity and honesty
3. Responsibility for work
4. Confidentiality of information
5. Public safety, health, and welfare
6. Participation in professional societies to improve standards of the profession
7. The notion that knowledge and access to technology is equivalent to social power

The canons of the ACM are summarized here. Those of the IEEE and DPMA can be found in Appendix E.

---

[3] C. Dianne Martin and David H. Martin, "Professional Codes of Conduct and Computer Ethics Education," *Computers and Society* 20 (1990), 18–29. (Reprinted from *Social Science Computer Review,* vol. 9, Duke University Press, 1990.)

ACM Canons of Conduct

Preamble: Recognition of professional status by the public depends not only on skill and dedication but also on adherence to a recognized Code of Professional Conduct. The following Code sets forth the general principles (Canons) followed by professional ideals (Ethical Considerations) . . . applicable to each member . . . An ACM member shall:

Canon 1. *Act at all times with integrity:*

EC1.1. . . . properly qualify expressed opinions outside the member's areas of competence.

EC1.2. . . . preface any partisan statement about information processing by indicating clearly on whose behalf they are made.

EC1.3. . . . act faithfully on behalf of employers or clients.

Canon 2. *Strive to increase competence and prestige of the profession:*

EC2.1. . . . encouraged to extend public knowledge, understanding, and appreciation of information processing, and to oppose any false or deceptive statements relating to information processing of which the member is aware.

EC2.2. . . . not use professional credentials to misrepresent the member's competence.

EC2.3. . . . undertake only those professional assignments and commitments for which the member is qualified.

EC2.4. . . . strive to design and develop systems that adequately perform the intended functions and that satisfy employer's or client's operational needs.

EC2.5. . . . maintain and increase competence through a program of continuing education encompassing the techniques, technical standards, and practices in the member's field of professional activity.

EC2.6. . . . provide opportunity and encouragement for professional development and advancement of both professionals and those aspiring to become professionals.

Canon 3. *Accept responsibility for own work:*

EC3.1. . . . accept only those assignments for which there is a reasonable expectancy of meeting requirements or specifications, and shall perform assignment in a professional manner.

Canon 4. *Act with professional responsibility:*

EC4.1. . . . not use ACM membership for professional advantage or to misrepresent the authority of the member's statements.

EC4.2. . . . conduct professional activities on a high plane.

EC4.3. . . . be encouraged to uphold and improve professional standards of the Association through participation in their formulation, establishment, and enforcement.

Canon 5. *Use special knowledge and skills for advancement of human welfare:*

EC5.1. . . . consider health, privacy, and general welfare of public in performance of work.

EC5.2. . . . whenever dealing with data concerning individuals, always consider the principle of the individual's privacy and seek the following:

- to minimize the data collected
- to limit authorized access to the data
- to provide proper security for the data
- to determine the required retention period of the data
- to ensure proper disposal of the data

In reading these canons you may note that they are not computer-specific codes but, rather, consist of general principles and guidelines that might apply to almost any profession. This is perhaps because computing is a relatively young discipline, which, unlike well-established professions such as medicine and law, has not benefited from hundreds and perhaps thousands of years of forming, analyzing, and interpreting ethical principles and practices. The development of specific ethical principles for computing has also been complicated by rapid advances in computer technology and the explosive growth of computer applications, several of which have raised new ethical problems and dilemmas. Since this trend will undoubtedly continue, the need to formulate and continually revise ethical guidelines is critical. It will be important for future computer professionals to gain not only technical expertise but also an awareness of ethical and moral issues and a commitment to responsible use of computers.

Exercises

1. Describe the importance of each of the following persons to the history of computing:

   (a) Charles Babbage   **(b)** Blaise Pascal
   (c) John von Neumann   **(d)** Herman Hollerith
   (e) Joseph Jacquard   **(f)** Gottfried Wilhelm von Leibniz
   (g) John Atanasoff   **(h)** Steven Jobs and Steve Wozniak
   (i) Robert Noyce   **(j)** J. P. Eckert
   (k) John Backus   **(l)** Ken Thompson
   (m) Dennis Ritchie   **(n)** Bjarne Stroustrup

2. Describe the importance of each of the following devices to the history of computing:

(a) ENIAC   (b) Analytical Engine
(c) Jacquard loom   (d) UNIVAC
(e) Mark I

3. Distinguish the four different generations of computers.

4. Briefly define each of the following terms:

(a) stored program concept   (b) FORTRAN
(c) C++   (d) CPU
(e) ALU   (f) peripheral devices
(g) bit   (h) byte
(i) word   (j) UNIX
(k) MS-DOS   (l) source program
(m) object program   (n) assembly language
(o) machine language   (p) K
(q) OOP   (r) GUI

5. What are the main functions of

(a) an operating system
(b) a compiler
(c) an assembler

6. Convert each of the following binary numerals to base 10:

(a) 1001   (b) 110010
(c) 1000000   (d) 111111111111111 (fifteen 1s)
(e) 1.1   (f) 1010.10101

7. Convert each of the following octal numerals to base 10:

(a) 123   (b) 2705   (c) 10000
(d) 77777   (e) 7.2   (f) 123.45

8. Convert each of the following hexadecimal numerals to base 10:

(a) 12   (b) 1AB   (c) ABC
(d) FFF   (e) 8.C   (f) AB.CD

9. Conversion from octal representation to binary representation is easy: We simply replace each octal digit with its three-bit binary equivalent. For example, to convert 617_8 to binary, replace 6 with 110, 1 with 001, and 7 with 111, to obtain 110001111_2. Convert each of the octal numerals in Exercise 7 to binary numerals.

10. Imitating the conversion scheme in Exercise 9, convert each of the hexadecimal numerals in Exercise 8 to binary numerals.

11. To convert a binary numeral to octal, place the digits in groups of three, starting from the binary point, or from the right end if there is no binary point, and replace each group with the corresponding octal digit. For example, $10101111_2 = 010\ 101\ 111_2 = 257_8$. Convert each of the binary numerals in Exercise 6 to octal numerals.

12. Imitating the conversion scheme in Exercise 11, convert each of the binary numerals in Exercise 6 to hexadecimal numerals.

13. One method for finding the **base-b** representation of a whole number given in base-10 notation is to divide the number repeatedly by b until a quotient of zero results. The successive remainders are the digits from right to left of the base-b representation. For example, the binary representation of 26 is 11010_2, as the following computation shows:

$$
\begin{array}{r}
0 \text{ R } 1 \\ \hline
2)\overline{1} \text{ R } 1 \\
2)\overline{3} \text{ R } 0 \\
2)\overline{6} \text{ R } 1 \\
2)\overline{13} \text{ R } 0 \\
2)\overline{26}
\end{array}
$$

Convert each of the following base-10 numerals to (i) binary, (ii) octal, and (iii) hexadecimal:

(a) 27   (b) 99   (c) 314   (d) 5280

14. To convert a decimal fraction to its base-b equivalent, repeatedly multiply the fractional part of the number by b. The integer parts are the digits from left to right of the base-b representation. For example, the decimal numeral 0.6875 corresponds to the binary numeral 0.1011_2, as the following computation shows:

$$
\begin{array}{r|l}
 & .6875 \\
 & \times 2 \\ \hline
1 & .375 \\
 & \times 2 \\ \hline
0 & .75 \\
 & \times 2 \\ \hline
1 & .5 \\
 & \times 2 \\ \hline
1 & .0
\end{array}
$$

Convert the following base-10 numerals to (i) binary, (ii) octal, (iii) hexadecimal:

(a) 0.5   (b) 0.25   (c) 0.625
(d) 16.0625   (e) 8.828125

15. Even though the base-10 representation of a fraction may terminate, its representation in some other base need not terminate. For example, the

following computation shows that the binary representation of 0.7 is $(0.1011001100110011001100110 \ldots)_2$, where the block of bits $\overline{0110}$ is repeated indefinitely. This representation is commonly written as $0.10\overline{110}_2$.

$$
\begin{array}{r|l}
 & .7 \\
 & \times 2 \\
\hline
1 & .4 \leftarrow \\
 & \times 2 \\
\hline
0 & .8 \\
 & \times 2 \\
\hline
1 & .6 \\
 & \times 2 \\
\hline
1 & .2 \\
 & \times 2 \\
\hline
0 & .4 \\
\end{array}
$$

Convert the following base-10 numerals to (i) binary, (ii) octal, (iii) hexadecimal:

(a) 0.3 **(b)** 0.6 **(c)** 0.05 **(d)** $0.\overline{3} = 0.33333 \cdots = 1/3$

16. Find the decimal value of each of the following 16-bit integers, assuming a two's complement representation:

(a) 0000000001000000 **(b)** 1111111111111110
(c) 1111111110111111 **(d)** 0000000011111111
(e) 1111111100000000 **(f)** 1000000000000001

17. Find the 16-bit two's complement representation for each of the following integers:

(a) 255 **(b)** 1K
(c) −255 **(d)** −256
(e) -34567_8 **(f)** $-3ABC_{16}$

18. Assuming two's complement representation, what range of integers can be represented in 8-bit words?

19. Assuming an 11-bit mantissa and a 5-bit exponent as described in the text and assuming that two's complement representation is used for each, indicate how each of the following real numbers would be stored in a 16-bit word if extra bits in the mantissa are: (i) truncated, or (ii) rounded:

(a) 0.375 **(b)** 37.375
(c) 0.03125 **(d)** 63.84375
(e) 0.1 **(f)** 0.01

20. Using the tables for ASCII and EBCDIC in Appendix A, indicate how each of the following character strings would be stored in 2-byte words using (i) ASCII or (ii) EBCDIC:

(a) TO **(b)** FOUR **(c)** AMOUNT
(d) ETC. **(e)** J. DOE **(f)** A#∗4−C

21. Using the instruction mnemonics and opcodes given in the text, write a sequence of (a) assembly language and (b) machine language instructions equivalent to the C++ statement

    ```
    X = (A + B) * C
    ```

    For the machine language instructions, assume that the values of **A**, **B**, and **C** are stored in memory words 15, 16, and 17, respectively, and the value of X is to be stored in memory word 23.

22. Repeat Exercise 21 for the C++ statement

    ```
    X = (A + B) * (C + D)
    ```

    assuming that the value of **D** is stored in memory word 18.

23. Examine recent issues of the *New York Times, Time, Newsweek,* or other newspapers and news magazines to find articles that describe the following:

    (a) A new or novel application of computing
    (b) A problem caused by a computer error, either in hardware or software
    (c) Difficulties caused by a computer virus, worm, or other scheme that causes a computer system to shut down or to function abnormally, that destroys or damages data stored in the computer, or that generally is intended to interfere with the normal operation of or use of one or many computer systems
    (d) A break-in by a hacker or a group of hackers to databases containing sensitive information

    Write a report that summarizes the article and your reaction to it, especially to any ethical and moral issues that are involved.

24. Many of the publications of the professional computing societies contain articles that are of interest to and can be understood by students. Select one or several of the publications in the following list, locate an article dealing with some current ethical issue, and prepare a written summary of the article, the ethical or moral problem/difficulty involved, suggestions for dealing with the problem/difficulty, and your reaction.

    Communications of the ACM
    Computers and Society, a publication of the ACM Special Interest Group on Computers & Society
    COMPUTERWORLD
    IEEE *Computer*
    IEEE *Software*
    IEEE *Spectrum*
    New Scientist
    SIGCAPH Newsletter, a publication of the ACM Special Interest Group on Computers and the Physically Handicapped
    SIGCHI bulletin, a publication of the ACM Special Interest Group on Computer & Human Interaction
    Software Engineering Notes, an informal newsletter of the ACM Special Interest Group on Software Engineering

PROGRAM DEVELOPMENT

If we really understand the problem, the answer will come out of it, because the answer is not separate from the problem.
KRISHNAMURTI

People always get what they ask for; the only trouble is that they never know, until they get it, what it actually is that they have asked for.
ALDOUS HUXLEY

CHAPTER CONTENTS

We noted in Chapter 1 that the computer has become an indispensable tool in many areas. Its applications are far too many to enumerate, and the following list is intended only to show some of the diverse uses of computers:

- Business and Finance
    Mailing lists and billings
    Payroll, accounts receivable, accounts payable
    Inventory control
    Reservations systems (airlines, car rentals, etc.)
    Word processing
    Data management
    Spreadsheets
    EFT (electronic funds transfer)
    ATMs (automatic teller machines)
    Electronic mail
    Home banking
    Financial planning
    Processing of insurance claims
- Industry
    Robots in assembly lines
    CAD (computer-aided design)
    CAM (computer-aided manufacturing)
    CIM (computer-integrated manufacturing)
    Market analysis
    Project management and control
    Production scheduling
- Government
    Defense systems
    Space programs
    Compilation of census data
    Weather forecasting by NOAA (National Oceanic and Atmospheric Administration)
    Automated traffic-control systems
    State and local lotteries
    The FBI's NCIS (national crime information system)
- Medicine
    CAT (computerized axial tomography) and MR (magnetic resonance) scans
    On-line access to patients' medical records
    Monitoring life-support systems
    Expert diagnosis systems
- Entertainment
    Animation, colorization, and creation of special effects in the film industry
    Video games
- Science
    Analysis of molecules
    Study of crystal structures
    Testing food quality
    Simulation of large dynamical systems

These and many other applications all require the development of software, and although the problems themselves and specific techniques used in their solutions vary, there are several phases or stages that are common in the software development process:

1. Problem analysis and specification
2. Design
3. Coding
4. Verification and validation
5. Maintenance

In this chapter we begin by describing and illustrating these stages of what is often referred to as the **software life cycle.** We then examine each stage in greater detail in the context of problems whose solutions are more difficult.

2.1   An Introduction to Software Development

We begin by considering a problem whose solution will illustrate the software life cycle.

PROBLEM 1: Revenue Calculation

Sam Splicer installs coaxial cable for the Metro City Cable Company. For each installation, there is a basic service charge of $25.00 and an additional charge of $2.00 for each foot of cable. The president of the cable company would like a program to compute the revenue generated by Sam in any given month. For example, if during the month of January, Sam installs a total of 263 yards of cable at 27 different locations, then he generates $2253.00 in revenue.

Stage 1: Problem Analysis and Specification

The first stage is to analyze the problem and precisely specify the information to be used in solving the problem. This information can usually be classified as follows:

- A value that must be supplied from outside the program is called an **input value.**
- A value that is given in the problem is called a **constant value.**
- A value that must be produced as part of the solution to the problem is called an **output value.**

The specification thus involves identifying the values in each of these categories, which is relatively easy in this textbook problem:

Input	Constants	Output
Number of installations	Basic service charge: $25.00	Revenue generated
Yards of cable	Cost of cable (per foot): $2.00	

The other items of information given—the employee's name, the name of the company, and the month—are not relevant (at least not for this problem) and can be ignored.

Once we have identified these values, which are sometimes called the **data objects** in the problem, the task of a program to solve this problem can be specified as follows:

Input: The number of installations and yards of cable used
Output: The total revenue generated

We now have a precise statement of the problem and are ready to begin designing its solution.

Stage 2: Design

The second stage consists of three steps:

2A. Describing the data objects used in solving the problem
2B. Describing the operations that must be applied to those objects to solve the problem
2C. Arranging those operations in an order that solves the problem

The sequence of operations that solves the problem is called an **algorithm** for the problem.

2A. Describing the Data Objects.   To accomplish step 2A, we must identify the various attributes of the data objects that we listed in stage 1, including their *kind* (variable or constant), their *type* (integer, real, etc.), and the *name* by which we will refer to that object. If the first stage has been done carefully, this step is usually quite easy.

To illustrate, the input for this problem consists of the number of installations and yards of cable used; the output to be produced is the amount of revenue generated. The data objects for input and output values must be **variables** (as opposed to **constants**) since their values will change between the time the program begins execution and its termination. The specification also stipulates that there are two constant values: the basic service charge and the cost of the cable (per foot). Finally, since the amount of cable used is measured in yards and the cost of the cable is given as cost per foot, we have added another data object (a variable) to hold the result of converting the yards of cable used into feet. This results in the following descriptions:

Data Object	Kind of Value	Type of Object	Name of Object[1]
Number of installations	Variable	Integer	*Installations*
Yards of cable used	Variable	Real	*YardsOfCable*
Feet of cable used	Variable	Real	*FeetOfCable*
Revenue	Variable	Real	*Revenue*
Basic service charge	Constant	Real	*ServiceCharge*
Cost of cable (per foot)	Constant	Real	*CostPerFoot*

Given such a list, we are ready to identify the operations that must be applied to these objects in order to solve the problem.

---

[1] In this text, we will display the names of data objects in italics during the design phase to more easily keep them distinct from the surrounding text.

2B. Describing the Operations.   It should be clear that the operations required to solve this problem are as follows:

- *Input* an integer value (*Installations*).
- *Input* a real value (*YardsOfCable*).
- Perform the numeric operations
    —*multiply* two real values (to convert yards into feet);
    —*multiply* a real and an integer value (to compute the value for *Revenue*);
    —*add* two real values (to compute the value for *Revenue*).
- *Assign* a value to a real variable (*FeetOfCable* and *Revenue*).
- *Output* a real value (*Revenue*).

Given this list, we are ready to arrange these operations in an order that solves the problem.

2C. Constructing an Algorithm.   The first step in an algorithm for solving this problem is to obtain the values for the input items—*Installations* and *YardsOf-Cable*—because without those values, we cannot perform any of the subsequent operations. Once we have those values, we compute *FeetOfCable* by multiplying *YardsOfCable* by 3.0, since *FeetOfCable* is needed in order to compute *Revenue*. We can then multiply *FeetOfCable* by the (per foot) cost of the cable; multiply the number of installations by the basic service charge; and add these two products to obtain the value for *Revenue*. As the last step, the output value (*Revenue*) must be displayed.

   This algorithm might be expressed more concisely as follows.

ALGORITHM FOR REVENUE CALCULATION

/* This algorithm calculates the revenue generated by the installation of a
   certain number of yards of cable at a number of locations. For each
   installation there is a fixed basic service charge and an additional charge for
   each foot of cable.

   Input: The number of *Installations* and *YardsOfCable* used
   Constants: A basic *ServiceCharge* and the *CostPerFoot* of cable
   Output: The *Revenue* generated

   ——*/

1. Enter *Installations* and *YardsOfCable*.
2. Calculate *FeetOfCable* = 3.0 * *YardsOfCable*.
3. Calculate

   Revenue = *Installations* * *ServiceCharge* + *CostPerFoot* * *FeetOfCable*.

4. Display *Revenue*.

Note that we have included a brief specification of the problem that the algorithm solves as a *comment* at the beginning of the algorithm (the part between the /* and */). Such **documentation** is important and should be included in every algorithm.

Once we have finished the algorithm, we are ready to proceed to the coding stage.

Stage 3: Coding

The third stage is simply a matter of implementing the data objects and the algorithm in some programming language. Figure 2.1 shows a C++ program for this example together with a sample execution. User input has been underlined to distinguish it from output produced by the program.

FIGURE 2.1 Revenue calculation.

```
/* This program calculates the revenue generated by an employee
   installing coaxial cable.

   Input (keyboard):   The number of installations
                       The yards of cable installed
   Constants:          The basic service charge for an installation
                       The cost per foot of the cable
   Output (screen):    The revenue generated
   --------------------------------------------------------------------*/

#include <iostream.h>

int main(void)
{
   const double
      ServiceCharge = 25.00,    // service charge per installation
      CostPerFoot = 2.00;       // unit cable cost

   int
      Installations;            // number of installations
   double
      YardsOfCable;             // yards of cable used

   cout << "\nPlease enter:"
        << "\n\tthe number of installations, and"
        << "\n\tthe yards of cable used.\n";

   cin >> Installations >> YardsOfCable;

   double
      FeetOfCable = 3.0 * YardsOfCable;

   double
      Revenue = Installations * ServiceCharge +
                CostPerFoot * FeetOfCable;

   cout << "The revenue generated = $" << Revenue << "\n\n";

   return 0;
}
```

FIGURE 2.1   Revenue calculation. (cont.)

Sample run:

```
Please enter:
   the number of installations, and
   the yards of cable used.
27 263.0 ←───────────────────────────── user input
The revenue generated = $2253
```

The program begins with **opening documentation** in the form of a comment that describes the program. This comment summarizes the purpose of the program and gives the specification of the problem the program is to solve.

Following the opening documentation is a special **compiler directive**

```
#include <iostream.h>
```

that instructs the compiler to include the declarations from the `iostream` library, which provides the capabilities needed to perform interactive I/O.

Following this directive is the actual C++ program. It begins with the lines

```
int main(void)
{
```

and ends with the closing brace

```
}
```

on the last line. Between the opening brace and closing brace are the declarations and statements that make up the **body** of the program.

Before we can use the name of a data object in a program, we must describe that name to the C++ compiler with a special statement called a **declaration.** The first items in the body of the program are the declarations of the two (real) constant data objects:

```
const double
   ServiceCharge = 25.00, // service charge per installation
   CostPerFoot = 2.00;    // unit cable cost
```

These are placed at the beginning of the program so that they can be easily found and modified, if necessary. Note that each declaration is followed by a comment (the part following the //) that explains its purpose.

Following the constant declarations are the declarations of the input variables:

```
int
   Installations;       // number of installations
double
   YardsOfCable;        // yards of cable used
```

As before, we have appended a comment to each declaration to explain its meaning more fully.

Once the input variables are declared, we are ready to perform the first step of the algorithm, which is to enter values from the keyboard and store them in the variables. We first display a **prompt for input** so that users will know how many and what kind of values should be entered:

```
cout << "\nPlease enter:"
     << "\n\tthe number of installations, and"
     << "\n\tthe yards of cable used.\n";
```

Within each of the character strings are some special **escape sequences,** which are used to control the placement of text. In particular, the escape sequence \n is used to insert a **newline character** (the character generated by the enter or return key) into the string, and the escape sequence \t is used to insert a **tab character** into the character string. A complete list of C++ escape sequences can be found in Section 3.3.

Note that even though all the output consists of characters, we have split these characters into three character strings (enclosed in double quotes) that are output separately. This gives the prompt the appearance of a *menu*

```
Please enter:
    the number of installations, and
    the yards of cable used.
```

and makes it easier to add or delete items if the need arises.

Following the prompt for input is a statement to input the two values:

```
cin >> Installations >> YardsOfCable;
```

In the sample run shown, the program displays the input prompt and then waits until the user enters values for the two variables:

```
27 263.0
```

These values are assigned to the variables **Installations** and **YardsOfCable,** respectively.

The next two steps in the algorithm,

2. Calculate *FeetOfCable* = 3.0 ∗ *YardsOfCable.*
3. Calculate
   Revenue = Installations ∗ ServiceCharge + CostPerFoot ∗ FeetOfCable.

translate into the C++ declarations (with initializations):

```
double
   FeetOfCable = 3.0 * YardsOfCable;

double
   Revenue = Installations * ServiceCharge +
             CostPerFoot * FeetOfCable;
```

For the values entered in the sample run, the first statement will multiply **YardsOfCable** (263.0) by 3.0, which yields 789.0; this value is then stored in the variable **FeetOfCable**. Similarly, the second statement will

A. Multiply **Installations** (27) by **ServiceCharge** (25.0), producing 675.0;
B. Multiply **CostPerFoot** (2.0) by **FeetOfCable** (789.0), producing 1578.0; and
C. Add the two products 675.0 and 1578.0, producing the value 2253.0;

which is then stored in the variable **Revenue**.

The output step

4. Display *Revenue.*

is translated into the C++ statement

```
cout << "The revenue generated = $" << Revenue << "\n\n";
```

In the sample run, execution of this statement displays the output

```
The revenue generated = $2253
```

The final statement in the program,

```
return 0;
```

is simply a mechanism used by C++ to indicate that the program terminated normally.

Stage 4: Verification and Validation

Once an algorithm has been encoded, the fourth step in the development cycle is to check that the algorithm and program are *correct*. One common way to do this is by testing the program with sample data for which the correct values are already known (or are easily calculated). In the sample execution in Figure 2.1, we tested the program by entering the values 27 and 263.0, since we had already determined that the correct answer for those inputs was 2253.0:

```
Please enter:
   number of installations, and
   yards of cable used.
27 263.0

The revenue generated = $2253
```

Similarly, the correct results for simple input values like 1 and 1.0 or 2 and 3.0 are easily calculated and can be used as a quick check of the answers produced by the program.

If a program compiles and executes normally but produces incorrect results, then it contains one or more **logical errors** stemming from faulty design or incorrect coding of the algorithm. For example, if the statement

```
FeetOfCable = 3.0 * YardsOfCable;
```

to compute `FeetOfCable` in the program of Figure 2.1 were mistakenly entered as

```
FeetOfCable = 3.0 + YardsOfCable;
```

with the addition symbol (+) substituted for the multiplication symbol (*), the compiler could not identify this substitution as an error, and so no error would be generated during compilation. However, the output produced by the program would not be correct, because an incorrect formula was used to calculate `FeetOfCable`. If the values 27 and 263.0 were entered for the variables `Installations` and `YardsOfCable`, respectively, the output produced would be

```
The revenue generated = $1207
```

instead of the correct output

```
The revenue generated = $2253
```

shown in the sample run in Figure 2.1.

Since it may not be obvious whether the results produced by a program are correct, *it is important that the user run a program several times with input data for which the correct results are known in advance.* This process of **program testing** is extremely important, as a *program cannot be considered to be correct until it has been checked with several sets of test data.* The test data should be carefully selected so that a program is thoroughly tested.

Stage 5: Maintenance

Suppose that a year after the program in Figure 2.1 was written, the Metro City Cable Company raises the basic service charge for an installation from $25.00 to $30.00. Obviously, the program will no longer compute the correct revenue. Although we could discard the program and write a new one, it is usually easier simply to modify the existing program to bring it up to date. In the program in Figure 2.1, this is easily done by changing the lines

```
const double
    ServiceCharge = 25.00, // service charge per installation
```

to

```
const double
    ServiceCharge = 30.00, // service charge per installation
```

and then recompiling the program. The program will then calculate `Revenue` using the new value of `ServiceCharge`, so that its output will reflect the new service charge.

As another example of program maintenance, suppose that the president of the Metro City Cable Company requested that exactly two decimal digits be displayed for revenue, since this is customary for monetary values. Formatting the output in this way requires using another C++ library named **iomanip** (described in detail in Section 3.6 and Chapter 8), and so we must add another compiler directive,

```
#include <iomanip.h>
```

near the beginning of the program (i.e., following the first directive). The items provided in this library can be used to modify the output statement

```
cout << "The revenue generated = $" << Revenue << "\n\n";
```

as follows:

```
cout << "The revenue generated = $"
     << setiosflags(ios::showpoint | ios::fixed)
            // display dec. point and use fixed-point format
     << setprecision(2)
            // display two decimal places
     << Revenue << "\n\n";
```

Then, when the program is compiled and executed, the results will be displayed in the desired format:

```
The revenue generated = $2253.00
```

For program segments whose purpose may not be clear, it is a good practice to add comments that explain why they are needed. This is the purpose of the comments in the preceding output statement. The effect of the new lines is best seen by considering what the output would be if they were omitted. If the second line (or just **ios::showpoint** |) were omitted, the output would be the same as before; if | **ios::fixed** were omitted, the value of **Revenue** would be displayed in exponential format:

```
The revenue generated = $2.25e+03
```

If we added the second line but not the third, the value of **Revenue** would be displayed using the default precision (which is often 6 decimal places):

```
The revenue generated = $2253.000000
```

None of these forms is quite appropriate for displaying a monetary value.

This completes our introduction to the software life cycle. In the sections that follow, we consider each of its five stages in greater detail.

Exercises

For each of the problems described in Exercises 1 and 2, identify the input values, constant values, and output values. Then describe the data objects and operations needed to solve the problem and design an algorithm for it.

1. Calculate and display the perimeter and area of a square with a given side.

2. Two common temperature scales are the Fahrenheit and Celsius scales. The boiling point of water is 212° on the Fahrenheit scale and 100° on the Celsius scale. The freezing point of water is 32° on the Fahrenheit scale and 0° on the Celsius scale. Assuming that the relationship between these two temperature scales is $F = \dfrac{9}{5}C + 32$, convert a temperature on the Celsius scale to the corresponding Fahrenheit temperature.

3. Enter and execute the following C++ program on your computer system:

```
/* This program adds the values of variables X and Y.
   Output (screen): The value X + Y

   ----------------------------------------------------------*/

#include <iostream.h>

int main(void)
{
   int
      X = 214,        // the first value
      Y = 2057,       // the second value
      Sum = X + Y;

   // output the resulting value
   cout << "\nThe sum of " << X << " and " << Y
        << " is " << Sum << "\n\n";
   return 0;
}
```

4. Make the following changes in the program in Exercise 3 and execute the modified program:

(a) Change **214** to **1723** in the statement assigning a value to **X**.
(b) Change the variable names **X** and **Y** to **Alpha** and **Beta** throughout.
(c) Add the comment

```
// find their sum
```

following the declaration of **Sum**.
(d) Change the variable declaration to

```
int
   Alpha = 214,              // the first value
   Beta = 2057,              // the second value
   Difference = Alpha - Beta, // find their difference
   Sum = Alpha + Beta;       // find their sum
```

and add the following statement after the output statement:

```
cout << "\nThe difference of " << Alpha << " and "
     << Beta << " is " << Difference << "\n\n";
```

5. Using the program in Figure 2.1 as a guide, write a C++ program to solve the problem in Exercise 1.

6. Using the program in Figure 2.1 as a guide, write a C++ program to solve the problem in Exercise 2.

2.2 Problem Analysis and Specification

Because the initial description of a problem may be somewhat vague and imprecise, the first stage in the development of a program to solve the problem is to analyze the problem and specify precisely what a solution to the problem requires. This **specification** must include

1. A list of the data values that must be *supplied from outside* the program;
2. A list of those constant values that are *given* or *assumed* by the problem;
3. A list of the values that must be *produced* in order to solve the problem.

We describe (1) as the problem's **input values,** (2) as the problem's **constant values,** and (3) as its **output values.** For a problem that appears in a programming text, input, constant, and output values are usually not too difficult to identify. However, in a real-world problem encountered by a professional programmer, the specification of the problem often includes extraneous items, and considerable effort may be required to formulate the problem specification completely. In this section we illustrate this first step of program development with two new examples that can be solved with relatively simple programs.

PROBLEM 2: The Pollution Index Problem—Specification

The Problem. The level of air pollution in the city of Dogpatch is measured by a pollution index. Readings are made at 12:00 P.M. at three locations: the Abner Coal Plant, downtown at the corner of Daisy Avenue and 5th Street, and at a randomly selected location in a residential area. The average of these three readings is the pollution index, and a value of 50.0 or greater for this index indicates a "hazardous" condition, whereas values lower than 50.0 indicate a "safe" condition. Because this index must be calculated daily, the Dogpatch environmental statistician would like a program that calculates the pollution index and then determines the appropriate condition, safe or hazardous.

Specification. The relevant given information consists of three pollution readings and the cutoff value used to distinguish between safe and hazardous conditions. A solution to the problem consists of the pollution index and a message indicating the condition. We can thus identify the following data objects in this problem:

Input	Constants	Output
Three air pollution readings	A cutoff value to distinguish between safe and hazardous conditions: 50.0	The pollution index: the average of the pollution readings A message: "safe condition" or "hazardous condition"

Given these data objects, we can write a more precise description of this problem, as follows:

Input: Three air pollution readings
Output: The average of the three readings;
         the string "safe condition" if the average is less than 50 and the string "hazardous condition" otherwise

PROBLEM 3: The Mean Time to Failure Problem—Specification

The Problem. One important statistic that is used in measuring the reliability of a component in a circuit is the *mean time to failure,* which can be used to predict the circuit's lifetime. This is especially important in situations in which repair is difficult or even impossible, such as a computer circuit in a space satellite. Suppose that an engineering laboratory has been awarded a contract by NASA to evaluate the reliability of a particular component for a future space probe to Jupiter. As part of this evaluation, an engineer at this laboratory has tested several of these circuits and recorded the time at which each failed. She now wishes to develop a program to process this data and determine the mean time to failure.

Specification. The input for this problem is a collection of failure times for the component being tested, and the output is the average or mean of these times:

Input	Constants	Output
An unknown number of numeric values	None	The number of values The mean of the values

To calculate this mean, we must know how many tests were conducted, but this information is not given in the statement of the problem. We may not assume that it is part of the input, and so the program will have to be flexible enough to process any number of measurements. We can thus specify this problem as follows:

Input: An unknown number of numeric values
Output: The number of values input;
         the mean (average) of the input values

A "Real-World" Problem: Payroll

Like the exercises and problems in most programming texts, the preceding problems are (we hope) clearly stated and involve simple data objects. Analyzing these problems to identify the data objects is, consequently, quite easy. This is not the case, however, with many real-world problems, which are often stated vaguely and imprecisely because the person posing the problem does not fully understand it. For example, the president of a land-development company might ask a programmer to "computerize the payroll system for the Metro City Construction Company."

In such situations, a number of questions must be answered before we can identify those data objects that are required to solve the problem: What information is available for each employee? How is the program to access this data? Has this information been validated, or must the program provide error checking? In what format should the output be displayed? Are paychecks being printed? Must additional reports be generated for company executives and/or government agencies?

Other questions deal more directly with the required processing. Are employees paid on an hourly or a salary basis, or are there some of each? What premium, if any, is paid for overtime? What items must be withheld—for federal, state, and city income taxes, retirement plans, insurance, and the like—and how are they to be computed? Answers to these questions must be obtained so that the basic data objects and the operations to be performed on them can be described. These descriptions are a critical part of the problem's specification.

Many other questions must be answered before the specification of the problem can be completed so that the design of the algorithms and programs can begin. Will the users be technically sophisticated, or will they be novices so that the software must be made extra user-friendly and robust? How often will the software be used? What are the response time requirements? How critical is the application in which the software is being used? If fault-free performance is required, must a proof of correctness accompany the software? As the specification of the problem is being formulated, decisions must be made regarding the feasibility of a computer solution. Is it possible to design programs to carry out the required processing? If so, is it economically feasible? What hardware and software are available? Could the problem be solved better manually? How soon must the software be ready? What is its expected lifetime; that is, how long will it be used, and what changes can be expected in the future?

Although this list is by no means exhaustive, it does indicate the wide range of information that must be obtained in analyzing and specifying the problem. In some situations this is done by a **systems analyst,** but in others it is part of the programmer's responsibility.

The statement of the specifications developed in this phase becomes the formal statement of the problem's requirements. This **problem specification** document serves as the major reference document that guides the development of the software, and it is the *standard,* or *benchmark,* used in validating the final system to determine whether it does in fact solve the problem. For this reason, a number of **formal methods** have been developed for writing such specifications. These methods are usually studied in more advanced software engineering courses, and in this text we will state the problem specifications somewhat less formally.

2.3 Design

Once the specification of a problem has been completed, the next step is to **design** a program or a system of programs that will satisfy that specification. As we have seen, such a design typically has three parts:

1. Identification of the attributes (*kind, type, name,* etc.) of the **data objects** that are required to solve the problem
2. Identification of the **operations** that must be applied to the data objects in order to solve the problem
3. Construction of a detailed sequence of simple steps (called an **algorithm**) that specifies how the operations can be applied to the data objects to solve the problem.

Object Attributes

If the problem has been carefully specified in terms of input, constant, and output values, then the data objects of the problem generally correspond to these values, although in some cases additional objects may be necessary to solve the problem (e.g., the variable *FeetOfCable* in the revenue calculation problem of the preceding section).

Whether these objects are variables or constants is largely determined by the problem statement; data objects whose values are given in the problem statement and remain unchanged throughout the program are generally represented using constants, whereas other data objects whose values change during execution are represented using variables.

The *types* of these objects are determined by the types of values to be stored in them. For the problems considered in the first several chapters of this text, the types of the data objects will for the most part be *numeric types* that are **predefined** in C++. In later chapters, we will consider more complex problems whose solutions may require that the programmer construct new types to describe and store the values of the problem's data objects.

The Pollution Index Problem.   Recall that the input for the pollution index problem consists of three real pollution readings. Since these values change, we will represent these readings with three real variable data objects: *Reading1, Reading2,* and *Reading3.* To compute the average, we will need the number of readings—the integer constant 3. There is also a single real constant cutoff value (50.0) that distinguishes between safe and hazardous conditions, which we will represent with the constant data object *CutOff.* The output to be produced consists of the real pollution index, which is the average of the three readings and which we will store in the real variable object *Index,* and one of two character string messages, "safe condition" or "hazardous condition", which indicate the condition determined by the value of *Index.* We thus have the following list of data objects for the pollution index problem:

Data Object	Kind of Value	Type of Object	Name of Object
The first reading	Variable	Real	*Reading1*
The second reading	Variable	Real	*Reading2*
The third reading	Variable	Real	*Reading3*
The number of readings	Constant	Integer	3
The pollution index	Variable	Real	*Index*
The cutoff value	Constant	Real	*CutOff*
Safe message	Constant	Character string	"safe condition"
Hazard message	Constant	Character string	"hazardous condition"

The Mean Time to Failure Problem.   Constructing the list of data objects in this problem is not quite so straightforward. We have already seen that the input is a sequence of numbers, each representing the failure time of a component in a circuit, and that the output is the number of data values and their average, which is the mean time to failure for this component. It is less clear what additional objects might be needed to solve the problem.

One useful method for designing an algorithm to solve a problem is to begin by considering how the problem could be solved without using a computer, perhaps instead using pencil and paper and/or a calculator. To solve the mean time to failure problem in this manner, we consider the values one at a time, counting each value as it is entered and adding it to the sum of the preceding values:

Data Value	Counter	Sum
	0	0.0
3.4	1	3.4
4.2	2	7.6
6.0	3	13.6
5.5	4	19.1
⋮	⋮	⋮

We see that this approach requires two additional data objects:

1. A counter that is incremented by 1 each time a value is entered
2. A running sum of the data values

We need, therefore, a total of four variable data objects: a real variable that we call *FailTime* to hold the current data value, an integer variable called *NumTimes* that will count the number of data values read, a real variable called *Sum* that will accumulate the sum of the data values, and a real variable called *MeanFailTime* that will store the mean of the failure times. We thus have the following list of objects:

Data Object	Kind of Value	Type of Object	Name of Object
Each failure time	Variable	Real	*FailTime*
The number of times	Variable	Integer	*NumTimes*
The sum of the times	Variable	Real	*Sum*
The mean of the times	Variable	Real	*MeanFailTime*

Operations

The operations that must be applied to the data objects clearly depend on the problem being solved. In the problems we consider initially, the operations on the numeric data objects will for the most part be the standard arithmetic operations used in algebraic formulas and equations. In the more complex problems of later chapters, in which the programmer constructs new types, it may be necessary to define new operations on these types.

The Pollution Index Problem. To solve the pollution index problem, we need the following operations:

- Input real values (*Reading1*, *Reading2*, and *Reading3*)

- Compute the average of three real values, which involves
  —Adding three real values (*Reading1, Reading2,* and *Reading3*); and
  —Dividing a real value by an integer value (3).
- Assign a value to a real variable (*Index*).
- Determine whether one real value is less than another real value (*Index* and *CutOff*).
- Output one character string ("safe condition") if *Index* is less than *CutOff* and a different character string ("hazardous condition") otherwise.

It is this last operation that distinguishes this problem from simpler problems such as the revenue problem considered in the previous section.

The Mean Time to Failure Problem. The operations needed to solve this problem are as follows:

- Input a real value (*FailTime*).
- Increment (add 1 to) an integer variable (*NumTimes*).
- Add two real values (*FailTime* and *Sum*).
- Change the value of a real variable (*Sum*).
- Repeat the preceding steps once for each component being tested.
- Halt the repetition when the last data value has been entered.
- Divide a real value and an integer value (*Sum* and *NumTimes*).
- Output a real value.

Algorithms

Once we have identified the operations necessary to solve the problem, the next step is to arrange those operations in an algorithm. Since programs to implement algorithms must be written in a programming language, it is natural to describe algorithms in a language that is similar to a programming language, that is, in a "pseudoprogramming language" or, as it is more commonly called, **pseudocode.**

Unlike the definitions of high-level programming languages such as C++, there is no set of rules that precisely define pseudocode. It varies from one programmer to another. Pseudocode is a mixture of natural language and symbols, terms, and other features commonly used in high-level languages. One typically finds the following features in various pseudocodes:

1. The standard computer symbols are used for arithmetic operations: + for addition, − for subtraction, * for multiplication, and / for division.
2. Symbolic names (identifiers) are used to represent the data objects being manipulated by the algorithm.
3. Some provision is made for including comments, often done by enclosing each comment between special symbols such as /* and */.
4. Certain key words that are common in high-level languages may be used, such as Read or Enter to indicate input operations and Display, Print, or Write for output operations.
5. Indentation is used to denote blocks of instructions that are controlled by other instructions.

The steps that comprise an algorithm must be organized in a logical and clear manner so that the solution to the problem is specified precisely and completely. Algorithms (and programs) are designed using three basic means of control:

1. *Sequential:* Steps are performed in a strictly sequential manner, each step being executed exactly once.
2. *Selection:* One of a number of alternative actions is selected and executed.
3. *Repetition:* One or more steps are performed repeatedly.

Individually, these three methods of control are quite simple, but they are, in fact, sufficiently powerful that any problem (that is solvable) can be solved using them exclusively.

Sequential execution is the default control mechanism—if the programmer does not stipulate selection or repetition, the statements in a program are executed in sequence from beginning to end. Our solution to the revenue calculation problem used only sequential control; the steps are simply executed in order, from beginning to end, with each step being performed exactly once.

For other problems, however, the solution may require that some of the steps be performed in some situations and bypassed in others. The pollution index problem is one such problem.

The Pollution Index Problem. An algorithm for this problem is as follows:

ALGORITHM FOR THE POLLUTION INDEX PROBLEM

/* This algorithm accepts three pollution readings, *Reading1*, *Reading2*, and *Reading3*.. It then calculates and outputs the pollution index as well as a message describing the air quality.

Input: Three pollution readings
Constants: *CutOff* = 50.0
Output: The pollution *Index* and a message indicating the air quality
                                                                        —*/

1. Enter *Reading1*, *Reading2*, and *Reading3*.
2. Calculate

$$Index = \frac{Reading1 + Reading2 + Reading3}{3}$$

3. Display *Index*.
4. If (*Index* < *CutOff*) then
     Display a "safe condition" message.
   Else
     Display a "hazardous condition" message.
   End If.

The solution begins in a sequential manner, inputting the values needed, computing the value of *Index*, and then displaying that value. Following this, one of two actions must be selected: either

a "safe condition" message must be displayed, or

a "hazardous condition" message must be displayed,

but not both. The appropriate action is selected by comparing the pollution index with the cutoff value. In the preceding algorithm, this selection is indicated by a **pseudocode if statement:**

4. If (*Index* < *CutOff*) then
   Display a "safe condition" message.
   Else
   Display a "hazardous condition" message.
   End If.

As we shall see in Chapter 5, such a statement is easily translated into a **C++ if statement.**

The Mean Time to Failure Problem.   In addition to the sequential and selective processing illustrated in the first two examples, the solution of a problem may require that a step or a collection of steps be repeated, as in the mean time to failure problem. We can express an algorithm for this problem as follows:

ALGORITHM TO CALCULATE MEAN TIME TO FAILURE

/* This algorithm reads a sequence of failure times, counts and sums them,
   and then finds the mean time to failure.

   Input: A sequence of failure times, each stored in *FailTime.*
   Constants: *Sentinel,* a value distinct from all possible failure times.
   Output: The mean time to failure, and the number of times entered.

---*/

1. Initialize *NumTimes* to 0 and *Sum* to 0.0.
2. Enter the first value for *FailTime.*
3. While *FailTime* is not equal to *Sentinel* do the following:
      a. Increment *NumTimes* by 1.
      b. Add *FailTime* to *Sum.*
      c. Enter next value for *FailTime.*
   End Loop.
4. If *NumTimes* ≠ 0 then
      a. Calculate *MeanFailTime* = *Sum* / *NumTimes.*
      b. Display *MeanFailTime* and *NumTimes.*
   Else
      Display a "No Data" message.
   End If.

The algorithm begins by initializing *NumTimes* and *Sum* with values 0 and 0.0, respectively, and reading the first data value for *FailTime.* We then (a) add 1 to the value of *NumTimes,* producing a new value for *NumTimes*; (b) add *FailTime* to

Sum, producing a new value for *Sum*; and (c) read a new data value for *FailTime*. These steps are repeated until all the data values have been processed. The value of *Sum* is then divided by the value of *NumTimes* to obtain the mean value, which is stored in the variable *MeanFailTime*. Finally, this mean failure time and the number of failure times are displayed or a "No Data" message is displayed in case no failure times were processed.

When one solves this problem by hand, it is clear when the last data value has been entered, but if this procedure is to be performed by a program, some method is needed to indicate that all of the data values have been processed. A common technique is to signal the end of the input data by having the user enter a special value called a **data flag** or **data sentinel** (which is distinct from any possible valid data item) after the last data value has been entered. By comparing each data value entered against this special value (which we shall call *Sentinel*), a program can determine when the repetition should be terminated.

In this algorithm, the repetition is indicated by:

3. While *FailTime* is not equal to *Sentinel* do the following:
    a. Increment *NumTimes* by 1.
    b. Add *FailTime* to *Sum*.
    c. Enter next value for *FailTime*.
   End Loop.

This specifies that steps 3a, 3b, and 3c are to be repeated as long as the value entered for *FailTime* is not the end-of-data flag. Thus, when the flag signaling the end of data is entered, this repetition is terminated, and step 4 of the algorithm is performed.

The three control structures in these examples, **sequential, selection,** and **repetition,** are used throughout this text in designing algorithms to solve problems. The implementation of each of them in the C++ language is considered in detail in later chapters.

Object-Oriented Design

The data objects in the preceding problems have all had numeric or character values, and so the predefined types of C++ could be used to represent such objects. However, representing the data objects in a real-world problem may be more difficult because the complexity of such objects surpasses the predefined types provided in C++.

To illustrate, consider the Metro City Construction Company payroll problem of processing a file containing a list of employee records, each containing information such as the employee's name, identification number, address, and number of dependents. A simple form of the problem is to compute and output the pay for each employee in that file.

One part of the solution to this problem involves repeatedly performing the following steps:

1. Read an employee's data from the file.
2. Compute the payroll information for that employee.
3. Output the results of step (2) to the appropriate place(s).

We thus need an *Employee* data object in which information about each employee can be stored, so that it can be processed quickly and efficiently. Some *Employee* information will be obtained from the file, while other information (such as hours worked for an hourly employee) will be entered during program execution, and an *Employee* data object must be able to store all of this information.

The operations on an *Employee* data object are not predefined in C++. The solution to this problem requires operations to input information into an *Employee* data object from the data file, manipulate the data stored in an *Employee* data object, and so on. To permit the definition of complex data objects like an *Employee,* some modern programming languages such as C++ provide a structure, called a **class,** in which both *data items* (such as name, address, etc.) and *operations* (such as input, compute pay, etc.) can be grouped.

class *Employee*

| Name |
| IDNumber |
| Address |
| $\vdots$ |
| Input (>>) |
| ComputePay( ) |
| Output (<<) |

A single class is usually sufficient to define such objects as long as the data items and operations required by the object are uniform (i.e., the same for all objects of that class). However this is not the case in many real-world problems. For example, if the Metro City Construction Company has both salaried and hourly workers, then its employees cannot be treated uniformly: The ComputePay( ) operation for salaried workers might utilize the formula

$$\text{Salary} / (\text{Number of Pay Periods per Year})$$

so that one variable data item (*Salary*) and one constant data item (*PayPeriodsPerYear*) are required to compute the pay for salaried workers. By contrast, the ComputePay( ) operation for an hourly worker might use a different formula,

$$(\text{Hourly Rate}) \times (\text{Hours Worked}) +$$
$$(\text{Overtime Hours}) \times (\text{Hourly Rate}) \times (\text{Overtime Factor})$$

and in this case three variable data objects (*HourlyRate, HoursWorked,* and *OverTimeHours*) and one constant data object (*OvertimeFactor*) are required. The data objects and operations that are needed for a salaried employee are different from the data objects and operations needed for an hourly employee.

These differences suggest that different classes of employees are needed, *SalariedEmployee* and *HourlyEmployee,* each containing the data objects and operations associated with a particular kind of employee. One approach would be to declare two independent classes, one for each kind of employee:

class *SalariedEmployee*
Name
IDNumber
Address
⋮
Salary
Input (**≫**)
ComputePay( )
Output (**≪**)

class *HourlyEmployee*
Name
IDNumber
Address
⋮
HourlyRate
HoursWorked
OverTimeHours
Input (**≫**)
ComputePay( )
Output (**≪**)

However, this approach is inefficient, since the two classes have a number of data objects and operations in common. An important key to **object-oriented design** is to

1. *Recognize the commonality in the data objects in a problem.*
2. *Declare a **base class** containing the common objects and operations.*
3. *Declare a **subclass** containing the special objects and operations for each kind of data object in the problem but which **inherits** the common objects and operations from the base class.*

For the Metro City Construction Company example, we might thus use a base class *Employee,* in which are stored all the data objects common to every employee, and two subclasses, *HourlyEmployee* and *SalariedEmployee,* each of which inherits all the objects and operations from the base class *Employee* and contains the special objects and operations needed for that kind of employee.

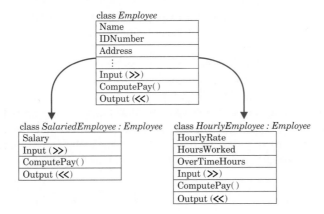

By doing so, we create two distinct **derived classes** that share a common base class in which is stored those data items the derived classes have in common.

Much of the modern practice of programming consists of class design and construction, in order that real-world objects can be modeled in software. Classes are introduced gradually in this text, beginning with the next chapter and studied in greater depth in Chapters 11–17. Derived classes and inheritance are discussed more fully in Chapters 14–17.

2.4 Coding

The first two steps of the program-development process are extremely important, because the remaining phases are much more difficult if the first two steps are skipped or are not done carefully. However, if the problem has been carefully analyzed and specified and if an effective design has been developed, the third step of program coding is usually straightforward.

Coding is the process of implementing the data objects and the algorithms for solving the problem in some programming language. In the design stage of program development, the data objects and algorithms may be described in a natural language or pseudocode, but the program that implements them must be written in the vocabulary of a programming language and must conform to the **syntax,** or grammatical rules, of that language. A significant portion of this text is concerned with the vocabulary and syntax of the programming language C++. In this section, we introduce some elementary features of this language and discuss them in the context of the program in Figure 2.1. We defer the solutions to the pollution index problem and the mean time to failure problem until Chapters 5 and 6, respectively, where selection and repetition are discussed in greater depth.

Types

In the examples we have been considering, two types of numbers have been used. The values of *Installations* in the first example and *NumTimes* in the third example are **integer** values, whereas the values of *YardsOfCable, FeetOfCable,* and *Revenue* in the first example, all the data objects in the second example, and *FailTime, Sum,* and *MeanFailTime* in the third example are **real** values; that is, they have fractional parts. In C++, these two types of numbers are called `int` and `double`, respectively.

Different types of data values have different memory storage requirements. For example, a value of type `int` is sometimes stored using 32 bits, and a value of type `double` is usually stored using 64 bits. In order to allocate the correct amount of memory for a data object, C++ requires that the type of values for the data object must be specified before that object is used. This is accomplished by using a special statement called a **declaration.** Variable data objects and constant data objects are declared differently, and so we examine each of these declarations separately.

Variable Data Objects

In the three examples we have considered, we used variables to store various quantities. In the first example, the variables *Installations* and *YardsOfCable* represented the number of installations and the yards of cable used, respectively. The output in this example was the revenue generated and was represented by the variable *Revenue.* In the second example, the variables *Reading1, Reading2, Reading3* and *Index* were used, and in the third example, the variables were *FailTime, NumTimes, Sum,* and *MeanFailTime.*

The names of C++ data objects should begin with a letter, which may be followed by any number of letters, or digits. Underscores (_) are also permitted and are sometimes used to separate the words in the name of a data object. C++ imposes no restriction on the length of a name, and this allows us to choose names that identify the object being represented; for example, `Installations`, `YardsOfCable`, `Revenue`, `Reading1`, `FailTime`, and `Sum` are all meaningful names for data objects. *Data objects should always be given meaningful names because they make a program easier to read and understand.*

To declare a variable data object, a **variable declaration** of the form

```
Type
    VariableList;
```

is used, where *Type* is the type of the variable(s) being declared and *VariableList* is a list of one or more names of variable data objects, separated by commas. A useful feature of C++ is that the variables in *VariableList* can optionally be initialized with an **initialization declaration** of the form:

```
Type
    Variable₁ = InitialValue₁,
    Variable₂ = InitialValue₂,
               .
               .
               .
    Variableₙ = InitialValueₙ;
```

In this text, we follow the convention of indenting the name of each variable data object on a separate line. Although this is not required, it improves the readability of a declaration.

The variables `Installations` and `YardsOfCable` in the program in Figure 2.1 are declared by:

```
int
    Installations;    // number of installations
double
    YardsOfCable;    // yards of cable used
```

and once a value has been entered for `YardsOfCable`, the variable `FeetOfCable` is declared and initialized in a single statement:

```
double
    FeetOfCable = 3.0 * YardsOfCable;
```

Unlike many other programming languages, *C++ permits a data object to be declared anywhere before its first use.* Thus, it is perfectly legitimate to defer declaring data objects such as `FeetOfCable` and `Revenue` until they are needed.

One way to think of a variable declaration is as a *definition for the compiler* in which the meaning (i.e., its type, such as `int`) is given for a word (e.g., `NumTimes`). In contrast, there are some words (such as `int` and `double`) for which the C++

compiler already has definitions. These words are called **keywords** in C++, and a *keyword may not be used as the name of a data object.* C++ keywords are all spelled with lowercase letters, and to make it easier to distinguish keywords from the names of data objects, we will follow the convention of capitalizing the first letter of each word in the names of our data objects.

Constant Data Objects

In each of the three examples in the preceding section, the specification of the problem listed certain values that were to remain constant during execution of the program. In the first problem, the data objects *ServiceCharge* and *CostPerFoot* were constants; in the second problem, the data object *CutOff* was a constant; and in the third problem, the data object *DataFlag* was a constant. Constant data objects must be declared using a **constant declaration** of the form

```
const Type
   ConstantName₁ = Value₁,
   ConstantName₂ = Value₂,
                .
                .
                .
   ConstantNameₙ = Valueₙ;
```

where **const** is a C++ keyword indicating that what follows is the declaration of a constant data object, **Type** is the type of the value of the data object, **ConstantName**ᵢ is the name of the data object being declared, and **Value**ᵢ is the value of that constant. For example, we used the constant declarations

```
const double
   ServiceCharge = 25.00, // service charge per installation
   CostPerFoot = 2.00;    // unit cable cost
```

to declare the constants in the revenue calculation problem. We could use the declaration

```
const double
   CutOff = 50.0;       // lower bound for safe pollution index
```

to declare the constant **CutOff** for the pollution index problem. Constants are discussed in more detail in Chapter 3.

You may have noticed that the declaration of a constant data object is essentially the declaration of a variable data object preceded by the word **const**. This one word makes a great deal of difference, however, because the compiler treats constant data objects as **read-only** objects: Their values can be used but not changed. If a program tries to change the value of a constant data object, the C++ compiler will generate an error when the program is compiled.

Numeric Operations

Addition and **subtraction** are denoted in C++ by the usual + and - symbols. **Multiplication** is denoted by * and **division** by the / symbol. For example, in the declaration

```
double
   FeetOfCable = 3.0 * YardsOfCable;
```

the expression

```
3.0 * YardsOfCable
```

is evaluated by multiplying **3.0** and the current value of the variable **YardsOfCable**. The resulting value is then used to initialize the variable **FeetOfCable**.

Input/Output

In the pseudocode descriptions of the algorithms in the preceding section, we used words such as Enter and Read for input operations and Display, Print, and Write for output operations. Unlike many languages, C++ has no predefined input/output (I/O) capabilities. To perform I/O, a program must direct the compiler to include a special **I/O library** such as **iostream**. This is done using a **directive** of the form

```
#include <LibraryName.h>
```

where ***LibraryName*** is the name of the library to be used. The **iostream** library contains all the declarations and definitions necessary to perform interactive I/O in C++. We can inform the C++ compiler that we wish to use this library with the directive

```
#include <iostream.h>
```

In subsequent chapters, we will examine many of the other libraries available in C++.

Output. The **iostream** output statement has the form

```
cout << Value₁ << Value₂ << ... << Valueₙ;
```

where **cout** is the name of an **output stream** associated with the screen and **<<** is an **output operator** that sends ***Value₁*** ... ***Valueₙ*** to the screen. For example, the statement

```
cout << "The revenue generated = $" << Revenue << "\n\n";
```

displays the string of characters

```
The revenue generated = $
```

followed by the value of the variable **Revenue** and then two advances to new lines.

Input. The **iostream** input statement has a slightly different form,

```
cin >> Variable₁ >> Variable₂ >> ... >> Variableₙ;
```

where **cin** is the name of an **input stream** associated with the keyboard and **>>** is the **input operator,** which causes the program to pause until values are entered for $Variable_1$, $Variable_2$, . . ., $Variable_n$. The first value entered is stored in $Variable_1$, the second value in $Variable_2$, and the nth value in $Variable_n$. For example, the statement

```
cin >> Installations >> YardsOfCable;
```

causes execution of the program to be suspended until the user enters two values from the keyboard, which are stored in the variables **Installations** and **YardsOfCable**, respectively.

A simple way to remember the input and output operators is to notice that the input operator points from the stream toward the variables, extracting values for the variables from the stream, whereas the output operator points from the values toward the stream, inserting values into the stream. These operators are therefore sometimes called **extraction** and **insertion** operators, respectively.

Comments

Comments can also be incorporated into C++ programs and may have one of two forms. The first form (carried over from C, the parent language of C++) begins with **/*** and is terminated by ***/**:

```
/* C style comment */
```

This form is most useful when a comment consists of several lines (such as opening documentation). The second form begins with **//** and terminates at the end of the line:

```
// C++ style comment
```

and is useful to document individual lines of a program.

Programming Style

In addition to the simple translation of an algorithm into a program, there are three programming practices that contribute to the development of *correct, readable, and understandable programs.* We conclude this section with a brief discussion of each of these.

1. The first such principle is that *programs should be well structured.* Two helpful guidelines in this regard are:

   - *Use an object-oriented approach when developing a program for a complex problem.* Identify the objects and operations needed to solve the problem. Then construct and encode an algorithm as operations on those objects.
   - *Strive for simplicity and clarity.* Avoid clever programming tricks intended only to demonstrate the programmer's ingenuity or to produce code that executes only slightly more efficiently.

2. The second principle is that *each program unit should be documented.* In particular:

   - *Each program unit should contain opening documentation.* Comments should be placed at the beginning of each program component to explain what that component does, how it works, any special algorithms it uses, a summary of the problem's specification, assumptions, and so on. They should also give other information such as the name of the programmer, the date the program was written and when it was last modified, and references to books and manuals that give additional information about the program.
   - *Comments should also be used to explain key program segments and/or segments whose purpose or design is not obvious.* However, too many detailed or unnecessary comments clutter the program and make it more difficult to read and understand.
   - *Meaningful identifiers should be used.* For example, the statement

     ```
     Wages = HoursWorked * HourlyRate;
     ```

     is more meaningful than

     ```
     W = H * R
     ```

     or

     ```
     X7 = R * ZEKE
     ```

     Don't use "skimpy" abbreviations just to save a few keystrokes when entering the program. Also, follow what has been called the "Shirley Temple principle" and avoid "cute" identifiers such as those in

     ```
     BaconBroughtHome = SlaveLabor * LessThanImWorth;
     ```

     In addition, it is a good practice to explain the constants and variables that are being used in the program.

3. The final principle has to do with a program's appearance. *A program should be aesthetic; it should be formatted in a style that enhances its readability.* The following are some guidelines for good program style:

   - *Use spaces between the items in a statement to make it more readable;* for example, use spaces before and after each operator (+, -, <, =, etc.).
   - *Insert a blank line between sections of a program and wherever appropriate in a sequence of statements to set off blocks of statements.*

- *Adhere rigorously to alignment and indentation guidelines to emphasize the relationship between various parts of the program.* For example, if an output statement requires several lines, indent the second (and subsequent) lines to show that they are part of the previous statement.

It is often difficult for beginning programmers to appreciate the importance of learning good programming habits that lead to the design of readable and understandable programs. The reason for this is that programs written in an academic environment are often quite different from those developed in real-world situations, in which program style and form are critical. Student programs are usually quite small (usually less than a few hundred lines of code); are executed and modified only a few times (almost never, once they have been handed in); are rarely examined in detail by anyone other than the student and the instructor; and are not developed within the context of budget constraints. Real-world programs, however, may be very large (several thousand lines of code); are developed by teams of programmers; are commonly used for long periods of time and thus require maintenance if they are to be kept current and correct; and are often maintained by someone other than the original programmer. As hardware costs continue to decrease and programmer costs increase, the importance of reducing programming and maintenance costs and the corresponding importance of writing programs that can be easily read and understood by others continue to grow.

As we discuss features of C++ in the following chapters, additional principles for program design will be given. It is important for beginning programmers to follow these guidelines, even in early, simple programs, so that good habits are established and carried on into the design of more complex programs.

2.5   Verification and Validation

Obviously the most important characteristic of any program is that it be *correct.* No matter how well structured a program is, how well it is documented, or how nice it looks, if it does not produce correct results, it is worthless. But as we have seen, the fact that a program executes without producing any error messages is no guarantee that it is correct. The results produced may be wrong because of logical errors that the computer system cannot detect.

The detection and correction of errors is an important part of software development and is known as validation and verification. **Validation** is concerned with checking that the algorithms and the program meet the problem's specification. **Verification** refers to checking that they are correct and complete. Validation is sometimes described as answering the question *Are we solving the correct problem?* and verification as answering the question *Are we solving the problem correctly?* In this section, we examine each of the distinct types of errors that can occur in developing software systems.

Compile-Time (Syntax) Errors

For beginning programmers, the most common type of error is the **syntax error,** in which a program contains a ''statement'' that violates one of the grammar or syntax rules of C++. Such errors are detected when the program is compiled.

For example, if the first output statement in Figure 2.1 (that prompts the user to enter values for **Installations** and **YardsOfCable**) were mistakenly entered as

```
cout << "\nPlease enter:"
     << "\n\tthe number of installations, and
     << "\n\tthe yards of cable used.\n";
```

with a missing quote in the second line, an attempt to compile the program may result in a message like the following, signaling a "fatal" error:

```
***** Error: Unterminated string constant
***** Line 23: Probable beginning of unterminated string
```

Although most beginning programmers are upset by syntax errors, they are actually the easiest errors to deal with. Correcting a syntax error is simply a matter of finding the point at which the program violates a C++ grammar rule and correcting the mistake:

```
cout << "\nPlease enter:"
     << "\n\tthe number of installations, and "
     << "\n\tthe yards of cable used.\n";
```

As programmers gain experience, their familiarity with the grammar rules of the programming language being used increases, so syntax errors occur less frequently; when they do occur, they are more easily corrected.

Linking Errors

Errors may also occur when a compiled program is linked to the libraries it uses. A common example occurs in programs on UNIX systems that use the square root function **sqrt()**, whose definition is stored in the math library. This function is declared in the file **<math.h>**, and so a directive

```
#include <math.h>
```

must be used in order for such a program to *compile* correctly. However, such a program will still not *link* correctly, because the (standard) UNIX linker does not automatically search the math library (where the definition of **sqrt()** is stored) but must be instructed to do so using the **-lm** switch (which must be placed at the end of the command line).

A different kind of linking error occurs in Symantec C++ (on the Macintosh), when the resulting executable program is too large. To correct this sort of error, it is usually necessary to move one of the standard libraries (usually **ANSI++** or **IOStream**) out of its segment (in the Project Manager Window) to a new one.

Correcting linking errors often requires more knowledge about the computing system than most beginning programmers have. If your program develops a linking error, find out how to correct the problem from your instructor or system administrator, since the error likely lies outside of your program.

Run-Time Errors

Other errors, such as an attempt to divide by zero in an arithmetic expression, may not be detected until execution of the program begins. Such errors are called **run-time errors** since they only occur when the program is running. Finding such errors is easiest using a symbolic debugger, such as **dbx** or **gdb** on a UNIX system. (Such debuggers are built into both Turbo C++ and Symantec C++ as an integrated part of the environment.) Using such a debugger, one can trace through the execution of the program one statement at a time until the statement generating the error is encountered.[2] In environments without a symbolic debugger, explanations of the run-time error messages displayed by the particular system being used can be found in the user manuals supplied by the manufacturer.

Once the errors have been identified, they must be corrected by replacing the incorrect statements with correct ones, and the modified program must be recompiled, relinked, and reexecuted.

Logical Errors

The most difficult errors to find are errors in the logic of the algorithm, because they stem from mistakes in reasoning about the solution to the problem. Such errors are thus called **logical errors.**

As we saw in Section 2.1, logical errors do not produce error messages—the program simply produces incorrect results. This necessitates **testing** the execution of the program with various sets of test data. It is only by thoroughly testing a program with a wide variety of data values that we can have any confidence that the program does not contain a logical error.

The easiest way to locate a logical error is to use a symbolic debugger to trace the execution of the program. Such debuggers can be used to display the value of a given variable (or expression) at any point during the execution. The correct values can be compared with the computed values, and when a mismatch is found, the source of the logical error has (probably) been found.

An alternative technique for programmers without access to a symbolic debugger is to insert output statements at key points throughout the program to display the values of the variables involved in the computation of the incorrect result. By tracing through the execution by hand (on a paper copy of the program), a mismatch between the output values and the predicted values can be used to find the source of the error.

Finding logical errors takes a great deal of patience. They are most easily avoided by devoting careful attention to the first three stages of the software life cycle: problem analysis and specification, design, and coding.

Life-Critical Systems

For some applications, such as flight-control software on an airliner or the device-control software on an X-ray machine, the occurrence of an error can have fatal consequences. Such software systems are accordingly described as **life-critical systems.**

---

[2] The statement that generates the error is not always the cause of the error. For example, in a divide-by-zero error, the fault typically lies in an earlier statement that resulted in the denominator having a zero value.

Prevention of errors in such systems is of the utmost importance. In some cases, the programmer may be required to provide a formal proof of the correctness of the software system. Constructing such proofs is a topic in upper-level computing courses and is beyond the scope of this introductory text.

2.6   Maintenance

The life cycle of a program written by a student programmer normally ends with the fourth phase; that is, once the program has been written, executed, and tested, the assignment is complete. Programs in real-world applications, however, are often used for several years and are likely to require some modification. Software systems, especially large ones developed for complex projects, often have obscure bugs that were not detected during testing and that surface after the software has been placed in use. One important aspect of software maintenance is fixing such flaws in the software.

It may also be necessary to modify software to improve its performance, to add new features, and so on. Other modifications may be required because of changes in the computer hardware and/or the system software such as the operating system. External factors may also force program modification; for example, changes in the tax laws may mean revising part of a payroll program. These changes are easier to make in systems that are developed as a group of independent (but interacting) components, because the changes can often be made by modifying only a few of the components or by adding new ones.

Software maintenance is an important aspect of the life cycle of software. Studies have shown that in recent years more than 50% of computer center budgets and more than 50% of programmer time have been devoted to software maintenance and that worldwide, billions and perhaps trillions of dollars have been spent on software maintenance. A major factor contributing to this high cost in money and time is that many of the original programs and systems had poor structure, documentation, and style. This problem is complicated by the fact that maintenance must often be done by someone not involved in the original design. It is mandatory, therefore, that programmers do their utmost to design programs and systems of programs that are readable, well documented, and well structured so that they are easy to understand and modify and are thus easier to maintain than is much of the software developed in the past.

Exercises

1. Consider the following algorithm:

1. Initialize X to 0, Y to 5, Z to 25.
2. While $X \leq 4$ do the following:
   a. Set $Y = Z - Y$, $A = X + 1$, and then increment X by 1.
   b. If $A > 1$ then
        Set $Z = Z - 5$, $A = A^2$, and then set $B = Z - Y$.
      End If.
   End Loop.
3. Display A, B, X, Y, and Z.

Complete the following **trace table** for this algorithm, which displays the labels of the statements in the order in which they are executed and the values of the variables at each stage:

Statement	A	B	X	Y	Z
1	?	?	0	5	25
2	''	''	''	''	''
2a	1	''	1	20	''
2b	''	''	''	''	''
2a	2	''	2	5	''
⋮	⋮	⋮	⋮	⋮	⋮
3	''	''	''	''	''

(? = undefined)

2. Construct a trace table similar to that in Exercise 1 for the following algorithm, assuming that the value entered for *A* is (a) 0.1, (b) 0.3, (c) 1.0:

1. Enter *A*.
2. While *A* ≤ 0.3 do the following:
    a. Increment *A* by 0.1.
    b. If *A* ≠ 0.3 then do the following:
        i. Set *S* and *X* to 0, *T* to 1.
        ii. While *T* ≤ 6 do the following:
            (a) Add *T* to *X* and then increment *T* by 2.
        End Loop.
    c. Else do the following:
        i. Set *T* to 0, *X* to 1, and *S* = 3 * *S*.
        ii. While *T* ≤ 5 do the following:
            (a) Increment *T* by 1 and then set *X* = *X* * *T*.
        End Loop.
    End If.
    d. Display *A*, *S*, and *X*.
End Loop.

3. Construct a trace table similar to that in Exercise 1 for the following algorithm, assuming the following data values are entered for *b*, *h*, and *k*:

b	h	k
3	6	1
4	3	2
5	2	0
2	6	2

1. Initialize I, A, and X to 0.
2. While $I \leq 4$ do the following:
   a. Increment I by 1.
   b. Enter b, h, k.
   c. If $k \geq 1$ then do the following:
      i. Set $A = \dfrac{bh}{2}$.
      ii. If $k \geq 2$ then do the following:
         (a) Set $X = \dfrac{bh^3}{36}$.
       End If.
     End If.
   d. Display I, b, h, A, and X.
 End Loop.

For each of the problems described in Exercises 4 through 11, identify the input values, constant values, and output values. Then describe the data objects and operations needed to solve the problem and design an algorithm for it.

4. Calculate and display the largest and the smallest of three given test scores.

5. Calculate and display the largest value, the smallest value, and the range (largest value minus the smallest value) for any given set of numbers.

6. The business manager of a certain company wants a program to calculate the wages for the company's employees. This program should accept an employee number, base pay rate per hour, and the number of hours worked. All hours above 40 are to be paid at the overtime rate of 1.5 times the base rate. For each employee, the program should print the employee number, total number of hours worked, base pay rate, and total wages, and it should also print the total of all wages paid by the company.

7. A certain city classifies a pollution index of less than 35 as pleasant, 35 through 60 as unpleasant, and above 60 as hazardous. The city's pollution control officer desires a program that will accept several values of the pollution index and produce the appropriate classification for each.

8. Suppose that a professor gave a quiz to her class and compiled a list of scores ranging from 50 through 100. She intends to use only three grades: A if the score is 90 or above, B if it is below 90 but above or equal to 75, and C if it is below 75. She would like a program to assign the appropriate letter grades to the numeric scores.

9. The "divide and average" algorithm for approximating the square root of any positive number A is as follows: Take any initial approximation X that is positive, and then find a new approximation by calculating the average of X and A/X, that is, $(X + A/X)/2$. Repeat this procedure with X replaced by this new approximation, stopping when X and A/X differ in absolute value by some specified error allowance, such as 0.00001.

10. Several quadratic equations of the form $Ax^2 + Bx + C = 0$ are to be solved or it is to be determined that no real solutions exist. If the discriminant $B^2 - 4AC$ is positive, the equation has two real solutions given by the quadratic formula

$$\frac{-B \pm \sqrt{B^2 - 4AC}}{2A}$$

If the discriminant is zero, the equation has one real solution, $-B/2A$, and if the discriminant is negative, there are no real solutions.

11. The Rinky Dooflingy Company currently sells 200 dooflingies per month, at a profit of $300 per dooflingy. The company now spends $2000 per month on advertising and has a fixed operating cost of $10,000 per month that does not depend on the volume of sales. If the company doubles the amount spent on advertising, its sales will increase by 20%. The company president would like to know, beginning with the company's current status and successively doubling the amount spend on advertising, at what point the net profit will "go over the hump," that is, begin to decline.

COMPUTING WITH SIMPLE OBJECTS

In Chapters 3 through 7, we begin our study of computing and programming in C++. These chapters introduce the basics of solving problems using simple data objects that can be represented using the C++ fundamental types. Chapter 3 introduces these types and the operations that can be applied to them to form expressions. Chapter 4 extends the discussion of expressions by showing how the programmer can define functions to implement operations not provided in C++. This chapter also introduces separately compiled libraries, which are used to store functions so that they can be easily reused. Chapter 5 introduces the C++ if and switch statements and illustrates how they can be used to solve problems that require selective execution of parts of a program. Chapter 6 introduces the for, while, do-while, and forever loops, and shows how they can be used to solve problems that require repetition of parts of a program. Finally, Chapter 7 presents an in-depth look at several function-related topics, including parameter passing, identifier scope, overloading function names with multiple definitions, and recursion. Together, these chapters provide an introduction to computational problem solving using simple data objects.

GETTING STARTED WITH EXPRESSIONS

Kindly enter them in your notebook.
And, in order to refer to them conveniently,
*   let's call them A, B, and Z.*
THE TORTOISE IN LEWIS CARROLL'S
What the Tortoise Said to Achilles

In language, clarity is everything.
CONFUCIUS

A little inaccuracy sometimes saves tons of explanation.
SAKI (H.H. MUNROE)

CHAPTER CONTENTS

An important part of using a computer to solve a problem is encoding the algorithm for solving that problem as a program. Whereas algorithms can be described somewhat informally in a pseudoprogramming language, the corresponding program must be written in strict compliance with the rules of some programming language. In this chapter, we begin a detailed study of the language C++.

As we noted in Chapter 1, C++, developed in the late 1970s and early 1980s by Bell Labs' scientist Bjarne Stroustrup, has become a popular programming language. For most languages (Pascal and C, for example), the American National Standards Institute (ANSI) has established language standards that precisely specify these languages. Unfortunately, as of this writing, the ANSI standard for C++ has not yet appeared.

In the absence of any official standard, we have prepared this text using two strategies:

1. We have used the latest editions of

   ■ *The C++ Programming Language,* 2nd ed. (1992), by Stroustrup
   ■ *The Annotated C++ Reference Manual* (1990), by Ellis and Stroustrup

   as principal references in preparing the text.[1]

2. The sample programs in this text have been tested in the following C++ environments:

   ■ GNU's g++ (for the UNIX environment), by The Free Software Foundation
   ■ Turbo C++® (for the IBM PC environment), by Borland
   ■ Symantec C++™ (for the Macintosh environment), by Symantec

One purpose of this text is to provide an introduction to the discipline of programming and problem solving using C++ as the programming language. Our descriptions of C++ are presented at a level that assumes no prior programming experience, and consequently, our descriptions of the language features are often simplified. The programs presented as examples (especially in the introductory chapters) have been chosen to illustrate particular constructs in the language. Wherever possible, such programs solve problems using the most appropriate features of C++. However, sometimes the C++ features that are most appropriate for solving a problem have not yet been introduced. In these cases, we solve the problem using features of C++ that have been discussed and defer a more appropriate solution until later.

3.1   C++ Programs

A **program** is a collection of statements written in a programming language. Just as there are English *grammar rules* that determine whether or not a sentence written in English is formed correctly, there are C++ grammar rules that determine whether or not C++ statements are well formed.

---

[1] B. Stroustrup, *The C++ Programming Language,* Second Edition, Addison-Wesley (1992).
M. A. Ellis, B. Stroustrup, *The Annotated C++ Reference Manual,* Addison-Wesley (1990).

Examples of Programs

The shortest syntactically correct C++ program is given in Figure 3.1.

 FIGURE 3.1 The null program.

```
main()
{
}
```

We call this program **the null program** because it contains no statements. The null program does nothing useful and is therefore not very interesting, except as an example of what components a C++ program minimally *must* contain and as a starting point for understanding the ideas behind C++ programs.

A more interesting program is given in Figure 3.2. This program computes the volume of a sphere with a given radius using the formula $V = 4\pi r^3/3$. We use these programs as illustrations in the sections that follow.

 FIGURE 3.2 Calculating the volume of a sphere.

```
/* This program computes the volume of a sphere.

    Input:  The radius of the sphere.
    Output: The volume of the sphere.
----------------------------------------------------------------*/

#include <iostream.h>
#include <math.h>

int main(void)
{
   const double
      Pi = 3.1416;                        // the mathematical constant

   cout << "\nPlease enter the radius of a sphere: ";

   double
      Radius;

   cin >> Radius;


   double
      Volume = 4.0 * Pi * pow(Radius, 3.0) / 3.0;

   cout << "\nThe volume of that sphere is " << Volume << "\n\n";

   return 0;
}
```

The Main Function

A C++ program is actually a **function.** The concept of function is a fundamental idea in mathematics. For example, the mathematical notation

$$f(x) = x^2$$

is used to describe the simple mathematical function of squaring a value x. In this example, f is the name of the function, and the variable x that appears inside the parentheses is called a **parameter** of the function. The *behavior* of the function is described in terms of its parameter x by "square the value of x." Thus, when $x = 2$, $f(x) = 4$; when $x = 3$, $f(x) = 9$, and so on. In the first case, we say that the **return value** of f is 4, whereas in the second case, the return value is 9. *The return value of a function is determined by its definition and by the values of its parameters.*

    C++ functions are like mathematical functions. They minimally consist of a name followed by a pair of parentheses, which enclose the parameters of the function. Following the parentheses is a pair of **braces.** The opening brace, {, marks the beginning of the statements that describe the function's behavior and the closing brace, }, marks the end of the statements.

    The program in Figure 3.1 consists of a single C++ function whose name is the keyword **main** and that has no parameters. This function, **main()**, which is required in all C++ programs, is called the **main function** of a program. Execution of a program begins at the first statement after the opening brace of the main function and proceeds through the statements that follow it. When the closing brace of the main function is reached, execution terminates. Thus, execution of the null program in Figure 3.1 produces nothing, since there are no statements within the braces.

    In contrast, the program in Figure 3.2 contains a main function with the form

```
int main(void)

{

    a list of C++ statements

}
```

Comparing this main function with that in Figure 3.1, we note three major differences:

1. The keyword **main** is preceded by the keyword **int**.
2. The keyword **void** appears inside the parentheses.
3. The braces have C++ statements between them (instead of being empty).

To understand these differences, we must know more about C++ functions.

    The general form of a C++ function definition is as follows.

C++ Function Definition

Form:

```
ReturnType FunctionName( ParameterList )
{
    StatementList
}
```

where:
> *ReturnType* is the type of value returned by the
> function or the keyword **void**;
> *FunctionName* is the name of the function;
> *ParameterList* is a list of the parameters of the
> function or the keyword **void**;
> *StatementList* is a sequence of statements de-
> scribing the behavior of the function.

Purpose:
Defines a function. A call to the function causes
execution of the statements in the statement list and
a return to the calling program unit after execution
of the function is terminated, usually by encountering a **return** statement.

In the program in Figure 3.2, the keyword **int** in the function heading

```
int main(void)
```

specifies the return type of the function and indicates to the compiler that the main
function returns an integer. (Although **int** is the default return type of the main
function in most implementations of C++, it is always a good idea to state this
return type explicitly.) The return value of a main function is used to indicate to the
operating system the program's *exit status,* that is, whether it terminated normally
or abnormally. In many operating systems, a return value of zero indicates that the
program terminated *normally,* and other return values (such as −1) indicate that it
terminated *abnormally.* The **return statement** at the end of the program in Figure
3.2,

```
return 0;
```

causes the main function to terminate and return the value zero.

The keyword **void** is a special C++ keyword that in this context indicates the
absence of parameters. When a function has no parameters, like **main()** in Figure
3.2, **void** is used for its parameter list to indicate this. For the present discussion,
leaving the parameter list empty and using **void** for the parameter list are equivalent. However, in some implementations of C++, there are advanced situations
where the two are not the same, and so the word **void** should always be used when
a function is to have no parameters.

The third major difference between the main functions in Figures 3.1 and 3.2 is
that the latter contains several statements between the braces. These statements are
described in the next several sections.

3.2 Programming with Libraries—Not Reinventing the Wheel

"Reinventing the wheel" refers to remaking something that has already been
made, redoing something that has already been done, resolving a problem that has

already been solved, and so on. In computer science the term usually refers to designing an algorithm, function, or program to solve a problem that has already been solved.

One of the major aims of the designers of C++ was to make it easy to reuse program components and thus avoid reinventing the wheel. The idea is to anticipate what parts of a program might be needed again and to store these components in a kind of software **library,** from which they can be retrieved and used when needed. This saves time and money in the development of software because it simplifies the task of programming by allowing programmers to reuse the work they or others have done.

Libraries

A library has two parts:

1. An **interface,** which specifies what items are in the library and how they are used. This part of the library is stored in a special file called a **header file.**
2. An **implementation,** which contains the definitions of most of the items in the library. These definitions are often stored in another file, called an **implementation file.** The contents of this file are usually not available to users of the library.

One of the convenient features of C++ is the large number of libraries provided with the language. There are literally dozens of libraries already written and available for use that put the objects and operations written by professional programmers at our fingertips. The header files for the libraries that are available are usually stored in a special directory named `include`. For example, in our Turbo C++ environment, they are stored in the directory

```
F:\TC\INCLUDE
```

In our GNU g++ environment, these files are stored in two directories:

```
/usr/local/lib/g++-include
```
 and
```
/usr/local/lib/gcc/include
```

In our Symantec C++ environment, these files are stored in the folder:

```
RC44:Development:Symantec C++:Standard Libraries:C++ headers
```

The contents of such libraries are more fully described in the C++ reference manuals for your system, and you should familiarize yourself with their capabilities, since they can save a great deal of time and effort in solving common problems.

Using a Library

A library whose header file is stored in the special `include` directory on your system can be used in a C++ program by using the **#include compiler directive** to insert the contents of that interface into the program. For example, the directive

```
#include <iostream.h>
```

in Figure 3.2 inserts the header file **<iostream.h>** into the program. This file contains the declarations of all the objects and operations required for interactive I/O in C++. (We discuss these objects and operations in greater detail in Section 3.6.) The angle brackets **<** and **>** surrounding the name of the header file inform the C++ compiler that the file **iostream.h** is located in the system's special **include** directory. In the same way, the other **#include** directive

```
#include <math.h>
```

inserts the header file **<math.h>** from the system's **include** directory into the program. This file contains the declarations of several mathematical functions, including the function **pow(x, n)** that computes the value x^n. The program in Figure 3.2 needs these declarations, since without them, function **pow** would be undefined.

Linking to a Library

Programs that do not use libraries can be translated into executable form simply by giving the appropriate compile command. Translating a program that uses one or more libraries, however, consists of two separate phases:

1. *Compiling* the program, which produces an **object program**
2. *Linking* any objects that are defined outside of the program with their definitions to produce an **executable program**

This linking phase involves two steps:

2a. Searching the libraries used by a program for the definitions of the objects the program uses
2b. Linking those objects with their definitions

For example, **cin** and **cout** are the names of objects that are used in the program in Figure 3.2 but that are defined outside the program in the **iostream** library. Translation of this program requires that these objects be linked to their definitions, since otherwise they will be undefined when the program uses them. Unfortunately, different C++ environments search libraries differently, and you should ask your instructor or system administrator about the search rules used on your system.[2]

---

[2] GNU C++ automatically searches its standard library (**libg++.a**) but (by default) does not search many of the other libraries. Because the program in Figure 3.2 uses a function from the math library (whose name is **libm.a**), the compile command must be modified to direct the linker to search this library. For example, in the command

```
g++ Figure3-2.C -o Figure3-2 -lm
```

the **-lm** switch directs the linker to search the math library **libm.a** as well as the standard libraries.

By contrast, the Turbo C++ **Make** facility (on the **Compile** menu) automatically searches its math library (**MATHx.LIB**) if a program includes its header file. Compiling the program in Figure 3.2 is thus the same as compiling any other program in the Turbo environment.

A still different approach is used by Symantec C++, which does not automatically search any standard libraries. Each library that you wish to use must be explicitly located and placed into the Project Manager Window (using the **Add Files...** choice from the **Source** menu). Most of the programs in this text require the presence of three libraries in the Symantec environment: **ANSI++**, **CPlusLib**, and **IOStreams**.

3.3 Declarations: Types of Objects

As we discussed in Chapter 2, the process of programming involves identifying the data objects used by a program, identifying what operations on those data objects are needed, and then constructing and encoding algorithms that manipulate those data objects. We also mentioned that C++ requires that the types of the data objects in a program be specified, or **declared,** before those objects are used. In this section, we examine the fundamental types provided by C++.

Fundamental Types

The fundamental data types provided by C++ are as follows:

- **Characters:** letters, digits, symbols and punctuation, declared as type `char`
- **Integers:** whole numbers and their negatives, declared as `int`
- **Integer variations**: variations such as `short`, `long`, and `unsigned`
- **Reals:** numbers with a decimal point, declared as `float`, `double`, or `long double`

C++ provides this diversity so that different types of data can be processed and memory can be used most efficiently. Table 3.1 shows the storage typically allocated for each of the fundamental types.

TABLE 3.1   The C++ Fundamental Types

Type	Number of Bits
`char`	8
`short int`	16
`int`	the word size of the machine
`long int`	32
`float`	32
`double`	64
`long double`	Implementation dependent (but commonly 96 or 128)

We now discuss these types in detail.

Character Values. The `char` type is used to process characters in the machine's character set (commonly the ASCII character set shown in Appendix A). This includes the uppercase letters **A** through **Z**; lowercase letters **a** through **z**; common punctuation symbols such as the semicolon (**;**), comma (**,**), and period (**.**); and special symbols such as +, =, >, and @.

As we saw in Chapter 1, characters are represented in memory by their numeric codes, and in C++, values of type `char` are stored using these integer codes. (See Potential Problem 2 at the end of this chapter to see how this can lead to confusion.) **Character constants** are usually written in C++ as single character symbols enclosed in single quotes (apostrophes). For example,

`'A', '+', '3', '@'`

are all examples of C++ character constants. The C++ compiler stores such constants using their numeric codes, which in ASCII are

65, 43, 51, and 124

respectively.

Using a single quote as a delimiter raises the question, What is the character constant for a single quote? A similar question arises for characters such as the newline character, for which there is no corresponding character symbol. As we mentioned in Chapter 2, C++ provides **escape sequences** for those characters that have a special purpose and cannot be described using the normal approach. For example, the character constant for a single quote can be written as

`'\''`

and the newline character by

`'\n'`

Table 3.2 lists the escape sequences provided in C++.

TABLE 3.2   C++ Character Escape Sequences

Character	C++ Escape Sequence
Newline	`\n`
Horizontal tab	`\t`
Vertical tab	`\v`
Backspace	`\b`
Form feed	`\f`
Alert	`\a`
Backslash	`\\`
Question mark	`\?`
Single quote	`\'`
Double quote	`\"`
Null character	`\0`
With octal code *ooo*	`\ooo`
With hexadecimal code **x*hhh***	`\x*hhh*`

As the last entries in the table indicate, any character in the character set can be described by an escape sequence using its octal or hexadecimal code (see Appendix A). For example, if ASCII is being used, the octal code for **A** is 101, so that

`'A'`

and

`'\101'`

refer to the same character constant (uppercase **A**). Similarly,

    '3'

and

    '\063'

represent the same character constant in ASCII (the digit **3**).

Character String Constants.   A different, but related, type of constant is the string constant, which consists of a sequence of characters enclosed in double quotes. For example,

```
"Hello, there"
"\nPlease enter the radius of a sphere: "
"\n\tThe revenue = $"
"Joe said to me, \"I have a cold today.\""
```

are all string constants. Note that escape sequences can be used within string constants. The double newline character string constant

```
"\n\n"
```

can be used to separate lines of output with blank lines, making the output more readable. For example, consider the output of a string constant of the form

```
"XXXXXXXX\n\n"
```

The first newline ends the line on which **XXXXXXXX** appears and the second newline makes the next line a blank line:

XXXXXXXX

Subsequent output starts on a new line.

Inserting blank lines into output is a simple way to make it easier to read.

Integer Values.   As indicated in Table 3.1, the number of bits used to store an **int** value depends on the word size of the machine: Usually, a 16-bit machine will store **int** values using 16 bits, whereas a 32-bit machine will use 32 bits. This can cause portability problems, because a program that uses **int** values may execute correctly on one machine and not on another. To deal with this problem, C++ allows **int** declarations to be modified with one of the key words **short** or **long**. These modifiers have the following effects:

- A **short int** is (usually) a 16-bit value, ranging from -32768 ($= -2^{15}$) through 32767 ($= 2^{15} - 1$).

- A **long int** is (usually) a 32-bit value,[3] ranging from -2147483648 $(= -2^{31})$ through 2147483647 $(= 2^{31} - 1)$.

Programmers who are concerned with efficiency and portability can use **short int** (or just **short**) for integer data objects with relatively small values and **long int** (or simply **long**) for those that may have larger values.

Recall from Chapter 1 that the internal representation of an integer typically uses one bit as a **sign bit,** so that the largest positive value of a 16-bit integer is $2^{15} - 1$ and not $2^{16} - 1$. However, some data objects never have negative values. For example, in the mean time to failure problem in Chapter 2, the number of failure times processed is always nonnegative. To avoid wasting the sign bit on data objects whose values are never negative, C++ provides the integer modifier **unsigned**:

- An **unsigned short int** is (usually) a 16-bit value, ranging from 0 through 65535 $(=2^{16} - 1)$.
- An **unsigned long int** is (usually) a 32-bit value, ranging from 0 through 4294967295 $(= 2^{32} - 1)$.
- An **unsigned int** is (usually) a nonnegative integer whose size is the word size of the particular machine being used.

In our discussion of number systems in Chapter 1, we noted the importance of base-2, base-8, and base-16 number systems in computing. To allow a programmer to use these systems, C++ provides different kinds of integer constants for these three number systems:

- A digit sequence that begins with a **0** (zero) is an **octal** (base-8) integer constant.
- A digit sequence that begins with **0x** is a **hexadecimal** (base-16) integer constant.
- Any other digit sequence is a **decimal** (base-10) integer constant.

For example, the constant

    12

has the decimal value $12_{10} = 1 \times 10^1 + 2 \times 10^0$, but the constant

    012

has the octal value $12_8 = 1 \times 8^1 + 2 \times 8^0 = 10_{10}$, and

    0x12

has the hexadecimal value $12_{16} = 1 \times 16^1 + 2 \times 16^0 = 18_{10}$. Table 3.3 is a quick guide to the C++ representation of integer values in the three bases.

---

[3] On some machines, a **long int** may be stored in 64 bits instead of 32.

TABLE 3.3   C++ Integer Constants

Decimal	Octal	Hexadecimal
0	0	0x0
1	01	0x1
2	02	0x2
3	03	0x3
4	04	0x4
5	05	0x5
6	06	0x6
7	07	0x7
8	010	0x8
9	011	0x9
10	012	0xA
11	013	0xB
12	014	0xC
13	015	0xD
14	016	0xE
15	017	0xF
16	020	0x10
17	021	0x11
18	022	0x12
19	023	0x13
20	024	0x14

Real Values. C++ provides three sizes of real values:

- **float**, (usually) a 32-bit real value
- **double**, (usually) a 64-bit real value
- **long double**, typically a 96-bit or a 128-bit real value[4]

The type used for a data object depends on the degree of precision required for that data object. The range of values and the precision of each of these types is implementation-dependent. They are defined in one of the standard header files **float.h** or **limits.h** that C++ implementations provide.

Like most programming languages, C++ provides two different ways of representing a real value, fixed-point notation and floating-point notation. A **fixed-point** real constant consists of

- An integer part,
- A decimal point, and
- A fractional part,

where either the integer part or the fractional part (but not both) can be omitted. For example,

```
5.0
0.5
5.
.5
```

are all valid fixed-point real constants in C++.

---

[4] There are also some C++ environments that implement long double as 80-bit values.

Scientists often write very large or very small real numbers using a special notation called *exponential, scientific,* or *floating-point* notation. For example, a scientist might write the number 12 billion (12,000,000,000) as:

$$0.12 \times 10^{11}$$

In C++, a **floating-point** real constant consists of

- An integer or fixed-point real constant, followed by
- Either the character **e** or **E**, and
- An integer exponent (that can be positive or negative).

For example, 12 billion,

$$0.12 \times 10^{11}$$

can be written in C++ in any of the following forms:

```
0.12e11
.12E11
12.0E9
12.e9
12E9
```

An unexpected feature of C++ is that all real constants (whether fixed or floating-point) are of type **double**. This means that if a value is computed using real constants and assigned to a **float** variable, then the value stored in the variable does not have the precision of the computed value. For this reason, many programmers never use the type **float** and instead always use the type **double** for real variables.

If, for some reason, it is necessary to have a real constant with a non**double** value, **f** or **F** can be appended to the constant to make it of type **float**, and **l** or **L** can be appended to make it a **long double**. Thus,

```
1.0F
0.1e1f
```

are both **float** constants, and

```
1.0l
0.1E1L
```

are both **long double** constants. (Note the difference between 1 (one) and l (ell).)

Identifiers

We have given *names* to most of the data objects used in the programs considered thus far. The names given to the various objects in a program are called **identifiers.**

C++ identifiers should begin with a letter, which may be followed by any number of letters, digits, or underscores.[5] *This allows the user to choose meaningful*

---

[5] Identifiers that begin with an underscore (_) or contain *consecutive* underscores (_ _) are reserved for special use and should be avoided.

identifiers that describe the data object being represented. For example, the identifier

    Radius

is more meaningful than the identifier

    R

which could stand for radius, reaction time, rate of pay, recycled material, roentgens, etc. Identifiers should be as descriptive as possible, because such identifiers make programs much easier to read.

C++ is case sensitive—that is, it distinguishes between uppercase and lowercase. For example,

    RADIUS
    radius
    Radius
    RaDiUs

are four different identifiers in C++. One must be careful to use the same name consistently.

Different programmers adopt different conventions regarding the use of uppercase, lowercase, and underscores in forming identifiers. For example, some programmers distinguish constant identifiers by writing them using all uppercase letters, whereas others use all lowercase. Some will write class names with their first letter capitalized, and others write them in all lowercase. Each person adopts a particular convention because he or she believes that it enhances the readability of the programs—an admirable goal. Unfortunately, what enhances the readability for one programmer makes reading a program more difficult for another programmer.

The convention that we use throughout this text is to capitalize the first letter of an identifier and write the rest of the letters in lowercase. If an identifier is made up of several words, we capitalize the first letter of each word. This practice makes it easy to distinguish the identifiers from the C++ keywords (**const**, **int**, **long**, etc.), which are lowercase and may not be used as identifiers (because they have a predefined meaning in C++). A complete list of the C++ keywords is given in Appendix B.

The keywords of a programming language (**int**, **const**, **double**, etc.) are words whose meanings are built into the compiler. An identifier is any word whose meaning is not built into the compiler, such as the names given to data objects in programs. If we wish to use a particular identifier in a program, we must provide the compiler with the meaning of that identifier before it is used for the first time. This is accomplished by using a **declaration statement.** Thus far, we have seen two kinds of identifiers, those for constant data objects and those for variable data objects, and we now examine their declarations in greater detail.

Named Constants

We have seen that C++ permits the declaration of data objects whose values are constant. This is particularly useful for universal constants, such as the geometric constant π or the base of natural logarithms, e,

```
const long double
    Pi = 3.141592653589793L;      // the geometric constant

const double
    e = 2.71828182846;            // the base for natural logs
```

but it is also useful for describing any data object whose value remains fixed during the execution of a program:

```
const int
    Year = 2001;                  // A Space Odyssey

const char                        // named char constants:
    MyMiddleInitial = 'C',        //     using a normal character
    FormFeed = '\f',              //     using form-feed's escape sequence
    SpaceBar = '\040';            //     using space's octal ASCII code

const double
    SpeedOfLight = 2.997925e8;    // real in scientific notation
```

In general, a **constant declaration** has the following form:

Constant Declaration

Form:

```
const Type
    ConstantName = Expression;
```

where:
  const is a C++ keyword;
  Type may be any type that is known to the compiler;
  ConstantName is a valid C++ identifier; and
  Expression is any valid expression (see Section 3.4) whose value is the same type as **Type**.

Purpose:
Declares and provides a value for a named constant. Any attempt to change this value within a program is an error.

There are two important reasons for using named constants instead of the constant values they represent. One reason is *improved readability*. To illustrate, consider which of the following statements is more readable:

```
PopulationChange = (0.1758 - 0.1257) * Population;
```

or

```
PopulationChange = (BirthRate - DeathRate) * Population;
```

If we define the named constants **BirthRate** and **DeathRate** by

```
const double
   BirthRate = 0.1758;      // rate at which people are born
   DeathRate = 0.1257;      // rate at which people die
```

we can use the second statement, and that part of the program becomes much easier to understand.

A second benefit of using named constants is that they *faciliate program modification.* To illustrate, suppose that you are solving a problem that uses a certain population's birth and death rates and that you use the values **0.1758** and **0.1257** throughout your program. Suppose further that new values are published for the birth and death rates of the population you are studying. To incorporate these new values into your program, you must find each occurrence of the old values and replace each of them with the new values.

If you had instead declared named constants such as **BirthRate** and **DeathRate** and used them throughout your program, you would simply change the declaration of **BirthRate** and **DeathRate**:

```
const double
   BirthRate = 0.1813;      // rate at which people are born
   DeathRate = 0.1195;      // rate at which people die
```

That's all there is to it: Changing the value of **BirthRate** and **DeathRate** in the declaration changes their values throughout the program, without any further effort on your part.

It is considered good programming practice to *place all declarations of named constants at the beginning of the function in which they are used.* This makes it easy to locate these declarations when it is necessary to modify the value of a named constant.

Named constants for character strings are slightly different from those for other types. To illustrate, consider the declarations

```
const char
   Name[] = "John D. Doe",
   Greeting[] = "Hi there !\n";
```

In these declarations, the identifiers **Name** and **Greeting** are followed by a pair of *brackets.* These brackets inform the compiler that the constant is not just a single character, but a string of characters.

In addition to programmer-defined named constants, C++ provides many predefined named constants in its various libraries. A few of these are listed in Table 3.4. This list is by no means exhaustive; for example, in addition to the minimum and maximum of each of the real types, **float.h** contains constants for the precision of each real type, the minimum and maximum exponent permitted in scientific notation, and so on.

TABLE 3.4 Some C++ Predefined Constants

Constant Name	Description	Header File
INT_MIN	Minimum **int** value	limits.h
INT_MAX	Maximum **int** value	limits.h
UINT_MIN	Minimum **unsigned int** value	limits.h
UINT_MAX	Maximum **unsigned int** value	limits.h
LONG_MIN	Minimum **long int** value	limits.h
LONG_MAX	Maximum **long int** value	limits.h
FLT_MIN	Minimum **float** value	float.h
FLT_MAX	Maximum **float** value	float.h
DBL_MIN	Minimum **double** value	float.h
DBL_MAX	Maximum **double** value	float.h
LDBL_MIN	Minimum **long double** value	float.h
LDBL_MAX	Maximum **long double** value	float.h

Variables

As scientists study the world, they discover relationships that exist between the objects they are studying. Such relationships can often be expressed by a *formula.* For example, the formula

$$V = \frac{4}{3}\pi R^3$$

describes the relationship between the volume (denoted by V) of a sphere and its radius (denoted by R). These symbolic names, V and R, are called **variables.** If a specific value is substituted for R, then this formula can be used to calculate V, the volume of a sphere with radius R.

Variables were used in Chapter 2 in our discussion of algorithms and programs. When a variable is used in a C++ program, the compiler associates it with a particular memory location. The value of a variable at any time is the value stored in the associated memory location at that time. One might think of a variable and its memory location as a mailbox, with the name of the variable on the outside and the values of the variable placed inside:

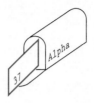

Variable names are identifiers and thus must follow the rules for forming valid identifiers.

As we saw in Chapter 2, a **variable declaration** indicates to the compiler the kind of data that a variable data object is to contain by associating a type with that variable. It has the following form.

Variable Declaration

Form:

> *Type*
>> *VariableName;*

where:
> *Type* may be any type that is known to the compiler; and
> *VariableName* is a valid C++ identifier.

Purpose:
Instructs the C++ compiler to reserve sufficient memory to store a value of type *Type* and associate that memory with the name *VariableName*.

For example, the following are all valid declarations of variables that might be used to store information about a student:

```
long int
   IdNumber;
double
   CumulativeHours,
   HoursThisTerm,
   GPA;
short int
   Year;
```

The type specified for a variable enables the compiler to associate the proper amount of memory with the variable. For example, it would be wasteful to use 4 bytes to store a character when a single byte is sufficient or 8 bytes to store a small integer when 2 are sufficient. Accordingly, the type of a C++ variable must be one of the data types described previously (or one of the other data types to be discussed later).

C++ allows variable declarations to be placed (almost) anywhere before their first use in a function body. Thus, in Figure 3.2, we wrote

```
   .
   .
   .
cout << "\nPlease enter the radius of a sphere: ";

double
   Radius;

cin >> Radius;

double
   Volume = 4.0 * Pi * pow(Radius, 3.0) / 3.0;
   .
   .
   .
```

in which we have

1. An output statement,
2. A declaration of the variable **Radius**,
3. An input statement, and
4. A declaration of the variable **Volume**.

Of course, C++ does not prohibit declaring all variables at the beginning of the function, as some programmers do, preferring to keep all their declarations together. As an example, consider

```
    .
    .
    .
int main(void)
{
    const double
        Pi = 3.14159;

    double
        Radius,
        Volume;

    cout << "\nPlease enter the radius of a sphere: ";

    cin >> Radius;

    Volume = 4.0 * Pi * pow(Radius, 3.0) / 3.0;
    .
    .
    .
```

Where variable declarations are placed is largely a matter of programming style. In this text, we usually declare variables just before they are first used rather than at the beginning of a function, because we find that in the process of coding a program, we occasionally require data objects beyond those anticipated in our original design. This practice also makes it easier to ensure that we are using the variable in a manner consistent with its type.

It is good programming practice to use meaningful variable names that suggest what they represent, since this makes the program more readable and easier to understand. It is also good practice to include a **data dictionary** *consisting of brief comments that indicate what the variables represent, how they are to be used, and so on.* The following declarations illustrate:

```
                                    Data dictionary
                                          ↓
long int
    IdNumber;               // Student Id Number
double
    CumulativeHours,        // Total credits earned to date
    HoursThisTerm,          // Credits this semester
    GPA;                    // Cumulative grade point average
short int
    Year;                   // 1 - freshman, 2 - sophomore
                            // 3 - junior, 4 - senior, 5 - continuing
```

Variable Initialization

We have seen that initial values may be assigned to variables when they are declared. The general form of an initialization declaration is as follows.

Initialization Declaration

Form:

> *Type*
>> *VariableName* = *Expression*;

where:

> ***Expression*** is any valid expression (see Section 3.4) whose value is the same type as ***Type***.

Purpose:
This statement declares and provides an intial value for a variable.

The following are thus valid variable initializations:

```
int
    i = 0,
    j = i + 1;
double
    GPA = 4.0;
char
    LetterGrade = 'A';
```

Variable initialization takes place when execution passes through the declarations. Thus, if the preceding declarations are in the main function of a program, `i` will be initialized with the integer value `1`, `j` with the integer value `1`, `GPA` with the real value `4.0`, and `LetterGrade` with the character `A` when execution passes through these declarations.

Exercises

1. Which of the following are valid C++ identifiers?

(a) XRay	**(b)** X-Ray	**(c)** Jeremiah	**(d)** R2D2
(e) 3M	**(f)** PDQ123	**(g)** PS.175	**(h)** x
(i) 4	**(j)** N/4	**(k)** $M	**(l)** ZZZZZZ
(m) night	**(n)** ngiht	**(o)** nite	**(p)** to day

2. Classify each of the following as an integer constant, real constant, or neither:

(a) 12	**(b)** 12.	**(c)** 12.0	**(d)** '12'
(e) 8+4	**(f)** -3.7	**(g)** 3.7-	**(h)** 1,024
(i) +1	**(j)** $3.98	**(k)** 0.357E4	**(l)** 24E0
(m) E3	**(n)** five	**(o)** 3E.5	**(p)** .000001
(q) 1.2 x 10	**(r)** -(-1)	**(s)** 0E0	**(t)** 1/2

3. Which of the following are valid string constants?

(a) "X"　　　　　(b) "123"　　　　(c) IS"　　　　　(d) "too yet"

(e) "DO\"ESNT"　(f) "isn't"　　　(g) "constant"　　(h) "$1.98"

(i) "DON\'T"　　(j) "12 + 34"　　(k) "\'twas"　　　(l) "\"A\"\"B\"\"C\""

4. For each of the following, write declarations to name each given constant with the specified name.

(a) 1.25 with the name **Rate**

(b) 40.0 with the name **RegHours** and 1.5 with the name **OvertimeFactor**

(c) 1776 with the name **Year**, the letter F with **Female**, and a blank character with **Blank**

(d) 0 with **Zero**, * with **Asterisk**, an apostrophe with **Apostrophe**, and the string **Computer Science** with **Course**

5. Write variable declarations for each of the following.

(a) **Item**, **Number**, and **Job** of type **double**

(b) **ShoeSize** of type **int**

(c) **Mileage** of type **double**, **Cost** and **Distance** of type **unsigned int**

(d) **Alpha** and **Beta** of type **long int**, **Code** of type **char**, and **Root** of type **double**

6. For each of the following, write declarations to declare each variable to have the specified type and initial value:

(a) **NumberOfDeposits** and **NumberOfChecks** to be of type **int**, each with an initial value of **0**; **TotalDeposits** and **TotalChecks** to be of type **double**, each with an initial value of **0.0**; and **ServiceCharge** to be of type **double** with an initial value of **0.25**

(b) **Symbol1** and **Symbol2** to be of type **char** and with a blank character and a semicolon for initial value, respectively; and **Debug** to be of type **char** with an initial value of **T**

7. Write constant declarations that associate the value **1900** with the name **Year** and the string **Nat'l Science** with **FieldOfStudy** and variable declarations that declare **Number** and **Prime** to be of integer type and **Initial** to be of character type.

3.4 Numeric Expressions

In the preceding section, we considered variables and constants of various types and saw that they can be initialized using expressions. In C++ an **expression** is a sequence of one or more data objects called *operands* and zero or more *operators* that combine to produce a value. For example, is an expression that consists of one data object (**12**) and no operators and has the integer value 12. Similarly,

     2.2 + 3.3

is an expression that consists of two operands, **2.2** and **3.3**, and one operator (**+**) and produces the real value 5.5.

     In this section, we examine the arithmetic operators and functions that are used in writing numeric expressions in C++ programs.

Operators

In C++, addition and subtraction are denoted by the usual plus (**+**) and minus (**-**) signs. Multiplication is denoted by an asterisk (*****). This symbol must be used to denote every multiplication. That is, to multiply **n** by **2**, we can write **2*n** or **n*2** but not **2n**. Division is denoted by a slash (**/**), which is used for both real and integer division. Another operation closely related to integer division is the **modulus** or **remainder** operation, denoted by percent (**%**), which gives the remainder in an integer division. The following table summarizes these operators.

Operator	Operation
+	Addition, unary plus
-	Subtraction, unary minus
*	Multiplication
/	Real and integer division
%	Modulus (remainder in integer division)

For the operators **+**, **-**, *****, and **/**, the operands may be of either integer or real type. If both are integer, the result is integer, but if either is of real type, the result is real:

```
2 + 3 = 5
2 + 3.0 = 5.0
2.0 + 3 = 5.0
2.0 + 3.0 = 5.0
7.0 / 2.0 = 3.5
7 / 2 = 3
```

It is important to note the difference between integer and real division. Consider the two expressions

     3 / 4

and

     3.0 / 4

Since both operands in the first expression, **3** and **4**, are integers, integer division is performed, producing the integer quotient **0**. By contrast, the second expression has a real operand, **3.0**, and so real division is performed, producing the real result **0.75**.

Integer division produces both a quotient and a remainder and C++ provides one operator (/) that gives the integer quotient and another operator (%) that gives the remainder from an integer division.[6] The following are some examples:

Integer Division	Modulus Operation
2 / 2 → 1	2 % 2 → 0
3 / 2 → 1	3 % 2 → 1
4 / 2 → 2	4 % 2 → 0
9 / 3 → 3	9 % 3 → 0
10 / 3 → 3	10 % 3 → 1
11 / 3 → 3	11 % 3 → 2
86 / 10 → 8	86 % 10 → 6
197 / 10 → 19	197 % 10 → 7

Type Conversions. We just saw that the division operation in the expression

```
3.0 / 4
```

performs real division and produces a real value as its result, even though only one of the operands is a real value. Some languages do not allow integer and real values to be intermixed within an expression in this manner. Although the extent to which mixed-type expressions are allowed is implementation-dependent in C++, most implementations will automatically *widen* the smaller of the values in such an expression. For example, suppose that in the expression

```
3.0 / 4
```

the **double** value **3.0** is stored in two words of memory and the **int** value **4** is stored in one word of memory. C++ will typically *widen* the smaller value (4) to a two-word value, so that the division can be performed on two two-word values, producing a two-word value as the result. No information or precision is lost, as it would be if the larger value were narrowed to the size of the smaller value.

This feature of automatically widening a smaller value to the size of a larger value in an expression is often described as **promotion** of the smaller value. Promotion is what permits **short**, **unsigned**, **int**, and **long** integer values to be freely intermixed in C++ expressions; most implementations of C++ will promote integer values to real values when necessary. For a type *T*, two values are said to be *T*-**compatible** if

- They are both of type *T*;
- One is of type *T* and the other can be promoted to type *T*; or
- The types of both can be promoted to *T*.

---

[6] Neither **i** / **j** nor **i** % **j** is defined if **j** is zero.

For example, `char` and `int` are `int`-compatible, since `char` can be promoted to `int`. In general, two values are **type-compatible** if they are *T*-compatible for some type *T*.

Operator Precedence.   The arithmetic operators can be grouped into two groups: the **additive** operators (+ and -) and the **multiplicative** operators (*, /, and %). These groupings are important because they are used to determine the order in which operators in an expression are applied. The order of evaluation in an expression is determined by **operator precedence** (or **priority**):

> *In an expression involving several operators, the multiplicative operators have higher precedence than (i.e., are applied before) the additive operators.*

Thus, in the expression

    2 + 3 * 5

* has higher precedence than +, so the multiplication is performed before the addition; therefore, the value of the expression is 17.

Operator Associativity.   In C++ the operators +, -, *, /, and % are all **left-associative** operators, which means that in an expression having two operators with the same priority, the left operator is applied first. Thus,

    9 - 5 - 1

is evaluated as

    (9 - 5) - 1 → 4 - 1 → 3

In the next section, we will see that some C++ operators are *right-associative.*
   Associativity is also used in more complex expressions containing different operators of the same priority. For example, consider

    7 * 10 - 5 % 3 * 4 + 9

There are three high-priority operators, *, %, and *, and so left associativity causes the leftmost multiplication to be performed first, giving the intermediate result

    70 - 5 % 3 * 4 + 9

% is performed next, giving

    70 - 2 * 4 + 9

and the second multiplication is performed last, yielding

    70 - 8 + 9

The two remaining operations, - and +, are equal in priority, and so left associativity causes the subtraction to be performed first, giving

    62 + 9

and then the addition is carried out, giving the final result

    71

Using Parentheses. Parentheses can be used to change the usual order of evaluation of an expression as determined by precedence and associativity. Parenthesized subexpressions are first evaluated in the standard manner, and the results are then combined to evaluate the complete expression. If the parentheses are "nested"— that is, if one set of parentheses is contained within another—the computations in the innermost parentheses are performed first.

To illustrate, consider the expression

    (7 * (10 - 5) % 3) * 4 + 9

The subexpression (10 - 5) is evaluated first, producing

    (7 * 5 % 3) * 4 + 9

Next the subexpression (7 * 5 % 3) is evaluated left to right, giving

    (35 % 3) * 4 + 9

followed by

    2 * 4 + 9

Now the multiplication is performed, giving

    8 + 9

and the addition produces the final result

    17

Care must be taken in writing expressions containing two or more operations to ensure that they are evaluated in the order intended. Even though parentheses may not be required, they should be used freely to clarify the intended order of evaluation and to write complicated expressions in terms of simpler expressions. It is important, however, that the parentheses balance (i.e., that they occur in pairs), since an unpaired parenthesis will result in a compilation error.

Unary Operators. The operators + and - can also be used as **unary operators** (i.e., they can be applied to a single operand); for example, -x and +34 are allowed. Similarly, the expression 3 * -4 is a valid C++ expression, producing the value

-12. Unary operations have higher priority than the binary operations +, -, *, /, and %.

Summary. In summary, the following rules govern the evaluation of arithmetic expressions.

Precedence Rules

Higher:	unary +, unary -
	*, /, and %
Lower:	binary +, binary -

1. Higher-priority operations are performed before lower-priority operations.
2. Operators having the same priority are applied using left associativity.
3. If an expression contains subexpressions enclosed within parentheses, these are evaluated first, using the standard order specified in Rules 1 and 2. If there are nested parentheses, the innermost subexpressions are evaluated first.

Other Operators. In addition to the basic arithmetic operations +, -, *, /, and %, C++ also provides bitwise operations that can be applied to integer data: ~ (negation), & (bitwise and), | (bitwise or), ^ (bitwise exclusive or), << (bitshift left), and >> (bitshift right). A complete list of the C++ operators (including the bitwise operators) can be found in Appendix C, and an example illustrating their use is given in Chapter 13.

Functions

In the expressions we have considered thus far, the operands have been simple objects like numbers and variables or the value of a subexpression within a larger expression. But an operand may also be a value returned by a function. Many languages provide predefined functions, such as square root, logarithm, and absolute value as part of the language. This is convenient, since a program can simply call such functions when they are needed. The problem is that these functions add to the size of the compiled program, regardless of whether the program uses them or not. This is a significant price (in terms of space) to pay for the convenience of built-in functions.

C++ provides so many predefined functions that even the simplest program (such as that in Figure 3.2) would be huge if all of the predefined functions were added to the program. Instead, C++ stores the most commonly used functions in a **standard library** (whose header file is `stdlib.h`). When a program is translated, the linker automatically searches this library, and thus the functions in this library may be used in any program simply by inserting the directive `#include<stdlib.h>`. The other C++ predefined functions are stored in several separate libraries. If a program uses only a few libraries, the executable program that results when it is translated is relatively small; but if it uses a large number of libraries, then the executable program is larger.

To *call* any of the functions from the standard library, we simply give the function name followed by its argument—the constant, variable, or expression to which the function is to be applied—enclosed within parentheses. For example, the notation

```
abs(X)
```

produces the *absolute value* of its argument **X**, which can be any numeric value. Similarly, if **i** is an integer variable and **d** is a `double` variable, then the expression

```
double(i)
```

produces the value equivalent to **i** but as a `double` instead of an integer. Similarly, the expression

```
int(d)
```

will truncate the fractional part and produce the integer part of **d** as its value. More generally, the type of an expression can be explicitly converted to a different type as follows:

Explicit Type Conversion

Form:

   Type(*Expression*)

where:
   Type is a valid C++ type; and
   Expression is any C++ expression.

Purpose:
The type of the value produced by *Expression* is converted to *Type* (if possible).

Explicitly converting the type of an expression is sometimes called **casting** the expression.[7]

Table 3.5 lists some of the functions provided by the math library; each of these functions takes one or more parameters of type `double` and returns a value of type `double`.

---

[7] A type cast can also be written in the form

   (*Type*) *Expression*

The form used in the text is sometimes referred to as *functional* notation and this form as *cast* notation.

TABLE 3.5   Math Library Functions

Function	Description
`sin(x)`	Sine of **x** (in radians)
`cos(x)`	Cosine of **x** (in radians)
`tan(x)`	Tangent of **x** (in radians)
`asin(x)`	Inverse sine of **x** (function value in radians)
`acos(x)`	Inverse cosine of **x** (function value in radians)
`atan(x)`	Inverse tangent of **x** (function value in radians)
`sinh(x)`	Hyperbolic sine of **x**
`cosh(x)`	Hyperbolic cosine of **x**
`tanh(x)`	Hyperbolic tangent of **x**
`exp(x)`	Exponential function e^x
`log(x)`	Natural logarithm of **x**
`log10(x)`	Base-10 logarithm of **x**
`pow(x,y)`	**x** raised to power **y**
`sqrt(x)`	Square root of **x**
`ceil(x)`	Smallest integer not less than **x**

Thus, to calculate the square root of 5, we can write

`sqrt(5.0)`

Most implementations will also allow us to write

`sqrt(5)`

since the **int** value **5** can be promoted to the **double** value **5.0**.
As a more complicated example, if we wish to calculate $\sqrt{b^2 - 4ac}$, we could write

`sqrt(pow(b, 2) - 4 * a * c)`

Note that if the value of the expression

`pow(b, 2) - 4 * a * c`

is negative, then an error results because the square root of a negative number is not defined.

Exercises

1. Find the value of each of the following expressions, or explain why it is not a valid expression:

   (a) `9 - 5 - 3`
   (b) `2 / 3 + 3 / 5`
   (c) `9.0 / 2 / 5`
   (d) `9 / 2 / 5`
   (e) `2.0 / 4`

(f) (2 + 3) % 2

(g) 7 % 5 % 3

(h) (7 % 5) % 3

(i) 7 % (5 % 3)

(j) (7 % 5 % 3)

(k) 25 * 1 / 2

(l) 25 * 1.0 / 2

(m) 25 * (1 / 2)

(n) -3.0 * 5.0

(o) 5.0 * -3.0

(p) 12 / 2 * 3

(q) ((12 + 3) / 2) / (8 - (5 + 1))

(r) ((12 + 3) / 2) / (8 - 5 + 1)

(s) (12 + 3 / 2) / (8 - 5 + 1)

(t) sqrt(pow(4.0, 2))

(u) sqrt(pow(-4.0, 2))

(v) pow(sqrt(4.0), 2)

(w) pow(sqrt(-4.0), 2)

(x) ceil(8.0 / 5.0)

2. If R1 and R2 are reals, I1, I2, I3 are integers, and R1 = 2.0, R2 = 3.0, I1 = 4, I2 = 5, and I3 = 8, find the value of each of the following:

(a) R1 + R2 + R2

(b) I3 / 3

(c) I3 / 3.0

(d) (R2 + R1) * I1

(e) I3 / I2 * 5.1

(f) pow(I1, 2) / pow(R1, 2)

(g) pow(I2, 2) / pow(R1, 2)

(h) sqrt(R1 + R2 + I1)

3. Write C++ expressions to compute the following.

(a) $10 + 5B - 4AC$

(b) Three times the difference $4 - n$ divided by twice the quantity $m^2 + n^2$

(c) The square root of $a + 3b^2$

(d) The square root of the average of m and n

(e) $|A/(m + n)|$ (where $|x|$ denotes the absolute value of x)

(f) a^x, computed as $e^{x \ln a}$ (where ln is the natural logarithm function)

(g) The real quantity *Amount* rounded to the nearest hundredth

4. (a) Verify that the statement

```
Cost = double(int(Cost * 100.0 + 0.5)) / 100.0;
```

can be used to convert a real value **Cost** to dollars, rounding to the nearest cent, using the following values of **Cost**:

(i) 12.342   (ii) 12.348   (iii) 12.345   (iv) 12.340   (v) 13.0

(b) Write an expression similar to that in part (a) that rounds a real amount **X** to the nearest tenth.

(c) Write an expression similar to that in part (a) that rounds a real amount **x** to the nearest thousandth.

3.5   Assignment Expressions

An **assignment expression** assigns a value to a variable.

Assignment Expression

Form:

> *Variable = Expression*

where:

Variable is a valid C++ identifier, declared as a variable;

Expression may be a constant, another variable to which a value has previously been assigned, or a formula to be evaluated, whose type is the same as that of *Variable*.

Behavior:

1. *Expression* is evaluated, producing a value *E*.
2. The value of *Variable* is changed to *E*.
3. The = operator produces the value *E*.

For example, suppose that **xCoord** and **yCoord** are real variables, **Number** and **Position** are integer variables, and **Code** is a character variable, declared as follows:

```
double
   xCoord, yCoord;
int
   Number, Position;
char
   Code;
```

These declarations associate memory locations with the four variables. This might be pictured as follows, with the question marks indicating that these variables are initially **undefined:**

xCoord	?
yCoord	?
Number	?
Position	?
Code	?

Now consider the following assignment statements:

```
xCoord = 5.23;
yCoord = sqrt(25.0);
Number = 17;
Code = 'M';
```

Note that the value of a variable of type **char** is a single character and not a string of characters.

The first assignment statement assigns the real constant **5.23** to the real variable **xCoord**, and the second assigns the real constant **5.0** to the real variable **yCoord**. The next assignment statements assign the integer constant **17** to the integer variable **Number** and the character **M** to the character variable **Code**. Thinking of variables as mailboxes, as described in Section 3.2, we might picture the results as follows:

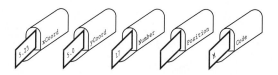

More precisely, when these assignment statements are executed, the values **5.23**, **5.0**, and **17** and the numeric code for **M** are stored in the memory locations associated with the variables **xCoord**, **yCoord**, **Number**, and **Code**, respectively. The variable **Position** is still undefined, and the content of the memory location associated with it is uncertain.

xCoord	5.23
yCoord	5.0
Number	17
Position	?
Code	M (77)

These values are substituted for the variables in any subsequent expression containing these variables. Thus, in the assignment statement

```
Position = Number / 3 + 2;
```

the expression **Number / 3 + 2** is evaluated (with the value **17** substituted for the variable **Number**) yielding **7**. This value is then assigned to the integer variable **Position**; the value of **Number** is unchanged.

xCoord	5.23
yCoord	5.0
Number	17
Position	7
Code	M (77)

Compare this with the assignment statement

```
xCoord = 2.0 * xCoord;
```

in which the variable **xCoord** appears on both sides of the assignment operator (=). In this case, the current value **5.23** for **xCoord** is used in evaluating the expression **2.0 * xCoord**, yielding the value **10.46**; this value is then assigned to **xCoord**. The old value **5.23** is lost because it has been replaced with the new value **10.46**.

xCoord	10.46
yCoord	5.0
Number	17
Position	7
Code	M (77)

In every assignment statement, the variable to be assigned a value must appear on the left of the assignment operator (=), a valid expression must appear on the right, and both the variable and the expression should be of the same type. Although mixing of numeric types is permitted in C++, the practice should be avoided, since assigning a real value to an integer variable truncates the real value (i.e., discards its fractional part). For example,

```
Number = 4 / yCoord;
```

will evaluate the expression **4 / yCoord**, and since **yCoord** is of type **double**, this expression produces the real result **0.8**. However, assigning this real value to the integer variable **Number** truncates the fractional part (**.8**), and assigns the integer part (**0**) to **Number**. Significant information can thus be lost through careless mixing of real and integer values.

An unusual feature of C++ is that it treats characters as 8-bit integers. This means that strange assignments like

```
Code = 65 + 1;
```

or

```
Number = 'A' + 'B';
```

are allowed in C++, the first assigning the value **66** (the numeric code for **'B'**) to **Code** and the second assigning the value **131** (**65 + 66**) to **Number**. Such statements are poor programming style and should be avoided. *Assign character values to character variables, integer values to integer variables, and real values to real variables.*

The following are examples of *invalid* assignment statements. A reason is given for each to explain why it is not valid. The variables in these statements are assumed to have the types specified earlier.

Statement	Error
5 = Number	Variable must appear on the left of the assignment operator.
xCoord + 3.5 = 2.7	Arithmetic expressions may not appear on the left of the assignment operator.
Code = "ABC"	Value of a **char** variable is a single character.
Number = "12" + "34"	"12" + "34" is not a valid expression.

It is important to remember that *the assignment statement is a replacement statement.* Some beginning programmers forget this and write an assignment statement like

    A = B;

when the statement

    B = A;

is intended. These two statements produce very different results: The first assigns the value of **B** to **A**, leaving **B** unchanged, and the second assigns the value of **A** to **B**, leaving **A** unchanged.

To illustrate further the replacement property of an assignment, suppose that the integer variables **Alpha** and **Beta** have values **357** and **59**, respectively, and that we wish to interchange these values. For this, we use an auxiliary integer variable **Temp** to store the value of **Alpha** while we assign **Beta**'s value to **Alpha**; then we can assign this stored value to **Beta**.

```
Temp  = Alpha;
Alpha = Beta;
Beta  = Temp;
```

Alpha	357		Alpha	357		Alpha	59		Alpha	59
-------	-----		-------	-----		-------	-----		-------	-----
Beta	59	Temp = Alpha →	Beta	59	Alpha = Beta →	Beta	59	Beta = Temp →	Beta	357
Temp	?		Temp	357		Temp	357		Temp	357

Assignment as an Operation

We have seen that an assignment

Variable = Expression

produces three actions:

1. *Expression* is evaluated, producing a value *E*.
2. The value of *Variable* is changed to *E*.
3. The = operator produces the value *E*.

Thus far in our discussion, we have concentrated on actions (1) and (2), and we now turn our attention to action (3) in this description.
   Just as the expression

```
2 + 2
```

produces the value 4, the assignment

```
Number = 4
```

is an expression that produces the value 4. The assignment operator = *is a binary infix operator whose result is the value being assigned.* For example, if the value of **Number** is 4, then in the expression

```
Number = Number * 2
```

the * is applied first (the precedence of the = operator is lower than almost all other C++ operators), producing the result 8. That value is then assigned to **Number**, producing the result 8 (again).
   It is important that you understand this concept: = *is a value-producing operator.*

Chaining Assignment Operators

Several assignment operators may be chained together in a single statement such as

```
xCoord = yCoord = 2.5;
```

which is equivalent to the two statements

```
yCoord = 2.5;
xCoord = yCoord;
```

The assignment operator = is *right-associative* (unlike the arithmetic operators we have seen), and hence the statement

```
xCoord = yCoord = 2.5;
```

is evaluated as though it were

```
xCoord = (yCoord = 2.5);
```

and since the = operator produces the value assigned (i.e., **2.5**), **2.5** is assigned to **xCoord** after it is assigned to **yCoord**.

Chaining assignment operators can be used to assign a group of variables the same value; for example,

```
a = b = c = d = 1;
```

will set **d** to **1**, **c** to **1**, **b** to **1**, and, finally, **a** to **1**. Similarly, in the statement

```
Area = (Length = 2.0) * (Width = 2.5);
```

Width is set to **2.5**, **Length** is set to **2.0**, and **Area** is set to the product **5.0** of these assignments.

The Increment and Decrement Operations

Algorithms often contain instructions of the form

"Increment *Counter* by 1."

The most straightforward way to encode this instruction in C++ is

```
Counter = Counter + 1;
```

Such a statement, in which the same variable appears on both sides of the assignment operator, often confuses beginning programmers. Although we read English sentences from left to right, execution of this statement *begins to the right of the assignment operator,* so that

1. The expression **Counter + 1** is evaluated, and
2. The resulting value is assigned to **Counter** (overwriting its previous value).

For example, if **Counter** has the value **16**, then

1. The value of **Counter + 1 = 16 + 1 = 17** is computed; and
2. That value is assigned as the new value for **Counter**:

Counter $\boxed{16}$ $\xrightarrow{\text{Counter = Counter + 1}}$ Counter $\boxed{17}$

Note that the old value of the variable is lost because it was replaced with a new value.

This kind of assignment (i.e., incrementing a variable) occurs so frequently that C++ provides a special unary **increment operator ++** for this operation. It can be used as a postfix operator,

```
VariableName++
```

or as a prefix operator,

```
++VariableName
```

where **VariableName** is an integer variable whose value is to be incremented[8] by 1. Thus, the assignment expression

```
Counter = Counter + 1
```

can also be written

```
Counter++
```

or

```
++Counter
```

The difference between the postfix and prefix use of the operator is subtle: Consider the assignments

```
Counter = 1;
Number = ++Counter;
```

and

```
Counter = 1;
Number = Counter++;
```

After execution of both sets of statements, the value of **Counter** will be 2. However, in the first set of assignments, the value assigned to **Number** will be 2, whereas in the second set of assignments, the value assigned to **Number** will be 1.

To understand this difference, we must remember that these increment expressions are assignment expressions and thus produce values. In the *prefix* expression

```
++Counter
```

Counter is incremented and *the value produced by the expression is **Counter** + 1*. By contrast, in the *postfix* expression

```
Counter++
```

---

[8] The name C++ stems from this operator—C++ is C that has been improved incrementally.

`Counter` is still incremented, but *the value produced by the expression is* `Counter`, *not* `Counter + 1`. That is, the assignment

```
Number = ++Counter;
```

is equivalent to

```
Counter = Counter + 1;
Number = Counter;
```

whereas the assignment

```
Number = Counter++;
```

is equivalent to

```
Number = Counter;
Counter = Counter + 1;
```

Note that if this operator is used simply to increment a variable as in

```
Counter++;
```

or

```
++Counter;
```

then the prefix and postfix forms produce exactly the same result.

Just as you can increment a variable's value with the ++ operator, you can also decrement (i.e., subtract 1 from the value of) a variable using the **decrement operator --**. For example, the assignment

```
Counter = Counter - 1;
```

can be written more compactly as

```
Counter--;
```

or

```
--Counter;
```

The prefix and postfix versions of the decrement operator behave in a manner similar to the prefix and postfix versions of the increment operator.

Other Assignment Shortcuts

The increment and decrement operations are special cases of a more general assignment that changes the value of a variable using some expression that involves its original value. For example, the pseudocode step

"Add *Counter* to *Sum*"

implicitly changes the value of *Sum* to the value *Sum + Counter*. This can be encoded in C++ as

```
Sum = Sum + Counter;
```

The following diagram illustrates this for the case in which the integer variables Sum and Counter have the values 120 and 16, respectively.

This operation occurs so frequently that C++ provides special operators for it. Instead of writing

```
Sum = Sum + Counter;
```

we can write

```
Sum += Counter;
```

to accomplish the same thing.

Each of the arithmetic operators can be used in this way. For example, the statement

```
xCoord = xCoord * yCoord;
```

can be written

```
xCoord *= yCoord;
```

In general, any statement of the form

```
Variable = Variable Δ Expression;
```

can be written :

```
Variable Δ= Expression;
```

where Δ is any of the operators +, -, *, /, or %. Each of the following is, therefore, an acceptable variation of the assignment operator:[9]

```
+=, -=, *=, /=, %=
```

---

[9] In addition to those listed here, the bitwise operators can be applied in this manner: << =, >> =, &=, |=, ^=.

Like the regular assignment operator, these are all right-associative. Thus, if **xCoord** has the value 4.0 and **yCoord** the value 2.5, then the statement

```
xCoord *= yCoord += 0.5;
```

has the effect of

1. Assigning **yCoord** the value **2.5 + 0.5 = 3.0** and then
2. Assigning **xCoord** the value **4.0 * 3.0 = 12.0**.

Chaining such operators together must be done carefully so that the readability of the program does not suffer. Programs that are cleverly written but are difficult to read are of little use because they are too costly to maintain.

Transforming Expressions into Statements—Semicolons

We are finally ready to understand the meaning of the semicolon in C++. It is used as a **statement terminator.** An expression followed by a semicolon becomes an *expression statement.* The semicolon can be thought of as an operator that causes the expression to its left to be evaluated and then discards the result of that expression. For example, in the statement

```
Number = 2 + 2;
```

the following actions occur:

1. The expression **2 + 2** is evaluated, producing the value 4.
2. The expression **Number = 4** is evaluated, which
   a. Changes the value of **Number** to 4; and
   b. Produces the value 4.
3. The semicolon terminates the statement, causing the value 4 (produced by the assignment operator) to be discarded.

This means that any C++ expression can become a statement simply by appending a semicolon. Thus, statements such as

```
2.5 + 0.5;
```

are valid; they just don't accomplish any useful work the way an assignment expression does.

Thinking of the semicolon as an operator gives a different (but equivalent) way to interpret an assignment statement:

```
Variable = Expression;
```

This is really an expression statement that returns the value of ***Expression*** and has the **side effect** of changing the value of ***Variable***.

A Final Word

In a C++ program, *variables are undefined until their values have been explicitly specified* by a declaration initialization, an input statement, an assignment statement, or by one of the other statements discussed later.[10] The results of attempting to use undefined variables are unpredictable.

Exercises

1. Assuming that **Number** is an integer, **xValue** and **yValue** are reals, and **Grade** is a character, determine which of the following are valid C++ assignment statements. If they are not valid, explain why they are not.

   (a) xValue = 2.17828;   (b) 3 = Number;
   (c) Grade = 'B+';   (d) Number = Number + 1;
   (e) xValue = 1;   (f) Grade = A;
   (g) Number + 1 = Number;   (h) xValue = '1';
   (i) xValue = yValue = 3.2;   (j) yValue = yValue;
   (k) xValue = A;   (l) Grade = Grade + 10;
   (m) xValue /= yValue;   (n) xValue = Number++;
   (o) Number = yValue;

2. Given that **R1**, **R2**, **R3**, and **xCoord** are real variables with **R1 = 2.0, R2 = 3.0**, and **R3 = 4.0**; **I1**, **I2**, and **I3** are integer variables with **I1 = 8**, and **I2 = 5**; and **Numeral** and **Symbol** are character variables with **Numeral = '2'**; find the value assigned to the given variable by each of the following, or indicate why the statement is not valid.

   (a) xCoord = (R1 + R2) * R2;
   (b) xCoord =(R2 + R1 / R3) * 2;
   (c) xCoord = I1 / I2 + 5;
   (d) I3 = I1 / I2 + 5;
   (e) xCoord = pow(I2, 2) / pow(I1, 2);
   (f) I3 = pow(I2, 2) / pow(I1, 2);
   (g) Symbol = 4;
   (h) Symbol = Numeral;
   (i) Symbol = '4';
   (j) Symbol = R3;
   (k) R1 = 2;
   (l) R1 = '2';
   (m) R1 = Numeral;
   (n) I1 = I1 + 2;
   (o) I3 = 1 + Numeral;
   (p) I3 = ceil(pow(I1 % I2, 2) / R3);

3. For each of the following, write an assignment statement that changes the value of the integer variable **Number** by the specified amount.

   (a) Increment **Number** by 77.
   (b) Decrement **Number** by 3.

---

[10] Variables of storage class **auto** (see Section 7.7) are undefined until explicitly given a value. However variables of storage class **static** are automatically initialized to zero when the program is loaded into memory.

(c) Increment **Number** by twice its value.

(d) Add the rightmost digit of **Number** to **Number**.

(e) Decrement **Number** by the integer part of the real value **X**.

4. Write a C++ assignment statement for each of the following that calculates the given expression and assigns the result to the specified variable. Assume that all variables are of type **double**, except where otherwise noted.

(a) **Rate** times **Time** to **Distance**

(b) **X** incremented by an amount **DeltaX** to **X**

(c) $\dfrac{1}{\dfrac{1}{\text{R1}} + \dfrac{1}{\text{R2}} + \dfrac{1}{\text{R3}}}$ to **Resistance**

(d) area of a triangle of base **b** and height **h** (one-half base times height) to **Area**

(e) the last three digits of the integer **StockNumber** with a decimal point before the last two digits to **Price** (e.g., if **StockNumber** is 1758316, **Price** is assigned the value of 3.16)

(f) **Tax** rounded to the nearest dollar to **Tax**

5. For each of the following, give values for the integer variables **a**, **b**, and **c** for which the two given expressions have different values.

(a) `a * (b / c)` and `(a * b) / c`

(b) `a / b` and `a * (1 / b)`

(c) `(a + b) / c` and `(a / c) + (b / c)`

3.6 Input/Output Expressions

In the preceding section we considered the assignment statement, which enables us to evaluate expressions and store the results by assigning them to variables. An assignment statement does not, however, display these results on some output device, nor does it allow the user to enter new values during execution. For example, a program to calculate the wages earned by John Doe, employee # 31564, for 38.5 hours of work at an hourly rate of $8.75 could contain the variable declarations

```
int
    EmpNumber = 31564;         // employee number
double
    Hours = 38.5,              // hours worked
    Rate = 8.75,               // hourly pay rate
    Wages = Hours * Rate;      // total earnings
```

The value of **Wages** is calculated as desired but is only stored internally in the memory location associated with **Wages** and is not displayed to the user. Moreover, if the same wage calculation is to be done for Mary Smith, employee #31565, who worked 37.5 hours at an hourly rate of $9.25, the initializations must be almost completely rewritten, as follows:

```
int
    EmpNumber = 31565;              // employee number
double
    Hours = 37.5,                  // hours worked
    Rate = 9.25,                   // hourly pay rate
    Wages = Hours * Rate;          // total earnings
```

The output expression that we consider in this section provides a method for easily displaying information. We also consider an input expression that provides a convenient method of assigning values from an external source to variables during execution of the program.

I/O Streams

The details of how input and output are performed differ according to whether you are working on a microcomputer, a microcomputer that is part of a network, a terminal that is hooked to a mainframe computer, or any number of other possibilities. In each different kind of system, the details of how input and output are performed are different. A programming language such as C++ must provide input/output (I/O) facilities that work in the same manner in any of these computing environments.

Rather than including in the language a multitude of I/O facilities for dealing with all the different kinds of computers, C++ treats input and output as simply as possible. When characters are entered from the keyboard, they enter an input stream called an **istream** that transmits the characters from the keyboard to the program. Similarly, when program output is to be displayed on the screen, the output characters are placed in an output stream called an **ostream** that transmits the characters to the monitor.[11]

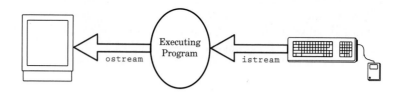

By dealing with **istream**s and **ostream**s, C++ can avoid the nitty-gritty details about how I/O is actually being performed on any particular machine.

As we noted in Chapter 2, C++ has no input or output facilities built into the language. Instead, **istream**s and **ostream**s are provided by a special library,

---

[11] The names **istream** and **ostream** are not a part of the C++ language but are the names of two *classes*. The ability to develop an entire I/O system using classes provides some indication of their powerful capabilities.

whose interface is in the header file **<iostream.h>**. This library defines three important data objects:

- An **istream** object named **cin**, which is associated with the *keyboard*
- An **ostream** object named **cout**, which is associated with the *monitor*
- An **ostream** object named **cerr**, which is associated with the *monitor* and is used to display error messages

Input and output are operations on these data objects.

Input Expressions

The program in Figure 3.2 contains the input statement

```
cin >> Radius;
```

where **Radius** is a real variable. We have seen that **cin** is the name of the **istream** data object defined in **<iostream.h>**, but what is the purpose of the **>>**? The answer is that **>>** is the operator that performs the input operation. Just as the expression

```
x + 2
```

consists of the *addition* operator (**+**) and two operands (**x** and **2**), and

```
y = 1
```

consists of the *assignment* operator (**=**) and two operands (**y** and **1**),

```
cin >> Radius
```

is an input expression in which the **input** (or **extraction**) **operator >>** is applied to the two operands **cin** and **Radius**. That is, the **>>** symbol is a binary operator that acts as follows.

Input Expression

Form:

> *IStream >> Variable*

where:
    IStream is the name of any declared C++ input stream; and
    Variable is any C++ variable for whose type the input operator **>>** is defined.

> **Behavior:**
>
> 1. A value *V* is read from *IStream*. (If there is none, program execution is suspended until one is entered.)
> 2. The value *V* is extracted from *IStream* and stored in *Variable*.
> 3. The **>>** operator produces the value *IStream*.

The **>>** operator is *left-associative,* which along with part 3 of its behavior allows input expressions to be chained together. For example,

```
cin >> Radius >> Height;
```

is evaluated as

```
(cin >> Radius) >> Height;
```

in the following manner:

1. The next value is read from **cin** and stored in **Radius** (if none is present, program execution is suspended until a value is entered), and the **>>** operator produces the value **cin**, giving

    ```
    cin >> Height;
    ```

2. The next value is read from **cin** and stored in **Height** (if none is present, program execution is suspended until a value is entered), and the **>>** operator produces the value **cin**, giving

    ```
    cin;
    ```

3. The expression **cin** is evaluated and discarded by the semicolon.

Note that just as a semicolon serves to make an assignment expression into an assignment statement, a semicolon serves to make an input expression into an input statement. We can thus describe a typical C++ (interactive) input statement as follows:

C++ Interactive Input Statement

> **Form:**
>
> ```
> cin >> Variable₁ >> Variable₂ >> . . . >> Variableₙ;
> ```
> where:
>   **cin** is the **istream** declared in **<iostream.h>**;

>> is the input operator; and
each *Variableᵢ* is a variable for whose type >> is defined.

Purpose:
Execution of an input statement reads a sequence of *n* values
from the input device with which **cin** is associated, storing them
in *Variable₁*, *Variable₂*, . . . , *Variableₙ*.

Note that the user must enter a value (of the appropriate type) for each variable
in the statement before execution of the program will resume. Thus, if **Alpha**,
Beta, **Gamma**, and **Delta** are real variables, the statement

```
cin >> Alpha >> Beta >> Gamma >> Delta;
```

is executed, and the user enters the values

```
1.0 2.0 3.0
```

then execution will not resume until the user enters a fourth value:

```
4.0
```

The first value is stored in the first variable, the second value in the second variable, and so forth. In our example, the value of **Alpha** will be 1.0, the value of
Beta will be 2.0, the value of **Gamma** will be 3.0, and the value of **Delta** will be
4.0. Program execution then resumes.

Any **white space** (spaces, tabs, or newlines) can be used to separate input
values. For example, the user could separate the values with newlines by entering
each data item on a separate line,

```
1.0
2.0
3.0
4.0
```

and produce the same result.

Because execution is suspended and because the correct number and types of
values must be entered before execution can resume, *it is good practice to provide
some message to prompt the user whenever it is necessary to enter data values.*
This is accomplished by preceding input statements with output statements that
display appropriate prompts. In the program in Figure 3.2, this was accomplished
by the statement

```
cout << "\nPlease enter the radius of a sphere: ";
```

We turn now to a study of such output statements.

Output Expressions

There is a natural correspondence between C++ input and output statements. To illustrate, consider the input statement

```
cin >> Radius;
```

and the output statement

```
cout << "\nPlease enter the radius of a sphere: ";
```

from the program in Figure 3.2. Just as `cin` is the name of an `istream` data object, `cout` is the name of an `ostream` data object defined in `<iostream.h>`. Similarly, just as `>>` is the `istream` input (or extraction) operator, `<<` is the `ostream` **output (or insertion) operator.** And just as the expression

```
cin >> Radius
```

performs the *input* operation (`>>`) using two operands (`cin` and `Radius`), the expression

```
cout << "\nPlease enter the radius of a sphere: "
```

performs the *output* operation (`<<`) using two operands (`cout` and `"\nPlease enter the radius of a sphere: "`). Thus, the `<<` symbol is a binary operator that behaves as follows.

Output Expression

Form:

> *OStream* `<<` *Expression*

where:
   OStream is the name of any declared C++
      output stream; and
   Expression is any C++ expression for whose
      type `<<` is defined.

Behavior:

1. *Expression* is evaluated, producing a value *E*.
2. The value of *E* is inserted into `OStream`.
3. The `<<` operator produces the value *OStream*.

Like `>>`, the `<<` operator is *left-associative,* which along with part 3 of its behavior allows output expressions to be chained together. Thus,

```
cout << "The hypotenuse = " << sqrt(a*a + b*b) << "\n\n";
```

is evaluated as

```
((cout << "The hypotenuse = " ) << sqrt(a*a + b*b) ) << "\n\n";
```

and its behavior is thus as follows:

1. The expression `"The hypotenuse = "` is evaluated and inserted into `cout`, and the `<<` operator produces the value `cout`, giving

```
cout << sqrt(a*a + b*b) << "\n\n";
```

2. The expression `sqrt(a*a + b*b)` is evaluated and inserted into `cout`, and the `<<` operator produces the value `cout`, giving

```
cout << "\n\n";
```

3. The expression `"\n\n"` is evaluated and inserted into `cout`, and the `<<` operator produces the value `cout`, giving

```
cout;
```

4. The expression `cout` is evaluated and discarded by the semicolon.

   Note that just as a semicolon serves to make an assignment operation into an assignment statement, a semicolon serves to make an output expression into an output statement. We can thus describe a typical C++ (interactive) output statement as follows.

C++ Interactive Output Statement

Form:

   cout << *Expr₁* << *Expr₂* << ... << *Exprₙ*;

where:
   `cout` is the `ostream` declared in `<iostream.h>`;
   `<<` is the output operator; and
   Each *Expr₁* is a C++ expression for whose type `<<` is defined.

Purpose:
Execution of an output statement displays the values of *Expr₁*, *Expr₂*, . . ., *Exprₙ* on the output device with which `cout` is associated.

For example, the statement

```
cout << Alpha << ' ' << Beta << '\n'
     << Gamma << ' ' << Delta << '\n';
```

displays the values of **Alpha** and **Beta** on one line and the values of **Gamma** and **Delta** on the next line. Subsequent output would begin on yet another line. Note that if white space is to appear in the output, it must be specified explicitly. For example, if the values of integer variables **A** and **B** are 2 and 3, respectively, then the output statement

```
cout << "\nThe sum of" << A << "and" << B
     << "is" << A + B;
```

will display the output

```
The sum of2and3is5
```

whereas the output statement

```
cout << "\nThe sum of " << A << " and " << B
     << " is " << A + B;
```

will display

```
The sum of 2 and 3 is 5
```

Newline escape sequences must be used to cause values being displayed to appear on separate lines. For example, the output statement

```
cout << "\nRats\nSnails\nPuppy Dog Tails\n";
```

will display the output

```
Rats
Snails
Puppy Dog Tails
```

Example: Calculating Wages

In an earlier example in this section, we considered the problem of calculating wages for an employee. Figure 3.3 presents a solution to this problem that uses output statements to prompt the user and display results, as well as input statements to enter values from the keyboard.

FIGURE 3.3   Calculating wages—version 1.

```
/* This program computes the wages of an employee.

    Input:    The employee's number, the hours worked, and hourly rate

    Output:   The employee's number, hours worked, hourly rate, and
              total wages
                                                                  --*/
```

FIGURE 3.3   Calculating wages—version 1. (cont.)

```cpp
#include <iostream.h>

int main(void)
{
    cout << "\nPlease enter the employee number: ";

    int
        EmpNumber;                          // employee number

    cin >> EmpNumber;

    cout << "\nPlease enter the hours worked, and the pay rate: ";

    double
        Hours,                              // hours worked by employee
        Rate;                               // employee's hourly rate

    cin >> Hours >> Rate;

    double
        Wages = Hours * Rate;               // gross wages earned by employee

    cout << "\nEmployee # " << EmpNumber
         << "\nHours Worked: " << Hours
         << "\nHourly Rate: $" << Rate
         << "\nTotal Wages: $" << Wages
         << "\n\n";

    return 0;
}
```

Sample run:

```
Please enter the employee number: 31564

Please enter the hours worked, and the pay rate: 38.5 8.75

Employee # 31564
Hours worked: 38.5
Hourly rate:  $ 8.75
Total Wages:  $ 336.875
```

Output Formatting

The output produced by the preceding program is not really satisfactory because the real values are displayed with a precision that is not suitable for monetary values. This can be remedied by inserting **format manipulators** from the header file **<iomanip.h>** as items in the output list. These format manipulators specify the appearance (or *format*) of the output. A few manipulators are given here; a more complete description of the capabilities provided by the **iostream** and **iomanip** libraries can be found in Chapter 8.

Format Manipulators

Manipulators:	Description:
setw(*Width*)	Display the next value in a field with the specified *Width* (1 is the default.)
setprecision(*Precision*)	Display values with the specified *Precision* (6 is a common default.)
setiosflags(*FlagList*)	Set the formatting flags in *FlagList*, where *FlagList* is a sequence of one or more flags, separated with the | symbol:

$$Flag_1 \mid Flag_2 \mid \ldots \mid Flag_n$$

The following are a few of the formatting flags available:

ios::showpoint
   Display decimal point and trailing zeros

ios::fixed
   Display real values in fixed-point form

ios::scientific
   Display real values in floating-point form

ios::left
   Display values left-justified within a field

ios::right
   Display values right-justified within a field

Purpose:
When inserted into an output list, these format manipulators specify the output format of subsequent item(s) in the list.

To illustrate the use of format manipulators, consider the statements

```
double
   Alpha = 8.0 / 3.0,
   Beta = 9.0 / 3.0;

cout << "\n(" << Alpha << ")"
     << "\n(" << Beta << ")\n";
```

While the default format depends on the particular C++ implementation, the output displayed by these statements might appear as

```
(2.666667)
(3)
```

because in this particular implementation

- The default precision is 6, so that (up to) six positions are provided to hold the digits after the decimal point,
- The value of **Alpha** is displayed in a field whose (default) width is 1, and C++ automatically widens fields that are too small to the minimum width required to display the value,
- By default, the flag **ios::showpoint** is not set, so that neither the decimal point nor the fractional values of **Beta** are displayed.

Using the **setiosflags()** manipulator to set the **ios::showpoint** flag will cause the decimal point and trailing zeros of **Beta** to be displayed, and using it to set the **ios::fixed** flag will ensure that values are displayed in fixed-point (rather than floating-point) form,

```
cout  << setiosflags(ios::showpoint | ios::fixed)
      << "\n(" << Alpha << ")"
      << "\n(" << Beta << ")\n";
```

so that the output appears as follows:

```
(2.66667)
(3.00000)
```

Suppose we wish to alter the precision to display only three decimal places. We can insert the **setprecision()** manipulator

```
cout  << setiosflags(ios::showpoint | ios::fixed)
      << setprecision(3)
      << "\n(" << Alpha << ")"
      << "\n(" << Beta << ")\n";
```

which will alter the output as follows:

```
(2.667)
(3.000)
```

Similarly, we can use the `setw()` manipulator to change the width of the field in which `Alpha` appears:

```
cout  << setiosflags(ios::showpoint | ios::fixed)
      << setprecision(3)
      << "\n(" << setw(10) << Alpha << ")"
      << "\n(" << Beta << ")\n";
```

The output will then appear as

```
(     2.667)
(3.000)
```

because

- The number of positions required to display the value of `Alpha` (5) is now smaller than the width of the field being used to display `Alpha` (10).
- By default, the flag `ios::right` is set (implying that `ios::left` is not set), causing the value of `Alpha` to be right justified in its (too-large) field.

Note that an important difference between `setw()` and the other manipulators is that `setw()` *affects the format of only the next value to be displayed,* whereas the other manipulators affect the appearances of all values that follow them in the statement.

The `setw()` manipulator can be used to align output right-justified values in a column (i.e., vertically). For example, inserting another `setw()` before outputting `Beta`,

```
cout << setiosflags(ios::showpoint | ios::fixed)
     << setprecision(3)
     << "\n(" << setw(10) << Alpha << ")"
     << "\n(" << setw(10) << Beta << ")\n";
```

changes the output to

```
(     2.667)
(     3.000)
```

We noted earlier that the output produced by the program in Figure 3.3 is not really satisfactory. The program in Figure 3.4 is a modification that uses format manipulators to display the results in a more acceptable format.

FIGURE 3.4   Calculating wages—Version 2.

```
/* This program computes the wages of an employee.

   Input:   The employee's number, the hours worked, and the hourly rate
   Output:  The employee's number, hours worked, hourly rate, and total
            wages.

---------------------------------------------------------------------*/
```

FIGURE 3.4 Calculating wages—Version 2. (cont.)

```cpp
#include <iostream.h>
#include <iomanip.h>

int main(void)
{
    cout << "\nPlease enter the employee number: ";

    int
        EmpNumber;                      // employee number

    cin >> EmpNumber;

    cout << "\nPlease enter the hours worked and the pay rate: ";

    double
        Hours,                          // hours worked by employee
        Rate;                           // employee's hourly rate

    cin >> Hours >> Rate;

    double
        Wages = Hours * Rate;           // gross wages earned by employee

    cout << "\nEmployee # " << EmpNumber
        << setprecision(2)              // precision for monetary values
        << setiosflags(ios::showpoint | ios::fixed)
                                        // force .00 to display
        << "\nHours Worked: " << setw(7) << Hours
        << "\nHourly Rate: $" << setw(7) << Rate
        << "\nTotal Wages: $" << setw(7) << Wages
        << "\n\n";

    return 0;
}
```

Sample run:

```
Please enter the employee number: 31564

Please enter the hours worked, and the pay rate: 38.5 8.75

Employee # 31564
Hours worked:    38.50
Hourly rate:  $   8.75
Total Wages:  $ 336.88
```

Exercises

1. Assuming that **Alpha** and **Beta** are real variables with values -567.392 and 0.0004, respectively, and that **Rho** is an integer variable with a value 436, show precisely the output that each of the following sets of statements produces, or explain why an error occurs.

   (a) cout << Rho << Rho + 1 << Rho + 2;

   (b) cout << "Alpha ="
           << setw(9) << setprecision(3) << Alpha << '\n'
           << setw(10) << setprecision(5) << Beta << '\n'
           << setw(7) << setprecision(4) << Beta << '\n';

   (c) cout << setprecision(1) << setw(8) << Alpha << '\n'
           << setw(5) << Rho << '\n'
           << "Tolerance:"
           << setw(8) << setprecision(5) << Beta << '\n';

   (d) cout << "Alpha =" << setw(12) << setprecision(5)
           << Alpha << '\n'
           << "Beta =" << setw(6) << setprecision(2)
           << Beta << '\n'
           << "Rho =" << setw(6) << Rho << '\n'
           << setw(15) << setprecision(3)
           << Alpha + 4.0 + Rho << '\n';

   (e) cout << "Tolerance =" << setw(5)
           << setprecision(3) << Beta;
      cout << setw(2) << Rho << setw(4) << Alpha;

   (f) cout << setw(8) << setprecision(1) << 10 * Alpha
           << setw(8) << ceil(10 * Alpha);
      cout << setprecision(3) << setw(5) << pow(Rho / 100, 2.0)
           << setw(5) << sqrt(Rho / 100);

   (g) cout << "Rho =" << setw(8) << setprecision(2) << Rho
           << '*****';

   (h) cout << setw(10) << Alpha << setw(10) << Beta;

2. Assuming that **I** and **J** are integer variables with **I** = 15 and **J** = 8, that **C** and **D** are character variables with **C** = 'C' and **D** = 'd', and that **X** and **Y** are real variables with **X** = 2559.50 and **Y** = 8.015, show precisely the output that each of the following sets of statements produces.

   (a) cout << setw(J) << setprecision(2) << "New balance ="
           << X << ' '
           << C << "an" << D << "y is" << setw(I % 10) << I
           << setw(J) << setprecision(J - 6) << Y;

   (b) cout << I =" << setw(I) << I
           << "J =" << setw(J) << setprecision(J) << J << '\n'
           << setw(J) << I << ' '
           << setw(I) << J;

3. Assume that **N1** and **N2** are integer variables with values 39 and −5117, respectively; that **R1** and **R2** are real variables with values 56.7173 and −0.00247, respectively; and that **C** is a character variable with value **F**. For each of the following, write a set of output statements that use these variables to produce the given output (without the underlines).

(a) _56.7173___F___39_
    -5117PDQ-0.00247

(b) __56.717____-0.0025***39_F
    ____56.72__39-5117_

(c) ROOTS_ARE__56.717_AND_-0.00247

(d) APPROXIMATE_ANGLES:__56.7_AND_-0.0
    MAGNITUDES_ARE_____39_AND_5117____

4. Assuming that **A**, **B**, and **C** are integer variables and **X**, **Y**, and **Z** are real variables, tell what value, if any, will be assigned to each of these variables, or explain why an error occurs, when each of the following sets of statements is executed with the given input data.

(a) `cin >> A >> B >> C`   Input: 1   2   3
        `>> X >> Y >> Z;`   4 5.5 6.6

(b) `cin >> A >> B >> C;`   Input: 1
    `cin >> X >> Y >> Z;`   2
                                         3
                                         4
                                         5
                                         6

(c) `cin >> A >> X;`   Input: 1 2.2
    `cin >> B >> Y;`   3 4.4
    `cin >> C >> Z;`   5 6.6

(d) `cin >> A >> B >> C;`   Input: 1 2.2
    `cin >> X >> Y >> Z;`   3 4.4
                                         5 6.6

(e) `cin >> A;`   Input: 1   2   3
    `cin >> B >> C;`   4 5.5 6.6
    `cin >> X >> Y;`
    `cin >> Z;`

(f) `cin >> A`   Input: 1   2   3
        `>> B >> C`   4 5.5 6.6
        `>> X >> Y`
        `>> Z;`

(g) `cin >> A >> B;`   Input: 1   2   3
    `cin >> C >> X >> Y >> Z;`   4   5.5 6.6
                                           7   8.8 9.9
                                          10 11.11 12.12
                                          13 14.14 15.15

3.7   Example: Truck Fleet Accounting

Problem

Suppose that a manufacturing company maintains a fleet of trucks to deliver its products. On each trip, the driver records the distance traveled in miles, the number of gallons of fuel used, the cost of the fuel, and other costs of operating the truck. As part of the accounting process, the controller needs to calculate and record for each truck and for each trip the miles per gallon, the total cost of that trip, and the cost per mile. A simple program is to be designed to carry out these calculations.

Specification

The input/output specifications for this problem are as follows:

> Input: the number of miles traveled
> the total number of gallons of fuel used
> the price of a gallon of fuel
> the per-mile cost of operating the vehicle
> Output: the number of miles driven per gallon
> the total cost of the trip
> the cost of the trip per mile

Design

The calculations required to solve this program are quite simple:

- The number of miles driven per gallon can be computed by dividing the number of miles traveled by the number of gallons of fuel used.
- The total cost of the trip can be computed by adding:
  a. The total cost of fuel (gallons used multiplied by price per gallon)
  b. The total operating costs (miles driven multiplied by cost per mile)
- The cost of the trip per mile can be computed by dividing the total cost of the trip by the number of miles traveled.

The solution thus requires only the standard arithmetic operations.

Expressing this algorithm in pseudocode is straightforward once we select the appropriate variable names to represent the quantities involved. Selecting names that are self-documenting, we use the following:

Data Object	Kind of Value	Type of Object	Name of Object
Total miles traveled	Variable	Real	*Miles*
Total gallons of fuel used	Variable	Real	*GallonsOfFuel*
Cost per gallon of fuel	Variable	Real	*UnitFuelCost*
Operating cost per mile	Variable	Real	*UnitOperatingCost*
Total fuel cost	Variable	Real	*TotalFuelCost*
Total operating cost	Variable	Real	*TotalOperatingCost*
Miles per gallon	Variable	Real	*MPG*
Total cost of the trip	Variable	Real	*TotalTripCost*
Cost per mile	Variable	Real	*CostPerMile*

A pseudocode description of the algorithm is the following:

ALGORITHM FOR TRUCK COST PROBLEM

/* This algorithm computes the costs of operating a fleet of trucks.

   Input: *Miles, GallonsOfFuel, UnitFuelCost, UnitOperatingCost*
   Output: *MPG, TotalTripCost, CostPerMile*
——*/

1. Enter *Miles, GallonsOfFuel, UnitFuelCost,* and *UnitOperatingCost.*
2. Calculate *MPG = Miles / GallonsOfFuel.*
3. Calculate:
     a. *TotalFuelCost = UnitFuelCost * GallonsOfFuel*
     b. *TotalOperatingCost = UnitOperatingCost * Miles*
     c. *TotalTripCost = TotalFuelCost + TotalOperatingCost*
4. Calculate *CostPerMile = TotalTripCost / Miles.*
5. Display *MPG, TotalTripCost,* and *CostPerMile.*

Coding and Testing

A C++ implemention of this algorithm and two sample runs are shown in Figure 3.5.

FIGURE 3.5 Trucking costs.

```
/* This program calculates the total cost and miles per gallon
   of a vehicle, based on the miles traveled, fuel consumed,
   cost per gallon of fuel, and operating cost per mile.

   Input: The total miles traveled, total fuel consumed,
          unit cost of the fuel, and operating cost per mile

   Output: The miles per gallon, total cost of the trip,
           and the cost per mile
-------------------------------------------------------------------*/

#include <iostream.h>
#include <iomanip.h>

int main(void)
{
   const int
      Width = 7;                        // width of output field
```

FIGURE 3.5 Trucking costs. (cont.)

```
cout << "\nPlease enter:\n\tthe total miles traveled,"
     << "\n\tthe gallons of fuel used,"
     << "\n\tthe total cost per gallon of the fuel, and"
     << "\n\tthe operating cost per mile."
     << "\n\t---> ";

double
   Miles,                       // total miles traveled
   GallonsOfFuel,               // total gallons used
   UnitFuelCost,                // fuel cost per gallon
   UnitOperatingCost;           // operating cost per mile

cin >> Miles >> GallonsOfFuel
    >> UnitFuelCost >> UnitOperatingCost;

double
   MPG = Miles / GallonsOfFuel,

   TotalFuelCost = UnitFuelCost * GallonsOfFuel,

   TotalOperatingCost = UnitOperatingCost * Miles,

   TotalTripCost = TotalFuelCost + TotalOperatingCost,

   CostPerMile = TotalTripCost / Miles;

cout << setiosflags(ios::showpoint | ios::fixed)
     << setprecision(2)
     << "\n\tMiles per gallon: " << setw(Width) << MPG
     << "\n\tTotal cost:      $" << setw(Width) << TotalTripCost
     << "\n\tCost per mile:   $" << setw(Width) << CostPerMile
     << "\n\n";
   return 0;
}
```

Sample runs:

```
Please enter:
   the total miles traveled,
   the gallons of fuel used,
   the total cost per gallon of the fuel, and
   the operating cost per mile.
   ---> 10.0 1.0 1.50 1.00

Miles per gallon:   10.00
Total cost:      $  11.50
Cost per mile:   $   1.15
```

FIGURE 3.5 Trucking costs. (cont.)

```
Please enter:
   the total miles traveled,
   the gallons of fuel used,
   the total cost per gallon of the fuel, and
   the operating cost per mile.
   ---> 500.0 55.5 1.25 .95

Miles per gallon:   9.01
Total cost:      $ 544.38
Cost per mile:   $   1.09
```

3.8 PART OF THE PICTURE: Syntax and Semantics

In this chapter we introduced enough of the basic features of the C++ language to allow us to write simple programs like that in the preceding section. We have described the general structure of a program as well as some of the declarations, operations, statements, and other items that make up a program. In each case we described the general form of these items and what they are intended to accomplish.

Recall from Section 1.2 that C++ programs must be compiled before they can be executed. A **compiler** is a system program that accepts as input the stream of characters that make up the C++ program and separates these characters into meaningful groups such as key words, constants, and identifiers. These groups are called *tokens,* and the compiler groups these tokens into larger structures such as arithmetic expressions and statements. If these tokens and structures are formed according to the rules of the C++ language, the compiler will be able to recognize them and translate them into machine instructions, which can then be executed.

The rules that specify the form of a C++ program and of each of its components are called the **syntax rules** of the language. These rules must be stated very clearly and precisely, and various methods have been used to accomplish this. Two of the most common methods are **Backus–Naur Form (BNF),** which uses an algebraic notation, and **syntax diagrams,** which present the rules graphically.

To illustrate, the syntax rule discussed in Section 3.2 for forming identifiers stated that an identifier consists of a letter or underscore followed by any number of letters, digits, or underscores. In BNF, this syntax rule would be stated as:

<identifier> ::= <letter> | _ [<letter> | <digit> | _]

The symbol ::= is read as "is defined as," the vertical bar (|) as "or," and the square brackets, [and], are used to enclose items that can be repeated zero or more times. Angular brackets, < and >, are used to enclose items like "letter" and "digit" that also must be defined:

<letter> ::= a | b | c | d | e | f | g | h | i | j | k | l | m |
         n | o | p | q | r | s | t | u | v | w | x | y | z |
         A | B | C | D | E | F | G | H | I | J | K | L | M |
         N | O | P | Q | R | S | T | U | V | W | X | Y | Z

<digit> ::= 0 | 1 | 2 | 3 | 4 | 5 | 6 | 7 | 8 | 9

The syntax rule for identifiers can also be given by the following syntax diagram:

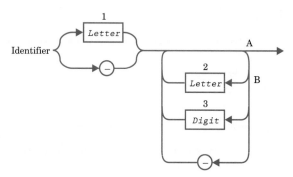

To use this diagram as a syntax rule for forming identifiers, we begin on the left and proceed to the right. Each time we pass through one of the boxes, we record a character of the specified type. At a junction in the diagram, any one of the paths may be followed. When we exit at the right, we will have formed a valid identifier. For example, the identifier **x14a** can be formed as follows: Beginning on the left and passing through the first box, we record the letter **x**. Moving to the right, at junction A we loop back, passing through box 3, and record the digit **1**. When we return to junction A, we loop back again and record the digit **4** when we pass through box 3. At junction A we loop back one final time, but this time at junction B we take the path through box 2 and record the letter **a**. Finally, at junction A we proceed to the right and exit, having formed the identifier **x14a**. (We labeled the boxes and junctions of the syntax diagram to facilitate our discussion, although normally such labels are not used.)

In a syntax diagram such as this one, the rectangular boxes indicate a language construct for which syntax rules must be specified. A syntax diagram for digits is

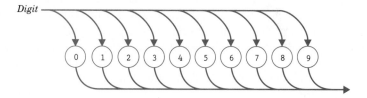

A syntax diagram for letters is similar. Circles and ovals indicate symbols or keywords in C++ that must appear exactly as shown.

The graphical representation of syntax rules afforded by syntax diagrams is easier to read than is the algebraic notation of BNF. Thus, we use syntax diagrams rather than BNF to present many of the syntax rules in this text.

A syntax diagram can be used to specify the form of any part of the constructs of C++. For example, we might specify the form of a variable declaration by

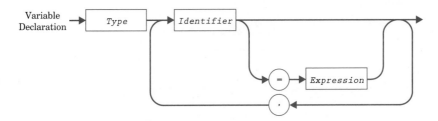

or the body of a C++ program (called a *compound statement*) by

As we have seen, one way that a statement can be formed is by terminating an expression with a semicolon. Each C++ expression can also be specified by a syntax diagram. For example, a syntax diagram specifying the correct form of an assignment expression is the following:

An input expression can be specifed as follows:

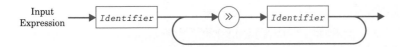

Here, the first identifier is the name of an **istream** object (e.g., **cin**), and each subsequent identifier encountered is one of the variables being filled with the input values.

Syntax diagrams provide a convenient mechanism for precisely defining the syntax rules for C++, and in subsequent chapters, we use them to summarize the syntax of many new C++ items.

Note that a syntax rule specifies only the *form* of an item and not its meaning. For example, the preceding syntax diagram specifies only the form of an input expression. As we saw, additional information must be given to describe the meaning of this statement, namely, that the first identifier must be an **istream** object, and each identifier subsequently encountered must be a variable for whose type the **>>** operator is defined. The interpretation or meaning of a language construct is called its **semantics** and must be specified by some means other than the syntax diagram. Although formal methods and notations analogous to BNF and syntax diagrams are available for specifying semantics, they are beyond the scope of this introductory text. Instead, we will describe the semantics of new items informally and illustrate them by means of examples.

Exercises

1. A "thing" is defined by the following syntax diagrams:

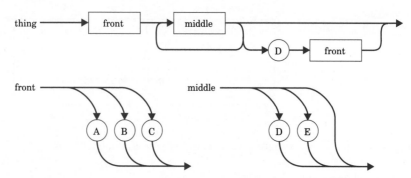

Determine which of the following are valid things:

(a) ADDDDDDA   **(b)** ADDA   **(c)** ADA   **(d)** ABC   **(e)** ADC   **(f)** A

2. Use BNF to state the syntax rules defined by the syntax diagrams in Exercise 1.

3. A widget is defined as follows.

   i. A widget is a jabber followed by a wocky followed by a slash (/).
  ii. A jabber is a thunk or a thunk followed by * or a thunk followed by a wocky.
 iii. A thunk is the letter T followed by one of the digits 1, 2, or 3.
 iv. A wocky is a thunk or a list of thunks separated by commas.

Give a complete set of syntax rules for widgets using **(a)** BNF and **(b)** syntax diagrams.

4. Describe the syntax errors in the following program:

```
{ 1}    #include >iostream,h<
{ 2}    int main(void)                \\ program's beginning
{ 3}    {
{ 4}        CONST int Year 1776;
{ 5}
{ 6}        int Add, Sub, Mult, Div, Rho
{ 7}
{ 8}
{ 9}        int Mult = 3.14;
{10}        cin >> Div;
{11}        real ALPha = 3,
{12}        Beta = Alpha + 1,
{13}        Rho % Beta = 3;
{14}        cout << 'Value is' << Alpha
{15}                << "Gamma isn\'t negative'
{16}                << Mult << '\n\n';
{17}        Year = Year + 1;
{18}        cout << Year
{19}    ]
```

Programming Pointers

In this section, we consider some aspects of program design and suggest guidelines for good programming style. We also point out some errors that may occur in writing C++ programs.

Program Design

1. *Programs cannot be considered to be correct if they have not been tested.* Test all programs with data for which the results are known or can be checked by hand calculations.

2. *Programs should be readable and understandable.*

   ■ *Use meaningful identifiers.* For example,

   ```
   Wages = Hours * Rate;
   ```

   is more meaningful than

   ```
   W = H * R;
   ```

   or

   ```
   Z7 = Alpha * X;
   ```

   Also, avoid "cute" identifiers, as in

   ```
   BaconBroughtHome = HoursWasted * Pittance;
   ```

   ■ *Use comments to describe the purpose of a program or other key program segments.* However, don't clutter the program with needless comments; for example, the comment in the statement

   ```
   Counter = Counter + 1;    // add 1 to counter
   ```

   is not helpful and should not be used.

   ■ *Label all output produced by a program.* For example,

   ```
   cout << "Employee # " << EmpNumber
        << " Wages = $ " << Wages;
   ```

   produces more informative output than does

   ```
   cout << EmpNumber << Wages;
   ```

3. *Programs should be general and flexible.* They should solve a class of problems rather than one specific problem. It should be relatively easy to modify a program to solve a related problem without changing much of the program. Using named constants as described in Section 3.3 is helpful in this regard.

Potential Problems

1. *Character constants must be enclosed in single quotes.*

2. *Values of type* char *are stored as their (integer) numeric codes.* This can be confusing if you mistakenly assign an integer value to a char variable, since the type char is equivalent to an 8-bit integer.[12] For example, strange things like the following are allowed in C++:

```
char
   LetterGrade = 65;
```

On machines using the ASCII character set, this causes **LetterGrade** to have exactly the same value as if it had been initialized to **'A'** (since 65 is the decimal ASCII code for **'A'**). Such mixing of integer and character values within an expression should normally be avoided.

3. *Character string constants must be enclosed within double quotes.* If either the beginning or the ending double quote is missing, an error will result. Escape sequences, such as \", are used to represent double quotes, single quotes, tabs, newlines, etc.

4. *Character string constants cannot be assigned to variables of type* char.

5. *The type of value stored in a variable should be the same as or promotable to the type of that variable.* For example, most implementations of C++ will not promote a chararacter value to a real value, so that if **Radius** is a real variable and the statement

```
Radius = 'z';
```

is executed, then a syntax error will be generated when this statement is compiled. By contrast, the statement

```
cin >> Radius;
```

is syntactically correct and will compile correctly. However, if the user should enter the character **z** when the program containing this statement is *executed,* then the language rules will prevent promotion and the value of **Radius** will be undefined.

   Although both assignments and input statements change the value of a variable, the compiler is able to check for incompatibility errors in an assignment but is unable to check incompatibility errors in input statements, since the input occurs at run time.

6. *If an integer value is to be stored in a real variable, then most implementations will automatically* **promote** *the integer to a real type. By contrast, if a real value is to be stored in an integer variable, then the real value is* **truncated,** *possibly resulting in the loss of information.*

7. *Parentheses within expressions must be paired.* That is, for each left parenthesis, there must be exactly one matching right parenthesis.

---

[12] A 7-bit integer, actualy, since $2^7 = 128$, but 8 bits (a byte) is the smallest piece of memory that can be accessed quickly. Some implementations have legal values ranging from 0 to 255 (unsigned chars), whereas others have legal values ranging from -128 to 127 (signed chars), and still others just ignore the whole question.

8. *Both real and integer division are denoted by /; which is used is determined by the type of the operands.* Thus, **8 / 5 = 1**, but **8.0 / 5.0 = 1.6**.

9. *All multiplications must be indicated by* *. For example **2 * n** is valid, but **2n** is not.

10. *A semicolon must appear at the end of each expression (assignments, input, output, etc.) that is meant to be a program statement.*

11. *Comments are enclosed within /* and */ or within // and the end of the line.* Each beginning delimiter **/*** must have a matching end delimiter ***/**. Failure to use these in pairs can produce strange results. For example, in the statement part

```
{
    /* Read employee data
    cin >> EmpNumber >> Hours >> Rate;
    /* Calculate wages */
    Wages = Hours * Rate;
}
```

everything from "Read employee data . . . " through "Calculate wages," including the input statement, is a single comment. No values are read for **EmpNumber**, **Hours**, and **Rate**, and so **Hours** and **Rate** are undefined when the statement **Wages = Hours * Rate**; is executed.

12. *Every { must be matched by a }.* Failure to include either one produces an error.

13. *All identifiers must be declared.* Failure to declare an identifier used in a program generates a syntax error.

14. *C++ distinguishes between uppercase and lowercase letters.* For example, **Sum**, **sum**, and **SUM** all represent different identifiers. Thus, variable declarations such as

```
int
    Sum;
double
    sum;
```

are allowed, since different identifiers are being declared. However, such declarations should be avoided, since the two data objects declared will be easily confused, forming a likely source for logical errors.

15. *Variables should be initialized at their declarations, unless they are going to be immediately changed by an input or assignment statement.* If a variable's value is going to be immediately changed, there is little point to giving it an initial value, since that value will be overwritten by the input value. However, other variables should be initialized appropriately, since the value of an uninitialized variable is *undefined*. This means that it is not possible to predict the contents of the memory location associated with a variable until a value has been explicitly assigned to that variable. For example, the statements

```
int
   x,
   y;

   .
   .
   .

y = x + 1;
```

will produce a ''garbage'' value for **y**, since **x** has not previously been initialized or assigned a value, as in

```
int
   x = 0,
   y;

   .
   .
   .

y = x + 1;
```

16. *Keywords, identifiers, and constants may not be broken at the end of a line, nor may they contain blanks (except, of course, a string constant may contain blanks).* Thus, the statements

```
EmpNumber = 12345;
cout << "The number of the current employee is "
     << EmpNumber;
```

are valid, whereas the statements

```
Emp Number = 12 345;
cout << "The number of the current employee
          is " << EmpNumber;
```

are not valid. If it is necessary to split a string over two lines, as in the second statement, one can split the string into two separate strings,

```
cout << "The number of the current employee "
     << "is " << EmpNumber;
```

or split the statement into two separate statements,

```
cout << "The number of the current employee ";
cout <<  "is " << EmpNumber;
```

17. *An equal sign* (=) *is used*

   ■ *In constant declarations to associate an identifier with a constant;*
   ■ *In variable declarations to provide a variable with an initial value;*
   ■ *In assignment statements to change the value of a variable.*

The actions produced by each of these uses occur at different times; do not confuse them.

Program Style

In the examples in this text, we adopt certain stylistic guidelines for C++ programs, and you should write your program in a similar style. In this text, the following standards are used; others are described in the Programming Pointers of subsequent chapters.

1. *Put each statement of the program on a separate line.*

2. *Use uppercase and lowercase letters in a way that contributes to program readability;* for example, put identifiers in lowercase, capitalizing the first letter of each word.

3. *Put each { and } on a separate line.*

4. *Each { and its corresponding } should be aligned. The statements enclosed by { and } are indented (usually 3 spaces).*

5. *When a statement is continued from one line to another, indent the continued line(s).*

6. *Indent each constant declaration and each variable declaration, placing them on separate lines;* for example,

```
const double
    TaxRate = 0.1963,
    InterestRate = 0.185;
int
    EmpNumber;
double
    Hours,
    Rate,
    Wages;
```

7. *Insert blank lines between declarations and statements and between blocks of statements (i.e., steps of your algorithm) to make clear the structure of your program.*

8. *Separate the operators and operands in an expression with spaces to make the expression easier to read.*

9. *Declare constants at the beginning of a function; declare variables near their first use.* This enables constants to be found easily, when their modification is needed. It also reduces the tendency to declare unused variables, since declarations are deferred until they are needed.

Programming Projects

1. Write a program that reads two three-digit integers and then calculates and prints their product and the quotient and the remainder that result when the first is divided by the second. The output should be formatted to appear as follows:

```
        739                              61 R 7
      x  12                            -----
      -----                       12 ) 739
       8868
```

2. Write a program to read the lengths of the two legs of a right triangle and to calculate and print the area of the triangle (one-half the product of the legs) and the length of the hypotenuse (square root of the sum of the squares of the legs).

3. Write a program to read values for the coefficients A, B, and C of the quadratic equation $Ax^2 + Bx + C = 0$, and then find the two roots of this equation by using the quadratic formula

$$\frac{-B \pm \sqrt{B^2 - 4AC}}{2A}$$

Execute the program with several values of A, B, and C for which the quantity $B^2 - 4AC$ is nonnegative, including $A = 4$, $B = 0$, $C = -36$; $A = 1$, $B = 5$, $C = -36$; and $A = 2$, $B = 7.5$, $C = 6.25$.

4. Write a program to convert a measurement given in feet to the equivalent number of (a) yards, (b) inches, (c) centimeters, and (d) meters (1 ft = 12 in, 1 yd = 3 ft, 1 in = 2.54 cm, 1 m = 100 cm).

5. Write a program to read a student's number, his or her old GPA (grade point average), and the number of old course credits (e.g., 31479, 3.25, 66) and to then print these with appropriate labels. Next, read the course credit and grade for each of four courses—for example, `Course1 = 5.0`, `Grade1 = 3.7`, `Course2 = 3.0`, `Grade2 = 4.0`, and so on. Calculate:

    # of old honor points = (# of old course credits) ∗ (old GPA)
    # of new honor points = `Course1` ∗ `Grade 1` +
                        `Course2` ∗ `Grade2` + · · ·
    # of new course credits = `Course1` + `Course2` + · · ·

$$\text{current GPA} = \frac{\text{\# of new honor points}}{\text{\# of new course credits}}$$

Print the current GPA with an appropriate label. Finally, calculate

$$\text{cumulative GPA} = \frac{(\text{\# of old honor points}) + (\text{\# of new honor points})}{(\text{\# of old course credits}) + (\text{\# of new course credits})}$$

and print this with a label.

6. The shipping clerk at the Rinky Dooflingy Company (Exercise 11 at the end of Chapter 2) is faced with the following problem: Dooflingies are very delicate and must be shipped in special containers. These containers are available in four sizes, huge, large, medium, and small, which can hold 50, 20, 5, and 1 dooflingy, respectively. Write a program that reads the number of dooflingies to be shipped and prints the number of huge, large, medium, and small containers needed to send the shipment in the minimum number of containers and with the minimum amount of wasted space. Use named constants for the number of

dooflingies each type of container can hold. The output should be similar to the following:

```
Container      Number
=========      ======
   Huge          21
   Large          2
   Medium         1
   Small          3
```

Execute the program for 3, 18, 48, 78, and 10,598 dooflingies.

7. Write a program that reads the amount of a purchase and the amount received in payment (both amounts in cents) and then computes the change in dollars, half-dollars, quarters, dimes, nickels, and pennies.

8. Angles are often measured in degrees (°), minutes ('), and seconds (''). There are 360 degrees in a circle, 60 minutes in one degree, and 60 seconds in one minute. Write a program that reads two angular measurements given in degrees, minutes, and seconds and then calculates and prints their sum. Use the program to verify each of the following:

$$74°29'13'' + 105°8'16'' = 179°37'29''$$
$$7°14'55'' + 5°24'55'' = 12°39'50''$$
$$20°31'19'' + 0°31'30'' = 21°2'49''$$
$$122°17'48'' + 237°42'12'' = 0°0'0''$$

9. Write a program that reads two three-digit integers and then prints their product in the following format:

```
        749
   x    381
   -------
        749
       5992
       2247
   -------
      285369
```

Execute the program with the following values: 749 and 381; −749 and 381; 749 and −381; −749 and −381; 999 and 999.

FUNCTIONS AND LIBRARIES

> *Great things can be reduced to small things, and small things can be reduced to nothing.*
> CHINESE PROVERB
>
> *From a little distance one can perceive an order in what at the time seemed confusion.*
> F. SCOTT FITZGERALD

CHAPTER CONTENTS

Most of us dislike unnecessary work, and one way to avoid unnecessary work in programming is to write code that is *reusable*. Showing how to do this is the theme of this chapter.

One basic idea noted in the preceding chapter is to *plan for the future*—that is, when writing a program to solve a particular problem, try to anticipate whether you (or anyone else) might someday want to reuse some parts of that program. If so, write those components of the program that you anticipate using again someday as *functions* and store them in a *library*. The program (and any program you write in the future) can then use those components by retrieving them from the library, just as the program in Figure 3.2 used the function `pow()` from `<math.h>`.

4.1   Computing with Formulas

There are many problems whose solutions involve the use of one or more formulas, such as the problem of computing the volume of a sphere that we examined in Section 3.1. Writing programs to solve such problems is usually straightforward, as long as we know the particular formula(s) that are required. For example, consider the following problem, that we will use as an example throughout this chapter:

Example: Temperature Conversion

Problem.   Suppose that we are studying chemistry in an antiquated lab whose thermometers measure temperature in Fahrenheit, and we wish to write a program to convert such temperatures to Celsius.

Specification.   From the statement of the problem, we can easily specify the problem precisely:

Input: A Fahrenheit temperature
Output: The equivalent Celsius temperature

Design.   The formula for converting temperature measured in Fahrenheit to Celsius can be found in any number of reference books:

$$C = (F - 32)/1.8$$

where F is the Fahrenheit temperature to be converted and C is the corresponding Celsius temperature. The following data objects are used in solving this problem:

Data Object	Kind of Value	Type of Object	Name of Object
A Fahrenheit temperature	Variable	Real	*FahrenheitTemp*
A Celsius temperature	Variable	Real	*CelsiusTemp*

In fact, this problem involves two additional data objects—the numeric values 32 and 1.8. For constant values such as these, which are unlikely to change in the foreseeable future, we neither name nor list them in our list of data objects.

The operations required to solve this problem are

- Input of a temperature, modeled as a real value;
- Conversion of a temperature from Fahrenheit to Celsius, which involves real subtraction and real division; and
- Output of a temperature, modeled as a real value.

As in all our programs thus far, each of these operations is provided in C++, and so the construction of an algorithm is straightforward:

ALGORITHM FOR TEMPERATURE CONVERSION PROBLEM

/* This algorithm converts a temperature from Fahrenheit to Celsius.

    Input: *FahrenheitTemp*
    Output: *CelsiusTemp*

——*/

1. Enter *FahrenheitTemp*.
2. Calculate *CelsiusTemp* = (*FahrenheitTemp* − 32)/1.8.
3. Display *CelsiusTemp*.

Coding and Testing. A C++ program that solves this problem is given in Figure 4.1.

    FIGURE 4.1 Converting a temperature—version 1.

```
/* This program converts a temperature from Fahrenheit to Celsius,
   using the standard Fahrenheit-to-Celsius conversion formula.

   Input:  FahrenheitTemp
   Output: CelsiusTemp
------------------------------------------------------------------*/

#include <iostream.h>

int main(void)
{
   cout << "\nThis program converts a temperature\n"
        << "\tfrom Fahrenheit to Celsius.\n";

   double
      FahrenheitTemp;
```

FIGURE 4.1   Converting a temperature—version 1. (cont.)

```
cout << "\nPlease enter a Fahrenheit temperature: ";
cin >> FahrenheitTemp;

double
   CelsiusTemp = (FahrenheitTemp - 32.0) / 1.8;

cout << "\n\t" << FahrenheitTemp
     << " in Fahrenheit is equivalent to "
     << CelsiusTemp << " in Celsius.\n\n";

return 0;
}
```

Sample runs:

```
This program converts a temperature
   from Fahrenheit to Celsius.

Please enter a Fahrenheit temperature: 212

   212 in Fahrenheit is equivalent to 100 in Celsius.

This program converts a temperature
   from Fahrenheit to Celsius.

Please enter a Fahrenheit temperature: 32

   32 in Fahrenheit is equivalent to 0 in Celsius.
```

4.2   Computing with Functions

While solving the temperature-conversion problem, we may have thought that it would be convenient if functions to convert a temperature from Fahrenheit to Celsius and from Celsius to Fahrenheit were in a library. Such a thought is exactly the theme of this chapter: *software reusability.* Instead of writing the program in Figure 4.1, we should anticipate that we (or someone else) might someday need to convert temperatures again. Accordingly, we should not simply build the formula into the program (the way we did in the program in Figure 4.1), but instead *construct a function that encodes the formula,* as illustrated in the program in Figure 4.2.

FIGURE 4.2   Converting a temperature—version 2.

```
/* This program converts a temperature from Fahrenheit to Celsius,
   using a conversion function named FahrToCelsius().

   Input:       FahrenheitTemp
   Output:      CelsiusTemp
------------------------------------------------------------------------*/

#include <iostream.h>

double FahrToCelsius(double);              // function declaration

int main(void)
{
   cout << "\nThis program converts a temperature\n"
        << "\tfrom Fahrenheit to Celsius.\n";

   double
      FahrenheitTemp;

   cout << "\nPlease enter a Fahrenheit temperature: ";
   cin >> FahrenheitTemp;

   double                                  // function call
      CelsiusTemp = FahrToCelsius(FahrenheitTemp);

   cout << "\n\t" << FahrenheitTemp
        << " in Fahrenheit is equivalent to "
        << CelsiusTemp << " in Celsius.\n\n";

   return 0;
}


/*------------------------------------------------------------------------
FahrToCelsius converts a temperature from Fahrenheit to Celsius.

   Receive: A Fahrenheit temperature
   Return:  The equivalent Celsius temperature
------------------------------------------------------------------------*/

double FahrToCelsius(double Temp)          // function definition
{
   return (Temp - 32.0) / 1.8;
}
```

The program in Figure 4.2 produces the same output as that in Figure 4.1, but the flow of execution is very different from that of the program in Figure 4.1. The second version of the program performs the Fahrenheit-to-Celsius conversion using a function that is defined following the main function. The following diagram illustrates the flow of control in this new program.

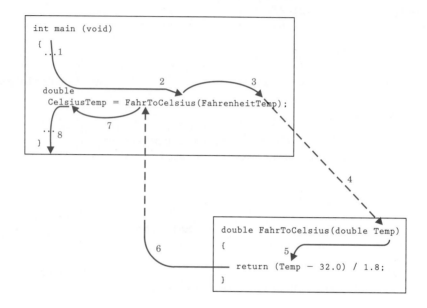

When this program is run, execution proceeds from the beginning of the program in the usual manner (1), until the assignment statement containing the **call** to function **FahrToCelsius()** is reached (2).[1] At that time, the function's **argument** **FahrenheitTemp** (3) is evaluated and copied into the **parameter Temp** in the function **FahrToCelsius()** (4). Control is then transferred from the main function to the function **FahrToCelsius()**, which begins execution (5). The expression

    (Temp - 32.0) / 1.8

is evaluated, and since **Temp** contains a copy of the value of **FahrenheitTemp**, the resulting value is the Celsius equivalent of the value of **FahrenheitTemp**. The **return** statement makes this value the **return value** of **FahrToCelsius()** and transfers execution back to the main function (6). There, the return value of **FahrToCelsius()** is assigned to **CelsiusTemp** (7), and execution proceeds normally through the remainder of the main function (8).

We now discuss the mechanics of constructing such C++ functions, using the program in Figure 4.2 to illustrate the discussion.

---

[1] We will use notation of the form **FunctionName()** for functions, with the parentheses used to distinguish them from identifiers that do not represent functions.

Defining a Function

In the program in Figure 4.2, the lines

```
double FahrToCelsius(double Temp)
{
    return (Temp - 32.0) / 1.8;
}
```

constitute the **definition** of function `FahrToCelsius()`. The syntax of a simplified C++ function definition is given by the following syntax diagram:

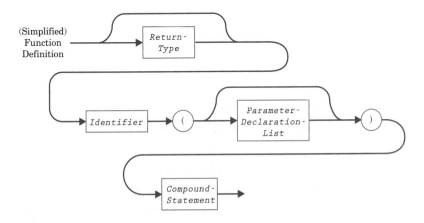

where

ReturnType is the type of value returned by the function (it is optional, and if it is omitted, the default *ReturnType* is `int`).
Identifier is the name of the function.
CompoundStatement is as described in Section 3.7.
ParameterDeclarationList is a sequence of parameter declarations separated by commas, as shown in the following syntax diagram:

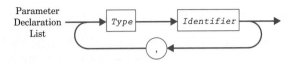

Thus, in the function defined in Figure 4.2,

```
double FahrToCelsius(double Temp)
{
    return (Temp - 32.0) / 1.8;
}
```

the first occurrence of **double** specifies the return type of the function; **FahrToCelsius** is the identifier naming the function; and inside the parentheses, the parameter declaration list declares a single parameter whose type is **double** and whose name is **Temp**. The compound statement of this function consists of braces surrounding a single **return** statement, whose syntax is

The type of the expression being returned should match the return type of the function.

Functions are often called **subprograms,** because defining a function is similar to defining a program. That is, the same steps used to design a program can be used to design a function:

1. Specification
2. Design
3. Coding
4. Verification and validation
5. Maintenance

Specification of a Function.   The specification of a function typically states

- The data objects that must be **received from** the calling function; and
- The data objects that must be **returned to** the calling function.

For example, the problem that **FahrToCelsius()** solves is the problem of converting a temperature from Fahrenheit to Celsius; we might, therefore, identify the following data objects:

Receive: A Fahrenheit temperature
Return: The equivalent temperature in Celsius

Designing a Function.   This specification provides two pieces of information that are critical in defining the function:

1. For each data object that is to be received, a *parameter* must be declared in the function definition to hold that data object; and
2. The *return type* of the function is the type of the data object being returned.

For example, the preceding specification for **FahrToCelsius()** tells us that

1. **FahrToCelsius()** requires one parameter, and its type should be **double** (since we are using the type **double** to represent a temperature); and
2. The return type of **FahrToCelsius()** should be **double**.

Such a specification allows us to begin defining the function. If we choose the name **Temp** for the parameter required by the specification, then we can construct the following **function stub** for **FahrToCelsius()**:

```
double FahrToCelsius(double Temp)
{
}
```

A function stub consists of the function's **heading**—its return type, name, and parenthesized parameter-declaration list—followed by a pair of braces. Once we have constructed such a stub, all that remains is to design an algorithm that solves the problem and then encode that algorithm within this stub.

Designing the algorithm for a function is almost the same as designing the algorithm for a program. The only differences are as follows:

- A program algorithm usually includes a step to *input* the data values required in the solution of the problem, but in a function algorithm, usually the *parameters already contain the data values* because the values of the arguments are copied into the function's parameters when the function is called.
- A program algorithm usually includes a step to *output* data values, but the function algorithm usually contains a step to *return* a data value to the function that calls it.

Thus, we might construct the following algorithm for function **FahrToCelsius()**:

ALGORITHM FOR FAHRENHEIT-TO-CELSIUS CONVERSION FUNCTION

/* This function converts a temperature from Fahrenheit to Celsius

Receive: *Temp,* a Fahrenheit temperature

Return: The Celsius equivalent of *Temp*

_____ *_/_

1. Return (*Temp* − 32.0)/1.8.

Coding a Function.   Given a C++ function stub and a pseudocode algorithm, encoding that algorithm in C++ consists of inserting appropriate C++ statements into the stub. In our example, the **return** statement can be used to code the single instruction in the algorithm for **FahrToCelsius()**:

```
double FahrToCelsius(double Temp)
{
    return (Temp-32.0) / 1.8;
}
```

Verification and Validation.   Just as a program must be tested to verify its correctness, a function should also be rigorously tested to ensure that it is correct. Unlike the simple example function **FahrToCelsius()**, the functions written for large software projects are often large and complex, and they must be thoroughly checked for logical errors before they are incorporated into the project.

However, testing a function is slightly more complicated than testing a program, because in order to execute a function, it must be **called by** another function. We can write a very simple program—actually a function named **main**—whose sole purpose is to test a function. Such a program is called a **driver program** because it "test drives" the function. Figure 4.3 shows a simple driver program that might be used to check the correctness of **FahrToCelsius()** and a sample run of the program. The sample run indicates that **FahrToCelsius()** is performing correctly for the test values we have chosen.

 FIGURE 4.3   A sample driver program.

```
#include <iostream.h>

double FahrToCelsius(double);              // function declaration

int main(void)
{
   cout << "\n212F => " << FahrToCelsius(212)
        << "C\n 32F => " << FahrToCelsius(32)
        << "C\n\n";

   return 0;
}

double FahrToCelsius(double Temp)          // function definition
{
   return (Temp - 32.0) / 1.8;
}
```

Sample run:

```
212F => 100C
 32F => 0C
```

Declaring a Function

The programs in Figures 4.2 and 4.3 each contain the line

```
        double FahrToCelsius(double);
```

before the main function. This line is called the **declaration, prototype,** or **signature,** of function **FahrToCelsius()**. Recall that C++ requires that objects be declared before they can be used so that the compiler can check that the object is being used in a manner consistent with its type. For the objects we have seen thus far (i.e., data objects), their declarations and definitions have been synonymous. However with functions, declarations and definitions are distinct. A function **definition** must *fully describe* the function, including its behavior, but a function **declaration** need only *specify the characteristics of the function,* in particular:

- The *return type* of the function
- The *name* of the function
- The *number of parameters* for the function
- The *type* of each of those parameters

The (simplified) syntax of a function declaration is given in the following syntax diagram:

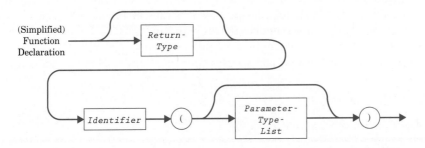

Here **ParameterTypeList** is the same as the parameter declaration list in the function heading except that only the types of the parameters are required. For example, in the declaration

```
double FahrToCelsius(double);
```

the return type of the function is **double**; the name of the function is **FahrToCelsius**; the function has one argument; and the type of that argument is **double**. Note that as with other declarations, a semicolon follows the function declaration to make it a *declaration statement.*

    C++ allows functions to be declared inside or outside the main function. In this text, we have chosen to declare functions outside the main function, because it leads naturally to the study of **libraries** in Section 4.3. Moreover, keeping the function declarations within the main function tends to clutter and obscure the program's structure. Externalizing the function declarations improves readability.

Calling a Function

Since a function returns a value, a function call is a kind of expression, which means that a function can be called at any point that an expression of the function's return type is permitted. Thus, because the return type of **FahrToCelsius()** is **double** and the syntax of a **double** variable declaration can be described by

> *double Identifier = Expression*

(where the type of *Expression* is or can be promoted to type **double**), a call to **FahrToCelsius()** can be used to initialize a variable of type **double** like **CelsiusTemp** in the program in Figure 4.2:

```
double
    CelsiusTemp = FahrToCelsius(FahrenheitTemp);
```

Similarly, the output statement in the driver program in Figure 4.3,

```
cout << "\n212F => " << FahrToCelsius(212)
     << "C\n 32F => " << FahrToCelsius(32)
     << "C\n\n";
```

containing two calls to **FahrToCelsius()**, is a valid statement, since the **<<** operator can be used to output a **double** expression to **cout**.

The ability to place a function call anywhere that an expression can appear is very powerful. To illustrate, consider the program in Figure 4.4. The program produces exactly the same output as the programs in Figures 4.1 and 4.2. However, this version solves the problem by encoding each nontrivial step of the algorithm in Section 4.1 as a function and so uses four functions (including **main**) instead of two.

 FIGURE 4.4 Converting a temperature—version 3.

```
/* This program converts a temperature from Fahrenheit to Celsius,
   using a variety of functions.

   Input:    FahrenheitTemp
   Output:   CelsiusTemp
--------------------------------------------------------------------*/

#include <iostream.h>

double GetFahrTemperature(void);        // \
double FahrToCelsius(double);           // function declarations
void DisplayResult(double, double);     // /

int main(void)
{
   cout << "\nThis program converts a temperature\n"
        << "\tfrom Fahrenheit to Celsius.\n";

   double
      FahrenheitTemp = GetFahrTemperature();

   double
      CelsiusTemp = FahrToCelsius(FahrenheitTemp);

   DisplayResult(FahrenheitTemp, CelsiusTemp);

   return 0;
}

/*-------------------------------------------------------------------
GetFahrTemperature is an operation to input a temperature.

   Output:   A prompt to the user
   Input:    A temperature
   Return:   The temperature that was input
--------------------------------------------------------------------*/

double GetFahrTemperature(void)
{
   double Temp;
```

FIGURE 4.4 Converting a temperature—version 3. (cont.)

```
    cout << "\nPlease enter a Fahrenheit temperature: ";
    cin >> Temp;
    return Temp;
}

/*-----------------------------------------------------------------
FahrToCelsius converts a temperature from Fahrenheit to Celsius.

    Receive:  A Fahrenheit temperature
    Return:   The equivalent Celsius temperature
-----------------------------------------------------------------*/

double FahrToCelsius(double Temp)
{
    return (Temp - 32.0) / 1.8;
}

/*-----------------------------------------------------------------
DisplayResult outputs the original and converted temperatures.

    Receive:  The Fahrenheit temperature and its Celsius equivalent
    Output:   The two temperatures and appropriate labels
-----------------------------------------------------------------*/

void DisplayResult(double OriginalTemp, double EquivalentTemp)
{
    cout << "\n\t" << OriginalTemp
         << " in Fahrenheit is equivalent to "
         << EquivalentTemp << " in Celsius.\n\n";
}
```

The first step in the temperature-conversion algorithm is to display a message explaining the purpose of the program. Since performing this step involves the construction of a single output expression, we simply encode it in the main function.

The second step of the algorithm is to input a Fahrenheit temperature. To accomplish this, a function named **GetFahrTemperature()** was constructed, whose specification is

Input: A Fahrenheit temperature
Output: A prompt for the Fahrenheit temperature
Return: The temperature that was input

This specification gives several important pieces of information:

1. The function receives no values from its caller and so requires no parameters (i.e., **void** should be used for the parameter list).
2. The function returns a temperature (implemented as type **double**) to its caller, and so its return type should be **double**.

`GetFahrTemperature()` can thus be declared as follows:

```
double GetFahrTemperature(void);
```

Designing an algorithm to solve this problem and coding it is then accomplished just as it would be for a main function.

The third step of the algorithm has already been studied, and we leave the analysis of the fourth step as an exercise.

From this example, we see that the specification of a function determines the form of a function's declaration and the algorithm determines the form of the function's body:

Design Component	Determines the Form of
Specification	The function declaration
Algorithm	The function body

The specification and design steps in developing a function may seem like extra work, but they will save time for any nontrivial problem. As the preceding example demonstrates, a well-defined specification makes the process of declaring a function almost mechanical, and a well-defined algorithm can make the process of coding the body of the function similarly straightforward.

Summary

Functions are an important part of C++, because as we shall see in the next section, they are the means for writing program components that are reusable. Because functions are so fundamental to C++ programming, we review a few important ideas that have emerged thus far:

- A *value* that is supplied to a function when it is called is an **argument** to that function call. For example, in the function call

  ```
  DisplayResult(FahrenheitTemp, CelsiusTemp);
  ```

  in Figure 4.4, the values of `FahrenheitTemp` and `CelsiusTemp` are arguments to the function `DisplayResult()`. When execution reaches this call, the values of the arguments `FahrenheitTemp` and `CelsiusTemp` are **passed** (i.e., transferred) from the main function to the function `DisplayResult()`, which begins to execute using those values.

- For each argument passed to a function, a *variable* must be provided in the function heading to hold that value. Such variables are called **parameters** of the function. For example, in the definition of `DisplayResult()`,

  ```
  void DisplayResult(double OriginalTemp,
                     double EquivalentTemp)
  {
     cout << "\n\t" << OriginalTemp
          << " in Fahrenheit is equivalent to "
          << EquivalentTemp << " in Celsius.\n\n";
  }
  ```

the variables **OriginalTemp** and **EquivalentTemp** are the parameters of the function **DisplayResult()**.

Finally, we also review the flow of execution when one function calls another. Specifically, consider again the main function's call of function **Display-Result()** in Figure 4.4:

```
         :
         :
int main(void)
{
         :
         :
    DisplayResult(FahrenheitTemp, CelsiusTemp);
         :
         :
}
```

When the call to **DisplayResult()** is encountered, execution proceeds as follows:

1. The values of the arguments **FahrenheitTemp** and **CelsiusTemp** are determined.
2. These values are passed from the main function to **DisplayResult()** and copied into the parameters **OriginalTemp** and **EquivalentTemp**.
3. Control is then transferred from the line containing the function call (in **main**) to the first statement of **DisplayResult()**, which begins execution using the values of its parameters.
4. When the final statement of the function (or a **return** statement) is executed, control is transferred back to the caller (i.e., the main function), and execution of the caller resumes at the point immediately following the function call.

The ability to define functions is a powerful tool in object-oriented programming. If the solution of some problem requires an operation on a data object that C++ does not provide (as an operator or a predefined function), we can simply

1. Define a function to perform that operation, and
2. Apply that function to the data object

as we did with the temperature-conversion operation **FahrToCelsius()**. As we shall see in the next section, such functions can then be stored in a library, from which they can be retrieved when needed. In Section 4.5, we extend these ideas by showing how functions can be used to define the operations for a class of objects.

Exercises

1. Write four functions **PrintZero()**, **PrintOne()**, **PrintTwo()**, and **Print-Three()** to produce "stick numbers" like those on a calculator display for the digits 0, 1, 2, and 3, respectively:

Then write a driver program to test the correctness of your functions.

2. Complete Exercise 1 by writing the additional functions needed for displaying all digits.

3. U.S. dollars are converted to Canadian dollars by multiplying the U.S. dollars by an *exchange rate,* which varies over time. For example, if on a given day, the exchange rate is 1.22, then $10.00 in U.S. currency can be exchanged for $12.20 in Canadian currency.

   (a) Write a function **USToCanadian()** that, given a dollar amount in U.S. currency and the exchange rate, returns the equivalent number of dollars in Canadian currency.
   (b) Write a function **CanadianToUS()** that, given a dollar amount in Canadian currency and the exchange rate, returns the equivalent number of dollars in U.S. currency.

   Then write a driver program to test the correctness of these functions.

4. Write a function **Range()** that, given two integers, returns the range between them—that is, the absolute value of their difference. Then write a driver program to test the correctness of the function.

5. Write a function **Wages()** that, given the number of hours worked and an hourly pay rate, returns the wages earned. Then write a driver program to test the correctness of the function.

6. Given the radius of a circle,

   (a) Write a function that returns its circumference.
   (b) Write a function that returns its area.

   Then write a driver program to test the correctness of the functions.

7. Given the lengths of the sides of a rectangle,

   (a) Write a function that returns its perimeter.
   (b) Write a function that returns its area.

   Then write a driver program to test the correctness of the functions.

8. Given the lengths of three sides of a triangle,

   (a) Write a function that returns its perimeter.
   (b) Write a function that returns its area. (The area of a triangle can be found by using **Hero's formula:**

   $$\sqrt{s(s-a)(s-b)(s-c)}$$

   where a, b, and c are the lengths of the sides and s is one-half of the perimeter.)

   Then write a driver program to test the correctness of the functions.

4.3 Computing with Libraries

In the last section, we saw that functions enable us to extend the operations provided in C++. If a problem requires some operation that C++ does not provide, we can define a function to perform that operation and then call that function, just as if C++ did provide it.

Although this is a significant improvement over computing with formulas, it does not by itself allow us (easily) to reuse our work. For example, if we need to use the function **FahrToCelsius()** from the program in Figure 4.2 in a different program, we could

1. Copy the program containing the declaration and definition of **FahrToCelsius()**;
2. Use a text editor to delete everything except the declaration and definition (in the copy); and
3. Write the new program between the declaration and definition of **FahrToCelsius()**.

Alternatively, we might use the *cut-and-paste* capabilities of a word processor to copy the function declaration from the first program, paste it into the appropriate position within the new program, and then copy the function definition from the first program and paste it into its appropriate place in the new program.

Although these approaches may be acceptable in languages that are not designed for reusability, C++ provides a better approach by supporting **libraries.** In Section 3.1 we saw examples of libraries that are provided in C++, and in this section we show how we can construct our own libraries.

Constructing a Library

If we examine the libraries of functions provided in the various C++ implementations, we see that the functions in each library are *related* in some way. For example, the **iostream** library provides functions for performing input and output. The **math** library provides functions that are commonly needed in mathematical computations. It would be silly (and confusing) to declare the **sin()** function in **<iostream.h>** or to declare one of the input functions in **<math.h>**.

The first step in constructing a library, therefore, is to identify its *organizing principle:* what kind of functions it should contain. For example, since we intend to store **FahrToCelsius()** (a temperature-conversion function) in this library and temperature measures heat, we might call the library **Heat**, so that its header file will be named **Heat.h**. The library will contain items that are in some way related to heat and temperature, just as the **iostream** library contains functions that are related to input and output streams.

Once we have decided what kind of items will be in the library, we must identify those particular items that we want it to provide. Here we must plan for the future and try to anticipate what items related to heat we (or anyone else) might need. By investing time now, we hope to save time in the future—long-term rather than short-term planning.

One way to select the functions to be stored in a library is to view them as the operations on a type of data object. For example, if the library is to contain functions that are related to temperature and we view temperature as a type, then the library should provide the commonly performed operations on that type. Thus, in addition to a Fahrenheit-to-Celsius conversion, we should perhaps also include the inverse operation of Celsius-to-Fahrenheit conversion. Functions to convert a temperature in each scale to Kelvin and back are other possible additions.

It is important to note that we are not limited to storing functions in a library. For example, we might also store important heat-related constants in our library, such as the heat of fusion of water (79.71 calories/gram) and the heat of vaporization of water (539.55 calories/gram). The important thing is to identify useful items that are related to heat or temperature and put them into the library, so that in the future, a user can retrieve and use these items (and thus avoid "reinventing the wheel").

Once the items that the library is to contain have been selected, we are ready to begin construction of the library. A library consists of two separate files:

- A **header file** that contains the *declarations* of the items in the library
- An **implementation file** that contains the *definitions* of those items

The header file serves as an *interface* between the library and a program that uses the library and is, therefore, sometimes called the library's **interface file.**

Building the Header File.   A header file contains all the information necessary to use the library. In particular, it should contain

1. A declaration of each item stored in the library;
2. Documentation that describes what those items in the library do and how they are used

For functions stored in the library, the header file contains the *declarations* of the functions but usually *not their definitions*. Thus, just as **iostream.h** is a file containing declarations of items needed to perform stream input and output, **Heat.h** will be a header file containing declarations of items needed for processing heat and temperatures. It might begin as shown in Figure 4.5.

 FIGURE 4.5 Header file for library **Heat**.

```
/* This file provides an interface for library Heat.

   Names declared:
      HeatOfFusion, the amount of heat needed to melt a gram of ice
      HeatOfVaporization, the amount of heat needed to boil a gram
        of water
      FahrToCelsius(), a Fahrenheit-to-Celsius conversion function
      CelsiusToFahr(), a Celsius-to-Fahrenheit conversion function
      ...
---------------------------------------------------------------*/
```

FIGURE 4.5 Header file for library **Heat**. (cont.)

```
const double HeatOfFusion = 79.71;          // calories per gram

const double HeatOfVaporization = 539.55;   // calories per gram

/*------------------------------------------------------------------
FahrToCelsius converts a temperature from Fahrenheit to Celsius.

   Receive:  A Fahrenheit temperature
   Return:   The equivalent Celsius temperature
------------------------------------------------------------------*/

double FahrToCelsius(double FTemp);

/*------------------------------------------------------------------
CelsiusToFahr converts a temperature from Celsius to Fahrenheit.

   Receive:  A Celsius temperature
   Return:   The equivalent Fahrenheit temperature
------------------------------------------------------------------*/

double CelsiusToFahr(double CTemp);

// . . . Declarations of other items might be added . . .
```

Each of the library's constants and functions must be declared in this file so that if a program includes this header file (using a `#include` directive) before its main function, the compiler will insert these declarations into the program at that point.

It is not necessary to compile the header file of a library (explicitly), because when a program that uses the `#include` directive is compiled, the named header file is *inserted* into the program. As a result, the contents of the header file are (inserted and) compiled whenever a program that names that file in a `#include` directive is compiled.

Building the Implementation File. As noted earlier, the *definitions* of a library's functions are stored in a file called the **implementation file** of the library.[2] The implementation file is so named because it implements (i.e., defines) the functions that are declared in the header file. Part of the implementation file for the library **Heat** is given in Figure 4.6.

---

[2] Although a library's header file always ends in the `.h` extension, the extension for an implementation file is the same as that of a source file in a given environment (for example, `.C` or `.cc` in UNIX, `.CPP` in the Turbo environment, and `.cpp` in the Symantec environment).

FIGURE 4.6 Implementation file for library **Heat**.

```
/* This file provides an implementation for library Heat.

   Names defined:
      FahrToCelsius(), a Fahrenheit-to-Celsius conversion function
      CelsiusToFahr(), a Celsius-to-Fahrenheit conversion function
------------------------------------------------------------------*/

#include "Heat.h"

//---------------------------------------------

double FahrToCelsius(double FTemp)
{
   return (FTemp - 32.0) / 1.8;
}

//---------------------------------------------

double CelsiusToFahr(double CTemp)
{
   return CTemp * 1.8 + 32.0;
}

// . . . Definitions of other items might be added . . .
```

It is important to note that, unlike the header file, a library's implementation file must be compiled. This is the reason that the implementation file contains the line

> #include "Heat.h"

in addition to the definitions of the various temperature-related operations. When the library's implementation file is compiled, the compiler will insert and process the library's declarations (from the header file), after which it will process the definitions in the library's implementation file. Because the compiler processes both the declarations and definitions of functions, it can check that these declarations and definitions are *consistent;* if it detects any inconsistencies, the compiler will display an error message.

It is also important to note that

- Items defined in the implementation file that were declared in the header file can be accessed in any program that uses the **#include** directive to insert the header file; but
- Items defined in the implementation file that were not declared in the header file cannot be accessed outside of the implementation file, even by a program that inserts the header file.

Stated differently, any information in the header file can be thought of as **public** information, whereas information in the implementation file is **private** within the library.

Using a Library in a Program

Once the library **Heat** has been constructed, it can be used in a program like that in Figure 4.7 for solving the temperature-conversion problem.

 FIGURE 4.7 Converting a temperature—version 4.

```
/* This program converts a temperature from Fahrenheit to Celsius,
   using function FahrToCelsius( ) that is stored in library Heat.

   Input:  FahrenheitTemp
   Output: CelsiusTemp
-----------------------------------------------------------------*/

#include <iostream.h>

#include "Heat.h"                          // the library's header file

int main(void)
{
   cout << "\nThis program converts a temperature\n"
        << "\tfrom Fahrenheit to Celsius.\n";

   double
      FahrenheitTemp;

   cout << "\nPlease enter a Fahrenheit temperature: ";
   cin >> FahrenheitTemp;

   double
      CelsiusTemp = FahrToCelsius(FahrenheitTemp);

   cout << "\n\t" << FahrenheitTemp
        << " in Fahrenheit is equivalent to "
        << CelsiusTemp << " in Celsius.\n\n";

   return 0;
}
```

Execution of this program is identical to that of the program in Figure 4.2. However, in this program, the line

```
#include "Heat.h"
```

is placed before the main function. The declaration and definition of **FahrToCelsius()** are not given in this file, because the declaration of **FahrToCelsius()** is in the header file of library **Heat**, and the definition of **FahrToCelsius()** is in the library's implementation file.

It is important to understand the difference between the notation

```
#include "Heat.h"
```

that is used to include the **Heat** library's header file and the notation

```
#include <iostream.h>
```

that is used to include the **iostream** library's header file. If the name of a library's header file is surrounded by *angle brackets* (**<** and **>**), the C++ compiler will search for that file in the special system **include** directory described in Chapter 3. By contrast, if the name of a library's header file is enclosed in *double quotes,* then the C++ compiler will search for that file in the current directory.

Most implementations of C++ permit the programmer to instruct the compiler to search alternate directories when looking for files named by **#include** directives. In the UNIX and DOS command-line environments, this can be done by invoking the compiler with a special *switch,*[3] whereas in the Turbo environment, this is done by adding the directory to the appropriate list of directories in the *Compile Options* window.

Translating a Library

As we have noted in Chapter 3, translation of a program consists of two separate steps:

1. **Compilation,** in which a source program is translated to an equivalent machine-language program, called an *object program,* which is stored in an *object file*[4]
2. **Linking,** in which any calls to functions that are defined within a library are linked to their definitions, creating an *executable program,* which is stored in an *executable file*

Since a programmer-defined library may also need to be compiled, translation of a program that uses a library may require three separate actions:

1. Separate compilation[5] of the program's source file, creating an object file
2. Separate compilation of the library's implementation file, creating a different object file (unless the library's implementation file has already been compiled)

---

[3] On UNIX systems, the **-I** switch is used. For example, the command

```
g++ -I/home/jdoe/MyLib Prog.C -o Prog
```

can be used when compiling a file **Prog.C** in the UNIX/GNU environment to instruct the compiler to search the directory **/home/jdoe/MyLib** when looking for files named in **#include** directives.

[4] UNIX object files have the extension **.o**, DOS object files have the extension **.OBJ**, and object files are stored within the project in the Symantec environment.

[5] In the UNIX environment, separate compilation requires that the compiler be invoked with the **-c** switch. An implementation module can be compiled in the usual manner in the Turbo and Symantec environments.

3. Linking the function calls in the program's object file to the function definitions in the library's object file, creating an executable program

It makes no difference whether the source program or the library's implementation file is compiled first, but *both source and library implementation files must be compiled before linking can be performed.* The following diagram illustrates this process:

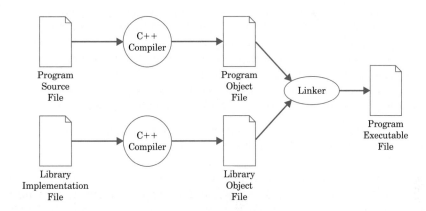

   Although the extra step of compiling a library separately from the source program may seem like an inconvenience, it has two significant benefits:

1. The compilation time for the source program is significantly reduced.
2. Any errors that occur are (most likely) confined to the source program.

These long-term advantages far outweigh the short-term inconvenience.
   To illustrate this, suppose that we have written a library containing a large number of functions that a friend wishes to use in a program she is writing. Because C++ allows us to link together separately-compiled files, translation of her program requires

1. Compilation of her source program; and
2. Linking the resulting object file to our library's object file.

By contrast, if it were necessary to recompile the library's implementation file each time she translated her program, then the translation would probably take much longer. Moreover, since our library is compiled separately (and, we hope, is error-free), any errors generated during compilation must lie in her source file. *Separate compilation and linking eliminate needless recompilation of a library and allow errors to be isolated in a file.*
   When a library has been completed and thoroughly tested so that no further changes are anticipated, a **library archive** can be created. How this is done depends on the environment being used and must be determined by consulting the documentation for that environment.

Summary

Libraries are fundamental to the object-oriented approach to programming, because they provide the following benefits:

Functions in a Library Are Reusable. A library *extends the language* by making additional items—functions, constants, and so on—available to any program (or other library). There is no need for a programmer to "reinvent the wheel" each time these items are needed.

Libraries Hide Implementation Details. To use the items in a library, the programmer needs to know only the information in the header file; the details in the implementation file are of no concern. The header file and other relevant documentation must be provided to users, but the source code in the implementation file need not be made available—only its compiled object file so that it can be linked to their programs. The details in the implementation file can thus remain "hidden" in the machine code of the object file provided to the user. This **information hiding** makes it possible to use the library without being concerned about these details. For example, one can use the square root function `sqrt()` from library `math` without worrying about the details of how the operation is being performed.

Libraries Make Programs Easier to Maintain. Information hiding is one of the most important benefits of using libraries, because it makes programs using the libraries easier to maintain. When programmers are permitted to access the contents of the implementation file, they may be tempted to use the implementation details in their programs. However, if the implementation file is subsequently changed (e.g., perhaps a faster square root function is devised and substituted for the old one), then such programs may no longer work correctly. Maintaining such programs requires that they be modified to remove the references to the obsolete details, recompiled, and relinked with the new implementation object file.

By contrast, if the implementation details are hidden in the implementation file, a programmer is unable to access those details and is thus forced to use the interface provided in the header file. The benefit is that if a library's implementation file changes (but its interface does not), then maintaining the program that uses the library requires only that it be relinked to the new implementation object file. By forcing programs to use the library's interface instead of the implementation details, no modification or recompilation of the program is necessary when those implementation details change.

Libraries Permit Separate Compilation. Another benefit that results from this separation of programs and libraries is that they can be compiled separately. **Separate compilation** makes it possible to change the implementation file of a library and recompile only the implementation file; programs or other libraries that use the library need not be changed or recompiled. For example, if function `FahrToCelsius()` in the implementation file of the library `Heat` is changed, then only the implementation file needs to be recompiled. A program using `FahrToCelsius()` need not be recompiled, because the declaration of `FahrToCelsius()` has not changed, only its definition. All that is needed is to relink the program to the new object file of library `Heat`. However, if the interface in the header file is altered, then both the library's implementation file and all programs and other libraries that name that header file in a `#include` directive must be recompiled.

Libraries Support Independent Coding. Libraries introduce a higher level of *modularity* into software design by allowing related functions to be grouped together into independent units. This is especially useful in large programming projects that involve several programmers. A team of programmers might jointly identify the objects (and operations) required to complete a large software project. By categorizing the operations according to the kind of object on which they operate, a library can be designed to house the operations on each particular kind of object. Once the needed libraries have been identified (as well as the operations they are to contain), the header files of these libraries can be easily constructed.

When the header files have been created, the work of the project can be divided among the programming team, with one group of programmers working on the program(s) that will use the functions in the libraries and different groups of programmers assigned to construct the implementation files of the various libraries. Because the work is partitioned into manageable "chunks," the entire project can be completed much more rapidly. Moreover, since the work in one portion of the project proceeds independently of the work in another portion of the project, the likelihood of errors is greatly diminished.

Libraries Simplify Testing.   Separate libraries can be developed and tested independently (using driver programs) by completely different programmers or teams of programmers. Again, because the project has been divided into smaller libraries, each library can be tested much more thoroughly (and rapidly) than can a project stored in a single, monolithic file.

Exercises

1. Construct a library **Digits** that contains the functions from Exercises 1 and 2 at the end of Section 4.2.

2. Construct a library **Exchange** that contains the functions from Exercise 3 at the end of Section 4.2.

3. Construct a library **Geometry** that contains the functions from Exercises 6 to 8 at the end of Section 4.2.

4.4   Example Program: Converting Days to Distance

Problem

You are the science officer on the USS Boobyprize, which is cruising the galaxy at the speed of light. Captain Quirk has asked you to write a program that will tell him how many kilometers you are from your home planet, given the number of days you have been traveling.

Specification

We can immediately identify the following data objects from the problem description:

Data Object	Kind of Value	Type of Object	Name of Object
Number of days	Variable	Real	*Days*
Speed of light	Constant	Real	*SpeedOfLight*
Distance traveled	Variable	Real	*Kilometers*

This list permits us to specify the problem more precisely:

Input: A number of days
Output: The distance traveled (at the speed of light)

Design

Solving this problem requires the following operations:

- Input a real value from the keyboard.
- Output a real value to the screen.
- Convert a number of days into a distance traveled at the speed of light.

Although input and output of an integer are provided by C++, a days-to-distance conversion operation is not provided. It is natural to encode this operation as a function. Given such a function, we might solve this problem with the following algorithm:

ALGORITHM FOR DAYS-TO-DISTANCE PROBLEM

/* This algorithm finds the distance traveled at the speed of light in a given number of days.

Input: *Days,* a number of days
Output: *Kilometers,* the distance traveled at the speed of light
——*/

1. Enter *Days.*
2. Compute *Kilometers,* the number of kilometers traveled in *Days* at the speed of light.
3. Output *Kilometers.*

Of course, Step 2 of this algorithm is somewhat complicated: The speed of light is approximately 2.997925×10^8 meters per second, but in this problem, time is measured in days (not seconds) and distance is measured in kilometers (not meters).

The subproblem that the days-to-distance conversion function must solve can be specified as follows:

Receive: *Days,* a number of days
Return: *Kilometers,* the kilometers traveled at the speed of light in *Days*

We might then use the following algorithm for this function:

2a. Compute *Seconds,* the number of seconds in *Days.*
2b. Compute *Meters* using the formula distance = rate × time:

$$Meters = Seconds \times SpeedOfLight$$

2c. Compute *Kilometers = Meters*/1000.
2d. Return *Kilometers.*

Steps 2b and 2c are formula-encoding steps for which C++ provides all of the required operations and encoding each of them as a function is almost trivial. However, Step 2a is still a bit complicated, and so we might construct a function to perform that step. We can specify its problem as

Receive: *Days,* a number of days
Return: *Seconds,* the equivalent number of seconds

and then use the following algorithm:

2a1. Compute *Hours = Days* × 24.
2a2. Compute *Minutes = Hours* × 60.
2a3. Compute *Seconds = Minutes* × 60.
2a4. Return *Seconds.*

Since each of these computations uses operators that are provided in C++, constructing functions to perform them is straightforward.

It is at this point that we want to consider what parts of the program might be reusable. Suppose we list and name the computations that will be performed:

Computation	Function Name
Convert days to kilometers	`DaysToKilometers()`
Convert days to seconds	`DaysToSeconds()`
Convert days to hours	`DaysToHours()`
Convert hours to minutes	`HoursToMinutes()`
Convert minutes to seconds	`MinutesToSeconds()`
Compute distance = rate × time	`RateTimesTime()`
Convert meters to kilometers	`MetersToKilometers()`

We can see that four of these functions involve various measurements of *time* and it thus makes sense to place these functions in a library **Times** and perhaps add other time-related functions.

Similarly, the function to convert meters to kilometers is one of many common metric conversions and we might construct a library **Metric** of metric conversion functions. This library can be expanded to include additional metric conversion functions as needed.

The remaining functions are either so specialized (or so trivial) that we will not construct a library for them in this example, although one could argue that the computation of distance = rate × time is used commonly enough to warrant consideration. This is left as an exercise.

It is important to note that the program is essentially done at this point. Because we have planned carefully at this (the design) stage of program development, the remaining task of coding the various functions can almost be done mechanically.

A programmer should take a long-term view at the design stage. Taking a short-term view and beginning a project by immediately writing code is unwise, because the resulting program is usually poorly thought out, must typically be

revised many times, and is not likely to be reusable. In constrast, a small investment of time in the specification and design phases has these benefits:

1. It makes the remainder of the project easy.
2. It results in reusable code, saving you (or your colleagues) work at some future
   time, when the solution to a different problem requires one of these functions.

Coding

Now that we have a design for the project, we can begin constructing the library
Times. Figure 4.8 shows the relevant portion of the header file for library **Times**. It
contains the specifications and declarations of the time-related functions listed
previously. It is important to note that in addition to the functions necessary to
solve this problem, we could also specify and declare other useful time-related
functions (see Exercise 4 at the end of this section) to make this library as complete
as possible.

FIGURE 4.8   Header file for library **Times**.

```
/* This file provides an interface for library Times.

   Names declared:
      DaysToSeconds, a function to compute the number of seconds,
                     given a number of days
      DaysToHours, a function to compute the number of hours,
                     given a number of days
      HoursToMinutes, a function to compute the number of minutes,
                     given a number of hours
      MinutesToSeconds, a function to compute the number of seconds,
                     given a number of minutes
      ...
-----------------------------------------------------------------*/

/*-----------------------------------------------------------------
DaysToSeconds computes the number of seconds in a given number of
   days.

   Receive:  Days, a (double) number of days
   Return:   The equivalent (double) number of seconds
-----------------------------------------------------------------*/

double DaysToSeconds(double Days);

/*-----------------------------------------------------------------
DaysToHours computes the number of hours in a given number of days.

   Receive: Days, a (double) number of days
   Return:  The equivalent (double) number of hours
-----------------------------------------------------------------*/

double DaysToHours(double Days);
```

FIGURE 4.8   Header file for library **Times**. (cont.)

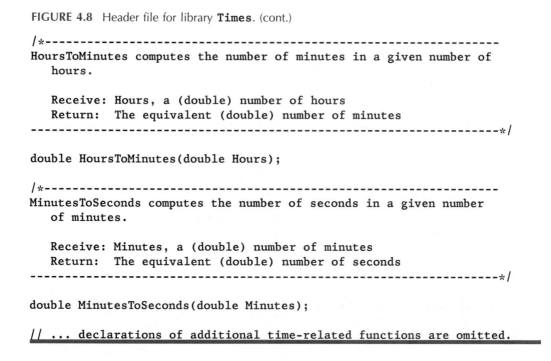

```
/*------------------------------------------------------------------
HoursToMinutes computes the number of minutes in a given number of
   hours.

   Receive: Hours, a (double) number of hours
   Return:  The equivalent (double) number of minutes
-----------------------------------------------------------------*/

double HoursToMinutes(double Hours);

/*------------------------------------------------------------------
MinutesToSeconds computes the number of seconds in a given number
   of minutes.

   Receive: Minutes, a (double) number of minutes
   Return:  The equivalent (double) number of seconds
-----------------------------------------------------------------*/

double MinutesToSeconds(double Minutes);

// ... declarations of additional time-related functions are omitted.
```

Note that a header file should be extensively documented so that a user of the library can determine exactly how to use each item stored in the library. This may be the only documentation to which a user of the library will have access.

Once we have constructed the interface to the library, constructing its implementation is simply a matter of defining each of the declared functions in an appropriately named implementation file (see footnote 2). Figure 4.9 shows a portion of the implementation file for the library **Times**.

   FIGURE 4.9   Implementation file for library **Times**.

```
/* This file provides an implementation for library Times.

   Names defined:
     DaysToSeconds, a function to compute the number of seconds,
                        given a number of days
     DaysToHours, a function to compute the number of hours,
                        given a number of days
     HoursToMinutes, a function to compute the number of minutes,
                        given a number of hours
     MinutesToSeconds, a function to compute the number of seconds,
                        given a number of minutes
     . . .
-----------------------------------------------------------------*/

#include "Times.h"
```

FIGURE 4.9 Implementation file for library **Times**. (cont.)

```
//----------------------------------------------

double DaysToSeconds(double Days)
{
    double
       Hours = DaysToHours(Days);

    double
       Minutes = HoursToMinutes(Hours);

    double
       Seconds = MinutesToSeconds(Minutes);

    return Seconds;
}

//----------------------------------------------

double DaysToHours(double Days)
{
    return Days * 24.0;
}

//----------------------------------------------

double HoursToMinutes(double Hours)
{
    return Hours * 60.0;
}

//----------------------------------------------

double MinutesToSeconds(double Minutes)
{
    return Minutes * 60.0;

}

// ... definitions of additional time-related functions are omitted.
```

As we have seen before, the library's implementation file must use the `#include` directive to insert the library's header file so that the compiler can verify that the functions are declared and defined consistently.

Once the library **Times** has been developed, it should be thoroughly tested with a simple driver program that simply inserts the header file, calls each function in the library, and outputs the result. By thoroughly testing **Times** at this point and ensuring that it is free of errors, we can have confidence that any errors we encounter later must lie elsewhere, rather than in this library.

We next turn our attention to the library **Metric**. As before, we specify each function that the library is to contain and then use that specification to construct a declaration for each function. Figure 4.10 shows the relevant portion of the header file for library **Metric**.

 FIGURE 4.10   Header file for library **Metric**.

```
/* This file provides an interface for library Metric.

   Names declared:
      MetersToKilometers, a function that converts meters
                          into kilometers.
      ...
------------------------------------------------------------------*/

/*---------------------------------------------------------------
MeterToKilometers converts a given number of meters into the
   equivalent number of kilometers.

   Receive: Meters, a (double) number of meters
   Return:  The equivalent (double) number of kilometers
------------------------------------------------------------------*/

double MetersToKilometers(double Meters);

// ... declarations of additional Metric items are omitted.
```

Completing the library **Metric** simply involves creating an implementation file for the library that contains a definition for each function declared in the library's header file. Figure 4.11 shows a partial listing of such an implementation file.

 FIGURE 4.11   Implementation file for library **Metric**.

```
/* This file provides an implementation for library Metric.

   Names defined:
      MetersToKilometers, a function that converts meters
                          into kilometers.
      ...
------------------------------------------------------------------*/

#include "Metric.h"

//----------------------------------------------------------

double MetersToKilometers(double Meters)
{
   return Meters / 1000.0;
}

// ... declarations of additional Metric items are omitted.
```

Using these two libraries, we can write a program that solves the days-to-distance problem. Figure 4.12 shows how the algorithm for this problem can be encoded.

FIGURE 4.12   Program to solve the days-to-distance problem.

```
/* This program computes the distance traveled (in kilometers)
   at the speed of light, given the number of days of travel.

   Input: Days, the number of days traveled
   Output: Kilometers, the distance traveled in Days days
   ----------------------------------------------------------------*/

#include <iostream.h>

double DaysToKilometers(double Days);
double RateTimesTime(double Velocity, double Time);

int main(void)
{
   cout << "\nThis program computes the distance traveled (in km) at"
        << "\n\tthe speed of light, given the number of days of "
        << "travel.\n";

   double
      Days;

   cout << "\nPlease enter the number of days: ";
   cin >> Days;

   double
      Kilometers = DaysToKilometers(Days);

   cout << "\nAt the speed of light, we have traveled\n\t"
        << Kilometers << " kilometers in " << Days << " days.\n\n";

   return 0;
}

/*----------------------------------------------------------------
DaysToKilometers computes the number of kilometers traveled during
   a given number of days of travel at the speed of light.

   Receive: Days, the number of days traveled at the speed of light
   Return:  Kilometers, the number of kilometers traveled
   ----------------------------------------------------------------*/

#include "Times.h"   // needed for converting days to seconds
#include "Metric.h"  // needed for converting meters to kilometers
```

FIGURE 4.12 Program to solve the days-to-distance problem. (cont.)

```
double DaysToKilometers(double Days)
{
   const double
      SpeedOfLight = 2.997925E8;              // meters per second

   double
      Seconds = DaysToSeconds(Days);          // from Times.h

   double
      Meters = RateTimesTime(SpeedOfLight, Seconds);

   double
      Kilometers = MetersToKilometers(Meters);  // from Metric.h

   return Kilometers;
}

/*-----------------------------------------------------------------
   RateTimesTime computes a distance, given a Velocity and a Time.

      Receive: Velocity, the speed at which travel is occurring
               Time, the time traveled
      Return:  the distance traveled

   --------------------------------------------------------------*/

double RateTimesTime(double Velocity, double Time)
{
   return Velocity * Time;
}
```

Sample run:

```
This program computes the distance traveled (in km) at
   the speed of light, given the number of days of travel.

Please enter the number of days: 1.1574074e-5

At the speed of light, we have traveled
   299792.498081 kilometers in 1.157407e-05 days.
```

Program Testing

As a simple test of the program, we use an input value for which the correctness of the output is easy to verify. Since we know that the speed of light is 2.997925×10^8 meters/second, we might calculate the number of days in one second as

$$(1/24.0/60.0/60.00) = 1.1574074 \times 10^{-5}$$

If we input this value, the program computes and outputs 2.99792×10^5 kilometers (which is the same as 2.99792×10^8 meters), the distance we would move in one second while traveling at the speed of light. For this input value, we can observe that the program produces the correct result.

Exercises

1. Describe the output produced by the following program, or explain why an error occurs:

```cpp
#include <iostream.h>

int Product(int);
int Sum(int);

int main(void)
{
    cout << Product(2) << ' ' << Sum(2) << '\n'
         << Sum(Product(3)) << ' '
         << Product(Sum(3)) << '\n';
}

int Product(int X)
{
    return 3 * X;
}

int Sum(int X)
{
    return 3 + X;
}
```

2. Describe the output produced by the following program, or explain why an error occurs:

```cpp
#include <iostream.h>

void P(int);

int main(void)
{
    int
        i = 1,
        Num = 3;

    cout << i << ' ' << Num << '\n'
         << P(i) << ' ' << P(Num) << '\n';
}

void P(int Num)
{
    Num *= 2;
    return Num;
}
```

3. Describe the output produced by the following program, or explain why an error occurs:

```
#include <iostream.h>

int Double(int);

int main(void)
{
    int
        Num = 4,
        HalfNum = 2;

    cout << HalfNum << ' ' << Num << '\n';

    Num = Double(HalfNum);

    cout << HalfNum << ' ' << Num << '\n'
         << Double(HalfNum) << ' '
         << Double(Num) << '\n';
}

int Double(int Num)
{
    Num *= 2;
    return Num;
}
```

4. Write functions that do the following:

   (a) Given a number of seconds, returns the equivalent number of minutes
   (b) Given a number of minutes, returns the equivalent number of hours
   (c) Given a number of hours, returns the equivalent number of days

   Then write a driver program to test the correctness of your functions.

5. Using the functions from Exercise 4, write a function that, given a number of seconds, returns the equivalent number of days. Then write a driver program to test the correctness of your function.

6. Extend the library **Times** to include the functions from Exercises 4 and 5.

7. Extend the library **Metric** to include functions that convert metric lengths, masses, and volumes.

4.5 Computing with Class Libraries

In the previous sections, we saw that functions can be used to implement operations that are not provided by C++. For example, because C++ does not provide a Fahrenheit-to-Celsius conversion operation, we wrote a function to perform that operation.

The use of functions as operations on a data type is a fundamental idea in object-oriented programming. In this section, we explore this capability further by examining **classes,** the C++ mechanism for defining new types, and **class member functions,** the C++ mechanism for building operations on such types.

Introduction to Classes

One of the chief advantages of the object-oriented programming approach is its emphasis on the creation of software models of data objects. In an object-oriented approach, a program is conceived as a series of interactions between the various data objects in the problem. As long as these data objects are relatively simple, they can usually be modeled using the predefined types of C++. For example, to model the real-world concept of a temperature, we used the C++ predefined type for real values: `double`. Many real-world measurements can be modeled in a similar fashion, since they have *a single (numeric) attribute*—the magnitude of the measurement.

However, as we saw in Chapter 2, many problems deal with data objects that are not simple measurements because they have *multiple data attributes.* For such data objects, which cannot be modeled with (individual) predefined C++ types, C++ provides *classes* that allow the programmer to *build types* to model such objects in software. A class can be thought of as a storage structure in which the programmer can declare

1. A component for each data attribute of the object being modeled; and
2. Operations on the object.

The components for the data attributes of a class are called the **data members** of the class, and the operations on the class are called the **member functions** of the class.

For example, a temperature actually has two data attributes: its *magnitude* (the `double` value we have been using) and its *scale* (either Fahrenheit or Celsius). We could design a class to model a `Temperature` data type by

1. Declaring a data member for its *magnitude* (modeled as a real value) and a data member for its *scale* (modeled using a character value: 'F' for Fahrenheit or 'C' for Celsius):

   ```
   double
      Magnitude;
   char
      Scale;
   ```

2. Declaring the operations (e.g., conversion functions) on a temperature as member functions:

   ```
   Temperature Celsius(void);       // return Cels-equivalent
   Temperature Fahrenheit(void);    // return Fahr-equivalent
   ```

We could then put these declarations in a class **declaration** that names the new type:

```
class Temperature
{                                      // data attributes
    double
        Magnitude;
    char
        Scale;
public:                                // operations
        Temperature Celsius(void);     // return Cels-equivalent
        Temperature Fahrenheit(void);  // return Fahr-equivalent
                                       // other operations...
};
```

This is a partial declaration of such a class. A complete declaration would contain the declarations of additional member functions such as an input function, an output function, other conversion functions, and so on. Once completed, this declaration would be stored in the header file of a library whose name is the same as that of the class (i.e., in **Temperature.h**). The definitions of the member functions would be stored in the library's implementation file.

Given a complete implementation of the class, we could use this new type **Temperature** to solve the temperature conversion problem, as shown in Figure 4.13.

 FIGURE 4.13   Program to solve the temperature-conversion problem.

```
/* This program converts a Fahrenheit temperature to a Celsius
   temperature, using class Temperature.

   Input:  A (Fahrenheit) Temperature
   Output: The equivalent Celsius Temperature
-----------------------------------------------------------------*/

#include <iostream.h>

#include "Temperature.h"

int main(void)
{
    cout << "\nThis program converts Fahrenheit temperatures"
         << " to Celsius.";

    Temperature
        FahrenheitTemp,
        CelsiusTemp;

    cout << "\nPlease enter a Fahrenheit temperature"
         << "\n\t(the number of degrees, followed by an F): ";

    cin >> FahrenheitTemp;
```

FIGURE 4.13 Program to solve the temperature-conversion problem. (cont.)

```
CelsiusTemp = FahrenheitTemp.Celsius();

cout << "\n\n" << FahrenheitTemp
     << " is equivalent to " << CelsiusTemp << ".\n\n";

return 0;
}
```

Sample run:

```
This program converts Fahrenheit temperatures to Celsius.

Please enter a Fahrenheit temperature
   (the number of degrees, followed by an F): 212 F

212 F is equivalent to 100 C.
```

The program begins by using the **#include** directive to insert the declaration of class **Temperature** (stored in the header file of library **Temperature**). We can then use the type **Temperature** to define one or more variable data objects, called **class objects,** or *instances* of the class:

```
    Temperature
       FahrenheitTemp,
       CelsiusTemp;
```

After the input of a **Temperature** value from the keyboard (performed using an input operator from class **Temperature**), the program performs a **Temperature** assignment:

```
    CelsiusTemp = FahrenheitTemp.Celsius();
```

The expression on the right-hand side of this assignment illustrates how a member function is called. Because the conversion function **Celsius()** was declared within class **Temperature**, **Temperature** objects (i.e., **FahrenheitTemp** and **CelsiusTemp**) can be thought of as having member functions like **Celsius()** *stored within them.* As a result, when we call a member function, we must tell the compiler the object whose member function we wish to call. The expression

```
    FahrenheitTemp.Celsius()
```

tells the compiler to call the function **Celsius()** associated with the object **FahrenheitTemp**. More generally, the notation:

```
    ObjectName.MemberFunction()
```

is used to access the member function named *MemberFunction()* associated with the class object named *ObjectName*. Because a *dot* (or period) is used to connect a class object and its member, this notation is sometimes referred to as **dot notation.**

Finally, an output statement (which uses an output operator from class **Temperature**) is used to display **FahrenheitTemp** and **CelsiusTemp**, along with appropriate labeling information.

Summary

The intent of this section has been to provide the reader with a working knowledge of how to use (but not necessarily write) class libraries. The points that should be understood at this time are as follows:

1. Classes are used by programmers to create a new data type when no existing C++ type is adequate to model some object in a problem (i.e., the object has multiple attributes).
2. Classes are generally stored in libraries, so that use of a particular class requires that the header file of its library be inserted in a source file using the **#include** directive.
3. Classes consist of data members and member functions stored within a single structure. Class objects thus contain multiple values together with operations on themselves.
4. Class members that are functions are accessed using dot notation of the form:

    ClassObject.MemberFunction( )

The implementation of classes is considered in detail in Chapter 11. In the intervening chapters, we make use of those classes that are available in most implementations of C++ as they prove useful in solving the problems we examine.

Programming Pointers

Program Design

1. *Once a problem has been specified in terms of its data objects and the operations needed to solve the problem, an algorithm should be constructed that specifies the order in which the operations are applied to the data objects.*

2. *Nontrivial operations should be encoded as functions separate from the main function.*

3. *In encoding an operation as a function, the problem it must solve should be specified and an algorithm constructed in exactly the same manner as the main problem.*

4. *A function that returns no values should have its return type declared as* `void`.

5. *A function that receives no values should have its parameter list declared as* `void`.

6. *If a function is sufficiently general that it might someday prove useful in solving a different problem, a library should be constructed to store that function, rather than declaring and defining it in the program's source file.*

7. *Libraries provide the following benefits:*

- *A library extends the language, since its objects can be made available to any program.*
- *The items in a library's interface can be used without being concerned about the details of their implementation.*
- *Programs and libraries can be compiled separately. Changing the implementation file of a library requires recompilation of only that implementation file.*
- *Libraries provide another level of modularity in software design; related functions and other objects can be grouped together in independent libraries.*

8. *When a problem involves one or more objects that cannot be adequately modeled by any available C++ type, classes allow the programmer to construct a new type to model the objects.*

Potential Problems

1. *When a function is called, the number of arguments must be the same as the number of parameters in the function heading, and the type of each argument must be compatible with the type of the corresponding parameter.* For example, consider the function with the heading

```
int F(int Number1, int Number2)
```

The statements

```
y = F(x);
```

and

```
y = F(2, 3.75);
```

are incorrect. In the first case, the number of arguments (1) does not agree with the number of parameters (2). In the second case, the real value **3.75** should not be passed to the integer parameter **Number2**.

2. *Identifiers defined within a function (e.g., parameters, local variables, and local constants) are defined only during the execution of that function; they are undefined both before and after its execution.* Any attempt to use such identifiers outside the function is an error. For example, in the function

```
void Calculate(int x, double y)
{
    int
        a, b;
        .
        .
        .
}
```

the local variables **x**, **y**, **a**, and **b** cannot be accessed outside the function **Calculate**.

3. *If a function changes the value of its parameter, the value of the corresponding argument is not altered.* A parameter is a completely separate variable into which the argument value is copied. Any change to the parameter thus changes the copy, not the corresponding argument. For example: if a function **F()** is defined as

```
void F(int X)
{
    X = X * 5;
}
```

and then called by

```
...
int
    Y = 1;

F(Y);
    .
    .
```

the value of **Y** is still 1 following the call to function **F()**.

4. *A function must be declared before it is called.* For example, if the function **FindTaxes()** needs to call the function **Calculate()**, then a declaration of **Calculate()** must precede its call in **FindTaxes()**:

```
void Calculate(...);  // declaration of function Calculate
    .
    .
void FindTaxes(...)    // definition of function FindTaxes
{
    .
    .
    Calculate(...); // call to function Calculate
    .
    .
}
```

5. *If a function needs data objects or functions from a library, the header file of that library must be inserted (using #include) before the definition of that function.* For example, if a function attempts to perform input using the `istream` data object `cin` and

    `#include <iostream.h>`

    does not precede the function's definition, then an error message such as the following is produced:

    `cin: Unknown identifier`

6. *The implementation file of a library should always insert the header file of that library (using #include) so that the compiler can verify that each function's declaration is consistent with its definition.*

7. *A function that is defined in the implementation file of a library but not declared in that library's header file cannot be called outside the library (but it can be called inside the library).* For example, if a library's implementation file contains the two function definitions

    ```
    void Calculate(...)
    {
        .
        .
        .
    }
    void FindTaxes(...)
    {
        .
        .
        .
    }
    ```

    and the library's header file declares `FindTaxes()` but does not declare `Calculate()`, then

    - `FindTaxes()` can be called by a program in which `#include` is used to insert the library's header file, but `Calculate()` cannot be called.
    - `Calculate()` can call `FindTaxes()` because there is a declaration of `FindTaxes()` before the definition of `Calculate()` in the header file, and `FindTaxes()` can call `Calculate()` because the definition of `Calculate()` precedes that of `FindTaxes()`.

8. *The variable data members and member functions of a class are accessed using the name of a class object and dot notation, but the constant data members of a class are accessed using the name of the class and the scoping operator (::).* For example, the statement

    `cout.setf(ios::fixed, ios::floatfield);`

    calls the `setf()` member function stored in the class `ostream` object named `cout` and passes it the two constant data members `ios::fixed` and `ios::floatfield` defined in class `ios`. This is an alternative to using the `setiosflags()` format manipulator for formatting output described in Section 3.6.

Program Style

1. *Functions should be documented in the same way as programs.* The documentation should include specifications and descriptions of

   - The *purpose* of the function
   - Any items *received by* the function
   - Any items *input to* the function
   - Any items *output by* the function
   - Any items *returned by* the function

2. *Functions are separate program components, and the format of a program should reflect this.* In this text, we

   - Insert appropriate documentation before each function definition to separate it from other program components.
   - Indent the declarations and statements within each function.

3. *All guidelines for programming style apply to libraries.* The stylistic standards described in earlier chapters for programs and functions should be applied to libraries as well.

4. *A library's files should be documented in much the same way as programs.* The documentation for a library should describe clearly, precisely, and completely the contents of the library and how to use items in it, any special algorithms it implements, and other useful information such as the author, a modification history, and so on. It is important to remember that the header file will often be the only documentation available to library users, and so it must contain complete documentation so that users can understand and use the objects and functions stored in the library.

5. *When the header file of a less commonly used class library is inserted in a program (using #include), a comment should be used to explain its purpose.* For example, simply writing

   ```
   #include <iomanip.h>
   ```

   tells the reader nothing about why the library is needed in this program. A simple comment

   ```
   #include <iomanip.h> // provides output-formatting functions
   ```

   provides the reader with such an explanation.

Programming Projects

1. Construct a library **Sphere** containing functions to compute the surface area and volume of a sphere. For a sphere of radius r, these values can be calculated using

$$\text{Surface Area} = 4\pi r^2$$
$$\text{Volume} = \frac{4\pi r^3}{3}$$

Write a driver program to test your library.

2. Construct a library **Cone** containing functions to compute the total surface area, lateral surface area, and volume of a right-circular cone. For a cone of radius r and height h, these can be calculated using:

$$\text{Total Surface Area} = 2\pi r(r + h)$$
$$\text{Lateral Surface Area} = 2\pi r\, h$$
$$\text{Volume} = \pi r^2 h.$$

Write a driver program to test your library.

3. Construct a library **Measures** containing functions that will allow a user to freely convert within the following categories of English-system measurement:

   Length: inches, feet, yards, miles
   Weight: ounces, pounds, tons
   Volume: teaspoons, tablespoons, cups, quarts, gallons

Write a driver program to test your library.

SELECTIVE EXECUTION

A journey of a thousand miles begins with a single step.
ANCIENT PROVERB

Then Logic would take you by the throat, and force you to do it!
ACHILLES IN LEWIS CARROLL'S
What the Tortoise Said to Achilles

If you can keep your head, when all about are losing theirs . . .
RUDYARD KIPLING

We are all special cases.
ALBERT CAMUS

CHAPTER CONTENTS

In Chapter 4, we saw that functions play an important role in programming in C++. Up to now, the problems we have considered and the functions we have designed to solve them have been quite simple, but as the problems become more complicated, the functions needed to solve also become more complex.

The logical flow of execution through a function is governed by three basic control mechanisms, **sequence, selection,** and **repetition.** The functions that we examined in Chapter 4 used only sequential execution; that is, they simply executed one or more statements *in sequence.* However, sequential execution is not sufficient to encode more complex operations. In this chapter, we review the sequence control mechanism and introduce another, *selection.* We will examine two C++ constructs that provide selection: the **if** statement and the **switch** statement. The C++ constructs that provide *repetition* are described in Chapter 6.

5.1   Sequential Execution

Sequential execution, as illustrated in the following diagram, refers to the execution of a sequence of statements in the order in which they appear so that each statement is executed exactly once. The arrows in this diagram, called **flow lines,** indicate the order in which the statements are executed. In the case of a sequential structure, they clearly show the ''straight-line'' pattern of execution. All the sample programs we have seen so far have been straight-line programs in which only sequential control is used.

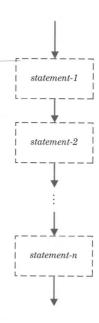

Compound Statements

In a C++ function, sequential execution is performed by a **compound statement** whose syntax diagram is

A compound statement consists of an opening brace ({), followed by a sequence of zero or more statements, followed by a closing brace (}).

Compound Statement

Form

```
{
      Statement₁
      Statement₂
           .
           .
           .
      Statementₙ
}
```

where:
   each *Statement*$_i$ is a C++ statement.

Purpose
The sequence of statements is treated as a single statement, in which *Statement*$_1$, *Statement*$_2$, . . . , *Statement*$_n$ are executed in order and each statement is executed exactly once.

Execution of the statements in a compound statement proceeds *in sequence*. The following compound statement (1) declares two variables, (2) displays a prompt to the user, (3) reads two values, (4) declares a variable and initializes it to the sum of the input values, and (5) displays the result.

```cpp
{
    int
        Number1, Number2;

    cout << "Enter two numbers: ";

    cin >> Number1 >> Number2 ;

    int
        Sum = Number1 + Number2;

    cout << "\nSum = " << Sum << "\n\n";
}
```

Recall that semicolons are used to transform declarations and expressions into statements. For example, in the preceding compound statement, the first statement is a declaration statement; the second statement is an (output) expression statement; the third statement is an (input) expression statement; the fourth statement is another declaration statement; and the fifth statement is another (output) expression statement. Thus, each of these declarations and expressions is terminated by a semicolon.

Sequence is a fundamental control mechanism, but it is not powerful enough to solve all programming problems. In the next section we present a problem that requires a control mechanism other than sequence.

5.2   Introducing Selective Execution

As usual, we begin with a problem.

Problem: Computing a Reciprocal

The Problem. Write a function to compute the reciprocal of a nonzero real value.

Specification. Examining this problem, we identify two data objects:

Data Object	Kind of Value	Type of Object	Name of Object
A nonzero input value	Variable	Real	*Val*
The reciprocal of the input value	Variable	Real	None

The problem can be specified in terms of these objects as follows:

Receive: A nonzero real value *Val*
Return: The reciprocal of *Val*

Design. Constructing an algorithm to solve this problem is straightforward, since the reciprocal of a nonzero value **X** is given by the expression **1 / X**:

ALGORITHM TO COMPUTE A RECIPROCAL—VERSION 1

/* This algorithm computes the reciprocal of an arbitrary nonzero value.

Receive: A nonzero real value *Val*
Return: The reciprocal of *Val*
———*/

1. Return the value of the expression 1 / *Val*.

Coding. Writing a function like that in Figure 5.1 to implement the preceding algorithm is straightforward.

FIGURE 5.1 A reciprocal function—version 1.

```
/* Recip computes the reciprocal of a nonzero real value.

   Receive: A nonzero real number Val
   Return:  The reciprocal of Val
-----------------------------------------------------------------------*/

double Recip(double Val)
{
   return 1.0 / Val;
}
```

Testing the Function. Although the function `Recip` is correct for nonzero values, it has the flaw that if it is passed the argument 0, then an attempt is made to evaluate the expression

```
1.0 / 0
```

and since the result of a division by zero is undefined, a run-time error message like the following may be produced:

```
Floating point error: Divide by 0.
Abnormal program termination
```

The difficulty here is not the encoding of the algorithm but the algorithm itself.

A Better Algorithm

A safer approach is to *guard* this division and perform it only if the value of `Val` is not zero. Thus, a safer algorithm is the following.

ALGORITHM TO COMPUTE A RECIPROCAL—VERSION 2

/* This algorithm computes the reciprocal of an arbitrary nonzero value.

Receive: A real number *Val*
Return: The reciprocal of *Val* if *Val* $\neq$ 0, 0 if *Val* = 0
Output: An error message if *Val* is 0

---*/

If *Val* $\neq$ 0 then
    Return the value of the expression 1 / *Val*.
Else
    a. Display an error message.
    b. Return 0 as a default value.
End If.

A Better Function

C++ provides a special statement that makes it easy to encode this algorithm, as illustrated in Figure 5.2. This modified version of the function **Recip** uses the C++ **if** statement, in which a statement is executed *selectively,* based on some *condition* (**Val** being nonzero, in this example). In the next section, we begin a careful study of selective execution by examining how conditions are constructed in C++.

 FIGURE 5.2 A reciprocal function—version 2.

```
/* Recip computes the reciprocal of a real value.

   Receive: A real number Val
   Return:  The reciprocal of Val if Val is nonzero, 0 otherwise
   Output:  An error message if Val is zero
--------------------------------------------------------------------*/

double Recip(double Val)
{
   if (Val != 0.0)
      return 1.0 / Val;
   else
   {
      cerr << "\n*** Error: Zero passed to function Recip!\n";
      return 0;
   }
}
```

5.3 Conditions

In the mid-1800s, a self-taught British mathematician, George Boole, developed an algebra of logic in which expressions could be formed to process logical values. Such logical expressions, which produce either the value *true* or the value *false,* have thus come to be known as **boolean expressions.** They are also often called **conditions,** and we will use the two terms interchangeably.

Every modern programming language provides some means for constructing boolean expressions, and in this section we consider how they are constructed in C++. We look first at simple boolean expressions and then at how logical operators can be used to combine boolean expressions to form compound expressions.

Simple Boolean Expressions

In C++, the value 0 is used to represent the logical value false, and the value 1 is generally used to represent the logical value true.[1] A boolean expression is thus a

---

[1] Actually, any nonzero value can be used to represent the logical value true, but 1 is the most commonly used nonzero value.

sequence of operands and operators that combine to produce one of the boolean values, true (1) or false (0).

The operators that are used in the simplest boolean expressions test some *relationship* between their operands. For example, the boolean expression

```
X == 5
```

tests the *equality* relationship between the (variable) operand **X** and the (constant) operand **5**. This expression evaluates to true (1) if the value of **X** is **5** and evaluates to false (0) if the value of **X** is not 5. The operators that test some relationship are called **relational operators** and they are used in boolean expressions of the form

Expression₁ RelationalOperator Expression₂

where *Expression₁* and *Expression₂* are two type-compatible expressions and the *RelationalOperator* may be any of the following operators:

Relational Operator	Relation Tested
<	Is less than
>	Is greater than
==	Is equal to
!=	Is not equal to
<=	Is less than or equal to
>=	Is greater than or equal to

These relational operators may be applied to operands of any of the standard data types: **char**, **int**, **float**, **double**, and so on. For example, if **x, a, b,** and **c** are of type **double**, **Number** is of type **int**, and **Initial** is of type **char**, then the following are valid boolean expressions formed using these relational operators:

```
x < 5.2
b * b >= 4.0 * a * c
Number == 500
Initial != 'Q'
```

For numeric data, the relational operators are the standard ones used to compare numbers. Thus, if **x** has the value 4.5, then the expression

```
X < 5.2
```

is true (producing the value 1). Similarly, if **Number** has the value 17, then the expression

```
Number == 500
```

is false (producing the value 0).

Characters are compared using their numeric codes (see Appendix A). Thus, if ASCII is used,

    `'A' < 'B'`

is a true boolean expression because the ASCII code of **A** (65) is less than the ASCII code of **B** (66). This expression thus produces the value 1 (true). Similarly, the expression

    `'a' < 'b'`

produces the value 1 (true), because the ASCII code of **a** (97) is less than the ASCII code of **b** (98). The boolean expression

    `'a' < 'A'`

is false (0), because the ASCII code of **a** (97) is not less than the ASCII code of **A** (65). Note that while the first two boolean expressions will produce the same values on a system using the EBCDIC character codes, this last expression evaluates to true (1), because the EBCDIC code for **a** (129) is less than the EBCDIC code for **A** (193).

Compound Boolean Expressions

Many relationships are too complex to be expressed using only the relational operators. For example, the mathematical relationship

$$5 \leq x \leq 10$$

is true if the value of x is between 5 and 10 (inclusive), and is false otherwise. However, this relationship cannot be represented by the boolean expression

    `5 <= x <= 10`

To see why, suppose that x has the value 15, which would mean that the inequality is false. Because `<=` is left-associative, the preceding expression is processed as

    `(5 <= x) <= 10`

Thus, if **x** has the value 15, this expression is evaluated as

    `(5 <= 15) <= 10`

The subexpression

    `(5 <= 15)`

is evaluated first, producing the value true (1). This value is then used as an operand for the second `<=` operator, so that the expression

    `1 <= 10`

is evaluated; it, of course, is true (1), which is not the value of the original mathematical expression.

To avoid this difficulty, we must represent the mathematical expression

$$5 \le x \le 10$$

by an expression of the form

$$(5 \le x) \quad \text{and} \quad (x \le 10)$$

This expression can be correctly coded in C++, because C++ provides a variety of **logical operators** that combine boolean expressions to form **compound boolean expressions.** These operators are defined as follows:

Logical Operator	Logical Expression	Name of Operation	Description
!	!*p*	*Not* (*Negation*)	!*p* is false if *p* is true; !*p* is true if *p* is false.
&&	*p* && *q*	*And* (*Conjunction*)	*p* && *q* is true if both *p* and *q* are true, it is false otherwise,
||	*p* || *q*	*Or* (*Disjunction*)	*p* || *q* is true if either *p* or *q* or both are true; it is false otherwise.

These definitions are summarized in the following **truth tables,** which display all possible values for two conditions **p** and **q** and the corresponding values of the logical expression:

p	!*p*
true	false
false	true

p	*q*	*p* && *q*	*p* || *q*
true	true	true	true
true	false	false	true
false	true	false	true
false	false	false	false

We can thus use the && operator to write the mathematical expression

$$(5 \le x) \quad \text{and} \quad (x \le 10)$$

as the compound boolean expression

$$(5 \texttt{ <= } x) \texttt{ \&\& } (x \texttt{ <= } 10)$$

In this case, if **x** has the value 15, the expression will be evaluated as follows

1. The relational expression **5 <= 15** is evaluated, giving true (1).
2. The relational expression **15 <= 10** is evaluated, giving false (0).
3. The && operator is applied to these two values, true && false (**1 && 0**), producing the correct value false (0).

Operator Precedence

A boolean expression that contains an assortment of arithmetic operators, boolean operators, and relational operators is evaluated using the following precedence (or priority) and associativity rules:[2]

Operator	Priority	Associativity
!	14	Right
/, *, %	13	Left
+, −	12	Left
<, >, <=, >=	10	Left
==, !=	9	Left
&&	5	Left
||	4	Left
=, +=, *=, . . .	2	Right

In C++, an operator with a higher priority number has higher precedence and is applied before an operator with a lower priority number.

To illustrate, consider the boolean expression

```
N != 0 && X < 1/N
```

The / operator has highest priority, and so this operator is applied first, producing an intermediate value **v1** and the expression

```
N != 0 && X < v1
```

Of the remaining operators, < has the highest priority, and so that operator is applied next, producing an intermediate (boolean) value **v2** and the expression

```
N != 0 && v2
```

Of the remaining two operators, != has the higher priority, and so that operator is applied next, producing an intermediate (boolean) value **v3** and the expression

```
v3 && v2
```

Finally, the && operator is applied to the two (boolean) intermediate values to produce the value of the expression.

Because it is difficult to remember so many precedence levels, it is helpful to remember the following:

- ! is the highest-priority operator (that we've seen so far).
- *, /, and % have higher priority than + and −.
- Every numeric operator has higher priority than every relational and/or logical operator (except !).
- Use parentheses to indicate clearly the order in which other operators are to be applied.

---

[2] The ''gaps'' in the priorities of the operators in this table occur because it lists only a few of the operators provided in C++; a complete table is given in Appendix C.

Short-Circuit Evaluation

An important feature of the **&&** and **||** operators is that they do not always evaluate their second operand. For example, if **p** is false, then the condition

    p && q

is false, regardless of the value of **q**, and so C++ does not evaluate **q**. Similarly, if **p** is true, then the condition

    p || q

is true, regardless of the value of **q**, and so C++ does not evaluate **q**. This approach is called **short-circuit evaluation** and has two important benefits:

1. One boolean expression can be used to *guard* a potentially unsafe operation in a second boolean expression.
2. A considerable amount of time can be saved in the evaluation of complex conditions.

   As an illustration of the first benefit, consider the boolean expression

    (N != 0) && (X < 1 / N)

No division-by-zero error can occur in evaluating this expression, because if **N** is 0, then the first expression,

    (N != 0)

is false and so the second expression,

    (X < 1 / N)

is not evaluated. Similarly, no division-by-zero error will occur in evaluating the condition

    (N == 0) || (X >= 1/N)

because if **N** is 0, the first expression

    (N == 0)

is true and so the second expression is not evaluated.

5.4 PART OF THE PICTURE: Computer Architecture

Architecture is the science (or art) of designing buildings and other structures. In the context of computing, the phrase *computer architecture* refers to the design of computers and their components.

In Section 1.3 we saw that the central processing unit (CPU) is one of a computer's components. The arithmetic operations performed by the CPU must be carried out using special electrical circuits called **logic circuits** that are used to implement boolean (or digital) logic in hardware. In this section we investigate the design of such circuits, which is one small part of the much broader area of computer architecture.

Since logic circuits use boolean logic, their behavior can be simulated using boolean expressions. To illustrate, consider the following logical circuit, called a **binary half-adder,** which adds two binary digits.

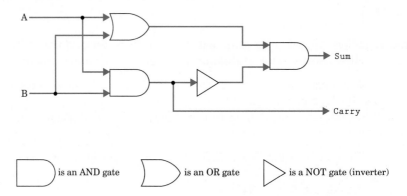

This circuit is designed to accept two inputs, **A** and **B**, and produce two outputs, **Sum** and **Carry**. It contains four basic electronic components called **gates,** two AND gates, one OR gate, and one NOT gate (also called an *inverter*). The inputs to and outputs from these gates are electrical voltages, where a voltage that exceeds a certain threshold value is interpreted as 1 and a voltage below that threshold is interpreted as 0. In the case of an AND gate, a 1 is produced only when there are 1s on both input lines. An OR gate produces a 1 only when there is a 1 on at least one of the input lines. The output of a NOT gate is the opposite of its input.

The boolean operators **&&**, **||**, and **!** can be used to model AND, OR, and NOT gates, respectively, and boolean expressions can thus be used to model logical circuits. For example, the output **Sum** in the circuit for a binary half-adder can be represented by the boolean expression

    (A || B) && !(A && B)

and the output **Carry** by

    A && B

The following truth table displays the values of these boolean expressions:

A	B	Carry	Sum
0	0	0	0
0	1	0	1
1	0	0	1
1	1	1	0

If we compare the values of **Sum** and **Carry** with the value produced when two binary digits are added (as specified by the following binary addition table),

+	0	1
0	0	1
1	1	10

we see that the circuit does, in fact, carry out this addition correctly.

The program in Figure 5.3 models a binary half-adder. It reads binary digits (0 or 1) for **A** and **B**. The (binary) values of the two boolean expressions representing the sum and carry outputs are then assigned to variables **Sum** and **Carry**, respectively, and are displayed. A *full-adder* for adding two binary digits and a carry bit and an *adder* for numbers having more than one binary digit are described in the Programming Projects at the end of this chapter.

 FIGURE 5.3 A binary half-adder.

```
/* This program calculates the outputs from a boolean expression
   that is equivalent to the logical circuit for a binary half-adder.

   Input (keyboard): Two binary digits
   Output (screen):  Two binary values representing the sum and
                     carry that result when the input values are
                     added
--------------------------------------------------------------------*/

#include <iostream.h>

int main(void)
{
   cout << "\nThis program simulates the execution of a "
        << "binary half-adder.\n";

   short
      A,                               // the two binary inputs
      B;

   cout << "\nPlease enter two binary inputs: ";
   cin >> A >> B;

   short
      Sum = (A || B) && !(A && B),     // the two circuit outputs
      Carry = (A && B);

   cout << "\n\tCarry = " << Carry << " Sum = " << Sum << "\n\n";

   return 0;
}
```

FIGURE 5.3 A binary half-adder. (cont.)

Sample runs:

```
This program simulates the execution of a binary half-adder.

Please enter two binary inputs: 0 0

  Carry = 0 Sum = 0

...

Please enter two binary inputs: 0 1

  Carry = 0 Sum = 1

...

Please enter two binary inputs: 1 0

  Carry = 0 Sum = 1

...

Please enter two binary inputs: 1 1

  Carry = 1 Sum = 0
```

Exercises

1. Use truth tables to display the values of the following boolean expressions for all possible (boolean) values of **a**, **b**, and **c**:

   (a) a || !b   (b) !(a && b)
   (c) !a || !b   (d) (a && b) || c
   (e) a && (b || c)   (f) (a && b) || (a && c)

2. Write C++ boolean expressions to express the following conditions:

   (a) **x** is greater than 3.
   (b) **y** is strictly between 2 and 5.
   (c) **r** is negative and **z** is positive.
   (d) Both **Alpha** and **Beta** are positive.
   (e) **Alpha** and **Beta** have the same sign (both are negative or both are positive).
   (f) $-5 < x < 5$.
   (g) **a** is less than 6 or is greater than 10.
   (h) **p** is equal to **q**, which is equal to **r**.
   (i) **x** is less than 3, or **y** is less than 3, but not both.

3. Given the boolean variables **a**, **b**, and **c**, write a C++ boolean expression that is

(a) True if and only if **a** and **b** are true and **c** is false
(b) True if and only if **a** is true and at least one of **b** or **c** is true
(c) True if and only if exactly one of **a** and **b** is true

4. In a certain region, pesticide can be sprayed from an airplane only if the temperature is at least 70°, the relative humidity is between 15% and 35%, and the wind speed is at most 10 miles per hour. Write a program that accepts three numbers representing temperature, relative humidity, and wind speed; assigns the value true or false to the boolean variable `OkToSpray` according to these criteria; and displays this value.

5. The Cawker City Credit Company will approve a loan application if the applicant's income is at least $25,000 or the value of his or her assets is at least $100,000; in addition, total liabilities must be less than $50,000. Write a program that accepts three numbers representing income, assets, and liabilities; assigns the value true or false to the boolean variable `CreditOK` according to these criteria; and displays this value.

5.5 Selection: The `if` Statement

The applications of boolean expressions that we considered in the preceding section are valid applications and are important in their own right, but boolean expressions are more commonly used to provide a mechanism for controlling program execution. In this section we consider a C++ **selection statement** that uses a boolean expression to implement a selection control mechanism.

To see the need for selection statements, we consider again the pollution index problem from Chapter 2.

Example: Pollution Index Problem

In this problem, as described in Section 2.1, a pollution index is to be calculated as the average of three air quality readings. If this index is less than some cutoff value, then a message indicating a safe condition must be displayed; otherwise, a message indicating a hazardous condition must be displayed.

The selection statement required to solve this problem was indicated in the algorithm for this problem (see Section 2.3) by the instruction:

> If (*Index* < *Cutoff*) then
>   Display a ''safe condition'' message.
> Else
>   Display a ''hazardous condition'' message.
> End If.

This selection structure can be implemented in C++ using the following `if` statement:

```
if (Index < Cutoff)
   cout << "Safe condition.\n";
else
   cout << "Hazardous condition!\n";
```

Figure 5.4 presents a complete solution to the problem.

 FIGURE 5.4 Pollution index.

```
/* This program reads 3 pollution levels, calculates an air
   pollution index as their average, and displays an appropriate
   air-quality message.

   Input:   Three pollution levels and a cutoff value
   Output:  The pollution index and a "safe condition"
            message if this index is less than the cutoff
            value, otherwise a "hazardous condition" message

   ----------------------------------------------------------------*/

#include <iostream.h>

int main(void)
{
   cout << "\nThis program processes pollution indices.\n";

   const int
      Cutoff = 50;                    // bottom line for a safe condition

   int
      Reading1, Reading2, Reading3;       // three pollution readings

   cout << "\nPlease enter 3 (integer) pollution readings: ";
   cin >> Reading1 >> Reading2 >> Reading3;

   int
      Index = (Reading1 + Reading2 + Reading3) / 3;

   cout << "\nPollution index = " << Index << ": ";

   if (Index < Cutoff)
      cout << "Safe condition.\n";
   else
      cout << "Hazardous condition!\n";

   return 0;
}
```

Sample runs:

```
This program processes pollution indices.

Please enter 3 (integer) pollution readings: 55 39 48

Pollution index = 47: Safe condition.
```

FIGURE 5.4   Pollution index. (cont.)

```
Please enter 3 (integer) pollution readings: 68 49 57

Pollution index = 58: Hazardous condition!
```

Having seen a simple problem whose solution requires selection and a C++ program that implements selection with an **if** statement, we now examine C++'s **if** statement in greater detail.

The Simple **if** Statement

In the simplest form of the C++ **if** statement, a sequence of statements is executed or bypassed, depending on whether a given boolean expression is true or false. This is pictured in the following diagram, where a diamond indicates the evaluation of a boolean expression, and the two possible execution paths are indicated using arrows.

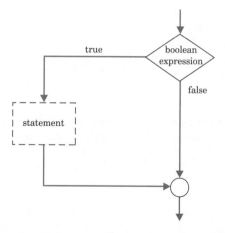

This selection structure can be implemented in C++ using a simple form of the **if** statement:

The **if** Statement (Simple Form)

Form

```
if (Condition)
    Statement
```

where:
  if is a keyword;
  Condition is a boolean expression; and
  Statement is a C++ statement (either simple or compound).

> **Purpose**
> If the *Condition* evaluates to true, then the speci-
> fied *Statement* is executed; otherwise it is by-
> passed. In either case, execution continues with the
> next statement in the program. Note that the
> *Condition* must be enclosed in parentheses.

For example, in the `if` statement

```
if (Score <= 60)
   cout << 'F';
```

the condition `Score <= 60` is evaluated, and if it is true, the letter `F` is displayed.
Otherwise, the output statement is bypassed. In either case, execution continues
with the statement following this `if` statement.

The statement that appears in an `if` statement may be a compound statement;
for example,

```
if (Hours > 40.0)
{
   Overtime = Hours - 40.0;
   OvertimePay = 1.5 * Overtime * Rate;
}
```

Here the values of `Overtime` and `OvertimePay` are calculated only in the case that
the boolean expression `Hours > 40.0` produces the value true. Similarly, for the
`if` statement

```
if ((1 < X) && (X < 3))
{
   Y = X * X;
   W = sqrt(x);
}
```

`Y` is assigned the square of `X` and `W` is assigned the square root of `X` only in the case
that `X` is strictly between 1 and 3; otherwise, these assignment statements are not
executed and the values of `Y` and `W` are unchanged.

Note that the `if` statement is an actual statement, as opposed to an expression.
This means that although an I/O expression or an assignment expression must be
terminated by a semicolon in order for it to "become" a statement, an `if` statement is already a statement, and so no semicolon should appear following its
closing brace.

The General `if` Statement

The simple `if` statement is used to select between (1) executing a given statement
and (2) bypassing this statement. In the two-way selection pictured in the follow-

ing diagram, the selection is between (1) executing one statement and (2) executing another statement:

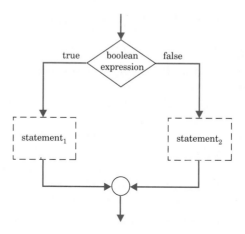

This selection structure is implemented in C++ by an **if** statement that allows the programmer not only to specify the statement selected for execution when the boolean expression is true but also to indicate an alternative statement for execution when it is false. This **if** statement (together with the earlier form) is specified by the following syntax diagram:

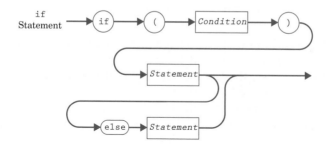

As the diagram clearly indicates, an **if** statement may contain an optional **else** part and thus may have two forms:

The if Statement (General Form)

Form

```
if (Condition)
    Statement
```

or

```
if (Condition)
    Statement₁
else
    Statement₂
```

where:

   if and **else** are keywords;

   Condition is a boolean expression; and

   Statement, *Statement₁*, and *Statement₂* are

      C++ statements (either simple or compound).

Purpose

In the first form, if the *Condition* is true, then the specified *Statement* is executed; otherwise it is bypassed, and execution continues with the next statement in the program.

   In the second form, if the *Condition* is true, then *Statement₁* is executed and *Statement₂* is bypassed; otherwise *Statement₁* is bypassed and *Statement₂* is executed. In either case, execution continues with the next statement in the program.

This more general form of the **if** statement selects one of two alternatives, as we saw in the program in Figure 5.4:

```
if (Index < Cutoff)
    cout << "Safe condition.\n";
else
    cout << "Hazardous condition!\n";
```

This statement evaluates the condition **Index < Cutoff**. If this condition is true, the first output statement is executed and the second output statement is bypassed; if this condition is false, the first output statement is bypassed, and the second output statement is executed.

   As with the simple **if** statement, either (or both) of the statements within the general **if** statement may be compound statements, as we saw in Figure 5.2:

```
if (Val != 0.0)
    return 1.0 / Val;
else
{
    cerr << "\n*** Error: Zero passed to function Recip!\n";
    return 0;
}
```

Or, we can accomplish the same thing by writing

```
if (Val == 0.0)
{
    cerr << "\n*** Error: Zero passed to function Recip!\n";
    return 0;
}
else
    return 1.0 / Val;
```

Example: Grade Computation

As another illustration of using an **if** statement to implement a two-alternative selection structure, suppose that students in a computer programming course will receive a passing grade if their final course average is 60 or above and will fail otherwise. The final average is computed as a weighted average of the homework average, the average on tests, and the exam score:

Average = 0.2 ∗ *HomeworkAverage* + 0.5 ∗ *TestAverage* + 0.3 ∗ *ExamScore*

A program is to be written to determine the pass/fail grade for a given student in this course. An algorithm for calculating grades is as follows:

GRADE COMPUTATION ALGORITHM

/* This algorithm determines the pass/fail *Grade* for a student, using a weighted *Average* of the student's *HomeworkAverage, TestAverage,* and *ExamScore.*

Input: A student's homework average, test average, and final exam score
Output: The weighted average and pass/fail grade
———*/

1. Enter *HomeworkAverage, TestAverage,* and *ExamScore.*
2. Calculate *Average* = 0.2 ∗ *HomeworkAverage* + 0.5 ∗ *TestAverage*
                         + 0.3 ∗ *ExamScore.*
3. Calculate *Grade,* according to the value of *Average.*
4. Display *Average* and *Grade.*

The problem is in computing Step 3: How can we assign *Grade* different values based on the value of *Average*? Recognizing that this is an operation that must select different letter grades for different averages, we might use the following algorithm for this subproblem:

LETTER GRADE COMPUTATION ALGORITHM—VERSION 1

/* This algorithm computes the appropriate grade for a given *Average.*

Receive: A weighted average
Return: A letter grade (P or F)
———*/

If *Average* ≥ 60 then
   Return 'P'.
Else
   Return 'F'.
End If.

A C++ program to implement this algorithm is given in Figure 5.5. An **if** statement is used to implement the selection structure that makes the appropriate grade assignment, depending on the boolean expression *Average* ≥ 60. Note the use of the four constant identifiers **HWWeight**, **TestWeight**, **ExamWeight**, and **PassFailLine** in place of the constants **0.2**, **0.5**, **0.3**, and **60**. These identifiers are defined early in the program and then used in place of the literal constants. If the program must be modified to use different weighting factors or a different pass/fail line, we need only change the definitions of these constant identifiers; the formula in the program need not be modified.

FIGURE 5.5   Grade computation—version 1.

```
/* This program computes a final course average using the homework
   average, the average on tests, and a final exam score; and
   assigns a pass/fail grade.

   Input:   Three real values representing a student's homework
               average, average on tests, and a final exam score
   Output:  The weighted average and the pass/fail grade

-----------------------------------------------------------------*/

#include <iostream.h>

char LetterGrade(double);

int main(void)
{
   const double
      HWWeight = 0.2,        // weight factors for homework,
      TestWeight = 0.5,      //      tests,
      ExamWeight = 0.3;      //      and the exam.


   cout << "\nThis program computes a final course average using the\n"
        << "\thomework average, test average, and a final exam "
        << "score.\n";

   cout << "\nPlease enter homework average, test average, "
        << "and exam score:\n";

   double
      HomeworkAverage,       // the average of the homework scores
      TestAverage,           // the average of the test scores
      ExamScore;             // the final exam score

   cin >> HomeworkAverage >> TestAverage >> ExamScore;

   double
      Average = HWWeight * HomeworkAverage + TestWeight * TestAverage +
                ExamWeight * ExamScore;
```

FIGURE 5.5 Grade computation—version 1. (cont.)

```
   char
      Grade = LetterGrade(Average);     // the grade received (P or F)

   cout << "Average = " << Average << ", Grade = " << Grade << "\n\n";

   return 0;
}

/*-------------------------------------------------------------------
LetterGrade computes a letter grade, given a weighted average.

   Receive:   A (double) weighted average
   Return:    The appropriate (char) letter grade
----------------------------------------------------------------*/

char LetterGrade(double Average)
{
   const double
      PassFailLine = 60.0;     // pass/fail line

   if (Average >= PassFailLine)
      return 'P';
   else
      return 'F';
}
```

Sample runs:

```
This program computes a final course average using the
   homework average, test average, and a final exam score.

Please enter homework average, test average, and exam score:
60 60 60
Average = 60, Grade = P

...

Please enter homework average, test average, and exam score:
60 70 80
Average = 71, Grade = P

...

Please enter homework average, test average, and exam score:
55.2 50.7 45.5
Average = 50.04, Grade = F

...

Please enter homework average, test average, and exam score:
99.5 58.3 75
Average = 71.55, Grade = P
```

Example: Grade Computation—Version 2

Recall that the general form of the **if** statement is

```
if (Condition)
    Statement₁
else
    Statement₂
```

where **Statement₁** and **Statement₂** can be any C++ statements. This means that **Statement₁** and **Statement₂** may themselves be **if** statements. In this case, an inner **if** statement is said to be **nested** within the outer **if** statement.

To illustrate, suppose that in the preceding example, students who pass are awarded a special honors grade if their average is 80 or above. This modification requires altering only the algorithm for computing letter grades:

LETTER GRADE COMPUTATION ALGORITHM—VERSION 2

/* This algorithm computes the appropriate letter grade for a given *Average*.

Receive: A weighted average
Return: A letter grade (P, H, or F)
——*/

If *Average* ≥ 60 then
  If *Average* ≥ 80 then
    Return 'H'.
  Else
    Return 'P'.
  End If.
Else
  Return 'F'.
End If.

The pseudocode description of this algorithm clearly shows the selection structure for determining honors designation based on the condition *Average* ≥ 80 nested within the larger selection structure based on the condition *Average* ≥ 60. This nested selection structure is implemented in the C++ function in Figure 5.6 by nested **if** statements.

FIGURE 5.6   Grade computation—version 2.

```
/*----------------------------------------------------------------
LetterGrade computes the appropriate Grade for a given Average.

   Receive: A (double) weighted average
   Return:  The appropriate (char) letter grade (P, H, or F)
----------------------------------------------------------------*/

char LetterGrade(double Average)
{
   const double
      PassFailLine = 60.0,         // pass/fail line
      HonorsLine = 80.0;           // honors/no honors line

   if (Average >= PassFailLine)    // outer if
      if (Average >= HonorsLine)   //    nested if
         return 'H';
      else
         return 'P';
   else
      return 'F';

}
```

Sample runs of program obtained by substituting this definition of `LetterGrade()` for that in Figure 5.5:

```
This program computes a final course average using the
   homework average, test average, and a final exam score.

Please enter homework average, test average, and exam score:
60 60 60
Average = 60, Grade = P.


...


Please enter homework average, test average, and exam score:
60 70 80
Average = 71, Grade = P.


...


Please enter homework average, test average, and exam score:
55.2 50.7 45.5
Average = 50.04, Grade = F.


...


Please enter homework average, test average, and exam score:
99 98 97
Average = 97.9, Grade = H.
```

When one **if** statement is nested within another, as in

```
if (x > 0)
   if (y > 0)
      z = sqrt(x) + sqrt(y);
 else
    cout << "\n*** unable to compute z!\n";
```

it may not be clear with which **if** the **else** is associated. This ambiguity is resolved in C++ by the following important rule:

In a nested **if** *statement, an* **else** *is matched with the nearest preceding unmatched* **if**.

Thus, in the preceding **if** statement, the **else** is associated with the inner **if** (the one containing the condition **y > 0**). Consequently, the output statement is executed only in the case that **x** is positive and **y** is nonpositive. If we wish to associate this else with the outer **if**, we can force the association by surrounding the inner **if** with braces, as follows:

```
if (x > 0)
{
   if (y > 0)
      z = sqrt(x) + sqrt(y);
}
else
   cout << "\n*** unable to compute z!\n";
```

This makes the inner **if** a complete statement inside a compound statement, so that the **else** must associate with the outer **if**. Thus the output statement is executed whenever **x** is nonpositive.

Note that in our examples each **else** is aligned with its corresponding **if**. This alignment improves readability by making clear the **if** with which a particular **else** is associated. We also indent the statements within an **if** to indicate that they are at a different level of control than the **if** statement controlling them (i.e., they may or may not be executed, based on the value of the condition).

The if-else-if Form

The selection statements considered thus far involve selecting one of two alternatives, but it is also possible to use the **if** statement to design selection statements that contain more than two alternatives. These **multialternative selection statements** can be constructed using nested **if** statements with the following form:

The `if` Statement (if-else-if Form)

Form

```
if (Condition₁)
    Statement₁
else if (Condition₂)
    Statement₂
       .
       .
       .
else if (Conditionₙ)
    Statementₙ
else
    Statementₙ₊₁
```

where:

   `if` and `else` are keywords;
   $Condition_1$, $Condition_2$, . . . , $Condition_{n+1}$
     are boolean expressions;
   $Statement_1$, $Statement_2$, . . . , $Statement_{n+1}$
     are C++ statements;
     and the `else` clause is optional.

Purpose

When an **if-else-if** is executed, each condition is evaluated in sequence, until some $Condition_i$ is found that is true. The associated $Statement_i$ is executed, and execution then continues with the statement following the end of the form.

   If no $Condition_i$ is true, then the statement associated with the `else` clause is executed, and execution then continues with the statement following the end of the form. (If the `else` clause is omitted, execution "falls through" to the next statement of the program.)

   This **if-else-if** form therefore implements a multialternative selection structure in which exactly one of $Statement_1$, $Statement_2$, . . . , $Statement_{n+1}$ is executed.

Note that this is not a new kind of `if` statement: We are simply writing

```
if (Condition₁)
    Statement₁
else Statement
```

where *Statement* happens to be an **if** statement that begins on the same line:

```
if (Condition₁)
    Statement₁
else if (Condition₂)
    Statement₂
else Statement
```

and so on. Each **if** in an **else if** clause is actually a new **if** statement (that is only executed if the conditions in all of the preceding **if** statements are false). Similarly, each **else** in an **else if** clause is actually associated with the **if** of the preceding **else if** clause (or the first **if**), as shown by the arrows in the following diagram:

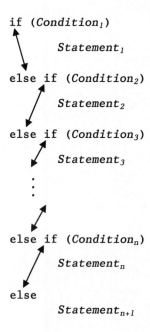

```
if (Condition₁)

        Statement₁

else if (Condition₂)

        Statement₂

else if (Condition₃)

        Statement₃
        .
        .
        .

else if (Conditionₙ)

        Statementₙ

else

        Statementₙ₊₁
```

Example: Grade Computation—Version 3

As an illustration of multialternative selection, suppose that the grade assignment program in Figure 5.5 must be modified so that letter grades are assigned as indicated in the following table:

Average	Letter Grade
Average ≥ 90	A
80 ≤ average < 90	B
70 ≤ average < 80	C
60 ≤ average < 70	D
Average < 60	F

As before, the only part of the program that must be altered to solve this problem is the definition of function `LetterGrade()`. The modified algorithm used by `LetterGrade()` is as follows.

LETTER GRADE COMPUTATION ALGORITHM—VERSION 3

/* This algorithm computes the appropriate grade for a given *Average.*

Receive: A weighted average
Return: A letter grade (A, B, C, D, or F)
——*/

If *Average* ≥ 90 then
   Return 'A'.
Else if *Average* ≥ 80 then
   Return 'B'.
Else if *Average* ≥ 70 then
   Return 'C'.
Else if *Average* ≥ 60 then
   Return 'D'.
Else
   Return 'F'.
End If-Else-if.

The function definition in Figure 5.7 implements this algorithm, using the following `if` statement to implement the five-way selection structure:

```
if (Average >= ABLine)
   Grade = 'A';
else if (Average >= BCLine)
   Grade = 'B';
else if (Average >= CDLine)
   Grade = 'C';
else if (Average >= DFLine)
   Grade = 'D';
else
   Grade = 'F';
```

 FIGURE 5.7 Grade computation—version 3.

```
/*-------------------------------------------------------------------
LetterGrade computes the appropriate Grade for a given Average.

   Receive: A (double) weighted average
   Return:  The appropriate (char) letter grade (A, B, C, D, or F)
   ----------------------------------------------------------------*/
```

FIGURE 5.7 Grade computation—version 3. (cont.)

```cpp
char LetterGrade(double Average)
{
    const double
        ABLine = 90.0,          // A/B cut-off
        BCLine = 80.0,          // B/C cut-off
        CDLine = 70.0,          // C/D cut-off
        DFLine = 60.0;          // D/F cut-off

    if (Average >= ABLine)
        return 'A';
    else if (Average >= BCLine)
        return 'B';
    else if (Average >= CDLine)
        return 'C';
    else if (Average >= DFLine)
        return 'D';
    else
        return 'F';
}
```

Sample runs of program obtained by substituting this definition of `LetterGrade()` for that in Figure 5.5:

```
Please enter homework average, test average, and exam score:
100 100 100
Average = 100, Grade = A.
```

. . .

```
Please enter homework average, test average, and exam score:
30 40 50
Average = 41, Grade = F.
```

. . .

```
Please enter homework average, test average, and exam score:
56.2 62.7 66.5
Average = 62.54, Grade = D.
```

. . .

```
Please enter homework average, test average, and exam score:
87.5 91.3 80
Average = 87.15, Grade = B.
```

The `if-else-if` form of the `if` statement thus provides the capability of constructing functions that implement more complicated operations. Such operations can often use some characteristic of their parameters to select from a number of alternative **return** statements.

Pitfall: Confusing = and ==

In this section, we discuss the most common source of errors in constructing **if** statements. We begin by reviewing two features of C++ that we have already seen:

1. *True and false in C++.* As we have seen, C++ interprets the value zero as the boolean value false and any nonzero value as the boolean value true. Thus, the statement

   ```
   if (0)
      cout << "T\n";
   else
      cout << "F\n";
   ```

   will always display **F**, because the condition controlling the selection is zero, which in C++ represents the boolean value false. Similarly, the statement

   ```
   if (23)
      cout << "T\n";
   else
      cout << "F\n";
   ```

   will always display **T**, because the condition controlling the selection is nonzero, which is interpreted as true in C++.

2. *Assignments are expressions.* We also saw in Chapter 3 that assignment (=) is an operator in C++ that returns the value being assigned as its result. For example, the assignment expression

   ```
   x = 32
   ```

   both assigns **x** the value **32** and produces the value **32** as its result. Similarly, the assignment

   ```
   x = 0
   ```

   both assigns **x** the value **0** and produces the value **0** as its result.

By themselves, neither C++'s representation of true and false nor its treatment of assignment as an expression is particularly troublesome. The problem is that these two features, coupled with the similarity of the assignment and equality operators, make it easy to write **if** statements that contain logical errors. As an example, suppose that a programmer encodes the instruction

> If x is equal to zero, then
>   Display the character string "Zero".
> Else
>   Display the character string "Nonzero".
> End If.

as follows:

```
if (x = 0)
   cout << "Zero\n";
else
   cout << "Nonzero\n";
```

This is functionally equivalent to

```
if (0)
   cout << "Zero\n";
else
   cout << "Nonzero\n";
```

because the condition in the **if** statement is an assignment expression

```
x = 0
```

instead of an equality comparison

```
x == 0
```

and the value produced by the assignment operator is the value that is assigned. Since this value is zero and zero is treated as false, the statement to output **Nonzero** will always be selected, regardless of the value of **x**.

Similarly, if a programmer writes

```
cout << Menu;           // display menu of choices: A, B, C
cin >> Choice;

if (Choice = 'A')
   Statement₁             // do something if Choice is A
else if (Choice = 'B')
   Statement₂             // do something else if Choice is B
else if (Choice = 'C')
   Statement₃             // do something else if Choice is C
else
   cout << Choice << " must be A, B, or C.\n";
```

then the statement associated with choice **A** will always be selected, regardless of the value entered by the user. The reason is that instead of the first condition testing whether **Choice** is equal to **A**,

```
Choice == 'A'
```

it assigns **Choice** the numeric code of **A** (the value 65 in ASCII). The result produced by the assignment operator is the value assigned (65), and so this **if-else-if** form is equivalent to

```
cout << Menu;           // display menu of choices: A, B, C
cin >> Choice;

if (65)
   Statement₁             // do something if Choice is A
else if (66)
   Statement₂             // do something else if Choice is B
else if (67)
   Statement₃             // do something else if Choice is C
else
   cout << Choice << " must be A, B, or C.\n";
```

Since nonzero values are treated as true, the value 65 is treated as true, and so *Statement₁* will be executed and *Statement₂*, *Statement₃*, and the output statement bypassed, regardless of the value of **Choice**.

This kind of error is one of the most frequent errors in writing **if** statements. Unfortunately, these errors can be difficult to find, because the equality operator (==) and the assignment operator (=) are similar in appearance. We recommend that any time an algorithm calls for an equality comparison, the resulting code should be double- and triple-checked to ensure that an assignment operator has not been inadvertently substituted for the equality operator.

Exercises

1. Write a C++ statement for each of the following:

   (a) If **TaxCode** is `'T'`, increase **Price** by adding **TaxRate** times **Price** to it.
   (b) If **Code** has the value 1, read values for **x** and **y**, and calculate and print the sum of **x** and **y**.
   (c) If **A** is strictly between 0 and 5, set **B** equal to $1/A^2$; otherwise set **B** equal to A^2.

2. Describe the output produced by the following poorly indented program segment:

   ```
   Number = 4;
   Alpha = -1.0;
   if (Number > 0)
      if (Alpha > 0)
         cout << "\nFirst\n";
   else
      cout << "\nSecond\n";
      cout << "\nThird\n";
   ```

3. A student used the following **if** statement in a program:

   ```
   if (Honors == 1)
      if (Awards == 1)
         GoodStudent = 1;
      else
         GoodStudent = 0;
   else if (Honors == 0)
      GoodStudent = 0;
   ```

   (a) Write a simpler **if** statement that is equivalent to this one.
   (b) Write a single assignment statement that is equivalent to this **if** statement.

4. Write a function that will

   (a) Return true (1) if the value of an **int** parameter **Year** is the number of a leap year (a leap year is a multiple of 4, and if it is a multiple of 100, it must also be a multiple of 400); and return false (0) otherwise.
   (b) Return the value **Cost** given an **int** parameter **Distance** according to the following table:

Distance	Cost
0 through 100	5.00
More than 100 but not more than 500	8.00
More than 500 but less than 1000	10.00
1000 or more	12.00

(c) Return the number of days in a given **int** parameter **Month** (1, 2, . . . , 12) of a given parameter **Year**. Use part (a) to determine the number of days if the value of **Month** is 2.

5. Write a function to check a quadratic equation of the form $Ax^2 + Bx + C = 0$ to see if it has real roots, and if so, find these roots. If there are no real roots, display an appropriate message (see Exercise 10 of Section 2.6). Construct a driver program that calls the function with the following values for A, B, and C: 1, −5, 6; 1, −2, 1; 1, 0, 4; 1, 1, 1; 2, 1, −3.

6. A certain city classifies a pollution index less than 35 as "pleasant," 35 through 60 as "unpleasant," and above 60 as "hazardous." Write a function that displays the appropriate classification of a number representing a pollution index. Construct a driver program that executes the function with the following data: 20, 45, 75, 35, 60.

7. Write a program that reads an employee's number, hours worked, and hourly rate and then calculates his or her wages. All hours over 40 are paid at 1.5 times the regular hourly rate. Execute the program with the following values for employee number, hours worked, and hourly rate: 123, 38, 7.50; 175, 39.5, 7.85; 223, 40, 9.25; 375, 44.5, 8.35.

8. Write a wage-calculation program like the one in Exercise 7, but with the following modification: If an employee's number is greater than or equal to 1000, the program should read an annual salary and calculate the employee's weekly pay as this salary divided by 52. If the employee's number is less than 1000, wages are calculated on an hourly basis, as described in Exercise 7. Execute the program with the data in Exercise 7 and the following data: 1217, 25500; 1343, 31775.

5.6   Selection: The **switch** Statement

In the preceding section, we saw that an **if** statement can be used to implement a multialternative selection statement in which exactly one of several alternative actions is selected and performed. In this **if-else-if** form of the statement, a selection is made by evaluating one or more boolean expressions. Since selection criteria can usually be formulated as boolean expressions, an **if-else-if** form can be used to implement virtually any multialternative selection.

In this section we describe a different multialternative selection statement called the **switch** statement. Although it is not as general as the **if** statement, it is a more efficient statement for implementing some kinds of selection.

As usual, we begin with an example that illustrates the use of the statement.

Example: Converting Year Names to Year Codes

Many colleges and universities store information about their students using numeric codes. For example, a university's records might store the following values:

1 if a student is a freshman
2 if a student is a sophomore
3 if a student is a junior
4 if a student is a senior
5 if a student is a graduate

When information about the freshman Jane Doe is displayed, output of the form

```
Doe, Jane D.     (1)
```

is less descriptive than

```
Doe, Jane D. (Freshman)
```

One way to produce the latter output is to construct a function that, for a given numeric year code, displays the appropriate year name. More precisely, the function should:

Receive: An integer year code (1–5)
Output: The character string corresponding to that year code ("Freshman"–"Graduate")

The following algorithm solves this problem.

ALGORITHM TO CONVERT A YEAR CODE

/* This algorithm displays a year name for a given year code.

Receive: An integer *YearCode* (1–5)
Output: The character string corresponding to that year code
          ("Freshman"–"Graduate")
——*/

If *YearCode* is 1 then
   Display "Freshman".
Else if *YearCode* is 2 then
   Display "Sophomore".
Else if *YearCode* is 3 then
   Display "Junior".
Else if *YearCode* is 4 then
   Display "Senior".
Else if *YearCode* is 5 then
   Display "Graduate".
Else
   Display an error message.
End If-Else-if.

Although we could clearly implement the algorithm using an **if-else-if**, the function in Figure 5.8 solves this problem using a **switch** statement.

FIGURE 5.8   Year code conversion.

```
/*---------------------------------------------------------------
 DisplayYearName displays the name of a year, given a year code.

    Receive: An int year code (1-5)
    Output:  The appropriate (char string) year name
             (Freshman - Graduate)
-------------------------------------------------------------*/

void DisplayYearName(int YearCode)
{
   switch (YearCode)
   {
      case 1:
              cout << "Freshman";  break;
      case 2:
              cout << "Sophomore"; break;
      case 3:
              cout << "Junior";    break;
      case 4:
              cout << "Senior";    break;
      case 5:
              cout << "Graduate";  break;
      default:
              cerr << "*** Year code error: " << YearCode;
   }
}
```

If this function is called by the statement

```
    DisplayYearName(1);
```

the character string

```
    Freshman
```

will be displayed. Similarly, if the function call

```
    DisplayYearName(4);
```

will display the character string

```
    Senior
```

Form of the `switch` Statement

A (simplified) syntax diagram for a **switch statement** is

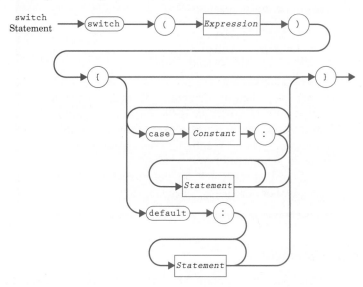

From this we see that a **switch** statement has the following form:

The `switch` Statement

Form

```
switch (Expression)
{
    CaseList₁ : StatementList₁
    CaseList₂ : StatementList₂
              ·
              ·
              ·
    CaseListₙ : StatementListₙ
    default:    StatementListₙ₊₁
}
```

where:

  switch and **default** are keywords;
  Expression is an integer (or integer-compatible) expression;
  each ***CaseListᵢ*** is a sequence of cases of the form

```
    case ConstantValue :
```

  the **default** clause is optional; and
  each ***StatementListᵢ*** is a sequence of statements.

Purpose

When the **switch** statement is executed, ***Expression*** is evaluated. If the value of

Expression is in *CaseList$_i$*, then execution begins in *StatementList$_i$* and continues until one of the following is reached:

A **break** statement
A **return** statement
The end of the **switch** statement

If the value of *Expression* is not in any *CaseList$_i$*, then the *StatementList$_{n+1}$* in the default clause is executed. If the **default** clause is omitted and the value of *Expression* is not in any *CaseList$_i$*, then execution "falls through" the **switch** statement.

Note that the values of the selector may not be real numbers or string constants.

The break Statement

As illustrated in the function in Figure 5.8, each of the statement lists in a **switch** statement usually ends with a **break statement** of the form

```
break;
```

When it is executed, this statement transfers control to the first statement following the **switch** statement. As we shall see in Chapter 6, the **break** statement can also be used in the statement lists of other statements. The effect of the **break** in these statements is the same, causing a transfer of control to the first statement following the statement in which it appears.

Choosing the Selection Statement to Use

Now that we have two different ways to perform multialternative selection, it is important to understand when an **if-else-if** should be used and when a **switch** statement should be used. If a selection step in an algorithm can be written in the form

If *Expression* is equal to *Constant$_1$*
  StatementList$_1$
Else if *Expression* is equal to *Constant$_2$*
  StatementList$_2$

$\vdots$

Else if *Expression* is equal to *Constant$_n$*
  StatementList$_n$
Else
  StatementList$_{n+1}$
End If-Else-if.

and if expression is an integer-compatible expression, then this selection step is most effectively coded as follows:

```
switch (Expression)
{
   case Constant₁ :
                    StatementList₁
                    break;
   case Constant₂ :
                    StatementList₂
                    break;
          .
          .
          .

   case Constantₙ :
                    StatementListₙ
                    break;
   default:
                    StatementListₙ₊₁
}
```

The reason is that in the **if-else-if** form, execution of *StatementList₁* requires the evaluation of one condition, execution of *StatementList₂* requires the evaluation of two conditions, . . . , and execution of *StatementListₙ* (or *StatementListₙ₊₁*) requires the evaluation of n conditions. Since evaluation of each condition requires time, there is a performance penalty associated with statements that occur later in an **if-else-if** construct.

For example, it would be correct to code function **DisplayYearName()** using an **if-else-if** as follows:

```
void DisplayYearName(int YearCode)
{
   if (YearCode == 1)
      cout << "Freshman";
   else if (YearCode == 2)
      cout << "Sophomore";
   else if (YearCode == 3)
      cout << "Junior";
   else if (YearCode == 4)
      cout << "Senior";
   else if (YearCode == 5)
      cout << "Graduate";
   else
      cerr << "*** Year code error: " << YearCode;
}
```

But this requires that four conditions be evaluated to display **Senior**, whereas only one must be evaluated to display **Freshman**.

By contrast, a **switch** statement is usually implemented so that each statement list requires (approximately) one comparison,[3] regardless of whether it is first or last. A **switch** statement is thus to be preferred over the **if-else-if** when

1. The equality (==) comparison is being performed;
2. The same expression (e.g., **YearCode**) is being compared in each condition; and
3. The type of value to which this expression is being compared is **int** (or **int**-compatible).

Drop-Through Behavior

An important feature to remember when using the **switch** statement is its *drop-through behavior*. To illustrate it, suppose the function **DisplayYearName()** is written

```
void DisplayYearName(int YearCode)
{
   switch (YearCode)
   {
      case 1:
              cout << "Freshman";
      case 2:
              cout << "Sophomore";
      case 3:
              cout << "Junior";
      case 4:
              cout << "Senior";
      case 5:
              cout << "Graduate";
      default:
              cerr << "*** Year code error: " << YearCode;
   }
}
```

(in which the **break** statements have been omitted). The output produced when this modified version is called may be rather unexpected. For example, the function call

```
DisplayYearName(2);
```

will produce the output

```
SophomoreJuniorSeniorGraduate*** Year code error: 2
```

Similarly, the function call

```
DisplayYearName(4);
```

---

[3] The mechanism by which this is accomplished is beyond the scope of this text. The interested reader should see "Compilers: Principles, Techniques and Tools" by Aho, Sethi, and Ullman (Reading, Mass.: Addison-Wesley, 1986).

will produce the output

```
SeniorGraduate*** Year code error: 4
```

The reason is that execution will proceed from the statement list associated with **case 2:** for the first function call and from the statement list associated with **case 4:** for the second call and then "drop through" into subsequent statement lists until a **break** statement (that transfers control from the **switch** statement) or a **return** statement (that terminates execution of the function containing the **switch** statement) or the end of the **switch** statement is encountered. To avoid this behavior, we must be certain to end each statement list in a **switch** statement with a **break** or **return** statement (except for the final statement list, where it is not necessary).

Occasionally, no action is required for certain values of the expression in a **switch** statement. In such situations, the statement lists associated with these values should consist of a single **break** statement, so that no action is taken. For example, a program to count aces and face cards might use the following **switch** statement where the **switch** expression **Card** is of type **char**:

```
switch (Card)
{
   case 'A':                     Ace++;
                                 break;

   case 'J': case 'Q': case 'K': FaceCard++;
                                 break;

   case '2': case '3': case '4':    // these 'cards' are
   case '5': case '6': case '7':    //   not being counted
   case '8': case '9': case 'T': break;

   default:
           cerr << "*** Error: Illegal card: "
                << Card << "\n";
}
```

Note that white space is ignored in the case lists and statement lists. Where these items are positioned is largely a matter of personal style, but the goal should be to write readable **switch** statements in which there is a clear association between a case list and its corresponding statement list.

It is important to remember that *the expression and the constants in the case lists in a* **switch** *statement must be integer-compatible.* In particular, they may not be a real or a character string expression. For example, *"ACE"*, *"JACK"*, *"QUEEN"*, and *"KING"* would not be allowed as constants in the case lists of the preceding **switch** statement.

Example: Grade Computation—Version 4

The function **LetterGrade()** in Figure 5.7 used an **if** statement to implement the multialternative selection structure required to assign a letter grade to a student's average, as specified in the following table:

Average	Letter Grade
Average ≥ 90	A
$80 \leq$ average < 90	B
$70 \leq$ average < 80	C
$60 \leq$ average < 70	D
Average < 60	F

If we assume that the value of **Average** does not exceed 100, we can use a **switch** statement to implement this five-way selection structure. There are, however, two problems:

1. The parameter **Average** is of type **double** (i.e., a real) and the type of the expression in a **switch** statement cannot be a real.

This problem can be solved by converting **Average** from a real to an integer value by casting **Average** as an **int** (see Section 3.4),

```
int(Average)
```

which truncates the decimal portion of **Average**, leaving the integer portion.

2. When **Average** has been converted from a real to an integer, there are still 10 or more values in each case list. For example, the values for a 'B' are

$$80, 81, 82, 83, 84, 85, 86, 87, 88, 89$$

This means that a case list like

```
case 80: case 81: case 82: case 83: case 84:
case 85: case 86: case 87: case 88: case 89:
```

would be required for each grade to be displayed.

One approach to solving this problem is to map the values

$$90, 91, 92, 93, 94, 95, 96, 97, 98, 99$$

to the value 9, map the values

$$80, 81, 82, 83, 84, 85, 86, 87, 88, 89$$

to the value 8, and so on. This can be accomplished by dividing **int(Average)** by 10,

```
int(Average) / 10
```

which performs *integer division* and achieves the desired result. The function in Figure 5.9 uses this approach.

FIGURE 5.9 Grade computation—version 4.

```
/*-------------------------------------------------------------------
LetterGrade computes the appropriate Grade for a given Average.

   Receive: A (double) weighted average
   Return:  The appropriate (char) letter grade (A, B, C, D, or F)
-----------------------------------------------------------------*/

char LetterGrade(double Average)
{
   switch (int(Average) / 10)
   {
      case 10:                   // int(100)/10 -> 10
      case 9:                    // int(90-99)/10 -> 9
              return'A';
      case 8:                    // int(80-89)/10 -> 8
              return 'B';
      case 7:                    // int(70-79)/10 -> 7
              return 'C';
      case 6:                    // int(60-69)/10 -> 6
              return 'D';
      default:                   // not so good!
              return 'F';
   }
}
```

Sample runs of program obtained by substituting this definition of `LetterGrade()`
for that in Figure 5.5:

```
This program computes a final course average using the
   homework average, test average, and a final exam score.


Please enter homework average, test average, and exam score:
100 100 100
Average = 100, Grade = A

...

Please enter homework average, test average, and exam score:
30 40 50
Average = 41, Grade = F

...

Please enter homework average, test average, and exam score:
56.2 62.7 66.5
Average = 62.54, Grade = D
```

FIGURE 5.9 Grade computation—version 4. (cont.)

...

```
Please enter homework average, test average, and exam score:
87.5 91.3 80
Average = 87.15, Grade = B
```

Exercises

1. Write a function that uses a **switch** statement for each of the following:

   (a) If the value of the character variable **TransCode** is **D**, increase **Balance** by adding **Amount** to it; if **TransCode** is **W**, decrease **Balance** by subtracting **Amount** from it; if **TransCode** is **P**, display the value of **Balance**.

   (b) Display the name of a month or an error message for a given value of the integer variable **Month**. Display an error message if the value of **Month** is less than 1 or greater than 12.

   (c) Returns the **Cost** corresponding to the value of the integer variable **Distance** given in the following table:

Distance	Cost
0 through 99	5.00
At least 100 but less than 300	8.00
At least 300 but less than 600	10.00
At least 600 but less than 1000	12.00
Otherwise (error)	0.00

   (d) Display the number of days in a month. (See Exercise 4a following Section 5.5 regarding the determination of leap years.)

2. Write a function that, given a number representing a TV channel, uses a **switch** statement to display the call letters of the station that corresponds to that number (or displays some message indicating that the channel is not used). Use the following channel numbers and call letters (or use those that are available in your locale):

2:	WCBS
4:	WNBC
5:	WNEW
7:	WABC
9:	WOR
11:	WPIX
13:	WNET

3. Locating avenues' addresses in mid-Manhattan is not easy; for example, the nearest cross street to 866 Third Avenue is 53rd Street, whereas the nearest cross street to 866 Second Avenue is 46th Street. To locate approximately the

nearest numbered cross street for a given avenue address, the following algorithm can be used:

Cancel the last digit of the address, divide by 2, and add or subtract the number given in the following (abbreviated) table:

1st Ave.	Add 3
2nd Ave.	Add 3
3rd Ave.	Add 10
4th Ave.	Add 8
5th Ave. up to 200	Add 13
5th Ave. up to 400	Add 16
6th Ave. (Ave. of the Americas)	Subtract 12
7th Ave.	Add 12
8th Ave.	Add 10
10th Ave.	Add 14

Write a function that uses a **switch** statement to determine the number of the nearest cross street for a given address and avenue number according to the preceding algorithm. Then write a driver program to test your function.

4. A wholesale office supply company discounts the price of each of its products depending on the number of units bought and the price per unit. The discount increases as the numbers of units bought and/or the unit price increases. These discounts are given in the following table:

Number Bought	Unit Price (Dollars)		
	0–10.00	10.01–100.00	100.01 or More
1–9	0%	2%	5%
10–99	5%	7%	9%
100–499	9%	15%	21%
500–999	14%	23%	32%
1000 or more	21%	32%	43%

Write a function that calculates the percentage discount for a specified number of units and unit price. Use this function in a program that reads the number of units bought and the unit price and then calculates and prints the total full cost, the total amount of the discount, and the total discounted cost.

*5.7   Selection: Conditional Expressions

The selection statements we have considered thus far (the **if** and **switch** statements) are similar to those provided by other languages. However, C++ also provides another selection mechanism: an expression that produces either of two values, based on the value of some condition.

To illustrate it, consider again the first grade-computation problem (see Section 5.5), in which we wish to determine whether a student is passing, based on a weighted average of homework average, test average, and final exam score. If **Average** is this weighted average, the output statement

```
cout << "You are "
     << ((Average >= PassFailLine) ? "passing." : "failing.");
```

will display

> **You are passing.**

if the condition (**Average >= PassFailLine**) is true (1), but it will display

> **You are failing.**

if the condition (**Average >= PassFailLine**) is false (0):

Because the value produced by such expressions depends on the value of their condition, they are called **conditional expressions,**[4] and have the general form described by the following syntax diagram:

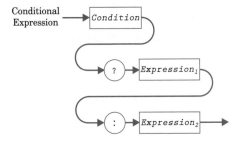

It follows that the general form of a conditional expression is as follows:

The Conditional Expression

Form

$$Condition \; ? \; Expression_1 \; : \; Expression_2$$

where:
  Condition is a boolean expression; and
  Expression₁ and **Expression₂** are type-compatible expressions.

---

[4] A conditional expression has the form **C ? A : B** and is actually a *ternary* (three-operand) operation, in which **C, A,** and **B** are the three operands and **? :** acts as the operator.

> **Behavior**
>
> *Condition* is evaluated.
>
> If the value of *Condition* is true (i.e., nonzero),
>   then the value of *Expression₁* is returned as the
>   result.
>
> If the value of *Condition* is false (i.e., zero),
>   then the value of *Expression₂* is returned as the
>   result.

As another example, recall that in Section 5.5, we used the statements

```
cout << "\nPollution index = " << Index << ": ";

if (Index < Cutoff)
    cout << "Safe condition.\n";
else
    cout << "Hazardous condition!\n";
```

to display a message like the following when the air quality **Index** was less than 50.0,

```
Pollution index = 38: Safe condition.
```

and to display a message like the following otherwise:

```
Pollution index = 62: Hazardous condition!
```

An alternative, simpler solution to this problem would be to write

```
cout << "\nPollution index = " << Index << ": "
     << ((Index < Cutoff) ? "Safe condition.\n"
                          : "Hazardous condition!\n");
```

which will produce exactly the same output.

Note that in a conditional expression, only one of *Expression₁* and *Expression₂* is evaluated. Thus, an assignment such as

```
Reciprocal = ( ( X == 0) ? 0 : 1 / X );
```

is safe because if the value of **X** is zero, then the expression 1 / **X** is not evaluated, and so no divide-by-zero error is produced. A conditional expression can thus be used instead of an **if** statement to guard a potentially unsafe operation against error.

When a conditional expression is used as a subexpression, it should be enclosed in parentheses, because its precedence is lower than most of the other operators (see Appendix C).

This mechanism has many different uses, because it can be used anywhere that an expression can appear. As one example, suppose that we wanted to write a function `LargerOf()` to find the maximum of two `int` values. Although we could do this with an `if` statement,

```
int LargerOf(int Value1, int Value2)
{
   if (Value1 > Value2)
      return Value1;
   else
      return Value2;
}
```

a conditional expression provides a simpler alternative:

```
int LargerOf(int Value1, int Value2)
{
   return ( (Value1 > Value2) ? Value1 : Value2 );
}
```

Using such a function, we can write

```
Max = LargerOf(X, Y);
```

and `Max` will be assigned the larger of the two values `X` and `Y`.

As a final example, suppose that `NumCourses` is an `int` variable containing the number of courses a student is taking in the current semester. Then the output statement

```
cout << "\nYou are taking " << NumCourses << " course"
     << ( (NumCourses == 1) ? "" : "s" )
     << " this semester.\n\n";
```

will display the following message if `NumCourses` has the value 3,

```
You are taking 3 courses this semester.
```

and will display an appropriately different message if `NumCourses` has the value 1:

```
You are taking 1 course this semester.
```

Exercises

1. Describe the operation that the following function performs:

```
int DoSomething1(int Value)
{
   return ( (Value >= 0) ? Value : -Value );
}
```

2. Describe the operation that the following function performs:

```
char DoSomething2(char Ch)
{
   return ( ( ('A' <= Ch) && (Ch <= 'Z') ) ? Ch+32 : Ch );
}
```

3. Rewrite function `Recip()` (from Section 5.2) using a conditional expression. (It need not display an error message.)

4. Write a function `SmallerOf()` that returns the smaller of two given integer values.

5. Using nested conditional expressions, write a function:

(**a**) `LargestOf()` that, given three `int` values, returns the largest of the three.
(**b**) `SmallestOf()` that, given three `int` values, returns the smallest of the three.

6. The mathematician Gauss discovered that the sum of the integers from 1 through n is given by the formula

$$\frac{n(n + 1)}{2}$$

Using a conditional expression, construct a function `Sum()` that returns the value according to Gauss's formula if the value of its parameter is positive and zero otherwise.

5.8   Example: A Menu-Driven Temperature Converter

In the last chapter, we used the example of converting temperatures from Fahrenheit to Celsius. In this section, we generalize that problem significantly.

Problem

Write a program that will allow a user to convert a temperature from Fahrenheit to Celsius, Celsius to Fahrenheit, Fahrenheit to Kelvin, Kelvin to Fahrenheit, Celsius to Kelvin, or Kelvin to Celsius.

Specification

The input for this problem is a temperature to be converted and an indication of the conversion to be carried out, and the output is the converted temperature.

One approach is to display a **menu** that lists

1. The conversions that the program can perform, and
2. A list of characters that can be used to select the desired conversion.[5]

For example, the program might display the following menu:

```
Please enter:
    A - to convert Fahrenheit to Celsius.
    B - to convert Celsius to Fahrenheit.
    C - to convert Fahrenheit to Kelvin.
    D - to convert Kelvin to Fahrenheit.
    E - to convert Kelvin to Celsius.
    F - to convert Celsius to Kelvin.

Your choice?
```

This menu lists each operation that the program performs and tells the user exactly what should be entered in order to select that operation.

We can, therefore, identify the following data objects in this problem:

Data Object	Kind of Value	Type of Object	Name of Object
An input temperature	Variable	Real	*Temperature*
A menu of conversions	Constant	Character string	*Menu*
The desired conversion	Variable	Character	*Conversion*
The output temperature	Variable	Real	*ConvertedTemperature*

We might then summarize the input/output specifications of the problem as follows:

Input:	A (real) temperature
Output:	A menu of conversion operations
Input:	A char representing a particular conversion operation
Output:	The (real) converted temperature

---

[5] Why have the user enter a character rather than an integer? The answer is that we want to begin thinking about using *space* efficiently in our programs. We (currently) have six possible menu options to represent (Fahrenheit to Celsius, Celsius to Fahrenheit, etc.). Three bits of memory are necessary to represent six values (e.g., 000 for the first value, 001 for the second, 010 for the third, etc.). Unfortunately, C++ does not provide a type consisting of 3 bits; the C++ type that is allocated the minimum number of bits is the **char** type (8 bits). Thus, if we want to represent our six values in a way that wastes the least amount of space, then using type **char** wastes only 5 bits, whereas using **int** would waste either 13 or 29 bits (depending on whether an **int** is allocated 16 or 32 bits, as discussed in Chapter 3).

Design

The operations required to solve this problem are as follows.

Operation	Provided in Library
Input a real value	`<iostream.h>`
Output a menu of conversions	Not provided (directly)
Input a character value, representing the conversion to be performed	`<iostream.h>`
Perform a particular conversion based on the character entered by the user	Not provided
Convert a temperature from	
Fahrenheit to Celsius,	`"Heat.h"`
Celsius to Fahrenheit,	`"Heat.h"`
and so on	
Output a real value	`<iostream.h>`

Note that most of the operations listed are either predefined in C++ or stored in library **Heat** developed in the last chapter. The only operations not provided are

Output a menu of conversions.
Perform the particular conversion selected by the user.

We begin by constructing an algorithm that specifies the order in which these operations are to be performed:

ALGORITHM TO PERFORM TEMPERATURE CONVERSIONS

/* This algorithm performs any of six temperature conversions.

Input: A (real) *Temperature*
Output: A (character string) *Menu*
Input: A (character) *Conversion*
Output: A (real) *ConvertedTemperature*
———*/

1. Enter the (real) *Temperature* to be converted.
2. Display a *Menu* of conversions.
3. Enter the (character) *Conversion* to be performed.
4. Convert *Temperature* from one scale to another, based on the char *Conversion* entered by the user, and store the result in *ConvertedTemperature*.
5. Output the (real) *ConvertedTemperature*.

Step 2 requires construction of a character string object to store the menu of conversions, but this is only slightly more complicated than displaying an introductory message. In the program in Figure 5.10, **Menu** is a character string constant that stores this menu and is displayed using the standard **<<** operator. One new C++ feature that should be noted is that because this menu (as a character string constant) is too long to fit on a single line, we simply broke it up into a series of shorter strings. When the C++ compiler processes these strings, they will be *concatenated* to form a single string constant.

Step 4 requires selection of a particular conversion function, based on the character entered by the user. Since C++ does not provide a predefined operator for this operation, we construct a function to perform this operation. This function requires the following data items:

Data Object	Kind of Value	Type of Object	Name of Object
The original temperature	Variable	Real	*Temperature*
The desired conversion	Variable	Character	*Conversion*
The converted temperature	Variable	Real	None

We can specify what this function must do as follows:

> Receive: A (real) temperature to be converted
>   A (character) conversion to be performed
> Return: The (real) converted temperature

This allows us to construct the following stub for the function, which we call **Convert()**:

```
double Convert(double Temperature, char Conversion)
{
}
```

In constructing an algorithm for a function, it is helpful to begin by simply listing what the function is to do. Clearly, for function **Convert()**:

> If a Fahrenheit-to-Celsius conversion is to be performed,
>   it should call **FahrToCelsius()** to perform it.
> If a Celsius-to-Fahrenheit conversion is to be performed,
>   it should call **CelsiusToFahr()** to perform it.
> If a Fahrenheit-to-Kelvin conversion is to be performed,
>   it should call **FahrToKelvin()** to perform it.
>
>   ⋮

From this, it should be evident that **Convert()** must *select* an appropriate function to carry out the conversion, based on the value of the parameter **Conversion**.

Thus, we might rephrase Step 4 of the algorithm as follows:

4. If the value of *Conversion* is 'A', then
    Return the result of the Fahrenheit-to-Celsius conversion.
Else if the value of *Conversion* is 'B', then
    Return the result of the Celsius-to-Fahrenheit conversion.

$$\vdots$$

Else if the value of *Conversion* is 'F', then
    Return the result of the Celsius-to-Kelvin conversion.
Else
    Display an error message (since the user didn't enter one of 'A'–'F').
End if-else-if.

Writing this step of the algorithm out in this way is important, because it allows us to recognize that it has the form:

If *Variable* is equal to *Constant$_1$*
    Statement$_1$
Else if *Variable* is equal to *Constant$_2$*
    Statement$_2$

$$\vdots$$

Else if *Variable* is equal to *Constant$_n$*
    Statement$_n$
Else
    Statement$_{n+1}$
End If-Else-if.

This in turn suggests that this step is better implemented by using a `switch` statement rather than by using an `if-else-if`.

Coding

Figure 5.10 shows the function `Convert()` that results when we use a `switch` statement to encode Step 4 of the algorithm for this function. Note that the `switch` statement makes it easy to deal with both upper- and lowercase values for `Conversion`.

 FIGURE 5.10 Function `Convert`.

```
/*-------------------------------------------------------------------
Convert converts a given Temperature from one scale to another,
   according to the value of Conversion.

Receive: Temperature, Conversion
Return:  The equivalent Temperature in the other scale
-------------------------------------------------------------*/
```

FIGURE 5.10   Function **Convert**. (cont.)

```
#include "Heat.h"        //    library of temperature-
                         //        conversion functions

double Convert(double Temperature, char Conversion)
{
   switch (Conversion)
   {
     case 'a': case 'A':
                       return FahrToCelsius(Temperature);
     case 'b': case 'B':
                       return CelsiusToFahr(Temperature);
     case 'c': case 'C':
                       return FahrToKelvin(Temperature);
     case 'd': case 'D':
                       return KelvinToFahr(Temperature);
     case 'e': case 'E':
                       return KelvinToCelsius(Temperature);
     case 'f': case 'F':
                       return CelsiusToKelvin(Temperature);
     default:
                       cerr << "\n*** Error: Illegal conversion: "
                            << Conversion
                            << " detected in function Convert.\n";
   }
   return 0.0; // default value in case of error
}
```

Once function **Convert()** has been encoded, writing the main function is straightfoward, as shown in Figure 5.11.

FIGURE 5.11   A temperature-conversion program.

```
/* This program converts a temperature between the Fahrenheit,
   Celsius, and Kelvin scales.

   Input:  A temperature (double) value
   Output: A menu of conversion choices
   Input:  The desired (char) conversion
   Output: The converted value
   --------------------------------------------------------------------*/

#include <iostream.h>

double Convert(double, char);
```

FIGURE 5.11   A temperature-conversion program. (cont.)

```cpp
int main(void)
{
   const char
      Menu[] = "\nPlease enter:\n"
                     "\tA - to convert Fahrenheit to Celsius.\n"
                     "\tB - to convert Celsius to Fahrenheit.\n"
                     "\tC - to convert Fahrenheit to Kelvin.\n"
                     "\tD - to convert Kelvin to Fahrenheit.\n"
                     "\tE - to convert Kelvin to Celsius.\n"
                     "\tF - to convert Celsius to Kelvin.\n\n"
                  "Your Choice ? ";

   cout << "\nThis program converts a temperature between the scales\n"
        << "\tFahrenheit, Celsius, and Kelvin.\n";

   double
      InTemp;

   cout << "\nPlease enter the temperature you wish to convert: ";
   cin >> InTemp;

   char
      Conversion;

   cout << Menu;
   cin >> Conversion;

   double
      OutTemp = Convert(InTemp, Conversion);

   cout << "\n--> The converted temperature is " << OutTemp << ".\n\n";

   return 0;
}

// ... definition of Convert() goes here ...
```

Sample runs:

```
This program converts a temperature between the scales
   Fahrenheit, Celsius, and Kelvin.

Please enter the temperature you wish to convert: 212

Please enter:
   A - to convert Fahrenheit to Celsius.
   B - to convert Celsius to Fahrenheit.
   C - to convert Fahrenheit to Kelvin.
   D - to convert Kelvin to Fahrenheit.
   E - to convert Kelvin to Celsius.
   F - to convert Celsius to Kelvin.
```

FIGURE 5.11   A temperature-conversion program. (cont.)

```
Your Choice ? a

--> The converted temperature is 100.

...

Please enter the temperature you wish to convert: -273

Please enter:
   A - to convert Fahrenheit to Celsius.
   B - to convert Celsius to Fahrenheit.
   C - to convert Fahrenheit to Kelvin.
   D - to convert Kelvin to Fahrenheit.
   E - to convert Kelvin to Celsius.
   F - to convert Celsius to Kelvin.

Your Choice ? f

--> The converted temperature is 0.

...

Please enter the temperature you wish to convert: 274

Please enter:
   A - to convert Fahrenheit to Celsius.
   B - to convert Celsius to Fahrenheit.
   C - to convert Fahrenheit to Kelvin.
   D - to convert Kelvin to Fahrenheit.
   E - to convert Kelvin to Celsius.
   F - to convert Celsius to Kelvin.

Your Choice ? e

--> The converted temperature is 1.
```

5.9   PART OF THE PICTURE: Computability Theory

Prior to this chapter, we were limited to designing functions that applied operations in a sequential fashion. By contrast, the statements presented in this chapter allow us to design functions that apply operations *selectively,* based on the value of some condition. This is important, because for any function **F()** that does not contain selection statements,

```
ReturnType F(Parameter-Declaration-List)
{
    Statement₁
          •
          •
          •
    Statementₙ
}
```

there is an equivalent function `G()` that does contain selection statements:

```
ReturnType G(Parameter-Declaration-List)
{
    if (1)
    {
        Statement₁
            •
            •
            •
        Statementₙ
    }
}
```

However, the converse is not true: There are functions `G()` that use selection statements for which there is no equivalent function `F()` that uses only sequential statements.

Stated differently, *the set of all operations that can be performed using only sequential statements is a proper subset of the set of all operations that that can be performed using sequential and selection statements,* as depicted in the following **Venn diagram:**

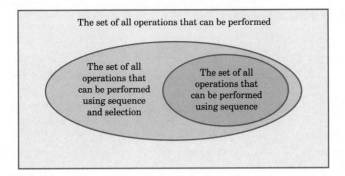

Selection statements allow us to design and implement operations that are more powerful than those we can design and implement using only sequence.

This is a simple result from *Computability Theory,* a branch of computer science that (from a theoretical viewpoint) investigates interesting questions such as the following:

■ What can (or cannot) be computed?

- How can functions be classified, and what relationships exist among those classes?
- What is the most efficient algorithm for solving a particular problem?

Rather than ask questions about programs written in an existing language (that becomes obsolete all too soon), theoreticians represent programs *abstractly,* using mathematical models (e.g., *the set of all functions that use only sequence*). The advantage of this is that when a theoretician discovers something that is true about the model, then that result is true for all programs that the model represents, regardless of the language in which those programs are written. This gives theoretical work a sense of *timelessness:* Although programming languages come and go, theoretical results endure.

Programming Pointers

Program Design

1. *Program defensively by using selection to guard against illegal values.* For example, some arithmetic functions are *partial functions* that are undefined for negative values. Defensive programming might implement such a function `F()` by writing

```
double F(double Val)
{
   if (Val < 0)
   {
      // ... display an error message ...
      // ... return some default value ...
   }
   else
   {
      // ... compute and return the value of F for Val...
   }
}
```

2. *Multialternative selection constructs can be implemented more efficiently with an* `if-else-if` *form than with a sequence of separate* `if` *statements.* For example, consider the function

```
char ScoreToGrade(int Score)
{
   if (Score > 100)
   {
      cout << "\nScore: " << Score << " exceeds maximum.\n";
      return '?';
   }
   if ((Score >= 90) && (Score <= 100))
      return 'A';
```

```
        if ((Score >= 80) && (Score < 90))
          return 'B';
        if ((Score >= 70) && (Score < 80))
          return 'C';
        if ((Score >= 60) && (Score < 70))
          return 'D';
        if (Score < 60)
          return 'F';
        if (Score < 0)
        {
            cout << "\nScore: " << Score << " less than minimum.\n";
            return '?';
        }
```

In this case, all the **if** statements are executed for each score processed and 3 of the boolean expressions are compound expressions, so that a total of 15 operations are performed, regardless of the score being processed. By contrast, consider the following statements:

```
        char ScoreToGrade(int Score)
        {
            if ((Score < 0) || (Score > 100))
            {
                cout << "\nScore: " << Score << " outside legal range.\n";
                return '?';
            }
            else if (Score >= 90)
                return 'A';
            else if (Score >= 80)
                return 'B';
            else if (Score >= 70)
                return 'C';
            else if (Score >= 60)
                return 'D';
            else
                return 'F';
        }
```

In this second case, most of the boolean expressions are simple, and not all of them are evaluated for each score, so that only three to seven operations are performed, depending on the score being processed.

3. *Multialternative selection statements of the form*

```
        if (Variable == Constant₁)
            Statement₁
        else if (Variable == Constant₂)
            Statement₂
              ⋮
        else if (Variable == Constantₙ)
            Statementₙ
        else
            Statementₙ₊₁
```

are usually more efficiently implemented using a switch *statement:*

```
switch (Variable)
{
    case Constant₁ :
                        StatementList₁
                        break;
    case Constant₂ :
                        StatementList₂
                        break;
            .
            .
            .
    case Constantₙ :
                        StatementListₙ
                        break;
    default:
                        StatementListₙ₊₁
}
```

For example, we might implement `ScoreToGrade()` even more efficiently as follows:

```
char ScoreToGrade(int Score)
{
    switch (Score / 10)
    {
        case 10:
        case 9:  return 'A';
        case 8:  return 'B';
        case 7:  return 'C';
        case 6:  return 'D';
        case 5:
        case 4:
        case 3:
        case 2:
        case 1:
        case 0:  return 'F';
        default: cout << "\nScore: " << Score
                     << " is outside the legal range.\n";
                 return '?';
    }
}
```

This version of `ScoreToGrade()` will perform the same number of operations regardless of the value of the score being processed.

A second advantage of the switch statement is that a problem solution implemented with a switch is often more readable than an equivalent solution implemented using an if statement. For example, consider the problem of classifying the value of a char variable Ch as an arithmetic operator (+, -, *, /, %), a relational operator (<, >), an assignment operator (=), or a punctuation symbol (semicolon or comma). Using the switch statement, we might write

```
switch (Ch)
{
  case '+': case '-':
  case '*': case '/':
  case '%':              cout << "Arithmetic operator";
                         break;

  case '<': case '>':    cout << "Relational operator";
                         break;

  case '=':              cout << "Assignment operator";
                         break;

  case ';': case ',':    cout << "Punctuation";
                         break;

  default:               cout << "identification of " << Ch
                              << " is not supported.";
}
```

which is far more readable than an equivalent implementation using an **if** statement:

```
if ((Ch == '+') || (Ch == '-')
    || (Ch == '*') || (Ch == '/')
    || (Ch == '%'))
      cout << "Arithmetic operator";
else if ((Ch == '<') || (Ch == '>'))
      cout << "Relational operator";
else if (Ch == '=')
      cout << "Assignment operator";
else if ((Ch == ';') || (Ch = ','))
      cout << "Punctuation";
else
      cout << "identification of " << Ch
           << " is not supported."
```

The potential error of inadvertently substituting the assignment operator (=) for one of the several equality operators (==) in this **if** statement is also avoided by the **switch** statement.

Potential Problems

1. *Semicolons are used to terminate expressions, forming statements.* Since C++ programs have no line structure, a missing semicolon at the end of an expression (on one line) will not be detected until the beginning of the next expression (on the next line). For example, in one of the C++ environments we examined, compiling the erroneous compound statement

```
{
   Number++
   Sum += Number;
}
```

produces an error message like the following

```
Error 85: ";" expected.
```

When this message is processed by the editor, the cursor is positioned at the beginning of the statement:

```
Sum += Number;
```

Because an expression may be spread over several lines, the absence of a semicolon at the end of the expression

```
Number ++
```

is not detected until the compiler determines that what follows,

```
Sum += Number;
```

is not a legal continuation of the first expression. This means that *syntax errors involving missing semicolons are often noted on the line following the line containing the error.*

2. *Each { must have a matching }.* To make it easier to find matching braces, we will align each { with its corresponding }.

3. *Parentheses should be used within boolean expressions to indicate those subexpressions that are to be evaluated first.* The precedence of the operators used thus far is as follows:

```
!                           Highest (performed first)
/, *, %
+, -
<<, >>
<, >, <=, >=
==, !=
&&
||
? :
=, +=, *=, etc.    Lowest (performed last)
```

However, there are so many operators in C++ (these are fewer than half of those available), that remembering their precedence levels is difficult. For this reason, we recommend using parentheses in boolean expressions to specify clearly the order in which the operators are to be applied.

4. *When real quantities that are algebraically equal are compared with* ==, *the result may be a false boolean expression, because most real numbers are not stored exactly.* For example, even though the two real expressions x * (1/x) and 1.0 are algebraically equal, the boolean expression x * (1/x) == 1.0 may be false for some real numbers x.

5. *In a nested* if *statement, each* else *clause is matched with the nearest preceding unmatched* if. For example, consider the following statements, which are given without indentation:

```
if (x > 0)
if (y > 0)
z = x + y;
else
z = x + abs(y);
w = x * y * z;
```

With which **if** is the **else** associated? According to the rule just stated, these statements are executed as

```
if (x > 0)
    if (y > 0)
        z = x + y;
    else
        z = x + abs(y);
w = x * y * z;
```

where the **else** clause matches the **if** statement containing the condition **y > 0**. Use indentation and alignment to show such associations.

6. *One of the most common errors in an* **if** *statement is using an assignment operator (=) when an equality operator (==) is intended.* It is very easy to forget that in C++, = is the assignment operator whose result is the value assigned and to encode an instruction of the form

> If *Variable* is equal to *Value,* then
> *Statement*

as

```
if (Variable = Value)
    Statement
```

perhaps because = is used in many programming languages to check equality. However, instead of testing whether **Variable** is equal to **Value**, the condition in this **if** statement assigns **Value** to **Variable**. If **Value** happens to be zero, then the result of the assignment is zero, which C++ interprets as false, and so the **Statement** will not be executed, regardless of the value of **Variable**. If **Value** is nonzero, then the result of the assignment is nonzero, which C++ interprets as true, and so **Statement** will be executed, regardless of the value of **Variable**. For example, execution of the following incorrect function for finding the reciprocal of a real number,

```
double Recip(double X)
{
    if (X = 0)
    {
        cerr << "\n***Error: Cannot divide by zero!\n";
        return 0.0;
    }
    else
        return 1.0 / X;
}
```

will always produce a division-by-zero error, regardless of the value of parameter **X**, because

- **X** is not compared to zero but is assigned the value zero, which changes the value of **X** to 0 and produces the value 0 as its result;
- The value 0 (produced by the assignment operator) is treated as false by the **if** statement, and so the statement

  ```
  return 1.0 / X;
  ```

  is selected; and

- The expression **1.0 / X** is evaluated, and since **X** was set to 0, a division-by-zero error occurs.

7. *Each* **switch** *statement must contain matching braces.* A missing **}** can be very difficult to locate. In certain situations, the compiler may not find that the **{** at the beginning of a **switch** is unmatched until it reaches the end of the file. In such cases, an unhelpful error message such as

   ```
   Error...: parse error at end of input
   ```

   may be generated,[6] which provides very little information about what is actually wrong.

8. *The selector in a* **switch** *statement must be integer-compatible.* In particular, the values of the selector in label lists

   - May *not* be real constants, such as **1.5**, **-2.3**, **3.414159**, or **2.998E8**; and
   - May *not* be string constants like **"JACK"**, **"QUEEN"**, or **"KING"**.

Program Style

In this text, we use the following conventions for formatting the statements considered in this chapter.

1. *In a compound statement,* **{** *and* **}** *are aligned, and the statements they enclose are indented.*

   ```
   {
       Statement₁
         .
         .
         .
       Statementₙ
   }
   ```

---

[6] This particular error message was generated by the GNU compiler in the UNIX environment. The Turbo environment gave a more helpful message:

```
Error...: Compound statement missing } in function ...
```

2. *For an* `if` *statement,* `if (Condition)` *is on one line, with its statement indented on the next line. If there is an* `else` *clause,* `else` *is on a separate line, aligned with* `if`, *and its statement is indented on the next line.*

```
if (...)
   Statement₁
else
   Statement₂


if (...)
{
   Statement₁

      .
      .
      .

   Statementₖ
}
else
{
    Statementₖ₊₁

      .
      .
      .

    Statementₙ
}
```

An exception is made when the `if-else-if` *form is used to implement a multialternative selection structure. In this case the format used is*

```
if (...)
   Statement₁
else if (...)
   Statement₂

      .
      .
      .

else if (...)
   Statementₙ
else
   Statementₙ₊₁
```

3. *For a* `switch` *statement, the* `switch (Expression)` *is on one line, with its braces aligned and on separate lines, each case list is indented within the braces, and each statement list and* `break` *statement is indented past their particular case list.*

```
switch (Expression)
{
   CaseList₁  StatementList₁
             break;

   CaseList₂  StatementList₂
             break;

         .
         .
         .
```

```
          CaseList_n   StatementList_n
                       break;

          default :    StatementList_n+1
      }
```

Each *StatementList_i* may be positioned on the line following *CaseList_i*.

Programming Projects

1. A *binary full-adder* has three inputs: the two bits **A** and **B** being added and a "carry-in" bit **CIn** (representing the carry bit that results from adding the bits to the right of **A** and **B** in two binary numbers). It can be constructed from two binary half-adders and an OR gate:

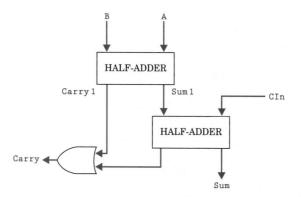

(a) Write boolean expressions for
   (i) **Sum1** and **Carry1** in terms of **A** and **B**.
   (ii) **Sum** and **Carry** in terms of **CIn**, **Sum1**, and **Carry1**.
(b) Write a program to implement this binary full-adder, and use it to verify the results shown in the following table:

A	B	CIn	Sum	Carry
0	0	0	0	0
0	0	1	1	0
0	1	0	1	0
0	1	1	0	1
1	0	0	1	0
1	0	1	0	1
1	1	0	0	1
1	1	1	1	1

2. An *adder* to calculate binary sums of two-bit numbers

$$\begin{array}{r} \texttt{A2 A1} \\ + \texttt{ B2 B1} \\ \hline \texttt{COut S2 S1} \end{array}$$

where **S1** and **S2** are the sum bits and **COut** is the carry-out bit, can be constructed from a binary half-adder and a binary full-adder:

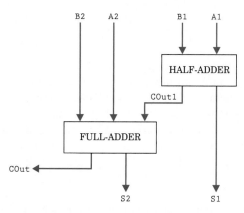

(a) Write logical expressions for
   (i) **S1** and **COut1** in terms of **A1** and **B1**.
   (ii) **S2** and **COut** in terms of **A2**, **B2**, and **COut1**.
(b) Write a program to implement this adder and use it to demonstrate that
   $00 + 00 = 000$, $01 + 00 = 001$, $01 + 01 = 010$, $10 + 01 = 011$, $10 + 10 = 100$, $11 + 10 = 101$, and $11 + 11 = 110$.

3. Write a program that reads three real numbers and assigns the appropriate boolean value to the following boolean variables:

Triangle:	true if the real numbers can represent lengths of the sides of a triangle (the sum of any two of the numbers must be greater than the third) and false otherwise.
Equilateral:	true if **Triangle** is true and the triangle is equilateral (the three sides are equal) and false otherwise.
Isosceles:	true if **Triangle** is true and the triangle is isosceles (at least two sides are equal) and false otherwise.
Scalene:	true if **Triangle** is true and the triangle is scalene (no two sides are equal) and false otherwise.

The output from your program should have a format like the following:

```
Enter 3 lengths: 2, 3, 3
Triangle is:      True
Equilateral is:   False
Isosceles is:     True
Scalene is:       False
```

4. Suppose that charges by a gas company are based on consumption according to the following table:

Gas Used	Rate
First 70 cubic meters	$5.00 minimum cost
Next 100 cubic meters	5.0¢ per cubic meter
Next 230 cubic meters	2.5¢ per cubic meter
Above 400 cubic meters	1.5¢ per cubic meter

Write a function that computes the charges for a given amount of gas usage. Use this function in a program in which the meter reading for the previous month and the current meter reading are entered, each a number with up to four digits and each representing cubic meters, and that then calculates and displays the amount of the bill. *Note:* The current reading may be less than the previous one; for example, the previous reading may be 9897, and the current one may be 103. Execute the program with the following meter readings: 3450, 3495; 8810, 8900; 9950, 190; 1275, 1982; 9872, 444.

5. An airline vice president in charge of operations needs to determine whether the current estimates of flight times are accurate. Because there is a larger possibility of variations due to weather and air traffic in the longer flights, he allows a larger error in the time estimates for them. He compares an actual flight time with the estimated flight time and considers the estimate to be too large, acceptable, or too small, depending on the following table of acceptable error margins:

Estimated Flight Time in Minutes	Acceptable Error Margin in Minutes
0–29	1
30–59	2
60–89	3
90–119	4
120–179	6
180–239	8
240–359	13
360 or more	17

For example, if an estimated flight time is 106 minutes, the acceptable error margin is 4 minutes. Thus, the estimated flight time is too large if the actual flight time is less than 102 minutes, or the estimated flight time is too small if the actual flight time is greater than 110 minutes; otherwise, the estimate is acceptable. Write a function that uses a **switch** statement to determine the acceptable error for a given estimated flight time, according to this table. Use your function in a program that reads an estimated flight time and an actual flight time and then prints whether the estimated time is too large, acceptable, or too small. If the estimated flight time is too large or too small, the program should also print the amount of the overestimate or underestimate.

REPETITION STATEMENTS 6

Progress might be a circle, rather than a straight line.
EBERHARD ZEIDLER

But what has been said once can always be repeated.
ZENO OF ELEA

Those who do not learn from history are doomed to repeat its mistakes.
UNKNOWN

CHAPTER CONTENTS

The basic control structures used in writing programs are **sequence, selection,** and **repetition.** In Chapter 5 we described the C++ compound statement, which specifies that a group of statements are to be executed *in sequence.* We also introduced the **if** and **switch** statements that specify that a group of statements are to be executed *selectively,* based on the value of some condition, and we introduced conditional expressions whose values are determined by *selecting* one of two expressions, based on a condition. In this chapter we examine the third control structure, repetition, and the statements (called **loops**) that cause a set of statements to be executed *repeatedly,* based on a condition.

6.1   Introduction to Repetition: The For Loop

Although sequence and selection are powerful control mechanisms, they are by themselves not powerful enough to solve all computing problems. In this section, we examine some problems that can be solved using repetition and introduce the most familiar of the repetition structures: the for loop.

The Summation Problem

Problem.   Our first problem begins with an incident in the life of Carl Friedrich Gauss, one of the greatest mathematicians ever to have lived. As a boy, Gauss attended a local school in Brunswick, Germany, and one day when the students were being particularly mischievous, their teacher gave them the problem of summing the numbers from 1 to 100, expecting this to keep them busy for quite some time. Gauss produced the correct answer to the problem (5050) almost immediately, using a particularly clever approach described in Section 6.9.

Although calculating the sum of the integers from 1 to 100 is not a particularly important computation, a generalization of this problem (called the *summation problem*) has many applications in computing. The problem is to construct a function **Sum(N)** that calculates the sum of the integers from 1 to **N**,

$$1 + 2 + \cdots + N$$

for a given positive integer **N** and returns the value of this sum. Thus, Gauss and his classmates were asked to compute a particular *instance* of the summation problem: **Sum(100)**.

Specification.   Obviously, the value *N* is required if we are to compute the sum of the integers from 1 to *N*. We can thus list the following data objects:

Data Object	Kind of Value	Type of Object	Name of Object
The limit value, *N*	Variable	Integer	*N*
$1 + 2 + \cdots + N$	?	Integer	?

This allows us to specify the problem as follows: Write a function `Sum()` that will

Receive: An integer value *N*
Return: $1 + 2 + \cdots + N$

This specification leads us to declare the function `Sum()` as follows:

```
int Sum(int N);
```

Design.   Since most of us do not have Gauss' ability, we will solve this problem using the approach probably used by his classmates (and intended by his teacher). We simply begin adding consecutive integers, keeping a running total as we proceed:

$$
\begin{array}{r}
0 \leftarrow \text{running total} \\
+ \; 1 \leftarrow \text{counter} \\
\hline
1 \leftarrow \text{running total} \\
+ \; 2 \leftarrow \text{counter} \\
\hline
3 \leftarrow \text{running total} \\
+ \; 3 \leftarrow \text{counter} \\
\hline
6 \leftarrow \text{running total} \\
+ \; 4 \leftarrow \text{counter} \\
\hline
10 \leftarrow \text{running total} \\
+ \; 5 \leftarrow \text{counter} \\
\hline
15 \leftarrow \text{running total}
\end{array}
$$

$$\vdots$$

This procedure consists of the following steps:

1. Initialize a *running total* to 0.
2. Initialize a *counter* to 1.
3. Cycle through the following steps:
   a. Add the *counter* to the *running total*.
   b. Add 1 to the *counter.*

The steps in the cycle must be repeated as long as the value of the *counter* is less than or equal to *N*. Thus, if *N* has the value 100, the cycle must be repeated as long as *counter* is less than or equal to 100:

$$\vdots$$

$$
\begin{array}{r}
4950 \leftarrow \text{running total} \\
+ \;\; 100 \leftarrow \text{counter} \\
\hline
5050 \leftarrow \text{running total}
\end{array}
$$

It is apparent that this procedure uses two previously unmentioned data objects; the *running total* and the *counter,* and that when the procedure is finished, the value of the *running total* is the sum of the integers from 1 to *N*—the value to be returned by the function. We can thus amend our list of data objects as follows:

Data Object	Kind of Value	Type of Object	Name of Object
The limit value, N	Variable	Integer	N
$1 + 2 + \cdots + N$	Variable	Integer	*RunningTotal*
A counter	Variable	Integer	*Counter*

The preceding description of how the problem can be solved suggests that the following operations are needed:

- Initialization of integer variables (*RunningTotal* to 0, *Counter* to 1)
- Addition of two integers (*Counter* and *RunningTotal*) and storage of the result
- Repetition of the preceding step for each value of *Counter* in the range 1 through N
- Return of an integer value (*RunningTotal*)

Aside from the "repetition" step, the C++ statements that implement each of these steps should be familiar by now. We use these operations in the following algorithm:

ALGORITHM FOR SUMMATION PROBLEM

/* This algorithm computes the summation from 1 through N using a loop.

  Receive: An integer N
  Return: $1 + 2 + \cdots + N$

───*/

1. Initialize *RunningTotal* to 0.
2. For each value of *Counter* in the range 1 through N:
     Add *Counter* to *RunningTotal*.
   End Loop.
3. Return *RunningTotal*.

Coding. Note that although our algorithm makes use of the two data objects, *RunningTotal* and *Counter,* these data objects are not part of the problem specification. It is important to understand that because these data objects are required only within the algorithm, they should be declared as *local variables within the definition of function* Sum(). By contrast, the specification tells us that the data object N must be *received* from whatever function calls Sum(), so that it is declared as a *parameter* of function Sum(). Figure 6.1 presents an implementation of function Sum().

FIGURE 6.1 Function **Sum()**—for loop version.

```
/* This function computes the summation from 1 to N, using a
   for loop.

   Receive: An integer N
   Return: The value 1 + 2 + ... + N
-----------------------------------------------------------------------*/

int Sum (int N)
{
   int
      RunningTotal = 0;

   for (int Counter = 1; Counter <= N; Counter++)
      RunningTotal += Counter;

   return RunningTotal;
}
```

Given this function, we could use the program in Figure 6.2 to solve any instance of the summation problem.

FIGURE 6.2 Driver program for function **Sum()**.

```
/* This is a simple driver program to test function Sum().

   Input:   An integer N
   Output:  Prompts for input,
            the sum of the integers from 1 through N
-----------------------------------------------------------------------*/

#include <iostream.h>
#include "MyMath.h"              // provides function Sum().

int main(void)
{
   cout << "\nThis program computes the sum of the integers from"
           " 1 through N.";
   int
      N;

   cout << "\nPlease enter a value for N: ";
   cin >> N;

   cout << "--> 1 + ... + " << N << " = " << Sum(N) << "\n\n";

   return 0;
}
```

FIGURE 6.2   Driver program for function **Sum()**. (cont.)

Sample runs:

```
This program computes the sum of the integers from 1 through N.
Please enter a value for N: 5
--> 1 + ... + 5 = 15
```

```
This program computes the sum of the integers from 1 through N.
Please enter a value for N: 100
--> 1 + ... + 100 = 5050
```

```
This program computes the sum of the integers from 1 through N.
Please enter a value for N: 0
--> 1 + ... + 0 = 0
```

This implementation of function **Sum()** uses a special kind of loop called a **counting loop.**

Counting Loops

Counting loops, or *counter-controlled loops,* are loops in which a set of statements is executed once for each value in a specified range:

> for each value of a counter-variable in a specified range
>   *Statement*

For example, the solution to the summation problem uses a counting loop, since it executes the statement

```
RunningTotal += Counter;
```

once for each value of **Counter** in the range 1 through **N**.

Counting loops are used so frequently that almost all programming languages provide a special statement, called a **for statement,** to implement them. These loops are thus commonly called **for loops.** The syntax of a **for** statement in C++ is given by the following syntax diagram:

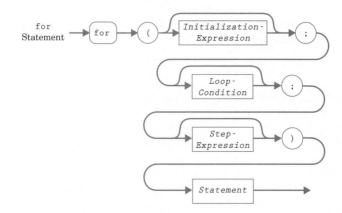

From this diagram, we see that a **for** statement has the following form:

The **for** Statement

Form

```
for (InitializationExpression;
        LoopCondition;
        StepExpression)
    Statement
```

where:
   for is a keyword;
   InitializationExpression, *LoopCondition*,
      and *StepExpression* are expressions; and
   Statement is a C++ statement (simple or compound).

Behavior
When execution reaches a **for** statement, the following actions occur:

(1) *InitializationExpression* is evaluated.
(2) *LoopCondition* is evaluated.
(3) If *LoopCondition* is true, then
      a. *Statement* is executed.
      b. *StepExpression* is evaluated.
      c. Control returns to step (2).
   Otherwise
      Control passes to the statement following the **for** statement.

The components of a for statement that implements a counting loop are usually these:

1. The *initialization expression,* which initializes a *loop control variable* (**Counter**, in the function in Figure 6.1)
2. The *loop condition,* which compares the value of the loop control variable with some *limit value* (**Counter <= N**)
3. The *step expression,* which specifies how the loop's control variable is to be changed before the next repetition (**Counter++**)
4. The *loop body,* which is a statement (either simple or compound) that is executed repeatedly, as long as the loop condition remains true (**RunningTotal += Counter;**)

For example, in the first sample run of Figure 6.2 in which the value 5 is entered for **N**, the loop counts through the values 1 through 5, so that the body of the for loop is executed five times. The following table shows the value of the various data objects as function **Sum()** executes:

Counter	N	Counter <= N	Action	RunningTotal
1	5	True	Execute loop body	1
2	5	True	Execute loop body	3
3	5	True	Execute loop body	6
4	5	True	Execute loop body	10
5	5	True	Execute loop body	15
6	5	False	Terminate repetition	15

A similar trace table for the second sample run (where **N** has the value 100) would show that the loop counts through the values 1 through 100, so that the loop body is executed 100 times.

In the third sample execution, **N** has the value 0. Because **Counter** is initialized to 1, its value is greater than **N** so that the loop condition

```
Counter <= N
```

is false the first time it is evaluated. Since this condition is evaluated before the statement

```
RunningTotal += Counter;      // add counter to running total
```

is reached, *this statement is not executed.* Control passes to the statement

```
return RunningTotal;
```

which causes the function to return 0, the initial value of **RunningTotal**.

In general, there are two common forms of **for** statements that implement counting loops: an ascending form, in which the step expression increments the loop control variable,

```
for ( int ControlVariable = InitialValue;
          ControlVarVariable <= LimitValue;
          IncrementExpression )
    Statement
```

and a descending form, in which the step expression decrements the loop control variable:

```
for ( int ControlVariable = InitialValue;
          ControlVarVariable >= LimitValue;
          DecrementExpression )
    Statement
```

The first form counts through an *ascending range,* and the second counts through a *descending range.*

To illustrate, consider the **for** statement

```
for (int Number = 1; Number <= 10; Number++)
    cout << '\t' << Number << '\t' << pow(Number, 2) << '\n';
```

Here, **Number** is the control variable, the initial value is 1, the limit value is 10, and the step expression is **Number++**. This for loop will execute the statement

```
cout << '\t' << Number << '\t' << pow(Number, 2) << '\n';
```

once for each value of **Number** in the ascending range 1 through 10. **Number** will have the value 1 on the first execution, the value 2 on the second execution, and so on, until the final execution, when **Number** will have the value 10. Thus, the output it produces will appear as follows:

```
1    1
2    4
3    9
4    16
5    25
6    36
7    49
8    64
9    81
10   100
```

The ascending form executes as shown in the following diagram:

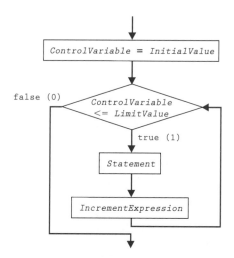

By using an appropriate step expression, a for loop can be used to step through a range of values in increments (or decrements) of size other than 1. For example, the **for** statement

```
for (int Number = 0; Number <= 100; Number += 20)
    cout << '\t' << Number << '\t' << pow(Number, 2) << '\n';
```

uses the step expression

```
Number += 20
```

to count upward in increments of 20, producing the output

```
0      0
20     400
40     1600
60     3600
80     6400
100    10000
```

The descending form of a for loop performs a decrement operation following each execution of the loop body. For example, the loop

```
for (int Number = 10; Number >=6; Number--)
    cout << '\t' << Number << '\t' << pow(Number, 2) << '\n';
```

will count downward from 10 to 6, producing the output

```
10     100
9      81
8      64
7      49
6      36
```

The descending form executes as shown in the following diagram:

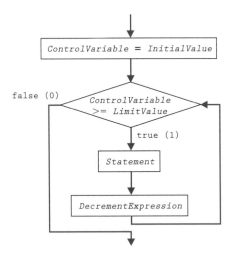

The **for** statement provides a convenient way of counting (upward or downward) by a fixed amount, on each trip through the loop.

Nested Loops: Displaying a Multiplication Table

The statement that appears within a **for** statement may itself be a **for** statement; that is, one for loop may be *nested within* another for loop. As an example, Figure 6.3 presents a program that displays a multiplication table by calculating and displaying products of the form **X * Y** for each **X** in the range 1 through **LastX** and each Y in the range 1 through LastY (where LastX and LastY are arbitrary integers). The multiplication table is generated by using nested **for** statements:

```
for (int X = 1; X <= LastX; X++)
   for (int Y = 1; Y <= LastY; Y++)
   {
      Product = X * Y;
      cout << setw(2) << X << " * "
           << setw(2) << Y << " = "
           << setw(3) << Product << '\n';
   }
```

The loop that has **X** as its control variable is referred to as the **outer loop,** and the loop that has **Y** as its control variable is referred to as the **inner loop.**

FIGURE 6.3 Printing a multiplication table.

```
/* This program calculates and displays a multiplication table.

   Input:  LastX and LastY, the largest numbers to be multiplied
   Output: A list of products: 1*1, ..., LastX * LastY
-----------------------------------------------------------------------*/

#include <iostream.h>
#include <iomanip.h>

int main(void)
{
   cout << "\nThis program constructs a multiplication table,\n"
        << "\tfor the values 1*1 through X*Y.\n";

   int
      LastX,           // the largest numbers being multiplied
      LastY,
      Product;         // the product of the two numbers

   cout << "\nPlease enter two integer limit values "
           "(one for X, one for Y): ";
   cin >> LastX >> LastY;

   for (int X = 1; X <= LastX; X++)
      for (int Y = 1; Y <= LastY; Y++)
      {
         Product = X * Y;
         cout << setw(2) << X << " * "
              << setw(2) << Y << " = "
              << setw(3) << Product << '\n';
      }

   return 0;
}
```

FIGURE 6.3   Printing a multiplication table. (cont.)

Sample run:

```
This program constructs a multiplication table,
    for the values 1*1 through X*Y.

Please enter two integer limit values (one for X, one for Y): 4 3
 1 * 1 =  1
 1 * 2 =  2
 1 * 3 =  3
 2 * 1 =  2
 2 * 2 =  4
 2 * 3 =  6
 3 * 1 =  3
 3 * 2 =  6
 3 * 3 =  9
 4 * 1 =  4
 4 * 2 =  8
 4 * 3 = 12
```

In the sample run, **LastX** is given the value 4 and **LastY** is given the value 3. When control reaches the outer loop,

```
for (int X = 1; X <= LastX; X++)
```

its control variable **X** is assigned its initial value 1. The statement it controls (the inner loop),

```
for (int Y = 1; Y <= LastY; Y++)
{
    Product = X * Y;
    cout << setw(2) << X << " * "
         << setw(2) << Y << " = "
         << setw(3) << Product << '\n';
}
```

is then executed. This inner loop counts through the values 1 through 3 and calculates and displays the first three products: 1 * 1, 1 * 2, and 1 * 3. Control then passes from the inner loop to the increment expression of the outer loop, where the value of **X** is incremented by 1 (to 2). The statement it controls (the inner loop) is then executed again. The inner loop again counts through the values 1 through 3, but since the value of **X** is now 2, this pass calculates and displays the next three products, 2 * 1, 2 * 2, and 2 * 3. The control variable **X** is then incremented again (to 3), so that when the inner loop is executed again, the next three products, 3 * 1, 3 * 2, and 3 * 3, are produced. **X** is then incremented again (to 4), and execution of the inner loop produces the last three products, 4 * 1, 4 * 2, and 4 * 3. **X** is then incremented again (to 5), making the loop condition **X <= LastX** false, so that repetition ceases. The statements

```
Product = X * Y;
cout << setw(2) << X << " * "
     << setw(2) << Y << " = "
     << setw(3) << Product << '\n';
```

is thus executed a total of 12 times, because the inner loop is executed 3 times for each of the 4 executions of the outer loop.

Words of Warning

A for loop must be constructed carefully to ensure that its initialization expression, loop condition, and increment expression will eventually cause the loop condition to become false. In particular:

> *If the body of a for loop alters the values of any variables involved in the loop condition, then the number of repetitions may be changed.*

It is generally considered poor programming practice to alter the value of any variables in the loop condition within the body of a for loop, because this can produce unexpected consequences. For example, execution of

```
int
   Limit = 1;

for (int i = 0; i <= Limit; i++)
{
   cout << i << '\n';
   Limit++;
}
```

produces an infinite sequence of integers[1]

```
0
1
2
3
.
.
.
```

because on each pass through the loop, the expression `Limit++` increments `Limit` by 1 before `i++` increments `i`. As a result, the loop condition `i <= Limit` remains true.

Similarly, the loop

```
for (int i = 0; i <= Limit; i++)
{
   cout << i << '\n';
   i--;
}
```

---

[1] In some environments execution will terminate when i is INT_MIN and LIMIT is INT_MAX+1 = INT_MIN.

will output infinitely many zeros,

```
0
0
0
.
.
.
```

because the expression `i--` in the body of the loop decrements `i` by 1 before the increment expression `i++` increments it by 1. As a result, `i` is always 0 when the loop condition is tested.

Exercises

1. Assuming that `I`, `J`, and `K` are integer variables, describe the output produced by each of the following program segments:

   (a)
   ```
   for (I = -2; I <= 3; I++)
       cout << I << " squared = " << I*I << '\n';
   ```

   (b)
   ```
   for (I = 1; I <= 5; I++)
   {
       cout << I << '\n';
       for (J = I; J >= 1; J--)
           cout << J << '\n';
   }
   ```

   (c)
   ```
   K = 5;
   for (I = -2; I <= 3; I++)
   {
       cout << (I + K) << '\n';
       K = 1;
   }
   ```

   (d)
   ```
   for (I = 1; I <= 3; I++)
       for (J = 1; J <= 3; J++)
           for (K = 1; K <= J; K++)
               cout << I << J << K << '\n';
   ```

   (e)
   ```
   for ( I = 1; I <= 3; I++)
       for (J = 1; J <= 3; J++)
       {
           for (K = I; K <= J; K++)
               cout << I << J << K << '\n';
           cout << '\n';
       }
   ```

2. The sequence of **Fibonacci numbers** begins with the integers

   $$1, 1, 2, 3, 5, 8, 13, 21, \ldots$$

   where each number after the first two is the sum of the two preceding numbers. Write a function that uses a for loop to generate the first *n* Fibonacci numbers.

Then write a driver program that tests the function by reading a positive integer *n,* calling the function with *n* as an argument, and outputting the result.

3. A certain product is to sell for **UnitPrice** dollars. Write a program that reads values for **UnitPrice** and **TotalNumber** and then produces a table showing the total price of from 1 through **TotalNumber** units. The table should have a format like the following:

```
Number of Units     Total Price
================     ===========
        1               $ 1.50
        2               $ 3.00
        3               $ 4.50
        4               $ 6.00
        5               $ 7.50
```

4. Suppose that at a given time, genotypes AA, AB, and BB appear in the proportions *x, y,* and *z,* respectively, where $x = 0.25$, $y = 0.5$, and $z = 0.25$. If individuals of type AA cannot reproduce, the probability that one parent will donate gene A to an offspring is

$$p = \frac{1}{2}\left(\frac{y}{y+z}\right)$$

since $y/(y + z)$ is the probability that the parent is of type AB and $\frac{1}{2}$ is the probability that such a parent will donate gene A. Then the proportions x', y', and z' of AA, AB, and BB, respectively, in each succeeding generation are given by

$$x' = p^2, \qquad y' = 2p(1 - p), \qquad z' = (1 - p)^2$$

and the new probability is given by

$$p' = \frac{1}{2}\left(\frac{y'}{y'+z'}\right)$$

Write a program to calculate and print the generation number and the proportions of AA, AB, and BB under appropriate headings for 30 generations. (Note that the proportions of AA and AB should approach 0, since gene A will gradually disappear.)

5. Write a program that uses nested for loops to print the following multiplication table:

```
    1  2  3  4  5  6  7  8  9
1   1
2   2  4
3   3  6  9
4   4  8 12 16
5   5 10 15 20 25
6   6 12 18 24 30 36
7   7 14 21 28 35 48 49
8   8 16 24 32 40 45 56 64
9   9 18 27 36 45 54 63 72 81
```

6.2   Repetition: The While Loop

The for loop provides a powerful tool for solving problems that involve counting through a range of values. It is a useful statement when the number of repetitions to be performed is known (or can be computed) in advance. There are, however, many problems whose solutions require repetitive execution, but the required number of repetitions cannot be determined easily in advance, as the next problem illustrates.

Example: Follow the Bouncing Ball

Problem.   Suppose that when a ball is dropped from the top of a building, it bounces from the pavement to a height one-half of its previous height. We want to write a program that will simulate the behavior of the ball when it is dropped from a given height. On each bounce, the program should display

- The number of the bounce, and
- The height of that bounce,

until the height of the bounce is very small (e.g., less than 1 millimeter).

Specification.   Given this description of the problem, we can identify the following data objects:

Data Object	Kind of Value	Type of Object	Name of Object
The current height	Variable	Real	*Height*
The bounce number	Variable	Integer	*Bounce*
A very small number	Constant	Real	*SmallNumber*

This list allows us to specify the problem as follows:

Input: The (starting) *Height* of a ball
Output: For each bounce of the ball:
    the number of the bounce and
    the height of that bounce
assuming that the height of each bounce is one-half the previous height

Design.   The following operations must be performed on these objects:

- Input a real value (the original *Height*)
- Initialize *Bounce* to zero
- Divide the *Height* by 2 (to compute the rebound height)
- Increment *Bounce*
- Display the current *Bounce* number and *Height* and
- Repeat the preceding steps as long as *Height* is at least *SmallNumber*

These operations are used in the following algorithm:

ALGORITHM FOR BOUNCING BALL PROBLEM

/* This algorithm displays the rebound heights of a dropped ball.

Input: A real *Height*
Output: For each bounce of the ball from the pavement below:
         the number of the bounce and
         the height of that bounce
         assuming that the height of each bounce is one-half the previous
         height.
                                                                      —*/

1. Initialize *Bounce* to 0.
2. Enter a value for *Height*.
3. Display original *Height* value with appropriate label.
4. Loop through the following steps while *Height* ≥ *SmallNumber:*
   a. Replace *Height* with *Height* divided by 2.
   b. Add 1 to *Bounce.*
   c. Display *Bounce* and *Height.*
   End Loop.

Coding.   Figure 6.4 presents a C++ program that implements this algorithm.

 FIGURE 6.4   Computing rebound height.

```
/* This program calculates and displays the rebound heights
   of a dropped ball.

   Input:   A real Height
   Output:  For each bounce of the ball from the pavement below:
            the number of the bounce and
            the height of that bounce
            assuming that the height of each bounce
            is one-half the previous height
   ------------------------------------------------------------*/

#include <iostream.h>

int main(void)
{
   const double
      SmallNumber = 1.0e-3;  // 1 millimeter.

   cout << "\nThis program computes the rebound height of a "
        << "dropped ball.\n";
```

FIGURE 6.4   Computing rebound height. (cont.)

```
int
    Bounce = 0;

double
    Height;

cout << "\nPlease enter the original height (in meters): ";
cin >> Height;

cout << "\nStarting height: " << Height << " meters.";

while (Height >= SmallNumber)
{
    Height /= 2.0;
    Bounce++;
    cout << "\nBounce # " << Bounce << ": " << Height << " meters.";
}

cout << "\n\n";

return 0;
}
```

Sample run:

```
This program computes the rebound height of a dropped ball.

Please enter the original height (in meters): 15.

Starting height: 15
Bounce # 1: 7.5 meters.
Bounce # 2: 3.75 meters.
Bounce # 3: 1.875 meters.
Bounce # 4: 0.9375 meters.
Bounce # 5: 0.46875 meters.
Bounce # 6: 0.234375 meters.
Bounce # 7: 0.117188 meters.
Bounce # 8: 0.0585938 meters.
Bounce # 9: 0.0292969 meters.
Bounce # 10: 0.0146484 meters.
Bounce # 11: 0.00732422 meters.
Bounce # 12: 0.00366211 meters.
Bounce # 13: 0.00183105 meters.
Bounce # 14: 0.000915527 meters.
```

The while Statement

The loop used in the preceding example is called a **while loop.** While loops are implemented in C++ using a **while statement,** whose syntax is given by the following diagram:

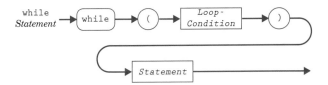

The **while** statement thus has the following form.

The **while** Statement

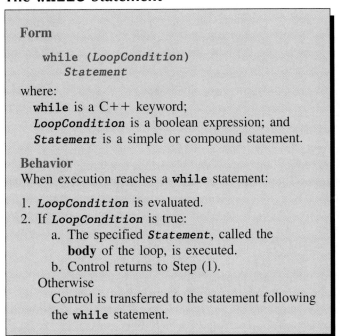

Form

```
while (LoopCondition)
    Statement
```

where:
  while is a C++ keyword;
  LoopCondition is a boolean expression; and
  Statement is a simple or compound statement.

Behavior
When execution reaches a **while** statement:

1. **LoopCondition** is evaluated.
2. If **LoopCondition** is true:
       a. The specified **Statement**, called the
          body of the loop, is executed.
       b. Control returns to Step (1).
   Otherwise
       Control is transferred to the statement following
       the **while** statement.

Like a for loop, a while loop has a loop condition that controls the execution of the loop. The placement of this loop condition before the body of the loop is significant because it means that when a while loop is executed, this condition is evaluated *before* the body of the loop is executed. This can be pictured as follows:

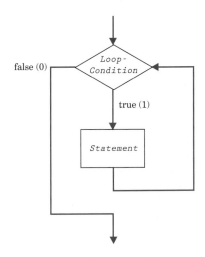

As this diagram indicates, execution of the specified statement continues as long as the loop condition remains true and terminates when it becomes false. For example, the following table provides a partial trace of the repetitions of the while loop in Figure 6.4, showing the values of the relevant data objects:

Height	Bounce	Height >= SmallNumber	Action
15.0	0	true	Execute loop body
7.5	1	true	Execute loop body
3.75	2	true	Execute loop body
1.875	3	true	Execute loop body
.	.	.	.
.	.	.	.
.	.	.	.
0.00183105	13	true	Execute loop body
0.000915527	14	false	Terminate repetition

As the preceding diagram also indicates, the condition in a while loop is evaluated before the loop body is executed; hence, a while loop is called a **pretest, or test-at-the-top loop.** This means that if the loop condition is initially false, the body of the loop will not be executed. Stated differently, the body of a pretest loop may be executed *zero or more times,* and so these loops are said to exhibit **zero-trip behavior.** Thus, in the program in Figure 6.4, if a nonpositive value were entered for **Height**, the statements in the while loop would not be executed, because the condition **Height >= SmallNumber** that controls repetition would be false the first time it is encountered. As we shall see, this zero-trip behavior distinguishes a while loop from other noncounting loops provided in C++. It is important to keep this characteristic in mind when designing a solution to a problem, because it influences the decision of which loop to use.

Words of Warning

It is important to ensure that the body of a while loop will eventually cause its loop condition to become false, since otherwise an *infinite loop* will result. To illustrate, consider the while loop

```
Counter = 1;
while (Counter < 100)
{
    cout << Counter << '\n';
    Counter--;
}
```

Counter is initially less than 100, and since **Counter--** decrements **Counter** by 1, the value of **Counter** will always be less than 100.[2] Thus, the condition **Counter < 100** will always be true, and so this loop is an infinite loop, producing the output

---

[2] In some environments, repetition will terminate when **Counter** becomes **INT_MIN** because the value of **Counter--** will then be **INT_MAX**.

```
    1
    0
   -1
   -2
   -3
    .
    .
    .
```

Another common mistake is illustrated by the following code segment:

```
Counter = 1;
while (Counter < 100)
    cout << Counter << '\n';
    Counter++;
```

This code segment will display the value 1 infinitely many times:

```
    1
    1
    1
    1
    1
    .
    .
    .
```

Errors of this kind can be difficult to find, because the indentation of the statements makes them appear correct. The problem here is that the loop body is a single statement. Thus, in the absence of braces, only the statement

```
cout << Counter << '\n';
```

is within the body of the loop. In order for the statement

```
Counter++;
```

to be within the loop body, both statements must be surrounded with braces.

Using Sentinel-Controlled While Loops to Input a List of Values

One common use of while loops is reading and processing a set of data values. Because it may not be possible or practical to determine beforehand how many data values must be processed, a general loop, such as a while loop, should be used rather than a counting loop.

One commonly used method is to use a **sentinel-controlled loop** and to append to the data an artificial data value called an **end-of-data flag** or **sentinel,** which is distinct from any possible data item. As each data item is read, it is checked to determine whether it is this end-of-data flag. If it is not, the value is processed. When the end-of-data flag is read, it is not processed as a regular data value. It serves only to terminate the repetition.

One way to implement this scheme is by using a sentinel-controlled while loop of the form:

1. Read the first data value.
2. While the data value is not the data sentinel, do the following:
    a. Process the data value.
    b. Read the next data value.

Note the presence of two input instructions, one before the while loop and one at the bottom of the while loop. The first data value must be read before the while loop is entered for the first time, since otherwise the condition that controls repetition may be undefined. After the current data value has been processed within the while loop, a new value must be read before the next pass through the loop. This standard technique for reading and processing data values is illustrated in the following example.[3]

Example: Calculating the Mean Time to Failure.   Consider again the mean time to failure problem of Chapter 2 in which failure times of some device must be read and counted and the mean time to failure calculated. The following specification was given for this problem:

Input: An unspecified number of failure times
Output: The number of values input and the mean (average) of the input
             values

Since the number of failure times is not known in advance, a sentinel-controlled while loop is an appropriate repetition structure to use. In fact, this kind of loop was used in the algorithm given in Section 2.2 for solving this problem:

ALGORITHM TO CALCULATE MEAN TIME TO FAILURE— SENTINEL-CONTROLLED WHILE LOOP VERSION

/* This algorithm reads a sequence of failure times, counts and sums them, and then finds the mean time to failure.

Input: A sequence of failure times, each stored in *FailTime*
Constants: *Sentinel,* a value distinct from all possible failure times
Output: The mean time to failure, and the number of times entered

——————————————————————————————————————*/

1. Initialize *NumTimes* to 0 and *Sum* to 0.0.
2. Enter the first value for *FailTime*.

---

[3] In Section 6.4 we describe an alternative loop that avoids this duplication: a *forever loop* containing an **if-break** *combination* to terminate repetition. Such a loop is considered by some, however, to violate principles of good program design because it is a "test-in-the-middle" loop rather than a "test-at-the-top" loop (i.e., a while loop) or a "test-at-the-bottom" loop (i.e., a do-while loop as described in the next section). Other programmers' design principles are not so severe, however, and require only that a loop *have exactly one exit.*

3. While *FailTime* is not equal to *Sentinel* do the following:
    a. Increment *NumTimes* by 1.
    b. Add *FailTime* to *Sum.*
    c. Enter next value for *FailTime.*
  End Loop.
4. If *NumTimes* ≠ 0 then
    a. Calculate *MeanFailTime = Sum / NumTimes.*
    b. Display *MeanFailTime* and *NumTimes.*
  Else
    Display a ''No Data'' message.
  End If.

Here Statements 3a, 3b, and 3c are to be repeated as long as the value of *FailTime* is not the sentinel value entered by the user to signal the end of data. When it is, so that the value of the boolean expression ''*FailTime* is not equal to *Sentinel*'' becomes false, repetition terminates, and execution continues with Statement 4.

In the C++ program in Figure 6.5 that implements this algorithm, the sentinel value −1 is used to signal the end of data because failure times can never be negative. Note that the program informs users of this sentinel value (when prompting them for input, as is customary). Note also that if the sentinel value were entered immediately, the while loop would be bypassed and *NumTimes* would remain zero and the computation of *MeanFailTime* would produce a divide-by-zero error. This computation is therefore *guarded* by placing it within an appropriate **if** statement.

FIGURE 6.5   Mean time to failure—sentinel-controlled while loop version.

```
/* This program computes the mean of a list of component failure
   times. It does so using a sentinel-controlled while loop with
   sentinel value -1.

   Input:   A list of fail times
   Output:  User prompts, number of failure times read, and their
            mean or a message indicating that no failure times
            were entered
--------------------------------------------------------------------*/

#include <iostream.h>

int main(void)
{
   const int
      Sentinel = -1;                 // the end-of-data indicator

   cout << "\nThis program computes the mean failure time\n"
        << "\tfor a list of component failure times.\n"
        << "\tEntering a failure time of " << Sentinel
        << " signals the end of data.\n\n";
```

FIGURE 6.5   Mean time to failure—sentinel-controlled while loop version. (cont.)

```
int
   NumTimes = 0;                    // number of failure times
double
   FailTime,                        // failure time being processed
   Sum = 0.0;                       // sum of the failure times

                                    // read first fail time
cout << "Please enter the first failure time ("
     << Sentinel << " to quit): ";
cin >> FailTime;

while (FailTime != Sentinel)    // while not end of data
{
   NumTimes++;                      //    process fail time
   Sum += FailTime;

   cout << "Please enter the next failure time ("
        << Sentinel << " to quit): ";
   cin >> FailTime;                 //    read next fail time
}                                   // end while loop

if (NumTimes > 0)
{
   double
      MeanFailTime = Sum / NumTimes;     // the mean failure time

   cout << "\n\t==> The mean of the " << NumTimes
        << " failure times is " << MeanFailTime << "\n\n";
}
else
   cout << "\n*** No fail times were entered !\n\n";

return 0;
}
```

Sample run:

```
This program computes the mean failure time
   for a list of component failure times.
   Entering a failure time of -1 signals the end of data.

Please enter the first failure time (-1 to quit): 127
Please enter the next failure time (-1 to quit): 123.5
Please enter the next failure time (-1 to quit): 155.4
Please enter the next failure time (-1 to quit): 99
Please enter the next failure time (-1 to quit): 117.3
Please enter the next failure time (-1 to quit): 201.5
Please enter the next failure time (-1 to quit): -1

   --> The mean of the 6 failure times is 137.283333
```

A while loop is a common way to implement a sentinel-controlled input loop. The usual pattern is as follows:

Pattern for Sentinel-Controlled While Loop

```
const ValueType
    Sentinel = NonDataValue;

        .
        .
        .
Enter the first data Value.
while (Value != Sentinel)
{
    Process the Value.

    Enter the next data Value.

}   // End while loop
```

Using End-of-File-Controlled While Loops to Input a List of Values

The chief drawback of a sentinel-controlled loop is that for some problems there is no appropriate sentinel. For example, if a problem processes values that may be any integers, then there is no suitable value to signal the end of data. One way to avoid this drawback is to use a special operating system character, called the **end-of-file mark,** as the sentinel value.[4] Because entering large sets of data from the keyboard is tiresome, data is often stored in files, and most operating systems use a special end-of-file character to mark the end of these files. Since indicating the end of a list of data items entered from the keyboard and indicating the end of a list of data items in a file are similar problems, most operating systems allow the user to enter a combination of keystrokes as an end-of-file mark for interactive input.

Most programming languages provide some means for detecting this end-of-file mark. Typically this is done with a boolean-valued function that returns true if the end-of-file mark has been read and returns false otherwise. In C++, this function is a member function of the class **istream** and is named **eof()**.[5] It returns true (1) if the last input operation attempted to read the end-of-file mark and returns false (0) otherwise. As we saw in Chapter 4, to call a member function, we must preface the name of the function with the name of the class object contain-

---

[4] In the MS-DOS environment, typing a `Control-Z` followed by the `Enter` key indicates end-of-file. In the Macintosh (Symantec) environment, a `Control-d` that follows a `Return` signals end-of-file. In the UNIX environment, simply type `Control-d` as the end-of-file mark (no `Enter` or `Return` is necessary).

[5] In Chapter 3 we noted that `istream` is a class in the `iostream` library and `cin` is an instance of this class; that is, it is of type `istream`.

ing it. Thus, since **cin** is an object of class **istream**, the member function **eof()** can be called by

```
cin.eof()
```

Such a call can be used as a termination condition in an input loop. To illustrate, consider the following alternative algorithm for the mean time to failure problem:

ALGORITHM TO CALCULATE MEAN TIME TO FAILURE— END-OF-FILE-CONTROLLED WHILE LOOP VERSION

/* This algorithm reads a sequence of failure times, counts and sums them, and then finds the mean time to failure.
The end-of-file mark is used for loop control.

Input: An arbitrary number of failure time values
Output: *MeanFailTime* and *NumTimes*

——*/

1. Initialize *NumTimes* to 0 and *Sum* to 0.0.
2. Enter the first value for *FailTime*.
3. While *EndofFileMark* has not been entered do the following:
      a. Increment *NumTimes* by 1.
      b. Add *FailTime* to *Sum*.
      c. Enter next value for *FailTime*.
   End Loop.
4. If *NumTimes* ≠ 0 then
      a. Calculate *MeanFailTime* = *Sum* / *NumTimes*.
      b. Display *MeanFailTime* and *NumTimes*.
   Else
      Display a "No Data" message.
   End If.

In this approach we must tell users what combination of keystrokes serves as the end-of-file mark in the current environment, since otherwise they will not know how to terminate the input loop. The program in Figure 6.6 uses the end-of-file mark for the UNIX environment. Note that it uses a named constant to represent the end-of-file mark, so that if we wish to port the program from the UNIX environment to the MS-DOS environment, all that is needed is to change the declaration of this constant.

FIGURE 6.6 Mean time to failure—end-of-file version.

```cpp
/* This program computes the mean of a list of component failure times.

   Input:    A list of fail times
   Output:   User prompts, number of fail times read, and mean or a
             message indicating that no failure times were entered

   Note: To port the program from UNIX to DOS,
             replace: EOFMarker[] = "Control-D";
             with     EOFMarker[] = "Control-Z";
----------------------------------------------------------------------*/

#include <iostream.h>

int main(void)
{
   const char
      EOFMark[] = "Control-D";

   cout << "\nThis program computes the mean failure time\n"
        << "\tfor a list of component failure times.\n"
        << "\tEntering a failure time of " << EOFMark
        << " signals the end of data.\n\n";

   int
      NumTimes = 0;                    // number of failure times
   double
      FailTime,                        // the fail time being processed
      Sum = 0.0;                       // sum of the failure times

                                       // read first fail time
   cout << "Please enter the first failure time ("
        << EOFMark << " to quit): ";
   cin >> FailTime;

   while (!cin.eof())                  // while not end of data
   {
      NumTimes++;                      //    process fail time
      Sum += FailTime;

      cout << "Please enter the next failure time ("
           << EOFMark << " to quit): ";
      cin >> FailTime;                 //    read next fail time
   }                                   // end while loop

   if (NumTimes > 0)
   {
      double
         MeanFailTime = Sum / NumTimes; // the mean of the fail times

      cout << "\n\t==> The mean of the " << NumTimes
           << " failure times is " << MeanFailTime << "\n\n";
   }
```

FIGURE 6.6   Mean time to failure—end-of-file version. (cont.)

```
    else
        cout << "\n*** No fail times were entered !\n\n";

    return 0;
}
```

Sample run:

```
This program computes the mean failure time
    for a list of component failure times.
    Entering a failure time of Control-D signals the end of data.

Please enter the first failure time (Control-D to quit): 127
Please enter the next failure time (Control-D to quit): 123.5
Please enter the next failure time (Control-D to quit): 155.4
Please enter the next failure time (Control-D to quit): 99
Please enter the next failure time (Control-D to quit): 117.3
Please enter the next failure time (Control-D to quit): 201.5
Please enter the next failure time (Control-D to quit): ^D

--> The mean of the 6 failure times is 137.283333
```

The end-of-file mark can thus be used as a special sentinel value for problems in which there are no data values to use as a sentinel. The general form of such end-of-file-controlled loops is as follows:

Pattern for End-of-File-Controlled While Loop

```
Read the first data Value.
while (!cin.eof())
{
    Process the Value.

    Input the next data Value to be processed.
}   // End while loop
```

As we noted, end-of-file-controlled input loops can be used in problems when there is no appropriate sentinel value. Another advantage they enjoy over sentinel-controlled input loops is that, with a little modification, the same loop can be used both for input from the keyboard and input from a file. File input is considered in Chapter 8.[6]

The main drawback of end-of-file-controlled loops is that (for interactive programs) they are not *portable,* because different environments use different special

_____

[6] This is particularly convenient in the UNIX environment, where the use of I/O redirection and pipes makes it easy for a program that normally reads from the keyboard to instead read from a text file.

characters for their end-of-file marks. If a program is written in the MS-DOS environment (and prompts the user to enter **Control-Z** to quit), then that prompt is incorrect in the UNIX environment (where the user should enter **Control-D**). (Of course, this is not a problem for noninteractive programs.)

A second drawback is that once the user enters the end-of-file mark, the **istream** named **cin** is *closed*, and no further input can be performed from the keyboard. This approach is thus limited to problems that require processing a single list of values, after which no further input is required.

Exercises

1. Assuming that **I** and **K** are integer variables, describe the output produced by each of the following program segments:

   (a)
   ```
   K = 5;
   I = -2;
   while (I <= K)
   {
       I += 2;
       K--;
       cout << (I + K) << '\n';
   }
   ```
   (b)
   ```
   I = 4;
   while (I >= 0)
   }
       I--;
       cout << I << '\n';
   }
   ```

2. Describe the output produced by the following poorly indented program segment:

   ```
   int
       Number = 4;
   while ( Number > 0 )
       Number--;
       cout << Number << '\n';
   ```

3. Write a program that uses a sentinel-controlled or end-of-file-controlled while loop to read data values shown in the following table, calculates the miles per gallon in each case, and displays the values with appropriate labels:

Miles Traveled	Gallons of Gasoline Used
231	14.8
248	15.1
302	12.8
147	9.25
88	7.0
265	13.3

4. Write a program that uses a sentinel-controlled or end-of-file-controlled while loop to read several values representing miles, converts miles to kilometers (1 mile = 1.60935 kilometers), and displays all values with appropriate labels.

5. Write a program that reads an exchange rate for converting English currency to U.S. currency and then reads several values in English currency and converts each amount to the equivalent U.S. currency. Display all amounts with appropriate labels. Use a sentinel-controlled or end-of-file-controlled while loop for the input.

6. Proceed as in the preceding exercise, but convert values from U.S. currency to English currency.

7. Write a program for the "divide-and-average" algorithm for approximating square roots (see Exercise 11 of Section 2.5). It should accept positive real values for the variables **PosReal**, **Approx**, and **Epsilon** and approximate the square root of **PosReal** by repeatedly replacing **Approx** by the average of **Approx** and **PosReal / Approx**, until **Approx** and **PosReal / Approx** differ in absolute value by less than **Epsilon**, where the value of **Epsilon** is a small real number. Have the program display each of the successive values of **Approx**.

8. Write a program that accepts a positive integer and gives its prime factorization, that is, expresses the integer as a product of primes or indicates that it is a prime.

6.3 Repetition: The Do-While Loop

In the last section, we saw that the **while** statement provides a general (i.e., non-counting) loop that evaluates its loop condition prior to executing the statement it controls. We also saw that such pretest loops are useful in solving problems where zero-trip behavior is required.

However, there are some repetition problems for which zero-trip behavior is not appropriate. To solve these problems, many languages provide a *posttest loop* called a *do-while loop,* which is described in this section.

Example: How Many Digits?

Problem.   When humans look at an integer, whether it be 12 or 135790246897531, it is relatively easy to determine the number of digits simply by scanning through the number and counting them. However, a computer program cannot simply "scan and count" the number of digits in a number. Our next problem is to write a function that, given an integer value, will count the digits in that value.

Specification.   From the problem description, we can identify the following data objects in this problem:

Data Object	Kind of Value	Type of Object	Name of Object
The integer value	Variable	Integer	*IntVal*
The number of digits in the integer value	Variable	Integer	*NumDigits*

This suggests the following specification for a function that solves this problem:

Receive: *IntVal,* an integer value
Return: *NumDigits,* the number of digits in *IntVal*

This specification allows us to declare a function, which we call `DigitsIn()`:

```
int DigitsIn(long int IntVal);
```

Design. One way to solve this problem is to count how many times *IntVal* must be divided by 10 to produce 0. For example, 12 has two digits, and two divisions by 10 are required to reach 0:

Repetition	Operation	*IntVal*	*NumDigits*	Action
0	None	12	0	Enter loop
1	12/10	1	1	Repeat execution
2	1/10	0	2	Terminate execution

Similarly, 5 has one digit, and one division by 10 gives 0:

Repetition	Operation	*IntVal*	*NumDigits*	Action
0	None	5	0	Enter loop
1	5/10	0	1	Terminate execution

The operations that `DigitsIn()` must perform are

1. Integer division (Divide *IntVal* by 10)
2. Integer addition (Add 1 to *NumDigits*)
3. Repetition of Steps (a) and (b) as long as *IntVal* is not 0

Each of these operations is provided in C++, either as an operator or a statement.
    There are two key observations in this solution:

1. Since every number has at least one digit, we must perform the integer division and assignment *at least once.*
2. We must *repeat* Steps 1 and 2 as long as *IntVal* is not 0.

The second observation implies the need of a loop, but the first observation suggests that the zero-trip behavior of a pretest loop is inappropriate. Instead, a loop that evaluates its loop condition at the "bottom" of the loop is required, as reflected in the following algorithm:

ALGORITHM TO COUNT DIGITS

/* This algorithm computes the number of digits in an integer value.

Receive: *IntVal,* an integer value
Return: *NumDigits,* the number of digits in *IntVal*
———*/

1. Initialize *NumDigits* to zero.
2. Loop through the following steps:
   a. Increment *NumDigits;*
   b. Divide *IntVal* by 10, storing the result in *IntVal.*
   as long as *IntVal* is not zero.
3. Return *NumDigits.*

Coding. Figure 6.7 presents an implementation of this algorithm as function `DigitsIn()`:

 FIGURE 6.7 Function `DigitsIn()`.

```
/* This function counts the digits in an integer value.

   Receive:    IntVal, an integer value
   Return:     NumDigits, the number of digits in IntVal
-----------------------------------------------------*/

int DigitsIn(longint IntVal)
{
   int
      NumDigits = 0;

   do
   {
      NumDigits++;
      IntVal /= 10;
   }
   while (IntVal != 0);

   return NumDigits;
}
```

A simple driver program to test function **DigitsIn()** is given in Figure 6.8.

FIGURE 6.8 Driver program for function **DigitsIn()**.

```
/* This program tests function DigitsIn.

   Input:  An integer value i
   Output: The number of digits in i
-----------------------------------------------------------------------*/

#include <iostream.h>

int DigitsIn(int IntVal);

int main(void)
{
   long int
      i;

   cout << "\nPlease enter an integer value: ";
   cin >> i;

   cout << '\n' << i << " contains " << DigitsIn(i) << " digit(s).\n\n";

   return 0;
}

/* ... Put definition of function DigitsIn() here ...
```

Sample runs:

```
Please enter an integer value: 5

5 contains 1 digit(s).

...

Please enter an integer value: 12

12 contains 2 digit(s).

...

Please enter an integer value: 12345678

12345678 contains 8 digit(s).
```

The following table traces execution of the loop in **DigitsIn()** during the last sample run in Figure 6.8, showing the values of **IntVal** and the loop condition on each pass through the loop:

Repetition	IntVal	NumDigits	IntVal != 0	Action
0	12345678	0	Not applicable	Enter loop
1	1234567	1	True	Execute loop body
2	123456	2	True	Execute loop body
3	12345	3	True	Execute loop body
4	1234	4	True	Execute loop body
5	123	5	True	Execute loop body
6	12	6	True	Execute loop body
7	1	7	True	Execute loop body
8	0	8	False	Terminate repetition

The function **DigitsIn()** returns the value of **NumDigits** (8) after execution leaves the loop.

A Posttest Loop

The function in Figure 6.8 uses a new C++ repetition statement—the **do-while statement,** whose form is given by the following syntax diagram:

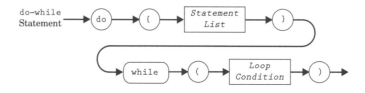

From this we see that a **do-while** statement has the following form:

The do-while Statement

Form

> do
> {
>   *Statement₁*
>   *Statement₂*
>   .
>   .
>   .
>   *Statementₙ*
> }
> while (*LoopCondition*);

where:

   do and **while** are C++ keywords;

   LoopCondition is a boolean expression;

   Statement₁, Statement₂, . . . , Statementₙ are
     statements; and a semicolon must follow the
     while clause at the end of the statement.

Behavior

When execution reaches a do-while loop:

   (1) *Statement₁, Statement₂, . . . , Statementₙ,*
      are executed.
   (2) *LoopCondition* is evaluated.
   (3) If *LoopCondition* is true, then
      Control returns to step (1).
     Otherwise
      Control passes to the first statement fol-
      lowing the do-while loop.

Note that the loop condition in a **do-while** statement appears *after* the body of the loop, which means that it is evaluated at the end, or ''bottom,'' of the loop. The do-while loop is thus a **posttest loop,** or **test-at-the-bottom loop,** in which execution flows as pictured in the following diagram:

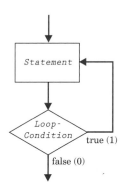

The fact that the loop condition is evaluated after the body of the loop has been executed guarantees that the body of the loop will be executed at least once. For this reason, posttest loops are said to exhibit **one-trip behavior,** just as pretest loops are said to exhibit zero-trip behavior.

Words of Warning

The syntax of the **do-while** statement is different from that of the **while** statement and is designed to indicate clearly that it is a posttest loop. However, there is another, less obvious difference between the **while** and **do-while** statements that is a common source of programming errors:

> *The* **do-while** *statement must be terminated with a semicolon, but it is an error to terminate a* **while** *statement with a semicolon.*

The reason is that the final component of a **do-while** statement is its loop condition, which, as an expression, must be terminated with a semicolon. By contrast, the loop condition in the **while** statement occurs at the beginning, and so no semicolon is needed.

As with while loops, it is important to ensure that the statements within a do-while loop will eventually cause repetition to terminate, because an infinite loop will result otherwise. For example, in the do-while loop

```
Counter = 1;
do
{
   cout << Counter << '\n';
   Counter--;
}
while (Counter < 100);
```

the termination condition is always true because **Counter** is initially less than 100 and **Counter--** decrements **Counter** by 1, causing the value of **Counter** to always be less than 100 (but see Footnote 2). Thus, this is an infinite loop, producing an unlimited amount of output:

```
 1
 0
-1
-2
-3
 .
 .
 .
```

Using a Do-While Loop to Input a List of Values

As we have seen, one common use of loops is to read and process a set of data values. Because it may not be possible or practical to determine beforehand how many data values must be processed, one of the general loops, rather than a counting loop, should be used.

As an example of such a problem, we reconsider the mean time to failure problem, for which the following specification was given in Chapter 2:

Input: An unspecified number of failure times
Output: The number of values input and the mean (average) of the input values

Design. In the preceding section, we showed how a sentinel-controlled while loop can be used to input an unspecified number of values. Another kind of loop in which the user is repeatedly asked whether there is more data is illustrated in the following algorithm:

ALGORITHM TO CALCULATE MEAN TIME TO FAILURE— QUERY VERSION

/* This algorithm reads a sequence of failure times, counts them, and finds their mean. Querying is used for loop control.

    Input: An arbitrary number of failure time values
    Output: *NumTimes* and *MeanFailTime*
    ———*/

0. Display instructions.
1. Initialize *NumTimes* to 0 and *Sum* to 0.0.
2. Loop through the following steps:
      a. Enter a value for *FailTime*.
      b. Increment *NumTimes* by 1.
      c. Add *FailTime* to *Sum*.
      d. Ask the user if there is more data (y or n).
      e. Input *Response;*
  as long as *Response* is not 'n'.
3. Calculate *MeanFailTime* = *Sum/NumTimes*.
4. Display *MeanFailTime* and *NumTimes*.

This approach assumes that there is at least one failure time to be processed. Consequently, we can omit the check for no data values that was done in the algorithm in Chapter 2. The program in Figure 6.9 uses a **do-while** statement to encode the posttest loop in Step 2.

 FIGURE 6.9 Mean time to failure—query version 1.

```
/* This program computes the mean of a list of component failure
   times, using a query controlled loop to input the values.

   Input:   A list of fail times and user responses
   Output:  User prompts, number of fail times read, and their mean
   -------------------------------------------------------------*/

#include <iostream.h>
```

FIGURE 6.9   Mean time to failure—query version 1. (cont.)

```cpp
int main(void)
{
    cout << "\nThis program computes the mean failure time,\n"
         << "\tgiven a list of component failure times.\n";

    int
        NumTimes = 0;           // number of failure times
    double
        FailTime,               // the failure time being processed
        Sum = 0.0;              // sum of the failure times
    char
        Response;               // user response

    do
    {
        cout << "\nPlease enter a failure time: ";
        cin >> FailTime;

        NumTimes++;
        Sum += FailTime;

        cout << "Do you have more data (y or n)? ";
        cin >> Response;
    }
    while ((Response != 'n') && (Response != 'N'));

    double
        MeanFailTime = Sum / NumTimes;     // the mean of the fail times

    cout << "\n\t--> The mean of the " << NumTimes
         << " failure times is " << MeanFailTime
         << "\n\n";

    return 0;
}
```

Sample run:

```
This program computes the mean failure time,
    given a list of component failure times.

Please enter a failure time: 127
Do you have more data (y or n)? y

Please enter a failure time: 123.5
Do you have more data (y or n)? y

Please enter a failure time: 155.4
Do you have more data (y or n)? y
```

FIGURE 6.9   Mean time to failure—query version 1. (cont.)

```
Please enter a failure time: 99
Do you have more data (y or n)? y

Please enter a failure time: 117.3
Do you have more data (y or n)? y

Please enter a failure time: 201.5
Do you have more data (y or n)? n

   --> The mean of the 6 failure times is 137.283333
```

The following table shows the values of the relevant objects on each trip through the loop:

FailTime	NumTimes	Sum	Response	Response == 'y'	Action
No value	0	0.0	No value	No value	Enter loop
127	1	127.0	y	True	Continue repetition
123.5	2	250.5	y	True	Continue repetition
155.4	3	405.9	y	True	Continue repetition
99	4	504.9	y	True	Continue repetition
117.3	5	622.2	y	True	Continue repetition
201.5	6	823.7	n	False	Terminate repetition

Queries.   The program in Figure 6.9 illustrates another of the standard techniques for using a loop to input a list of values. This general approach is simply to ask the user (at the end of each repetition) whether there is more data to process. The question is called a **query,** and this technique is called **querying the user.** Typical queries include

```
   Do you have more data to process (y or n)?
```

or

```
   Do you wish to continue (y or n)?
```

The user's response (i.e., presumably the character **y** or **n**) is entered and stored in a character variable and a boolean expression of the form

```
   CharVariable != 'n'
```

or

```
   CharVariable == 'y'
```

is used as the loop condition. Execution of such a loop will continue until the user enters a response indicating no further input.

If it is reasonable to assume that at least one data value will be entered and processed, then the query and corresponding test of the loop condition should be placed at the bottom of the loop. A do-while loop is, therefore, appropriate. This suggests the following pattern for a query-controlled input loop:

Pattern for Query-Controlled Input Loop

```
char
    Response;
       .
       .
       .
do
{
    Display a Prompt (for a data value).
    Input the Value to be processed.
    Process the Value.

    Display a Query (asking if there is more data).
    Input the user's Response (y or n).
}
while ((Response != 'n') && (Response != 'N'));
```

Query Functions.   The code to perform a query tends to clutter a loop, and this may obscure the program's structure. This can be avoided by constructing a **query function** like the following to perform the query and to return true (1) or false (0) based on the user's response:

```
int MoreData(void)
{
    char
        Answer;

    cout << "Do you have more values to enter (y or n)? ";
    cin >> Answer;

    return (Answer != 'n') && (Answer != 'N');
}
```

Note that because C++ represents the boolean values true and false with the integer values 1 and 0, respectively, the return type of **MoreData()** is **int**.[7]

---

[7] Although the type char might be used instead of int to save space, machines that allocate values on *word boundaries* may effectively use an entire word of memory to store a single char value. Moreover, many machines are able to access an int value faster than a char value, since an int is usually the word size of the machine.

A call to such a **query function** can then be used as the loop condition controlling the do-while loop. For example, Figure 6.10 presents a program that solves the mean time to failure problem with the help of the preceding query function `MoreData()`, which is stored in a library named `Query`.

FIGURE 6.10   Mean time to failure—query version 2.

```
/* This program computes the mean of a list of component failure
   times, using a query-function controlled loop to input the values.

   Input:    A list of fail times and user responses (via MoreData())
   Output:   User prompts, number of fail times read, and their mean
             or a message indicating that no failure times were
             entered
-----------------------------------------------------------------*/

#include <iostream.h>
#include "Query.h"                    // provides function MoreData()

int main(void)
{
   cout << "\nThis program computes the mean failure time,\n"
        << "\tgiven a list of component failure times.\n";

   int
      NumTimes = 0;                    // number of failure times
   double
      FailTime,                        // failure time being processed
      Sum = 0.0;                       // sum of the failure times

   do
   {
      cout << "\nPlease enter a failure time: ";
      cin >> FailTime;

      NumTimes++;
      Sum += FailTime;
   }
   while (MoreData());                 // call to query function

   double
      MeanFailTime = Sum / NumTimes;// the mean of the fail times

   cout << "\n\t--> The mean of the " << NumTimes
        << " failure times is " << MeanFailTime
        << "\n\n";

   return 0;
}
```

When execution reaches the loop condition of the do-while loop in this program, evaluation of the loop condition causes the function **MoreData()** to be called. This function queries the user, reads the response, and returns true (1) if the response was neither **n** nor **N** and returns false (0) otherwise. If **MoreData()** returns true, then the body of the do-while loop is repeated, but if it returns false, repetition is terminated.

This version of a query-controlled loop is easier to read than the earlier version, because the statements that perform the querying (including the declaration of variable **Response**) are now hidden in the function **MoreData()**.

The other advantage of this approach is that a query function can be stored in a library, from which it can be accessed by any program requiring a query-controlled loop. Since this particular query,

```
Do you have more values to enter (y or n)?
```

may be inappropriate for a different program, such a library might contain a variety of query functions:

    MoreData():   Asks if there are more values
    Continue():   Asks if the user wants to continue
    NotDone():   Asks if the user is finished

and so on. A program that uses the **#include** directive to insert the library's header file can use whichever query function is most appropriate.

A pattern for a loop controlled by a query function is as follows:

Pattern for Input Loop Controlled by a Query Function

```
int QueryFunction();        // or #include "Query.h"
     .
     .
     .
do
{
      Display a Prompt (for a data value).
      Input the Value to be processed.
      Process the Value.

}
while (QueryFunction());
```

Exercises

1. Assuming that **I**, **J**, and **K** are integer variables, describe the output produced by each of the following program segments:

(a)
```
I = 0;
do
{
   K = I * I * I - 3 * I + 1;
   cout << I << K << '\n';
   I++;
}
while (I <= 2);
```

```
(b) I = -2;
    do
    {
        K = I * I * I - 3 * I + 1;
        cout << I << K << '\n';
    }
    while (I <= 2);
(c) I = 0;
    do
    {
        J = I * I * I;
        cout << I;
        do
        {
            K = I + 2 * J;
            cout << J << K;
            J += 2;
        }
        while ( K <= 10);
        cout << '\n';
        I++;
    }
    while (J <= 5);
```

2. Exercise 13 of Chapter 1 describes the method of repeated division for converting a nonnegative integer n from base 10 to another base b. Since this method
   requires at least one division by b to produce the digits in the base-b representation, a do-while loop is a natural repetition structure to use. Write a program to
   accept various integers and bases and display the digits of the base-b representation (in reverse order) for each integer. You may assume that each base is in the
   range 2 through 10.

3. Proceed as in Exercise 2, but convert integers from base 10 to hexadecimal
   (base 16). Use a `switch` statement to display the symbols A, B, C, D, E, and F
   for 10, 11, 12, 13, 14, and 15, respectively.

*6.4   Repetition: The Forever Loop

In the preceding sections, we have seen that C++ provides the `for` statement to
implement counting loops, the `while` statement for pretest loops, and the `do-
while` statement for posttest loops. In addition to these three loops, most modern
programming languages provide a fourth loop, which, like the while and do-while,
is a general (i.e., noncounting) loop.[8] However, unlike those loops (in which the
loop condition is located at the beginning and end of the loop, respectively), this
fourth loop permits the programmer to place the loop condition at any point in the
loop. To see how this can be useful, we consider a new problem.

---

[8] For example, Ada, FORTRAN 90, and Modula-2.

Example: The ATM Menu-Choice Problem

Problem. Most banks provide automated teller machines (ATMs), both as a convenience to their customers and as a cost-saving measure. After an initial greeting,

```
Welcome to the BankNet ATM!

Please enter your ATM Card in the provided slot,
    and then enter your Personal Identification Number.
```

a typical ATM might present the user with a *menu* such as the following:

```
Please enter:
    A - to make a withdrawal from your account.
    B - to make a deposit to your account.
    C - for other transactions.
    D - to quit.
```

The customer then presses one of the buttons provided to select the desired transaction.

Our next problem involves this input operation. The ATM keyboard contains other buttons besides A–D (e.g., number buttons for entering dollar amounts, a period button for entering a decimal point, etc.) and the user may mistakenly press one of these buttons. If this occurs, an error message should be displayed, after which the menu should be redisplayed and another input accepted. These actions must be repeated until the button pressed is a valid menu choice (i.e., one of A–D).

Specification. Ignoring the initial greeting message, we can identify the following data objects in this problem:

Data Object	Kind of Value	Type of Object	Name of Object
Menu of choices	Constant	Character string	*Menu*
The user's choice	Variable	Character	*Choice*
The valid choices	Constants	Character	A, B, C, and D

This suggests the following specification for a function to solve this problem:

> Output: *Menu,* a character string,
>   and an error message, if necessary
> Input: *Choice,* a character
> Return: A value of *Choice,* guaranteed to be a valid menu option

This specification allows us to declare the function, which we call `GetMenuChoice()`:

```
char GetMenuChoice(void);
```

Design. The operations that `GetMenuChoice()` must perform are

1. Display the menu (output a character string);
2. Get the user's choice (input a character);
3. Display an error message if the user's choice was not valid; and

4. Repeat the whole set of operations (using some kind of loop) if the user's choice was not valid (compare characters).

Each of these operations—output, input, looping, and comparison—is provided in C++, either as an operator or a statement.

The key observations are the following:

1. We must display the menu object *at least once* in order to solve the problem.
2. We must also repeat steps 1, 2, and 3 as long as the user's choice is invalid.
3. We should not display the error message (Step 3) if the user's choice is valid.

The second observation implies the need for a loop, and the first observation suggests that the zero-trip behavior exhibited by a pretest loop is inappropriate. Moreover, the third observation suggests that we want to perform Step 3 only if the value input in Step 2 is invalid.

We could satisfy these requirements with the following algorithm:

1. Loop through the following steps:
   a. Display *Menu*.
   b. Input the user's *Choice*.
   c. If (*Choice* is invalid), then
         Display an error message.
   as long as (*Choice* is invalid).
2. Return *Choice*.

However, this algorithm requires that the condition (*Choice* is invalid) be evaluated twice—once in Step 1c and once in the loop condition at the ''bottom'' of the loop. The following algorithm demonstrates how a test-in-the-middle loop can be used to eliminate this duplication:[9]

ALGORITHM TO DISPLAY AND INPUT AN ATM MENU CHOICE

/* This algorithm displays a menu of four choices, repeatedly, if necessary, and returns the user's choice when it is a valid menu option.

Output: *Menu,* a character string
Input: *Choice,* a character
Return: A valid menu option

———*/

1. Loop through the following steps:
   a. Display *Menu*.
   b. Input the user's *Choice*.
   c. If Choice is valid, then terminate repetition.
   d. Display an error message.
   forever, if necessary.
2. Return *Choice*.

---

[9] As we noted in Section 6.2, those who view good program design as allowing only test-at-the-top (while) loops and test-at-the-bottom (do-while) loops consider use of such test-in-the-middle loops as a bad programming practice. Others, however, require only that a loop *have exactly one exit* and thus program freely with such loops (provided they have a *single exit point*). We leave it to the reader to choose between the two viewpoints.

Coding.   The function **GetMenuChoice()** in Figure 6.11 implements this algorithm. The loop condition

the user's choice is valid

is encoded as

(Choice >= 'A') && (Choice <= 'D')

 FIGURE 6.11   Function **GetMenuChoice()**.

```
/* This function simulates the input of an ATM transaction choice,
   using a forever loop.

   Output: A Menu of choices (A-D)
   Input:  Choice, a char indicating the transaction selected
           by the user
   Return: A valid menu option
---------------------------------------------------------------------*/

char GetMenuChoice(void)
{
   const char
      Menu[] = "\nPlease enter:"                    // the transaction menu
               "\n\tA - to make a withdrawal from your account."
               "\n\tB - to make a deposit to your account."
               "\n\tC - for other transactions."
               "\n\tD - to quit.n";
   char
      Choice;                                       // the transaction

   for (;;)                                         // Forever loop:
   {
      cout << Menu;                                 //    display the menu
      cin >> Choice;                                //    input Choice (A-D)

      if ((Choice >= 'A') && (Choice <= 'D'))       // if a valid Choice:
         break;                                     // exit the loop

      cout << "\nI'm sorry, but " << Choice         // else display
           << " is not a valid menu"                //    an error message
           << " choice.\n";
   }                                                // End loop

   return Choice;                                   // return (valid) choice
}
```

Given such a function, we can test its correctness and simulate the action of an ATM machine with a driver program like that in Figure 6.12.

FIGURE 6.12 Driver program for function **GetMenuChoice()**—version 2.

```
/* This is a simple driver program to test function GetMenuChoice().

   Input:  Characters Ch (via GetMenuChoice())
   Output: The menu produced by GetMenuChoice and the value of Ch
   ------------------------------------------------------------------------*/

#include <iostream.h>

char GetMenuChoice(void);

int main(void)
{
   cout << "\nThis program tests function GetMenuChoice.\n";

   char
      Ch;

   Ch = GetMenuChoice();

   cout << "\nThank you for selecting transaction "
        << Ch << ", which ...\n\n";

   return 0;
}

// ... Insert function GetMenuChoice() definition here...
```

Sample runs:

```
Please enter:
   A - to make a withdrawal from your account.
   B - to make a deposit to your account.
   C - for other transactions.
   D - to quit.
E

I'm sorry, but E is not a valid menu choice.

Please enter:
   A - to make a withdrawal from your account.
   B - to make a deposit to your account.
   C - for other transactions.
   D - to quit.
Y

I'm sorry, but Y is not a valid menu choice.
```

FIGURE 6.12   Driver program for function **GetMenuChoice()**—version 2. (cont)

```
Please enter:
   A - to make a withdrawal from your account.
   B - to make a deposit to your account.
   C - for other transactions.
   D - to quit.
B
```

```
Thank you for selecting transaction B, which ...
```

The following table traces the execution of the loop in **GetMenuChoice()** during the sample run shown in Figure 6.13, showing the values of **Choice** and the loop condition on each pass through the loop:

Repetition	Choice	(Choice >= 'A') && (Choice <= 'D')	Action
1	E	False	Continue repetition
2	Y	False	Continue repetition
3	B	True	Terminate repetition

An Unrestricted Loop

As mentioned previously, many modern programming languages provide a general loop statement that is not restricted to being a pretest or posttest loop. This loop is usually implemented by a language statement that is different from the statements for other loops.

C++, however, does not provide a syntactically distinct statement, but instead allows the programmer to construct such a loop from other loops. One way this can be done[10] is by removing the initialization expression, the loop condition, and the step expression from the for statement, as illustrated in the following syntax diagram:

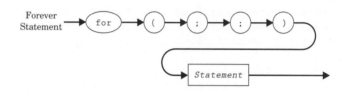

---

[10] Alternatively, we might achieve the same effect by writing either

```
while (1) Statement  or  do { StatementList } while (1)
```

Because such a loop contains no loop condition specifying the condition under which repetition continues, it is an **infinite loop** that executes the statements in its body forever. We shall call such a loop a **forever loop.**

The Forever Loop

Form

```
for (;;)            // forever loop
    Statement
```

where:

for is a C++ keyword; and

Statement is a simple or compound statement.

Behavior

The specified *Statement* is executed infinitely many times, unless it contains a **break** or **return** statement (usually an **if-break** or **if-return** combination).

In the case that a **break** statement is encountered, execution of the loop will terminate and execution will continue with the next statement after the loop.

If a **return** statement is encountered, the loop and the function containing it are terminated and control returns to the calling function.

To illustrate, consider the following forever loop:

```
for (;;)                        // forever loop
    cout << "Help! I'm caught in a loop!\n";
```

This statement will produce the output

```
Help! I'm caught in a loop!
Help! I'm caught in a loop!
Help! I'm caught in a loop!
        .
        .
        .
```

an unlimited number of times, unless the user *interrupts* execution (usually by typing **Control-C**).

To avoid this, the body of a forever loop is usually a compound statement, containing

1. Those statements that must be repeatedly executed in order to solve the problem; and
2. A statement that will *terminate* execution of the loop, when some condition is satisfied.

The terminating statement is usually an **if** statement combined with a **break** statement:

```
if (Condition) break;
```

We call this pairing of the two statements an **if-break combination.** Just as a **break** statement within a **switch** statement transfers control to the first statement following the **switch** statement, execution of a **break** statement within a loop terminates execution of the loop by transferring control to the statement following the loop.

Note that unlike the other loops, repetition continues as long as the condition in the **if-break** combination is false—repetition terminates when the condition becomes true. We therefore distinguish this condition from the loop conditions of the other loops by calling it a *termination condition* instead of a *loop condition.*

Most forever loops are thus organized as follows:

```
for (;;)                          // forever loop:
{
    StatementList₁
    if (TerminationCondition) break;
    StatementList₂
}                                 // end loop
```

This pattern can be seen in the forever loop used by function **GetMenuChoice()**:

```
for (;;)                          // forever loop:
{
                                  //   StatementList₁
    cout << Menu;
    cin >> Choice;
                                  //   if-break combination
    if ((Choice >= 'A') && (Choice <= 'D'))
        break;
                                  //   StatementList₂
    cout << "\nI'm sorry, but " << Choice
        << " is not a valid menu choice.\n";
}                                 // End loop

return Choice;
```

When the user enters an invalid menu choice, the termination condition is false. As a result, the **break** statement is not executed, and execution "falls through" to the statement that displays the error message. That statement is the last statement in the loop, and so control returns to the beginning of the loop for the next repetition.

By contrast, when the user enters a valid choice, the termination condition evaluates to true, so that the **break** statement is executed. This transfers control to the statement following the loop, the **return** statement in this case.

In situations like this where the statement following a forever loop is a **return** statement, it is slightly more efficient to replace the **break** statement with the **return** statement:

```
    for (;;)                              // forever loop:
    {
                                          //    StatementList₁
        cout << Menu;
        cin >> Choice;
                                          //    if-break combination
        if ((Choice >= 'A') && (Choice <= 'D'))
            return Choice;
                                          //    StatementList₂
        cout << "\nI'm sorry, but " << Choice
             << " is not a valid menu choice.\n";
    }                                     // End loop
```

Execution of the **return** statement causes the termination of the function containing the loop and so terminates the loop, but it takes one less step to do so.

Input Loops Using Sentinels

In the last section we saw that a do-while loop coupled with a query provides a means of inputting a list of values. In Section 6.2 we saw that a while loop provides another way to input a list of values by having the use enter an end-of-data sentinel value. However, this mechanism requires the use of *two* input steps (and two prompts for input), one before the loop and one at the bottom of the loop. The forever loop makes it possible to control an input loop with a sentinel, using a single input statement (and prompt).

To illustrate, consider again the mean time to failure problem. An alternative way to view the repetition required to solve this problem is as follows:

Loop through the following steps:
    a. Enter a value for *FailTime*.
    b. Increment *NumTimes* by 1.
    c. Add *FailTime* to *Sum*.
End Loop.

It is clear that Steps b and c must not be performed when *FailTime* is equal to the sentinel value. This means that we need to terminate repetition in the middle of the loop (immediately following the input step), which suggests the use of a forever loop. The following algorithm adopts this approach:

===

ALGORITHM TO CALCULATE MEAN TIME TO FAILURE— SENTINEL-CONTROLLED FOREVER LOOP VERSION

/* This algorithm reads a sequence of failure times, counts and sums them, and then finds the mean time to failure.

    Input: A sequence of failure times, each stored in *FailTime*
    Constants: *Sentinel,* a value distinct from all possible failure times
    Output: The mean time to failure, and the number of times entered

0. Display instructions.
1. Initialize *NumTimes* to 0 and *Sum* to 0.0.
2. Forever loop:
      a. Enter a value for *FailTime*.
      b. If *FailTime* is equal to the *Sentinel*,
          Exit the loop.
      c. Increment *NumTimes* by 1.
      d. Add *FailTime* to *Sum*.
    End Loop.
3. If *NumTimes* ≠ 0 then
      a. Calculate *MeanFailTime* = *Sum/NumTimes*.
      b. Display *MeanFailTime* and *NumTimes*.
    Else
      Display a "No Data" message.
    End If.

The program in Figure 6.13 implements this algorithm.

FIGURE 6.13   Mean time to failure—sentinel-controlled forever loop version.

```
/* This program computes the mean of a list of component failure
   times. It does so using a sentinel-controlled forever loop
   with sentinel value -1.

   Input:   A list of fail times
   Output:  User prompts, number of fail times read, and their
            mean or a message indicating that no failure times
            were entered
------------------------------------------------------------------*/

#include <iostream.h>

int main(void)
{
   const int
      Sentinel = -1;                  // the end-of-data indicator

   cout << "\nThis program computes the mean failure time,\n"
        << "\tfor a list of component failure times.\n"
        << "\tEntering a failure time of " << Sentinel
        << " signals the end of data.\n\n";

   int
      NumTimes = 0;                   // number of failure times
   double
      FailTime,                       // the fail time being processed
      Sum = 0.0;                      // sum of the failure times
```

FIGURE 6.13 Mean time to failure—sentinel-controlled forever loop version. (cont.)

```
for (;;)                          // forever loop
{
    cout << "Please enter a failure time ("
        << Sentinel << " to quit): ";
    cin >> FailTime;

    if (FailTime == Sentinel)   //   if-break combination, that
        break;                  //      tests the sentinel value

    NumTimes++;
    Sum += FailTime;
}                                 // end loop

if (NumTimes > 0)
{
    double
        MeanFailTime = Sum / NumTimes; // the mean failure time

    cout << "\n\t--> The mean of the " << NumTimes
        << " failure times is " << MeanFailTime << "\n\n";
}
else
    cout << "\n*** No fail times were entered !\n\n";

return 0;
}
```

Sample run:

```
This program computes the mean failure time,
    given a list of component failure times.
    Entering a failure time of -1 signals the end of data.

Please enter a failure time (-1 to quit): 127
Please enter a failure time (-1 to quit): 123.5
Please enter a failure time (-1 to quit): 155.4
Please enter a failure time (-1 to quit): 99
Please enter a failure time (-1 to quit): 117.3
Please enter a failure time (-1 to quit): 201.5
Please enter a failure time (-1 to quit): -1

    --> The mean of the 6 failure times is 137.283333
```

The following trace table shows the values of the various objects on each iteration of the loop:

FailTime	FailTime == Sentinel	Action	NumTimes	Sum
No value	No value	Entry to the loop	0	0.0
127	False	Continue repetition	1	127
123.5	False	Continue repetition	2	250.5
155.4	False	Continue repetition	3	405.9
99	False	Continue repetition	4	504.9
117.3	False	Continue repetition	5	622.2
201.5	False	Continue repetition	6	823.7
−1	True	Terminate repetition	6	823.7

In general, the pattern of a forever loop used to implement a sentinel-controlled input loop is as follows:

Pattern for Sentinel-Controlled Forever Loop

```
const ValueType
   Sentinel = NonDataValue;

      .
      .
      .

for (;;)                    // forever loop
{
   Enter a Value to be processed.

   if (Value == Sentinel)
      break;

   Process the Value.
}                           // end loop
```

Input Loops Using End-of-File

An end-of-file condition can also be used with a forever loop to read and process input values. In the program in Figure 6.13, we would simply replace the declaration of the constant **Sentinel** with

```
const char
   EOFMark[] = "Control-D";
```

for a UNIX environment,

```
const char
    EOFMark[] = "Control-Z";
```

for a DOS environment, and replace the forever loop with

```
for (;;)                          // forever loop
{
    cout << "Please enter a failure time ("
        << EOFMark << " to quit): ";
    cin >> FailTime;

    if (cin.eof())                //   if-break combination, that

        break;                    //       checks for end of file

    NumTimes ++;
    Sum += FailTime;
}                                 // end loop
```

The following pattern for a general forever loop can be used to design end-of-file-controlled loops for input.

Pattern for End-Of-File-Controlled Forever Loop

```
for (;;)                    // forever loop
{
    Enter a Value to be processed.

    if (cin.eof())
        break;

    Process the Value.
}                           // end loop
```

Words of Warning

As with other loops, it is the programmer's responsibility to ensure that the statements within a forever loop eventually cause the termination condition to become true, since an infinite loop will result otherwise.

It might also be noted that a forever loop may contain multiple termination combinations:

```
for (;;)
{
    StatementList₁
    if (TerminationCondition₁) break;
    StatementList₂
    if (TerminationCondition₂) break;
    StatementList₃

        .
        .
        .

    StatementListₙ
    if (TerminationConditionₙ) break;
    StatementListₙ₊₁
}
```

However, multiple-exit loops make it more difficult to trace the flow of control through a program, since any of the termination conditions can cause control to exit the loop. For this reason, this practice should be avoided.

Exercises

1. Assuming that I, J, and K are integer variables, describe the output produced by each of the following program segments:

   (a)
   ```
   I = 0;
   J = 0;
   for (;;)
   {
       K = 2 * I * J;
       if (K > 10)
           break;
       cout << I << J << K << '\n';
       I++;
       J++;
   }
   cout << K << '\n\;
   ```

   (b)
   ```
   I = 0;
   J = 0;
   for (;;)
   {
       K = 2 * I * J;
       if (K > 10)
           break;
       cout << I << J << K << '\n';
       if (I + J > 5)
           break;
       I++;
       J++;
   }
   cout << K << '\n\;
   ```

(c)
```
I = 5;
for (;;)
{
   cout << I;
   I -= 2;
   if (I < 1)
      break;
   J = 0;
   for (;;)
   {
      J++;
      cout << J;
      if (J >= I)
         break;
   }
   cout << "###\n"
}
cout << "***\n"
```

2. Consider the following three program segments for finding the smallest value of *Number* for which the sum $1 + 2 + \cdots + Number$ is greater than *Limit:*

```
/* Using a while loop */
   Number = 0;
   Sum = 0;
   while (Sum <= Limit)
   {
      Number++;
      Sum += Number;
   }
/* Using a do-while loop */
   Number = 0;
   Sum = 0;
   do
   {
      Number++;
      Sum += Number;
   }
   while (Sum <= Limit);


/* Using a test-in-the middle loop */
   Number = 0;
   Sum = 0;
   for (;;)
   {
      Number++;
      if (Sum > Limit)
         break;
      Sum += Number;
   }
```

Make three trace tables, one for each of these program segments, each of which displays the values of **Number** and **Sum** for the following values of **Limit**:

(a) 10   (b) 1   (c) 0

3. Write a program that uses a sentinel-controlled or end-of-file-controlled forever loop to read data values as shown in the following table, calculates the miles per gallon in each case, and displays the values with appropriate labels:

Miles Traveled	Gallons of Gasoline Used
231	14.8
248	15.1
302	12.8
147	9.25
88	7
265	13.3

4. Write a program that uses a sentinel-controlled or end-of-file-controlled forever loop to read several values representing miles, converts miles to kilometers (1 mile = 1.60935 kilometers), and displays all values with appropriate labels.

5. Write a program that reads an exchange rate for converting English currency to U.S. currency and then reads several values in English currency and converts each amount into the equivalent amount in U.S. currency. Display all amounts with appropriate labels. Use a sentinel-controlled or end-of-file-controlled forever loop for the input.

6. Proceed as in the preceding exercise, but convert several values from U.S. currency to English currency.

6.5 Guidelines for Using Loops

In this section, we present a number of guidelines for using loops. Following these guidelines can prevent many of the common logic errors involving loops.

Choosing the Right Loop

With so many different kinds of loops, it can be difficult for a programmer (beginning or otherwise) to choose the kind of loop best suited for solving a particular problem. One simple guideline to follow in this decision is the following:

> The choice of a loop should be determined by the **nature of the problem being solved.**

This means that determining which kind of loop to use is part of the design phase of program development. If the algorithm is developed in sufficient detail, it will provide clues as to which loop to use. For example, if a set of instructions must be performed for all values in some range of values, then a counting loop is needed, implying that a for loop is the appropriate loop to use. However, if solving the problem does not involve counting through a fixed range of values or repeating the execution of statements a fixed number of times, then one of the more general loops—while, do-while, or forever—is a better choice.

The obvious next question is: If one of the more general loops should be used, on what basis do we choose the appropriate kind? One way to proceed is to use a *generic loop* of the form

Loop
    body-of-the-loop
End Loop.

in constructing the algorithm. We then develop the algorithm, adding any necessary initialization statements before the loop together with the statements that make up the body of the loop:

Initialization-statements
Loop
    Statement-1

         :
         :

    Statement-n
End Loop.

We must then formulate an appropriate termination condition and determine where in the loop it should be placed. Where it is placed determines which "standard" loop to use. If the termination condition is placed

- At the beginning of the loop, the loop is a pretest loop, that is, a while loop;
- At the bottom of the loop, the loop is a posttest loop, that is, a do-while loop;
- Within the list of statements, the loop is a test-in-the-middle loop; use a forever loop with an **if-break** (or **if-return**) combination.

To illustrate, consider again the problem of designing an algorithm for the bouncing ball problem. Using a generic loop, we might write a first version of the algorithm as follows:

1. Initialize *Bounce* 0.
2. Enter a value for *Height*.
3. Display original *Height* value with appropriate label.
4. Loop
    Replace *Height* with *Height* divided by 2.
    Add 1 to *Bounce*.
    Display *Bounce* and *Height*.
  End Loop.

Since repetition is to stop when *Height* is less than some *SmallNumber*, the condition

    Height < *SmallNumber*

can be used as a termination condition for the loop. However, the user could have entered zero or a negative value for *Height*, in which case none of the statements in the body of the loop should be executed. Thus, we should evaluate this condition immediately upon entering the loop:

1. Initialize *Bounce* to 0.
2. Enter a value for *Height*.
3. Display original *Height* value with appropriate label.
4. Loop
       If *Height* < *SmallNumber,* then exit the loop.
       Replace *Height* with *Height* divided by 2.
       Add 1 to *Bounce.*
       Display *Bounce* and *Height.*
    End Loop.

This is a pretest loop; therefore, we should use a while loop for Step 4, as we did in Section 6.2.

    By contrast, if we reconsider the ATM menu-choice problem using this approach, we construct the generic loop

    Loop
       Display the *Menu.*
       Input the user's *Choice.*
       Display an error message (if *Choice* is invalid);
    End Loop.

Since the purpose of this loop is to guarantee that the user enters a valid menu choice, an appropriate termination condition is

    Choice is a valid menu choice

Before this termination condition can be evaluated, *Choice* must have a value, and this value is obtained in the input statement; thus, the termination condition should be placed after this input statement:

    Loop
       Display the *Menu.*
       Input the user's *Choice.*
       If *Choice* is a valid menu choice, then exit from the loop.
       Display an error message.
    End Loop.

This is most conveniently implemented using a forever loop, as we did in the preceding section. If preferred, it can also be implemented as a pretest (while) loop:

> Set *Terminate* to false.
> While not *Terminate* do the following:
> > Display the *Menu.*
> > Input the user's *Choice.*
> > If *Choice* is a valid menu choice,
> > > Set *Terminate* to true.
> > Else
> > > Display an error message, and
> > > Set *Terminate* to false.
> End While.

It can also be implemented as a posttest (do-while) loop:

> Do
> > Display the *Menu.*
> > Input the user's *Choice.*
> > If *Choice* is a valid menu choice,
> > > Set *Terminate* to true.
> > Else
> > > Display an error message, and
> > > Set *Terminate* to false.
> While not *Terminate*.

Confusing = and ==

Loops are controlled by conditions, and as we have seen before, C++ conditions are simply expressions, in which a value of zero (0) is interpreted as the boolean value false, and a nonzero value is interpreted as the boolean value true. We have also seen that the assignment operator in C++ is an actual operator that returns a value. These two facts, combined with the ease with which the equality operator == can accidently be typed as an assignment operator = in a loop condition, can lead to loops that do not perform as expected.

To illustrate, consider a query-controlled loop of the form

```
do
{
    // ... perform some action that needs to be repeated

    cout << "\nDo you want to quit (y or n)? ";
    cin >> Response;
}
while (Response = 'n');
```

This loop will never terminate. The problem lies in the loop condition, where there is an assignment statement

```
Response = 'n'
```

instead of a comparison:

```
Response == 'n'
```

Regardless of what the user enters, the loop condition will assign the value **n** to **Response**, which on an ASCII system sets the value of **Response** to 110 (the ASCII value of **n**). This is then the value of the assignment expression and is interpreted as true. Consequently, the loop condition is never false, and the loop never terminates.

The similarity between the assignment operator and the equality operator makes these kinds of errors extremely difficult to find. We recommend double- and triple-checking any condition that is supposed to perform an equality comparison to make certain that an assignment is not inadvertently being performed.

Exercises

1. Write a C++ statement to

   (a) Print the value of **x** and decrease **x** by 0.5 as long as **x** is positive.
   (b) Read values for **a**, **b**, and **c** and print their sum, repeating this as long as none of **a**, **b**, or **c** is negative.
   (c) Print the squares of the first 100 positive integers in increasing order.
   (d) Print the cubes of the first 50 positive integers in decreasing order.
   (e) Print the square roots of the first 25 odd positive integers.
   (f) Calculate and print the squares of consecutive positive integers until the difference between a square and the preceding one is greater than 50.
   (g) Print a list of points (x, y) on the graph of $y = x^3 - 3x + 1$ for x ranging from -2 to 2 in steps of 0.1.

2. Write a program to read a set of numbers, count them, and calculate and display the mean, variance, and standard deviation of the set of numbers. The **mean** and **variance** of numbers $x_1, x_2, \ldots, x_n$ can be calculated using the formulas

$$\text{Mean} = \frac{1}{n}\sum_{i=1}^{n} x_i \qquad \text{Variance} = \frac{1}{n}\sum_{i=1}^{n} x_i^2 - \frac{1}{n^2}\left(\sum_{i=1}^{n} x_i\right)^2$$

The **standard deviation** is the square root of the variance.

6.6   Techniques for Testing and Debugging Loops

In Section 2.5 we noted that four types of errors may occur when we develop a program: syntax, or compile-time, errors, run-time errors, linking errors, and logical errors. **Syntax errors,** such as incorrect punctuation, unbalanced parentheses, and misspelled keywords, are detected during the program's compilation, and an appropriate error message is usually displayed. **Run-time errors,** such as division by zero, are detected during the program's execution; again, a suitable error message is often displayed. **Linking errors,** such as an incorrectly named library module, are detected during the linking phase. These three types of errors are, for the most part, relatively easy to correct, because the system error messages often indicate the type of error and where it occurred. **Logical errors,** however, are usually more difficult to detect, because they arise in the design of the algorithm or in coding the algorithm as a program, and in most cases, no error messages are displayed to assist the programmer in identifying such errors.

The "Programming Pointers" at the ends of the chapters of this book include warnings about some of the more common errors. As programs become increasingly complex, however, the logical errors that occur may be more subtle and consequently more difficult to identify and correct. In this section we consider a program that contains logical errors and describe techniques that are useful in detecting them.

An Example

Suppose that, as a programming exercise, your programming class has been asked to write a program to read a list of positive integers representing employee salaries in thousands of dollars and determine the salary range—that is, the difference between the largest salary and the smallest. The following opening documentation and declarations were given, and your task is to complete the program:

```
/* This program reads a list of salaries and determines the
   salary range.  (A sentinel salary value of 0 is used to
   indicate end-of-input).

   Input:   A list of salaries in thousands of dollars
   Output:  User prompts, labels, and the salary range
   ------------------------------------------------------------*/


#include <iostream.h>

int main(void)
{
   int
      Salary,          // the current salary being processed
      MaxSalary,       // largest salary read so far
      MinSalary;       // smallest salary read so far
}
```

Suppose that a classmate (not following the advice of the preceding sections) wrote the following program (lines have been numbered for easy reference):

```
 1   /* This program reads a list of salaries and determines the
 2       salary range.  (A sentinel salary value of 0 is used to
 3       indicate end-of-input).
 4
 5       Input:    A list of salaries in thousands of dollars.
 6       Output:   User prompts, labels, and the salary range.
 7   ------------------------------------------------------------*/
 8
 9   #include <iostream.h>
10   #include <limits.h>              // needed for INT_MAX to be defined
11
12   int main(void)
13   {
14       const int
15          Sentinel = 0;            // the end-of-data indicator
16       int
17          Salary,                  // the current salary being processed
18          MaxSalary = 0,           // largest salary read so far
19          MinSalary = INT_MAX;     // smallest salary read so far
20
21       cout << "Enter salaries in thousands of dollars (0 to stop).\n";
22
23       while (Salary != Sentinel)
24       {
25          cout << "\nEnter salary: ";
26          cin >> Salary;
27          if (Salary > MaxSalary)
28             MaxSalary = Salary;
29          else if (Salary < MinSalary)
30             MinSalary = Salary;
31       }
32
33       cout << "\nSalary range = " << MaxSalary - MinSalary
34             << " thousand dollars.\n\n";
35   }
```

Execution of the program produced the output

```
Enter salaries in thousands of dollars (0 to stop).
Salary range = 32767 thousand dollars.
```

and your classmate has brought the program to you to find out what is wrong. Since the prompt

```
Enter salary:
```

was never displayed, it is clear that the body of the while loop was not entered. This suggests that the loop condition

```
Salary != 0
```

that controls repetition was initially false, causing immediate termination.

This is, in fact, what happened. Since **Salary** had not been assigned a value before the while loop was encountered, **Salary** had an undefined value when the loop condition `Salary != Sentinel` was evaluated. The particular system in which the program was executed auto-initialized `Salary` with the value 0, making this loop condition false and causing the while loop to terminate immediately.

Ignoring the suggested pattern for a sentinel-controlled loop, the student modified the declaration of `Salary` to give it the initial value of 1 (ahead of the while loop) to force execution to enter the loop:

```
1    /* This program reads a list of salaries and determines the
2       salary range. (A sentinel salary value of 0 is used to
3       indicate end-of-input.)
4
5       Input:   A list of salaries in thousands of dollars.
6       Output:  User prompts, labels, and the salary range.
7       -----------------------------------------------------------*/
8
9    #include <iostream.h>
10   #include <limits.h>            // needed for INT_MAX to be defined
11
12   int main(void)
13   {
14      const int
15         Sentinel = 0;           // the end-of-data indicator
16      int
17         Salary = 1,             // the current salary being processed
18         MaxSalary = 0,          // largest salary read so far
19         MinSalary = INT_MAX;    // smallest salary read so far
20
21      cout << "Enter salaries in thousands of dollars (0 to stop).\n";
22
23      while (Salary != Sentinel)
24      {
25         cout << "\nEnter salary: ";
26         cin >> Salary;
27         if (Salary > MaxSalary)
28            MaxSalary = Salary;
29         else if (Salary < MinSalary)
30            MinSalary = Salary;
31      }
32
33      cout << "\nSalary range = " << MaxSalary - MinSalary
34           << " thousand dollars.\n\n";
35   }
```

This "quick and dirty solution" fixed the problem of premature termination of the while loop; after recompiling, execution of this revised program produced

```
Enter salaries in thousands of dollars (0 to stop).

Enter salary: 10
Enter salary: 7
Enter salary: 15
Enter salary: 0
Salary range = 15 thousand dollars.
```

Data values are read and processed, and the loop terminates when the sentinel 0 is read. Unfortunately, the correct salary range for this set of data is $8000, not the $15,000 computed by the program.

Trace Tables

In several of our examples of the preceding section, we used **trace tables** to trace the execution of an algorithm or part of a program. These trace tables may also be used to locate logical errors in a program by manually tracing execution through the segment of the program that is suspect. This technique is also known as **desk checking** and consists of recording in a table the values of all or certain key variables in the program segment, step by step. In this example, the following trace table for the while loop might be obtained:

Statements	Salary	MaxSalary	MinSalary	
	1	0	32767	←Initial values
23	1	0	32767	
26	10	0	32767	First pass through the loop
27–28	10	10	32767	
23	10	10	32767	
26	7	10	32767	Second pass through the loop
29–30	7	10	7	
23	7	10	7	
26	15	15	7	Third pass through the loop
27–28	15	15	7	
23	15	15	7	
26	0	15	7	Fourth pass through the loop
29–30	0	15	0	

The last line in this trace table shows why the salary range was incorrect: The value of **MinSalary** became 0 on the last pass through the loop, and this occurred because the sentinel value 0 was erroneously read and processed as a salary.

Debugging

An alternative way to trace the execution of a program segment is by using a special system program called a **debugger.**[11] If no debugger is available in the environment in which you are working, the same effect can be (less conveniently) achieved by inserting temporary output statements into your program to display the

---

[11] The Turbo and Symantec environments each provide an integrated set of debugging tools for tracing execution. Most UNIX environment provide the symbolic debugger **dbx**, but users of GNU emacs and **g++** will want to utilize **gdb**, GNU's symbolic debugger that is nicely integrated with emacs and the **g++** compiler.

values of key variables at selected stages of program execution. For example, we might insert the output statement

```
cout << "Salary = " << Salary << '\n';
```

after the input statement to echo the data values as they are entered and the statement

```
cout << "Max = " << MaxSalary
     << ", Min = " << MinSalary << '\n';
```

at the bottom of the loop in order to display the values of these variables at the end of each pass through the loop. The resulting output is then

```
Enter salaries in thousands of dollars (0 to stop).

Enter salary: 10
Salary = 10
Max = 10, Min = 32767

Enter salary: 7
Salary = 7
Max = 10, Min = 7

Enter salary: 15
Salary = 15
Max = 15, Min = 7

Enter salary: 0
Salary = 0
Max = 15, Min = 0

Salary range = 15 thousand dollars.
```

By displaying relevant information on each trip through the loop, it is possible to deduce that execution is proceeding correctly until the final trip. However, the word *relevant* is key: Displaying every value in the program, regardless of its significance, can make it harder to find an error. Similarly, unless these statements are placed at strategic points in the loop (e.g., the beginning and/or end of the loop), the information they display may provide little insight into the problem.

Modifying and Testing the Program

Either manual or automatic tracing of this program reveals that the source of difficulty is that the sentinel value 0 is being processed as an actual salary. A first reaction might be to fix this error by using a nested **if** statement:

```
if (Salary != Sentinel)
   if (Salary > MaxSalary)
      MaxSalary = Salary;
   else if (Salary < MinSalary)
      MinSalary = Salary;
```

Patches like this one and the one used earlier are not recommended, however, because they often fail to address the real source of the problem and make the program unnecessarily complicated and messy.

The real source of difficulty in the preceding example is that the student did not use the correct technique for reading and processing data. Using one of the recommended patterns of the preceding sections for a sentinel-controlled loop will solve the problem in the first version of the program.

Using the standard form of a sentinel-controlled while loop for reading and processing data, the student modified the program as follows:

```
1   /* This program reads a list of salaries and determines the
2       salary range. (A sentinel salary value of 0 is used to
3       indicate end-of-input.)
4
5       Input:    A list of salaries in thousands of dollars.
6       Output:   User prompts, labels, and the salary range.
7   ------------------------------------------------------------*/
8
9   #include <iostream.h>
10  #include <limits.h>           // needed for INT_MAX to be defined
11
12  int main(void)
13  {
14 const int
15     Sentinel = 0;             // the end-of-data indicator
16 int
17     Salary = 1,               // the current salary being processed
18     MaxSalary = 0,            // largest salary read so far
19     MinSalary = INT_MAX;      // smallest salary read so far,
20
21 cout << "Enter salaries in thousands of dollars (0 to stop).\n";
22
23 cout << "\nEnter first salary: ";
24 cin >> Salary;               // read first salary before while loop
25
26 while (Salary != Sentinel)
27 {
28     if (Salary > MaxSalary)
29         MaxSalary = Salary;
30     else if (Salary < MinSalary)
31         MinSalary = Salary;
32
33     cout << "\nEnter next salary: ";
34     cin >> Salary;           // read next salary at bottom of loop
35 }
36
37 cout << "\nSalary range = " << MaxSalary - MinSalary
38         << " thousand dollars.\n\n";
39  }
```

A sample run using the same data values now produced the correct output:

```
Enter salaries in thousands of dollars (0 to stop).

Enter first salary: 10
Enter next salary: 7
Enter next salary: 15
Enter next salary: 0
Salary range = 8 thousand dollars.
```

The student may now be tempted to conclude that the program is correct. However, to establish confidence in the correctness of a program, it is necessary to test it with several sets of data. For example, the following sample run reveals that the program still contains a logical error:

```
Enter salaries in thousands of dollars (0 to stop).

Enter first salary: 7
Enter next salary: 10
Enter next salary: 15
Enter next salary: 0
Salary range = -32752 thousand dollars.
```

Tracing the execution of the while loop produces the following:

Statements	Salary	MaxSalary	MinSalary	
	?	0	32767	←Initial values
25	7	0	32767	
27–28	7	7	32767	First pass through the loop
31–32	7	7	32767	
25	10	7	32767	
27–28	10	10	32767	Second pass through the loop
31–32	10	10	32767	
25	15	10	32767	
27–28	15	15	32767	Third pass through the loop
31–32	15	15	32767	

This trace table reveals that the value of **MinSalary** never changes, suggesting that the statement

```
MinSalary = Salary;
```

is never executed. This is because the boolean expression **Salary > MaxSalary** is true for each data value, since these values are entered in increasing order;

consequently the **else if** part of the **if** statement is never executed. This error can be corrected by replacing the **if-else-if** with two **if** statements:

```
if (Salary > MaxSalary)
    MaxSalary = Salary;
if (Salary < MinSalary)
    MinSalary = Salary;
```

The resulting program is then correct but is not as efficient as it could be, since the boolean expressions in both of these **if** statements must be evaluated on each pass through the loop. Constructing an alternative that avoids this inefficiency is described in Exercise 1.

Summary

Logical errors may be very difficult to detect, especially as programs become more complex, and so it is important that test data be carefully selected so that each part of the program is thoroughly tested. The program should be executed with data values entered in several different orders, with both large and small data sets, with extreme values, and with "bad" data. For example, entering the salaries in increasing order revealed the existence of a logical error in the program considered earlier. Also, even though the last version of the program will produce correct output if legitimate data values are read, the output

```
Salary range = -32767 thousand dollars.
```

would be produced if the value 0 were entered immediately. Although it may not be necessary to guard against invalid data input in student programs, those written for the general public, especially programs used by computer novices, should be as **robust** as possible and should not "crash" or produce "garbage" results when unexpected data values are entered.

When a logical error is detected, a trace table is an effective tool for locating the error. Once it has been found, the program must be corrected and then tested again. It may be necessary to repeat this cycle of testing, tracing, and correcting many times before the program produces correct results for a wide range of test data, allowing us to be reasonably confident of its correctness. It is not possible, however, to check a program with every possible set of data, and thus obscure bugs may still remain. In some applications, this may not be critical, but in others, for example, in programs used to guide a space shuttle, errors cannot be tolerated. Certain **formal verification techniques** have been developed for proving that a program is correct and will always execute correctly (assuming no system malfunction), but a study of these techniques is beyond the scope of this introductory text.

Exercises

1. Write a program that solves the salary range problem discussed in this section but is more efficient than those described in the text. (*Hint:* Initialize **MaxSalary** and **MinSalary** to the first data value after it has been read.)

2. For each of the following data sets, construct a trace table for the repetition structure used in the program of Exercise 1 and determine the salary range that will be computed by your program:

(a) 7, 15, 10, −1   (b) 7, 10, 15, −1   (c) 15, 10, 7, −1
(d) 7, −1   (e) −1

6.7   Example: Depreciation Tables

We have now considered all the statements provided in C++ for implementing the basic control structures:

Control Structure	C++ Implementation
Sequential	Compound statement
Selection	**if** statement **switch** statement
Repetition	**for** statement **while** statement **do-while** statement forever loop

We are also familiar with functions and libraries, which play an important role in the modular design of software. In this section we demonstrate how these are used in a program that solves the problem of calculating depreciation.

Problem: Depreciation Tables

Depreciation is a decrease in the value over time of some asset due to wear and tear, decay, declining price, and so on. For example, suppose that a company purchases a new computer system for $200,000 that will serve its needs for 5 years. After that time it can be sold at an estimated price of $50,000. Thus, the value of the computing equipment will have depreciated $150,000 over the 5-year period.

The calculation of depreciation tables that display the value lost in each of several years is an important accounting problem, and there are several ways of calculating depreciation. One of the simplest methods is the **straight-line method,** in which the amount to be depreciated is divided evenly over the specified number of years. For example, straight-line depreciation of $150,000 over a 5-year period gives an annual depreciation of $150,000/5 = $30,000. An algorithm for calculating depreciation using this method is simple:

ALGORITHM FOR STRAIGHT-LINE DEPRECIATION

/* This algorithm depreciates a given amount over a given number of years, using the straight-line method of calculating depreciation.

Receive: An *Amount* and number of years (*NumYears*)
Output: A depreciation table
——*/

1. Calculate *Depreciation* = *Amount/NumYears*.
2. For *Year* ranging from 1 through *NumYears* do the following:
   Display *Year* and *Depreciation*.
   End For.

The C++ function in Figure 6.14 implements this algorithm. (The header file **<iomanip.h>** must be inserted using the **#include** directive in any program or library that contains this function in order for the **setw()** manipulator to be defined.)

 FIGURE 6.14   Straight-line depreciation.

```
/*-------------------------------------------------------------
StraightLine computes the depreciation of Amount over NumYears,
   using the straight-line method.

   Receive: A (double) Amount, and (int) NumYears
   Output:  A depreciation table
-------------------------------------------------------------*/

void StraightLine(double Amount, int NumYears)
{
   double
      Depreciation = Amount / NumYears;

   cout << "\nYear - Depreciation"
        << "\n------------------\n";

                                      //set up format for $$
   cout << setiosflags(ios::showpoint | ios::fixed)
        << setprecision(2);

   for (int Year = 1; Year <= NumYears; Year++)
      cout << setw(3) << Year
           << setw(11) << Depreciation << '\n';
}
```

Another common method of calculating depreciation is the **sum-of-the-years-digits method.** To illustrate it, consider again depreciating $150,000 over a 5-year period. We first calculate the "sum of the years," $1 + 2 + 3 + 4 + 5 = 15$. In the first year, 5/15 of \$150,000 (\$50,000) is depreciated; in the second year, $\frac{4}{15}$ of \$150,000 (\$40,000) is depreciated; and so on, giving the following depreciation table:

Year	Depreciation
1	\$50,000
2	\$40,000
3	\$30,000
4	\$20,000
5	\$10,000

An algorithm for calculating depreciation using this method is as follows:

ALGORITHM FOR SUM-OF-THE-YEARS-DIGITS DEPRECIATION

/* This algorithm depreciates a given amount over a given number of years, using the sum-of-the-years-digits method of calculating depreciation.

Receive: An *Amount* and number of years (*NumYears*)
Output: A depreciation table
_____ */

1. Calculate *Sum* = $1 + 2 + \cdots + NumYears$.
2. For *Year* ranging from 1 through *NumYears* do the following:
   a. Calculate
      Depreciation = (*NumYears* − *Year* + 1) ∗ *Amount*/*Sum*
   b. Display *Year* and *Depreciation*.
   End For.

Figure 6.15 presents a function that implements this algorithm.

FIGURE 6.15 Sum-of-years-digits depreciation.

```
/*------------------------------------------------------------
SumOfYears displays the depreciation of Amount over NumYears,
   using the sum-of-years-digits method.

   Receive: A (double) Amount, and (int) NumYears
   Output:  A depreciation table
------------------------------------------------------------*/
```

FIGURE 6.15   Sum-of-years-digits depreciation. (cont.)

```
void SumOfYears(double Amount, int NumYears)
{
   double
      Depreciation;
   int
      Sum = 0;

   for (int Year = 1; Year <= NumYears; Year++)
      Sum += Year;

   cout << "\nYear - Depreciation"
        << "\n-------------------\n";

                                       //set up format for $$
   cout << setiosflags(ios::showpoint | ios::fixed)
        << setprecision(2);

   for (Year = 1; Year <= NumYears; Year++)
   {
      Depreciation = (NumYears - Year + 1) * Amount / Sum;
      cout << setw(3) << Year
           << setw(11) << Depreciation << '/n';
   }
}
```

A third method of calculating depreciation is the **double-declining balance method.** In this method, if an amount is to be depreciated over n years, $2/n$ times the undepreciated balance is depreciated annually. For example, in the depreciation of \$150,000 over a 5-year period using the double-declining balance method, $\frac{2}{5}$ of \$150,000 (\$60,000) would be depreciated the first year, leaving an undepreciated balance of \$90,000. In the second year, $\frac{2}{5}$ of \$90,000 (\$36,000) would be depreciated, leaving an undepreciated balance of \$54,000. Since only a fraction of the remaining balance is depreciated in each year, the entire amount will never be depreciated. Consequently, it is permissible to switch to the straight-line method at any time. Developing an algorithm and function for this method of calculating depreciation is left as an exercise.

Using the Depreciation Functions

The program in Figure 6.16 is a menu-driven program for computing depreciation tables. A **DisplayMenu()** function is used to display the menu

```
Please enter:
    A - to enter a new Amount and/or Number of Years,
    B - to use the straight-line method,
    C - to use the sum-of-years-digits method,
    D - to re-display this menu, or
    Q - to quit.
```

A do-while loop is used to read menu choices from the user until **Q** is selected.

```
do
{
   Option = GetMenuChoice();        // get user's choice
      .
      .
      .
   // perform the option selected
      .
      .
      .
}
while (Option != 'Q');
```

The user may enter either lower- or uppercase menu choices. To simplify the processing of the choice, a lowercase choice is converted to uppercase using the character-processing capabilities provided by the **islower()** and **toupper()** functions available in the file **<ctype.h>**.[12]

A **switch** statement is used to process that option:

```
switch (Option)       // perform the option selected
   {
   case 'A':             // get new Amount & NumYears
      cout << "\nHow much money is to be depreciated? ";
      cin >> Amount;
      cout << "Over how many years? ";
      cin >> NumYears;
      break;
   case 'B':             // do straight-line method
      StraightLine(Amount, NumYears);
      break;
   case 'C':             // do sum-of-years-digits method
      SumOfYears(Amount, NumYears);
      break;
   case 'D':             // redisplay the menu
      DisplayMenu();
      break;
   case 'Q':             // do nothing -- stop procession
      break;
   default:              // execution should never get here
      cerr << "*** Invalid menu choice: "  << Option << ".\n";
      DisplayMenu();
   }
```

Here, **StraightLine()** and **SumOfYears()** are the functions defined previously. Because these functions might also prove useful in some other program, they were stored in a module **Deprec**, from which a program can access them. The remaining

---

[12] The functions islower() and toupper() are from the C library ctype.h. A program or library that contains this function must use the #include directive to insert the header file < ctype.h> . The character-processing operations provided by this file are extremely useful; see < ctype.h> for a complete list.

functions, `DisplayMenu()` and `GetMenuChoice()`, simply carry out the operations selected by the user, and since it is unlikely that they will be reused, they are stored in the same file as the main function.

FIGURE 6.16 Methods of depreciation (driver program).

```
/* This program calculates and displays depreciation tables
   using various methods of computing the depreciation.

   Input:   User-selected options, amounts to be depreciated,
            and number of years
   Output:  User prompts, menu of options, and depreciation tables


---------------------------------------------------------------*/

#include <iostream.h>

#include "Deprec.h"               // module of depreciation functions

void DisplayMenu(void);           // function to display the menu
char GetMenuChoice(void);         // function to input user choice

int main(void)
{
    cout << "\nThis program computes depreciation tables,\n"
         << "\tusing various methods of depreciation.\n";

    char
        Option;                   // menu option selected by user
    int
        NumYears = 0;             // number of years
    double
        Amount = 0.0;             // amount to be depreciated

    DisplayMenu();                // show the menu at the outset

    do
    {
        Option = GetMenuChoice(); // get user's choice

        switch (Option)           // perform the option selected
        {
            case 'A':             // get new Amount & NumYears
                cout << "\nHow much money is to be depreciated? ";
                cin >> Amount;
                cout << "Over how many years? ";
                cin >> NumYears;
                break;
            case 'B':             // do straight-line method
                StraightLine(Amount, NumYears);
                break;
```

FIGURE 6.16 Methods of depreciation (driver program). (cont.)

```
        case 'C':                  // do sum-of-years-digits method
          SumOfYears(Amount, NumYears);
          break;
        case 'D':                  // redisplay the menu
          DisplayMenu();
          break;
        case 'Q':                  // do nothing--stop procession
          break;
        default:                   // execution should never get here
          cerr << "*** Invalid menu choice: " << Option << ".\n";
          DisplayMenu();
      }
   }
   while (Option != 'Q');

   return 0;
}


/*--------------------------------------------------------------------
DisplayMenu outputs the menu of operations supported by the program.

   Output: The menu of options
----------------------------------------------------------------------*/

void DisplayMenu(void)
{
   cout << "\nPlease enter:\n"
        << "\tA - to enter a new Amount and/or Number of Years,\n"
        << "\tB - to use the straight-line method,\n"
        << "\tC - to use the sum-of-years-digits method,\n"
        << "\tD - to re-display this menu, or\n"
        << "\tQ - to quit.\n";
}


/*-----------------------------------------------------------------
GetMenuChoice reads and returns a menu choice.

   Output:  prompts for input.
   Input:   the user's (char) Choice.
   Return:  that choice.
------------------------------------------------------------------*/

#include <ctype.h>               // provides islower(), toupper()

char GetMenuChoice(void)
{
   char
      Choice;                    // the user\'s menu choice
```

FIGURE 6.16   Methods of depreciation (driver program). (cont.)

```
    cout << "\nOption? ";        // prompt the user
    cin >> Choice;               // input their choice
    if (islower(Choice))         // if choice is uppercase
      Choice = toupper(Choice);  //   convert it to lowercase

    return Choice;
}
```

Sample run:

```
This program computes depreciation tables,
   using various methods of depreciation.

Please enter:
   A - to enter a new Amount and/or Number of Years,
   B - to use the straight-line method,
   C - to use the sum-of-years-digits method,
   D - to re-display this menu, or
   Q - to quit.

Option? a

How much money is to be depreciated? 1500.00
Over how many years? 5

Option? b

Year - Depreciation
-------------------
   1        300.00
   2        300.00
   3        300.00
   4        300.00
   5        300.00

Option? c

Year - Depreciation
-------------------
   1        500.00
   2        400.00
   3        300.00
   4        200.00
   5        100.00

Option? x

*** Invalid menu choice: x
```

FIGURE 6.16 Methods of depreciation (driver program). (cont.)

```
Please enter:
    A - to enter a new Amount and/or Number of Years,
    B - to use the straight-line method,
    C - to use the sum-of-years-digits method,
    D - to re-display this menu, or
    Q - to quit.

Option? a

How much money is to be depreciated? 1000.00
Over how many years? 3

Option? b

Year - Depreciation
-------------------
    1       333.33
    2       333.33
    3       333.33

Option? q
```

Exercises

1. Develop an algorithm for the third method of calculating depreciation (double-declining balance combined with straight-line) described in this section.

2. Modify the program in Figure 6.14 so that it includes this third method of calculating depreciation as one of the options. Also, modify the output so that the year numbers in all the depreciation tables begin with the current year rather than with year number 1.

6.8 PART OF THE PICTURE: Introduction to Numeric Computation

Mathematical models are used to solve problems in a wide variety of areas including science, engineering, business, and the social sciences. Many of these models consist of ordinary algebraic equations, differential equations, systems of equations, and so on, and the solution of the problem is obtained by finding solutions of these equations. Methods for solving such equations that can be implemented in a computer program are called **numerical methods,** and the development and analysis of such numerical methods is an important area of study in computer science.

Some of the major types of problems in which numerical methods are routinely used include the following.

1. *Curve fitting.* In many applications, the solution of a problem requires analyzing data consisting of pairs of values to determine whether the items in these pairs are related. For example, a sociologist might wish to determine whether there is a linear relationship between educational level and income level.

2. *Solving equations.* Such problems deal with finding the value of a variable that satisfies a given equation.

3. *Integration.* The solution of many problems such as finding area under a curve, determining total revenue generated by sales of an item, calculating probabilities of certain events, and calculating work done by a force require the evaluation of an integral. Often these integrals can be evaluated only by using numerical techniques.

4. *Differential equations.* Differential equations involve one or more derivatives of functions and play an important role in many different applications. Several effective and efficient numerical methods for solving these equations have been developed.

5. *Solving linear systems.* Linear systems consist of several linear equations, each of which has several unknowns. A solution of such a system is a collection of values for these unknowns that satisfies all of the equations simultaneously.

The numerical methods for all of these problems use repetition. In this section, we consider simple numerical methods for two of these areas: curve fitting and solving equations. Numerical methods for performing integration, solving differential equations, and solving linear systems are either described in the exercises or considered in subsequent chapters.

Curve Fitting: Least Squares Line

Suppose the following table contains a small part of the data collected in an survey designed to determine what relationship (if any) exists between the annual income of a student's parents and the composite score earned by the student on a series of college entrance exams:

Income ($ thousands)	Composite Score
20.0	761
31.5	817
50.0	874
71.8	917
91.3	1018

The plot of this data in Figure 6.17 indicates a linear relationship between income and score. We wish to find the equation of the line that ''best fits'' this data.

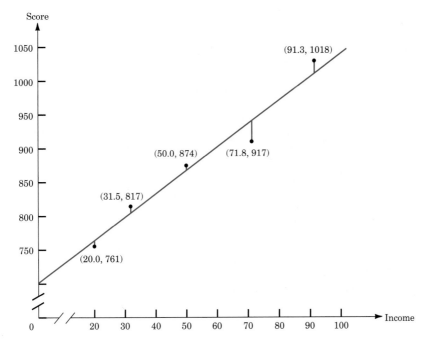

FIGURE 6.17   Least squares line.

In general, whenever the relation between two quantities x and y appears to be roughly linear—that is, when a plot of the points (x, y) indicates that they tend to fall along a straight line—one can ask for the equation

$$y = mx + b$$

of the line that best fits these points. This equation (called a **regression equation**) can then be used to predict the value of y corresponding to a given value of x by evaluating the equation at that point.

A standard method for finding the **regression coefficients** m and b is the **method of least squares,** so named because it produces the line $y = mx + b$, for which the sum of the squares of the deviations of the observed y values from the predicted y values (using the equation) is as small as possible (see Figure 6.17); that is, values of m and b are found to minimize the sum

$$\sum_{i=1}^{n} [y_i - (mx_i + b)]^2 = [y_1 - (mx_1 + b)]^2 + [y_2 - (mx_2 + b)]^2 + \cdots + [y_n - (mx_n + b)]^2$$

Using the methods of calculus for minimizing a function of two variables, we obtain the following formulas for the slope m and the y-intercept b:

$$\text{Slope} = m = \frac{(\Sigma xy) - (\Sigma x)\bar{y}}{(\Sigma x^2) - (\Sigma x)\bar{x}}$$

$$y\text{-intercept} = b = \bar{y} - m\bar{x}$$

where

Σx is the sum of the x values.
Σx^2 is the sum of the squares of the x values.
Σxy is the sum of the products xy of corresponding x and y values.
$\bar{x}$ and $\bar{y}$ are the means of the x and y values, respectively.

The program in Figure 6.18 calls function **DoLeastSquares()**, which uses these formulas to find the equation of the least squares line for a given set of data points. Note that this program uses the end-of-file marker to control the repetition. It implements the following algorithm:

ALGORITHM FOR LEAST SQUARES LINE

/* Find the equation of the least squares line for a set of n data points (x, y). *Slope* is its slope, and *YIntercept* is its y intercept. *SumX, SumY, SumX2,* and *SumXY* are the sums of the xs, the ys, the squares of the xs, and the products $x*y$. *XMean* and *YMean* are the means of the xs and the ys, respectively.

Input: A collection of data points (x, y)
Output: The equation of the least squares line

———*/

1. Initialize n, *SumX, SumY, SumX2,* and *SumXY* all to 0.
2. Read the x-coordinate of the first data point x.
3. While the end of data has not been encountered, do the following:
    a. Read the y-coordinate of the data point, y.
    b. Increment n by 1.
    c. Add x to *SumX*.
    d. Add x^2 to *SumX2*.
    e. Add y to *SumY*.
    f. Add $x*y$ to *SumXY*.
    g. Read the next data point x, y.
    End While.
4. If $n > 0$ then
    a. Calculate:

$$XMean = \frac{SumX}{n}$$

    and

$$YMean = \frac{SumY}{n}$$

    b. Calculate:

$$Slope = \frac{SumXY - SumX*YMean}{SumX2 - SumX*XMean}$$

and

$$YIntercept = YMean - Slope * XMean$$

    c. Display *Slope* and *YIntercept.*
Else
    Display a message that no data points were read.
End If.

The function `DoLeastSquares()` in the program in Figure 6.18 implements this algorithm.

    FIGURE 6.18   Least squares line.

```
/* Find the equation of the least squares line, given a set of
   data points.

   Input:    A set of data points
   Output:   User prompts and equation of least squares line
-----------------------------------------------------------------*/

#include <iostream.h>

void DoLeastSquares(void);

int main(void)
{
   cout << "\nGiven a set of data points, this program finds the"
        << "\n\tequation of the least squares line to fit that data "
        << "set.\n\n";

   DoLeastSquares();

   return 0;
}

-----------------------------------------------------------------*/
DoLeastSquares performs the least squares algorithm.

   Input:    A set of data points
   Output:   User prompts and equation of least squares line
-----------------------------------------------------------------*/

void DoLeastSquares(void)
{
   const char
      EOFMarker[] = "Control-D";
```

FIGURE 6.18 Least squares line. (cont.)

```
int
   n = 0;                           // number of data points

double
   x,                               // x-coordinate of current data point
   y,                               // y-coordinate of current data point
   SumX = 0.0,                      // sum of the xs
   SumY = 0.0,                      // sum of the ys
   SumX2 = 0.0,                     // sum of the squares of the xs
   SumXY = 0.0;                     // sum of the x*y products

cout << "Enter x, y of data point ("    // prompt for input
     << EOFMarker << " to quit) ? ";
cin >> x;                          // get first x-coordinate

while (!cin.eof())                 // while not end-of-data
{
   cin >> y;                       //    get the y-coord

   n++;                            //    update the count
   SumX += x;                      //    update the sums
   SumY += y;
   SumX2 += (x * x);
   SumXY += (x * y);
   cout << "Enter x, y of data point (" //   prompt for input
        << EOFMarker << " to quit) ? ";
   cin >> x;                       //    get next x-coordinate
}                                  // end-of-while

if (n > 0)                         // if positive n,
{                                  //    compute &
   double                          //      output results:
      XMean = SumX / n,            //      mean of the xs
      YMean = SumY / n,            //      mean of the ys
      Slope = (SumXY - SumX * YMean)   //    slope, and
              / (SumX2 - SumX * XMean),
      YIntercept = (YMean - Slope * XMean);
                                   //      y intercept
                                   //    of least squares line

   cout << "\n\n--> The least squares line equation is y = mx + b"
        << "\n\t whose Slope = m = " << Slope
        << ", and Y-intercept = b = " << YIntercept
        << "\n\n";

}
else
   cout << "\n--> No data points to process! \n\n";
}
```

FIGURE 6.18   Least squares line. (cont.)

Sample run:

```
Given a set of data points, this program finds the equation
   of the least squares line to fit that data set.

Enter x, y of data point (Control-D to quit) ? 20 761
Enter x, y of data point (Control-D to quit) ? 31.5 817
Enter x, y of data point (Control-D to quit) ? 50 874
Enter x, y of data point (Control-D to quit) ? 71.8 917
Enter x, y of data point (Control-D to quit) ? 91.3 1018
Enter x, y of data point (Control-D to quit) ? ^D

--> The least squares line equation is y = mx + b
     whose Slope = m = 3.33658, and Y-intercept = b = 700.828
```

Solving Equations

In many applications, it is necessary to solve an equation of the form

$$f(x) = 0$$

For some functions f, it may be very difficult or even impossible to find an exact solution. Examples include the equation

$$50 \cdot 10^{-9}(e^{40v} - 1) + v - 20 = 0$$

which may arise in a problem of determining the dc operating point in an electrical circuit, or the equation

$$A - P\frac{(1 + r)^n - 1}{r(1 + r)^n} = 0$$

which can be solved to find the monthly interest rate r for a loan amount A, where P is the payment to be made for a period of n months.

   For such equations, a repetitive numerical method may be used to find an approximate solution. One such method is the **bisection method.** In this method, we begin with two numbers a and b, where the function values $f(a)$ and $f(b)$ have opposite signs. If f is continuous between $x = a$ and $x = b$—that is, if there is no break in the graph of $y = f(x)$ between these two values—then the graph of f must cross the x-axis at least once between $x = a$ and $x = b$; thus, there must be at least one solution of the equation $f(x) = 0$ between a and b. To locate one of these solutions, we first bisect the interval $[a, b]$ and determine in which half f changes sign, thereby locating a smaller subinterval containing a solution of the equation. We bisect this subinterval and determine in which half of it f changes sign; this gives a still smaller subinterval containing a solution.

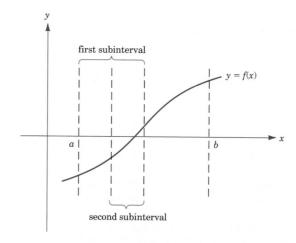

Repeating this process gives a sequence of subintervals, each of which contains a solution of the equation and has a length one-half that of the preceding interval. Note that at each step, the midpoint of a subinterval of length L is within $L/2$ of the exact solution:

The program in Figure 6.19 calls the function **Bisector()**, which uses the bisection method to find an approximate solution of

$$f(x) = x^3 + x - 5 = 0$$

It begins by having the user enter the accuracy desired in the answers, and this is followed by a do-while loop that asks the user to enter values of **a** and **b** for which **f(a)** and **f(b)** have opposite signs, terminating when such values are entered. It then calls function **Bisector()**, which generates successive approximations to a solution using the bisection method, terminating when **Length** is less than or equal to **DesiredAccuracy**, where **Length** is the length of the subinterval containing a solution and **DesiredAccuracy** is a value entered by the user to specify how accurate the approximation should be. The midpoint of this subinterval is the approximate solution of the equation.

FIGURE 6.19 Bisection method.

```
/* Find an approximate solution of the equation F(x) = 0 in a given
   interval, using the bisection method.

   Input:   Desired accuracy of approximation, endpoints of an
            interval containing a solution
   Output:  Prompts to the user and the approximate solution

Notes:
   1. The solution will be within DesiredAccuracy of the exact
      solution.
   2. To find the solution for a different F(x), redefine F() below.
-------------------------------------------------------------------*/

double F(double x)
{
   return x*x*x + x - 5;        // the function F for which the
}                               // equation F(x) = 0 is being solved

//------------------------------------------------------------------

#include <iostream.h>

double Bisector(double, double, double);

int main(void)
{
   cout << "\nThis program uses the bisection method to find an\n"
        << "\tapproximate solution to the equation F(x) = 0.\n";

   double
      DesiredAccuracy;        // the accuracy desired

   cout << "\nEnter the accuracy desired (e.g. .001): ";
   cin >> DesiredAccuracy;

   double
      Left,
      Right;

   do                         // get the interval containing a solution
   {
      cout << "Enter the x-values of interval containing solution: ";
      cin >> Left >> Right;
   }
   while (F(Left) * F(Right) >= 0.0);

   double                     // solve the equation
      Solution = Bisector(Left, Right, DesiredAccuracy);
```

FIGURE 6.19   Bisection method. (cont.)

```
   cout << "\n--> "<< Solution
       << " is an approximate solution of F(x) = 0, to within "
       << DesiredAccuracy << ".\n\n";

   return 0;
}
```

```
--------------------------------------------------------------------*/
Bisector performs the bisection algorithm.

   Receive: Left, the left endpoint of the original interval
            Right, the right endpoint of the original interval
            Accuracy, the desired accuracy of the approximation
   Return:  MidPt, the middle of the final interval
--------------------------------------------------------------------*/

double Bisector(double Left, double Right, double Accuracy)
{
   double
      Width = Right - Left,          // the interval width
      MidPt,                         // the midpoint of the interval
      fMid;                          // value of F at Midpoint

   while (Width/2.0 > Accuracy)      // While loop
   {
      MidPt = (Left + Right) / 2.0;  //    compute midpoint
      fMid = F(MidPt);               //    compute function at midpoint

      if (F(Left) * fMid < 0.0 )     //    solution is in left half
         Right = MidPt;
      else                           //    solution is in right half
         Left = MidPt;

      Width /= 2.0;                  //    split the interval
   }                                 // End While

   return MidPt;
}
```

Sample run:

```
This program uses the bisection method to find an
        approximate solution to the equation F(x) = 0.

Enter the accuracy desired (e.g. .001): 1E-4
Enter the x-values of interval containing solution: 0 1
Enter the x-values of interval containing solution: 1 2

--> 1.51599 is an approximate solution of F(x) = 0, to within 0.0001.
```

1. The infinite series

$$\sum_{k=0}^{\infty} \frac{1}{k!}$$

converges to the number e, whose approximate value is 2.71828. (See Programming Project 1 at the end of this chapter for a definition of $k!$, the factorial of k.) The nth *partial sum* of such a series is the sum of the first n terms of the series; for example,

$$\frac{1}{0!} + \frac{1}{1!} + \frac{1}{2!} + \frac{1}{3!}$$

is the fourth partial sum. Write a program to calculate and print the first 10 partial sums of this series.

2. In this section we considered the problem of fitting a line to a set of data points. In some situations, a better fit is obtained by using an exponential function

$$y = ae^{bx}$$

One common method for determining the constants a and b is to take logarithms of both sides of the exponential equation to obtain

$$\ln y = \ln a + bx$$

and then use the method of least squares to find values of the constants b and $\ln a$. Write a program that uses this method to fit an exponential curve to a set of data points. Run it for the values in the following table, which gives the barometric pressure readings, in millimeters of mercury, at various altitudes:

Altitude (Meters) x	Barometric Pressure (Millimeters) y
0	760
500	714
1000	673
1500	631
2000	594
2500	563

3. Related to the least squares method is the problem of determining whether there is a linear relationship between two quantities x and y. One statistical measure used in this connection is the *correlation coefficient*. It is equal to 1 if there is a perfect positive linear relationship between x and y, that is, if y increases linearly as x increases. If there is a perfect negative linear relationship between x and y—that is, if y decreases linearly as x increases—then the correlation coefficient has the value -1. A value of zero for the correlation coefficient indicates that there is no linear relationship between x and y, and nonzero values between -1 and 1 indicate a partial linear relationship between the two quantities. The correlation coefficient for a set of n pairs of x and y values is calculated by

$$\frac{n(\Sigma xy) - (\Sigma x)(\Sigma y)}{\sqrt{(n\Sigma x^2 - (\Sigma x)^2)(n\Sigma y^2 - (\Sigma y)^2)}}$$

where

Σx is the sum of all the x values.
Σy is the sum of all the y values.
Σx^2 is the sum of the squares of the x values.
Σy^2 is the sum of the squares of the y values.
Σxy is the sum of the products xy of corresponding x and y values.

Write a program to calculate the correlation coefficient of a set of data points. Run it for the data points used in the sample run in Figure 6.18 and for several data sets of your own.

4. Another method for finding an approximate solution of an equation $f(x) = 0$ is **Newton's method.** This method consists of taking an initial approximation x_1 to the solution and constructing the tangent line to the graph of f at point $P_1(x_1, f(x_1))$. The point x_2 at which this tangent line crosses the x-axis is the second approximation to the solution. Another tangent line may be constructed at point $P_2(x_2, f(x_2))$, and the point x_3 where this tangent line crosses the x-axis is the third approximation. For many functions, this sequence of approximations $x_1, x_2, x_3, \ldots$ converges to the solution, provided that the first approximation is sufficiently close to the solution. The following diagram illustrates Newton's method:

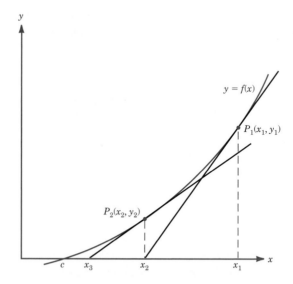

If x_n is an approximation to the solution of $f(x) = 0$, then the formula for obtaining the next approximation x_{n+1} by Newton's method is

$$x_{n+1} = x_n - \frac{f(x_n)}{f'(x_n)}$$

where f' is the derivative of f. Note that Newton's method will fail if $f'(x_n)$ is 0 at some approximation x_n. Write a program to find an approximate solution of an equation $f(x) = 0$ using Newton's method. The process should terminate when the difference $|x_{n+1} - x_n|$ between two successive approximations is sufficiently small or when the number of iterations exceeds some upper limit. Display the sequence of successive approximations.

5. The Cawker City Cookie Company can purchase a new microcomputer for $4440 cash or by paying $141.19 per month for the next 36 months. You are to determine what annual interest rate is being charged in the monthly payment plan.

    The equation that governs this calculation is the *annuity formula*

$$A = P \cdot \left[\frac{(1 + R)^N - 1}{R(1 + R)^N} \right]$$

where A is the amount borrowed, P is the monthly payment, R is the monthly interest rate (annual rate/12), and N is the number of payments. In this problem, this equation is to be solved for R. Write a program that uses the bisection method or Newton's method (see Exercise 4) to find an approximate solution of the equation

$$A - P \cdot \left[\frac{(1 + x)^N - 1}{x(1 + x)^N} \right] = 0$$

6.9 PART OF THE PICTURE: Introduction to Algorithm Analysis

As we mentioned in Section 6.1, Gauss solved the problem of summing the numbers from 1 through 100 almost immediately. The simplicity and efficiency of his method in comparison to the repetitive algorithm we have used is an indication of his genius, and we would be remiss if we did not mention his algorithm.

    To compute the summation from 1 through 100, Gauss perhaps noted that if he wrote the sum

$$\text{Sum} = 1 + 2 + 3 + \cdots + 98 + 99 + 100$$

backward,

$$\text{Sum} = 100 + 99 + 98 + \cdots + 3 + 2 + 1$$

and then added corresponding terms of these two equations to obtain

$$2 \times \text{Sum} = 101 + 101 + 101 + \cdots + 101 + 101 + 101$$
$$= 100 \times 101$$

and thus the sum is equal to

$$\frac{100 \times 101}{2} = 5050$$

Applying his algorithm to the more general summation from 1 through *n,* we have

$$Sum = 1 + 2 + 3 + \cdots + (n - 2) + (n - 1) + n$$

which we rearrange as

$$Sum = n + (n - 1) + (n - 2) + \cdots + 3 + 2 + 1$$

Adding these two equations gives

$$2 \times Sum = (n + 1) + (n + 1) + (n + 1) + \cdots + (n + 1) + (n + 1) + (n + 1)$$
$$= n \times (n + 1)$$

and thus the sum is equal to

$$\frac{n \times (n + 1)}{2}$$

This formula implies that function **Sum()** can be written without using a loop, as shown in Figure 6.20.

 FIGURE 6.20   Function **Sum()**—no-loop version.

```
/* This function computes the summation from 1 to N,
   using Gauss' formula.

   Receive:   An integer N
   Return:    The value 1 + 2 + ... + N
-----------------------------------------------------------*/

int Sum(int N)
{
   return N * (N + 1) / 2;
}
```

This solution is better than one that uses a loop, because it solves the same problem *more quickly.* For example, suppose we want to compute the sum of the integers from 1 through 1000. A version of **Sum()** that uses a loop (such as that in Figure 6.1) must repeat the body of the loop 1000 times. That means it must perform:

   1000 additions of **Counter** to **RunningTotal**,
   1000 assignments of that result to **RunningTotal**,
   1000 increments of **Counter**, and
   1000 comparisons of **Counter** to **N**,

for a total of 4000 operations. For an arbitrary value of **N**, each of these operations would be performed **N** times, for a total 4N operations. We say that the number of operations performed by the loop version of **Sum()** **grows linearly** with the value of its parameter **N**.

By contrast, the final version of **Sum()** always does

1 addition,
1 multiplication, and
1 division,

for a total of 3 operations, *regardless of the value of* **N**. The time taken by the last version of **Sum()** thus is **constant,** no matter what the value of its parameter **N**.

This introduces an important area of computer science called **analysis of algorithms.** We have just seen two algorithms for the summation problem, both of which correctly solve the problem. To determine which of them is "better," we analyze the number of operations each performs to solve the problem. This analysis tells us that since the algorithm using Gauss' formula solves the problem in constant time, whereas the algorithm using a loop solves the problem in time proportional to the value of **N**, the Gauss algorithm is to be preferred. We will consider the analysis of algorithms in more detail in Section 12.5.

Programming Pointers

Program Design

1. *Anything that can be computed can be computed using (only) the three control structures:* sequence, selection, *and* repetition.

2. *Repetition structures can be implemented in C++ using the for, while, do-while, and forever loops, and it is important to select the one that best implements the repetition structure required in a given problem.* Some guidelines for choosing the appropriate loop are as follows:

   - *The for loop is most appropriate for performing repetition when the number of repetitions can be determined before the loop is entered.*
   - *The while loop is most appropriate for performing repetition when zero-trip behavior is desired.* Since the loop condition appears at the top of the loop, the body of the loop will not be entered inadvertently if the loop condition is false initially.
   - *The do-while loop is most appropriate for performing repetition when one-trip behavior is desired.* Since the loop condition appears at the bottom of the loop, the body of the loop will be executed at least once before repetition is terminated.
   - *The forever loop can be used to perform repetition when neither zero-trip nor one-trip behavior is desired.* An **if-break** (or **if-return**) combination is usually used to terminate repetition.

Potential Problems

1. *Care must be taken to avoid infinite looping.*

   ■ The body of a for, while, or do-while loop should always contain statements that cause its loop condition eventually to become *false*. For example, the code segment

   ```
   x = 0.0;
   do
   {
       cout << x << '\n';
       x += 0.3;
   }
   while (x != 1.0);
   ```

   produces an infinite loop:

   ```
   0.0
   0.3
   0.6
   0.9
   1.2
   1.5
   1.8
     .
     .
     .
   ```

   Since the value of x is never equal to 1.0, repetition is not terminated.

   ■ The body of a forever loop should always contain an **if-break** (or **if-return**) combination and statements that ensure that the termination condition of the loop will eventually become *true*.

2. *In a while loop, the loop condition that controls repetition is evaluated before execution of the body of the loop. In a do-while loop, the loop condition that controls repetition is evaluated after execution of the body of the loop.* Thus, the body of a while loop will not be executed if the loop condition is false, but the statements within a do-while loop are always executed at least once.

3. *For, while, do-while and forever loops control a single statement.* For example, the poorly indented segment

   ```
   for (i = 1; i <= 10; i++)
      j = i*i;
      cout << j;
   ```

   will display only the single value

   ```
   100
   ```

   because the output statement is outside the body of the loop. Likewise, the segment

```
Count = 1;
while (Count <= 10)
   cout << Count << '\t' << Count*Count << '\n';
   Count++;
```

will produce an infinite loop

```
1        1
1        1
1        1
   .
   .
   .
```

because the statement to increment **Count** is outside the body of the loop.

4. *The loop condition of a do-while loop must be followed by a semicolon, or a syntax error will result.*

5. *In a for loop, neither the control variable nor any variable involved in the loop condition should be modified within the body of the for loop, because it is intended to run through a specified range of consecutive values.* Strange or undesirable results may be produced otherwise. To illustrate, the statement

```
for (i = 1; i <= 4; i++)
{
      cout << i << '\n';
      i++;
}
```

produces the output

```
1
3
```

The statement

```
for (i = 1; i <= 4; i++)
{
      cout << i << '\n';
      i--;
}
```

results in an infinite loop, displaying the output

```
1
1
1
1
   .
   .
   .
```

6. *Each use of the equality operator in a loop condition should be double-checked to make certain that the assignment operator is not being used.* Using = instead of == is one of the easiest errors to make, as illustrated by the following code fragment:

```
do
{
    ...
    cout << "\nDo you wish to continue (y or n) ? ";
    cin >> Answer;
}
while (Answer = 'y');
```

This loop will be executed infinitely many times, regardless of what the user enters, because

- Its loop condition is an *assignment* that sets **Answer** to **y**, instead of a *comparison;*
- The assignment operator (=) produces the value that was assigned as its result;
- This assignment thus produces the nonzero decimal code for **y** (121 in ASCII); and
- C++ treats any nonzero value as true.

Similarly, the forever loop:

```
for
{
    cout << "\nPlease enter an integer value (0 to quit): ";
    cin >> Value;

    if (Value = 0) break;

    // ... do something with Value ...
}
```

is an infinite loop, because the termination condition in its **if-break** combination is an *assignment,* not a *comparison.* Because the result of that assignment is zero and C++ uses zero to represent the value false, this termination condition will always be false, and so the **break** statement will never be executed.

Program Style

In this text, we use the following conventions for formatting the control statements considered in this chapter:

1. *In each of the loops, the opening brace (*{*) and closing brace (*}*) are placed on separate lines and are aligned; the lines within the loop body are indented.*

```
for (...)
    Statement
```

```
for (...)
{
    Statement₁
       .
       .
       .
    Statementₙ
}
```

2. *In a do-while loop,* **do** *is aligned with its corresponding* **while**, *and the body of the loop is indented.*

```
do
{
    Statement₁;
    .
    .
    .
    Statementₙ
}
while ( Loop Condition );
```

Programming Projects

1. For a positive integer *n*, *n* **factorial** is denoted by *n*! and is defined to be the product of the integers from 1 through *n*; 0! is defined as 1. A for loop is the natural repetition structure to use in calculating factorials. Write a program that reads several nonnegative integers and calculates and displays the factorial of each. Use a function to calculate the factorials.

2. The proper divisors of an integer *n* are the positive divisors less than *n*. A positive integer is said to be a **deficient, perfect,** or **abundant** number if the sum of its proper divisors is less than, equal to, or greater than the number, respectively. For example, 8 is deficient because its proper divisors are 1, 2, and 4, and $1 + 2 + 4 < 8$; 6 is perfect, because $1 + 2 + 3 = 6$; 12 is abundant, because $1 + 2 + 3 + 4 + 6 > 12$. Write a program that classifies *n* as being deficient, perfect, or abundant for *n* = 20 to 30, then for *n* = 490 to 500, and finally for *n* = 8120 to 8130.
Extra: Find the smallest odd abundant number. *Warning:* An attempt to find an odd perfect number will probably fail, because none has yet been found, although it has not been proven that such numbers do not exist.

3. In the Fibonacci sequence (see Exercise 2 of Section 6.1), the ratios of consecutive Fibonacci numbers ($\frac{1}{1}, \frac{1}{2}, \frac{2}{3}, \frac{3}{5}, \ldots$) approach the "golden ratio"

$$\frac{\sqrt{5} - 1}{2}$$

Write a program to calculate and display all Fibonacci numbers less than 5000 and the decimal values of the ratios of consecutive Fibonacci numbers.

4. The Rinky Dooflingy Company (Exercise 13 of Section 2.5) currently sells 200 dooflingies per month at a profit of $300 per Dooflingy. The company now spends $2000 per month on advertising and has fixed operating costs of $1000 per month that do not depend on the volume of sales. If the company doubles the amount spent on advertising, sales will increase by 20%. Write a program that prints, under appropriate headings, the amount spent on advertising, the number of sales made, and the net profit. Begin with the company's current status and successively double the amount spent on advertising until the net profit "goes over the hump," that is, begins to decline. The output should include the amounts up through the first time that the net profit begins to decline.

5. Write a program that reads the amount of a loan, an annual interest rate, and a monthly payment and then displays in a table with appropriate headings the payment number, the interest for that month, the balance remaining after that payment, and the total interest paid to date. (The monthly interest is $R/12$ percent of the unpaid balance after the payment is subtracted, where R is the annual interest rate.) Use a function to display these tables. Design the program so it can process several different loan amounts, interest rates, and monthly payments, including at least the following triples of values: $100, 18%, $10 and $500, 12%, $25. (*Note:* In general, the last payment will not be the same as the monthly payment; the program should show the exact amount of the last payment due.)

6. Proceed as in Exercise 5 but with the following modifications: During program execution, have the user enter a payment amount and a day of the month on which this payment was made (see Exercise 4(c) of Section 5.5 regarding leap years). The monthly interest is to be calculated on the *average daily balance* for that month. (Assume that the billing date is the first of the month.) For example, if the balance on June 1 is $500 and a payment of $20 is received on June 12, the interest will be computed on $(500 \cdot 11 + 480 \cdot 19)/30$ dollars, which represents the average daily balance for that month.

7. Suppose that on January 1, April 1, July 1, and October 1 of each year, some fixed *Amount* is invested and earns interest at some annual interest rate R compounded quarterly (that is, $R/4$ percent is added at the end of each quarter). Write a program that reads a number of years and that calculates and displays a table showing the year, the yearly dividend (total interest earned for that year), and the total savings accumulated through that year. Design the program to process several different inputs and to call a function to display the table for each input.

     A *possible modification or addition to your program:* Instead of investing *Amount* dollars each quarter, invest *Amount*/3 dollars on the first of each month. Then, in each quarter the first payment earns interest for 3 months ($R/4$ percent), the second for 2 months ($R/6$ percent), and the third for 1 month ($R/12$ percent).

FUNCTIONS: AN IN-DEPTH LOOK

Fudd's Law states: 'What goes in must come out.' Aside from being patently untrue, Fudd's Law neglects to mention that what comes out need not bear any resemblance to what went in.
V. OREHCK III (fictitious)

So, Naturalists observe, a flea
Hath smaller fleas that on him prey;
And these have smaller fleas to bite 'em
and so proceed ad infinitum.
JONATHAN SWIFT

CHAPTER CONTENTS

355

We have seen that designing a solution to a problem involves the identification of the *data objects* needed to solve the problem as well as the *operations* that must be applied to those objects. Thus far the problems we have examined have required operations that were either provided by the language C++ or were such that a function could easily be constructed to perform that operation. Functions are thus one mechanism by which operations not provided in C++ can be implemented.

In this chapter, we study C++ functions in greater detail. We begin by reexamining the binary half-adder problem from Chapter 5 and solve it in a way that, unlike the earlier version, allows our work to be reused. This will require the introduction of a new mechanism, called *reference parameters,* which we consider in detail. After presenting several examples that can easily be solved using reference parameters, we consider other properties of parameters in C++ functions. We conclude the chapter with an introduction to recursion and apply that technique to a classic problem in artificial intelligence.

7.1 Returning Multiple Values from a Function

Example: The Half-Adder Revisited

Problem. In Chapter 5, we considered a logical circuit called a **binary half-adder** that can be used to add two binary digits:

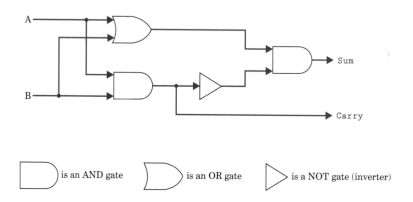

When we wrote a program to implement this half-adder, we did not encode the half-adder circuit as a function, even though it is clearly an operation on the two binary inputs **A** and **B**. Furthermore, such a function would clearly be one that we might wish to use again in the future, perhaps in constructing a full-adder (see Programming Project 1 at the end of Chapter 5). To understand why we did not encode a half-adder as a function, we must look at what the specification of such a function would be.

Specification. Four data objects are involved in the operation of a binary half-adder: the two inputs, **A** and **B**, and the two outputs, **Sum** and **Carry**. Since these values are binary digits, they can be implemented as integers:

Data Object	Kind of Value	Type of Object	Name of Object
The first input bit	Variable	Integer	A
The second input bit	Variable	Integer	B
The sum bit	Variable	Integer	Sum
The carry bit	Variable	Integer	Carry

Recognizing that the function must receive A and B from its caller and return Sum and Carry to its caller gives the following specification:

Receive: A binary digit A
           A binary digit B
Return: The Sum bit of A + B
           The Carry bit of A + B

This specification makes clear why we could not encode the half-adder operation as a function: such a function would have to return *two* values to its caller, but as we have seen, a function's **return** statement has the form

```
return Expression;
```

and is thus able to return only a *single* value. To make it possible for a function to return multiple values, C++ provides **reference parameters.** In this section we show how such parameters can be used to design a half-adder function, and in the next section we discuss them in greater detail.

Design.   As we saw in Chapter 5, the values of Sum and Carry in the circuit for a binary half-adder are given in the following table:

A	B	Carry	Sum
0	0	0	0
0	1	0	1
1	0	0	1
1	1	1	0

We showed that the value of Sum is given by the boolean expression:

```
(A || B) && !(A && B)
```

and the output Carry by

```
A && B
```

so that the function need only evaluate and return the results of these expressions. We now show how this is done by assigning those results to reference parameters.

Coding.   The function `HalfAdd()` in Figure 7.1 performs the binary half-adder operation. The parameters `Sum` and `Carry` are reference parameters.

FIGURE 7.1   A binary half-adder function.

```
/* This function implements the binary half-adder operation.

   Receive: Two binary inputs A and B
   Return:  The Sum and Carry bits of A + B
------------------------------------------------------------------*/

void HalfAdd(int A, int B, int& Sum, int& Carry)
{
   Sum = (A || B) && !(A && B);
   Carry = (A && B);
}
```

The program in Figure 7.2 reads two binary digits and calls function `HalfAdd()` to add them.

FIGURE 7.2   Driver program for the binary half-adder function.

```
/* This program calculates -- via HalfAdd() -- the outputs from a
   boolean expression that is equivalent to the logical circuit for
   a binary half-adder.

   Input:  Two binary digits

   Output: Two binary values representing the sum and
           carry that result when the input values are added
------------------------------------------------------------------*/

#include <iostream.h>

void HalfAdd(int, int, int&, int&);

int main(void)
{
   cout << "\nThis program simulates the execution of "
        << "a binary half-adder.\n";
```

FIGURE 7.2   Driver program for the binary half-adder function. (cont.)

```
int
   ABit,                     // the two binary inputs
   BBit,
   SumBit,                   // the sum bit
   CarryBit;                 // the carry bit
char
   Answer;                   // for the user's query response

do
{
   cout << "\nPlease enter two binary inputs: ";
   cin >> ABit >> BBit;

   HalfAdd(ABit, BBit, SumBit, CarryBit);

   cout << "\n\tCarry = " << CarryBit
        << " Sum = " << SumBit << '\n';

   cout << "\nDo you have more additions to perform (y or n) ? ";
   cin >> Answer;
}
while (Answer != 'n');

return 0;
}

// ... Insert definition of function HalfAdd() here.
```

Sample runs:

This program simulates the execution of a binary half-adder.

Please enter two binary inputs: <u>0 0</u>

        Carry = 0 Sum = 0

Do you have more additions to perform (y or n) ? <u>y</u>

Please enter two binary inputs: <u>0 1</u>

        Carry = 0 Sum = 1

Do you have more additions to perform (y or n) ? <u>y</u>

Please enter two binary inputs: <u>1 0</u>

        Carry = 0 Sum = 1

Do you have more additions to perform (y or n) ? <u>y</u>

FIGURE 7.2 Driver program for the binary half-adder function. (cont.)

```
Please enter two binary inputs: 1 1

        Carry = 1 Sum = 0

Do you have more additions to perform (y or n) ? n
```

Of course, the function **HalfAdd()** could be stored in a library (perhaps one called **BinaryOps**) for reuse by other programs. Such programs would need to include the header file (**BinaryOps.h**) of that library.

7.2 Reference Parameters

In this section, we examine the C++ mechanism that function **HalfAdd()** uses to return multiple values to its caller.

If we examine the definition of function **HalfAdd()** in Figure 7.1,

```
void HalfAdd(int A, int B, int& Sum, int& Carry)
{
   Sum = (A || B) && !(A && B);
   Carry = (A && B);
}
```

we see that its parameters are defined in two different ways:

1. **A** and **B** are declared in the same way that parameters have been declared earlier.
2. **Sum** and **Carry** are declared with an ampersand (**&**) following their types.

These two pairs of parameters illustrate two different mechanisms for declaring parameters. Parameters whose declarations have the form

Type Identifier

are called **value** (or **in-only** or **copy**) parameters, whereas those having the form

Type& Identifier

are called **reference** (or **in-and-out**) parameters. Thus, in function **HalfAdd()**, **A** and **B** are value parameters, whereas **Sum** and **Carry** are reference parameters. As we shall see, the simple appending of an ampersand to the type specifier in a parameter declaration significantly changes the properties of the parameter.

Value Parameters

All the parameters that we have seen in earlier chapters have been value parameters. To contrast value parameters and reference parameters, suppose that all four parameters in the half-adder function were defined as value parameters, as in **HalfAdd2()**,

```
void HalfAdd2(int A, int B, int Sum, int Carry)
{
    Sum = (A || B) && !(A && B);
    Carry = (A && B);
}
```

and consider a program like that in Figure 7.2, in which variables **ABit**, **BBit**, **SumBit**, and **CarryBit** are defined with **ABit** and **BBit** each having the value 1 and **SumBit** and **CarryBit** undefined:

ABit	1
BBit	1
SumBit	?
CarryBit	?

When this program calls the function **HalfAdd2()**,

```
HalfAdd2(ABit, BBit, SumBit, CarryBit);
```

the following actions occur:

1. Memory is allocated for the parameters **A**, **B**, **Sum**, and **Carry**. (Memory was allocated for **ABit**, **BBit**, **SumBit**, and **CarryBit** when these arguments were declared.)

ABit	1	?	A
BBit	1	?	B
SumBit	?	?	Sum
CarryBit	?	?	Carry

2. The values of the arguments **ABit**, **BBit**, **SumBit**, and **CarryBit** are copied into their corresponding parameters **A**, **B**, **Sum**, and **Carry**:

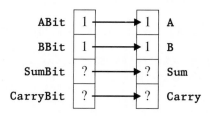

3. The body of `HalfAdd2()` is executed, changing the values of `Sum` and `Carry`:

ABit	1		1	A
BBit	1		1	B
SumBit	?		0	Sum
CarryBit	?		1	Carry

4. The function terminates, and the memory of parameters `A`, `B`, `Sum`, and `Carry` is released.

ABit	1
BBit	1
SumBit	?
CarryBit	?

This example illustrates the fundamental characteristic of value parameters:

Value Parameters

> Value parameters are variables for which *new memory locations are allocated when the function is called* and into which the values of the corresponding arguments are *copied*. Therefore, any change to the value of a value parameter within the body of a function *has no effect on the value of its corresponding argument.*

Thus, even though parameters `Sum` and `Carry` were changed by `HalfAdd2()`, the values of arguments `SumBit` and `CarryBit` were unchanged following the function call, because these are four distinct variables associated with four distinct memory locations.

Reference Parameters

Now compare the execution of `HalfAdd2()` with that of `HalfAdd()` (where `Sum` and `Carry` are declared to be reference parameters):

```
void HalfAdd(int A, int B, int& Sum, int& Carry)
{
    Sum = (A || B) && !(A && B);
    Carry = (A && B);
}
```

Suppose again that a program defines variables **ABit**, **BBit**, **SumBit**, and **CarryBit**, and initializes **ABit** and **BBit** with the values 1 and 1.

ABit | 1
BBit | 1
SumBit | ?
CarryBit | ?

When this program calls the function **HalfAdd()**,

    HalfAdd(ABit, BBit, SumBit, CarryBit);

the following actions occur:

1. The value parameters **A** and **B** are allocated new memory locations. However, the reference parameters **Sum** and **Carry** are associated with the same memory locations as their corresponding arguments **SumBit** and **CarryBit** instead of receiving their own new memory locations:

ABit | 1   ? | A
BBit | 1   ? | B
SumBit | ? | Sum
CarryBit | ? | Carry

2. The values of the arguments **ABit** and **BBit** are copied into the corresponding parameters **A** and **B**:

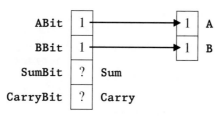

3. The body of **HalfAdd()** is executed, changing the values of **Sum** and **Carry** (which are alternative names for the arguments **SumBit** and **CarryBit**):

ABit | 1   1 | A
BBit | 1   1 | B
SumBit | 0 | Sum
CarryBit | 1 | Carry

4. The function terminates, and the memory associated with parameters **A** and **B** is released.

ABit	1
BBit	1
SumBit	0
CarryBit	1

This example illustrates the fundamental characteristic of reference parameters:

Reference Parameters

> Reference parameters are *aliases of* (alternative names for) their corresponding arguments. Therefore, any change to the value of a reference parameter within the body of a function *changes the value of* its corresponding argument.

Thus, because the values of parameters **Sum** and **Carry** were changed by **HalfAdd()**, the values of the corresponding arguments **SumBit** and **CarryBit** are changed by the function call

```
HalfAdd(ABit, BBit, SumBit, CarryBit);
```

The reason is that as reference parameters, **Sum** and **Carry** are simply alternative names for (and thus share memory locations with) their corresponding arguments, **SumBit** and **CarryBit**.

Using reference parameters thus makes it possible for a function to return multiple values to its caller by changing the values of argument variables that are defined in the caller. For example, the function **HalfAdd()** returns the two values 1 and 0 to the program that calls it with

```
HalfAdd(1, 1, SumBit, CarryBit);
```

by changing the value of argument **SumBit** to 0 and the value of the argument **CarryBit** to 1.

Since the purpose of a reference parameter is to permit the value of its argument to be changed, it follows that the corresponding argument must be a data object whose value can be changed. Thus, whereas the argument corresponding to a value parameter can be a constant, *the argument corresponding to a reference parameter must be a variable whose type is the same as that parameter.* For example, if **SumBit** and **CarryBit** are defined as **int** variables, then the call

```
HalfAdd(1, 1, SumBit, CarryBit);
```

is valid, but it would not be valid if `SumBit` or `CarryBit` were of a type other than `int`. By contrast, the call:

```
HalfAdd(1, 1, 0, 1);
```

will result in a syntax error (because reference parameters cannot have constant arguments), as would

```
HalfAdd(1, 1, SumBit, CarryBit);
```

if `SumBit` and `CarryBit` were defined as named constants.

Using Reference Parameters

Learning to use reference parameters correctly is not difficult, but it does require expanding the way we think about constructing functions.

As we have seen, the fundamental rule in constructing a function is:

> *The form of a function is determined by the specification of the problem it must solve.*

Jumping in and writing a function without a clear specification of the problem to be solved often leads to wasted work. Instead, one should begin by formulating a precise specification for the function because such a specification provides all the information necessary to declare that function. To illustrate the importance of this relationship between a function and its specification, we present three general *specification patterns* and show how they determine the form of the resulting function.

Pattern 1: A Single Return Value. Suppose that a problem requires a function `F()` whose specification is as follows:

Receive: V_1 of type *Type$_1$*
V_2 of type *Type$_2$*

$\vdots$

V_n of type *Type$_n$*
Return: *RV* of type *RType*

This specification provides two important pieces of information:

1. Function `F()` must have n value parameters, of types *Type$_1$*, *Type$_2$*, . . . , *Type$_n$*.
2. The return type of function `F()` is type *RType*.[1]

---

[1] We could use a single reference parameter to return the function value and make the return type of the function `void`. This, however, is not the commonly accepted way to return a single value, since the usual mathematical concept of function is that it returns a single value, namely, the value of the function at the arguments passed to it.

This, in turn, requires that function `F()` have the following form:

```
RType F(Type₁ V₁, Type₂ V₂, ..., Typeₙ Vₙ)
{
    // ... function body ...

    RType RV;

    // ... compute return value RV

    return RV;
}
```

The specification thus provides important information that enables us to identify (1) how many parameters the function requires, (2) their types, and (3) the return type of the function. This function can then be called in a statement such as

```
RType
    Variable = F(Arg₁, Arg₂, ..., Argₙ);
```

where $Arg_1, Arg_2, \ldots, Arg_n$ are expressions that are type-compatible with $Type_1$, $Type_2, \ldots, Type_n$, respectively.

Pattern 2: No Return Value. In contrast to Pattern 1, suppose that a problem requires a function `G()` whose specification has the form:

> Receive: V_1 of type $Type_1$
> V_2 of type $Type_2$
>
> $\vdots$
>
> V_n of type $Type_n$
>
> Output: Something depending on V_1, V_2, $\ldots$, V_n
> Returns: Nothing

This specification gives two important pieces of information:

1. Function `G()` must have n value parameters, of types $Type_1, Type_2, \ldots, Type_n$.
2. The return type of `G()` is type **void** because `G()` returns no values to its caller.

Thus, the function `G()` will have the following form:

```
void G(Type₁ V₁, Type₂ V₂, ..., Typeₙ Vₙ)
{
    ... // perform required output
}
```

Again, the specification indicates (1) how many parameters the function requires, (2) the types of those parameters, and (3) the return type of the function, which is **void**, because the function returns no values to its caller. Because the function does not return a value, it can be called as follows:

```
G(Arg₁, Arg₂, ..., Argₙ);
```

where $Arg_1, Arg_2, \ldots, Arg_n$ are expressions that are type-compatible with $Type_1$, $Type_2, \ldots, Type_n$, respectively.

Pattern 3: Multiple Return Values.   Finally, suppose that the problem requires a function H() whose specification has the form:

Receive only: V_1 of type $Type_1$
               V_2 of type $Type_2$

$\vdots$

               V_m of type $Type_m$
Return: RV_1 of type $RType_1$
               RV_2 of type $RType_2$

$\vdots$

               RV_n of type $RType_n$

(Note: We also allow that items that return values may also receive values.) This specification tells us the following:

1. Function H() needs m value parameters of types $Type_1$, $Type_2$, . . . , $Type_m$.
2. Function H() needs n reference parameters of types $RType_1$, $RType_2$, . . . , $RType_n$.
3. The return type of H() is type **void**.

Thus the function H() will have the form

```
void H(Type₁ V₁, Type₂ V₂, ..., Typeₘ Vₘ,        // value params
       RType₁& RV₁, RType₂& RV₂, ..., RTypeₙ& Rₙ) // ref. params
{
    // ... compute each return value
}
```

The function H() can then be called as follows:

```
H(Arg₁, Arg₂, ..., Argₘ, Var₁, Var₂, ..., Varₙ);
```

where Arg_1, Arg_2, . . ., Arg_m are expressions that are type-compatible with $Type_1$, $Type_2$, . . ., $Type_m$, and Var_1, Var_2, . . ., Var_n must be variables of types $RType_1$, $RType_2$, . . ., $RType_n$, respectively. Following the call, the value of Var_1 will have been changed to RV_1, Var_2 to RV_2, and so on. We see, therefore, that when the specification of a function requires that multiple values be returned, the function can be implemented by

1. Declaring a value parameter for each receive-only value,
2. Declaring a reference parameter for each value that must be returned, and
3. Assigning the value to be returned to that parameter within the function.

Summary.   We can summarize these observations in the following guidelines:

Guidelines for Declaring Function Parameters

Given a specification for a function F():

1. A **value parameter** should be declared for each *receive-only* value.

> 2. If `F()` is to return a single value *V* of type *T*, then the return type of `F()` is type *T*.
> Otherwise
> a. the return type of `F()` is **void**, and
> b. **reference parameters** should be declared for each value `F()` is to return.

In the next section, we present some additional examples in which these guidelines are used in the construction of functions that return multiple values.

7.3   Examples Using Reference Parameters

There are many problems that can be solved using functions that return multiple values. In this section we consider three such problems: making change; swapping values of variables; and finding the maximum, minimum, and average of a list of data values.

Example 1: Making Change

Problem. Design and test a function that, given the amount of a purchase and the amount given as payment, will compute and return the change in dollars, half-dollars, quarters, dimes, nickels, and pennies.

Specification.   Identifying the data objects in this problem is easy:

Data Object	Kind of Value	Type of Object	Name of Object
The amount of the purchase	Variable	Real	*PurchaseAmount*
The amount of the payment	Variable	Real	*Payment*
The dollars in change	Variable	Integer	*Dollars*
The half-dollars in change	Variable	Integer	*HalfDollars*
The quarters in change	Variable	Integer	*Quarters*
The dimes in change	Variable	Integer	*Dimes*
The nickels in change	Variable	Integer	*Nickels*
The pennies in change	Variable	Integer	*Pennies*

Once we have identified these objects, we can specify the function as follows:

Receive: *PurchaseAmount,* the (real) amount of the purchase
         Payment, the (real) amount of the payment
Return: *Dollars,* the (integer) number of dollars in change
         HalfDollars, the (integer) number of half-dollars in change
         Quarters, the (integer) number of quarters in change
         Dimes, the (integer) number of dimes in change
         Nickels, the (integer) number of nickels in change
         Pennies, the (integer) number of pennies in change

Note that this specification fits Pattern 3 of the preceding section, in which multiple values are returned by the function. As we noted in the discussion of Pattern 3, a value parameter should be defined for each of the (two) values being received, and a reference parameter should be defined for each of the (six) values being returned. We can, therefore, construct the following stub for the function, which we call `MakeChange()`:

```
void MakeChange(double PurchaseAmount,  // the amount of the purchase
                double Payment,         // the amount of the payment
                int& Dollars,           // dollars of change
                int& HalfDollars,       // half-dollars of change
                int& Quarters,          // quarters of change
                int& Dimes,             // dimes of change
                int& Nickels,           // nickels of change
                int& Pennies )          // pennies of change
{
}
```

Design. To determine what sequence of operations is needed to make change, consider a specific example. Suppose the amount of a purchase is $8.49 and we pay with a $10.00 bill. We clearly must begin by subtracting the purchase amount from the payment to get the total amount of change ($1.51). This is a real value but our return values are integers, and so we must at some point convert this real value to an integer value. One approach would be to store the total amount of change (1.51) as a real value and perform a separate conversion as each return value is computed. However, this requires doing (essentially) the same thing six times—an indication that there is probably a better way. Also, real values are not stored exactly (e.g., 1.51 might be stored as 1.50999. . .) and thus it is better to convert the real amount of change (1.51) into an integer value (151) at the outset, ensuring that no significant digits are lost. This can be done by multiplying the real amount of change by 100, adding 0.5, and then truncating the fractional part of the result. The following examples illustrate this computation:

$$1.50993 \rightarrow \boxed{* \ 100} \rightarrow 150.993 \rightarrow \boxed{+ \ 0.5} \rightarrow 151.493 \rightarrow \boxed{\text{truncate}} \rightarrow 151$$

$$1.51002 \rightarrow \boxed{* \ 100} \rightarrow 151.002 \rightarrow \boxed{+ \ 0.5} \rightarrow 151.502 \rightarrow \boxed{\text{truncate}} \rightarrow 151$$

The result of this computation is the total amount of change in pennies, and we will store this value in a local (variable) object `Change`.

We can now construct the following algorithm to solve the problem:

ALGORITHM FOR MAKING CHANGE

/* This algorithm computes the number of dollars, half-dollars, quarters, dimes, nickels, and pennies needed to make change for a given purchase amount and a payment.

Receive: *PurchaseAmount*, the (real) amount of the purchase
           Payment, the (real) amount of the payment

Return: *Dollars*, the (integer) number of dollars in change
           HalfDollars, the (integer) number of half-dollars in change
           Quarters, the (integer) number of quarters in change
           Dimes, the (integer) number of dimes in change
           Nickels, the (integer) number of nickels in change
           Pennies, the (integer) number of pennies in change

———*/

1. Compute *Change*, the difference of *Payment* and *PurchaseAmount*, in pennies.
2. If *Change* is positive, then
   a. Compute *Dollars* in *Change* and remove *Dollars* from *Change*.
   b. Compute *HalfDollars* in *Change* and remove *HalfDollars* from *Change*.
   c. Compute *Quarters* in *Change* and remove *Quarters* from *Change*.
   d. Compute *Dimes* in *Change* and remove *Dimes* from *Change*.
   e. Compute *Nickels* in *Change* and remove *Nickels* from *Change*.
   f. Compute *Pennies* in *Change*.
   Otherwise
       Set each of *Dollars, HalfDollars, Quarters, Dimes, Nickels,* and *Pennies* to zero.

Once we have computed **Change** as the amount of change in pennies, the number of dollars of change can be computed using integer division, by dividing the value of **Change** by 100:

```
Dollars = Change / 100;       // for Change = 151, Dollars equals 1
```

We next remove **Dollars** from **Change** by using the modulus operation to find the remainder of **Change** divided by 100:

```
Change %= 100;                // for Change = 151, Change becomes 51
```

The number of half-dollars remaining in **Change** can then be computed by dividing **Change** by 50,

```
    HalfDollars = Change / 50;
```

and then removing the number of half dollars from **Change**:

```
    Change %= 50;
```

Similar calculations are used to determine the number of quarters, dimes, nickels, and pennies. The complete function is given in Figure 7.3.

FIGURE 7.3   Making change.

```
/* This function computes the dollars, half-dollars, etc. of
   change given the amount of a purchase and the payment made.

      Receive: PurchaseAmount, the (real) amount of the purchase
               Payment, the (real) amount of the payment

      Return:  Dollars, the (integer) number of dollars in change
               HalfDollars, the (integer) number of half-dollars in
                  change
               Quarters, the (integer) number of quarters in change
               Dimes, the (integer) number of dimes in change
               Nickels, the (integer) number of nickels in change
               Pennies, the (integer) number of pennies in change
-----------------------------------------------------------------*/

void MakeChange(double PurchaseAmount, // the amount of the purchase
                double Payment,        // the amount of the payment
                int& Dollars,          // dollars of change
                int& HalfDollars,      // half-dollars of change
                int& Quarters,         // quarters of change
                int& Dimes,            // dimes of change
                int& Nickels,          // nickels of change
                int& Pennies )         // pennies of change
{
   int                               // total change in pennies
      Change = int(100.0 * (Payment - PurchaseAmount) + 0.5);

   if (Change > 0)
   {
      Dollars = Change / 100;        // 100 pennies per dollar
      Change %= 100;                 // compute remaining change

      HalfDollars = Change / 50;     // 50 pennies per half dollar
      Change %= 50;                  // compute remaining change

      Quarters = Change / 25;        // 25 pennies per quarter
      Change %= 25;                  // compute remaining change

      Dimes = Change / 10;           // 10 pennies per dime
      Change %= 10;                  // compute remaining change

      Nickels = Change / 5;          // 5 pennies per nickel
      Pennies = Change % 5;          // pennies are all that's left
   }
   else
      Dollars = HalfDollars = Quarters
            = Dimes = Nickels = Pennies = 0;
}
```

To test this function we might write a driver program that simply reads two amounts `ItemCost` and `AmountPaid`, calls `MakeChange()` to calculate the change that must be given and then displays the amounts returned by `MakeChange()`. Figure 7.4 presents such a driver program.

 FIGURE 7.4   Making change—driver program.

```
/* This is a driver program to test function MakeChange().

   Input:   The cost of an item, and the amount paid
   Output:  The change in terms of numbers of dollars, half-dollars,
            quarters, dimes, nickels, and pennies
   ----------------------------------------------------------------*/

#include <iostream.h>

void MakeChange(double, double, int&, int&, int&, int&, int&, int&);

int main(void)
{
   const char
      Sentinel[] = "a negative value ";

   cout << "\nThis program tests a change-making function...\n";

   double
      ItemCost,          // a purchase
      AmountPaid;        // what was paid
   int                   // the amount of change
      NumDollars,
      NumHalfDollars,
      NumQuarters,
      NumDimes,
      NumNickels,
      NumPennies;

   cout << "\nEnter item cost, and amount paid ("
        << Sentinel << "to quit): ";
   cin >> ItemCost;

   while (ItemCost >= 0)
   {
      cin >> AmountPaid;

      MakeChange(ItemCost, AmountPaid, NumDollars, NumHalfDollars,
                 NumQuarters, NumDimes, NumNickels, NumPennies);

      cout << "\nThe change from this purchase is:\n"
           << NumDollars << " dollars,\n"
           << NumHalfDollars << " half-dollars,\n"
           << NumQuarters << " quarters,\n"
           << NumDimes << " dimes,\n"
           << NumNickels << " nickels, and\n"
           << NumPennies << " pennies.\n";
```

FIGURE 7.4 Making change—driver program. (cont.)

```
        cout << "\nEnter item cost, and amount paid ("
             << Sentinel << "to quit): ";
        cin >> ItemCost;
    }

    return 0;
}
```

...Insert definition of MakeChange() here.

Sample run:

```
This program tests a change-making function...

Enter item cost, and amount paid (a negative value to quit): 1.01 2.00

The change from this purchase is:
0 dollars,
1 half-dollars,
1 quarters,
2 dimes,
0 nickels, and
4 pennies.

Enter item cost, and amount paid (a negative value to quit): 1.09 3.00

The change from this purchase is:
1 dollars,
1 half-dollars,
1 quarters,
1 dimes,
1 nickels, and
1 pennies.


Enter item cost, and amount paid (a negative value to quit): 9.99 10.00

The change from this purchase is:
0 dollars,
0 half-dollars,
0 quarters,
0 dimes,
0 nickels, and
1 pennies.


Enter item cost, and amount paid (a negative value to quit): -1
```

Example 2: Exchanging the Values of Two Variables

Problem. There are certain problems in which it is useful to be able to exchange the values of two variables. This "swap" operation is needed so frequently that it is useful to construct a function to perform it and store the function in a library.

Specification.   The swap operation involves two data objects: the two variables whose values are being exchanged. If we assume for this example that these are integer variables, then we can list the data objects needed to perform this operation as follows:

Data Object	Kind of Value	Type of Object	Name of Object
The first variable	Variable	Integer	*First*
The second variable	Variable	Integer	*Second*

If we consider how this operation must affect these two variables, we can specify its behavior as follows:

Receive: *First,* an (int) variable
                 Second, another (int) variable
Return: *First,* containing the value of *Second,* and
                 Second, containing the value of *First*

Note that since this specification indicates that multiple values must be returned in order to perform the operation, Pattern 3 can be applied with *First* and *Second* as reference parameters, because they are receive-and-return parameters. This allows us to construct the following stub for our function, which we call **Swap()**:

```
void Swap(int& First, int& Second)
{
}
```

Design.   We cannot simply assign the value of **Second** to **First** (or vice versa) to solve this problem, because the value of **First** will be overwritten and lost. Instead, we introduce a third (local, variable) data object, which we call **Temporary**, in which the value of **First** can be stored while we assign **First** the value of **Second**. We can then assign **Second** the value of **Temporary**, completing the operation. This gives the following algorithm:

ALGORITHM TO EXCHANGE THE VALUES OF TWO VARIABLES

/* This algorithm exchanges the values of two variables.

Receive: *First,* an (int) variable,
                 Second, another (int) variable

Return: *First,* containing the value of *Second,* and
                 Second, containing the value of *First*

——*/

1. Store the value of *First* in *Temporary.*

2. Assign the value of *Second* to *First*.
3. Assign the value of *Temporary* to *Second*.

Coding. Encoding this algorithm is straightforward, as shown in Figure 7.5.

 FIGURE 7.5 Exchanging the values of two variables.

```
/* Swap() exchanges the values of two variables.

   Receive: First, an (int) variable
            Second, an (int) variable

   Return:  First, containing the value of Second, and
            Second, containing the value of First
-----------------------------------------------------------------------*/

void Swap(int& First, int& Second)
{
   int
      Temporary = First;

   First = Second;
   Second = Temporary;
}
```

Other functions can use **Swap()** to exchange the values of two integer variables. For example, suppose that function **Swap()** is called in the following context:

```
int
   Alpha,
   Beta;

cout << "\nPlease enter the two values to be processed: ";
cin >> Alpha >> Beta;

Swap(Alpha, Beta);      // exchange them

cout << "\nAlpha = " << Alpha
     << ", and Beta = " << Beta << endl;
```

Now suppose that the user enters 11 and 22 for the values of **Alpha** and **Beta**. Then memory appears as

Alpha	11
Beta	22

The function call

```
Swap(Alpha, Beta);
```

is then performed, which causes the following actions to occur:

1. The parameters **First** and **Second** are associated with **Alpha** and **Beta**, respectively; and a new memory location is allocated for the local variable **Temporary**:

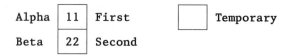

2. Function **Swap()** executes, exchanging the values of **First** and **Second** and thus, the values of **Alpha** and **Beta** also, because **First** and **Second** are reference parameters.

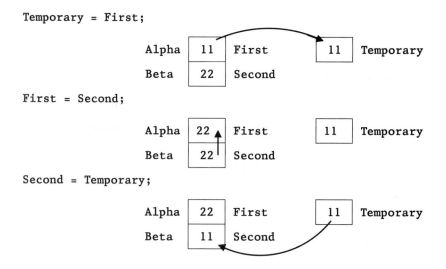

3. Function **Swap()** terminates and the memory allocated to **Temporary** is released:

Alpha | 22
Beta | 11

Overloading. The **Swap()** function is useful in many problems such as sorting a list of values (Section 12.5) and operating on a matrix (Section 14.4) that we consider later. However, the function we have written can be used only to exchange the values of two **int** variables, whereas lists may contain **char** values, matrices may contain **double** values, and so on. Constructing a library, perhaps named **Swap**, whose header file contains the following declarations will make **Swap()** especially easy to use:

```
/* This (header) file presents the interface to library Swap,
   a collection of functions for exchanging the values of two variables.

Names Declared:
   Swap(), a function for exchanging the values of two
           char, short, int, long, float, double, or long double
           variables.
-------------------------------------------------------------------*/
```

```
                                         // exchange the values of:
void Swap(char& First, char& Second);    //    chars
void Swap(short& First, short& Second);  //    shorts
void Swap(int& First, int& Second);      //    ints
void Swap(long& First, long& Second);    //    longs
void Swap(float& First, float& Second);  //    floats
void Swap(double& First, double& Second); //   doubles
void Swap(long double& First, long double& Second);//  long doubles
```

For each of these declarations, we place a corresponding definition (similar to that in Figure 7.5) in the library's implementation file. Our library `Swap` thus contains multiple functions, each with the same name but having parameters with different types. This phenomenon, in which a name like `Swap` is given multiple definitions that can be distinguished by their parameter types,[2] is called **overloading** that name. Overloading allows us to use the same name (`Swap`) for the same operation (exchanging the values of two variables) for a variety of different types.

Given such a library, any program can use these functions simply by inserting its header file `Swap.h` with the `#include` directive and linking the compiled implementation file to the compiled program, as discussed in Section 4.3. For example, consider the following simple program:

```
#include <iostream.h>

#include "Swap.h"

int main(void)
{
   int
      i1 = 11,
      i2 = 22;
   double
      d1 = 11.1,
      d2 = 22.2;
   char
      c1 = 'A',
      c2 = 'B';

   Swap(c1, c2);
   cout << c1 << ' ' << c2 << endl;
```

---

[2] Names can also be overloaded by providing definitions in which the *number* of parameters differ. For example, we could declare `void Swap(int& First, int& Second, int& Third);` that shifts the value of `First` to `Second`, `Second` to `Third`, and `Third` to `First`. Its three `int&` parameters would enable the C++ compiler to distinguish a call to this version of `Swap()` from a call to the version with two `int&` parameters.

```
    Swap(i1, i2);
    cout << i1 << ' ' << i2 << endl;

    Swap(d1, d2);
    cout << d1 << ' ' << d2 << endl;
}
```

When executed, this program produces the output

```
B A
22 11
22.2 11.1
```

It is important to understand what is happening in this program. The first call to Swap(),

```
Swap(c1, c2);
```

has two **char** arguments, and so the C++ compiler applies the version of **Swap()** having the declaration:

```
void Swap(char& First, char& Second);
```

However, the second call to **Swap()**,

```
Swap(i1, i2);
```

has two **int** arguments, and so the compiler applies a different version of the function:

```
void Swap(int& First, int& Second);
```

Similarly, the third call to **Swap()**,

```
Swap(d1, d2);
```

has two **double** arguments, and so the compiler applies yet another version of the function:

```
void Swap(double& First, double& Second);
```

It should be evident that we have been using overloading all along. For example, the operators +, -, *, and / are all overloaded so that they can be applied to any of the numeric types. In the expression

```
2.0 / 3.0
```

the C++ compiler uses the real division operation (which produces the value 0.666666. . .), whereas in the expression

```
2 / 3
```

the C++ compiler uses the integer division operation (which produces the value 0). Many of the other operators we have used frequently, including `<<`, `>>`, `=`, `+=`, `-=`, `*=`, `/=`, `<`, `>`, `==`, `<=`, `>=`, `!=`, and others, are similarly overloaded with multiple definitions. Given an expression

> `Operand₁ Operator Operand₂`

the compiler simply uses the types of **Operand₁** and **Operand₂** to determine which definition of **Operator** to apply. If no suitable definition exists, a compilation error is generated.

Example 3: Analyzing a List of Data Values

Problem.   A common computing problem is analyzing a list of data values, calculating various statistics such as the minimum, maximum, and average values. For example, a teacher might wish to find the minimum, maximum, and average of a set of exam scores. A meterologist might wish to know the minimum, maximum, and average of sequences of temperature readings. The president of a business would be interested in the minimum, maximum, and average of a sequence of monthly earnings. If we solve this problem in general, then the solution can be applied to any of these particular instances of the problem.

Specification.   Considering this general problem, we can identify the following data objects:

Data Object	Kind of Value	Type of Object	Name of Object
A sequence of data values	Variable	Real	*Value*
The minimum value	Variable	Real	*Min*
The maximum value	Variable	Real	*Max*
The average value	Variable	Real	*Average*

A specification of the function is straightforward:

> Input: A sequence of values
> Return: The minimum, maximum, and average of the values

Since the function is to return multiple values, a reference parameter must be declared for each value to be returned. This allows us to construct the following stub for the function, which we call **FindMinMaxAverage()**:

```
void FindMinMaxAverage(double& Min, double& Max, double& Average)
{
}
```

Design.   Clearly, one of the operations required to solve this problem is inputting a list of values. To find the average value, we must sum the input values and then divide by the number of values in the list. This means that the function must count the values as they are entered. To find the minimum value, we compare each value as it is entered with the minimum value *Min* found so far, and if the new value is smaller, we update the value of *Min* to this new value. The maximum value is found in a similar manner. This leads to the following algorithm:

ALGORITHM TO FIND THE MIN, MAX, AND AVERAGE VALUE IN A LIST OF VALUES

/* This algorithm finds the smallest, largest, and average value in a sequence of values. It assumes there is at least one value in the sequence.

    Input: A sequence of an arbitrary number of real values
    Return: The minimum, maximum, and average values
    ——*/

1. Enter the first *Value*.
2. Set *Min* and *Max* to *Value*, *Sum* to 0, and *Count* to 1.
3. While the end of data has not been reached do the following
    a. Increment *Count*.
    b. Add *Value* to *Sum*.
    c. If *Value* < *Min*, then
        Set *Min* to *Value*.
      Else if *Value* > *Max*, then
        Set *Max* to *Value*.
    d. Enter the next *Value*.
    End while.
4. Compute *Average* by dividing *Sum* by *Count*.

Coding. The preceding algorithm can be encoded in C++, as shown in Figure 7.6. Here we have used the end-of-file mark to control the loop.

 FIGURE 7.6 Finding the min, max, and average value in a list.

```
/* This function finds the smallest, largest, and average values
   in a list.

   Input:  A sequence of real values
   Return: Min, the smallest value in the sequence,
           Max, the largest value in the sequence, and
           Average, the average of the values in the sequence
   ------------------------------------------------------------------*/

   void FindMinMaxAverage(double& Min, double& Max, double& Average)
   {
      int
         Count = 0;
      double
         Value,
         Sum = 0.0;
```

FIGURE 7.6   Finding the min, max, and average value in a list. (cont.)

```
cout << "\nFirst value ("          // get the first value
    << EOFMarker << " to quit): ";
cin >> Value;

Min = Max = Value;                 // initialize the params

while (!cin.eof())                 // while more data
{
   Count++;                        // increment Count

   Sum += Value;                   // add Value to Sum

   if (Value < Min)                // compare Value to Min
      Min = Value;                 // save it if it's smaller
   else if (Value > Max)           // compare Value to Max
      Max = Value;                 // save it if it's larger

   cout << "Next value ("          // get the next value
      << EOFMarker << " to quit): ";
   cin >> Value;
}

   Average = Sum / Count;          // compute Average
}
```

If we store this function definition in a library, perhaps named **MyStats**, and declare it (and **EOFMarker**) in **MyStats.h**, then a driver program such as that in Figure 7.7 can use this function.

 FIGURE 7.7   A driver program for **FindMinMaxAverage()**.

```
/* This program processes a list of monthly profits.

   Input:  A sequence of monthly profits
   Output: The minimum, maximum, and average of the profits
-------------------------------------------------------------------------*/

#include <iostream.h>
#include <iomanip.h>

#include "MyStats.h"

int main(void)
{
   cout << "\nThis program processes a list of monthly profits.\n";
```

FIGURE 7.7 A driver program for **FindMinMaxAverage()**. (cont.)

```
double
   MinProfit,
   MaxProfit,
   AverageProfit;

FindMinMaxAverage(MinProfit, MaxProfit, AverageProfit);

cout << setprecision(2) << setiosflags(ios::fixed)
     << "\n\nThe worst month was:     " << setw(8) << MinProfit
     << ",\nthe best month was:       " << setw(8) << MaxProfit
     << ", and\nthe average profit was: " << setw(8) << AverageProfit
     << "\n\n";

return 0;
}
```

Sample run (UNIX environment):

```
This program processes a list of monthly profits.

First value (Control-D to quit): 12345.66
Next value (Control-D to quit):  9802.32
Next value (Control-D to quit): 14121.78
Next value (Control-D to quit): 12121.94
Next value (Control-D to quit):  9798.13
Next value (Control-D to quit): 14156.64
Next value (Control-D to quit):  ^D

The worst month was:     9798.13,
the best month was:     14156.64, and
the average profit was: 12057.75
```

Exercises

1. Consider the following program skeleton:

```
void Calculate(double a, double& b,
               int m, int& k, int& n, char& c);

int main(void)
{
   const double
      pi = 3.14159;
   const int
      two = 2;
   const char
      Initial = 'N';
   int
      Month, Day, Year, p, q ;
   double
      Hours, Rate, Amount, u, v;
```

```
char
    Code, Class;
}
```

Determine whether each of the following statements can be used to call this function. If it cannot be used, explain why.

(a) `Calculate(u, v, two, p, q, Code);`
(b) `Calculate(pi, u, two, p, v, Class);`
(c) `Calculate(Hours, pi, two, Day, Year, Class);`
(d) `Calculate("16", Hours, pi, 13, Year, Class);`
(e) `Calculate(pi * Hours, pi, two, Day, Year, Class);`
(f) `Calculate(pi, pi * Hours, two, Day, Year, Class);`
(g) `while (u > 0)`
`        Calculate(u, v, two, p, q, Code);`
(h) `Calculate(0, Hours, (p + 1) / 2, Day, Year, Code);`
(i) `Calculate(sqrt(Amount), Rate, 7, p, q, Init);`
(j) `while (Amount > 0)`
`        Calculate(two, Amount, Day, p + q, Day, Class);`
(k) `cout << Calculate(u, v, two, p, q, Code);`

2. Write a function that accepts a time in military format and returns the corresponding time in the usual representation in hours, minutes, and A.M./P.M. For example, a time of 100 should be returned as 1 hour, 0 minutes, and 'A' to indicate A.M.; a time of 1545 should be returned as 3 hours, 45 minutes, and 'P' to indicate P.M.

3. Write a function that accepts a time in the usual representation of hours, minutes, and a character value that indicates whether this is A.M. ('A') or P.M. ('P') and displays the corresponding military time. (See Exercise 2.)

4. Write a program that reads two positive integers **n** and **b** and then calls a function **ChangeBase()** to calculate and display the base-b representation of **n**. Assume that **b** is not greater than 10. (See Exercise 13 of Chapter 1 for one method for converting from base 10 to another base. Displaying the digits in reverse order as generated by this method is acceptable.)

5. Write a program that reads a positive integer **n** and then calls a function **Hexadecimal()** to display the base-16 representation of **n**. The symbols A, B, C, D, E, and F should be displayed for 10, 11, 12, 13, 14, and 15, respectively. (See Exercise 13 of Chapter 1 and the preceding exercise.)

6. (a) Write a function **ConvertLength()** that accepts a real **Value** and two characters **InUnits** and **OutUnits** and then converts **Value** given in **InUnits** to the equivalent metric value in **OutUnits** and displays this value. The function should carry out the following conversions:

InUnits	OutUnits	
I	C	(inches to centimeters; 1 in = 2.54001 cm)
F	C	(feet to centimeters; 1 in = 30.4801 cm)
F	M	(feet to meters; 1 ft = 0.304801 m)
Y	M	(yards to meters; 1 yd = 0.914402 m)
M	K	(miles to kilometers; 1 mi = 1.60935 km)

(b) Write a driver program that reads several values to be converted and the units and then calls this function to perform the specified conversion. What happens if you enter units other than those listed?

(c) Write a function `ConvertWeight()` that carries out the following conversions:

InUnits	OutUnits	
O	G	(ounces to grams; 1 oz = 28.349527 g)
P	K	(pounds to kilograms; 1 lb = 0.453592 kg)

(d) Write a function `ConvertVolume()` that carries out the following conversions:

InUnits	OutUnits	
P	L	(pints to liters; 1 pt = 0.473167 L)
Q	L	(quarts to liters; 1 qt = 0.94633 L)
G	L	(gallons to liters; 1 gal = 3.78541 L)

(e) Write a menu-driven program to test the three functions `ConvertLength()`, `ConvertWeight()`, and `ConvertVolume()`. It should allow the user to select one of three options according to whether lengths, weights, or volumes are to be converted, read the value to be converted and the units, and then call the appropriate function to carry out the conversion.

7. With **polar coordinates** (r, θ) of a point P, the first polar coordinate r is the distance from the origin to P, and the second polar coordinate θ is the angle from the positive x axis to the ray joining the origin with P.

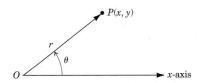

The formulas that relate polar coordinates of a point to its **rectangular coordinates** (x, y) are

$$x = r \cos \theta$$
$$y = r \sin \theta$$

Write a function `Convert()` that converts polar coordinates to rectangular coordinates. Use it in a program that reads the polar coordinates for several points and calls `Convert()`, which calculates and returns the rectangular coordinates for each point. The program should display both pairs of coordinates.

8. Write a function `CalculateTaxes()` that calculates and returns the amount of city income tax and the amount of federal income tax to be withheld from an employee's pay for one pay period. Assume that city income tax withheld is computed by taking 1.15% of gross pay on the first $15,000 earned per year and that federal income tax withheld is computed by taking the gross pay less $15 for each dependent claimed and multiplying by 20%.

Use this function in a program that, for each of several employees, reads the employee's number, number of dependents, hourly pay rate, city income tax withheld to date, federal income tax withheld to date, and hours worked for this period and then calls function `CalculateTaxes()` to find the amount of taxes to be withheld. The program should then display the employee number, gross pay and net pay for this pay period, the amount of city income tax and the amount of federal income tax withheld for this pay period, and the total amounts withheld through this pay period.

9. The **greatest common divisor** of two integers a and b, GCD(a, b), not both of which are zero, is the largest positive integer that divides both a and b. The **Euclidean algorithm** for finding this greatest common divisor of a and b is as follows: Divide a by b to obtain the integer quotient q and remainder r, so that $a = bq + r$. (If $b = 0$, GCD(a, b) = a.) Then GCD(a, b) = GCD(b, r). Replace a with b and b with r, and repeat this procedure. Since the remainders are decreasing, eventually a remainder of 0 will result. The last nonzero remainder is GCD(a, b). For example,

$$1260 = 198 \cdot 6 + 72 \qquad \text{GCD}(1260, 198) = \text{GCD}(198, 72)$$
$$198 = 72 \cdot 2 + 54 \qquad\qquad\qquad\quad = \text{GCD}(72, 54)$$
$$72 = 54 \cdot 1 + 18 \qquad\qquad\qquad\quad = \text{GCD}(54, 18)$$
$$54 = 18 \cdot 3 + 0 \qquad\qquad\qquad\quad = 18$$

(*Note:* If either a or b is negative, replace it with its absolute value.) The **least common multiple** of a and b, LCM(a, b), is the smallest nonnegative integer that is a multiple of both a and b and can be calculated using

$$\text{LCM}(a, b) = \frac{|a \cdot b|}{\text{GCD}(a, b)}$$

Write a program that reads two integers and then calls two functions, one to calculate and return the greatest common divisor of the integers and the other to calculate their least common multiple. The program should then display the two integers together with their greatest common divisor and their least common multiple.

7.4 Default Values for Parameters

As we have mentioned previously, the most useful functions are those that are general enough to solve a variety of instances of the same problem. Nevertheless, it is often the case that the most common uses of functions do not require full generality—the generality is most useful for less-common cases. To see an example of this, consider the following problem.

Example: Evaluating 4th-Order Polynomials

Problem. We are to construct a function that will evaluate any real-valued polynomial function of degree 4 or less for a given real value X. The general form of such a polynomial is

$$a + bX + cX^2 + dX^3 + eX^4$$

where the coefficients a, b, c, d, and e are real constants.

Specification.   For such a function, we clearly need the data objects *a*, *b*, *c*, *d*, *e*, and *X*, all of which will have real values. We can thus specify the function as follows:

Receive: The real values *a*, *b*, *c*, *d*, *e*, and *X*
Return: The real value $a + bX + cX^2 + dX^3 + eX^4$

Based on this specification, we can construct the following stub:

```
double Polynomial(double X, double a, double b,
                  double c, double d, double e)
{
}
```

Design.   Designing an algorithm for this function is straightforward. It need only return the value of an appropriate C++ expression for

$$a + bX + cX^2 + dX^3 + eX^4$$

Coding.   Figure 7.8 shows the complete function `Polynomial()`.

FIGURE 7.8   Evaluating fourth-order polynomials.

```
/* This function will evaluate any polynomial, up to degree 4.

   Receive: The real values X, a, b, c, d, and e
   Return:  The real value a + bX + cX^2 + dX^3 + eX^4
-------------------------------------------------------------------*/

#include <math.h>

double Polynomial(double X, double a, double b,
                  double c, double d, double e)
{
    return a + b*X + c*pow(X, 2.0) + d*pow(X, 3.0) + e*pow(X, 4.0);
}
```

If we store this function in a library `MyMath` and store its declaration

```
double Polynomial(double, double, double, double, double, double);
```

in `MyMath.h`, then any program can use `Polynomial()` by simply including the file `MyMath.h`.

The Difficulty

The difficulty with `Polynomial()` is that in common usage, its generality may not be needed very often. That is, suppose that in some application, `Polynomial()` is used mostly to evaluate quadratic polynomials, that is, those of degree 2. Then because `Polynomial()` is declared as

```
double Polynomial(double, double, double, double, double, double);
```

a function call to evaluate a quadratic with `Polynomial()` must have the form:

```
yVal = Polynomial(xVal, aVal, bVal, cVal, 0.0, 0.0);
```

For example to calculate the value of

$$P(x) = 4 + 4x + x^2$$

when x is 12, we can use the function call

```
yVal = Polynomial(12.0, 4.0, 4.0, 1.0, 0.0, 0.0);
```

and to compute the value of the linear function

$$Q(x) = 3 - 4x$$

when x is 7, we would use the call

```
yVal = Polynomial(7.0, 3.0, -4.0, 0.0, 0.0, 0.0);
```

The problem should be evident: To make `Polynomial()` a (relatively) general function, we used six parameters. In applications that involve lower-degree polynomials, however, this generality becomes a nuisance, because we must pass arguments for all the parameters each time that we call `Polynomial()`.

The Solution

To avoid this inconvenience, C++ allows the programmer to *specify a default value for a parameter.* If a function with default-valued parameters is called and no arguments are passed to these parameters, they receive their specified default values.

Providing a default value for a parameter is easy. We simply use the assignment operator (=) to give the parameter its default value, usually in the declaration of the function. For example, we can change the declaration of `Polynomial()` as follows:

```
double Polynomial(double X, double a = 0.0, double b = 0.0,
                  double c = 0.0, double d = 0.0, double e = 0.0);
```

Now if we need to compute the value of

$$P(x) = 4 + 4x + x^2$$

when x is 12, we can use the function call

```
yVal = Polynomial(12.0, 4.0, 4.0, 1.0);
```

Because only four arguments are passed, the last two parameters (**d** and **e**) are given their default values (0.0). Similarly, to compute the value of

$$Q(x) = 3 - 4x$$

when x is 8, we can use the function call

```
yVal = Polynomial(8.0, 3.0, -4.0);
```

Because only three arguments are passed, the last three parameters (**c**, **d**, and **e**) will be given their default values.

Limitations of Default Parameter Values

There are several restrictions imposed on the use of parameters with default values:

1. *Default values for parameters of a function can be given only once.* The practical implication of this rule is that *a parameter should be given a default value in the declaration of the function or in its definition, but not both.* For example, if we were to declare **Polynomial()** to have default-valued parameters in a library's header file named **MyMath.h**,

```
double Polynomial(double X, double a = 0.0,
                  double b = 0.0, double c = 0.0,
                  double d = 0.0, double e = 0.0);
```

   and also in the implementation file of library **MyMath**,

```
#include "MyMath.h"

double Polynomial(double X, double a = 0.0,
                  double b = 0.0, double c = 0.0,
                  double d = 0.0, double e = 0.0)
{
    return a + b*x + c*pow(X, 2.0)
         + d*pow(X, 3.0) + e*pow(X, 4.0);
}
```

   then the compilation of the implementation file of **MyMath** would produce a syntax error.

2. *If the default parameter values are given in the declaration of the function and that declaration is stored in the header file of a library, then any program that uses the* **#include** *directive to insert that header file can use the default values.* This is the recommended approach.

3. *If the default values are given in the definition of the function and the function's definition is stored in the implementation file of a library, then the default values cannot be used by a program that inserts the header file of that library (using the* **#include** *directive).* This is because a program that uses a library (by inserting its header file) ''sees'' the declarations in the header file of the library but never ''sees'' the function definitions in the implementation file. Consequently, we suggest that the default values be given in the function declaration, since otherwise the default parameter values cannot be used outside the library.

4. *If an argument is supplied for a parameter P that has a default value, then an argument must be supplied for every parameter that precedes P in the parameter list.* For example, suppose that we wish to evaluate

$$P(x) = 2 + 3x^2$$

when x is 1. Then we are unable to take advantage of the default value of parameter **b** and must use the expression

```
Polynomial(1.0, 2.0, 0.0, 3.0)
```

to call **Polynomial()**. The reason for this is that in determining which argument goes with which parameter, C++ matches from left to right, associating the first argument with the first parameter, the second argument with the second parameter, and so on. Thus, the expression

```
Polynomial(1.0, 2.0, 3.0)
```

evaluates the polynomial

$$2 + 3x$$

instead of the polynomial $2 + 3x^2$. Note that this mistake results in a *logic* error, not a *syntax* error. The compiler will process such calls without generating an error.

5. *Parameters that receive default values must be declared at the end of the parameter list.* Stated differently, a parameter that does not receive a default value must precede all parameters that do. For example, if we try to declare **Polynomial()** as

```
double Polynomial(double X, double a = 0.0,
                  double b, double c = 0.0,
                  double d = 0.0, double e = 0.0);
```

a syntax error results because parameter **a**, which has a default value, precedes parameter **b**, which does not have a default value. Again, this rule makes sense, since otherwise a call like

```
Polynomial(3.0, 2.0, 1.0);
```

is ambiguous because it is not clear which default values the programmer intended to use. Although **X** is clearly meant to be 3.0, the programmer could have intended that **a** be 2.0 and **b** be 1.0; or that **a** be 0.0, **b** be 2.0, and **c** be 1.0; or that **a** be 0.0, **b** be 2.0, **c** be 0.0, and **d** be 1.0; and so on. C++ avoids such ambiguities by stipulating that all parameters with default values must follow all parameters without default values in the parameter list.

Summary

Whereas the normal parameter mechanism requires that a function that has n parameters must be called with n arguments, supplying a function with default parameter values allows it to be called with fewer than n arguments. Thus, we were able to construct function **Polynomial()** to compute the value of any polynomial of degree 4 *or less.*

The default parameter value mechanism allows us to call a function with *fewer* arguments than the specified number of parameters. In the next section, we consider the problem of constructing a function that can be called with *more* arguments than the number specified.

*7.5 Varying the Number of Arguments

Sometimes the problem that a function solves requires function calls with different numbers of parameters. As an example, we consider the general polynomial-evaluation problem.

Example: Evaluating Polynomials of Any Degree

Problem. We wish to construct a function that will evaluate a polynomial of degree n for any positive integer n.

We cannot solve this problem with the normal parameter mechanism, since if we construct a function that has the $n + 1$ parameters needed for a polynomial of degree n, then it cannot be used for a polynomial of degree greater than n. The default parameter value mechanism is also of no use because it only allows us to compute polynomials of order less than n. What is needed is some means of *passing different numbers of arguments to the function*, depending on the degree of the polynomial we want to evaluate.

Specification. Identifying the data objects required to evaluate a polynomial gives the following list:

Data Object	Kind of Value	Type of Object	Name of Object
The degree of the polynomial	Variable	Integer	*Degree*
The polynomial's x value	Variable	Real	X
The coefficient of x^0	Variable	Real	a
The coefficient of x^1	Variable	Real	?
$\vdots$	$\vdots$	$\vdots$	$\vdots$

Using this list, we can construct the following specification for the function:

Receive: *Degree*, the degree of the polynomial
X, the value at which the polynomial is to be evaluated
a, the constant term in the polynomial
The coefficients of higher-order terms (if any)
Return: The value of the polynomial at X

Solving this problem requires construction of a function with no limit on the number of its arguments. A stub for a function that accomplishes this is as follows:

```
#include <stdarg.h>   /* declarations to permit
                          varying numbers of arguments */

double Polynomial(int Degree, double X, double a, ...)
{
}
```

The declarations in **<stdarg.h>** allow the use of **ellipses** (. . .) within the parameter list to inform the C++ compiler that if this function is called with more than three arguments, the extra parameters should not be treated as errors. The compiler thus "turns off" argument-checking when processing such calls. It is left to programmers that use this **ellipses mechanism** to ensure that the number and types of arguments are correct.

Design.   An algorithm for evaluating an arbitrary polynomial is as follows:

ALGORITHM FOR EVALUATING A POLYNOMIAL

/* This algorithm can be used to evaluate a polynomial of any degree.

Receive: *Degree,* the degree of the polynomial
X, the value at which the polynomial is to be evaluated
a, the constant term in the polynomial
The coefficients of higher-order terms (if any)

Return: The value of the polynomial at *X*

———————————————————————————————————*/

1. Initialize *PolyValue* to *a,* and *PowerOfX* to 1.0.
2. For each value *i* in the range 1 through *Degree*:
   a. Get the *i*th coefficient of the polynomial, storing it in *NextCoef.*
   b. Multiply *PowerOfX* by *X.*
   c. Multiply *NextCoef* by *PowerOfX* and add the product to *PolyValue.*
3. Return the value of *PolyValue.*

Coding.   When a function whose parameter list includes ellipses is called, any additional arguments that are present are placed into a special type of list, called a **va_list** (for *varying-argument list*). The type **va_list** and the operations for manipulating it are declared in the header file **<stdarg.h>**, so this file must be inserted (using the **#include** directive) before the function definition.

There are three basic operations for manipulating a varying-argument list. In the following descriptions of these operations, **List** is of type **va_list**:

- **va_start(List, LastParam):**   Initializes **List** for processing; **LastParam** is the name of the last parameter in the function declaration before the ellipsis.
- **va_arg(List, Type):** Retrieves and returns the next value of the specified **Type** from **List** (assuming **List** has been initialized with **va_start()**).
- **va_end(List):** "Cleans up" **List** after processing is completed.

This type **va_list** and the preceding operations are used in the program of Figure 7.9 to implement the polynomial-evaluation algorithm.

FIGURE 7.9   Evaluating polynomials.

```
/* This function will evaluate a polynomial of any degree.

   Receive: The int Degree, a real value X, and the real
            coefficients a, ... of a polynomial
   Return:  The real value of the polynomial at X
-----------------------------------------------------------------------*/

#include <stdarg.h>

double Polynomial(int Degree, double X, double a, ...)
{
   double
      PowerOfX = 1.0,                  // powers of X
      NextCoef,                        // next coefficient
      PolyValue = a;                   // polynomial's value at X

   va_list
      ArgList;

   va_start(ArgList, a);              // ArgList begins after a

   for (int i = 1; i <= Degree; i++)
   {
      NextCoef = va_arg(ArgList, double); // get the ith coefficient
      PowerOfX *= X;                       // i-th power of X

      PolyValue += NextCoef * PowerOfX;   // ith term of polynomial

   }

   va_end(ArgList);                    // clean up the list

   return PolyValue;
}
```

Two comments should be made about this function. The first is that unlike the earlier examples of polynomial evaluation, we have calculated the powers of **X** in successive terms using the property that

$$X^i = X^{i-1} * X$$

This is more efficient than using **pow(X, i)**, which would calculate each power of **X** "from scratch." Also, we have used the local variable **NextCoef** for clarity, although it could have been eliminated and the last two statements of the **for** loop replaced by

```
PolyValue += va_arg(ArgList, double) * PowerOfX;
```

If we store this function in the implementation file of the library **MyMath** and store its declaration

```
double Polynomial(int Degree, double X, double a = 0, ...);
```

in the header file **MyMath.h**, then any program can use this version of **Polynomial()** simply by including the file **MyMath.h**. Figure 7.10 shows a simple driver program for testing the correctness of **Polynomial()** on polynomials of degree three or less.

FIGURE 7.10   A driver program for **Polynomial()**.

```
/* This program is a driver program to test function Polynomial().

   Output: The value of Polynomial() for polynomials of various degrees
--------------------------------------------------------------------------*/

#include <iostream.h>

#include "MyMath.h"

int main(void)
{
   cout // P(1.0) for P(x) = 2
        << Polynomial(1, 1.0, 2.0) << endl

        // P(1.0) for P(x) = 2 + 3x
        << Polynomial(2, 1.0, 2.0, 3.0) << endl

        // P(1.0) for P(x) = 2 + 3x + 4x^2
        << Polynomial(3, 1.0, 2.0, 3.0, 4.0) << endl

        // P(1.0) for P(x) = 2 + 3x + 4x^2 + 5x^3
        << Polynomial(4, 1.0, 2.0, 3.0, 4.0, 5.0)

        << "\n\n";

   return 0;
}
```

Sample runs:

```
2
5
9
14
```

Note that it is the programmer's responsibility to ensure that **Polynomial()** is called correctly. If **int** values instead of **double** values were passed to **Polynomial()**,

```
Polynomial(4, 1, 2, 3, 4, 5)
```

then the arguments would be stored as **int** (instead of **double**) values within the **va_list**. If **int** values are stored in one memory word and **double** values in two memory words, then the first call to **va_arg()**,

>   va_arg(ArgList, double)

would interpret the two (**int**) words storing 3 and 4 as a **double** value and, consequently, would return an incorrect result. This is one situation where different types of numeric data cannot be freely intermixed: If a function that uses this ellipses mechanism is expecting a series of arguments of a particular type, then it must receive arguments of that type.

7.6   Inline Functions

We have seen that, when a function **F()** calls another function **G()**, execution is transferred from **F()** to **G()**. When **G()** terminates, a second transfer of control is necessary to return execution back to **F()**. Each of these transfers takes time—a great deal of time compared to the speed at which a computer normally operates. *Each function call increases the amount of time required for a program to execute.*

In many situations, the *overhead* associated with function calls is perfectly acceptable, but there are other problems in which time is so important that the overhead associated with function calls cannot be tolerated. For these problems, C++ provides a way to avoid the overhead normally associated with the function call: the **inline** specifier.[3]

In Section 4.2, we described the syntax of a function declaration using a syntax diagram. As we noted there, that syntax diagram was *simplified,* omitting certain details that would have been confusing at that time. A more complete syntax diagram for a function declaration is

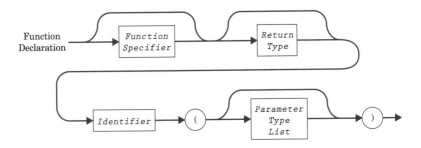

where *FunctionSpecifier* is an optional C++ keyword that directs the compiler to translate the function in a special way. Similarly, a more accurate general form for a function definition is:

FunctionSpecifier ReturnType Identifier(ParameterDeclarationList)

CompoundStatement

---

[3] The **inline** specifier effectively provides a third parameter passing mechanism that is known as *call-by-name,* or *macro-substitution.* See *Compilers: Principles, Techniques and Tools,* by Aho, Sethi, and Ullman (Reading, Mass.: Addison-Wesley, 1986) for a discussion of the limitations of this mechanism.

The C++ mechanism for avoiding the overhead of normal function calls is to declare and define a function using the keyword `inline` as the function specifier. For example, we could declare a Fahrenheit-to-Celsius conversion function `FahrToCelsius()` as

```
inline double FahrToCelsius(double);
```

and define it as

```
inline double FahrToCelsius(double Temp)
{
    return (Temp - 32.0) / 1.8;
}
```

The `inline` specifier suggests[4] to the C++ compiler that it *replace each call to this function with the body of the function, with the arguments for that function call substituted for the function's parameters.* That is, if the compiler treats `FahrToCelsius()` as `inline`, then it will replace the function call in the statement

```
CelsiusTemp = FahrToCelsius(FahrenheitTemp);
```

with the body of the function, but with the argument `FahrenheitTemp` substituted for parameter `Temp`:

```
CelsiusTemp = (FahrenheitTemp - 32.0) / 1.8;
```

The effect of the `inline` specifier is to ask the compiler to take the additional time (at *compile-time*) to perform this substitution *for each call* to the function. This subsequently saves time at *run-time,* because the elimination of each function call means that no transfers of execution need be performed, eliminating the overhead incurred by those function calls.

Note that *both* the function declaration and definition should be labeled as `inline`. Otherwise, there will be a mismatch between the declaration and the definition of the function. For example, in the Turbo C++ environment, defining but not declaring a function as `inline` produces an error message like the following at its definition,

```
Error... 39: Function defined inline after use as extern
```

whereas declaring it but not defining it as `inline` produced the following error message at its declaration:

```
Error... 23: No body defined for this inline function ...
```

To Inline or Not to Inline: A Space–Time Tradeoff. Since `inline` functions eliminate the overhead of function calls and make programs run faster, it may be

---

[4] It is important to realize that this *request* may be ignored by the compiler if it judges the function definition to be too complicated to be efficiently inlined.

tempting to make all functions **inline**. There is, however, a *space–time tradeoff* in the use of **inline** functions: A program that uses **inline** functions may indeed run *faster* than its non-**inline** equivalent, but it may also require more memory.

To see why this is the case, we must realize that, in contrast to the simple examples we have been using, functions written for a real-world software project typically

1. Contain many statements instead of a single **return** statement and
2. May be called at many different places in a program, rather than just one.

When such a function is specified to be **inline**, *each substitution of the function's body for its call replaces a single statement (the call) with multiple statements (the body),* which increases the size of the program.

More generally, suppose that we are working on a software project and write a function **F()**, which is called in *N* different places in a program. Let S_P be the size of the space required by our program (including the definition and call of **F()**) and S_F be the size of function **F()**. Then if **F()** is not implemented as an **inline** function, the total space for the program is simply

$$S_P,$$

but if **F()** is implemented as an **inline** function, then the program's total space is roughly

$$S_P + N \times S_F$$

That is, if the size of function **F()** is more than a few operations and **F()** is called many times, then substituting the body of **F()** at each call significantly increases the size of the program.

We recommend that **inline** be used *with restraint:* If a function is truly trivial (such as **FahrToCelsius()**) and uses just a few operations, then declare and define it as **inline**. Otherwise, avoid using **inline** in order to avoid increasing the memory requirements of the program.[5]

7.7 Object Lifetime and Storage Classes

As we have seen in almost every program we have written, data objects such as parameters and variables can be declared within functions. An important question that we have not yet considered is:

What happens to an object declared within a function when that function terminates?

The answer to this question depends on an attribute called the *storage class* of the object. In this section, we examine storage classes and a related attribute called the *lifetime* of an object.

---

[5] There are actually situations where the use of **inline** will increase the size of a program without producing any gain in its execution speed. See *Effective C++*, by Scott Meyers (Reading, Mass.: Addison-Wesley, 1992), pp. 107–110.

First Things First

A C++ compound statement,

```
{
    Statement-List
}
```

is sometimes called a block of statements, or simply a **block.** Blocks are important to our discussion because they are the means by which C++ determines the lifetime of most objects.

Object Lifetime

At some point during the *execution* of a program, the data objects it uses must be defined. This involves two actions:

1. The data object becomes associated with a particular portion of memory.
2. (Optionally) The data object is initialized to a particular value.

The performance of these two actions is called the **construction** of the object. The symmetric act of disassociating a data object from its portion of memory is called the **destruction** of that object. The period of time from the construction of an object until its destruction is called the **lifetime** of that object.

For example, consider the following code fragment that prints a small multiplication table:

```
{
    .
    .
    .

    for (int i = 1; i <= 3; i++)
        for (int j = 1; j <= 3; j++)
            cout << i << '\t' << j << '\t' << i*j << endl;
    .
    .
    .

}
```

The construction of the data object i involves two actions:

1. A word of memory is associated with the name i.
2. That memory word is initialized to the value 1
   (e.g., 0000000000000001 on a 16-bit machine).

When i is destroyed, the name i is no longer associated with this memory word.

In order to determine the lifetime of i, we must know the times at which the construction and destruction of i occur. This is determined by an attribute of i called its *storage class.*

Storage Classes

There are two different classifications, called **storage classes,** for C++ data objects:

1. Data objects that are

   a. Constructed when the program begins execution and
   b. Destroyed when the program terminates

   are called **static** objects. *The lifetime of a static object is the lifetime of the program.* None of the examples we have seen thus far has used static objects.
2. Data objects that are

   a. Constructed when execution enters the block in which they are declared and
   b. Destroyed when execution leaves the block in which they are declared

   are called **automatic** objects. *The lifetime of an automatic object is the period of time between when execution enters the block in which that object is declared and when execution leaves that block.* All the examples we have seen thus far have used automatic objects. Because an automatic object exists only when execution is in the block in which it was declared, such objects can only be accessed by statements within that block.[6] For this reason, automatic objects are sometimes described as **local** to the block in which they are declared.

Nothing special needs to be done to make the storage class of a data object automatic, because *automatic is the default storage class* for parameter objects and variable objects declared within a block. For example, in the code fragment

```
{
    int
        i = 1;
        .
        .
        .
}
```

the storage class of object `i` is automatic. Each time execution enters this block, object `i` is constructed anew. Each time execution leaves this block, object `i` is destroyed. Thus, if this block is the body of a while loop,

```
while ( SomeCondition )
{
    int
        i = 1;
        .
        .
        .
}
```

then at the beginning of each repetition of the loop body, `i` is constructed, and at the end of each repetition, `i` is destroyed. For this reason, it is usually a good idea

---

[6] This is the reason that an error is generated by any attempt to access an object outside of the block in which it is declared—the object does not exist to be accessed.

to avoid declaring automatic objects within the body of a loop—the time required to construct and destroy such objects can significantly slow execution of the loop.

All that is required to declare an object whose storage class is static is to precede its declaration with the keyword **static**. Thus, if we change the preceding code fragment to

```
{
    static int
        i = 1;
        .
        .
        .
}
```

then the storage class of **i** is static instead of automatic. This means that **i** is constructed once, when the program begins execution, and remains in existence until the program terminates, even if control leaves the block in which **i** is declared. Moreover, if control returns to the block in which **i** is declared, **i** is not reinitialized (because initialization is a part of construction, and **i** is constructed only once); rather it retains its value from the previous execution of the block. The value of **i** thus *persists* between executions of the block.

The static storage class allows us to define objects within a function whose values will persist between executions of that function. This capability is useful in any function that must retain some value between executions, as illustrated by the following example.

Example: Computing Sums

Suppose that we are asked to write a function **NextSumTerm()** with the following property:

- When invoked the first time, the function returns the sum of the integers from 1 to 1.
- When invoked the second time, the function returns the sum of the integers from 1 to 2.

    .
    .
    .

- When invoked the *n*th time, the function returns the sum of the integers from 1 to *n*.

Note that the problem description does not allow passing any information (such as the number of the invocation). The function must somehow keep track of how many times it has been called. The function in Figure 7.11 accomplishes this by using a static object named **CallNumber**.

 FIGURE 7.11 Computing sums.

```
/* This function returns the sum of the integers from 1 to n, where n
   number of times the function has been called.

   Precondition: The function has been called for the n-th time
   Return:       The summation from 1 to n
   ------------------------------------------------------------------*/
```

FIGURE 7.11   Computing sums. (cont.)

```
int NextSumTerm(void)
{
    static int
        CallNumber = 0;

    CallNumber++;

    return CallNumber * (CallNumber + 1) / 2;   // Gauss' formula
                                                 //   see Section 6.9
}
```

Because **CallNumber** has been declared to be a static object, it will be constructed (i.e., defined and initialized to 0) whenever a program that uses this function begins execution. The first time such a program calls **NextSumTerm()**, the function will

a. Increment **CallNumber** (from 0 to 1), and
b. Return the result of applying Gauss' summation formula to **CallNumber**.

Each subsequent call will in turn

a. Increment **CallNumber** by 1, and
b. Return the result of applying Gauss' summation formula to **CallNumber**.

Thus, the first call will compute the sum from 1 to 1, the second call will compute the summation from 1 to 2, and so on. Figure 7.12 presents a simple driver program that can be used to test function **NextSumTerm()**:

FIGURE 7.12   Driver program for **NextSumTerm()**.

```
/* This program tests function NextSumTerm().

   Output: The summation from 1 through i, for all i from 1 to 100
----------------------------------------------------------------*/

#include <iostream.h>

int NextSumTerm(void);

int main(void)
{
    for (int i = 1; i <= 100; i++)
        cout << i << ": " << NextSumTerm() << endl;

return 0;
}

// ... definition of NextSumTerm() omitted
```

FIGURE 7.12 Driver program for **NextSumTerm()**. (cont.)

Sample run:

```
1:  1
2:  3
3:  6
4:  10
    .
    .
    .
97:  4753
98:  4851
99:  4950
100:  5050
```

Static data objects can be used to write an alternative version of **NextSumTerm()** that will execute even faster. Gauss' formula uses a multiplication, an addition, and a division:

```
return CallNumber * (CallNumber + 1) / 2;
```

However, since the sum of the integers from 1 to *n* can be obtained simply by adding *n* to the summation from 1 to $n - 1$, a more efficient approach would be to have the function

a. Maintain a static data object (e.g., **LastSum**) containing the return value of the previous call to the function; and
b. Compute its return value by adding **CallNumber** to **LastSum**.

This improvement is left as an exercise.

Using the register Specifier

In Chapter 1, a **register** was described as a one-word high-speed memory unit within the CPU. The time to access a value stored in a register is far less than the time to access a value stored in memory. It thus makes sense to store object values that will be accessed frequently (such as loop control variables) in registers because each access will require far less time.

Although an optimizing compiler will do its best to keep heavily used variables in registers, C++ allows the programmer to use a **register specifier** to suggest to the compiler that the value of an automatic object be stored in a register (instead of in memory). This is accomplished by preceding the declaration of an automatic object with the keyword **register**. For example, the execution time of the function

```
int Factoriall(register int Limit)
{
   register int
      Fact = 1;
```

```
    for (register int i = Limit; i > 1; i--)
        Fact *= i;

    return Fact;
}
```

could be a fraction of the time required by the following equivalent function:

```
int Factorial2(int Limit)
{
    int
        Fact = 1;

    for (int i = Limit; i > 1; i--)
        Fact *= i;

    return Fact;
}
```

Only automatic objects (variables declared in a block, and parameters) can be declared using the **register** specifier. An attempt to apply the register specifier to a static object, such as

```
register static int i;
```

or

```
static register int j;
```

will generate a syntax error. Note also that because every CPU has only a finite number of registers, the use of the **register** specifier should be limited to heavily used numeric variables, such as variables accessed frequently within a loop.

7.8   PART OF THE PICTURE: Simulation

The term **simulation** refers to modeling a dynamic process and using this model to study the behavior of the process. The behavior of some **deterministic** processes can be modeled with an equation or a set of equations. For example, processes that involve exponential growth or decay are commonly modeled with an equation of the form

$$A(t) = A_0 e^{kt}$$

where $A(t)$ is the amount of some substance A present at time t, A_0 is the initial amount of the substance, and k is a rate constant.

In many problems, however, the process being studied involves **randomness**—for example, Brownian motion, the arrival of airplanes at an airport, the number of defective parts manufactured by a machine, and so on. Computer programs that simulate such processes use a **random number generator,** which produces a number selected from some fixed range in such a way that a sequence of these numbers tends to be uniformly distributed over the given range. Although it is not possible to develop an algorithm that produces truly random numbers, there are some methods that produce sequences of **pseudorandom numbers** that are adequate for most purposes.

Although C++ does not provide a random number generator, its parent language, C, does. We have used this random number generator to construct a class `RandomInt`, that can be used to define integer data objects whose values are pseudorandom numbers. (See Appendix F and the distribution diskette accompanying this text for more information about this class.)

There are two basic operations on a `RandomInt` object:

- Construction (i.e., declaration), which initializes the object to a random number
- Generation, which replaces the object's value with a new random number

Additional operations, such as assignment (=) and output (<<) are also provided. The class is designed so that any of the operations (numeric, relational, etc.) that can be applied to integers can also be applied to class objects, although the result is an `int` (as opposed to a `RandomInt`).

Construction. We can construct a `RandomInt` object by writing a declaration of the form

```
RandomInt
    VariableName(LowerBound, UpperBound);
```

Such a declaration constructs an object named *VariableName* whose value is a random number in the range *LowerBound* to *UpperBound*. If *LowerBound* and *UpperBound* are omitted, a random number is generated in the range **0** to **RAND_MAX** (the bound on random integers), which is declared in `<stdlib.h>`.

Generation. The second operation is to generate a new random number. Given a `RandomInt` object constructed as described previously, a new random integer can be generated by using the member function `Generate()`, as follows:

```
VariableName.Generate();
```

The effect of this call is that the value of *VariableName* is changed to another random integer (from the range specified when *VariableName* was constructed).[7] In addition to changing the value of *VariableName*, `Generate()` returns that value to the function that called it.

Example: Modeling a Dice Roll

Suppose we wish to model the random process of tossing a pair of dice. Using the `RandomInt` class, we can define the objects

```
RandomInt
    Die1(1, 6),
    Die2(1, 6);
```

---

[7] Optional arguments *LowerBound* and *UpperBound* can be used with the `Generate()` function to alter the range in which the random number is to be generated.

to initialize the random number generator and construct the objects `Die1` and `Die2` as random integers in the range 1 through 6. We can then use the statements

```
Die1.Generate();
Die2.Generate();

int
    Pair = Die1 + Die2;
```

to simulate one roll of two dice; the value of `Pair` is the total number of dots showing. The program in Figure 7.13 uses statements similar to these in its simulation.

If the random number generator is suitably constructed, the relative frequency of each value from 2 through 12 for `Pair` should correspond to the probability of that number occurring on one throw of a pair of dice. These probabilities (rounded to three decimal places) are given in the following table:

Outcome	Probability
2	0.028
3	0.056
4	0.083
5	0.111
6	0.139
7	0.167
8	0.139
9	0.111
10	0.083
11	0.056
12	0.028

The program in Figure 7.13 reads an integer `NumRolls` indicating the number of times that two dice are to be tossed. It then repeatedly asks the user to enter a possible outcome of a roll of the dice, simulates `NumRolls` dice rolls, and then displays the relative frequency of this outcome. For each outcome, a for loop is used to perform the required number of dice rolls.

 FIGURE 7.13 Dice-roll simulation.

```
/* This program simulates a given number of pairs of dice rolls,
   and counts the number of times a specified number occurs.

   Input:   Number of dice rolls, the number to be counted,
            and user's response to "More rolls?" query
   Output:  User prompts, and the relative frequency of
            the number of spots
------------------------------------------------------------*/

#include <iostream.h>
```

FIGURE 7.13 Dice-roll simulation. (cont.)

```cpp
#include "RandomInt.h"

int main(void)
{
    cout
        << "This program simulates a given number of dice-pair rolls,\n"
        << "\tcounting the number of times a given number occurs.\n";

    int
        NumRolls;                          // number of rolls of dice

    cout << "\nHow many times are the dice to be rolled ? ";
    cin >> NumRolls;

    RandomInt
        Die1(1, 6),                        // the first die
        Die2(1, 6);                        // the second die

    int
        Pair,                              // the sum of the dice
        NumberBeingCounted,                // the number we want to count
        Occurrences;                       // the counter variable

    char
        Response;                          // user's query response

    do                                     // repeat the following:
    {                                      //    get outcome to count
        cout << "\nWhich number do you want counted (2-12)? ";
        cin >> NumberBeingCounted;

        Occurrences = 0;                   //    set counter to zero

                                           //    for loop to repeat
        for (int RollCount = 1;            //       the following
             RollCount <=  NumRolls;       //       NumRolls times:
             RollCount++)
        {                                  //          roll the dice
            Pair = Die1.Generate() + Die2.Generate();

            if (Pair == NumberBeingCounted)//       if the number came up
                Occurrences++;             //          increment the counter
        }                                  //    end for loop
                                           //    display the result
        cout << "\nThe relative frequency of " << NumberBeingCounted
             << " was " << double(Occurrences) / double(NumRolls)
             << "\n\n";
                                           //       query the user
        cout << "Do you want to do another (y or n) ? ";
        cin >> Response;
    }                                      // until ready to quit
    while ((Response == 'y') || (Response == 'Y'));

    return 0;
}
```

FIGURE 7.13   Dice-roll simulation. (cont.)

Sample run:

```
This program simulates a given number of dice rolls,
    counting the number of times a given number occurs.

How many times are the dice to be rolled ? 10000

Which number do you want counted (2-12)? 2

The relative frequency of 2 was 0.0281

Do you want to do another (y or n) ? y

Which number do you want counted (2-12)? 7

Which number do you want counted (2-12)? 6

The relative frequency of 6 was 0.1365

Do you want to do another (y or n) ? y

Which number do you want counted (2-12)? 7

The relative frequency of 7 was 0.1691

Do you want to do another (y or n) ? y

Which number do you want counted (2-12)? 8

The relative frequency of 8 was 0.141

Do you want to do another (y or n) ? y

Which number do you want counted (2-12)? 11

The relative frequency of 11 was 0.0543

Do you want to do another (y or n) ? n
```

By comparing the generated relative frequencies against the entries in the probability table given previously, we can see that the **RandomInt** class provides a reasonable simulation of a dice roll.

Most random number generators generate random numbers having a **uniform distribution,** but they can also be used to generate random numbers having other distributions. The **normal distribution** is especially important because it models many physical processes. For example, the heights and weights of people, the lifetimes of light bulbs, the tensile strengths of steel produced by a machine, and, in general, the variations in parts produced in almost any manufacturing process have normal distributions. The normal distribution has the familiar bell-shaped curve,

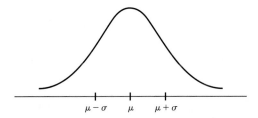

where μ is the mean of the distribution, σ is the standard deviation, and approximately two-thirds of the area under the curve lies between $\mu - \sigma$ and $\mu + \sigma$.

A normal distribution having $\mu = 0$ and $\sigma = 1$ is called a **standard normal distribution,** and random numbers having approximately this distribution can be generated quite easily from a uniform distribution using the following algorithm:

ALGORITHM FOR THE STANDARD NORMAL DISTRIBUTION

/* This algorithm generates random numbers having an approximate standard normal distribution from a uniform distribution.

Return: A random number Z from a standard normal distribution
——*/

1. Set *Sum* equal to 0.
2. Do the following 12 times:
   a. Generate a random number X from a uniform distribution.
   b. Add X to *Sum*.
3. Calculate $Z = Sum - 6$.

The numbers Z generated by this algorithm have an approximate standard normal distribution. To generate random numbers Y having a normal distribution with mean μ and standard deviation σ, we simply add the following step to the algorithm:

4. Calculate $Y = \mu + \sigma * Z$.

Implementing this algorithm as a program is left as an exercise.

Exercises

1. A coin is tossed repeatedly, and a payoff of 2^n dollars is made, where n is the number of the toss on which the first head appears. For example, TTH pays \$8, TH pays \$4, and H pays \$2. Write a program to simulate playing the game several times and to print the average payoff for these games.

2. Suppose that a gambler places a wager of \$5 on the following game: A pair of dice is tossed, and if the result is odd, the gambler loses the wager. If the result

is even, a card is drawn from a standard deck of 52 playing cards. If the card drawn is an ace, 3, 5, 7, or 9, the gambler wins the value of the card (with ace counting as 1, Jack as 11, Queen as 12, and King as 13); otherwise, the gambler loses. What will be the average winnings for this game? Write a program to simulate the game.

3. Johann VanDerDoe, centerfielder for the Klavin Klodhoppers, has the following lifetime hitting percentages:

Out	63.4%
Walk	10.3%
Single	19.0%
Double	4.9%
Triple	1.1%
Home run	1.3%

Write a program to simulate a large number of times at bat, for example, 1000, for Johann, counting the number of outs, walks, singles, and so on, and calculating his

$$\text{Batting Average} = \frac{\text{Number of Hits}}{\text{Number of Times at Bat} - \text{Number of Walks}}$$

4. The classic **drunkard's walk problem** is as follows: Over an 8-block line, the home of an intoxicated person is at block 8, and a pub is at block 1. Our poor friend starts at block n, $1 < n < 8$, and wanders at random, one block at a time, either toward or away from home. At any intersection, the person moves toward the pub with a certain probability, say $\frac{2}{3}$, and toward home with a certain probability, say $\frac{1}{3}$. Having gotten either home or to the pub, the person remains there. Write a program to simulate 500 trips in which the person starts at block 2, another 500 in which the person starts at block 3, and so forth up to block 7. For each starting point, calculate and print the percentage of time the person ends up at home and the average number of blocks walked on each trip.

5. A slab of material is used to shield a nuclear reactor, and a particle entering the shield follows a random path by moving forward, backward, left, or right with equal likelihood, in jumps of one unit. A change of direction is interpreted as a collision with an atom in this shield. Suppose that after 10 such collisions, the particle's energy is dissipated and that it dies within the shield, provided that it has not already passed back inside the reactor or outside through the shield. Write a program to simulate particles entering this shield and to determine what percentage of them reaches the outside.

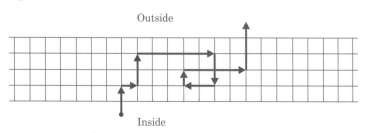

6. Consider a quarter circle inscribed in a square whose sides have length 1:

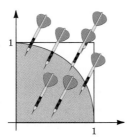

Imagine throwing q darts at this square and counting the total number p that hit within the quarter circle. For a large number of throws, we would expect

$$\frac{p}{q} \sim \frac{\text{Area of Quarter Circle}}{\text{Area of Square}} = \frac{\pi}{4}$$

Write a program to approximate π using this method. To simulate throwing the darts, generate two random numbers X and Y and consider point (X, Y) as being where the dart hits.

7. The famous **Buffon needle problem** is as follows: A board is ruled with equidistant parallel lines, and a needle of length equal to the distance between these lines is dropped at random on the board. Write a program to simulate this experiment and estimate the probability p that the needle crosses one of these lines. Display the values of p and $2/p$. (The value of $2/p$ should be approximately equal to a well-known constant. What constant is it?)

7.9   Introduction to Recursion

We have seen that when one function A calls another function B, the execution of the calling function A is interrupted, and execution begins at the first statement in B. Then, when execution of B is completed, execution resumes in A, at the point immediately following the call to B. This restoration is possible because the values of the variables, constants, parameters, and all other items that are defined within A are stored before B begins to execute. When execution of B has completed, these stored values can be retrieved, and execution can be resumed at the point at which it was interrupted. A function call can thus be viewed as a control mechanism that interrupts execution of the calling function, saves its execution environment, initiates execution of the called subprogram and upon completion of that subprogram, restores the execution environment of the calling function and resumes its execution.

All the examples of function calls considered thus far have involved one function A calling a different function B (with the calling function A often being the main function). However, a function F may also *call itself*, a phenomenon known as **recursion,** and in this section, we show how recursion is implemented in C++.

Examples: Factorial, Exponentiation, and Number Reversal

To illustrate the basic idea of recursion, we consider the problem of calculating the factorial function. The first definition of the factorial $n!$ of a nonnegative integer n that one usually learns is

$$n! = 1 \times 2 \times \cdots \times n, \qquad \text{for } n > 0$$

and that 0! is 1. In calculating a sequence of consecutive factorials, however, it would be foolish to calculate each one using this definition—that is, to multiply together the numbers from 1 through n each time:

$$
\begin{aligned}
0! &= 1 \\
1! &= 1 \\
2! &= 1 \times 2 = 2 \\
3! &= 1 \times 2 \times 3 = 6 \\
4! &= 1 \times 2 \times 3 \times 4 = 24 \\
5! &= 1 \times 2 \times 3 \times 4 \times 5 = 120
\end{aligned}
$$

It is clear that once a factorial has been calculated, it can be used to calculate the next factorial; for example, given the value $4! = 24$, we can use this value to calculate 5! simply by multiplying the value of 4! by 5:

$$5! = 4! \times 5 = 24 \times 5 = 120$$

This value can then be used to calculate 6!:

$$6! = 5! \times 6 = 120 \times 6 = 720$$

and so on. Indeed, to calculate $n!$ for any positive integer n, we need only know the value of 0!,

$$0! = 1$$

and the fundamental relation between one factorial and the previous factorial:

$$n! = n \times (n - 1)!$$

This approach to calculating factorials leads to the following recursive definition of $n!$:

$$
n! = \begin{cases} 1 & \text{if } n = 0 \\ n \times (n - 1)! & \text{if } n > 0 \end{cases}
$$

Another classic example of a function that can be calculated recursively is the power function that calculates x^n, where x is a real value and n is a nonnegative integer. The first definition of x^n that one learns is usually an iterative (nonrecursive) one:

$$x^n = \underbrace{x \times x \times \cdots \times x}_{n \ x\text{'s}}$$

and later one learns that x^0 is defined to be 1. (For convenience, we assume here that x^0 is 1 also when x is 0, although 0° is usually left undefined.)

In calculating a sequence of consecutive powers of some number, however, it would again be foolish to calculate each one using this definition—that is, to multiply the number by itself the required number of times:

$$3.0^0 = 1$$
$$3.0^1 = 3.0$$
$$3.0^2 = 3.0 \times 3.0 = 9.0$$
$$3.0^3 = 3.0 \times 3.0 \times 3.0 = 27.0$$
$$3.0^4 = 3.0 \times 3.0 \times 3.0 \times 3.0 = 81.0$$
$$3.0^5 = 3.0 \times 3.0 \times 3.0 \times 3.0 \times 3.0 = 243.0$$

Once again, the value of this function for a given integer can be used to calculate the value of the function for the next integer. For example, to calculate 3.0^4, we can simply multiply the value of 3.0^3 by 3.0:

$$3.0^4 = 3.0 \times 3.0^3 = 3.0 \times 27.0 = 81.0$$

Similarly, we can use the value of 3.0^4 to calculate 3.0^5:

$$3.0^5 = 3.0 \times 3.0^4 = 3.0 \times 81.0 = 243.0$$

and so on. We need only know the value of 3.0^0,

$$3.0^0 = 1$$

and the fundamental relation between one power of 3.0 and the next:

$$3.0^n = 3.0^{n-1} \times 3.0$$

This suggests the following recursive definition of x^n:

$$x^n = \begin{cases} 1 & \text{if } n = \text{zero} \\ x^{n-1} \times x & \text{if } n > 0 \end{cases}$$

In general, a function is said to be **defined recursively** if its definition consists of two parts:

1. An **anchor** or **trivial case,** in which the value/action of the function is specified for one or more values of the parameter(s).
2. An **inductive** or **nontrivial case,** in which the function's value/action for the current value(s) of the parameter(s) is defined in terms of currently available parameter values and function values/actions.

Constructing a recursive solution to a problem involves identifying these two components. For example, in the factorial function, we have the components

$$n! = \begin{cases} 1 & \text{if } n = 0 \quad \text{(the anchor, or trivial, case)} \\ n \times (n-1)! & \text{if } n > 0 \quad \text{(the inductive, or nontrivial, case)} \end{cases}$$

and in the power function, we have the components

$$x^n = \begin{cases} 1 & \text{if } n = 0 \quad \text{(the anchor, or trivial, case)} \\ x^{n-1} \times x & \text{if } n > 0 \quad \text{(the inductive, or nontrivial, case)} \end{cases}$$

In each definition, the first statement specifies a particular value of the function when the solution to the problem is trivial, and the second statement defines the value of the function for nontrivial values of n in terms of its value for $n - 1$.

As we noted in these examples, such recursive definitions are useful in calculating function values $f(n)$ for a sequence of consecutive values of n. Using them to calculate any one particular value, however, requires computing earlier values. For example, consider using the recursive definition of the factorial function to calculate 5!. We must first calculate 4! because 5! is defined as the product of 5 and 4!. But to calculate 4! we must calculate 3! because 4! is defined as $4 \times 3!$. And to calculate 3!, we must apply the inductive step of the definition again, $3! = 3 \times 2!$, then again to find 2!, which is defined as $2! = 2 \times 1!$, and once again to find $1! = 1 \times 0!$. Now we have finally reached the anchor case:

$$5! = 5 \times 4!$$
$$4! = 4 \times 3!$$
$$3! = 3 \times 2!$$
$$2! = 2 \times 1!$$
$$1! = 1 \times 0!$$
$$0! = 1$$

Since the value of 0! is given, we can now backtrack to find the value of 1!,

$$5! = 5 \times 4!$$
$$4! = 4 \times 3!$$
$$3! = 3 \times 2!$$
$$2! = 2 \times 1!$$
$$1! = 1 \times 0! = 1 \times 1 = 1$$
$$0! = 1$$

and then backtrack again to find the value of 2!,

$$5! = 5 \times 4!$$
$$4! = 4 \times 3!$$
$$3! = 3 \times 2!$$
$$2! = 2 \times 1! = 2 \times 1 = 2$$
$$1! = 1 \times 0 = 1 \times 1 = 1$$
$$0! = 1$$

and so on until we eventually obtain the value 120 for 5!:

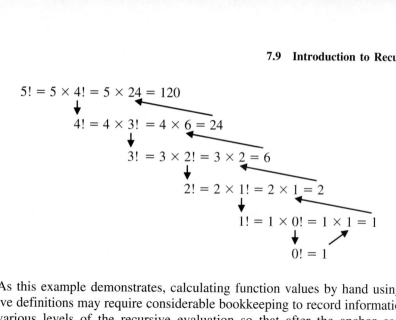

As this example demonstrates, calculating function values by hand using recursive definitions may require considerable bookkeeping to record information at the various levels of the recursive evaluation so that after the anchor case is reached, the information can be used to backtrack from one level to the preceding one. Fortunately, most modern high-level languages (including C++) support recursive functions, and all the necessary bookkeeping and backtracking is performed automatically by the computer.

To illustrate, consider the factorial function again. The recursive definition of this function:

$$n! = \begin{cases} 1 & \text{if } n = 0 \text{ (the anchor, or trivial, case)} \\ n \times (n-1)! & \text{if } n > 0 \text{ (the inductive or nontrivial case)} \end{cases}$$

is itself an algorithm,[8] which is quite easy to encode in C++, as shown in Figure 7.14.

 FIGURE 7.14 Computing $n!$ recursively.

```
/* Factorial computes n! recursively.

   Receive:   n, an integer
   Return:    n! (or -1 in case of error -- n is negative)
-----------------------------------------------------------*/

int Factorial(int n)
{
   if (n == 0)
      return 1;                        // trivial case
   else if (n > 0)
      return n * Factorial(n-1);       // inductive step
```

---

[8] Note that a recursive definition that has a slightly different anchor case can be constructed by observing that $0! == 1! == 1$. Although this alternate definition leads to a slightly more efficient implementation of `Factorial()`, we have chosen this definition for its simplicity in introducing the concepts of recursion.

FIGURE 7.14 Computing *n*! recursively. (cont.)

```
    else                            // check that parameter is valid
    {
        cerr << "n! is not defined for negative n\n";
        return -1;
    }
}
```

When this function is called with a positive argument, the inductive step

```
        else if (n > 0)
            return n * Factorial(n-1);
```

causes the function to call itself repeatedly, each time with a smaller parameter, until the anchor case

```
        if (n == 0)
            return 1;
```

is reached.

To illustrate, suppose that some function issues the call

```
        int
            Fact = Factorial(5);
```

to calculate 5!. Since the value of **n** (which is 5) is not 0, the inductive step generates another recursive call to **Factorial** with parameter n - 1 = 4. Before execution of the original function call is suspended, the current value 5 of the parameter **n** is saved so that the value of **n** can be restored when execution resumes. This might be pictured as follows:

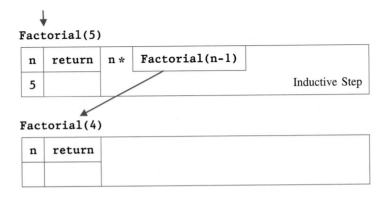

Since the value of **n** (4) in this function call is not 0, the inductive step in this second call to **Factorial()** generates another call **Factorial(n - 1)**, passing it the argument 3. Once again, the value of **n** (4) is saved so that it can be restored later:

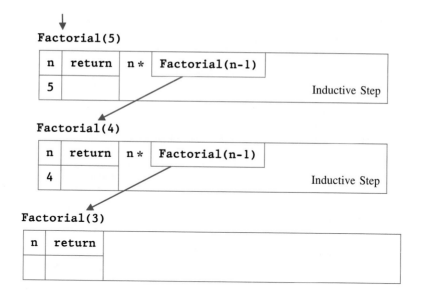

Since the value of **n** (3) in this function call is not 0, the inductive step in this third call to **Factorial()** generates another call **Factorial(n - 1)**, passing it the argument 2. Once again, the value of **n** (3) is saved so that it can be restored later. The call **Factorial(2)** in turn generates another call **Factorial(1)**, which, in turn, generates another call **Factorial(0)**:

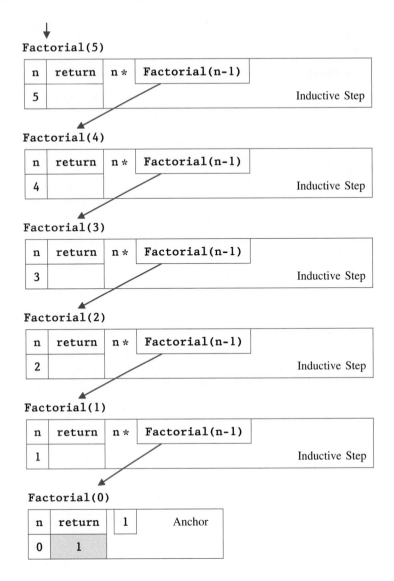

Because the anchor condition

```
if (n == 0)
    return 1;
```

is now satisfied in this last function call, no additional recursive calls are generated. Instead, the value 1 is returned as the value for **Factorial(0)**, and execution resumes in the preceding recursive call, in which **n** has the value 1. That value for **n** is restored, and the value

```
n * Factorial(n - 1) = 1 * Factorial(0) = 1 * 1 = 1
```

is computed as the value of **Factorial(1)**:

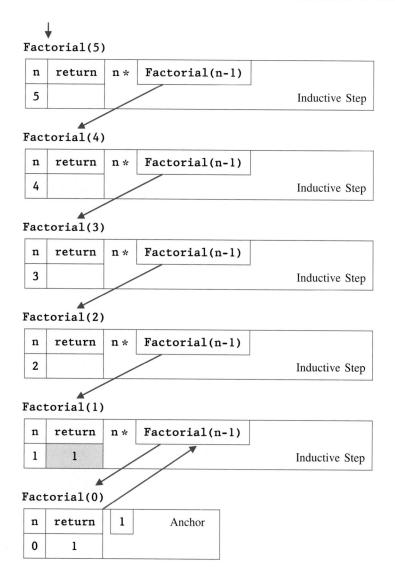

Execution of **Factorial()** with argument 1 is thus complete, and execution resumes in the preceding recursive call, in which **n** has the value 2. The value of **n** is restored; and the value

```
n * Factorial(n - 1) = 2 * Factorial(1) = 2 * 1 = 2
```

is computed for **Factorial(2)**.

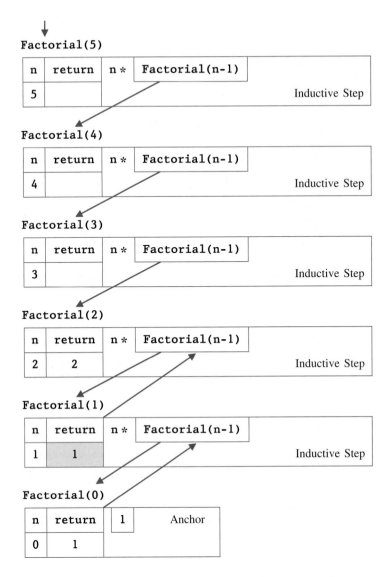

This completes the call to **Factorial(2)**, and so execution resumes in **Factorial(3)**, which computes and returns the value

```
n * Factorial(n - 1) = 3 * Factorial(2) = 3 * 2 = 6
```

This completes the function call to **Factorial(3)**, and so execution resumes in the call to **Factorial(4)**, which computes and returns the value:

```
n * Factorial(n - 1) = 4 * Factorial(3) = 4 * 6 = 24
```

This completes the call to **Factorial(4)**, and so execution resumes in the original function call, in which **n** has the value 5. There, the value

```
n * Factorial(n - 1) = 5 * Factorial(4) = 5 * 24 = 120
```

is computed and returned by `Factorial(5)`:

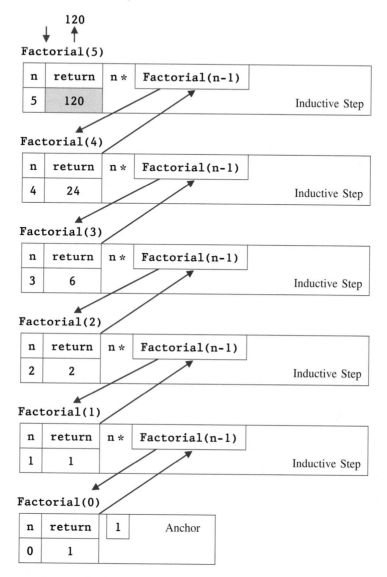

The value 120 is thus returned as the value for `Factorial(5)`.

Note that in the definition of `Factorial()` we have included a test that the parameter is a nonnegative integer. To see the reason for this, consider what would happen if it had been omitted and the function were called with a negative integer, as in

```
int
    Fact = Factorial(-1);
```

Since −1 is not equal to 0, the inductive step

```
else
    return n * Factorial(n-1);
```

would be performed, recursively calling **Factorial(-2)**. Execution of this call would begin, and because -2 is not equal to 0, the inductive step

```
else
   return n * Factorial(n-1);
```

would be performed, recursively calling **Factorial(-3)**. This behavior would continue until memory was exhausted, at which point the program would terminate abnormally, possibly producing an error message such as

Stack overruns Heap.

Such behavior is described as **infinite recursion** and is obviously undesirable. To avoid this, we programmed defensively by including the parameter-validity check so that **Factorial(n)** is defined over all integer values.

As a second example of a recursive function, consider again the exponentiation operation defined recursively by

$$x^n = \begin{cases} 1 & \text{if } n \text{ is 0} \quad \text{(the anchor, or trivial, case)} \\ x^{n-1} \times x & \text{if } n > 0 \quad \text{(the inductive, or nontrivial, case)} \end{cases}$$

Like the factorial function, this definition is an algorithm, from which a recursive function can be written, as shown in Figure 7.15.

FIGURE 7.15   Performing exponentiation recursively.

```
/* Power computes X raised to the power n recursively.

   Receive:  X, a real value, and
             n, an integer
   Return:   X raised to the power n
-------------------------------------------------------*/

double Power(double X, int n)
{
   if (n == 0)
      return 1.0;                    // anchor case
   else if (n > 0)
      return Power(X, n - 1) * X;// inductive step (n > 0)
   else
   {
      cerr << "\n*** Power has received a negative exponent.\n";
      return -1.0;
   }
}
```

The following diagram pictures the five levels of function references generated by the initial call **Power(3.0, 4)**:

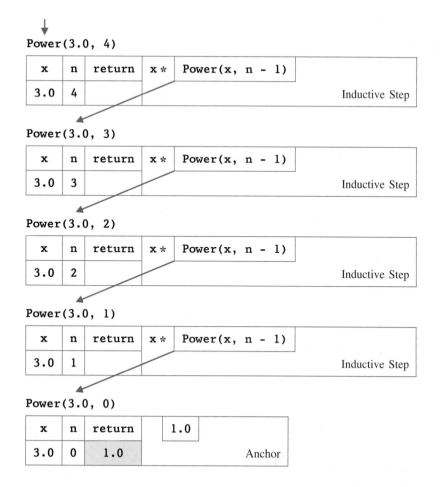

In the final call (with arguments 3.0 and 0), the value 1.0 is computed and returned by `Power()`. That completes the fifth call; and control returns to the preceding call, in which **n** has the value 1. This fourth call then computes and returns

Power(x, n-1) * x = Power(3.0, 0) * 3.0 = 1.0 * 3.0 = 3.0

as the value of **Power(3.0, 1)**, and this value is returned to the previous call, in which **n** has the value 2. There, the value

Power(x, n-1) * x = Power(3.0, 1) * 3.0 = 3.0 * 3.0 = 9.0

is computed and returned to the previous call, in which **n** has the value 3. There, the value

Power(x, n-1) * x = Power(3.0, 2) * 3.0 = 9.0 * 3.0 = 27.0

is computed and returned to the previous call, in which **n** has the value 4. There, the value

Power(x, n-1) * x = Power(3.0, 3) * 3.0 = 3.0 * 27.0 = 81.0

is computed and returned as the value for the initial function call **Power(3.0, 4)**. The following diagram summarizes these actions.

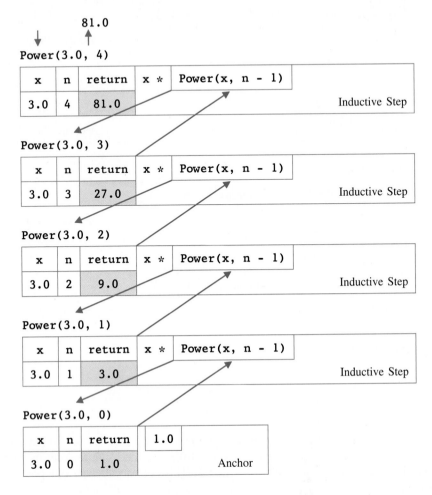

Functions that do not return a value but simply perform some action may also be recursive. To illustrate, consider the problem of printing the digits of a nonnegative integer in order from right to left. Although this problem can easily be solved without recursion (as the exercises ask you to do), it can also be solved by a recursive function.

The recursive approach to solving this problem is motivated by considering how the problem would be solved by hand. To write the digits of the number 6385 in reverse order, we first look at the last digit 5 and write it. Next we look to the left and consider the number formed by the remaining digits and process it *in exactly the same way* (inductive step). We continue in this way until we reach the left end of the number (anchor step). Viewed in this way, the processing is recursive and leads naturally to the recursive function for solving this problem given in Figure 7.16.

FIGURE 7.16 Printing a number's digits in reverse order.

```
/* This function displays a number's digits in reverse order.

   Receive:  An integer Number >= 0
   Output:   The digits of Number in reverse order
-----------------------------------------------------------*/

void PrintReverse(int Number)
{
   cout << Number % 10;          // output the rightmost digit

   int
      LeftDigits = Number / 10;  // leftmost part of Number

   if (LeftDigits)               // inductive step:
      PrintReverse(LeftDigits);  // ... output the rest recursively
   else                          // anchor case:
      cout << '\n';              // ... generate a new line
}
```

To show how this function solves the problem, we will trace the execution of the function call **PrintReverse(6285)**. The statement

```
cout << Number % 10;
```

displays the rightmost digit (5), and the number that remains when this last digit is removed is calculated by the statement

```
LeftDigits = Number / 10;
```

which produces the nonzero value 628. Since this is treated as true in the test

```
if (LeftDigits)
```

the inductive step generates another call to **PrintReverse()** with argument **LeftDigits** = 628:

PrintReverse(6285)

Number	LeftDigits	PrintReverse(LeftDigits)	**Output**
6285	628	Inductive Step	5

PrintReverse(628)

Number	LeftDigits	PrintReverse(LeftDigits)	Output
628	62	Inductive Step	5

This new call, **PrintReverse(628)**, displays the rightmost digit 8 and calculates **LeftDigits** = 62, which is treated as true in the condition

```
if (LeftDigits)
```

and so a new function call **PrintReverse(62)** is generated:

PrintReverse(6285)

Number	LeftDigits	PrintReverse(LeftDigits)	**Output**
6285	628	Inductive Step	5

PrintReverse(628)

Number	LeftDigits	PrintReverse(LeftDigits)	Output
628	62	Inductive Step	5 8

PrintReverse(62)

Number	LeftDigits	PrintReverse(LeftDigits)	Output
62		Inductive Step	5 8

This function call displays the rightmost digit 2 and generates another function call with argument **LeftDigits** = 6, and this call displays the digit 6. This time, **LeftDigits** is assigned the value **Number** / **10**, which is zero, and is thus treated as false in the condition

```
if (LeftDigits)
```

and so the output statement

```
cout << '\n';
```

is executed, which terminates output on the current line:

PrintReverse(6285)

Number	LeftDigits	PrintReverse(LeftDigits)	**Output**
6285	628	Inductive Step	5

PrintReverse(628)

Number	LeftDigits	PrintReverse(LeftDigits)	Output
628	62	Inductive Step	5 8

PrintReverse(62)

Number	LeftDigits	PrintReverse(LeftDigits)	Output
62	6	Inductive Step	5 8 2

PrintReverse(6)

Number	LeftDigits	cout << '\n'	Output
6	0	Anchor	5 8 2 6

Control then resumes in the preceding call to **PrintReverse()**. However, execution of that function is complete, so control simply returns to the preceding call, which terminates in the same way. This continues until the original call has terminated. The following diagram summarizes this execution trace of **PrintReverse(6285)**:

PrintReverse(6285)

Number	LeftDigits	PrintReverse(LeftDigits)	**Output**
6285	628	Inductive Step	5

PrintReverse(628)

Number	LeftDigits	PrintReverse(LeftDigits)	Output
628	62	Inductive Step	5 8

PrintReverse(62)

Number	LeftDigits	PrintReverse(LeftDigits)	Output
62	6	Inductive Step	5 8 2

PrintReverse(6)

Number	LeftDigits	cout << '\n'	Output
6	0	Anchor	5 8 2 6

Thus, a recursive function need not return a value in order for it to be useful in solving a problem.

Recursion versus Iteration

Many problems can be solved with equal ease using either a recursive or an iterative algorithm. For example, we implemented the factorial and power functions in this section as recursive functions, but these functions can be written nonrecursively just as easily. What factors should determine the method to use for such functions?

Nonrecursive functions may execute more rapidly and use memory more efficiently than do their recursive counterparts, unless the C++ compiler is instructed to perform **optimization** when compiling the function.[9] A good optimizing C++ compiler can be thought of as an "expert system" in programming and will replace inefficient (but intuitive) recursive definitions with more efficient definitions that use loops. An optimizing compiler thus frees the programmer to write intuitive (if inefficient) source code and leaves the task of ensuring that the binary executable code is efficient to the compiler.

Given a compiler capable of optimization, the following rule of thumb is one approach to deciding whether to use recursion or iteration:

> If there is little difference in the effort to define a function recursively or iteratively, then
>   if the C++ compiler will perform optimization, then
>   the recursive definition can be used;
>   otherwise,
>   the iterative definition should be used;
> otherwise, if the function is substantially easier to implement recursively, then
>   the recursive definition can be used;
> otherwise
>   the iterative definition should be used.

Optimization, however, will increase compilation time, because the compiler must check the source program for inefficiencies and translate them into equivalent but more efficient binary statements. As a result, the time required to compile and optimize programs can increase significantly. To avoid this delay, programs are typically compiled without optimization during their development. Once a program is completed and in its final form, it is recompiled using optimization, so that

---

[9] Turning on optimization for GNU's g++ compiler is simply a matter of invoking `g++` with the `-O` switch (for simple optimization) or `-O2` (for highly optimized code). In the Turbo environment, programmers can customize their optimizations in an `Optimization Settings Window`, accessed via the `Options-Compiler-Optimizations` menu path. Similarly, programmers in the Symantec environment can customize their optimizations in an `Optimizations Window` that is accessed via the `Edit-Options-Symantec C++ ...` menu path.

the added compile-time cost of optimization is only incurred once, on the final compilation.

For some problems, such as the Towers of Hanoi problem described in the next section, recursion is the most natural and straightforward technique. For these problems, nonrecursive algorithms may not be obvious, may be more difficult to develop, and may be less readable than recursive ones. For such problems, the simplicity of the recursive algorithms compensates for any inefficiency that might remain after optimization. Recursion is also appropriate when the problem's data is organized in a data structure that is defined recursively. Such data structures are considered in Chapter 17.

The examples of recursion in this section have illustrated **direct recursion,** in which a function calls itself directly. There are other situations in which a function calls another function, and after a chain of function calls, the first function is eventually called again. For example, one function *A* may call another function *B*, which calls function *C*. If C subsequently calls *A* again, then this chain of function calls is said to exhibit **indirect recursion.**

Exercises

1. Consider the following function F:

```
void F(int Num)
{
   if ((1 <= Num) && (Num <= 8))
   {
      F(Num - 1);
      cout << Num;
   }
   else
      cout << endl;
}
```

   (a) What output is produced by each of the following calls?
   (i) F(3)   (ii) F(7)   (iii) F(10)
   (b) If Num - 1 is replaced by Num + 1 in the function, what output will be produced by the function calls in (a)?
   (c) If the cout << Num; statement and the recursive call to F() are interchanged, what output will be produced by the calls in (a)?
   (d) If a copy of the statement cout << Num; is inserted before the recursive call to F(), what output will be produced by the calls in (b)?

2. Given the following function F(), use the method illustrated in this section to trace the sequence of function calls and returns in evaluating F(1, 5) and F(8, 3).

```
int F(int Num1, int Num2)
{
   if (Num1 > Num2)
      return 0;
   else if (Num2 == Num1 + 1)
      return 1;
   else
      return F(Num1 + 1, Num2 - 1) + 2;
}
```

3. Consider the following function G():

```
void G(int Num1, int Num2)
{
    if (Num2 <= 0)
        cout << endl;
    else
    {
        G(Num1 - 1, Num2 - 1);
        cout << Num1;
        G(Num1 + 1, Num2 - 1);
    }
}
```

(a) What output is produced by the function call G(14, 4)? (*Hint:* First try G(14, 2); then try G(14, 3)).

(b) How many letters are output by the call G(14, 10)?

(c) If the **cout << Num1;** statement is moved before the first recursive call to G(), what output will be produced by G(14, 4)?

4. Determine what is calculated by the following recursive functions:

(a)
```
void F(unsigned n)
{
    if (n == 0)
        return 0;
    else
        return n * F(n - 1);
}
```

(b)
```
double F(double x, unsigned n)
{
    if (n == 0)
        return 0;
    else
        return x + F(x, n - 1);
}
```

(c)
```
unsigned F(unsigned n)
{
    if (n < 2)
        return 0;
    else
        return 1 + F(n / 2);
}
```

(d)
```
unsigned F(unsigned n)
{
    if (n == 0)
        return 0;
    else
        return F(n / 10) + n % 10;
}
```

(e)
```
unsigned F(int n)
{
    if (n < 0)
        return F(-n);
    else if (n < 10)
        return n;
    else
        return F(n / 10);
}
```

5. Write nonrecursive versions of the functions in Exercise 4.

6. Write a nonrecursive version of the recursive function `PrintReverse()` given in the text.

7. Write a test driver for one of the functions in Exercise 4. Add output statements to the function to trace its actions as it executes. For example, the trace displayed for `F(19)` for the function `F()` in part (c) should have a form like

```
F(19) = 1 + F(10)
    F(10) = 1 + F(5)
        F(5) = 1 + F(2)
            F(2) = 1 + F(1)
                F(1) returns 0
            F(2) returns 1
        F(5) returns 2
    F(10) returns 3
F(19) returns 4
```

where the indentation level reflects the depth of the recursion. (*Hint:* You might use a static variable `Level`, initially zero, that is incremented when the function is entered and decremented when execution is finished.)

8. Modify the recursive exponentiation function in the text so that it works for negative exponents also. One approach is to modify the recursive definition of x^n so that for negative values of n, division is used instead of multiplication and n is incremented rather than decremented:

$$x^n = \begin{cases} 1 & \text{if } n = \text{zero} \\ x^{n-1} * x & \text{If } n > 0 \\ x^{n+1}/x & \text{otherwise} \end{cases}$$

9. Write a test driver for the function `PrintReverse()` in this section, and add output statements to the function to trace its actions as it executes. For example, the trace displayed for `PrintReverse (9254)` might have a form such as

```
PrintReverse (9254): Output 4, then call PrintReverse (925).
    PrintReverse (925): Output 5, then call PrintReverse (92).
        PrintReverse (92): Output 2, then call PrintReverse (9).
            PrintReverse (9): Output 9 and \n.
            PrintReverse (9) returns.
        PrintReverse (92) returns.
    PrintReverse (925) returns.
PrintReverse (9254) returns.
```

where the indentation level reflects the depth of the recursion. (See the hint in Exercise 7.)

10. **(a)** Write a recursive function that returns the number of digits in a nonnegative integer.
    (b) Write a driver program to test the function of part (a).

11. **(a)** Write a recursive function to convert an integer from base 10 to base b (see Exercise 9 of Section 7.4).
    (b) Write a driver program to test the function of part (a).

12. The **Euclidean algorithm** for finding the **greatest common divisor** of two integers (not both zero) was described in Exercise 9 of Section 7.3.)

    (a) Write a recursive function that calculates the greatest common divisor using the Euclidean algorithm.
    (b) Write a program that uses the function of part (a) to find the greatest common divisors of several pairs of numbers.

13. Proceed as in Exercise 12, but write a nonrecursive function.

14. **Binomial coefficients** can be defined recursively as follows:

$$\left.\begin{array}{r}\binom{n}{0} = 1 \\ \binom{n}{n} = 1\end{array}\right\} \quad \text{(anchor)}$$

$$\text{For } 0 < k < n, \quad \binom{n}{k} = \binom{n-1}{k-1} + \binom{n-1}{k} \qquad \text{(inductive step)}$$

    (a) Write a recursive function to calculate binomial coefficients.
    (b) Draw a diagram like that in this section showing the recursive function calls and returns involved in calculating the binomial coefficient $\binom{4}{2}$.
    (c) Use your recursive function in a program that reads values for n and k and displays the value of $\binom{n}{k}$, using the function to obtain this value.

15. Binomial coefficients can also be defined as follows:

$$\binom{n}{k} = \frac{n!}{k!(n-k)!}$$

    (a) Write a nonrecursive function for calculating binomial coefficients using this definition.
    (b) If possible with your version of C++, write a program to compare the computing time of this nonrecursive function for calculating binomial coefficients with the recursive function developed in Exercise 14.

16. **(a)** Write a recursive function that prints a nonnegative integer with commas in the correct locations. For example, it should print 20131 as 20,131.
    (b) Write a program to test the function of part (a).

7.10 PART OF THE PICTURE: **Artificial Intelligence**

Artificial intelligence (AI) is the part of computer science concerned with designing computer systems that exhibit characteristics associated with human intelligence; for example, learning, deductive reasoning, problem solving, language understanding, and the recognition of visual images. Because of the nature of its subject matter, it is necessarily interdisciplinary in its approach, using ideas and techniques drawn from philosophy, psychology, linguistics, mathematics, physics, electrical engineering, and computer science. The history of research in AI is marked by some controversy, due at least in part to grandiose claims made early in its history about what AI could and would accomplish. Although many of these goals have not been reached, progress has been made in a number of areas. The discipline continues to change and grow as applications in new areas are studied. Currently, areas studied in AI include the following:

- *Search techniques:* Searching for solutions to problems such as airline scheduling and routing problems in which the number of possible search paths is so large that it is not feasible to examine them all.
- *Game playing:* Devising programs that play board games and solve puzzles such as tic-tac-toe, chess, and checkers.
- *Automated reasoning:* Making logical inferences like those needed to prove mathematical theorems or discover new results; in general, attempting to automate the process of reasoning.
- *Computational linguistics:* Using computational techniques to generate languages and analyze their structures such as in the design of lexical analyzers, parsers, and code generators.
- *Natural language processing:* Recognizing and translating natural languages such as English. Applications include the design of style and spelling checkers, verification of authorship, and intelligent user interfaces for complex software such as database-management systems.
- *Expert systems:* Designing systems that use a knowledge base of information obtained from a human expert in some area and logical rules to answer questions, analyze problems, and provide advice, much as a human expert would. Successful expert systems include MYCIN for medical consultations, DENDRAL for chemical inference, PROSPECTOR for dealing with geological data, and XCON to configure computer systems.
- *Pattern recognition:* Recognizing speech, handwriting, patterns of amino acids in DNA strands, and so on.
- *Computer vision:* Designing machines that can accept input in visual form and can recognize and classify the images they receive.
- *Robotics:* Attempting to build machines that have sensing capabilities (vision, force, touch), can manipulate objects (grasp them, pick them up, put them down), and solve various object- and space-oriented problems (moving without bumping into things, fitting parts together).

Recursion is an important technique used in many of these areas of AI. In fact, it is the basic repetitive control structure in the programming language LISP, which is one of the major programming languages in AI. In this section we consider one problem from the area of game playing that can easily be solved using recursion, but for which a nonrecursive solution is quite difficult.

Example: The Towers of Hanoi

The **Towers of Hanoi** problem is to solve the puzzle shown in the following figure, in which one must move the disks from the left peg to the right peg according to the following rules:

1. When a disk is moved, it must be placed on one of the three pegs.
2. Only one disk may be moved at a time, and it must be the top disk on one of the pegs.
3. A larger disk may never be placed on top of a smaller one.

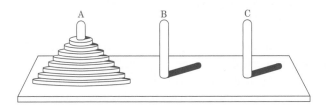

The following *game tree* shows the various configurations that are possible in the problem with two disks; the highlighted path in the tree shows a solution to the two-disk problem:

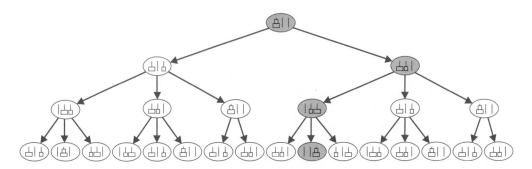

Legend has it that the priests in the Temple of Bramah were given a puzzle consisting of a golden platform with the three diamond needles on which were placed 64 golden disks. The priests were to move one disk per day, following the preceding rules, and when they had successfully finished moving the disks to another needle, time would end. (*Question:* If the priests moved one disk per day and began their work in year 0, when would time end?)

Novices usually find the puzzle easy to solve for a small number of disks, but they have more difficulty as the number of disks grows to seven, eight, and beyond. To a computer scientist, however, the Towers of Hanoi puzzle is easy: We begin by identifying a base case, for which the problem is trivial to solve:

If there is one disk, then move it from Peg A to Peg C.

The puzzle is thus easily solved for $n = 1$ disk. We then seek an inductive solution for $n > 1$ disks, in which we assume that a solution exists for $n - 1$ disks:

1. *Move the topmost n − 1 disks from Peg A to Peg B, using Peg C for temporary storage.*
2. *Move the final disk remaining on Peg A to Peg C.*
3. *Move the n − 1 disks from Peg B to Peg C, using Peg A for temporary storage.*

This scheme is implemented by the recursive function **Move()** in Figure 7.17, which solves the Towers of Hanoi puzzle for *n* disks.

 FIGURE 7.17   Solving the Towers of Hanoi problem recursively.

```
/* Move is a recursive function to solve the Hanoi Towers puzzle.

   Receive: N, the number of disks to be moved,
            Source, the needle the disks are to be moved from,
            Destination, the needle the disks are to be moved to, and
            Spare, the needle that can be used to store disks
               temporarily
------------------------------------------------------------------*/

void Move(int N, char Source, char Destination, char Spare)
}
   if (N <= 1)                              // base case
      cout << "\nMove the top disk from " <<  Source << " to "
           << Destination;
   else
   {                                        // inductive case
      Move(N-1, Source, Spare, Destination);
      Move(1, Source, Destination, Spare);
      Move(N-1, Spare, Destination, Source);
   }
}
```

Figure 7.18 presents a driver program that uses **Move()** to solve the Towers of Hanoi problem and an execution in which the problem is solved for four disks.

 FIGURE 7.18   Towers of Hanoi driver program.

```
/* This program solves the Towers of Hanoi puzzle recursively.

   Input:  NumDisks, the (int) number of disks to be moved
   Output: A sequence of moves that solves the puzzle
------------------------------------------------------------------*/

#include <iostream.h>
```

FIGURE 7.18   Towers of Hanoi driver program. (cont.)

```cpp
void Move(int, char, char, char);     // the function to solve the puzzle

int main(void)
{
   const char                         // the three pegs
      Peg1 = 'A',
      Peg2 = 'B',
      Peg3 = 'C';

   cout << "\nThis program solves the Hanoi Towers puzzle.\n";

   int
      NumDisks;                        // the number of disks to be moved

   cout << "\nPlease enter the number of disks: ";
   cin >> NumDisks;

   Move(NumDisks, Peg1, Peg3, Peg2); // the solution

   cout << endl;
   return 0;
}

// ... definition of Move() goes here ...
```

Sample run:

```
This program solves the Hanoi Towers puzzle.

Please enter the number of disks: 4

Move the top disk from A to B
Move the top disk from A to C
Move the top disk from B to C
Move the top disk from A to B
Move the top disk from C to A
Move the top disk from C to B
Move the top disk from A to B
Move the top disk from A to C
Move the top disk from B to C
Move the top disk from B to A
Move the top disk from C to A
Move the top disk from B to C
Move the top disk from A to B
Move the top disk from A to C
Move the top disk from B to C
```

The key observation is that each recursive call has distinct values for its parameters **N**, **Source**, **Destination**, and **Spare**, and the particular combination of these values in one call is completely different from the combination of values in any other call.

Exercises

1. Trace the execution of the call

```
Move(4, 'A', 'B', 'C');
```

far enough to produce the first five moves. Does your answer agree with the program output in Figure 7.18? Do the same for the call

```
Move(5, 'A', 'B', 'C');
```

2. Modify the program in Figure 7.18 so that it displays a picture of each move rather than a verbal description.

Programming Pointers

Program Design

1. *Programs for solving complex problems should be designed as interactions among objects.*

   - *A problem should be constructed as a series of operations on a set of objects.*
   - *A complicated operation on an object should be broken down into a sequence of less-complicated operations, until such operations are trivial.*
   - *All variable objects should be defined within a function (either as a local variable or as a parameter) so that the function is as self-contained as possible.*

2. *Parameters should be declared as determined by the* **specification** *of a function: If the specification for a function stipulates that*

   - *The function* **receive and not return** *a value,*
     then a **value** *parameter should be defined to hold that value.*
   - *The function* **receive and return a value,**
     then a **reference** *parameter should be defined to hold that value.*
   - *The function* **receive a value that is often the same,**
     then a **default value** *should be supplied for that parameter.*
   - *Different function calls may* **require differing numbers of arguments,**
     then the **ellipses mechanism** *should be used so that the number of arguments can vary.*

3. *Only simple functions should be specified as being* `inline` *functions.* Substitution of an inline function's body for each of its calls can cause a program's size to increase considerably if the function is nontrivial and/or it is called at several places in the program.

4. *Heavily used (automatic) numeric variables, such as loop control variables, can be declared to be register variables to speed up execution.*

5. *Automatic data objects should not, in general, be defined within a loop.* Such objects will be constructed and destroyed during each repetition of the loop, greatly slowing its execution.

6. *Unless they are optimized, recursive functions typically execute slower than their nonrecursive counterparts.* Because of this, a file containing a recursive function definition should be compiled with optimization turned on.

Potential Problems

1. *When a function is called, the number of arguments must be the same as the number of parameters in the function heading,* unless the default-value mechanism or the ellipses mechanism is in use. For example, consider a function with heading:

```
int Maximum(int Number1, int Number2)
```

If i, j, and k are integer variables, the statement

```
Larger1 = Maximum( i, j, k );
```

will generate an error, because the number of arguments does not match the number of parameters.

2. *When a function with value parameters is called, the type of each argument must be type-compatible with the type of the corresponding parameter.* For example, consider again the function with the heading

```
int Maximum(int Number1, int Number2)
```

The statement

```
Larger2 = Maximum(Number, 3.75);
```

is incorrect, because a real value such as 3.75 should not be passed to the integer parameter **Number2**, since a loss of precision will occur.

3. *Parameters that are to return values from a function must be declared as reference parameters using the indicator &. The arguments that correspond to reference parameters must be variables; they may not be constants or expressions.* For example, the function heading

```
void FindTaxes(double Income,
               double& NetIncome, double& Tax)
```

can return only values of **NetIncome** and **Tax** to the calling program unit, and it cannot be called by the statement

```
FindTaxes( Salary, 3525.67, IncomeTax );
```

because the constant **3525.67** cannot be associated with the reference parameter **NetIncome**.

4. *For a function with reference parameters, the type of each argument that corresponds to a reference parameter must be the same as the type of that parameter.*

For example, consider the function with the heading

```
int Swap(int& First, int& Second)
```

If `Ch1` and `Ch2` are character variables, then the statement

```
Swap(Ch1, Ch2)
```

will generate a syntax error, because the types of arguments `Ch1` and `Ch2` differ from their corresponding parameters `First` and `Second`.

5. *A function's parameters (and local variables) are allocated memory only during execution of that function; there is no memory associated with them either before or after execution of that function.* Any attempt to use these parameters outside the function will generate an error. Declaring an object within a function to be `static` will cause its value to persist from one execution of that function to the next, but that object still cannot be accessed outside the function.

6. *A function must be declared before it can be called.* For example, if the function `FindTaxes()` calls the function `Calculate()`, then a declaration of `Calculate()` must precede the definition of `FindTaxes()`.

```
void Calculate(ParameterList);
     ⋮
     ⋮

void FindTaxes();
{
     ⋮
     ⋮

    Calculate(ArgumentList);
     ⋮
     ⋮
}
```

7. *Parameters with default values must be defined at the (rightmost) end of the parameter list.* This enables the C++ compiler to associate each argument with the appropriate parameter, since arguments are matched against parameters from left to right.

8. *The variable-number-of-arguments mechanism should be used with caution.* The effect of this mechanism is to turn off type-checking for the rest of the argument list. It follows that if a value of the incorrect type is passed to a function using this mechanism, the C++ compiler is unable to identify the error.

Program Style

1. *Functions should be documented in the same way that programs are.* The documentation should include specifications and descriptions of

- The *purpose* of the function.
- Any items that must be *received by* the function from its caller.

- Any items that must be *input to* the function.
- Any items that are *returned by* the function to its caller.
- Any items that are *output by* the function.

2. *The layout of a program should clearly indicate the relationship of each line to its surrounding context.* In this text we do the following:

   - Insert blank lines and documentation before each function definition to separate it from other functions.
   - Indent the declarations and statements within each function.
   - Follow the same stylistic standards for functions as we do for main programs.

3. *Libraries should be documented in much the same way that programs are.* The initial documentation for a library should describe clearly, precisely, and completely what the contents of the library are and how to use items in it, any special algorithms it implements, and other useful information such as the author, when it was last modified, and so on.

4. *All guidelines for programming style apply to libraries.* The stylistic standards described in earlier chapters for functions in a program should also be followed for the functions defined in a library.

Programming Projects

1. (a) Write a function **DaysIn()** that returns the number of days in a given month and year. (See Exercise 4 of Section 5.5, which describes which years are leap years.)

   (b) Write a function **Ndays()** that returns the number of days between two given dates.

   (c) A person's biorhythm index on a given day is the sum of the values of his or her physical, intellectual, and emotional cycles. Each of these cycles begins at birth and forms a sine curve having an amplitude of 1 and periods of 23, 33, and 28 days, respectively. Write a program that accepts the current date, a person's name, and his or her birthdate and then calculates the biorhythm index for that person.

2. Write a program for the nuclear shield problem described in Exercise 5 of Section 7.8, but allow the particle to travel in any direction rather than simply left, right, forward, or backward. Choose a direction (angle) at random, and let the particle travel a random distance in that direction.

3. Write a program to simulate the random path of a particle in a box. A direction (angle) is chosen at random and the particle travels a fixed (or random) distance in that direction. This procedure is repeated until the particle either passes out through the top of the box or collides with one of the sides or the bottom and stops. Calculate the average number of times the particle escapes from the box and the average number of jumps needed for it to get out.

Some modifications are as follows: Use a two-dimensional box if a three-dimensional one seems too challenging. Let the particle bounce off the sides or the bottom of the box at the same angle with which it hits rather than stop when it collides with these boundaries.

4. Consider a network of streets laid out in a rectangular grid, for example,

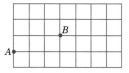

In a *northeast path* from one point in the grid to another, one may walk only to the north (up) and to the east (right). For example, there are four northeast paths from *A* to *B* in the preceding grid:

Write a program that uses a recursive function to count the number of northeast paths from one point to another in a rectangular grid.

5. Write a recursive function to find the prime factorization of a positive integer—that is, to express the integer as a product of primes or indicate that it is a prime. Display the prime factors in descending order.

6. Develop a recursive function to generate all of the *n!* permutations of the set $\{1, 2, \ldots, n\}$. (*Hint:* The permutations of $\{1, 2, \ldots, k\}$ can be obtained by considering each permutation of $\{1, 2, \ldots, k - 1\}$ as an ordered list and inserting *k* into each of the *k* possible positions in this list, including at the front and at the rear.) For example, the permutations of $\{1, 2\}$ are (1, 2) and (2, 1). Inserting 3 into each of the three possible positions of the first permutation yields the permutations (3, 1, 2), (1, 3, 2), and (1, 2, 3) of $\{1, 2, 3\}$, and using the second permutation gives (3, 2, 1), (2, 3, 1), and (2, 1, 3). Write a program to test your function.

COMPUTING WITH
CLASS OBJECTS

III

In Chapters 8 through 11, we begin the transition from computing with simple objects to computing with objects whose representation involves multiple attributes. We begin in Chapter 8 by examining *files* and how `fstream` objects can be used to perform I/O operations on files. Chapter 9 presents the type `Strings`—a class we have provided for storing and manipulating *character strings*. In Chapter 10, we introduce *enumerations*—our first look at programmer-defined types. Chapter 11 extends this idea by introducing the *class*, which is the primary C++ mechanism for defining new types and their operations. In Chapter 12, we introduce the *array* and see how a `List` class containing an array can be used to store and process lists of data. Chapter 13 presents a case study in which we apply the ideas of Chapter 12 and the *bitwise operators* in implementing a `Set` class. Finally, Chapter 14 presents *multidimensional arrays* and uses them in constructing `Table` and `Matrix` classes. Together, these chapters provide an introduction to the solution of problems involving data objects with multiple attributes.

FILES AND STREAMS

> . . . it became increasingly apparent to me that, over the years, Federal agencies have amassed vast amounts of information about virtually every American citizen. This fact, coupled with technological advances in data collection and dissemination, raised the possibility that information about individuals conceivably could be used for other than legitimate purposes and without the prior knowledge or consent of the individuals involved.
> PRESIDENT GERALD R. FORD

> The rights of the people to be secure in their persons, houses, papers, and effects against unreasonable searches and seizures, shall not be violated. . . .
> FOURTH AMENDMENT OF THE U. S. CONSTITUTION

CHAPTER CONTENTS

Most programmers have had the unfortunate experience of being in the process of editing a program when the text editor unexpectedly terminates. This is especially inconvenient, because all the changes made since the program was last saved are lost. This happens because the text editor is an executable program, and the source program being edited is stored in main memory allocated to the text editor. When the text editor terminates, this memory is deallocated and its contents are lost.

To avoid this problem we must be able to *save* the edited program in some *stable* memory (such as a secondary memory) so that it is not lost even if a power outage should occur. Examples of secondary memory include hard disks, floppy disks, floptical disks, and magnetic tapes.

When a program is saved in secondary memory, it must be stored in such a way that

1. It can be retrieved in the future, and
2. It is kept distinct from all other programs that are saved.

To achieve these goals, secondary memory is organized into distinct containers called **files,** in which information (i.e., programs and data) can be stored. Then when a program must be edited, the text editor *loads* the program from secondary memory into its memory by *reading* from the file in which that program is stored. *Saving* the program from main memory to secondary memory involves *writing* that program to a file.

A compiler is another program that performs input by reading from a file and performs output by writing to a file. For example, in the command-line environment, the C++ compiler is a program that might be specified by

Input (command-line):	*InFile,* a file containing a C++ source program;
	OutFile, a file that will store an executable program;
Input (*InFile*):	*P,* the source C++ program stored in *InFile;*
Output (*OutFile*):	*B,* a binary executable program equivalent to *P;* or
Output (*Screen*):	a listing of the syntax errors in *P.*

Files are important in computing because they provide a stable place to store programs (both source and binary) indefinitely. Files can also be used to store *data.* If a large set of data values is to be processed, then those values can be stored in a file, and a program can be written to read these values from the file and process them. This is especially useful in testing and debugging a program because the data does not have to be reentered each time the program is executed. In this chapter, we examine how file input and output can be performed in C++.

Files can be classified by the kind of data that is stored in them. Those that contain textual characters (such as the source code for a program, numbers entered with a text editor, etc.) are called **text files.** By contrast, files that contain non-ASCII/EBCDIC characters (such as the binary code for a compiled program or the control codes for a word processor) are called **binary files.** In this chapter, we discuss input and output using text files.

8.1 Computing with Files

Until now our programs have been *interactive,* meaning that the user interacted with them directly by entering data from the keyboard in response to prompts and/or queries displayed on the screen. However, there are many problems in which the sheer volume of data to be processed makes entering the data from the keyboard impractical. For such problems, the data can be stored in a file and the program designed to read the data values from that file. To illustrate, consider the following problem.

Example: Processing Meteorological Data

Problem. A meteorologist, Dr. Blitzen, must record and process large amounts of weather-related data. One part of this data consists of thousands of atmospheric pressure readings that were recorded every 15 minutes for (approximately) the past year. This data has been stored in a file named **pressure.dat**. The statistics that Dr. Blitzen needs are the minimum, maximum, and average of these readings.

Specification. The relevant objects in the preceding description of the problem are the pressure readings, the name of the file in which they are stored, and the three statistics to be calculated. Since the number of readings is not available, a fourth statistic that must be computed is the number of these readings. Also, to illustrate file output, we will write the results to a file rather than to the screen. The list of data objects for this problem is thus as follows:

Data Object	Kind of Value	Type of Object	Name of Object
The pressure readings	Sequence	Real	*Reading*
The name of the file in which the readings are stored	Constant	Character string	*InputFileName*
The number of readings	Variable	Integer	*Count*
The minimum reading	Variable	Real	*Min*
The maximum reading	Variable	Real	*Max*
The sum of the readings	Variable	Real	*Sum*
The average reading	Variable	Real	*Sum/Count*
The name of the file to which the results are to be written	Constant	Character string	*OutputFileName*

This list allows us to specify the problem as follows:

Input (*InputFileName*):   A sequence of pressure readings
Output (*OutputFileName*):   The minimum, maximum, and average of the input values

Design. This problem is similar to problems we have considered earlier, so we will omit the customary list of operations. Obviously, a loop is required because there are many data values, each of which must be processed using the same sequence of steps. Finding the minimum and maximum values involves saving the smallest and largest of the values that have been examined thus far, comparing each new value to those values, and updating them as necessary. Similarly, finding the average value requires keeping a running total of all the values as well as counting the values; then, after all the values have been read, the sum of the data values must be divided by the count. We might use the following algorithm to solve the problem.

ALGORITHM FOR PROCESSING METEOROLOGICAL DATA

/* This algorithm reads real values from a file, counts them, and computes the minimum, maximum, and average values.

Input (File): A sequence of real values
Output (File): The minimum, maximum, and average of those values ————————————*/

1. Open the input file for reading. If this fails, display an error message and terminate the algorithm. Otherwise proceed as follows.
2. Initialize (integer) *Count* to 0; (real) *Sum* to 0.0.
3. Read the first *Reading* from the input file.
4. Initialize (real) *Max* to *Reading* and (real) *Min* to *Reading*.
5. While the end of the input file has not been reached:
    a. Increment *Count*.
    b. Add *Reading* to *Sum*.
    c. If *Reading* is less than *Min*, then
        Set *Min* to *Reading*.
    Else if *Reading* is greater than *Max*, then
        Set *Max* to *Reading*.
    End If.
    d. Read the next *Reading* from the input file.
    End While.
6. Close the input file.
7. Open a file for output. If this fails, display an error message and terminate the algorithm. Otherwise proceed as follows.
8. Write *Count* to the output file.
9. If *Count* is greater than zero, then
    Write *Min, Max,* and *Sum/Count* to the output file.
10. Close the output file.

Coding. Once we become familiar with the file-processing capabilities provided in C++, encoding the preceding algorithm is straightforward. A program that implements this algorithm is shown in Figure 8.1. The file-processing features used in this program are described in the following section.

 FIGURE 8.1 Reading a file of meteorological data.

```
/* This program processes meteorological data stored in a file named
   "pressure.dat".

   Input(File):  A sequence of meteorological readings
   Output(File): The number of readings, the minimum reading,
                 the maximum reading, and the average reading
-------------------------------------------------------------*/
```

FIGURE 8.1   Reading a file of meteorological data. (cont.)

```cpp
#include <iostream.h>              // contains ios
#include <fstream.h>              // contains fstream
#include <stdlib.h>               // contains exit()

int main(void)
{
   const char
      InputFileName[] = "pressure.dat",   // name of the input file
      OutputFileName[] = "pressure.out",  // name of the output file
      ErrorMsg[] = "\n*** main: unable to open file: ";

   cout << "\nThis program computes the number, maximum, minimum, and"
        << "\n\taverageof an input list of numbers in the file '"
        << InputFileName << "'\n\t\and places its results in the file '"
        << OutputFileName << "'.\n";

   // ----------- Input Section ----------------------------------------
   fstream
      InStream;                            // a stream to the input file

   InStream.open(InputFileName, ios::in);
                                           // establish the connection

   if (InStream.fail())                    // if stream cannot be opened
   {
      cerr << ErrorMsg << InputFileName //  display error msg, and
           << "\n\n";
      exit(-1);                           //  terminate abnormally
   }
                                           // otherwise declare
   int                                     //    and initialize vars:
      Count = 0;                           //    number of values
   double
      Reading,                             //    value being processed
      Sum = 0.0;                           //    running total

   InStream >> Reading;                    // read a value from fstream

   double
      Max = Reading;                       // largest seen so far
      Min = Reading;                       // smallest seen so far

   while (!InStream.eof())                 // while there is more data
   {
      Count++;                             //   update: Count,
      Sum += Reading;                      //           Sum, and
      if (Reading < Min)
         Min = Reading;                    //           Min or
      else if (Reading > Max)
         Max = Reading;                    //           Max
      InStream >> Reading;                 //   read next value from fstream
   }                                       // end while

   InStream.close();                       // close the connection
```

FIGURE 8.1   Reading a file of meteorological data. (cont.)

```
// ------------ Output Section ----------------------------------

fstream
   OutStream(OutputFileName, ios::out);
                                      // open fstream for output
if (OutStream.fail())                 // if stream cannot be opened
{
   cerr << ErrorMsg << OutputFileName//   display error message
         << "\n\n";
   exit (-1);                         //   and terminate.
}                                     // otherwise:
                                      //   output results
                                      //   (to fstream)
OutStream << "\n-->There were " << Count << " values,";

if (Count > 0)
   OutStream << "\n\tranging from " << Min
             << " to " << Max
             << "\n\tand their average is " << Sum / Count
             << ".\n\n";

return 0;
}
```

As we shall see, this program writes its results to a file named **pressure.out**. When it is executed, it simply displays its opening message and seems to terminate, because all subsequent output goes to **pressure.out**. If we were to replace the ''Output Section'' of the program with the statements

```
cout << "\n--> There were  " << Count << " values,";

if (Count > 0)
   cout << "\n\tranging from " << Min << " to " << Max
         << "\n\tand their average is " << Sum / Count
         << ".\n\n";
```

then the program would display its results on the screen. These sets of statements illustrate the differences (and similarities) between interactive and file I/O.

Testing and Verification.   To test the correctness of the program, we construct several **test files,** in which we place a small set of data values that will be used to check whether the program is performing correctly. For example, we might place an ascending sequence of numbers

```
11
12
13
14
15
```

in one such file **test1.dat**, a descending sequence

> 99 98 97 96 95 94 93 92 91

in another file **test2.dat**, two sets of numbers separated by a blank line

> 4 5 6
> 1 2 3
>
> 9 8
> 7

in yet another file **test3.dat**, and so on. We thus create test files that *exercise* the program, looking for conditions under which it fails to work properly.

Figure 8.2 shows several sample runs of the program (named **pressure**) using these test files in a UNIX environment. The UNIX command **cp** is used to copy each of the test files into the file named **pressure.dat** (being careful to not destroy Dr. Blitzen's original file) and the **more** command is used to list the output file produced by each execution.[1] Once the program has been thoroughly tested, we can execute it using Dr. Blitzen's original data file and be confident that the results it produces are correct.

FIGURE 8.2   Testing file I/O.

```
% cp test1.dat pressure.dat
% pressure

This program computes the number, maximum, minimum, and
    average of an input list of numbers in the file 'pressure.dat'
    and places its results in the file 'pressure.out'.

% more pressure.out

-->There were 5 values,
   ranging from 11 to 15
   and their average is 13.

% cp test2.dat pressure.dat
% pressure

This program computes the number, maximum, minimum, and
    average of an input list of numbers in the file 'pressure.dat'
    and places its results in the file 'pressure.out'.

% more pressure.out

-->There were 9 values,
   ranging from 91 to 99
   and their average is 95.
```

---

[1] DOS users can enter TYPE PRESSURE.OUT|MORE to accomplish the same thing.

FIGURE 8.2 Testing file I/O. (cont.)

```
% cp test3.dat pressure.dat
% pressure
```

```
This program computes the number, maximum, minimum, and
    average of an input list of numbers in the file 'pressure.dat'
    and places its results in the file 'pressure.out'.
```

```
% more pressure.out
```

```
-->There were 9 values,
    ranging from 1 to 9
    and their average is 5.
```

As the preceding example demonstrates, ''hard-wiring'' the names of the input and output files into the program by using string constants **"pressure.dat"** and **"pressure.out"** makes it clumsy to execute the program with files having other names. In Chapter 9, we will see an easier way to do this.

8.2 fstream Objects and Operations

In this section, we examine the types and operations provided by the **iostream** library for performing file I/O.

Declaring fstream Objects

With interactive I/O, **<iostream.h>** automatically establishes the following connections (among others) between programs executing in main memory and I/O devices:

1. An **istream** object named **cin** connects the program and the keyboard.
2. An **ostream** object named **cout** connects the program and the screen.[2]

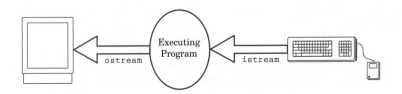

These streams are automatically constructed for interactive programs. However, if a program is to perform input from and/or output to a text file, then a stream must

---

[2] The **ostream** object **cerr** is also established as a second connection between the program and the screen.

be established between that program (in main memory) and the text file (stored on some secondary memory device such as a disk drive).

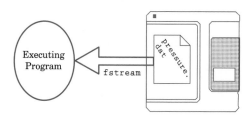

As illustrated by the program in Figure 8.1, this can be accomplished by using the **fstream** class. This class is declared in the header file **<fstream.h>**, so that any program that uses this class must insert that file using the **#include** directive.

Declaring an fstream Object.   Before a program can read values from or write values to a text file, it must construct an **fstream** object to act as a connection between the program and the file. This is accomplished with a declaration of the form

```
fstream
    ObjectName;
```

For example, the program in Figure 8.1 uses the declaration

```
fstream
    InStream;
```

to construct an **fstream** object named **InStream**. Once an **fstream** object has been constructed, the various **fstream** operations can be applied to that object. These operations are the subject of the remainder of this section.

The Basic fstream Operations

It is important to understand that the class **fstream** is *derived from* the class **iostream**, meaning that **fstream** has been written as an extension of the **iostream** class. The immediate implication of this is that all the operations on **iostream** objects can also be performed on **fstream** objects, along with some new operations that are limited to **fstream** objects. Of these operations, the five most common are the following:

open()	A function that establishes a connection between a program and a file
>>	An operator that inputs an object from a file (opened for input)
<<	An operator that outputs an object to a file (opened for output)
eof()	A boolean function that returns true if the last input operation read the end-of-file mark, and returns false otherwise
close()	A function that terminates a connection between a program and a file

We now examine each of these operations in greater detail.

The open( ) Member.   Just as the declaration

```
int
    i;
```

declares object **i** as an uninitialized **int** variable, the declaration

```
fstream
    InStream;
```

declares the object **InStream** as an uninitialized **fstream**—a *potential* connection between the program and a file. This potential connection becomes an actual connection by using the **open()** function, which is a member of class **fstream**. In the program in Figure 8.1, the statement

```
InStream.open(InputFileName, ios::in);
```

initializes the **fstream** object **InStream** by establishing it as a connection between the program and the file named **InputFileName**. (Recall that **InputFileName** is a named constant associated with the character string constant **"pressure.dat"**.)

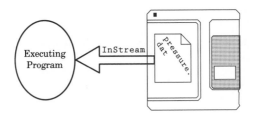

The second argument, **ios::in**, of the **open()** function specifies that **InStream** is being opened for input; an error will be generated if an attempt is made to output something to **InStream**.

To illustrate, suppose that the file **pressure.dat** contains the following values:

```
11.1 22.2 33.3 44.4
55.5 66.6 77.7
88.8 99.9
```

It is important to realize that a **text file** such as **pressure.dat** is simply a *sequence of characters*. Such files are created by the operating system, which automatically places an end-of-file mark at the end of the file. If we use the symbol ƀ to represent a blank, the symbol ↵ to represent a newline, and the symbol ◊ to represent the end-of-file mark, then after the statement

```
InStream.open(InputFileName, ios::in);
```

has been executed, **InStream** may be visualized as

11.1♭22.2♭33.3♭44.4↵55.5♭66.6♭77.7↵88.8♭99.9↵◊

InStream

where the down arrow (↓) indicates the **read position,** denoting the location of the next character to be read.

The **open()** member-function can also be used to open **fstream** objects as connections to output files. For example, given the declaration

```
fstream
    OutStream;
```

then the statement

```
OutStream.open("NewFile.out", ios::out);
```

creates a new file named **NewFile.out** containing only the end-of-file mark and then establishes **OutStream** as a connection between the program and the file:

OutStream

In this diagram, the down arrow (↓) represents the **write position**—the position at which the next output value will be placed in the stream.

Opening a file with the argument **ios::out** is *destructive:* If a file named **NewFile.out** exists prior to execution of the **open()** function, then the contents of that file are lost. By contrast, opening a file with the argument **ios::app** is *nondestructive:*

```
OutStream.open("ExistingFile.out", ios::app);
```

Any values output to **ExistingFile.out** will be *appended* to the file.

In general, the **open()** function can be described as follows.

The open() Member

> Use
>
>   *FStreamName*.open(*FileName, Mode*);
>
> where:
>   *FStreamName* is the name of the stream being
>   initialized;

> *FileName* is the (character string) name of a data file stored on a secondary memory device; and
>
> *Mode* is one or more of the following
>
> > `ios::in` if *FileName* is to be opened for reading,
> >
> > `ios::out` if *FileName* is to be (destructively) opened for writing, and
> >
> > `ios::app` if *FileName* is to be (nondestructively) opened for appending
>
> with multiple modes being separated by the | operator.
>
> **Action**
>
> The object *FStreamName* is initialized as a connection between the executing program and the secondary memory file named *FileName*.

For example, the function call

```
IOStream.open("MyData", ios::in|ios::app);
```

initializes an **fstream** object named **IOStream** as a connection to a file named **MyData** from which data can be read and to which data can be written.[3]

Initialization at Declaration. It is also possible to initialize an **fstream** object *when it is declared.* In the program in Figure 8.1, we used the declaration statement

```
fstream
    Outstream(OutputFileName, ios::out);
```

in place of the equivalent statements

```
fstream
    OutStream;
       .
       .
       .
OutStream.open(OutputFileName, ios::out);
```

---

[3] In addition to these modes, the modes `ios::ate`, `ios::trunc`, `ios::nocreate`, and `ios::noreplace` can be used with the `open()` function. See the documentation for `< streambuf.h>` for a description of how they work on your system.

Both of these construct **OutStream** and initialize it as a connection to **OutputFileName**:

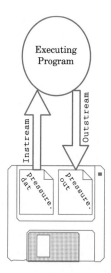

The trade-offs in these two initialization mechanisms are as follows:

- The **open()** operation is a common one in programming languages, and the initialization

    ```
    InStream.open(OutputFileName, ios::out);
    ```

    could be considered to be more readable than the second mechanism, since it explicitly states the operation being performed.
- The initialization of an **fstream** object is an easily forgotten detail, since we do not need to initialize **cin** or **cout** before we use them. It might thus be argued that initializing an object at its declaration

    ```
    fstream
        InStream(InputFileName, ios::in);
    ```

    is less prone to error, since it eliminates the (additional) **open()** operation.

Regardless of the approach used, the two mechanisms are functionally equivalent. The choice is largely a matter of programming style.

Programming Defensively. There are a number of errors that can occur in a call to the function **open()**. To illustrate, consider the following attempt to initialize a stream to an input file:

```
InStream.open(FileName, ios::in);
```

If the file **FileName** does exist and **Instream** is established as a connection to it, then **open()** is said to **succeed,** but if **FileName** does not exist, then **open()** is said to **fail.** Obviously, if `open()` should fail, any subsequent attempts to perform input from that file also will fail. Consequently,

> *The success or failure of a call to open a file should always be **tested** before proceeding with any additional operations on the file.*

This testing is easily done using the member function `fail()`. In the program in Figure 8.1, the `if` statement,

```
if (InStream.fail())
{
  cerr << ErrorMsg << InputFileName
       << "\n\n";
  exit(-1);
}
```

uses the function `fail()` to test the success of the `open()` call. The function `fail()` returns false (zero) if `open()` was successful and true (nonzero) if it failed. Of course, if a call to `open()` fails, an informative error message should be displayed, as illustrated. The function call

```
exit(-1);
```

can be used by any function to terminate the execution of the program in the event of an error. The argument to `exit()` will be the value returned to the operating system by the main function, so a negative argument is typically given to indicate abnormal termination. The header file `<stdlib.h>` contains the declaration of `exit()`, and so this file must be inserted using the `#include` directive.

The `fail()` Member

> **Use**
>
>   *FStreamName*.`fail();`
>
> where:
>   *FStreamName* is the name of an `fstream` object that serves as a connection to some secondary memory file.
>
> **Action**
> `fail()` returns:
>
>   True (nonzero) if the last operation on
>   *FStreamName* failed;
>   False (zero) if that operation was successful.

The Input Operator. One of the most elegant features of C++ is its *consistency*—its use of the same operators to perform tasks that are functionally similar. The task of performing input from a file is an example of this consistency, because

fstream input is performed in the same manner as **istream** input. That is, once an **fstream** has been established as a connection to some file **F**, the same input operator (**>>**) that we have used to input data from the keyboard using an **istream** (i.e., **cin**) can now be used to input data from a file via the **fstream** to that file. Thus, in the program in Figure 8.1, the first input statement

    InStream >> Reading;

reads the first value from the file **pressure.dat** (through the **fstream** object **Instream**) and stores it in the variable **Reading**. For example, given the **In-Stream** described earlier,

       ↓
    | 11.1♭22.2♭33.3♭44.4↵55.5♭66.6♭77.7↵88.8♭99.9↵◊ |

         InStream

execution of the statement

    InStream >> Reading;

reads the characters **'1'**, **'1'**, **'.'**, **'1'** and then stops upon encountering the blank. The characters are then converted to the real value **11.1**, which is stored in variable **Reading**:

                      ↓
| 11.1 | | 11.1♭22.2♭33.3♭44.4↵55.5♭66.6♭77.7↵88.8♭99.9↵◊ |

Reading   **InStream**

At the end of the loop, execution of the statement:

    InStream >> Reading;

skips the blank, reads the characters **'2'**, **'2'**, **'.'**, **'2'** and then stops upon encountering the next blank. The characters are converted to the real value **22.2**, which is stored in variable **Reading**.

                      ↓
| 22.2 | | 11.1♭22.2♭33.3♭44.4↵55.5♭66.6♭77.7↵88.8♭99.9↵◊ |

Reading   **InStream**

In subsequent repetitions of the loop, the value **33.3** is read in exactly the same way,

                      ↓
| 33.3 | | 11.1♭22.2♭33.3♭44.4↵55.5♭66.6♭77.7↵88.8♭99.9↵◊ |

Reading   **InStream**

as is the value **44.4**, except that reading stops at the newline character instead of a blank:

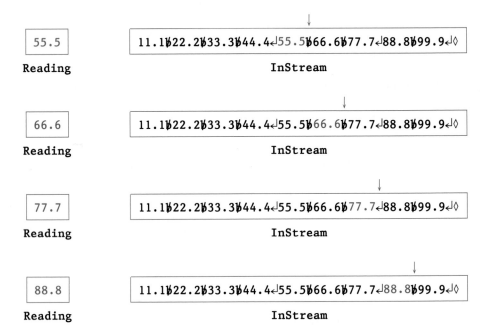

(Recall that any *white-space* character—blank, tab, or newline—serves to delimit numbers.) Subsequent repetitions of the loop input the remaining values in the same way until only the **99.9** remains unread:

The next repetition reads the four characters **'9'**, **'9'**, **'.'**, **'9'** and stops when the newline is encountered:

On the final trip through the loop, the input statement finds no data before encountering the end-of-file mark, and so the member function **eof()** returns the value true, terminating the loop (see the following discussion).

Note that this is similar to what would happen if we were to use the statement

```
cin >> Reading;
```

to get the next **double** value from the keyboard and store it in the variable **Reading**. The only difference is that the input operator would extract values from the **istream** named **cin** instead of from the **fstream** named **InStream**.

Input is consistent in the **iostream** library because the same operator (**>>**) is used to input a **double** value from an **istream** object such as **cin** and to input a **double** value from an **fstream** object named **InStream**. The only difference in these operations is the type of their first operand.

When the same operator (such as **>>**) can be applied to operands of different types, that operator is said to be **overloaded.** Just as we overloaded the function **Swap()** in Section 7.3 by defining its behavior for a variety of types, the designer(s) of **<fstream.h>** overloaded the **>>** operator so that it can be applied to **fstream** objects as well as **istream** objects.

As noted in Section 7.3, we have been using overloaded operators all along. For example, the expressions

```
cin >> CharVariable
```

and

```
cin >> DoubleVariable
```

show that the input operator in **<iostream.h>** is overloaded, since the first expression gets the next (non–white-space) **char** value from the keyboard, whereas the second gets the next **double** value from the keyboard. Overloading will prove increasingly important as we continue.

The eof() Member. We saw in Section 6.2 that a loop of the form

```
// ... input first value from istream cin

while (!cin.eof())      // while more data
{
    // ... process the input value

    // ... input next value from istream cin

}                       // end while
```

can be used to input a sequence of values. This loop will continue to execute until the user enters an end-of-file mark to indicate that no more data is to be input.

In the program in Figure 8.1, the main processing loop has a similar form

```
InStream >> Reading;

while (!InStream.eof())
{
    // ...process Reading

    InStream >> Reading;
}
```

Here, the function call

```
InStream.eof()
```

behaves exactly like

```
cin.eof()
```

except that the user need not enter an end-of-file mark to make the function return true, because the file from which we are reading already contains such a mark:

$$\downarrow$$

11.1ɓ22.2ɓ33.3ɓ44.4↵55.5ɓ66.6ɓ77.7↵88.8ɓ99.9↵◊

InStream

`InStream.eof()` returns true (nonzero) following execution of the statement

```
InStream >> Reading;
```

if there is no data between the read position and the end-of-file mark.

The eof() Member

> **Use**
>
>   *FStreamName*.eof();
>
> where:
>   *FStreamName* is the name of an **fstream** that
>   serves as a connection to some secondary
>   memory file.
>
> **Action**
> **eof()** acts as a boolean function, returning
>   True (nonzero) if the last input operation on
>   *FStreamName* failed because the end of the
>   secondary memory file was reached;
>   False (zero) otherwise.

Again, we see a pleasing consistency in the I/O facilities of the **iostream** library, because **eof()** is a member function of **fstream** objects just as it is of **istream** objects. This is an example of the usefulness of the C++ *inheritance* mechanism—**eof()** is actually a member of the class **ios**, from which the other **iostream** classes are derived. These other classes (such as **fstream**) thus inherit **eof()** from the base class **ios** (which all of them hold in common) and avoid the redundant redefinition of their own **eof()** functions.

The Output Operator. Just as the input operator is overloaded to perform consistently with both **istream** and **fstream** objects opened using **ios::in**, the output operator (**<<**) is overloaded to behave consistently with both **ostream** and **fstream** objects opened using **ios::out** or **ios::app**. For example, as we saw in Figure 8.1 we can declare

```
fstream
   OutStream(OutputFileName, ios::out);
```

to open an output connection between the program and a file named **OutputFileName**. The **fstream** object **OutStream** is initially empty, containing only the end-of-file marker:

OutStream

The program in Figure 8.1 contains statements to write the results to **pressure.out** via **OutStream**:

```
OutStream << "\n--> There were " << Count << " values,";

if (Count > 0)
   OutStream << "\n\tranging from " << Min
             << " to " << Max
             << "\n\tand their average is " << Sum / Count
             << ".\n\n";
```

Execution of the first statement inserts the appropriate characters into **OutStream**:

OutStream

Execution of the output statement within the **if** statement inserts the remaining characters:

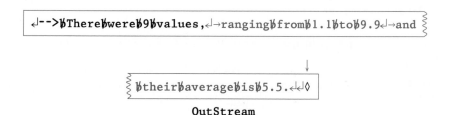

OutStream

[Here we have used the right-arrow symbol (→) to represent a tab character.]

Execution of the program simply displays the introductory message and then seems to terminate; all other output has been sent to **pressure.out** via **OutStream** instead of to the screen via **cout**.

The close() Member. We have seen that the initialization of an **fstream** object establishes that object as a connection between a program and a file. Generally, this **fstream** is disconnected when the program terminates, just as a variable's value is lost when the program using that variable terminates. Nevertheless, it is good programming practice to disconnect the **fstream** explicitly, using the **close()** member function. In the program in Figure 8.1, the statements

```
InStream.close();
```

and

```
OutStream.close();
```

sever the connection between the program and the secondary memory files **pressure.dat** and **pressure.out**, respectively. We can describe the **close()** operation as follows.

The close() Member

> **Use**
>
> > *FStreamName*.close();
>
> where:
> >   *FStreamName* is the name of an **fstream** that
> >   serves as a connection to some secondary
> >   memory file.
>
> **Action**
> The executing program and the secondary memory
> file named *FileName* are disconnected, and
> *FStreamName* becomes undefined.

In the program in Figure 8.1, the effect of the statement

```
OutStream.close();
```

is to write the contents of the **fstream** named **OutStream**,

⏎-->◊There◊were◊9◊values,⏎→ranging◊from◊1.1◊to◊9.9⏎→and

↓

◊their◊average◊is◊5.5.⏎⏎◊

OutStream

to the file **pressure.out**, which we might visualize as

```
-->There were 9 values,
   ranging from 1.1 to 9.9
   and their average is 5.5.
```

It is important to use the **close()** function when a program uses many different files because many operating systems place a limit on the number of files a program may have open simultaneously.[4] This means that if a program tries to open more files than allowed, the operating system will terminate the program (abnormally). This problem can be avoided by always using the **close()** function to sever the connection between a program and a file when the program is done using it. This keeps the number of open files associated with the program from growing beyond the limit allowed by the operating system.

Summary

The following points summarize some of the important ideas regarding file I/O in C++.

- A text file is simply a container for characters stored on a secondary memory device.
- A text file cannot be accessed directly from a program but must be accessed indirectly through an **fstream**—a connection between the program and the file through which the program can perform input to and/or output from the file.
- Either the **open()** member function or the initialization-at-declaration mechanism can be used to connect an **fstream** to a text file.
- If a file is opened using the mode **ios::in**, then the **fstream** is initialized with the contents of that file with the read position at the first character in the **fstream**.
- If a file is opened using the mode **ios::out**, then the **fstream** is initialized as empty (containing only the end-of-file mark) with the write position at the beginning of the file. Any previously existing file with the same name is lost.
- If a file is opened using the mode **ios::app**, then the file being opened must exist, and the **fstream** is initialized with the contents of that file with the write position at the end of the file.
- The input operator (**>>**) can be used to extract the value that begins at the read position in the **fstream** (opened in **ios::in** mode). The read position is advanced to the first character past the input value. Any initial white space characters are skipped. Numeric values are delimited by nonnumeric characters.

---

[4] For example, UNIX systems allow a program to have a maximum of 15 files open simultaneously.

- The output operator (`<<`) can be used to insert a value into an `fstream` (opened in `ios::out` or `ios::app` mode) at the write position. The write position is advanced to the point immediately following the value.
- An `fstream` should be disconnected from a text file using the `close()` member when that file is no longer needed.

Exercises

1. Suppose that `Num1`, `Num2`, `Num3`, and `Num4` are integer variables and that for each of the following input statements, the following data is entered:

   ```
   1   -2 3↵
   4 -5 6↵
   7        -8       9↵
   ```

   What values will be assigned to these variables when each of the following statements is executed?

   (a) `cin >> Num1 >> Num2 >> Num3 >> Num4;`

   (b) `cin >> Num1 >> Num2;`
       `cin >> Num3;`
       `cin >> Num4;`

   (c) `cin >> Num1 >> Num2 >> Num3 >> Num4;`
       `cin >> Num4 >> Num3 >> Num2 >> Num1;`

2. Using both the `open()` function and the initialization-at-declaration mechanism, write statements to declare and open

   (a) An `fstream` named `Instream` as a connection to an input file named `In-Data`.
   (b) An `fstream` named `OutStream` as a connection to an output file named `OutData`.

3. Assume that `Instream` has been opened as a connection to an input file and that the following declarations are in effect:

   ```
   int
       N1, N2, N3;
   double
       R1, R2, R3;
   char
       C1, C2, C3, C4;
   ```

   Suppose also that the input file contains the following data:

   ```
   123   45.6↵
   X78 -909.8 7↵
   -65 $   432.10↵
   ```

List the values that are assigned to each of the variables in the input list, or explain why an error occurs:

(a) `Instream >> N1 >> R1 >> C1 >> N2 >> R2`
`>> C2 >> N3 >> C3 >> C4 >> R3;`

(b) `Instream >> N1 >> C1 >> C2 >> R1 >> R2`
`>> N2 >> N3 >> C3;`

(c) `Instream >> N1 >> R1 >> C1 >> C2 >> C3`
`>> N2 >> R2 >> C4 >> R3 >> N3;`

(d) `Instream >> C1 >> N1 >> R1 >> R2`
`>> N2 >> C2 >> C3 >> R3;`

(e) `Instream >> N1 >> R1 >> C1 >> C2`
`>> C3 >> N2 >> C4;`

4. Assume the declarations

```
int
    N1, N2, N3;
double
    R1, R2, R3;
char
    C1, C2, C3;
```

and that the contents of an `fstream` named `InStream` are as follows:

↓

♭54♭32E1↵-6.78♭$90↵↵♭1↵◊

InStream

List the values that are assigned to each of the variables in the input list for each of the following statements, or explain why an error occurs. Also, show the location of the read position after each of the sequences of statements is executed:

(a) `InStream >> N1 >> R1 >> R2 >> C1 >> N2 >> N3;`

(b) `InStream >> N1 >> R1 >> R2 >> C1 >> C2 >> C3 >> N2 >> N3;`

(c) `InStream >> N1 >> C1 >> C2 >> C3 >> C4 >> R1 >> R2`
`>> N2 >> R2;`

(d) `InStream >> R1 >> R2 >> R3 >> C1 >> N1 >> N2;`

(e) `InStream >> N1 >> N2 >> C1 >> N3 >> C2 >> R1`
`>> C3 >> N3 >> R2;`

8.3   Examples: Employee File Processing and Payroll Computation

Problem 1: Processing a File of Employee Data

Suppose that your employer has a file named **emp.dat** that contains information about the company's employees. Each line in the file contains an employee's identification number and hourly rate:

```
123456789     7.50
234567891     8.75
345678912     9.35
456789123    10.50
        ⋮
```

Your employer would like a program that will construct a new file **newemp.dat** that contains the same information as **emp.dat** but is easier to read. For example, the preceding lines might appear as

```
123-45-6789      7.50
234-56-7891      8.75
345-67-8912      9.35
456-78-9123     10.50
        ⋮
```

Column headings should be placed at the beginning of the file and the average hourly wage at the end.

This problem is very similar to the one given in Section 8.1. Both use a main loop in which file input is performed; however, this problem requires that *both* file input and file output be performed within the same loop:

> Read a line from **emp.dat**, obtaining *EmpIdNumber* and *HourlyWage*.
> While the end of the file hasn't been reached, do the following
> > Process and output *EmpIdNumber* and *HourlyWage* to **newemp.dat**.
> > Read the next line from **emp.dat**, obtaining *EmpIdNumber* and
> > *HourlyWage*
> End While.

The program in Figure 8.3 uses this approach to read the contents of **emp.dat**, display it in a more readable format, and calculate the average hourly rate of all employees. Note that the formatting capabilities provided by **<iomanip.h>** are applicable to **fstream** objects as well as **ostream** objects. Note also that the program informs the user not only that processing is complete, but also where to find the results. Without such information, the program simply terminates without displaying any output on the screen, which might be baffling to the user.

FIGURE 8.3 Reading an employee file.

```
/* This program reformats the data from the file "emp.dat" and
   writes it to the file "newemp.dat" in an easier-to-read format.

   Input (emp.dat):     A sequence of lines of the form:

                            employee-id-number      hourly-rate

   Output (newemp.dat): Column headings, and a sequence of lines:

                            employee-id-number      hourly-rate

                        in an easy-to-read format, followed by
                        the average hourly rate
-----------------------------------------------------------------*/

#include <iostream.h>                  // for terminal I/O
#include <fstream.h>                   // for file I/O
#include <iomanip.h>                   // for formatted I/O
#include <stdlib.h>                    // for exit()

int main(void)
{
   const char
      InFile[] = "emp.dat",            // name of input file
      OutFile[] = "newemp.dat",        // name of output file
                                       // error messages:

   cout << "\nThis program reformats the data from the file '"
        << InFile << "'\n\tand writes it to the file '"
        << OutFile << "'.\n\n";

   OpenFailedMsg[] = "\n*** main: unable to open file: ",
   NoValuesMsg[] = "\n*** main: no values to process!\n";

   fstream
      InStream(InFile, ios::in),       // stream to input file
      OutStream(OutFile, ios::out);    // stream to output file

   if (InStream.fail())                // check for
   {                                   //    successful opens
      cerr << OpenFailedMsg << InFile << endl;
      exit (-1);
   }
   else if (OutStream.fail())
   {
      cerr << OpenFailedMsg << OutFile << endl;
      exit (-1);
   }
```

FIGURE 8.3   Reading an employee file. (cont.)

```
long
    Count = 0,                          // number of employees
    EmpIdNumber;                        // an ID number
double
    HourlyRate,                         // hourly rate
    RateSum = 0.0;                      // total of hourly rates

                                        // write column headings
OutStream << "\n\t" << "  Employee  " << '\t' << " Hourly Rate "
          << "\n\t" << "============" << '\t' << "============="
          << endl;

OutStream << setprecision(2)            // 2 dec. places
          << setiosflags(ios::showpoint | ios::fixed);
                                        // fixed, not scientific

InStream >> EmpIdNumber >> HourlyRate;  // get first line
                                        //    from the file
while (!InStream.eof())                 // while more values
{
    Count++;                            //     increment Count
    RateSum += HourlyRate;              //     keep running total
                                        //     reformat the lines
    OutStream << "\t "
              << EmpIdNumber / 1000000 << '-'
              << EmpIdNumber % 1000000 / 10000 << '-'
              << EmpIdNumber % 10000
              << '\t'
              << setw(9) << HourlyRate
              << endl;
                                        //    get next line
    InStream >> EmpIdNumber >> HourlyRate;//    from the file
}                                       // end while

InStream.close();                       // close the input file

                                        // output summary info
if (Count > 0)
    OutStream << "\n\nThere are " << Count
              << " employees, averaging $" << RateSum / Count
              << " per hour.\n\n";
else
    cerr << NoValuesMsg;

OutStream.close();                      // close the output file

cout << "\nDone. Results are in the file" //   and tell user where
     << " '" << OutFile << "'.\n\n";    //    to find the results

return 0;
}
```

FIGURE 8.3 Reading an employee file. (cont.)

Listing of emp.dat:

```
123456789    7.50
234567891    8.75
345678912    9.35
456789123    10.50
567891234    6.35
678912345    10.85
789123456    7.15
891234567    9.15
912345678    8.75
987654321    11.60
```

Sample run:

```
This program reformats the data from the file 'emp.dat'
    and writes it to the file 'newemp.dat'.

Done. Results are in the file 'newemp.dat'.
```

Listing of newemp.dat:

```
        Employee         Hourly Rate
    ============      =============
    123-45-6789          7.50
    234-56-7891          8.75
    345-67-8912          9.35
    456-78-9123          10.50
    567-89-1234          6.35
    678-91-2345          10.85
    789-12-3456          7.15
    891-23-4567          9.15
    912-34-5678          8.75
    987-65-4321          11.60
```

```
There are 10 employees, averaging $9.00 per hour.
```

Problem 2: Payroll Computation (fstream Objects as Parameters)

Like any other types of objects, objects of type **fstream** may be used as arguments to user-defined functions. In this case, however, *the parameters corresponding to* **fstream** *arguments must be reference parameters,* because

- Reading from an **fstream** opened for input alters the read position within that **fstream**;
- Writing to an **fstream** opened for output alters the write position within that **fstream**.

The parameter must be defined as a reference parameter so that these alterations are propagated back to the caller of the function. To illustrate the use of **fstream**s as parameters, consider the following problem:

Problem: Wages are to be calculated for employees whose employee numbers and hourly rates are contained in the file **emp.dat** described earlier. For each of these employees, this information is to be read from the file, but the hours worked are to be entered by the user during program execution, because this value is usually not the same for all pay periods. The total of all employees' wages is also to be calculated and displayed.

The program in Figure 8.4 solves this problem. The primary difference between this program and the one in Figure 8.3 is that function **GetEmployeeInfo()** is called within the loop to extract the next employee number and hourly rate from the **fstream**. One of its parameters is an **fstream** reference parameter named **InS** that denotes the **fstream** from which this information is to be obtained. In the statement that calls **GetEmployeeInfo()**, the corresponding argument is the **fstream** object **InStream**. As a result, the statement

```
InS >> EmpIdNumber >> HourlyRate;
```

in **GetEmployeeInfo()** actually reads this information from the **fstream** object **InStream** (which is, of course, connected to the file **emp.dat**). The function then prompts the user to enter the hours worked for this employee, calls **ComputeWages()** to calculate wages, and returns this value together with the employee's number to the main program. The main program then displays the wages for that employee and, after processing all employees, displays the total payroll.

 FIGURE 8.4 Calculating payroll.

```
/* This program reads employee numbers and hourly rates from the file
   "emp.dat", hours worked from the keyboard, and calculates employee
   wages, writing them and the total of all wages to the file
   "payroll.dat".

   Input (emp.dat):      A sequence of lines of the form:

                              employee-id-number   hourly-rate

   Input (keyboard):     For each employee, the number of hours worked

   Output (payroll.dat): Column headings, and a series of lines with:

                              employee-id-number   wages

                         in an easy-to-read format; also, the total
                         wages for all employees
-------------------------------------------------------------------*/
```

FIGURE 8.4   Calculating payroll. (cont.)

```
#include <iostream.h>                    // for terminal I/O
#include <fstream.h>                     // for file I/O
#include <iomanip.h>                     // for formatted I/O
#include <stdlib.h>                      // for exit()

void GetEmployeeInfo(fstream&, long&, double&);

int main(void)
{
   const char
      InFile[] = "emp.dat",              // name of input file
      OutFile[] = "payroll.dat",         // name of output file
                                         // error messages
      OpenFailedMsg[] = "\n*** main: unable to open file: ";

   cout << "\nThis program gets data from the user and from a file"
        << "\n\t'" << InFile
        << "', computes each employee's pay, and displays"
        << "\n\tthis information and the total of all wages in a "
        << "\n\treadable format in the file '"
        << OutFile << ".\n\n";

   fstream
      InStream(InFile, ios::in),         // stream to input file
      OutStream(OutFile, ios::out);      // stream to output file
   if (InStream.fail())                  // check for
                                         //   successful opens
   {
      cerr << OpenFailedMsg << InFile << endl;
      exit (-1);
   }
   else if (OutStream.fail())
   {
      cerr << OpenFailedMsg << OutFile << endl;
      exit (-1);
   }

   long
      EmpIdNumber;                       // employee's ID number
   double
      Pay,                               // employee's pay
      TotalPay = 0.0;                    // running pay-total

                                         // write column headings
   OutStream << "\n\t" << "  Employee  " << '\t' << "     Pay     "
             << "\n\t" << "============" << '\t' << "============="
             << endl;

   OutStream << setprecision(2)          // 2 dec. places
             << setiosflags(ios::showpoint | ios::fixed);
                                         // fixed, not scientific
```

FIGURE 8.4   Calculating payroll. (cont.)

```
      GetEmployeeInfo(InStream, EmpIdNumber, Pay);
                                               // get 1st set of info
      while (!InStream.eof())                  // while more values left,
      {
         TotalPay += Pay;                      //   keep running total
                                               //   format the lines
         OutStream << "\t "
                   << EmpIdNumber / 1000000 << '_'
                   << EmpIdNumber % 1000000 / 10000 << '_'
                   << EmpIdNumber % 10000
                   << '\t'
                   << setw(9) << Pay
                   << endl;
                                               //  get next set of info
            GetEmployeeInfo(InStream, EmpIdNumber, Pay);
      }                                        // end while

      InStream.close();                        // close the input file

                                               // output summary info
      OutStream << "\n\nThe total payroll comes to $"
                << TotalPay << "\n\n";

      OutStream.close();                       // close the output file

      cout
         << "\nDone. Results are in the file '"  // and tell user where
         << OutFile << "'.\n\n";                 // to find the results

      return 0;
}

/*-------------------------------------------------------------------
ComputeWages determines the pay for a rate and time,
   including overtime.

   Receive: HourlyRate, the hourly rate for an employee;
            Hours, the number of hours that employee worked
   Return:  The pay earned by that employee
-------------------------------------------------------------------*/

double ComputeWages(double HourlyRate, double Hours)
{
   const double
      OverTimeFactor = 1.5,                 // bonus for OT hours
      RegularLimit = 40.0;                  // cutoff for OT
   double
      RegularWages,                         // non-OT earnings
      OverTimeWages = 0.0;                  // OT earnings
```

FIGURE 8.4 Calculating payroll. (cont.)

```
   if (Hours <= RegularLimit)              // if no OT,
      RegularWages = HourlyRate * Hours;   //    just compute non-OT
   else                                    // otherwise
   {                                       //    compute OT & non-OT
      RegularWages = HourlyRate * RegularLimit;
      OverTimeWages = HourlyRate * OverTimeFactor
                  * (Hours - RegularLimit);
   }
   return RegularWages + OverTimeWages;    // return non-OT + OT
}
/*-------------------------------------------------------------------
GetEmployeeInfo inputs all necessary information for an employee,
   and uses ComputeWages to compute the amount that employee is
   to be paid.

   Receive:         InS, an fstream to a file containing
                        employee data
   Input(InS):      An employee Id number (EmpId) and HourlyRate
   Output(Screen):  A prompt for keyboard input
   Input(keyboard): HoursWorked by the employee
   Return:          EmpId and the Pay earned by the employee
-------------------------------------------------------------------*/

void GetEmployeeInfo(fstream& InS, long& EmpId, double& Pay)
{
   double
      HoursWorked,
      HourlyRate;

   InS >> EmpId >> HourlyRate;             // get emp# and pay rate

   if (! InS.eof())                        // if there was data left
   {                                       //    get hours worked
      cout << "\nHow many hours did employee "
           << EmpId << " work? ";
      cin >> HoursWorked;
                                           //    calculate wages
      Pay = ComputeWages(HourlyRate, HoursWorked);
   }
   else
      Pay = 0.0;                           // use when end of file
}
```

FIGURE 8.4 Calculating payroll. (cont.)

Listing of emp.dat:

```
123456789    7.50
234567891    8.75
345678912    9.35
456789123    10.50
567891234    6.35
678912345    10.85
789123456    7.15
891234567    9.15
912345678    8.75
987654321    11.60
```

Sample run:

This program gets data from the user and from a file
'emp.dat', computes each employee's pay, and displays
this information and the total of all wages in a
readable format in the file 'payroll.dat'.

How many hours did employee 123456789 work? <u>38.5</u>

How many hours did employee 234567891 work? <u>40.0</u>

How many hours did employee 345678912 work? <u>43.5</u>

How many hours did employee 456789123 work? <u>45</u>

How many hours did employee 567891234 work? <u>39</u>

How many hours did employee 678912345 work? <u>0</u>

How many hours did employee 789123456 work? <u>20</u>

How many hours did employee 891234567 work? <u>50</u>

How many hours did employee 912345678 work? <u>40</u>

How many hours did employee 987654321 work? <u>44</u>

Done. Results are in the file 'payroll.dat'.

FIGURE 8.4   Calculating payroll. (cont.)

Listing of payroll.dat:

```
      Employee            Pay
   ============     ==============
   123-45-6789          288.75
   234-56-7891          350.00
   345-67-8912          423.09
   456-78-9123          498.75
   567-89-1234          247.65
   678-91-2345            0.00
   789-12-3456          143.00
   891-23-4567          503.25
   912-34-5678          350.00
   987-65-4321          533.60


The total payroll comes to $3338.09
```

Note that in function **GetEmployeeInfo()**, **InS** is a reference parameter corresponding to argument **InStream**. This means that the expression

```
InS.eof()
```

returns exactly the same result as the expression

```
InStream.eof()
```

in the main program.

8.4   Additional fstream Operations

In addition to the basic operations on **fstream** objects (**open()**, **<<**, **>>**, **eof()**, and **close()**), there are many other useful I/O-related operations. We have already seen that the functions from **<iomanip.h>** can be applied to **fstream** objects as well as to **ostream** objects. In fact, most of the operations that can be applied to the **istream** object **cin** can be applied to an **fstream** object opened for input and most of the operations that can be applied to the **ostream** object **cout** can be applied to an **fstream** object opened for output, and vice versa.

In this section, we examine a few of these additional operations. The I/O facilities provided by the **iostream** library are too extensive to do more than scratch the surface, but we will give a sampling of the capabilities that are available. The reference manuals for your implementation of C++ can be consulted for further information.

The get() and put() Members

get(). The member function **get()** provides an alternative way to perform character input: Given the objects **InStream** and **Ch** declared by

```
fstream
   InStream("SomeFile", ios::in);
char
   Ch;
```

an input statement of the form

```
InStream >> Ch;
```

behaves as follows:

1. While the character at the read position in **InStream** is a white-space character, advance the read position in **InStream** ahead one character.
2. Store the character at the read position in **InStream** in **Ch**.
3. Advance the read position in **InStream** ahead one character.

The critical observation here is that any leading white space is skipped by the >> operator, which is desirable in most applications. However, sometimes white space should not be skipped, and the **get()** function can be used in these situations. The statement

```
InStream.get(Ch);
```

performs two actions:

1. Store the character at the read position in **InStream** in **Ch**.
2. Advance the read position in **InStream** ahead one character.

The function **get()** does not skip white-space characters the way the input operator does.

To see how this can be useful, consider the word-processing problem of counting the number of lines in a document (i.e., a file). Since lines are delimited by newline characters, solving this problem consists of counting the number of newline characters. The basic algorithm is as follows.

ALGORITHM TO COUNT LINES IN A FILE

/* This algorithm counts the lines in a file.

    Input(File):   A sequence of characters
    Output(Screen): The number of lines in the file

———*/

1. Open the file for input.
2. Initialize *NumberOfLines* to zero.

3. Read the first character from *InStream,* storing it in *Ch.*
4. While the end of file has not been reached:
    a. If *Ch* is a newline character,
       Increment *NumberOfLines.*
    b. Read the next character from *InStream,* storing it in *Ch.*
   End While.
5. Close the file.
6. Display *NumberOfLines.*

In Step 3 of the preceding algorithm, each individual character of the file must be read and checked to see if it is the newline character. It is impractical to use the **>>** operator for this because newline characters are white-space characters, and **>>** skips all white-space characters. Function **get()** is precisely what is needed, and the function **LineCount()** in the program in Figure 8.5 uses it in implementing this algorithm.

 FIGURE 8.5 Counting lines in a file.

```
/* This program counts the lines in a file named "Document".

   Input(Document):   A sequence of characters
   Output(Screen):    The number of lines in Document
-----------------------------------------------------------------*/

#include <iostream.h>
#include <fstream.h>
#include <stdlib.h>

unsigned LineCount(const char[]);

int main(void)
{
   const char
      InputFileName[] = "Document";

   unsigned
      NumberOfLines = LineCount(InputFileName);

   cout << "\nThe file named '" << InputFileName
        << "' contains " << NumberOfLines << " lines.\n\n";

   return 0;
}
```

FIGURE 8.5 Counting lines in a file. (cont.)

```
/*-------------------------------------------------------------------
LineCount counts the number of lines in a file named FileName.

   Receive: FileName, the name of the file whose lines are to
            be counted.
   Return:  LCount, the number of lines in the file.
--------------------------------------------------------------------*/

unsigned LineCount(const char FileName[])
{
   const char
      OpenFailedMsg[] = "\n*** LineCount: unable to open file: ";

   fstream                   // open stream to FileName
      InStream(FileName, ios::in);

   if (InStream.fail())
   {
      cerr << OpenFailedMsg << FileName << endl;
      exit (-1);
   }

   unsigned
      LCount = 0;            // counter variable
   char
      Ch;                    // input character container

   InStream.get(Ch);        // get first character
   while (!InStream.eof())// while more data:
   {
      if (Ch == '\n')       //    if Ch is a newline
         LCount++;          //       increment the counter
      InStream.get(Ch);     //    get next character
   }                        // end while

   InStream.close();

   return LCount;
}
```

Listing of Document:

```
This is a test.

For the next 60 seconds,
   this station will conduct a test
   of the emergency broadcast system.

In the event of a real emergency,
   you will be informed of where you should go.

This is only a test.
```

FIGURE 8.5   Counting lines in a file. (cont.)

Sample run:

```
The file named 'Document' contains 10 lines.
```

put(). The output operation complementary to the function `get()` is the function `put()`, which is a member of both `ostream` objects and `fstream` objects that are opened with mode `ios::out` or `ios::app`. The `put()` function is quite general and can be used to output numeric values, character strings, and character values.[5] For example, the output produced by

```
cout << "\nA + B = " << A + B << '\n';
```

is also produced by the statements

```
cout.put("\nA = B = ");
cout.put(A + B);
cout.put('\n');
```

In fact, one way of implementing the `<<` operator is to use the more primitive `put()` function.[6] However, `put()` is inconvenient compared with `<<`, and since `put()` provides no real advantage over `<<`, it is rarely used.

The seekg(), tellg(), seekp(), and tellp() Members

The file-processing programs we have considered thus far have used **sequential access,** which means that the values in the file are accessed and processed sequentially, from beginning to end. To access any item in the file, one must pass through all those that precede it. It obviously takes more time, therefore, to access a value near the end of the file than one near the beginning.

For an `fstream` opened for input, sequential input is accomplished by

- Initializing the read position to the first character in the file;
- Ensuring that an input operation always begins at the read position; and
- After each input operation, advancing the read position to the first character after the input value.

Similarly, sequential processing in an `fstream` opened for output is accomplished by

- Initializing the write position to the end-of-file mark;
- Ensuring that an output operation inserts characters at the write position; and
- After each output operation, advancing the write position to the first position after the output value (i.e., back to the end-of-file mark).

---

[5] The `put()` function is overloaded with multiple definitions, and the compiler chooses the appropriate definition based on the type of the argument.

[6] In the same manner, `get()` can be thought of as a more primitive input operation from which the higher-level `>>` can be implemented.

It should be clear that sequential I/O is accomplished simply by ensuring that the read/write positions are advanced continually in the stream and are never moved backward.

Sequential processing is sufficient to solve most problems involving files, but there are some problems whose solutions require that the data in a file be accessed and processed in a nonsequential manner. Such access is called **direct** or **random access** because each item can be accessed directly by specifying its location in the file. For such problems, **<iostream.h>** provides the member functions **seekg()**, **tellg()**, **seekp()**, and **tellp()**, which make it possible to manipulate a stream's read position and write position directly.

seekg(). If an **fstream** named **InStream** has been opened for input, the function call

```
InStream.seekg(Offset, Base);
```

can be used to alter the read position within **InStream**,[7] where **Base** is one of the following:

- **ios::beg** causes the read position to move **Offset** bytes from the beginning of the stream.
- **ios::cur** causes the read position to move **Offset** bytes from its current position.
- **ios::end** causes the read position to move **Offset** bytes from the end of the stream.

The arguments **ios::beg** and **ios::end** set the read position relative to the beginning and end of the stream, respectively, whereas **ios::cur** sets the read position relative to the current position.

To illustrate, suppose that **InStream** has the following contents:

InStream

Then the call

```
InStream.seekg(-2, ios::end);
```

can be used to move the read position to 2 bytes before the end-of-file mark in **InStream**:

InStream

---

[7] The **g** in **seekg()** and **tellg()** refers to the fact that one *gets* values from the stream being manipulated (i.e., that it is an input stream).

Regardless of the read position, the call:

```
InStream.seekg(0, ios::beg);
```

will reset the read position to the first character in **InStream**:

InStream

After this, the call

```
InStream.seekg(3, ios::cur);
```

will advance the read position 3 bytes from its current position:

InStream

and the call

```
InStream.seekg(-1, ios::cur);
```

will move the read position backward 1 byte from its current position:

InStream

This is useful when a program must reread some value earlier in the stream.

The **seekg()** function is most useful when a file consists of a series of lines or records, each having a fixed length. As a simple example, suppose that a file named **Friends** contains the first names of some friends, each on a separate line, and padded with blanks so that each line is eight characters long:

Friends

The statement

```
fstream
    InStream("Friends", ios::in);
```

initializes InStream:

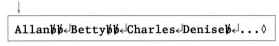

InStream

If LineLength has been defined by

```
const int
    LineLength = 8;
```

we can move the read position to the beginning of the first name with the statement

```
InStream.seekg(0*LineLength, ios::beg);
```

to the beginning of the second name with

```
InStream.seekg(1*LineLength, ios::beg);
```

and in general, to the beginning of the ith name with the statement

```
InStream.seekg((i - 1)*LineLength, ios::beg);
```

Thus, the statement

```
InStream.seekg(2*LineLength, ios::beg);
```

will move the read position 16 bytes from the beginning of the file:

AllanÞÞ↵BettyÞÞ↵Charles↵DeniseÞ↵...◊

InStream

Similarly, the statement

```
InStream.seekg(LineLength, ios::cur);
```

can be used to move the read pointer from the beginning of one line to the beginning of the next line:

InStream

The function **seekg()** thus allows us to adjust the read position in any way that is useful in solving a particular problem.

It should be apparent that seeking with a negative offset from the base **ios::beg**, or seeking with a positive offset from the base **ios::end** is not desirable. Such operations will cause the member function **fail()** to return true.

tellg(). It is sometimes convenient to think of a stream as a *list* of characters, in which each position has its own number, or *index:*

A	♭	B	♭	C	♭	D	↵	◊
0	1	2	3	4	5	6	7	8

InStream

The **tellg()** function can be used to find the index of the read position. For example, the statements

```
InStream.seekg(0, ios::end);

long
   LastPosition = InStream.tellg();
```

move the read position to the end-of-file mark

A	♭	B	♭	C	♭	D	↵	◊
0	1	2	3	4	5	6	7	8

InStream

and store the index of the end-of-file mark (8) in **LastPosition**. Note that because the index of the first character is always zero, the index of the end-of-file mark is always the number of characters in the file (not counting the end-of-file mark). A text-processing program can use this fact to determine how many characters are in a file, rather than counting them character by character.

Knowing the index of the last character allows us to find the middle of a file. For example, the statements

```
InStream.seekg(0, ios::end);

long
   LastPosition = InStream.tellg(),
   MiddlePosition = (LastPosition + 1) / 2;

InStream.seekg(MiddlePosition, ios::beg);
```

can be used to move the read position to the middle character in `InStream`:

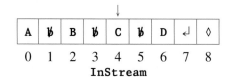

0 1 2 3 4 5 6 7 8

InStream

It should be evident that like `seekg()`, `tellg()` is most useful for files that are organized into lines or records of fixed lengths. To illustrate, suppose that in the previous example with the file **Friends**, the read position has moved away from the beginning of a line,

```
Allanℬℬ⏎Bettyℬℬ⏎Charles⏎Deniseℬ⏎...◊
```

InStream

and we want to advance it to the next line. Since `InStream.tell()` returns the index of the current read position (11), the statement

```
long
    OffBy = InStream.tellg() % LineLength;
                    // how far past beginning of line
```

can be used to compute the number of characters (`OffBy` = 3) that the read position is past the beginning of the current line; and the statement

```
InStream.seekg(LineLength - OffBy, ios::cur);
                    // go to beginning of next line
```

can then be used to move the read position forward `LineLength - OffBy` = 5 bytes, thus advancing it to the beginning of the next line.

`seekp()` and `tellp()`. The functions `seekg()` and `tellg()` can only be used with input streams, because they only manipulate the read position within a stream. The write position within an output stream can be manipulated by using the functions `seekp()` and `tellp()` provided in `<iostream.h>`.[8] These functions behave in the same manner as `seekg()` and `tellg()`, respectively, but for output streams.

Controlling I/O State Flags

We have seen that the function `eof()` can be used to determine whether there is more data in an input stream, and we have also seen that the function `seekg()` can

---

[8] The `p` in `seekp()` and `tellp()` refers to the fact that one *puts* values into the stream being manipulated (i.e., that it is an output stream).

be used to change the read position. These properties make these two functions useful in solving problems that require that a data set be processed in a series of *passes*.

To illustrate, consider the following code segment:

```
fstream
   InStream("Data", ios::in|ios::out);

InStream >> Value;
while (!InStream.eof())  // loop ... first pass
{
   // ... process Value (possibly writing to InStream) ...
   InStream >> Value;
}                        // end loop

InStream.seekg(0, ios::beg);    // reset read position to 0

InStream >> Value;
while (!InStream.eof())  // loop ... second pass
{
   // ... process Value (from InStream modified by 1st pass) ...
   InStream >> Value;
}                        // end loop
```

This code fragment looks fine—we make one pass through **InStream**, reposition the read position to the beginning of the buffer, and then make the second pass.

When this code is executed, however, the first pass proceeds as expected, but the second pass is never made. In fact, if we trace the execution (with output statements or a debugger), we will find that the first loop executes perfectly, but as execution approaches the second loop, execution of the input statement seems to have no effect and the loop terminates immediately.

To see why this is happening, it is necessary to understand that a stream object is not only a connection between a program and a file, but it also stores additional information that indicates the **state** of the stream. This state information is used to answer questions like:

- Is everything all right?
- Has the end of the file been reached?
- Did the last operation fail?

The state information is encoded as a series of bits:

State Bits

where

The *good* bit is 1 if everything is all right and 0 otherwise;
The *eof* bit is 1 if the end-of-file mark has been read and 0 otherwise;
The *fail* bit is 1 if the last operation failed and 0 otherwise;

and so on. Normally, the bits have the following values:

fail eof good

... | 0 | 0 | 1 |

State Bits

However, suppose the following statements are executed:

```
double
   DoubleVar;

cin >> DoubleVar;
```

If the user enters the end-of-file mark, the *eof* bit is set:

fail eof good

... | 0 | 1 | 1 |

State Bits

Or, if the user enters some value whose type is incompatible with **double** (e.g., a character value), then the *fail* bit is set and the *good* bit is cleared:

fail eof good

... | 1 | 0 | 0 |

State Bits

The state bits thus describe the current state of the stream, and the stream member functions **eof()** and **fail()** simply return the current value of the *eof* and *fail* bits, respectively.[9] Beyond this, the various stream operations use these bits as follows:

> *If any of the state bits of a stream other than* good *are set to 1, then no subsequent input operations on that stream will be performed.*

This explains the problem in the earlier attempt to make two passes through a file. In the first part of the code

```
fstream
   InStream("Data", ios::in|ios::out);

InStream >> Value;
while (!InStream.eof())   // loop ... first pass
{
    // ... process Value (possibly writing to InStream) ...
    InStream >> Value;
}                         // end loop
```

---

[9] Streams also have a member function **good()** that returns the value of the *good* bit.

the loop executes normally, and when the end-of-file mark is encountered, the *eof* bit is set:

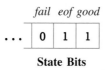

State Bits

The statement

```
InStream.seekg(0, ios::beg);  // reset read position to 0
```

in the second part of the code does reset the read position to the beginning of the stream, but it does not clear the *eof* bit. Consequently, when the second loop,

```
InStream >> Value;
while (!InStream.eof())  // loop ... second pass
{
    // ... process Value (from InStream modified by 1st pass) ...
    InStream >> Value;
}                              // end loop
```

is encountered, the *eof* bit is still set, so the input statement has no effect and the `eof()` function returns true, and the while loop is never entered.

The solution is to use another member function `clear()`, which resets the state bits to their normal values. Thus, we simply add a call to `clear()` before the second part of the code:

```
fstream
    InStream("Data", ios::in|ios::out);

InStream >> Value;
while (!InStream.eof())  // loop ... first pass
{
    // ... process Value (possibly writing to InStream) ...
    InStream >> Value;
}                              // end loop

InStream.seekg(0, ios::beg);  // reset read position to 0

InStream.clear();                // reset state bits

InStream >> Value;
while (!InStream.eof())  // loop ... second pass
{
    // ... process Value (from InStream modified by 1st pass) ...
    InStream >> Value;
}                              // end loop
```

When executed, the `clear()` function resets the state bits to their normal values, allowing the second pass to proceed as intended.

The peek(), putback(), and ignore() Members

The final set of functions that we discuss allows the programmer to do some useful, if unconventional, manipulations of an input stream. These functions are named **peek()**, **putback()**, and **ignore()**, and their names describe the operations they perform.

peek(). The **peek()** member is used to *look ahead* in an input stream. This operation is similar to the **get()** function, in that both return the next character in the stream, but whereas **get()** advances the read position, **peek()** does not.

To illustrate, consider the problem of the C++ compiler reading a C++ program from a stream. One of the tasks of a compiler is **lexical analysis** (see Section 13.4), which breaks the source program down into a sequence of indivisible symbols, called **tokens.** This task is accomplished by a special function called the **lexical analyzer,** which the compiler calls whenever it needs the next token. Each identifier, each keyword, operator, and punctuation mark has its own token.

Suppose, for example, that the compiler's input stream is named **InStream** and appears as follows:

InStream

Suppose further that the compiler is ready for the next token and calls the lexical analyzer, which executes the statement

```
Ch = InStream.get();
```

Clearly, this will retrieve the character **+** and advance the read position:

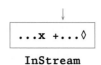

InStream

In order to determine which operation the programmer specified, the lexical analyzer needs more information: If the next character is an equal sign (=), then the operator is +=; if the next character is another +, the operator is the increment operator ++; and if the next character is a letter, a digit, or a white-space character,[10] then the operator is simply the addition operator +. The **peek()** function makes it possible to look ahead at the next character without actually moving the read position:

---

[10] The function **isalnum(Ch)** returns true if and only if its argument **Ch** is an alphanumeric character. Similarly, **isspace(Ch)** returns true if and only if its argument **Ch** is a white-space character. These useful character-processing functions (along with many others) are available in the header file **< ctype.h>** .

```
NextCh = InStream.peek();               // look ahead at next char

if (NextCh == '=')                      // if it's an =
{
   InStream.get(Ch);                    //    get the char
   return PlusEqualToken                //    and return +=
}
else if (NextCh == '+')                 // else if it's another +
{
   InStream.get(Ch);                    //    get the char
   return IncrementToken                //    and return ++
}
else if (isalnum(NextCh) || isspace(NextCh)) // else if it's valid here
   return AdditionToken                 //    just return +
else                                    // else
   // ... generate error message ...
```

Thus, if

```
InStream.peek()
```

returns the character **y**, then the lexical analyzer can infer that `InStream` contains

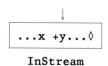

InStream

allowing it to conclude that the addition operator + was specified, and not ++ or +=. The **y** is left in the stream, so it can be processed the next time the compiler calls the lexical analyzer.

putback(). An alternative approach is provided by the **putback()** function, whose effect is to cause its character argument to be put back into the input stream, so that the next call to **get()** will input that character.

As an example, consider again the compiler problem, where the lexical analyzer has used **get()** to retrieve the character + from `InStream`:

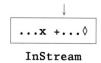

InStream

An alternative to using **peek()** would be to use **get()** to retrieve the next character

```
NextChar = InStream.get();
```

and then use `putback()` to return it to `InStream`, if that is the appropriate action:

```
if (NextCh == '=')                          // if it's an =
   return PlusEqualToken                    //    just return +=
else if (NextCh == '+')                     // else if it's another +
   return IncrementToken                    //    just return ++
else if (isalnum(NextCh) || isspace(NextCh)) // else if it's a delimiter
{
   InStream.putback(NextChar);              //    put it back for now
   return AdditionToken                     //    and return +
}
else                                        // else
   // ...generate error message ...
```

Thus, if the value of `NextChar` were `y`, the `putback()` function would put that character back into the stream so that the next time the lexical analyzer is called, its call to `get()` will retrieve that character.

`ignore()`. The function `ignore()` is another useful operation that makes it possible to skip over a portion of an input stream. More precisely, the call

> `InStream.ignore(ThisMany, StopChar);`

can be used to skip over up to *ThisMany* characters or until *StopChar* is encountered, whichever comes first. For example, if `InStream` is a connection to a file in which the maximum line length is 80 characters, then the call

> `InStream.ignore(80, '\n');`

can be used to skip over the rest of the characters on the current line.

To illustrate the use of `ignore()`, consider again the lexical analyzer function of a compiler. Since comments are ignored by the compiler, if the lexical analyzer has recognized the beginning of a C++ comment (the symbol //), it must skip the remainder of that line. By selecting some suitably large value for *ThisMany*, the `ignore()` function makes this easy.

The definition of the `ignore()` function provides the default arguments 1 for *ThisMany* and `EOF` for *StopChar*, so that if `ignore()` is called with no arguments,

> `InStream.ignore();`

a single character will be skipped over, and if it is called with one argument,

> `InStream.ignore(n);`

then `n` characters will be skipped, unless the end-of-file mark is encountered first.

Example: A Goof-Proof Numeric Input Function

Consider the problem of getting a real number from the keyboard, but in a "goof-proof" fashion. The function should prompt the user to input a value and then attempt to input that value. However, if the user enters some invalid value (such as a character, punctuation mark, or operator), then the function should display an error message and try again, repeating this procedure as long as the user continues to enter invalid values. The basic algorithm is as follows.

ALGORITHM FOR GOOF-PROOF NUMERIC INPUT

/* This algorithm will reliably input a real value from the keyboard.

   Receive: *Number,* a real variable for which a value is to be input
   Input: A real value, stored in *Number*
   Return: *Number,* guaranteed to be input by the user and a valid real
               value (exception: unless the end-of-file mark was entered) ——*/

1. Prompt for a number.
2. Read the user's response, storing it in *Number.*
3. While neither the end-of-file mark nor a valid value was entered:
      a. Display an error message.
      b. Reset the stream status bits.
      c. Move the read position past the erroneous value in the stream (to the newline).
      d. Prompt for a number.
      e. Read the user's response, storing it in *Number.*
   End While.

In encoding Step 3 of this algorithm, the **eof()** function can be used to check for the end-of-file mark and the **fail()** function can be used to check for an invalid input value. Resetting the status bits as required in Step 3-b and ignoring the rest of the input in Step 3-c can be accomplished using the **clear()** function and the **ignore()** function, respectively. The function **GetNumber()** in Figure 8.6 uses these functions to implement the algorithm.

FIGURE 8.6   Goof-proof numeric input.

```
/* This function reliably inputs a real value from the keyboard.

   Receive:   Number, a (reference to a) real variable
   Input:     The user's value, stored in Number
   Return:    Number, guaranteed to be a user response AND a real
              value
              (Exception: if the user enters the end-of-file mark)
------------------------------------------------------------------*/

#include <iostream.h>
#include <limits.h>                    // provides INT_MAX
```

FIGURE 8.6   Goof-proof numeric input. (cont.)

```
void GetNumber(double& Number)
{
   const char                        // error message
      InvalidValue[] =
         "\n*** GetNumber: input value must be numeric.\n",
      Prompt[] = "\nNumber ? ";

   cout << Prompt;                    // prompt for a number
   cin >> Number;                     // input the user's response
   while(!cin.eof() && cin.fail())    // trap the user--while neither
   {                                  // end-of-file nor valid input:
      cerr << InvalidValue;           //    display the error msg
      cin.clear();                    //    reset the state bits
      cin.ignore(INT_MAX, '\n');      //    skip the invalid entry
      cout << Prompt;                 //    prompt for a number
      cin >> Number;                  //    input the user's response
   }
}
```

If we store the declaration

> `void GetNumber(double& Number);`

in the header file of one of our libraries (e.g., **Query**) and the preceding definition in its implementation file, then this function can be reused whenever the need arises. We can also overload the name **GetNumber()** by constructing additional declarations and definitions in which the type of parameter **Number** is a numeric type other than **double**.[11]

8.5   PART OF THE PICTURE: Databases

Data stored more or less permanently in a computer forms a **database,** and the software that allows users to access and modify this data is called a **database-management system.** Databases, like crabgrass, are almost everywhere, and we come into contact with them in a wide variety of situations:

- When we purchase groceries at most supermarkets, a scanner reads the universal product code and searches a database to determine the name of the item and its price so that this information can be printed on the register tape. The inventory information stored in this database may also be updated to reflect the sale of this item.

---

[11] This is the reason that we define `GetNumber()` as a `void` function that returns its value via a `double` parameter instead of defining `GetNumber()` as a `double` function and having it return the value. C++ uses parameter types and not return types to resolve overloaded references. Thus, `GetNumber(double&)` and `GetNumber(int&)` are valid overloadings of the name `GetNumber`, but `double GetNumber()` and `int GetNumber()` are not.

- If we pay for a purchase using a charge or debit card, it is quite likely that the items we have purchased, along with our name, address, and/or phone number (obtained from our card), are recorded in a database maintained by that store. Many stores routinely sell this information to telemarketing services. Such services then begin calling or mailing us information (commonly known as **junk mail**) about products related to those we purchased.

- When we charge a purchase using a bank card, a database of credit information must be searched to locate our account number and to determine whether this charge should be approved. If it is, the amount of the purchase is recorded for billing purposes, and the amount of available credit is reduced.

- When we make travel arrangements, we might use the databases maintained by airlines, hotel chains, and rental car agencies. For example, an airline reservation system maintains a database of information about flight schedules, number of seats available in various fare categories, seat assignments, type of aircraft, and so on.

- A computerized card catalog in a library is a database that contains information about the library holdings and allows the user to search for books and articles by title, by author, and by subject area, to determine whether a given book is available for checking out, and so on.

As we noted in Section 1.4, the ubiquity of databases makes many people worry about an invasion of their privacy. In a recent article, one information technology professional expressed her concern as follows:

> The violation of personal privacy, which today is possible through the use of customer databases, ISDN source telephone number recognition, personnel files, insurance records, and so on, is staggering.
>
> Even if you pay cash, you cannot shop at some stores without giving your home phone number. From your number, the merchant can determine your name and address.
>
> If you are a credit card user, your credit card vendor can compile a list of your favorite restaurants, the trips you have taken, the hotels you have stayed at and the gifts you purchased while traveling. The hotel companies' databases will know that you requested an iron, a makeup mirror and extra towels, that you ordered room service for two and that you had an 8 A.M. wake-up call.
>
> If you call to make a catalog purchase and get a busy signal, the vendor may call you back. You don't even have to leave a message. The new ISDN source-routing tags source phone numbers and registers them, so the company's phone switch can later retrieve and display them. . . .
>
> All of that information is in the hands of total strangers. You, as an individual, have no way of knowing the level of integrity of the people handling your information. Moreover, the firms with which you do business have no way of knowing the level of integrity of their employees. . . .
>
> "I like people and I like to interact with them, but there is virtually no way to do this without being put in a database somewhere.
>
> As a professional, I feel strongly that we need to build provisions into the databases we create to flag those subscribers, customers and clients who choose not to be included in mailings, who choose not to have their names sold and so on. And, of course, we must give those individuals the opportunity to designate their preference . . . we can actively build in the security and take the measures required to safeguard one another's privacy."[12]

---

[12] Corinne Chaves, "The Death of Personal Privacy," *Computerworld* (January 27, 1992): 25.

Files are the basic building blocks of databases, and the study of files is therefore necessary to understanding the basic principles of database design and management. The files that make up the database may be very large, and the information contained in them may be interrelated and linked together in intricate ways. For example, a file that maintains credit information on consumers would contain names, addresses, phone numbers, records of loan applications, payment defaults, credit approvals and denials, records of charge accounts, balances in these accounts, balances in banks, credit unions, investments, and so on. Keeping such information up to date and accurate is a complex task, and news reports frequently tell of complaints from consumers about inaccuracies in their credit reports and their resulting poor credit ratings.

Files are usually stored on magnetic disks, tapes, or some other form of secondary memory, and accessing and retrieving data from such devices is slower than for data stored in internal memory. It is important, therefore, that this data be organized in such a way that any item of information can be located quickly and the data retrieved, displayed, and perhaps updated with more current information.

The basic operation required to retrieve information from a file is that of searching the file to determine where that information is stored. Each search is based on some **key** that is part of the information stored in the records of the file; records are examined to locate a particular record or perhaps several records that contain this key. For example, a person's social security number might be the search key for a file whose records contain credit information about individuals. If the file is being searched to locate the records of all persons living in a particular city, the key field will be the name of that city. Or if all records of customers having charge accounts with that company are to be retrieved, the search key might be the name of a particular company. We consider the searching problem and the information-retrieval problem in detail in Sections 12.4 and 12.5.

Exercises

1. Suppose that `InFile` contains the following:

```
I think that I shall never see
A poem lovely as a tree

         -JOYCE KILMER (1914)
```

and that a program begins with

```
#include <iostream.h>
#include <fstream.h>

int main(void)
{
   fstream
      InStream("InFile", ios::in);
   char
      Ch;
```

What output will be produced by each of the following code fragments?

(a) ```
InStream >> Ch;
while (!InStream.eof())
{
    cout << Ch;
    InStream >> Ch;
}
InStream.close();
```

(b) ```
InStream.get(Ch);
while (!InStream.eof())
{
    cout << Ch;
    InStream.get(Ch);
}
InStream.close();
```

2. Write a program to copy one text file into another text file in which the lines are numbered 1, 2, 3, . . . with a number at the left of each line.

3. Write a program that reads a text file and counts the vowels in the file.

4. Write a program that reads a text file and counts the occurrences in the file of specified characters entered during execution of the program.

5. People from three different income levels, A, B, and C, rated each of two different products with a number from 0 through 10. Construct a file in which each line contains the income level and product rankings for one respondent. Then write a program that reads this information and calculates

   (a) For each income bracket, the average rating for Product 1
   (b) The number of persons in Income Bracket B who rate both products with a score of 5 or higher
   (c) The average rating for Product 2 by persons who rated Product 1 lower than 3

   Label all output and design the program so that it automatically counts the number of respondents.

Programming Pointers

Program Design

1. *If a program is to read data from or write data to a file, an* fstream *must be declared and initialized as a connection between the program and the file.* The three basic steps in such programs are thus

   (a) Declare an fstream object and open it to establish a connection between it and the file;

(b) Perform the desired processing of the file via the **fstream**;

(c) Close the **fstream** object, severing the connection with the file.

2. *To read data from a file via an* **fstream**, *a while loop controlled by the* **fstream** *member* **eof()** *may be used:*

Read the first data value from the **fstream**.
While end-of-file is false, do the following:
{
    Process the data value.
    Read the data value from the **fstream**.
}

Some programmers prefer a forever loop because it avoids the duplicate input code:

```
for(;;)
{
    Read a data value from the fstream.
    If end-of-file is true, then exit the loop.
    Process the data value.
}
```

Potential Problems

1. *The operations performed on an* **fstream** *must be consistent with the mode by which it was initialized:*

   ■ Applying the input operator to an **fstream** not opened using **ios::in**, or
   ■ Applying the output operator to an **fstream** not opened using **ios::out** or **ios::app** will generate an error.

2. *When inputting character values, the input operator "skips over" any leading white-space characters (blanks, tabs, and newlines), whereas the member function* **get()** *does not.* For example, if the user enters:

    A⏎
    B⏎
    C⏎

then the **istream** named **cin** can be visualized as follows:

cin

Now, if the statements

```
cin >> Letter1;
cin >> Letter2;
cin >> Letter3;
```

are executed, then 'A' is read and stored in `Letter1`:

cin

The newline (as white space) is skipped, and the value 'B' is read and stored in `Letter2`:

cin

Also, the newline (as white space) is skipped and the value 'C' is read and stored in `Letter3`:

cin

leaving the final newline unread. By contrast, if the statements

```
cin.get(Letter1);
cin.get(Letter2);
cin.get(Letter3);
```

are executed, then the value 'A' is read and stored in `Letter1` as before,

cin

but the newline value '\n' is read and stored in `Letter2`,

cin

and the value 'B' is read and stored in `Letter3`,

cin

leaving the second newline, 'C', and third newline unread.

3. *In reading a value for a numeric variable with the input operator, if an end-of-file mark is encountered while the operator is skipping leading white space, the value of that variable is undefined.* For this reason, the **eof()** function should always be evaluated following an input statement to prevent an undefined variable from being processed.

4. *An* fstream *should always be closed using the member* close() *once use of that* fstream *has been completed.*

5. *The parameters to hold stream arguments must be reference parameters, because an input or output operation changes the stream's read or write position, respectively.*

6. *Once the eof or fail state bits have been set in a stream, no subsequent operations can be performed on that stream until those bits have been cleared (using the* clear() *member).*

Programming Projects

For descriptions of the files **USER.DAT** and **INVEN.DAT**, see Appendix D.

1. Write a program to search the file **USERS.DAT** to find and display the resources used to date for specified users whose identification numbers are entered during execution of the program.

2. Write a program to search the file **INVEN.DAT** to find an item with a specified item number. If a match is found, display the item number and the number currently in stock; otherwise, display a message indicating that it was not found.

3. At the end of each month, a report is produced that shows the status of each user's account in **USER.DAT**. Write a program to accept the current date and produce a report of the following form:

```
                USER ACCOUNTS--1/31/94

   USER-ID          RESOURCE LIMIT          RESOURCES USED
   ------------------------------------------------------------
   10101                $750                     $381
   10102                $650                     $599***
     :                    :                        :
     :                    :                        :
     :                    :                        :
```

where the three asterisks (***) indicate that the user has already used 90% or more of the resources available to him or her.

4. Write a program that reads a text file and counts the characters in each line. The program should display the line number and the length of the shortest and longest lines in the file, as well as the average number of characters per line.

5. Write a program that reads a text file and writes it to another text file, but with leading blanks and blank lines removed. Run this program using as input files the last two C++ programs you have written, and comment on whether you think indenting C++ programs makes them more readable.

6. Write a file pagination program that reads a text file and prints it in blocks of 20 lines. If there still are lines in the file after a block of lines is printed, the program should allow the user to indicate whether more ouput is desired. If so, the next block should be printed; otherwise, execution of the program should terminate.

7. Write a program that reads a text file; counts the nonblank characters, the non-blank lines, the words, and the sentences; and calculates the average number of characters per word and the average number of words per sentence. You may assume the following: The file contains only letters, blanks, commas, periods, semicolons, and colons; a word is any sequence of letters that begins a line or is preceded by one or more blanks and that is terminated by a blank, comma, semicolon, colon, period, or the end of a line; and a sentence is terminated by a period.

CHARACTER STRINGS 9

An average English word is four letters and a half. By hard, honest labor I've dug all the large words out of my vocabulary and shaved it down till the average is three and a half. . . .
MARK TWAIN

CHAPTER CONTENTS

The word *compute* usually suggests arithmetic operations performed on numeric data; thus, computers are sometimes thought to be mere "number crunchers," devices whose only purpose is to process numeric information. This is not the case, however, for in Chapter 1 we considered coding schemes used to represent characters, and in subsequent chapters we introduced some of C++'s capabilities for processing characters and strings.

We have not, however, described how character strings can be stored in variables, and many problems require this capability. For example, in processing employee information it might be convenient to store the name of each employee along with other information. A program for maintaining an inventory might require processing product names, names of manufacturers, their addresses, and so on. Also, as we noted in Chapter 8, files can be processed more conveniently if we can input file names interactively, rather than "hard-wiring" their names into programs as character string constants. What is needed are *character string variables;*—that is, objects that are capable of storing a character string and whose values can change during program execution.

Unfortunately, C++ has no predefined string type, and although every implementation of C++ (that we have seen) provides a string class that can be used to define character string variables, each of these implementations is somewhat different from the others. For example, Microsoft C/C++ names this class **CString**, whereas Turbo and Borland C++ name the class **String**. Similar differences arise in the names and/or functionality of the string operations. This disparity stems from the absence of an ANSI standard for C++, which would specify precisely the name, operations, and functionality of such a class. At the time of this writing, a committee is working on such a standard, but it is not yet available.

The result is that programs that use the string class provided in a particular implementation are not portable. Although they may compile and execute perfectly in the environment in which they were written, they may not even compile when ported to a different environment.

For this text, we have developed a string class named **Strings** that allows the definition of character string variables. In the absence of an ANSI standard, this chapter uses class **Strings** to introduce the concepts of computing with strings. We have provided the source code for class **Strings** (in Appendix F and on the disk that accompanies this text), so that programs written using this class can be ported from one machine to another (by porting class **Strings** along with them).

9.1 A Sample Problem

As usual, we begin by looking at a simple problem that involves processing character strings.

Problem: Reversing a String

Construct a program that, for a given character string, will display the reversal of the string. For example, for the string

```
sdrawkcab
```

the program should display the string:

    backwards

Specification.   The problem statement suggests that we need a data object in which to store the character string:

Data Object	Kind of Value	Type of Object	Name of Object
The string to be reversed	Variable	Character string	*StringIn*

The problem can be specified in terms of this object as follows:

> Input: *StringIn,* the character string to be reversed.
> Output: The reversal of this character string.

Design.   The first step in solving this problem is to recognize that reversing a character string such as

    sdrawkcab

implies that the last character of the input string must be read before the first character of the output string can be displayed. This, in turn, implies that all the characters prior to that last character must also be stored, so that they can be subsequently displayed.

Although we could declare enough character variables to hold a line of input,

```
char
    Ch1, Ch2, Ch3, Ch4, Ch5, Ch6, Ch7, Ch8, Ch9, Ch10, Ch11,
    Ch12, Ch13, Ch14, Ch15, Ch16, Ch17, Ch18, Ch19, Ch20, Ch21,
        :
        :
    Ch112, Ch113, Ch114, Ch115, Ch116, Ch117, Ch118, Ch119, Ch120;
```

this is surely clumsy and inconvenient. Fortunately, there is a better approach, namely, declaring a single object that can hold all of the characters from a line of input:

```
#include "Strings.h"

Strings
    StringIn;
```

This declaration creates a **Strings** object named **StringIn** that can store a string of characters. This object provides an easy way to solve the string-reversal problem, because we can input the string to be reversed, store it in **StringIn**, and process the individual characters. The following algorithm describes this approach in more detail.

ALGORITHM TO REVERSE A STRING

/* This algorithm displays an input string in reverse order.

    Input: A sequence of characters, stored in *StringIn*
    Output: The characters from *StringIn* in reverse order

    ——*/

1. Input a character string, storing it in *StringIn.*
2. Determine *LastPosition,* the position of the last character in *StringIn.*
3. For each integer *i* in the range *LastPosition* down to 0:
    Output the character at position *i* in *StringIn.*

Coding. The program in Figure 9.1 implements this algorithm. It uses the (over-loaded) input operator **>>**, the member function **Length()** and the subscript operator **[ ]** provided in the class **Strings** to carry out the required string operations in Steps 1, 2, and 3, respectively. Besides the **Strings** object **StringIn** that stores the string to be reversed, it also uses a **Strings** object **Response** to store the user's response to the query in the query-controlled do-while loop and the (overloaded) operator **==** from the class **Strings** to compare **Response** with the character strings **"yes"** and **"YES"**.

FIGURE 9.1 Reversing a string.

```
/* This program displays a character string in reverse order.

   Input:   StringIn, a character string up to 120 characters in
            length (the max. length is set in Strings.h)
   Output: The characters from StringIn in reverse order
-----------------------------------------------------------------------*/

#include <iostream.h>
#include "Strings.h"                         // class Strings

int main(void)
{
   cout << "\nThis program reverses a character string...\n";

   Strings
      StringIn,                              // string to be reversed
      Response;                              // query-response variable

   do                                        // loop:
   {
      cout << "\nPlease enter the string you wish reversed: ";

      cin >> StringIn;

      int                                    // find the position of
         LastPosition = StringIn.Length() - 1; //   its last character
```

FIGURE 9.1 Reversing a string. (cont.)

```
    cout << "\n'" << StringIn << "' reversed is: ";

    for (int i = LastPosition; i >= 0; i--)  // output its characters,
        cout << StringIn[i];                  //     from last to first

    cout << "\n\nWant to do another (yes or no)? ";
    cin >> Response;
  }
  while ((Response == "yes") || (Response == "YES"));

    return 0;
}
```

Sample run:

This program reverses a character string...

Please enter the string you wish reversed: <u>sdrawkcab</u>

'sdrawkcab' reversed is: backwards

Want to do another (yes or no)? <u>yes</u>

Please enter the string you wish reversed: <u>drawn</u>

'drawn' reversed is: nward

Want to do another (yes or no)? <u>no</u>

Note that in the sample run, only one word was entered on each line of input. This is because the input operator **>>** stops reading characters when it encounters a white-space character (blank, tab, or newline). Had the string **"drawn onward"** been entered, only the first word **drawn** would have been read and assigned to **StringIn**. The rest of the string would have remained in the **istream** and read as the value for **Response**, causing repetition to terminate. To read an entire line of characters that may contain white space, we can use the **GetLine()** member function from the class **Strings** described in Section 9.3.

9.2 Declaring Strings

In several examples of earlier chapters we used *named character string constants,* such as

```
    char
        ErrorMsg[] = "\n*** Invalid Menu Choice!\n";
```

The declaration

```
Strings
   StringIn;
```

of object **StringIn** in the program of Figure 9.1, however, is new. Although both **ErrorMsg** and **StringIn** are objects associated with a character string, the character string associated with **ErrorMsg** is a constant, whose value cannot be changed during program execution. For example, if we were to (later in the program) try to assign **ErrorMsg** a different string,

```
ErrorMsg = "\n*** Unable to open input file!\n";
```

an error would result when the program is compiled.

By contrast, **StringIn** is a **character string variable**—an object that can store a character string whose value can change as the program executes. Moreover, **Strings** objects use memory efficiently by growing and shrinking dynamically according to the size of the character string stored in them. (The implementation of class **Strings** is given in Appendix F, but the class can be used without knowledge of that implementation.)

There are several ways to declare a **Strings** object. One common form of declaration is similar to the string declarations seen before:

```
Strings
   StringName = StringConstant;
```

This declaration constructs *StringName* as a **Strings** object whose value is the character string *StringConstant*. For example, the declaration

```
Strings
   Play = "The Tempest";
```

constructs a **Strings** object named **Play**, whose value is the string **The Tempest**:

Play: | T | h | e | | T | e | m | p | e | s | t |

The number of characters in a **Strings** object is its **length.** The entries in the object in which individual characters are stored are called its **elements,** and these elements are numbered, beginning with zero. For the object **Play**, element 0 contains the character **T**, element 1 contains the character **h**, element 2 contains the character **e**, element 3 contains the space character, and so on. We can visualize **Play** as follows:

	0	1	2	3	4	5	6	7	8	9	10
Play:	T	h	e		T	e	m	p	e	s	t

Similarly, the declaration

```
Strings
    Name = "Prospero";
```

declares the `Strings` object `Name` and initializes it to the string `"Prospero"`:

<pre>
            0   1   2   3   4   5   6   7
Name: │ P │ r │ o │ s │ p │ e │ r │ o │
</pre>

In general, if a `Strings` object contains n elements (i.e., its length is n), then those elements are numbered from 0 through n − 1.

Another common form of declaration for a `Strings` object is

```
Strings
    StringName;
```

This declaration constructs an object named *StringName* that is initially **empty.** It contains no elements, and so its length is zero. As we shall see, a `Strings` object can grow and shrink dynamically so that an assignment statement or an input statement will cause *StringName* to grow to the appropriate size to hold the value being assigned or input.

The general form of a `Strings` object declaration can thus be given as follows:

Strings Object Declaration

Forms

```
    Strings
        StringName = CharacterString;
```

where:
StringName is the `Strings` object being declared; and
`=` *CharacterString* is an optional initialization of the object.

Purpose
Constructs an object named *StringName* that is capable of storing a string of `char` values. If the `=` *CharacterString* is present, then the elements of *StringName* are initialized to the characters in *CharacterString*.

Note: The directive `#include "Strings.h"` must be used to insert the definition of the class `Strings` before this declaration can be used. The program must also be linked to the `Strings` object file.

9.3 String I/O

The I/O operators **>>** and **<<** have been overloaded in class **Strings** so that their application to a **Strings** objects is consistent with that of other objects we have seen thus far. Remember that to use these operators, the declaration of the class **Strings** (see Appendix F or the disk that accompanies this text) must be inserted into a program (e.g., with the compiler directive **#include "Strings.h"**) and linked to the **Strings** object file.

Input

As we noted in Section 9.1, the class **Strings** provides two ways to input a character string. The first is to use the input operator **>>** and the second is to use the member function **GetLine()** in the class **Strings**.

Using the Input Operator >>. Suppose that **Name** is declared by

```
Strings
    Name;
```

and that the statement

```
cin >> Name;
```

is executed. If the user enters

<u>A1</u>

then execution proceeds as expected and **A1** is assigned to **Name**:

```
       0   1
Name:  A | 1
```

If, however, the user enters

<u>A1 E Cat</u>

the value of **Name** will also be **A1**, the same as before!

The reason for this is that in an input expression of the form

```
cin >> StringsObject
```

the input operator **>>** gets the next *word* from **cin**. That is, *the input operator extracts characters from the* **istream** *and transfers them into* **StringsObject** *until the character being read is a white-space character (space, tab, or newline).* The unread characters

```
E Cat
```

remain in the **istream** and will be read by subsequent input statements (which is probably not what the programmer wants), unless these characters are ignored. For example, if the input lines contain at most 80 characters, the **fstream** member function **ignore()** could be called with the statement

```
cin.ignore(80, '\n');
```

to skip over the rest of the characters on the current line. (See Section 8.4 for a description of the **ignore()** function.)

The general form of the input expression is as follows.

Strings Input Expression

Form

   StreamName >> *StringName*

where:
   StreamName is the name of an **istream** or
      fstream opened for input;
   StringName is the name of a **Strings** object.

Purpose

Read a word from a stream, as long as its length does not exceed the maximum allowed (as defined in the class **Strings**).[1] Characters are read from *StreamName* until either

- A white-space character (blank, tab, end-of-line) has been read, or
- the maximum length allowed is reached,

whichever comes first. In the first case, the white-space character is read but is not stored in *StringName*.

Although getting the next word from an **istream** is very useful in solving many problems, the **Strings** class also provides a member function for reading an entire line of input.

GetLine().   The class **Strings** also includes a member function named **GetLine()** that can be used to input a line of text from an **istream** passed as an argument.[2] For example, suppose that **Name** is the **Strings** object declared earlier

---

[1] The maximum length allowed for input values of strings can be determined by using the statement

   `cout << Strings::MaxLength;`

[2] Class **istream** has a similar member function **getline()** that can be used to fill a character array with a line from an input file. The words in the **Strings** member **GetLine()** are capitalized to keep it distinct.

and the statement

```
Name.GetLine(cin);
```

is executed. If the user enters

A1

then the contents of **Name** is the same as before:

```
          0   1
Name:  | A | 1 |
```

If the user enters

A1 E Cat

however, then the entire line is read by **GetLine()** and placed into **Name**:

```
          0   1   2   3   4   5   6   7
Name:  | A | 1 |   | E |   | C | a | t |
```

Similarly, the input statement

```
cin >> StringIn;
```

in the program in Figure 9.1 could be replaced by

```
StringIn.GetLine(cin);
```

Then if the user enters a line containing more than one word such as

drawn onward

the entire line of input is read and stored in **StringIn**,

```
            0   1   2   3   4   5   6   7   8   9  10  11
StringIn: | d | r | a | w | n |   | o | n | w | a | r | d |
```

whereas only the string **"drawn"** would be read and assigned to **StringIn** with the input statement

```
cin >> StringIn;
```

The rest of the input string would remain in the input stream.

The general form of a call to the `GetLine()` member function is as follows:

Strings Member GetLine()

Form

StringName.GetLine(*StreamName, MaxChars, UntilChar*);

where:

StringName is the name of a `Strings` object;

StreamName is the name of an `istream` or `fstream` opened
for input;

MaxChars is an optional integer bound on the number of chars
to be read; its default value is a maximum length specifier
defined in the class `Strings` (see Footnote 1); and

UntilChar is an optional character that, if read, terminates the
function; its default value is `'\n'`.

Purpose

Read characters from *StreamName* until either

- *MaxChars* characters have been read, or
- The character *UntilChar* has been read,

whichever comes first. In the second case, the character
UntilChar is not stored in *StringName*. If the default value
(newline) is used for *UntilChar*, this function can be used to
input a line of text from a stream.

Output

As we have seen several times, character string constants can be output to an
`ostream` object using the output operator `<<`. For example, the statement

```
cout << "Hi There!";
```

outputs `Hi There!` to the `ostream` named `cout`, and the statement

```
cerr << "*** Illegal Menu Choice!";
```

outputs `*** Illegal Menu Choice!` to the `ostream` named `cerr`.

The output operator `<<` can also be used to output a string that is stored in a
`Strings` object. For example, if we declare

```
Strings
   Name = "John Doe";
```

then the statement

```
cout << "\nMy name is " << Name << ".\n\n";
```

will display

```
My name is John Doe.
```

The general form of an output expression involving **Strings** is as follows:

Strings Output Expression

Form

    StreamName << *StringName*

where:
    StreamName is the name of an **istream** or
        fstream opened for output;
    StringName is the name of a **Strings** object.

Purpose
Output characters from *StringName* to
StreamName. This function can be used to output a
Strings object either to the screen or to a file.

Example: Copying a File

One kind of name that we frequently use in programs is the name of an input or output file. In the examples that used files in earlier chapters, we had to hard-wire the name of each file into the program by defining it as a named constant such as

```
char const
   InputFileName[] = "Document.txt";
```

and then open the file with

```
fstream
   InStream(InputFileName, ios::in);
```

The problem with this approach is that if a different file must be processed, then there are only two options:

1. Change the names of files to be processed to match the name of the input file (e.g., **Document.txt**).
2. Modify the program, changing the character string constant associated with **InputFileName** to the names of the files (and then recompiling the program).

Clearly, neither of these approaches is convenient. It would be much better to declare

```
Strings
   InputFileName;
```

get the name of the input file from the user,[3]

```
cout << "\nPlease enter the name of the input file: ";
InputFileName.GetLine(cin);
```

and then open the file as usual:

```
fstream
   InStream(InputFileName, ios::in);
```

The program in Figure 9.2 uses this approach to make a copy of a file. It reads lines from the input file using the **GetLine()** member of class **Strings** and outputs them to the output file using the output operator **<<**.

FIGURE 9.2 Copying a file.

```
/* This program uses class Strings to copy a file.

   Output(screen):        Prompts for input
   Input(keyboard):       The name of an input file, stored in
                          InputFileName; and the name of an output
                          file, stored in OutputFileName
   Input(InputFileName):  Characters in the file, line by line
   Output(OutputFileName): All the input characters
--------------------------------------------------------------------*/

#include <iostream.h>                  // cin, cout, <<, >>
#include <fstream.h>                   // fstream, <<, >>
#include <stdlib.h>                    // exit()

#include "Strings.h"                   // class Strings

int main(void)
{                                      // introductory message
   cout << "\nThis program prompts for the name of an input file"
        << "\n\tand the name of an output file and makes a"
        << "\n\tcopy of the input file in the output file.\n";
```

---

[3] We use `InputFileName.GetLine(cin)` to input a file name because in many computing environments (e.g., UNIX and Macintosh), file names may consist of multiple words.

FIGURE 9.2 Copying a file. (cont.)

```
Strings
   InputFileName,                      // user-entered input file
   OutputFileName;                     // user-entered output file

cout << "\nPlease enter the name of the input file: ";
InputFileName.GetLine(cin);           // get name of input file

fstream
   InStream(InputFileName, ios::in);  // open it for input

if (InStream.fail())                  // check that it worked
{
   cerr << "\n*** Unable to open file '"
        << InputFileName << "'!\n";
   exit (-1);
}

cout << "\nPlease enter the name of the output file: ";
OutFileName.GetLine(cin);             // get name of output file

fstream
   OutStream(OutputFileName, ios::out);// open if for output...

if (OutStream.fail())                 // checking, as always
{
   cerr << "\n*** Unable to open file '"
        << OutputFileName << "'!\n";
   exit (-1);
}

Strings
   Line;                              // container for a line of input

Line.GetLine(InStream);              // read the first line

while (!InStream.eof())              // while not end-of-file
{
   OutStream << Line << endl;        //    write the line
   Line.GetLine(InStream);           //    read the next line
}                                    // end while

InStream.close();                   // close input and output files
OutStream.close();
cout << "\nCopy completed.\n";       // user feedback

return 0;                           // successful termination
}
```

FIGURE 9.2   Copying a file. (cont.)

Listing of file `Lincoln.txt`

```
Four score and seven years ago
our fathers brought forth on this continent a new nation
conceived in liberty
and dedicated to the proposition
that all men are created equal.
```

Sample run:

```
This program prompts for the name of an input file
   and the name of an output file, and makes a
   copy of the input file in the output file.

Please enter the name of the input file: Lincoln.txt

Please enter the name of the output file: Lincoln.bak

Copy completed.
```

Listing of file `Lincoln.bak`

```
Four score and seven years ago
our fathers brought forth on this continent a new nation
conceived in liberty
and dedicated to the proposition
that all men are created equal.
```

Note that class **Strings** allows us to view a file abstractly as a sequence of lines. Note also that it is necessary to output a newline character following each line, because although **GetLine()** reads the newline character from **InStream**, it does not store it in **Line**.

Exercises

1. Write a program that reads the name of a file and then determines how many lines are in the file.

2. Write a program that reads the name of a file and then determines how many words are in the file, where a "word" is any string of characters delimited by white space but containing no white-space characters.

3. Modify the program in Figure 9.1 so that it makes a copy of the input file, but with its lines numbered.

4. The local chapter of the Know-Nothing political party maintains a file of names and addresses of its contributors. Each line of the file contains a contributor's last name, first name, middle initial, street address, city, state, and zip code. These items are separated by white space but none contains any white-space characters; for example,

```
Doe John Q 123_SomeStreet AnyTown AnyState 12345
```

Write a program that reads the name of this file, opens it for input, reads this information from the file, and produces mailing labels having the format

```
John Q. Doe
123_SomeStreet
AnyTown, AnyState 12345
```

9.4   More Operations on `Strings` Objects

In addition to input and output, there are a number of fairly standard operations on character strings. In the following list of operations for the class `Strings`, `Str`, `Str1`, and `Str2` are `Strings` objects:

- `Str.Length()` returns the number of characters in `Str`.
- `Str[i]` returns the `i`th character in `Str` (numbered from zero).
- `Str1 = Str2` assigns `Str2` to `Str1`, replacing the contents of `Str1` with those of `Str2`.
- The relational operators `==`, `!=`, `<`, `>`, `<=`, and `>=` can be used to compare `Str1` and `Str2` (e.g., `Str1 != Str2`).
- `Str1 & Str2` returns the concatenation of `Str1` and `Str2`.
- `Str(a, b)` returns the substring of `Str` starting at position **a** and ending at position **b**.
- `Str1.Replace(a, b, Str2)` replaces the characters at positions **a** through **b** in `Str1` with `Str2`, if possible; it returns true (1) if successful and false (0) otherwise.
- `Str.Delete(a, b)` removes the characters at positions **a** through **b** from `Str`, if possible; it returns true (1) if successful and false (0) otherwise.
- `Str1.Insert(Str2, Pos)` inserts `Str2` into `Str1` at index `Pos`.
- `Str1.Pos(Str2)` returns the index of the first occurrence of `Str2` within `Str1`, if possible; it returns true (1) if successful and false (0) otherwise.

In the remainder of this section, we discuss each of these operations in greater detail. Again, remember that to use any of these string operators, the declaration of the class `Strings` must be inserted into a program (e.g., with the compiler directive `#include "Strings.h"`) and that program must be linked to the `Strings` object file.

String Length

The `Length()` function is a member of class `Strings` that returns the number of characters in the object of which it is a member. Thus, if `StringIn` contains the string `"drawn onward"`,

	0	1	2	3	4	5	6	7	8	9	10	11
StringIn:	d	r	a	w	n		o	n	w	a	r	d

there are 12 characters in `StringIn` (numbered from 0 to 11) and so the value of

```
StringIn.Length()
```

is 12.

The general form of a call to the `Length()` member function is as follows.

Strings Member Length()

Form

StringName`.Length();`

where:
  StringName is the name of a `Strings` object.

Purpose
Returns the number of characters stored in *StringName*.

Note that because the numbering of a `Strings` object begins with zero, the expression

StringName`.Length() - 1`

can be used to find the position of the last character of *StringName:*

```
int
    LastPosition = StringIn.Length() - 1;
```

The Subscript Operator

The variables of previous chapters are called **scalar** variables to indicate that they can only store single values. In contrast, a `Strings` object can be viewed as a container for storing a sequence of values. Each *element* of a `Strings` object is like a scalar character variable in that it can store a single character, and anything that can be done to a character variable can be done to an element of a `Strings` object.

The character stored in a particular element of a `Strings` object can be accessed using the number of that element and the **subscript operator** [ ]. For example, suppose that `Name` is declared by

```
Strings
    Name = "John Doe";
```

so that the character string **"John Doe"** is stored in the **Strings** object **Name**:

```
      0   1   2   3   4   5   6   7
Name: J   o   h   n       D   o   e
```

The number of an element, called its **subscript** or **index,** provides us with a means of accessing the character stored in that particular element. For example, consider the following assignment statements:

```
Name[1] = 'a';
Name[2] = Name[3];
Name[3] = 'e';
Name[5] = 'R';
```

The first assignment changes the value of the element whose index is 1 to the character **'a'**. The second assignment changes the value of the element whose index is 2 to the value of the element whose index is 3. The third assignment changes the value of the element whose index is 3 to the character **'e'**. The final assignment changes the value of the element whose index is 5 to the character **'R'**. The **Strings** object **Name** is thus changed to:

```
      0   1   2   3   4   5   6   7
Name: J   a   n   e       R   o   e
```

As a second example, recall that the program in Figure 9.1 contained

```
int
   LastPosition = StringIn.Length() - 1;
      .
      .
      .
for (int i = LastPosition; i >= 0; i--) // output its characters,
   cout << StringIn[i];                  //    from last to first
```

Here, the statement

```
cout << StringIn[i];
```

is used to access and output the character in position **i** of **StringIn**. Since the value of **i** in the for loop ranges from the index of the last character in **StringIn** down to 0, the characters of **StringIn** are output in reverse order.

The general form of a subscript expression is as follows.

`Strings` **Subscript Expression**

> **Form**
>
> $\quad$ *StringName*[*i*]
>
> where:
> $\quad$ *StringName* is the name of a `Strings` object.
>
> **Purpose**
> Returns the character from the element within
> *StringName* whose index is *i*, provided
> $0 \leq i < StringName.\texttt{Length()}$.

Note that the subscript operator for a `Strings` object performs **range checking,** so that an attempt to access the character in position *i*,

$\quad$ *StringName*[*i*]

will generate a run-time error if the value of *i* is outside the range of valid indices for *StringName*.

Assignment

The assignment operator (=) can be used to assign a value to a `Strings` variable. It uses dynamic sizing, so that a `Strings` object on the left side of an assignment automatically grows or shrinks to the appropriate size to hold the value it is being assigned. For example, consider the declaration

```
Strings
    Quote = "To be is to do - Aristotle.";
```

When this statement is executed, the `Strings` object `Quote` is initialized to the indicated character string of length 27. The subsequent assignment statement

```
Quote = "To do is to be - Sartre.";
```

assigns this new character string to `Quote` and changes its length to 24. Similarly, the assignment statement

```
Quote = "Doobee-Doobee-Doo - Sinatra.";
```

assigns a character string of length 28 to `Quote`.

The **Strings** class also permits a character string named constant to be assigned to a **Strings** object; for example,

```
Strings
   Quote;
const char
   Aesop[] = "Familiarity breeds contempt.";
      .
      .
      .
Quote = Aesop;
```

Note that the value of the constant object **Aesop** has a fixed length 27 (fixed when the program is compiled), but the **Strings** object **Quote** has length 0 initially and, following execution of the assignment statement, has length 27. These examples show that **Strings** objects *grow and shrink as the program executes,* a feature sometimes called **dynamic sizing.**

The value of any **Strings** object may be assigned to a **Strings** variable. For example, the statements

```
Strings
   Quote,
   MarkTwain;

MarkTwain = "Familiarity breeds contempt - and children.";
Quote = MarkTwain;
```

will store the character string constant

```
Familiarity breeds contempt - and children.
```

in the two **Strings** objects **Quote** and **MarkTwain**. Assignments of **Strings** objects may also be chained. For example, the two preceding assignment statements could be replaced by

```
Quote = MarkTwain = "Familiarity breeds contempt - and children.";
```

The general form of a **Strings** assignment expression is as follows.

Strings Assignment

Form

> *StringName* = *StringExpression*

where:
   StringName is the name of a **Strings** object;
      and
   StringExpression is an expression of type
      Strings or a character string.

> **Purpose**
> Copy the value of *StringExpression* as a
> `Strings` object into *StringName*, whose size
> grows or shrinks as necessary to hold this value.
>
> *Note:* Unlike input string values described in the
> preceding section, there is no preset limit on the
> length of a value being assigned to a `Strings` vari-
> able.

The Relational Operators

The relational operators have all been overloaded in class `Strings` so that two
`Strings` objects can conveniently be compared. In each operation, the elements of
the `Strings` operands are compared element by element until a mismatch occurs
or the end of either string is encountered.

To illustrate, consider the declarations

```
Strings
    HisName = "James",
    HerName = "Jane";
```

The objects produced are

```
            0  1  2  3  4              0  1  2  3
HisName:  | J | a | m | e | s |   HerName:  | J | a | n | e |
```

The expression

```
HisName < HerName
```

evaluates to true (nonzero) because in comparing the character strings element by
element, the first characters match, as do the second characters; but in comparing
the third characters, 'm' is less than 'n', and so the < operator returns true (nonzero). Similarly, the expresssions

```
HisName == HerName

HisName != HerName

HisName > HerName

HisName <= HerName

HisName >= HerName
```

evaluate to false (zero), true (nonzero), false (zero), true (nonzero), and false (zero), respectively.

If the end of one of the strings is reached in the character-by-character comparison without a mismatch, the shorter string is considered to be less than the longer string. For example, if the string in **HisName** was *"Janus"* instead of *"James"* and the string in **HerName** was *"Jan"* instead of *"Jane"*,

	0	1	2	3	4
HisName:	J	a	n	u	s

	0	1	2
HerName:	J	a	n

then the values of the conditional expressions

    HisName > HerName

and

    HisName != HerName

would be true (nonzero).

The general form of a **Strings** conditional expression is as follows.

Strings Conditional Expression

Form

StringExpression₁ RelationalOperator StringExpression₂

where:
  Each of *StringExpression₁* and *StringExpression₂* is an expression of type **Strings** or a character string; and
  RelationalOperator is one of the relational operators

    <, <=, ==, !=, >=, >

Purpose
Compare *StringExpression₁* to *StringExpression₂* and return the boolean value determined by a character-by-character comparison, as illustrated in the preceding examples.

Note that **Strings** objects and character string constants can be mixed in conditional expressions. For example, if Jane Doe is the designer of a program and wishes to keep others from executing her program, she might use a simple password scheme like the following to control access to the program:

```
const char
   Password[] = "Prospero!";
Strings
   PassString;

cout << "\nEnter the password: ";
PassString.GetLine(cin);

if (PassString != Password)
{
   cout << "\nSorry, password is incorrect!\n";
   exit (-1);
}
```

Concatenation

Another useful string operation is **concatenation**—combining two strings into a single string. For example, the concatenation of the string `"list"` and the string `"en"` is the string `"listen"`. Ordering is important in concatenation—if we concatenate the string `"en"` and the string `"list"`, the result is the string `"enlist"`. The concatenation operation can be thought of as forming a string whose value is the second string *appended* to the first string.

The ampersand symbol (**&**) is overloaded in class **Strings** so that when its operands are two **Strings** objects (or character strings or a mixture), the result is the concatenation of these operands. For example, given the declarations

```
Strings
   State = "Michigan",
   GreatLake;
```

the expression

```
GreatLake = "Lake " & State;
```

concatenates the character string `"Lake"` and the string stored in the **Strings** object **State** and stores the result in **GreatLake**:

	0	1	2	3	4	5	6	7	8	9	10	11	12
GreatLake:	L	a	k	e		M	i	c	h	i	g	a	n

Concatenation thus builds a (larger) string out of two (smaller) strings. The concatenation operator in the class **Strings** returns the **Strings** object it produces, and so multiple concatenations can be chained together, as in

```
Strings
   FirstName = "Popeye",
   MiddleName = "the",
   LastName = "Sailor",
   FullName = FirstName & " " & MiddleName & " " & LastName;
```

which initializes **FullName** to be a **Strings** object containing the character string

```
"Popeye the Sailor"
```

Following this initialization, **FullName.Length()** will return the value 17.
The general form of a concatenation expression is as follows.

Strings Concatenation Expression

Form

   StringExpression₁ & *StringExpression₂*

where:
   StringExpression₁ and *StringExpression₂*
   are expressions of type **Strings** or character
   strings.

Purpose
Create the **Strings** value obtained by appending
the string from *StringExpression₂* to the string
from *StringExpression₁*.

Note: The length of the **Strings** value produced
by concatenation is not subject to the limit described earlier for input strings.

The concatenation and assignment operations can be used to circumvent the
limitation on the length of an input string. To illustrate how this is done, suppose
that the length of an input string is three times the limit set in the class **Strings**.
The following statements can be used to input that string piece by piece and then
concatenate the pieces together.

```
fstream
    InStream(FileName, ios::in);
Strings
    FirstPart,
    SecondPart,
    ThirdPart,
    WholeThing;
       .
       .
       .

FirstPart.GetLine(InStream);
SecondPart.GetLine(InStream);
ThirdPart.GetLine(InStream);

WholeThing = FirstPart & SecondPart & ThirdPart;
```

The Substring Operation

The subscript operator provides access to a particular character in a string, but sometimes it is useful to access a *substring* of characters. To illustrate, suppose that the following **Strings** objects have been declared:

```
Strings
    FullName = "John Quincy Doe",
    FirstName,
    MiddleName,
    LastName;
```

```
          0   1   2   3   4   5   6   7   8   9   10  11  12  13  14
FullName: | J | o | h | n |   | Q | u | i | n | c | y |   | D | o | e |
```

Also suppose that we want to access the first, middle, or last name from within **FullName**. The class **Strings** provides a substring operation that makes this easy. The assignments

```
FirstName = FullName(0, 3);
MiddleName = FullName(5, 10);
LastName = FullName(12, 14);
```

set the value of **FirstName** to the string **"John"**, the value of **MiddleName** to the string **"Quincy"**, and the value of **LastName** to the string **"Doe"**, leaving **FullName** unchanged. Note the differences between this substring operation and the subscript operation:

Subscript Operation	Substring Operation
Uses square brackets: **[ ]**	Uses parentheses: **( )**
Uses one index	Uses two indices
Returns a **char** value	Returns a **Strings** object

The general form of the substring operation is as follows.

Strings Substring Expression

Form

> *StringName(First, Last)*

where:

> *StringName* is a **Strings** object; and
> *First* and *Last* are nonnegative integers with
> *First* ≤ *Last* < *StringName*.Length().

> **Purpose**
> length *Last* - *First* + 1 consisting of the charac-
> Create a **Strings** value containing the substring of
> length *Last* - *First* + 1 consisting of the charac-
> ters in positions *First* through *Last* of
> *StringName*.

Note that bounds checking is performed to ensure that *First* and *Last* are valid indices of *StringName* and that *First* ≤ *Last*. The substring that this operation produces is itself a **Strings** object, and so assignment, comparison, and any of the other **Strings** operations may be applied to it.

It should be emphasized that the substring operation is a read-only, or nondestructive, operation that does not modify the **Strings** object to which it is applied. For example, the statement

```
FullName(0, 3) = "Jane";
```

will not change the first four characters in **FullName** to *"Jane"* because the substring operation builds and returns a new **Strings** object that is distinct from the **Strings** object to which the substring operator was applied. Thus, the effect of such an assignment statement is that

1. The expression **FullName(0, 3)** returns a new **Strings** object containing *"John"* that is completely distinct from the **Strings** object named **FullName**;
2. The value of this new **Strings** object is changed to *"Jane"* (leaving the value of **FullName** unchanged).

The ability to alter a substring of a **Strings** object is provided by the function **Replace()** that we describe next.

Substring Replacement

We have seen that the substring operation does not modify the **Strings** object to which it is applied. However, it is sometimes necessary to modify some portion of a string, leaving the rest of it unaltered. The **Strings** class provides a member function named **Replace()** to perform this operation. To illustrate, suppose the following declaration is given:

```
Strings
    FullName = "John Quincy Doe";
```

	0	1	2	3	4	5	6	7	8	9	10	11	12	13	14
FullName:	J	o	h	n		Q	u	i	n	c	y		D	o	e

Then the function call

```
FullName.Replace(0, 3, "Jane");
```

changes the first name in **FullName** to *"Jane"*:

	0	1	2	3	4	5	6	7	8	9	10	11	12	13	14
FullName:	J	a	n	e		Q	u	i	n	c	y		D	o	e

Similarly,

    FullName.Replace(12,12, "R");

changes the last name in **FullName** to *"Roe"*:

	0	1	2	3	4	5	6	7	8	9	10	11	12	13	14
FullName:	J	a	n	e		Q	u	i	n	c	y		R	o	e

In the preceding examples, the length of the **FullName** did not change, because the replacement string and the substring being replaced had the same length. In general, however, the replacement string and the substring being replaced may have different lengths. For example, execution of the statement:

    FullName.Replace(5, 10, "Eyre");

will replace the 6-character substring *"Quincy"* with the 4-character string *"Eyre"*. As a result, the length of **FullName** decreases from 15 to 13:

	0	1	2	3	4	5	6	7	8	9	10	11	12
FullName:	J	a	n	e		E	y	r	e		R	o	e

Note that the indices of the substring *"Roe"* that were 12 through 14 change to 10 through 12 when **FullName** shrinks. If we subsequently execute the statement

    FullName.Replace(10, 12, "Roebuck");

then the 3-character substring *"Roe"* will be replaced with the 7-character string *"Roebuck"*, giving *"Jane Eyre Roebuck"* (length 17) as the value of **FullName**:

	0	1	2	3	4	5	6	7	8	9	10	11	12	13	14	15	16
FullName:	J	a	n	e		E	y	r	e		R	o	e	b	u	c	k

The general form of the **Strings** replacement operation is as follows.

Strings Replacement Expression

Form

    StringName.Replace(*First*, *Last*, *Replacement*)

where:
  StringName is a **Strings** object;
  First and *Last* are nonnegative integers with

   First ≤ *Last* < *StringName*.Length()

  Replacement is a **Strings** object or character string.

Purpose
Modify the **Strings** object *StringName* by replacing the substring *StringName(First, Last)* with *Replacement*; the
length of *StringName* increases or decreases as necessary.
Bounds checking is performed to ensure that *First* and *Last* are
valid indices of *StringName* and that *First* ≤ *Last*.
Replace() returns true (1) or false (0) according to whether or
not replacement is successful.

Substring Deletion

Another useful string operation is deletion of a substring. To perform this operation, the class **Strings** provides a member function named **Delete()**.[4] For example, consider the declaration

```
Strings
    CommonName = "John Quincy Doe";
```

which initializes the **Strings** object **CommonName** as

	0	1	2	3	4	5	6	7	8	9	10	11	12	13	14
CommonName:	J	o	h	n		Q	u	i	n	c	y		D	o	e

The statement

```
CommonName.Delete(5, 11);
```

---

[4] The similarity of replacement and deletion would make it easy to combine the two operations so that a call
with the form Str1.Replace(a, b, Str2) would replace the characters at positions a through b, and a call
with the form Str1.Replace(a, b) would delete those characters. For the sake of readability, we have opted
to keep these operations distinct.

deletes the middle name from `CommonName`

	0	1	2	3	4	5	6	7
CommonName:	J	o	h	n		D	o	e

and the length of `CommonName` decreases to 8.

The general form of the `Strings` deletion operation is as follows.

Strings Deletion Expression

Form

> *StringName*`.Delete(`*First, Last*`)`

where:

StringName is a `Strings` object; and
First and *Last* are nonnegative integers with

> *First* ≤ *Last* < *StringName*`.Length()`

Purpose

Modify the `Strings` object *StringName* by removing the substring *StringName*`(`*First, Last*`)`. The length of *StringName* decreases by *Last* - *First* + 1 characters. Bounds checking is performed to ensure that *First* and *Last* are valid indices of *StringName* and that *First* ≤ *Last*. `Delete()` returns true (1) or false (0) according to whether deletion is successful.

Substring Insertion

The inverse of the deletion operation for a `Strings` object is insertion of a substring into a string. The `Strings` class provides the member function `Insert()` to perform this operation. For example, consider the declaration

```
Strings
    Signature = "Jane Roe";
```

which initializes `Signature` to `"Jane Roe"`:

	0	1	2	3	4	5	6	7
Signature:	J	a	n	e		R	o	e

The function reference

```
Signature.Insert("E. ", 5);
```

can be used to insert the character string *"E. "* into **Signature** beginning at position 5, giving

	0	1	2	3	4	5	6	7	8	9	10
Signature:	J	a	n	e		E	.		R	o	e

The length of **Signature** increases to 11.

The general form of the **Strings** insertion operation is as follows.

Strings Insertion Expression

Form

    StringName.Insert(*Insertion, Position*)

where:

  StringName is a **Strings** object;

  Insertion is a **Strings** object or character string;

  Position is a nonnegative integer with

    Position ≤ *StringName*.Length()

Purpose

Modify the **Strings** object *StringName* by inserting the string *Insertion* with its first character at *Position*. The length of *StringName* increases by *Insertion*.Length() characters. Bounds checking is performed to ensure that *Position* is a valid index of *StringName*. Insert() returns true (1) or false (0) according to whether insertion is successful (i.e., the indices are valid).

Substring Pattern Matching

Another common string operation is finding the location of a given substring within a string, an operation known as **pattern matching.** The **Strings** class provides a member function named **Position()** that provides this capability. For example, given the declaration

```
Strings
    Quote = "If it walks like a duck, and quacks like a duck, "
            "then it just may be a duck - Reuther";
```

the call

```
Quote.Position("duck")
```

returns the value 19, since 19 is the index of the first occurrence of the substring *"duck"* within the **Strings** object **Quote**. The positions of different occurrences of the substring `"duck"` can be found by adding enough characters to distinguish these occurrences from those preceding them. For example, the call

```
Quote.Position("duck, then")
```

returns the value 43, whereas

```
Quote.Position("duck - ");
```

returns the value 71.

The general form of the `Strings` pattern-matching operation is as follows.

Strings Pattern-Matching Expression

Form

   StringName.`Position`(*Pattern*)

where:
   StringName is a `Strings` object; and
   Pattern is a `Strings` object or character string.

Purpose
Returns the index in *StringName* at which the substring *Pattern* begins. If *Pattern* does not occur within *StringName*, then the value −1 is returned.

In general, it is good programming practice to check the return value of operations that can easily fail (like the pattern-matching operation) to ensure that they were successful before continuing. For example, instead of simply writing

```
int
   Location = Quote.Position(SomeString);
```

and then using `Location`, the value of `Location` should be checked before continuing:

```
int
   Location = Quote.Position(SomeString);

if (Location < 0)
   cerr << SomeString << " does not occur within Quote";
else
{
   // ... process using valid Location value ...
}
```

Otherwise, if *SomeString* is a value that does not occur within `Quote` (e.g., `"chicken"`), `Position()` will return the value −1, causing subsequent accesses to `Quote[Location]` to generate a range error.

Numeric Conversion Operations

We have seen that the subscript operator provides a way to access the individual characters stored in a `Strings` object. Now consider the declaration

```
Strings
   NumString = "3.14159";
```

Here, we have a `Strings` object whose value is a sequence of digit characters, but those characters taken together represent a number:

```
                    0   1   2   3   4   5   6
     NumString:   | 3 | . | 1 | 4 | 1 | 5 | 9 |
```

The class `Strings` provides three member functions that can be used to convert such strings to numbers.

`Double()`. The member function `Double()` attempts to convert a string into a double value. For the preceding object `NumString`, the expression

```
NumString.Double()
```

returns the `double` value 3.14159. The `Double()` function skips over leading white space in the string until it encounters a non-white-space character. If that character is not a number (or a sign character), the conversion fails and `Double()` returns zero. Otherwise, `Double()` scans the characters, combines them into a real numeric value until a real value delimiter is encountered, and then returns the accumulated real value.

`Long()`. The second conversion function attempts to extract a `long` (integer) value from a string. For example, given the preceding value of `NumString`, the call

```
NumString.Long()
```

returns the value 3, since the decimal point is not part of an integer value and thus acts as an integer delimiter. Like `Double()`, the `Long()` function skips leading white space and returns zero if the first non-white-space character is not a sign character or a digit. Otherwise, it scans the digits, combining them into an integer value until an integer-value delimiter is encountered, and then returns the accumulated integer value.

The `Long()` function will also convert strings containing hexadecimal and octal values. For example, given the declaration

```
Strings
   HexString = "0x1f";
```

the call

```
HexString.Long()
```

returns the hexadecimal value `0x1f` (= 31 in base 10).

`Unsigned()`. The third conversion function is the `Unsigned()` function, which behaves in exactly the same manner as the `Long()` function, except that the value it returns is an **unsigned** value. Thus, the call

> `NumString.Unsigned()`

also returns the value 3. However, if we declare

> `Strings`
> `   NumString = "-3.14159";`

then the call `String.Double()` will return the value `-3.14159` and the call `String.Long()` will return the value `-3`, but the call `String.Unsigned()` will return the value `0`.

Exercises

1. Write a function to convert a string of lowercase and uppercase letters into all lowercase letters. (*Hint:* Use the functions provided in `<ctype.h>`.)

2. Write a function that, given the three components of a name (the first name, a middle name or initial, and a last name, returns the single `Strings` object consisting of the last name, followed by a comma and then the first and middle initials, each followed by a period. For example, given the strings: `"John"`, `"Henry"`, and `"Doe"`, the function should produce `"Doe, J. H."`.

3. Proceed as in Exercise 2, but design the function to accept a single `Strings` object consisting of a first name, a middle name or initial, and a last name and that returns the single `Strings` object consisting of the last name, followed by a comma and then the first and middle initials, each followed by a period. For example, given the string `"John Henry Doe"`, the function should produce `"Doe, J. H."`.

4. Write a function to convert ordinary Hindu-Arabic (integer) numerals into Roman numerals and an inverse function that converts Roman numerals into Hindu-Arabic numerals. (I = 1, V = 5, X = 10, L = 50, C = 100, D = 500, and M = 1,000.)

5. A string is said to be a **palindrome** if it does not change when the order of characters in the string is reversed. For example,

   MADAM
   463364
   ABLE WAS I ERE I SAW ELBA

   are palindromes. Write a function to determine if a string is a palindrome.

6. Repeat Exercise 5, but this time use a recursive function to determine if a string is a palindrome.

9.5   Using Strings Objects

In this section, we present some examples to illustrate the use of the class **Strings**.

Example 1: Scanning for a Virus

A computer **virus** is a piece of software that, when executed, attempts to hide itself within other executable programs. When it succeeds, the executable program becomes a **host** for the virus, so that when that program containing the virus is executed, the virus tries to ''infect'' other programs. That is, if the programs on one computer are infected with a virus and a user copies one of those programs onto a floppy disk and then takes the floppy disk to another computer to execute that program, the virus will try to replicate itself by infecting the programs on the second computer. A computer virus can thus spread quickly among a community of computer users if they share infected software applications.

There are a number of organizations that write software products to combat viruses. These products use two basic approaches:

- Virus *detection and recovery* to identify those viruses in a system and remove them (hopefully, without damaging their hosts)
- Virus *prevention* to keep new viruses from infecting a computer's programs, by watching for behaviors characteristic of viruses

The behavior of a virus can be malicious. An example is the infamous Michelangelo virus, which is programmed to do nothing (but replicate itself) until March 6 (the birthday of Michelangelo), when it erases the hard disk of the computer whose software it infects. By contrast, the CODE 252 virus activates itself whenever an infected system or application is executed and displays the following annoying message:

```
You have a virus
Ha Ha Ha Ha Ha Ha Ha
Now erasing all disks...
Ha Ha Ha Ha Ha Ha Ha
P.S. Have a nice day
Ha Ha Ha Ha Ha Ha Ha
(Click to continue...)
```

Fortunately, this message is a ''practical joke,'' because the virus does not actually delete any files or directories.

For viruses that display such messages, the character string being displayed is typically stored within the virus as a constant. Thus, to determine whether a program is a host for a virus, a virus-detection program can simply scan the suspected host for the appropriate string. This is the approach used to detect the ANTI virus; virus-detection programs simply scan executable programs suspected of being infected for the string ''ANTI.''

The program in Figure 9.3 simulates this detection technique. It uses the capabilities provided by the **Strings** class and an end-of-file controlled loop to repeatedly

- Read a line from a file.
- Scan that line for a given string.
- If the string is found, display a message to that effect.

The sample run in Figure 9.3 uses a text file named **binary.sim**, in which we have
simulated the appearance of a binary file infected with the ANTI virus.

FIGURE 9.3   Scanning for a virus.

```
/* This program uses class Strings to scan a file for a given string,
   simulating the behavior of a virus detection program.

   Input:   The name of the input file; the string to be checked
   Output:  A message indicating whether the input string occurs
            in the input file
   -----------------------------------------------------------------*/

#include <iostream.h>
#include <fstream.h>
#include <stdlib.h>
#include "Strings.h"

int main(void)
{
   cout << "\nThis program searches a file for a given string.";

   Strings
      FileName,                      // the input file name
      SearchString,                  // the string being sought
      InputString;                   // a line from input file

                                     // get name of input file
   cout << "\nPlease enter the name of the file to be searched: ";
   FileName.GetLine(cin);

   fstream
      InStream(FileName, ios::in);   // open a stream to it

   if (InStream.fail())             // check for successful open
   {
      cerr << "\n*** main: unable to open " << FileName
           << " for input!\n";
      exit(-1);
   }
```

FIGURE 9.3   Scanning for a virus. (cont.)

```
                                                // get the search string
    cout << "\nPlease enter the string being sought: ";
    SearchString.GetLine(cin);

    InputString.GetLine(InStream);           // get the first line
    while (!InStream.eof())                   // while not end-of-file
    {                                         // if line contains string
                                              //   display a "found" msg.
        if (InputString.Position(SearchString) >= 0)
            cout << "\n***" << SearchString
                << " found in this file.\n";

        InputString.GetLine(InStream);       // get the next line
    }

    cout << "\nProcessing complete.\n\n";    // message to user
    InStream.close();                        // close the file
    return 0;
}
```

Listing of simulated virus-infected file:

```
aisjdfklasdjfklasjfljasdfljasdas;l
zzmANTIkladfklajsdfklajsdfkjasdljaslkdfj
kasjfklasdjfklajsdfkljasdflkalskdf
kjavjdfjoiwjefmm,.xmcjeoieCewmp.EM
,mckwjoaejcccnmeyquvhi hnrefnnfhDKFa
nacjksnfhean, ae lcajwefawefmaklmefl;m
ckmadjeoiemaamcl;maelalskmclamsl;k
```

Sample run:

```
This program searches a file for a given string.
Please enter the name of the file to be searched: binary.sim

Please enter the string being sought: ANTI

***ANTI found in this file.

Processing complete.
```

Example 2: Global Replacement of a String

It is common for text editors and word processors to provide an operation that allows a user to replace all occurrences of a given string in a document with an alternative string. Such an operation is called a **global replacement** operation.

The `Strings` class makes it easy to implement this operation. We simply search the file line by line, seeking occurrences of the first string (using the

Position() member) and then replacing those occurrences with the second string (using the **Replace()** member). Since a given line may have zero or more occurrences of the first string, this search and replacement is done in a pretest loop in which repetition continues as long as **Position()** finds occurrences of the first string within the line of text.

The function in Figure 9.4 uses this approach to implement a global replacement function named **ReplaceAll()**, which counts and returns the number of replacements it performs.

FIGURE 9.4 A global replacement function.

```
/* This function uses class Strings to replace all occurrences
   of a string in a given input file with another string.

   Receive:                 Target, the string to be replaced;
                            InFileName, the name of the input file;
                            Replacement, the replacement string;
                            OutFileName, the name of the output file
   Input(InFileName):       The characters in the file, line by line
   Output(OutFileName):     The input characters, with occurrences of
                            Target replaced by Replacement
   Return:                  The number of replacements performed
-----------------------------------------------------------------*/

int ReplaceAll(const Strings& Target,
               const Strings& InFileName,
               const Strings& Replacement,
               const Strings& OutFileName)
{
   if (Target == Replacement)              // no change required
      return 0;

   int
      Occurrences = 0;                     // replacement counter

   fstream                                 // open files for I/O
      InStream(InFileName, ios::in),
      OutStream(OutFileName, ios::out);

   if (InStream.fail())                    //  check for success
   {
      cerr << "\n*** Unable to open file ' "
           << InFileName << "'!\n";
      exit (-1);
   }
   else if (OutStream.fail())
   {
      cerr << "\n*** Unable to open file ' "
           << OutFileName << "'!\n";
      exit (-1);
   }
```

FIGURE 9.4   A global replacement function. (cont.)

```
Strings
   Line;                              // stores a line of input
int
   Location,                         // position of Target in Line
   TargetLength = Target.Length();    // length of Target

Line.GetLine(InStream);              // get the first Line

while (!InStream.eof())               // while not end-of-file,
{
   Location = Line.Position(Target);  //    search Line for Target

   while (Location >= 0)              //    while Target in Line
   {
      Occurrences++;                 //       increment counter
      Line.Replace(Location,         //       replace Target
               Location + TargetLength - 1,
               Replacement);
      Location = Line.Position(Target);//    search Line for Target
   }                                 //    end while

   OutStream << Line << endl;        //    send the line to OutStream
                                     //    reset for next repetition
   Line.GetLine(InStream);           //    get the next Line
}                                    // end while

InStream.close();                    // close the two streams
OutStream.close();

return Occurrences;                  // return # of replacements
}
```

In constructing this function, we could declare **Target**, **InFileName**, **Replacement**, and **OutFileName** as value parameters, but then each call to this function will copy the members of the corresponding arguments into the members of these parameters. We can avoid wasting this time by defining these parameters as *reference* parameters,

```
int ReplaceAll(const Strings& Target,
               const Strings& InFileName,
               const Strings& Replacement,
               const Strings& OutFileName)
```

rather than value parameters. But this opens the possibility of accidently altering the values of the corresponding arguments within the body of the function **ReplaceAll()**. To guard against this, these parameters are declared as *constant reference* parameters:

```
int ReplaceAll(const Strings& Target,
               const Strings& InFileName,
               const Strings& Replacement,
               const Strings& OutFileName)
```

This allows the compiler to generate an error if the function attempts to change their values.

A driver program to test function **ReplaceAll()** is shown in Figure 9.5, along with a sample run using the quote from Walter Reuther used previously.

FIGURE 9.5   Driver for function **ReplaceAll()**.

```
/* This program tests function ReplaceAll().

   Input(keyboard): The names of the input and output files, and
                    the names of the target and replacement strings
   Output(screen):  Prompts for input, confirmation message
-------------------------------------------------------------------*/

#include <iostream.h>                   // cin, cout, <<, >>
#include <fstream.h>                    // fstream, <<, >>
#include <stdlib.h>                     // exit()

#include "Strings.h"                    // class Strings

int ReplaceAll(const Strings&,         // ReplaceAll() declaration
               const Strings&,
               const Strings&,
               const Strings&);

int main(void)
{
   cout << "\nThis program tests function ReplaceAll.\n";

   Strings
      InFileName,
      OutFileName,
      OldString,
      NewString;

   cout << "\nEnter name of input file: ";  // get input file name
   InFileName.GetLine(cin);

   cout << "\nReplace what string? ";       // get target string
   OldString.GetLine(cin);
```

FIGURE 9.5 Driver for function `ReplaceAll()`. (cont.)

```
cout << "\nReplace it with what? ";       // get replacement string
NewString.GetLine(cin);

cout << "\nEnter name of output file: ";  // get output file name
OutFileName.GetLine(cin);

int                                       // replace all occurrences
   NumReplaced = ReplaceAll(OldString,    //   of OldString
                            InFileName,    //   in InFileName
                            NewString,     // with NewString
                            OutFileName);  // in OutFileName

cout << "\nThere were a total of "        // report results
     << NumReplaced << " occurrences replaced.\n\n";

return 0;
}

// ... definition of ReplaceAll() omitted ...
```

Listing of Input File `reuther.txt`

```
If it walks like a duck, and quacks like a duck,
then it just may be a duck - Reuther.
```

Sample run:

```
This program tests function ReplaceAll.

Enter name of input file: reuther.txt

Replace what string? a duck

Replace it with what? an aardvark

Enter name of output file: mangle.txt

There were a total of 3 occurrences replaced.
```

Listing of Output File `mangle.txt`

```
If it walks like an aardvark, and quacks like an aardvark,
then it just may be an aardvark - Reuther.
```

*Example 3: Varying Arguments of Arbitrary Types—Finding Minimum Value

In Section 7.5, we saw that the ellipses mechanism (. . .) can be used to define a function with a varying number of arguments. In the examples presented to illustrate this mechanism, the types of arguments passed to the function had to be of the same type. However, there are some problems for which this requirement is too restrictive—it may be necessary to pass a varying number of arguments of varying types to a function.

To solve such problems, a mechanism must be devised to pass the types of the arguments in addition to the arguments themselves. One such mechanism is to pass a special character string as the first argument, whose characters indicate the types of the subsequent arguments. That is, if a particular call to a function `F()` needs to pass to `F()` an integer value `I`, a character value `C`, and a real value `D`, then we might call `F()` with

```
F("icr", I, C, D);
```

where the character string `"icr"` encodes the following information:

    `i` indicates that the first argument is an integer.
    `c` indicates that the second argument is a character.
    `r` indicates that the third argument is a (`double`) real value.

This mechanism is general enough to encode the types of any particular sequence of arguments, because C++ will automatically convert the types of arguments with the ellipses for their parameter, as follows:

- Any `float` argument is converted to type `double`.
- Any integer-compatible argument (e.g., `char`, `short`, etc.) is converted to type `int`.

To illustrate the use of this mechanism, we consider the following problem.

Problem.   Construct a function that returns the minimum of an arbitrary number of values of arbitrary numeric types. Since a function can have only one return type, the minimum of the argument numbers should be returned as a `double` value.

Specification.   We can encode the types of the arguments described in the problem in a character string, as described earlier. We also have an arbitrary number of input values, as well as the value to be returned. We can thus identify the following data objects:

Data Object	Kind of Value	Type of Object	Name of Object
An encoding of the argument types	Constant	Character string	*TypeString*
An arbitrary sequence of values	Variables	?	. . .
The minimum of those values	Variable	Real	*CurrentMin*

This leads to the following specification of this problem:

Receive: *TypeString,* a character string encoding the types of the subsequent arguments; a sequence of values (one for each character in *TypeString*)

Return: The minimum value from that sequence, as a real

Since **double** is the most general of the numeric types, we can use this specification to construct the following stub:

```
double Minimum(const Strings& TypeString ...)
{
}
```

Note that the parameter **TypeString** has been declared to be a constant reference parameter. (See the discussion following Figure 9.4 for an explanation of why this is done.)

Design.   To solve this problem, we must process each argument in the argument list as follows:

1. Identify the type of the argument.
2. Retrieve the argument from the argument list.
3. Compare the argument to the smallest one seen thus far.
4. Store the current argument if it is smaller than the smallest one seen thus far.

The first two steps are the most difficult, and the key is to remember that there is one character in the **TypeString** for each argument and that the first character in the string is **TypeString[0]**, the second is **TypeString[1]**, and so on. Taken together, these indicate that we can use a for loop to process the arguments:

```
int
   NumArgs = TypeString.Length();

for (int i = 0; i < NumArgs; i++)
{
   // based on the value of TypeString[i], retrieve argument i
}
```

This leads to the following algorithm to solve the problem.

ALGORITHM TO FIND THE MINIMUM OF A SEQUENCE OF ARBITRARY VALUES

/* This algorithm finds the minimum of arbitrarily many values of arbitrary types.

Receive: *TypeString,* a character string encoding the types of the arguments ('c' for char, 'i' for int, 'd' for double, etc.)
          A sequence of values, one for each character in *TypeString,* such that the type of the *i*th value is indicated by *TypeString[i]*

Return: The minimum of the sequence of values

──*/

1. Initialize the argument list *ArgList;*
2. Initialize *CurrentMin* to the maximum value of type **double**.
3. For each character in *TypeString:*
    a. If that character is 'i', 'c', or 's':
        Retrieve an int value from *ArgList,* convert it to a double, and store it in *CurrentArg.*
    Else if that character is 'l' (in case longs are bigger than ints):
        Retrieve a long value from *ArgList,* convert it to double, and store it in *CurrentArg;*
    Else if that character is 'f', 'd', or 'r':
        Retrieve a double value from *ArgList* and store it in *CurrentArg.*
    b. If *CurrentArg* is less than *CurrentMin:*
        Replace the value in *CurrentMin* with the value in *CurrentArg.*
4. Clean up *ArgList.*
5. Return *CurrentMin.*

Coding.   Given this algorithm, we can construct the function shown in Figure 9.6.

FIGURE 9.6   A minimum-value function.

```
/* This function finds the minimum of an arbitrary sequence of values.

Receive: TypeString, an encoding of the argument types
         an arbitrary sequence of variables
Return:  The (double) smallest of all of the values passed
---------------------------------------------------------------------*/

#include <stdarg.h>
#include <float.h>                  // contains DBL_MAX

#include "Strings.h"

double Minimum(const Strings& TypeString ...)
{
   va_list
      ArgList;

   va_start(ArgList, TypeString);// ArgList begins after TypeString

   double
      CurrentMin = DBL_MAX,       // initially, the largest double
      CurrentArg;                 // stores value being processed

   int
      NumArgs = TypeString.Length();
```

FIGURE 9.6 A minimum-value function. (cont.)

```
for (int i = 0; i < NumArgs; i++)
{
    switch(TypeString[i])
    {
      case 'c': case 's':      // char, short come through as ints
      case 'i':
         CurrentArg = double( va_arg(ArgList, int) );
         break;

      case 'l':                // in case sizeof int < sizeof long
         CurrentArg = double( va_arg(ArgList, long) );
         break;

      case 'f': case 'd':      // float comes through as double
      case 'r':                // allow 'r' for any real value
         CurrentArg = double( va_arg(ArgList, double) );
         break;

      default:
         cerr << "\n*** Minimum: unknown type indicator: "
              << TypeString[i] << endl;
    }

    if (CurrentArg < CurrentMin)//  smaller number found
       CurrentMin = CurrentArg;
  }

  va_end(ArgList);

  return CurrentMin;
}
```

If `Minimum()` is invoked with

```
float
   fl = 75.4;

cout << endl
     << Minimum("idif", 93, 3.0e3, 68, fl)
     << "\n\n";
```

the value **68** will be displayed, whereas

```
float
   fl = 0.75;

cout << endl
     << Minimum("idif", 93, 3.0e3, 68, fl)
     << "\n\n";
```

will display the value **0.75**.

In summary, the variable argument mechanism allows an arbitrary number of arguments to be passed to a function. Encoding the types of the arguments in a character string also allows the types of the arguments to be arbitrary.

9.6   PART OF THE PICTURE: Data Encryption

The basic string operations of input, output, subscript, substring, length, position, concatenate, copy, insert, delete, and replace are adequate for most applications that use strings. There are, however, some important kinds of string processing that require other operations. One such application is data encryption, in which the basic operations are *replacement* and *permutation.*

Encryption refers to the coding of information in order to keep it secret. The string of characters comprising the information is transformed into another string that is a coded form of the information. This is called a **cryptogram,** or **ciphertext,** and may be safely stored or transmitted. At a later time it can be deciphered by reversing the encrypting process to recover the original information, which is called **plaintext.**

Data encryption has been used to send secret military and political messages from the days of Julius Caesar to the present. More recent situations in which the transmission of secret data was crucial include the Washington–Moscow hotline of the cold-war era, electronic funds transfer, electronic mail, and database security. Less serious applications include the Captain Midnight secret decoder rings that could be obtained in the 1950s for 25¢ and two Ovaltine labels, puzzles appearing in the daily newspaper, and a number of other frivolous applications.

Example: The Caesar Cipher

The simplest encryption schemes are based on the string operation of **replacement,** in which each character in the plaintext string is replaced by some other character according to a fixed rule. For example, the **Caesar cipher** scheme consists of replacing each character by the character that appears k positions later in the character set for some integer k. In the original Caesar cipher, k was 3, so that each occurrence of A in the plaintext was replaced by D, each B by E, each C by F, and so on, with "wraparound" at the end of the character set. For example, we would encrypt the string "IDESOFMARCH" as follows:

Message:	I D E S O F M A R C H
	↓ ↓ ↓ ↓ ↓ ↓ ↓ ↓ ↓ ↓ ↓
Cryptogram:	L G H V R I P D U F K

The function `CaesarCipher()` in Figure 9.8 implements the Caesar cipher encryption scheme. Its basic approach is to examine each character in the character string, and if it is a *printable* character (i.e., its ASCII value is in the range 32 through 126), then it is shifted k positions. This shifting is accomplished by adding the offset k to the numeric code (e.g., ASCII) of the character. For example, suppose that k is 3 and the character being examined is 'A'. The ASCII code of 'A' is 65, and adding 3 gives 68, which is the ASCII code of 'D', the coded value of 'A'.

The shifting is complicated by the wraparound required for values near the end of the character set. For example, suppose that k is 10 and the character being examined is 'z', whose ASCII value is 122. If we simply add 10 to 122, we get 132, which is not the ASCII code of a printable character. Instead, the values must wrap around to the beginning of the printable characters,

$$
\begin{array}{llllllllll}
\text{ASCII value:} & 32, & 33, & 34, \ldots, & 116, & 117, & 118, & 119, \ldots, & 126 \\
k = 10 & \downarrow & \downarrow & \downarrow & \downarrow & \downarrow & \downarrow & \downarrow & \downarrow \\
\text{Shifted value:} & 42, & 43, & 44, \ldots, & 126, & 32, & 33, & 34, \ldots, & 41
\end{array}
$$

so that the value that is 10 positions from 'z' is 37, the ASCII value of the percent character (%). This wraparound effect can be accomplished by processing a character as follows:

1. Scale the value from the range 32 through 126 into the range 0 through 94, by subtracting 32 (allowing us to use the remaindering operator in Step 3 to achieve the wraparound effect).
2. Add the value of the offset k.
3. Since the resulting value may be outside the range 0 through 94, wrap it around by finding the remainder when it is divided by 95, the number of printable characters.
4. Scale the resulting value from the range 0 through 94 back into the range 32 through 126 by adding 32.

The function in Figure 9.7 implements these steps.

 FIGURE 9.7 The Caesar cipher.

```
/* This function encodes/decodes a character string with the Caesar
   cipher, assuming ASCII codes for character representation. It
   uses the function isprint() from <ctype.h> to determine if a
   character is an ASCII printable character.

   Receive: A, a character array
            k, an integer, assumed to be in the range -94 to 94
   Return:  A, with each char changed to the char k positions away
   ----------------------------------------------------------------*/

#include <ctype.h>
#include "Strings.h"

void CaesarCipher(Strings& A, int k)
{
   const int
      FirstPrintableChar = 32,      // printable range is
      NumPrintableChars = 95;       // 32 through 126;

   while (k < 0)                     // if k is negative, % won't work
      k += NumPrintableChars;        //    get it in the range 0 to 94

   int
      LengthA = A.Length();
```

FIGURE 9.7   The Caesar cipher. (cont.)

```
for (int i = 0; i < LengthA; i++) // for each char in the string:
   if (isprint(A[i]))               //    if it's in 32-126,
      A[i] =
         ((((A[i] - FirstPrintableChar) //    scale into 0-94
            + k)                         //    add the offset
            % NumPrintableChars)        //    wrap-around, and
            + FirstPrintableChar);      //    scale back into 32-126
}
```

Note that the offset k may be negative, which permits **CaesarCipher()** to be used both to encode and decode messages. For example, we can use the negative offset $k = -3$ to decrypt the message we encrypted earlier with an offset of 3:

Cryptogram: L G H V R I P D U F K
             ↓ ↓ ↓ ↓ ↓ ↓ ↓ ↓ ↓ ↓ ↓
Message: I D E S O F M A R C H

Figure 9.8 presents a program that uses **CaesarCipher()** to encode/decode character strings.

FIGURE 9.8   Encrypting/decrypting a message.

```
/* This program encodes/decodes multiple messages of up to 1024
   characters using the Caesar cipher.

   Input:  A sequence of characters, stored in S
           An integer, stored in k
   Output: The sequence of characters that are k positions away
           from the input characters in the ASCII ordering
   ----------------------------------------------------------------*/

#include <iostream.h>

#include "Ciphers.h"        // contains declaration of CaesarCipher()
#include "Query.h"          // contains declaration of NotDone()
#include "Strings.h"        // class Strings

int main(void)
{
   cout << "\nThis program encodes/decodes a line of text,\n"
        << "\t using the Caesar cipher.\n";

   Strings
      S;
   int
      k;
```

FIGURE 9.8   Encrypting/decrypting a message. (cont.)

```
  do
  {
     cout << "\nPlease enter your string: ";
     S.GetLine(cin);                            // get the whole line

     cout << "Offset (an integer)? ";           // get the offset
     cin >> k;

     CaesarCipher(S, k);

     cout << "\n--> Your message is: " << S << "\n\n";

  }
  while (NotDone());

  return 0;
}
```

Sample run:

```
This program encodes/decodes a line of text,
   using the Caesar cipher.

Please enter your string: THE IDES OF MARCH
Offset (an integer)? 3

--> Your message is: WKH#LGHV#RI#PDUFK


Are you done (y or n)? n

Please enter your string: WKH#LGHV#RI#PDUFK
Offset (an integer)? -3

--> Your message is: THE IDES OF MARCH


Are you done (y or n)? n

Please enter your string: One if by land, two if by sea !
Offset (an integer)? 27

--> Your message is: j*!;%";}5;(|* G;03+;%";}5;/!|;<
```

FIGURE 9.8   Encrypting/decrypting a message. (cont.)

```
Are you done (y or n)? n

Please enter your string: j*!;%";}5;(|* G;03+;%";}5;/!|;<
Offset (an integer)? -27

--> Your message is: One if by land, two if by sea !


Are you done (y or n)? y
```

Although the function **CaesarCipher()** correctly encodes and decodes a message, it obviously does not provide a very secure scheme, since it is easy to ''break'' a coded message simply by trying all the possible values for the key *k* (which is the sort of task that is easily programmed):

```
SavedMsg = Message;                    // save a copy of Message

for (int k = -95; k <= 95; k++)        // for each possible k value:
{
    CaesarCipher(Message, k);          //     try k
    cout << "\nk = " << k << ": "      //     display the result
        << Message;
    Message = SavedMsg;                //     restore Message
}
```

Substitutions and Permutations

An improved substitution operation is to use a *keyword* to specify several different displacements of letters rather than the single offset *k* of the Caesar cipher. In this **Vignère cipher** scheme, a keyword is added character by character to the plaintext string, where each letter is represented by its position in the character set and wrap around occurs as with the Caesar cipher scheme. For example, if the positions of A, B, C, . . . , Z are given by 0, 1, 2, . . . , 25, respectively, and the keyword is DAGGER, the message ''IDESOFMARCH'' is encrypted as follows:

```
         Message:   I D E S O F M A R C H
                    ↓ ↓ ↓ ↓ ↓ ↓ ↓ ↓ ↓ ↓ ↓
Repeated keyword:   D A G G E R D A G G E
                    ↓ ↓ ↓ ↓ ↓ ↓ ↓ ↓ ↓ ↓ ↓
      Cryptogram:   L D K Y S W P A X I L
```

The receiver recovers the message by subtracting the characters in this keyword from those in the cryptogram.

A different substitution operation is to use a **substitution table,** for example:

Original character:	A	B	C	D	E	F	G	H	I	J	K	L	M
Substitute character:	Q	W	E	R	T	Y	U	I	O	P	A	S	D

	N	O	P	Q	R	S	T	U	V	W	X	Y	Z
	F	G	H	J	K	L	Z	X	C	V	B	N	M

The string "IDESOFMARCH" would then be encoded using this substitution table as follows:

Message: I D E S O F M A R C H
            ↓ ↓ ↓ ↓ ↓ ↓ ↓ ↓ ↓ ↓ ↓
Cryptogram: O R T L G Y D Q K E I

To decode the cryptogram, the receiver simply uses the substitution table in reverse.

Since there are 95! (approximately 10^{148}) possible substitution tables, this scheme is considerably more secure than the simple Caesar cipher scheme. Experienced cryptographers can easily break the code, however, by analyzing frequency counts of certain letters and combinations of letters.

Another basic string operation in some encryption schemes is **permutation,** in which the characters in the plaintext or in blocks of the plaintext are rearranged. For example, we might divide the message into blocks (substrings) of size 3 and permute the characters in each block as follows:

Original position: 1   2   3
Permuted position: 3   1   2

Thus, the message "IDESOFMARCH" would be encrypted (after the addition of a randomly selected character X so that the string length is a multiple of the block length) as

Message: I D E S O F M A R C H X
Cryptogram: D E I O F S A R M H X C

To decode the cryptogram, the receiver must know the key permutation and its inverse:

Original position: 1   2   3
Permuted position: 2   3   1

DES

Many modern encryption schemes combine several substitution and permutation operations. Perhaps the best known is the **Data Encryption Standard (DES)** developed in the early 1970s by researchers at the IBM Corporation. The scheme is described in *Federal Information Processing Standards Publication 46* (FIPS Pub 46).[5] It consists essentially of a permutation followed by a sequence of 16 substitutions and a final permutation. The substitution operations are similar to those in earlier examples. Some are obtained by the addition of keywords (16 different ones) and others use substitution tables.

DES was adopted in 1977 by the National Institute of Standards and Technology (formerly the National Bureau of Standards) as the standard encryption scheme for sensitive federal documents. It has been the subject of some controversy, however, because of questions about its security. In fact, two Israeli scientists, E. Biham and A. Shamir (one of the developers of the popular public-key encrpytion scheme described later), recently announced a mathematical technique that makes it possible to break the DES code under certain circumstances.

Public-Key Encryption

Each of the preceding encryption schemes requires that both the sender and the receiver know the encryption key or keys. This means that although the cryptogram may be transmitted through some public channel such as a telephone line that is not secure, the keys must be transmitted in some secure manner, for example, by a courier. This problem of maintaining secrecy of the key is compounded when it must be shared by several persons.

Recently developed encryption schemes eliminate this problem by using two keys, one for encryption and one for decryption. These schemes are called **public-key encryption schemes,** because the encryption key is made public by the receiver to all those who will transmit messages to him or her; the decryption key, however, is known only to the receiver. The security of these schemes depends on it being nearly impossible to determine the decryption key if one knows only the encryption key.

In 1978, R. L. Rivest, A. Shamir, and L. Adelman proposed one method of implementing a public-key encryption scheme.[6] The public key is a pair (e, n) of integers, and one encrypts a message string M by first dividing M into blocks M_1, $M_2, \ldots, M_k$ and converting each block M_i of characters to an integer P_i in the range 0 through $n - 1$ (e.g., by concatenating the ASCII codes of the characters). M is then encrypted by raising each block to the power e and reducing modulo n:

$$\text{Message:} \quad M = M_1 M_2 \cdots M_k \rightarrow P_1 P_2 \cdots P_k$$
$$\text{Cryptogram:} \quad C = C_1 C_2 \cdots C_k, \qquad C_i = P_i^e \ \text{modulo } n$$

(Here x modulo n is the remainder when x is divided by n.) The cryptogram C is decrypted by raising each block C_i to the power d and reducing modulo n, where d is a secret decryption key.

---

[5] Copies of this publication can be obtained from the National Institute of Standards and Technology of the U.S. Department of Commerce.

[6] R. L. Rivest, A. Shamir, and L. Adelman, ''A Method for Obtaining Digital Signatures and Public-Key Cryptosystems,'' *Communications of the ACM* (February 1978): 120–126.

To illustrate, suppose that characters are converted to numeric values using the codes 0, 1, 2, . . . , 25 for the letters A, B, C, . . . , Z, respectively, and that $(17, 2773)$ is the public encryption key. To encrypt the message $M =$ "IDESOFMARCH" using the RSA algorithm, we divide M into two-character blocks $M_1, M_2, \ldots, M_6$ (after appending a randomly selected character X) and represent each block M_i as an integer P_i in the range 0 through $2773 - 1 = 2772$ by concatenating the numeric codes of the characters that comprise the block:

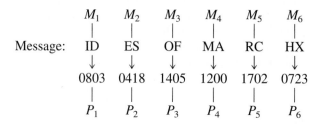

Each of these blocks P_i is then encrypted by calculating $C_i = P_i^{17}$ modulo 2773:

$$\text{Cryptogram:} \quad \underset{C_1}{0779} \quad \underset{C_2}{1983} \quad \underset{C_3}{2641} \quad \underset{C_4}{1444} \quad \underset{C_5}{0052} \quad \underset{C_6}{0802}$$

For this encryption key, the corresponding decrypting key is $d = 157$. Thus, we decode the cryptogram by calculating C_i^{157} modulo 2773 for each block C_i. For the preceding cryptogram, this gives

Decoded cryptogram: 0803   0418   1405   1200   1702   0723

which is the numeric form of the original message.

The number n is the product of two large "random" primes p and q,

$$n = p \cdot q$$

In the preceding example, we used the small primes 47 and 59 to simplify the computations, but Rivest, Shamir, and Adelman suggest that p and q have several hundred digits. The decrypting key d is then selected to be some large integer that is relatively prime to both $p - 1$ and $q - 1$—that is, one that has no factors in common with either number. In our example, $d = 157$ has this property. The number e is then selected to have the property that

$$e \cdot d \text{ modulo } ((p - 1) \cdot (q - 1)) \text{ is equal to 1}$$

To break this code, one must be able to determine the value of d from the values of n and e. Because of the manner in which d and e are selected, this is possible if n can be factored into a product of primes. Thus, the security of the RSA encryption scheme is based on the difficulty of determining the prime factors of a large integer. Even with the best factorization algorithms known today, this is a prohibitively time-consuming task. A study a few years ago gave the following table displaying some estimated times, assuming that each operation required one microsecond:

Number of Digits in Number Being Factored	Time
50	4 hours
75	104 days
100	74 years
200	4 billion years
300	5×10^{15} years
500	4×10^{25} years

Although research on factorization continues, no efficient algorithms have been found that significantly reduce the times in the preceding table. Improved algorithms and the use of high-speed computers have made factorization possible in less time than the table shows, but not significantly less for large numbers. This public-key encryption scheme thus appears (so far) to be quite secure and is being endorsed by a growing number of major computer vendors; the adoption of a public-key encryption standard is being considered by the National Institute of Standards and Technology.

Exercises

1. A pure permutation encryption scheme is very insecure. Explain why by describing how an encryption scheme that merely permutes the bits in an n-bit string can easily be cracked by studying how certain basic bit strings are encrypted. Show this for $n = 4$.

2. Using the character codes 0, 1, . . . , 25 given in the text and the message "PUBLIC":

   (a) Find the cryptogram produced by the Caesar cipher scheme with key = 3.
   (b) Find the cryptogram produced by the Vignère cipher scheme with keyword "AND".
   (c) Find the cryptogram produced using the substitution table given in the text.
   (d) Find the cryptogram produced using the permutation given in the text:

        Original position: 1   2   3
      Permuted position: 3   1   2

   (e) Find the cryptogram produced using the RSA scheme with encryption key $(e, n) = (5, 2881)$.
   (f) One decrypting key for the RSA scheme in part (d) is $d = 1109$. Use it to decode the cryptogram obtained in part (e).

3. Write a program to encrypt and decrypt a message using the Vignère cipher scheme.

4. Write a program to encrypt and decrypt a message using a substitution table.

5. Write a program to encrypt and decrypt a message using a permutation scheme.

6. Write a program that implements the RSA scheme.

7. The Morse code is a standard encoding scheme that uses substitutions similar to those in the scheme described in this section. The substitutions used in this case are shown in the following table. Write a program to read a message either in plaintext or in Morse code and then to encode or decode the message.

A ·–	M ––	Y –·––
B –···	N –·	Z ––··
C –·–·	O –––	1 ·––––
D –··	P ·––·	2 ··–––
E ·	Q ––·–	3 ···––
F ··–·	R ·–·	4 ····–
G ––·	S ···	5 ·····
H ····	T –	6 –····
I ··	U ··–	7 ––···
J ·–––	V ···–	8 –––··
K –·–	W ·––	9 ––––·
L ·–··	X –··–	0 –––––

Programming Pointers

Program Design

1. *Strings objects are useful for storing names as well as lines of text.* **Strings** objects are generally the most convenient way to store names and other character strings. They are also useful for storing lines of text. For example, if a file contains addresses, such as

       1313 Mockingbird Lane
       2000 Pennsylvania Avenue
          ⋮
          ⋮

   and if *StreamName* has been associated with the file, then statements such as

       Strings
           StreetAddress;

       StreetAddress.GetLine(StreamName);

   can be used to input such addresses.

2. *Strings objects are dynamic structures that grow and shrink according to the size of the character string stored in them.* Thus **Strings** objects use memory efficiently. In particular, a declaration of the form

       Strings
           StringVariable = StringExpression;

or an assignment statement like

    StringVariable = *StringExpression*;

or input statements of the form

    cin >> *StringVariable*;

and

    StringVariable.GetLine(cin);

will produce a **Strings** object *StringVariable* whose size is exactly tailored to the string stored within it.

3. *The* **Strings** *class provides a case study for class design.* The operations provided by class **Strings** can be grouped as follows:

- Operations required by any class object (class-constructor)
- Operations required by dynamic class objects (copy-constructor, destructor)
- Standard operations on most data objects (assignment, comparison, i/o, extraction, conversion)
- Operations particular to this class of objects (subscript, length, concatenation, insertion, deletion, replacement)

Students are encouraged to study class **Strings** as a model for designing their own classes in the chapters that follow.

Potential Problems

1. *The* **Strings** *subscript operation uses square brackets containing an index,*

    StringVariable[i]

whereas the **Strings** *substring operation uses parentheses containing a pair of indices,*

    StringVariable(i, j)

These must not be confused because they have very different effects.

2. *The index of the first character in a* **Strings** *object is always zero.* This zero-relative indexing is a legacy from C, the parent language of C++, that simplifies the mapping of a subscript access

    StringVariable[i]

to an actual memory location, as we shall see in Chapter 12.

3. *Run-time bounds checking is performed on* **Strings** *objects.* In general, the compiler cannot determine whether a subscript access

    StringVariable[i]

is valid, because the value of **i** is typically unknown when the program is compiled. The value of **i** cannot be known until run-time, and hence **Strings** operations that use indices (i.e., the *subscript, substring, insert, delete, replace,* and *position* operations) check to ensure that subscript accesses are valid. An invalid access will produce a **run-time error.**

4. *To fill a* `Strings` *object* `StringVariable` with a line of input from a stream, the call

> `StringVariable.GetLine(StreamName)`

should be used. We have used the name `GetLine()` to try to distinguish this line-input function from the `getline()` function (a member of class `istream` objects).

5. *A bound on the length of the character string that can be input and stored in a* `Strings` *object using* `GetLine()` *or* `>>` *is given by the constant* `MaxLength` *defined in the class* `Strings`. Although the value of the constant is quite large in the implementation of class `Strings` on the disk distributed with this text, there may be situations that require the input of character strings whose length exceed this bound. In such circumstances, simply increase the value of the constant in the declaration of class `Strings` (in `Strings.h`).

6. *The input operator* `>>` *and the input member function* `GetLine()` *treat newline characters differently:* `>>` skips leading white space and then reads a sequence of characters until it encounters another white-space character, leaving that character unread; `GetLine()` does not skip leading white space and terminates on the first newline it encounters. This means that if the statements

```
int
    Year;
Strings
    Title;

cin >> Year;
Title.GetLine(cin);
```

are executed and **cin** contains

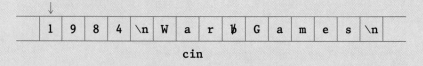

then execution of the input statement

> `cin >> Year;`

will read the value 1984 from **cin**, halting when it encounters the newline and leaving the newline unread:

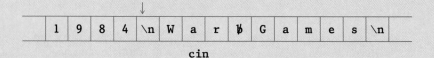

The subsequent execution of the statement

```
Year.GetLine(cin);
```

will read that newline from **cin** and halt, leaving the remainder of the text unread:

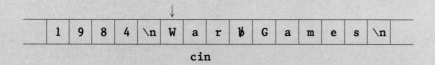

cin

To avoid such problems, the **get()** function (a member of **cin**) can be used to explicitly consume the newline. If we add

```
char
   ReturnChar;
```

```
cin >> Year;
cin.get(ReturnChar);      // clean out the newline char
Title.GetLine(cin);
```

then execution of the first input statement will proceed as it did before, leaving the newline as the next character to be read:

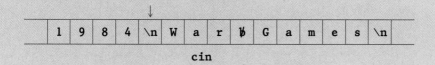

cin

Execution of the statement

```
cin.get(ReturnChar);
```

will then consume the newline character:

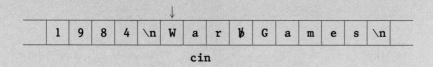

cin

Following this, execution of the **GetLine()** will read the remaining text into **Title**:

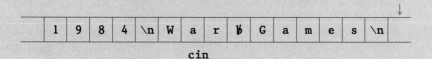

cin

Programming Projects

1. There are 3 teaspoons in a tablespoon, 4 tablespoons in a quarter of a cup, 2 cups in a pint, and 2 pints in a quart. Write a program to convert units in cooking. The program should call for the input of the amount, the units, and the new units desired. For example, the input **0.5**, **CUPS**, **TEASPOONS** asks for the conversion of ½ cup to teaspoons.

2. The game of Hangman is played by two persons. One person selects a word and the other person tries to guess the word by guessing individual letters. Design and implement a program to play Hangman. You might store a list of words in a file and have the program randomly select a word for the user to guess (see Section 7.8).

3. Write a program that, given the name of an input file and a search string, determines whether the search string occurs in the input file. If not, the program should simply display a message to that effect. Otherwise, the program should output a copy of the input file in which each line containing the search string is followed by a line containing blanks and dashes that "underline" the occurrence of the search string.

4. Write a program to produce mailing labels as in Exercise 4 of Section 9.3 but assume that the items in the file may contain white space and are separated by some delimiter such as #; for example,

   Doe#John#Q#123 SomeStreet#Any Town#Any State#12345

5. Write a program to print a "personalized" contest letter like those frequently received in the mail. It might have a format like that of the following sample, with the underlined locations filled in with appropriate data:

   ```
   Mr. John Q. Doe
   123 SomeStreet
   AnyTown, AnyState 12345

   Dear Mr. Doe:

       How would you like to see a brand new Cadillac parked in
   front of 123 SomeStreet in AnyTown, AnyState? Impossible,
   you say? No, it isn't, Mr. Doe. Simply keep the enclosed
   raffle ticket and validate it by sending a $100.00 tax-
   deductible political contribution and 10 labels from
   Shyster & Sons chewing tobacco. Not only will you become
   eligible for the drawing to be conducted on February 29 by
   the independent firm of G. Y. P. Shyster, but you will also
   be helping to reelect Sam Shyster. That's all there is to
   it, John. You may be a winner!!!
   ```

6. Graphs of equations also can be plotted by using the computer. For example, Figure 9.9 shows computer-generated plots of

$$Y = X^2 \quad \text{for} \quad -3 \le X \le 3$$

and

$$Y = X^3 \quad \text{for} \quad -2 \le X \le 2$$

using an X increment of 0.25 in each case. Note that for convenience, the X-axis has been printed vertically and the Y-axis, horizontally.

Write a program to produce a similar plot of a given equation, using a string whose length is equal to the width of the page. For each X value, set all the string elements equal to blanks or equal to the marks comprising the Y axis if $X = 0$; then set one string element equal to the X-axis mark and another equal to the plotting character; the position of this latter element should correspond to the Y-coordinate of the point on the graph for that X value.

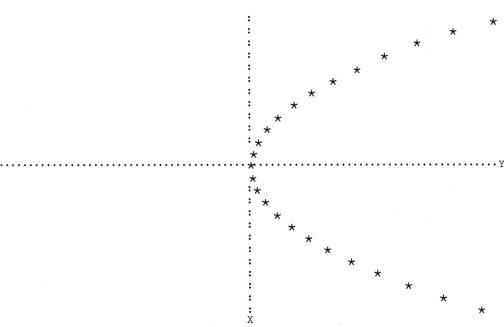

FIGURE 9.9   Plots of $Y = X^2$ and $Y = X^3$.

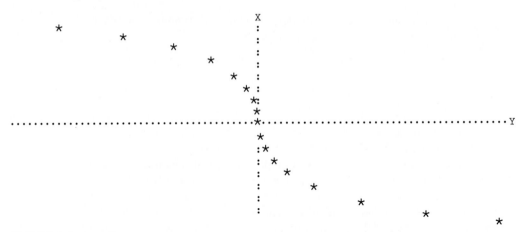

FIGURE 9.9   (cont.)

7. Write a function that accepts two character strings and determines whether one is an anagram of the other—that is, whether one character string is a permutation of the characters in the other string. For example, "dear" is an anagram of "read," as is "dare."

TYPES

> *God created the integers; all the rest is the work of man.*
> LEOPOLD KRONECKER

CHAPTER CONTENTS

In Chapter 2 we considered in detail the program-development process. In Section 2.3 we considered the design phase in which the objects and operations needed to solve a particular problem are identified. These objects and operations were then organized into an algorithm.

For most of the problems we have considered until now, the predefined types provided by C++ were adequate to design the objects needed to solve the problems. However, as problem solutions require objects that are increasingly complex, the predefined types may be inadequate to represent these objects. Modeling these complex objects can be more easily done if programmers can *construct new types.* We saw, for example, in Chapter 9 how the **Strings** class provides a very useful type for processing character strings. We did not, however, show how this new type was constructed. In this chapter, we begin our study of the mechanisms provided by C++ for type construction.

10.1   Using Real-World Values: Enumerations

We have seen that C++ provides a number of predefined types, such as **int**, which is used for integer values, and **double**, which is used for real values. The type of a data item often determines the operations that can be applied to that data item. For example, we have seen that the division operator (*/*) can be applied to integer or real values but it makes no sense to apply it to two character values. A type is thus a way of classifying data items—of specifying what operations can be performed on them.

In the real world, data types are ubiquitous. For example:

- People are sometimes typed by their gender: *female* or *male.*
- Automobiles are often typed by their manufacturer: *BMW, Chevrolet, Chrysler, Ferrari, Ford, Mercedes Benz, Oldsmobile, Saab, Toyota,* or *Volkswagen* (to name just a few).
- Craftsmen are sometimes typed by their expertise: *apprentice, journeyman,* and *master.*
- Athletic shoes are typed by the sport for which they are designed: *running shoes, tennis shoes, cross-trainers, volleyball shoes,* or *basketball shoes* (this is another long list).

We use types every day.

Suppose that a problem involves a data object whose type is not predefined. As a simple example, suppose that a problem requires a variable object named **Hue**, whose values are the seven colors *red, orange, yellow, green, blue, indigo,* and *violet.* One approach is to represent such real-world values as integers:

```
int
   Hue;          // 1 - Red, 2 - Orange, ..., 7 - Violet

if (Hue == 4)
   DoSomethingWith(Hue);
```

The problem with this approach is remembering which integer is associated with which color. Is red represented by 0 or 1? Which is the fourth color? The programmer is forced to remember this object-to-integer mapping and use it consistently. This is annoying, because maintaining this mapping is a mechanical process and could just as well be done by the computer. It would be much more convenient simply to write

```
if (Hue == Green)
   DoSomethingWith(Hue);
```

Fortunately, C++ provides a mechanism for doing this, allowing the programmer to construct objects whose values are names of real-world entities like colors, genders, days, and so on.

Declaring Enumerated Types

One of the mechanisms provided by C++ for constructing new types is an **enumeration,** in which the programmer

1. Provides a name for the new type; and
2. Explicitly lists all the values (called **enumerators**) of this new type.

For example, to declare a type **Color** consisting of the values **Red**, **Orange**, **Yellow**, **Green**, **Blue**, **Indigo**, and **Violet**, we could write:

```
enum Color {Red, Orange, Yellow, Green, Blue, Indigo, Violet};
```

The effect of this declaration is to make the name **Color** a new type whose values are the identifiers **Red**, **Orange**, **Yellow**, **Green**, **Blue**, **Indigo**, and **Violet**. The compiler performs the object-to-integer mapping referred to earlier, associating the integer 0 with the first identifier in this list, the integer 1 with the second, and so on. Thus, for the preceding declaration, the compiler associates 0 with **Red**, 1 with **Orange**, 2 with **Yellow**, 3 with **Green**, 4 with **Blue**, 5 with **Indigo**, and 6 with **Violet**.

As another example, the declaration

```
enum Gender {Female, Male};
```

declares a new type **Gender** whose values are the identifiers **Female** and **Male**; the compiler will associate the integer 0 with **Female** and the integer 1 with **Male**. Similarly, the declaration

```
enum HandTool {Hammer, Pliers, Saw, Screwdriver};
```

constructs a new type **HandTool** whose values are **Hammer**, **Pliers**, **Saw**, and **Screwdriver** and associates the integers 0, 1, 2, and 3 with these identifiers, respectively. Many programmers use the declaration

```
enum Boolean {False, True};
```

to construct a new type **Boolean**, whose values are the identifiers **False** and **True**. The compiler will associate the integer 0 with **False** and the integer 1 with **True**.

By contrast, neither of the declarations

```
enum Zipcodes {12531, 14405, 21724, 30081};  // ERROR!

enum LetterGrades {A, A-, B+, B, B-, C+, C,   // ERROR!
                   C-, D+, D, D-, "FAIL"};
```

is a valid enumeration, because each contains items that are not valid identifiers.

C++ also allows the programmer to specify explicitly the integer values associated with the identifiers that make up the values of an enumerated type. For example, the declaration

```
enum NumberBase {Binary = 2,
                 Octal = 8,
                 Decimal = 10,
                 Hex = 16, Hexadecimal = 16};
```

associates the identifiers **Binary**, **Octal**, **Decimal**, **Hex**, and **Hexadecimal** with the integers 2, 8, 10, 16, and 16, respectively. Similarly, a more explicit declaration of the type **Boolean** might be given by

```
enum Boolean {True = 1, False = 0};
```

If we wish to have the integers 1, 2, . . . , 7 (instead of 0 through 6) associated with the seven colors given earlier, we could use the declaration

```
enum Color {Red = 1, Orange = 2, Yellow = 3, Green = 4,
            Blue = 5, Indigo = 6, Violet = 7};
```

or, more compactly,

```
enum Color {Red = 1, Orange, Yellow, Green, Blue, Indigo, Violet};
```

The declaration

```
enum HandTools {Hammer, Pliers = 2, Saw, Screwdriver = 10};
```

associates 0 with **Hammer**, 2 with **Pliers**, 3 with **Saw**, and 10 with **Screwdriver**.

These examples illustrate the flexibility of C++—the integers associated with the names need not be distinct, nor do they need to be given in ascending order, although it is good programming style to do so. It should be clear that the form of an enumeration declaration is as follows.

Enumeration Declaration Statement

Form

```
    enum TypeName { List };
```
where:
   TypeName is an identifier naming a new type;
      and

> *List* is a list of items, separated by commas, each of which is a valid
>
> *Identifier*
>
> or an initialization expression of the form
>
> *Identifier* = *IntegerConstant*
>
> **Purpose**
> Define a new data type whose values are the identifiers in *List*. Each identifier is associated with an integer as follows:
>> If an item in *List* has the form *Identifier* = *IntegerConstant*, then *IntegerConstant* is associated with *Identifier*;
>> otherwise if it is the first item in the list, 0 is associated with the *Identifier*;
>> otherwise,
>>> 1 + (the integer associated with the preceding identifier) is associated with the *Identifier*.

Using an Enumeration

To illustrate how enumerations are used, consider the following enumeration **Day**, whose values are the days of the week:

```
enum Day {DayUnderflow = -1,              // too-low error
          Sunday, Monday, Tuesday, Wednesday,// 0-3
          Thursday, Friday, Saturday,     // 4-6
          NumberOfDays,                   // 7
          DayOverflow = 7};               // too-high error
```

Here, we added the identifiers **DayUnderflow** and **DayOverflow** as values to indicate error conditions. As we will see later, these values can be used to keep from "falling off the ends of a list" when iterating through the **Day** values (e.g., in a loop). We also added the identifier **NumberOfDays**, whose value is the number of values in the list, since it appears at the end of the list. An identifier whose value is the number of enumeration values is often useful.

Given this type, we can declare and initialize a variable **Today** as an object of type **Day**:

```
Day
  Today = Sunday;
```

Such a variable can be assigned, used as a parameter, compared using the relational operators, and so on. For example, consider the following function **Next()**:

```
/* This function returns the Day that follows its argument.

   Receive: A Day DayVal
   Return:  The successor of DayVal (or DayOverFlow if
            DayVal is not a valid Day value)
   Output:  Error message if DayVal is not a legal value
-------------------------------------------------------*/

Day Next(Day DayVal)
{
   const char
      ErrorMsg[] = "\n*** Next: invalid Day value received!\n";

   switch (DayVal)
   {
      case Sunday:
         return Monday;
      case Monday:
         return Tuesday;
      case Tuesday:
         return Wednesday;
      case Wednesday:
         return Thursday;
      case Thursday:
         return Friday;
      case Friday:
         return Saturday;
      case Saturday:
         return Sunday;
      default:
         cerr << ErrorMsg;
         return DayOverflow;       // error indicator
   }
}
```

Given such a function, the statement

```
Day
   Tomorrow = Next(Today);
```

can be used to initialize a **Day** object named **Tomorrow** to the day after **Today**.
A problem occurs with I/O of an enumeration object. The statements

```
Today = Wednesday;
cout << Today;
```

will either generate an error or display the value 3, depending on the implementation. The reason for this latter possibility is that the compiler associates integers
with the enumeration values: 0 with the identifier **Sunday**, 1 with the identifier
Monday, . . . , 6 with the identifier **Saturday**. Thus, in some environments, as far
as the compiler is concerned, the statement

```
Today = Wednesday;
```

assigns the integer 3 to **Today** and the output statement

```
cout << Today;
```

then simply displays this value of **Today**. In the next section, we show how this problem can be remedied.

Overloading the Output Operator

Recall that in Section 7.3, we saw that many of the C++ operators are **overloaded,** meaning that

1. They have multiple definitions that are distinguished by the types (or number) of their parameters; and
2. When the operator is used, the C++ compiler uses the types (or number) of the operands to determine which definition is to be used.

We have seen that the output operator (**<<**) is one of the overloaded operators and we have used this same operator to output integers, to output reals, to output character strings, and to output other types of data.

One of the powerful features of C++ is that *the programmer is allowed to overload operators,* and this feature can be used to solve the problem of displaying a value of type **Day**. When the statement

```
cout << Today;
```

is executed, the current value of **Today** (e.g., **Wednesday**) should be displayed. Although we cannot actually display the identifier **Wednesday**, we can display the character string **"Wednesday"** that corresponds to that identifier. To do this, we must overload **<<** with a new definition that specifies the action to be taken when it is given a **Day** value. To overload an operator, we construct a function definition in which we

1. Name the operator being overloaded;
2. Specify the (new) types of parameters (operands) the operator is to receive;
3. Specify the type of value returned by the operator; and
4. Specify what action the operator is to perform.

We consider these steps in order.

Step 1. Naming an Operator.   This is the easiest part, because C++ allows us to use the name

```
operator<<
```

to overload the **<<** operator. In general, if we wish to overload any operator **Δ** with a new definition, the name of **Δ** is given by

```
operatorΔ
```

Thus, the name of the *assignment* operator is `operator=`, the name of the *addition* operator is `operator+`, the name of the *increment* operator is `operator++`, the name of the *input* operator is `operator>>`, and so on. All but a few of the C++ operators may be overloaded in this fashion[1]—a feature we use several times later in this text.

Step 2. Specifying the Parameter Types.   We first examine a familiar output operation:

```
cout << 12;
```

Just as the operands in the expression

```
2 + 3
```

are the integers **2** and **3**, the operands in the expression

```
cout << 12
```

are the `ostream` object `cout` and the `int` object **12**. The addition expression

```
2 + 3
```

can be thought of as a call to the function `operator+` with the arguments **2** and **3**:

```
operator+(2, 3)
```

Similarly, the output expression

```
cout << 12
```

can be thought of as calling the function `operator<<` with the arguments `cout` and **12**:

```
operator<<(cout, 12)
```

This means that the expression

```
cout << Today
```

has two operands: the `ostream` object `cout` and a `Day` object `Today`. Moreover, since displaying something on an `ostream` alters that `ostream`, the parameter corresponding to `cout` must be a reference parameter. We therefore declare two parameters to hold the values of these arguments (operands):

```
operator<<(ostream& Out, Day DayVal)
```

---

[1] The only operators that *cannot* be overloaded are `.`, `.*`, `::`, `?:` and `sizeof`. Overloading the preprocessing symbols `#` and `##` is also not permitted.

We use new names for the parameters so that they are clearly distinguished from the arguments. Also, note that because the *left* operand of **<<** is almost always an **ostream** object (usually **cout**), the first parameter of **operator<<** will usually be an **ostream** reference parameter.

Step 3. Specifying the Return Type.   Recall (from Section 3.6) that the output operator is left associative. This means that in a statement such as

        cout << 12 << 13 << endl;

the order of evaluation is

        (((cout << 12) << 13) << endl);

That is, the expression

        cout << 12

is evaluated first, which inserts **12** into the **ostream** and returns some value *ReturnValue1*. Then the expression

        ReturnValue1 << 13

is evaluated, which inserts **13** into the **ostream** and returns some value *ReturnValue2*. Then the expression

        ReturnValue2 << endl;

is evaluated, which inserts **endl** into the **ostream** and returns some value *ReturnValue3*. The semicolon then causes this final *ReturnValue3* to be discarded. In order for the expression

        (((cout << 12) << 13) << endl);

to function correctly, it must be evaluated as

        cout << 12

followed by

        cout << 13

followed by

        cout << endl

followed by

        cout;

Thus, each of the return values *ReturnValue1*, *ReturnValue2*, and *ReturnValue3* must be the **ostream** object received as a parameter. Consequently, the ≪ operator must return the **ostream** that was passed to it. This means that the function **operator≪** must have the form

```
ostream& operator<< (ostream& Out, Day DayVal)
{
    // ... action that << must take

    return Out;
}
```

That leaves only the problem of specifying the action to be taken to perform the operation.

Step 4. Specifying the Action. As stated previously, we want the expression

```
cout << Today
```

to display the string corresponding to the **Day** value **Today**. Since this value might be any of **Sunday, Monday, . . . , Saturday** and the string to be displayed is different for each value, the function **operator≪** must use the value of the parameter **DayVal** to select a statement that outputs the corresponding character string. The complete definition of **operator≪** is shown in Figure 10.1.

FIGURE 10.1 Overloading ≪ for an enumeration value.

```
/* This function displays a Day value.
   Receive: Out, an ostream reference
            DayVal, a Day value
   Output:  the character string corresponding to DayVal onto Out
   Return:  ostream reference Out
-------------------------------------------------------------------*/

ostream& operator<< (ostream& Out, Day DayVal)
{
    const char
        ErrorMsg[] = "\n*** <<: invalid Day value received!\n";

    switch (DayVal)
    {
        case Sunday:        Out << "Sunday";
                            break;
        case Monday:        Out << "Monday";
                            break;
        case Tuesday:       Out << "Tuesday";
                            break;
        case Wednesday:     Out << "Wednesday";
                            break;
        case Thursday:      Out << "Thursday";
                            break;
        case Friday:        Out << "Friday";
                            break;
```

FIGURE 10.1   Overloading **<<** for an enumeration value. (cont.)

```
        case Saturday:        Out << "Saturday";
                              break;
        case DayOverflow:     Out << "Day Overflow";
                              break;
        case DayUnderflow:    Out << "Day Underflow";
                              break;
        default:
                              cerr << ErrorMsg;
    }

    return Out;
}
```

Given this function definition, the statements

```
Today = Wednesday;
cout << Today;
```

will display the output

```
Wednesday
```

The expression

```
cout << Today
```

corresponds to the function call

```
operator<<(cout, Today)
```

so that the argument corresponding to parameter **Out** is **cout** and the argument corresponding to parameter **DayVal** is **Today**. Since the value of **Today** is **Wednesday**, the value of parameter **DayVal** is **Wednesday**, so that the statement

```
Out << "Wednesday";
```

in **operator<<** is executed, causing the character string **"Wednesday"** to be written to **cout**.

Overloading the Input Operator

The complement of output is input, and so the complement of **operator<<** is **operator>>**. The statement

```
cin >> Today;
```

will generate a compiler error because no definition of **operator>>** exists for a **Day** operand. However, the input operator can be overloaded, just as the output operator was overloaded. The important points are as follows:

1. `cin` is an `istream` object, so the first parameter of `operator>>` is an `istream`.
2. `>>` changes its `istream` operand, so the first parameter of `operator>>` is an `istream` reference parameter.
3. Input expressions can be chained, so the return value of `operator>>` is its `istream` reference parameter.
4. Whereas `operator<<` does not change the value of parameter `DayVal`, `operator>>` must return a value via the second parameter `DayVal`, which must therefore be a `Day` reference parameter.

These observations permit us to construct the following stub for `operator>>`:

```
istream& operator>> (istream& In, Day& DayVal)
{
    // action >> must take
    return In;
}
```

The obvious strategy is to input a character string, one of `"Sunday"`, `"Monday"`, `"Tuesday"`, . . . , `"Saturday"`; store that string in a `Strings` object `Str`; and then set the value of parameter `DayVal` to the `Day` value corresponding to that string. If the character string does not correspond to a `Day` value, then an error message should be displayed. To make the function a bit more user-friendly, we will make it *case-insensitive*, so that the user can enter `monday`, `MONDAY`, `Monday`, `MoNdaY`, etc., for the `Day` value `Monday`. This is easily done by first converting the characters in the input string to lowercase and then using the lowercase character string equivalents of the `Day` values to determine the input value. For this, we use the functions `isupper()` and `tolower()` from `<ctype.h>`. The function in Figure 10.2 uses this approach to overload `>>`.

FIGURE 10.2 Overloading `>>` for an enumeration value.

```
/* This function inputs a Day value.

   Receive: In, an istream reference
            DayVal, a Day reference
   Input:   A character string, from In
   Output:  An error message, if there is no Day value that
               corresponds to the input string
   Return:  If there is a Day value corresponding to the string,
               return that Day value via parameter DayVal
            istream In
------------------------------------------------------------------*/

#include <ctype.h>
#include "Strings.h"                          // class Strings
```

FIGURE 10.2 Overloading **>>** for an enumeration value. (cont.)

```
istream& operator>> (istream& In, Day& DayVal)
{
   Strings
     Str;                                    // the input string
   const char
     ErrorMsg[] = "\n*** >>: invalid Day value input!\n";

   In >> Str;                               // 1. Input the string

   for (int i = 0; i < Str.Length(); i++)  // 2. Convert it
     if (isupper(Str[i]))                   //        to lowercase
        Str[i] = tolower(Str[i]);

   if (Str == "sunday")                     // 3. Set DayVal to the
     DayVal = Sunday;                       //        value corresponding
   else if (Str == "monday")               //        to the string Str
     DayVal = Monday;
   else if (Str == "tuesday")
     DayVal = Tuesday;
   else if (Str == "wednesday")
     DayVal = Wednesday;
   else if (Str == "thursday")
     DayVal = Thursday;
   else if (Str == "friday")
     DayVal = Friday;
   else if (Str == "saturday")
     DayVal = Saturday;
   else
   {
     DayVal = DayOverflow;                  // Return error value
     cerr << ErrorMsg;                      // Display error msg
   }

   return In;                               // 4. Return In
}
```

Note that a **switch** statement cannot be used to implement the selection statement in this function, because a **Strings** value is not integer-compatible (see Section 5.6).

Libraries and Types

Thus far, we have used libraries only to store related sets of functions. However, given the capability of constructing our own types, the true purpose of the library can be explained:

> *The purpose of a library is to store*
>
> *1. A type declaration; and*
> *2. The operations on objects of that type.*

That is, a library is intended to be a container for a type, together with the collection of functions that define the basic operations on that type. In the case of the type **Day**, we would define a library named **Day**. In its interface file **Day.h**, we would store the declarations of **Day**, **operator<<**, **operator>>**, and function **Next()**, as shown in Figure 10.3.

FIGURE 10.3   Storing types in a library.

```
/* This file contains the interface for library Day.

   Names Declared:
      Day, an enumeration of the values Sunday through Saturday
      operator<<, a function to output a Day value
      operator>>, a function to input a Day value
   ------------------------------------------------------------------*/


#include <iostream.h>
#include <fstream.h>

/********** the enumeration type **********/

enum Day {DayUnderflow = -1, Sunday, Monday, Tuesday, Wednesday,
          Thursday, Friday, Saturday, NumberOfDay, DayOverflow = 7};

/********** output function **********

   Receive: Out, an ostream reference
            DayVal, a Day value
   Output:  The character string corresponding to DayVal onto Out
   Return:  Ostream reference Out
   ------------------------------------------------------------------*/

ostream& operator<< (ostream& Out, Day DayVal);

/********** input function **********

   Receive: In, an istream reference
            DayVal, a Day reference
   Input:   A character string, from In
   Output:  An error message, if there is no Day value that
               corresponds to the input string
   Return:  If there is a Day value corresponding to the string,
               return that Day value via parameter DayVal
            istream In
   ------------------------------------------------------------------*/

istream& operator>> (istream& In, Day& DayVal);
```

FIGURE 10.3   Storing types in a library. (cont.)

```
/********** file output function **********

   Receive: Out, an fstream reference
            DayVal, a Day value
   Output:  The character string corresponding to DayVal onto Out
   Return:  fstream reference Out


----------------------------------------------------------------*/

fstream& operator<< (fstream& Out, Day DayVal);

/********** file input function **********

   Receive: In, an fstream reference
            DayVal, a Day reference
   Input:   A character string, from In
   Output:  An error message, if there is no Day value that
              corresponds to the input string
   Return:  If there is a Day value corresponding to the string,
              return that Day value via parameter DayVal
            fstream In
----------------------------------------------------------------*/

fstream& operator>> (fstream& In, Day& DayVal);


/********** successor function **********

   Receive: DayVal, a Day value
   Return:  The following Day value, with Saturday followed
            by Sunday
----------------------------------------------------------------*/

Day Next (Day DayVal);
```

We would then store the corresponding definitions of **operator<<**, **operator>>**, and **Next()** in the implementation file of library **Day**.[2]

Given this library, a program can now use the type **Day** and its operations by inserting the library's header file **(Day.h)**. The resulting executable program must then be linked with the definitions in the compiled implementation files of *all* libraries whose header files are used in the program, either directly or indirectly. For example, a program that uses library **Day** must also be linked to library **Strings**, since the **Day** input operation uses class **Strings**. Note that since the header file is all that most users of the library will ever see, it is important to document thoroughly the items that are being declared in it.

---

[2] Recall that although a library's header file always ends in the **.h** extension, the extension for its implementation file is the same as that of a source file in a given environment (e.g., **.C** or **.cc** in UNIX, **.CPP** in the Turbo environment, and **.cpp** in the Symantec environment).

Another Example: A Boolean Type

In Section 5.3, we discussed the *boolean* data type, consisting of the values *true* and *false*. We saw that C++ does not have a predefined boolean type but treats the integer value 0 as false and any nonzero integer value as true. As we noted earlier in this section, enumerations make it possible to represent these boolean values directly. The declaration

```
enum Boolean {False, True};
```

makes the name **Boolean** a new type with values **False** and **True**. Given such a type, an assignment such as

```
Done = 1;
```

can be replaced with a more readable assignment:

```
Done = True;
```

because the compiler represents the name **False** with 0 and the name **True** with 1. Note that the ordering of **False** and **True** is significant in the declaration of **Boolean**—in order for the compiler to associate 0 with **False** and 1 with **True**, **False** should occur first and **True** second in the declaration (unless we explicitly specify the integers to be associated with them, as illustrated earlier).

Similarly, we can declare functions that return a true or false value as **Boolean** functions. For example, in Section 6.4, we examined the ATM menu-choice problem, one part of which was determining whether the choice entered by the user was a valid menu choice. Figure 10.4 presents a simple **Boolean** function **ValidMenuChoice()** that returns **True** if its argument is one of **A–D** or **a–d** and **False** otherwise:

 FIGURE 10.4   A Boolean function.

```
/* This function returns True if its argument is a valid menu
   choice and False otherwise.

   Receive: Ch, a char
   Return:  True, if and only if Ch is one of A-D (upper- or
            lowercase)
------------------------------------------------------------------*/

Boolean ValidMenuChoice(char Ch)
{
   switch (Ch)
   {
      case 'A': case 'B': case 'C': case 'D':
      case 'a': case 'b': case 'c': case 'd':
         return True;
      default:
         return False;
   }
}
```

The statement

```
if (ValidMenuChoice(Choice))
```

can then be used to check if **Choice** was a valid menu option.

To maximize the reusability of the type **Boolean**, we could store its declaration in a library **Boolean**, along with I/O operations on that type. Figure 10.5 presents the header file for such a library.

 FIGURE 10.5   A Boolean library.

```
/* This file contains the interface for library Boolean.

Names Declared:

   Boolean, a type whose values are True and False
   <<, the output operator
   >>, the input operator
-----------------------------------------------------------------------*/

/********** input function **********
#include <iostream.h>
#include <fstream.h>

/********** the type Boolean **********/

enum Boolean {False, True};

/********** output function **********

   Receive: Out, an ostream reference
            BoolVal, a Boolean value
   Output:  The character string corresponding to BoolVal
               onto Out
   Return:  ostream reference Out
----------------------------------------------------------------*/

ostream& operator<< (ostream& Out, Boolean BoolVal);

/********** input function **********

   Receive: In, an istream reference
            BoolVal, a Boolean reference
   Input:   A character string, from In
   Output:  An error message, if there is no Boolean value that
               corresponds to the input string
   Return:  If there is a Boolean value corresponding to the string,
               return that Boolean value via parameter BoolVal
            istream In
----------------------------------------------------------------*/

istream& operator>> (istream& In, Boolean& BoolVal);
```

FIGURE 10.5   A Boolean library. (cont.)

```
/********** file output function **********

   Receive: Out, an fstream reference
            BoolVal, a Boolean value
   Output:  The character string corresponding to BoolVal
              onto Out
   Return:  fstream reference Out
-----------------------------------------------------------------*/

fstream& operator<< (fstream& Out, Boolean BoolVal);


/********** file input function **********

   Receive: In, an fstream reference
            BoolVal, a Boolean reference
   Input:   A character string, from In
   Output:  An error message, if there is no Boolean value that
              corresponds to the input string
   Return:  If there is a Boolean value corresponding to the string,
              return that Boolean value via parameter BoolVal
            fstream In
-----------------------------------------------------------------*/

fstream& operator>> (fstream& In, Boolean& BoolVal);
```

Construction of the corresponding implementation file is left as an exercise.

Exercises

   1. (a) Write an enumeration **MonthAbbrev**, whose values are abbreviations of the months of the year and consist of the first three letters of the months' names.
      (b) Write a function whose parameter is the number of a month and whose return value is the corresponding value of type **MonthAbbrev**.
      (c) Design a header file for the type **MonthAbbrev** that defines it and I/O operations.

   2. Write a function whose parameters are a nonnegative integer **n** and a month abbreviation **Abbrev**, like that in Exercise 1, and that finds the ''nth successor'' of **Abbrev**. The 0th successor of **Abbrev** is **Abbrev** itself; for **n** > 0, the nth successor of **Abbrev** is the nth month following **Abbrev**. For example, the fourth successor of **Aug** is **Dec**, and the sixth successor of **Aug** is **Feb**.

   3. Repeat Exercise 2, but define the function recursively.

   4. Write an implementation file for the type **Boolean** described in the text.

5. Write an implementation file for the type **MonthAbbrev** of Exercise 1.

6. Using the enumerated type **Day** in the text, write a program to read a customer's account number and current balance; then for each weekday (Monday through Friday), read a series of transactions by that customer of the form D (deposit) or W (withdrawal) followed by an amount, and update the balance with this amount. Display the new balance after all transactions for the week have been processed.

7. (a) Write a function whose parameters are a month of type **MonthAbbrev** (see Exercise 1) and a year in the range from 1538 through 1999 and whose value is the number of days in the month. Remember that February has 28 days, except in a leap year, when it has 29. A leap year is one in which the year is divisible by 4 except for centesimal years (those ending in 00); these centesimal years are not leap years unless the year number is divisible by 400. Thus 1950 and 1900 are not leap years, but 1960 and 1600 are.

(b) Use the function of part (a) in a program to read two dates and calculate the number of days that have elapsed between them.

10.2   Example: A Classification Program

Objects are often organized into groups that share similar characteristics. To illustrate:

- A doctor might be described as an internist, a pediatrician, a surgeon, a gynecologist, a family practitioner, or some other specialty, according to his or her area of training.
- Members of the animal kingdom are organized into groups (called phyla) according to whether they have vertebrae, the relative positions of their nervous and digestive systems, and their outer covering.
- The elements are organized into groups according to the number of electrons in the outermost shell of their atoms.

These are just a few of the many cases in which we **classify** objects. By classifying objects into groups according to their characteristics, objects that are in some way similar become *related* by their group membership.

In this section, we develop a simple library that illustrates how enumerations can be used to simulate classifications from the real world in software.

Problem: Geological Classification

In geology, rocks are classified according to the nature of their origin. More precisely, a given rock is described as

- *Igneous*, if it is volcanic in origin (i.e., formed as the result of cooling magma);
- *Metamorphic*, if the rock was formed under conditions of high temperature and pressure; and
- *Sedimentary*, if the rock was formed from the laying down of deposits of sediment.

Igneous rocks include basalt, granite, and obsidian. Metamorphic rocks include marble, quartzite, and slate. Sedimentary rocks include dolomite, limestone, sandstone, and shale.

Knowing the different categories of rocks can make outdoor activities (such as backpacking and canoeing) more interesting. For example, if one is hiking through a valley whose walls contain layers of sandstone, then one can conclude that the walls of the valley were probably once under water and may contain fossils of water creatures. By contrast, a valley whose walls consist of granite indicates that there was once a volcano in the vicinity, and finding it can be an interesting diversion in the hike.

For those who find it difficult to memorize such things, it is relatively easy to write a program that, given the name of a rock, describes some of its characteristics. Figure 10.6 gives an example of such a program.

 FIGURE 10.6   A rock-classification program.

```
/* This program allows a user to retrieve information about a
   given rock.

   Receive: The name of a rock
   Output:  The known information about that rock
   ------------------------------------------------------------------*/

#include <iostream.h>

#include "Rock.h"    // various rock-related types and functions

int main(void)
{
   cout << "\nThis program provides information about ";
       << "specific rocks.\n";

   RockName
      Rock;          // the rock about which information is needed
   char
      Response;      // loop-control (query) variable

   do
   {
      cout << "\nEnter the name of a rock: ";
      cin >> Rock;

      cout << endl << Rock
           << " is classified as a(n) " << Kind(Rock)
           << " rock, and\n its texture is " << Texture(Rock) << ".\n";

      cout << "\nEnter 'c' to continue, anything else to quit: ";
      cin >> Response;
   }
   while (Response == 'c');

   return 0;
}
```

FIGURE 10.6   A rock-classification program. (cont.)

Sample run:

```
This program provides information about specific rocks.

Enter the name of a rock: sandstone

Sandstone is classified as a(n) Sedimentary rock, and
  its texture is Coarse.

Enter 'c' to continue, anything else to quit: c

Enter the name of a rock: obsidian

Obsidian is classified as a(n) Igneous rock, and
  its texture is Fine.

Enter 'c' to continue, anything else to quit: q
```

The interesting thing about the preceding program is that it allows the user to communicate in real-world terms (the names of rocks) rather than through some artificial mechanism (a menu). This is accomplished by declaring the type **RockName** as an enumeration, whose values are the names of common rocks:

```
enum RockName {Basalt, Dolomite, Granite,
               Limestone, Marble, Obsidian,
               Quartzite, Sandstone, Shale, Slate,
               NameError};
```

Since there are three real-world kinds of rocks, these are also easily represented using an enumeration **RockKind**, whose values are the kinds of rocks:

```
enum RockKind {Igneous, Metamorphic, Sedimentary, KindError};
```

The declaration of the type **RockTexture** is similar and can be seen in Figure 10.8.

In order to determine the category to which a given rock belongs, a mapping function is needed that, given a **RockName**, returns its **RockKind**. This is easily done using a **switch** statement and the categories described earlier, as shown in Figure 10.7.

FIGURE 10.7   Mapping a rock to a **RockKind**.

```
RockKind Kind(RockName Rock)
{
   switch (Rock)                    // if the rock is...
   {
      case Basalt: case Granite:    //    any of these, then
      case Obsidian:                //        its an igneous rock
         return Igneous;
      case Marble: case Quartzite:  //    any of these, then
```

FIGURE 10.7   Mapping a rock to a **RockKind**. (cont.)

```
      case Slate:                   //      it's a metamorphic rock
         return Metamorphic;
      case Dolomite: case Limestone: //    any of these, then
      case Sandstone: case Shale:   //      it's a sedimentary rock
         return Sedimentary;

      default:                      //    just in case...
         cerr << "\n*** Kind received invalid RockName: "
              << Rock << endl;
   }
   return KindError;
}
```

Other useful functions, such as those to perform I/O of a **RockName** value, perform I/O of a **RockKind** value, and map a **RockName** value to a **RockTexture** value, are similar to those we have seen previously and are left as exercises.

Since it might be useful for other geological programs to be able to use these types and their related functions, they should be stored in a library to facilitate their reuse. Figure 10.8 gives a header file for such a library.

   FIGURE 10.8   Header file of library **Rock**.

```
/* This file contains the declarations for library Rock.

   ...
   -----------------------------------------------------------*/


#include <iostream.h>

enum RockKind {                   // classification by origin:
               Igneous,           //     volcanic
               Metamorphic,       //     high temp/pressure
               Sedimentary,       //     deposits of sediment
               KindError};        //     none of the above

/* --- The iostream operations for a RockKind value -------------*/
ostream& operator<< (ostream& Out, RockKind Kind);
istream& operator>> (istream& In, RockKind& Kind);


enum RockTexture {                // classification by texture:
               Coarse,            //     rough
               Intermediate,      //     less rough
               Fine,              //     smooth
               TextureError};     //     none of the above

/* --- The iostream operations for a RockTexture value ----------*/
ostream& operator<< (ostream& Out, RockTexture Texture);
istream& operator>> (istream& In, RockTexture& Texture);
```

FIGURE 10.8   Header file of library **Rock**. (cont.)

```
enum RockName {                      // some common rocks, in
            Basalt, Dolomite, //    alphabetical order
            Granite, Limestone,
            Marble, Obsidian,
            Quartzite, Sandstone,
            Shale, Slate,
            NameError};

/*--- The iostream operators for a RockName value ---------------*/
ostream& operator<< (ostream& Out, RockName Rock);
istream& operator>> (istream& In, RockName& Rock);


/* --- Map a rock to its kind -------------------------------------

   Receive: Rock, a RockName value.
   Return:  The (RockKind) classification of Rock.
-----------------------------------------------------------------
RockKind Kind(RockName Rock);


/* --- Map a rock to its texture ---------------------------------*/

   Receive: Rock, a RockName value.
   Return:  The (RockTexture) classification of Rock.
-----------------------------------------------------------------*/
RockTexture Texture(RockName Rock);
```

   Enumerations together with functions that provide useful operations on them thus allow objects from the real world to be represented using their real-world names, both by *programmers* as they write programs and by *users* as they execute programs.

Exercises

1. Write a function that overloads **operator<<** for each of the following types:

   (a) **RockName**
   (b) **RockKind**
   (c) **RockTexture**

2. Write a function that overloads **operator>>** for each of the following types:

   (a) **RockName**
   (b) **RockKind**
   (c) **RockTexture**

3. Implement the function **Texture()** that, given a **RockName** value, returns the corresponding **RockTexture** value, assuming that the rocks

- **Granite**, **Sandstone**, **Dolomite**, and **Limestone** are **Coarse** in texture;
- **Basalt**, **Shale**, **Slate**, and **Quartzite** are **Intermediate** in texture; and
- **Obsidian** and **Marble** are **Fine** in texture.

10.3 Synonym Types: Using `typedef`

The second mechanism that C++ provides for declaring types is the **typedef** facility, so named because its declarations have the form

```
typedef ExistingTypeName NewTypeName;
```

The effect of such a declaration is to make the name *NewTypeName* a **synonym** for *ExistingTypeName*, which is some existing type. For example, if we preferred to use the word **real** instead of **double**, we could write

```
typedef double real;
```

Once such a declaration has been made, the word **real** may be used any place that the word **double** is used. For example, constants and variables can be declared to be of type **real**:

```
const real
   Pi = 3.14159;
real
   Sum = 0.0,
   Rate1,
   Rate2;
```

Functions and parameters can be defined using the new name:

```
real Cube(real X)
{
   return X*X*X;
}
```

Or an argument of the new type can be passed to a function (predefined or otherwise) in place of a parameter of the old type:

```
Rate2 = sqrt(Rate1);
```

In summary, the two names are interchangeable; objects declared using the new name can be used to do anything that is permitted with objects declared using the old name, and vice versa. Thus, to perform I/O with a **real** value, it is not necessary to overload the **<<** or **>>** operator. For example, in the statement

```
cout << Rate2;
```

the C++ compiler will use the existing definition of **<<** (for a **double** object) to output the **real** object **Rate2**.

The **typedef** facility can be applied to any existing type, not just the predefined types. For example, suppose that the following declaration is in the header file of a library named **Color**:

```
enum Color {Red, Orange, Yellow, Green, Blue, Indigo, Violet};
```

In a program for maintaining an inventory of art supplies, one might find it more desirable to insert the header file **Color.h**, declare

```
typedef Color Pigment;
```

and then use the name **Pigment** throughout the program, rather than **Color**.

Note that if the **typedef** is omitted, a variable declaration results:

```
Color Pigment;   // Here, Pigment is a variable of type Color
```

The following observation is the key to using **typedef** effectively:

When a variable declaration

>   *Type Name*;

is preceded with the keyword **typedef**,

>   **typedef** *Type Name*;

Name is declared as a synonym for *Type* rather than as a *Type* object.

For example, consider the following function that displays the error message (a character string constant) passed to it and then terminates the program that calls it:

```
#include <stdlib.h>

void FatalError(const char ErrorMsg[])
{
   cerr << "\n\n" << ErrorMsg << "\n\n";
   exit(-1);
}
```

If we store this function in a library, then the header file for that library contains the declaration

```
void FatalError(const char []);
```

in which the parameter type is not very readable. To declare a more readable synonym for the type **const char []**, we could precede a character string constant object declaration

```
const char StringConstant[];
```

with the word **typedef**

```
typedef const char StringConstant[];
```

and thus declare the name **StringConstant** as a synonym for the type **const char []**. We can then use this synonym to declare the function with a (more readable) parameter type:

```
void FatalError(StringConstant);
```

In the implementation file, the function can be defined as

```
void FatalError(StringConstant ErrorMsg)
{
   cerr << "\n\n" << ErrorMsg << "\n\n";
   exit (-1);
}
```

The primary use of the **typedef** mechanism is to *improve the readability of a program* by defining more meaningful type names. As we shall see in Chapter 15, the **typedef** facility can be used to significantly improve the readability of some of the types C++ has inherited from its parent language C.

Exercises

1. Declare the name **Letter** as a synonym type for the predefined type **char**. Then construct a function **GetLetter()** that repeatedly

   - Reads a character from the keyboard and
   - Displays an error if that character is not an alphabetic character

   as long as the input character is not an alphabetic character.

2. Declare the name **Digit** as a synonym type for the predefined type **char**. Then construct a function **GetDigit()** that repeatedly

   - Reads a character from the keyboard and
   - Displays an error if that character is not a numeric character

   as long as the input character is not a numeric character.

3. Construct a library **CharTypes** that stores the definitions from Exercises 1 and 2, and write a driver program to test their correctness.

10.4   PART OF THE PICTURE: The Type Hierarchy

At this point, we have examined many of the types available in C++. Figure 10.9 presents a diagram in which these types are organized into a **type hierarchy** that shows their relationships to one another.

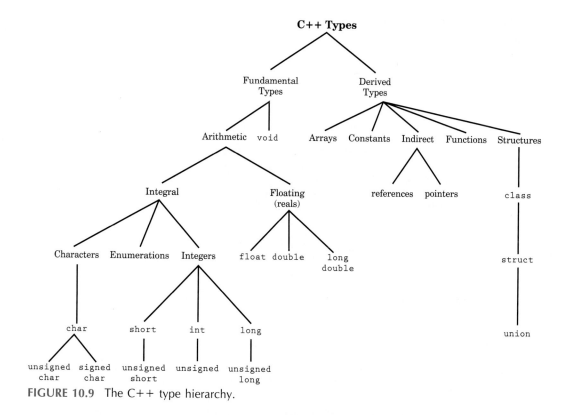

FIGURE 10.9 The C++ type hierarchy.

Note that the **typedef** mechanism does not appear anywhere within the hierarchy. The reason is that **typedef** is not a facility for creating a new type; instead, it is designed to provide a new name for an existing type.

The hierarchy provides a map of the richness of the C++ language that shows where we have been and where we have not yet explored. Part II of this text introduced the process of programming when the objects in one's program were limited to the fundamental types, constants, and functions that dealt with such objects, classes that are provided by the standard libraries, and a few nonstandard classes. Part III of this text expands on the ideas of Part II by introducing enumerations (this chapter) and derived types, such as classes (Chapter 11), and arrays (Chapters 12 through 14). Part IV introduces objects that are constructed using indirection (Chapters 15 through 17). These final chapters of the text apply what we have learned to the creation of data objects of significant complexity.

Programming Pointers

Program Design

1. *Use enumerations to improve program readability and to make the program easier to understand and use.* For example, using enumerated values such as

```
enum Color {Black, Blue, Red, Orange, Yellow, Green,
            Brown, Violet, Gray, White};
```

to represent colors in a program instead of cryptic codes 0, 1, 2, 3, 4, 5, 6, 7, 8, and 9 obviously makes the program easier to read and understand.

2. *Use* `typedef` *to improve program readability by replacing predefined types with names that are easier to understand and use.* To the casual reader, the declaration

```
DisplayError( StringConstant ErrorMsg );
```

is more meaningful than

```
DisplayError( char ErrorMsg [] );
```

3. *Type identifier declarations should be stored in a header file, together with operations on that type, so that other programs needing that type can reuse the declarations (instead of reinventing the wheel).*

4. *The definitions of operations on a new type should be stored in a separately compiled implementation file so that different programs can reuse the same definitions.* To see why, suppose that the compiled definitions take up 1K bytes. Suppose also that five programs are using the type and each inserts the header file. If the definitions are stored in the header file, then each program has its own separate copy of those definitions, so the total space devoted to them is 5K.

   By contrast, if each program is linked to a separately compiled file containing the definitions, then those definitions are shared by the programs, so the total space devoted to the definitions is only 1K.

   Using separately compiled files of function definitions almost always speeds compilation as well, since any files that have not been modified since they have been compiled need not be recompiled.

Potential Problems

1. *Values listed in an enumeration must be legal identifiers and may not be overloaded.* For example, the declaration

```
enum PassengerType { first-class, coach, standby };    // ERROR!
```

is not allowed because `first-class` is not a legal identifier. The declarations

```
enum Weekday { Monday, Tuesday, Wednesday, Thursday, Friday };
enum VacationDay { Friday, Saturday, Sunday, Monday }; // ERROR!
```

are not allowed because the same identifiers (**Friday** and **Monday**) may not be used in two declarations.

2. *Values of an enumerated data type cannot be input or output unless the I/O operators are overloaded.*

3. *Arithmetic operators such as* **++** *cannot be applied to or overloaded for an enumeration object.* This is the primary motivation for implementing enumerations as a class, as described in the next chapter.

4. *A synonym type for any type T is constructed using* **typedef** *by*

   (a) *Declaring an object of type T and*
   (b) *Preceding that declaration with the word* **typedef**.

   What was an object declaration is now a synonym-type declaration. For example, to declare a synonym type named **StringConstant** for character string constants, we do the following:

   (a) Declare a character string constant object named **StringConstant**:

   ```
   const char StringConstant[];
   ```

   (b) Precede that declaration with the word **typedef**:

   ```
   typedef const char StringConstant[];
   ```

The identifier **StringConstant** is then a synonym type for the type **const char []**. It is especially important to remember this when using **typedef** to declare character string types.

Forgetting the keyword **typedef** can lead to subtle errors. For example, omitting the **typedef** in the declaration

```
typedef double real;
```

yields a declaration of a **double** variable named **real** instead of a synonym type:

```
double real;
```

Programming Projects

1. Construct a library **PlayingCard** containing a declaration of the name **PlayingCard** as an enumeration whose values are the 52 playing cards as well as I/O operations on a **PlayingCard** value. Using the **RandomInt** class from Section 7.8, write a function **BuildHand()** that, for a given integer **n**, deals two "random" hands of **n** cards, making certain that none of the cards have been dealt already. Write a driver program that tests your library and plays a simple card game (e.g., Go Fish!).

2. Construct a library **PeriodicTable** in which the name **ChemicalSymbol** is declared as an enumeration whose values are the element abbreviations (e.g., **H**,

He, Li, ...). Construct I/O operations for a **ChemicalSymbol** value, and add functions that, for a given **ChemicalSymbol** value, return

- The atomic number of the element,
- The atomic weight of the element,
- The number of protons (and/or neutrons) in the nucleus of the element,
- The period of the element,
- The group of the element,

and any other useful operations that represent information that can be extracted from the periodic table. Then write a menu-driven program that allows users to obtain the information about any element whose symbol they input.

3. Construct a library **Temperature** in which the name **Temperature** is declared as a synonym type for the predefined type **double**. Write a function **GetTemperature()** that, for a given **Strings** object **Scale** (either "**Fahrenheit**" or "**Celsius**"), prompts for, inputs, and returns a **Temperature** of the indicated scale. Write conversion functions to convert a **Temperature** value from Fahrenheit to Celsius, and vice versa. Write a function **PrintTemp()** that, given a **Temperature** and its **Scale**, displays that **Temperature** (and its scale) in an easy-to-read format. Write a driver program that uses this library to convert a temperature from Fahrenheit to Celsius, or vice versa.

4. Construct a library in which the name **Sword** is declared as a type having the values **Short, Broad, Long**, and **TwoHanded**, as well as **iostream** operations for the type **Sword**. Include a function **Reach()** that, for a given **Sword** value, returns its length (e.g., 18 inches, 24 inches, 36 inches, and 48 inches, respectively). Include another function **Speed()** that, for a given **Sword** value, returns the time required to swing that sword as a value inversely proportional to its length. Write a program that allows its user to pick the weapons of two duelists and then incorporates a random number generator (see Section 7.8) and the **Reach()** and **Speed()** functions of those weapons to provide a blow-by-blow simulation of their duel.

5. (Group Project) Have one group member proceed as in Project 4, but have a second group member build another library that defines the type **Armor**, consisting of the values **None, Leather, Chain**, and **Plate**, as well as **iostream** operations on the type **Armor**. Add a function **Protection()** that, for a given **Armor** value, returns the degree to which it protects its wearer (e.g., 0.0, 0.50, 0.75, and 0.95, respectively). Add a function **Weight()** that, for a given **Armor** value, returns the degree to which a wearer of the armor is slowed in swinging a weapon (e.g., 0, 2, 4, 8). Write the duel-simulation program so that the user can choose both the duelists' weapons and armor and that both are considered in the simulation.

INTRODUCTION TO CLASSES

11

> *The old order changeth, yielding place to new.*
> ALFRED, LORD TENNYSON

CHAPTER CONTENTS

The word *class* is often used to group or categorize objects that have a common set of attributes. For example, the high school football teams in one state are described as

- *Class A*, if they have fewer than 100 students in three grades;
- *Class AA*, if they have fewer than 500 students in three grades;
- *Class AAA*, if they have fewer than 1000 students in three grades; and
- *Class AAAA*, if they have 1000 or more students in three grades.

The U.S. Navy describes ships as belonging to certain *classes;* for example, *Skipjack class, Thresher class,* and *Sturgeon class* have been used to classify different kinds of submarines.[1] Economists describe families as *lower class, middle class,* or *upper class,* based on their annual income. Karl Marx described history as a *class struggle* between the workers and the bourgeoisie.

Used in this way, the word *class* is a synonym for the word *type,* since it provides a name for a group of related objects, and the C++ mechanism for creating a new type is called the *class.* This chapter examines the C++ class mechanism, showing how it can be used to represent objects too complicated to be modeled using the C++ fundamental types.

11.1 Nonscalar Types: The Class

Most of the types considered prior to Chapter 9 were **scalar** types, meaning that objects of those types can store a single value at a time. For example, the types **char**, **int**, and **double** are all scalar types, since a variable of type **char** can store a single character value, a variable of type **int** can store a single integer value, and a variable of type **double** can store a single real value. Similarly, enumerations are scalar types, since the value of an enumeration variable is a single value of that type.

Scalar types allow us to solve a wide variety of computational problems that involve objects that have a single *attribute,* or characteristic. If we represent that attribute with a scalar variable, that variable becomes a model for the object. For example, if the object we wish to model is a Fahrenheit temperature, then that temperature has a single attribute (the number of degrees), and so we can model it with a scalar (real) variable:

```
double
    Temp1 = 0.0;  // Brrrr!
```

However, an arbitrary temperature has two attributes—*number of degrees* and *scale* (Fahrenheit or Celsius). Of course, we could model this using two variables:

```
char
    Scale = 'F';
double
    Degrees = 0.0;
```

But this requires two data items (**Scale** and **Degrees**) in order to model a single real-world object (temperature). If we wish to perform some function **G()** on a

---

[1] To carry on this theme, the Enterprise on the popular television show *Star Trek* was described as a Constitution class starship. On the succeeding show, *Star Trek: The Next Generation,* the (new and improved) Enterprise is a Galaxy class starship.

temperature, we must pass to `G()` each of the data items used in our model,

    G(Scale, Degrees);

instead of being able to pass a single object:

    G(Temp);

Similarly, in order to output a temperature, we must use an output statement such as

    cout << Degrees << Scale;

instead of simply being able to write

    cout << Temp;

Although this approach to modeling is not too inconvenient for objects that can be described with two attributes, it quickly becomes unmanageable as the complexity of the object being modeled increases. How would we model a tax form like that shown in Figure 11.1?

1 Control number ABC-123		**Copy C** For EMPLOYEE'S RECORDS OMB No. 12-34-56-78	
2 Employer's name, address, and ZIP code Dinoville Rock Quarry 1212 T-Rex Ave. Bedrock, Prehistoria 00001		6 Statutory Deceased Pension Legal 942 Defered employee plan rep. emp. compensation	
		7 Allocated tips	8 Advance EIC payment
		9 Federal income tax withheld .00	10 Wages, tips, other compensation 1111.11
3 Employer's identification number 12-345-6-789	4 Employer's state I.D. number	11 Social security tax withheld 11.22	12 Social security wages
5 Employee's social security number 987-65-4321		13 Social security tips	14 Medicare wages and tips
19 Employee's name, address, and ZIP code Fred Flintstone 123 Cave A Bedrock, Prehistoria 00001		15 Medicare tax withheld 22.11	16 Nonqualified plans
		17 See Instrs. for Box 17	18 Other Country Club 10.00 Tax Dodge 50.00 Loop Hole 100.00
20	21	22 Dependent care benefits	23 Benefits included in Box 10
24 State income tax .00	25 State wages, tips, etc. 1111.11	26 Name of state PREH	27 Local income tax 28 Local wages, tips, etc. 29 Name of locality .00 1111.11 Dinoville

Form W-2 Wage and Tax Statement—1994

FIGURE 11.1 A W-2 income tax form.

C++ provides better mechanisms to model objects with multiple attributes, one of which is the **class.** Classes allow the programmer to declare new types capable of storing multiple values. Since Chapter 2, we have been using classes *provided in C++* (e.g., `istream`, `ostream`, and `fstream`). This chapter is devoted to learning how to *build our own* classes.

A First Example: Modeling Temperature

To introduce the key concepts of class design, we begin with a familiar example. Figure 11.2 presents a program that uses a class `Temperature` to solve a variation of the temperature-conversion problem.

 FIGURE 11.2   A temperature-conversion program.

```
/* This program converts a temperature to Fahrenheit and/or Celsius,
   using class Temperature.

   Input:  An arbitrary Temperature
   Output: The Fahrenheit and Celsius equivalents of that Temperature
-------------------------------------------------------------------*/

#include <iostream.h>

#include "Temperature.h"

int main(void)
{
   cout << "\nThis program converts a temperature "
        << "to Fahrenheit and/or Celsius.\n";

   char
      Response;
   Temperature
      TempVar;                                    // construction

   do
   {
      cout << "\nPlease enter a temperature\n"
           << "(degrees, followed by F or C): ";

      cin >> TempVar;                             // input

      cout << "\n\t" << TempVar.Fahrenheit()      // conversion
           << " is equivalent to "                // and
           << TempVar.Celsius() << endl;          // output
```

FIGURE 11.2   A temperature-conversion program. (cont.)

```
      cout << "\nMore temperatures (y or n)? ";
      cin >> Response;
   }
   while ((Response == 'y') || (Response == 'Y'));

   return 0;
}
```

Sample run:

```
This program converts a temperature to Fahrenheit and/or Celsius.

Please enter a temperature
(degrees, followed by F or C): 212 F

   212 F is equivalent to 100 C

More temperatures (y or n)? y

Please enter a temperature
(degrees, followed by F or C): 0c

   32 F is equivalent to 0 C

More temperatures (y or n)? y

Please enter a temperature
(degrees, followed by F or C): 100 C

   212 F is equivalent to 100 C

More temperatures (y or n)? n
```

This program uses a class named **Temperature** to construct an object named
TempVar:

```
   Temperature
      TempVar;
```

The program proceeds to input a **Temperature** value from the keyboard with the
statement

```
   cin >> TempVar;
```

which uses an overloaded definition for the input operator from class

Temperature. The program then calls each of the two conversion member functions,

```
TempVar.Fahrenheit()
```

and

```
TempVar.Celsius()
```

which return the equivalent **Temperature** value in Fahrenheit and Celsius, respectively. These values are displayed using the statement

```
cout << "\n\t" << TempVar.Fahrenheit()      // conversion
     << " is equivalent to "                // and
     << TempVar.Celsius() << endl;          // output
```

which uses an overloaded definition of the output operator from class **Temperature**.

These statements illustrate some of the basic operations provided by most classes. We examine classes in greater detail in the remainder of this section.

Declaring Class Temperature

Figure 11.3 presents a declaration of class **Temperature**.

FIGURE 11.3   The **Temperature** class declaration.

```
/* This file contains the interface for class Temperature.

-----------------------------------------------------------------*/

#ifndef TEMPERATURE
#define TEMPERATURE

#include <iostream.h>
#include "Boolean.h"

class Temperature
{
    double
        Degrees_;
    char
        Scale_;
```

FIGURE 11.3 The **Temperature** class declaration. (cont.)

```
public:

    /********** Class Constructor *********************************

        Precondition:  A Temperature object has been declared.
        Receive:       The (optional) initialization values
                          InitDegrees (a double, default 0.0)
                          InitScale (a char, default 'C')
        Postcondition: The declared Temperature object has its
                          Degrees_ member initialized to InitDegrees
                          and its Scale_ member initialized to
                          InitScale.
    -------------------------------------------------------------*/

    Temperature(double InitDegrees = 0.0, char InitScale = 'C');


    /********** Assignment ****************************************

        Receive: The Temperature object Temp being assigned
        Return:  The Temperature object containing this function,
                    its members as copies of those of Temp
    -------------------------------------------------------------*/

    Temperature& operator=(const Temperature& Temp);


    /********** Degrees Extraction ********************************

        Return: The value stored in the Degrees_ member of the
                   Temperature object containing this function
    -------------------------------------------------------------*/

    double Degrees(void) const { return Degrees_; };


    /********** Scale Extraction **********************************

        Return: The value stored in the Scale_ member of the
                   Temperature object containing this function
    -------------------------------------------------------------*/

    char Scale(void) const { return Scale_; };


    /********** Fahrenheit Conversion *****************************

        Return: The Fahrenheit equivalent of the Temperature object
                   containing this function
    -------------------------------------------------------------*/

    Temperature Fahrenheit(void) const;
```

FIGURE 11.3   The **Temperature** class declaration. (cont.)

```
/*********** Celsius Conversion *******************************

    Return: The Celsius equivalent of the Temperature object
            containing this function
    -----------------------------------------------------------*/

Temperature Celsius(void) const;


/*********** Output ******************************************

    Receive: An ostream Out, and a Temperature Temp
    Output:  A Temperature value (a double Degrees and char Scale)
    Return:  Out
    -----------------------------------------------------------*/

friend ostream& operator<<(ostream& Out, const Temperature& Temp);


/*********** Input *******************************************

    Receive: An istream In, and a Temperature (reference) Temp
    Input:   A Temperature value (a double Degrees and char Scale)
    Return:  Temp, its members containing the input values
             In
    -----------------------------------------------------------*/

friend istream& operator>>(istream& In, Temperature& Temp);

/********* Relational Operators ****************************/

/**** Equality ****

    Receive: Temp1 and Temp2, two Temperature objects
    Return:  True if and only if corresponding data members of
             Temp1 and Temp2 are the same
    -----------------------------------------------------------*/

friend Boolean operator==(const Temperature& Temp1,
                          const Temperature& Temp2);


/**** Inequality ****

    Receive: Temp1 and Temp2, two Temperature objects
    Return:  True if and only if at least one data member of
             Temp1 is different from the corresponding data
             member of Temp2
    -----------------------------------------------------------*/

friend Boolean operator!=(const Temperature& Temp1,
                          const Temperature& Temp2);
```

FIGURE 11.3 The **Temperature** class declaration. (cont.)

```
/**** Less than ****

   Receive: Temp1 and Temp2, two Temperature objects
   Return:  True if and only if the Degrees_ member of Temp1
            is less than the Degrees_ member of Temp2
            (and their Scale_ members are equal)
   ----------------------------------------------------------*/

   friend Boolean operator<(const Temperature& Temp1,
                            const Temperature& Temp2);

};

#endif
```

The first part of this declaration,

```
class Temperature
{
  double
    Degrees_;
  char
    Scale_;
```

creates a new type called **Temperature**, which has two **data members** (sometimes called **fields,** or **instance variables**):

- **Degrees_**, which can store a real value, and
- **Scale_**, which can store a character value.[2]

This new type **Temperature** is similar to all the other types we have seen before, in that it allows us to declare objects. For example, the program in Figure 11.2 uses it to declare a variable named **TempVar**:

```
Temperature
   TempVar;
```

which might be visualized as follows:

```
        TempVar
     Degrees_ [      ]
       Scale_ [      ]
```

---

[2] We follow the convention of naming data members with names ending in an underscore (_) so that the same names can be used for member functions that extract the values of those data members.

TempVar is a single (variable) object, but it is not scalar, because it can hold two data values: a real value in its **Degrees_** member and a character value in its **Scale_** member.

Encapsulation.   The object **TempVar** illustrates one of the benefits of using classes:

> Classes make it possible to *store multiple data values of different types* in a single object.

This property of storing multiple values in a single object is known as **data encapsulation** and is provided by virtually all modern programming languages.
But classes go further:

> A class makes it possible to *store the operations on objects of that type* within its objects.

For example, if we want to be able to assign a **Temperature** value to a **Temperature** variable, then we must store a declaration of the assignment operator within the class declaration, as shown in Figure 11.4.

FIGURE 11.4   The assignment declaration in class **Temperature**.

```
class Temperature
{
  double
    Degrees_;
  char
    Scale_;
      .
      .
      .

  /*********** Assignment ***************************************

      Receive: The Temperature object Temp being assigned
      Return:  The Temperature object containing this function,
               its members as copies of those of Temp
      ------------------------------------------------------------*/

  Temperature& operator=(const Temperature& Temp);

      .
      .
      .
};
```

This ability to store operations within a class means that these operations, as well as the data members, are stored within objects of that class type. As we have noted, these operations are called **member functions** (or sometimes **methods**).

To illustrate, suppose we define a function that receives a parameter of type `Temperature`:

```
void DoSomething(Temperature Temp)
{
    // ... do something using parameter Temp ...
}
```

Then in a call to this function,

```
DoSomething(TempVar);
```

not only are the data members (**Degrees_** and **Scale_**) of **TempVar** passed to **DoSomething()**, but all its member functions (such as **operator=**) are also passed and can be used within **DoSomething()** without having to be redeclared.

Class Structure and Design

Every class has two parts:

- The **public** portion of the class, consisting of those members (data or functions) that are accessible outside of the class
- The **private** portion of the class, consisting of those members (data or functions) that can be accessed only within the class

Typically, all data members are declared in the private portion of the class and the operations on the class are declared in the public section.

The data members of a class are kept private because over the years, people have found that **maintenance** of a real-world software system often requires modification of the way that one or more of the system's objects are modeled. Now, suppose that

A program uses a class in which the data members are public;
The program has access to the data members of that class; and
Maintenance of the class requires that its data members be modified.

Because the program accesses the data members of the class, it *depends on* those particular data members. Thus, when those data members are modified, the program must also be modified. This means that the time to maintain the system is the sum of the time to modify the object and the time to modify the programs that access its data members.

By contrast, if all the data members of a class are concealed in the private section, then programs are forced to interact with a class object through its public member functions. The set of public member functions can thus be thought of as an **interface** between programs and the class. As long as this interface remains stable, any program that uses the class solely through the interface need not be modified, even if the private part of the class (the data members) is modified extensively. This means that the time to maintain such a system is only the time to modify the class. That, in turn, means that such systems can be maintained more easily, which saves time and money.

The keyword **public:** is used to mark the end of the declarations of private members of a class and the beginning of the declarations of the public members. The most common form of a class is thus

```
class ClassName
{
    PrivateDeclarationList

public:

    PublicDeclarationList
};
```

where ***PrivateDeclarationList*** contains the declarations of the data members of the class and any class member functions that are not to be part of its interface, and ***PublicDeclarationList*** contains the declarations of the class member functions that make up its interface. Thus, we would partition the class **Temperature** into a private section and a public section by inserting the keyword **public:**, as shown in Figure 11.5.

FIGURE 11.5   The sections of class **Temperature**.

```
class Temperature
{
//****************** data members -- PRIVATE **********************
    double
        Degrees_;
    char
        Scale_;

public:
//***************** member functions -- PUBLIC ********************

        .
        .
        .


    /*********** Assignment *****************************************

        Receive: The Temperature object Temp being assigned
        Return:  The Temperature object containing this function,
                 its members as copies of those of Temp
        -------------------------------------------------------------*/

    Temperature& operator=(const Temperature& Temp);

        .
        .
        .

};
```

The members **Degrees_** and **Scale_** are private and are, therefore, accessible only to the member functions of the class. The member functions such as **operator=** are public and so can be used outside of the class.

Although most of our classes will have this structure, a class may have multiple public and private sections:

Class Declaration Statement

Form

```
class ClassName
{
    PrivatePart₁
    PublicPart₁
    PrivatePart₂
    PublicPart₂
        .
        .
        .
    PrivatePartₙ
    PublicPartₙ
```

where:

ClassName is an identifier naming the class;

each *PrivatePart₁* consists of the keyword **private:** (optional for the first) and a list of declarations of members of the class; and

each *PublicPart₁* consists of the keyword **public:** and a list of declarations of members of the class.

Purpose

Define a new data type *ClassName*, which is a class consisting of the specified private parts and public parts. Each member (data or function) of each private part is accessible only within the class. Each member (data or function) of each public part is accessible outside the class.

As we have seen before, the public members of a class can be accessed using **dot notation:**

ObjectName.PublicMemberName

For example, the function **get()** is a public member of class **istream** objects, so that

```
cin.get(Ch);
```

calls the **get()** member function stored within the object **cin**.

Selecting Member Functions

One of the most difficult parts of building a good class is designing its interface—identifying the operations that are needed by objects of the class. The reason is that these operations vary with the kind of object being defined. For example, if we try to anticipate what operations might be useful for an object of type **Temperature**, we might identify

- The assignment operator (=);
- Two *extraction* operations, **Degrees()** and **Scale()**, to retrieve the values of the data members **Degrees_** and **Scale_**, respectively;[3]
- Conversion functions **Fahrenheit()** and **Celsius()** that return the equivalent **Temperature** in the indicated scale;
- The I/O operators (<< and >>); and
- The relational operators (==, !=, <, <=, >, and >=).

In addition to these, there is a special member called the **class constructor** that is used to initialize a class object when it is declared. In the remainder of this section, we complete the class **Temperature** by constructing these functions.

Declaring and Defining Member Functions

Once we have identified the operations a class is to provide, we must declare and define those operations as functions. Usually, member functions are declared in much the same manner as other functions, except that their declarations occur within the class rather than outside of it.[4]

However, the definitions of member functions are slightly different from other function definitions in that the name of the function must be **qualified** with the name of the class of which the function is a member. This qualification is accomplished by preceding the function name with the class name and the **scope operator ::**, giving the general form

```
ReturnType ClassName::FunctionName( ParameterDeclarationList )
{
    StatementList
}
```

As an example, consider the problem of assigning a **Temperature** value to a **Temperature** object. Figure 11.6 gives a definition of the function **operator=** that implements the assignment operation for **Temperature** objects. This definition is stored in the implementation file of the library **Temperature**:

---

[3] To expand upon an earlier footnote, we append underscores to the names of data members (such as **Scale_**) so that extraction functions (like **Scale()**) can be used without generating a name conflict.

[4] If a function is *defined* (instead of *declared*) within the class, the C++ compiler treats it as an **inline** function, as discussed in Section 7.6.

FIGURE 11.6 Defining assignment for class **Temperature**.

```
/*-----------------------------------------------------------------
 This function performs the assignment operation.

   Receive: The Temperature object Temp being assigned
   Return:  The Temperature object containing this function,
            its members as copies of those of Temp
 ---------------------------------------------------------------*/

Temperature& Temperature::operator=(const Temperature& Temp)
{
   Degrees_ = Temp.Degrees_;
   Scale_   = Temp.Scale_;

   return *this;            // return this Temperature object
}
```

In constructing this function, there are a number of issues to address:

1. Since **operator=** is being defined as a member function of class **Temperature**, its name must be qualified with the name of the class and the scope operator, as described earlier:

   Temperature& Temperature:: operator=(const Temperature& Temp)

2. We could declare **Temp** as a value parameter, but then each call to this function would spend time copying the members of the argument into the members of parameter **Temp**. We can avoid this by defining **Temp** as a *reference* parameter,

   Temperature& Temperature::operator=(const Temperature& Temp)

   rather than a value parameter. But this opens the possibility of accidently altering the value of **Temp** within the body of the function **operator=**. To guard against this, **Temp** is declared as a *constant reference* parameter:

   Temperature& Temperature::operator=(const Temperature& Temp)

   This allows the compiler to generate an error if the function attempts to change the value of **Temp**.

3. Similarly, we could make **Temperature** the return type of the function, but then whenever the function returns, time will be wasted copying the members of the return value. By convention, this is avoided by making the return type a *reference* to a **Temperature** object,

   Temperature& Temperature::operator=(const Temperature& Temp)

   rather than a **Temperature** object.

4. The final problem is determining what value the function should return in order to permit assignments to be chained together. Since assignment is right-associative, a statement such as

   TempVar1 = TempVar2 = TempVar3 = TempVar4;

is evaluated as

```
TempVar1 = (TempVar2 = (TempVar3 = TempVar4));
```

so the value returned by the rightmost = should be the value of **TempVar3**, and the value returned by the middle = should be the value of **TempVar2**. This implies that the return value of an assignment operation should be the **Temperature** object to which a value is being assigned.

To access a class object, every member function of a class has access to a (hidden) named constant whose name is **this** and whose value is the address of that class object. For example, if the **Temperature** object named **TempVar1** is stored at address **0x24**, then the value of **this** is **0x24** within the member functions of **TempVar1**; and if another **Temperature** object named **TempVar2** is stored at address **0x32**, then the value of **this** is **0x32** within the member functions of **TempVar2**. We might visualize this as follows:

TempVar1

Degrees_		0x24
Scale_		
	⋮	
this	0x24	

TempVar2

Degrees_		0x32
Scale_		
	⋮	
this	0x32	

The value of **this** is the same in all member functions for a particular object but is different in different objects.

> The **dereferencing operator** (∗) is used to access the object stored at a given address. When ∗ is applied as a prefix operator to a variable whose value is the address of an object (such as **this**), *the object at that address is accessed.*

Thus, in the preceding example, the expression ∗**this** within a member function of **TempVar1** refers to **TempVar1**, whereas the expression ∗**this** within a member function of **TempVar2** refers to **TempVar2**. The constant **this** can thus be used to return the object to which a member function refers, since execution of the statement

```
return *this;
```

within a member function causes the function to return the class object containing that function.

To illustrate how the function **operator=** executes, consider the chained assignment statement given earlier:

```
TempVar1 = TempVar2 = TempVar3 = TempVar4;
```

This statement is executed as

```
TempVar1.operator=(TempVar2.operator=(TempVar3.operator=(TempVar4)));
```

so that the following actions are taken:

1. The `operator=` in `TempVar3` assigns its `Degrees_` and `Scale_` members the values of the corresponding members of `TempVar4` and returns a reference to itself (the `Temperature` object `TempVar3`).
2. That return value is passed as an argument to the `operator=` in `TempVar2`, which assigns its `Degrees_` and `Scale_` members the values of the corresponding members of `TempVar3` and returns a reference to itself (`TempVar2`).
3. That return value is passed as an argument to the `operator=` in `TempVar1`, which assigns its `Degrees_` and `Scale_` members the values of the corresponding members of `TempVar2` and returns a reference to itself, `TempVar1`, which is then discarded by the semicolon.

We complete our work on the assignment operator by storing its declaration in the public portion of class `Temperature` (see Figure 11.3).

The Class Constructor

In Section 7.7, we saw that the construction of an object involves two actions:

1. The allocation of memory for the object
2. The (optional) initialization of the object

As the name implies, a **constructor** is a function that is used to construct an object. In C++, the name of a constructor is easy to remember:

> *The name of a C++ constructor function is always the same as the name of the class.*

Thus, in our example, since the name of the class is `Temperature`, its constructor functions must be named `Temperature()`.

One of the places an object can be constructed is at its declaration. For example, the declaration

```
double
   R1;
```

constructs a real object named `R1` without initializing it, whereas the declaration

```
char
   Letter = 'A';
```

constructs a character object named `Letter` and initializes it to the character `'A'`. The problem is that although the types `double` and `char` are predefined for the

C++ compiler, the new type **Temperature** is not, and the compiler may not take the right actions with a declaration such as

```
Temperature
   TempVar;
```

To specify exactly what actions are to be taken when an object of a particular class is declared, one or more constructor functions, called **class constructors,** can be written.

> *The primary role of a class constructor is to initialize each of the data members of the class with values (either default or provided in the declaration).*

For example, we might define the class constructor shown in Figure 11.7 and store this definition in the implementation file of library **Temperature**.

 FIGURE 11.7 Defining a **Temperature** class constructor.

```
/*********** Class Constructor **********************************

   Precondition:   A Temperature object has been declared.
   Receive:        The (optional) initialization values:
                      InitDegrees, for the Degrees (a double,
                         default 0.0), and
                      InitScale, for the Scale (a char, default 'C')
   Postcondition:  The declared Temperature object has
                      its Degrees member initialized to InitDegrees
                      and its Scale member initialized to InitScale
                      (provided InitScale is 'C', 'c', 'F', or 'f').
--------------------------------------------------------------*/

#include <stdlib.h>            // provides exit()

Temperature::Temperature(double InitDegrees, char InitScale)
{
   Degrees_ = InitDegrees;

   switch (InitScale)
   {
      case 'C': case 'c':   // InitScale must represent one of
      case 'F': case 'f':   //    Celsius or Fahrenheit, to be valid
            Scale_ = InitScale;
            break;
      default:
            cerr << "\n*** Illegal scale: " << InitScale
                 << " received by Temperature constructor!\n";
            exit (-1);
   }
}
```

Note that the class constructor is a member function, and so its name must be qualified with the name of its class (**Temperature::Temperature**), as described previously. Note also that a **switch** statement is used to guard against receiving an invalid scale through parameter **InitScale**. This is necessary because a programmer might erroneously pass some character other than ′**C**′, ′**c**′, ′**F**′, or ′**f**′ as an argument for **InitScale**.

Note finally that the documentation of this function describes the behavior of a constructor using a **precondition,** which describes what condition(s) must be true before the function is called, and a **postcondition,** which describes what condition(s) must be true when the function terminates. We use preconditions and postconditions to describe the behavior of constructor functions, because such functions have no return type or value.

As shown in Figure 11.3, we complete the class constructor by declaring this function in the public section of class **Temperature** (in the header file **Temperature.h**), with the default values of **0.0** and ′**C**′ for parameters **InitDegrees** and **InitScale**, respectively:

```
Temperature(double InitDegrees  = 0.0, InitScale = 'C');
```

A programmer can then declare a **Temperature** object such as **TempVar** as follows:

```
#include "Temperature.h"
     .
     .
     .
Temperature
   TempVar(212.0, 'F');
```

When this statement is encountered,

1. The function call **Temperature::Temperature(212.0, ′F′)** is executed;
2. The arguments **212.0** and ′**F**′ are copied into parameters **InitDegrees** and **InitScale**, respectively; and
3. The body of **Temperature::Temperature()** executes, initializing the **Degrees_** and **Scale_** data members of **TempVar** to the values of **InitDegrees** and **InitScale**, respectively:

TempVar

Degrees_	212.0
Scale_	′F′

By contrast, if the programmer should declare

```
Temperature
   TempVar;
```

then

1. The function **Temperature::Temperature()** is called with no arguments;
2. The default arguments **0.0** and ′**C**′ are given to parameters **InitDegrees** and **InitScale**, respectively; and

3. The body of `Temperature::Temperature()` executes, initializing the `Degrees_` and `Scale_` data members of `TempVar` to the values of `InitDegrees` and `InitScale`, respectively:

TempVar

Degrees_	0.0
Scale_	'C'

Designing a constructor to perform **default initialization** is a good practice to follow, because it ensures that a class object always contains a valid value, even if the programmer neglects to initialize the object. It also provides the user of the class with considerable flexibility. For example, the declaration

```
Temperature
   TempVar(100.0);
```

is a simple way to initialize **Temperature** to the value 100.0° C, since the default argument of `'C'` is used as the value for parameter **InitScale** when the constructor executes.

In summary, the constructor for a class is called whenever an object of that class is declared and should perform any actions the designer of the class wishes to be taken at that point. As a programming convention, we list all class constructors first in the public section of the class, so that they can be found easily.

Other Member Functions

We now consider the remaining members of class **Temperature**.

Data-Extraction Functions. Given what we now know, the construction of functions to extract the individual data members of a **Temperature** object is straightforward. It is common practice to store the definitions of such simple functions in the class declaration itself rather than separating the definition of the function from its declaration. This is illustrated by the extraction functions **Degrees** and **Scale** in Figure 11.8.[5]

FIGURE 11.8 The class **Temperature** extractor functions.

```
class Temperature
{
   //********** data members **********
   double
      Degrees_;
   char
      Scale_;

public:
   //******** member functions ********
      .
      .
      .
```

---

[5] Note: To save space, we will omit some of the documentation in preliminary versions of classes.

FIGURE 11.8   The class **Temperature** extractor functions. (cont.)

```
/*********** Degrees Extraction ****************************/

    Return:   The value stored in the Degrees_ member of the
              Temperature object containing this function
-----------------------------------------------------------*/

double Degrees(void) const {return Degrees_;}

/*********** Scale Extraction ******************************/

    Return:   The value stored in the Scale_ member of the
              Temperature object containing this function
-----------------------------------------------------------*/

char Scale(void) const {return Scale_;}
    .
    .
    .
};
```

The effect of such a definition is that the member functions are treated as **inline** functions, as discussed in Section 7.6. In addition to the definition of these functions in the class body, these functions illustrate another new characteristic—each has the keyword **const** following its parameter list:

```
double Degrees(void) const  {return Degrees_;}

char Scale(void) const  {return Scale_;}
```

The difference between these member functions and those we have seen previously is that these member functions access, but *should not modify,* the data members of the class. This raises a potential problem: If we were to mistakenly modify the value of one of the members **Degree_** or **Scale_** in either of these functions, how would the compiler detect such a mistake?

The answer is that it cannot, unless the following rule is observed:

> *Any member function that is not to modify the data members of a class should be declared as a* **const** *function by placing the keyword* **const** *after its parameter list.*

In this way, a program informs the compiler that although the member function has access to the members of the class, it may not modify those members.

The Conversion Functions.   The final member function that we present is **Fahrenheit()**, a member function that will return the Fahrenheit **Temperature** equivalent to the **Temperature** value stored in the object containing this function. We might define this function in the implementation file of library **Temperature**, as shown in Figure 11.9.

FIGURE 11.9 Defining function **Fahrenheit()**.

```
/*-------------------------------------------------------------------
  This function returns the Fahrenheit equivalent of the
    Temperature stored within the object containing this function.

    Return: The Fahrenheit equivalent of the value of this object,
            if the value of this object is a Celsius Temperature,
            the value of this object, otherwise
  ----------------------------------------------------------------*/

Temperature Temperature::Fahrenheit(void) const
{
    switch (Scale_)
    {
      case 'f': case 'F':
         return *this;
      case 'c': case 'C':
         return Temperature(Degrees_ * 1.8 + 32.0, 'F');
      default:
         cerr << "\n*** Fahrenheit: Temperature has invalid scale of "
             << Scale_ << ".\n\n";
         exit(-1);
    }
}
```

Here, we see that if **TempVar** is a Celsius **Temperature**, then the expression

```
TempVar.Fahrenheit();
```

will execute the function **Fahrenheit()** that is a member of **TempVar**. Since **TempVar** is a Celsius **Temperature**, **Fahrenheit()** will construct and return the equivalent Fahrenheit **Temperature**. By contrast, if **TempVar** is a Fahrenheit **Temperature**, then the value of this expression is simply the value of **TempVar**.

To complete function **Fahrenheit()**, we must declare it in class **Temperature**, as shown in Figure 11.3. The other conversion operation **Celsius()** is similar to **Fahrenheit()** and is left as an exercise.

Friend Functions

The remaining operators that we want to include in the class **Temperature** are the I/O operators and the relational operators. As we will see, including these requires a mechanism for making the private members of a class accessible to objects outside the class. C++ allows a class to name certain functions as *friend functions* to provide them with this access privilege.

I/O Operators. The next two operations to be implemented for the class **Temperature** are input and output. As usual, we will implement these operations by overloading the **>>** and **<<** operators. However, if we examine typical I/O statements

    `cin >> TempVar;`

and

    `cout << TempVar;`

we see that there is a difficulty. Both **<<** and **>>** are binary operators, but neither of their left operands is a **Temperature** object. This means that we cannot make **<<** or **>>** a member function of **Temperature**, because when **operatorΔ** is a member function for some binary operator Δ, an expression of the form

    Left Δ *Right*

(where *Left* and *Right* are class objects) is evaluated as the function call

    Left.operatorΔ(*Right*)

That is, the **operatorΔ** member function in the left operand *Left* is called, not the **operatorΔ** function in the right operand *Right*. This means that an expression such as

    `cin >> TempVar;`

will call the **operator>>** defined as a member of **cin**, not a definition of **operator>>** defined as a member function of **TempVar**.

    The correct way to define these functions is to overload the **<<** and **>>** operators, as shown in Figure 11.10.

FIGURE 11.10 Overloading the I/O operators.

```
/*-------------------------------------------------------------------
 This function outputs a Temperature value.

    Receive: An ostream reference, Out
             A Temperature object, Temp
    Output:  The Degrees_ and Scale_ members of Temp, in readable
             format
    Return:  Out (for chaining)
-------------------------------------------------------------------*/

ostream& operator<<(ostream& Out, const Temperature& Temp)
{
   Out << Temp.Degrees_;
```

FIGURE 11.10   Overloading the I/O operators. (cont.)

```
   switch (Temp.Scale_)
   {
      case 'C': case 'c':
         Out << " C";
         break;
      case 'F': case 'f':
         Out << " F";
         break;
      default:
         cerr << "\n*** << received Temperature with invalid scale "
              << T.Scale_ << ".\n\n";
         exit (-1);
   }

   return Out;                    // to allow << chaining
}
```

```
/*------------------------------------------------------------------
 This function inputs a Temperature value.

    Receive: An istream reference, In
             A Temperature object, Temp
    Input:   A real value, to be stored in the Degrees_ member
               of Temp,
             A char value, to be stored in the Scale_ member
               of Temp
    Return:  Temp, containing the input values
             In (for chaining).
 -----------------------------------------------------------------*/

#include <limits.h>              // provides INT_MAX

istream& operator>>(istream& In, Temperature& Temp)
{
   Boolean
      Valid;                     // to check for valid input

   In >> Temp.Degrees_;          // get the degrees

   do                            // loop
   {
      In >> Temp.Scale_;         //    get the scale

      switch (Temp.Scale_)       //    check that it's valid
      {
         case 'C': case 'c':
         case 'F': case 'f':
            Valid = True;
            break;
```

FIGURE 11.10 Overloading the I/O operators. (cont.)

```
        default:
            cerr << "\n*** >> received invalid scale " << Temp.Scale_
                << " from keyboard.\n\n";
            Valid = False;
        }
        In.clear();                    // clear state flags
        In.ignore(INT_MAX, '\n');  // ignore remainder of line
    }
    while Valid;
    return In;
}
```

However, these functions cannot be successfully compiled because they are not member functions; and nonmember functions are not permitted to access the private members (e.g., **Degrees_** and **Scale_**) of a class object.

To solve this problem, C++ provides a mechanism whereby a class can grant a nonmember function access to the private members in the class. This is done by naming that function as a **friend function** when it is declared within the class by prefacing that declaration with the keyword **friend**. Figure 11.3 illustrates this for the **operator<<** and **operator>>** functions in class **Temperature**:

```
friend  ostream& operator<<(ostream& Out, const Temperature& Temp);
    .
    .
    .
friend  istream& operator>>(istream& In, Temperature& Temp);
```

The declarations tell the C++ compiler that although **<<** and **>>** applied to a **Temperature** object are not member functions, they are nevertheless permitted to access the private members of a **Temperature** object.

The friend mechanism thus permits *the designer of the class* to allow nonmember functions to have access to the private portion of the class while still maintaining its security. *Users of the class* are prohibited from writing functions that can access its private portion unless they are able to alter the class declaration itself.

The Relational Operators. We were forced to use the friend mechanism for I/O operators, because the left operands of I/O expressions are not **Temperature** objects. The friend mechanism can also be used advantageously for most of the operations that take two **Temperature** operands. For example, Figure 11.11 presents definitions of the relational operators for class **Temperature**, as they would appear in the library's implementation file.[6]

---

[6] These functions are sufficiently simple that they may instead be defined within the class declaration, as we did with the extractor functions.

FIGURE 11.11 Defining **Temperature** relational operators.

```
/*------------------------------------------------------------------
  This function defines the Temperature equality operation.

     Receive: Two Temperature objects Temp1 and Temp2
     Return:  True if and only if corresponding data members of
                 Temp1 and Temp2 are the same
  ------------------------------------------------------------------*/

Boolean operator== (const Temperature& Temp1,
                    const Temperature& Temp2)
{
   return ((Temp1.Degrees_ == Temp2.Degrees_) &&
           (Temp1.Scale_ == Temp2.Scale_));
}


/*------------------------------------------------------------------
  This function defines the inequality Temperature operation.

     Receive: Two Temperature objects named Temp1 and Temp2
     Return:  True if and only if at least one data member of
                 Temp1 is different from the corresponding data
                 member of Temp2
  ------------------------------------------------------------------*/

Boolean operator!= (const Temperature& Temp1,
                    const Temperature& Temp2)
{
   return ((Temp1.Degrees_ != Temp2.Degrees_) ||
           (Temp1.Scale_ != Temp2.Scale_));
}

/*------------------------------------------------------------------
  This function defines the less than operation on a Temperature
  object.

     Receive: Two Temperature objects named Temp1 and Temp2
     Return:  True, if and only if the Degrees_ member of Temp1
                 is less than the Degrees_ member of Temp2
                 (and their Scale_ members are equal)
  ------------------------------------------------------------------*/

Boolean operator< (const Temperature& Temp1,
                   const Temperature& Temp2)
{
   return (Temp1.Degrees_ < Temp2.Degrees_) &&
          (Temp1.Scale_ == Temp2.Scale_);
}
   // ... definitions of remaining relational operators >, <=, >=
```

The definitions of the remaining relational operators are similar to these and are left as exercises.

These operators can be declared as friend functions in the class `Temperature` as shown in Figure 11.3. A program using this class can then construct expressions such as

```
Temperature
   Temp1,
   Temp2,
   MinTemp;                   // some temperatures
       .
       .
       .
   if (Temp1 < Temp2)
      MinTemp = Temp1;
```

In particular, the expression

```
Temp1 < Temp2
```

is equivalent to the function call

```
operator<(Temp1, Temp2)
```

This is a general pattern for binary friend operations on objects of the same class: An expression of the form

```
Object1 Δ Object2
```

where Δ is a binary operator, is actually evaluated as

```
operatorΔ(Object1, Object2)
```

Now suppose that a program that uses class `Temperature` contains the statements

```
if (Temp1 < 0.0)
   cout << "\nBrrr! It's cold out there!\n";
```

The expression

```
Temp1 < 0.0
```

will be evaluated as

```
operator<(Temp1, 0.0)
```

and `operator<` is the friend function from class `Temperature`. Now here is the crucial point: When `operator<` receives the real argument `0.0`, the corresponding parameter `Temp2` is a `Temperature` object that must be constructed, and so

1. The class constructor `Temperature(0.0)` is called;

2. The argument **0.0** is copied into the constructor's parameter **InitDegrees** (while its parameter **InitScale** receives its default value **'C'**; and
3. The body of the constructor executes and constructs a **Temperature** object whose value is 0° C.

The friend function **operator<** can then compare **Temp1** with this newly constructed **Temperature** object. All this happens automatically, without any further work by the programmer. This illustrates the power of constructors, especially those that have been carefully designed with default arguments.

Friends Versus Members. It is worth noting that any of the operations that we have implemented on two **Temperature** values could have been implemented as member functions. For example, we could have defined the equality operation as

```
Boolean Temperature::operator==(const Temperature& Temp) const
{
    return (Degrees_ == Temp.Degrees_) && (Scale_ == Temp.Scale_);
}
```

and this version of **operator==** could also have been used to compare two **Temperature** objects (once we declare this function within **Temperature** as a member rather than as a friend):

```
Boolean operator==(const Temperature& Temp) const;
```

This raises the important question: When should an operation be implemented as a member function, and when should it be implemented as a friend? Three guidelines are as follows:

- Some operators, such as assignment (**=**), must be implemented as member functions.[7]
- If the left operand of the operator *must* be of a type different from the class, then a friend function *must* be used. The I/O operators (**<<** and **>>**) are examples.
- If the left operand may or may not be of a type different from the class, then a friend function is usually the best choice. To see why, consider the expression

```
0.0 < Temp1
```

If **operator<** is implemented as a friend function, then this is evaluated as

```
operator<(0.0, Temp1)
```

and so the **0.0** will pass to parameter **Temp1** of **operator<**, whose constructor will convert the **0.0** into a **Temperature** value, as described before. By contrast, if **operator<** is implemented as a member function, then the compiler is unable to evaluate this expression as

```
(0.0).operator<(Temp1)
```

(since **0.0** is not a class object, it cannot contain a definition of **operator<**), and so a compilation error will result.

---

[7] The others are subscript **[]**, call **()**, and member selection **->** (see Chapter 14).

Conditional Compilation

The code presented in Figure 11.3 contains one other significant new feature: The class is "wrapped" within the odd-looking lines

```
#ifndef TEMPERATURE
#define TEMPERATURE
     .
     .
     .
#endif
```

Whenever a program stored in a file is compiled, it is first examined by a special program called the **preprocessor,** which scans through the file doing some rudimentary analysis before the file is passed on to the compiler itself. For example, the preprocessor strips all comments out of the program so that the compiler need not spend time finding them and can instead devote its time to translation.

Another task performed by the preprocessor is to process all **preprocessor directives,** such as

```
#include FileName
```

When it encounters this directive, the preprocessor finds the file named *FileName* and inserts it at that point in the program. All lines that begin with a # character are preprocessor directives. For example,

```
#define Symbol
```

is a directive that defines the identifier *Symbol*.[8] The directive

```
#ifndef Symbol
```

tests to see whether the identifier *Symbol* has been defined. If *Symbol* has not been defined, processing proceeds as normal. If it has been defined, then all ensuing code is stripped (just like a comment) until another directive beginning with **#elif**, **#else**, or **#endif** is encountered. Thus, whenever the preprocessor encounters these directives in Figure 11.3 for the *first time,* the symbol **TEMPERATURE** is undefined, and so processing proceeds as normal to the second directive, which defines **TEMPERATURE**. Processing then continues as normal to the **#endif** and beyond.

Now, suppose that the preprocessor somehow encounters this class declaration again. Once again, the directive

```
#ifndef TEMPERATURE
```

is encountered, but this time the symbol **TEMPERATURE** has been defined. As a result, all code between the **#ifndef** directive and the **#endif** directive is stripped by the preprocessor instead of being passed on to the compiler.

---

[8] More precisely, the preprocessor associates the value 1 (true) with *Symbol* from this point onward.

The reason for including these directives is that C++ does not allow redundant definitions within the same file, and it is surprisingly easy for a class to be defined twice, especially when we are designing objects that are reusable. To see how this can happen, consider the **iostream** library. We inserted its header file in the program in Figure 11.1, but we also inserted that header file in the header file of class **Temperature**. This means that if the declarations in the **iostream** library were not "wrapped" in preprocessor directives to prevent the file from being processed more than once, an error like

```
In included file <iostream.h>: Redeclaration of class ...
```

would be generated when the program is compiled. The net effect of using the **#ifndef** and **#endif** directives is thus to ensure that the compiler processes a class only once, regardless of how many times the header file (and therefore the class) is inserted in a program.[9]

Using Class Temperature

Once the implementation file containing the definitions of all the members functions for the class **Temperature** has been developed, it can be used in any program to model temperatures. As we saw in Figure 11.2, the statement

```
Temperature
    TempVar;
```

uses the constructor for class **Temperature**; the statement

```
cin >> TempVar;
```

uses the definition of the friend function **operator>>**; the expression

```
TempVar.Fahrenheit()
```

uses the definition of the member function **Fahrenheit()**, which returns the Fahrenheit equivalent of **TempVar**; and, since this is a **Temperature** value, the expression

```
cout << TempVar.Fahrenheit()
```

uses the definition of the friend function **operator<<** from class **Temperature**.

---

[9] Some C++ implementations (e.g., Symantec C++) support the use of the directive

```
#pragma once
```

which, when placed at the beginning of a header file, guarantees that that header file will be inserted only once. Using this directive, however, produces programs that are not as easily ported from one machine to another.

Exercises

1. Add (or modify) functions (member or friend) to class **Temperature** to

   (a) Allow a **Temperature** value to be input from a file that has been opened for input.
   (b) Allow a **Temperature** value to be output to a file that has been opened for output.
   (c) Allow a **Temperature** value to be increased by a given amount.
   (d) Allow a **Temperature** value to be decreased by a given amount.
   (e) Model temperatures from the Kelvin scale.

2. Modify the less than relational operator in class **Temperature** to allow comparison of two **Temperature** values whose scales are different.

3. For each of the following, define the private portion of a class to model the given item.

   (a) A card in a deck of playing cards
   (b) Time measured in hours, minutes, and seconds
   (c) A telephone number as area code, local exchange, and number
   (d) Position of a checker on a board
   (e) A point (x, y) in a Cartesian coordinate system
   (f) A point (r, θ) in a polar coordinate system

4. Completely implement a class for one of the objects in Exercise 2, supplying a complete set of operations for the class.

5. For each of the following, develop a class for the given information, and then write operations appropriate for an object of that type.

   (a) Information about a person: name, birthday, age, gender, social security number, height, weight, hair color, eye color, and marital status
   (b) Statistics about a baseball player: name, age, birthdate, position (e.g., pitcher, catcher, infielder, outfielder), batting average, stolen bases
   (c) Weather statistics: date; city and state, province, or country; time of day; temperature; barometric pressure; weather conditions (e.g., clear skies, partly cloudy, cloudy, stormy)

6. The data files **StudentFile**, **InventoryFile**, and **UsersFile** are described in Appendix F. Write appropriate class declarations to describe the information in these files.

11.2 Enumerations, Classes, and Structs

As we saw in Section 10.1, the arithmetic operators (including increment and decrement) cannot be applied to an enumeration. For example, if we were to write

```
#include "Day.h"

for (Day Today = Monday; Today <= Friday; Today++)
   cout << Today << endl;
```

then the expression **Today++** would cause a compilation error. In this section, we show how a class can be used to solve this problem.

Replacing an Enumeration with a Class

We have seen that most operators can be overloaded for classes, and this feature provides a solution to the problem of performing arithmetic operations on enumerations. We replace the enumeration type **Day** with a class **Day** containing an enumeration data member and then overload whatever (numeric) operators we want to use for a (class) **Day** object.

Figure 11.12 gives the header file for such a class. It begins with a declaration of the enumeration type **DayName**, in which the values of the enumeration are listed. The class named **Day** then follows, in which a private data member named **DayValue** of type **DayName** and the various operations we wish to perform on **Day** values are declared.

 FIGURE 11.12   Redeclaring **Day** as a class.

```
/* This file contains the interface for class Day.

   NOTE:   Because of similarities to other classes, some
           documentation has been omitted to save pages.
           See the data disk for full documentation.
--------------------------------------------------------------------*/

#include <iostream.h>

#include "Boolean.h"

#ifndef DAY
#define DAY

enum DayName { DayUnderflow = -1,                  // too-low error
               Sunday, Monday, Tuesday, Wednesday,// 0-3
               Thursday, Friday, Saturday,         // 4-6
               NumberOfDays,                       // 7
               DayOverflow = 7};                   // too-high error
class Day
{
// -- the private section --
/********** the data member **********/

DayName
  DayValue_;
```

FIGURE 11.12 Redeclaring **Day** as a class. (cont.)

```
public:
/********** member functions **********/
   /*----- Class constructor -----
      To initialize a declaration of a Day object.

      Receive: DayName value InitDay (default value of Sunday)
      Return:  This Day object with its data member initialized
               to InitDay
      --------------------------------------------------------------*/

   Day(DayName InitDay = Sunday) {DayValue_ = InitDay;}

   /*----- Data member extractor ----- . . . */
   DayName DayValue(void) const {return DayValue_;}

   /*----- Assignment ----- . . . */
   Day& operator=(const Day& DayExp);

   /*----- In-/De-crement -----
      Operations that (destructively) increment/decrement
      a Day object . . . */

   Day operator++(void);                   // prefix increment
   Day operator++(int);                    // postfix increment
   Day operator--(void);                   // prefix decrement
   Day operator--(int);                    // postfix decrement

   /*----- Suc-/Prede-cessor -----
      Functions that find the successor/predecessor of
      a Day object . . . */

   Day Next(void) const;                   // next day (wraps)
   Day Previous(void) const;               // previous day (wraps)

   /*----- Relational Operators ----- . . . */

   friend Boolean operator==(               // equality
                        const Day& LeftDay,
                        const Day& RightDay);
   friend Boolean operator!=(               // inequality
                        const Day& LeftDay,
                        const Day& RightDay);
   friend Boolean operator<(                // less than
                        const Day& LeftDay,
                        const Day& RightDay);
   friend Boolean operator<=(               // less or equal
                        const Day& LeftDay,
                        const Day& RightDay);
   friend Boolean operator>(                // greater than
                        const Day& LeftDay,
                        const Day& RightDay);
```

FIGURE 11.12 Redeclaring **Day** as a class. (cont.)

```
    friend Boolean operator>=(                        // greater or equal
                           const Day& LeftDay,
                           const Day& RightDay);

    /*----- Input/Output ----- . . . */
    /* Interactive */
    friend ostream& operator<< (ostream& Out, const Day& DayOut);
    friend istream& operator>> (istream& In, Day& DayIn);

    /* File */
    friend fstream& operator<< (fstream& Out, const Day& DayOut);
    friend fstream& operator>> (fstream& In, Day& DayIn);

};
#endif
```

Several things should be noted about this class declaration:

- The class constructor takes a **DayName** argument (with default value of **Sunday**) and initializes the **DayValue** member to that argument. Thus, a declaration such as

  ```
  Day
      Today,
      Tomorrow(Monday);
  ```

  will autoinitialize **Today** to **Sunday** and explicitly initialize **Tomorrow** to **Monday**.
- The assignment, increment, and decrement member functions each change the object of which they are members, and so they are not declared as **const** functions.
- The argument to the assignment function is a class object, and so we pass it as a constant reference, rather than as a value parameter.
- The **Next()** and **Previous()** functions do not change the object of which they are members (see their implementations that follow), and so they are declared as **const** functions.
- The relational operators might be used to compare two **Day** values,

  ```
  if (Today == Tomorrow)
  ```

  or a **Day** value and a **DayName** value:

  ```
  if ((Today == Monday) || (Monday == Tomorrow))
  ```

  Since the left operand may or may not be a **Day** value, we declare these functions as friend, rather than member, functions. In each case, both their arguments are declared as constant reference parameters.

- The left operand of each of the I/O operators cannot be a **Day** value, and so they must be declared as friend functions, rather than members. The output function does not change its **Day** argument, and so a constant reference parameter is declared for that argument. The input function changes its **Day** argument, and so a reference parameter is declared for that argument.

Figure 11.13 gives a partial listing of the implementation file for class **Day**.

FIGURE 11.13 Partial implementation of class **Day**.

```
/* This file provides the implementation for class Day.

    ----------------------------------------------------------------*/

#include "Day.h"

         .
         .
         .

/* ---------------------------------------------------------------
    This function overloads the assignment operator for Day values.

    Receive: DayExp, the Day value being assigned
    Return:  The Day object with its data member set equal to
             the data member in DayExp.
    ----------------------------------------------------------------*/

Day& Day::operator=(const Day& DayExp)
{
    DayValue_ = DayExp.DayValue_;  // set DayValue_ member in this
                                   //   object to that in DayExp
    return *this;                  // return this object
}


/*---------------------------------------------------------------
    This function (destructively) prefix-increments a Day object.

    Return:  The Day object containing this function,
             with DayValue changed to the next value
    ----------------------------------------------------------------*/

Day Day::operator++(void)
{
  switch(DayValue_)                // change DayValue to its successor ...
  {
    case Sunday:
      DayValue_ = Monday;
      break;
    case Monday:
      DayValue_ = Tuesday;
      break;
```

FIGURE 11.13 Partial implementation of class **Day**. (cont.)

```
      case Tuesday:
        DayValue_ = Wednesday;
        break;
      case Wednesday:
        DayValue_ = Thursday;
        break;
      case Thursday:
        DayValue_ = Friday;
        break;
      case Friday:
        DayValue_ = Saturday;
        break;
      case Saturday:                   // unless it's the final valid DayName
        DayValue_ = DayOverflow;
        break;
      default:
        cerr << "*** ++: erroneous Day value received!\n";
    }
    return *this;
}


/*------------------------------------------------------------------
    This function (destructively) postfix-increments a Day object.

    Return:   The Day object containing this function,
              with DayValue changed to the next value
   --------------------------------------------------------------*/

Day Day::operator++(int)
{
    switch(DayValue_)                 // change DayValue to its successor ...
    {
      case Sunday:
        DayValue_ = Monday;
        return Sunday;
      case Monday:
        DayValue_ = Tuesday;
        return Monday;
      case Tuesday:
        DayValue_ = Wednesday;
        return Tuesday;
      case Wednesday:
        DayValue_ = Thursday;
        return Wednesday;
      case Thursday:
        DayValue_ = Friday;
        return Thursday;
      case Friday:
        DayValue_ = Saturday;
        return Friday;
```

FIGURE 11.13 Partial implementation of class **Day**. (cont.)

```
      case Saturday:              // unless it's the final valid DayName
        DayValue_ = DayOverflow;
        return Saturday;
      default:
        cerr << "*** ++: erroneous Day value received!\n";
        return DayOverflow;
    }
}


/*-----------------------------------------------------------------
    This function (nondestructively) returns the day after its
        Day object, wrapping around from Saturday to Sunday.

    Return:  The Day value that follows the value of this
             Day object
-----------------------------------------------------------*/
Day Day::Next(void) const
{
  switch(DayValue_)         // return the DayName that follows DayValue_
  {
    case Sunday:
      return Monday;
    case Monday:
      return Tuesday;
    case Tuesday:
      return Wednesday;
    case Wednesday:
      return Thursday;
    case Thursday:
      return Friday;
    case Friday:
      return Saturday;
    case Saturday:
      return Sunday;        // ...wrapping around for the last DayName
    default:
      cerr << "*** Next: erroneous Day value received!\n";
      return DayOverflow;
    }
}

// ... remaining definitions are left as exercises ...
```

Note that Figure 11.13 has two different definitions for the increment operator. The reason for this is that the increment operator can be used as either a prefix or a postfix operator. When **operator++** is declared and defined without parameters, as in the first definition,

```
    Day Day::operator++(void)
```

the C++ compiler associates that function with the *prefix* operation, so that a prefix increment expression

    ++DayVariable

will call the first function. By contrast, when the increment operator is defined with a single **int** parameter, as in the second definition,

    Day Day::operator++(int)

the C++ compiler associates that definition with the *postfix* operation, so that a postfix increment expression

    DayVariable++

will call the second function. Note that no **int** parameter is used by this second definition—its sole purpose is to allow the C++ compiler to distinguish between the two different definitions.

    Figure 11.14 presents a simple program to test the class **Day**.

  FIGURE 11.14   A program to test class **Day**.

```
/* This program tests class Day.

   Output: A simple Day-dependent message
   ----------------------------------------------------------------*/

#include <iostream.h>

#include "Day.h"

void Child(const Day&);

int main(void)
{
   for (Day D = Monday; D <= Saturday; D++)
      Child(D);

   Child(Sunday);

   return 0;
}
```

FIGURE 11.14   A program to test class **Day**. (cont.)

```
//-------------------------------------------------------------------

void Child(const Day& Birth)
{
   switch(Birth.DayValue())
   {
      case Sunday:
         cout << "But the child that is born on the Sabbath day\n"
              << "  is bonny and blithe, and good and gay.\n";
         break;
      case Monday:
         cout << Birth << "'s child is fair of face.\n";
         break;
      case Tuesday:
         cout << Birth << "'s child is full of grace.\n";
         break;
      case Wednesday:
         cout << Birth << "'s child is full of woe.\n";
         break;
      case Thursday:
         cout << Birth << "'s child has far to go.\n";
         break;
      case Friday:
         cout << Birth << "'s child is loving and giving.\n";
         break;
      case Saturday:
         cout << Birth << "'s child works hard for its living.\n"
         break;
      default:
         cerr << "*** Child: invalid Day value received: "
              << Birth << endl;
   }
}
```

Sample run:

```
Monday's child is fair of face.
Tuesday's child is full of grace.
Wednesday's child is full of woe.
Thursday's child has far to go.
Friday's child is loving and giving.
Saturday's child works hard for its living.
But the child that is born on the Sabbath day
   is bonny and blithe, and good and gay.
```

In the implementations of the **Day** member functions, note that **Next()** simply returns the next valid value without altering the **DayValue_** member. It is thus declared and defined as a **const** member function. By contrast, **operator++** is *destructive* in that it changes the value of the **DayValue_** member to the next valid value. Accordingly, **operator++** is not declared or defined as a **const** member.

Note also the difference in the behavior of the two functions. Suppose that the objects **Today** and **Tomorrow** have been declared and initialized as follows:

```
Day
    Today = Saturday,
    Tomorrow;
```

Then in the statement

```
Tomorrow = Today.Next();
```

the call to **Next()** returns the wraparound value **Sunday** (which is assigned to **Tomorrow**), leaving the value of **Today** unchanged. By contrast, in the statement

```
Tomorrow = Today++;
```

the increment operator changes the value of **Today** to **DayOverflow** (without wrapping around) and then returns **Saturday**, the original value of **Today**, so that the value assigned to **Tomorrow** is **Saturday**.

To see why this is useful, consider what would happen if we changed the for loop in Figure 11.14 as follows:

```
for (Day D = Monday; D <= Saturday; D = D.Next())
    Child(D);
```

Consider what happens at the end of the repetition when the value of **D** is **Saturday** (which is intended to be the final repetition). The assignment

```
D = D.Next()
```

will change the value of **D** to **Sunday**, which is less than **Saturday**, and so the loop will continue to execute, resulting in an infinite loop! By contrast, in the same repetition of the for loop in Figure 11.14, the increment operation

```
D++
```

changes the value of **D** from **Saturday** to **DayOverflow**, which is not less than or equal to **Saturday**, and so the loop terminates.

The C++ Struct

The class is just one of the mechanisms C++ provides to allow programmers to create their own types. Another mechanism is the **struct.** Like a class, it allows the programmer to make a new type in which data members, member functions, and friend functions are encapsulated. In fact, a struct is like a class, except that:

> *Whereas the members of a class are (by default) private unless they are explicitly made public, the members of a struct are (by default) public unless they are explicitly made private.*

Stated differently, a class usually has the form

```
class NewTypeName
{
    PrivateDeclarationList

public:

    PublicDeclarationList
};
```

but a struct typically has the form

```
struct NewTypeName
{
    PublicDeclarationList

private:

    PrivateDeclarationList
};
```

We could have used a struct instead of a class to declare the new type **Day**, as shown in Figure 11.15. The implementation file containing the definitions of the member and friend functions of struct **Day** would be exactly the same as that for the class **Day**.

 FIGURE 11.15   Redeclaring **Day** as a struct.

```
/* This file contains the interface for struct Day.

    NOTE:   Because of similarities to class Day, most documentation
            has been omitted to save pages. See the data disk for
            full documentation.
-------------------------------------------------------------------*/

#include <iostream.h>

#include "Boolean.h"

#ifndef DAY
#define DAY
```

FIGURE 11.15 Redeclaring **Day** as a struct. (cont.)

```
enum DayName {DayUnderflow = -1,                    // too-low error
              Sunday, Monday, Tuesday, Wednesday,// 0-3
              Thursday, Friday, Saturday,          // 4-6
              NumberOfDays,                         // 7
              DayOverflow = 7};                     // too-high error

struct Day
{
// -- the public section --

/********** member functions **********/
   /*----- Class constructor -----
      To initialize a declaration of a Day object.

      Receive:  DayName value InitDay (default value of Sunday)
      Return:   This Day object with its data member initialized
                to InitDay
      ----------------------------------------------------------------*/

   Day(DayName InitDay = Sunday) {DayValue_ = InitDay;}

   /*----- Data member extractor ----- . . . */
   DayName DayValue(void) const {return DayValue_;}

   /*----- Assignment ----- . . . */
   Day& operator=(const Day& DayExp);

   /*----- In-/De-crement -----
      Operations that (destructively) increment/decrement
      a Day object . . . */

   Day operator++(void);                   // prefix increment
   Day operator++(int);                    // postfix increment
   Day operator--(void);                   // prefix decrement
   Day operator--(int);                    // postfix decrement

   /*----- Suc-/Prede-cessor -----
      Functions that find the successor/predecessor of
      a Day object . . . */

   Day Next(void) const;                   // next day (wraps)
   Day Previous(void) const;               // previous day (wraps)

   /*----- Relational Operators ----- . . . */

   friend Boolean operator==(               // equality
                      const Day& LeftDay,
                      const Day& RightDay);
   friend Boolean operator!=(               // inequality
                      const Day& LeftDay,
                      const Day& RightDay);
```

FIGURE 11.15 Redeclaring **Day** as a struct. (cont.)

```
    friend Boolean operator<(                        // less than
                            const Day& LeftDay,
                            const Day& RightDay);
    friend Boolean operator<=(                       // less or equal
                            const Day& LeftDay,
                            const Day& RightDay);
    friend Boolean operator>(                        // greater than
                            const Day& LeftDay,
                            const Day& RightDay);
    friend Boolean operator>=(                       // greater or equal
                            const Day& LeftDay,
                            const Day& RightDay);

    /*----- Input/Output ----- . . . */
    /* Interactive */
    friend ostream& operator<< (ostream& Out, const Day& DayIn);
    friend istream& operator>> (istream& In, Day& DayOut);

    /* File */
    friend fstream& operator<< (fstream& Out, const Day& DayIn);
    friend fstream& operator>> (fstream& In, Day& DayOut);

// -- the private section --
 private:

/********** the data member **********/

  DayName
    DayValue_;
};
#endif
```

The struct is another of the significant differences between C++ and its parent language C—in C, the struct can contain only data members, whereas a C++ struct can contain data members *and operations* on those members.

Using the Struct Versus Using the Class.   If the class and the struct are essentially the same in C++, except that the members of one are by default private and the members of the other are by default public, what circumstances dictate the use of one mechanism instead of the other?

In practice, the class is used more frequently than the struct because its members are private by default. That is, programmers mentally associate the class with the notion of private members and the struct with the notion of public members. Since current programming practice is to prevent users of a new type from (directly) accessing its data members, the default privacy of the class makes it the more commonly chosen mechanism for implementing new types. In this text, we only use the struct where we feel it provides a clear advantage over the class and will always try to explain the circumstances that led to our choice of the struct.

Exercises

1. Complete the implementation of class **Day**, using the preceding section as a starting point.

2. Construct a class **Boolean** that has a data member whose type is an enumeration with values **True** and **False**. Overload the I/O, assignment, and relational operators for objects of class **Boolean**.

3. **(a)** Write a class **Month** that has a data member whose type is an enumeration **MonthAbbrev**, whose values are abbreviations of the months of the year and consist of the first three letters of the months' names.
   (b) Overload the I/O operators for objects of this class.
   (c) Overload the increment and decrement operators to (destructively) change the value of a **Month** object to the next or previous month without wrapping around at the year's end.
   (d) Add **Next()** and **Previous()** members to **Month**, that will (nondestructively) return the next or previous month and wrap around at the year's end.
   (e) Write two constructors for a **Month** object, one taking a parameter that is the number of a month and the other taking a parameter that is a **MonthAbbrev** value.
   (f) Overload the relational operators for objects of this class.
   (g) Write a member function whose parameter is a nonnegative integer **n** that nondestructively finds the ''nth successor'' of **Month**. The 0th successor of **Month** is **Month** itself; for **n** > 0, the nth successor of **Month** is the nth month following **Month**. For example, the fourth successor of **Aug** is **Dec**, and the sixth successor of **Aug** is **Feb**.
   (h) Write a member function **DaysIn()** whose parameter is a year in the range from 1538 through 1999 and whose return value is the number of days in the month. Remember that February has 28 days, except in a leap year, when it has 29. A leap year is one in which the year number is divisible by 4 except for centesimal years (those ending in 00); these centesimal years are not leap years unless the year number is divisible by 400. Thus, 1950 and 1900 are not leap years, but 1960 and 1600 are.
   (i) Use the class in a program that read two dates and calculates the number of days that have elapsed between them.

4. Using an enumeration **ColorName**, construct a class **Color** whose values are **Red**, **Orange**, **Yellow**, **Green**, **Blue**, **Indigo**, and **Violet**, along with appropriate operations on a **Color** object.

5. Using the class **Color** defined in Exercise 4:
   (a) Design a class **Shirt** described by its color, neck size, and an enumeration whose values are **LongSleeve** and **ShortSleeve**.
   (b) Design a class **Flower** described by its color, its height, and an enumeration whose values are **Annual** and **Perennial**.
   (c) Design a class **HousePaint** described by its color, an enumeration whose values are **Indoor** and **Outdoor**, and an enumeration whose values are **Latex**, **Oil**, and **Enamel**.

6. Using the class **Day** in the text, write a program to read a customer's account number and current balance; then for each weekday (Monday through Friday) read a series of transactions by that customer of the form D (deposit) or W (withdrawal) followed by an amount, and update the balance with this amount. Display the new balance after all transactions for the week have been processed.

11.3   Example: The Dean's List

To reinforce what we have learned about classes and to see their use in a slightly different context, we consider another problem that is conveniently solved using classes.

Problem.   The registrar at IO-U has a data file named **student.dat**:

```
111223333 Bill Board
Freshman    16.0   3.15

666554444 Jose Canusee
Sophomore   16.0   3.25

444556666 Ally Cat
Senior      16.0   3.125

777889999 Ben Dover
Junior      16.0   2.5

333221111 Stan Dupp
Senior       8.0   3.75

999887777 Isabelle Ringing
Junior      16.0   3.8
       .
       .
       .
```

The lines in this file have the form

StudentNumber FirstName LastName
StudentYear   Credits   GPA

where
StudentNumber is a 9-digit (integer) student ID number,
FirstName and *LastName* are character strings,
StudentYear is one of the enumeration values

Freshman, Sophomore, Junior, Senior, Graduate

Credits is the (real) number of credits this student carried this semester, and
GPA is the (real) grade point average of this student this semester.

The problem is to write a program that the registrar can use to generate a file containing the records of all students who made the dean's list; that is, all full-time students (*Credits* $\geq$ 9.0) whose *GPA* is at least 3.0.

Specification and Design. The key to solving this problem is (as always) to recognize the objects in the problem and the operations on those objects. In particular, the program must construct a model of a student, consisting of the attributes

StudentNumber   Name   Year   Credits   GPA

Given such a model, we can construct the following algorithm to solve the problem:

ALGORITHM FOR CONSTRUCTING THE DEAN'S LIST

/* This algorithm uses the registrar's data file and creates another file
   containing the records of all students on the dean's list.

    Input(the registrar's file):   A sequence of student data records
    Output(an output file):   The records of full-time students whose
                                   GPA ≥ 3.0

--- */

1. Get the name of the input file and open it for input.
2. Get the name of the output file and open it for output.
3. Input the first student record from the input file.
4. While the end of the file has not been reached:
       a. If *GPA* ≥ 3.0 and *Credits* ≥ 9.0 then
               Write the student record to the output file.
       b. Input the next student record from the input file.
     End While.
5. Close the input and output files.

The key to solving this problem clearly lies in being able to model a student. Since a student is described by multiple attributes (*StudentNumber, Name, Year, Credits, GPA*) and these attributes are of different types, a class is the natural mechanism to use. However, one of these attributes (*Year*) is an enumeration, not a predefined type, and the class provides the best way to implement a new type whose values are enumerators. Although file I/O functions are the only operations required to solve this problem, designing with an eye toward the future suggests that we add a full range of **Year** operations, as shown in Figure 11.16.

FIGURE 11.16 The header file for class **Year**.

```
/* This file contains the interface for class Year.

   NOTE:   Some documentation has been omitted to save pages.
           See the data disk for full documentation.
------------------------------------------------------------*/

#ifndef YEAR
#define YEAR
```

FIGURE 11.16   The header file for class **Year**. (cont.)

```
#include <iostream.h>                          // interactive I/O
#include <fstream.h>                           // file I/O
#include "Boolean.h"

enum YearName {YearUnderflow = -1,            // too-low error
               Freshman, Sophomore,           // 0-1
               Junior, Senior, Graduate,      // 2-4
               NumberOfYears,                  // 5
               YearOverflow = 5};             // too-high error

class Year
{              // -- the private section --
  YearName
    YearValue_;                                // the data member

  public:      // -- the public section --

/********** member functions **********/
   /*----- Class constructor -----
      To initialize a declaration of a Day object.

      Precondition:  A Day object has been declared.
      Receive:       YearName value InitYear (default value of
                        Freshman)
      Postcondition: The data member of this Day object has been
                        initialized to InitYear.
      -----------------------------------------------------------*/

   Year(YearName InitYear = Freshman) {YearValue_ = InitYear;}

   /*----- Data member extractor ----- . . . */

   YearValue(void) const {return YearValue_;}

   /*----- Assignment ----- . . . */

   Year& operator=(const Year& YearExp);

   /*----- In-/De-crement -----
      Operations that (destructively) increment/decrement
      a Years object . . . */

   Year operator++(void);                     // prefix increment
   Year operator++(int);                      // postfix increment
   Year operator--(void);                     // prefix decrement
   Year operator--(int);                      // postfix decrement

   /*----- Suc-/Prede-cessor -----
      Nondestructive functions that find the successor/predecessor of
      a Years object . . . */

   Year Next(void) const;                     // next year
   Year Previous(void) const;                 // previous year
```

FIGURE 11.16 The header file for class **Year**. (cont.)

```
/*----- Relational Operators ----- . . . */

friend Boolean operator==(                          // equality
                    const Year& Left, const Year& Right);
friend Boolean operator!=(                          // inequality
                    const Year& Left, const Year& Right);
friend Boolean operator<(                           // less-than
                    const Year& Left, const Year& Right);
friend Boolean operator<=(                          // less-or-equal
                    const Year& Left, const Year& Right);
friend Boolean operator>(                           // greater-than
                    const Year& Left, const Year& Right);
friend Boolean operator>=(                          // greater-or-equal
                    const Year& Left, const Year& Right);

/*----- Input/Output ----- . . . */

/* Stream I/O */
friend ostream& operator<< (ostream& Out, const Year& OutYear);
friend istream& operator>> (istream& In, Year& InYear);

/* File I/O */
friend fstream& operator<< (fstream& Out, const Year& OutYear);
friend fstream& operator>> (fstream& In, Year& InYear);
};
#endif
```

The definitions of these functions are similar to those we have seen previously and are left as exercises.

Once we can declare objects of type **Year**, the implementation of a class named **Student** is straightforward, as shown in Figure 11.17.

FIGURE 11.17 The header file for class **Student**.

```
/* This file contains the interface for class Student.
   NOTE:  Because of similarities to other classes, some
          documentation has been omitted to save pages.
          See the data disk for full documentation.
   -------------------------------------------------------------*/

#ifndef STUDENT
#define STUDENT

#include <iostream.h>              // interactive I/O
#include <fstream.h>               // file I/O

#include "Year.h"
#include "Strings.h"
#include "Boolean.h"
```

FIGURE 11.17   The header file for class **Student**. (cont.)

```
class Student
{
// -- the private section --
/********** the data members **********/

   Strings
      FirstName_,
      LastName_;
   long
      StudentNumber_;
   Year
      StudentYear_;
   double
      Credits_,
      GPA_;

public:
/********** member functions **********/
   /*----- Class constructor ----- */

   /* To initialize a declaration of a Student object
        with individual values for the data elements.

      Precondition:  A Student object has been declared.
      Receive:       Strings FName (default "")
                        and LName (default "")
                     long integer SNumb (default 0)
                     Year object StuYear (default Freshman)
                     double Creds (default 0.0)
                        and GPA (default 0.0)
      Postcondition: The data members of this Student object have
                     been initialized to FName, LName, SNumb,
                     StuYear, Creds, and GPA, respectively.
      ------------------------------------------------------------*/

   Student(const Strings& FName = "", const Strings& LName = "",
           long SNumb = 0, Year StuYear = Freshman,
           double Creds = 0.0, double GPA = 0.0);

   /*----- Equality ----- . . . */
   friend Boolean operator==(const Student& Left, const Student& Right);

   /*----- Inequality ----- . . . */
   friend Boolean operator!=(const Student& Left, const Student& Right);

   /*----- Less than ----- . . . */
   friend Boolean operator<(const Student& Left, const Student& Right);

   /*----- Greater than ----- . . . */
   friend Boolean operator>(const Student& Left, const Student& Right);
```

FIGURE 11.17 The header file for class **Student**. (cont.)

```
/*----- Less than or equal ----- . . . */
friend Boolean operator<=(const Student& Left, const Student& Right);

/*----- Greater than or equal ----- . . . */
friend Boolean operator>=(const Student& Left, const Student& Right);

/*----- Data member extractors ----- . . . */
Strings FirstName(void) const              // extract first name
{
    return FirstName_;
}

Strings LastName(void) const               // extract last name
{
    return LastName_;
}

long StudentNumber(void) const             // extract number
{
    return StudentNumber_;
}

Year StudentYear(void) const               // extract year
{
    return StudentYear_;
}

double Credits(void) const                 // extract credits
{
    return Credits_;
}

double GPA(void) const                     // extract GPA
{
    return GPA_;
}

/*----- Input/Output ----- . . . */

/* Stream I/O */
  friend istream& operator>> (istream& In, Student& S);
  friend ostream& operator<< (ostream& Out, const Student& S);

/* File I/O */
  friend fstream& operator>> (fstream& InF, Student& S);
  friend fstream& operator<< (fstream& OutF, const Student& S);
};

#endif
```

Note that in addition to the assignment operation for **Student** values, we also provide the six relational operations (equality, inequality, less than, and so on). The implementation of these operations is discussed in the exercises at the end of this section.

Note also that the class **Year** is used to declare the member **StudentYear_** within class **Student**. This ability to **nest** one class object within another is extremely powerful, since a "bigger" class (like **Student**) can be built as a collection of "smaller" classes (such as **Year**). Since a **Year** object carries its operations within it, all those operations can be applied to the **StudentYear_** data member of a **Student**.

Figure 11.18 presents a partial listing of the implementation file for class **Student**.

 FIGURE 11.18 A (partial) implementation file for class **Student**.

```
/* This file implements the operations on a Student.

... Most documentation omitted to save pages ...
----------------------------------------------------------*/

# include "Student.h"

# include <iomanip.h>

/*----- Class constructor ----- */

/* To initialize a declaration of a Student object
      with individual values for the data elements.

   Precondition:  A Student object has been declared.
   Receive:       Strings FName (default "")
                      and LName (default "")
                  long integer SNumb (default 0)
                  Year object StuYear (default Freshman)
                  double Creds (default 0.0)
                      and GPA (default 0.0)
   Postcondition: The data members of this Student object have
                      been initialized to FName, LName, SNumb,
                      StuYear, Creds, and GPA, respectively.
----------------------------------------------------------*/

Student(const Strings& FName, const Strings& LName,
        long Snumb, Year StuYear, double Creds,
        double GPA)
```

FIGURE 11.18   A (partial) implementation file for class **Student**. (cont.)

```
{
   FirstName_ = FName;
   LastName_ = LName;
   StudentNumber_ = SNumb;
   StudentYear_ = StuYear;
   Credits_ = Creds;
   GPA_ = GPA;
}

// ... various function definitions omitted ...

/*-----------------------------------------------------------
   This function inputs a Student from a file.

   Receive:   InFile, the fstream being read from
              InStu, the Student being filled with data
   Return:    InStu, filled with the input data
              InFile
   -------------------------------------------------------*/

fstream& operator>> (fstream& InFile, Student& InStu)
{
   InFile >> InStu.StudentNumber_ >> InStu.FirstName_
          >> InStu.LastName_ >> InStu.StudentYear_
          >> InStu.Credits_ >> InStu.GPA_;

   return InFile;
}

/*-----------------------------------------------------------
   This function outputs a Student to a file.

   Receive:   OutFile, the fstream being written to
              OutStu, Student being written
   Output:    OutStu to OutFile
   Return:    OutFile
   -------------------------------------------------------*/

fstream& operator<< (fstream& OutFile, const Student& OutStu)
{
   OutFile << setw(10) << OutStu.StudentNumber_ << '\t'
           << OutStu.FirstName_ << ' ' << OutStu.LastName_ << endl
           << setw(12) << OutStu.StudentYear_
           << setprecision(4)
           << setiosflags(ios::showpoint | ios::fixed)
           << setw(8) << OutStu.Credits_
           << setw(8) << OutStu.GPA_ << endl;

   return OutFile;
}
```

It should be noted that the layout of the input file determines the arrangement of the input expressions within **operator>>**. In particular, the input function assumes that the student's student ID comes first, followed by the student's name (first, then last), followed by the remainder of the student's data (year, semester hours, and GPA) on the next line. The output function produces output with the same format.

Once we have constructed class **Student**, encoding the algorithm for the dean's list problem is quite simple, as shown in Figure 11.19.

 FIGURE 11.19   The dean's list program.

```
/* This program uses the data file 'student.dat' and creates a file
   'deans.dat' containing all students making the dean's list.

   Input(student.dat):  A sequence of student data records
   Output(deans.dat):   All student IDs whose GPA >= 3.0
---------------------------------------------------------------*/

#include <iostream.h>
#include <fstream.h>
#include <stdlib.h>

#include "Student.h"

int main(void)
{
   const double
      DeanListCutoff = 3.0,                  // min. Dean's List GPA
      FullTime = 9.0;                        // min. full-time credits

   cout << "\nThis program reads the records in the file "
        << " 'student.dat',"
        << "\n\tand displays the dean's list in the file "
        << " 'deans.dat'.\n";

   fstream
      InStream("student.dat", ios::in),      // open input file
      OutStream("deans.dat", ios::out);      // open output file

   if (InStream.fail())                      // check for success
   {
      cerr << "\n*** Unable to open 'student.dat' for input!\n";
      exit (-1);
   }
```

FIGURE 11.19   The dean's list program. (cont.)

```
else if (OutStream.fail())
{
   cerr << "\n*** Unable to open 'dean.dat' for output!\n";
   exit (-1);
}

OutStream << "\n\tThe Dean's List\n\n";   // print a heading

Student
   Stu;                                   // Student being processed

InStream >> Stu;                          // input first Student

while (!InStream.eof())                   // while not end-of-file:
{
   if ((Stu.GPA() >= DeanListCutoff) &&   //    if high-enough GPA
         (Stu.Credits() >= FullTime))     //       and full-time,
      OutStream << Stu << endl;           //       output the Student
   InStream >> Stu;                       //    input next Student
}

InStream.close();                         // close the files
OutStream.close();

return 0;
}
```

Sample input file listing: "student.dat":

```
111223333 Bill Board
Freshman    16.0 3.15

666554444 Jose Canusee
Sophomore   16.0 3.25

444556666 Ally Cat
Senior      16.0 3.125

777889999 Ben Dover
Junior      16.0 2.5

333221111 Stan Dupp
Senior       8.0 3.75

999887777 Isabelle Ringing
Junior      16.0  3.8
```

FIGURE 11.19   The dean's list program. (cont.)

Sample run:

```
This program reads the records in the file 'student.dat',
   and displays the dean's list in the file 'deans.dat'.
```

Output file listing: `"deans.dat"`:

```
   The Dean's List

 111223333    Bill Board
     Freshman 16.0000   3.1500

 666554444    Jose Canusee
    Sophomore 16.0000   3.2500

 444556666    Ally Cat
       Senior 16.0000   3.1250

 999887777    Isabelle Ringing
       Junior 16.0000   3.8000
```

Note that the main program is relatively simple, since most of the work went into implementing the classes **Year** and **Student**. The time spent implementing an object as a class is, in a sense, an *investment for the future*—when the registrar asks us to write a program to create a list of all part-time students, class **Student** makes this easy:

```
// ...open InStream and OutStream...

InStream >> Stu;
while (!eof())
{
   if (Stu.Credits() < FullTime)
      OutStream << Stu << endl;
   InStream >> Stu;
}

// ... close InStream and OutStream ...
```

By planning for the future when we design classes, we can save ourselves and others a great deal of time and effort.

Exercises

1. Suppose that a **Student** value *S1* will be considered to be less than another **Student** value *S2* if:

   > The **LastName_** member of *S1* is less than the **LastName_** member of *S2*; or
   > The **LastName_** member of *S1* is equal to the **LastName_** member of *S2* and the **FirstName_** member of *S1* is less than the **FirstName_** member of *S2*.

   A rule for the greater than relationship between two **Student** values is similar. Provide definitions for **operator<** and **operator>** that implement these relationships.

2. A **Student** value *S1* can be described as equal to another **Student** value *S2* if the **LastName_** member of *S1* is equal to the **LastName_** member of *S2* and the **FirstName_** member of *S1* is equal to the **FirstName_** member of *S2*. A rule for the inequality relation of two **Student** values is similar. Provide definitions for **operator==** and **operator!=** that implement these relationships, being sure to state clearly the assumptions made.

3. If it is possible for two different students to have the same first and last name, a **Student** value *S1* can be described as equal to another **Student** value *S2* if the **StudentNumber_** member of *S1* is equal to the **StudentNumber_** member of *S2*. A rule for the inequality relation of two **Student** values is similar. Provide definitions for **operator==** and **operator!=** that implement these relationships. What advantages are there to implementing these operations in this way rather than as described in Exercise 2? What are the disadvantages? (*Hint:* Consider the problem of searching for a particular student in the registrar's file.)

4. Using the functions defined in Exercises 1 and 2 (or 3), provide definitions for **operator<=** and **operator>=** that implement the less than or equal and greater than or equal relations on two **Student** values.

Programming Pointers

Program Design

1. *Use classes to define scalar types whose values are enumeration types.* This permits the arithmetic operators to be overloaded for such types, so that readable statements such as:

```
for (Year Y = Freshman; Y <= Senior; Y++)
    // ... do something with Year ...
```

can be used.

2. *Use classes to define new types whose values consist of multiple attributes of differing types.* One of the purposes of the class is to permit different data types to be encapsulated in a single object. For example, to model a playing card, we might declare

```
enum SuitName {Clubs, Diamonds, Hearts, Spades};

enum RankName {Ace, Two, Three, Four, Five, Six, Seven,
               Eight, Nine, Ten, Jack, Queen, King};
```

from which the classes **Suit** and **Rank** can be constructed. Given these classes, a playing card can then be modeled as follows:

```
class PlayingCard
{
   SuitName
      SuitValue_;
   RankName
      RankValue_;
public:
   // ... operations on a PlayingCard object ...
};
```

3. *Keep all data members of a class private, and provide extraction/insertion functions to manipulate those members.* One purpose of a class is to prevent programs that use an object from accessing its data members directly. By providing a carefully designed set of interface functions and keeping programs from accessing the data members except through this interface, classes encourage the writing of maintainable programs.

4. *If a function requires a class argument and the function alters that argument, then the corresponding parameter should be declared as a reference parameter (as usual). However, if the function does not alter that argument, then the parameter for that argument should be declared as a **constant reference** parameter instead of as a value parameter.* The reasons are (1) efficiency and (2) safety.

More precisely, passing a class object as a value parameter is time-consuming because all of the data members of the argument must be copied into the parameter:

```
class X { ... };

void F(X Param);
```

A reference to a class object is only a single value (its address), and so passing a reference to a class object can be much more time-efficient than passing its value:

```
void F(X& Param);
```

However, this causes a safety problem if the function is not to modify the class object, since a programmer might mistakenly modify the parameter within the function and, in so doing, modify its argument. This can be prevented by declaring the reference parameter as a constant reference parameter by preceding the declaration with the keyword **const**.

```
void F(const X& Param);
```

5. *Member functions that do not modify the object containing them should be declared and defined as constant functions.* This is accomplished by placing the keyword **const** after the closing parentheses that follow the parameter list. For example, if we were to add a function to a **Point** class to extract its **X_** member, that function would be reading from, not writing to, its object and so should be declared as a constant function:

```
class Point
{
    double
        X_,
        Y_;
public:
    // ...
    double X(void) const { return X_; }
};
```

6. *Every member function of a class object contains the named constant* **this**, *whose value is the address of that object.* The object can be accessed by applying the dereferencing operator (*) to **this**. For example, in any member function of class **Point**, the notation *this can be used to access the particular **Point** object containing that function. Functions that need to return the object containing them can do so by returning the value *this.

7. *It is good practice to surround a class declaration with the preprocessor directives*

```
#ifndef CLASSNAME
#define CLASSNAME

ClassDeclaration

#endif
```

to avoid generating errors if multiple files should insert that declaration using the #include *directive.* To illustrate, suppose that the class **Point** described previously has been declared and we use it to create two new classes **Line** and **Rectangle**:

```
#include "Point.h"        #include "Point.h"

class Line                class Rectangle
{                         {
   double                    Point
      Slope;                    UpperLeft,
   Point                        LowerRight;
      YIntercept;         // ...
// ...                    };
};
```

Now if a program should use the **#include** directive to insert both **Line.h** and **Rectangle.h**, then **Point** is defined twice, generating an error. By surrounding **Point** as follows,

```
#ifndef POINT
#define POINT

class Point
{
   // ...
};

#endif
```

the code declaring class **Point** will be processed in whichever header file is processed first but skipped over in the header file that is processed second, eliminating the error.

Some compilers allow the directive

```
#pragma once
```

to be placed at the beginning of a header file to achieve this same objective:

```
#pragma once

class Point
{
   // ...
};
```

However, this directive is not universally supported, and so programs relying upon it may not be portable.

Potential Problems

1. *Arithmetic operators such as* + + *cannot be applied to or overloaded for an enumeration object.* This is the primary motivation for implementing enumerations as a class, as presented in Section 11.2.

2. *In order to access an enumerator of an enumeration declared publicly within a class, the enumerator must be qualified with the name of the class.* For example,

if we were to declare

```
class Boolean
{
public:
    enum BoolNames {False, True};
private:
    BoolNames
        BoolVal;
public:
    // ... Boolean operations ...
};
```

then the enumerators `False` and `True` must be accessed with the notation

```
Boolean::False
```

and

```
Boolean::True
```

If this is too inconvenient, the enumeration can be declared outside the class,

```
enum BoolNames {False, True};
```

```
class Boolean
{
    BoolNames
        BoolVal;
public:
    // ...
};
```

so that the enumerators `False` and `True` can be freely accessed.

3. *All members of a class that are declared prior to the keyword* `public:` *are private.* Private members of a class can be accessed only by member functions and friend functions.

4. *When defining the member functions of a class, the function's name must be qualified with the name of the class and the scope operator (*`::`*). For example,* given a class declaration

```
class Point
{
    double
        X_,
        Y_;
public:
    Point(double X = 0.0, double Y = 0.0);
};
```

the constructor for this class could be defined as:

```
Point::Point(double X, double Y)
{
    X_ = X;
    Y_ = Y;
}
```

The assignment operator *must* be implemented as a member function.

5. *A friend function must be named as such by the class of which it is a friend.* This is accomplished by preceding its declaration with the keyword **friend** in the class declaration. For example, in the class **Point** given earlier, we might declare:

```
class Point
{
    double
        X_,
        Y_;
public:
    // ...

    friend ostream& operator<< (ostream& Out, const Point& P);
};
```

The I/O operators *must* be implemented as friend functions.

6. *A function cannot return a reference to a local class object.* A common mistake is to construct a function **F()** as follows:

```
class C1 { ... };

C1& F(...)
{
    C1
        LocalObject;
    ...
    return LocalObject;        // Error !
}
```

The class object **LocalObject** is defined within function **F()** and thus ceases to exist when **F()** terminates. It is, therefore, an error for **F()** to return the reference (address of) a **C1** object that no longer exists once **F()** has terminated. This is easily corrected, simply by returning the value of a local **C1** object instead of its reference:

```
C1 F(...)                      // Slow, but Ok.
{
    C1
        LocalObject;
    ...
    return LocalObject;
}
```

However, a function can return the reference of a constructed class object:

```
Cl& F(...)
{
    ...
    return CL(Args);
}
```

and/or a reference to the class object containing it:

```
Cl& F(...)
{
    ...
    return *this;
}
```

Programming Projects

1. The **point-slope** equation of a line having slope m and passing through point P with coordinates (x_1, y_1) is

$$y - y_1 = m(x - x_1)$$

   (a) Write a class **CartesianPoint** to model points, described by their x- and y-coordinates, with appropriate operations on such objects.
   (b) Write a **LineSegment** class, described by two **CartesianPoint** endpoints. In addition to the usual operations, this class should provide operations to compute
      (i) The midpoint of the line segment joining two points;
      (ii) The equation of the perpendicular bisector of this line segment.
   (c) Write a class for a **Line**, described by its slope and a point on the line, with functions that
      (i) Find the point-slope equation of the line;
      (ii) Find the slope-intercept equation of the line.
   (d) Write a program to read the point and slope information for two lines and to determine whether they intersect or are parallel. If they intersect, find the point of intersection and also determine whether they are perpendicular.

2. Write a program that accepts a time of day in military format and finds the corresponding standard representation in hours, minutes, and A.M./P.M. or accepts the time in the usual format and finds the corresponding military representation. For example, the input 100 should produce 1:00 A.M. as output, and the input 3:45 P.M. should give 1545. Use a class to store the time, and provide extraction or conversion functions to display the time in either format.

3. A **complex number** has the form $a + bi$, where a and b are real numbers and $i^2 = -1$. The four basic arithmetic operations for complex numbers are defined as follows:

$$\text{Addition:} \quad (a + bi) + (c + di) = (a + c) + (b + d)i$$

$$\text{Subtraction:} \quad (a + bi) - (c + di) = (a - c) + (b - d)i$$

$$\text{Multiplication:} \quad (a + bi) * (c + di) = (ac - bd) + (ad + bc)i$$

$$\text{Division:} \quad \frac{a + bi}{c + di} = \frac{ac + bd}{c^2 + d^2} + \frac{bc - ad}{c^2 + d^2}i$$

$$\text{provided } c^2 + d^2 \neq 0$$

Write a program to read two complex numbers and a symbol for one of these operations and to perform the indicated operation. Use a class to model complex numbers, and use member functions to implement the operations.

4. A rational number is of the form *a/b*, where *a* and *b* are integers with $b \neq 0$. Write a program to do rational number arithmetic, storing the numerator and the denominator of each rational number. The program should read and display all rational numbers in the format *a/b* or simply *a* if the denominator is 1. The following examples illustrate the menu of commands that the user should be allowed to enter:

Input	Output	Comments
3/8 + 1/6	13/24	*a/b* + *c/d* = (*ad* + *bc*)/*bd* reduced to lowest terms
3/8 − 1/6	5/24	*a/b* − *c/d* = (*ad* − *bc*)/*bd* reduced to lowest terms
3/8 * 1/6	1/16	*a/b* * *c/d* = *ac/bd* reduced to lowest terms
3/8 / 1/6	9/4	*a/b* / *c/d* = *ad/bc* reduced to lowest terms
3/8 I	8/3	*a/b* inverted
8/3 M	2 + 2/3	*a/b* written as a mixed number
6/8 R	3/4	*a/b* reduced to lowest terms
6/8 G	2	Greatest common divisor of numerator and denominator
1/6 L 3/8	24	Lowest common denominator of *a/b* and *c/d*
1/6 < 3/8	True	*a/b* < *c/d*?
1/6 <= 3/8	True	*a/b* ≤ *c/d*?
1/6 > 3/8	False	*a/b* > *c/d*?
1/6 >= 3/8	False	*a/b* ≥ *c/d*?
3/8 = 9/24	True	*a/b* = *c/d*?
2/3 X + 2 = 4/5	X = −9/5	Solution of linear equation (*a/b*)X + *c/d* = *e/f*

ONE-DIMENSIONAL ARRAYS

12

With silver bells, and cockle shells,
And pretty maids all in a row.
MOTHER GOOSE

There is nothing more difficult to take in hand, more perilous to conduct, or
more uncertain in its success, than to take the lead in the introduction of a
new order of things.
NICCOLO MACHIAVELLI
The Prince

CHAPTER CONTENTS

In this chapter, we combine two ideas that, at first glance, might seem unrelated. The first of these ideas is *list processing*. There are many problems whose solutions involve processing a list of values. For example, in Section 8.1, we examined the meteorological problem of finding the minimum, maximum, and average pressure from a list of pressure readings.

The second idea is that of an *indexed* (or *subscripted*) *variable.* In Chapter 9, we presented a class named `Strings` that makes it possible to store a collection of characters (i.e., a character string) within a single object. A `Strings` object named `Str` is an *indexed* object for which the notation `Str[i]` can be used to access the character of `Str` whose index is `i`.

It should be clear that it would be convenient to combine these ideas. Problems that involve lists of noncharacter data (e.g., the meteorological problem) can be solved more conveniently if the entire list of values can be stored in an indexed variable `ValueList` so that the value stored in location `i` can be accessed with the notation `ValueList[i]`.

An **array** is such a variable. It is a more general object than a `Strings` object, because a `Strings` object can only store `char` values, but arrays can be defined to store scalar values, including `char`, `int`, and `double` values, as well as nonscalar values such as `Strings`, `Student`, and `Day` values. (In fact, class `Strings` uses an array data member to store character strings.[1]) In short, an array can be defined to store any type that has been declared prior to the definition of the array.

In the first section of this chapter, we introduce a simple form of array, in which the programmer specifies the size of the array in the array declaration. Once the program is compiled, the size of such an array cannot be changed without changing the array declaration and recompiling the program. Such arrays are thus called **fixed-size arrays.** In Sections 12.2 and 12.3, we present a class `List` that contains a fixed-size array as a data member.

12.1 An Introduction to Arrays

We begin with a simple list-processing problem to motivate our study of arrays.

Problem: Processing Test Scores

To help with processing the grades for one of her classes, Professor von Neuperson would like a program that will do the following:

1. Input a list of up to 32 (real) test scores from the keyboard.
2. Output the average score.
3. Display each score and the difference between it and the average score.

For example, if the average score is 75, the program should display something like

```
... 82 (7)
```

---

[1] The size of the array member of a `Strings` object is not fixed at compile-time, but it is an array nonetheless. Arrays whose sizes can vary at run-time are described in Chapter 14.

for a score of 82 but

   ... 69 (-6)

for a score of 69.

Solving this problem requires that the input data be processed twice. Finding the average value requires one pass through the list to sum and count its values. Once we have the average value, finding the difference between each value and that average value requires a second pass through the list. Although the **seekg()** member of **cin** could be used to read the list twice (see Section 8.4), it is more efficient to declare an array data object that can store the entire list of values and read the list into this array.[2] A value from the list can then be processed simply by accessing the element in which that value is stored, using its index.

The program in Figure 12.1 solves this problem, using an array. Note that no header files need to be included to use an array. Unlike **Strings** (a class that *we* wrote), arrays are a part of the C++ language, and so no files or libraries need to be included to declare array objects.

 FIGURE 12.1   Processing test scores.

```
/* This program inputs a sequence of test scores, finds their mean,
   and displays the scores together with their differences from
   the mean.

   Input:   A sequence of test scores
   Output: The mean of the test scores, all scores with their
           differences from the mean, and prompts for input
   -----------------------------------------------------------------*/

#include <iostream.h>
#include <iomanip.h>

double Mean(const double[], unsigned);     // function to compute
                                           //    the mean
int main(void)
{
   const int
      ArraySize = 32;                       // number of array elements
   double
      Score[ArraySize];                     // the array of scores

   cout << "\nThis program processes a sequence of up to "
        << ArraySize <<" test"
        << "\n\t scores.  It finds the average of the scores and"
        << "\n\tthe differences of the scores from the average.\n\n"
        << "How many scores are there to process? ";
```

---

[2] Using an array is more time-efficient because an array is stored in *main memory,* whereas a file is stored in *secondary memory,* and the time to access main memory is far less than the time to access secondary memory.

FIGURE 12.1 Processing test scores. (cont.)

```
   int
      NumScores;                              // number of scores
   cin >> NumScores;

   for (int i = 0; i < NumScores; i++)     // loop to input scores
   {
      cout << "Please enter score "         //   display prompt
           << (i + 1) << ": ";
      cin >> Score[i];                       //   store score in array
   }

   double
      MeanScore = Mean(Score, NumScores);  // find the mean score

   cout << "\n\nThe mean score is "         // display the mean
        << MeanScore << ".\n\n";
   cout.setf(ios::showpoint | ios::fixed);
   cout.precision(1);

   cout << "Scores and (differences):\n";  // display scores and
   for (i = 0; i < NumScores; i++)         //   differences from mean
      cout << "\tScore " << (i + 1)
           << ": " << Score[i]
           << "\t(" << Score[i] - MeanScore
           << ")\n";

   return 0;
}


/*-------------------------------------------------------------------
This function computes the mean of values stored in an array.

   Receive: Array, an array of double values
            NumValues, the number of values stored in the array
   Return:  The mean of the values
-------------------------------------------------------------------*/

double Mean(const double Array[], unsigned NumValues)
{
   if (NumValues <= 0)                        // avoid division by zero
   {
      cerr << "\n*** No elements passed to Mean!\n";
      return 0.0;
   }

   double
      Sum = 0.0;                              // sum of the scores

   for (int i = 0; i < NumValues; i++)      // sum the array elements
      Sum += Array[i];

   return Sum / NumValues;                    // compute the mean value
}
```

FIGURE 12.1   Processing test scores. (cont.)

Sample run (UNIX system):

```
This program processes a sequence of up to 32 test
   scores.  It finds the average of the scores and
   the differences of the scores from the average.

How many scores are there to process? 9
Please enter score 1: 55
Please enter score 2: 22
Please enter score 3: 77
Please enter score 4: 66
Please enter score 5: 99
Please enter score 6: 44
Please enter score 7: 33
Please enter score 8: 88
Please enter score 9: 11

The mean score is 55.0

Scores and (differences):
   Score 1: 55.0    (0.0)
   Score 2: 22.0    (-33.0)
   Score 3: 77.0    (22.0)
   Score 4: 66.0    (11.0)
   Score 5: 99.0    (44.0)
   Score 6: 44.0    (-11.0)
   Score 7: 33.0    (-22.0)
   Score 8: 88.0    (33.0)
   Score 9: 11.0    (-44.0)
```

Declaring Arrays

The declarations

```
const int
   ArraySize = 32;        // the number of array elements

double
   Score[ArraySize];      // the array of scores
```

in the program of Figure 12.1 instruct the compiler to reserve a block of memory large enough to hold 32 **double** values. The name **Score** is associated with this block of memory, and the elements of **Score** are indexed from 0 through 31:

	0	1	2	3	4	5	6	7	8	9	10	11	...	31
Score	?	?	?	?	?	?	?	?	?	?	?	?		?

An array element may be of any type. For example, the declarations

```
const int
   Size = 4;
char
   CharList[Size];        // array of 4 character elements
long
   IntList[Size];         // array of 4 integer elements
Strings
   StringList[Size];      // array of 4 Strings elements
```

declare four arrays, each having four elements. The first is an array **CharList** of four characters (stored in 4 bytes); the second is an array **IntList** of four integers (usually stored in 4×4 bytes = 16 bytes); and the third array **StringList** is an array of four **Strings** objects (for which the storage requirements vary with the string sizes).

The preceding declarations are examples of the following simplified form of a fixed-size array declaration:

```
Type
   ArrayName[Size];
```

Here *Type* is any defined type (predefined, or programmer-defined), *ArrayName* is the name of the array object being declared, and *Size* is the number of values the object can contain. Such a declaration instructs the compiler to reserve sufficient memory locations to hold *Size* objects of type *Type* and associates the name *ArrayName* with that block of locations.

To understand what this means, it is useful to contrast the following declarations of **CharArray** and **String**:

```
const int
   Size = 16;
char
   CharArray[Size];
Strings
   String;
```

The object **CharArray** is a 16-byte **fixed-size array,** whose size can not change. By contrast, the object **String** contains a **varying-size array** (initially of length zero) that will automatically grow or shrink, according to the size of the character string stored in it.

Using Named Constants.   It is good programming practice to provide flexibility and generality in a program involving arrays by using named constants rather than literals to specify the size of the arrays, as in

```
const int
   Size = 16;
double
   Array[Size];
       .
       .
       .
for (int i = 0; i < Size; i++)
   cin >> Array[i];
       .
       .
       .
Mean(Array, Size);
```

This is because it is often necessary to adjust the size of a fixed-size array several times while developing a program. Also, it may be necessary to modify the size of the array later after the program has been in use for some time. If literals are used, then these modifications require finding and changing each of these literals, but if a named constant (such as **Size**) is used throughout the program, then modifying the size of the array requires only a single modification — to the declaration of the named constant:

```
const int
   Size = 24;
double
   Array[Size];
       .
       .
       .
for (int i = 0; i < Size; i++)
   cin >> Array[i];
       .
       .
       .
Mean(Array, Size);
```

When the program is recompiled, the compiler updates all occurrences of **Size** with the new value, saving time and aggravation.

Using Enumerations.   In some situations, it can be useful to declare an array using an enumeration type. For example, suppose that a particular problem requires storing the number of hours an employee worked on each day of the week. We could simply declare an array of 7 real values,

```
const int
   NumDays = 7;
double
   HoursWorked[NumDays];
```

which would give an array with indices 0, 1, . . . , 6.

An alternative approach is to use the **#include** directive to insert the library **Day** described in Chapter 11, which contains a **DayName** enumeration data member:

```
enum DayName { DayUnderflow = -1,          // too-low error
               Sunday, Monday, Tuesday, Wednesday,// 0-3
               Thursday, Friday, Saturday,  // 4-6
               NumberOfDays,                // 7
               DayOverflow = 7 };           // too-high error
```

The enumerator value **NumberOfDays** can then be used to declare the array:

```
double
    HoursWorked[NumberOfDays];
```

Like the preceding declaration, this constructs an array of 7 real values, indexed from 0 through 6, but because the compiler associates 0 with **Sunday**, 1 with **Monday**, and so on, the array **HoursWorked** can also be viewed as having its elements indexed by **Sunday, Monday, . . . , Saturday**:

	Sunday	Monday	Tuesday	Wednesday	Thursday	Friday	Saturday
HoursWorked							

The first element of this array can be accessed using

```
HoursWorked[Sunday]
```

the second element, using

```
HoursWorked[Monday]
```

and so on.

We can thus use an enumeration to make programs more readable than they would be if we simply used integer indices. For example, a payroll program might process the array **HoursWorked** using a **for** loop, as follows:

```
double
    Total = 0.0;

for (Day WorkDay = Sunday; WorkDay <= Saturday; WorkDay++)
{
    cout << "On " << Day << ", you worked "
         << HoursWorked[WorkDay.DayValue]
         << " hours.\n";
    Total += HoursWorked[WorkDay.DayValue];
}

cout << "\n\t... for a total of " << Total << " hours.\n";
```

If the values in **HoursWorked** are

	Sunday	Monday	Tuesday	Wednesday	Thursday	Friday	Saturday
HoursWorked	0.0	8.0	8.0	0.0	8.0	8.0	8.0

then the preceding code fragment would output

```
On Sunday, you worked 0 hours.
On Monday, you worked 8 hours.
On Tuesday, you worked 8 hours.
On Wednesday, you worked 0 hours.
On Thursday, you worked 8 hours.
On Friday, you worked 8 hours.
On Saturday, you worked 8 hours.

... for a total of 40 hours.
```

When an array is used to store a *table* in which the rows (or columns) are labeled with some real-world names, enumerations provide a convenient means of making the operations on that table more readable.

Initialization of Arrays

The declarations of numeric and character arrays thus far have had the form

```
Type
    ArrayName[Size];
```

Both character and numeric arrays can also be initialized when they are declared, but they differ in *how* this is done. An array of characters can be initialized with a character string:

```
const int
    NameLength = 10;
char
    Name[NameLength] = "John Doe";
```

This initialization sets the elements of **Name** to the individual characters in **"John Doe"** and adds an invisible **null character,** the NUL character **'\0'**, whose numeric code is 0, that C++ uses as an "end-of-string" mark:[3]

	0	1	2	3	4	5	6	7	8	9
Name	J	o	h	n		D	o	e	\0	0

Space must always be provided for this null character if character arrays are used to store character strings (instead of using a class like **Strings**).

---

[3] **\0** is the escape sequence for the NUL character (just as **\n** is the escape sequence for the newline character). Since its octal numeric code is 000, it could also be written as **\000**. We will use the customary short version **\0** throughout this text.

A numeric array, however, cannot be initialized with a character string. Instead, the initial values for a numeric array must be listed in braces, { and }, separated by commas:

```
const int
   ListLength = 10;
double
   NumList[ListLength] = {9,8,7,6,5,4,3,2,1,0};
```

This declaration will construct an object named **NumList**, initialized as follows:

	0	1	2	3	4	5	6	7	8	9
NumList	9	8	7	6	5	4	3	2	1	0

If fewer values are supplied than the number of elements declared for an array, those elements for which no initial values were provided are each set to zero. (Uninitialized non-static arrays will usually contain "garbage" values.) For example, the declarations

```
const int
   ListLength = 10;
double
   NumList[ListLength] = {9,8,7,6,5,4};        // Okay!
```

will construct the object **NumList** as follows:

	0	1	2	3	4	5	6	7	8	9
NumList	9	8	7	6	5	4	0	0	0	0

Similarly, a list of characters can be used to initialize a character array. In this case, the zeros assigned to unspecified array elements are interpreted as null characters. For example, the declaration

```
const int
   NameLength = 10;
char
   Name[NameLength] = {'J','o','h','n',' ','D','o','e'};
```

will construct an object **Name** that is equivalent to that constructed previously,

	0	1	2	3	4	5	6	7	8	9
Name	J	o	h	n		D	o	e	\0	\0

because the last 2 elements will be set to zero. Using a string constant is simpler, however, and is the preferred method of initializing a character array.

Accessing Array Elements

As earlier examples have demonstrated, the individual elements of an array can be accessed by using an **indexed variable** with the notation:

```
Array[index]
```

For example, if **Score** is a **double** array, **Name** is a **char** array, and **HoursWorked** is a **double** array indexed by the enumeration type **DayName**, then the statement

```
Score[i] = DoubleValue;
```

can be used to assign *DoubleValue* to the element of **Score** whose index is **i**;

```
if (Name[0] == 'J')
   // ... do something appropriate ...
```

can be used to compare the first element of **Name** with the character '**J**'; and

```
cout << HoursWorked[Wednesday]
```

can be used to output the element of **HoursWorked** whose index is **Wednesday** (i.e., 3).

It is also worth noting that any operation that is defined for a given type can be applied to an array element of that type. For example, any operation that can be applied to the type **double** can be applied to an element of **Score**, as in

```
#include <math.h>
        .
        .
        .
ScoreSquared = pow(Score[i], 2.0);
```

or to an element of **HoursWorked**:

```
WeeklyTotal += HoursWorked[Day];
```

And any operation that is defined for the type **char** can be applied to any of the elements of **Name**:

```
#include <ctype.h>
        .
        .
        .
for (int i = 0; Name[i] != '\0'; i++)
   if (islower(Name[i]))
      Name[i] = toupper(Name[i]);
```

Array Input

Values that are to be input and stored in an array must be read one at a time. For example, the following for loop was used in the program in Figure 12.1 to read and store `NumScores` scores in the array `Score`:

```
for (int i = 0; i < NumScores; i++)
{
   cout << "Please enter score "    //    display prompt
        << (i + 1) << ':';
   cin >> Score[i];                  //    store score in array
}
```

In this loop the first value is read and stored in `Score[0]`, the second value in `Score[1]`, the third in `Score[2]`, and so on.

In some situations, the number of values to be stored in the array is not known in advance or may be too difficult to determine. Such problems can, in general, be solved with an end-of-file controlled loop or a query-controlled loop. However, if the values to be stored in the array are restricted in some manner (e.g., to nonnegative values), then we might use a sentinel-controlled loop like that in the following code segment to read and count the values and store them in the array:

```
int
   NumScores = 0;
double
   Value;

cout << "Enter first score (negative value to stop): ";
cin >> Value;

while ((NumScores < ArraySize) && (Value >= 0))
{
   Score[NumScores++] = Value;
   cout << "Enter next score (negative value to stop): ";
   cin >> Value;
}
```

Here each value is read and temporarily stored in `Value`. If it is not the end-of-data sentinel, `Value` is stored in the `NumScore`-th location of the array `Score` and the index `NumScores` is incremented by 1.

There are two ways such a loop can terminate:

1. If there are fewer data values than there are elements in the array, the sentinel value will be entered to signal the end of input, and the condition `Value >= 0` will become false and terminate repetition.
2. The array becomes filled with values when the number of values entered reaches the size `ArraySize` specified for the array `Score`. In this case, the condition `NumScores < ArraySize` will become false, and repetition will terminate.

In either case, the value of `NumScores` will be the number of values stored in the array `Score`.

Since numeric arrays are useful in solving a wide variety of problems, a general function to perform the operation of array input is likely to be used many times. The class `List` described in the next section provides such a function.

Operating on an Array

Once we have a list of values stored in an array, a function can be constructed to operate on the list by operating on individual array elements. For example, in the introductory problem for this section, the mean value of a list of scores must be calculated. The program in Figure 12.1 uses the array-processing function `Mean()` for this purpose:

```
/* -----------------------------------------------------------------
   This function computes the mean of values stored in an array.

      Receive: Array, an array of double values;
               NumValues, the number of values stored in the array
      Return:  The mean of the values
   --------------------------------------------------------------*/

double Mean(const double Array[], unsigned NumValues)

{
   if (NumValues <= 0)                    // avoid division by zero
   {
      cerr << "\n*** No elements passed to Mean!\n";
      return 0.0;
   }

   double
      Sum = 0.0;                          // sum of the scores

   for (int i = 0; i < NumValues; i++) // sum the array elements
      Sum += Array[i];

   return Sum / NumValues;                // compute the mean value
}
```

As we have seen with character string parameters, placing a pair of empty brackets after the name of a parameter indicates that the parameter is an array. The fact that the brackets are empty is significant:

> *If a length is not specified for an array parameter (brackets are empty), then there is no restriction on the length of the array that can be passed to the function.*

It is also important to remember that

> *An array is automatically passed as a reference object.*

That is, simply specifying that a parameter is an array makes it a reference parameter, without having to use the usual ampersand notation. If the function modifies the array, then the corresponding argument will also be modified. In functions where this should be prevented, we specify that the parameter is a *constant reference parameter* by prefacing the parameter declaration with the keyword **const**:

```
double Mean(const double Array[], unsigned NumValues)
```

The compiler will then generate an error if an attempt is made to modify the array within the function.

Function **Mean()** uses a for loop to calculate the sum of the values stored in **Array**:

```
for (int i = 0; i < NumValues; i++)
    Sum += Array[i];
```

This is a standard technique for processing arrays:

> *Each of an array's elements can be accessed in sequence by varying an array index variable within a loop (e.g., a for loop).*

In the sample run in Figure 12.1, the program calls

```
MeanScore = Mean(Score, NumScores);
```

with a value of 9 for **NumScores**, so the value of parameter **NumValues** is 9 and parameter **Array** refers to **Score**:

	0	1	2	3	4	5	6	7	8	9	10	11	...	31
Score	55	22	77	66	99	44	33	88	11	0	0	0		0

It should be clear that when the for loop terminates, the value of **Sum** is

$$(55.0 + 22.0 + 77.0 + \cdots + 11.0) = 495.0$$

so that the statement

```
return Sum / NumValues;
```

divides 495.0 by 9 and returns the value 55.0. Note that if the named constant **ArraySize** were the second argument to **Mean()** instead of variable **NumScores**, the result would be incorrect, since the default (zero) values in elements 9 through 31 of **Score** would be used in computing the average.

Array Output

An array cannot be output using the **iostream** output operator,[4] but must be displayed element by element. Once again, it is convenient to use a for loop that

---

[4] Again, character arrays are an exception. The **iostream** operators will treat the sequence of characters within a character array as a character string.

varies an array index. A general form for a loop that displays the first **n** elements of **Array** on the same line and separated by spaces is

```
for (int i = 0; i < n; i++)
    cout << Array[i] << ' ';
```

The first repetition displays the value of **Array[0]** followed by a space; the second repetition displays the value of **Array[1]** followed by a space; and so on, until all the values **Array[0]**, **Array[1]**, . . . , **Array[n-1]** have been displayed. Note again that the variable **n** must be used to control this loop, not the named constant **Size** that specifies the size of the array in its declaration.

A general function to perform array output is likely to be used many times. The class **List** described in the next section includes such a function.

Predefined Array Operations

As a legacy from C, the parent language of C++, the files **<string.h>** and **<stdlib.h>** contain many predefined functions that operate on arrays of characters. However there are virtually *no* analogous libraries of standard predefined functions for operating on numeric arrays. For example, the **iostream** operators have been overloaded in these files to operate on arrays of characters, allowing us to write

```
cin >> Name;
```

to fill a character array **Name** with characters from the keyboard, but there is no corresponding provision for numeric arrays. Similarly, we can simply write

```
cout << Name;
```

to display a character array **Name**, but there is no corresponding function to output a numeric array. We must implement all such operations ourselves.

One of the reasons for this is that a character-processing function can find the end of a character string simply by comparing the value of each element with the null character, which is used as an *end-of-string mark,* just as the end-of-file mark is used to denote the end of a file. By contrast, there is no numeric value equivalent to the null character that can be used to mark the end of a sequence of numbers. Functions to process numeric arrays thus need the number of values in the array so that the end of the sequence of numbers can be found. That means that in order for the output operator to display a numeric array, it would require *three* operands (the **ostream**, the array, and its length) instead of the usual two. Since C++ does not permit an operator to be overloaded with a definition in which the number of operands differs from the original definition, we cannot simply overload the output operator **<<** for numeric arrays.[5]

Usually *we* must construct a function for any operation we wish to perform on a numeric array. Because

---

[5] Such a definition would change the *arity* of the operator—for example, changing **<<** from a *binary* to a *ternary* operator. Accordingly, this restriction applies only to *operators*—it is permitted to overload *function names* with definitions in which the number of operands differs from previous definitions.

- Processing a numeric array requires at least two pieces of information, the array and the number of values in it, and
- A class allows us to store multiple data members in a single object along with the operations on that object,

classes provide a natural and convenient way to encapsulate an array, the number of values in that array, and the operations on that array. In the next section, we construct a class **List** to illustrate these capabilities.

Exercises

1. Assume that the following declarations have been made:

```
const int
   Little = 6,
   Medium = 10,
   Big = 128;
int
   i,
   Number[Medium];
char
   Ch,
   LetterCount[Big];
```

For each of the following, tell what value (if any) will be assigned to each array element, or explain why an error occurs.

(a)
```
for (i = 0; i < Medium; i++)
   Number[i] = i / 2;
```

(b)
```
for (i = 0; i < Little; i++)
   Number[i] = i * i;
for (i = Little; i < Medium; i++)
   Number[i] = Number[i - 5];
```

(c)
```
i = 0;
while (i != 10 )
{
   if ((i % 3) == 0)
      Number[i] = 0;
   else
      Number[i] = i;
   i++;
}
```

(d)
```
Number[0] = 1;
i = 1;
do
{
   Number[i] = 2 * Number[i - 1];
   i++;
}
while (i < Medium);
```

(e) for (Ch = 'A'; Ch <= 'F'; Ch++)
       if (Ch == 'A')
          LetterCount[Ch] = 1;
       else
          LetterCount[Ch] = LetterCount[Ch-1] + 1;

2. For each of the following, write appropriate declarations and statements to construct the specified array.

   (a) An array whose indices are the integers from 0 through 5 and in which each element is the same as the index

   (b) An array whose indices are the integers from 0 through 20 and for which an array element has the value true if the corresponding index is even and false otherwise

   (c) An array whose indices are the decimal ASCII values (0–127) such that the value of each element is the letter preceding the index, except that the array element corresponding to 0 is 127

   (d) An array whose indices are the decimal ASCII values (0–127) such that the value of each element is true (1) if the index is that of a vowel and false (0) otherwise

3. Assuming that values of type **char** are stored in 1 byte, values of type **int** are stored in 4 bytes, and values of type **double** are stored in 8 bytes, find the address of element **A[4]** if the address of the first element in **A** is b and **A** is declared as follows:

   (a) int A[5];

   (b) double A[5];

   (c) char A[5];

12.2 Designing a **List** Class

Many problems involve processing **lists** of information: a list of test scores, a list of names, a list of employee records, and so on. Since most programming languages do not provide a predefined list type (LISP, an acronym for LISt Processing, is one exception), lists must be processed using some other structure. This is usually done by storing the list in an array so that the ith list item is stored in the ith element of the array.

In Figure 12.1, we defined such an array inside the main function, since we wanted to keep our introduction to the topic of arrays simple. In general, however, this practice should be discouraged, because (1) the array definition and any operations on it (e.g., **Mean()**) cannot be easily reused, and (2) any functions that operate on such an array require (at least) two arguments: the array to be processed and the number of elements in the array. Both these difficulties can be avoided by defining the array in a class instead of in a main function. The number of elements in the array can be stored inside the class, along with the array itself, and the operations on the array can be defined as class members (or friends) making them easy to reuse.

In this and in the following section, we begin the construction of a general class named **List**, in which we store some of the common operations used to process lists. These operations include displaying the items in the list, searching the list for a specified item, and sorting the list so that the items are in a certain order.

Designing the Data Members

As usual, careful design of the class **List** will save time in the future. Clearly, if the class is to store a list, then it must have a data member capable of storing a list; that is, an array. However, before we declare this array, two decisions must be made:

1. How big should the array be?
2. What should be the type of the array elements?

Sizing the Array.   Answering the first question is difficult, because determining the appropriate array size depends on the problem to be solved. We will, therefore, simply choose a number (256) large enough to hold moderately sized lists. To facilitate changing this size should it become necessary, we use a named constant **MaxLength** (whose value is 256) to size the array, rather than using the literal **256**. For reasons beyond the scope of this discussion, C++ does not permit *definitions* within its classes, and so we cannot define **MaxLength** using a **const** declaration. Enumeration values can be initialized within a class, however, and so we can declare **MaxLength** and associate it with the value 256 using an **enum** declaration:

```
enum { MaxLength = 256 };
```

This declaration should, of course, be public, so that it can be accessed by any program.

Element Types.   The second question is somewhat easier. We cannot anticipate what types of data values users of the class will wish to store in a **List**, and so it should be easy for them to change the type of the array's elements, as easy as it is to change the number of elements. One way to do this is to use the **typedef** facility discussed in Section 10.3, which allows us to create an alias or alternative name for a given type. If we preface the class declaration with

```
typedef double ListElement;
```

then **ListElement** can be used throughout the class to specify the type of the array's elements. If the user of the class needs an array of a different type (say **Strings**), the only modification required is to change the **typedef** statement, replacing **double** with the new type:

```
typedef Strings ListElement;
```

When the class is recompiled, the type of the array's elements will be **Strings** instead of **double**.[6]

---

[6] A preferable approach (but one that is beyond the scope of our discussion) is to use the *template* mechanism to build a **List** whose element type is left unspecified. The template mechanism is an advanced feature of C++, and is described in Appendix G.

Figure 12.2 contains our initial declaration of class **List**, using these observations.

FIGURE 12.2 Class **List**—version 1.

```
typedef double ListElement;        // type of array elements

class List
{
public:

    enum { MaxLength = 256 };       // number of array elements

private:

    ListElement
        Array[MaxLength];           // declare the array
};
```

As we saw in Section 12.1, the definitions of the operations on an array usually depend on the number of values in the array. One of the advantages of designing a list as a class is that this number can be stored within the class, simply by declaring a data member to hold that number and ensuring that any operation that changes the number of values in the array adjusts this number accordingly. For example, a data member **Length_** can be added to class **List**, as illustrated in Figure 12.3.

FIGURE 12.3 Class **List**—version 2.

```
typedef double ListElement;        // type of array elements

class List
{
public:

    enum { MaxLength = 256 };       // number of array elements

private:

    ListElement
        Array[MaxLength];           // declare the array

    unsigned
        Length_;                    // number of array elements
};
```

Designing the List Operations

The operations performed on a list often depend on the particular problem in which the list is being used. Nevertheless, there are some operations that are sufficiently general to warrant inclusion in almost any list class:

- **Construction:** Declaring and initializing a list object
- **I/O:** Input and output of a list, both interactively and using a file
- **Assignment:** Making a copy of a list using the assignment operator
- **Subscript:** Accessing a particular element using the subscript operator
- **Length:** Determining the number of values in a list
- **Searching:** Finding a particular value in a list
- **Sorting:** Arranging the elements of a list in ascending (or descending) order

Once the operations to be included in the class have been identified, functions can be defined to perform those operations, as described in the next section.

12.3   Implementing `List` Operations

In this section, we construct operations for each of the class **List** operations identified in the preceding section.

Constructor

Recall that a constructor is a function that is called to initialize a class object when it is created. For a **List** object, construction involves the initialization of its two data members, **Length_** and **Array**, to values (possibly) supplied by the caller. Figure 12.4 shows one approach:

FIGURE 12.4   Class constructor for the class **List**.

```
/* This function is the class constructor for class List.

   Precondition:   A List object has been declared.
   Receive:        Len, the length of the array (default 0)
                   InitVal, the initial value of the array's
                     elements
   Output:         An error message if Len > MaxLength
   Postcondition:  The List has been initialized as a list of
                     Len elements, each with the value InitVal.
---------------------------------------------------------------*/

List::List(unsigned Len, ListElement InitVal)
{
   if (Len > MaxLength)
   {
      cerr << "\n*** List: Length value " << Len
           << " exceeds limit - using 0!\n";
      Length_ = 0;
   }
```

FIGURE 12.4   Class constructor for the class **List**. (cont.)

```
    Length_ = Len;

    for (int i = 0; i < Length_; i++)
        Array[i] = InitVal;
}
```

This constructor must be declared within class **List**:

```
List(unsigned Len = 0; ListElement InitVal);
```

Once this has been done, **List** objects can be declared and initialized as follows:

```
List
    Alpha,
    Beta(20),
    Gamma(10, 1.0);
```

This will construct **Alpha**, **Beta**, and **Gamma** as **List** objects of length 0, 20, and 10, respectively. The elements of **Alpha** and **Beta** are not initialized (and thus will contain garbage values) but all the elements of **Gamma** will be initialized to 1.0.

Input

The next step is to store values in **List** objects. One way to do this is to overload the input operator for **List** variables that permit **List** values to be input either interactively or from a file, as shown in Figure 12.5. The interactive version assumes that the list's length has been specified previously, whereas the file version assumes nothing about the list's previous state.

 FIGURE 12.5   Input functions for class **List**.

```
/* --- This function performs interactive input of a List object.
   It assumes that the length of the List has been previously
   initialized.

   Receive: An istream (reference) object In
            A List (reference) object InList
   Input:   A sequence of InList.Length_ ListElement values
                from In
   Return:  InList, with the input values stored in its Array
                elements
            In
---------------------------------------------------------------*/

istream& operator>>(istream& In, List& InList)
{
    for (int i = 0; i < InList.Length_; i++)
        In >> InList.Array[i];
```

FIGURE 12.5 Input functions for class **List**. (cont.)

```
   return In;
}
/* --- This function performs file input of a List object.

   Receive: An fstream (reference) object InFile
            A List (reference) object InList
   Input:   A sequence of n ListElement values, 0 < n <= MaxLength,
              from InFile
   Return:  InList, with the input values stored in its Array
              elements, its Length_ member set to n
            InFile
-----------------------------------------------------------------*/

fstream& operator>>(fstream& InFile, List& InList)
{
   InList.Length_ = 0;

   InFile >> InList.Array[InList.Length_];

   while (!(InFile.eof()) && (InList.Length_ < List::MaxLength))
   {
      InList.Length_ ++;
      InFile >> InList.Array[InList.Length_];
   }

   if (InList.Length_ >= List::MaxLength)
   {
      cerr << "\nWarning: List filled ! Values may be unread...\n";
      break;
   }

   return InFile;
}
```

Once the declarations of these (friend) functions have been stored in the class, statements such as

```
int
   NumValues;              // number of values

cout << "How many values are to be read? ";
cin >> NumValues;

List
   Alpha(NumValues);

cout << "\n\nPlease enter the list of "
     << NumValues << " values:\n\n-->";
cin >> Alpha;
```

can be used. Execution of these statements might proceed as follows:

How many values are to be read? <u>18</u>

Please enter the list of 18 values:

-> <u>11 22 33 44 55 66 77 88 99 99 88 77 66 55 44 33 22 11</u>

The **Length_** member of **Alpha** will be initialized to 18, and the 18 input values will then be stored in elements 0 through 17 of **Alpha**'s **Array** member.

Output

The output operation is relatively straightforward. The function in Figure 12.6 can be used to display the values stored in a **List** object on the screen. For output to a file simply replace the **ostream** object **Out** with an **fstream OutFile**. If it is preferable to have each number displayed on a separate line, the space character in the output statement can be replaced with a newline (e.g., **endl**).

 FIGURE 12.6 Output functions for class **List**.

```
/* This function performs screen output for a List object.

   Receive:  An ostream (reference) object Out
             A List (reference) object OutList
   Output:   The values stored within OutList, separated by spaces,
             to out
   Return:   Out
------------------------------------------------------------------*/

ostream& operator<<(ostream& Out, const List& OutList)
{
   for (int i = 0; i < OutList.Length_; i++)
      Out << OutList.Array[i] << ' ';

   return Out;
}
```

Once the declarations of these (friend) functions have been stored in class **List**, an output statement such as

cout << "\nAlpha contains: " << Alpha << endl;

can be used to display the list stored in a **List** object **Alpha**.

Assignment

Assignment is not defined for array objects in C++.[7] However, for an array within a class, we can overload the assignment operator with a definition that permits the assignment of a class object by having the **operator=** member function copy the array's values element by element. Figure 12.7 presents such a function for **List** class objects.

FIGURE 12.7   Assignment for class **List** objects.

```
/* operator= makes a copy of a List object.

   Receive: Original, a List object
   Return:  The object containing this function, with its members
            as copies of those of Original, and a reference to
            this List (for chained assignments)
            -------------------------------------------------------*/

List& List::operator=(const List& Original)
{
   Length_ = Original.Length_;          // copy scalar member

   for (int i = 0; i < Length_; i++) //  copy array member
      Array[i] = Original.Array[i];

   return *this;                        // return this object
}
```

Given this definition, the statements

```
List
   Alpha,
   Beta;
        .
        .
        .
Beta = Alpha;
```

effectively call **Beta.operator=(Alpha)** and thus assign **Beta** the values from **Alpha**.

Subscripting

Although it is important to be able to manipulate entire lists of data with operations like input, output, and assignment, it is also important to be able to access the

---

[7] As mentioned earlier, the reason is that the value of an array object is not its sequence of elements but the *address* of its first element. The array name can be thought of as a named constant whose value is this address, and so an assignment, by attempting to change the value of that constant, generates an error.

individual values stored in the **Array** member of a **List**. Fortunately, the brackets
(**[ ]**) used to access array elements are not simply punctuation but denote an actual
operator called the **subscript operator,** which can be overloaded. Like the assignment operator, the subscript operator must be defined as a member function for a
class. Figure 12.8 presents such a definition.

 FIGURE 12.8 Subscript operation for class **List**.

```
/* This function provides access to the values stored within a List.

    Receive: i, an index for a List element
    Return:  The value of the element in member Array whose index
             is i
--------------------------------------------------------------------*/

ListElement& List::operator[] (unsigned i)
{
   if (i < Length_)
      return Array[i];

   cerr << "\n***Subscript: invalid attempt to access element "
        << i << " !\n";
   exit (-1);
}
```

Note that *we* must explicitly check that the value of the argument **i** is a valid index
for **Array**. This is done through two separate actions:

1. Declaring **i** as an **unsigned** parameter (ensuring that its value is nonnegative);
   and
2. Checking that the value of **i** is less than the number of values in the list.

If these conditions are met, the function can access and return the appropriate value
from the **Array** member. Otherwise, an informative (fatal) error message is displayed.

Once this function is declared within the class, if **Beta** is a **List** object, the
familiar notation **Beta[i]** can be used to access the element whose index is **i** in
the **Array** member of **Beta**.

Another point concerns the return type of **operator[ ]**. If the return type were
simply **ListElement**, then the statement

```
   return Array[i];
```

would return a copy of the value of **Array[i]**. By making the return type of
operator[ ] a *reference* to a **ListElement**, the actual reference (address) of the
ith element of **Array** is returned. The difference is significant, because an assignment statement such as

```
   Beta[0] = 3.14159;
```

is intended to change the value of element **0** of the **Array** member of **Beta**. If **operator[]** returns the reference of that element, then such an assignment correctly modifies the value of that element. However, if **operator[]** returns *a copy* of that element, then the assignment statement (erroneously) modifies this copy, leaving **Beta** as it was.

The definition of **operator[]** in Figure 12.9 is sufficient if **operator[]** is never applied to a constant **Array**. However, this cannot be assumed, and so a second definition is needed with logic identical to the version in Figure 12.9. Not only must this new version be a **const** function, but it must return a **const ListElement** reference to inform the compiler that it is to be applied to **const Array** objects. The declaration of this version can be seen in Figure 12.16.

Length

Another useful list operation is to determine the number of values in a list. This function is trivial to write, since the data member **Length_** contains this value. The extraction function **Length()** determines the number of values in the list by extracting and returning the value of the **Length_** member:

```
unsigned Length(void) const { return Length_; }
```

As usual, such a simple function should be defined within the class itself, as in Figure 12.16. Once defined, the number of values in a **List** object **Beta** is easily determined by calling this function:

```
unsigned
    ValuesInBeta = Beta.Length();
```

Searching 1: Linear Search

Another important problem in list processing is **searching** a list of data items for a specified item and retrieving some information associated with that item. For example, we search a telephone directory for a specific name in order to retrieve the phone number listed with that name, a dictionary for a word in order to retrieve its meaning, and a file of student records in order to find the record of a student with a specified student number.

A **linear search** of a list begins with the first item in the list and searches sequentially until either the desired item is found or the end of the list is reached. The following algorithm is a general description of this method of searching:

LINEAR SEARCH ALGORITHM

/* This algorithm searches an arbitrary list for a given value.

    Receive: *SearchVal,* a value;
                a list of values
    Return: The index of *SearchVal,* if it is present in the list;
               −1, otherwise

                                                                        */

1. For each index *i* of the list:
   If element *i* of the list is equal to *SearchVal*
      Return *i*;

2. Return −1; // This happens only if we fail to find *SearchVal* in step 1.

The return value of −1 is used to indicate that the search failed (*SearchVal* is not found in the list).

Figure 12.9 presents a member function `LSearch()` for class `List` that performs a linear search on the `List` object of which it is a member. Note that the function's return type must be `int`, not `unsigned`, since the return value may be negative. Note also that this function assumes that the equality operator is defined for comparing objects of type `ListElement`.

FIGURE 12.9 Linear search for class **List**.

```
/* LSearch finds the index of a value SearchVal in a List.

   Receive:  SearchVal, a (ListElement) value
   Return:   The index of SearchVal, if it is present in member
             Array, and -1 otherwise
-------------------------------------------------------------------*/

int List::LSearch (const ListElement& SearchVal) const
{
   for (int i = 0; i < Length_; i++)  // for each element:
      if (Array[i] == SearchVal)      //   if SearchVal at location i
         return i;                    //      return its index

   return -1;                         // SearchVal not found
}
```

Given such a function, we can find a given `Value` in a `List` object `Beta` with the call:

```
int
   Position = Beta.LSearch(Value);      // search Beta for Value

if (Position < 0)                       // if the search failed
   cerr << "\n*** " << Value            //    take an appropriate
        << " is not in the List!\n";    //       action
else                                    // otherwise
   // ... do something with Beta[Position] //    proceed
```

The linear search technique is important because it can be used for *any* list. Unlike other search algorithms, linear search is not restricted to lists whose elements have some special organization or arrangement.

Sorting 1: Simple Selection Sort

Sorting is the problem of arranging the items in a list so that they are in either ascending or descending order. There are literally dozens of sorting methods of varying complexity and efficiency. We start by examining one of the simplest sorting methods, called **simple selection sort.** Although it is not an efficient sorting method for large lists, it does perform reasonably well for small lists, and it is easy to understand. More efficient sorting schemes are described later in this section and in the exercises.

The basic idea of selection sort is to process a list by making a number of passes through the list, correctly positioning one item on each pass. For example, one approach is to

Find the smallest entry in the list and move it to the first position;
Find the second-smallest entry in the list and move it to the second position;
Find the third-smallest entry in the list and move it to the third position;

$$\vdots$$

and so on, until all the entries are in order. To illustrate, suppose that the following list is to be sorted into ascending order:

$$67 , 33 , 21 , 84 , 49 , 50 , 75$$

We first scan the list to locate the smallest item and find it in position 3:

$$67 , 33 , \boxed{21} , 84 , 49 , 50 , 75$$

We interchange this item with the first item, thus properly positioning the smallest item at the beginning of the list:

$$\boxed{21} , 33 , 67 , 84 , 49 , 50 , 75$$

Next, we scan the sublist of the items from position 2 onward to find the smallest item,

$$21 , \boxed{33} , 67 , 84 , 49 , 50 , 75$$

and exchange it with the second item (itself in this case), thus properly positioning the second-smallest item in position 2:

$$21 , \boxed{33} , 67 , 84 , 49 , 50 , 75$$

We continue in this manner, locating the smallest item in the sublist of items from position 3 on and interchanging it with the third item, then properly positioning the smallest item in the sublist of items from position 4 on, and so on, until we eventually do this for the sublist consisting of the last two items:

21 , 33 , 49 , 84 , 67 , 50 , 75

21 , 33 , 49 , 50 , 67 , 84 , 75

21 , 33 , 49 , 50 , 67 , 84 , 75

21 , 33 , 49 , 50 , 67 , 75 , 84

Positioning the smallest item in this last sublist obviously also positions the last item correctly and thus completes the sort.

An algorithm for this simple selection sort is as follows:

SIMPLE SELECTION SORT ALGORITHM

/* This algorithm sorts a list of items into ascending order.

Receive: A list of n items $L[0], \ldots, L[n-1]$
Return: The list with its elements arranged in ascending order

——*/

For each index i in the range 0 through $n - 2$:
a. On the ith pass, find the index Pos of the smallest item in the sublist $L[i], \ldots, L[n]$.
b. Exchange the item in $L[i]$ with the item in $L[Pos]$.

Refinement of (a). Step a of this algorithm is to find the index of the smallest item in a portion of the list. This is a searching problem that can be solved using an approach similar to the approach used in **LSearch()**.

The subtle part of this problem is that we must locate the smallest value in *a portion of the list*, as opposed to the entire list. A general function to find the index of the smallest value in a sublist needs an index at which to begin the search and an index at which to end the search, as shown in the following algorithm:

ALGORITHM TO FIND THE SMALLEST VALUE IN A LIST

/* This algorithm finds the index of the smallest value in a list.

Receive: *L*, a (sub)list of items;
First, the index of the element where the search is to begin; and
Last, the index of the element where the search is to end
Return: The index of the smallest element in the examined elements

——*/

1. Set *MinPos* equal to *First;*
2. For each index *j* in the range from *First* + 1 through *Last*:
    If element *L*[*j*] is less than element *L*[*MinPos*], then
        Set *MinPos* equal to *j*;
3. Return *MinPos.*

By encoding this function as a member of `List`, we can avoid passing the list to be searched. Figure 12.10 shows such a function, with bounds checking added.

FIGURE 12.10   Searching a list for its smallest value.

```
/* IndexOfMin finds the index of the smallest value in a List.

   Receive: First, the index of the first element to be examined
            Last, the index of the last element to be examined
   Return:  The index of the smallest value in the examined elements
   ------------------------------------------------------------------*/

unsigned List::IndexOfMin(unsigned First, unsigned Last) const
{
   if ((First > Last) || (Last >= Length_))
   {
      cerr << "\n*** IndexOfMin: invalid index(s) received: "
           << First << ':' << Last << "!\n";
      exit (-1);
   }

   unsigned
      MinPos = First;

   for (int j = First+1; j <= Last; j++)  // for each j > First:
      if (Array[j] < Array[MinPos])       //    if j-th elem. is smaller
         MinPos = j;                      //       save value of j

   return MinPos;                         // return index of smallest
}
```

Given this function, the statement

```
unsigned
   NumValues = Beta.Length(),
   Pos = Beta.IndexOfMin(i, NumValues-1);
```

can be used to find the index of the smallest element in the sublist that begins with the element whose index is `i` and ends with the element whose index is `NumValues - 1`. Note that this function assumes that `operator<` is defined for the type `ListElement`. If `ListElement` is a class, then `operator<` must be overloaded to specify the less-than relation for such objects.

Refinement of (b). Step b of the selection-sort algorithm is to exchange the item in position *i* with the item in position *Pos*. This can be done with a `ListElement` version of the `Swap()` function given in Section 7.3:

```
void Swap(ListElement& A, ListElement& B)
{
    ListElement
        Temp;

    Temp = A; A = B; B = Temp;
}
```

Given this definition, the call

```
Swap(Beta[i], Beta[Pos]);
```

will exchange the values of `List` elements `Beta[i]` and `Beta[Pos]` as long as the assignment operator is defined for the type `ListElement`.

The function `SSort()` in Figure 12.11 uses the functions `IndexOfMin()` and `Swap()` to implement the simple selection sort algorithm.

FIGURE 12.11 Simple selection sort for class `List`.

```
/* SSort sorts a List into ascending order using simple selection sort.

    Return: The List containing this function,
            its Array member sorted into ascending order
-----------------------------------------------------------------*/

void List::SSort(void)
{
    int
        MinPos;

    for (int i = 0; i < Length_ - 1; i++)
    {
        MinPos = IndexOfMin(i, Length_ - 1);
        Swap(Array[i], Array[MinPos]);
    }
}
```

If we then declare these member functions within the class `List`, they can be applied to any `List`, as illustrated in the program in Figure 12.12.

FIGURE 12.12 Using selection sort.

```
/* This program illustrates the use of function SSort.

    Input:   A sequence of double values
    Output:  User prompts and the input sequence in ascending order
-----------------------------------------------------------------*/
```

FIGURE 12.12 Using selection sort. (cont.)

```cpp
#include <iostream.h>
#include "List.h"

int main(void)
{
    cout << "\nThis program inputs and sorts"
         << " a sequence of numeric values.\n\n";

    int
        NumValues;                      // number of values

    cout << "How many values are to be read? ";
    cin >> NumValues;

    List
        OriginalList(NumValues),
        SortedList;                     // declare some lists

    cout << "\nPlease enter the list of "
         << NumValues << " values:\n--->";

    cin >> OriginalList;                // fill List from keyboard

    SortedList = OriginalList;          // work with a copy of the list
    SortedList.SSort();                 // sort the list

    cout << "\n\nOriginal List: " << OriginalList << endl
         << " Sorted list: " << SortedList << "\n\n";
    return 0;
}
```

Sample run:

```
This program inputs and sorts a sequence of numeric values.

How many values are to be read? 9
Please enter the list of 9 values:

---> 55 88 34 84 21 99 5 83 71

Original List: 55 88 34 84 21 99 5 83 71
  Sorted List: 5 21 34 55 71 83 84 88 99
```

Searching 2: Binary Search

One of the reasons that sorting is important is that it imposes an *ordering* on a list. This ordering makes it possible to perform certain other list operations more efficiently. An example of this is the *search* operation, which we have already implemented using the linear search algorithm. Although linear search may be an adequate method for small data sets, it is quite time-consuming for large lists. For certain kinds of lists, more efficient methods are available.

One such method is the **binary search** algorithm, which may be used if the list to be searched has been sorted. With this method, we begin by examining the middle element of the list. If that element contains the value for which we are searching, then the search is successful. Otherwise, if the item for which we are searching is less than the middle element of the list, we repeat the procedure ignoring the second half of the list. Otherwise, the item for which we are searching must be greater than the middle element of the list, so we repeat the procedure ignoring the first half of the list.

To illustrate, suppose that the list to be searched is as follows

1331, 1373, 1555, 1624, 1682, 1755, 1889, 2002, 2335, 2665, 3103

and that we are looking for 1889. Binary search begins by examining the middle number, 1755.

1331, 1373, 1555, 1624, 1682, 1755 , 1889, 2002, 2335, 2665, 3103

This is not the item being sought, but because 1889 is greater than 1755 and the list values are in ascending order, the first half of the list can now be ignored, leaving

1889, 2002, 2335, 2665, 3103

The middle number in this sublist is 2335

1889, 2002, 2335 , 2665, 3103

and the item sought, 1889, is less than 2335, so the second half of this sublist can be ignored, leaving:

1889, 2002

Since there is no middle number in this half, we examine the number immediately preceding the middle position, that is, 1889.

1889 , 2002

In this example, we have located the desired entry with only three comparisons, rather than the seven required by a linear search.

In general, the algorithm for binary search of an array can be described as follows:

BINARY SEARCH ALGORITHM

/* This algorithm searches a sorted array for a given value.

Receive: *SearchVal,* the value being sought;
        Array, an array whose elements are in ascending order
Returns: The index of *SearchVal* within *Array,* if *SearchVal* is present;
        −1, otherwise

——*/

1. Initialize *First* to the index of the first element, and
        Last to the index of the last element (*NumItems*−1).
2. While (*First* ≤ *Last*):
    a. Find the middle position in the sublist by setting *Middle* equal to the integer quotient of (*First* + *Last*) divided by 2.

b. Compare *SearchVal* with element *Middle* of *Array*. There are three possibilities:

    (i) *SearchVal* = *Array*[*Middle*]: *SearchVal* has been found; return *Middle*.

    (ii) *SearchVal* < *Array*[*Middle*]: *SearchVal* is in the first half of the sublist; set *Last* equal to *Middle* − 1.

    (iii) *SearchVal* > *Array*[*Middle*]: *SearchVal* is in the last half of the sublist; set *First* equal to *Middle* + 1.

End While.

3. Return −1; // This happens only if *SearchVal* is not found in step 2.

Since the `Array` member of class `List` is an array, this algorithm can be applied to `Array`. Figure 12.13 shows an implementation of the algorithm as a member function of class `List`.

FIGURE 12.13   Binary search for class **List**.

```
/* BSearch finds the index of a value SearchVal in a List.

   Receive: SearchVal, a (ListElement) value
   Return:  The index of SearchVal, if it is present in this List,
            and -1 otherwise.
-------------------------------------------------------------------*/

int List::BSearch(const ListElement& SearchVal) const
{
   int
      First = 0,                        // index of first value
      Last = Length_ - 1,               // index of last value
      Middle;                           // index of middle value

   while (First <= Last)                // while sublist is not empty
   {
      Middle = (First + Last) / 2;      //    find middle element

      if (SearchVal == Array[Middle])   //    if it's the value sought
         return Middle;                 //       return its index
      else if (SearchVal < Array[Middle])//   else if it's in 1st half
         Last = Middle - 1;             //       adjust value of Last
      else                              //    else (it's in 2nd half)
         First = Middle + 1;            //       adjust value of First
   }
                                        // if we reach this point,
   return -1;                           //    SearchVal is not in
                                        //    the Array
}
```

With each repetition of the while loop, the size of the list to be searched decreases by approximately one-half. As we shall see, this allows **BSearch()** to search a list quite rapidly.

*Sorting 2: Quicksort

The **quicksort** method of sorting is more efficient than simple selection sort. It is, in fact, one of the fastest methods of sorting and is most often implemented by a recursive algorithm. The basic idea of quicksort is to choose some element called a **pivot** and then to perform a sequence of exchanges so that all elements that are less than this pivot are to its left and all elements that are greater than the pivot are to its right. This correctly positions the pivot and divides the (sub)list into two smaller sublists, each of which may then be sorted independently in the *same* way. This **divide-and-conquer** strategy leads naturally to a recursive sorting algorithm.

To illustrate this splitting of a list into two sublists, consider the following list of integers:

$$50, \ 30, \ 20, \ 80, \ 90, \ 70, \ 95, \ 85, \ 10, \ 15, \ 75, \ 25$$

If we select the first number as the pivot, we must rearrange the list so that 30, 20, 10, 15, and 25 are placed before 50 and 80, 90, 70, 95, 85, and 75 are placed after it. To carry out this rearrangement, we search from the right end of the list for an element less than 50 and from the left end for an item greater than 50.

This locates the two numbers 25 and 80, which we now interchange to obtain

We then resume the search from the right for a number less than 50 and from the left for a number greater than 50:

This locates the numbers 15 and 90, which are then interchanged:

A continuation of the searches locates 10 and 70:

Interchanging these gives

When we resume our search from the right for a number less than 50, we locate the value 10, which was found on the previous left-to-right search. This signals the end of the two searches, and we interchange 50 and 10, giving

$$\underline{10\,,\,30\,,\,20\,,\,25\,,\,15}\,,\, \boxed{50}\,,\, \underline{95\,,\,85\,,\,70\,,\,90\,,\,75\,,\,80}$$

The two underlined sublists now have the required properties: All elements in the first sublist are less than 50, and all those in the right sublist are greater than 50. Consequently, 50 has been properly positioned.

Both the left sublist,

$$10,\ 30,\ 20,\ 25,\ 15$$

and the right sublist,

$$95,\ 85,\ 70,\ 90,\ 75,\ 80$$

can now be sorted independently in the same way. Each must be split by choosing and correctly positioning one pivot element (the first) in each of them. For this, a function is needed to split a list of items in the array positions given by two parameters **Low** and **High**, denoting the beginning and end positions of the sublist, respectively. The member function in Figure 12.14 carries out the desired splitting of a **List**.

 FIGURE 12.14   Splitting a list into two sublists.

```
/* This function splits a List into two subLists, using the first
   element as pivot, and returns the index of the element about
   which the List was divided.

   Receive:  Low, the index of the first element
             High, the index of the last element
   Return:   The List containing this function,
                with all elements < the pivot to the left of the pivot
                and all elements > the pivot to the right of the pivot
             The index of the element about which L was split
-----------------------------------------------------------------*/

unsigned List::Split(unsigned Low, unsigned High)
{
   int
      Left = Low,                      // index of first element
      Right = High;                    // index of last element
   ListElement
      Pivot = Array[Low];              // pivot element

   while (Left < Right)                // while indices haven't met
   {
      while (Array[Right] > Pivot)     // scan right to left to find
         Right--;                      //    elem smaller than pivot

      while ((Left < Right) &&         // scan left to right to find
         (Array[Left] <= Pivot))       //    elem larger than pivot
         Left++;
```

FIGURE 12.14   Splitting a list into two sublists. (cont.)

```
    if (Left < Right)                   // if indices haven't met
        Swap(Array[Left], Array[Right]);//   exchange the two elems
}

    Array[Low] = Array[Right];          // switch element in split
    Array[Right] = Pivot;               //    position with pivot

    return Right;                       // return split position
}
```

Given this function, a recursive function to sort a list is now easy to write.

- The trivial case occurs when the **List** being examined is empty or contains a single element, in which case the **List** is in order, and nothing needs to be done.
- The nontrivial case occurs when the **List** contains multiple elements, in which case the **List** can be sorted by
  a. Splitting the **List** into two sublists;
  b. Recursively sorting the left sublist; and
  c. Recursively sorting the right sublist.

This algorithm is encoded as function **QuickSort()** in Figure 12.15.

 FIGURE 12.15   Quicksort for class **List**.

```
/* This function sorts a list using the quicksort method.

   Receive: Low, the index of the first element
            High, the index of the last element
   Return:  The List containing this function, in ascending order
   -------------------------------------------------------------*/

void List::QuickSort(int Low, int High)
{
    int
        Mid;                            // index of split point

    if (Low < High)                     // if list has 2 or more items
    {
        Mid = Split(Low, High);         // split the list
        QuickSort(Low, Mid-1);          // recursively sort left half
        QuickSort(Mid+1, High);         // recursively sort right half
    }
}

/* This function is the interface to QuickSort(), so that programs
   using the function need not pass the indices of the first and
   last elements.

   Return: The List containing this function, in ascending order
   -------------------------------------------------------------*/
```

FIGURE 12.15 Quicksort for class **List**. (cont.)

```
void List::QSort(void)
{
   QuickSort(0, Length_ - 1);
}
```

The only subtle point in Figure 12.15 is that we defined two functions:

- **QuickSort()**, which (because it recursively sorts **sublists**) requires the indices of the first and last elements of the sublist being sorted; and
- **QSort()**, which (because it is not recursive and sorts the entire list) simply calls **QuickSort()** and passes it the indices of the first and last value in the list.

In the declaration of these functions, **QuickSort()** and **Split()** are declared in the private portion of the class, so that only members like **QSort()** and friends of the class can call them. **QSort()** is placed in the public portion of the class so that a **List** named **Beta** can be sorted with the following call:

> **Beta.QSort();**

To demonstrate how Quicksort works, suppose that **Beta** is list of the following integers:

$$8, 2, 13, 5, 14, 3, 6$$

Then the call

> **Beta.QSort();**

simply calls

> **Beta.QuickSort(0, 6);**

The following table traces the action of **Quicksort()** as it sorts this list. An underlined (sub)list in the first column indicates the current (sub)list being sorted; the values for parameters **Low** and **High** are given in the second and third columns. List elements in color have been correctly positioned.

(Sub)List Being Sorted	Low	High	Mid	Action
8, 2, 13, 5, 14, 3, 6	0	6		Call **Quicksort()** with original list.
3, 2, 6, 5, 8, 14, 13			4	**Split()** positions the pivot 8 in location 4.
3, 2, 6, 5, 8, 14, 13	0	3		Call **Quicksort()** with left sublist.
2, 3, 6, 5, 8, 14, 13			1	**Split()** positions the pivot 3 in location 1.

(Sub)List Being Sorted	Low	High	Mid	Action
2, 3 , 6, 5, 8 , 14, 13	0	1		Call **Quicksort()** with left (one-element) sublist. **Low ≮ High**, so sublist is already sorted. Return to previous reference to **Quicksort()**.
2 , 3 , 6, 5, 8 , 14, 13	0	3	1	Left sublist is now sorted.
2 , 3 , 6, 5, 8 , 14, 13	2	3		Now call **Quicksort()** with right sublist.
2 , 3 , 5, 6, 8 , 14, 13			2	**Split()** positions the pivot 5 in location 2.
2 , 3 , 5 , 6, 8 , 14, 13	3	2		Call **Quicksort()** with left (empty) sublist. **Low ≮ High**, so sublist is already sorted. Return to previous reference to **Quicksort()**.
2 , 3 , 5 , 6, 8 , 14, 13	2	3	2	Left (empty) sublist has been sorted.
2 , 3 , 5 , 6, 8 , 14, 13	3	3		Call **Quicksort()** with right (one-element) sublist. **Low ≮ High**, so sublist is already sorted. Return to previous reference to **Quicksort()**.
2 , 3 , 5 , 6 , 8 , 14, 13	2	3	2	Right sublist has been sorted, so return to previous reference to **Quicksort()**.
2 , 3 , 5, 6 , 8 , 14, 13	0	3	1	Right sublist has been sorted, so return to previous (original) reference to **Quicksort()**.
2, 3, 5, 6 , 8 , 14, 13	0	6	4	Left sublist has been sorted.
2, 3, 5, 6 , 8 , 14, 13	5	6		Now call **Quicksort()** with right sublist.
2, 3, 5, 6 , 8 , 13 , 14			5	**Split()** positions the pivot 13 in location 5.
2, 3, 5, 6 , 8 , 13 , 14	6	5		Call **Quicksort()** with left (empty) sublist. **Low ≮ High**, so sublist is already sorted. Return to previous reference to **Quicksort()**.
2, 3, 5, 6 , 8 , 13 , 14	5	6	5	Left sublist has been sorted.
2, 3, 5, 6 , 8 , 13 , 14			6	Call **Quicksort()** with right (one-element) sublist. **Low ≮ High**, so sublist is already sorted. Return to previous reference to **Quicksort()**.
2, 3, 5, 6 , 8 , 13, 14,	5	6	5	Right sublist has been sorted, so return to previous (original) reference to **Quicksort()**.
2, 3, 5, 6, 8, 13, 14	0	6	4	Original reference to **Quicksort()** is complete, so entire list has been sorted.

The Class Declaration

Once all these operations on a `List` have been defined and their declarations stored within class `List`, the class declaration appears as shown in Figure 12.16.

 FIGURE 12.16   Header file for class `List`.

```
/* This file contains the declaration of class List.
   NOTE:  Because of similarities to other classes, some documentation
          has been omitted to save space. See the data disk for full
          documentation and for the corresponding implementation file.
----------------------------------------------------------------*/

#ifndef LIST
#define LIST

#include <iostream.h>              // interactive I/O
#include <fstream.h>               // file I/O

typedef double ListElement;        // array element type

class List
{

// -- the public section --

public:
    enum { MaxLength = 256 };      // number of array elements

    /***** Constructor *****/

/* This function is the class constructor for class List.

   Precondition:  A List object has been declared.
   Receive:       Len, the length of the array (default 0)
                  InitVal, the initial value of the array's
                  elements
   Output:        An error message if Len > MaxLength
   Postcondition: The List has been initialized as a list of
                  Len elements, each with the value InitVal.
----------------------------------------------------------------*/

List(unsigned Len = 0, ListElement InitVal);


    /***** Operations *****/
    /***---Input---***/
    /*-----Interactive -----
       Receive: An istream (reference) object In
                A List (reference) object InList
       Input:   A sequence of InList.Length_ ListElement values,
                from In
```

FIGURE 12.16 Header file for class **List**. (cont.)

```
    Return:   InList, with the input values stored in its Array
              elements
              In
-----------------------------------------------------------------*/
friend istream& operator>>(istream& In, List& InList);


/*-----File -----
   Receive: An fstream (reference) object InFile, presumably
            opened for input
            A List (reference) object InList
   Input:   A sequence of n numbers, 0 < n <= MaxLength,
            from InFile
   Return:  InList, with the input values stored in its Array
            elements, its Length_ member set to n
            InFile
-----------------------------------------------------------------*/
friend fstream& operator>>(fstream& InFile, List& InList);



/***---Output---***/
/***---Screen ---
   Receive: An ostream (reference) object Out
            A List (reference) object OutList
   Output:  The values stored within OutList to Out, separated
            by spaces
   Return:  Out
-----------------------------------------------------------------*/
friend ostream& operator<<(ostream& Out, const List& L);


/***---File ---
   Receive: An ostream (reference) object OutFile, presumably
            opened for output
            A List (reference) object OutList
   Output:  The values stored within OutList to OutFile,
            separated by spaces
   Return:  OutFile
-----------------------------------------------------------------*/
friend fstream& operator<<(fstream& OutFile, const List& OutList);



/***---Assignment---
   Receive:  Original, a List object
   Return:   The object containing this function, with its
             members as copies of those of Original, and a
             reference to this List (for chained assignments)
-----------------------------------------------------------------*/
   List& operator=(const List& Original);


/***---Subscript---
   Receive: i, an index for a List element
   Return:  The value of the element in member Array with index i
   Note: Two forms are provided, the first for nonconstant
         arrays and the second for constant arrays.
-----------------------------------------------------------------*/
```

```
ListElement& operator[](unsigned i);

const ListElement& operator[](unsigned i) const;
```

FIGURE 12.16 Header file for class **List**. (cont.)

```
/***---Length---
   Return:  The length of the list (the value stored in field
               Length_).
-----------------------------------------------------------------*/

unsigned Length(void) const
   { return Length_; }

/***---Searches---***/
/***---Linear search ---
   Receive:  SearchVal, a (ListElement) value
   Return:   The index of SearchVal, if it is present in
               member Array, and -1 otherwise
-----------------------------------------------------------------*/
int LSearch (const ListElement& SearchVal) const;

/***---Binary search ---
   Receive:  SearchVal, a ListElement value
   Return:   The index of SearchVal, if it is present in
               member Array, and -1 otherwise
-----------------------------------------------------------------*/
int BSearch(const ListElement& SearchVal) const;

/***---Find smallest value in a sublist ---
   Receive:  First, the index of the first element to be examined
             Last, the index of the last element to be examined
   Return:   The index of the smallest value in the examined
               elements
-----------------------------------------------------------------*/
unsigned IndexOfMin(unsigned First, unsigned Last) const;

/***---Sorts---***/
/***---Simple Selection Sort ---

   Return:  The List containing this function, its Array
               member sorted into ascending order by simple
               selection sort
-----------------------------------------------------------------*/
void SSort(void);

/***---Quicksort ---

   Return:  The List containing this function, its Array
               member sorted into ascending order by
               quicksort
-----------------------------------------------------------------*/
void QSort(void);
```

FIGURE 12.16   Header file for class **List**. (cont.)

```
// -- the private section --
private:

/********** data members **********/
   ListElement
      Array[MaxLength];                 //      the array

   unsigned
      Length_;                          //      array value counter

/********** private functions **********/
   unsigned Split(                      //      quicksort utility
            unsigned Low,               //         sublist beginning
            unsigned High);             //         sublist end
   void QuickSort(                      //      quick sort
            unsigned Low,               //         sublist beginning
            unsigned High);             //         sublist end
};

#endif
```

There are many decisions to be made when deciding how to organize the declarations within a class. For example, some might argue that function **IndexOfMin()** is just a utility function used by **SSort()** and so should be private, not public. Others would disagree, believing that the operation performed by **IndexOfMin()** is sufficiently useful that it deserves to be made publicly available, as we have done in class **List**. By contrast, **Split()** is a utility function that seems to have little use outside of **QuickSort()**, and so we store it as a private function. Similarly, we view **QuickSort()** as a utility function that has little use outside of **QSort()** and so make it a private member of **List**.

Exercises

1. Write a **List** member function **Insert()** for inserting an item at a specified position.

2. Write a **List** member function **Delete()** for deleting an item at a specified position.

3. Write **List** member functions **Max()** and **Min()** that find the largest and smallest values in a **List**, respectively; assume that the relational operators are overloaded for a **ListElement**.

4. Write a member function to find and return the range of values in a **List**, that is, the difference between the largest value and the smallest.

5. The Cawker City Candy Company records the number of cases of candy produced each day over a 4-week period. Write a program that reads these production numbers and stores them in an array. The program should then accept a week number and a day number from the user and should display the production level for that day. Assume that each week consists of 5 workdays.

6. The Cawker City Candy Company maintains two warehouses, one in Chicago and one in Detroit, each of which stocks at most 25 different items. Write a program that first reads the product numbers of items stored in the Chicago warehouse and stores them in an array **Chicago** and then repeats this for the items stored in the Detroit warehouse, storing these product numbers in an array **Detroit**. The program should then find and display the **intersection** of these two lists of numbers—that is, the collection of product numbers common to both lists. The lists should not be assumed to have the same number of elements.

7. Repeat Exercise 7, but find and display the **union** of the two lists—that is, the collection of product numbers that are elements in at least one of the lists.

8. Peter the postal worker became bored one night, and to break the monotony of the night shift, he carried out an experiment with a row of mailboxes in the post office. These mailboxes were numbered 1 through 150, and beginning with mailbox 2, he opened the doors of all the even-numbered mailboxes. Next, beginning with mailbox 3, he went to every third mailbox, opening it if it was closed and closing it if it was open. Then he repeated this procedure with every fourth mailbox, then every fifth mailbox, and so on. When he finished, he was surprised at the distribution of closed mailboxes. Using class **List**, write a program to determine which ones these were.

12.4 Example: Information Retrieval

Once we have constructed an array-based class like **List**, we can use that class, either on its own or to build more complex objects. In this section, we present an information-retrieval system that makes direct use of class **List**.

Problem: Retrieving Student Information

In Section 11.3, we built a class **Student** to model the information for a typical student (Name, ID Number, Year, Credits, and GPA). In that class, we built operations to input and output a **Student**, permit the assignment of a **Student**, and so on. The problem of overloading the relational operators so that two students could be compared using their names was described in the exercises at the end of that section.

In this section, we reuse the work done in developing the **List** and **Student** classes by building a list of student objects. This is surprisingly easy. All that is necessary is to modify the header file for class **List** as follows:

```
#include "Student.h"

typedef Student ListElement;
```

The effect of these lines is to make the name **ListElement** a synonym for
Student rather than for **double**. As a result, when the implementation file for
class **List** is recompiled, the member **Array** within **List** (whose elements are of
type **ListElement**) becomes an array of **Student**s,

Array	0	1	2	3	...	MaxLength-1
FirstName_						
LastName_						
StudentNumber_						
Year_						
Credits_						
GPA_						

and all the operations that are defined for **ListElements** become defined for
Students.

Figure 12.17 presents a program that uses the resulting **List** of **Student**
values for information retrieval. It uses the **#include** directive to insert the **List**
declaration described in the previous section, and then defines a **List** named
StudentList. The program fills **StudentList** with the sequence of **Student** data
records from a file **"Registrar.Dat"**; then (since this is a small file) it uses the
member function **SSort()** to arrange these records in ascending order, by their
names. Once the elements of **StudentList** are in order, the program retrieves the
information for any particular student, using binary search.

FIGURE 12.17 Student information retrieval.

```
/* This program inputs student numbers, class codes, and test
   scores.  A student number can then be input and the
   corresponding class code and test score are retrieved.

   Input (file):     A list of Student records
   Input (keyboard): One or more student ID numbers
   Output:           The student data corresponding to the
                     input ID number
   -----------------------------------------------------------*/
```

FIGURE 12.17 Student information retrieval. (cont.)

```
#include <iostream.h>
#include <stdlib.h>
#include "Student.h"
#include "List.h"                        // list of Student records
#include "Strings.h"

int main(void)
{
  const char
     EOFMark[] = "Ctrl-D",
     InputFile[] = "Registrar.Dat";

  cout
     << "\nThis program simulates an information retrieval system"
     << "\n\tby reading a series of student records from"
     << '\'' << InputFile << '\''
     << "\n\tand then allowing retrieval of any student's data.\n";

  fstream
     InStream(InputFile, ios::in);       // open the input file

  if (InStream.fail())                   // check for failure
  {
     cerr << "\n*** Main: unable to open '"
          << InputFile << "'!\n";
     exit (-1);
  }

  int
     NumValues;
  InStream >> NumValues;

  List
     StudentList(NumValues);             // list of Student records

  InStream >> StudentList;               // fill the list
  StudentList.SSort();                   // sort the list (by name)

  long
     Pos;                                // index of ID in List
  Strings
     FirstName,                          // the names of the
     LastName;                           // student being sought

  cout <<"\nEnter a student's name ("    // prompt for input
       << EOFMark << " to quit): ";
  cin >> FirstName >> LastName;          // get first name
  while (!cin.eof())                     // while more data:
  {
     Pos = StudentList.BSearch(          // binary search for
           Student(FirstName, LastName));//   this student
     if (Pos >= 0)                       // if search successful
        cout << endl                     //    display the data
             << StudentList[Pos] << endl;
```

FIGURE 12.17   Student information retrieval. (cont.)

```
      else                                    // otherwise, tell user
         cerr << "\nThere is no student whose name is "
              << FirstName << ' ' << LastName << ".\n";
      cout <<"\nEnter a student's name ("    // get next name
           << EOFMark << " to quit): ";
      cin >> FirstName >> LastName;
   }
   return 0;
}
```

Listing of input file `Registrar.Dat`:

```
6
777889999 Ben Dover
Junior    16.0   2.5

333221111 Stan Dupp
Senior    8.0 3.75

999887777 Isabelle Ringing
Junior    16.0   3.8

444556666 Ally Cat
Senior    16.0 3.125

111223333 Bill Board
Freshman  16.0 3.15

666554444 Jose CanuSee
Sophomore 16.0 3.25
```

Sample run:

```
This program simulates an information retrieval system
   by reading a series of student records from 'Registrar.Dat'
   and then allowing retrieval of any student's data.

Enter a student's name (Ctrl-D to quit): Stan Dupp

 333221111 Stan Dupp
     Senior 16.0000 3.7500

Enter a student's name (Ctrl-D to quit): Joe Blow

There is no student whose name is Joe Blow.

Enter a student's name (Ctrl-D to quit): Isabelle Ringing

 999887777 Isabelle Ringing
     Junior  8.0000  3.8000

Enter a student's name (Ctrl-D to quit): ^D
```

There are a few important observations about this program:

1. The `SSort()` function calls function `IndexOfMin()`, which executes the statement:

    ```
    if (Array[j] < Array[MinPos])
    ```

    This statement applies an overloaded definition of `operator<` that compares two `Student` objects, which was described Exercise 1 following Section 11.3. Similarly, the `SSort()` function calls function `Swap()`, which executes the statements

    ```
    Temp = A; A = B; B = Temp;
    ```

    where `A`, `B`, and `Temp` are all `ListElement` objects. It should be clear that the assignment performed is the `operator=` in class `Student`. Also, function `BSearch()` contains statements that utilize the relational operators, such as

    ```
    if (SearchVal == Array[Middle])
    ```

    Since both `SearchVal` and `Array[Middle]` are of type `ListElement` (which is a synonym for type `Student`), the equality operator that is applied is `operator==` from class `Student`, which was described in Exercise 2 following Section 11.3.

2. The program in Figure 12.17 calls `BSearch()` as follows:

    ```
    Pos = StudentList.BSearch(Student(FirstName, LastName));
    ```

    Recall that the parameter `SearchVal` in `BSearch()` is a `ListElement`, and so the argument to `BSearch()` must be a `ListElement`. This means that the strings that make up a student's name must be converted to a `Student` object. One way to do this is to use an explicit call to the `Student` class constructor, whose declaration has the form

    ```
    Student(const Strings& FName = "", const Strings& LName = "",
            long SNumb = 0, Year StuYear = Freshman,
            double Creds = 0.0, double GPA = 0.0);
    ```

    The default argument values in this declaration mean that the call:

    ```
    Student(FirstName, LastName)
    ```

    builds a `Student` object whose `FName` parameter has the value `FirstName` and whose `LName` parameter has the value `LastName`. As long as the relational operators for class `Student` only compare these members, this object contains all the information required for `BSearch()` or `LSearch()` to find the index of the element containing this student, if it is present in the list.

Some Limitations of Fixed-Size Arrays

The examples in this section demonstrate that arrays are very useful for storing lists of values, whether those values are simple (like a number), or complicated (like a `Student` or `String`). There are some drawbacks, however, to using arrays to model lists. One is that whereas a list need not have a fixed length, an array must have a fixed number of elements. This means that it is possible to declare the array to have exactly the right size for storing the list only if the size of the list is fixed (which is rarely the case). The common approach for lists of varying sizes is to guess the maximum size of the list and to declare the array to have this number of components. There are two significant drawbacks to this approach:

1. If we make the array too small, we may be unable to process some of the list elements because there is no room for them in the array (an **overflow error**).
2. If we make the array too large, then we may be wasting a considerable part of the memory allocated to it.

Another weakness of the array implementation of lists is that although algorithms for the insertion and deletion operations are quite easy to write (as the exercises following Section 12.3 ask you to do), they are not very efficient. For example, consider the following ordered list of ten integers:

$$23, 34, 48, 55, 68, 80, 82, 89, 91, 97$$

If these values are stored in an array and we wish to insert the value 75 into its proper position, then the sixth through the tenth elements must be shifted one position to the right to make room for the new value:

$$23, 34, 48, 55, 68, 80, 82, 84, 91, 97$$

$$23, 34, 48, 55, 68, 75, 80, 82, 84, 91, 97$$

Deleting an item from the list also requires moving array elements; for example, to remove the second number in the list, we must shift the third through the eleventh array elements one position to their left to "close the gap":

$$23, 34, 48, 55, 68, 75, 80, 82, 84, 91, 97$$

$$23, 48, 55, 68, 75, 80, 82, 84, 91, 97$$

If insertions and deletions are restricted to the ends of the list, then array implementations that do not require moving array elements are possible. Two important special cases are stacks and queues. A **stack** is a list in which elements may be inserted (**pushed**) and deleted (**popped**) at only one end, called the **top** of the stack. By contrast, if elements may be inserted only at one end (the **rear** or **tail**) and deleted only at the other (the **front** or **head**), the list is called a **queue**. Array implementation of stacks and queues are described in the exercises.

In summary, arrays work very well for fixed-size lists and reasonably well for lists whose maximum sizes can be estimated and for which insertions and deletions are infrequent or are restricted to the ends of the list. **Dynamic** lists whose sizes may vary greatly during processing and those in which items are frequently inserted and/or deleted anywhere in the list are better implemented using a varying-size structure, as described in Chapter 16.

Exercises

1. For each of the following arrays X, show X after each of the first four passes of simple selection sort:

(a)

i	0	1	2	3	4	5	6	7
$X[i]$	30	50	80	10	60	20	70	40

(b)

i	0	1	2	3	4	5	6	7
$X[i]$	20	40	70	60	80	50	30	10

(c)

i	0	1	2	3	4	5	6	7
$X[i]$	80	70	60	50	40	30	20	10

(d)

i	0	1	2	3	4	5	6	7
$X[i]$	10	20	30	40	50	60	70	80

2. One variation of simple selection sort for a list stored in an array $X[0], \ldots,$ $X[n-1]$ is to locate both the smallest and the largest elements while scanning the list and to position them at the beginning and the end of the list, respectively. On the next scan, this process is repeated for the sublist $X[1], \ldots,$ $X[n-2]$, and so on.

    (a)–(d)   Using the arrays X in Exercise 1, show X after each of the first four passes of this double-ended simple selection sort.
    (e) Write an algorithm to implement this double-ended selection sort.

3. Write a recursive function that implements simple selection sort.

4. For the following array X, show its contents after the function **Split()** operates on it using **First** $= 0$ and **Last** $= 9$:

i	0	1	2	3	4	5	6	7	8	9
$X[i]$	45	20	50	30	80	10	60	70	40	90

5.   Construct a trace table like that in the text to trace the action of **QuickSort()** as it sorts the following lists:

    (a) 5, 1, 6, 4, 3, 2   **(b)** 1, 2, 3, 6, 5, 4
    (c) 6, 5, 4, 3, 2, 1   **(d)** 1, 2, 3, 4, 5, 6

6. One of the lists in Exercise 5 shows why the condition **Low < High** is needed to control the search from the left in function **Split()**. Which is it? What would happen if this condition were omitted?

7. **Insertion sort** is an efficient sorting method for small data sets. It begins with the first item, x_1, then inserts x_2 into this one-item list in the correct position to form a sorted two-element list, then inserts x_3 into this two-element list in the correct position, and so on. For example, to sort the list 7, 1, 5, 2, 3, 4, 6, 0, the steps are as follows (the element being inserted is highlighted):

List

7

↘

1 , 7   (shift 7 one position to the right)

↘

1, 5 , 7   (shift 7 to the right again)

↘ ↘

1, 2 , 5, 7   (shift 5 and 7 to the right)

↘ ↘

1, 2, 3 , 5, 7   (shift 5 and 7 to the right)

↘ ↘

1, 2, 3, 4 , 5, 7   (shift 5 and 7 to the right)

↘

1, 2, 3, 4, 5, 6 , 7   (shift 7 to the right)

↘ ↘ ↘ ↘ ↘ ↘

0 , 1, 2, 3, 4, 5, 6, 7   (shift all of 1 through 7 to the right)

Write a function to sort a list of items using this insertion sort method, and then write a driver program to test its correctness.

8. The investment company of Shyster and Shyster has been recording the trading price of a particular stock over a 15-day period. Write a program that reads these prices and sorts them into increasing order, using the insertion sort scheme described in the preceding exercise. The program should display the trading range, that is, the lowest and the highest prices recorded, and also the median price.

9. Insertion sort (see Exercise 7) performs best for small lists or partially sorted lists. **Shell sort** (named after Donald Shell) is a more efficient scheme that uses insertion sort to sort small sublists to produce larger partially ordered sublists. Specifically, one begins with a "gap" of a certain size g and then uses insertion sort to sort sublists of elements that are g apart, first $X[0]$, $X[0 + g], X[0 + 2g], \ldots$, then the sublist $X[1], X[1 + g], X[1 + 2g], \ldots$, then $X[2], X[2 + g], X[2 + 2g], \ldots$, and so on. Next the size of the gap g is reduced, and the process is repeated. This continues until the gap g is 1, and the final insertion sort results in the sorted list. Write a program to sort a list of items using this Shell sort method, beginning with a gap g of the form $\dfrac{3^k - 1}{2}$ for some integer k and dividing it by 3 at each stage.

10. The function **QuickSort()** always sorts the left sublist before the right. Its performance will improve slightly if the shorter of the two sublists is sorted first. Modify **QuickSort()** to sort the shorter sublist first.

11. Another improvement of the quicksort method is to use some other sorting algorithm to sort small sublists. For example, insertion sort is usually better than quicksort when the list has fewer than 20 items. Modify the quicksort

scheme to use insertion sort (see Exercise 7) if the sublist has fewer than **LBound** items for some constant **LBound** and, otherwise, use quicksort.

12. The function **Split()** in the quicksort method of sorting always selects the first element of the sublist to position. Another common practice is to use the "median-of-three" rule in which the median of the first, last, and middle elements of the array is selected. (The median of three numbers a, b, and c, arranged in ascending order, is the middle number b.) Modify **Split()** to use this median-of-three rule.

13. Design and write a function to linear search a **List** recursively.

14. The Cawker City Candy Company manufactures different kinds of candy, each identified by a product number. Write a program that reads in two arrays, **Number** and **Price**, where **Number[0]** and **Price[0]** are the product number and unit price for the first item, **Number[1]** and **Price[1]** are the product number and unit price for the second item, and so on. The program should then allow the user to select one of the following options:

(a) Retrieve and display the price of a product whose number is entered by the user.
(b) Print a table displaying the product number and the price of each item.

15. Design and write a function to binary search a **List** recursively.

16. One possible implementation of a stack is to use an array **Stack** indexed **0** through **StackLimit**, with the top of the stack always at position 0 of the array.

(a) Why isn't this a good implementation?
(b) A better implementation is to let the stack grow from position 0 toward position **StackLimit** and to maintain an integer variable **Top** to "point" to the current top of the stack. Write functions for the push and pop operations in this implementation.
(c) Use the functions of part (b) in a program that reads a command I (Insert) or D (Delete); for I, read an integer and push it onto the stack, and for D, pop an integer from the stack and display it.

17. For a queue, we might imitate the array implementation of a stack in Exercise 16, using an array **Queue** indexed **0** through **QueueLimit-1** and maintaining two "pointers," **Front** to the item at the front of the queue and **Rear** to the item at the rear. To add an item to the queue, simply increment **Rear** by 1 and store the item in **Queue[Rear]**; to remove an item, simply increment **Front** by 1.

(a) Describe the inadequacies of this implementation. Consider, for example, an integer array with five elements and the following sequence of queue operations: Insert 37, Insert 82, Insert 59, Delete an item, Delete an item, Insert 66, Insert 13, Insert 48.

(b) A better implementation is to think of the array as being circular, with the first element following the last. For this, index the array beginning with 0 and increment `Front` and `Rear` using addition `% QueueLimit`. Write functions for the insertion and deletion operations, assuming this implementation. Use these functions in a program that reads a command I (Insert) or D (Delete); for I, read an integer and add it to the queue and, for D, remove an integer from the queue and display it.

12.5   PART OF THE PICTURE: Analysis of Algorithms

We have seen that there may be several different algorithms for solving a particular problem; for example, either selection sort or quicksort can be used to arrange a list of values in ascending order. When there are several solutions for a problem, it is important to be able to compare the performance of these solutions so that the most efficient solution can be used. In this section, we look more carefully at how algorithms are analyzed and at some of the techniques for measuring their efficiency.

An algorithm's efficiency is usually measured according to two criteria. The first is **space efficiency,** the amount of memory required to store the data, and the second is **time efficiency,** the amount of time required to process the data. Unfortunately, these two criteria are often in conflict with one another. Algorithms that require the least memory are often slower than those that use more memory. For such problems, the programmer is faced with a **space-time trade-off:** Should the space efficiency be improved at the expense of time efficiency, or vice versa? An algorithm's time efficiency is usually considered the more important of the two, and in this section we consider how it can be measured.

The execution time of an algorithm is influenced by several factors. Obviously, one factor is the size of the input, since the number of input items usually affects the time required to process these items. For example, the time it takes to sort a list of items surely depends on the number of items in the list. Thus, the execution time T_A of an algorithm A is a function $T_A(n)$ of the size n of the input.

In many cases, T_A depends not only on the size of the input but also on the arrangement of the input items. For example, it may take less time to sort a list of items that are nearly in order initially than to sort a list in which the items are in reverse order. Thus, we might attempt to measure T_A in the **worst case** or in the **best case,** or we might attempt to compute the **average** value of T_A over all possible cases. The best-case performance of an algorithm is usually not very informative, and the average performance is often quite difficult to determine; thus, $T_A(n)$ is commonly taken as a measure of the algorithm's performance in the worst case.

The kind of instructions and the speed with which the machine can execute them also influence execution time. These factors, however, depend on the particular computer being used; consequently, we cannot expect to express meaningfully the value of $T_A(n)$ in real time units such as seconds. Instead, $T_A(n)$ will be an approximate count of the number of instructions executed. Doing so provides a measure of the time to execute algorithm A that is independent of any particular machine.

Another factor that influences computing time is the quality of the source code that implements the algorithm and the quality of the machine code generated from this source code by a compiler. Some languages are better suited than others for certain algorithms; some programmers write better programs than others; and some compilers generate more efficient code than others. This means, in particular, that $T_A(n)$ cannot be computed as the number of machine instructions executed; instead it is taken to be the number of times the instructions in the *algorithm* are executed. In the following discussion, we use the syntax of C++ to express the algorithms we examine.

To illustrate how the computing time of an algorithm is measured, we first examine the two methods for searching a list described in Section 12.3, linear search and binary search. There we claimed that binary search is more efficient than linear search, and we now substantiate this claim.

Linear Search

Recall that a linear search is carried out by examining each element in a list sequentially, beginning with the first element, until either the desired item is found or the end of the list is reached. The following function for linear search was constructed in the preceding section:

LINEAR SEARCH FUNCTION

```cpp
int List::LSearch (const ListElement& SearchVal) const
{
    for (int i = 0; i < Length_; i++)       // 1
        if (Array[i] == SearchVal)           // 2
            return i;                        // 3

    return -1;                               // 4
}
```

(The statements have been numbered for easy reference.)

The worst case for the linear search algorithm occurs when **SearchVal** is not in the list; thus, to measure the performance of this algorithm, we count the number of times that each statement is executed in this case. Statement 1 actually consists of three separate expressions:

```cpp
int i = 0;           // 1a
i < Length_;         // 1b
i++                  // 1c
```

Expression 1a is executed once, on entry to the loop. By contrast, expression 1b is executed once for each element in the list, plus the final time that terminates the loop, a total of $n + 1$ times, where $n =$ **Length_**; and expression 1c is executed n times (at the end of each iteration). The condition in statement 2,

```
if (Array[i] == SearchVal)              // 2
```

is also evaluated n times, once for each element in the list. Statement 3, by contrast will never be executed, since the value is never found. It should be clear that statement 4 will be executed once, since it causes the function to terminate. The following table summarizes these statement counts:

Statement	No. of Times Executed
1a	1
1b	$n + 1$
1c	n
2	n
3	0
4	1
Total:	$3n + 3$

Thus the total number of statements executed, expressed as a function of the size n of input, is

$$T_{LSearch}(n) = 3n + 3$$

For sufficiently large values of n ($n \geq 3$), we see that

$$T_{LSearch}(n) \leq 4n$$

and so we say that $T_{LSearch}(n)$ has **order of magnitude** n and denote this using the "big Oh" notation:

$$T_{LSearch}(n) = O(n)$$

In general, the execution time $T_A(n)$ of an algorithm is said to have **order of magnitude $g(n)$,** denoted by

$$T_A(n) = O(g(n))$$

if there exists some constant C so that

$$T_A(n) \leq C \cdot g(n)$$

for all sufficiently large values of n. The interpretation of this is that for a list of length n, linear search requires time that is proportional to n. Put differently, the time to perform this search grows **linearly** as the length of the list increases.

Binary Search

The following function implements the binary search algorithm for ordered lists.

BINARY SEARCH FUNCTION

```
int List::BSearch(const ListElement& SearchVal) const
{
```

```
int
   First = 0,                                        // 1
   Last = Length_-1,                                 // 2
   Middle;                                           // 3

while (First <= Last)                                // 4
{
   Middle = (First + Last) / 2;                      // 5

   if (SearchVal == Array[Middle])                   // 6
       return Middle;                                // 7
   else if (SearchVal < Array[Middle])               // 8
       Last = Middle - 1;                            // 9
   else                                              // 10
       First = Middle + 1;                           // 11
}

return -1;                                           // 12
}
```

It is clear that in this algorithm, Statements 1, 2, and 3 are executed exactly once, and to determine the worst-case performance, we must determine the number of times the loop composed of Statements 4 through 11 is executed when **SearchVal** is not in the list. This is not as easy to determine as it is for linear search, and so we first consider some particular values of $n =$ **Length_**.

First, suppose that **Array** contains only one element **Array[0]**, and suppose that **SearchVal** is greater than **Array[0]**. After Statements 1, 2, and 3 are executed, the boolean expression in Statement 4 is evaluated and found to be true (**First** = 0, and **Last** = 0). Thus the body of the while loop is executed; Statement 5 calculates the value 0 for **Middle**, the condition in statement 6 is evaluated as false, as is the condition in Statement 8, and so Statement 11 sets **First** equal to 1. The boolean expression in Statement 4 is then evaluated again and found to be false (**First** = 1, **Last** = 0), causing repetition to terminate. Thus, we see that for $n = 1$, one pass through the loop is made, and one additional evaluation of the boolean expression is made to terminate repetition.

Next, consider a list of size $n = 2$, **Array[0]**, **Array[1]**, and suppose that **SearchVal** is greater than both elements of this list. A first pass through the loop sets **First** equal to 1, so that the unsearched sublist is reduced from 2 elements to 1, **Array[1]**. As we have just seen, a list of size 1 requires one pass through the loop and one more evaluation of the boolean expression in Statement 4 to terminate repetition. Thus, for $n = 2$, the loop is executed twice and Statement 4, one additional time.

Now consider a list of size $n = 4$, **Array[0]**, **Array[1]**, **Array[2]**, **Array[3]**, with **SearchVal** greater than each list element. A first pass through the loop reduces the list to one of size 2, **Array[2]**, **Array[3]**. We have just determined that two passes are required to search a list of 2 elements, and thus we see that for a list of size 4, the loop is executed three times, and the boolean expression in Statement 4 is evaluated one additional time.

Continuing this analysis with values 8, 16, . . . for n, we obtain the following table:

n	Number of Passes Through the Loop
$1 = 2^0$	1
$2 = 2^1$	2
$4 = 2^2$	3
$8 = 2^3$	4
$\vdots$	$\vdots$
2^k	$k + 1$

Thus, we see that a list of size 2^k requires $k + 1 = \log_2(2^k) + 1$ passes through the loop. In general, a list of size n requires no more than $\log_2 n + 1$ passes through the loop.

Since only Statements 5, 6, 8, and 11 are executed in the worst case and Statement 4 is executed one more time than the number of loop repetitions, we obtain the following (approximate) counts for executions of the statements in the binary search algorithm:

Statement	No. of Times Executed
1	1
2	1
3	1
4	$\log_2 n + 2$
5	$\log_2 n + 1$
6	$\log_2 n + 1$
7	0
8	$\log_2 n + 1$
9	0
10	0
11	$\log_2 n + 1$
12	1
Total:	$5 \log_2 n + 10$

Thus, we see that in the worst case, the computing time of binary search is

$$T_{BSearch}(n) = 5 \log_2 n + 10$$

and since

$$T_{BSearch}(n) \leq 6 \log_2 n$$

for large n $(n \geq 2^{10})$, we see that $T_{BSearch}(n)$ has order of magnitude $\log_2 n$,

$$T_{BSearch}(n) = O(\log_2 n)$$

That is, binary search requires time that is proportional to the base-2 logarithm of n, the number of values in the list. Put differently, the time to perform this search grows **logarithmically** with the length of the list.

If we compare our two searching algorithms, we have the following measures of worst-case performance of the linear search and binary search algorithms (which also measure the average case performance):

Linear search: $O(n)$
Binary search: $O(\log_2 n)$

Because the function $\log_2 n$ grows less rapidly than n as the list length n increases (see Figure 12.18), it follows that binary search is more efficient than linear search for large lists. For small lists, however, linear search may—and, in fact, does—outperform binary search. Empirical studies indicate that linear search is usually more efficient than binary search for lists of up to 20 elements. Moreover, binary search can be used only for ordered lists; consequently, the list must be in sorted order before that approach can be used.

Simple Selection Sort

The computing time of simple selection sort is $O(n^2)$, where n is the size of the list. To see this, consider the following function that implements the algorithm for this sorting scheme:

SIMPLE SELECTION SORT FUNCTION

```
void List::SSort(void)
{
   int
      MinPos;

   for (int i = 0; i < Length_ -1; i++)    // 1
   {
      MinPos = IndexOfMin(i, Length_ -1); // 2
      Swap(Array[i], Array[MinPos]);      // 3
   }
}
```

---

where the function **IndexOfMin()** in Statement 2 (minus its bounds-checking code) is defined as follows:

INDEX OF MINIMUM VALUE FUNCTION

```
unsigned List::IndexOfMin(unsigned First, unsigned Last) const
{
   unsigned
      MinPos = First;                         // 1
```

```
    for (int j = First+1; j <= Last; j++)   // 2a, 2b, 2c
        if (Array[j] < Array[MinPos])        // 3
            MinPos = j;                       // 4

    return MinPos;                            // 5
}
```

It should be clear from the preceding examples that the order of magnitude of an algorithm is determined by the statements executed most often, and for simple selection sort these are Statements 2b, 2c, and 3 in the **IndexOfMin()** function. The first time **IndexOfMin()** is called (with $j = 1$), these statements are each executed $n - 1$ times. On the second call (with $j = 2$), they are executed $n - 2$ times, and so on. Thus, these statements are executed a total of $(n - 1) + (n - 2) + \cdots + 1$ times. As we saw in Section 6.9,

$$1 + 2 + \cdots + k = \frac{k(k + 1)}{2}$$

or in the usual summation notation,

$$\sum_{i=1}^{k} i = \frac{k(k + 1)}{2}$$

Substituting $k = n - 1$, we find that Statements 2b, 2c, and 3 are each executed

$$\sum_{i=1}^{n-1} i = \frac{n - 1(n - 1 + 1)}{2} = \frac{n(n - 1)}{2} = \frac{n^2 - n}{2}$$

times, from which it follows that the computing time of selection sort is given by $T_{SSort}(n) = O(n^2)$.

By contrast, quicksort is a more time-efficient sorting algorithm, because although its worst-case computing time is $O(n^2)$, its average computing time is $O(n \cdot \log_2 n)$. A rigorous derivation of these times is considerably more difficult than for simple selection sort, and we leave it for more advanced courses in analysis of algorithms.

Complexity Measures

Besides $O(\log_2 n)$, $O(n)$, $O(n \cdot \log_2 n)$, and $O(n^2)$, other computing times that frequently arise in algorithm analysis are $O(\log_2(\log_2 n))$, $O(n^3)$, and $O(2^n)$. The following table displays values of these functions for several values of n:

$\log_2\log_2 n$	$\log_2 n$	n	$n \log_2 n$	n^2	n^3	2^n
—	0	1	0	1	1	2
0	1	2	2	4	8	4
1	2	4	8	16	64	16
1.58	3	8	24	64	512	256
2	4	16	64	256	4,096	65,536
2.32	5	32	160	1,024	32,768	4,294,967,296
2.6	6	64	384	4,096	2.6×10^5	1.85×10^{19}
3	8	256	2.05×10^3	6.55×10^4	1.68×10^7	1.16×10^{77}
3.32	10	1,024	1.02×10^4	1.05×10^6	1.07×10^9	1.8×10^{308}
4.32	20	1,048,576	2.1×10^7	1.1×10^{12}	1.15×10^{18}	$6.7 \times 10^{315,652}$

Graphs of these functions are shown in Figure 12.18.

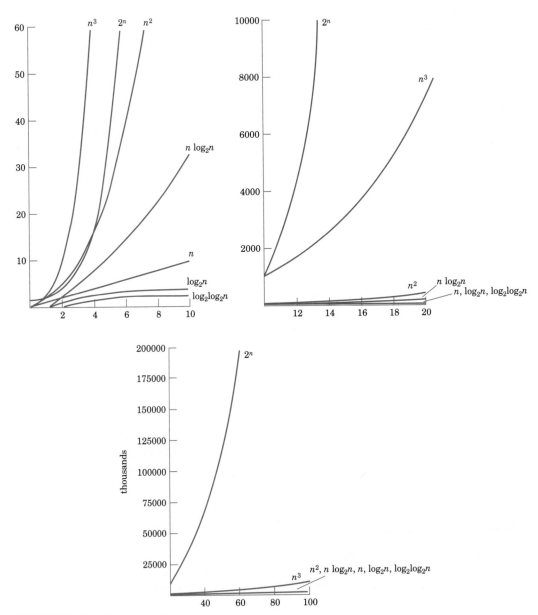

FIGURE 12.18   Computing times.

It should be clear from the preceding table and graphs that algorithms with exponential complexity are practical only for solving problems in which the number of inputs is small. To emphasize this, suppose that each instruction in some function can be executed in 1 microsecond (0.000001 second). The following table shows the time required to execute $f(n)$ instructions for the common complexity functions f with $n = 256$ inputs:

Function	Time
$\log_2\log_2 n$	0.000003 seconds
$\log_2 n$	0.000008 seconds
n	0.0025 seconds
$n\log_2 n$	0.002 seconds
n^2	0.065 seconds
n^3	17 seconds
2^n	3.7×10^{61} centuries

Exercises

1. Which of the orders of magnitude given in this section is the best O notation to describe the following computing times?

   (a) $T_A(n) = n^3 + 100n \cdot \log_2 n + 5000$
   (b) $T_A(n) = 2^n + n^{99} + 7$
   (c) $T_A(n) = \dfrac{n^2 - 1}{n + 1} + 8\log_2 n$
   (d) $T_A(n) = 1 + 2 + 4 + \cdots + 2^{n-1}$

2. What would it mean to say that an algorithm has computing time $T_A(n) = O(1)$? Give an example of such an algorithm.

3. For each of the following code fragments, determine which of the orders of magnitude given in this section is the best O notation to use for expressing the worst-case computing time as a function of **n**:

   (a)
   ```
   // Calculate mean
   n = 0;
   Sum = 0;
   cin >> x;
   while (x != -999)
   {
      n++;
      Sum += x;
      cin >> x;
   }
   Mean = Sum / n;
   ```

   (b)
   ```
   // Calculate array sums
   Sum1 = 0;
   for (i = 0; i < n; i++)
     Sum1 += A[i];
   Sum2 = 0;
   for (j = 0; j < n; j++)
     Sum2 += B[j];
   ```

(c)
```cpp
// Print sums of elements of two arrays
for (i = 0; i < n; i++)
{
  for (j = 0; j < n; j++)
    cout << A[i] + B[j];
  cout << endl;
}
```

(d)
```cpp
// Print sums of elements of three arrays
for (i = 0; i < n; i++)
{
  for (j = 0; j < n; j++)
  {
    for (k = 0; k < n; k++)
      cout << A[i] + B[j] + C[k];
    cout << endl;
  }
  cout << endl;
}
```

(e)
```cpp
// Bubble sort
for (i = 0; i < n - 1; i++)
{
  for (j = i; j < n - 1; j++)
    if (X[j] > X[j + 1])
    {
      Temp   = X[j];
      X[j] = X[j + 1];
      X[j + 1] = Temp;
    }
}
```

(f)
```cpp
// Repeated division
while (n >= 1)
    n /= 2;
```

(g)
```cpp
// Repeated multiplication
x = 1;
for (i = 1; i <= n - 1; i++)
{
  for (j = 1; j <= x; j++)
    cout << j;
  x *= 2;
}
```

Program Design

1. *Arrays can be used to store lists of values.* The elements of an array are all the same type, so that if an object can be described by a set of attributes that are all of the same type, then an array is a reasonable choice for modeling that object. By contrast, if the attributes are not all the same type, then an array is not an appropriate structure to model the object (which should be modeled using a class).

2. *Avoid writing programs that define and manipulate arrays directly.* Instead, store the array and its length in a class as data members, and then construct member functions that operate on the array. This approach produces functions that are reusable and programs that are more easily read (and, therefore, easier to debug), because the "normal" operators can be overloaded for the class.

3. *Always use named constants in referring to the number of elements in an array.* For example, code such as

```
class ShortString
{
   enum {Size = 10};      // declare Size as a named constant,
   char                   // and use it wherever the array's
      A[Size];            // length must be referred to...
   // ...
   cin.getline(A, Size);
   // ...
};
```

is far easier to modify and maintain, since only the value of **Size** needs to be changed to change the size of the array throughout the class.

Potential Problems

1. *In C++ the subscript operator is a pair of square brackets, not a pair of parentheses.* Trying to access element **i** of an array **A** by using

```
A(i)
```

is interpreted by the C++ compiler as an attempt to call a function named **A**, passing it the argument **i**. A compile-time error will result unless such a function happens to exist, in which case a logical error will result.

2. *The first element of any C++ array has the index value 0, not 1.* Forgetting this can produce some puzzling results. For example, consider the loop

```
for (int i = 1, i < Length_ ; i++)
   // ... do something with Array[i]
```

Such a loop will "skip over" the first element in the array, since **Array[0]** is never accessed. To illustrate, recall that the system initializes array elements to zero and suppose that a programmer were to attempt to fill and output a character array named **Array** as follows:

```
cout >> "? ";                        // prompt for input
for (int i = 1, i < Length_; i++)    // read in elem-by-elem
   cin.get(Array[i]);
//...
cout << Array;                       // display A
```

If the user enters:

<u>WXYZ</u>

then the contents of **Array** appear as follows:

	0	1	2	3	4	5	6	...	9
Array	\0	W	X	Y	Z	\0	\0		\0

Because the array elements have been initialized to zero (the same as '\0', the null character) the output statement will display nothing. The reason is that if the first element of the array contains the null character (which is used to terminate character strings), then all predefined operations will treat that array as though it contains the empty string.

3. *No checking is performed to ensure that array indices stay within the range specified in an array's declaration.* Out-of-range errors occur when an index variable is given a value outside the range specified for the indices in the array declaration. To illustrate, consider the declarations

```
const int
   ListLimit = 10;
   EndOfDataFlag = -999;
int
   Number[ListLimit],
   i, Value;
```

and consider the following statements designed to read and count the elements of this array:

```
i = 0;
cin >> Value;
while (Value != EndOfDataFlag)
{
   Number[i] = Value;
   i++;
   cin >> Value;
}
```

These statements correctly read values for the entries of **Number**, provided that there are no more than 10 values preceding the end-of-data flag. But if there are more than 10 values, an out-of-range error may result when the value of i reaches 10, because an attempt is made to read a value for **Number[10]**, but the indices of **Number** range from 0 through 9.

As this example demonstrates, it is important to check **boundary conditions** when processing the elements of arrays—that is, to check to make sure that the index is not out of range. Thus, the preceding set of statements could better be written as

```
i = 0;
cin >> Value;
while ((Value != EndOfDataFlag) && (i < ListLimit))
{
    Number[i] = Value;
    i++;
    cin >> Value;
}
```

Strange results may be obtained when an index is allowed to get out of bounds. In this case, the memory location that is being accessed is typically determined by simply counting forward or backward from the **base address** of the array, which is the address of the first element in the array. This is illustrated by the program in Figure 12.19. Here **A**, **B**, and **C** are arrays declared by

```
const int
    ArrayLimit = 4;
int
    A[ArrayLimit],
    B[ArrayLimit],
    C[ArrayLimit];
```

and the illegal array references **B[-3]** and **B[6]** access the memory locations associated with **A[1]** and **C[2]**:

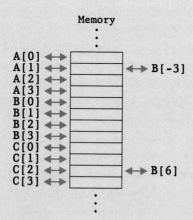

Thus modifying **B[-3]** and **B[6]** changes **A[1]** and **C[2]**, respectively. This change is obviously undesirable.

FIGURE 12.19 Why array indices must stay in bounds.

```
/* This program demonstrates aberrant behavior resulting from
   range errors.

   Output: arrays A, B, and C
---------------------------------------------------------------*/

#include <iostream.h>
#include <iomanip.h>

void PrintArray(const char[], const int[], int);

int main(void)
{
   const int
      ArrayLimit = 4;
   int
      A[ArrayLimit] = {0, 1, 2, 3},
      B[ArrayLimit] = {4, 5, 6, 7},
      C[ArrayLimit] = {8, 9, 10, 11},
      below = -3,
      above = 6;

   PrintArray("A", A, ArrayLimit);
   PrintArray("B", B, ArrayLimit);
   PrintArray("C", C, ArrayLimit);

   B[below] = -999;
   B[above] = 999;

   cout << endl;
   PrintArray("A", A, ArrayLimit);
   PrintArray("B", B, ArrayLimit);
   PrintArray("C", C, ArrayLimit);
   return 0;
}

/*-------------------------------------------------------------*/
void PrintArray(const char Name[], const int L[], int N)
{
  cout << Name << " = ";
  for (int i = 0; i < N; i++)
    cout << setw(5) << L[i];
  cout << endl;
}
```

FIGURE 12.19 Why array indices must stay in bounds. (cont.)

Sample run:

```
A =       0    1    2   3
B =       4    5    6   7
C =       8    9   10  11

A =       0  -999   1   2
B =       4    5    6   7
C =       8    9  999  11
```

An array reference such as **B[5000]** that is very much out of range may cause the program to crash. Consequently, *when writing functions that receive indices of arrays as arguments, it is important to check the validity of those indices.*

4. *Array arguments are automatically passed by reference.* If a function has an array parameter through which a value is being returned to its caller, it is not necessary to declare the array as a reference parameter. If a function has an array parameter that is being received but not returned, that parameter should be declared as a **const** parameter.

5. *A character string must be terminated with the null character '\0' and a character array must provide room for this character.* Virtually all of the C-language operations in **<string.h>** depend upon the null character to terminate a character string. If a program mistakenly

   - Constructs a string that has no terminating null character or
   - Somehow overwrites the terminating null character of a string with some nonnull value,

   then the results are unpredictable but can easily produce a run-time error. Similarly, an array used to store such a string must leave room for the null character to avoid an overflow error.

Programming Projects

1. Using class **List** as a model, build a class **Vector** for processing real vectors. In the following descriptions of the operators to be included, **A** and **B** are the vectors:

$$\mathbf{A} = (a_1, a_2, \ldots, a_n)$$
$$\mathbf{B} = (b_1, b_2, \ldots, b_n)$$

■ **operator+** is overloaded to perform **Vector** addition:

$$\mathbf{A} + \mathbf{B} = (a_1 + b_1, a_1 + b_2, \ldots, a_n + b_n)$$

■ **operator-** is overloaded to perform **Vector** subtraction:

$$\mathbf{A} - \mathbf{B} = (a_1 - b_1, a_1 - b_2, \ldots, a_n - b_n)$$

■ **operator*** is overloaded to find the product of a scalar and a vector,

$$c\mathbf{A} = (ca_1, ca_2, \ldots, ca_n)$$

or to find the inner (or dot) product of two vectors (which is a scalar):

$$\mathbf{A} \cdot \mathbf{B} = a_1 * b_1 + a_2 * b_2 + \cdots + a_n * b_n = \sum_{i=1}^{n} a_i * b_i$$

■ the member function **Magnitude()** finds the magnitude of a vector:

$$|\mathbf{A}| = \sqrt{a_1^2 + a_2^2 + \cdots + a_n^2}$$

■ **operator>>** and **operator<<** are overloaded to perform vector I/O.

Write a menu-driven **Vector** calculator program that allows a user to perform these operations on vectors that are entered from the keyboard.

2. If $\bar{x}$, denotes the mean of the numbers $x_1, x_2, \ldots, x_n$, the **variance** is the average of the squares of the deviations of the numbers from the mean:

$$\text{Variance} = \frac{1}{n} \sum_{i=1}^{n} (x_i - \bar{x})^2$$

and the **standard deviation** is the square root of the variance. Extend class **Vector** with member functions that calculate the mean, variance, and standard deviation of the components of the vector. Then extend the **Vector** calculator program to use these functions.

3. Letter grades are sometimes assigned to numeric scores by using the grading scheme commonly called "grading on the curve." In this scheme, a letter grade is assigned to a numeric score according to the following table:

x = Numeric Score	Letter Grade
$x < m - \frac{3}{2}\sigma$	F
$m - \frac{3}{2}\sigma \le x < m - \frac{1}{2}\sigma$	D
$m - \frac{1}{2}\sigma \le x < m + \frac{1}{2}\sigma$	C
$m + \frac{1}{2}\sigma \le x < m + \frac{3}{2}\sigma$	B
$m + \frac{3}{2}\sigma \le x$	A

where m is the mean score and σ (sigma) is the standard deviation. Write a program that uses class **Vector** from Project 2 to read a list of real numbers representing numeric scores, calculate their mean and standard deviation, and display the letter grade corresponding to each numeric score.

4. Construct a class **BigInt** whose values are large integers with up to 300 digits. Overload the addition and subtraction operators for class objects. (Suggestion: Treat each number as a list, each of whose elements is a block of digits of the number. For example, the integer 179,534,672,198 might be stored with **Block[0]** = 198, **Block[1]** = 672, **Block[2]** = 534, and **Block[3]** = 179. Then add the integers (lists) element by element, carrying from one element to the next when necessary.) Write a two-function **BigInt** calculator program to test your class.

5. Extend class **BigInt** from Exercise 4 by overloading the multiplication and division operators to multiply and divide two large integers of length up to 300 digits.

6. A **prime number** is an integer greater than 1 whose only positive divisors are 1 and the integer itself. The Greek mathematician Eratosthenes developed an algorithm, known as the **Sieve of Eratosthenes,** for finding all prime numbers less than or equal to a given number n—that is, all primes in the range 2 through n. Consider the list of numbers from 2 through n. Two is the first prime number, but the multiples of 2 (4, 6, 8, . . .) are not, and so they are crossed out in the list. The first number after 2 that was not crossed out is 3, the next prime. We then cross out from the list all higher multiples of 3 (6, 9, 12, . . .). The next number not crossed out is 5, the next prime, and so we cross out all higher multiples of 5 (10, 15, 20, . . .). We repeat this procedure until we reach the first number in the list that has not been crossed out and whose square is greater than n. All the numbers that remain in the list are the primes from 2 through n. Write a program that uses this sieve method and class **List** to find all the prime numbers from 2 through n. Run it for $n = 50$ and for $n = 500$.

7. Develop a recursive function to generate all of the $n!$ permutations of the set $\{1, 2, \ldots, n\}$. (*Hint:* The permutations of $\{1, 2, \ldots, k\}$ can be obtained by considering each permutation of $\{1, 2, \ldots, k - 1\}$ as an ordered list and inserting k into each of the k possible positions in this list, including at the front and at the rear.) For example, the permutations of $\{1, 2\}$ are $(1, 2)$ and $(2, 1)$. Inserting 3 into each of the three possible positions of the first permutation yields the permutations $(3, 1, 2)$, $(1, 3, 2)$, and $(1, 2, 3)$ of $\{1, 2, 3\}$, and using the second permutation gives $(3, 2, 1)$, $(2, 3, 1)$, and $(2, 1, 3)$. Write a program to test your function.

*ARRAY APPLICATION: IMPLEMENTING A Set CLASS

13

No one shall expel us from the paradise which Cantor has created for us.
DAVID HILBERT

CHAPTER CONTENTS

In mathematics and computer science the term **set** denotes an unordered collection of objects called the **elements,** or **members,** of the set. A set is commonly denoted by listing the elements enclosed in braces, { and }. For example, the set of decimal digits contains the elements 0, 1, 2, 3, 4, 5, 6, 7, 8, and 9 and is denoted {0, 1, 2, 3, 4, 5, 6, 7, 8, 9}. The set of uppercase letters is {A, B, C, . . . , Z}. The set of even prime numbers, {2}, contains the single element 2; and the set of female U.S. presidents before 1994 is the empty set, denoted by $\varnothing$ or { }—that is, the set containing no elements.

Sets differ from arrays in that the entries of an array are ordered in a certain sequence, but the elements of a set are unordered. Thus we can speak of the first, second, third, . . . entries of an array, but it does not make sense to refer to the first, second, third, . . . elements of a set. For example, the set whose elements are the even digits 0, 2, 4, 6, and 8 is the same as the set whose elements are 4, 8, 0, 2, and 6 or the set whose elements are 8, 0, 6, 4, and 2. The ordering of array entries makes it possible to access an entry directly by specifying its location in the array, but because sets are unordered, no such direct access to the elements of a set is possible.

Unlike some programming languages, C++ does not provide a predefined set type. However, the C++ bitwise operators and arrays can be used to implement a **Set** class whose member functions provide the standard set operations: union, intersection, difference, the membership relation, and the set relations of subset and superset (in addition to the ''standard'' operations such as assignment, equality, and so on). In this chapter, we describe such a class and see how it can be used in problem solving.

13.1 Using Set Objects

As usual, we begin with an example.

Problem: The ATM Menu-Choice Problem (Revisited)

In Section 6.4, we examined the automated teller machine (ATM) menu-choice problem, in which the user is prompted with a menu of choices,

```
Please enter:
   A - to make a withdrawal from your account.
   B - to make a deposit to your account.
   C - for other transactions.
   D - to quit.
```

and the user enters a (character) value. If some value other than A, B, C, or D is entered, we want to prevent execution from proceeding further. As we saw in Chapter 6, one way to do so is to use a loop to confine users to this portion of the program, continuing to display the menu and input values as long as they are invalid:

1. Cycle through the following steps:
   a. Display *Menu*;
   b. Input the user's *Choice*;
   as long as (*Choice* is not a valid menu option).
2. Return *Choice*.

In Figure 13.1, we implement the function `GetMenuChoice()` using the `Set` class.

 FIGURE 13.1 Getting a valid menu choice.

```
/* This function simulates the input of an ATM transaction choice,
   using a Set and some of its operations.

   Output: A Menu of choices (A-D)
   Input:  The user's Choice
   Return: Choice, guaranteed to be one of {A, B, C, D}
--------------------------------------------------------------------*/

#include "Set.h"

char GetMenuChoice(void)
{
   const char                              // the prompt
      Menu[] = "\nPlease enter:\n"
         "A - to make a withdrawal from your account.\n"
         "B - to make a deposit to your account.\n"
         "C - for other transactions.\n"
         "D - to quit.\n--->";
   Set                                     // declare the Set
      ValidChoices(4, 'A', 'B', 'C', 'D');

   char
      Response;                            // the user's response

   do                                      // Loop:
   {
      cout << Menu;                        //    display the menu
      cin >> Response;                     //    get their response
   }                                       // until response is valid
   while (!ValidChoices.Contains(Response));

   return Response;                        // return the valid response
}
```

Sample run:

```
Please enter:
         A - to make a withdrawal from your account.
         B - to make a deposit to your account.
         C - for other transactions.
         D - to quit.
--->Q
```

FIGURE 13.1   Getting a valid menu choice. (cont.)

```
Please enter:
        A - to make a withdrawal from your account.
        B - to make a deposit to your account.
        C - for other transactions.
        D - to quit.
--->Z

Please enter:
        A - to make a withdrawal from your account.
        B - to make a deposit to your account.
        C - for other transactions.
        D - to quit.
--->D
```

A `Set` class provides an alternative way to check the validity of a value at the end of Step 1. More precisely, the `Set` class we implement in the next section allows us to build a set `ValidChoices` of valid menu choices:

{A, B, C, D}

This set is constructed by the definition

```
Set
    ValidChoices(4, 'A', 'B', 'C', 'D');
```

which constructs a set containing the four values `'A'`, `'B'`, `'C'`, and `'D'`. The constructor that performs this operation uses the ellipsis mechanism discussed in Section 7.5.

Given this set and the user's response assigned to the character variable `Response`, we can use the `Set` member function `Contains()` to build the boolean expression

```
ValidChoices.Contains(Response)
```

which will evaluate to true if and only if the set `ValidChoices` contains the value of `Response`. Since we want the do-while loop to repeat its execution as long as the user's choice is invalid, we negate (i.e., apply `!` to) this expression to form the loop condition.

13.2   Designing a `Set` Class

As with the other classes we have seen, designing a `Set` class involves (1) selecting some mechanism for representing the data members; and (2) selecting the operations for `Set` objects that the class is to provide.

Data Members of a `Set`

The first task in designing a set class is to determine what data members are required in order to represent a set in memory. One common technique is the **bitset** approach, in which each possible member of the set is represented by a distinct bit in some string of bits. The first bit in the string represents the value zero, the second bit represents the value one, the third bit represents the value 2, . . . , and the ith bit represents the value $i - 1$. If there are a total of N values being represented, then the set

$$\{0, 1, 2, \ldots, N - 1\}$$

is called the **universal set**—the set of all possible elements.

To indicate that an element is in a set, its corresponding bit is set to 1, and to indicate that the element is not in the set, the bit representing that element is set to 0. To illustrate with a simple example, suppose that the universal set is

$$\{0, 1, 2, 3, 4, \ldots, 29, 30, 31\}$$

Since there are 32 possible elements, 32 bits are required to represent those elements. Since the universal set contains every possible element, it is represented by thirty-two **1** bits:

11111111111111111111111111111111

By contrast, an **empty set** is represented by thirty-two **0** bits:

00000000000000000000000000000000

If the rightmost bit represents the element 0 and the leftmost bit represents the element 31, then the set

$$\{2, 3, 5, 9, 31\}$$

is represented by the bit string:

10000000000000000000001000101100

Making the value of a bit 1 is called **setting** that bit, and making it 0 is called **clearing** that bit. In the bitset approach, a set contains a given element if its corresponding bit has been set, and a set does not contain a given element if its corresponding bit has been cleared. We can thus add elements to and remove elements from a set simply by setting and clearing the appropriate bits.

To design the class `Set` we must decide how big the universal set should be. We have chosen 256 for the number of elements in the universal set of class `Set` because (1) sets of characters are often useful, (2) characters are stored in 8 bits, and (3) a total of $2^8 = 256$ values can be stored in 8 bits. As we did with the class `List`, we declare a named constant for this value,

```
enum {MaxElements = 256};
```

which is then used throughout the class, rather than the literal **256**, so that the size of the universal set can be easily modified, if necessary (for instance, to $2^{10} = 1024$).

The bitset approach then requires constructing a data member that consists of 256 bits. None of the predefined data types provide this much storage, but we can declare this data member as an array with sufficient capacity to store 256 bits. If we assume that as usual, a **long** value has 32 bits, then an array of **long** values will require 256/32 = 8 entries. To simplify maintenance of the class, we use named constants in declaring such an array instead of literals:

```
enum { BitsPerEntry = 32,        // a long has 32 bits
       ArrayLength =             // # of array elems needed
          MaxElements / BitsPerEntry};
long
   Array[ArrayLength];           // container for the bits
```

Since the named constants **BitsPerEntry** and **ArrayLength** are details of the particular technique being used to implement sets, these names should be declared privately. However, the constant **MaxElements** is a characteristic of a set, not its implementation, and so it should be declared publicly. Since **MaxElements** must be declared prior to **ArrayLength**, we organize the data members of the class as shown in Figure 13.2.

FIGURE 13.2   Data members of class **Set**.

```
/* This file contains the declaration of class Set.

... Most documentation omitted to save pages.
   (see the data disk that accompanies this text.)...
-----------------------------------------------------*/

#ifndef SET
#define SET

class Set
{
public:
   enum {MaxElements = 256};        // U = {0, 1, ..., 255}

   // ... public member functions

private:
   enum { BitsPerEntry = 32,        // number of bits in a long
          ArrayLength =             // #array elements needed
             MaxElements/BitsPerEntry};

   long
      Array[ArrayLength];           // container for the bits

};
#endif
```

In this case, **ArrayLength** is 8, so that the **Array** member in which we store the values of the **Set** can be visualized as

Array   0   1   2   3   4   5   6   7

with each entry of **Array** containing 32 bits. By applying the C++ bitwise operations to the appropriate entry of this array, we can set an individual bit to 1 and/or clear a bit to 0 and so represent a set of up to 256 values. For example, as we shall see, the set

{0, 2, 4}

will be represented by setting the appropriate bits in the first entry of **Array** to the bit string

00000000000000000000000000010101

Since the base-10 representation of this binary value is 21, the **Array** member can be visualized as follows:

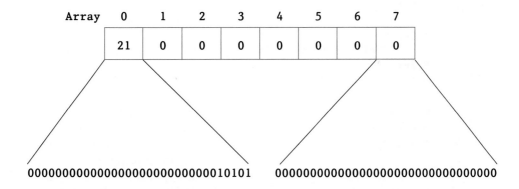

Note that since the elements in a **Set** range in value from 0 to 255, sets of up to 256 enumeration values can be represented. For example, the set

{Red, Green}

can be represented by declaring an enumeration

```
enum Colors { Red, Orange, Yellow, Green, Blue, Indigo, Violet };
```

whose values can be the values in a **Set**. Since **Red** is a symbolic name for 0, **Orange** is a symbolic name for 1, and so on, the preceding set can be represented by setting the bits corresponding to 0 and 3 in entry 0 of the **Array** member:

00000000000000000000000000001001

Using the constructors for class `Set` (described later), the preceding set can be built with the declaration

```
Set
    ChristmasColors(2, Red, Green);
```

Set Operations

The second task in designing the class is to identify the operations to be implemented for class `Set`. The standard set operations include

- `S1 + S2`   Compute the union of two sets `S1` and `S2`
- `S1 * S2`   Compute the intersection of two sets `S1` and `S2`
- `S1 - S2`   Compute the difference of two sets `S1` and `S2`
- `S1 == S2`   Determine if sets `S1` and `S2` are equal
- `S1 != S2`   Determine if sets `S1` and `S2` are not equal
- `S1 <= S2`   Determine if set `S1` is a subset of set `S2`
- `S1 >= S2`   Determine if set `S1` is a superset of set `S2`
- `S1 < S2`   Determine if set `S1` is a proper subset of set `S2`
- `S1 > S2`   Determine if set `S1` is a proper superset of set `S2`
- `S.Contains(E)`   Determine whether set `S` contains a given element `E`

In addition to these standard operations, there are others that are useful for a `Set` class:

- `Set`
     `S;`   Construct set `S` as the empty set
- `Set`
     `S(Set::MaxElements);`   Construct set `S` as the universal set
- `Set`
     `S(N, Val1, Val2, ..., ValN);`   Construct set `S` from a list of N values
- `S1 = S2;`   Assign set `S2` to set `S1`
- `cout << S;`   Display the elements of set `S`
- `cin >> S;`   Input a sequence of elements, storing them in set `S`
- `S.Insert(E);`   Insert element `E` into set `S`
- `S.Delete(E);`   Delete element `E` from set `S`

The data disk that accompanies this text provides the source code for many of these operations, and others are left as exercises. Some of the operations are implemented in the next section.

13.3   Implementing Set Operations

In this section, we present the implementation of a number of the operations on a `Set`, assuming that the bitset implementation is used to represent sets. The operations that are presented have been chosen for their diversity, some operating on pairs of sets, others on a set and an element of a set, and still others that do neither. Each of the other operations is similar to one or more of those we present.

Because we are implementing class `Set` using the bitset approach, these operations rely heavily on the bitwise operators. Since these operators have not been discussed before, we will describe them in detail as they arise.

A Class Constructor for the Empty Set

We begin with an operation to construct an empty set. Since the empty set is represented by zero values in every bit, an empty set can be constructed by setting each entry of **Array** to zero, as shown in Figure 13.3.

 FIGURE 13.3 The empty set class constructor.

```
/* This function constructs a Set as the empty set.

   Precondition:  A Set has been defined with no arguments.
   Postcondition: That Set is initialized as an empty set.
--------------------------------------------------------------*/

Set::Set(void)
{                                // initialize Array as an empty set
   for (int i = 0; i < Set::ArrayLength; i++)
      Array[i] = 0;
}
```

Once we have declared this constructor in the public section of class **Set**, we can write a declaration such as

```
Set
    EmptySet;
```

and every bit in the **Array** member of **EmptySet** will be initialized to zero.

Set Union

The **union** of two sets *Set1* and *Set2* is the set of elements that are in *Set1* or *Set2* or both and is denoted by a set expression of the form

```
Set1 + Set2
```

This can be pictured by the following **Venn diagram:**

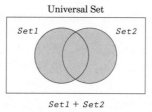

Universal Set

Set1   *Set2*

Set1 + Set2

To implement this operation, we overload **operator+** as a friend function of class **Set**. The definition of the union operation is shown in Figure 13.4.

FIGURE 13.4 The union operation.

```
/* This function returns the union of two Set objects.

   Receive: S1 and S2, two Set objects
   Return: The union of S1 and S2
-----------------------------------------------------------*/

Set operator+(const Set& S1, const Set& S2)
{
   Set
      Result;

   for (int i = 0; i < Set::ArrayLength; i++)
      Result.Array[i] = S1.Array[i] | S2.Array[i];

   return Result;
}
```

This function performs the union operation by applying the **bitwise OR operator** (|) to the corresponding entries in the **Array** members of its operands. The effect of this operator is to produce a result whose value is the OR of the individual bits of each operand.

To illustrate, suppose that **S1** represents the set $\{0, 2, 4, 6, 8\}$ and **S2** represents the set $\{1, 3, 5, 6, 7\}$. Then **Array[0]** in **S1** is

00000000000000000000000101010101

and **Array[0]** in **S2** as

00000000000000000000000001101010

Then the computation

```
Result.Array[0] = S1.Array[0] | S2.Array[0];
```

performs a bitwise OR on these two bitstrings:

```
S1.Array[0]  <───────>       00000000000000000000000101010101
| S2.Array[0]  <───────> OR  00000000000000000000000001101010

Result.Array[0]  <───────>   00000000000000000000000111111111
```

Array[0] of **Result** thus represents the set $\{0, 1, 2, 3, 4, 5, 6, 7, 8\}$.

The bitwise OR operator can be used to *set a bit* by ORing the bit with the value 1:

```
Bit |= 1;
```

Bit will have the value 1 following the execution of the statement. In general, the bitwise OR operator behaves as follows:

The Bitwise OR Operator

Form

> $IntExpression_1$ | $IntExpression_2$

where:

each **IntExpression$_i$** is an integer-compatible expression.

Behavior

Bit 1 of the result =
  (bit 1 of **IntExpression$_1$**) OR (bit 1 of **IntExpression$_2$**);
Bit 2 of the result =
  (bit 2 of **IntExpression$_1$**) OR (bit 2 of **IntExpression$_2$**);
  .
  .
  .

To illustrate, the expression

    6 | 4

produces the value 6, as follows:

```
  6 = 0110
| 4 = 0010
    0110 = 6
```

It is important to understand the difference between this *bitwise* OR operator (|) and the *relational* OR operator (||), which always produces a boolean value. For example:

    6 || 4

produces the value 1, because a nonzero operand (such as **6** or **4**) is treated as true. As a result, this expression is treated as

  true OR true

which produces the value true.

Set Intersection

The **intersection** of **Set1** and **Set2** is the set of elements that are in both **Set1** and **Set2** and is denoted by

  *Set1 * Set2*

It can be pictured as

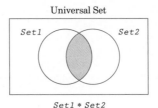

Universal Set

*Set1 * Set2*

The intersection of **Set1** and **Set2** is the set of values that are in **Set1** *and* in **Set2**. The intersection operation is implemented by applying the bitwise AND operation to the corresponding elements of each operand's **Array** member. Figure 13.5 presents an implementation of this operation.

FIGURE 13.5   The intersection operation.

```
/* This function returns the intersection of two Set objects.
   Receive: S1 and S2, two Set objects
   Return:  The intersection of S1 and S2
--------------------------------------------------------------*/

Set operator*(const Set& S1, const Set& S2)
{
   Set
      Result;

   for (int i = 0; i < Set::ArrayLength; i++)
      Result.Array[i] = S1.Array[i] & S2.Array[i];

   return Result;
}
```

This function uses the **bitwise AND operator** (**&**), which produces a value that is the AND of the bits of its operands. To illustrate, suppose that **S1** represents the set {4, 5, 6} and **S2** represents the set {1, 3, 5, 7, 9}. Then the computation

```
Result.Array[0] = S1.Array[0] & S2.Array[0];
```

performs a bitwise AND on these two bitstrings:

```
    S1.Array[0]  ⟷        00000000000000000000000001110000
  * S2.Array[0]  ⟷   AND  00000000000000000000001010101010
Result.Array[0]  ⟷        00000000000000000000000000100000
```

Thus, **Array[0]** of **Result** correctly represents the set {5}, since 5 is the only element that **S1** and **S2** have in common.

One use of the bitwise AND operator is to *check the value of a bit* by ANDing it with the value 1. This can be done with an expression of the form:

```
Bit & 1
```

since the result will be 1 if the value *Bit* is 1, and the result will be 0 if the value of *Bit* is 0. Another use is to *clear a bit* by ANDing it with the value 0:

```
Bit & 0
```

The bitwise AND operator can be described more generally as follows:

The Bitwise AND Operator

Form

$$IntExpression_1 \ \& \ IntExpression_2$$

where:
   each *IntExpression$_i$* is an integer-compatible expression.

Behavior
   Bit 1 of the result =
         (bit 1 of *IntExpression$_1$*) AND (bit 1 of *IntExpression$_2$*),
   Bit 2 of the result =
         (bit 2 of *IntExpression$_1$*) AND (bit 2 of *IntExpression$_2$*),

                        .
                        .
                        .

To illustrate, the value of the expression

```
6 & 4
```

is 4, since

```
    6 = 0110
& 4 = 0100
    0100 = 4
```

It is important to understand the difference between the bitwise AND operator (&) and the relational AND operator (&&), which always produces a boolean value. For example:

```
6 && 4
```

produces the value 1, because a nonzero operand is taken as true. For this reason, this expression is treated as

   true AND true

which produces the result true.

Set Difference

The **difference** of two sets,

> *Set1* - *Set2*

is the set of elements that are in *Set1* but not in *Set2*:

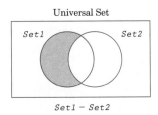

For example,

$$\{1, 3, 5, 7, 9\} - \{3, 4\ 5, 6, 7\} = \{1, 9\}$$

The difference operation is slightly more difficult to implement than the union or intersection operations, because we must identify those elements that are in **S1** but not in **S2**. The preceding diagram suggests thinking of this operation as removing from **S1** those elements that are in the intersection of **S1** and **S2**. One way to do this is

1. Build **ResultSet**, a set containing a copy of **S1**;
2. Build **CommonSet**, the set of elements that are common to both **S1** and **S2**; and
3. In **ResultSet**, clear those bits that are 1s in both **ResultSet** and **CommonSet**.

Figure 13.6 presents an implementation of **operator-** using this approach. An alternative approach that is somewhat more efficient because it does not require computing the intersection of **S1** and **S2** is described in the exercises.

FIGURE 13.6   The difference operation.

```
/* This function returns the difference of two Set objects.

   Receive: S1 and S2, two Set objects
   Return:  The difference of S1 and S2
--------------------------------------------------------------*/

Set operator-(const Set& S1, const Set& S2)
{
   Set
      Result = S1,
      CommonSet = S1 * S2;
```

FIGURE 13.6   The difference operation. (cont.)

```
for (int i = 0; i < Set::ArrayLength; i++)
    Result.Array[i] ^= CommonSet.Array[i];

return Result;
}
```

This function begins by initializing its local **Set** object **Result** as a copy of **S1**, the left operand. It then uses the intersection operation to build a second local **Set** named **CommonSet**, whose value is the intersection of **S1** and **S2**. **CommonSet** thus contains all the elements that **S1** and **S2** have in common. A for loop then processes each entry in the **Array** member of **Result** by clearing those bits that are set in both **Result** and **CommonSet**. The implementation in Figure 13.6 clears these bits using the **bitwise exclusive-OR operator** (^) which, applied to two bits, produces a 1 if *either but not both* of those bits are 1 and produces a 0 otherwise. Exclusive-OR is sometimes abbreviated as **XOR.**

To illustrate, suppose that **S1** represents the set $\{1, 3, 5, 7, 9\}$, **S2** represents the set $\{3, 4, 5, 6, 7\}$, and that **long** values have 32 bits. Thus, **S1.Array[0]** is

00000000000000000000001010101010

and **S2.Array[0]** is

00000000000000000000000011111000

Result.Array[0] is then constructed as a copy of **S1.Array[0]**, and **CommonSet.Array[0]** is constructed using the intersection of **S1.Array[0]** and **S2.Array[0]**:

00000000000000000000000010101000

Within the for loop, the statement

```
Result.Array[i] ^= CommonSet.Array[i];
```

is executed, which applies a bitwise XOR operation to **Result.Array[0]** and **CommonSet.Array[0]**:

```
      Result.Array[0] ⟷          00000000000000000000001010101010
  ^ CommonSet.Array[0] ⟷   XOR 00000000000000000000000010101000
                                 00000000000000000000001000000010
```

This result represents the set $\{1, 9\}$, which is the difference of $\{1, 3, 5, 7, 9\}$ and $\{3, 4, 5, 6, 7\}$, and this is then written to **Result.Array[0]**.

The general form of the bitwise XOR operator can be described as follows:

The Bitwise XOR Operator

> **Form**
>
> $IntExpression_1 \; \wedge \; IntExpression_2$
>
> where:
>   each **IntExpression₁** is an integer-compatible
>   expression.
>
> **Behavior**
> For each bit in the resulting value, the bit is
>
>   0, if the corresponding bits in **IntExpression₁**
>   and **IntExpression₂** are both 0 or both 1;
>   1, otherwise.

To illustrate, the value of the expression:

    6 ^ 4

is 2, since

```
    6 = 0110
^   4 = 0100
        0010 = 2
```

It is important to remember the difference between the XOR and OR operators, since XOR produces a 1 if *either but not both* of its operand bits are 1,
whereas the OR operator produces a 1 if *either or both* of its operand bits are 1.

Set Membership

Another standard set operation is the set membership operation. This is a boolean
relation that, given an element and a set, returns true if and only if the element is
a member of the set. In our class, we have implemented this operation as a **Set**
member function named **Contains()**. The expression

    SetName.Contains(Element)

returns true if **Element** is a member of **SetName** and returns false otherwise. This
operation is somewhat more complicated than the previous ones, because we must
deal with an individual element of the set. The basic approach is to write a function
that returns

    True, if the bit corresponding to the given element is set; and
    False, if that bit is clear.

The function must, therefore,

1. Determine which entry of the **Array** member contains the corresponding bit;

2. Determine the position of the bit in that `Array` entry;
3. Examine that bit, and return true if it is set and return false otherwise.

The fact that `BitsPerEntry` was defined to be 32 implies that

If *Element* is between 0 and 31, then the appropriate entry is 0;
If *Element* is between 32 and 63, then the appropriate entry is 1;

.

.

.

If *Element* is between 224 and 255, then the appropriate entry is 7.

Because each range contains 32 values, the appropriate entry is easily computed using an integer division:

> *Entry* = *Element* / Set::BitsPerEntry;

The second step of finding the position of the appropriate bit in that entry is also easy:

If *Element* is one of 0, 32, 64, 96, 128, 160, 192, or 224, then the bit position is 0.
If *Element* is one of 1, 33, 65, 97, 129, 161, 193, or 225, then the bit position is 1.

.

.

.

If *Element* is one of 31, 63, 95, 127, 159, 191, 223, or 255, then the bit position is 31.

Because each of the values for bit position i is a multiple of 32 plus i, the position of the appropriate bit is the remainder from an integer division:

> *BitPosition* = *Element* % Set::BitsPerEntry;

The third step is accomplished using the bitwise operators as follows:

3a. Define a 32-bit value, consisting of thirty-one 0 bits followed by a 1 bit:

> 00000000000000000000000000000001

3b. Use the **bitwise left-shift operator** (`<<`) to shift the 1 bit to the position corresponding to the element in question (the resulting string of bits is called a **mask**); and

3c. Apply the bitwise AND operator (`&`) to the mask and the array entry containing the bit. The result of this operation will be true (nonzero) if and only if that bit is set in the array entry.

The function `Contains()` in Figure 13.7 uses these techniques to implement the set membership operation.

FIGURE 13.7 The membership operation.

```
/* This function performs the set membership operation.

   Receive: Elem, an element
   Return:  True if Elem is a member of the Set
             containing this function and False otherwise
-----------------------------------------------------------------*/

Boolean Set::Contains(unsigned Elem) const
{
   int
      Index = Elem / Set::BitsPerEntry;       // find index of Elem

   if (Index >= Set::ArrayLength)             // if it's invalid
   {                                          //   display error msg
      cerr << "\n*** Contains: Set is too small to hold "
           << Elem << endl;
      return False;                           // indicate failure
   }

   int
      BitPosition = Elem % Set::BitsPerEntry;// find the bit to set

   long
      Mask = 1;                               // 31 0s and a 1.

   Mask = Mask << BitPosition;                // left-shift the mask

   return (Array[Index] & Mask) != 0;         // see if the bit is 1
}
```

To illustrate this implementation, suppose that the argument 34 is passed to parameter **Elem**. After checking that 34 lies in the range of values for the set, the statement

```
   Index = Elem / Set::BitsPerEntry;
```

computes the index of the appropriate **Array** entry as 1. The statement

```
   BitPosition = Elem % Set::BitsPerEntry;
```

computes the value 2 as the position of the bit corresponding to 34. After constructing a 32-bit object named **Mask** with the value 1,

```
   00000000000000000000000000000001
```

the statement

```
   Mask = Mask << BitPosition;
```

uses the bitwise left-shift operator (**<<**) to shift each bit of **Mask** to the left by two positions, filling the vacated rightmost positions with zeros. This has the effect of shifting the 1 in the mask from where it was (position 0) to the position corresponding to **Elem** (position 2):

00000000000000000000000000000100

Once **Mask** has been constructed and its 1 bit has been properly positioned, the statement

```
return (Array[Index] & Mask) != 0;
```

returns the result of the bitwise AND of these operands, so that a nonzero value is returned if the bit at position 2 of entry 1 of the **Array** member is set; and the value 0 is returned otherwise.

In general, the bitwise shift operators can be described as follows.

The Bitwise Shift Operators

Form

  $IntExpression_1$ **<<** $IntExpression_2$

or

  $IntExpression_1$ **>>** $IntExpression_2$

where:

  each **IntExpression**$_i$ is an integer-compatible expression.

Behavior
The bits of the value **IntExpression**$_1$ are shifted **IntExpression**$_2$ positions

- To the left by the **<<** operator; and
- To the right by the **>>** operator.

The shift operators also provide a quick way to multiply or divide by any power of two. The expression

  IntegerExpression **<<** *i*

to compute the square of *IntegerExpression* can be computed faster than the expression

  IntegerExpression * pow(2.0, *i*)

because it avoids the function call overhead; and evaluating the expression

  IntegerExpression **>>** *i*

takes less time than does the expression

```
IntegerExpression / pow(2.0, i)
```

Deleting an Element from a Set

The last operation we consider is the operation to delete an element from a set. We must do the following:

1. Compute the entry in **Array** containing the bit corresponding to the deleted value.
2. Compute the position of the appropriate bit in that entry.
3. Clear that bit.

The first two steps are identical to those of the membership operation, and the third step is similar. Figure 13.8 presents one possible implementation.

 FIGURE 13.8   The **Delete()** operation.

```
/* This function removes an element from a Set.

   Receive: Elem, a set element
   Return:  The Set containing this function, without Elem as a
               member
            True if successful and False otherwise
   ----------------------------------------------------------------*/

Boolean Set::Delete(unsigned Elem)
{
   int
      Index = Elem / Set::BitsPerEntry;       // find index for Elem

   if (Index >= Set::ArrayLength)             // if it's invalid
   {                                          //    display error msg
      cerr << "\n*** Delete: Set is too small to hold "
           << Elem << endl;
      return False;                           // indicate failure
   }

   int
      BitPosition = Elem % Set::BitsPerEntry; // find the bit to set

   long
      Mask = 1;                               // the mask to set it

   if (BitPosition > 0)                       // if not the first bit
      Mask <<= BitPosition;                   //    left-shift the mask

   Array[Index] &= (~Mask);                   // clear the bit

   return True;                               // indicate success
}
```

Here, we see that the function begins like the membership operation, checking the validity of **Elem**, computing **Entry** and **BitPosition**, and then constructing a **Mask** object using the left-shift operator. In this function, we use one of the "short-cut" operators to position the 1 in the mask:

```
Mask <<= BitPosition;
```

Once **Mask** has been constructed, the statement

```
Array[Index] &= ~Mask;
```

uses the bitwise AND operator and the (unary) **bitwise negation operator** (~).

As mentioned previously, a bit can be cleared by ANDing it with 0. Here, however, we must clear only the bit corresponding to **Elem**; all of the other bits of **Array[Index]** must remain unchanged. We can accomplish this by building a mask that has a single 0 at the position we wish to clear and has thirty-one 1 bits at the other positions (since a value ANDed with 1 is that value). Such a mask can be constructed by

1. Building a mask with a single, correctly positioned 1 and thirty-one 0s elsewhere; and
2. Applying the bitwise negation operator (~) that inverts the bits of its operand, turning all its 1 bits to 0s and all its 0 bits to 1s.

Given such a mask, the bitwise AND operator (**&**) can be applied to it and the selected array entry using

```
Array[Index] &= (~Mask);
```

To illustrate, suppose that a **Set** named **S** represents the set {32, 34, 36} so that **S.Array[1]** is:

```
00000000000000000000000000010101
```

The call

```
S.Delete(36);
```

will pass the value 36 to **Elem** and then compute

```
Index = Elem / Set::BitsPerEntry;
```

which assigns **Index** the value 1. After checking its validity, the statement

```
BitPosition = Elem % Set::BitsPerEntry;
```

computes the value 4 as the position of the bit corresponding to 36. The object `Mask` is then constructed,

Mask: 00000000000000000000000000000001

and its bits are shifted left by four positions:

Mask: 00000000000000000000000000010000

When the negation operator is applied to `Mask`, its bits are inverted,

~Mask: 11111111111111111111111111101111

and this value is ANDed with the bit string in `S.Array[1]`:

```
S.Array[1]  ⟷         00000000000000000000000000010101
     ~Mask  ⟷     AND 11111111111111111111111111101111
                      00000000000000000000000000000101
```

When the result is stored into `S.Array[1]`, `S` subsequently represents the set {32, 34}.

The bitwise negation operator can be described more generally as follows.

The Bitwise Negation Operator

Form

   ~IntExpression

where:

   IntExpression is an integer-compatible expression.

Behavior
Each bit of *IntExpression* is inverted, meaning that

   Any 0 bit in *IntExpression* is a 1 bit in
      ~IntExpression, and
   Any 1 bit in *IntExpression* is a 0 bit in
      ~IntExpression.

Other Operations

The remaining `Set` operations are variations of those just described, and additional operations are described in the exercises.

1. Given that A, B, C, and D are set variables declared as follows:

```
Set
   A(7, 3, 5, 6, 7, 8, 9, 11),
   B(7, 1, 2, 3, 4, 5, 11, 12),
   C(4, 2, 4, 6, 8),
   D(5, 6, 7, 8, 9, 10);
```

Calculate the following.

(a) A * B
(b) A + B
(c) A - B
(d) B - A
(e) A + D
(f) A - D
(g) A * D
(h) D - A
(i) C + C
(j) C * C
(k) C - C
(l) C - [ ]
(m) A + B + C + D
(n) (A - B) - C
(o) A - (B - C)
(p) A * B * C * D
(q) A + B * C
(r) A * B + C
(s) A * B - C * D
(t) (A - (B + C)) * D
(u) A * B - (A + B)
(v) A - B - C - D
(w) B - B - C
(x) B - (B - C)

2. Write appropriate declarations for the following set identifiers:

(a) **SmallIntegers**: set of integers from 1 through 9
(b) **LowerCaseLetters**: set of lowercase letters
(c) **Days**: the set of names of days of the week
(d) **Suit**: set of 13 cards in a suit

3. Write appropriate variable declarations for the following set variables, and write statements to give each the specified values:

(a) **Evens**: the set of all even integers from 1 through 99; and **Odds**: the set of all odd integers in the range from 1 through 99
(b) **OneModThree**: the set of the numbers of the form $3k + 1$ in the range from 1 through 99, with k an integer
(c) **LargeFactors**: the set of all numbers in the range 1 through 99 that are not divisible by 2, 3, 5, or 7
(d) **Divisors**: the set of all divisors of a given integer **Number**
(e) **Vowels**: the set of all vowels; and **Consonants**: the set of all consonants
(f) **WeekDays**: the set of all weekdays
(g) **FaceCards**: the set of all face cards in a suit; and **NumberCards**: the set of all number cards in a suit.

4. Extend class **Set** by adding functions to

(a) Overload **operator!=** to return true if and only if its first operand is not equal to its second operand.
(b) Define **Insert()** as a member function that, given an element, inserts that value into its **Set**.
(c) Overload **operator>=** to return true if and only if its first operand is a superset of its second operand.
(d) Overload **operator>** to return true if and only if its first operand is a proper superset of its second operand.

5. Add a member function **Cardinality()** to class **Set** to calculate the cardinal number of a set, that is, the number of elements in the set.

6. In the implementation file of class **Set**, modify the definition of **operator<<** (see the disk that accompanies this text) to display any set using the usual mathematical notation in which the elements are enclosed in braces, { and }, and are separated by commas. For example, the set of numbers 2, 5, and 7 should be displayed as {2, 5, 7}, the set whose element is 4, as {4}, and the empty set, as { }.

7. Assuming the universal set is {0, 1, . . . , 31}, give the bit string representations of the following sets:

   (a) The set of odd digits
   (b) The set of prime digits
   (c) The set of digits divisible by 1
   (d) The set of digits not divisible by 1

8. For the universal set {'A', 'B', . . . , 'Z'}, describe the bit strings for the following sets:

   (a) The set of vowels
   (b) {'A', 'B', 'C', 'D', 'E', 'X', 'Y', 'Z'}

9. Modify the implementation of set difference in Figure 13.5 so that it uses the bitwise AND and negation operators and does not require computing the intersection of **S1** and **S2**.

13.4   PART OF THE PICTURE:
Automata and Language Translation

In our discussion of system software in Chapter 1, we mentioned **compilers,** which are programs whose function is to translate a source program written in some high-level language such as C++ into an object program in machine language. After this object program has been linked to any external definitions it uses, the resulting executable program can be executed by the computer.

The basic components of the compiler are summarized in the following diagram:

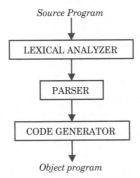

The input to a compiler is a stream of characters that comprise the source program. Before the translation can actually be carried out, these characters must be grouped into meaningful units, such as identifiers, reserved words, constants, and operators. For example, when a program segment such as

```
{
    Var1 = Var2 + 256;
    if (Var1<500)
        Var1 += Num;
}
```

is read by the compiler as a "stream" of characters

{⏎ɓɓɓVar1ɓ=ɓVar2ɓ+ɓ256;⏎ɓɓɓifɓ(Var1<500)⏎ɓɓɓɓɓVar1ɓ+=ɓNum;⏎}⏎

(where ɓ) is a blank and ⏎ is a newline character), the lexical analyzer must identify the following units:

{	Left brace
Var1	Identifier
=	Assignment operator
Var2	Identifier
+	Addition operator
256	Integer constant
;	Semicolon
if	Reserved word
(	Left parenthesis
Var1	Identifier
<	Relational operator
500	Integer constant
)	Right parenthesis
Var1	Identifier
+=	Addition-assignment operator
Num	Identifier
;	Semicolon
}	Right brace

These units are called **tokens,** and the part of the compiler that recognizes these tokens is called the **lexical analyzer.**

Given a sequence of tokens, it is the task of the **parser** to group the tokens together to form the basic **syntactic structures** of the language as determined by the syntax rules. For example, it must recognize that the three consecutive tokens

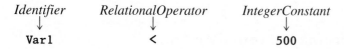

can be grouped together to form a valid *BooleanExpression.* Similarly it must recognize that the three consecutive tokens

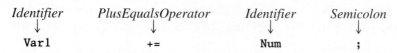

form a valid *Statement*. It must also recognize that the word **if** is a reserved word and that opening and closing parentheses are separate tokens:

Finally, it must recognize that the sequence

ReservedWordIf   *OpenParen*   *BooleanExpression*   *CloseParen*   *Statement*

forms a valid **if** statement. The complete **parse tree** constructed during the compilation of this **if** statement is

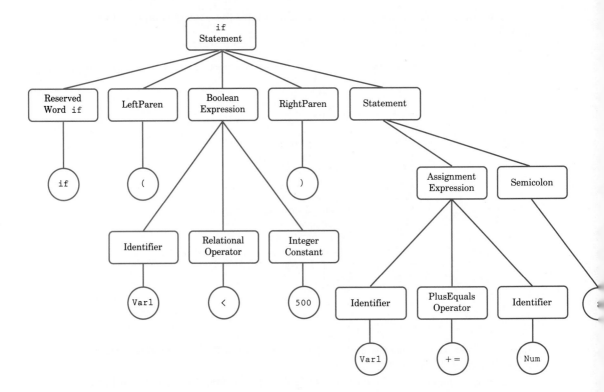

Later phases of the compilation process then generate the machine code for this **if** statement.

Finite-State Automata and Lexical Analysis

When designing a lexical analyzer to recognize various tokens, one can begin by designing a **finite-state automaton,** also called a **finite-state machine,** to recognize each token. A finite-state automaton consists of a finite number of states, together with a function that defines transitions from one state to another, depending on the current machine state and the current input character. One state is designated as the *start state* and is the state of the automaton when it begins processing an input string of characters. If the machine is in one of the special states called *accepting states* after an input string is processed, then that string is said to be *recognized,* or *accepted,* by the automaton. For example, a finite automaton to recognize strings of A's and B's that contain AB is

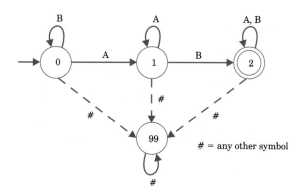

Here, the arrow pointing to state 0 indicates that this is the start state. The automaton begins processing input characters in state 0 and makes transitions from one state to another state or remains in the current state, as specified by the labels on the arrows.

To illustrate, consider the input string AABB. The finite-state automaton begins in state 0, and because the first input symbol is A, it transfers to state 1. Since the next input symbol is an A, it remains in state 1. However, the third symbol is a B, which causes a transition to state 2. The final symbol is a B and does not cause a state change. When the end of the input string is reached, and the automaton is in an accept state (as indicated by the double circle), we say that it accepts the string AABB. It is easy to see that any string containing AB will be processed in a similar manner and lead to an accept state and that only such strings will cause the automaton to terminate in state 2. For example, the string BBAAA is not accepted, since the automaton will be in state 1 after processing this string, and state 1 is not an accept state. The string BAACAB also is not accepted, since the "illegal" symbol C causes a transition from state 1 to state 99, which is not an accept state.

Because 99 is a "reject," or "dead," state, once it is entered, it is never exited. The transitions to this state are shown as dashed lines, since the existence of such a state is usually assumed and transitions are not drawn in the diagram. For any state and any input symbol for which no transition is specified, it is assumed that the transition is to such a reject state. Thus, the finite-state automaton is usually drawn as

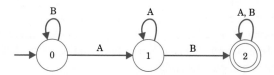

Another example is the following finite-state automaton that recognizes the reserved word **if** (followed by some delimiter *delim,* which is any character that can legally follow **if**):

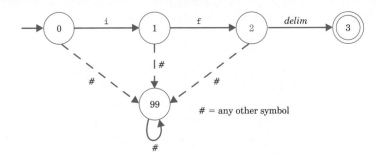

A finite-state automaton to recognize a C++ identifier (followed by a delimiter) is

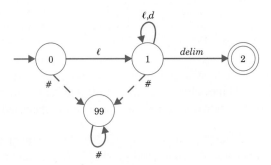

where ℓ denotes a letter (including underscores), d denotes a digit and *delim* is a delimiter.

Example: Recognizing a Decimal Integer

To show how a finite-state automaton can aid in the design of lexical analyzers, we consider the problem of recognizing C++ (unsigned) decimal integer constants. A finite-state automaton that does this is

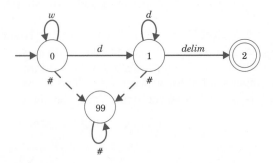

where d denotes one of the digits 0, 1, . . . , 9, w denotes any whitespace character, *delim* is a delimiter and state 2 is the only accepting state. The machine begins in state 0, where it behaves as follows:

- If the first input symbol is a whitespace character, it stays in state 0, "gobbling up" leading white space.
- If the first input symbol is a digit, it goes to state 1.
- Any other input sends the machine to the "reject" state.

In state 1, the machine reads the next symbol and behaves as follows:

- If that symbol is a digit, it remains in state 1.
- If that symbol is a delimiter, it passes to the "accept" state.
- Any other input is invalid and sends the machine to the "reject" state.

A delimiter is a character that can legally follow the object we are seeking to recognize (an integer in this case), so that our machine can safely accept the input only when a delimiter follows a sequence of digits.

Writing program statements that simulate such a finite-state automaton is straightforward. The function in Figure 13.9 illustrates this. It reads a string of characters and determines whether it represents valid C++ unsigned decimal integers, assuming that they are delimited by newline characters. The function `IntRecognized()` implements the preceding finite state automaton.

FIGURE 13.9   Lexical analysis.

```
/*----- This function simulates the behavior of a finite state
          automaton that recognizes decimal integer constants.

   Input (keyboard):  A line of characters
   Return:            True iff that line comprises a valid
                      decimal integer constant
------------------------------------------------------------*/

#include <limits.h>                          // INT_MAX

Boolean IntRecognized(void)
{
  const int                                  // constant values:
    AcceptState = 2,                         //    accept state
    RejectState = 99;                        //    reject state

  char
    Symbol;                                  // input symbol
  int                                        // current state,
    State = 0;                               //    initially the
                                             //    start state
  Set
    WhiteSpaceSet(3, ' ', '\t', '\n'),       // set of white spaces
    DigitSet(10, '0', '1', '2', '3', '4',    // set of digit chars
               '5', '6', '7', '8', '9'),
    DelimiterSet(1, '\n'),                   // valid int followers
    FinalStateSet(2, AcceptState, RejectState);// terminal states
```

FIGURE 13.9 Lexical analysis. (cont.)

```
do                                              //  Loop:
{
  cin.get(Symbol);                              //    get the next char

  switch (State)                                //    if in:
  {
    case 0:                                     //      State 0:
      if (WhiteSpaceSet.Contains(Symbol))       //        if white space
        State = 0;                              //          stay here
      else if (DigitSet.Contains(Symbol))       //        if it's a digit
        State = 1;                              //          goto state 2
      else                                      //        otherwise
      {
        cin.ignore(INT_MAX, '\n');              //          skip the line
        State = RejectState;                    //          REJECT
      }
      break;

    case 1:                                     //      State 1:
      if (DigitSet.Contains(Symbol))            //        if it's a digit
        State = 1;                              //          stay in 1
      else if (DelimiterSet.Contains(Symbol))   //        if it's a delim
        State = AcceptState;                    //          ACCEPT
      else                                      //        otherwise
      {
        cin.ignore(INT_MAX, '\n');              //          skip the line
        State = RejectState;                    //          REJECT
      }
      break;

    default:                                    //      shouldn't happen
      cerr << "\n*** Main error: invalid state "
           << State << "entered!\n";            //        but just in case
      State = RejectState;                      //        REJECT
  }
}                                               // until State is
while (!FinalStateSet.Contains(State));         //    a final state

return (State == AcceptState);
}
```

A driver program to test the operation of this function is presented in Figure 13.10.

FIGURE 13.10 Recognizing an integer constant.

```
/* This program determines if a sequence of characters represents a
   valid C++ decimal integer, by simulating a finite state automaton.

   Input (keyboard): A sequence of characters
   Output (screen): User prompts and messages indicating whether
                    inputs represent valid integers
--------------------------------------------------------------------------*/

#include <iostream.h>

#include "Set.h"
#include "Boolean.h"

Boolean IntRecognized(void);                            // the recognizer

int main(void)
{
   char
      Response;                                          // query response
   Set
      YesResponsesSet(2, 'y', 'Y');                      // "Yes" responses

   do                                                    // Loop:
   {
      cout << "\nEnter the string to be analyzed: ";//    input prompt

      if (IntRecognized())                              //    scan string
         cout << "--Valid integer recognized.\n";       //      and display
      else                                              //      appropriate
         cout << "--Not a valid integer.\n";            //      message
      cout << "More data (y or n)? ";                   //      query user
      cin >> Response;                                  //      get response
   }
   while (YesResponsesSet.Contains(Response));          // as long as
                                                        // user wants

   return 0;
}

// ... definition of IntRecognized() omitted ...
```

Sample run:

```
Enter the string to be analyzed: 1234
--Valid integer recognized.
More data (y or n)? y

Enter the string to be analyzed: 12+
--Not a valid integer.
More data (y or n)? y
```

FIGURE 13.10   Recognizing an integer constant. (cont.)

```
Enter the string to be analyzed: -12
--Not a valid integer.
More data (y or n)? y

Enter the string to be analyzed: 12345678987654321234567898765321
--Valid integer recognized.
More data (y or n)? y

Enter the string to be analyzed: R2D2
--Not a valid integer.
More data (y or n)? n
```

The sample run shows that in C++, a signed constant such as

-12

is not an integer constant. The reason for this is that C++ treats such signed values as two separate tokens: a minus sign (-) and an integer constant (12).

Exercises

1. Design a finite state automaton to recognize bit strings satisfying the following conditions.

   (a) Containing 00 or 11
   (b) Containing an even number of 1s
   (c) Containing an even number of 0s and an even number of 1s
   (d) In which n % 3 = 1, where n is the number of 1s

2. Design a finite state automaton to recognize valid C++:

   (a) Character constants
   (b) Character string constants
   (c) Operators beginning with + (+, ++, +=)
   (d) Operators beginning with < (<, <<, <=)

3. A **double** constant in C++ consists of an integer part, a decimal point, a fraction part, an **e** or **E**, an optionally signed integer exponent, and an optional type suffix. The integer and fractional parts are each (decimal) digit sequences. Either the integer or the fractional part (but not both) can be omitted, and either the decimal point or the letter **e** (or **E**) and the exponent (not both) can be omitted. For example, **1.0, 1., 0.1e1** and **10E-1** are all **double** constants. Write a program that analyzes a string of characters and checks to see whether it represents a valid **double** constant.

4. Write a program for a lexical analyzer to process assignment statements of the form *Identifier = StringConstant*. Have it recognize the following tokens: identifier, assignment operator (=), and string constant.

Program Design

1. *A set can be used to store data values that are all of the same (integer-compatible) type if the order in which they are stored is not important.* For example, a set is an appropriate storage structure in a problem that involves determining whether each item in a certain collection of data values also belongs to some other collection of like values, because the order of the data items is irrelevant and one need only determine whether the first collection is a subset of the second.

2. *The* Contains() *relation for set membership can be used to simplify complex boolean expressions.* To illustrate, the function in Figure 13.9 defines the Set

```
Set
   WhiteSpaceSet(3, ' ', '\t', '\n');
      .
      .
      .
```

and later uses the if statement:

```
if (WhiteSpaceSet.Contains(Symbol))
      .
      .
      .
```

Alternatively, the condition in this if statement could have been written as follows:

```
if ((Symbol == ' ') || (Symbol == '\t')
   || (Symbol == '\n'))
      .
      .
      .
```

The Contains() relation thus provides an alternative means of writing conditions that can be more easily read and are more intuitive than the equivalent condition written using relational operators, particular if the Set involved is given a properly descriptive name.

3. *A set value can be displayed using a normal output statement.* This is accomplished by using an overloaded definition of operator<< from class Set.

4. *A set can be filled with input values using a normal input statement.* This is accomplished by using an overloaded definition of **operator>>** from class **Set**.

5. *The binary set operations include + (union), * (intersection), and - (difference).* These operations map from a pair of **Set** objects to a **Set** value.

6. *The binary set relational operators include* **<=** *(subset),* **<** *(proper subset),* **>=** *(superset),* **>** *(proper superset),* **==** *(equal), and* **!=** *(not equal).* These operations map from a pair of **Set** objects to a boolean value.

7. *The set operations on an element include* **Insert()** *and* **Delete()**. These operations map from a **Set** and an **Element** to a **Set** value.

8. *The set relational operation on an element is* **Contains()**. This operation maps from a **Set** and an **Element** to a boolean value.

Potential Problems

1. *All the elements of a* **Set** *must be of an integer-compatible type, with a maximum value less than* **Set::MaxElements**. Consequently, collections of real numbers, collections of strings, collections of records, and so on, cannot be stored in a **Set**.

2. *Class* **Set** *limits the number of elements that a set may contain to 256 and requires that the minimum and maximum values be in the range 0 through 255.* In particular, negative integers or integers greater than 255 cannot be inserted into a **Set**. This restriction can be circumvented to some degree by increasing the value of **Set::MaxElements** and recompiling the implementation file.

3. *When using* **Set** *operations, make certain that the operands for an operation have the appropriate types.* For example, trying to use a binary **Set** operation such as union to "add" an element to a **Set**,

```
Set1 = Set1 + 32;
```

or trying to remove an element from a **Set** using the difference operator,

```
Set1 = Set1 - 45;
```

will generate compilation errors, since the union and difference operations are defined on two **Set** values, not on a **Set** and an element. The members **Insert()** and **Delete()** are designed for this purpose, so that the calls

```
Set1.Insert(32);
Set1.Delete(45);
```

can be used.

Programming Projects

1. Write a program to read several lines of text, and find all words having three or more distinct vowels.

2. Write a program to deal two 10-card hands from a standard deck of 52 cards. Use a random number generator (see Section 7.8), and use sets to ensure that the same card is not dealt twice.

3. The **Sieve of Eratosthenes** algorithm from Programming Project 6 in Chapter 12 can be rephrased using sets as follows:

ALGORITHM FOR THE SIEVE METHOD

1. Initialize the set *Sieve* to contain the integers from 2 through n.
2. Select the smallest element *Prime* in *Sieve*.
3. While $Prime^2 \leq n$, do the following:

   a. Remove from *Sieve* all elements of the form $Prime * k$ for $k > 1$.
   b. Replace *Prime* with the smallest element in *Sieve* that is greater than *Prime*.

The elements remaining in *Sieve* when this algorithm terminates are the primes in the range 2 through n. Write a program that implements this algorithm using class **Set** to find all the prime numbers from 2 through n. Run it for $n = 50$ and for $n = 255$.

4. Because the value of **MaxElements** in the **Set** class allows only relatively small sets to be represented, the Sieve of Eratosthenes for finding prime numbers described in Project 3 cannot be used to find large primes. Write a program that can. (*Hint*: Use an array **Sieve** of sets **Sieve[0]**, **Sieve[1]**, **Sieve[2]**, . . . whose elements are integers in the range 0 through 99. Each element of **Sieve[1]** must be interpreted as 100 plus its value, each element of **Sieve[2]** as 200 plus its value, and so on.)

5. Write a program for a lexical analyzer that recognizes input statements of the form

   StreamName Operator Object

   Have it recognize the following tokens: identifier, I/O operator (<< or >>), and literal (integer constants, real constants, character constants, and string constants).

6. Proceed as in Project 5, but recognize input statements that utilize *chaining*:

   StreamName Operator Object$_1$ Operator Object$_2$ . . . Operator Object$_n$

MULTIDIMENSIONAL ARRAYS

14

Everyone knows how laborious the usual Method is of attaining to Arts and Sciences; whereas by his Contrivance, the most ignorant Person at a reasonable Charge, and with a little bodily Labour, may write Books in Philosophy, Poetry, Politicks, Law, Mathematicks, and Theology, without the least Assistance from Genius or Study. He then led me to the Frame, about the sides whereof all his Pupils stood in Ranks. It was Twenty Foot square . . . linked by slender Wires. These Bits . . . were covered on every Square with Paper pasted upon them; and on These Papers were written all the Words of their Language. . . .

The Professor then desired me to observe, for he was going to set his Engine at work. The Pupils at this Command took each of them hold of an Iron Handle, whereof there were Forty fixed round the Edges of the Frame; and giving them a sudden Turn, the whole Disposition of the Words was entirely changed. . . .
JONATHAN SWIFT
Gulliver's Travels

CHAPTER CONTENTS

In Chapter 12, we introduced one-dimensional arrays and used them to store lists of values. C++ also allows arrays of more than one dimension. As we shall see, a two-dimensional array can be used to store a data set whose values are arranged in rows and columns. Similarly, a three-dimensional array is an appropriate storage structure when the data can be arranged in rows, columns, and ranks. When there are several characteristics associated with the data, still higher dimensions may be useful, with each dimension corresponding to one of these characteristics. In this chapter, we consider the use of multidimensional arrays in C++ programs.

14.1   Introduction to Multidimensional Arrays

There are many problems in which the data being processed can be naturally organized as a table. For such problems, a two-dimensional array provides a way to build a software model of a table.

Declaring a Two-Dimensional Array

As a first example, consider the screen on a standard computer monitor. A typical screen can display 24 lines, with 80 characters on each line. The standard way to describe the screen is in terms of horizontal rows and vertical columns, with the rows numbered from 0 through 23 and the columns numbered from 0 through 79. The position at row 0 and column 0 is usually at the upper left corner of the screen, giving the screen the following layout:

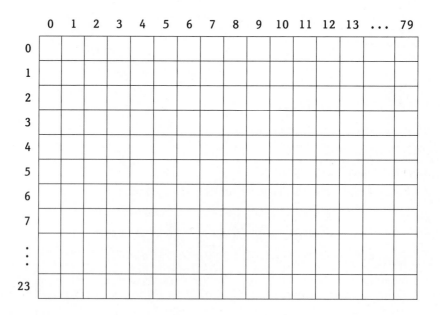

It should be clear that the screen is a **two-dimensional structure** and that two indices, the row number and the column number, provide a way to identify uniquely each position on the screen.

Such a screen can be modeled in software using a **two-dimensional** array, declared by placing two separate subscript operators after the name of the array being defined. This particular screen might be modeled using a two-dimensional array whose elements are of type `char`, whose row indices range from 0 through 23 and whose column indices range from 0 through 79. Such an array can be declared as follows:

```
const int
   NumRows = 24,
   NumColumns = 80;

char
   Screen[NumRows][NumColumns];
```

The variable `Screen` is a **two-dimensional array** in which the notation

```
Screen[0][0]
```

represents the position at row 0 and column 0. C++ allocates the memory for a two-dimensional array like `Screen` row by row and, within each row, from left to right. Thus, the second element of `Screen` is the second column of the first row and so is denoted by

```
Screen[0][1]
```

The third element of `Screen` is

```
Screen[0][2]
```

and so on. The 80th element of `Screen` is, thus,

```
Screen[0][79]
```

Since this is the last element of the first row, the next element is the first element of the second row,

```
Screen[1][0]
```

It is followed by

```
Screen[1][1]
```

and so on. We can thus visualize the software object named `Screen` as follows:

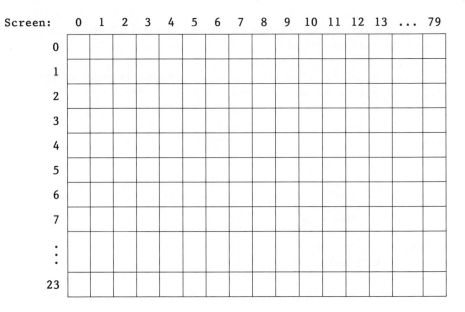

Declaring Two-Dimensional Arrays Using `typedef`. To improve the readability of a program, it is a good practice to use `typedef` to associate a type name with two-dimensional arrays. For example, given the preceding declarations of `NumRows` and `NumColumns`, we could declare the name `MonitorScreen` as a type denoting a two-dimensional array of character values

```
typedef char MonitorScreen[NumRows][NumColumns];
```

and then define `Screen` to be an object of type `MonitorScreen`:

```
MonitorScreen
   Screen;
```

Functions can then be written to operate on a `MonitorScreen` value, and when the object `Screen` is passed to such a function, the operation encoded in the function will be performed on `Screen`. For example, the following function initializes the elements of a `MonitorScreen` object with blank characters:

```
void Initialize(MonitorScreen Screen)
{
   for (int row = 0; row < NumRows; row++)
      for (int col = 0; col < NumColumns; col++)
         Screen[row][col] = ' ';
}
```

As another example, consider the following function, which uses the `ostream` member function `put()` to display a `MonitorScreen` to `cout`:

```
void Display(MonitorScreen Screen)
{
   for (int row = 0; row < NumRows; row++)
   {
      for (int col = 0; col < NumColumns; col++)
         cout.put(Screen[row][col]);
      cout.put('\n');
   }
}
```

Primitive "graphics" functions can also be designed. For example, the following simple function can be used to draw a box of arbitrary size at an arbitrary position on a **MonitorScreen**:

```
void DrawBox(MonitorScreen Screen,            // 2-D array
            int TopRow, int LeftColumn,       // upper left corner
            int BottomRow, int RightColumn,   // bottom right corner
            char FillChar = 'X')              // optional fill char
{
   // do top & bottom edges
   for (int col = LeftColumn; col <= RightColumn; col++)
      Screen[TopRow][col] = Screen[BottomRow][col] = FillChar;

   // do left & right edges
   for (int row = TopRow; row <= BottomRow; row++)
      Screen[row][LeftColumn] = Screen[row][RightColumn] = FillChar;
}
```

Other functions can use primitive graphics functions like **DrawBox()** to draw more complex patterns on a **MonitorScreen**. For example, the following function fills a **MonitorScreen** with nested boxes:

```
void DrawNestedBoxes(MonitorScreen Screen)
{
   for (int offset = 0; offset < NumRows/2; offset += 2)
      DrawBox(Screen, offset, offset,
             NumRows - offset - 1, NumColumns - offset - 1);
}
```

Given the **MonitorScreen** object named **Screen** defined previously, the following sequence of function calls can be used to initialize, draw on, and display **Screen**:

```
   Initialize(Screen);
   DrawNestedBoxes(Screen);
   Display(Screen);
```

When executed, the output from function **Display()** appears as follows:

```
XXXXXXXXXXXXXXXXXXXXXXXXXXXXXXXXXXXXXXXXXXXXXXXXXXXXXXXXXXXXXXXXXXXXXXXXXXXXXX
X                                                                          X
X XXXXXXXXXXXXXXXXXXXXXXXXXXXXXXXXXXXXXXXXXXXXXXXXXXXXXXXXXXXXXXXXXXXXXXXXXX X
X X                                                                      X X
X X XXXXXXXXXXXXXXXXXXXXXXXXXXXXXXXXXXXXXXXXXXXXXXXXXXXXXXXXXXXXXXXXXXXX X X X
X X X                                                                X X X
X X X XXXXXXXXXXXXXXXXXXXXXXXXXXXXXXXXXXXXXXXXXXXXXXXXXXXXXXXXXXXXXXXX X X X
X X X X                                                            X X X X
X X X X X XXXXXXXXXXXXXXXXXXXXXXXXXXXXXXXXXXXXXXXXXXXXXXXXXXXXXXX X X X X
X X X X X                                                      XX X X X
X X X X X XXXXXXXXXXXXXXXXXXXXXXXXXXXXXXXXXXXXXXXXXXXXXXXXXXXX X X X X X
X X X X X X                                              X X X X X X
X X X X X X                                              X X X X X X
X X X X X XXXXXXXXXXXXXXXXXXXXXXXXXXXXXXXXXXXXXXXXXXXXXXXXXXX X X X X X
X X X X X                                                      XX X X X
X X X X X XXXXXXXXXXXXXXXXXXXXXXXXXXXXXXXXXXXXXXXXXXXXXXXXXXXXXXX X X X X
X X X X                                                            X X X X
X X X XXXXXXXXXXXXXXXXXXXXXXXXXXXXXXXXXXXXXXXXXXXXXXXXXXXXXXXXXXXXXXXX X X X
X X X                                                                X X X
X X XXXXXXXXXXXXXXXXXXXXXXXXXXXXXXXXXXXXXXXXXXXXXXXXXXXXXXXXXXXXXXXXXXXXXX X X
X X                                                                      X X
X XXXXXXXXXXXXXXXXXXXXXXXXXXXXXXXXXXXXXXXXXXXXXXXXXXXXXXXXXXXXXXXXXXXXXXXXXX X
X                                                                          X
XXXXXXXXXXXXXXXXXXXXXXXXXXXXXXXXXXXXXXXXXXXXXXXXXXXXXXXXXXXXXXXXXXXXXXXXXXXXXX
```

Using Enumerations. As a second application of two-dimensional arrays, suppose that four times a day, water temperatures are recorded at each of three discharge outlets of the cooling system of a nuclear power plant. These temperature readings can be arranged in a table having four rows and three columns:

Time	Location		
	Outlet1	Outlet2	Outlet3
12 A.M.	65.5	68.7	62.0
6 A.M.	68.8	68.9	64.5
12 P.M.	70.4	69.4	66.3
6 P.M.	68.5	69.1	65.8

In this table, the three temperature readings at 12 A.M. are in the first row, the three temperatures at 6 A.M. are in the second row, and so on. We might model such a table by first declaring an enumeration for the row indices,

```
enum Row {Midnight, SixAM, Noon, SixPM, NumTimes};
```

and another enumeration for the indices of the columns,

```
enum Column {Outlet1, Outlet2, Outlet3, NumOutlets};
```

Recall that the C++ compiler treats **Midnight** and **Outlet1** as 0, **SixAM** and

Outlet2 as 1, **Noon** and **Outlet3** as 2, **SixPM** and **NumOutlets** as 3, and **Num-Times** as 4. This means that the declaration

```
double
    TempTable[NumTimes][NumOutlets];
```

defines **TempTable** as a two-dimensional array consisting of four rows and three columns. The C++ compiler reserves 12 memory locations for this object and associates **TempTable** with these memory locations:

TempTable:	Outlet1	Outlet2	Outlet3
Midnight			
SixAM			
Noon			
SixPM			

The notation

```
TempTable[Noon][Outlet2]
```

refers to the element in row **Noon** and column **Outlet2** of **TempTab**. In general, the notation

```
TempTable[r][c]
```

refers to the entry in the **r**th row and **c**th column—that is, to the temperature recorded at time r at location **c**.

Using typedef for Readability. As before, the **typedef** mechanism can be used to declare the name **TemperatureTable** as a type denoting a two-dimensional array of real values,

```
typedef double TemperatureTable[NumTimes][NumOutlets];
```

and this type can then be used to declare **TempTable** to be an object whose type is **TemperatureTable**:

```
TemperatureTable
    TempTable;
```

Declaring Three-Dimensional Arrays

To illustrate the use of an array with more than two dimensions, suppose that the temperatures in the last example are recorded for 1 week, so that seven such tables are collected:

Time	Location Outlet1	Outlet2	Outlet3
12A.M.	66.5	69.4	68.4
6A.M.	68.4	71.2	69.3
12P.M.	70.1	71.9	70.2
6P.M.	69.5	70.0	69.4

Saturday

.

Time	Location Outlet1	Outlet2	Outlet3
12A.M.	63.7	66.2	64.3
6A.M.	64.0	66.8	64.9

Monday

Time	Location Outlet1	Outlet2	Outlet3	
12A.M.	65.5	68.7	62.0	66.3
6A.M.	68.8	68.9	64.5	65.8
12P.M.	70.4	69.4	66.3	
6P.M.	68.5	69.1	65.8	

Sunday

The collection of these tables can be modeled with a **three-dimensional array**
`Temperature` declared by

```
enum DayName {Sunday, Monday, Tuesday, Wednesday,
              Thursday, Friday, Saturday, NumDays};

typedef double
    TempArray3D[NumDays][NumTimes][NumOutlets];

TempArray3D
    Temperature;
```

The object `Temperature` can then be used to store these 84 temperature readings.
The notation

```
Temperature[Monday][Midnight][Outlet3]
```

refers to the temperature recorded on Monday at 12 A.M. at the third outlet—that is,
the value 64.3 in the second table, first row, and third column. In general,

```
Temperature[d][r][c]
```

is the temperature recorded on day `d` at time `r` at location `c`.

Declaring Higher-Dimensional Arrays

In some problems, arrays with even more dimensions may be useful. For example,
suppose that a retailer maintains an inventory of jeans. She carries several different
brands of jeans; for each brand she stocks a variety of styles, waist sizes, and
inseam lengths. A four-dimensional array can be used to record the inventory, with

each element of the array being the number of jeans of a particular brand, style, waist size, and inseam length currently in stock. The first index represents the brand; thus, it might be of type

```
enum BrandType {Levi, Wrangler, CalvinKlein, Lee, BigYank, NumBrands};
```

The second index represents styles and is of type

```
enum StyleType {Baggy, Tapered, StraightLeg, Designer, NumStyles};
```

The third and fourth indices represent waist size and inseam length, respectively. For waist sizes ranging from 28 through 48 and inseam lengths ranging from 26 through 36, we might declare enumerations as follows:

```
enum WaistType {w28, w29, w30, w31, w32, w33, w34, w35, w36,
               w37, w38, w39, w40, w41, w42, w43, w44, w45,
               w46, w47, w48, NumWaistSizes};
enum InseamType {i26, i27, i28, i29, i30, i31, i32, i33, i34,
                i35, i36, NumInseamSizes};
```

A program to maintain inventory can then declare the type

```
typedef int
   JeansArray[NumBrands][NumStyles][NumWaistSizes][NumInseamSizes];
```

and then use this type to declare a four-dimensional array **JeansInStock** having indices of the types just described:

```
   JeansArray
      JeansInStock;
```

The value of the expression

```
   JeansInStock[Levi][Designer][w32][i31]
```

is the number of Levi's designer 32 × 31 jeans that are in stock. The statement

```
   JeansInStock[Brand][Size][Waist][Inseam]--;
```

can be used to record the sale (i.e., decrement the inventory) of one pair of jeans of a specified **Brand**, **Style**, **Waist** size, and **Inseam** length.

As the following syntax diagram for array declarations indicates, C++ places no limit on the number of dimensions of an array, but the maximum value of each index must be specified:

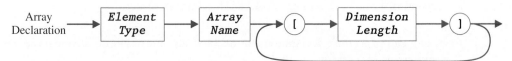

From this we see that the general form of an array declaration is as follows:

Array Declaration

Form

ElementType
   ArrayName[*DimLength₁*][*DimLength₂*]...[*DimLengthₙ*];

where:
   ElementType is any type;
   ArrayName is the name of the array being defined; and
   each *DimLengthᵢ* must be a nonnegative integer (constant)
      value.

Purpose
Defines an *n*-dimensional object whose elements are of type
ElementType, in which *DimLength₁*, *DimLength₂*, . . . ,
DimLengthₙ are the numbers of elements in each dimension.

Array of Arrays Declarations.   One way to view a multidimensional array is as an **array of arrays**—that is, an array whose elements are other arrays. For example, reconsider the nuclear power plant's temperature table described earlier. The table can be thought of as a list of 4 rows, and, from this perspective, the diagram can be viewed as a one-dimensional array with 4 elements, each of which is a list of 3 real values:

The entire temperature table can thus be viewed as a one-dimensional array whose components are also one-dimensional arrays.

C++ allows array declarations to be given in a form that reflects this perspective. If we first define the type **TemperatureList** as an array of temperature readings

```
enum Column {Outlet1, Outlet2, Outlet3, NumOutlets};

typedef double TemperatureList[NumOutlets];
```

then we can use this declaration to declare an array whose elements are **TemperatureList** objects:

```
enum Row {Midnight, SixAM, Noon, SixPM, NumTimes};

typedef TemperatureList TemperatureTable[NumTimes];
```

the resulting type can then be used to define an object with two dimensions, as before:

```
TemperatureTable
   TempTable;
```

Regardless of which approach is used, the notation

```
TempTable[SixAM]
```

refers to the second row of temperatures in the table,

	Outlet1	Outlet2	Outlet3
SixAM			

and the notation

```
TempTable[SixAM][Outlet2]
```

refers to the second entry in this row.

This idea can be extended to higher-dimensional arrays. For example, the three-dimensional array of temperature tables considered earlier can also be thought of as an array of arrays. In particular, since one temperature table was recorded for each day, the entire three-dimensional array can be viewed as a list of temperature tables, that is, as a one-dimensional array whose components are two-dimensional arrays. If we adopt this point of view, we might declare the three-dimensional array **Temp** by adding the declarations

```
enum Days {Sunday, Monday, Tuesday, Wednesday,
           Thursday, Friday, Saturday, Sunday, NumDays};

typedef TemperatureTable
   TemperatureTableList[NumDays];

TemperatureTableList
   Temp;
```

to the preceding declarations. This may make it clearer that the notation

```
Temp[Monday]
```

refers to the temperature table recorded on Monday:

Time	Location Outlet1	Outlet2	Outlet3
12 A.M.	63.7	66.2	64.3
6 A.M.	64.0	66.8	64.9
12 P.M.	72.7	69.9	66.3
6 P.M.	66.6	68.0	65.8

To access the temperature at 12 A.M. at outlet 3 in this table (i.e., 64.3), we still use the notation

`Temp[Monday][Midnight][Outlet3]`

Note that as in the previous example, each row in a temperature table can be viewed as a one-dimensional array of temperatures, and each table can, therefore, be viewed as a one-dimensional array of temperature arrays. The doubly-indexed variable

`Temp[Monday][Midnight]`

thus refers to the first row in the temperature table for Monday,

63.7	66.2	64.3

and

`Temp[Monday][Midnight][Outlet3]`

denotes the third temperature in this row:

64.3

Initialization of Arrays

In Chapter 12 we saw that one-dimensional arrays can be initialized when they are declared. Multidimensional arrays may also be initialized using this same technique. For example, we might initialize the 4 × 3 array **TempTable** as follows:

```
TemperatureTable
    TempTable = { 65.5, 68.7, 62.0, 68.8, 68.9, 64.5,
                  70.4, 69.4, 66.3, 68.5, 69.1, 65.8};
```

To improve the readability of such declarations, C++ permits the values to be grouped using braces:

```
TemperatureTable
    TempTable = { {65.5, 68.7, 62.0},      //row1: Midnight
                  {68.8, 68.9, 64.5},      //row2: 6 A.M.
                  {70.4, 69.4, 66.3},      //row3: Noon
                  {68.5, 69.1, 65.8} };    //row4: 6 P.M.
```

This latter form makes it clear that the list used to initialize `TempTab` has 4 elements, each of which is a triple of numbers: the three values in the first row followed by the three values in the second row, then those in the third row, and, finally, those in the fourth row. Note that this is precisely the form required for initializing a one-dimensional array having 4 elements, each of which is a one-dimensional array having 3 elements. Also, consistent with initialization of one-dimensional arrays described in Chapter 12, if a row's initialization has fewer values than row elements, the remaining elements in that row will be set to zero.

Higher-dimensional arrays may also be initialized by using additional nested brackets. For example, if `TempTableList` is the three-dimensional array type declared previously, then an object `Temp` could be defined and initialized as follows:

```
TempTableList
  Temp = {
            { {65.5, 68.7, 62.0},      // Sunday
              {68.8, 68.9, 64.5},
              {70.4, 69.4, 66.3},
              {68.5, 69.1, 65.8}
            },
            { {63.7, 66.2, 64.3},      // Monday
              {64.0, 66.8, 64.9},
              {65.7, 67.2, 66.3},
              {66.4, 65.7, 65.8}
            },
              // ... Tuesday-Friday omitted ...

            { {66.5, 69.4, 68.4},      // Saturday
              {68.4, 71.2, 69.3},
              {70.1, 71.9, 70.2},
              {69.5, 70.0, 69.4}
            }
          };
```

Exercises

1. Consider the following declarations:

```
enum Color{red, yellow, blue, green, white, black, NumColors};
enum Boolean{false, true};

typedef int BigTable[50][100];
typedef char CharTable[26][26];
typedef Boolean BooleanTable[2][2];
typedef Boolean BitArray[2][2][2][2];
typedef int Shirt[NumColors][18][48];
typedef Shirt ShirtStock[5];
```

How many elements can be stored in an array of each of the following type names?

(a) `BigTable`   (b) `CharTable`   (c) `BooleanTable`
(d) `BitArray`   (e) `Shirt`   (f) `ShirtStock`

2. Assume that the following declarations have been made:

2. Assume that the following declarations have been made:

```
typedef int Array3x3[3][3];

Array3X3
   Matrix;
```

For each of the following, tell what value (if any) is assigned to each array element, or explain why an error occurs.

(a)
```
for (int i = 0; i < 3; i++)
    for (int j = 0; j < 3; j++)
        Matrix[i][j] = i + j;
```

(b)
```
for (int i = 0; i < 3; i++)
    for (int j = 2; j >= 0; j--)
        if (i == j)
            Matrix[i][j] = 0;
        else
            Matrix[i][j] = 1;
```

(c)
```
for (int i = 0; i < 3; i++)
    for (int j = 0; j < 3; j++)
        if (i < j)
            Matrix[i][j] = -1;
        else if (i == j)
            Matrix[i][j] = 0;
        else
            Matrix[i][j] = 1;
```

(d)
```
for (int i = 0; i < 3; i++)
{
    for (int j = 0; j < i; j++)
        Matrix[i][j] = 0;
    for (j = i; j < 3; j++)
        Matrix [i][j] = 2
}
```

3. Assume that the following declarations have been made:

```
const char
   TextLine[2][7] = {"ABCDEFG", "HIJKLMN"};
```

For each of the following, tell what output will be produced or explain why an error occurs.

(a)
```
for (int i = 0; i < 2; i++)
{
    for (int j = 0; j < 7; j++)
        cout << TextLine[i][j];
    cout << endl;
}
```

(b)
```
for (int j = 0; j < 7; j++)
{
    for (int i = 0; i < 2; i++)
        cout << TextLine[i][j];
    cout << endl;
}
```

(c)
```
for (int i = 0; i < 2; i++)
{
    for (int j = 0; j < 7; j++)
        cout << TextLine[j][i];
    cout << endl;
}
```

(d)
```
for (int i = 0; i < 2; i++)
{
    for (int j = 6; j >= 0; j--)
        cout << TextLine[i][j];
    cout << endl;
}
```

4. Write a function that, given a `TemperatureTable` (as declared in this section) will calculate and return the average temperature at each of the three locations.

5. Like one-dimensional arrays, multidimensional arrays are stored in a block of consecutive memory locations, and address translation formulas are used to determine the location in memory of each array element. To illustrate, consider a 3×4 array A of integers, and assume that an integer can be stored in one memory word. If A is allocated memory in a rowwise manner and b is its base address, then the first row of A, `A[0][0]`, `A[0][1]`, `A[0][2]`, `A[0][3]`, is stored in words b, $b + 1$, $b + 2$, $b + 3$, the second row in words $b + 4$ through $b + 7$, and the third row in words $b + 8$ through $b + 11$.

Address	Memory	Array Element
	⋮	
b		A[0][0]
$b + 1$		A[0][1]
$b + 2$		A[0][2]
$b + 3$		A[0][3]
$b + 4$		A[1][0]
$b + 5$		A[1][1]
$b + 6$		A[1][2]
$b + 7$		A[1][3]
$b + 8$		A[2][0]
$b + 9$		A[2][1]
$b + 10$		A[2][2]
$b + 11$		A[2][3]
	⋮	

In general, $A[i][j]$ is stored in word $b + 4i + j$.

(a) Give a similar diagram and formula if A is a 3×3 array of integer values.
(b) Give a similar diagram and formula if A is a 3×4 array of **double** values, where **double** values require two words for storage.

14.2   Multidimensional Arrays and Classes

Like one-dimensional arrays, multidimensional arrays can be explicitly defined and processed within a main function. However, building such definitions inside a main function rather than in a class makes it more difficult to reuse those definitions. Consequently, it is preferable to define a multidimensional array in a class and then build the common operations on the array as class member (or friend) functions. In this section, we construct a general two-dimensional numeric array class named **Table**. We then define a number of useful operations on a **Table** object, including a constructor, I/O, assignment, and functions to sum the rows and/or columns of a **Table**.

Designing and Declaring the Class **Table**

To model a table in software, we must first identify the **attributes** of a table—that is, the key characteristics that completely describe a table. It may be helpful to recall the **List** class from Chapter 12, where a one-dimensional array was used to store the elements of the list. Because arrays have a fixed size, we had to declare (1) an array member **Array** that was large enough to hold most lists of values, and (2) a member **Length_** to indicate the length of the particular list being stored in the array. Since a **List** object is a one-dimensional object, no additional data members are needed to store the dimensional attributes of a **List**.

Table objects, however, must model two-dimensional tables and thus require a two-dimensional array data member in which the values of a table can be stored. In our implementation of class **Table**, this data member is a 10×10 array named **Grid**. In addition to **Grid**, we also need two data members to hold the two-dimensional attributes of the table. In our implementation of class **Table**, these data members are named **Rows_** and **Columns_** and hold the number of rows and columns, respectively, of the table being stored in **Grid**. These allow us to declare the data members of class **Table**, as shown in Figure 14.1.

 FIGURE 14.1 Class **Table**—version 1.

```
typedef double TableElement;          // array element type

class Table
{
public:

   enum {MaxRows = 10, MaxCols = 10}; // bounds on the two dimensions
```

FIGURE 14.1 Class **Table**—version 1. (cont.)

```
protected:

    unsigned
        Rows_,                          // number of rows in use
        Columns_;                       // number of columns in use

    TableElement
        Grid[MaxRows][MaxCols];         // the 2-dim array member

// ...
};
```

Note that we used the keyword **protected** instead of **private** to designate the data members of **Table**. We have seen that a **public** class member can be accessed outside of the class and a **private** member cannot be accessed outside of the class (except by class members and friends). A **protected** member is between these two extremes. More precisely, a **protected class member** is like a **private** class member, except that such a member can also be accessed by the members and friends of any class that is *derived from* this class (a property that we use in the next section).

Given this declaration, a **Table** object **T** can be defined with the statement

```
Table
    T;
```

This object consists of three data members:

- **Grid**, a **MaxRows** × **MaxCols** two-dimensional array
- **Rows_** and **Columns_**, to hold the dimensions of the particular table stored in **Grid**

We can visualize the data portion of **T** as follows:

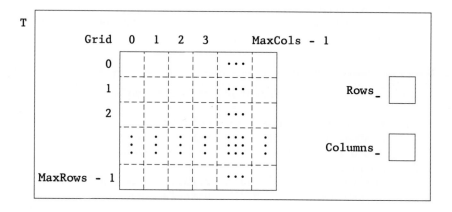

Operations on a `Table` Object

We turn now to constructing some of the member functions of a **Table** object. There are many operations that might be performed on **Table** objects, but the common operations include the following:

- Construct a **Table** object.
- Input.
- Output.
- Assign (copy) one **Table** object to another.
- Find the number of rows or columns.
- Sum the values in a specified row or column.
- Retrieve the value from a specified row and column.

In the remainder of this section, we construct functions to perform these operations.

Note that we do not list the subscript operation that allows a particular value within a **Table** to be accessed. As we shall see in Section 14.6, this can be done, but it complicates the design of the class, and the same effect can be achieved through other member functions, which are described in the exercises at the end of this section. We therefore defer the implementation of a **Table** subscript operator until Section 14.6 in order to keep the initial implementation simple and straightforward.

The Table Class Constructor.　The first operation we wish to implement is that of constructing a **Table** object. This operation initializes the data members of a **Table**, in particular, the **Rows_** and **Columns_** members. This means that this constructor function must have parameters to receive initial values for these members. An additional parameter **InitValue** (with default value zero) is used to initialize the elements of a **Table** when it is constructed.

As usual, we should anticipate what might go wrong. One obvious possibility is that the caller of the function might pass invalid initial values for **Rows_** and **Columns_**, values that are negative or that exceed the bounds **Table::MaxRows** or **Table::MaxCols**. The constructor function should check therefore that these parameter values are valid before using them to initialize the **Rows_** and **Columns_** members. Figure 14.2 presents one possible implementation for this constructor: It checks the validity of the initial values for **Rows_** and **Cols_** by

1. Declaring **RowVal** and **ColVal** as **unsigned** parameters (ensuring that their values are nonnegative); and
2. Checking that the value of each does not exceed the maximum value allowed.

FIGURE 14.2　Table class constructor.

```
/* This function is the class constructor for class Table.

   Precondition:  A Table object has been declared.
   Receive:       NumRows (optional), the number of rows in the Table
                  NumCols (optional), the number of columns in the
                     Table
                  InitValue (default value zero), to initialize
                     the values of the Table's elements
```

FIGURE 14.2 **Table** class constructor. (cont.)

> Postcondition: The declared Table object containing this function
>   has its Rows_ member initialized to NumRows,
>   and its Columns_ member initialized to NumCols.
> --*/

```
Table::Table(unsigned NumRows, unsigned NumCols,
         TableElement InitValue)
{
   if (NumRows > Table::MaxRows)                  // if NumRows too big
   {
      cerr << "\nConstructor warning - rows received: "
           << NumRows << " exceed Table maximum!\n";
      Rows_ = Table::MaxRows;                     //   use maximum
   }
   else                                           // else
      Rows_ = NumRows;                            //   use value passed

   if (NumCols > Table::MaxCols)                  // if NumCols too big
   {
      cerr << "\nConstructor warning - columns received: "
           << NumCols << " exceed Table maximum !\n";
      Columns_ = Table::MaxCols;                  //   use maximum
   }
   else                                           // else
      Columns_ = NumCols;                         //   use value passed

   for (int row = 0; row < NumRows; row++)        // for each row:
      for (int col = 0; col < NumCols_; col++) //   for each column:
         Grid[row][col] = InitValue;             //     initialize array
                                                  //      element
}
```

To provide default values for the constructor's parameters, we might declare this constructor in the public section of the class declaration as follows:

```
Table(unsigned NumRows = 0, unsigned NumCols = 0,
      TableElement InitValue = 0);
```

Note that the task of setting each element of **Grid** to **InitValue** is accomplished by using two **nested for loops**—the outer loop is used to pass through the rows of **Grid**, and the inner loop is used to pass through the columns. This use of nested for loops is a standard technique for processing two-dimensional arrays.

It is important that the outer loop be used to process the rows and the inner loop to process the columns, and not vice versa. To see why, suppose that a 2×3 **Table** named **T** is being processed. The following table traces the action of the function as the two loops execute:

Step	Value of Row	Value of Col	Element Accessed
1	0	0	`T.Grid[0][0]`
2	0	1	`T.Grid[0][1]`
3	0	2	`T.Grid[0][2]`
4	1	0	`T.Grid[1][0]`
5	1	1	`T.Grid[1][1]`
6	1	2	`T.Grid[1][2]`

The memory associated with `Grid` is typically allocated row by row as a block. If the base address of `T.Grid` is b, then the access pattern to `T.Grid` is as follows:

Iteration	Element Accessed	Address
1	`Grid[0][0]`	b
2	`Grid[0][1]`	$b + 1$
3	`Grid[0][2]`	$b + 2$
4	`Grid[1][0]`	$b + 3$
5	`Grid[1][1]`	$b + 4$
6	`Grid[1][2]`	$b + 5$

Thus, if the outer for loop runs through the rows and the inner for loop runs through the columns, the elements of the array are processed in the order in which they are stored in memory. By contrast, if we were to organize the for loops in the opposite arrangement,

```
for (c = 0; c < Columns_; c++)
   for (r = 0; r < Rows_; r++)
      Grid[r][c] = T.Grid[r][c];
```

then the elements of the array would not be accessed sequentially. Instead, the accesses would ''ping-pong'' back and forth between the rows, in the following pattern:

Iteration	Element Accessed	Address
1	`Grid[0][0]`	b
2	`Grid[1][0]`	$b + 3$
3	`Grid[0][1]`	$b + 1$
4	`Grid[1][1]`	$b + 4$
5	`Grid[0][1]`	$b + 2$
6	`Grid[1][2]`	$b + 5$

For large arrays, the time to access an array's elements in such a nonsequential pattern can be significantly greater than the time to access the array's elements in a sequential pattern. In general, if an array is declared as

```
ElementType
   ArrayName [DimA][DimB][DimC] ... [DimN];
```

and some operation requires that every element of the array be accessed, then that operation can be most efficiently implemented using nested for loops that vary the dimensions from first to last:

```
for (int a = 0; a < DimA; a++)
   for (int b = 0; b < DimB; b++)
      for (int c = 0; c < DimC; c++)
            .
            .
            .
            for (int n = 0; n < DimN; n++)
               // do something with ArrayName[a][b][c]...[n]
```

Once a constructor is defined, we can define **Table** objects such as

```
Table
   T1,
   T2(2, 2, 1),
   T3(3, 2);
```

The first declaration uses the default arguments for all parameters and constructs a **Table** object **T1** that is an empty table having zero rows and zero columns:

The second declaration constructs the **Table** object **T2** as a table with two rows and two columns with each of its elements initialized to 1:

The final **Table** object constructed by this declaration is **T3**, with three rows and two columns, using the default value for parameter **InitValue**:

It is important to note the differences between the declaration of a 2 × 3 **Table** object

```
Table
    T(2,3);
```

and the declaration of a 2 × 3 two-dimensional array:

```
double
    Array2x3[2][3];
```

One difference is that the **Table** definition is a *function call* to the class constructor (to which the arguments 2 and 3 are passed) and so uses a pair of *parentheses,* whereas the array definition uses a separate *subscript operator* for each *dimension* of the array being defined.

A second difference is that when the compiler processes the array definition, it allocates space sufficient to store six (2 × 3) **double** values. By contrast, when the compiler processes the **Table** definition, it allocates space sufficient to store 100 (10 × 10) **double** values (of which only 6 are used), as well as the space to store the **Rows_** and **Columns_** data members. Significant memory is thus wasted for small tables. In Chapter 15, we present an alternative implementation of class **Table** that avoids this waste.

A Table Input Operation.   The input operator can be overloaded and used to fill a **Table** object with interactive or file input. However, because a **Table** may be quite large, entering its data interactively can be tedious, and filling a **Table** from an **fstream** requires that the **fstream** has been previously opened. To avoid these difficulties, we define a member function **Fill()**, which, given the name of a file, attempts to open that file and read data from it into its **Table**. Figure 14.3 presents an implementation of this function.

FIGURE 14.3 File input of a table.

```
/* This function fills a Table object with data from a file,
     assuming that the Table has been constructed with the
     number of rows and columns for the Table in the file.

   Receive: FileName, a Strings object containing the name of an
                input file
   Input:   A table of values from the input file
   Return:  False, if the file could not be opened; otherwise, true
                and the Table object containing this function, its
                Grid member containing the input values
   ----------------------------------------------------------------*/

Boolean Table::Fill(const Strings& FileName)
{
   fstream
      InStream(FileName, ios::in);             // open the stream

   if (InStream.fail())                        // check for failure...
   {
      cerr << "\n*** Fill: Unable to open "    //    display message
         << FileName << " for input!\n";       //    and
      return False;                            //    indicate failure
   }

   for (int row = 0; row < Rows_; row++)       // for each row:
      for (int col = 0; col < Columns_; col++) //   for each column:
         InStream >> Grid[row][col];           //     fill
                                               //       Grid[row][col]
   InStream.close();                           // close the stream

   return True;                                // indicate success
}
```

Note that the function uses the values of **Rows_** and **Columns_** to control its nested for loops, and it assumes that the **Rows_** and **Columns_** members have been initialized with the number of rows and columns of the table in **FileName** before the function is called. To illustrate how this might be done, consider the following loop to process a series of tables stored in separate input files:

```
char
   Response;
int
   Row,
   Col;
Strings
   FileName;
```

```
do
{
   cout << "\nHow many rows are in the file (0 to quit) ? ";
   cin >> Row;                  // get number of rows

   cout << "How many columns are in the file ? ";
   cin >> Col;                  // get number of columns

   Table                        // build Row x Col Table
      Tab(Row, Col);
                                // get name of input file
   cout << "What is the name of the file? ";
   cin >> FileName;
                                // fill Table from file
   if (Tab.Fill(FileName))
      // ... do something with the Row x Col table in Tab ...

   cout << "More data (y or n)? "
   cin >> Response
}
while (Response = 'y');
```

Note that by interactively inputting **Row** and **Col**, the two dimensions of the table, and declaring **Tab** as a **Row** × **Col** **Table** *within the loop,* each repetition of this loop can construct **Tab** as a different-sized **Table** object. That is, if a file **Data1** contains a 3 × 3 table, then the user can enter 3 for the number of rows (**Row**), 3 for the number of columns (**Col**), and **Data1** for the name of the input file. The definition

```
Table
   Tab(Row, Col);
```

will then construct **Tab** as a 3 × 3 **Table**, after which the call

```
Tab.Fill(FileName);
```

will read the nine values from **Data1** into **Tab**. To process a different file **Data2** containing a 2 × 4 table, the user can (on the next repetition) enter 2 for the number of rows, 4 for the number of columns, and **Data2** for the name of the input file. **Tab**'s definition will construct it as a 2 × 4 **Table**, after which the call to **Fill()** will fill **Tab** with the values from **Data2**.

Note also that the return value of **Fill()** should be checked, so that **Tab** is processed only if **Fill()** indicates successful execution by returning the value true (1).

An Alternative Input Operation.   An alternative solution to the problem of inputting a table from a file is to store the number of rows and columns in the file along with the table itself. For example, rather than storing a 2 × 4 table in a file as

```
99 88 77 66
11 22 33 44
```

this approach stores the number of rows and columns in the table on the first line of the file:

```
2 4
99 88 77 66
11 22 33 44
```

A **Table** input function can then read these first two values and use them to set the values of the **Rows_** and **Columns_** members, respectively. Once these values have been read, the remainder of the input function is similar to function **Fill()**. The **Load()** function in Figure 14.4 uses this approach.

  FIGURE 14.4   File input of a table (alternative version).

```
/* This function fills a Table object with data from a file,
   and assumes that the first two values in the file
   give the number of rows and columns in the Table.

   Receive:      FileName, a Strings object containing the name of
                    an input file
   Input (File): The number of rows and columns and a table
                    of values
   Return:       False, if the file could not be opened; otherwise,
                    true and the Table object containing this
                    function, its Grid member containing the
                    input values
   --------------------------------------------------------------*/

Boolean Table::Load(const Strings& FileName)
{
   fstream
      InStream(FileName, ios::in);              // open the stream

   if (InStream.fail())                         // check for failure...
   {
      cerr << "\n*** Load: Unable to open "  //    display message
           << FileName << " for input!\n";   //    and
      return False;                           //    indicate failure
   }

   InStream >> Rows_ >> Columns_;               // get # rows and columns

   if (Rows_ > Table::MaxRows)                  // check their validity
   {
      cerr << "\nLoad: " << Rows_ <<
             " exceeds maximum number of rows for a Table!\n";
      exit (-1);
   }
```

FIGURE 14.4 File input of a table (alternative version). (cont.)

```
else if (Columns_ > Table::MaxCols)
{
   cerr << "\nLoad: " << Columns_ <<
        " exceeds maximum number of columns for a Table!\n";
   exit (-1);
}

for (int row = 0; row < Rows_; row++)        // for each row:
   for (int col = 0; col < Columns_; col++)  //   for each column:
      InStream >> Grid[row][col];            //     fill [row,col]

InStream.close();                            // close the stream

return True;                                 // indicate success
}
```

Once such a function is declared, a program can use it to fill a **Table** object with values from a file by passing the function the name of the input file, just as before. However, it is no longer necessary for the user to input the number of rows and columns for the table, since these values are now read from the input file by **Load()**:

```
Strings
   FileName;
Table
   Tab;

cout << "\nPlease enter the name of the input file: ";
cin >> FileName;

if (Tab.Load(FileName))
   //... process Tab
```

Of course, function **Load()** will not work correctly for files in which the first two values are not the number of rows and columns in the table.

The Table Output Operation. A function **Write()** that complements function **Fill()** or **Load()** by writing a **Table** to a file is easy to construct and is left as an exercise. Instead, we will overload the output operator, so that a statement such as:

```
cout << Tab << endl;
```

can be used to display a **Table** object **Tab** on the screen. Such a function is shown in Figure 14.5.

FIGURE 14.5 Screen output of a table.

```
/* This function overloads the output operator for a Table object.

    Receive: Out, an ostream (reference) object
             Tab, a (const reference) Table object
    Return:  Out, containing the data from Tab
-----------------------------------------------------------------*/

#include <iomanip.h>

ostream& operator<< (ostream& Out, const Table& Tab)
{
   Out << setprecision(2)                         // 2 decimal places
       << setiosflags(ios::showpoint | ios::fixed); // non-scientific

   for (int row = 0; row < Tab.Rows_; row++)      // for each row:
   {
      for (int col = 0; col < Tab.Columns_; col++) //  for each column:
         Out << setw(8) << Tab.Grid[row][col];    //    display
                                                  //      Grid[row][col]
      Out << endl;                                //    add a newline
   }

   return Out;                                     // allow chaining
}
```

Note that unless a newline is output at the end of each row, all the values will be displayed on the same (possibly very long) line.

Note also that, as described in Section 11.1, **operator<<** cannot be implemented as a member function (since its left operand is not a **Table**) but must be declared as a *friend* within the class:

```
friend ostream& operator<< (        // interactive output
                   ostream& Out,     // the ostream
                   const Table& Tab); // the Table
```

Once this has been done, a statement such as

```
cout << Tab << endl;
```

can be used to display a **Table** object **Tab** on the screen. The formatting employed by this function is arbitrary and can be altered as appropriate for different kinds of tables.[1]

---

[1] To allow different **Table** objects to have different formats without editing the function, simply define a data member in **Table** for each format attribute (precision, field width, etc.). Then add parameters to the class constructor so that these data members can be initialized when a **Table** object is defined.

The Table Assignment Operator.   The final operator that we overload for class **Table** is the assignment operator. Assignment must be implemented as a member function, and its task is to make the **Table** containing it a copy of the **Table** it receives as an argument. Figure 14.6 presents an implementation.

FIGURE 14.6   Assignment of a **Table**.

```
/* This function overloads the assignment operator for a Table object.

   Receive: Tab, a (const reference) Table object
   Return:  The Table containing this function, its data members
            containing copies of those of Tab, and a reference
            to the object assigned.

---------------------------------------------------------------------*/

Table& Table::operator= (const Table& Tab)
{
   if (Rows_ != Tab.Rows_)                       // check row equality
      cerr << "\nAssignment warning: number of rows not equal!\n";

   Rows_ = Tab.Rows_;                            // update row size

   if (Columns_ != Tab.Columns_)                 // check col. equality
      cerr << "\nAssignment warning: number of columns not equal!\n";

   Columns_ = Tab.Columns_;                      // update column size

   for (int row = 0; row < Rows_; row++)         // for each row:
      for (int col = 0; col < Columns_; col++)   //   for each column:
         Grid[row][col] = Tab.Grid[row][col];    //     copy
                                                 //       Grid[row][col]

   return *this;                                 // return copy
}
```

Once the declaration corresponding to this function has been placed in class **Table**, a statement such as

```
Table2 = Table1;
```

can be used to store a copy of the **Table** object **Table1** in the **Table** object **Table2**.

An interesting question arises concerning an assignment

```
Table2 = Table1;
```

in which **Table1** and **Table2** differ in their number of rows or columns. Some programmers view this as a logical error that is so severe that program execution should not continue. Other programmers think such assignments are perfectly fine, since **Table2** can ''grow'' or ''shrink'' to the size of **Table1** simply by setting its **Rows_** and **Columns_** members to those of **Table1**. The implementation in Figure 14.6 takes a middle-of-the-road approach by generating a *nonfatal warning* if an assignment is performed between two **Table** objects of unequal sizes. A less strict implementation might simply proceed without bothering to compare their sizes, and a more strict implementation might treat this as a fatal error by calling the function **exit()**.

Extracting the Number of Columns or Rows in a Table. The operation to find the number of columns or rows in a **Table** object is easy to implement, because it is simply an extraction operation that returns the value of the **Columns_** or **Rows_** member. As we have seen before, such a trivial function should be defined within the declaration of class **Table**, for example,

```
unsigned Columns(void) const {return Columns_;}
```

so that the compiler will treat it as an inline definition. Given this definition, the call

```
int
    Width = Tab.Columns()
```

can be used to find the number of columns of any **Table** object **Tab**. The operation to find the number of rows in a **Table** object **Tab** is similar and is given in Figure 14.8.

Summing a Row of a Table. Another useful operation on a table of numbers is to compute the sum of a specified row in the table. For example, suppose that the rows in a table represent students, and the columns represent their exam percentages:

	Exam I	Exam II	Exam III
Board, Bill			
Canusee, Jose			
Cat, Ally			
⋮	⋮	⋮	⋮
Ringing, Isabelle			

Then the sum of a given row is the sum of the exam scores for that particular student and could be used, for example, in the computation of a student's average grade.

We might specify this problem more precisely, as follows:

Receive: A **Table** object *Tab*
           A row subscript *row*
Return: The sum of the elements in the specified *row* of *Tab*

Figure 14.7 presents an implementation of such a function as a member function of class **Table**.

 FIGURE 14.7   Summing a row in a table.

```
/* This function sums the elements of a given row in a Table object.

   Receive: Integer row, the row number
   Return:  The sum of the elements in the row-th row of the Table
            object containing this function
-----------------------------------------------------------------*/

TableElement Table::RowSum(unsigned row) const
{
   if (row >= Rows_)                          // check index validity
   {
      cerr << "\n*** RowSum: invalid row index "
           << row << " received !\n";
      return 0;
   }

   TableElement                               // running total
      Sum = 0;

   for (int col = 0; col < Columns_; col++)   // for each column:
      Sum += Grid[row][col];                  //    add Grid[row][col]
                                              //        to total

   return Sum;                                // return total
}
```

As usual, the function consists of two parts: the first part, which checks for potential errors, and the second part, which solves the problem. Because the function receives an index, a possible error would be an invalid index passed to the function. The error-checking part of the function thus checks that the row number received is a valid index for a row, displaying an error message (and returning zero) if the row number is not valid.

Note that all that is needed is a single for loop to pass through the columns, because a single row is being processed. The first pass through the for loop in Figure 14.7 accesses **Grid[row][0]**, the second pass accesses **Grid[row][1]**, the third pass accesses **Grid[row][2]**, and so on, until the final pass accesses **Grid[row][Columns_-1]**.

Once the corresponding declaration of **RowSum** has been placed in class **Table**, a call of the form

```
double
   SumOfFirstRow = Tab.RowSum(row);
```

can be used to find the sum of the elements in a specified *row* of a **Table** object **Tab**.

The problem of summing a given column in a table is similar and is left as an exercise.

Retrieving the Value at a Given Row and Column.   In Chapter 12, we saw that the subscript operator is a binary operator (having an array and an index as operands) and that a **Table** is an object whose elements are accessed using two indices (a row and a column). However, **operator[]** is one of the operators that must be overloaded as a member function, so that if the usual subscript notation is applied to a **Table** named **Tab**

```
Tab[row][col]               // ERROR!
```

the second application of **operator[]** generates a compilation error, because although its second operator (**col**) is a valid index, its first operand (**Tab[row]**) is not a valid **Table**, but is a *row* of a **Table**.

We cannot use the notation

```
Tab[row, col]               // ERROR!
```

because this would involve three operands (**Tab**, **row**, and **col**), which would change the *arity* of **operator[]**, which, as we have seen, is not permitted in C++.[2]

What can be done, however, is to define a **Table** member function **GetElem()** that, given two valid indices *row* and *col,* returns the element stored in **Grid[row][col]**. Such a function is easily defined, as shown in Figure 14.8.

 FIGURE 14.8   Accessing a **Table** element.

```
/* This function accesses the element at a given row & column in
   a Table.

   Receive: row, a row index
            col, a column index
   Return:  The element at Grid[row][col]
---------------------------------------------------------------*/
```

---

[2] The difficulty actually lies in our simple implementation of class **Table**, not in **operator[]**. In Section 14.6, we see an alternate implementation of class **Table** that eliminates this handicap.

FIGURE 14.8   Accessing a **Table** element. (cont.)

```
TableElement Table::GetElem(unsigned row, unsigned col) const
{
   if ((row < Rows_) && (col < Columns_))
      return Grid[row][col];
   cerr << "\n*** GetElem - invalid index received - row: " << row
      << " column: " << col << endl;
   exit (-1);
}
```

Once this function has been declared within class **Table**, a call such as

```
TableElement
   Value = Tab.GetElem(row, col);
```

can be used to retrieve the element at row *row* and column *col* within a **Table** object **Tab**.

A complementary function **SetElem()** that can be used to change the value at a given row and column within a **Table** object is described in the exercises.

The Final **Table** Class Declaration

Once we have completed the definitions of the operations on a **Table** object and inserted their declarations into class **Table**, the class is complete. Figure 14.9 presents a partial listing of the header file of this class.

 FIGURE 14.9   Header file for class **Table**.

```
/* This file contains the declaration of class Table.

   NOTE:  Because it has appeared earlier or is similar to certain
          other classes, some documentation has been omitted to
          save pages. See the data disk for full documentation.
   -------------------------------------------------------------*/

#include <iostream.h>
#include <fstream.h>
#include <stdlib.h>
#include "Boolean.h"
#include "Strings.h"
#ifndef TABLE
#define TABLE

typedef double TableElement;                    // array element type
```

FIGURE 14.9   Header file for class **Table**. (cont.)

```
class Table
{
protected:

   enum { MaxRows = 10, MaxCols = 10 }; // bounds on the 2 dimensions

private:
/********** data members **********/

   unsigned
      Rows_,                           // the number of rows in use
      Columns_;                        // the number of columns in use

   TableElement
      Grid[MaxRows][MaxCols];          // the 2-D array member


public:
   /***** Constructor *****/
   /*-----Class-----
      Initializes a declaration of a Table object.

      Precondition:  A Table object has been declared.
      Receive:       NumRows (optional), the number of rows in the
                        Table
                     NumCols (optional), the number of columns in the
                        Table
                     InitValue (default value zero), to initialize
                        the values of the Table's elements
      Postcondition: The declared Table object containing this
                        function has its Rows_ member initialized to
                        NumRows, and its Columns_ member initialized
                        to NumCols.
   ------------------------------------------------------------------*/

   Table(unsigned NumRows = 0, unsigned NumCols = 0,
         TableElement InitialValue = 0);


   /***** Operations *****/
   /***---Input---***/
   /*-----File - Version 1 -----
      Fills a Table object with data from a file, assuming
         that the Table has been constructed with the number of
         rows and columns for the Table in the file.

      Receive:       FileName, a Strings object containing the name
                        of an input file
      Input (file):  A table of values from the input file
      Return:        The Table object containing this function, its
                        Grid member containing the input values
                     True if operation successful, false otherwise
   ------------------------------------------------------------------*/

   Boolean Fill( const Strings& FileName);
```

FIGURE 14.9 Header file for class **Table**. (cont.)

```
/*-----File - Version 2 -----
   Fills a Table object with data from a file FileName,
      assuming that the first two values in the file give
      the number of rows and columns of the Table.
   ...
   -----------------------------------------------------------*/


Boolean Load(const Strings& FileName);


/***--- Output ---***/
/*----- File -----
Boolean Write(                          // write Table to a file
         const Strings& FileName);  //   the file

/***--- Overloaded I/O Operations ---***/

/* --- interactive output */
friend ostream& operator<<(ostream& Out, const Table& Tab);

/* --- interactive input */
friend istream& operator>>(istream& In, Table& Tab);

/***---Overloaded Assignment Operator---***/
Table& operator=(const Table& Tab)

/*----- Data member extractors ----- . . . */

unsigned Rows(void) const           // how many rows?
   { return Rows_;}
unsigned Columns(void) const        // how many columns?
   { return Columns_;}


/*----- Row and Column Sums ----- . . . */
TableElement RowSum(                 // sum elements in a row
             unsigned row) const;//   the row
TableElement ColumnSum(              // sum elements in a column
             unsigned col) const;//   the column


/*----- Retrieving/Setting A Table Element ----- . . . */
TableElement GetElem(                // retrieve the element
             unsigned row,       //    at this row
             unsigned col) const;//    and this column

void SetElem(                        // set the element
          unsigned row,           //    at this row
          unsigned col,           //    and this column
          TableElement Elem);     //    equal to Elem
};
#endif
```

Given such a class, we can model tables of data, as illustrated in the next section.

Exercises

1. Complete the I/O functions of class **Table** by writing functions that do the following.

   (a) Overload **operator>>** to fill a **Table** interactively, assuming that the **Table** has been constructed with the number of rows and columns appropriate for the table being input.

   (b) Overload **operator <<** to output a **Table** to a specified **ostream**.

   (c) Given a character string, open an output file by that name, write the **Table** object's **Grid** values to that file, and then close the file.

   (d) Given a character string, open an output file by that name, write the number of rows and columns on the first line of the file, write **Table** object's **Grid** values on subsequent lines, and close the file.

2. Write the definition of the member function **ColumnSum()** that sums the values in a given column of a **Table**.

3. Write a **Table** member function **SetElem()** that, for a given row **r**, column **c**, and **TableElement Elem**, sets the value in **Grid[r][c]** to **Elem**.

4. Add member functions to class **Table** that

   (a) Given a row index, computes the average of the values in that row;

   (b) Given a row index, computes the standard deviation of the values in that row (see Programming Project 2 at the end of Chapter 12);

   (c) Given a column index, computes the average of the values in that column;

   (d) Given a column index, computes the standard deviation of the values in that column.

14.3 Example: Automobile Sales

Suppose that a certain automobile dealership sells ten different models of automobiles and employs eight salespersons. A record of sales for each month can be represented by a table in which each row contains the number of sales of a given model by each salesperson and each column contains the number of sales of each model by a given salesperson. For example, suppose that the sales table for a certain month is as follows:

```
0  0  2  0  5  6  3  0
5  1  9  0  0  2  3  2
0  0  0  1  0  0  0  0
1  1  1  0  2  2  2  1
5  3  2  0  0  2  5  5
2  2  1  0  1  1  0  0
3  2  5  0  1  2  0  4
3  0  7  1  3  5  2  4
0  2  6  1  0  5  2  1
4  0  2  0  3  2  1  0
```

A program is to be written to produce a monthly sales report, displaying the monthly sales table in the form

```
                                Salesperson
    Models :    1    2    3    4    5    6    7    8    : Totals
            --------------------------------------------------
       1    :    0    0    2    0    5    6    3    0    :   16
       2    :    5    1    9    0    0    2    3    2    :   22
       3    :    0    0    0    1    0    0    0    0    :    1
       4    :    1    1    1    0    2    2    2    1    :   10
       5    :    5    3    2    0    0    2    5    5    :   22
       6    :    2    2    1    0    1    1    0    0    :    7
       7    :    3    2    5    0    1    2    0    4    :   17
       8    :    3    0    7    1    3    5    2    4    :   25
       9    :    0    2    6    1    0    5    2    1    :   17
      10    :    4    0    2    0    3    2    1    0    :   12
            --------------------------------------------------
   Totals :   23   11   35    3   15   27   18   17
```

As indicated, the report should also display the total number of automobiles sold by each salesperson and the total number of each model sold by all salespersons.

The input to the program is a sales table as just described, and the output is to be a report of the indicated form. The required processing is given by the following algorithm:

ALGORITHM FOR SALES REPORT

/* This algorithm reads a sales table and displays a sales report consisting of the sales table and the total sales for each salesperson and model.

Input (keyboard): The name of the file containing the sales table
Input (file):   The number of rows and number of columns in the sales table and the sales table itself
Output (screen):   The sales table and the total sales for each salesperson and for each model in easy-to-read format

───*/

1. Read the name of the input file.
2. Read the sales table into a two-dimensional array *SalesTable* so that each of the rows contains the sales information for one of the models, and each of the columns contains the information for one of the salespersons.
3. Print the array *SalesTable* with appropriate headings, and column and row summaries.

Implementing this algorithm is quite easy because class **Table** contains general table-processing operations. For example, if the file containing the sales table begins with the number of rows and columns in the sales table, then function **Load()** can be used to fill a **Table** with the sales table. Otherwise, function **Fill()** can be used.

Unfortunately, the generality of the functions in **Table** also works against us, because none of the general output functions will display a sales table and summary information with the desired format. We describe two approaches to overcoming this difficulty.

Approach 1: Using a Local Output Function

One approach is to write a program that uses class **Table** and that defines and calls its own local output function to display the sales table with row and column summaries in the required format. This approach might be taken, for example, if there are no plans to reuse this function because the particular format of the report is a "one-time thing."

The structure of such a function is similar to that of **operator<<**. The primary difference lies in the various formatting expressions used to display the **Table** in the format required by the problem. For example, whereas the index of the first row or column of a **Table** is zero, the first row of a sales table represents the first model of automobile and should be labeled with 1 instead of 0. Figure 14.10 presents the implementation of such a function, along with a main function that uses it and the members of class **Table** to solve the sales report problem.

   FIGURE 14.10   Reporting automobile sales.

```
/* This program provides a monthly sales report, given a sales table.

    Input (keyboard): Name of file containing sales table
    Input (file):     The dimensions and entries of the sales table
    Output (screen):  User prompts and a monthly sales report

-----------------------------------------------------------------*/

#include <iostream.h>
#include <iomanip.h>

#include "Table.h"
#include "Strings.h"

void DisplayReport(const Table& Tab);

int main(void)
{                                           // explain the program
    cout << "\nThis program generates a monthly sales report,\n"
         << "\tgiven a file of the month's sales figures,\n"
         << "\torganized as a table whose rows are the auto models\n"
         << "\tand whose columns are the salespersons.\n";
```

FIGURE 14.10   Reporting automobile sales. (cont.)

```
                                            // get the input file name
    cout << "\nPlease enter the name of the input file: ";
    Strings
        FileName;
    cin >> FileName;

    Table                                   // declare a Table
        SalesTable;

    SalesTable.Load(FileName);              // fill it from the input file

    DisplayReport(SalesTable);              // display the report

    return 0;
}

/*----- This function displays a Table as a summary report.

Receive:          A Table named Tab
Output (screen):  Tab, in easy-to-read format,
                     with column and row headings, and
                     with column and row summaries
-----------------------------------------------------------------*/

void DisplayReport(const Table& Tab)
{
    const int                               // column width
        Width = 5;

    cout << setprecision(0);                // integer display

                                            // column headings
    cout << "\n                    Salesperson\n";
    cout << " Models :    1    2    3    4    5    6    "
         << "7    8 :  Totals\n";
    cout << "-----------------------------------------"
         << "----------------\n";

    for (int row = 0; row < Tab.Rows(); row++)   // for each row:
    {
        cout << setw(Width) << (row + 1) << "  :";   // label the row

                                            //  for each column:
        for (int col = 0; col < Tab.Columns(); col++)
            cout << setw(Width)             //     display
                 << Tab.GetElem(row, col);  //      Grid[row,col]

        cout    << " :" << setw(Width)
                << Tab.RowSum(row) << endl;     //     summarize row
    }
```

FIGURE 14.10   Reporting automobile sales. (cont.)

```
cout << "----------------------------------------"
     << "------------------------\n";
cout << " Totals : ";                               // label Totals row

for (int col = 0; col < Tab.Columns(); col++)       // for each column:
   cout << setw(Width) << Tab.ColumnSum(col);        //   summarize col.

cout << "\n\n";
}
```

Listing of file sales.dat used in sample run:

```
10 8
0      0      2      0      5      6      3      0
5      1      9      0      0      2      3      2
0      0      0      1      0      0      0      0
1      1      1      0      2      2      2      1
5      3      2      0      0      2      5      5
2      2      1      0      1      1      0      0
3      2      5      0      1      2      0      4
3      0      7      1      3      5      2      4
0      2      6      1      0      5      2      1
4      0      2      0      3      2      1      0
```

Sample run:

```
This program generates a monthly sales report,
   given a file of the month's sales figures,
   organized as a table whose rows are the auto models
   and whose columns are the salespersons.

Please enter the name of the input file: sales.dat
```

				Salesperson						
Models :	1	2	3	4	5	6	7	8	:	Totals
1 :	0	0	2	0	5	6	3	0	:	16
2 :	5	1	9	0	0	2	3	2	:	22
3 :	0	0	0	1	0	0	0	0	:	1
4 :	1	1	1	0	2	2	2	1	:	10
5 :	5	3	2	0	0	2	5	5	:	22
6 :	2	2	1	0	1	1	0	0	:	7
7 :	3	2	5	0	1	2	0	4	:	17
8 :	3	0	7	1	3	5	2	4	:	25
9 :	0	2	6	1	0	5	2	1	:	17
10 :	4	0	2	0	3	2	1	0	:	12
Totals :	23	11	35	3	15	27	18	17		

Approach 2: Deriving a Class **SalesTable** from the Class **Table**

An alternative approach to displaying a sales table is to use a feature of C++ that allows us to build one class that reuses the work done by another class. When one object *is a specialized instance of* another object (as a sales table is of a **Table**), a class for the specialized object can be *derived from* the more general class. The general class is called the **base class,** and the specialized class is called a **derived class.** Figure 14.11 shows a declaration of class **SalesTable** as a derived class whose base class is **Table**.

 FIGURE 14.11   Deriving **SalesTable** from **Table**.

```
/* This file declares class SalesTable, derived from class Table.

   ...
------------------------------------------------------------*/

#include "Table.h"
class SalesTable : public Table
{
 public:

    SalesTable(unsigned rows = 0, unsigned cols = 0)
       : Table(rows, cols)
    {}

    void DisplayReport(ostream& Out = cout) const;
};
```

Appending the symbols

> : public Table

to the name **SalesTable** informs the C++ compiler that **SalesTable** is a derived class whose base class is **Table**.

The relationship between a derived class and a base class can be described as the **is a** relationship. That is, a **SalesTable** *is a* **Table** that has one or more additional members. This relationship is important, because it implies that

> *A derived class* **inherits** *all members of its base class except for constructors and destructors.*

More precisely, the class **SalesTable** declared in Figure 14.11 contains data members **Rows_**, **Columns_**, and **Grid**, as well as most of the member functions from class **Table**, without our having to redeclare or redefine them!

The only member function in class **Table** that is not inherited by class **SalesTable** is its constructor (class **Table** has no destructors), so class **SalesTable** must provide its own function for this operation. In order for this constructor to initialize the data members of the base class, C++ permits the class constructor of a derived class to invoke the constructor of its base class with the notation:

DerivedClassConstructor(DerivedClassConstructorParameterList)

   : BaseClassConstructor(BaseClassConstructorArgumentList)

{ StatementList }

That is, we can build a **SalesTable** class constructor by writing

```
SalesTable(unsigned rows = 0, unsigned cols = 0)
   : Table(rows, cols)
{}
```

In this definition, the statement list is empty, because a **SalesTable** has no data members to be initialized beyond those it inherits from class **Table**. (If **SalesTable** did have its own data members, they would be initialized in the statement list, as normal.) Invoking the **Table** constructor is all that is needed to initialize the data members of a **SalesTable**.

Given such a definition, we can declare

```
SalesTable
   ST;
```

and the constructor for a **SalesTable** is called (with default arguments), which passes those default arguments to the **Table** constructor to initialize the (inherited) data members of **ST**. This **base class member initialization mechanism** is described in more detail in Section 16.4.

Derivation is the reason why (in Section 14.2) the data members of class **Table** were declared using the phrase **protected:** instead of **private:**

> *A derived class cannot access the private members of its base class, but it can access the protected and public members of its base class.*

Thus, making **Rows_**, **Columns_**, and **Grid** *protected* data members instead of private members in class **Table** allows the derived class **SalesTable** to access those members, as shown in the definition of **DisplayReport()** in Figure 14.12.

FIGURE 14.12 `SalesTable` Member `DisplayReport()`.

```
/* This file contains the definition of the function for SalesTable.

   ...
   -----------------------------------------------------------------*/

#include "SalesTable.h"

/*------------------------------------------------------------------
 This function displays a SalesTable as a report, including row
   and column labels, plus row and column summaries.

   Receive: An ostream (default value cout)
   Output:  The SalesTable containing this function, with row
            and column labels, and row and column summaries
   -----------------------------------------------------------------*/

#include <iomanip.h>

void SalesTable::DisplayReport(ostream& Out) const
{
  const int
    Width = 5;

  Out << setprecision(0);                          // integer display

  Out << "\n                        Salesperson\n";
  Out << " Models :    1    2    3    4    5    6    "
      << "7    8    : Totals\n";
  Out << "-----------------------------------------"
      << "---------------\n";

  for (int row = 0; row < Rows_; row++)
  {
    Out << setw(Width) << row + 1 << " : ";

    for (int col = 0; col < Columns_; col++)
      Out << setw(Width) << Grid[row][col];

    Out << "    :" << setw(Width) << RowSum(row) << endl;
  }

  Out << "----------------------------------------"
      << "----------------\n";
  Out << " Totals : ";
  for (int col = 0; col < Columns_; col++)
    Out << setw(Width) << ColumnSum(col);
  Out << "\n\n";
}
```

Once this function has been defined and declared, a program can make use of class **SalesTable** and all its public members (including those it inherited from class **Table**), as illustrated by the program in Figure 14.13. The differences between this program and that of Figure 14.10 are shown in color for easy comparison. Execution of this program produces output identical to that shown in Figure 14.10.

 FIGURE 14.13 Reporting automobile sales (version 2).

```
/* This program provides a monthly sales report, given a sales table.

   Input (keyboard): Name of file containing sales table
   Input (file):     The dimensions and entries of the sales table
   Output (screen):  User prompts and aa monthly sales report
-------------------------------------------------------------------*/

#include <iostream.h>

#include "SalesTable.h"
#include "Strings.h"

int main(void)
{                                       // explain the program
   cout << "\nThis program generates a monthly sales report,\n"
        << "\tgiven a file of the month's sales figures,\n"
        << "\torganized as a table whose rows are the auto models\n"
        << "\tand whose columns are the salespersons.\n";

   Strings                              // get the input file name
      FileName;

   cout << "\nPlease enter the name of the input file: ";
   cin >> FileName;
                                        // declare a Table
   SalesTable
      SalesTab;

   SalesTab.Load(FileName);             // fill it from the input file

   SalesTab.DisplayReport();            // display w/ report format

   return 0;
}
```

Note that the call

```
SalesTab.Load(FileName);
```

invokes the general-purpose function **Load()** that **SalesTab** inherits from class **Table**, whereas the call

```
SalesTab.DisplayReport();
```

involves the special-purpose function **DisplayReport()** declared in class **SalesTable**.

Derivation and inheritance are two very powerful aspects of object-oriented programming. However, to make use of these features, one must design and plan for the future by constructing classes that are *as general as possible,* as we have attempted to do with classes **List** and **Table**. Once a set of general-purpose classes has been built, more specialized classes can be built that reuse the features of the general-purpose classes, saving a great deal of time and effort. Derived classes are discussed in greater detail in the next section and in Sections 16.4 and 16.5.

Exercises

1. Construct two enumeration classes: **AutoModel**, whose values are the ten different automobile models, and **EmployeeName**, whose values are the names of eight employees of the auto dealership. Overload the I/O operators with definitions to perform **AutoModel** and **EmployeeName** I/O. Using these types, rewrite function **DisplayReport()** to display a sales table with the rows labeled with the automobile models and the columns labeled with the employee's names, instead of numbers.

2. A certain professor has a file containing a table of student grades, where the first line of the file contains the number of students and the number of scores in the table; each row of the table represents the exam scores of a given student; and each column represents the scores on a given exam. The maximum possible score on each exam is 100 points. Write a program that, given the name of such a file, generates a report summarizing the overall percentage for each student and the average score on each exam.

3. The group CAN (Citizens Against Noise) has collected some data on the noise level (measured in decibels) produced at seven different speeds by six different models of cars. This data is summarized in the following table:

Car	20	30	40	Speed(mi/h) 50	60	70	80
0	88	90	94	102	111	122	134
1	75	77	80	86	94	103	113
2	80	83	85	94	100	111	121
3	68	71	76	85	96	110	125
4	77	84	91	98	105	112	119
5	81	85	90	96	102	109	120

Write a program that will read the data for this table from a file and display this table in easy-to-read format and that will calculate and display the average noise level for each car model, the average noise level at each speed, and the overall average noise level.

4. Suppose that the prices for the ten automobile models in the example of this section are as follows:

Model No.	Model Price
0	$ 7,450
1	$ 9,995
2	$26,500
3	$ 5,999
4	$10,400
5	$ 8,885
6	$11,700
7	$14,440
8	$17,900
9	$ 9,550

Write a program to read this list of prices and the sales table given in this section and calculate the total dollar sales for each salesperson and the total dollar sales for all salespersons.

5. A certain company has a product line that includes five items that sell for $100, $75, $120, $150, and $35. There are four salespersons working for this company, and the following table gives the sales report for a typical week:

Salesperson Number	Item Number				
	1	2	3	4	5
1	10	4	5	6	7
2	7	0	12	1	3
3	4	9	5	0	8
4	3	2	1	5	6

Write a program to

(a) Compute the total dollar sales for each salesperson.
(b) Compute the total commission for each salesperson if the commission rate is 10%.
(c) Find the total income for each salesperson for the week if each salesperson receives a fixed salary of $200 per week in addition to commission payments.

6. A number of students from several different engineering sections performed the same experiment to determine the tensile strength of sheets made from two different alloys. Each of these strength measurements is a real number in the range 0 through 10. Write a program to read several lines of data, each consisting of a section number and the tensile strength of the two types of sheets recorded by a student in that section, and store these values in a two-dimensional array. Then calculate

(a) For each section, the average of the tensile strengths for each type of alloy.
(b) The number of persons in a given section who recorded strength measures of 5 or higher.
(c) The average of the tensile strengths recorded for alloy 2 by students who recorded a tensile strength lower than 3 for alloy 1.

7. A magic square is an $n \times n$ table in which each of the integers 1, 2, 3, ... , n^2 appears exactly once and all column sums, row sums, and diagonal sums are equal. For example, the following is a 5×5 magic square in which all the rows, columns, and diagonals add up to 65:

17	24	1	8	15
23	5	7	14	16
4	6	13	20	22
10	12	19	21	3
11	18	25	2	9

The following is a procedure for constructing an $n \times n$ magic square for any odd integer n. Place 1 in the middle of the top row. Then after integer k has been placed, move up one row and one column to the right to place the next integer $k + 1$, unless one of the following occurs:

(i) If a move takes you above the top row in the jth column, move to the bottom of the jth column and place the integer $k + 1$ there.
(ii) If a move takes you outside to the right of the square in the ith row, place $k + 1$ in the ith row at the left side.
(iii) If a move takes you to an already filled square or if you move out of the square at the upper right-hand corner, place $k + 1$ immediately below k.

Write a function to construct an $n \times n$ magic square for any odd value of n and a driver program to test your function.

8. Consider a square grid, with some cells empty and others containing an asterisk. Define two asterisks to be *contiguous* if they are adjacent to each other in the same row or in the same column. Now suppose we define a *blob* as follows:

(i) A blob contains at least one asterisk.

(ii) If an asterisk is in a blob, then so is any asterisk that is contiguous to it.

(iii) If a blob has more than two asterisks, then each asterisk in it is contiguous to at least one other asterisk in the blob.

For example, there are four blobs in the partial grid

*			*	*			*		*	*
							*		*	*

seven blobs in

*		*		*			*	*	*
				*				*	
*			*						

and only one in

		*	*	*		*	*	*		
				*		*		*		
			*	*	*					

Write a program that uses a recursive function to count the number of blobs in a square grid. Input to the program should consist of the locations of the asterisks in the grid, and the program should display the grid and the blob count.

14.4 PART OF THE PICTURE: Numeric Computation

A two-dimensional numeric array having *m* rows and *n* columns is called an *m* × *n* **matrix.** In this section, we briefly examine how to build a `Matrix` class, together with a sample `Matrix` operation: **matrix multiplication.** There are a wide variety of additional matrix operations, some of which are described in the exercises. We also describe one of the many important applications that involve the manipulation of matrices.

Matrix Multiplication

Suppose that *Mat1* is an $m \times n$ matrix and *Mat2* is an $n \times p$ matrix. The product *Mat3* of *Mat1* and *Mat2* is then an $m \times p$ matrix with the entry *Mat3*[*i*][*j*], which appears in the *i*th row and the *j*th column given by

$Mat3[i][j]$ = the sum of the products of the entries in row *i* of
Mat1 with the entries of column *j* of *Mat2*

$$= Mat1[i][1] \cdot Mat2[1][j] + Mat1[i][2] \cdot Mat2[2][j]$$
$$+ \cdots + Mat1[i][n] \cdot Mat2[n][j]$$

Note that the number of columns (*n*) in *Mat1* must equal the number of rows in *Mat2* for the product of *Mat1* with *Mat2* to be defined.

As an example, suppose that *Mat1* is the 2×3 matrix

$$\begin{bmatrix} 1 & 0 & 2 \\ 3 & 0 & 4 \end{bmatrix}$$

and that *Mat2* is the 3 x 4 matrix

$$\begin{bmatrix} 4 & 2 & 5 & 3 \\ 6 & 4 & 1 & 8 \\ 9 & 0 & 0 & 2 \end{bmatrix}$$

Because the number of columns (3) in *Mat1* equals the number of rows in *Mat2*, the product matrix *Mat3* is defined. The entry in the first row and first column is

$$1 \cdot 4 + 0 \cdot 6 + 2 \cdot 9 = 22$$

Similarly, the entry in the first row and second column is

$$1 \cdot 2 + 0 \cdot 4 + 2 \cdot 0 = 2$$

The complete product matrix *Mat3* is the 2×4 matrix given by

$$\begin{bmatrix} 22 & 2 & 5 & 7 \\ 48 & 6 & 15 & 17 \end{bmatrix}$$

In general, the algorithm for multiplying matrices is as follows:

MATRIX MULTIPLICATION ALGORITHM

/* This algorithm computes the product of two matrices *Mat1* and *Mat2*, if the number of columns in *Mat1* equals the number of rows in *Mat2*. The operation is undefined, otherwise.

Receive: A *Rows1* $\times$ *Cols1* matrix *Mat1*, and
           A *Rows2* $\times$ *Cols2* matrix *Mat2*

Return: The product matrix *Mat3*, provided it is defined
———*/

1. If the number of columns in *Mat1* ≠ the number of rows in *Mat2,* then the product *Mat3* = *Mat1*∗*Mat2* is not defined; terminate the algorithm.
2. For each row *i* in *Mat1,* do the following:
    For each column *j* in *Mat2* do the following:
        a. Set *Sum* equal to 0.
        b. For each column *k* in *Mat1* (= the number of rows in *Mat2*):
            Add *Mat1*[*i*][*k*]∗*Mat2*[*k*][*j*] to *Sum.*
        c. Set *Mat3*[*i*][*j*] equal to *Sum.*

This is the general algorithm for matrix multiplication. However, before we can encode this algorithm, we need a **Matrix** class in which to store this operation.

Building a **Matrix** Class

As we have noted several times, it is always worthwhile to spend some time carefully designing a class before jumping in and writing code. It is especially worthwhile for the class **Matrix**, because with a bit of thought, it becomes evident that a matrix *is a* table that has some specialized operations (such as multiplication). The fact that a matrix and a table can be related using the *is a* relation means that we do not have to build class **Matrix** from the beginning but can instead construct it as a derived class from the base class **Table**. The derived class **Matrix** will then inherit all the members from the base class **Table** (except the constructor), saving a great deal of work. Figure 14.14 shows the declaration of class **Matrix**, together with its declaration that overloads **operator∗**.

FIGURE 14.14   Deriving **Matrix** from **Table**.

```
/* This file declares class Matrix, derived from class Table.

   ...
   ------------------------------------------------------------------*/

#include "Table.h"

class Matrix : public Table
{

public:

   Matrix(unsigned rows = 0, unsigned cols = 0, TableElement val = 0)
     : Table(rows, cols, val)
   {}

   friend Matrix operator*(const Matrix& Mat1, const Matrix& Mat2);
   // ...
};
```

As we saw in the last section, the constructors of base classes are not inherited by classes derived from it, and so a class constructor should be provided for the class **Matrix** to ensure that the data members it inherits from class **Table** are properly initialized. As we saw previously, C++ permits the definition of a derived class constructor to invoke the constructor of its base class with the notation:

DerivedClassConstructor(DerivedClassConstructorParameterList)

: *BaseClassConstructor(BaseClassConstructorArgumentList)*

{ *StatementList* }

We thus create the **Matrix** class constructor definition by writing

```
Matrix(unsigned rows = 0, unsigned cols = 0,
       TableElement val = 0)
   : Table(rows, cols, val)
{}
```

which invokes the **Table** class constructor, and passes the values **rows**, **cols**, and **val**, which the **Table** class constructor then uses to initialize its members. Since class **Matrix** has no additional data members beyond those of **Table**, the *StatementList* of its class constructor has no additional initializations to perform, and is thus empty. The base class member initialization mechanism is discussed in greater detail in Section 16.4.

After we have declared class **Matrix**, we must define its specialized operations. Figure 14.15 shows an implementation of the matrix multiplication algorithm for **Matrix** objects.

 FIGURE 14.15 **Matrix** multiplication.

```
/* This file defines the operations on class Matrix, which is
   derived from class Table.

...
-----------------------------------------------------------------*/

#include "Matrix.h"

/*-----------------------------------------------------------------
This function multiplies two matrices.

   Receive: Matrix Mat1 and Mat2
   Return:  Mat3, containing the product of Mat1 and Mat2.
-----------------------------------------------------------------*/
```

FIGURE 14.15 **Matrix** multiplication. (cont.)

```
#include <stdlib.h>                          // provides exit()

Matrix operator*(const Matrix& Mat1, const Matrix& Mat2)
{
  if (Mat1.Columns_ != Mat2.Rows_)          // check argument
  {                                         //  validity
     cerr << "\n*** Mat1*Mat2: columns of Mat1 "
          << "must equal rows of Mat2\n";
     exit (-1);
  }

  Matrix                                    // use Table constructor
     Mat3(Mat1.Rows_, Mat2.Columns_);       // declare result Matrix

  TableElement                              // stores the sum of
     Sum;                                   //  pairwise products

  for (int i = 0; i < Mat1.Rows_; i++)      // for each row in M1:
     for (int j = 0; j < Mat2.Columns_; j++)  //  for each col in M2:
     {
        Sum = 0;                            //    initialize Sum
                                            //    for each col in M1:
        for (int k = 0; k < Mat1.Columns_; k++)//    sum products
           Sum += Mat1.Grid[i][k]
                 * Mat2.Grid[k][j];

        Mat3.Grid[i][j] = Sum;              //    store Sum in M3
     }
  return Mat3;                              // return result matrix
}
```

Once **Matrix** operations have been defined, a program can make use of these operations in the same manner as those of any other class, as illustrated in Figure 14.16.

 FIGURE 14.16 Demonstration of matrix multiplication.

```
/* This program demonstrates matrix multiplication, using class
   Matrix.

   Input (keyboard): Names of files containing matrices
   Input (files):    Two matrices, with number of rows and columns
                     listed first
   Output (screen):  The matrices together with their product
-----------------------------------------------------------------*/
```

FIGURE 14.16 Demonstration of matrix multiplication. (cont.)

```cpp
#include <iostream.h>

#include "Strings.h"
#include "Matrix.h"

int main(void)
{
  cout << "\nThis program demonstrates matrix multiplication,\n"
       << "\tby multiplying two matrices stored in separate files.\n"
       << "\nA file must list the # of rows and columns of its "
       << "matrix.\n";

  Strings                             // file names
    File1,
    File2;
                                      // get the names of the files
  cout << "\nPlease enter the name of the first file: ";
  cin >> File1;

  cout << "The name of the second file ? ";
  cin >> File2;

  Matrix                              // declare two matrices
    Matrix1,
    Matrix2;

  Matrix1.Load(File1);                // load Matrix1 from File1
  Matrix2.Load(File2);                // load Matrix2 from File2
                                      // use Table's operator<<
                                      //   to display the matrices
  cout << "\n- Matrix1 -------------------------------------\n";
  cout << Matrix1;
  cout << "- Matrix2 ---------------------------------\n";
  cout << Matrix2;

  Matrix                              // declare result matrix
    Matrix3(Matrix1.Rows(), Matrix2.Columns());
                                      // mult. Matrix1 and Matrix2,
  Matrix3 = Matrix1 * Matrix2;        //   giving Matrix3
                                      // display Matrix3
  cout << "- Matrix3 --------------------------------------\n";
  cout << Matrix3 << endl;

  return 0;
}
```

FIGURE 14.16   Demonstration of matrix multiplication. (cont.)

Listing of Input File mat2x3.dat

```
2 3
1 0 2
3 0 4
```

Listing of Input File mat3x4.dat

```
3 4
4 2 5 3
6 4 1 8
9 0 0 2
```

Sample run:

```
This program demonstrates matrix multiplication,
   by multiplying two matrices stored in separate files.

A file must list the # of rows and columns of its matrix.

Please enter the name of the first file: mat2x3.dat
The name of the second file ? mat3x4.dat

- Matrix1 ---------------------------------------
        1.00       0.00       2.00
        3.00       0.00       4.00
- Matrix2 ---------------------------------------
        4.00       2.00       5.00       3.00
        6.00       4.00       1.00       8.00
        9.00       0.00       0.00       2.00
- Matrix3 ---------------------------------------
       22.00       2.00       5.00       7.00
       48.00       6.00      15.00      17.00
```

It is important to understand that the statement

```
Matrix
    Matrix1,
    Matrix2;
```

uses the **Matrix** constructor to build **Matrix1** and **Matrix2**, by invoking the **Table** constructor to initialize each of their **Rows_** and **Columns_** members to the constructor's default arguments (zeros). By the same token, the statements

```
Matrix1.Load(File1);
Matrix2.Load(File2);
```

use the definition of function **Load()** from class **Table**, and the statements

```
cout << Matrix1;
cout << Matrix2;
```

apply the definition of **operator<<** from class **Table**. The declaration of the result matrix

```
Matrix
    Matrix3(Matrix1.Rows(), Matrix2.Columns());
```

also invokes the class constructor from class **Table** but passes its arguments other than the default arguments. These arguments are the values returned by the **Table** extractor functions **Rows()** and **Columns()**, applied to **Matrix1** and **Matrix2**, respectively. Thus, in our sample execution, **Matrix1** is a 2×3 matrix and **Matrix2** is a 3×4 matrix, so that **Matrix3** is constructed as a 2×4 matrix and is thus the same size as that returned by **operator***.

The statement

```
Matrix3 = Matrix1 * Matrix2;
```

applies the overloaded definition of **operator*** from **Matrix** to **Matrix1** and **Matrix2**, returning a result matrix. This result matrix is then assigned to **Matrix3** using the definition of **operator=** from class **Table**. The definition of **operator<<** from class **Table** is then used a third time to display **Matrix3**.

Solving Linear Systems

A linear system is a set of linear equations, each of which involves several unknowns; for example,

$$5x_2 - x_2 - 2x_3 = 11$$
$$-x_1 + 5x_2 - 2x_3 = 0$$
$$-2x_1 - 2x_2 + 7x_3 = 0$$

is a linear system of three equations involving the three unknowns x_1, x_2, and x_3. A solution of such a system is a collection of values for these unknowns that satisfies all of the equations simultaneously.

One method for solving a linear system is called **Gaussian elimination.** In this method, we first eliminate x_1 from the second equation by adding $\frac{1}{5}$ times the first equation to the second equation and from the third equation by adding $\frac{2}{5}$ times the first equation to the third equation. This yields the linear system

$$5x_1 - x_2 - 2x_3 = 11$$
$$4.8x_2 - 2.4x_3 = 2.2$$
$$-2.4x_2 + 6.2x_3 = 4.4$$

which is equivalent to the first system because it has the same solution as the original system. We next eliminate x_2 from the third equation by adding $2.4/4.8 = \frac{1}{2}$ times the second equation to the third, giving the new equivalent linear system

$$5x_1 - x_2 - 2x_3 = 11$$
$$4.8x_2 - 2.4x_3 = 2.2$$
$$5x_3 = 5.5$$

Once the original system has been reduced to such a *triangular* form, it is easy to find the solution. It is clear from the last equation that the value of x_3 is

$$x_3 = \frac{5.5}{5} = 1.100$$

Substituting this value for x_3 in the second equation and solving for x_2 gives

$$x_2 = \frac{2.2 + 2.4(1.1)}{4.8} = 1.008$$

Substituting these values for x_2 and x_3 in the first equation gives

$$x_1 = \frac{11 + 1.008 + 2(1.100)}{5} = 2.842$$

The original linear system can also be written as a single matrix equation

$$Ax = b$$

where A is the 3×3 **coefficient matrix,** b is the 3×1 **constant vector,** and x is the 3×1 **vector of unknowns:**

$$A = \begin{bmatrix} 5 & -1 & -2 \\ -1 & 5 & -2 \\ -2 & -2 & 7 \end{bmatrix}, \quad x = \begin{bmatrix} x_1 \\ x_2 \\ x_3 \end{bmatrix}, \quad b = \begin{bmatrix} 11 \\ 0 \\ 0 \end{bmatrix}$$

The operations used to reduce the original linear system to triangular form use only the coefficient matrix A and the constant vector b. Thus, if we combine these into a single matrix by adjoining b to A as a last column,

$$Aug = \begin{bmatrix} 5 & -1 & -2 & 11 \\ -1 & 5 & -2 & 0 \\ -2 & -2 & 7 & 0 \end{bmatrix}$$

we can carry out the operations on this new matrix, called the **augmented matrix,** without writing down the unknowns at each step. Thus we add $-Aug[1][0]/Aug[0][0] = \frac{1}{5}$ times the first row of Aug to the second row and $-Aug[2][0]/Aug[0][0] = \frac{2}{5}$ times the first row of Aug to the third row to obtain the new matrix

$$Aug = \begin{bmatrix} 5 & -1 & -2 & 11 \\ 0 & 4.8 & -2.4 & 2.2 \\ 0 & -2.4 & 6.2 & 4.4 \end{bmatrix}$$

Then adding $-Aug[2][1]/Aug[1][1] = \frac{1}{2}$ times the second row to the third row gives the following *triangular* matrix, which corresponds to the final triangular system of equations:

$$Aug = \begin{bmatrix} 5 & -1 & -2 & 11 \\ 0 & 4.8 & -2.4 & 2.2 \\ 0 & 0 & 5 & 5.5 \end{bmatrix}$$

From this example, we see that the basic row operation performed at the ith step of the reduction process is:

For $k = i + 1, i + 2, \ldots, n$

Replace row_k by $\text{row}_k - \dfrac{Aug[k][i]}{Aug[i][i]} \times \text{row}_i$

Clearly, for this to be possible, the element $Aug[i][i]$, called a **pivot** element, must be nonzero. If it is not, we must interchange the ith row with a later row to produce a nonzero pivot.

An algorithm and a program for solving linear systems using Gaussian elimination is given in Appendix H. To minimize the effect of roundoff error in the computations, it selects as a pivot at each stage in the reduction the candidate that is largest in absolute value.

Exercises

1. Write and test a function to **add** two matrices. If A_{ij} and B_{ij} are the entries in the ith row and jth column of $m \times n$ matrices A and B, respectively, then $A_{ij} + B_{ij}$ is the entry in the ith row and jth column of the sum, which is also an $m \times n$ matrix. For example,

$$\begin{bmatrix} 1 & 0 & 2 \\ -1 & 3 & 5 \end{bmatrix} + \begin{bmatrix} 4 & 2 & 1 \\ 7 & 0 & 3 \end{bmatrix} = \begin{bmatrix} 5 & 2 & 3 \\ 6 & 3 & 8 \end{bmatrix}$$

2. Write and test a function to find the **transpose** of a matrix. Suppose that A is an $m \times n$ matrix and that A_{ij} is the entry in the ith row and jth column of A. Then T, the transpose of A, is an $n \times m$ matrix in which $T_{ji} = A_{ij}$, for all indices i and j. For example, if A is the 2×3 matrix

$$\begin{bmatrix} 1 & 0 & 2 \\ -1 & 3 & 5 \end{bmatrix}$$

then T, the transpose of A, is the 3×2 matrix

$$\begin{bmatrix} 1 & -1 \\ 0 & 3 \\ 2 & 5 \end{bmatrix}$$

3. A certain company manufactures four electronic devices using five different components that cost $10.95, $6.30, $14.75, $11.25, and $5.00, respectively. The number of components used in each device is given in the following table:

Device Number	Component Number				
	1	2	3	4	5
1	10	4	5	6	7
2	7	0	12	1	3
3	4	9	5	0	8
4	3	2	1	5	6

Write a program that uses matrix multiplication to do each of the following.

(a) Calculate the total cost of each device.
(b) Calculate the total cost of producing each device if the estimated labor cost for each device is 10 percent of the cost in part (a).

4. The vector-matrix equation

$$
\begin{bmatrix} N \\ E \\ D \end{bmatrix} = \begin{bmatrix} \cos \alpha & -\sin \alpha & 0 \\ \sin \alpha & \cos \alpha & 0 \\ 0 & 0 & 1 \end{bmatrix} \begin{bmatrix} \cos \beta & 0 & \sin \beta \\ 0 & 1 & 0 \\ -\sin \beta & 0 & \cos \beta \end{bmatrix} \begin{bmatrix} 1 & 0 & 0 \\ 0 & \cos \gamma & -\sin \gamma \\ 0 & \sin \gamma & \cos \gamma \end{bmatrix} \begin{bmatrix} I \\ J \\ K \end{bmatrix}
$$

is used to transform local coordinates (I, J, K) for a space vehicle to inertial coordinates (N, E, D). Write a program that reads values for α, β, and γ and a set of local coordinates (I, J, K) and then uses matrix multiplication to determine the corresponding inertial coordinates.

5. A Markov chain is a system that moves through a discrete set of states in such a way that when the system is in state i there is probability P_{ij} that it will next move to state j. These probabilities are given by a transition matrix P, whose (i, j) entry is P_{ij}. It is easy to show that the (i, j) entry of P^n then gives the probability of starting in state i and ending in state j after n steps.

To illustrate, suppose there are two urns A and B containing a given number of balls. At each instant, a ball is chosen at random and is transferred to the other urn. This is a Markov chain if we take as a state the number of balls in urn A and let P_{ij} be the probability that a ball is transferred from A to B if there are i balls in urn A. For example, for four balls, the transition matrix P is given by

$$
\begin{bmatrix} 0 & 1 & 0 & 0 & 0 \\ \frac{1}{4} & 0 & \frac{3}{4} & 0 & 0 \\ 0 & \frac{1}{2} & 0 & \frac{1}{2} & 0 \\ 0 & 0 & \frac{3}{4} & 0 & \frac{1}{4} \\ 0 & 0 & 0 & 1 & 0 \end{bmatrix}
$$

Write a program that reads a transition matrix P for such a Markov chain and calculates and displays the value of n and P^n for several values of n.

6. A directed graph, or digraph, consists of a set of vertices and a set of directed arcs joining certain of these vertices. For example, the following diagram pictures a directed graph having five vertices numbered 1, 2, 3, 4, and 5, and seven directed arcs joining vertices 1 to 2, 1 to 4, 1 to 5, 3 to 1, 3 to itself, 4 to 3, and 5 to 1:

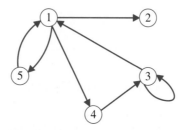

A directed graph having n vertices can be represented by its adjacency matrix, which is an $n \times n$ matrix, with the entry in the ith row and jth column a 1 if vertex i is joined to vertex j and 0 otherwise. The adjacency matrix for this graph is

$$\begin{bmatrix} 0 & 1 & 0 & 1 & 1 \\ 0 & 0 & 0 & 0 & 0 \\ 1 & 0 & 1 & 0 & 0 \\ 0 & 0 & 1 & 0 & 0 \\ 1 & 0 & 0 & 0 & 0 \end{bmatrix}$$

If A is the adjacency matrix for a directed graph, the entry in the ith row and jth column of A^k gives the number of ways that vertex j can be reached from the vertex i by following k edges. Write a program to read the number of vertices in a directed graph and a collection of ordered pairs of vertices representing directed arcs, construct the adjacency matrix, and then find the number of ways that each vertex can be reached from every other vertex by following k edges for some value of k.

7. A company produces three different products. They are processed through four different departments, A, B, C, and D, and the following table gives the number of hours that each department spends on each product.

14.5   PART OF THE PICTURE: Computer Graphics

Computer graphics is the area of computing that studies how information can be modeled and manipulated using pictures on a computer screen. To provide graphics capabilities, a computer screen is usually organized as a two-dimensional array (e.g., 480×640) of picture elements, called **pixels**. Primitive graphics operations include the ability to set a particular pixel to a given color (black or white on a monochrome screen). From these primitive operations, higher-level graphics operations can be implemented to draw lines, boxes, circles, text, and so on.

Functions that perform graphics operations are typically stored in *graphics libraries* to make them easy to access. However, in order for such functions to be as efficient as possible, they are often written as low-level (e.g., assembly language) functions. Because of this, graphics functions cannot usually be ported between different hardware platforms or operating systems. Different implementations of C++ thus have different graphics libraries:

- For C++ implementations on most UNIX systems, the X-windows environment provides graphics libraries such as *Xlib* and *Xt*, which provide low-level and high-level graphics functions, respectively,
- On the Macintosh, Symantec C++ provides the THINK Class Library, which provides a rich set of graphics objects (e.g., *Window, Pane, Button, ScrollBar, CheckBox,* etc.), and functions to manipulate them.
- On IBM PCs running MS-DOS, Turbo/Borland C++ provides the library **GRAPHICS.LIB** that provides a graphics window (e.g., a *viewport*) and a wide assortment of functions to draw graphics objects (e.g., *arc, circle, polygon, ellipse, line, rectangle,* etc.) within that window.
- On IBM PCs running MS-Windows, Borland C++ and MS C/C++ provide libraries (*ObjectWindows* and the *MS Foundation Classes,* respectively) that provide graphics objects and operations similar to those available on the Macintosh.

Unfortunately, none of these libraries is compatible with the others, and so C++ programs that employ them are limited to that particular environment.

To illustrate the use of a graphics library, we have implemented a class named **CartesianSystem**, whose source code can be found in Appendix G. Graphics operations (e.g., **DrawAxes()**, **Graph()**, **DensityPlot()**, etc.) are provided as member functions of class **CartesianSystem**. Although this **CartesianSystem** class is implemented using the Turbo C++ graphics library **GRAPHICS.LIB**, the class can be implementated using any of the other graphics libraries.

Examples: Function Graphing and Density Plots

Function Graphing. The number and quality of software packages and hand-held calculators that can be used to generate high-resolution graphs of functions are increasing rapidly. For example, Figure 14.17a shows the graph of $y = x * \cos(x)$ for $-8 \le x \le 8$ as plotted on a Texas Instruments TI-85 Advanced Scientific Cal-

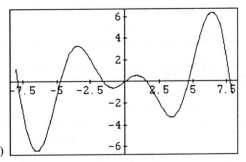

(a)　　　　(b)

FIGURE 14.17　(a) Plot of $y = x * \cos(x)$ on a Texas Instruments TI = 85 calculator. (b) Plot of $y = x * \cos(x)$ produced by Mathematica.

culator, and Figure 14.17b shows the same graph as produced by the powerful software package Mathematica™.

Similar to the two-dimensional character array **Screen** presented in Section 14.1, the window containing each of the plots shown in Figure 14.17 is simply a two-dimensional array of points (pixels) on the window, some of which (those corresponding to points on the graph of the function) are ''on'' (black) and the rest of which are ''off'' (white). The following enlarged view of the portion of the graphics window near the origin shows clearly the grid structure of this part of the window:

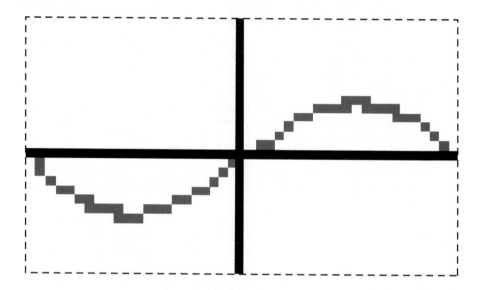

Class **CartesianSystem** contains a member function **Graph()** that, given a function $f(x)$, draws the graph of $f(x)$. To plot a function $y = f(x)$, **Graph()** uses a loop to iterate through the x values. For each such x value, the y value nearest the actual function value $y = f(x)$ is determined and the point (x, y) is mapped into the appropriate pixel in the window. This pixel is then set to a color different from the background by using a primitive graphics command.

The program in Figure 14.18 uses the **Graph()** member of class **CartesianSystem** to plot graphs of some functions in the Turbo C++ environment.

FIGURE 14.18 Plotting a function.

```
/* This program can be used to graph an arbitrary function(s)
   using class CartesianSystem.

   Output: Prompts for input
   Input:  Values for the endpoints of the x and y axes
   Output: The graphs of f(x) and g(x)

   Note:   In this example, two functions f(x) and g(x) are plotted.
   ---------------------------------------------------------------*/
```

FIGURE 14.18   Plotting a function. (cont.)

```cpp
#include <iostream.h>
#include <math.h>

#include "CartSys.h"                  // declaration of CartesianSystem


double f(double x)                    // a function to be plotted
{
    return x * cos(x);
}

double g(double x)                    // another function to be plotted
{
    return x;
}

int main(void)
{
    cout << "\nThis program plots some functions..."
         << "\n(currently y = x*cos(x) and y = x.)\n";

    double                            // endpoints of the axes
        xMin, xMax,
        yMin, yMax;
    char
        ReturnChar;                   // the newline

    do                                // get the x bounds
    {
        cout << "\nPlease enter the minimum and maximum x values: ";
        cin >> xMin >> xMax;
    }
    while (xMin >= xMax);

    do                                // get the y bounds
    {
        cout << "\nPlease enter the minimum and maximum y values: ";
        cin >> yMin >> yMax;
    }
    while (yMin >= yMax);
    cin.get(ReturnChar);              // clean out the newline

    CartesianSystem                   // construct a Cartesian system
        CoordinateSys(xMin, xMax, yMin, yMax);

    CoordinateSys.DrawAxes();         // draw the axes

    CoordinateSys.Graph(f);           // graph f

    CoordinateSys.Graph(g, CYAN);     // graph g in a different color


    return 0;
}
```

FIGURE 14.18   Plotting a function. (cont.)

Sample run:

```
This program plots some functions...
(currently y = x*cos(x) and y = x.)

Please enter the minimum and maximum x values: -8 8

Please enter the minimum and maximum y values: -7 7
```

The sample run of this program produced the following output:

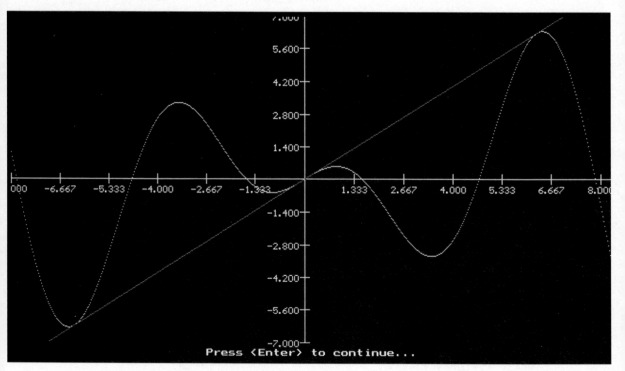

Density Plots.   We have just seen how a function $y = f(x)$ of a single variable x can be plotted. Graphs of functions $z = f(x, y)$ of two variables x and y are surfaces in three dimensions and are considerably more difficult to display on a two-dimensional screen. Some software packages are able to generate good two-dimensional representations of many three-dimensional surfaces. For example, the following is a graph produced by Mathematica of the surface defined by

$$z = e^{-(x^2+y^2)}$$

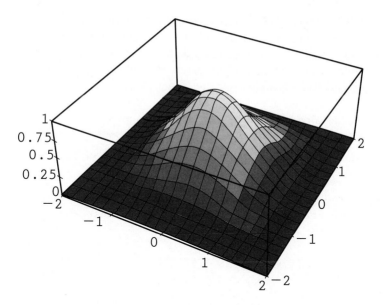

Note that in this representation, shading is used to represent the height of the function, with lighter shades for larger values and darker shades for smaller values. This shading, together with the curved grid lines and the enclosing box, produces a visual illusion of a three-dimensional surface.

Another representation of a surface that also uses shading but not perspective is a **density plot** obtained by projecting onto a plane a representation like the preceding one. The following is the density plot generated by Mathematica for this surface. The various densities of gray again indicate different heights of the function.

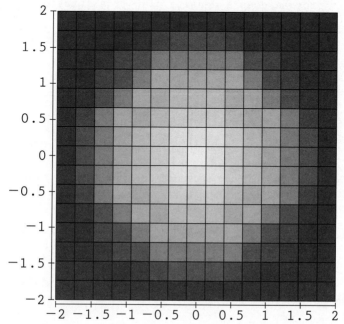

To generate a density plot, class **CartesianSystem** provides a member function named **DensityPlot()**. This function sets each pixel to a color, based on the value of z (i.e., smaller z values produce darker colored pixels and larger z values produce lighter colored pixels). The program in Figure 14.19 uses this function to produce the density plot of the function $z = e^{-(x^2+y^2)}$.

 FIGURE 14.19 Plotting a contour plot.

```
/* This program can be used to draw a control plot of an arbitrary
   function z = f(x, y) using class CartesianSystem.

   Output: Prompts for input
   Input:  Values for the endpoints of the x and y axes
   Output: The graphs of f(x) and g(x)

-------------------------------------------------------------------*/

#include <iostream.h>
#include <math.h>

#include "CartSys.h"              // declaration of CartesianSystem

double f(double x, double y)      // f(x,y)
{
    return exp( -(x*x + y*y) );
}

int main(void)
{
    cout << "\nThis program does a density plot of a function..."
         << "\n\t(currently z = e^(-x^2 + y^2).)\n";

    double                        // axes endpoints
        xMin, xMax,
        yMin, yMax,
        zMin, zMax;
    char
        ReturnChar;               // the newline

    do                            // get x-axis endpoints
    {
        cout << "\nPlease enter the minimum and maximum x values: ";
        cin >> xMin >> xMax;
    }
    while (xMin >= xMax);

    do                            // get y-axis endpoints
    {
        cout << "\nPlease enter the minimum and maximum y values: ";
        cin >> yMin >> yMax;
    }

    while (yMin >= yMax);

    do                            // get z-axis endpoints
    {
```

FIGURE 14.19   Plotting a contour plot. (cont.)

```
        cout << "\nPlease enter the minimum and maximum z values: ";
        cin >> zMin >> zMax;
    }
    while (zMin >= zMax);
    cin.get(ReturnChar);              // clean out the newline

    CartesianSystem                   // construct the cartesian system
        CoordinateSys(xMin, xMax, yMin, yMax, zMin, zMax);

    CoordinateSys.DensityPlot(f); // plot the function

    return 0;
}
```

Sample run:

```
This program does a density plot of a function...
    (currently z = e^(-x^2 + y^2).)

Please enter the minimum and maximum x values: -2 2

Please enter the minimum and maximum y values: -2 2

Please enter the minimum and maximum z values: 0 1
```

The sample run shown produced the following output for the function $f(x, y) = e^{-(x^2+y^2)}$:

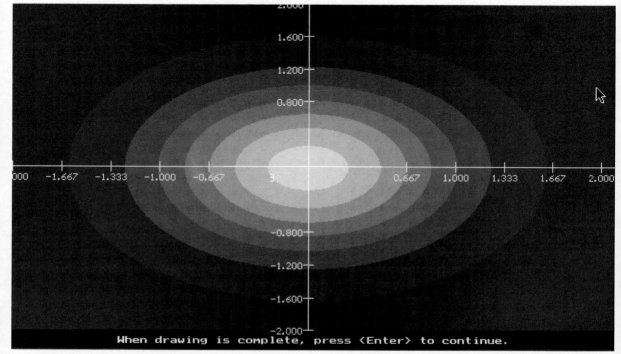

The ideas in these examples can be modified to display an image that is represented in digitized form and to enhance this image. This digitized representation might be a table of light intensities transmitted from a remote sensor, such as a television camera in a satellite. This problem of visual image processing and enhancement is described in the exercises.

Exercises

1. Add a member function to class **CartesianSystem** (Appendix G) to plot graphs of parametric equations of the form

$$x = x(t), \qquad y = y(t), \qquad a \leq t \leq b$$

2. A **scatterplot** of a set of data pairs (x, y) of real numbers is obtained simply by plotting these points. Add a member function to class **Cartesian System** (Appendix G) to produce a scatter plot of a set of data pairs read from a file. Execute your program using **LeastSquaresFile** (see Appendix D).

3. At the end of this section, we noted that the ideas there can be modified to carry out *visual image processing* and *enhancement.* Make a file that represents light intensities of an image in digitized form, say, with intensities from 0 to 9. Write a program that reads these intensities from the file and then reconstructs and displays them using a different color for each intensity. This image might then be enhanced to sharpen the contrast. For example, ''gray'' areas might be removed by replacing all intensities in the range 0 through some value by 0 (light) and intensities greater than this value by 9 (dark). Design your program to accept a threshold value that distinguishes light from dark and then enhances the image in the manner described.

4. An alternative method for enhancing an image (see Exercise 3) is to accept three successive images of the same object and, if two or more of the intensities agree, to use that value; otherwise, the average of the three values is used. Modify the program of Exercise 3 to use this enhancement technique.

*14.6 Subscripting Operation for Multidimensional Arrays

In constructing the class **Table** in Section 14.2, we decided against overloading the subscript operator for accessing the elements of the table because that would have complicated the design of the class. Instead, we included member functions **GetElem()** and **SetElem()** so that a call of the form

```
Tab.GetElem(row, col)
```

could be used to retrieve the element at row *row* and column *col* of a `Table` object `Tab`.

As we noted there, we could not simply overload the subscript operator to permit a call of the form

```
Tab[row, col]
```

because doing so would require that `operator[]` be redefined as a *ternary* (three-operand) operator, taking `Tab`, *row*, and *col* as its arguments. That is, the subscript operator is normally a *binary* operator, and this approach would overload the subscript operator with a definition with different *arity* (number of operands). As we noted in Section 14.2, C++ does not permit an overloaded operator definition to change the arity of an operator.

Instead, we can construct a definition for the subscript operator so that the element at row *row* and column *col* of a `Table` object `Tab` can be accessed using the usual two-dimensional array notation:

```
Tab[row][col]
```

This requires, however, that the `Table` class be redesigned. To see why, consider the expression

```
Tab[row][col]
```

In such an expression, the binary operator `[]` is being applied *twice:* first with the operands `Tab` and *row,*

```
Tab[row]
```

and then with the value returned by the first operator as one operand and *col* as the other:

```
ReturnValue[col]
```

One way of understanding this is to note that `operator[]` is left associative, so that the expression `Tab[row][col]` is evaluated as

```
(Tab[row])[col]
```

where the `Tab[row]` part of the expression returns **the entire row** whose index is *row*. The `[col]` part then simply accesses the element of that row whose index is *col*.

This behavior complicates the definition of the subscript operator for a class containing a multidimensional array, because two separate overloaded definitions are needed:

1. Given a `Table` object as its first argument and an index `i` as its second argument, `operator[]` should return the `i`th row of that `Table`;
2. Given a `Row` object as its first argument and an index `j` as its second argument, `operator[]` should return the `j`th element in that `Row`.

These observations provide the insight needed to redesign the `Table` class. The member `Grid` must be restructured as an array of `Row` objects, where a `Row` is a distinct class, separate from class `Table`. Figure 14.20 shows this alternative structure.

FIGURE 14.20 Redesigning class `Table`.

```
/* This file contains the declaration of class Table.

 ...

 ----------------------------------------------------------------*/

// ... preprocessor directives omitted ...


typedef double TableElement;

   class Row
   {
   public:
      enum {MaxLength = 20};              // maximum length of a Row

   protected:
      TableElement                       // declare one-dim array
         Array[MaxLength];               //    of TableElements

   public:
      TableElement& operator[] (unsigned j) // overload [] so that
         {return Array [j];}             //    (Row) [j]accesses
                                         //    element j of Row

      const TableElement& operator[] (unsigned j) const
         {return Array [j];}             //    for const objects
   };

   class Table
   {
   public:
     enum {MaxRows = 20,
           MaxCols = Row::MaxLength};    // define Table::MaxCols
                                         //    using length bound
                                         //    from Row
```

FIGURE 14.20 Redesigning class **Table**. (cont.)

```
protected:
  Row                             // restructure Grid as a
  Grid[MaxRows];                  //   one-dim array of Rows

  unsigned
    Rows_,
    Columns_;

public:
  Table(                          // the class constructor
        unsigned NumRows = 0,     //   the number of rows
        unsigned NumCols = 0,     //   the number of columns
        TableElement InitValue = 0);  //   initialization value

  Row& operator[] (unsigned i)    // overload [] so that T[i]
    {return Grid[i];}             // accesses Row i of Grid

  const Row& operator[] (unsigned i) const
    {return Grid[i];}             // for const objects

  // ... remaining members of Table omitted ...
};
```

No changes are required to the other members of class **Table**, and because each of the subscript operators is defined as an *inline* function, all of the changes needed to restructure class **Table** are contained in this file.

The resulting **Table** class behaves exactly like the earlier version, except that an expression like

```
Tab[i][j]
```

can now be used to access the element in row **i** and column **j** of the table stored within a **Table** object **Tab**. The expression **Tab[i][j]** is evaluated from left to right, so that the left subscript operator is applied first,

```
Tab[i]
```

using the **Table** definition of **operator[]**. This function returns **Tab.Grid[i]**, which is a **Row** object. That means that when the second subscript operator is applied to that return value,

```
Tab.Grid[i][j]
```

the **Row** definition of **operator[]** is used, which returns the element whose index is **j** in that **Row**.

As with the subscript operator for the class **List** in Chapter 12, two forms are given for each of the **Table** definition and the **Row** definition of **operator[]**, one for constant objects and one for nonconstant objects. (See Figure 12.16 and the discussion following the definition of **operator[]** for nonconstant arrays in Figure 12.8.) Note also that in all these definitions of **operator[]**, for example,

```
Row& operator[] (unsigned i) {return Grid[i];}
```

and

```
TableElement& operator[] (unsigned j) {return Array[j];}
```

the return type of each function should be a *reference* to a **Row** or **TableElement**, rather than simply a **Row** or **TableElement**. This is important, because it causes the return value of the subscript operator to actually refer to **Grid[i]** and/or **Grid[i][j]**—if the return type were simply **Row** or **TableElement**, then a *copy* of **Grid[i]** or **Grid[i][j]** would be returned instead. The difference is significant when these operators appear on the left-hand side of an assignment:

```
Tab[i][j] = 11;
```

In order for this assignment to alter the element in the **i**th row and the **j**th column of **Tab**, the subscript operators must return the references of the **i**th row and the **j**th element in that row, respectively. If either of those operators returns a copy of their value, then the assignment will change that copy, rather than the actual element.

Programming Pointers

Many of the programming pointers given for one-dimensional arrays at the end of Chapter 12 also apply to multidimensional arrays, and the reader should refer to those for an expanded discussion.

Program Design

1. *Like one-dimensional arrays, multidimensional array objects should be stored in a class, so that*

   - *The number of elements in each dimension and*
   - *The operations on the object*

   can be encapsulated within a single package. This makes it easier to reuse that object and its operations.

2. *Use of a multidimensional array is appropriate when a table of data values, a list of tables, and so on, must be stored in main memory for processing.* Using a multidimensional array when it is not necessary, however, can tie up a large block of memory locations. The amount of memory required to store a multidimensional array may be quite large, even though each index is restricted to a small range of values. For example, the three-dimensional array `ThreeD` declared by

```
typedef int
    ThreeDimArray[20][20][20];

ThreeDimArray
    ThreeD;
```

requires $20 \times 20 \times 20 = 8000$ memory locations.

3. *Design classes as generally as possible, so that they can be used as base classes from which more specialized classes can be derived.* This can save much time and effort, because the members of the base class are **inherited** by the derived class and thus need not be recoded. The keys to designing a good base class are as follows:

1. Try to anticipate what special-purpose instances of a class may be needed later.
2. Identify the *attributes* these special-purpose instances have *in common*.

These common attributes indicate what should appear in the *base* class; attributes that are not common to all instances are specialized and so should appear in *derived* classes.

4. *If a function must receive a class object as an argument, then the parameter to hold that object should be declared as a reference parameter.* It is especially important that class objects be passed as constant reference parameters rather than value parameters, since copying such class objects as value parameters can greatly slow the execution of a function.

Potential Problems

1. *Arrays cannot be input/output simply by including the array name in an input/output list.* This is one significant reason for storing arrays in classes, since this allows the I/O operators to be overloaded with definitions to input/output the array.

2. *Array indices are not (by default) checked for validity.* Any array-manipulating functions that accept indices as arguments should check their validity to avoid **out-of-range** errors. Such errors occur most often when a variable being used as an index takes on values outside the valid range of index values.

3. *Assignment of one array to another is not permitted.* This is another significant reason for storing arrays in classes, since the assignment operator can be overloaded to permit the assignment of class objects containing array members.

4. *Each element in an array has the same type.* Whereas the class and struct can be defined to store related values of differing types, all the values stored in an array must have the same type.

5. *When processing the elements of a multidimensional array using nested loops, the loops must be arranged so that the indices vary in the appropriate order.* To illustrate, suppose that the two-dimensional array **Table** is declared by

```
typedef int
    Array3x4[3][4];

Array3x4
    Table;
```

and the following data values are to be read into the array:

```
11 22 27 35 39 40 48 51 57 66 67 92
```

If these values are to be read and assigned in a rowwise manner so that the value is the matrix

```
11 22 27 35
39 40 48 51
57 66 67 92
```

then the following nested for loops are appropriate:

```
for (int row = 0; row < 3; row++)
    for (int col = 0; col < 4; col++)
        cin >> Table[row][col];
```

If the order of these loops is reversed,

```
for (int col = 0; col < 4; col++)
    for (int row = 0; row < 3; row++)
        cin >> Table[row][col];
```

then **Table** will be loaded column by column instead of row by row,

```
11 35 48 66
22 39 51 67
27 40 57 92
```

and operations applied to **Table** will generate incorrect results.

6. *When overloading the subscript operator for a multidimensional array, a separate class must be declared for each dimension, containing its own definition of the subscript operator.* To illustrate, suppose that we wish to build a class

named **RubixCube** containing a three-dimensional array member, and we wish to overload the subscript operator so that for a **RubixCube** object **RCube**, the expression

    RCube[i][j][k]

can be used to access a particular element of **RCube**. Then class **RubixCube** might be implemented by defining

- An enumeration named **Color**, whose values are the six colors of a **RubixCube**;
- A class named **Row** containing a one-dimensional array of **Color** objects;
- A class named **Side** containing a one-dimensional array of **Row** objects;
- A class named **RubixCube** as a one-dimensional array of **Side** objects.

The subscript operators are then overloaded in each class as follows:

- In class **RubixCube**, [i] returns the **Side** element whose index is i.
- In class **Side**, [j] returns the **Row** element whose index is j.
- In class **Row**, [k] returns the **Color** element whose index is k.

Given these definitions, the expression

    RCube[i][j][k]

will be evaluated as

    (((RCube[i]) [j]) [k])

More precisely, applying [i] to **RCube** returns a **Side** value, to which [j] is applied returning a **Row** value, to which [k] is applied returning a **Color** value.

Programming Projects

1. Write a program to calculate and display the first ten rows of Pascal's triangle. The first part of the triangle has the form

```
            1
          1   1
        1   2   1
      1   3   3   1
    1   4   6   4   1
```

in which each row begins and ends with 1, and each of the other entries in a row is the sum of the two entries just above it. If this form for the output seems too challenging, you might display the triangle as

```
    1
    1  1
    1  2  1
    1  3  3  1
    1  4  6  4  1
```

2. A demographic study of the metropolitan area around Dogpatch divided it into three regions, urban, suburban, and exurban, and published the following table showing the annual migration from one region to another (the numbers represent percentages):

↱	Urban	Suburban	Exurban
Urban	1.1	0.3	0.7
Suburban	0.1	1.2	0.3
Exurban	0.2	0.6	1.3

For example, 0.3% of the urbanites (0.003 times the current population) move to the suburbs each year. The diagonal entries represent internal growth rates. Using a two-dimensional array with an enumerated type for the indices to store this table, write a program to determine the population of each region after 10, 20, 30, 40, and 50 years. Assume that the current populations of the urban, suburban, and exurban regions are 2.1, 1.4, and 0.9 million, respectively.

3. The famous mathematician G. H. Hardy once mentioned to the brilliant young Indian mathematician Ramanujan that he had just ridden in a taxi whose number he considered to be very dull. Ramanujan promptly replied that on the contrary, the number was very interesting because it was the smallest positive integer that could be written as the sum of two cubes (that is, written in the form $x^3 + y^3$, with x and y integers) in two different ways. Write a program to find the number of Hardy's taxi.

4. The game of *Life,* invented by the mathematician John H. Conway, is intended to model life in a society of organisms. Consider a rectangular array of cells, each of which may contain an organism. If the array is assumed to extend indefinitely in both directions, each cell will have eight neighbors, the eight cells surrounding it. Births and deaths occur according to the following rules:

(a) An organism is born in an empty cell that has exactly three neighbors.
(b) An organism will die from isolation if it has fewer than two neighbors.
(c) An organism will die from overcrowding if it has more than three neighbors.

The following display shows the first five generations of a particular configuration of organisms:

Write a program to play the game of *Life* and investigate the patterns produced by various initial configurations. Some configurations die off rather quickly; others repeat after a certain number of generations; others change shape and size and may move across the array; and still others may produce "gliders" that detach themselves from the society and sail off into space.

5. The game of *Nim* is played by two players. There are usually three piles of objects, and on his or her turn, each player is allowed to take any number (at least one) of objects from one pile. The player taking the last object loses. Write a program that allows the user to play *Nim* against the computer. You might have the computer play a perfect game, or you might design the program to "teach" the computer. One way for the computer to "learn" is to assign a value to every possible move, based on experience gained from playing games. The value of each possible move is stored in some array; initially, each value is 0. The value of each move in a winning sequence of moves is increased by 1, and those in a losing sequence are decreased by 1. At each stage, the computer selects the best possible move (that having the highest value).

6. Write a program that allows the user to play tic-tac-toe against the computer.

IV

COMPUTING WITH ADVANCED OBJECTS

In Chapters 15 through 17, we examine the design and implementation of dynamic objects whose memory is allocated during program execution instead of during compilation. Chapter 15 begins this investigation by introducing indirection, pointer variables, and arrays whose storage is allocated at run time, and how these can be used to create a List class that uses memory efficiently. Chapter 16 introduces self-referencing nodes—structures that can be linked together to form a linked list. This idea is illustrated in the implementation of the LinkedList, Stack, and Queue classes. Finally, Chapter 17 shows how self-referencing nodes can be organized into a tree structure and presents a class BST (binary search tree)—a linked structure that can be searched efficiently using a binary search. Together, these chapters provide an introduction to the study of data structures and serve as the basis for more advanced courses.

POINTERS AND RUN-TIME ALLOCATION

[Pointers] are like jumps, leaping wildly from one part of a data structure to another. Their introduction into high-level languages has been a step backward from which we may never recover.
C. A. R. HOARE

He's making a list, and checking it twice, gonna' find out who's naughty or nice...
Santa Claus Is Coming To Town

... is the sort of person who keeps a list of all of his lists.
V. OREHCK III

CHAPTER CONTENTS

The arrays we have considered until now have one property that limits their usefulness in some problems: Their sizes must be declared in advance, before compilation, so that the compiler can determine how much storage to allocate for them. This fixed-size requirement can result in very inefficient memory usage. For example, reconsider the following sample run of the matrix multiplication program in Figure 14.16:

```
This program demonstrates matrix multiplication,
   by multiplying two matrices stored in separate files.

A file must list the # of rows and columns of its matrix.

Please enter the name of the first file: mat2x3.dat
The name of the second file? mat3x4.dat

- Matrix1 ------------------------------------------
      1.00       0.00       2.00
      3.00       0.00       4.00
- Matrix2 ------------------------------------------
      4.00       2.00       5.00       3.00
      6.00       4.00       1.00       8.00
      9.00       0.00       0.00       2.00
- Matrix3 ------------------------------------------
     22.00       2.00       5.00       7.00
     48.00       6.00      15.00      17.00
```

Matrix1 contains $2 \times 3 = 6$ values, **Matrix2** contains $3 \times 4 = 12$ values, and **Matrix3** contains $2 \times 4 = 8$ values. However, the values of the **MaxRows** and **MaxCols** in the **Matrix** class are 10, which means that each of **Matrix1**, **Matrix2**, and **Matrix3** contains space for $10 \times 10 = 100$ values. If each **Matrix** element uses one memory location, then the three matrices together use $100 \times 3 = 300$ memory locations, of which $6 + 12 + 8 = 26$ contain values. Put differently, $(300 - 26)/300 \times 100\% = 91.3\%$ of the memory allocated to these three **Matrix** objects is being wasted!

There is another problem with fixed-size arrays. Suppose that solving a problem requires multiplying two 12×12 matrices. We cannot use the class **Matrix** to do this without increasing the values of **MaxRows** and **MaxCols** from 10 to 12 and then recompiling the class. Of course, once we have done that, small matrices like **Matrix1**, **Matrix2**, and **Matrix3** will waste even more memory.

This kind of catch-22 problem is typical of fixed-size arrays, both one-dimensional and multidimensional. If a problem involves a small data set, memory is wasted; but if it involves a large data set, we must increase the size of the array to avoid overflowing the array. When we declare an array and specify its dimensions, we are instructing the compiler to allocate a fixed number of memory locations, each of which is the size of an array element. The real problem is that the dimensions must be specified using expressions whose values can be determined *at compile time*. Consequently, C++ does *not* allow us to write

```
unsigned
   N;                                    // declare a variable
```

```
cout << "\nHow many elements ? ";  // at run-time, let the user
cin >> N;                          //    input the size of the array

ListElement                        // and then allocate storage
    Array[N];                      //    for the array
```

which would tailor the size of the array to the number of values being stored.
    C++ does provide a solution for this problem, by providing a way to allocate an array's storage as a program executes. To understand this facility and how to use it we must first study the seemingly unrelated topics of *pointers and indirection.*

15.1   Introduction to Pointer Variables

As usual, we begin with a program that illustrates the topic at hand. The program in Figure 15.1 uses several new features, which we discuss in turn.

 FIGURE 15.1 Using indirection.

```
/* This program illustrates indirection and pointer variables.

   Output: Addresses of memory locations and the integers
           stored there
----------------------------------------------------------------*/
#include <iostream.h>

int main(void)
{
   int
      i = 11,
      j = 22,
      k = 33;

   int
      *iPtr = &i,
      *jPtr = &j,
      *kPtr = &k;

   cout << "\nAt address " << iPtr
        << ", the value " << *iPtr << " is stored.\n\n"

        << "\nAt address " << jPtr
        << ", the value " << *jPtr << " is stored.\n\n"

        << "\nAt address " << kPtr
        << ", the value " << *kPtr << " is stored.\n\n";

   return 0;
}
```

FIGURE 15.1   Using indirection. (cont.)

Sample run:

```
At address 0x0053AD78, the value 11 is stored.


At address 0x0053AD7C, the value 22 is stored.


At address 0x0053AD80, the value 33 is stored.
```

Declaring and Initializing Pointers

We begin with the declarations in this program. The declarations of integer variables i, j, and k are straightforward, so we proceed to the next set of declarations:

```
int
    *iPtr = &i,
    *jPtr = &j,
    *kPtr = &k;
```

There are two new items in this declaration statement:

1. An asterisk (*) before the name of an object in a declaration of the form

    ```
    Type
        *VariableName;
    ```

    declares that the name *VariableName* is an object that can store *the address of* an object of the specified *Type*. Such variables are often called **pointer variables,** or simply **pointers.** Thus, the declarations

    ```
    int
        *iPtr,
        *jPtr,
        *kPtr;
    ```

    declare that iPtr, jPtr, and kPtr are pointer variables, each of which can store the address of an integer variable. The type of each of these variables is int*.

2. The ampersand (&) can be used as a unary prefix operator that, when applied to an object,

    ```
    &VariableName
    ```

    returns the address with which *VariableName* is associated, and & thus is called the **address-of operator.** Thus, the expressions &i, &j, and &k return the addresses (or references[1]) associated with variables i, j, and k, respectively.

---

[1] The word *reference* is used as a synonym for *address.* In fact, this is the origin of the phrase *reference parameter*—the value of a reference parameter is actually the address of its argument, rather than a copy of the argument.

When we combine these two pieces of information, we see that the declarations

```
int
    *iPtr = &i,
    *jPtr = &j,
    *kPtr = &k;
```

declare **iPtr**, **jPtr**, and **kPtr** as pointer variables, each of which can store the address of an integer, and initialize **iPtr** to the address of variable **i**, **jPtr** to the address of variable **j**, and **kPtr** to the address of variable **k**. In the sample run in Figure 15.1, the address associated with variable **i** is the hexadecimal value **0x0053AD78**, the address of **j** is **0x0053AD7C**, and the address of **k** is **0x0053AD80**. We can thus visualize the layout of the program's data in memory as follows:[2]

0x0053AD78	11	i
0x0053AD7C	22	j
0x0053AD80	33	k
	0x0053AD78	iPtr
	0x0053AD7C	jPtr
	0x0053AD80	kPtr

It is important to remember that:

> In a declaration, *the asterisk operator* ∗ *must be attached to each identifier that is to serve as a pointer.*

Thus,

```
double *Ptr1, *Ptr2;
```

is a correct declaration of **Ptr1** and **Ptr2** as pointers to **double**s. Had we used

```
double *Ptr1, Ptr2;
```

or, equivalently,

```
double* Ptr1, Ptr2;
```

only **Ptr1** would be a pointer variable; **Ptr2** would be an ordinary **double** variable.

---

[2] Note that (using hexadecimal arithmetic)

```
0x00537C - 0x005378 = 4
```

and

```
0x005380 - 0x00537C = 4
```

which indicates that the size of an **int** on this particular machine is 4 bytes (32 bits).

Using `typedef` for Readability.   An alternative approach that does not require the repeated use of the asterisk is to use the **`typedef`** facility to rename a pointer type. For example, we could first declare

```
typedef double *DoublePointer;
```

and then use **DoublePointer** to declare **Ptr1** and **Ptr2**:

```
DoublePointer
    Ptr1,
    Ptr2;
```

Similarly, to declare the pointers in Figure 15.1, we could have written:

```
typedef int *IntPointer;
IntPointer
    iPtr = &i,
    jPtr = &j,
    kPtr = &k;
```

Such declarations tend to improve the readability of pointer declarations, especially when pointer parameters are being declared.

Pointer Operations

C++ supports a variety of operations on pointers, including initialization, dereferencing, I/O, assignment, comparison, and arithmetic. We examine each of these in turn.

Initialization.   We have already seen that a pointer variable can be initialized to an address,

```
int
    *iPtr = &i;
```

but this address must be the address of an object whose type is the same as the type specified in the pointer's declaration. For example, the declarations

```
double
    DoubleVar;

int
    *iPtr = &DoubleVar; // not valid
```

will generate a compilation error, because an integer pointer may only store addresses of integer objects.

One important exception is the address 0, often called the **NULL address,** which can be assigned to any pointer variable. Thus, the declarations

```
char
    *cPtr = 0;
```

```
int
    *iPtr = 0;
double
    *dPtr = 0;
```

are all valid initializations using the NULL address. Since it can be assigned to any pointer variable, the NULL address can be thought of as being *type-independent*.

The NULL address is often depicted graphically using the electrical engineering ground symbol

To illustrate, the pointer `iPtr` declared by

```
int
    *iPtr = 0;
```

can be pictured as:

iPtr

The NULL address is a special value that can be assigned to a pointer to indicate that it is not currently pointing to any memory location. This is not the same as the pointer variable being undefined. A pointer variable whose value is the NULL address has a value, so that a comparison can be used to indicate whether the pointer is pointing to anything:

```
if (iPtr == 0)
    // iPtr is not currently pointing to anything,
else
    // iPtr is pointing to a memory location
```

This technique is especially important when pointers are used to store the addresses of blocks of memory allocated at run-time, as we shall see in subsequent sections.

Indirection and Dereferencing.   Pointer variables not only store addresses but also provide access to the values stored at those addresses. An expression of the form

```
*PointerVariable
```

can be used to access the value at the address stored in `PointerVariable`. It can be thought of as going to the reference (address) given by `PointerVariable` and accessing the value stored at that address. To illustrate, in the sample run of Figure 15.1, the value of

```
iPtr
```

is **0x0053AD78**, and the value of the expression

    *iPtr

is 11, because 11 is the value stored at address **0x0053AD78**. We can visualize this situation as follows:

For the same reason, the values of the expressions ***jPtr** and ***kPtr** are 22 and 33, respectively, so that the output statement

```
cout << "\nAt address " << iPtr
     << ", we have the value " << *iPtr << "\n\n"

     << "\nAt address " << jPtr
     << ", we have the value " << *jPtr << "\n\n"

     << "\nAt address " << kPtr
     << ", we have the value " << * kPtr << "\n\n";
```

in Figure 15.1 displays both the value of the address in each pointer variable and the value stored at that address. The value of variable **i** can be accessed via the expression ***iPtr**, the value of **j** via ***jPtr**, and the value of **k** via ***kPtr**. The value of a variable **v** can thus be **accessed indirectly** by applying the ***** operator to a pointer variable **vPtr** whose value is the address of **v**. For this reason, the ***** operator is called the **indirection operator.** Since reference is another name for address, applying the indirection operator to a pointer variable to access the value at the address stored in that pointer variable is called **dereferencing** that pointer variable.

    The indirection operator can be used on either side of an assignment statement. If the statement

    i = *jPtr;

were added to Figure 15.1, then the value of **i** would be changed from 11 to 22 by dereferencing **jPtr** and assigning **i** the value 22 stored at address **0x0053AD7C**. The same effect can be achieved with the statement

    *iPtr = j;

which dereferences **iPtr**, yielding the address **0x0053AD78**, and copies the value of **j** (22) into the memory location with that address. Since this address is associated with the name **i**, the effect is to change the value of **i**.

    In most applications, pointers are not used to store addresses that are associated with names, as was done in the first program. We did this only to introduce the basics of indirection. Instead, pointers are used to store and retrieve values in memory locations with which no name has been associated. One example of this is the predefined name **this**, which is a member of every class. Recall that each of our overloaded definitions of **operator=** have ended with the statement

```
return *this;
```

It should now be clear that the name **this** is in fact a pointer member whose value is the address of the object containing it. By returning the expression *this, the function dereferences that pointer and thus returns the object to which it points (which is the object containing the **operator=** function).

In summary, the value of an expression

PointerVariable

is simply the reference (i.e., address) stored in ***PointerVariable***, whereas the expression

*PointerVariable

uses the reference stored in the pointer to access (indirectly) the value at that reference.

I/O.   In the program in Figure 15.1, we were able to determine the addresses of **i**, **j**, and **k**, by using an output statement to display the values of **iPtr**, **jPtr**, and **kPtr**,

```
cout << "\nAt address " << iPtr
     ...
     << "\nAt address " << jPtr
     ...
     << "\nAt address " << kPtr
     ...
```

because the output operation is defined for pointer variables. Another way to display the same information would be to write

```
cout << "\nAt address " << &i
     ...
     << "\nAt address " << &j
     ...
     << "\nAt address " << &k
     ...
```

Similarly, to find the particular addresses associated with **iPtr**, **jPtr**, and **kPtr**, we could write

```
cout << "\n iPtr is stored at address " << &iPtr
     << ",\n jPtr is stored at address " << &jPtr
     << ", and\n kPtr is stored at address " << &kPtr
     << "\n\n";
```

The address-of operator allows us to determine exactly where in memory an object is stored, whereas pointer variables allow us to store this information.

Just as the value of a pointer can be output using ≪, an address can be input and stored in a pointer variable using ≫. However, this is rarely done, because the user is usually not interested in the address of the word storing a value, only in the value itself. In fact, it is dangerous to input address values because an attempt to access a memory address outside of the space allocated to an executing program may result in a fatal error.

Assignment.   Although the program in Figure 15.1 does not illustrate it, pointer variables can be assigned the values of pointer variables that point to the same type. Also, since the NULL address is type-independent, it can be assigned to any pointer variable. For example, if we were to add the statement

```
jPtr = iPtr;
```

to the program, then the value of **iPtr** would be copied to **jPtr** so that both have the same memory address as their value; that is, both point to the same memory location, as the following diagram illustrates.

Before the assignment:

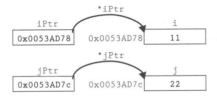

After the assignment **jPtr = iPtr;**

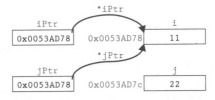

After the assignment statement is executed, **jPtr** no longer points to **j**, but now points to **i**. Thus, applying the indirection operator to **jPtr** will access the memory location associated with **i**. For example, the output statement

```
cout ≪ *jPtr
```

will display the value 11 instead of 22, and the statement

```
*jPtr = 44;
```

will change the value at address **0x0053AD78** (i.e., the value of **i**) from 11 to 44:

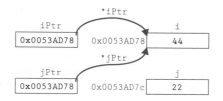

We have included this example to show that pointers are a very powerful (and dangerous) feature of programming languages. Statements that change the value of a variable in a statement in which that variable is not named are generally considered to be poor programming practice, because they make programs more difficult to debug by hiding such changes to the variable. In the preceding example, the expressions *iPtr and *jPtr are alternative names for variable i and are sometimes called **aliases** for i. A function that changes a variable's value through an alias for that variable is said to exhibit **the aliasing problem.**

Comparison.   The relational operators can be used to compare two pointers that *point to the same type.* The most common operation is to use the equality or inequality operators to determine if two pointer variables both point to the same memory location. For example, the condition

    iPtr == jPtr

is valid and returns true if and only if the address in iPtr is the same as the address in jPtr. However, the type to which they point must be the same. Thus, if iPtr and jPtr are declared by

```
int
    *iPtr;
double
    *dPtr;
```

then the comparison

    iPtr == dPtr   // not valid

will result in a compilation error.
    Since the NULL address is type-independent, it can be compared with any pointer variable, so that the conditions

    iPtr != 0

and

    dPtr == 0

are both valid boolean expressions.

Pointer Arithmetic. Before examining the arithmetic operations on pointers, it is helpful to introduce a new C++ operator that we have not used until now. The **sizeof operator** is an operator that, applied to a type T or an object O, returns

- The number of bytes of storage the compiler allocates for an object of type T, or
- The number of bytes of storage the compiler has allocated for object O.

The **sizeof** operator can be applied to either objects or types:

```
sizeof(type-specifier)
```

```
sizeof expression
```

Note that in the first case, the type specifier is enclosed within parentheses, but no parentheses are used to enclose the expression in the second form.

To illustrate, the expression

```
sizeof(char)
```

evaluates to 1, since objects of type **char** are allocated one byte. Similarly, if **LongVar** is a long variable declared by

```
long
    LongVar;
```

and **long** objects are allocated four bytes, the expression

```
sizeof LongVar
```

will evaluate to 4. Finally, since **int** objects are usually allocated one word of memory, the expression

```
sizeof(int)
```

will (usually) return the word size of the machine (in bytes).

Knowing about the **sizeof** operator makes it a bit easier to understand pointer arithmetic. The *increment* operation is perhaps the most commonly used arithmetic operation on pointer variables. Given a pointer variable **Ptr** declared by

```
Type
    *Ptr;
```

the increment statement

```
Ptr++;
```

adds the value **sizeof(Type)** to the address in **Ptr**. Similarly, the decrement statement

```
Ptr--;
```

subtracts the value `sizeof(Type)` from the address in `Ptr`. If *IntExpr* is an integer expression, a statement of the form

```
Ptr += IntExpr;
```

adds the value *IntExp* `* sizeof(Type)` to `Ptr`, and

```
Ptr -= IntExp;
```

subtracts the value *IntExp* `* sizeof(Type)` from `Ptr`.

To illustrate how these operations are used, suppose that `Ptr` is a pointer whose value is the address of the first element of an array of **double** elements:

```
double
   D[10],          // an array of 10 doubles
   *Ptr = &(D[0]); // a pointer to the first element of D
```

or equivalently,

```
double
   D[10],          // an array of 10 doubles
   *Ptr = D;       // a pointer to the first element of D
```

Now consider the following loop:

```
for (int i = 0; i < 10; i++)
{
   *Ptr = 0;
   Ptr++;
}
```

On the first pass through the loop, `Ptr` is dereferenced and the value 0 is assigned to the memory location at that address. `Ptr` is then incremented, which adds `sizeof(double)` to its value. Since array elements are allocated adjacent memory locations, this effectively makes `Ptr` point to the second element of the array:

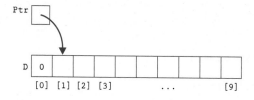

The next pass again dereferences `Ptr`, sets that memory location to zero, and increments `Ptr`:

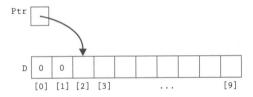

This continues with each subsequent iteration. On the final pass, the last element of the array is set to zero and `Ptr` is again incremented, so that it points to the first address past the end of the array:

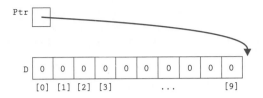

A pointer can thus be used to move through consecutive blocks of memory, accessing those blocks in whatever way a particular problem requires.

Pointers as Arguments and Parameters.   Pointers may also be passed as arguments to functions. The parameters corresponding to such arguments may be either value or reference parameters, but the type of value pointed to by a pointer argument must be the same as the type of value pointed to by its corresponding parameter. The return type of a function may also be a pointer.

Exercises

1. Using the `sizeof` operator, determine how many bytes your C++ compiler allocates for

(a) An `int`   (b) A `float`
(c) A `double`   (d) A `long double`
(e) The character string `"Hello!"`   (f) The character string `"Hi!"`

2. Using the `sizeof` operator, determine how many bytes your C++ compiler allocates for *a pointer* to each of the types listed in Exercise 1.

3. Using the address-of operator, find the starting addresses of each of the objects in the following declaration:

```
const int
    Size = 10;
char
    CharArray[Size];
int
    IntArray[Size];
```

```
double
   DoubleArray[Size];
char
   CharVar;
```

4. Use the **sizeof** operator to find the number of bytes your C++ compiler allocates for each object defined in Exercise 3.

5. Suppose that the starting address of the first object in a block is *b*. Using the results from Exercises 3 and 4, construct an expression that, using *b* and the **sizeof** operator, can be used to find the address of any subsequent object declared in that same block.

6. Using **typedef**, create an alias type **CharPointer** for the type **char***.

7. Given an array declaration like the following:

```
char
   Array[10];
```

   (a) Use the address-of operator to find the address of the first element of **Array**.
   (b) Display the value associated with the name **Array**.
   (c) What inference can you make from the results of (a) and (b)?

15.2   Run-Time Allocation: The new and delete Operations

A variable declaration of the form

```
Type
   VariableName;
```

instructs the compiler to

1. Allocate a block of memory large enough to store a value of the specified *Type*.
2. Associate the name *VariableName* with the address of that block.

As we have seen, the value of the expression

```
&VariableName
```

is the address of this block. The memory block associated with a variable name is allocated *when the program is compiled* and cannot be changed without editing and recompiling the program.

It is this **compile-time allocation** that is the root of the problem discussed at the beginning of this chapter. A declaration of the form

```
const int
   Length = 10;
double
   ArrayName[Length];
```

causes a block of memory large enough to hold ten **double** values to be allocated and associates the starting address of that block with the name *ArrayName*. The size of this block cannot be changed, except by editing the declaration and then recompiling the program. As we saw in the chapter introduction, such fixed-size arrays suffer from two problems:

- If the size of the array exceeds the number of values to be stored in it, then memory is wasted by the unused elements.
- If the size of the array is smaller than the number of values to be stored in it, then array overflow may occur.

Both of these problems would be solved if memory could be allocated to an object while the program executes (i.e., **run-time allocation**) instead of when it is compiled (i.e., compile-time allocation). At its simplest, such a mechanism would involve two operations:

1. A means of acquiring additional memory locations as they are needed
2. A means of releasing memory locations when they are no longer needed

C++ provides the predefined operations **new** and **delete** to perform these two operations of memory allocation and deallocation during program execution.

The new Operation

The **new** operation is used to request additional memory from the operating system during program execution. The general form of such a request is as follows.

The new Operation

Form

   new *Type*

Purpose
Issue a run-time request for a block of memory large enough to hold an object of the specified *Type*. If the request can be granted, **new** returns the address of the block of memory; otherwise, it returns the NULL address 0.

Since the **new** operation returns an address and addresses can be stored in pointer variables, this operation is almost always used in conjunction with a pointer. For example, when the statements

```
int
    *IntPtr;

IntPtr = new int;
```

are executed, the expression

```
new int
```

issues a request to the operating system for a memory block large enough to store an integer value (or put differently, for **sizeof(int)** bytes of memory). If the operating system is able to grant the request, **IntPtr** will be assigned the address of this memory block. Otherwise, if all available memory has been exhausted, it will be assigned the value 0. Because of this possibility, the value returned by **new** should always be tested before it is used:

```
if (IntPtr == 0)
{
    cerr << "\n*** No more memory!\n";
    exit (-1);
}
```

A more convenient way to test for such potentially fatal errors is to use the C++ **assert()** **mechanism.** The statement

```
assert(IntPtr != 0);
```

checks the condition **IntPtr != 0**, called an *assertion,* and permits the program to continue execution if and only if the assertion is true. If the assertion is false, execution is terminated and an appropriate error message is displayed. The header file **<assert.h>** must be inserted using the **#include** directive if **assert()** is to be used.

Once we have verified that **IntPtr** contains a nonzero value, the newly allocated memory location is an **anonymous variable,** meaning that it is an allocated memory location that has no name associated with it. For example, if **new** returns the address **0x020**, we can picture the situation as follows:

```
        IntPtr
     ┌─────────┐        ┌─────────────┐
     │  0x020  │  0x020 │             │
     └─────────┘        └─────────────┘
```

Since there is no name associated with this newly allocated memory, it *cannot be accessed directly,* the way other variables are accessed. However, its address is stored in **IntPtr**, so that this anonymous variable can be *accessed indirectly* by dereferencing **IntPtr**:

Statements such as the following can be used to operate on this anonymous variable:

```
cin >> *IntPtr;     // store an input value in the new integer

if (*IntPtr < 100) // apply relational operators to the new integer
    (*IntPtr)++;    // apply arithmetic operators to the new integer
else
    *IntPtr = 100;  // assign values to the new integer
```

In short, anything that can be done with an ''ordinary'' integer variable can be done with this anonymous integer variable by accessing it indirectly via `IntPtr`.

Allocating Arrays with new.   In practice, `new` is rarely used to allocate space for scalar values like integers. Instead, it is used to allocate space for arrays of values. To illustrate, consider an integer array object `Beta` declared as follows:

```
int
    Beta[10];
```

The value associated with the name `Beta` is the address of the first element of the array.[3] The type of object `Beta` is `int[10]`. Such a type can be used with `new` to allocate memory for arrays. For example, the statements

```
int
    *BetaPtr;

BetaPtr = new int[10];
```

allocate space for an array of ten integers. Before the latter statement is executed, `BetaPtr` is simply a pointer variable whose value is undefined. After it is executed (assuming that sufficient memory is available), `BetaPtr` contains the address of the first element of the *newly allocated* array. If that address is **0x032**, we might picture this as follows:

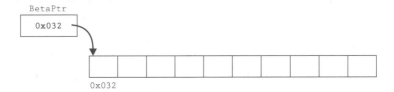

We just noted that the value of a compile-time allocated array is the address of the first element of the array. This means that

> *If the address of the first element of a run-time allocated array is stored in a pointer variable, then the elements of that array can be accessed via the pointer in exactly the same manner as the elements of compile-time allocated array are accessed via its name, using the subscript operator ([ ]).*

That is, the first element of the new array can be accessed using the notation `BetaPtr[0]`, the second element, using `BetaPtr[1]`, the third element, using

---

[3] This was one reason that the assignment operator cannot be used to copy a ''normal'' array—the statement

```
Alpha = Beta;
```

would attempt to copy the starting address of `Beta` into `Alpha`, as opposed to copying the elements of `Beta`.

BetaPtr [2], and so on:

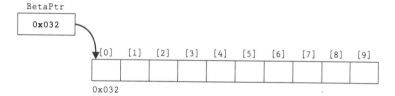

Note that this is consistent with our description of array-address mapping described in the third potential problem in the "Programming Pointers" section of Chapter 12. The value of the pointer variable **BetaPtr** is the **base address** of the array. For a given index **i**, the subscript operator

```
BetaPtr[i]
```

simply accesses the memory location **BetaPtr + i**.

The benefit of run-time allocation is that it is not necessary to know the size of the array at compile-time. For example, we can now write:

```
cout << "\nHow many entries in your list? ";   // find how big the
cin >> NumEntries;                             //    array should be

double                                         // allocate an array
   *DPtr = new double[NumEntries];             //    exactly that size

assert(DPtr != 0)                              // check for success

cout << "\nOk, enter your values now.\n";      // fill it with values

for (int i = 0; i < NumEntries; i++)
   cin >> DPtr[i];
   ...
```

Unlike arrays that are allocated memory at compile-time, arrays whose sizes are specified at run-time can be tailored to the exact size of the lists to be stored in them. The wasted memory problem is solved because the array will not be too large. The overflow problem is solved because the array will not be too small.

In summary, the **new** operator can be used to allocate anonymous variables at run time, including arrays, whose sizes can be tailored to the number of values to be processed. By storing the base address of an array in a pointer variable, most things that can be done with a compile-time allocated array can be done with the run-time allocated array using the pointer.[4]

---

[4] In fact, some programmers like to think of the name of a compile-time allocated array as a *constant pointer,* because like a pointer, the evaluation of such a name produces the array's base address, and like a constant, C++ does not allow that value to be altered.

The delete Operation

When execution of a program begins, the program has a "pool" of available unallocated memory locations, called the **free store** or **heap.** The effect of the **new** operation is to request the operating system to

1. Remove a block of memory from the free store; and
2. Allocate that block to the executing program.

The block can be accessed by the executing program if it stores the address of that block (the return value of **new**) in a pointer variable.

Since the size of the free store is limited, each execution of **new** causes the pool of available memory to shrink. If a call to **new** requests more memory than is available in the free store, so that the operating system is unable to fulfill the request, **new** returns the value zero.

Memory that is no longer needed can be returned to the free store by using the **delete operation.** Just as **new** is a request by the executing program for memory from the free store, the **delete** operation is a request to return memory to the free store. Such memory can then be reallocated to the program by a subsequent **new** operation. The **new** and **delete** operations are thus complementary:

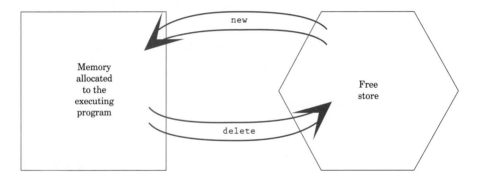

The general form of the **delete** operation is as follows:

The delete Operation

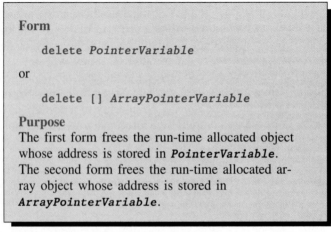

Form

    delete *PointerVariable*

or

    delete [] *ArrayPointerVariable*

Purpose
The first form frees the run-time allocated object whose address is stored in ***PointerVariable***. The second form frees the run-time allocated array object whose address is stored in ***ArrayPointerVariable***.

For example, if `IntPtr` has been allocated a word of memory from the free store with

```
int
    *IntPtr = new int;
```

then the statement

```
delete IntPtr;
```

releases the memory location pointed to `IntPtr`, making it available for allocation at a later time. Following the operation, the value of `IntPtr` is undefined, and so the result of any attempt to dereference it,

```
*IntPtr
```

is unpredictable, possibly producing a run-time error. To avoid such problems, it is good programming practice always to set the value of such pointers to zero,

```
delete IntPtr;
IntPtr = 0;
```

so that a statement such as

```
if (IntPtr != 0)
    // ... ok - IntPtr can be safely dereferenced
else
    // ... not ok - IntPtr's memory has been deallocated
```

can be used to guard access to the memory pointed to by `IntPtr`.

Similarly, if `DPtr` is a pointer to the first element of an array allocated at run-time,

```
        ⋮

cin >> N;

double
    *DPtr = double[N];
```

then that array's memory can be returned to the free store with the statements

```
delete [] DPtr;
DPtr = 0;
```

Exercises

1. Write C++ statements to

   (a) Allocate an anonymous **char** variable, storing its address in a **char** pointer variable named **CharPtr**.

(b) Input a character value and store it in the anonymous variable from (a).

(c) Display the value of the anonymous variable from (a).

(d) Convert the case of the value of the anonymous variable from (a) using character-processing functions such as `isupper()` and `tolower()` from `<ctype.h>`.

2. Write C++ statements that

(a) Allow the user to enter *N*, the number of values to be processed.

(b) Allocate an anonymous array of *N* `double` values, storing its address in a `double` pointer variable `DoublePtr`.

(c) Fill the anonymous array with *N* input values, entered from the keyboard.

(d) Compute and display the average of the values in the anonymous array.

(e) Deallocate the storage of the anonymous array.

3. Find the base address of the anonymous array allocated in Exercise 2 and draw a memory map showing the addresses of its first few elements.

4. Class `Strings`, described in Chapter 9, uses the `new` and `delete` operators extensively to allocate and deallocate storage at run-time.

(a) What data members are needed by class `Strings` and why?

(b) What `Strings` operations require the use of the `new` operator and why?

(c) What `Strings` operations require the use of the `delete` operator and why?

(d) Give an algorithm that describes the behavior of the `Strings` class constructor.

15.3 A Run-Time Allocated List Class

In Chapter 12, we constructed a class `List` that contained a member named `Array`, which was a fixed-size array. We then defined various members and overloaded various operators so that data sets could be stored and manipulated within a `List` object. The deficiency of this class is that its member `Array` suffers from the drawbacks of any array for which memory is allocated at compile time: Storage is wasted if the data set to be stored in `Array` is smaller than the size of `Array`; and overflow occurs if the data set to be stored in `Array` is larger than the size of `Array`. These deficiencies can be avoided by replacing the compile-time allocated `Array` member with a pointer named `Array` that stores the address of an array to be allocated at run-time. In this section, we rebuild class `List` using this approach. Since much of the code in this rebuilt class `List` is identical to that of the original class `List`, we examine only those declarations and functions that are significantly different in the new version. Readers may wish to review Sections 12.2 and 12.3 to reacquaint themselves with the original class.

The Declaration of Class List

Since the `Array` member in class `List` was an array whose elements are of type `ListElement`, we begin by replacing `Array` with a member that is a pointer to a `ListElement`. To minimize the number of changes to the rest of the class, we use the same name, **Array**, for this pointer. Figure 15.2 shows a portion of our new **List** class with this change.

FIGURE 15.2 Class **List** (with run-time allocation).

```
/* This file contains the declaration of class List,
   using run-time allocation.
   ...
------------------------------------------------------------------*/

//...

typedef double ListElement;              // array element type

class List
{
protected:
   ListElement                           // Array is a pointer
       *Array;                           //   to a ListElement

   unsigned
     Length_;                            // array value counter

   // ...

};
```

The only other change we make to this part of the class is to remove the declaration of the enumerator **MaxLength**. Since the storage for our improved **List** class will be allocated at run-time instead of compile-time, it is no longer needed.

Once we have redesigned the data members of class **List**, all that remains is to modify or add those operations that involve the construction or destruction of **List** objects. These include the following:

- The class constructor, because it builds a **List** object
- The copy constructor, because it builds a copy of a **List** object
- The assignment operator, because it destroys a **List** object, replacing that object with a copy of another **List** object
- Any input operations, which destroy a **List** object and replace that object with a copy of another **List** object

In addition to these, we must provide a special new function called a *destructor* that will reclaim the memory allocated at run time whenever this is appropriate.

The Class Constructor

The class constructor is called whenever a **List** object is declared, and so it must do everything necessary to initialize the members of a **List** object. To take advantage of run-time allocation, we design the constructor so that the declaration

```
List
   L;
```

will construct an empty **List** (i.e., one in which member **Array** is set to the NULL address and member **Length_** is zero), and

```
        ⋮

cin >> N;
```

```
List
   L(N);
```

will construct a **List** that can store an arbitrary number **N** values of type **ListElement**. Figure 15.3 gives a definition of this constructor.

FIGURE 15.3   **List** class constructor.

```
/* This function constructs a List object.

   Precondition:  A List object has been declared.
   Receive:       NumValues, the size of the list (default 0)
   Postcondition: In the List object containing this function,
                  Length_ is equal to NumValues, and
                  the Array member is either a NULL pointer,
                  or points to an array of NumValues elements.
------------------------------------------------------------------------*/

List::List(unsigned NumValues)
{
   Length_ = NumValues;          // set List length indicator

   if (Length_ == 0)             // if default length
      Array = 0;                 //    set ptr to NULL address
   else                          // otherwise, allocate anonymous array
   {                             //    of the specified length
      Array = new ListElement [NumValues];
      assert(Array != 0);
   }
}
```

Note that since the constructor uses the **assert()** mechanism (but none of the declarations in **List.h** do), the **#include** directive should be used to insert the file **<assert.h>** in the implementation file of class **List**.

We can then declare this constructor in class **List** (i.e., in **List.h**) as

```
List(unsigned NumValues = 0);
```

to provide a default value for parameter **NumValues**. Then, when execution reaches a declaration of the form

```
List
    L;
```

the parameter **NumValues** gets its default value 0, so that the statement

```
Array = 0
```

will be executed, setting the **Array** member to the NULL address and producing the following **List**:

By contrast, when execution reaches the declaration

```
List
    L(2048);
```

then parameter **NumValues** has the value 2048, and the statement

```
Array = new ListElement [NumValues];
```

is executed. This statement

1. Allocates an array capable of holding **NumValues** values of type **ListElement**; and
2. Sets the **Array** member to point to the first element of that array.

Execution of the constructor function thus builds **L** as a **List** whose **Array** member points to a run-time allocated array capable of holding 2048 elements:

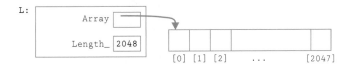

The key observation is that these actions are taken *when execution reaches the declaration* (i.e., at run time, not at compile time).

The Copy Constructor

There are certain situations where a *copy* of a class object is needed, such as:

- When a class object is passed to a function via a value parameter;
- When a function returns a class object as its return value; and
- When the result of a subexpression is a class object that must be held temporarily, until the result of another subexpression has been computed.

In each of these situations, the compiler must construct a copy of the class object. To do so, it uses a special constructor function called the **copy constructor.**

Whenever a programmer defines a class, the C++ compiler provides a *default copy constructor* that essentially performs a bitwise copy of each of the data members of the class. In each of the classes we have written thus far, copying the bits of each data member has been sufficient to make a distinct copy of a class object.

However, when a class contains a data member that is a pointer to run-time allocated memory, then copying the bits of that data member copies the pointer but does not copy the allocated memory.

To illustrate, suppose that a `List` object named `L` appears as follows:

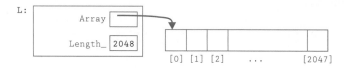

Then if the default copy constructor makes a copy of `L`, it simply copies the bits of `L`, producing the following situation:

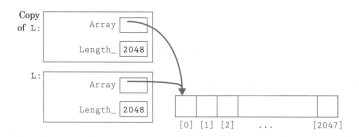

The problem of course is that the copy of `L` is not a distinct copy—what is needed is for copying to occur as follows:

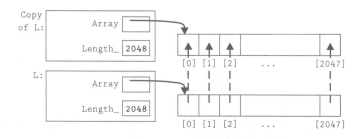

For class `List`, this problem can be specified as follows:

Precondition: The compiler needs a copy of a `List` object.
Receive: *Original*, the `List` object being copied.
Postcondition: A distinct copy of the members of *Original* has been made.

To solve this problem, we must provide our own `List` copy constructor, whose declaration is as follows:

```
List(const List& Original);
```

When the compiler needs a copy of a `List` object L, it will call this constructor (instead of the default copy constructor) and pass it the object to be copied:

```
List(L);
```

Parameter `Original` is thus a constant reference to L, the object being copied.

If `Original` is an empty list, then the `Array` and `Length_` members should be given the NULL address and 0, respectively, as in the class constructor. However, if `Original` is not an empty `List`, then two steps must be taken:

1. An array must be allocated to hold a copy of the array in `Original`; and
2. The values in the array of `Original` must be copied into that array.

Figure 15.4 presents such a constructor function:

 FIGURE 15.4 Class **List** copy constructor.

```
/* This function is the copy constructor for class List.

   Precondition:    The compiler needs a copy of a List.
   Receive:         Original, the List object to be copied
   Postcondition:   The List containing this function is a complete
                    copy of the List named Original.
------------------------------------------------------------------*/

List::List(const List& Original)
{
   Length_ = Original.Length_;          // copy the scalar member
                                        // copy the array member
   if (Length_ > 0)                     // if Original has an array:
   {                                    //    allocate a new array
      Array = new ListElement [Length_];
      assert(Array != 0);               //    verify success
                                        //    copy the array member
      for (int i = 0; i < Length_; i++)
         Array[i] = Original.Array[i];
   }
   else                                 // else
      Array = 0;                        //    set Array to
}                                       //       null address
```

This function makes a copy of `Original` by copying its `Length_` member and then using the statement

```
Array = new ListElement[Length_];
```

to allocate a new array. It then uses a for loop to copy the values from the array of `Original` into the newly allocated array:

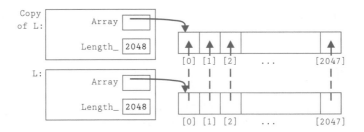

Note that because **Array** is a pointer whose value is the address of the first element of the run-time allocated array, the subscript operator can be used,

```
Array[i]
```

to access the element of the run-time allocated array whose subscript is **i**, just as if **Array** were a compile-time allocated array.

The general form of a copy constructor for an arbitrary class is:

Class Copy Constructor Declaration

Form:

   ClassName(const *ClassName*& *Original*);

where:
   ClassName is the name of the class containing this function; and
   Original is a reference to the object being copied.

Purpose:
This function is used by the compiler to construct a copy of the argument corresponding to *Original*. The compiler calls this function whenever such a copy is needed, such as:

   ■ When an object of type *ClassName* is passed as a value parameter;
   ■ When the return value of a function is a value of type *ClassName*; or
   ■ When the evaluation of an expression produces an intermediate (or temporary) value of type *ClassName*.

Note that the parameter of a copy constructor *must* be a reference parameter (and should be a **const** reference parameter, as well) because if it is defined as a value parameter, then a call to the function will

1. Pass a value parameter, which makes a copy of its argument.
2. But to copy that argument, the copy constructor is called again (with that argument as a value parameter).
3. Passing a value parameter, makes a copy of its argument.
4. But to copy that argument, the copy constructor is called again (with that argument as a value parameter).

resulting in an infinite recursion! Defining *Original* as a reference parameter avoids this infinite recursion because the reference (address) of the argument is passed, which involves no copying.

The Class Destructor

With the ability to build objects whose memory is allocated at run-time comes the responsibility of making certain that the memory allocated to those objects is properly reclaimed. Just as a constructor is used to build such objects, a function called a **destructor** is used to "tear down" such objects. Destructor functions are the complement of constructor functions.

Destructor functions are needed for classes that use pointers and memory allocated at run-time. To see why, suppose that a **List** is defined in a function **F()**:

```
void F(void)
{
        .
        .
        .
    cin >> N;

    List
        L(N);
        .
        .
        .
}
```

When execution reaches the declaration of **L**, the constructor will build **L** as a **List** whose **Array** member is a pointer to a run-time allocated array with **N** elements:

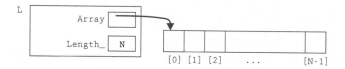

The difficulty occurs when function **F()** terminates and **L** must be destroyed. The immediate storage used to define **L** is automatically reclaimed, but the array itself is not, because it was allocated at run-time:

It is clearly undesirable to "maroon" blocks of memory in this way, because

1. They are no longer pointed to by a pointer and thus cannot be accessed by the program.

2. They are not in the free store, so they cannot be allocated by subsequent calls to **new**.

If we wish to avoid depleting the free store prematurely, a run-time allocated array should be returned to the free store when the object pointing to it is destroyed. The destructor function can be used for this, since it allows us to specify the actions that should be taken when the lifetime of a **List** object like **L** ends.

The name of a destructor function is always the name of the class in which it is declared, preceded by the tilde (~) symbol:

The Class Destructor

Form:

~*ClassName*( )

Purpose:
The compiler calls this function to destroy objects of type *ClassName* whenever such objects should no longer exist:

- At the end of the main function, for *ClassName* objects that are defined within the main function, as static, or globally
- At the end of each block in which a non-static *ClassName* object is defined
- At the end of each function containing a *ClassName* parameter
- When a *ClassName* object allocated at run-time is destroyed using **delete**
- When an object with a *ClassName* data member is destroyed
- When an object *derived from* type *ClassName* is destroyed (see Section 14.3)
- When a *ClassName* compiler-generated copy (made by the copy constructor) is no longer needed

Note that like a constructor, a destructor has no return type. However, unlike a constructor, a destructor cannot have parameters and thus cannot be overloaded.

The destructor for class **List** needs to use the **delete** operation to reclaim the storage allocated to the **List** object in which it is declared. Figure 15.5 presents such a function.

FIGURE 15.5 Class **List** destructor.

```
/* This function reclaims the memory for a List object.

   Precondition:   The List containing this function should no
                   longer exist.
   Postcondition: The run-time allocated memory of the List
                   containing this function has been deallocated.
   -----------------------------------------------------------------*/

List:: ~ List(void)
{
   delete [] Array;    // reclaim the run-time allocated storage

   Array = 0;          // set data members to indicate List is
   Length_ = 0;        //   empty (in case we call it explicitly).
}
```

Alternatively, this function is simple enough that it could be defined within class **List**:

```
~List(void)
{
   delete [] Array;
   Array = 0;
   Length_ = 0;
}
```

Although it is not strictly necessary, we reset the data members of the **List** to the values that indicate an empty list, so that a function that needs to reinitialize a **List** object to be an empty list can do so by calling the destructor explicitly.

The Assignment Operator

From our experience with the assignment operator, we know that for two integer objects **x** and **y**, the assignment

```
x = y;
```

destroys the previous contents of **x** and replaces those contents with a copy of **y**. In exactly the same manner, an assignment involving two **List** objects L1 and L2, such as

```
L1 = L2;
```

must destroy the previous contents of **L1**, and replace them with a copy of **L2**. If **L1** is a **List** with **M** elements and **L2** is a **List** with **N** elements,

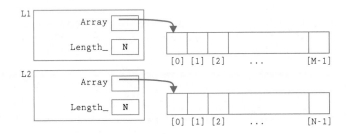

then the following actions must be taken:

1. Set **L1**'s member **Length_** to that of **L2**:

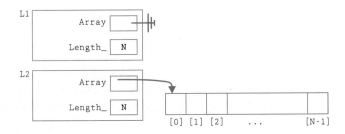

2. Deallocate the array pointed to by **L1**'s **Array** member using the **delete** operation:

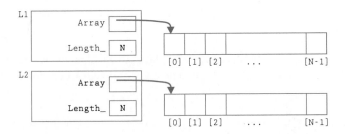

3. Allocate a new array the size of **L2**'s **Length_** member, storing its address in **L1**'s **Array** member:

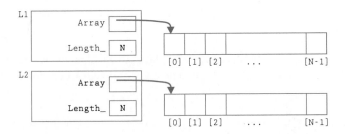

4. Copy the values from array pointed to by **L2**'s **Array** member into the array pointed to by **L1**'s **Array** member:

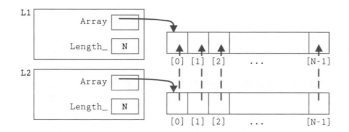

Of course, the last two steps should not be performed if **L2** is empty, as shown in Figure 15.6.

FIGURE 15.6   Class **List** assignment operator.

```
/* This function permits the assignment of a List object.

   Receive:  Original, a List object
   Return:   The object containing this function, with its members
             as copies of those of Original, and a reference to
             this List (for chained assignments)
-----------------------------------------------------------------*/

List& List::operator=(const List& Original)
{
   if (this != &Original)                 // check if L != Original;
   {
      delete [] Array;                    //    destroy previous array
      Length_ = Original.Length_;         // copy scalar member
      if (Length_ > 0)                    //    copy Array member
      {                                   // allocate a new array
         Array = new ListElement [Length_];
         assert(Array != 0);              //   verify success
                                          // copy the array member
         for (int i = 0; i < Length_; i++)
            Array[i] = Original.Array[i];
      }
      else
         Array = 0;                       // set Array to NULL
   }
   return *this;                          // return this object
}
```

Note that this function only performs the assignment operation if the condition

```
   (this != &Original)
```

is true. A check like this is necessary for assignments involving pointer members, since otherwise, a (valid) assignment of the form

```
L1 = L1;
```

would destroy the contents of **L1**, which is incorrect, regardless of the usefulness of the statement.

As this function illustrates, if an operation resizes an object whose memory is allocated at run-time, then the object's run-time allocated memory should be deallocated, and new memory (of the appropriate size) should be allocated to hold the operation result. Thus, in this example, the **delete** operation is used to deallocate the (old) run-time allocated array, after which the **new** operation is used to allocate the appropriate amount of memory for the new array.

As with any assignment operation, the function should return a reference to the object being assigned (i.e., ***this**) so that assignments can be chained:

```
L1 = L2 = L3;
```

The Input Operation

We know that an input operation such as

```
cin >> x;
```

destroys the previous contents of the object **x** and replaces those contents with the input value. In exactly the same way, an input statement involving a **List** object **L1**, such as

```
cin >> L1;
```

must destroy the previous contents of **L1** and replace them with the input values.

A function for input must determine the number of values in the list, in order to know how big an array should be allocated. We present a number of different approaches to solving this problem.

Interactive Input. Since interactive input is usually performed using an **istream** and **operator>>**, we will write a definition of **operator>>** to input a **List** from an **istream** that assumes that the **List** being filled has been constructed interactively, with statements such as the following:

```
unsigned
   N;

cout << "\nHow many values are in your list? ";
cin >> N;

List
   L(N);

cout << "\nPlease enter your list: ";
cin >> L;
```

The class constructor will construct L, initializing its **Length_** member to the value N. It will also initialize L's **Array** member as a pointer to a run-time allocated array of N elements. Since we are assuming that N is the number of elements in the input list, the array pointed to by **Array** is exactly the right size to hold the input list, so no deallocation/reallocation is necessary. The function can use a for loop (controlled by the value of **Length_**) to read the values in the input list into successive elements of the array, as seen in Figure 15.7.

 FIGURE 15.7   Class **List** interactive input (unbounded version).

```
/* This function performs keyboard input for a List object,
   assuming that it has been constructed to hold the number of
   values in the input list.

   Receive: An istream (reference) object In containing n values
            A List (reference) object InList, with
                its Length_ member equal to n, and
                its Array member pointing to an array of n elements
   Input:   A sequence of n ListElement values, from In
   Return:  InList, with the input values stored in the array
                pointed to by Array
-----------------------------------------------------------------*/

istream& operator>>(istream& In, List& InList)
{
   for (int i = 0; i < InList.Length_; i++)   // fill existing array
      In >> InList.Array[i];

   return In;
}
```

This function requires users to enter the size of the lists before memory is allocated. This permits the entry of **List**s whose size is bounded only by the amount of memory available in the free store. The disadvantage is that the user must know how many values are in their list before input begins.

A variation on this approach is to place the statements that query the user for the number of elements as well as the call to the constructor in the input function itself:

```
istream& operator>>(istream& In, List& L)
{
   cout << "\nHow many values are in your list ? ";
   In >> N;

   delete [] L.Array;

   L = List(N);
```

```
   cout << "\nPlease enter your list: ";

   for (int i = 0; i < L.Length_; i++)    // fill existing array
       In >> L.Array[i];

   return In;
}
```

Note that since the **List** corresponding to the parameter **L** may be nonempty, the function must deallocate any run-time–allocated storage for a nonempty **List** to avoid marooning such storage.

This approach is somewhat simpler for the programmer, since an arbitrary **List** can be passed to the function. However, the approach suffers the same disadvantage as the previous approach, since the number of values in the list must be known before these values can be entered.

A third approach is to assume a (large) bound on the number of values in the input list. In this case, the input function can define a local fixed-size array of that many elements (named **Buffer** in Figure 15.9) in which to store the input values while the values are counted. After the number of values has been determined, an array of appropriate size can be allocated (during execution) and the input values copied from **Buffer** into that array. Since the default storage class of local objects is automatic, memory will be allocated for the array **Buffer** when the input function is called and deallocated when execution of the function is finished.

In this approach, it is unlikely that the number of elements in the array pointed to by **Array** will be the same as the number of values in the input **List**. Hence **delete** must be used to deallocate the array pointed to by **Array** and then **new** used to allocate a new array of the appropriate length, whose address must be stored in **Array**. **Length_** must be similarly updated. The input function in Figure 15.8 uses this approach.

 FIGURE 15.8   Class **List** interactive input (bounded version).

```
/* This function performs keyboard input for a List object, assuming
   that a bound exists on the number of values in the input list.

   Receive: An istream (reference) object In
            A List (reference) object InList
   Input:   A sequence of n numbers, 0 < n <= MaxLength, from In
   Return:  InList, with the input values stored in the first n
            array elements, its Length_ member set to n
-------------------------------------------------------------*/

istream& operator>>(istream& In, List& InList)
{
   ListElement
      Buffer[List::MaxLength];                 // fixed-size array
```

FIGURE 15.8 Class **List** interactive input (bounded version). (cont.)

```
    InList.Length_ = 0;                       // initialize counter
    In >> Buffer[InList.Length_];             // read a value into Buffer
    while (!In.eof() &&                        // while more data
        (InList.Length_ < List::MaxLength))   //    and Buffer not full:
    {
        InList.Length_++;                     //    update counter
        In >> Buffer[InList.Length_];         //    read next value
    }                                         //        into Buffer

    if (InList.Length_ == List::MaxLength)
        cerr << "\nWarning: List filled ! Values may be unread...\n";

    delete [] InList.Array;                   // deallocate old array

    InList.Array =
        new ListElement[InList.Length_];      // allocate new array
    assert(InList.Array != 0);                // verify success

    for (int i = 0; i < InList.Length_; i++)// copy values from Buffer
        InList.Array[i] = Buffer[i];          //    into the new array

    return In;
}
```

Using this approach, a programmer need only write:

```
List                                          // declare an empty List
    L;
                                              // fill the List with values
cout << "\nPlease enter your List (Ctrl-D to quit): ";
cin >> L;
```

This approach is somewhat more convenient than the previous approach because the user does not need to know ahead of time how many values are in the list. The disadvantages are that the user cannot enter a list with more than **MaxLength** values and cannot enter any more values without clearing the state bits of **cin**.

Whichever approach is used, the documentation in the **.h** file of class **List** must clearly describe how to use the function and any assumptions that are made.

File Input. As with interactive input, filling a **List** with values from a file can be done in any of several ways. The approach we develop here is to assume that the first line of the file contains the number of values in the list, which can be read into the **Length_** member of the **List**. Because this approach does not assume that the anonymous array pointed to by the **Array** member of the **List** has been preallocated to the correct size, any previous array must be deallocated and a new array allocated with the correct size. The values in the file can then be read directly into the elements of this newly allocated array using a for loop.

To allow the caller of this function to avoid the inconvenience of having to open and close an **fstream** to the file containing the **List**, the function (defined as a member named **Load()**) is designed to receive the name of the file containing the list as a parameter. The function then opens an **fstream** to that file, reads the values from the **fstream** into the **List**, and closes the **fstream**. Since opening files is susceptible to failure, **Load()** has been written as a **Boolean** function that returns true if it completes its task successfully and false otherwise. This function is given in Figure 15.9.

 FIGURE 15.9 File input for class **List** (unbounded version).

```
/* This function fills a List object with data from a file,
   assuming that the first line of the file is the number of values
   in the list.

   Receive:      FileName, a Strings object containing the name of
                    an input file
   Input (File): The number of list values and the values
   Return:       The List object containing this function, its
                    Length_ member containing the number of input
                    values and its Array member containing the
                    input values
                 True if operation successful, false otherwise
---------------------------------------------------------------*/

Boolean List::Load(const Strings& FileName)
{
    fstream
       InStream(FileName, ios::in);      // open stream to input file

    if (InStream.fail())                 // if not successful
    {
       cerr << "\n*** Load: Unable to open "
            << FileName << ".\n";
       return False;                     // ... indicate failure
    }

    InStream >> Length_;                 // read the number of values

    delete [] Array;                     // deallocate old array

    Array = new ListElement[Length_];    // allocate right-sized array
    assert(Array != 0);                  // verify success

    for (int i = 0; i < Length_; i++)    // fill it with input values
       InStream >> Array[i];

    InStream.close();                    // close the stream

    return True;                         // indicate success
}
```

Given this function as a member of class `List`, the programmer can write

```
Strings
    FName;
```

```
cout << "\nPlease enter the name of the file containing your list: ";
cin >> FName;
```

```
List
    L;
```

```
L.Load(FName);
```

Note that this approach is essentially a file-I/O version of the interactive-I/O function in which the user is queried for the number of values in the list. The primary difference is that the file, rather than the user, must supply the number of values in the list.

An alternative approach that works in some versions of C++ is to overload the input operator for an `fstream` and a `List` and adapt one of the `istream` functions described previously. This is left as an exercise.

This completes the restructuring of class `List`. All the remaining members presented in Sections 12.2 and 12.3 can be used exactly as implemented there, because none of these operations require the construction or destruction of a `List`. Although some of these members (e.g., `QSort()`) alter the contents of a `List`, none of them changes the number of elements in the `List`.

Figure 15.10 presents a declaration of class `List`. To save space, we have included documentation only for the `List` functions that differ from those in Figure 12.17. Additional `List` operations that change the size of a list (insert, delete, concatenate, etc.) are left as exercises.

FIGURE 15.10   Final declaration of class `List`.

```
/* This file contains the declaration of class List.
   NOTE:  Most documentation is omitted here to save pages.
          See Figure 12.16 for complete documentation.
--------------------------------------------------------------------*/
```

```
#include <iostream.h>              // interactive i/o
#include <fstream.h>               // file i/o
#include "Boolean.h"
#include "Strings.h"
```

```
typedef double ListElement;        // array element type
```

```
class List
{
protected:
```

```
    ListElement                    // a pointer to a run-time
        *Array;                    // allocated array
```

FIGURE 15.10 Final declaration of class **List**. (cont.)

```
unsigned
   Length_;                              // # values in List

enum
   {MaxLength = 1024};                   // maximum list length

unsigned Split(int Low, int High);

void QuickSort(int First, int Last);

public:

   /****** Constructors and Destructor ******/
   /*----- Class -----
      Precondition:  A List object has been declared.
      Receive:       NumValues, the size of the List being defined
                     (default 0)
      Postcondition: The List has been appropriately initialized
                     as a list that can hold NumValues values.
   --------------------------------------------------------------*/
   List(unsigned NumValues = 0);

   /*----- Copy -----
      Precondition:   The compiler needs a copy of a List.
      Receive:        Original, the List being copied
      Postcondition:  The scalar and array members of this List are
                      distinct copies of the data members of
                      Original.
   --------------------------------------------------------------*/
   List(const List& Original);

   /*----- Destructor -----
      Precondition:  A List object's lifetime is over.
      Postcondition: The storage allocated to that List is
                     deallocated; and its data members are
                     reset as an empty List.
   --------------------------------------------------------------*/
   ~List(void)
     {
        delete [] Array;
        Array = 0;
        Length_ = 0;
     }


   /****** Operations and Members *****/
   /*----- Assignment -----

      Receive: A List object Original
      Return:  The List containing this function, its members
               as distinct copies of those of Original
   --------------------------------------------------------------*/
   List& operator=(const List& Original);
```

FIGURE 15.10   Final declaration of class **List**. (cont.)

```
/*--- Interactive Input ---
    Receive:     An istream (reference) object In
                 A List (reference) object InList
    Input:       A sequence of n numbers, 0 < n <= MaxLength,
                    from In
    Return:      InList, with the input values stored in the first
                    n array elements, its Length_ member set to n
                 In
    Assumption: The number of values in the input list
                    is <= MaxLength.
    ----------------------------------------------------------------*/
    friend istream& operator>>(istream& In, List& InList);

/*--- File Input -----

    Receive:        FileName, a Strings object containing the name
                       of an input file
    Input (File):   The number of list values and the values
    Return:         The List object containing this function, its
                       Length_ member containing the number of
                       inputvalues and its Array member containing
                       the input values
                    True if operation successful, false otherwise
    Assumption:     The first line of the file has the number of
                       values in the list.
    ----------------------------------------------------------------*/
    Boolean Load(const Strings& FName);

    Boolean Write(const Strings& FName) const;

    friend ostream& operator<<(ostream& Out, const List& L);

    ListElement& operator[] (unsigned i);

    unsigned Length(void) const { return Length_; }

    int LSearch(ListElement SearchVal) const;

    int BSearch(ListElement SearchVal) const;

    unsigned SubscriptOfMin(unsigned First, unsigned Last);

    void SSort(void);

    void QSort(void);
};
```

Example: Finding the Median of a List of Numbers

The *median* of a list of n values is a value such that $n/2$ of the values are greater than that value, and $n/2$ of the values are less than that value. For example, the median of the following list:

$$11\ 99\ 22\ 88\ 33\ 77\ 44\ 66\ 55$$

is 55, because $9/2 = 4$ of the values are less than 55 and 4 of the values are greater than 55. An easy technique for finding the median of a list is to first sort the list; the middle element then contains the median value:

$$11\ 22\ 33\ 44\ 55\ 66\ 77\ 88\ 99$$
$$\uparrow$$

The preceding list contains an odd number of elements and so has a unique middle element. However, lists containing an even number of elements have two middle elements:

$$11\ 22\ 33\ 44\ 55\ 66\ 77\ 88$$
$$\uparrow\ \uparrow$$

For such lists the median value is usually computed as the average of the middle two elements.

The following algorithm finds the median of an arbitrary list of values:

ALGORITHM TO FIND THE MEDIAN OF A LIST OF VALUES

/* This algorithm finds the median value of a list of values stored in a file.

Input (keyboard):	The name of a file containing a list of values.
Input (file):	A sequence of values, stored in a *List* named *L*.
Output (screen):	The median value of that sequence.

—————————————————————————————————————*/

1. Input the name of the file.
2. Input the sequence of values from the file, storing them in a *List* named *L*.
3. Sort *L* into ascending order.
4. If the number of values in *L* is even, then
    Output the average of the two middle elements in *L*;
  Otherwise
    Output the middle element of *L*.
  End If.

The program in Figure 15.11 encodes this algorithm.

FIGURE 15.11   Finding the median of a list of values.

```
/* This program finds the median of a list of values.

    Input (keyboard):   Name of a file containing a list; the first line
                        of the file contains the number of list
                        elements
    Input (file):       Number of list elements, and the list elements
    Output:             User messages and prompts; the median of the
                        values in the list
 --------------------------------------------------------------------*/

#include <iostream.h>

#include "List.h"
#include "Strings.h"

int main(void)
{

    cout << "\nThis program finds the median of a list of values stored"
         << "\n\tin a file. The first number in the file must be the"
         << "\n\tnumber of values in the list.\n";

    Strings
        FName;                          // get the input file name

    cout << "\nPlease enter the name of the file containing your list: ";
    cin >> FName;

    List                                // load the input file list
        L;                              //    into a List object

    L.Load(FName);

    L.SSort();                          // sort the List

    int
        N = L.Length();                 // find # values in List

    ListElement
        Median;                         // container for the answer

    if (N % 2 == 1)                     // if # values is odd
        Median = L[N/2];                //    median = middle element
    else                                // otherwise
        Median = (L[N/2 - 1] + L[N/2]) / 2;// median = average of
                                        //    middle elements
    cout << "\nThe median of the list is "// output result
         << Median << "\n\n";

    return 0;
}
```

FIGURE 15.11 Finding the median of a list of values. (cont.)

Listing of input file `list.dat`:

```
8
11  12  13  14  15  16  17  18
```

Sample run:

```
This program finds the median of a list of values stored
   in a file. The first number in the file must be the
   number of values in the list.

Please enter the name of the file containing your list: list.dat

The median of the list is 14.5
```

In summary, class `List` can be used to store one-dimensional lists of data without wasting memory. The number of elements in the array allocated to hold a list is exactly the same as the number of values in that list.

Specialized one-dimensional list classes that use memory efficiently can be constructed by deriving them from the class `List`. Since such classes will inherit the operations from the class `List`, these derived classes need only provide whatever specialized operations they require beyond those already defined in `List`.

Exercises

1. Define a `List` member function `Insert()` that, given a `ListElement Elem` and an index `i`, inserts `Elem` into the `List` at position `i`, without overwriting the value at that position.

2. Define an overloaded `List` member function `Delete()` that

   (a) Given an index `i`, deletes and returns the `ListElement` at position `i`.
   (b) Given a `ListElement Elem`, deletes the first occurrence of `Elem` from the `List` without leaving any gaps in the list.

3. Overload `operator&` with a definition that, given two `List` objects, returns the `List` consisting of their concatenation.

4. Improve the efficiency of `List::operator=` by modifying its definition, so that it only deallocates its anonymous array and allocates a new array if the length of the lists on the right-hand and left-hand sides of the assignment differ in length.

5. Add a definition to class `List` that overloads `operator>>` to perform interactive input.

15.4   A Run-Time Allocated Table Class

In Chapter 13, we constructed a general class named Table that provided a set of basic operations on two-dimensional arrays of numbers. Table contained a two-dimensional array member named Grid, for which memory was allocated at compile-time. As a result, this Table class suffers from the usual limitations of all compile-time allocated arrays: overflow if the number of values is larger than the Table capacity and waste of memory if it is smaller. Imitating what we did with the class List in the last section, in this section we restructure the class Table as an object whose storage is allocated at run-time instead of compile-time.

Our approach will follow that in Section 12.6, where we designed a separate class named Row, containing a one-dimensional array member, and the Grid member of class Table was then defined as a one-dimensional array of Row objects. By defining two separate subscript functions (one in Row and one in Table), we were able to use the notation

```
Tab[i][j]
```

to access the jth element in the ith Row of a Table object Tab. To restructure class Table as a run-time allocated object, we will first build class Row as a class containing a run-time allocated array of TableElement objects and then build class Table as a class containing a run-time allocated array of Row objects.

The Class Row

Class Row is like class List in the preceding section in that it is a class containing a pointer member to store the address of a run-time allocated one-dimensional array. As before, we also define a member in which to store the number of elements in the row. It is clear from the preceding discussion that class Row must contain a definition for the subscript operator. Because Row will employ run-time allocation, we must also define constructors and a destructor to allocate and deallocate the space for a Row object.

These are the only operations that are strictly necessary on a Row object. However, some of the operations on class Table will require the row-wise copying of a table. This copying can be simplified if we provide a Row assignment operator that will make a copy of a given row.

Using class List as a model, we can declare class Row as shown in Figure 15.12.

FIGURE 15.12   Class Row declaration.

```
/* Declaration of class Row.
   NOTE:   Because it has appeared earlier or is similar to that in
           Chapter 14, additional documentation and preprocessor
           directives have been omitted to save pages. See the
           data disk for full documentation.
--------------------------------------------------------------------*/
```

FIGURE 15.12   Class **Row** declaration. (cont.)

```
typedef double TableElement;            // simplify changing
                                        //     element type
class Row
{
   TableElement                         // pointer to one-dim array
       *Array;

   unsigned                             // length of the array
     Length_;

public:
   Row(unsigned N = 0);                 // class constructor
   Row(const Row& R);                   // copy constructor
   ~Row(void);                          // destructor
   TableElement& operator[](unsigned i); // subscript operator
   Row& operator=(const Row& R);        // assignment operator
};
```

This leaves the task of defining each of the operations.

The Row Class Constructor.   A constructor for class Row is much like that for class **List** in that it must initialize both of the data members of class **Row**. A declaration of the form

```
     Row
        R;
```

should initialize **R** as an empty **Row** (i.e., with **Array** set to the NULL address and **Length_** set to zero), and a declaration of the form

```
     Row
        R(N);
```

should initialize **R** as a **Row** of **N** elements (i.e., **Array** pointing to a run-time allocated array of **N** elements and **Length_** set to **N**). Figure 15.13 presents such a function.

 FIGURE 15.13   **Row** class constructor.

```
/* This function constructs a Row.

   Precondition:    A Row object has been declared.
   Receive:         N, the number of elements to be allocated
                       (default 0)
   Postcondition:   In the Row containing this function the Length_
                       member is set to N, and the Array member
                       contains the address of an array of N
                       elements (or the NULL address).
---------------------------------------------------------------*/
```

FIGURE 15.13 **Row** class constructor. (cont.)

```
Row::Row(unsigned N)                          // N has default value zero
{
   Length_ = N;                               // set Length_ member
                                              // set Array member:
   if (Length_ > 0)                           //    if N is not zero
   {
      Array = new TableElement[Length_];      //       allocate a new array
      assert(Array != 0);                     //       verify success
   }
   else                                       //    otherwise
      Array = 0;                              //       set Array to NULL
}
```

The Row Copy Constructor. Since class **Row** uses run-time allocation, the constructor that makes a copy of a **Row** must explicitly allocate a new array of the appropriate size and then copy the array values from that **Row** into the newly allocated **Array** (assuming that the **Row** being copied is not empty). Figure 15.14 presents such a function.

 FIGURE 15.14 **Row** copy constructor.

```
/* This function makes a copy of a Row.

   Precondition:  The compiler needs a copy of a Row.
   Receive:       OrigRow, the Row being copied
   Postcondition: In the Row containing this function,
                  the Length_ member is set to OrigRow.Length_,
                  and the Array member contains the address of
                  an array that is a copy of OrigRow's array
                  (or the NULL address).
--------------------------------------------------------------------*/

Row::Row(const Row& OrigRow)
{
   Length_ = OrigRow.Length_;                     // copy Length_ member
                                                  // copy Array member:
   if (Length_ > 0)                               // if OrigRow is not empty
   {
      Array = new TableElement [Length_];         //    allocate a new array
      assert(Array != 0);                         //    verify success
      for (int i = 0; i < Length_; i++)           //    copy the elements
         Array[i] = OrigRow.Array[i];             //       from OrigRow
   }                                              //       into the array
   else                                           // otherwise
      Array = 0;                                  //    set Array to NULL
}
```

The Row Destructor.   As with class **List**, the **Row** destructor must deallocate the array pointed to by the **Array** member. We also reset the two data members to indicate that the **Row** is now empty, as shown in Figure 15.15.

FIGURE 15.15   **Row** destructor.

```
/* This function tears down a Row.

   Precondition:   The Row containing this function should cease to
                   exist.
   Postcondition: The run-time storage of this Row has been
                  deallocated, and its members are set
                  appropriately as an empty Row.
   ------------------------------------------------------------------*/

Row:: ~ Row(void)
{
   delete [] Array;
   Array = 0;
   Length_ = 0;
}
```

The Row Subscript Operator.   Given an integer **i**, the **Row** subscript operator must return the element of the run-time allocated array whose index is **i**. This is easily done with the expression

        Array[i]

because **Array** is a pointer containing the address of the first element of the run-time allocated array. However, **i** is being received as a parameter, and so we must guard against the possibility that the value of **i** is outside the range of valid array indices. Figure 15.16 contains a function that does this.

FIGURE 15.16   **Row** subscript.

```
/* This function performs the subscript operation on a Row object.

   Receive: i, an integer value;
   Return:  The element of the array pointed to by Array whose
            index is i (assuming that i is a valid index).
   ------------------------------------------------------------------*/

TableElement& Row::operator[](unsigned i)
{
   if (i < Length_)                                 // if access is valid
      return Array[i];                              //    return element
                                                    // otherwise
   cerr << "\n*** Row Subscript: invalid index " // fatal error msg
      << i << " received!\n";
   exit (-1);
}
```

Note that we do not explicitly test **Array** to ensure that it contains a non-NULL address. Thanks to the constructors, if **Length_** is greater than zero then **Array** contains a non-NULL address. The condition

   (i < Length_)

thus serves a dual purpose. The condition will be false if either

- **Array** contains a non-NULL address and **i** is an invalid index; or
- **Array** contains the NULL address—**Length_** is then equal to zero (since **i** is an **unsigned** integer).

Row Assignment. The operation to assign a **Row** object is much like the operation to assign a **List**. Figure 15.17 shows the definition of **operator=** for class **Row**.

 FIGURE 15.17 **Row** assignment.

```
/* This function assigns a Row.

   Receive: RowObj, a Row object
   Return:  The Row containing this function, as a distinct copy of
            RowObj
   ------------------------------------------------------------------*/
Row& Row::operator=(const Row& RowObj) const
{
   if (this != &RowObj)
   {
      Length_ = RowObj.Length_;              // copy # values

      delete [] Array;                       // deallocate old storage

      if (Length_ > 0)                       // if R not empty
      {
         Array = new TableElement [Length_];//   allocate new array
         assert(Array != 0);                 //   verify success
         for (int c = 0; c < Length_; c++)   //   and copy RowObj
            Array[c] = RowObj.Array[c];       //     into it
      }
      else                                   // otherwise
         Array = 0;                          //   set Array to NULL
   }
   return *this;                             // permit chaining
}
```

This completes the implementation of the class **Row**. Other operations could be defined for a **Row**, but these are sufficient for the task at hand, namely, the implementation of class **Table**, which we present next.

The Class `Table`

Our purpose in building class **Row** was to allow us to restructure class **Table** to use
run-time allocation. Thus, we begin by replacing **Table**'s compile-time allocated
array member **Grid** with a pointer to a **Row** (which we shall name **Grid**), as shown
in Figure 15.18.

 FIGURE 15.18   Restructuring class **Table**.

```
/*
   ... */

class Table
{
protected:              // hide the data members, but allow
                        //    access to derived classes

   unsigned
      Rows_,            // the number of rows in use
      Columns_;         // the number of columns in use

   Row
      *Grid;            // pointer to run-time allocated array

         .
         .
         .
};
```

We must then update those operations that create or destroy a **Table** object, including:

- The constructors (class and copy)
- Assignment
- Input

We must also add a destructor to deallocate the memory of a **Table** object.

The Table Class Constructor.   As before, the class constructor should allow
programmers to use

```
    Table
       T;
```

to define an empty **Table** and

```
    Table
       T(R, C);
```

to allocate a **Table** of R **Row** objects, each of length C. The class constructor thus
needs two parameters **NumRows** and **NumCols**, each having default values of zero.
    The class constructor begins much as before, by setting the row and column
counters **Rows_** and **Columns_** to the values of parameters **NumRows** and **NumCols**,

respectively. If **NumRows** is zero, then we can simply set **Grid** to the NULL address. However, if **NumRows** is not zero, then the constructor must allocate an array of **Row** objects and store its address in the pointer **Grid**. Moreover, for each of these **Row** objects, the **Row** constructor must be called to build each **Row**, so that it contains **NumCols** elements. The class constructor in Figure 15.19 shows one way that this can be done using the **Row** assignment operator.

 FIGURE 15.19   **Table** class constructor.

```
/* This function is the class constructor for class Table.

   Precondition:  A Table object has been declared.
   Receive:       NumRows (optional), the number of rows in the Table
                  NumCols (optional), the number of columns in the
                     Table
                  InitValue (default value zero), to initialize
                     the values of the Table's elements
   Postcondition: The declared Table object containing this function
                     has its Rows_ member initialized to NumRows
                     and its Columns_ member initialized to NumCols.
----------------------------------------------------------------*/

Table::Table(unsigned NumRows, unsigned NumCols,
             TableElement InitValue)

{
   Rows_ = NumRows;                      // set the scalar members
   Columns_ = NumCols;

   if (NumRows > 0)                      // if not empty
   {
      Grid = new Row[NumRows];           //    allocate array of Rows
      assert(Grid != 0);                 //    verify success
      for (int r = 0; r < NumRows; r++)  //    build NumRows Rows,
         Grid[r] = Row(NumCols);         //       each of length NumCols

                                         //    now fill the 2-dim array
      for (int row = 0; row < NumRows; row++)
         for (int col = 0; col < NumCols; col++)
            Grid[row][col] = InitValue;
   }
   else                                  // otherwise
      Grid = 0;                          //    set Grid to NULL address
}
```

Once this function is declared in class **Table** (i.e., in **Table.h**) with its default arguments,

```
Table(unsigned NumRows = 0, unsigned NumCols = 0);
```

a declaration of the form

```
Table
    T;
```

can be used to build a **Table** object, which we might picture as

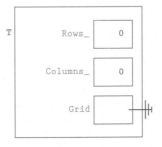

By contrast, a declaration of the form

```
Table
    T(2,3);
```

will build a **Table** object that we can picture

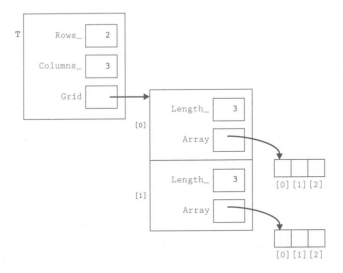

The Copy Constructor.   The copy constructor for a **Table** must do everything necessary to make a copy of the **Table** it receives as an argument. It must replicate the functionality of the class constructor by building a new **Table** whose **Rows_** and **Columns_** members are identical to those of its parameter **Original** and ensure that its **Grid** member points to an array of **Rows_** **Row** objects, each of length **Columns_**. In addition, each **Row** in this array must be a copy of the corresponding **Row** in **T**. Fortunately, this is quite easy, using the assignment operator in class **Row**, as illustrated in Figure 15.20.

FIGURE 15.20 **Table** copy constructor.

```
/* This function makes a copy of a Table object.

   Precondition:   The compiler needs a copy of a table object.
   Received:       The Table (reference) object Original to be copied
   Postcondition:  The members of the object containing this function,
                   are copies of those of Original.
-----------------------------------------------------------------*/

Table::Table(const Table& Original)
{
   Rows_ = Original.Rows_;              // copy Rows_
   Columns_ = Original.Columns_;        // copy Columns_
                                        // copy Grid member:
   if (Rows_ > 0)                       // if Original is not empty
   {
      Grid = new Row[Rows_];            //    allocate new Row array
      assert (Grid != 0);              //    verify success
      for (int r = 0; r < Rows_; r++) //    for each Row:
         Grid[r] = Original.Grid[r];   //       make it a copy of
   }                                    //          that in Original
   else                                 // otherwise
      Grid = 0;                         //    set Grid to NULL
}
```

In this function, each repetition of the loop

```
for (int r = 0; r < Rows_; r++)
   Grid[r] = Original.Grid[r];
```

uses the **Row** assignment operator to build **Row r** in **Grid** as a copy of **Row r** in **Original**—if we had not overloaded that operator, then everything that it does would have to be done in this loop:

```
for (int r = 0; r < Rows_; r++)
   if (Columns_ > 0)
   {
      Grid[r] = Row(Columns_);
      for (int c = 0; c < Columns_; c++)
         Grid[r][c] = Original.Grid[r][c];
   }
   else
      Grid = 0;
}
```

The assignment operator thus hides all of the details of allocating and copying a **Row**, greatly improving the readability of the function.

The Table Destructor. Recall that the **Table** constructor first allocates an array of **Row** objects and then uses the **Row** constructor to build each row. The **Table** destructor must "undo" these actions by using the delete operator, as shown in Figure 15.21.

  FIGURE 15.21 Table destructor.

```
/* This function tears down a Table.

    Precondition:  This Table object should no longer exist.
    Postcondition: The run-time storage of this Table has been
                   reclaimed, and its members reset as an
                   empty Table.
------------------------------------------------------------------*/

Table:: ~ Table(void)
{
    delete [] Grid;        // reclaim the array
                           //   (and its Rows)
    Rows_ = 0;             // set scalars for empty Table
    Columns_ = 0;
    Grid = 0;
}
```

It is important to understand the steps being taken by the statement:

```
delete [] Grid;
```

Suppose that before it is executed, **T** is a 2 × 3 **Table**:

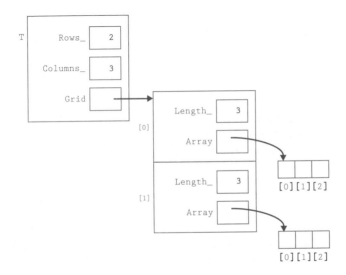

The **delete** statement clearly reclaims the array pointed to by **Grid**. However, calling the array form of **delete**,

> delete [] *PointerVariable;*

automatically invokes the destructors of the elements in the array pointed to by *PointerVariable*. That is, because **Grid** is an array of **Row** objects, the statement

> delete [] **Grid;**

automatically invokes **~Row()** for each element of the array pointed to by **Grid**, and thus reclaims the run-time storage of each **Row**:

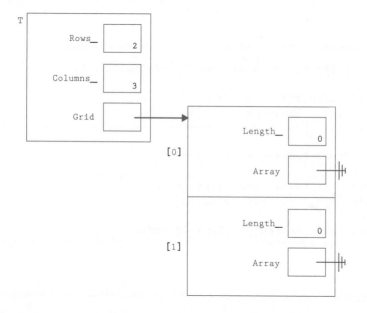

Once these destructors are done executing, **delete** reclaims the array of (now empty) **Row** objects,

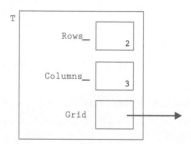

so that once the final statements have executed, **T** is an empty **Table**:

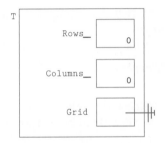

Table Subscript. The **Table** subscript operation is fairly straightforward, because the subscript operation in class **Row** was overloaded. This operation simply checks the validity of the index received as a parameter (the row index) and, if it is valid, accesses and returns the corresponding row of the array pointed to by **Grid**, as shown in Figure 15.22.

 FIGURE 15.22 **Table** subscripting.

```
/* This function performs the subscript operation on a Table.

   Receive: i, an index into the Table
   Return:  That row in Table whose index is i
----------------------------------------------------------------*/

Row& Table::operator[] (unsigned i)
{
   if (i < Rows_)          // if subscript is valid
      return Grid[i];      //    return Row i

   cerr << "\n*** Table Subscript: invalid index "
        << i << " received!\n";
   exit (-1);
}
```

Given this function, an entry in a **Table** object **T** can be accessed using the notation

   T[r][c]

Since its order of evaluation is

   (T[r]) [c]

the operation **T[r]** accesses the **Row** whose index is *r* in the array pointed to by **T.Grid**, to which the **Row** operation **[c]** is applied, accessing the **TableElement** in that **Row** whose index is *c*.

Table Assignment. The **Table** assignment operation is similar to the **Table** copy constructor, since each makes a copy of its argument. One difference is that whereas the copy constructor builds a new **Table** object, the target of an assignment operation may be a nonempty **Table** object. This means that although it was not necessary for the copy constructor to reclaim the run-time allocated memory pointed to by **Grid**, the assignment operator must do so. In Figure 15.23, the assignment function explicitly invokes the **Table** destructor to deallocate its memory:

FIGURE 15.23 **Table** assignment.

```
/* This function overloads the assignment operator for a Table object.

   Receive: Tab, a (const reference) Table object
   Return:  The Table containing this function, its data members
            containing copies of those of Tab, and a reference
            to the object assigned.
-----------------------------------------------------------------*/
Table& Table::operator= (const Table& Tab)
{
   if (this != &Tab)
   {
      delete [] Grid;                       // deallocate old storage
      Rows_ = Tab.Rows_;                    // copy scalar members of Tab
      Columns_ = Tab.Columns_;

      if (Rows_ > 0)                        // if Tab is not empty
      {
         Grid = new Row[Rows_];             //    allocate new Row array
         assert(Grid != 0);                 //    verify success
         for (int r = 0; r < Rows_; r++)    //    for each row r
            Grid[r] = Tab.Grid[r];          //       copy row r from Tab
      }
      else                                  // otherwise
         Grid = 0;                          //    set Grid to NULL
   }
   return *this;                            // to allow chaining
}
```

Note that the **Table** assignment operator makes use of the **Row** assignment operator in the for loop

```
for (int r = 0; r < Rows_; r++)
   Grid[r] = Tab.Grid[r];
```

Since **operator=** is a member of class **Row**, each of the assignments

```
Grid[r] = Tab.Grid[r];
```

can be thought of as calling

```
Grid[r].operator=(Tab.Grid);
```

which

1. Allocates a new **Row** the length of the array pointed to by **Tab.Grid[r].Array**;

2. Stores the address of that **Row** in **Grid[r].Array**;

3. For each **i** from **0** to **Length_**, copies **Tab.Grid[r].Array[i]** into **Grid[r].Array[i]**.

Once this function has been declared as a member of class **Table**, it can be used to assign **Table** objects. To illustrate, let **Tab1**, **Tab2**, and **Tab3** be three **Table** objects. Then the statement

    Tab1 = Tab2 = Tab3;

will begin by invoking

    Tab2.operator=(Tab3)

(since **operator=** is *right associative*), which stores a copy of **Tab3** into **Tab2** and returns a reference to **Tab2**, after which

    Tab1.operator=(Tab2)

is invoked, which stores a copy of the newly updated **Tab2** into **Tab1**.

The Input Operation. We have seen that the number of input values must be determined when filling an object whose memory is allocated at run-time. As we saw with class **List**, one reasonable approach for inputting values from a file is to assume that the file contains the information necessary for memory allocation. For class **Table**, this information would be the number of rows and columns of the table stored in the file. This information can be read into the **Rows_** and **Columns_** members of the **Table** and then used to control nested for loops to read the values. Figure 15.24 presents the implementation of the **Table** member **Load()**, which uses this approach.

FIGURE 15.24   **Table** input (file).

```
/* This function loads a Table object with data from a file,
    and assumes that the first two values in the file
    give the number of rows and columns of the Table.

   Receive:      FileName, a Strings object containing the name of
                    an input file
   Input (File): The number of rows and columns and a table
                    of values
   Return:       False, if the file could not be opened; otherwise,
                    true and the Table object containing this
                    function, its Grid member containing the
                    input values
   --------------------------------------------------------------*/
```

FIGURE 15.24 **Table** input (file). (cont.)

```
Boolean Table::Load(const Strings& FileName)
{
    fstream
        InStream(FileName, ios::in);         // open the stream

    if (InStream.fail())                     // check for failure...
    {
        cerr << "\n*** Load: Unable to open "// ...displaying msg, and
            << FileName << " for input !\n";
        return False;                        // ...indicate failure
    }

    delete [] Grid                           // deallocate old storage

    InStream >> Rows_ >> Columns_;           // get # rows and columns

    if (Rows_ > 0)                           // if the file isn't empty
    {
        Grid = new Row[Rows_];               //   allocate new Row array
        assert (Grid != 0);                  //   verify success
        for (int r = 0; r < Rows_; r++)      //   for each Row r:
        {
            Grid[r] = Row(Columns_);         //      build Row of correct
                                             //      number of elements
            for (int c = 0; c < Columns_; c++)//     for each column c:
                InStream >> Grid[r][c];      //      read value from file
        }                                    //      into element [r][c]
    }
    else                                     // otherwise
        Grid = 0;                            //   set Grid to NULL

    InStream.close();                        // close the stream

    return True;                             //   indicate success
}
```

Alternative approaches in which the user (interactively) sets the values of **Rows_** and **Columns_** can also be used for file input but are more appropriate for interactive input functions. The development of these functions is left as an exercise.

This completes the restructuring of class **Table**. The remaining operations described in Section 14.2 do not modify the size of a **Table** and so can be used as described there. A partial declaration of the class (with preprocessor directives, opening documentation, etc., omitted) is shown in Figure 15.25, showing several of its members. Additional operations that can be added to class **Table** are described in the exercises.

FIGURE 15.25 Class `Table` declaration.

```
/* Declaration of class Table.
   Note: Class Row, redundant documentation and preprocessor
          directives are omitted to save pages. See the data
          disk for additional documentation.
-------------------------------------------------------------------*

#include "Row.h"
#include "Boolean.h"
#include "Strings.h"
#include <iostream.h>
#include <fstream.h>


class Table
{
protected:                          // hide the data members:

   unsigned
       Rows_,                       //    the number of rows
       Columns_;                    //    the number of columns

   Row                              //    pointer to a Row array,
       *Grid;                       //       allocated at run-time

public:                             // the public operations:

   /***** Constructors and Destructors *****/
   /*----- Class Constructor -----

       Precondition:   A Table object has been declared.
       Receive:        NumRows (optional), the number of rows in the Table
                         NumCols (optional), the number of columns in the
                         Table
                         InitValue (default value zero), to initialize
                         the values of the Table's elements
       Postcondition:  The declared Table object containing this
                         function has its Rows_ member initialized to
                         NumRows and its Columns_ member initialized
                         to NumCols.
   -----------------------------------------------------------------*/
   Table(unsigned NumRows = 0, unsigned NumCols = 0,
        TableElement InitValue);
   /*----- Copy Constructor -----

       Precondition:   The compiler needs a copy of a table object.
       Received:       The Table (reference) object Original to be
                         copied
       Postcondition:  The members of the object containing this
                         function, are copies of those of Original.
   -----------------------------------------------------------------*/
   Table(const Table& Original);
```

FIGURE 15.25   Class **Table** declaration. (cont.)

```
/*----- Destructor -----

   Precondition:  This Table object should no longer exist.
   Postcondition: The run-time storage of this Table has been
                  reclaimed, and its members reset as an
                  empty Table.
-------------------------------------------------------------------*/
~Table(void);


/****** Operations ******/
/*----- Subscript -----

   Receive: i, an index into the Table
   Return:  That Row in Table whose index is i
-------------------------------------------------------------------*/
Row& operator[](unsigned i);

/*----- Assignment -----

   Receive: Tab, a (const reference) Table object
   Return:  The Table containing this function, its data members
            containing copies of those of Tab, and a reference
            to the object assigned.
-------------------------------------------------------------------*/
Table& operator=(const Table& Tan);

TableElement RowSum(unsigned r) const;

TableElement ColumnSum(unsigned c) const;

unsigned NumberOfRows(void) const { return Rows_;}

unsigned NumberOfColumns(void) const { return Columns_;}

friend ostream& operator<<(ostream& Out, const Table& T);

/*----- Interactive Input -----

   Receive:    In, an istream
               InTab, a (reference) Table object
   Input (In): A table of values.
   Return:     The Table object containing this function,
               filled with the input values
   Assumption: InTab has been initialized appropriately with the
               number of rows and columns needed to store the
               input values.
-------------------------------------------------------------------*/
friend istream& operator>>(istream& In, Table& InTab);
```

FIGURE 15.25   Class **Table** declaration. (cont.)

```
/*----- File Input -----
   Receive:      FileName, a Strings object containing the name of
                    an input file
   Input (File): The number of rows and columns and a table
                    of values
   Return:       False, if the file could not be opened; otherwise,
                    true and the Table object containing this
                    function, its Grid member containing the
                    input values
   Assumption:   The first two values in FileName are the number of
                    rows and columns, respectively.
   --------------------------------------------------------------*/
Boolean Load(const Strings& FileName);

Boolean Write(const Strings& FileName) const;
};
```

Sample Program: Filling Order Forms

Mail-order catalogues contain order forms, which are essentially tables, with each row representing an item being ordered and the columns labeled item code, cost per item, number of items, item total, and so on:

Transaction	Item Code	Unit Cost	No. of Items	Item Total
1	12345	2.50	2	5.00
2	98765	3.25	1	3.25
3	01011	8.50	1	8.50
.	.	.	.	.
.	.	.	.	.
.	.	.	.	.

If such order forms were stored in files whose first line had the number of transactions (i.e., rows) in the order and 5 (the number of columns), then class **Table** could be used in a program to check the arithmetic on such forms. The program in Figure 15.25 uses the following algorithm to do this processing:

ALGORITHM FOR PROCESSING ORDER FORMS

/* This algorithm checks the arithmetic on mail order forms stored in a file.

Input (keyboard): The name of a file containing an order form
Input (file):   The order form
Output (screen):   The order form, any arithmetic errors detected, and
                     the total charge for the order
                                                                    */

1. Input the name of a file containing an order form.
2. While the name is not the end-of-data sentinel
   - a. Load a **Table** T with the data from the form.
   - b. Display T on the screen.
   - c. For each row in T:
   Check that the value in the *Unit Cost* column multiplied by the value in the *No. of Items* column is equal to the value in the *Item Total* column, noting and correcting any discrepancies.
   - d. Output the column sum for the *Item Total* column of T.

   End While.

The program in Figure 15.26 encodes this algorithm.

FIGURE 15.26   Processing order forms.

```
/* This program processes order forms, checking their arithmetic.

Input (keyboard): names of file containing the order forms.
Input (file):     an order form. Each file begins with the number
                  of transactions and the number of columns in
                  the order form.
Output:           Instructions and prompts for the user, a copy of
                  each order, a list of the arithmetic errors in
                  each, and the total amount of the order.

-----------------------------------------------------------------*/

#include <iostream.h>
#include <iomanip.h>
#include "Strings.h"
#include "Table.h"

int main(void)
{
   cout
      << "\nThis program processes M X N order forms stored in files\n"
      << "\twhere M is the number of items ordered and N is the\n"
      << "\tnumber of columns on the form.  It assumes that each\n"
      << "\tfile begins with the numbers M and N.\n";

   Strings
      FName;

   enum {                                  // The column headings:
           Transaction,                    //   0
           ItemCode,                       //   1
           UnitCost,                       //   2
           NumItems,                       //   3
           ItemTotal};                     //   4
```

FIGURE 15.26   Processing order forms. (cont.)

```cpp
TableElement
    TransactionTotal;

cout
    << "\nPlease enter the name of an order file (QUIT to quit): ";
cin >> FName;

while (FName != "QUIT")
{
    Table
        OrderForm;

    OrderForm.Load(FName);

    cout << "\nProcessing each transaction in the order:\n"
    for (int r = 0; r < OrderForm.NumberOfRows(); r++)
    {
        cout << setiosflags(ios::fixed)
             << resetiosflags(ios::showpoint)
             << setprecision(2)
             << OrderForm[r][Transaction] << setw(7)
             << OrderForm[r][ItemCode]
             << setiosflags(ios::showpoint)
             << setw(8) << OrderForm[r][UnitCost]
             << resetiosflags(ios::showpoint)
             << setw(3) << OrderForm[r][NumItems]
             << setiosflags(ios::showpoint)
             << setw(8) << OrderForm[r][ItemTotal] << '\n';

        TransactionTotal = OrderForm[r][UnitCost]
                        * OrderForm[r][NumItems]);

        if (TransactionTotal != OrderForm[r][ItemTotal])
        {
            cout << "*** Error in the preceding transaction: "
                 << "Item Total should be $" <<
                 << setiosflags(ios::showpoint | ios::fixed)
                 << setprecision(2)
                 << TransactionTotal << "\n\n";
            OrderForm[r][ItemTotal] = TransactionTotal;
        }
    }

    OrderForm.Write(FName);

    cout << "The correct total charge for this order is: $"
         << OrderForm.ColumnSum(ItemTotal) << "\n\n";

    cout
         << "\n\nPlease enter the name of an order file (QUIT to quit): ";
    cin >> FName;

}
return 0;
}
```

FIGURE 15.26   Processing order forms. (cont.)

Listing of input file `Order1.dat`:

```
4 5
1   13579    2.39    2     4.78
2   24680    4.99    3    12.98
3   97531    1.49    2     1.98
4   08642    1.99    3     3.98
```

Sample run:

```
This program processes M X N order forms stored in files
    where M is the number of items ordered and N is the
    number of columns on the form.   It assumes that each
    file begins with the numbers M and N.

Please enter the name of an order file: Order1.dat

Processing each transaction in the order:
1   13579    2.39    2     4.78
2   24680    4.99    3    12.98
*** Error in the preceding transaction: Item Total should be $14.97

3 97531    1.49    2     1.98
*** Error in preceding transaction: Item Total should be $2.98

4 8642     1.99    3     3.98
*** Error in preceding transaction: Item Total should be $5.97

The correct total charge for this order is: $28.70


Please enter the name of an order file: QUIT
```

*15.5   Pointers and Command-Line Arguments

In Section 3.1, we saw that every C++ program has a function whose name is **main**. The main function differs from other programmer-defined functions in a number of ways. One of the differences is that arguments are passed to the main function by using an array of pointers. How this is done is the topic of this section.

The main function cannot be called directly. Instead, we can think of a main function as being *called* when a program is *executed*. In **command-line environments** such as the UNIX and MS-DOS operating systems, a program is executed by entering its name following the operating system prompt. For example, if we are working on a computer running the MS-DOS operating system and wish to execute the program for Turbo C++ (its name is **TC**), we might enter the command

TC

and the program would begin executing. Similarly, to invoke the text editor **emacs** on a computer running the UNIX operating system, we might enter the command

```
emacs
```

In any command-line environment, entering the name of a C++ program on the command-line can be thought of as issuing a call to the main function of that program.

To edit a C++ source file with Turbo C++ in the MS-DOS environment we can enter the command

```
TC SourceFileName
```

and in the UNIX environment, we can use

```
emacs SourceFileName
```

When invoked in this way, the program (**TC** or **emacs**) begins execution, searches for the file named *SourceFileName*, and (assuming that it is found) opens it for editing. In this example, the file *SourceFileName* is an example of a **command-line argument.** Just as entering the name of the program (**TC** or **emacs**) is like calling the main function of a program, entering the name of the program followed by *SourceFileName* is like calling the main function of a program and passing *SourceFileName* to it as an argument.

Command-line arguments are used by many of the system commands in a command-line environment such as UNIX or MS-DOS. For example, in the UNIX operating system, the command

```
mkdir projects
```

is used to create a new subdirectory named **projects**. (The same command is used in MS-DOS.) Similarly, the command

```
cd projects
```

will change "location" in the directory structure to the subdirectory **projects**. In each case, a program is being executed (one corresponding to **mkdir**, the other to **cd**), and the name **projects** is passed to that program as an argument. In this section, we examine the mechanism by which a main function can receive and process command-line arguments. The techniques discussed can be used in any C++ command-line environment.

Parameters of the Main Function

The general form of the main function is

```
int main( Parameter-List )
{
    Statement-List
}
```

In all the programs we have seen to this point, the parameter list has been **void**:

```
int main(void)
{
    // ... body of the main function ...
}
```

But this need not be the case. A main function can be declared with a parameter list consisting of two predefined parameters:

- argc (the argument count), an integer
- argv (the argument vector), an array of character strings (pointers to characters)

The standard way to declare these parameters in a main function is

```
int main( int argc, char *argv[] )
{
    // ... body of the main function ...
}
```

When a C++ program with the parameters **argc** and **argv** declared in the parameter list of its main function is executed from the command line, two things occur automatically:

1. If **n** character strings were entered on the command-line, then the value of **argc** is set to **n**.
2. The value of **argv[0]** is the address of the first character string of the command-line (the name of the program).
   The value of **argv[1]** is the address of the second character string of the command-line.

$$\vdots$$

   The value of **argv[n-1]** is the address of the nth character string of the command-line.

To illustrate, consider the simple C++ program in Figure 15.27.

   FIGURE 15.27   Introducing **argc** and **argv**.

```
/* This program introduces the predefined parameters argc and argv.

   Output: The value of argc, followed by each character string
           in argv
-----------------------------------------------------------------*/

#include <iostream.h>

int main(int argc, char* argv[])
{
    cout << "\nThere are " << argc
         << " strings on the command line:\n";
```

FIGURE 15.27 Introducing **argc** and **argv**. (cont.)

```
for (int i = 0; i < argc; i++)
   cout << '\t' << "argv[" << i << "] contains: "
        << argv[i] << endl;

return 0;
}
```

In this program the parameter list of the main function contains declarations of **argc** and **argv**. If the compiled version of this program is stored in a file named **example**, then **example** can be executed by entering the command

    <u>**example**</u>

which produces the output

```
There are 1 strings on the command line:
   argv[0] contains: example
```

Thus, within **example**, **argc** has the value 1, and **argv[0]** refers to the character string **example**. If we execute **example** by entering the command

    <u>**example Argument**</u>

then the output produced will be

```
There are 2 strings on the command line:
   argv[0] contains: example
   argv[1] contains: Argument
```

In this execution, we see that **argc** has the value **2**, **argv[0]** contains the character string **example**, and **argv[1]** contains the character string **Argument**. If we execute **example** by

    <u>**example I want an argument**</u>

then the output will be

```
There are 5 strings on the command line:
   argv[0] contains: example
   argv[1] contains: I
   argv[2] contains: want
   argv[3] contains: an
   argv[4] contains: argument
```

From these sample runs it should be evident that the values of **argc** and **argv** depend on what the user enters on the command line when invoking the program. If the user enters the name of the program followed by *i* arguments, then the value of `argc` will be *i* + 1, the number of character strings entered on the command-line; `argv[0]` will refer to the name of the program; and `argv[1]` through `argv[i]` will refer to the *i* arguments that were entered.

Example: A Square Root Calculator

As a simple illustration of the use of `argv` and `argc`, consider the problem of designing a square root calculator that allows the user to enter the value(s) to be processed on the command-line.

Problem.   Construct a program `sroot` that, given a real value, displays the square root of that value; the input value is to be entered on the command-line. For example, if the command

   <u>sroot 4</u>

is entered, the value **2** will be displayed; and if

   <u>sroot 4 9 16 25</u>

is entered, the values **2**, **3**, **4**, and **5** will be displayed.

Specification.   From the problem description, we can identify the following data objects:

Data Object	Kind	Type
A sequence of command-line arguments	Variable	Real
The square roots of those arguments	Variable	Real

Since the program must process command-line arguments, it *receives* the arguments through the parameters of the main function (i.e., `argc` and `argv`). We can thus specify the problem as follows:

   Receive: One or more real values
   Output: The square roots of those values

On the basis of this specification, we can construct the following stub for the program:

```
#include <iostream.h>

int main(int argc, char* argv[])
{
}
```

Design.   In designing the solution, we identify the following operations:

- Retrieve any command-line arguments.
- Take the square root of each argument.
- Output the resulting value(s).

Taking the square root of each argument and outputting the resulting value are straightforward, but retrieving the arguments requires the use of **argc** and **argv**. Consider what the user might enter:

<u>sroot</u>	// error—no data to process (**argc** is 1)
<u>sroot A</u>	// error—nonnumeric data (**argc** is 2, **argv[1]** is *"A"*)
<u>sroot 9</u>	// one value (**argc** is 2, **argv[1]** is *"9"*)
<u>sroot 4 9</u>	// two values (**argc** is 3, **argv[1]** is *"4"*, **argv[2]** is *"9"*)

Generalizing, we see that if the user supplies **i** values to be processed, then **argc** will equal **i** + 1, **argv[1]** will refer to the first value, **argv[2]** will refer to the second value, and so on. We can thus use **argv[i]** to retrieve the **i**th value, with **i** varying from 1 through **argc** - 1.

However, each **argv[i]** contains the address of the first character in a character sequence, and we must take the square root of a value of type **double**. This means that the character sequence beginning at **argv[i]** must be converted to the corresponding **double** value. Fortunately, C++ provides the **strtod()** function in **<stdlib.h>** that performs this operation.[5] That function can also be used to make our program more foolproof by checking its return value (**strtod()** returns 0 if it is unable to convert the string to a numeric value, which will be the case if the user supplies a nonnumeric value on the command-line).

Once we have converted the character sequence to its **double** value, all that remains is to find its square root, which is easy, using the **sqrt()** function declared in **<math.h>**. We then simply display the value and its square root.

We can thus construct the following algorithm, which checks that at least one command-line argument has been given and, if so, uses a loop to sequence through those arguments.

ALGORITHM FOR SROOT

/* This algorithm displays the square roots of a sequence of values
   given by the user on the command-line.

   Receive: A sequence of real values
   Output: The square roots of the values received
                                                                    */

1. If *argc* < 2, display an "incorrect usage" error message and quit.
2. For each integer *i* in the range 1 through argc − 1:
   a. Get *Value*, the double equivalent to argument *i*;
   b. If *Value* > 0
      Display the square root of *Value*.
   Else
      Display an "invalid data" error message.
   End If.
   End For.

---

[5] More accurately, the **strtod()** function is a legacy from C, the parent language of C++.

Coding. This algorithm can be encoded in C++ as shown in Figure 15.28.

 FIGURE 15.28 Encoding **sroot**.

```cpp
/* This program displays the square roots of a sequence of values,
    specified by the user on the command-line.

    Receive: One or more numeric (double) values
    Output:  The square roots of the input values
--------------------------------------------------------------------*/

#include <iostream.h>
#include <math.h>
#include <stdlib.h>

int main(int argc, char* argv[])
{
    if (argc < 2)
    {
        cout << "\n*** Usage: sroot List-of-Positive-Numbers \n\n";
        return -1;
    }

    double
        SqRoot,             // square root of one of the numbers
        Value;              // double equivalent of an argument

    for (int i = 1; i < argc; i++)
    {
        Value = strtod(argv[i], 0);

        if (Value > 0)
            cout <<"\n--> The square root of " << Value
                << " is " << sqrt(Value) << "\n";
        else
            cout << "\n*** " << argv[i] << " is not a valid data item;"
                << "\n*** must be numeric and greater than 0.\n";
    }

    return 0;
}
```

Sample runs:

<u>sroot</u>

*** Usage: sroot List-of-Positive-Numbers

<u>sroot 4</u>

--> The square root of 4 is 2

FIGURE 15.28   Encoding **sroot**. (cont.)

```
sroot 4 ABC 7 9
--> The square root of 4 is 2

*** ABC is not valid data item;
*** must be numeric and greater than 0

--> The square root of 7 is 2.64575

--> The square root of 9 is 3
```

The program in Figure 15.28 is a simple illustration of how **argc** and **argv** can be used, but it barely scratches the surface of the powerful capabilities they provide. We now describe a few of these capabilities.

Command-Line Arguments: Files and Switches

The main function parameters **argc** and **argv** permit the programmer to retrieve whatever arguments were entered on the command line and then use those arguments to determine how the program should behave. For example, suppose that we are working on a UNIX system. To remove several files from the file system, we might enter the command

```
rm FileName1 FileName2 FileName3
```

In this usage of the **rm** command (which is equivalent to **DEL** in MS-DOS), the files to be removed, *FileName1*, *FileName2*, and *FileName3*, are the arguments to the command. It should be clear that the **rm** command can retrieve these files using **argc** and **argv**.

As mentioned earlier, a common text editor used on UNIX systems is the **emacs** editor. One feature of the **emacs** editor is that if you are editing a file named *FileName*, **emacs** creates a backup file named *FileName* ~ . Because such files take up disk space, they should be removed periodically. To remove all such files from the current directory, one can use the command

```
rm * ~
```

Because UNIX (and MS-DOS) treats the asterisk (*) as a **wild card** that matches any character string, the arguments to the **rm** command become all files of the form *FileName* ~ . The **rm** command then removes all such files from the file system.

Using wild cards can be risky, because it is easy to remove files inadvertently. To reduce this risk, an alternative form of the **rm** command can be used:

```
rm -i * ~
```

Instead of blindly removing all files that end in tilde, the command-line argument **-i** causes the **rm** command to query the user before removing each file (i.e., to remove files interactively). For example, execution of this command might produce the following queries from the operating system and user replies:

```
rm: remove MyStats.C ~ ?y
rm: remove change.C ~ ?y
rm: remove minimum.C ~ ?y
rm: remove minmax.C ~ ?y
rm: remove polyN.C ~ ?y
rm: remove sroot.C ~ ?y
```

It should be clear that the **rm** command can use **argc** and **argv** to check for the presence of the **-i** argument and behave interactively if it is present but noninteractively if it is absent.

Command-line arguments like **-i** that alter the behavior of a program are called **switches** and are common in command-line operating systems. For example, switches are used in the MS-DOS operating system, where the **DEL** command is used to remove files. To remove all the backup files created by the Turbo C++ editor (i.e., saved as *FileName*.**BAK**), we could enter the command

```
DEL *.BAK
```

but again, we run the risk of deleting files inadvertently. To make **DEL** remove files interactively, we can enter

```
DEL *.BAK /p
```

where the /**p** switch causes the **DEL** command to prompt the user before deleting each file:

```
MYSTATS.BAK: Delete (Y/N)?y
CHANGE.BAK: Delete (Y/N)?y
MINIMUM.BAK: Delete (Y/N)?y
MINMAX.BAK: Delete (Y/N)?y
POLYN.BAK: Delete (Y/N)?y
SROOT.BAK: Delete (Y/N)?y
```

In summary, most command-line arguments fall into one of three categories:

1. *Values* that the program processes
2. *Files* that the program reads from or writes to (see Chapter 8)
3. *Switches* that in some way alter the behavior of the program

The main function parameters **argc** and **argv** provide a mechanism whereby a program can receive such arguments from a command-line environment.

Exercises

1. Write a program **binary** so that the command

```
binary DecimalValue
```

will calculate and display the binary representation of *DecimalValue*.

2. Rewrite the program to find the median of a list (Figure 15.11) so that the command

     `median ` *`FileName`*

will calculate and display the median of the values in file *`FileName`*, but the command

     `median`

will calculate and display the median of a list of numbers entered from the keyboard.

3. Write a program so that the command

     `number ` *`File1 File2`*

will copy *`File1`* into *`File2`* but with the lines numbered.

4. Write a program so that the command

     `page ` *`File`*

will display the specified file on the screen, one page (23 lines) at a time, waiting between pages until the user presses a key.

*15.6   Pointers and Passing Functions as Arguments

In this section, we examine a different use of pointers: storing the address of a function in a pointer variable and invoking the function by using the pointer.

Functions as Arguments

The functions we have used thus far have taken *values* as their arguments. For example, the call

     `sqrt(4.0)`

passes the value `4.0` to `sqrt()`. Similarly, if `CurrentArg` is a variable and we call

     `sqrt(CurrentArg)`

then the value of `CurrentArg` is passed to `sqrt()`. If we call

     `sqrt(abs(CurrentArg))`

then something slightly more complicated occurs:

1. In determining the value of the argument of `sqrt()`, function `abs()` is called.
2. The value `CurrentArg` is passed to `abs()`.
3. `abs()` computes and returns its value.

4. The return-value of **abs()** is passed to **sqrt()**, which then performs the square root computation.

Thus, in this function call, we are not actually passing the function **abs()** to **sqrt()**, but are instead passing the value returned by the function call **abs(CurrentArg)** to **sqrt()**.

This distinction is important, because there are some situations where it is useful to *pass a function* as an argument to another function. For example, we shall see shortly that any numerical method that involves processing a function can be written most generally if the function is passed to it as an argument.

Pointers to Functions

To permit one function to be passed to another function as an argument, C++ stipulates that

> *The value of a function's* **name** *is the* **starting address** *of that function.*

That is, just as the value of an array name is the base address of that array, for any function **F()**, the value of the name **F** is the starting address of that function. If we declare a type **FunctionPtr** capable of storing *the address of a function* and then declare a variable **FPtr** of that type,

```
FunctionPtr
    FPtr;
```

then the assignment statement

```
FPtr = F;
```

can be used to store the starting address of function **F()** in the variable **FPtr**. Because the value of **FPtr** is a valid address, **FPtr** can be dereferenced using the indirection operator (∗), just like any other pointer variable. That means that the expression

```
(*FPtr)(ArgumentList)
```

dereferences **FPtr**, which (since function **F()** is at that address) calls function **F()**, passing it **ArgumentList**.[6] In fact, we need not even use the indirection operator, since attaching an argument list to **FPtr** automatically dereferences **FPtr**,

```
FPtr(ArgumentList)
```

(much like attaching a list of subscripts to a pointer to an array).

---

[6] The parentheses around ∗**FPtr** are necessary because the dereferencing operator ∗ has lower priority than the function-call operation, (). See Appendix C for a complete table of operator priorities.

Similarly, we can declare **FPtr** as a parameter of a function **G()** and then use **FPtr** to call **F()** from within **G()**:

```
void G(FunctionPtr Fptr)
{
   ...
   Fptr(ArgumentList);
   ...
}
```

Then, we could call **G()** and pass the name of function **F()** as an argument,

```
G(F);
```

and **G()** will call function **F()**.

The **typedef** mechanism can be used to declare **FunctionPtr** as a type whose objects can store the address of a function:

```
typedef ReturnType (*FunctionPtr)(ParameterTypeList);
```

which declares the name **FunctionPtr** as a type whose objects can store the address of any function whose return type is **ReturnType** and whose parameter types match those in **ParameterList**. For example, the declaration

```
typedef double (*FunctionPtr)(double);
```

can be used to declare **FunctionPtr** as a pointer to a function having a single parameter of type **double** and whose return type is **double**. In the discussion that follows, we apply this technique to a numerical method for approximating integrals: the rectangle method.

The Rectangle Method for Approximating a Definite Integral

Students who have had a course in calculus will be familiar with the concept of a *definite integral:*

$$\int_a^b f(x)\, dx$$

For a nonnegative function f, the definite integral gives the area of the region bounded by this graph, the x-axis, and the vertical lines $x = a$ and $x = b$:

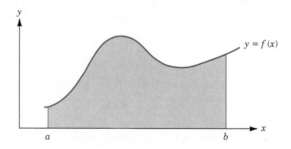

One simple method of approximating this area, called the *rectangle method,* is to divide the interval $[a, b]$ into n subintervals, each of length $\Delta x = (b - a)/n$, and then form rectangles having these subintervals as bases and with altitudes given by the values of the function at the midpoints (or left or right endpoints) $x_1, x_2, \ldots,$ x_n of the subintervals, as illustrated in the following diagram:

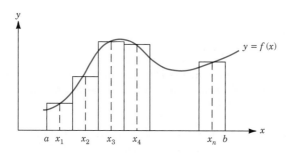

The sum of the areas of these rectangles

$$f(x_1)\Delta x + f(x_2)\Delta x + \cdots + f(x_n)\Delta x$$

which is the same as

$$[f(x_1) + f(x_2) + \cdots + f(x_n)]\Delta x$$

or, written more concisely using Σ (sigma) notation,

$$\left[\sum_{i=1}^{n} f(x_i) \right] \Delta x$$

is then an approximation to the area under the curve.

The preceding figure shows this method for a curve lying above the x-axis. It may also be used to approximate the definite integral of a function whose graph falls below the x axis. In this case, the integral does not give the total area between the curve and the axis but, rather, gives the area of the region(s) above the axis minus the area of the region(s) below the axis.

Figure 15.29 presents a function `RectangleMethod()` that uses this rectangle method to approximate the area under the graph of an arbitrary function $f(x)$ from $x = a$ to $x = b$. The address of the function to be processed, the endpoints a and b of the interval of integration, and the number n of rectangles are each received by `RectangleMethod()` as parameters. We would store this function in the implementation file of an appropriately named library such as `NumMethods`.

FIGURE 15.29 **NumMethods** Implementation File.

```
/* This file contains the definitions of some numerical methods
   functions.

   ...
   ----------------------------------------------------------------*/

#include "NumMethods.h"

/*----------------------------------------------------------------
RectangleMethod approximates the definite integral of a function
   using the rectangle method with altitudes chosen at the
   midpoints of the subintervals.

   Receive: FPtr, a pointer to the function being integrated
            Left, Right, the endpoints of the integration
            n, the number of rectangles to be used
   Return:  The approximate value of the definite integral of the
            function over the interval [Left, Right]
   ----------------------------------------------------------------*/

double RectangleMethod(FunctionPtr FPtr,
                       double Left, double Right, int n)
{
   double
      DeltaX = (Right - Left) / n,
      MidPt = Left + DeltaX / 2.0,
      Sum = 0.0;

   for (int i = 1; i <= n; i++)       // for each rectangle
   {
      Sum += FPtr(MidPt);             // add f(midpoint) to Sum
      MidPt += DeltaX;                // move to next rectangle
   }

   return Sum * DeltaX;               // compute area approximation
}

// ... additional numerical methods function definitions
```

We would declare this function along with the name **FunctionPtr** in the header file of **NumMethods**. To declare **FunctionPtr** as a pointer to an arbitrary function **F()**, the parameter-type list should contain a single entry of type **double**, and the return type should be **double**, as shown in Figure 15.30. Default values can be provided for parameters **a** (**0**), **b** (**1**), and **n** (**100**), if desired.

FIGURE 15.30   **NumMethods** header file.

```
/* This file contains the declarations for NumMethods.
 ...
 ---------------------------------------------------------------*/

typedef double (*FunctionPtr)(double);    // pointer to function f(x)

double RectangleMethod(                    // integral approximation
        FunctionPtr FPtr,                  //    the function
        double a,                          //    left endpoint
        double b,                          //    right endpoint
        int n);                            //    number of rectangles

// ... additional numerical methods function declarations
```

Given such a function, we can use function **RectangleMethod()** to approximate the definite integral of an arbitrary function. Figure 15.31 presents a program that uses function **RectangleMethod()** to approximate the area under the graph of $y = x^2 + 1$ from $x = a$ to $x = b$. The program queries the user for the endpoints a and b of the interval of integration and n, the number of rectangles to be used in the approximation. Once these values have been received, they and the function to be integrated are passed as arguments to function **RectangleMethod()**.

FIGURE 15.31   Numerical integration of a function.

```
/* This program approximates the definite integral of a function
       F(x) from x = a to x = b using the rectangle method.

    Input:    Endpoints a and b and the number n of rectangles
    Output:   Prompts to the user and the approximation of the integral

Note: To find the integral of a different F(x), redefine
      function F().
 ---------------------------------------------------------------*/

double F(double x)                         // the function being integrated
{
   return x*x + 1;                         // change here as desired...
}

//-------------------------------------------------------------------

#include <iostream.h>

#include "NumMethods.h"
```

FIGURE 15.31 Numerical integration of a function. (cont.)

```cpp
int main(void)
{
    cout << "\nThis program approximates the definite integral of a"
            "\n\tfunction using the rectangle method.\n";

    int
        n;                              // the number of rectangles

    double
        a,                              // left endpoint of integral
        b,                              // right endpoint of integral
        ApproximateInt;                 // the approximate integral

    char
        Answer;                         // query response variable

    do
    {
        do                              // get the endpoints
        {
            cout << "\nEnter the endpoints (a & b) of the integral: ";
            cin >> a >> b;
        }
        while (a >= b);

        do                              // get the number of rectangles
        {
            cout << "Enter the number of rectangles to be used: ";
            cin >> n;

            ApproximateInt = RectangleMethod(F, a, b, n);

            cout << "--> An approximation to the integral using "
                 << n << " rectangles is " << ApproximateInt << "\n\n";

            cout << "\nChange the number of rectangles (y or n)? ";
            cin >> Answer;
        }
        while ((Answer == 'y') || (Answer == 'Y'));

        cout << "\nChange the starting interval (y or n)? ";
        cin >> Answer;
    }
    while ((Answer == 'y') || (Answer == 'Y'));

    return 0;
}
```

FIGURE 15.31   Numerical integration of a function. (cont.)

Sample run:

```
This program approximates the definite integral of a
   function using the rectangle method.

Enter the endpoints (a & b) of the interval: 0 1
Enter the number of rectangles to be used: 20
--> An approximation to the integral using 20 rectangles is 1.333125

Change the number of rectangles (y or n)? y
Enter the number of rectangles to be used: 100
--> An approximation to the integral using 100 rectangles is 1.333325

Change the number of rectangles (y or n)? n

Change the starting interval (y or n)? y

Enter the endpoints (a & b) of the interval: -1 2
Enter the number of rectangles to be used: 10
--> An approximation to the integral using 10 rectangles is 5.9775

Change the number of rectangles (y or n)? y
Enter the number of rectangles to be used: 20
--> An approximation to the integral using 20 rectangles is 5.99437

Change the number of rectangles (y or n)? y
Enter the number of rectangles to be used: 50
--> An approximation to the integral using 50 rectangles is 5.9991

Change the number of rectangles (y or n)? n

Change the starting interval (y or n)? n
```

This technique can be used to implement any of the function-processing numerical methods, such as the bisection method discussed in Section 6.8 and results in a library of general and powerful functions that are easily reused.

Exercises

1. Rewrite function **Bisection()** in Figure 6.19 so that it receives the function f via a function pointer parameter and finds an approximate solution of $f(x) = 0$ using the bisection method.

2. Another method for finding an approximate solution of an equation $f(x) = 0$ is Newton's method, described in Exercise 4 of Section 6.8. Write a function **Newton()** that, given a function f via a parameter, finds an approximate solution of an equation $f(x) = 0$ using Newton's method.

3. In this section, we considered the numerical approximation of integrals using rectangles. As the following figure indicates, a better approximation can usually be obtained by using trapezoids rather than rectangles:

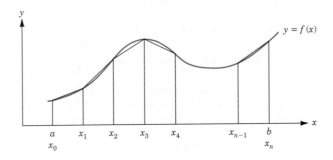

The sum of the areas of these trapezoids is given by

$$\sum_{i=1}^{n} [\, f(x_{i-1}) + f(x_i)]\frac{\Delta x}{2}$$

which can also be written

$$\frac{\Delta x}{2}[\, f(x_0) + 2f(x_1) + 2f(x_2) + \cdots + 2f(x_{n-1}) + f(x_n)]$$

or

$$\Delta x\left[\frac{f(a) + f(b)}{2} + \sum_{i=1}^{n-1} f(x_i)\right]$$

Write a function **Trapezoid()** that, given a function f via a parameter, approximates the integral of f using this *trapezoidal method.*

4. Another method of numerical integration that generally produces better approximations than either the rectangle method described in this section or the trapezoidal method described in Exercise 3 is based on the use of parabolas and is known as *Simpson's rule.* In this method, the interval $[a, b]$ is divided into an even number n of subintervals, each of length Δx, and the sum

$$\frac{\Delta x}{3}[\, f(x_0) + 4f(x_1) + 2f(x_2) + 4f(x_3) + 2f(x_4) + \cdots$$
$$+ 2f(x_{n-2}) + 4f(x_{n-1}) + f(x_n)]$$

is used to approximate the integral of f over the interval $[a, b]$. Write a function **Simpson()** that, given a function f via a parameter, uses Simpson's rule to approximate the integral of f.

Program Design

The values of the variables that we have considered in previous chapters have been specific data items such as integers, real numbers, characters, and strings. Pointer variables, however, have memory addresses as values. Consequently, the manner in which pointer variables are used is quite different from that in which other kinds of variables are processed, and this can cause special difficulties for both beginning and experienced programmers. Pointers are used to store the addresses of objects whose memory is allocated at run-time. As a result, operations on such objects that

- Create the object require that its memory be explicitly allocated using **new**;
- Destroy the object require that its memory be explicitly deallocated using **delete**; or
- Modify the size of the object require that its old memory be deallocated and then new memory of the correct size be reallocated.

When used in conjunction with the run-time allocation/deallocation commands **new** and **delete**, pointers allow the construction of objects whose memory requirements are tailored to the size of the data stored in them, eliminating the problems of wasted memory and overflow that characterize objects built using fixed-size objects.

Potential Problems

The operations used to process pointers are quite different from those used to process objects whose memory is allocated at compile time. Some of the main features to remember when using pointer variables and run-time allocation in C++ programs are these:

1. *Use the* **typedef** *mechanism to declare pointer types.* This greatly increases the readability of programs, which reduces the likelihood of errors and makes errors easier to find when they do occur.

2. *Each pointer variable is bound to a type; a pointer is the address of a memory location in which only a value of that type can be stored.* For example, if **P** and **Q** are pointer variables declared by

   ```
   int
       *P;
   double
       *Q;
   ```

   then **P** is bound to the type **integer** and **Q** to the type **double**. Memory locations pointed to by **P** can store only integer values, whereas those to which **Q** points can store only real values.

3. *Care must be used when operating on pointers because they have memory addresses as values.* In particular:

■ *A pointer* **P** *can be assigned a value in the following ways:*

```
P = &V;        (where V is a variable of the type to which P points)
P = 0;         (the NULL address)
P = Q;         (where Q is a pointer to the same type as P)
P = new Type;  (where Type is the type to which P points)
```

■ *Arithmetic operations on pointers are restricted.* For example, two pointer values (memory addresses) cannot be added, subtracted, multiplied, or divided. However, an integer value **i** can be added to or subtracted from the value of a pointer variable, which changes the address in the pointer by **i * sizeof(Type)**, where *Type* is the type to which the pointer is bound.

■ *Relational operators can be used to compare pointers, but the two pointers must be bound to the same type or one or both may be the NULL address.*

■ *Pointers may be used as parameters in functions, but corresponding parameters and arguments must be bound to the same type.* A function may also return a pointer as its return-value, but the type to which that pointer is bound must be the same as the type to which the function points.

4. *Don't confuse memory locations with the contents of memory locations.* If **P** is a pointer, its value is the address of a memory location; ***P** refers to the contents of that location. Both **P++** and **(*P)++** are valid (if **P** is bound to type **int** or **double**), but the first increments the address in **P**, whereas the second simply adds 1 to the contents of the memory location at that address.

5. *The NULL address ≠ undefined.* A pointer becomes defined when it is assigned the address of a memory location or the NULL address. Assigning a pointer the NULL address is analogous to initializing a numeric variable to zero.

6. *If the value of a pointer* **P** *is undefined or is the NULL address, then an attempt to dereference* **P** *is an error.* On UNIX systems, doing so may produce one of the infamous "segmentation fault" or "bus error" run-time error messages.

7. *When memory is allocated at run time with the* **new** *operation, the value returned by* **new** *should be tested before proceeding, to ensure that the operation was successful.* The **assert()** mechanism provides a convenient way to do this. For example, if **P** is a pointer in which we are storing the address of a newly allocated block of memory

```
P = new SomeType;
```

then the assertion

```
assert(P != 0);
```

can be used to verify that the **new** operation returned a valid (non-NULL) address.

8. *Memory locations that were once associated with a pointer variable and that are no longer needed should be returned to the free store by using the function* **delete**. Special care is required so that memory locations are not rendered

inaccessible. For example, if **P** and **Q** are pointer variables bound to the same type, the assignment statement

```
P = Q;
```

causes **P** to point to the same memory location as that pointed to by **Q**. If the program should execute

```
delete Q;
```

then the memory previously pointed to by **Q** is deallocated, leaving an invalid address in **P**, so that any attempt to dereference **P** (i.e., *P) will usually generate a run-time error. This problem occurs so frequently, it has a special name—the **dangling pointer problem.**

Programming Projects

Virtually any of the exercises and projects from Chapters 12 and 13 can be redone using run-time allocation. Suggestions include the following:

1. Design and implement a **Vector** class (see Project 1 in Chapter 12) that provides the addition, subtraction, sum, and inner product functions for **Vector** objects of "arbitrary" length. Write a menu-driver program that operates as a **Vector** calculator.

2. Design and implement a class **BigInt** whose values are integers (see Project 4 in Chapter 12), where the user of the program can specify the number of digits in each integer.

3. Design and implement a program that acts as a screen-oriented text editor. (*Hint:* Assume that the first line of the file to be edited contains the number of lines in the file, and build a class containing a run-time allocated array of **Strings** to store the file.) The editor should display

- Fifteen to twenty numbered lines at a time,
- The current "cursor" position (line and column), and
- A menu of the commands that allow the user to replace, insert, delete, and find the position of text strings in the file, as well as load and store a file.

Optionally, allow the user to enter the name of the file to be edited on the command-line.

4. In Chapter 13, a **Set** class was implemented, in which the maximum number of elements was bounded by the constant **Set::MaxElements**. Rewrite class **Set** to eliminate this limitation by replacing its fixed-size array with a run-time allocated array. In particular, declarations like the following:

```
Set
    S1(M),
    S2(N, N);
```

should initialize **S1** as a set that can store *M* values in the range 0 through *M* - 1 and is initialized to the empty set; and **S2** as a set that can store *N* elements and is initialized to the universal set.

5. A certain professor maintains a file containing a table of student grades for each class she teaches. The first line of the file contains the number of rows and columns in the table. Each row of the table represents the exam scores of a given student, and each column represents the scores on a given exam. The maximum possible score on each exam is 100 points. Write a program that, given the name of such a file (optionally on the command-line), generates a report summarizing the overall percentage for each student and the average score on each exam.

6. Rewrite class **Matrix** from Section 14.4 as a class derived from class **Table** in this chapter, and include functions to perform **Matrix** addition, subtraction, and transposition (see the exercises at the end of Section 14.4). Then write a menu-driven program that operates as a **Matrix** calculator.

7. Trans-Fryslan Airlines has three different models of passenger planes:

   - The 101 is a charter plane that carries up to 10 passengers, with the seats arranged in five rows of two seats each.
   - The 202 is a commuter plane that carries up to 40 passengers, with the seats arranged in ten rows of four seats each.
   - The 404 is a wide-body plane that carries up to 160 passengers, with the seats arranged in twenty rows of eight seats each.

   Write a reservation system for TFA that, given a flight number (the name of a file), displays the seating chart for that flight, displaying Xs for seats that have been booked and leaving blank those seats that are not booked. For example, if flight 1234 is a model 101 plane with five passengers, its seating chart might appear as follows:

	A	B
1	X	
2		X
3	X	
4		X
5	X	

   indicating that seats 1A, 2B, 3A, 4B, and 5A have been booked, and that the other five seats are available. The program should allow the agent to reserve seats on the flight, cancel reservations, and change to a different flight. Assume that the reservations for each flight are stored in a separate file and that the first line of each file is the airplane model of that flight.

LINKED LISTS, STACKS, AND QUEUES

16

I've got a little list, I've got a little list.
GILBERT AND SULLIVAN
The Mikado

CHAPTER CONTENTS

In Chapter 15, we saw how the **new** and `delete` operations can be used to allocate and deallocate storage for an array at run-time. By allocating and deallocating memory at run-time, the `List` and `Table` classes we constructed in Chapter 15 allow us to construct data objects whose memory requirements are determined by the amount of data to be stored. Such objects avoid the wasted memory and over-flow problems that characterize arrays whose memory is allocated at compile-time.

For a list or table whose size is relatively constant, run-time allocation offers a convenient way to tailor the size of the object to the quantity of data stored in it. However, in programs that process lists or tables whose sizes change frequently during program execution, any array-based structure—whether allocated at com-pile-time or run-time—suffers from a significant drawback. Enlarging an array so that new values can be added requires that

- A new larger array be allocated;
- The elements of the old array be copied into the new array;
- The new elements be written into the new array; and
- The old array be deallocated.

A similar sequence of steps is required to decrease the size of an array.

Processing lists whose sizes change frequently can thus involve extensive copying of elements. The time to perform this copying, coupled with the time to allocate the new array and deallocate the old array, can make these operations very time-consuming.

One way to avoid this problem is to use run-time allocation to implement an object as a collection of structures (called nodes), each of which contains at least two members: one to store a data value and one to store a *link* to the next node:[1]

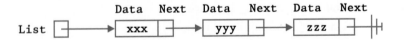

As indicated by the diagram, a node's link consists of a pointer containing the address of the next node in the list. A list can be formed as a series of linked nodes, producing a structure called a *linked list*. In this chapter, we consider the imple-mentation of linked objects in C++.

16.1   Introduction to Linked Lists

In Chapters 12 through 15, we described how an array can be used to store and process a list. Although this array-based implementation of a list works well for lists whose sizes remain quite constant, it is not an efficient way of processing *dynamic lists* that grow and shrink because elements are inserted and/or deleted. The reason is that each time a new element is inserted into such a list, array elements may have to be shifted to make room for it.

---

[1] This use of the word *link* refers to a member of a structure that is a pointer and should not be confused with the translation phase called *linking*.

To illustrate the problem, suppose we wish to insert the new value 56 after the element 48 in the list of integers

23, 25, 34, 48, 61, 79, 82, 89, 91, 99

to produce the new list

23, 25, 34, 48, 56, 61, 79, 82, 89, 91, 99

If the list elements are stored in an array, the array elements in positions 5 through 10 must first be shifted into positions 6 through 11 before the new element can be inserted at position 5:

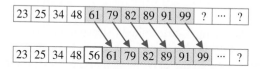

Removing a list element also requires shifting array elements. For example, to delete the second item in the list

23, 25, 34, 48, 56, 61, 79, 82, 89, 91, 99

we must shift the array elements in positions 3 through 11 into locations 2 through 10 to "close the gap" in the array:

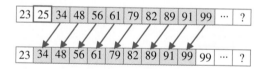

A linked list is an alternative structure for storing the elements of a list, and, as we will see, it provides a better way to implement a dynamic list. A **linked list** consists of a collection of elements called **nodes,** each of which stores two items of information:

1. A data value of the list
2. A **pointer,** whose value is the address of the node containing the next data value in the list

This second item is called a **link;** hence the name linked list.

There are different approaches to implementing a linked list, but one approach is to maintain pointers to the first and last nodes in the list. For example, a linked list named **L** storing the list of names **Brown, Jones,** and **Smith** might be pictured as follows:

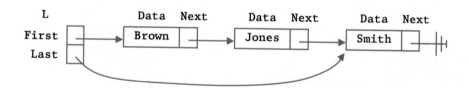

In this diagram, arrows represent links, so that **L.First** points to the first node in the list and **L.Last** points to the last node in the list. The **Data** member of each node stores one of the names in the list, and a node's **Next** member stores a pointer to the node containing the next value in the list. The ''ground'' symbol in the **Next** member of the last node represents the NULL (zero) address, indicating that the **Data** value in that node is the final value in the list.

Inserting Items into a Linked List

One of the features of a linked list is that no list elements need be moved when an element is inserted into or removed from the list. We demonstrate this first for the insertion operation.

To insert a new data value into a linked list, we must first use the **new** operation to obtain a new node and store the data value in its **Data** member. The second step is to connect this new node to the existing list, and for this, there are three cases to consider: (1) insertion at the beginning of the list, (2) insertion at the end of the list, and (3) insertion after some element in the list.

To illustrate the first case, suppose that we wish to insert the name **Adams** at the beginning of the preceding linked list. We first obtain a new node and store the name **Adams** in its data part.

Get a node pointed to by **NewNodePtr.**
Store **"Adams"** in the **Data** part of this node.

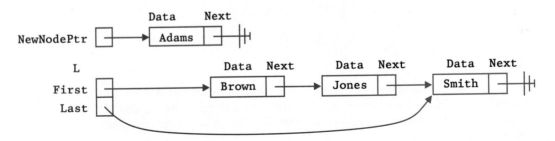

We then insert this node into the list by setting its link part to point to the first node in the list, and then setting the **First** member of **List** to point to this new first node:

Set the **Next** part of the node pointed to by
NewNodePtr equal to **L.First.**

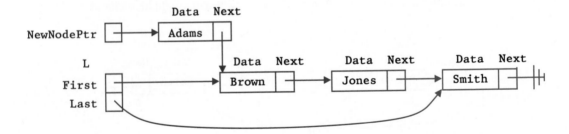

Set **L.First** equal to **NewNodePtr**.

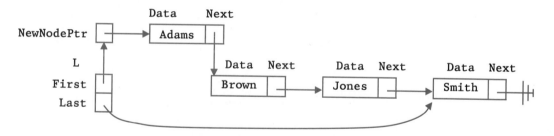

To illustrate the second case, suppose that we wish to insert the name **Wagner** at the end of the list. We allocate a new node and store the name **Wagner** in it:

Get a node pointed to by **NewNodePtr**.
Store **"Wagner"** in the **Data** part of this node.

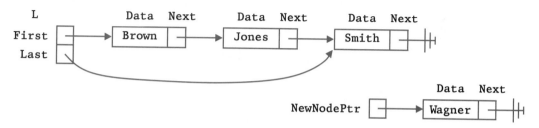

We then make the **Next** member of the last node point to this new node, and then update the **Last** member of **L**:

Set the **Next** member of the node pointed to by
L.Last equal to the value in **NewNodePtr**.

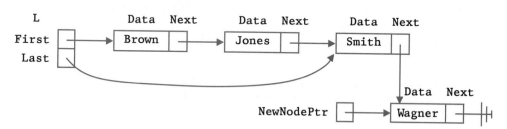

Set the **Last** member of **L** to the value in **NewNodePtr**.

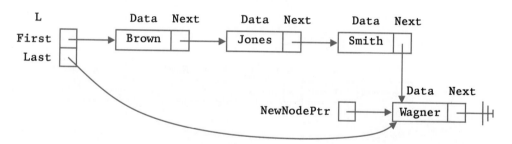

To illustrate the third case, suppose that we wish to insert the name **Lewis** after the node containing **Jones** and that **PredPtr** is a pointer to this predecessor.

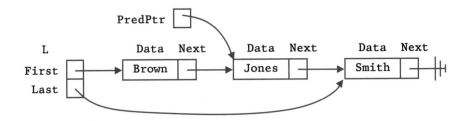

We begin as before by obtaining a new node in which to store the name **Lewis**:

Get a node pointed to by **NewNodePtr**.
Store **"Lewis"** in the **Data** part of this node.

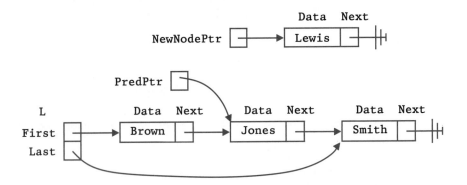

We insert this node into the list by first setting its link part equal to the pointer in the **Next** part of the node pointed to by **PredPtr** so that it points to its successor, and then resetting the link part of the predecessor node to point to this new node:

Set the **Next** part of the node pointed to by **NewNodePtr**
equal to the **Next** part of the node pointed to by **PredPtr**.

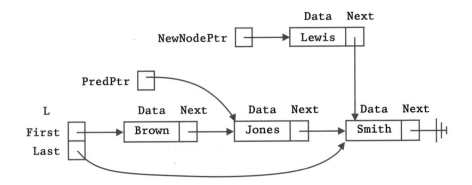

Set the **Next** part of the node pointed to
by **PredPtr** equal to **NewNodePtr**:

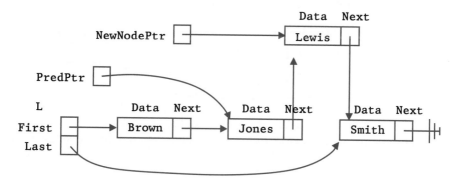

These examples demonstrate that each of the insertions into a linked list can be
done with only three assignments.

Deleting Items from a Linked List

Deleting an item from a linked list can also be done without the extensive copying
required for an array-based list. With deletion, there are only two cases to consider:
(1) deleting the first element in the list, and (2) deleting an element that has a
predecessor. To illustrate the first case, suppose that we have the list

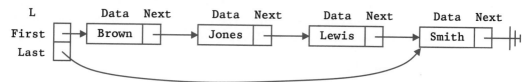

and we wish to delete the name **Brown** from the list. This case is easy—we simply
make **TempPtr** point to the node we intend to delete:

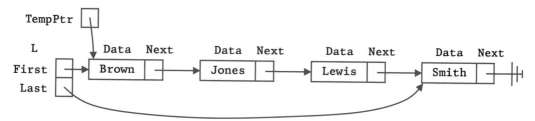

We next set the **First** member of **L** to point to the second node in the list,

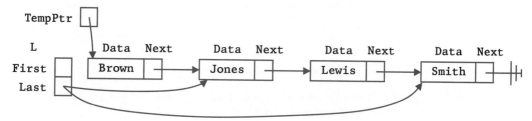

and then deallocate the node pointed to by `TempPtr`:

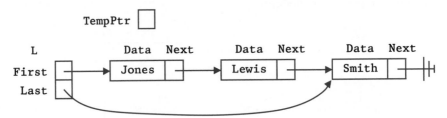

The second case is almost as easy as the first. For example, suppose we wish to delete the node containing `Lewis` from the preceding list, and that `PredPtr` points to the predecessor of this node. We first set `TempPtr` to point to the node we wish to delete:

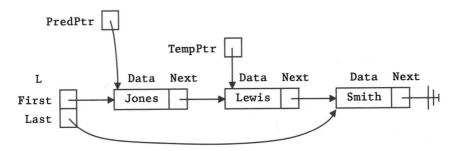

We then set the `Next` member of the node pointed to by `PredPtr` to the `Next` member of the node pointed to by `TempPtr`,

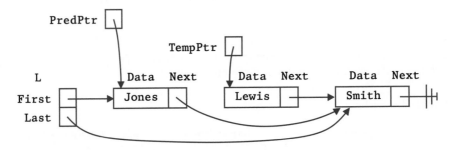

and then deallocate the node pointed to by `TempPtr`:

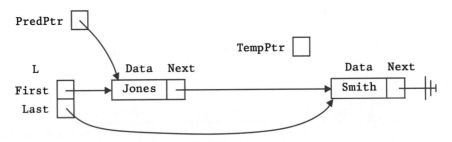

In the special case that the last element of the list is being deleted, we must also set the `Last` member of `L` equal to `PredPtr`.

As the preceding examples demonstrate, it is possible to insert or delete items in a linked list without shifting list elements as required in the array-based implementation of a list. In the next section, we examine how a linked list can be implemented in C++.

Exercises

1. Design an operation to count the nodes in a linked list **L**.

2. Design an operation to determine the average of a linked list **L** of real numbers.

3. Design an operation to concatenate two linked lists to yield a new linked list.

4. Design an operation to determine whether the data items in a linked list **L** are in ascending order.

5. Suppose the items stored in two linked lists are in ascending order. Design an operation to merge these two lists to produce a new list with the items in ascending order.

6. Design an operation to reverse a linked list **L**. Do not copy the list elements; rather, reset links and pointers so that **L.First** points to the last node, **L.Last** points to the first node, and all links between nodes are reversed.

16.2 Implementing Linked Lists

At this stage, we have described linked lists at an abstract, logical level. Although there are a few programming languages (such as LISP, an acronym for LISt Processing) that provide dynamic lists as predefined objects, most languages require the programmer to implement such lists using other predefined data types. In this section, we show how they can be implemented in C++ using the class and pointer mechanisms.

Declaring a Linked List

The examples of the last section indicate that two different declarations are useful in implementing linked lists:

1. A **ListNode** object with a **Data** and a **Next** member
2. A **LinkedList** object with (at least) a **First** and a **Last** member

In our implementation of linked lists, we have added a third data member named **NumNodes**, in which the number of nodes in the linked list (i.e., the *length* of the list) is stored. Figure 16.1 shows the data members of this implementation.

FIGURE 16.1   The data members of class **LinkedList**.

```
/* This is part of the header file for the LinkedList library.
-------------------------------------------------------------*/

#include "Strings.h"

typedef Strings ListElement;    // make a 'generic' ListElement type

class LinkedList
{                      // LinkedList data members are protected, to allow
protected:             //   them to be accessed by derived classes

   struct ListNode // use a struct so that LinkedList member functions
   {                //   can access the ListNode members
      ListElement
         Data;      // the value being stored
      ListNode
         *Next;     // the link to the next list node

      // ... ListNode member functions omitted ...
   }
      *First,       // a pointer to the first node in the linked list
      *Last;        // a pointer to the last node in the linked list

   int
      NumNodes;     // the length of the linked list


public:

   // ... LinkedList member functions omitted ...

};
```

Once again, we use the **typedef** mechanism to create a synonym type
ListElement:

> ```
> #include "Strings.h"
> ```
>
> ```
> typedef Strings ListElement;
> ```

This declaration of **ListElement** is appropriate for a linked list of names,

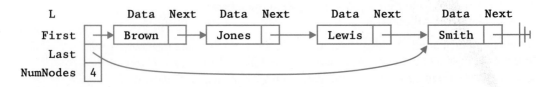

whereas for a linked list of employee records,

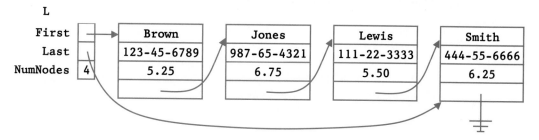

we would use the declaration:

```
#include "Employee.h"

typedef Employee ListElement;
```

From the preceding discussion of the insert and delete operations, it should be evident that the operations on a **LinkedList** must be able to access the **Data** and **Next** members of a **ListNode**. Thus, it seems that a struct is the natural structure to use for implementing a **ListNode**. However, a **ListNode** is simply a detail of the implementation of a **LinkedList**—a program using a **LinkedList** should not be able to directly access a **ListNode** (or its members), and this suggests that a **ListNode** should be protected as a class. Both of these seemingly contradictory objectives can be achieved by

1. Declaring a **ListNode** as a struct; but
2. Nesting the declaration of that struct within a declaration of class **LinkedList**.

This gives the following nested structure for class **LinkedList**:

```
class LinkedList
{
    ...
    struct ListNode
    {
        ...
    };
    ...
};
```

A struct declaration creates a type, and this allows us to declare the **First** and **Last** members as pointers to a **ListNode** by naming them as such after the **ListNode** declaration:

```
struct ListNode
{
    ...
}
    *First,
    *Last;
```

The type `ListElement` can then be used to declare the `Data` member in a `ListNode` within `LinkedList`:

```
ListElement
   Data;
```

Because the `Next` member of a `ListNode` must store the address of a `ListNode`, it is declared as a pointer to a `ListNode`:

```
ListNode
   *Next;
```

This declaration is unusual in that it contains a `ListNode` member named `Next` whose type is `ListNode*`. That is, the declaration of type `ListNode` uses the name `ListNode`, making it a *recursive declaration*. Objects such as `ListNode`, whose declarations refer to themselves, are called **self-referencing objects** and are commonly used in implementing linked objects.

Last but not least, we declare the `NumNodes` member of `LinkedList` to be an integer.

`ListNode` Operations

As mentioned in the preceding section, each `ListNode` will be created and destroyed dynamically using the `new` and `delete` operations, respectively. Its members will also be accessed directly by the operations on (i.e., the member functions of) a `LinkedList`. It might seem at first glance that no operations on a `ListNode` are required. Although this is technically true, there are two constructors that will allow us to create `ListNode` objects far more conveniently—one that initializes a `ListNode` with default values and one that initializes a `ListNode` with provided values. We describe these operations next.

A Default-Value Constructor. A `ListNode` can be created by using the expression

```
new ListNode
```

As we shall see shortly, it is convenient if this statement can be used to autoinitialize the `Next` member of the `ListNode` to the null pointer. We can accomplish this by defining the following `ListNode` constructor:

```
ListNode(void)
{
   Next = 0;
}
```

The simplicity of this constructor suggests that it be defined in the struct `ListNode`.

An Explicit-Value Constructor. A second useful operation is a constructor that initializes the members of a `ListNode` using values passed as arguments. This can be accomplished with the following `ListNode` constructor:

```
ListNode(ListElement E, ListNode *Ptr = 0)
{
   Data = E;
   Next = Ptr;
}
```

If `ListElement` is a synonym for `Strings`, then this constructor can be invoked with an expression such as

```
new ListNode("Lewis");
```

which will construct a new `ListNode` whose `Data` member contains the string `"Lewis"` and whose `Next` member contains the NULL address:

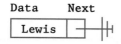

Alternatively, a pointer value may be passed as a second argument to the constructor to set the `Next` member of the new `ListNode` to some non-NULL address.

Note that two separate class constructors must be provided to perform these operations because we are unable to provide a default value for the ''generic'' `ListElement` parameter `InitVal`. A default value for parameter `InitVal` must be of type `ListElement`, which could be a synonym for any predefined or programmer-defined type, and there is no default value that is appropriate for every possible type. Because of this, two separate constructors for a `ListNode` are needed—one that initializes the `Data` member and one that leaves it undefined.

LinkedList Operations

The operations on a `LinkedList` object are similar to those on a `List` object from earlier chapters. They include the following:

- Constructing an empty `LinkedList` (initialization)
- Outputting a `LinkedList` (either interactively or to a file)
- Constructing a copy of a `LinkedList`
- Determining the length of a `LinkedList`
- Finding the value at a given index in a `LinkedList`
- Searching a `LinkedList` for a given value
- Inserting an item into a `LinkedList`
- Deleting an item from a `LinkedList`
- Destroying a `LinkedList`

In the remainder of this section, we implement these operations. Other operations, such as assignment, input, subscript, and concatenation are left as exercises.

Constructing an Empty Linked List. To construct a linked list, we must design a constructor function that initializes a `LinkedList` as an empty list. This is easily done by setting the `First` and `Last` members to the NULL pointer and setting the `NumNodes` member to zero. Figure 16.2 presents a constructor function definition that does this:

FIGURE 16.2 **LinkedList** class constructor.

```
/* This function initializes a LinkedList to be empty.

   Precondition:  The LinkedList containing this function has been
                  declared.
   Postcondition: That LinkedList is initialized as an empty list.
-------------------------------------------------------------------*/

LinkedList(void)
{
   First = 0;
   Last = 0;
   NumNodes = 0;
}
```

Because of the relative simplicity of this function, we store its definition in the public section of class **LinkedList**.

Given such a definition, the declaration

```
LinkedList
   L;
```

can be used to construct and initialize an empty **LinkedList** object named L:

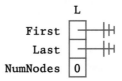

Displaying a Linked List. To display each element in the list, we traverse the list, "visiting" each node, using **operator<<** to display its **Data** member (assuming that **operator<<** is defined for the type **ListElement**), and then moving to the next node, until the end of the list is reached. As usual, we implement this output function by overloading **operator<<** as shown in Figure 16.3.

FIGURE 16.3 Displaying a **LinkedList**.

```
/* This function displays a LinkedList on the screen.
   Receive: Out, the stream to which the values are to be sent;
            L, the list of values
   Output:  The values from L
   Return:  Out
-----------------------------------------------------------*/

ostream& operator<<(ostream& Out, const LinkedList& L)
{
   LinkedList::ListNode
      *TempPtr = L.First;                 // start at the list's beginning
```

FIGURE 16.3 Displaying a **LinkedList**. (cont.)

```
    while (TempPtr != 0)                 // while there are unvisited nodes:
    {
        Out << TempPtr->Data << ' ';     //    display the node's data
        TempPtr = TempPtr->Next;         //    advance TempPtr to next node
    }

    return Out;                          // return ostream for chaining
}
```

Note that in order for a friend function to access the name of a type declared in the private section of the class (e.g., **ListNode**), the fully qualified name of that type must be given:

LinkedList::ListNode

As usual, **operator<<** should be declared as a friend function in the public section of class **LinkedList**:

friend ostream& operator<<(ostream& Out, const LinkedList& L);

This function can then be invoked with the statement

cout << L << endl;

If **L** is the **LinkedList** considered earlier,

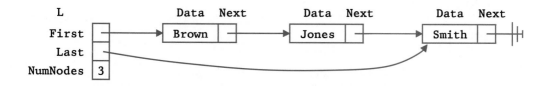

then the function begins by setting **TempPtr** to point at the first node in the list:

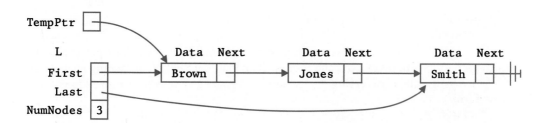

Control then reaches the while loop,

```
while (TempPtr != 0)
{
    Out << TempPtr->Data << ' ';
    TempPtr = TempPtr->Next;
}
```

and because the loop condition is initially true, execution passes through the body of the loop, which uses the **Strings** definition of **operator<<** to display the name **Brown**, and then advances **TempPtr** to the next node in the list:

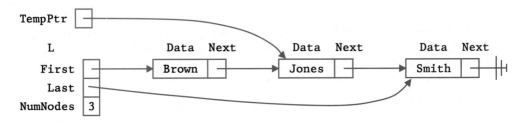

The loop condition evaluates to true, and so the loop body is executed again, which displays the name **Jones**, and advances **TempPtr** to the next node:

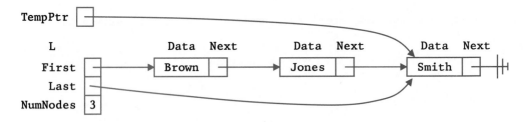

The loop condition again evaluates to true, and so the loop body is executed again, which displays the value **Smith** and replaces the pointer in **TempPtr** with the NULL pointer:

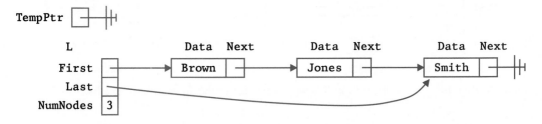

At that point, the loop condition evaluates to false and the loop (and function) terminates.

Many of the operations on a linked list require this approach in which a loop is used to pass through a list and process its nodes. This action of visiting each node in a list is called **traversing** the list and is typically accomplished with a loop of the form

```
TempPtr = L.First;                    // start at the beginning

while (TempPtr != 0)                   // while nodes remain unvisited
{
    // ... statements to "visit" the node pointed to by TempPtr

    TempPtr = TempPtr->Next;           // proceed to the next node
}
```

The last statement in the while loop uses the **class pointer selector** (->), whose left operand is a *pointer* to a class object and whose right operand is a *member* of a class object. The effect of this statement is to set `TempPtr` to point to the next node in the list. Note that when `TempPtr` points to the last node in the list, this statement will set its value to the NULL pointer, since NULL is the value of the `Next` member of the final node. In general, if *Ptr* is a pointer to a structure with a link named *Next*,

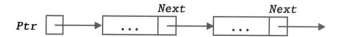

then the statement

```
Ptr = Ptr->Next;
```

can be used to "advance" *Ptr* to the node that follows it in the list,

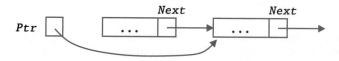

or to set *Ptr* to NULL if the node it pointed to was the final node. Note that the notation *Ptr->Member* is equivalent to the more cumbersome *(*Ptr).Member*.

Copying a Linked List.   To copy a linked list (e.g., when it is passed as a value parameter), we must provide a copy constructor for class `LinkedList`. If the list being copied is empty, we simply make the copy of the list an empty list. Otherwise, we make a copy of the first node and then traverse the list, copying the remaining nodes and attaching the new node to the node that was most recently added to the new list. Two pointers are needed: `OldNode` to move through the original list and `NewNode` to keep track of the last node added to the new list.

The function in Figure 16.4 uses this approach. The statement

```
NewNode->Next = new ListNode(OldNode->Data);
```

constructs a new `ListNode`, copies the data value stored in the node pointed to by `OldNode` into it, and attaches it to the last node in the new list by setting the `Next` field in `NewNode` to point to this new node.

FIGURE 16.4   Copy constructor for a **LinkedList**.

```
/* This function constructs a copy of a LinkedList.

   Receive: L, a LinkedList to be copied
   Return:  the LinkedList containing this function, as a copy of L
--------------------------------------------------------------------*/

LinkedList::LinkedList(const LinkedList& L)
{
   ListNode
      *OldNode = L.First,          // Ptr to node being copied
      *NewNode = 0;                // Ptr to copied node

   NumNodes = L.NumNodes;          // copy scalar field

                                   // COPY L'S FIRST NODE:
   if (NumNodes == 0)              // if L is empty
      First = 0;                   //    set First to NULL
   else                            // otherwise
   {                               //
      NewNode =
         new ListNode(OldNode->Data);  //    make a copy of OldNode
      assert(NewNode != 0);        //    verify
      OldNode = OldNode->Next;     //    move OldNode to next node
      First = NewNode;             //    set First to new Node
   }
                                   // COPY THE REMAINING NODES:
   while (OldNode != 0)            //    while not at end-of-list
   {
      NewNode->Next =
         new ListNode(OldNode->Data);  //    make a copy of OldNode
      assert(NewNode->Next != 0);  //    verify
      NewNode = NewNode->Next;     //    move NewNode to next node
      OldNode = OldNode->Next;     //    move OldNode to next node
   }

   Last = NewNode;                 // update Last
}
```

Since this is not a trivial function, we store its definition in the implementation file for library **LinkedList** and declare it in the public section of class **LinkedList**:

```
LinkedList(const LinkedList& L);
```

Finding the Length of a Linked List.   A function to determine the length of a **LinkedList** is easy to write, since it can simply extract and return the value of the **NumNodes** member, as shown in Figure 16.5.

FIGURE 16.5   Finding the length of a **LinkedList**.

```
/* This function finds the length of a LinkedList.

   Return: The number of values in the LinkedList containing
              this function
-------------------------------------------------------------------*/

int Length(void)const
{
   return (NumNodes);
}
```

Because this function is so simple, we define it within the class **LinkedList** (that is, in **LinkedList.h**). Given such a definition and a **LinkedList** object named **L**, the expression

L.Length()

will return the number of values in **L**. With this function, a condition such as

(L.Length() == 0)

can be used to determine whether a **LinkedList L** is empty.

Subscripting.   As we have seen before, the subscript operation is used to access the list element at a particular position or index in the list. An array-based list provides access to any list element directly, but a linked list does not permit such direct access. To see why, consider the structure of a linked list such as the following:

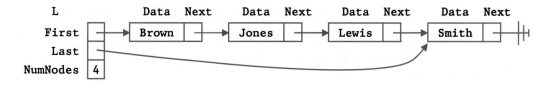

The pointer members of **L** point only to the first and last nodes in its list—to access a middle node, such as the node whose **Data** value is **Lewis**, we must start at the first node, follow its **Next** member to the second node, and then follow its **Next** member to the third node, and so on until we reach the node we are seeking.

Note also that links point in only one direction—we cannot, for example, start at the last node and move backward, since the last node contains no pointer to its predecessor. In general, to access any node, we must traverse all the nodes that precede it. The function in Figure 16.6 implements the subscript operation for a **LinkedList** using this approach.

FIGURE 16.6 The **LinkedList** subscript operation.

```
/* This function accesses the ith element of a LinkedList.

   Receive: i, an (unsigned) list index
   Return:  (a reference to) the element at index i
---------------------------------------------------------------*/

ListElement& LinkedList::operator[] (unsigned i)
{
   if (i >= NumNodes)                  // check for range error
   {
      cerr << "\n*** LinkedList Subscript: index " << i
         << " is outside of List !\n";
      exit (-1);
   }

   ListNode
      *Position = First;               // pointer to first node

   for (int j = 0; j < i; j++)         // move through the list
      Position = Position->Next;       //    to the i-th node

   return Position->Data;
}
```

After this definition is stored in the implementation file of library **LinkedList**, the function should be declared as a member function in the public section of class **LinkedList**:

    ListElement& operator[] (unsigned i);

To illustrate how this function works, consider the list:

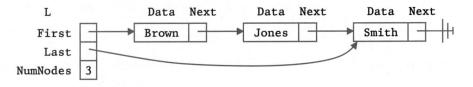

The function **operator[]** allows us to write the statement

    L[1] = "Clark";

which changes the **Data** member of the node whose index is 1 to **"Clark"**. This statement assigns the string **"Clark"** to L[1], which calls **L.operator[]** and passes it the argument **1**, storing that argument in parameter **i**. The function first checks the validity of **i**, after which a pointer named **Position** is initialized to point to the first node in the list:

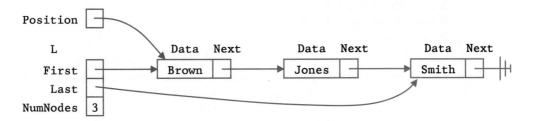

Control then enters the loop

```
for (int j = 0; j < i; j++)
    Position = Position->Next;
```

which advances **Position** to the node whose index is **i** (one node, in this case):

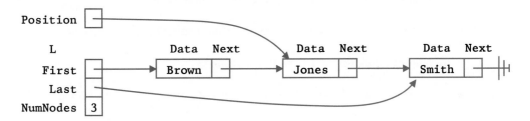

Control then leaves the loop and reaches the statement

```
return Position->Data;
```

which, since the return type of **operator[]** is a *reference* to a **ListElement**, returns a reference to the **Data** member of the node pointed to by **Position**. The assignment operation changes the value at that reference to the string **"Clark"**:

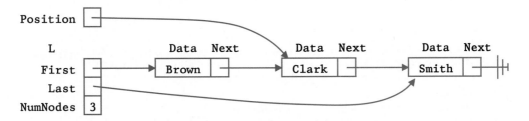

Note that this subscript operation is significantly more complicated than the same operation for an array-based list. If there is an equal probability of accessing any of the n nodes in a list, this subscript operation will, on average, have to traverse $n/2$ of those nodes. The subscript operation is thus extremely slow for large linked lists.

Inserting Items into a Linked List.   One of the primary advantages of the linked list is the relative ease and efficiency with which a value may be inserted into the list. As we noted in the previous section, there are three cases to consider when inserting a value:

- Insertion at the beginning of the list
- Insertion at the end of the list
- Insertion within the list

The function **Insert** in class **LinkedList** allows the caller to specify any of these three cases. The caller must pass the value to be inserted as the first argument and the index of the position at which the value is to be inserted as a second argument. Named constants **LinkedList::Beginning** and **LinkedList::End** are defined in the public section of class **LinkedList**,

```
enum {Beginning = 0, End = INT_MAX};
```

and may be used to specify the beginning and end of the linked list, respectively. For example, the call

```
L.Insert("Adams", LinkedList::Beginning);
```

can be used to insert the string **"Adams"** at the beginning of **L**; the call

```
L.Insert("Wagner", LinkedList::End);
```

can be used to insert the string **"Wagner"** at the end of **L**; and the call

```
L.Insert("Lewis", 2);
```

can be used to insert the string **"Lewis"** into the position whose index is 2. As with array-based lists, the index of the first node is 0, the index of the second node is 1, and so on. The calls

```
L.Insert("Adams", LinkedList::Beginning);
```

and

```
L.Insert("Adams", 0);
```

thus are equivalent. Figure 16.7 gives an implementation of **Insert()**.

 FIGURE 16.7   Inserting an item into a **LinkedList**.

```
/*---------------------------------------------------------------------
 This function inserts a ListElement into a LinkedList at a given
    index.

    Receive: A ListElement Elem
             An index Pos
    Return:  The LinkedList containing this function, with Elem
             inserted at index Pos in it
 ---------------------------------------------------------------------*/
```

FIGURE 16.7   Inserting an item into a **LinkedList**. (cont.)

```
void LinkedList::Insert(const ListElement& Elem, int Pos)
{
  if ((Pos >= NumNodes) &&
      (Pos != LinkedList::End))        // check for range error
    {
      cerr << "\n*** LinkedList Insert: index " << Pos
           << " is past the end of the list!\n";
      Pos = LinkedList::End;
    }
  else if (Pos < LinkedList::Beginning)
    {
      cerr << "\n*** LinkedList Insert: index " << Pos
           << " is before the beginning of the list!\n";
      Pos = LinkedList::Beginning;
    }

  ListNode                             // build new Node
    *NewPtr = new ListNode(Elem);      //    containing Elem

  assert(NewPtr != 0);                 // verify

  if  (Pos == LinkedList::Beginning)   // if inserting at beginning
  {
      NewPtr->Next = First;            //    set Next to first Node
      First = NewPtr;                  //    make First point to NewPtr
      if (NumNodes == 0)               //    if List is empty
         Last = NewPtr;                //       update Last as well
  }
  else if ((Pos == LinkedList::End) || // else if inserting at the end
           (Pos == NumNodes))
  {
      if (NumNodes == 0)               //    if List is empty
         First = NewPtr;               //       update First
      else                             //    otherwise
         Last->Next = NewPtr;          //       attach to end of list
      Last = NewPtr;                   //    update Last
  }
  else
    {
      ListNode
        *PrevPtr = First;              // start at the beginning

      for (int i = 0; i < Pos - 1; i++)// find the node just before
         PrevPtr = PrevPtr->Next;      //    the insertion point

      NewPtr->Next = PrevPtr->Next;    // append trailing nodes to new node
      PrevPtr->Next = NewPtr;          // append new node to prior nodes
  }

  NumNodes++;                          // increment NumNodes;
}
```

Returning to our discussion in Section 16.1, consider again the linked list of names:

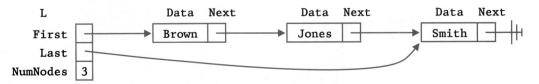

To add **Adams** at the front of this list, we use the call

```
L.Insert("Adams", LinkedList::Beginning);
```

which passes the argument **"Adams"** to parameter **Elem**, and the argument **LinkedList::Beginning** to the parameter **Pos**. After checking to ensure that the argument for **Pos** is valid, the **new** operator and the class constructor are used:

```
ListNode
    *NewPtr = new ListNode(Elem);
```

This statement constructs a new **ListNode**, initializes its **Data** member to the value **"Adams"**, initializes its **Next** member to the NULL pointer (by default), and then stores the address of that **ListNode** in the pointer **NewPtr**:

Since the value of **Pos** is **LinkedList::Beginning**, the following statements are executed:

```
if (Pos == LinkedList::Beginning)
{
    NewPtr->Next = First;
    First = NewPtr;
    if (NumNodes == 0)
        Last = NewPtr;
}
```

The first statement places the new node at the front of the list by making its **Next** member point to the first node:

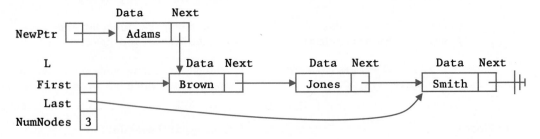

The second statement sets the **First** member of **L** to point to this new first node. The third statement checks whether the new value is the only value in the list, in which case the `Last` member would also be set to point to the new node. The function ends by incrementing `NumNodes`.

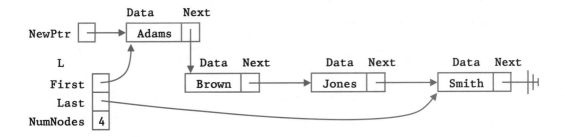

By contrast, consider the call

```
L.Insert("Wagner", LinkedList::End);
```

Here, `"Wagner"` is passed to the parameter `Elem` and `LinkedList::End` is passed to `Pos`. As before, the function checks the validity of the value for `Pos` and then constructs a new node with `"Wagner"` as its `Data` value:

Since the value of `Pos` is `LinkedList::End`, the statements that insert at the beginning of the list are bypassed and the following statements are executed:

```
else if ((Pos == LinkedList::End) ||
         (Pos == NumNodes))
{
   if (NumNodes == 0)
      First = NewPtr;
   else
      Last->Next = NewPtr;
   Last = NewPtr;
}
```

The first of these statements checks whether the list is empty. If so, it updates the `First` member of the `LinkedList`; otherwise, it appends this node to the list by setting the `Next` member of the last node in the list to point to the new node:

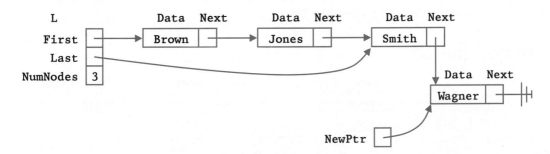

The final statement in this block updates the **Last** member of the **LinkedList**, so that it points to the new final node, and the last statement in the function increments the value of **NumNodes**.

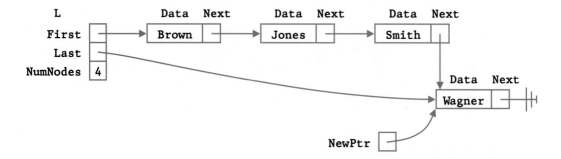

To illustrate the final case, the call

```
L.Insert("Lewis", 2);
```

passes the argument **"Lewis"** to **Elem** and the value **2** to **Pos**. After checking that the value of **Pos** is valid, a new node is constructed with **"Lewis"** as its **Data** value:

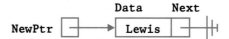

The sections of code that perform insertion at the beginning and the end of the list are bypassed and the following statements are executed:

```
else
{
    ListNode
        *PredPtr = First;

    for (int i = 0; i < Pos - 1; i++)
        PredPtr = PredPtr->Next;

    NewPtr->Next = PredPtr->Next;
    PredPtr->Next = NewPtr;
}
```

The first statement constructs a new pointer named **PredPtr** and initializes it to point to the first node in the list.

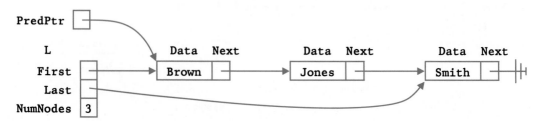

The next statement is a for loop that advances **PredPtr** to the node immediately preceding the insertion position:

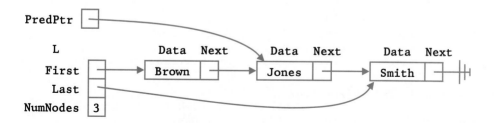

Once **PredPtr** is correctly positioned, the next statement makes the **Next** member of the new node point to the node that is currently "in its place":

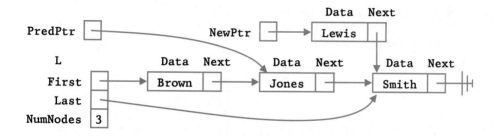

The final statement in the block makes the link portion of the predecessor node point to this new node after which the function updates the value of **NumNodes**.

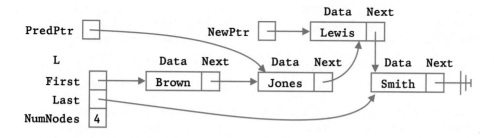

Deleting Items from a Linked List.   As we saw in Section 16.1, there are two cases to consider for deletion:

- Deleting the first element in the list
- Deleting an element that has a predecessor

Figure 16.8 presents a function that deletes the node at a given index.

FIGURE 16.8 Deleting an item from a **LinkedList**.

```
/*-------------------------------------------------------------------
 This function deletes the Node at position Pos from a LinkedList.

    Receive: Pos, an index value
    Return:  The LinkedList containing this function, with the
             Node whose index is Pos removed
-----------------------------------------------------------------*/

Boolean LinkedList::Delete(int Pos)
{                                       // check if valid index
   if ((Pos >= NumNodes) && (Pos != LinkedList::End))
   {
      cerr << "\n*** LinkedList Delete: index " << Pos
           << " is past the end of the list!\n";
      Pos = LinkedList::End;
   }
   else if (Pos < LinkedList::Beginning)
   {
      cerr << "\n*** LinkedList Delete: index " << Pos
           << " is before the beginning of the list!\n";
      Pos = LinkedList::Beginning;
   }

   ListNode                             // pointer to node
      *DelPtr;                          //    being deleted

   if ((Pos == LinkedList::Beginning) ||    // if deleting first node
       ((Pos == LinkedList::End) && (NumNodes == 1)))
   {
      DelPtr = First;                   //    save the node
      First = First->Next;              //    remove it from list
      DelPtr->Next = 0;
   }
   else                                 // otherwise
   {
      if (Pos == LinkedList::End)       //    if deleting last node
         Pos = NumNodes - 1;            //       reset Pos correctly

      ListNode
         *PredPtr = First;              //    start at beginning

      for (int Pred = 1; Pred < Pos; Pred++)// find predecessor of
         PredPtr = PredPtr->Next;       //       node being removed
```

FIGURE 16.8 Deleting an item from a **LinkedList**. (cont.)

```
    DelPtr = PredPtr->Next;              // save node
                                         //   being removed
    PredPtr->Next = DelPtr->Next;        // remove node from list
    DelPtr->Next = 0;

    if (Pos == NumNodes - 1)
       Last = PredPtr;
}

delete DelPtr;                           // deallocate node
NumNodes--;                              // update node counter

return True;
}
```

To see how **Delete()** works, let us begin with the first case in which the first node is to be deleted. Consider the following **LinkedList** L:

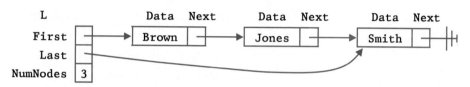

In the call

```
    L.Delete(LinkedList::Beginning);
```

the argument **LinkedList::Beginning** is passed to parameter **Pos**. After the validity of this value is checked, the statements

```
    if ((Pos == LinkedList::Beginning) ||
        ((Pos == LinkedList::End) && (NumNodes == 1)))
    {
       DelPtr = First;
       First = First->Next;
       DelPtr->Next = 0;
    }
```

are executed. The first statement in the block saves the address of the node being deleted in **DelPtr**:

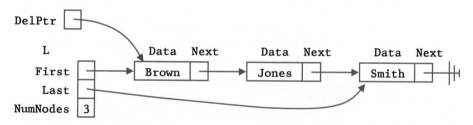

The second statement advances the **First** member of L to the second node in the list, thereby removing the first node from the list.

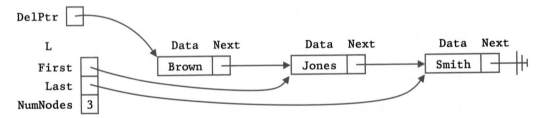

Control then leaves the block and passes to the statements

```
delete DelPtr;
NumNodes--;
```

which deallocate the node and decrement the **NumNodes** counter.

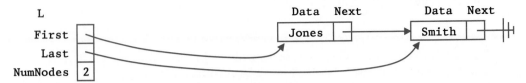

The second case is slightly more complicated than the first. For example, given the list,

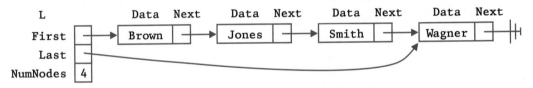

execution of the statement

```
L.Delete(2);
```

passes the value **2** to the parameter **Pos**. After its validity is checked, the statements that delete the first node are bypassed and the following statements are executed:

```
else
{
   if (Pos == LinkedList::End)
      Pos = NumNodes - 1;

   ListNode
      *PredPtr = First;

   for (int Prev = 1; Prev < Pos; Prev++)
      PredPtr = PredPtr->Next;

   DelPtr = PredPtr->Next;
   PredPtr->Next = DelPtr->Next;
   DelPtr->Next = 0;

   if (Pos == NumNodes - 1)
      Last = PredPtr;
}
```

The first statement checks whether the value of **Pos** is **LinkedList::End**, and if it is, resets **Pos** to the index of the new last element (2). The next statement initializes a pointer named **PredPtr** to point to the first node in the list:

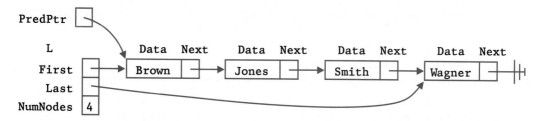

The for loop then advances **PredPtr** until it reaches the node preceding the node that is to be deleted:

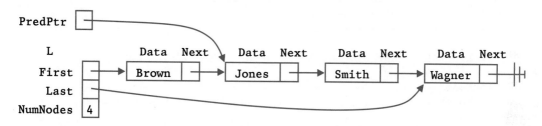

The next statement uses **PredPtr** to set the pointer **DelPtr** to point to the node to be deleted:

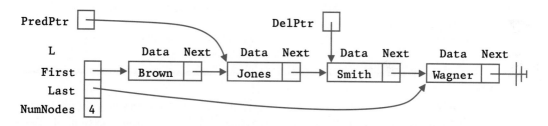

That node is then separated from the list by resetting the **Next** member of **PredPtr** to the **Next** member of the node being deleted:

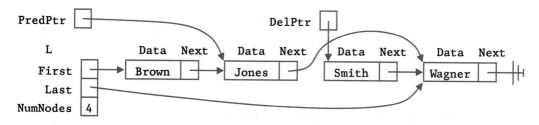

The final statement in the block updates the value of the **Last** member of **L** if necessary (i.e., if the last node was being deleted), after which the last statements in the function deallocate the memory of the node being deleted and decrement **NumNodes**.

Searching a Linked List.   Another standard operation on a list is to search the list for a particular element. Recall from Section 12.3 that the technique of searching a list by starting at the beginning of the list and checking each element in sequence is called **linear search.** Figure 16.9 presents a function **LSearch()** that, given a **ListElement** named **SearchVal**, returns the index of the node whose **Data** value is equal to **SearchVal** if there is such a node and returns the value −1 otherwise.

 FIGURE 16.9   Searching a **LinkedList** for an item.

```
/*----------------------------------------------------------------
 This function searches a LinkedList for a given ListElement.

    Receive: SearchVal, a ListElement
    Return:  The index of SearchVal within the LinkedList
             containing this function, if it is present,
             -1 otherwise
-----------------------------------------------------------------*/

int LinkedList::LSearch(const ListElement& SearchVal) const
{
    ListNode
       *NodePtr = First;                // start at the beginning

    for (int i = 0; i < NumNodes; i++)  // check each node in sequence
       if (NodePtr->Data == SearchVal)  // if it's the one we seek
          return i;                     //    return its index
       else                             // otherwise
          NodePtr = NodePtr->Next;      //    move on to the next node

    return -1;                          // indicate search failure
}
```

Once this definition has been stored in the implementation file of library **LinkedList**, the function should be declared in the public section of class **LinkedList**.

It should be noted that a binary search cannot be used (efficiently) for a linked list, even if the list elements are in order as in the list:

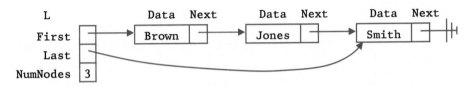

The reason is that it is not possible to access *directly* the middle node in a linked list. The pointer members of **L** point only to the first and last nodes in its list—to access any other node, we must start at the first node, follow its **Next** member to the second node, and continue following **Next** members until we reach the node we are seeking.

> *One of the main drawbacks of linked lists is that their elements must be accessed sequentially.*

In Section 17.3, we describe a **multiply linked structure** called a **binary search tree** that does allow a binarylike search to be performed efficiently.

Destroying a Linked List.   The final operation we consider is "tearing down" a linked list. The basic idea is to use a loop that repeatedly deallocates the first node in the list. Some care must be taken, however, to avoid losing access to nodes, since such nodes cannot be deallocated. To illustrate, consider the following list:

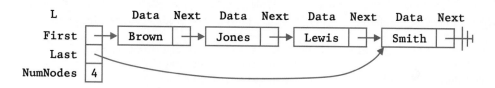

If we simply deallocate the first node,

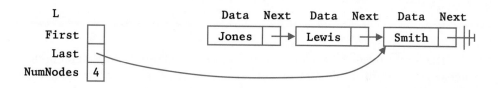

then all the nodes from there until the last node will have been "marooned," because our only access to them was via the **Next** member of the first node. We therefore need a local pointer variable **TempPtr** to keep track of the node we wish to deallocate while the **First** member is advanced to the next node in the list:

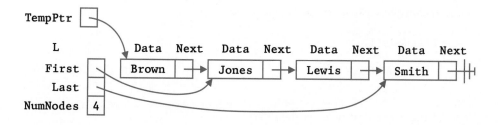

We can then safely deallocate the node pointed to by **TempPtr** without losing the remainder of the list and then repeat the process until all the nodes have been reclaimed. The function in Figure 16.10 presents a destructor function for class **LinkedList** that uses this approach.

FIGURE 16.10 Destroying a **LinkedList**.

```
/* This function tears down a LinkedList.

   Precondition:   The lifetime of the LinkedList containing this
                   function is over.
   Postcondition:  The memory allocated to this LinkedList has been
                   reclaimed.
-----------------------------------------------------------------*/

LinkedList::~LinkedList(void)
{
   ListNode
      *TempPtr = First;          // set TempPtr to first node

   while (TempPtr != 0)          // while there are nodes to be deleted:
   {
      First = First->Next;       //    move First to the next node
      delete TempPtr;            //    delete the current node
      TempPtr = First;           //    update TempPtr
   }

   NumNodes = 0;                 // set NumNodes to zero
   Last = 0;                     // set Last to NULL
}
```

Due to the relative complexity of this function, we store its definition in the implementation file of library **LinkedList** and declare it in the public section of class **LinkedList**:

```
~LinkedList(void);
```

Given such a function, the memory allocated to a **LinkedList** declared locally within a function will be reclaimed when that function terminates.

A more elegant but less efficient version of **~LinkedList()** presented in Figure 16.10 is obtained by defining a separate **ListNode** destructor (which can be done within the class **ListNode**):

```
~ListNode()
{
   delete Next;
}
```

The **LinkedList** destructor is then very simple:

```
~LinkedList()
{
   delete First;
   First = Last = 0;
   NumNodes = 0;
}
```

These two functions together are sufficient to deallocate the memory of an entire linked list. The trick is to remember that when an object is destroyed using **delete**, its destructor is invoked. The **ListNode** destructor uses this to generate an *indirect recursion* that destroys all of the nodes in the list.

To illustrate, suppose that the lifetime of the following **LinkedList** object L is over, and the compiler has invoked its destructor:

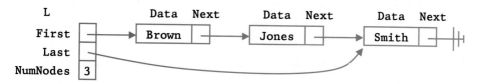

When the **LinkedList** destructor executes the statement

    delete First;

this causes the **ListNode** destructor in the first node (**Brown**) to begin execution. However, the first thing it does is execute the statement

    delete Next;

which causes the **ListNode** destructor in the second node (**Jones**) to begin execution (an indirect recursive call). But the first thing that destructor does is execute the statement

    delete Next;

causing the **ListNode** destructor in the final node (**Smith**) to begin execution (an indirect recursive call). That destructor executes the statement

    delete Next;

but since the value of **Next** is the NULL address in that node, the statement has no effect (halting the recursion). The storage of the node containing **Smith** is then reclaimed,

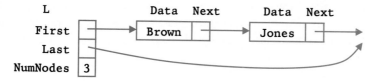

after which control returns to the destructor in the node containing **Jones**. It has now finished its execution, and so the storage of the node containing **Jones** is reclaimed:

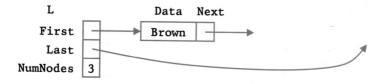

afterwhich control returns to the destructor in the node containing **Brown**. It has now finished its execution, and so that node's storage is reclaimed:

Control then returns to the **LinkedList** destructor, which sets the data members of L appropriately for an empty list:

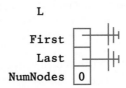

While this solution seems far more elegant than the iterative version in Figure 16.10, it is significantly less time-efficient due to the overhead of the recursive calls, and so we favor the iterative version.

Note that a third approach would be to implement the destructor using the **Delete()** and **Length()** members, as follows:

```
LinkedList::~LinkedList(void)
{
    while (Length() != 0)                    // while this LinkList is not empty:
        Delete(LinkedList::Beginning);  //    remove its first node
}
```

This implementation reuses our work in implementing the **Delete()** and **Length()** members. Its disadvantage is that it performs two function calls for each node being deleted and thus may be slower than the function in Figure 16.10.

Other Operations. These are just a few of the possible operations on a linked list. Other common operations include interactive input and output of a list, file I/O, sorting, and concatenation. Some of these operations are discussed in the exercises.

Exercises

1. Assume the following declarations:

```
int
    X,
    *P1, *P2;
double
    *Q1, *Q2;
```

What (if anything) is wrong with each of the following statements?

(a) `cout << P1;`
(c) `P1 = Q1;`
(e) `if (*P1 = 0)`
　　　`Q1 = Q2;`

(b) `cin >> P1;`
(d) `new X;`
(f) `{`
　　　　`*P1 = 17;`
　　　　`P1 = new int;`
　　`}`

2. Assume the following declarations:

```
struct NumberNode
{
   int Data;
   NumberNode *Next;
};

typedef NumberNode *NodePointer;


NodePointer
   P1, P2;
int
   *P3;
```

Also assume that the following three statements have already been executed:

```
P1 = new NumberNode;
P2 = new NumberNode;
P3 = new int;
```

Tell what will now be displayed by each of the following program segments or explain why an error occurs:

(a) `P1->Data = 123;`
　　`P2->Data = 456;`
　　`P1->Next = P2;`
　　`cout << P1->Data;`
　　`cout << P1->Next->Data;`

(b) `P1->Data = 12;`
　　`P2->Data = 34;`
　　`P1 = P2;`
　　`cout << P1->Data );`
　　`cout << P2->Data );`

(c) `P1->Data = 123;`
　　`P2->Data = 456;`
　　`P1->Next = P2;`
　　`cout << P2->Data;`
　　`cout << P2->Next->Data;`

(d) `P1->Data = 12;`
`P2->Data = 34;`
`P3->Data = 34;`
`P1->Next = P2;`
`P2->Next = P3;`
`cout << P1->Data;`
`cout << P2->Data;`
`cout << P3->Data;`

(e) `P1->Data = 111;`
`P2->Data = 222;`
`P1->Next = P2;`
`P2->Next = P1;`
`cout << P1->Data, P2->Data;`
`cout << P1->Next->Data;`
`cout << P1->Next->Next->Data;`

(f) `P1->Data = 12;`
`P2->Data = 34;`
`P1 = P2;`
`P2->Next = P1;`
`cout << P1->Data;`
`cout << P2->Data;`
`cout << P1->Next->Data;`
`cout << P2->Next->Data;`

3. Given the following linked list and node pointers **P1**, **P2**, **P3**, and **P4**:

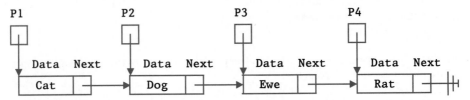

Draw a similar diagram for each of the following to show how this configuration changes when the given program segment is executed or explain why an error occurs:

(a) `P1 = P2->Next;`

(b) `P4 = P1;`

(c) `P4->Data = P1->Data;`

(d) `P4->Next->Data = P1->Data;`

(e) `P2->Next = P3->Next;`

(f) `P4->Next = P1;`

(g) `P1->Next = P3->Next;`
`P1 = P3;`

(h) `P1 = P3;`
`P1->Next = P3->Next;`

(i) `P4->Next = P3->Next;`
     `P3->Next = P2->Next;`
     `P2->Next = P1->Next;`

(j) `P4->Next = P3;`
     `P4->Next->Next = P2;`
     `P4->Next->Next->Next = P1;`
     `P1 = 0;`

4. Suppose that linked lists are implemented without the `NumNodes` member. Write a

(a) Nonrecursive function
(b) Recursive function

that counts the nodes in such a linked list.

5. Write a function to reverse a linked list; that is, the last node becomes the first node and all links between nodes are reversed.

6. Write a

(a) Nonrecursive boolean-valued function
(b) Recursive boolean-valued function

that determines whether the data items in a linked list are arranged in ascending order.

7. Add a boolean data member named `InOrder` to class `List`, and modify all necessary operations to ensure that the value of `InOrder` is true if and only if the elements of the `List` are in ascending order.

8. If the elements in a list are ordered, then a linear search function for an element not in the list can halt as soon as it encounters an element larger than the element being sought and so avoid searching the entire list. Proceed as in Exercise 7 and modify `LSearch()` so that it takes advantage of this approach if the list is ordered but performs a "normal" linear search if the list is not ordered.

16.3   Example: Maintaining Employee Records

As an example of processing linked lists, suppose we wish to create and maintain a linked list of employee records ordered by employee age. Each employee record contains an employee's number, age, number of dependents, and hourly pay rate. These records are stored in a file, so we assume the existence of a class `Employee` with the appropriate data members and member functions to permit file I/O, relational operators, and so on. Given such a class, the first step is to create an initial (empty) linked list and then read each record from the file and insert it at the end of the list. The second step is to update this list by adding new records to the list, deleting records, and modifying existing records. Finally, after all the updating is complete, the list must be copied back to the file. An algorithm for solving this problem is as follows:

ALGORITHM TO MAINTAIN A LINKED LIST OF EMPLOYEE RECORDS

1. Construct the initial linked list.
2. Fill the list by reading employee records from a file and inserting them into the list, beginning with an empty list.
3. Repeat the following so long as *Option* ≠ 'Q':
    a. Read an *Option*.
    b. If *Option* is
        A: Read a new employee record and add it into the list.
        D: Read an employee number and delete the record for that employee.
        M: Modify an existing record.
        Q: Quit.
4. Copy the list to a file and terminate processing.

The program in Figure 16.11 implements this algorithm.

 FIGURE 16.11   Maintaining a linked list of employee records.

```
/* This program maintains a list of Employee records.

   Input(EmpFile):  A list of employee records
   Input(keyboard): Modifications, insertions, and deletions to
                    the list
   Output(EmpFile): The updated list
---------------------------------------------------------------*/

#include <iostream.h>

#include "LinkedList.h" // ListElement = Employee

void Update(LinkedList& L);

int main(void)
{
   LinkedList
       L;                 // an empty list

   L.Load("EmpFile");    // fill it with data from EmpFile

   Update(L);            // allow user to update the list

   L.Write("EmpFile");   // write the updated list back to EmpFile

   return 0;
}
```

FIGURE 16.11 Maintaining a linked list of employee records. (cont.)

```cpp
/* This function updates the linked employee list.

   Receive: L, a linked list of employees
   Input:   Modifications, insertions, and/or deletions for the list
   Return:  L, updated as specified
-----------------------------------------------------------------------*/

void AddEmployee(LinkedList& L);    // add a new employee to the list

void DeleteEmployee(LinkedList& L);// delete an employee from the list

void ModifyEmployee(LinkedList& L);// modify an employee's record

void Update(LinkedList& L)
{
   const Strings
      Menu = Strings("\nPlease enter:\n") &
               "\tA - to add a new employee to the list\n" &
               "\tD - to delete an employee\n" &
               "\tM - to modify an employee's record\n" &
               "\tQ - to quit.\n--> ";
   char
      Choice;                       // the user's menu choice

   do                              // Loop1: perform multiple updates
   {
      do                           //    Loop2: get a valid menu choice
      {
         cout << Menu;
         cin >> Choice;
      }
      while ((Choice != 'A') && (Choice != 'D') &&
            ( Choice != 'M') && (Choice != 'Q'));

      switch (Choice)              //      perform their choice
      {
      case 'A': AddEmployee(L);
               break;
      case 'D': DeleteEmployee(L);
               break;
      case 'M': ModifyEmployee(L);
               break;
      case 'Q': // do nothing
               break;
      default: cerr << "\n*** " << Choice
                    << " is not a valid option!\n";
      }
   }
   while (Choice != 'Q');                // until 'quit' is chosen
}
```

FIGURE 16.11   Maintaining a linked list of employee records. (cont.)

```
/* This function adds a new employee to the linked list.

   Receive: L, the linked list of employees
   Output:  Prompts for input
   Input:   An employee's data
   Return:  L, with the new employee record appended
-----------------------------------------------------------------------*/

void AddEmployee(LinkedList& L)
{
   int
      EmpNumber,
      EmpAge,
      EmpDependents;
   double
      EmpWage;
                                              // get the new emp's data
   cout << "\nEnter new employee's ...\n";
   cout << "\tNumber: ";
   cin >> EmpNumber;
   cout << "\tAge: ";
   cin >> EmpAge;
   cout << "\tNumber of Dependents: ";
   cin >> EmpDependents;
   cout << "\tand Wage: ";
   cin >> EmpWage;

   Employee                                   // build an Employee object
      Emp(EmpNumber, EmpAge, EmpDependents, EmpWage);

   if (L.LSearch(Emp) >= 0)
      cout << "\nAdd: this employee is already in the list!\n";
   else
      L.Insert(Emp, LinkedList::End);    // append it to L
}

/* This function removes an employee from the linked list.

   Receive: L, the linked list of employees
   Output:  Prompts for input
   Input:   An employee's number
   Return:  L, with the employee's record removed
-----------------------------------------------------------------------*/

void DeleteEmployee(LinkedList& L)
{
   int
      EmpNumber;
                                           // get their number
   cout << "\nNumber of employee to be deleted? ";
   cin >> EmpNumber;

   Employee                                   // build an Employee object
      Emp(EmpNumber);
```

FIGURE 16.11   Maintaining a linked list of employee records. (cont.)

```
   int                              // search for them
      Pos = L.LSearch(Emp);
   if (Pos >= 0)                    // if they're found
      L.Delete(Pos);               //    remove them
   else
      cout << "\n*** DeleteEmployee: no employee found with "
           << EmpNumber << " as their number!\n";
}


/* This function modifies an employee's record in the linked list.

   Receive: L, the linked list of employees
   Output:  Prompts for input
   Input:   The updates to the data
   Return:  L, with the employee's record updated
-----------------------------------------------------------------*/

void ModifyEmployee(LinkedList& L)
{
   int
      EmpNumber,
      EmpAge,
      EmpDependents;
   double
      EmpWage;
                                    // get their number
   cout << "\nNumber of employee whose data is to be modified? ";
   cin >> EmpNumber;

   Employee                         // build an Employee object
      Emp(EmpNumber);

   int                              // search the list for them
      Pos = L.LSearch(Emp);

   if (Pos >= 0)                    // if they're found
     {                              //    do modification
       cout << "\nCurrent Data:  " << L[Pos] <<     endl;
       cout << "Enter new Data: ";
       cin >> EmpNumber >> EmpAge >> EmpDependents >> EmpWage;

       L[Pos] = Employee(EmpNumber, EmpAge, EmpDependents, EmpWage);
     }
   else
     cout << "\n*** Sorry - no employee with number "
          << EmpNumber << " is listed.\n";
}
```

FIGURE 16.11   Maintaining a linked list of employee records. (cont.)

Listing of EmpFile used in sample run:

```
2100 17 0  9.60
3889 19 1 10.25
2222 65 3 16.05
1801 39 4 14.15
4144 31 2 12.85
1111 39 3 13.50
1357 25 2 12.50
2534 40 5 14.95
3011 21 0 12.75
2888 29 1 13.95
3414 22 2 12.80
```

Sample run:

```
Please enter:
        A - to add a new employee to the list
        D - to delete an employee
        M - to modify an employee's record
        Q - to quit.
--> M

Number of employee whose data is to be modified? 1112

*** Sorry - no employee with number 1112 is listed.

Please enter:
        A - to add a new employee to the list
        D - to delete an employee
        M - to modify an employee's record
        Q - to quit.
--> M

Number of employee whose data is to be modified? 1111

Current Data:    1111 39 3 13.50
Enter new Data: 1111 40 4 13.75

Please enter:
        A - to add a new employee to the list
        D - to delete an employee
        M - to modify an employee's record
        Q - to quit.
--> A

Enter new employee's ...
        Number: 3137
        Age: 44
        Number of Dependents: 2
        and Wage: 11.25
```

FIGURE 16.11 Maintaining a linked list of employee records. (cont.)

```
Please enter:
        A - to add a new employee to the list
        D - to delete an employee
        M - to modify an employee's record
        Q - to quit.
--> D

Number of employee to be deleted? 2222

Please enter:
        A - to add a new employee to the list
        D - to delete an employee
        M - to modify an employee's record
        Q - to quit.
--> Z

*** Z is not a valid option!


Please enter:
        A - to add a new employee to the list
        D - to delete an employee
        M - to modify an employee's record
        Q - to quit.
--> Q
```

Listing of `EmpFile` following sample run:

```
2100 17 0  9.60
3889 19 1 10.25
1801 39 4 14.15
4144 31 2 12.85
1111 40 4 13.75
1357 25 2 12.50
2534 40 5 14.95
3011 21 0 12.75
2888 29 1 13.95
3414 22 2 12.80
3137 44 2 11.25
```

Exercises

1. Suppose that processes in a computer system are assigned a process number and a priority from 0 through 9. The numbers of processes awaiting execution by the system are kept in a **priority queue.** A process entered into this queue is placed ahead of all processes of lower priority but after all those of equal or higher priority. Write a program to read one of the letters **R** (remove), **A** (add),

or **L** (list). For **R**, remove the first item in the queue; for **A**, read a process number and priority and then add it to the priority queue in the manner just described; and for **L**, list all the process numbers in the queue. Maintain the priority queue as a linked list.

2. A limited number of tickets for the Frisian Folk Singers concert go on sale tomorrow, and ticket orders are to be filled in the order in which they are received. Write a program that reads the names and addresses of the persons ordering tickets, together with the number of tickets requested, and stores these in a linked list. The program should then produce a list of names, addresses, and number of tickets for orders that can be filled.

3. Modify the program in Exercise 2 so that multiple requests from the same person are not allowed.

4. Write a program to read the records from **StudentFile** (see Appendix D) and construct five linked lists of records containing a student's name, number, and cumulative GPA, one list for each class. Each list is to be an ordered linked list in which the student numbers are in ascending order. After the lists have been constructed, print each of them with appropriate headings.

5. Write a menu-driven program that allows at least the following options:

GET: Read the records from **StudentFile** (see Appendix D) and store them in five linked lists, one for each class, with each list ordered so that the student numbers are in ascending order.

INS: Insert the record for a new student, keeping the list sorted.

RET: Retrieve and display the record for a specified student.

UPD: Update the information in the record for a specified student.

DEL: Delete the record for some student.

LIS: List the records (or perhaps selected items in the records) in order. This option should allow the following suboptions:

    A: List for all students.

    C: List for only a specified class.

    G: List for students with GPAs above/below a specified value.

    M: List for a given major.

    G: List for a given gender.

SAV: Save the updated list of records by writing them to **NewStudentFile**.

6. A **polynomial of degree n** has the form

$$a_0 + a_1 x + a_2 x^2 + \cdots + a_n x^n$$

where $a_0, a_1, \ldots, a_n$ are numeric constants called the **coefficients** of the polynomial and $a_n \neq 0$. For example,

$$1 + 3x - 7x^3 + 5x^4$$

is a polynomial of degree 4 with integer coefficients 1, 3, 0, -7, and 5.

(a) Develop an ordered linked list that can represent any such polynomial. Let each node store a nonzero coefficient and the corresponding exponent.

(b) Write a program to read the nonzero coefficients and exponents of a polynomial, construct its linked representation, and print the polynomial using the usual mathematical format with x^n written as $x \uparrow n$ or $x \; \hat{} \; n$. The program should then read values for x and evaluate the polynomial for each of them.

7. Write a program that reads the nonzero coefficients and exponents of two polynomials, possibly of different degrees, stores them in linked lists (as described in Exercise 6), and then calculates and displays their sum and product.

8. The Cawker City Candy Company maintains two warehouses, one in Chicago and one in Detroit, each of which stocks at most 25 different items. Write a program that first reads the product numbers of items stored in the Chicago warehouse and stores them in a linked list `Chicago` and then repeats this for the items stored in the Detroit warehouse, storing these product numbers in a linked list `Detroit`. The program should then find and display the **intersection** of these two lists of numbers, that is, the collection of product numbers common to both lists. Do not assume that the lists have the same number of elements.

9. Repeat Exercise 8, but find and display the **union** of the two lists, that is, the collection of product numbers that are elements of at least one of the lists.

10. The number of elements in an ordered list may grow so large that searching the list, always beginning with the first node, is not efficient. One way to improve efficiency is to use an array of several smaller linked lists. Write a program to read several lines of uppercase text and to produce a **text concordance,** which is a list of all distinct words in the text. Store distinct words beginning with **A** alphabetically ordered in one linked list, those beginning with **B** in another, and so on. Use an array whose elements are these linked lists of words. After all the text lines have been read, print a list of all the words in alphabetical order.

11. Modify the program of Exercise 10 so that the concordance also includes the frequency with which each word occurs in the text.

12. In addition to the words in a section of text, a concordance usually stores the numbers of selected pages on which there is a significant use of the word. Modify the program of Exercise 10 so that the line numbers of the first ten or fewer references to a word are stored along with the word itself. The program should display each word together with its references in ascending order.

13. Proceed as in Exercise 12, but modify the data structure used for the text concordance so that the numbers of *all* lines in which a word appears are stored.

14. **Directed graphs** and their representations using adjacency matrices were described in Exercise 6 of Section 14.4.

(a) Imitating the construction in Exercise 10, develop a representation of a directed graph by using an array of linked lists (one for each vertex) containing the vertices that can be reached directly (following a single directed arc) from the vertex corresponding to the index.

(b) Draw a diagram showing the linked representation for the following directed graph:

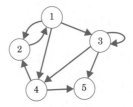

(c) Write a program to read the numbers (or names) of the vertices of a directed graph and ordered pairs of vertices representing the directed arcs, construct the linked representation for the digraph, and then use it to display the adjacency matrix.

15. In Chapter 14 we represented matrices by two-dimensional arrays. But for a **sparse matrix,** that is, one with only a few nonzero entries, this is not an efficient representation.

(a) Imitating the construction in Exercise 10, develop a representation for a sparse matrix by using an array of ordered linked lists, one for each row. Do not store zero entries of the matrix. (*Hint:* Store a matrix entry and the number of the column in which it appears.)

(b) Write a program to read the nonzero entries of a sparse matrix and their locations in the matrix, and construct its linked representation. Then print the matrix in the usual table format with all entries (including 0s) displayed.

16. Extend the program of Exercise 15 to read two sparse matrices and calculate their sum and product (see Section 14.4).

16.4   A Special-Purpose List: The Stack

There are a number of problems whose solutions involve special lists—lists in which we always insert or delete at the *ends* of the list. A list in which values are always added and removed from the same end is called a *stack*. In this section, we examine how stacks can be implemented as linked lists.

Problem: Displaying a Number's Binary Representation

In Chapter 1, we saw that data items are stored in computer memory using a binary representation. In particular, positive integers are commonly stored using the base-2 representation described in Section 1.2. This means that the base-10 representation of an integer that appears in a program or in a data file must be converted to a base-2 representation. One algorithm for carrying out this conversion, described in the exercises following Section 1.2, uses repeated division by 2, with the successive remainders giving the binary digits in the base-2 representation from right to left. For example, the following computation shows that the base-2 representation of 26 is 11010:

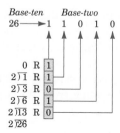

The problem is to write a function that will output the base-2 representation of a given base-10 number.

One of the difficulties in this problem is that the *first* remainder computed,

$$26 \% 2 = 0$$

is the *last* binary digit displayed. Similarly, the *second* remainder computed,

$$13 \% 2 = 1$$

produces the *next-to-the-last* binary digit displayed. This pattern continues until we generate the final remainder,

$$1 \% 2 = 1$$

which produces the first binary digit to be displayed.

Stacks

One approach to solving this problem uses a special kind of list into which values can be inserted and from which values can be deleted but where the delete operation always removes the value that was most recently inserted into the list. The values in such a list are maintained in **last-in-first-out** (**LIFO**) order; that is, the last item inserted is the first item to be removed. Such a list is called a **stack** (or a **push-down stack**) because it functions in the same manner as does a spring-loaded stack of plates or trays used in a cafeteria:

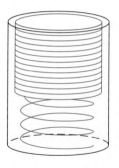

In a cafeteria, plates are added to the stack by *pushing* them onto the **top** of the stack. When a plate is removed from the top of the stack, the spring causes the next plate to *pop* up. For this reason, the insert and delete operations are commonly called **push** and **pop,** respectively. If the stack contains no plates, then it is described as **empty;** and if no more plates can be added to the stack, it is described as **full.** These illustrate the four standard stack operations:

1. *Empty( )* is a boolean function that returns true if and only if there are no values on the stack.
2. *Full( )* is a boolean function that returns true if and only if no values can be added to the stack.
3. *Push(v)* is an operation to push a value *v* onto the top of the stack.
4. *Pop(v)* is a value to pop the value from the top of the stack, returning it in variable *v*.

A stack can be used to solve the base-conversion problem. To display the base-2 representation of an integer like 26 in the usual left-to-right sequence, we must "stack up" the remainders generated during the repeated division by 2 by pushing them onto a stack. When the division process terminates, we can retrieve the remainders from this stack in the required "last-in-first-out" order by popping them from the stack.

Given a stack object, we can use the following algorithm to convert from base 10 to base 2 and to display the result:

BASE-CONVERSION ALGORITHM

/* This algorithm displays the base-2 representation of a base-10 number.

Receive: a positive integer *Number*
Output: the base-two representation of *Number*
——*/

1. Create an empty stack to hold the remainders.
2. While *Number* $\neq$ 0 do the following:
    a. Calculate the *Remainder* that results when *Number* is divided by 2.
    b. Push *Remainder* onto the stack of remainders.
    c. Replace *Number* by the integer quotient of *Number* divided by 2.
   End While.
3. While the stack of remainders is not empty do the following:
    a. Remove the *Remainder* from the top of the stack of remainders.
    b. Display *Remainder*.
   End While.

The following diagram traces this algorithm for the integer 26:

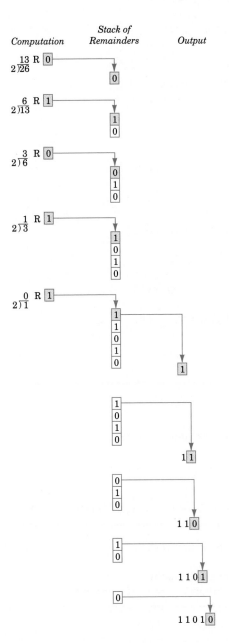

Figure 16.12 presents a function **DisplayBinary()** that implements this algorithm.

FIGURE 16.12   Converting base 10 to base 2.

```
/* This function displays the base-2 equivalent of a base-10 number.

   Receive: Number, a base-10 (positive) integer
   Output:  The base-2 equivalent of Number
-----------------------------------------------------------------*/
```

FIGURE 16.12   Converting base 10 to base 2. (cont.)

```
#include "Stack.h"

void DisplayBinary(unsigned Number)
{
   Stack
      StackOfRemainders;
   int
      Remainder;

   while (Number != 0)
   {
      Remainder = Number % 2;
      StackOfRemainders.Push(Remainder);
      Number /= 2;
   }

   while (! StackOfRemainders.Empty())
   {
      StackOfRemainders.Pop(Remainder);
      cout << Remainder;
   }
}
```

Figure 16.13 presents a simple program that uses function **DisplayBinary()** to translate numbers.

 FIGURE 16.13   A driver program for **DisplayBinary()**.

```
/* This program tests DisplayBinary().

   Input:  A positive integer, Number.
   Output: The base-2 representation of Number.
------------------------------------------------------------------*/

#include <iostream.h>

void DisplayBinary(unsigned);

   int main(void)
   {
      int
         Number;

      cout << "\nPlease enter a (base-10) integer (-1 to quit): ";
      cin >> Number;
```

FIGURE 16.13   A driver program for **DisplayBinary()**. (cont.)

```
    while(Number >= 0)
    {
      if (Number < 0)
        break;

      cout << "\n-->The binary representation of " << Number << " is ";

      DisplayBinary(Number);

      cout << ".\n\n";
      cout << "\nPlease enter a (base-10) integer (-1 to quit): ";
      cin >> Number;

    }

    return 0;
}

// ... definition of DisplayBinary() omitted ...
```

Sample run:

```
Please enter a (base-10) integer (-1 to quit): 16

-->The binary representation of 16 is 10000.


Please enter a (base-10) integer (-1 to quit): 17

-->The binary representation of 17 is 10001.


Please enter a (base-10) integer (-1 to quit): 63

-->The binary representation of 63 is 111111.


Please enter a (base-10) integer (-1 to quit): 64

-->The binary representation of 64 is 1000000.


Please enter a (base-10) integer (-1 to quit): -1
```

Implementing a Stack Class

We have noted that a stack is simply a special kind of list—one in which elements
are added and deleted at the same end. This suggests that we can use the C++

inheritance mechanism to implement a **Stack** as a class derived from one of our list classes. The fact that the two primary stack operations (push and pop) change the size of the list suggests that we derive our stack from class **LinkedList**, as opposed to class **List**. Figure 16.14 presents the declaration of the class, including the public member functions **Empty()**, **Full()**, **Push()**, and **Pop()**, as well as the appropriate constructors and destructors. Thanks to the inheritance mechanism, each of these operations is simple enough that it can be defined within class **Stack**.

 FIGURE 16.14   Declaring class **Stack**.

```
/* This is the header file for the Stack library.

...
----------------------------------------------------------------------*/

#ifndef STACK
#define STACK

#include <assert.h>

#include "LinkedList.h"

#include "Boolean.h"

class Stack : private LinkedList
{

public:

  /* --- Class Constructor ---

     Precondition:  A stack has been defined.
     Postcondition: The stack has been constructed as an
                    empty stack.
     ------------------------------------------------------------*/

  Stack(void) : LinkedList()
  {}

  /* --- Copy Constructor ---

     Precondition:  The compiler needs a copy of a Stack S.
     Receive:       S, the Stack to be copied
     Postcondition: The Stack containing this function is
                    a copy of S.
     ------------------------------------------------------------*/

  Stack(const Stack& S) : LinkedList(S)
  {}
```

FIGURE 16.14   Declaring class **Stack**. (cont.)

```
/* --- Is the Stack empty? ---

   Return: True iff the Stack containing this function is empty
--------------------------------------------------------------*/

Boolean Empty(void) const
{ return (NumNodes == 0); }


/* --- Is the Stack full? ---

   Return: True iff the Stack containing this function is full
--------------------------------------------------------------*/

Boolean Full(void) const
{ return False; }      // a run-time allocated stack is "never" full

/* --- Add an element to the stack ---

   Receive: Elem, the Element to be added
   Return:  The Stack containing this function, with Elem
            added at its top
--------------------------------------------------------------*/

void Push(const ListElement& Elem)
{ Insert(Elem, Stack::Beginning); }// prepend Elem to the stack

/* --- Remove the most-recently added element from the stack. ---

   Return: Elem, the top (most recently added) element
           The Stack containing this function, with Elem
           removed
--------------------------------------------------------------*/

void Pop(ListElement& Elem)
{
   assert(NumNodes > 0);      // check that stack isn't empty
   Elem = First->Data;        // return first node's Data via Elem
   Delete(Stack::Beginning);  // remove top node
}
};

#endif
```

Declaring the Stack.   We declare the **Stack** class using the inheritance mechanism we have seen before:

```
class Stack : private LinkedList
{
    // ...
};
```

The specifier **private** before naming **LinkedList** stipulates that the public operations on a **LinkedList** are not to be public for a **Stack**, unless we explicitly overload them. We do this because virtually all the **LinkedList** operations (input, output, assignment, subscripting, and so on) are not valid operations for a stack.

The next noteworthy item is that the **Stack** class contains no data members. Because a **Stack** is simply a list with a restricted access requirement and a **LinkedList** is a completely functional list, there is no need to store any further information beyond what is already present in a **LinkedList**.

The Constructors.   Since a **Stack** contains no data members beyond those of a **LinkedList**, the constructor for a **Stack** does nothing but ensure that the members it inherits from class **LinkedList** are properly initialized. To allow a constructor in a derived class to initialize the members of its base class, C++ provides a mechanism called a **member initialization list** by which it can invoke the constructor of its base class. This member initialization list can be described as follows:

Class Construction Using Member Initialization

Form

>   *ClassName(ParameterList) : MemberInitializationList*
>   *{ StatementList }*

where
   ClassName() is the class constructor being defined;
   ParameterList is an optional list of parameters to the constructor;
   MemberInitializationList is a list of *Initializers,* separated by commas; and
   StatementList is an optional list of statements within the constructor.

An *Initializer* can have either (or both) of the following forms:

Form1

>   *BaseClass(ParameterList)*

where
   BaseClass() is the constructor of a base class from which *ClassName* is derived; and
   ParameterList is an optional list of parameters to that constructor.

> *Form2*
>
>   *Member(InitialValue)*
>
> where
>   *Member* is a data member of *ClassName*; and
>   *InitialValue* is a value to which *Member* should be initial-
>   ized.

The definition of the **Stack** class constructor illustrates the first form:

```
Stack(void) : LinkedList()
{}
```

Here, the **LinkedList()** portion of the definition is a member initialization list in which the **Stack** constructor simply names the default-value constructor of its base class **LinkedList**. Since this constructor initializes all the data members of class **LinkedList** and class **Stack** has no data members beyond those it inherits from class **LinkedList**, the statement-list portion of the constructor is left empty.

The **Stack** copy constructor is another example of the first form. The definition

```
Stack(const Stack& S) : LinkedList(S)
{}
```

defines the **Stack** copy constructor, but as with the class constructor, its only task is to ensure that the data members of its base class **LinkedList** are copied properly. To do this, it simply uses the initializer

```
LinkedList(S)
```

Since parameter **S** is a **Stack** object and a **Stack** is a **LinkedList**, this invokes the **LinkedList** copy constructor,

```
LinkedList(const LinkedList&)
```

which correctly copies the members of **S** that are inherited from **LinkedList**. Since **S** contains no other data members, there is nothing more for the **Stack** copy constructor to do, and so its statement list is empty. Note that if a derived class contains data members in addition to those it inherits from its base class, then those members can be initialized in the usual manner. That is, if class **Stack** were declared to contain data members besides those in class **LinkedList**, those members could be initialized in the statement lists of the two constructors.

The second form of initializer provides an alternate means of writing constructors. For example, instead of writing the **LinkedList** class constructor of Figure 16.2,

```
LinkedList(void)
{
    First = 0;
    Last = 0;
    NumNodes = 0;
}
```

we could have used a member initialization list of the second form,

```
LinkedList(void) : First(0), Last(0), NumNodes(0)
{}
```

or a combination of the two forms:

```
LinkedList(void) : First(0), NumNodes(0)
{
    Last = 0;
}
```

Both of these would achieve the same effect. For the purposes of this text, initializing data members via assignments or via a member initialization list are functionally equivalent.[2] However, we believe that initializing data members via assignments is more readable and is therefore preferred.

The Boolean Functions.   Since a **Stack** has a **NumNodes** member that it inherits from **LinkedList**, the boolean **Empty()** operation is easily implemented by checking this value:

```
Boolean Empty(void) const
{
    return (NumNodes == 0);
}
```

Moreover, since a **LinkedList** object's memory is allocated dynamically, a **Stack** that is derived from a **LinkedList** can never be full (assuming that memory has not been exhausted). Our **Full()** function thus simply returns the value **False**:

```
Boolean Full(void) const
{
    return False;
}
```

The Push and Pop Operations.   The **Push()** and **Pop()** operations give a **Stack** its LIFO character. We must ensure that the pop operation removes the last element that was pushed onto the stack. One easy way to accomplish this is to *add and delete elements from the same end of the list*. That is, if we always insert at one end

---

[2] The initializations in a constructor's initialization list are always performed first, before the execution of any statements in its statement list. As a result, any data members that must be initialized before the execution of a constructor's statements (e.g., const or reference data members) *must* be initialized using an initialization list.

of the list and delete from that same end, then an element removed from the stack will be the last element added to the stack.

We can utilize the `Insert()` operation that `Stack` inherits from `LinkedList` to implement the `Push()` operation and use the inherited `Delete()` operation to implement the `Pop()` operation. However, we can insert or delete at either end of a `LinkedList`, so we must decide whether we want to add new elements at the beginning or end of the list.

If we examine the definitions of the `Insert()` and `Delete()` functions in `LinkedList`, we see the following:

- The time to insert an element at the beginning of the list is independent of the list length.
- The time to delete the element at the beginning of the list is independent of the list length.
- The time to insert an element at the end of the list is independent of the list length.
- The time to delete the element at the end of the list increases with the length of the list.

We should, therefore, choose the beginning of the list as the top of our stack and insert values there to implement the `Push()` operation,

```
void Push(const ListElement& Elem)
{
    Insert(Elem, Stack::Beginning);
}
```

and delete values from there to implement the `Pop()` operation:

```
void Pop(ListElement& Elem)
{
    assert(NumNodes > 0);
    Elem = First->Data;
    Delete(Stack::Beginning);
}
```

Note that we check to ensure that the list is not empty before proceding with the `Pop()` operation, because if the value of **First** is the NULL pointer, then attempting to dereference **First** to access the (nonexistent) **Data** member it points to will likely produce a fatal error.

The Destructor. Note that Figure 16.14 contains no **Stack** destructor. To see why none is necessary, recall (from Section 15.3) that the destructor for a class *C* is called any time an object *derived from* **C** is destroyed. More specifically, class **Stack** is derived from class **LinkedList** and contains no data members beyond those of **LinkedList**. This means that no **Stack** destructor is needed, since the destruction of a **Stack** will automatically invoke the **LinkedList** destructor, because **Stack** is *derived from* class **LinkedList**.

Exercises

1. The following outline of a declaration of a **linked stack** class is similar to that
   for a linked list and is more space-efficient than the derived class described in
   this section:

```
typedef int StackElement;

class LinkedStack
{
   struct StackNode
   {
      StackElement
         Data;
      StackNode
         *Next;
      // ...
   };

   StackNode
      *Top;

   // ... basic operations
};
```

If the linked stack **Stack** is then declared by

```
LinkedStack
   Stack;
```

the value of **Stack.Top** will be a pointer to the top of the stack (NULL, if the
stack is empty). For example, a linked stack of integers might be pictured as

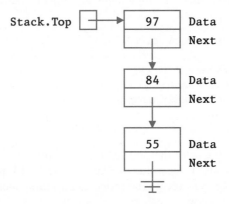

(a) Design and implement a class constructor that will initialize a
   LinkedStack as an empty stack.
(b) Design and implement boolean member functions **Empty()** and **Full()**
   that will return the status of a **LinkedStack** object.
(c) Design an algorithm to pop an element from this linked stack. Draw a
   picture of the modified stack. Implement this operation as a member of
   class **LinkedStack**.
(d) Design an algorithm to push an element onto the linked stack. Draw a
   picture of the modified stack. Implement this operation as a member of
   class **LinkedStack**.

(e) Design and implement a class destructor that the compiler can call to reclaim the storage of a `LinkedStack` when its lifetime has ended.

(f) Use class `LinkedStack` in a program like that in Figure 16.13 to convert integers from base-10 to base-2 notation.

2. To facilitate the debugging of programs that use a `LinkedStack`, modify class `LinkedStack` by adding a definition for `operator<<` to display a `LinkedStack`, as described here:

```
/**** operator<< displays the contents of a LinkedStack.

     Receive: An ostream (reference) and a LinkedStack.
     Output : A list of the elements in the LinkedStack,
              top to bottom.
     ---------------------------------------------------------*/

ostream& operator<< (ostream& Out, const LinkedStack& S);
```

3. Add a member function named `Top()` to class `LinkedStack` that retrieves the element at the top of the stack but without removing it from the stack.

16.5   A Special-Purpose List: The Queue

In the preceding section, we examined the stack—a special kind of list in which values are always inserted and removed from the same end. In this section, we examine another special-purpose list called a **queue,** in which values are always added at one end, called the **front** or **head,** and removed from the opposite end, called the **rear** or **tail.**

Queues abound in everyday life, because they provide a way to schedule things that are waiting for some kind of service. For example,

- A line of persons waiting to check out at a supermarket,
- A line of vehicles at a toll booth,
- A line of planes waiting to take off at an airport, and
- A line of persons waiting to purchase a ticket for a movie

are all examples of queues. Arriving customers, vehicles, planes, and the like enter the line at the rear and are removed from the line and served when they reach the front of the line, so the first object to enter the queue is the first object served.

Because the first thing to enter the queue has been waiting the longest, it seems *fair* that it should be the first one served. (People get irritated when other people "cut ahead" of them in a line, because this *fairness principle* is violated.) Stated differently, whereas a stack exhibits LIFO behavior, a queue exhibits **first-in-first-out,** or **FIFO**, behavior.

Examples of Queues in Computer Systems

In addition to lines of people, vehicles, and planes waiting for service, queues are also commonly used to model waiting lines that arise in the operation of computer systems. These queues are formed whenever more than one process requires a particular resource that cannot be shared, such as a printer, a disk drive, the central processing unit, and so on. As processes request a particular resource, they are placed in a queue to wait for service by that resource.

For example, if several personal computers are sharing the same printer, a **spool queue** may be used to schedule output requests in a first-come, first-served manner. If a print job is requested and the printer is free, it is immediately given to this job. While this output is being printed, other jobs may need the printer, and so they are placed in a spool queue to await their turns. When the current job is finished printing, the printer is released from that job and the first job in the spool queue is removed and scheduled.

Another important use of queues in computing systems is **input/output buffering.** The transfer of information from an input device or to an output device is relatively slow, and if a program must be suspended while data is transferred, then its execution is slowed dramatically. One common solution to this problem uses sections of main memory known as **buffers** and transfers data between the program and these buffers rather than directly between the program and the input/output device.

In particular, consider a problem in which data being processed by a program is to be read from a disk file. This information is transferred from the disk file to an input buffer in main memory while the central processing unit (CPU) is performing some other task. When data is required by the program, the next value stored in this buffer is retrieved. While this value is being processed, additional data values can be transferred from the disk file to the buffer. Clearly, the buffer must be organized as a FIFO structure, that is, as a queue. A queue-empty condition indicates that the input buffer is empty, and program execution is suspended while the operating system attempts to load more data into the buffer or signals the end of input. Of course, such a buffer has a limited size, and thus a queue-full condition must also be used to signal when the buffer is full and no more data is to be transferred from the disk file to it.

Queue Operations

Just as there were four standard operations on a stack, there are four operations used to manipulate a queue:

1. *Empty*(), a boolean operation that returns true if and only if the queue is empty;
2. *Full*(), a boolean operation that returns true if and only if the queue is full;

3. *Append*(*v*), an operation to add a new value *v* to the queue; and

4. *Delete*(*v*), an operation to remove the oldest value *v* from the queue.

In the next section, we present a **Queue** class, where these operations are implemented.

Implementing a Queue Class

Like a stack, the queue is a special kind of list, and so the inheritance mechanism can be used to implement a **Queue** class. However, values must be inserted at one end of the list and deleted from the other end. We must, therefore, decide which operation should be performed at which end. As with the **Stack** class, this decision should be determined by the relative efficiency of choosing one end over the other.

    When we examined the **LinkedList Insert()** and **Delete()** operations, we saw that the time to insert at the beginning of the list is independent of the length of the list but that deleting from its end requires that we traverse the length of the list—a time-consuming operation for long lists. The time to delete the first element, however, is independent of the list's length, as is the time to insert an element at the end of the list, and we therefore choose this latter strategy: Delete from the list's beginning and insert at the list's end to implement the **Queue** class. Figure 16.15 presents a declaration of class **Queue** that uses this approach.

 FIGURE 16.15   Declaring class **Queue**.

```
/* This is the header file for the Queue library.

...
-----------------------------------------------------------------*/

#ifndef QUEUE
#define QUEUE

#include "LinkedList.h"

#include <assert.h>

#include "Boolean.h"

class Queue : private LinkedList
{
public:

   /* --- Class Constructor ---

      Precondition:  A queue has been defined.
      Postcondition: The queue has been constructed as an empty queue.
      -----------------------------------------------------------*/

   Queue(void) : LinkedList()
   {}
```

FIGURE 16.15   Declaring class **Queue**. (cont.)

```
/* --- Copy Constructor ---

    Precondition:  The compiler needs a copy of a Queue Q.
    Receive:       Q, the Queue to be copied
    Postcondition: The Queue containing this function is
                   a copy of Q.
------------------------------------------------------------*/

  Queue(const Queue& Q) : LinkedList(Q)
  {}


/* --- Is the Queue empty? ---

    Return: True iff the Queue containing this function is empty
------------------------------------------------------------*/

Boolean Empty(void) const
{
   return (NumNodes == 0);
}


/* --- Is the Queue full? ---

    Return: True iff the Queue containing this function is full
------------------------------------------------------------*/

  Boolean Full(void) const
   { return False; }     // a run-time allocated queue is "never" full


/* --- Add an element to the queue ---

    Receive:  Elem, the Element to be added
    Return:   The Queue containing this function, with Elem added
              at the rear
------------------------------------------------------------*/

void Add(const ListElement& Elem)
{
   Insert(Elem, Queue::End);
}


/* --- Remove the element first added to the queue. ---

    Return: Elem, the element first added to the queue;
            The Queue containing this function with Elem removed
------------------------------------------------------------*/
```

FIGURE 16.15   Declaring class **Queue**. (cont.)

```
   void Remove(ListElement& Elem)
   {
      assert(NumNodes != 0);
      Elem = First->Data;
      Delete(Queue::Beginning);
   }
};

#endif
```

As with class **Stack**, class **Queue** needs no additional data members beyond those inherited from class **LinkedList**. As a result, no destructor is needed for class **Queue**—the **LinkedList** destructor will be invoked whenever a **Queue** is destroyed, which suffices to reclaim a **Queue**'s run-time allocated memory.

In a similar way, the constructors for class **Queue** need take no actions beyond those taken by the constructors for class **LinkedList**, which are invoked via member initialization lists:

```
   Queue(void) : LinkedList()
   {}

   Queue(const Queue& Q) : LinkedList(Q)
   {}
```

Given these definitions, a declaration

```
   Queue
      Q;
```

constructs a **Queue** object named **Q** and uses the default-value constructor for class **LinkedList** to initialize its members as an empty queue.

The boolean functions **Empty()** and **Full()** are similar to those of a **Stack**. The expression

```
   Q.Empty()
```

will return true if and only if there are no values in the queue, and the expression

```
   Q.Full()
```

will never return true, unless memory has been exhausted.

Thanks to the inheritance of the **Insert()** and **Delete()** operations from class **LinkedList**, the **Add()** and **Remove()** operations are easy to implement. The function call

```
   Q.Add(SomeValue);
```

can be used to add a **ListElement** named *SomeValue* to the queue. If it is the first element added to the queue, then it will be the first element removed from the queue by the **Remove()** function, which utilizes the **Delete()** function inherited from class **LinkedList**.

Exercises

1. Like stacks, queues also can be implemented directly as linked lists, instead of using the inheritance mechanism. A **linked queue** class **LinkedQueue** might contain two pointer members: **FrontPtr**, which points to the node at the front of the queue, and **RearPtr**, which points to the node at the rear. For example, a linked queue containing the integers 573, −29, and 616 in this order, might be pictured as

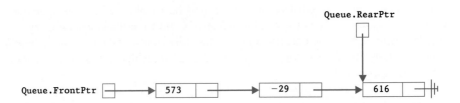

   (a) Design and implement a class constructor that will initialize a **LinkedQueue** as an empty queue.
   (b) Design and implement boolean member functions **Empty()** and **Full()** that will return the status of a **LinkedQueue** object.
   (c) Design an algorithm to remove an element from this linked queue. Draw a picture of the modified queue. Implement this operation as a member of class **LinkedQueue**.
   (d) Design an algorithm to add an element at the rear of this linked queue. Draw a picture of the modified queue. Implement this operation as a member of class **LinkedQueue**.
   (e) Design and implement a class destructor that the compiler can call to reclaim the storage of a **LinkedQueue** when its lifetime has ended.

2. To simplify debugging programs that use class **LinkedQueue**, add to the class a definition for the function **operator<<** to display a **LinkedQueue**:

```
/* operator<< displays the contents of a LinkedQueue.

   Receive: An ostream (reference) and a LinkedQueue.
   Output : A list of the elements in the LinkedQueue.
----------------------------------------------------------*/

ostream& operator<< (ostream& Out, const LinkedQueue& Q);
```

3. Add a member function to class **LinkedQueue** named **First()** that retrieves the element at the front of the queue without removing it from the queue.

4. Add a member function to class **LinkedQueue** named **Last()** that retrieves the element at the rear of the queue without removing it from the queue.

Program Design

1. *If a problem solution involves a list that frequently changes in size, then a* **linked list** *may be a more time-efficient way to store and process that list.* In an array-based list, the values are stored in adjacent memory locations. This means that when values are inserted into (or deleted from) an array-based list of *n* values, an average of *n*/2 of the values will have to be shifted to make room for the new value (or to close the gap left by the deleted item). The time required to shift these values makes insertion (and deletion) a time-expensive operation on an array-based list. By contrast, the values in a liked list are stored in non-adjacent nodes, which are attached to one another using pointers. Inserting a value at a given point in the list simply involves altering the values of at most three of these pointers.

2. *If a problem solution involves many accesses to the interior values of a list, then an* **array-based list** *may be a more time-efficient way to store and process the list.* In a linked list, all interior values (i.e., all but the first and last) must be accessed **sequentially.** That is, a value in a linked list can only be accessed from the pointer in the preceding node, which can only be accessed from the pointer in the node that precedes this node, . . . , which can only be accessed from the pointer in the first node. An average of *n*/2 accesses are required to access an interior node in a linked list of length *n.* By contrast, all values of an array-based list can be accessed **directly,** which means that such lists can be processed more quickly.

3. *If a problem solution requires that multiple values of the same type be stored temporarily, and the values stored more recently will be needed before those stored less recently, then a* **stack** *is an appropriate structure for storing these values.* Stacks are LIFO (last-in-first-out) lists, since the operation to remove a value from a stack will always retrieve the value that was inserted most recently.

4. *If a problem solution requires that multiple values of the same type be stored temporarily, and the values will be needed in the order in which they were stored, then a* **queue** *is an appropriate structure for storing these values.* Queues are FIFO (first-in-first-out) lists, since the operation to remove a value from a queue will always retrieve the value that was inserted least recently.

Potential Problems

The following are some of the main features to remember when using pointer variables and dynamic objects in C++ programs:

1. *If* P *is a pointer whose value is undefined or NULL, then an attempt to dereference* P *is an error.*

2. *Memory locations that were once associated with a pointer variable and that are no longer needed should be returned to the free store by using the* `delete` *operation.* Special care is required to avoid marooning memory locations. For example, if **P** and **Q** are pointer variables bound to the same type, the assignment statement

```
P = Q;
```

causes **P** to point to the same memory location as that pointed to by **Q**. Any memory location previously pointed to by **P** becomes inaccessible and cannot be disposed of properly unless it is pointed to by some other pointer. Temporary pointers should be used to maintain access, as the following statements demonstrate:

```
TempPtr = P;
P = Q;
delete TempPtr;
```

3. *Pay attention to special cases in processing linked lists, and be careful not to lose access to nodes.* In particular, remember the following "programming proverbs":

■ *Don't take a long walk off a short linked list.* It is an error to attempt to process elements beyond the end of the list. As an example, consider the following incorrect attempts to search a linked list with first node pointed to by **List** for some **ItemSought**:

Attempt 1:

```
CurrentPtr = List.First;
while (CurrentPtr->Data != ItemSought)
   CurrentPtr = CurrentPtr->Next;
```

If the item is not present in any node of the linked list, **CurrentPtr** will eventually reach the last node in the list. **CurrentPtr** then becomes NULL, and an attempt is made to examine the **Data** field of a nonexistent node, resulting in an error.

Attempt 2:

```
/* This time I'll make sure I don't fall off the end
   of the list by stopping if I find ItemSought
   or reach a node whose link field is NULL. */

Found = False;
CurrPtr = List.First;
while ((! Found) && (CurrentPtr->Next != 0))
   if (CurrentPtr->Data == ItemSought)
      Found = True;
   else
      CurrentPtr = CurrentPtr->Next;
```

Although this avoids the problem of moving beyond the end of the list, it will fail to locate the desired item (that is, set **Found** to true) if the item sought is the last one in the list. When **CurrentPtr** reaches the last node, the value of `CurrentPtr->Next` is NULL, and repetition is terminated without examining the `Data` field of this last node. Another problem is that if the item is found in the list, the remaining nodes (except the last) will also be examined.

Attempt 3:

```
// Another attempt to avoid running
   past the end of the list.

CurrentPtr = List.First;
while ((CurrentPtr->Data != ItemSought)
   && (CurrentPtr != 0))
   CurrentPtr = CurrentPtr->Next;
```

This solution is almost correct, but like the first attempted solution, it results in an error if the item is not in the list. The reason is that boolean expressions are evaluated from left to right. Thus, when the end of the list is reached and `CurrentPtr` becomes NULL, the first part of the boolean expression controlling repetition is evaluated, and the result of dereferencing a null pointer is unpredictable as we noted earlier.

Attempt 4:

```
// Okay, so I'll just reverse the two parts
   of the boolean expression

CurrentPtr = List.First;
while ((CurrentPtr != 0)
   && (CurrentPtr->Data != ItemSought))
   CurrentPtr = CurrentPtr->Next;
```

This is a correct solution, thanks to the short-circuit evaluation of conditions in C++. That is, if `CurrentPtr` is NULL, then the first part of the condition,

```
(CurrentPtr != 0)
```

evaluates to false, and so the condition "short-circuits," leaving the second condition,

```
(CurrentPtr->Data != ItemSought)
```

unevaluated. Note that if short-circuit evaluation were not utilized, this second condition would be evaluated, and the attempt to dereference `CurrentPtr` (whose value is NULL) would result in an error.

■ *You can't get water from an empty well.* Don't try to access elements in an empty list; this case usually requires special consideration. For example, if `List.First` is NULL, then initializing `CurrentPtr` to `List.First` and attempting to access `CurrentPtr->Data` or `CurrentPtr->Next` is an error. In the same manner, trying to pop an element from an empty stack or to delete an element from an empty queue produces a fatal error. To avoid such errors, such operations should be guarded with an `if` statement; for example,

```
if (!S.Empty())
    S.Pop(v);
else
    // .. take some remedial action ...
```

will perform the pop operation only if there are values to be popped from the stack **S**.

■ *Don't burn bridges before you cross them.* Be careful to change links in the correct order, or you may lose access to a node or to many nodes. For example, in the following attempt to insert a new node at the beginning of a linked list,

```
List.First = NewNodePtr;
NewNodePtr->Next = List.First;
```

the statements are not in correct order. As soon as the first statement is executed, **List.First** points to the new node, and access to the remaining nodes in the list (those formerly pointed to by **List.First**) is lost. The second statement then simply sets the link field of the new node to point to itself:

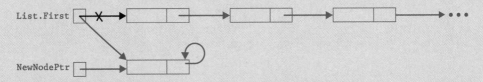

The correct sequence is to first connect the new node to the list and then reset **List.First**:

```
NewNodePtr->Next = List.First;
List.First = NewNodePtr;
```

Programming Projects

1. In an ordered list, all operations that modify the list are designed to ensure that its elements remain in ascending order. Build a class **OrderedList** derived from class **LinkedList** that exhibits this characteristic.

2. In a **doubly,** or **symmetrically, linked list,** each node has two link fields, one containing a pointer to the predecessor of that node and the other containing a pointer to its successor. It might be pictured as follows:

This design is especially useful when it is necessary to traverse a linked list or a part of it in either direction.

(a) Write the necessary class declarations, constructors, and destructors for such a list.

(b) Define a member function for displaying the list from left to right.

(c) Define a member function for displaying the list from right to left.

(d) Define a member function for inserting an item at a specified index in a doubly linked list.

(e) Define a member function to delete the item at a specified index from a doubly linked list.

3. A **doubly linked ring,** or **doubly linked circular list,** is a doubly linked list in which the NULL right pointer in the last node is replaced with a pointer to the first node, and the NULL left pointer in the first node is replaced with a pointer to the last node.

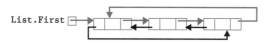

This design eliminates the need for a `Last` member, since the last node in the list can be accessed via `List.First->BLink`.

(a) Write the necessary class declarations, constructors and destructors for such a list.

(b) Define a function for displaying the list from left to right.

(c) Define a function for displaying the list from right to left.

(d) Define a function for inserting an item at a specified index in a doubly linked ring.

(e) Define a function to delete the item at a specified index from a doubly linked ring.

4. A **deque** (pronounced "deck") is a double-ended queue—that is, a list into which items may be inserted and from which items may be removed at either end.

(a) Write a function for adding an element to a deque; one of the parameters should specify the end at which the item is to be added.

(b) Write a function for removing an element from a deque; one of the parameters should specify the end from which the item is to be removed.

5. An application of multiply linked lists is to maintain a list sorted in two or more different ways. For example, consider the following multiply linked list having two links per node:

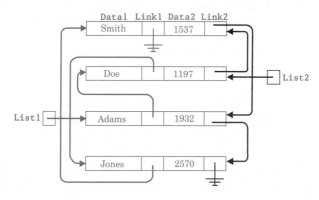

If this list is traversed and the data fields are displayed by using `List1` to point to the first node and following the pointers in the field `Link1`, the names will be in alphabetical order:

Adams	1932
Doe	1197
Jones	2570
Smith	1537

A traversal using `List2` to point to the first node and following pointers in the field `Link2` gives the identification numbers in ascending order:

Doe	1197
Smith	1537
Adams	1932
Jones	2570

This list is logically ordered, therefore, in two different ways. Write a program to read the first ten records from `UsersFile` (see Appendix D) and store them in a multiply linked list that is logically sorted so that the user identification numbers are in ascending order and the resources used to date are in descending order. Traverse the list and display the records so that the identification numbers are in ascending order. Then traverse the list and display the records so that the resources used to date are in descending order.

6. In Exercise 6 of Section 16.3, a linked list representation for a polynomial in x,

$$P(x) = a_0 + a_1x + a_2x^2 + \cdots + a_nx^n$$

was described. A **polynomial in two variables,** x and y, can be viewed as a polynomial in one variable, y, with coefficients that are polynomials in x; that is, it has the form

$$P(x, y) = A_0(x) + A_1(x)y + \cdots + A_{m-1}(x)y^{m-1} + A_m(x)y^m$$

where each $A_i(x)$ is a polynomial in x. For example,

$$6 + 8x^4 + y^2 - 3xy^2 + 4x^5y^2 + 5x^2y^3 + 7x^5y^3$$

can be rewritten as

$$(6 + 8x^4) + (1 - 3x + 4x^5)y^2 + (5x^2 + 7x^5)y^3$$

A multiply linked representation for such polynomials is obtained by representing each term of the form $A_k(x)y^k$ by a node that stores the exponent of y and two links, one containing a pointer to a linked list representing the polynomial $A_k(x)$ and the other a pointer to the next term. For example, the first term in the preceding example can be represented as

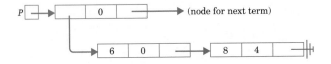

(a) Draw a multiply linked representation for

$$P(x, y) = 1 + 4x + x^2 + 9y + 2xy + xy^4 + 6x^2y^4 - 7xy^5 + 5x^7y^5 + 3x^9y^5$$

(b) Design and implement a class to represent such polynomials.

(c) Write a program that uses the class in (b) to read a triple of the form

(coefficient, x exponent, y exponent)

for a polynomial in x and y and constructs its linked representation. Then read values for x and y and evaluate the polynomial.

(d) Modify the program in part (b) so that the exponents of x and the exponents of y need not be read in increasing order.

7. Write a "quiz-tutor" program, perhaps on a topic from one of the early chapters or some other topic about which you are knowledgeable. The program should read a question and its answer from a file, display the question, and accept an answer from the user. If the answer is correct, the program should go on to the next question. If it is not correct, the question should be put into a queue. When the file of questions is exhausted, the questions that were missed should be displayed again. The program should keep a count of the correct answers and display the final count. Also, it should display the correct answer when necessary in the second round of questioning.

TREES

> *I think that I shall never see,*
> *A poem lovely as a tree.*
> **JOYCE KILMER**
>
> *Woodman, spare that tree!*
> **GEORGE POPE MORRIS**

CHAPTER CONTENTS

In Chapter 16, we saw how lists can be implemented by linking together self-referencing structures called nodes. The main advantage of linked lists over array-based lists is that values can be inserted at any point in the list without having to move list values to "make room" for the new value, and items can be deleted without having to move list values to "close the gaps."

The primary weakness of linked lists is that values cannot be accessed directly (except those at the ends of the list). If an array has n values and these are ordered, then the direct access property of an array makes it possible to use binary search to locate a value in the list in $O(\log_2 n)$ time as opposed to the $O(n)$ time required for linear search. Unfortunately, the binary search technique provides no such improvement over linear search for a linked list because the items in a linked list cannot be accessed directly. To access the middle value in a linked list, as required in a binary search, one-half of that list must be traversed. As a result, the time to perform a binary search of a linked list is much greater than the time required for a linear search.

In this chapter, we examine the **tree**—an object made up of nodes linked together to form a nonlinear structure. After a general introduction to trees, we consider **binary search trees,** in which, as the name suggests, the elements are arranged in such a way that a binary search technique can be used to search the structure efficiently.

17.1   PART OF THE PICTURE: Expert Systems

Example: The Game of Animal

The game of *animal* is an old children's game. There are two participants in the game—the *player* and the *guesser*. The player is asked to think of an animal, which the guesser will try to guess. The guesser asks the player a series of yes-or-no questions, such as

```
Guesser: Does it live on land?
```

If the player answers yes, then the guesser can eliminate from consideration those animals that do not live on land and use this information in formulating the next question, such as

```
Guesser: Does it have four feet?
```

Again, the answer to the question allows the user to eliminate from consideration either the animals with four feet or those that do not have four feet.

Carefully formulating each question allows the guesser to eliminate a large group of animals from consideration, based on the player's response. Eventually, the guesser knows of only a single animal with the given characteristics:

```
Guesser: Is it an elephant?
```

If the guesser is correct, then he or she wins the game. Otherwise, the player wins the game, and the guesser asks the player:

> *Guesser:* What is your animal?
> *Player:* An aardvark
> *Guesser:* How does an elephant differ from an aardvark?
> *Player:* An elephant has a trunk, but an aardvark does not.

By remembering the new animal and the difference between his or her animal and the new animal, the guesser learns to distinguish between the two animals.

A computer program that plays the animal game provides a classic example of a situation in which a program can seemingly *learn* and thus display **artificial intelligence.** The user of the program assumes the role of player and the program assumes the role of guesser.

The program maintains a **knowledge base** of questions, each of which allows it to eliminate animals from consideration. When the program has narrowed its search to a single animal, it guesses that animal. If the guess is correct, the program wins. Otherwise, the program asks the player to name the animal of which he or she was thinking and then asks how to distinguish between this new animal and the animal it guessed. It then stores this question and the animal in its knowledge base for the next time the game is played. The program thus exhibits some of the characteristics of learning each time it adds a new animal to its knowledge base.

As time passes and the program's knowledge base grows, it becomes more and more difficult for the player to think of animals that are not in the knowledge base— the program becomes an *expert* at guessing animals. Programs that exhibit expertise in some area through the use of a knowledge base are called **expert systems,** and the study of such systems is one of the branches of artificial intelligence. Examples of such systems range from welding experts that control welding robots on an automotive assembly line to legal experts that can help draw up standard legal documents.

Although most expert systems utilize fixed knowledge bases that the program is unable to modify, a program that plays the animal game is an example of a special *adaptive expert system,* because it adds new animals to its knowledge base as they are encountered. It is this ability to adapt its knowledge base that enables the animal program to simulate the process of learning.

Figure 17.1 presents a simple program that plays the animal game using a library named **DecisionTree**.

 FIGURE 17.1 Driver for the game of *animal.*

```
/* This program plays the game of animal, in which the player
   thinks of an animal, and the program tries to guess it. If the
   program is unable to guess the player's animal, it "learns" to
   distinguish the player's animal from its animal.
   ...
-----------------------------------------------------------------*/

#include <iostream.h>
#include "DecisionTree.h"

int PlayMore(void);
```

FIGURE 17.1   Driver for the game of *animal*. (cont.)

```
int main(void)
{
    cout << "\nWelcome to the game of Animal!\n";

    DecisionTree
        Tree;

    Tree.Load("Animal.data");

    int
        Winner;                     // 0 = the player, 1 = the program

    do
    {
        cout << "\nThink of an animal, and I will try to guess it...\n";

        Winner = Tree.Descend();

        if (Winner)
            cout << "\nHa! Even a computer program can beat you...\n";
        else
            cout << "\nYou're just lucky...\n";
    }
    while (PlayMore());

    Tree.Write("Animal.data");

    return 0;
}

int PlayMore(void)
{
    char
        Answer;

    cout << "\nWant to play again (y or n)? ";
    cin >> Answer;

    return ((Answer == 'y') || (Answer == 'Y'));
}
```

Sample run:

```
Welcome to the game of Animal!

Think of an animal, and I will try to guess it.

Does it live on land (y or n)? y
```

FIGURE 17.1   Driver for the game of *animal*. (cont.)

```
Does it have wings (y or n)? n

Is it a(n) elephant (y or n)? y

Ha! Even a computer program can beat you...

Want to play again (y or n)? y

Think of an animal, and I will try to guess it.

Does it live on land (y or n)? n

Is it a(n) whale (y or n)? n

What animal are you thinking of? shark

Please enter a question, such that the answer is
        yes - for a(n) shark, and
        no - for a(n) whale
--> Is it cold-blooded

You're just lucky...

Want to play again (y or n)? y

Does it live on land (y or n)? n

Is it cold-blooded (y or n)? y

Is it a(n) shark (y or n)? n

What animal are you thinking of? electric eel

Please enter a question, such that the answer is
        yes - for a(n) electric eel, and
        no - for a(n) shark
--> Can meeting it be a shocking experience

You're just lucky...

Want to play again (y or n)? n
```

The program plays the game by building a special linked structure in which it stores the questions and the animals that it "knows." For example, when this program was first written, it "knew" only three animals: a duck, an elephant, and a whale. The structure it used to distinguish these animals was as follows:

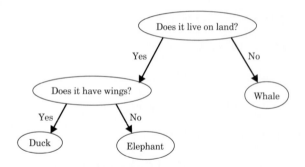

Such a structure is called a **decision tree**—each node in the tree contains the information needed to make a decision between its two subtrees. The guesser begins by asking the topmost question and, based on the player's response, follows the Yes branch or the No branch to the next question. The guesser continues this process, descending through the tree until it reaches the end of a line of questioning, in which case it guesses the animal whose name is stored in that node.

By implementing such a tree as a linked structure, new nodes can be easily inserted (or deleted). Thus, in the first repetition of our program's main loop, the program "got lucky" because it happened that the animal of which the player was thinking (an elephant) was one it knew about. However, on the second repetition, the user was thinking of a shark—an animal the program did not know about. Using the information it received from the player, the program learned to distinguish between a whale and a shark by creating and inserting the nodes needed to distinguish the two animals:

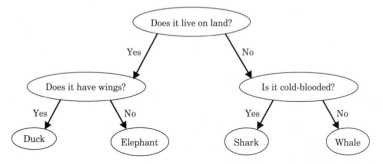

Similarly, the next repetition of its main loop, the program learned to distinguish between a shark and an electric eel:

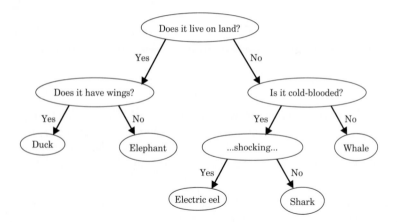

The program thus learns by adding to its decision tree each time it encounters an animal that is not in its knowledge base. By saving its decision tree in a file when the program terminates and then rebuilding the tree from that file when the program is run again, the program can "remember" what it has "learned" in previous games. Over the course of time, such a program can become quite adept at identifying animals, based on the characteristics it is taught.[1] The source code for this program is included on the distribution diskette, and the reader is invited to examine it for further details.

17.2 An Introduction to Trees

In the introduction to this chapter, we argued that binary search could not be used efficiently with an ordered linked list because the nodes in a linked list must be accessed in a sequential fashion. The problem lies in the *linear organization* of a linked list—the one-directional nature of its links requires that we start at the beginning and examine each element of the list in sequence.

This raises an interesting question: Is it possible to organize a linked structure in some other way so that its elements can be searched more quickly than is possible in a linearly linked structure? Ideally, such a structure would provide for easy insertion/deletion as in linked lists but permit the access of individual elements in less than O(n) time. Happily, the answer is *yes*—it is possible to store the elements of an ordered list in a linked structure that can be searched in a binary-search-like manner.

To illustrate, consider the following ordered list of integers:

13, 28, 35, 49, 62, 66, 80

The first step in a binary search requires examining the middle element in the list. Direct access to this element is possible if we maintain a pointer to the node storing it:

For the next step, one of the two sublists, the left half or the right half, must be searched, and so both must be accessible from this node. This is possible if we maintain two pointers, one to each of these sublists. Since these sublists are searched in the same manner, these pointers should point to nodes containing the middle elements in these sublists:

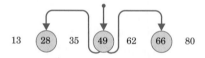

---

[1] Note that in employing such a simple model of knowledge, our program can show no *discernment* and "believes" whatever it is taught. The program cannot reconcile (or even detect) contradictory information. Whether such a program truly exhibits *intelligence* is a continuing subject of debate in the computing community.

By the same reasoning, in the next step, pointers from each of these "second-level" nodes are needed to access the middle elements in the sublists:

The resulting structure is usually drawn so that it has a treelike shape:

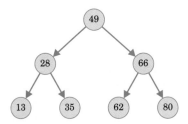

This structure is called a *binary search tree* and is a special kind of *binary tree,* which is a special instance of a more general structure called a *tree.*

Trees

A **tree** consists of a finite set of elements called **nodes,** or **vertices,** and a finite set of **directed arcs** that connect pairs of nodes. If the tree is not empty, then one of the nodes, called the **root,** has no incoming arcs, but every other node in the tree can be reached from the root by following a unique sequence of consecutive arcs.

Trees derive their names from the treelike diagrams that are used to picture them. For example,

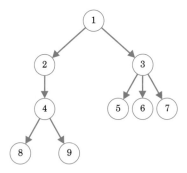

shows a tree with nine vertices, in which vertex 1 is the root. As this diagram indicates, trees are usually drawn upside down, with the root at the top and the **leaves**—that is, vertices with no outgoing arcs—at the bottom. Nodes that are directly accessible from a given node (by using only one directed arc) are called the **children** of that node, and a node is said to be the **parent** of its children. For example, in the preceding tree, vertex 3 is the parent of vertices 5, 6, and 7, and these vertices are the children of vertex 3 and are called **siblings.**

Applications of trees are many and varied. For example, a **genealogical tree** such as the following is a convenient way to picture a person's descendants:

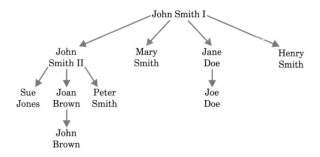

Game trees like the following, which shows the various configurations possible in the towers of Hanoi problem with two disks (see Section 7.10), are used to analyze games and puzzles.

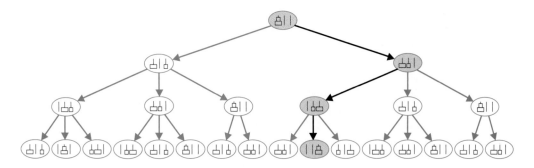

Parse trees constructed during the compilation of a program are used to check the program's syntax. For example, the following is a parse tree for the expression $2 * (3 + 4)$:

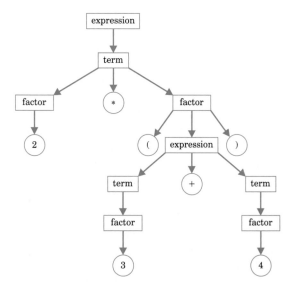

Binary Trees

Binary trees are trees in which each node has at most two children. Such trees are especially useful in modeling processes in which some experiment or test with two possible outcomes (for example, off or on, 0 or 1, false or true, down or up, yes or no) is performed repeatedly. For example, the following binary tree might be used to represent the possible outcomes of flipping a coin three times:

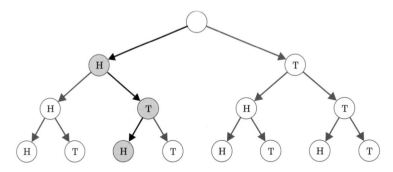

Each path from the root to one of the leaf nodes corresponds to a particular outcome, such as HTH (a head followed by a tail followed by another head), as highlighted in the diagram.

Similarly, a binary tree can be used in coding problems such as in encoding and decoding messages transmitted in Morse code, a scheme in which characters are represented as sequences of dots and dashes, as shown in the following table (see Exercise 7 of Section 9.6):

A • −	M − −	Y − • − −
B − • • •	N − •	Z − − • •
C − • − •	O − − −	1 • − − − −
D − • •	P • − − •	2 • • − − −
E •	Q − − • −	3 • • • − −
F • • − •	R • − •	4 • • • • −
G − − •	S • • •	5 • • • • •
H • • • •	T −	6 − • • • •
I • •	U • • −	7 − − • • •
J • − − −	V • • • −	8 − − − • •
K − • −	W • − −	9 − − − − •
L • − • •	X − • • −	0 − − − − −

In this case, the nodes in a binary tree are used to represent the characters, and the arcs from a node to its children are labeled with a dot or a dash, according to whether they lead to a left child or to a right child, respectively. Thus, part of the tree for Morse code is

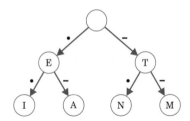

The sequence of dots and dashes labeling a path from the root to a particular node corresponds to the Morse code for that character; for example, · · is the code for I, and −· is the code for N.

In the preceding section we saw that when a decision-making process can be modeled as a series of yes-or-no questions, a binary tree can be used to model that process. Each nonleaf node is used to store a question, and if an affirmative answer to a question leads to another question, then the two nodes are connected with an arc labeled Yes. Similarly, if a negative answer to a question leads to another question, then the two nodes are connected with an arc labeled No. Since there are only two choices for each question, the resulting structure is a binary tree with decisions at its leaf nodes. The problem of choosing a single choice from among many choices is solved simply by descending through the tree until a leaf node (i.e., a decision) is reached.

Decision trees can be designed to mimic the choices made by experts in a given field, and programs that utilize them are thus sometimes called expert systems. For example, programs to help a person prepare an income tax return (such as *MacinTax*™ or *TurboTax*™)[2] have some of the expertise of a tax accountant encoded within them. Similarly, programs that lead a person through the steps of writing a will (such as *WillMaker*™)[3] have some of the expertise of an estate lawyer encoded within them.

In this chapter, we confine our attention to binary trees. This is not a serious limitation, however, because any tree can be represented by a binary tree, using a technique described in the exercises.

A binary tree can be represented by a multiply linked structure in which each node has two link fields, one being a pointer to the left child of that node and the other a pointer to the right child. Such nodes can be represented in C++ by a struct whose declaration has the following form:

```
typedef SomeType BinTreeElement;

struct Node
{
   BinTreeElement
      Data;
   Node
      *LChild,
      *RChild;

   // ... member functions omitted ...
};
```

The two link fields **LChild** and **RChild** are pointers to nodes representing the left and right child, respectively,

---

[2] The software products *MacinTax* and *TurboTax* are trademarks of ChipSoft (ChipSoft, 1993).

[3] *WillMaker* is a trademark of Nolo Press/Legisoft (Nolo Press, 1991).

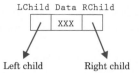

or are NULL if the node does not have a left or right child. A leaf node is character-ized by having NULL values for *both* **LChild** and **RChild**:

This declaration of a **Node** can then be placed within a binary tree class so that the implementation details of a **Node** and its members are hidden from programs using the binary tree. Figure 17.2 gives a declaration of the data members of such a class.

 FIGURE 17.2   Data members of a binary tree class.

```
typedef SomeType BinTreeElement;

class BinaryTree
{
protected:

  struct Node                  // a binary tree node
  {
    BinTreeElement
      Data;
    Node
      *Left,
      *Right;

      // ... member functions omitted...
  };

typedef Node *NodePtr;         // an easy-to-read alias type

NodePtr                        // pointer to the root node
  Root;

// ...
};
```

Given such a class, the binary tree

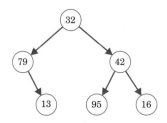

can be represented as the following linked tree of structures:

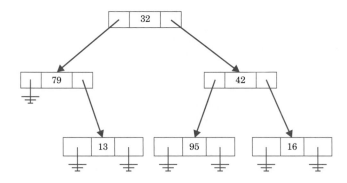

The root node of this binary tree contains the integer 32 and has pointers to the nodes containing 79 and 42, each of which is itself the root of a binary **subtree:**

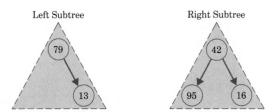

Now consider the left subtree. Its root node contains the integer 79 and has a right child but no left child. Nevertheless, we can still regard this node as having pointers to two binary subtrees, a left subtree and a right subtree, since an empty (sub)tree is still a tree:

Both the left and right subtrees of the one-node tree containing 13 are empty binary trees.

This leads to the following recursive definition of a binary tree:

RECURSIVE DEFINITION OF A BINARY TREE

A binary tree either

    a. Is empty ◄────────────────────────── Anchor

or

    b. Consists of a node called the root,
       which has pointers to two disjoint
       binary subtrees called the **left** ◄──────── Inductive step
       subtree and the **right subtree.**

Because of the recursive nature of binary trees, many of the basic operations on them can be implemented most simply and elegantly using recursive algorithms. These algorithms are typically anchored by the special case of an empty binary tree, and the inductive step specifies how a binary tree is to be processed in terms of its root and either or both of its subtrees.

The first operation for binary trees that we consider is **traversing** the tree, that is, visiting each node in the binary tree exactly once. Suppose for the moment that the order in which the nodes are visited is not relevant but that it is important that we visit each node, not missing any, and that the information in each node is processed exactly once.

One simple scheme is to traverse the binary tree recursively, as follows:

If the binary tree is empty, then ◄────────────── Anchor case
    Do nothing.
Else ◄──────────────────────────── Inductive step
    1. Visit the root and process its contents.
    2. Traverse the left subtree (recursively).
    3. Traverse the right subtree (recursively).
End if.

Thus, in our example, if visiting a node means displaying the information it contains, then this scheme begins by displaying the value 32 in the root of the binary tree. Next, we must traverse the left subtree, and after this traversal is finished, we must traverse the right subtree. When this traversal is completed, we will have traversed the entire binary tree.

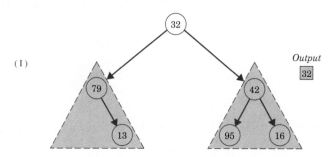

(I)

Output
32

The problem has thus been reduced to the traversal of two smaller binary trees, each of which is processed in exactly the same way. The scheme processes the left subtree first and displays the value in its root node (79). In processing this subtree, its left subtree must be traversed, followed by its right subtree.

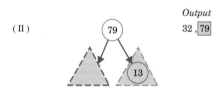

Output

(II)   32 , 79

The left subtree is empty, and so we have reached the anchor case of the recursion; hence, there is nothing to be done, which terminates the recursive traversal of that subtree.

Since traversal of the empty left subtree is finished, the scheme next recursively traverses the right subtree, displaying the value in its root, after which its left subtree and then its right subtree must be traversed:

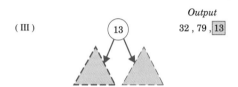

Output

(III)   32 , 79 , 13

Because both subtrees are empty, no action is required to traverse them. Consequently, traversal of the binary tree in diagram III is complete, and since this was the right subtree of the tree in diagram II, traversal of this tree is also complete.

This means that the traversal of the left subtree of the root in the original binary tree in diagram I has been completed, and so the right subtree remains to be traversed. This traversal proceeds in a similar manner. Its root is visited, which displays the value 42 stored there; then its left and right subtrees are recursively traversed:

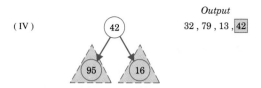

Output

(IV)   32 , 79 , 13 , 42

The left subtree consists of a single node with empty left and right subtrees and is traversed as described earlier for a one-node binary tree:

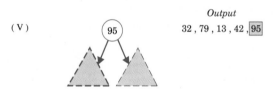

Output

(V)   32 , 79 , 13 , 42 , 95

The right subtree is traversed in the same way:

Output

(VI)

$32 , 79 , 13 , 42 , 95 , \boxed{16}$

This completes the traversal of the binary tree in diagram IV and thus completes the traversal of the original tree in diagram I.

As this example demonstrates, traversing a binary tree recursively requires three basic steps, which we shall denote V, L, and R:

V: Visit a node.
L: Traverse the left subtree of a node.
R: Traverse the right subtree of a node.

We performed these steps in the order listed here, but in fact, there are six different orders in which they can be carried out:

LVR, VLR, LRV, VRL, RVL, RLV

For example, the ordering LVR corresponds to the following traversal algorithm:

LVR BINARY TREE TRAVERSAL ALGORITHM

/* This algorithm traverses a binary tree using the LVR scheme.

Receive: A binary tree.
Behavior: Process the values in the binary tree, in LVR order.
——*/

If the binary tree is empty then   // anchor
    Do nothing.
Else do the following: // inductive step
    L: Traverse the left subtree.
    V: Visit the root.
    R: Traverse the right subtree.
End if.

For the preceding binary tree, LVR traversal visits the nodes in the order 79, 13, 32, 95, 42, 16.

The first three orders, in which the left subtree is traversed before the right, are the most important of the six traversals and are commonly called by other names:

LVR ↔ Inorder traversal
VLR ↔ Preorder traversal
LRV ↔ Postorder traversal

To see why these names are appropriate, consider the following **expression tree,** a binary tree used to represent the arithmetic expression

$$A - B * C + D$$

in which each operand is stored in a leaf node, whose parent node contains the operator to be applied to that operand:

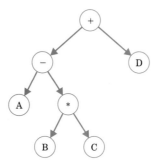

An **inorder** traversal of this expression tree produces the **infix** expression

$$A - B * C + D$$

A **preorder** traversal gives the **prefix** expression

$$+ - A * B C D$$

and a **postorder** traversal yields the **postfix** (Reverse Polish Notation) expression:

$$A B C * - D +$$

A binary tree is, in general, an unordered structure. That is, the definition of a binary tree does not specify any relationship between the values of the nodes in a binary tree and their positions in the tree. Consequently, an access operation such as searching for a given value may have to traverse the entire tree in order to find that value.

ALGORITHM TO SEARCH A BINARY TREE (PREORDER)

/* This algorithm searches a binary tree using the VLR scheme.

    Receive: A binary tree.
                  A value *Val.*
    Return: True if and only if *Val* is present in the binary tree.
    ——*/

If the binary tree is empty then   // anchor
   Return False.
Else do the following: // inductive step
   V: If the value in the root node is equal to *Val*, then
      Return True.
   L: Else if the result of recursively searching the left subtree is true, then
      Return true.
   R: Else if the result of recursively searching the right subtree is true, then
      Return true.
   Else
      Return false.
   End if.
End if.

Of course, to determine that a value is not present in the tree (the worst case), the entire tree must be traversed. That is, the time to access an arbitrary node in a binary tree is proportional to the number of values in the tree, which provides no improvement over the time to search a linked list.

This situation is similar to the problem of searching an array for a value—if the values in the array are unordered, then linear search must be used; but if the values in the array are ordered, then a more efficient approach such as binary search can be employed. In the same manner, searching a binary tree whose values are unordered requires the traversal of the entire tree, in the worst case. However, if the values in the tree are ordered, then a more efficient approach can be employed. One such ordering is used in a binary search tree, which we discuss next.

Binary Search Trees

Consider the following binary tree:

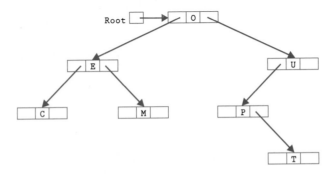

If a function **InOrder()** is used to perform an inorder traversal of this tree, then its nodes will be processed as follows:

Contents of Current Node	Level in the Tree	Action	Visit
Not applicable	0	Call **InOrder()**, passing it the pointer to the root node (**O**).	
O	1	Call **InOrder()**, passing it the pointer to root of the left subtree (**E**).	
E	2	Call **InOrder()**, passing it the pointer to root of the left subtree (**C**).	
C	3	Call **InOrder()**, passing it the pointer to root of the left subtree (null).	
None	4	None; return to the parent node.	
C	3	Visit the current node.	C
C	3	Call **InOrder()**, passing it the pointer to root of the right subtree (null).	
None	4	None; return to the parent node.	
C	3	Return to the parent node.	
E	2	Visit the current node.	E
E	2	Call **InOrder()**, passing it the pointer to root of the right subtree (**M**).	
M	3	Call **InOrder()**, passing it the pointer to root of the left subtree (null).	
None	4	None; return to the parent node.	
M	3	Visit the current node.	M
M	3	Call **InOrder()**, passing it the pointer to root of the right subtree (null).	
None	4	None; return to the parent node.	
M	3	Return to the parent node.	
E	2	Return to the parent node.	
O	1	Visit the current node.	O
O	1	Call **InOrder()**, passing it the pointer to root of the right subtree (**U**).	
U	2	Call **InOrder()**, passing it the pointer to root of the left subtree (**P**).	
P	3	Call **InOrder()**, passing it the pointer to root of the left subtree (null).	
None	4	None; return to the parent node.	
P	3	Visit the current node.	P
P	3	Call **InOrder()**, passing it the pointer to root of the right subtree (**T**).	
T	4	Call **InOrder()**, passing it the pointer to root of left subtree (null).	

Contents of Current Node	Level in the Tree	Action	Visit
None	5	None; return to the parent node.	
T	4	Visit the current node.	T
T	4	Call `InOrder()`, passing it the pointer to root of the right subtree (null).	
None	5	None; return to the parent node.	
T	4	Return to the parent node.	
P	3	Return to the parent node.	
U	2	Visit the current node.	U
U	2	Call `InOrder()`, passing it the pointer to root of the right subtree (null).	
None	3	None; return to the parent node.	
U	2	Return to the parent node.	
O	1	Function terminates; traversal complete.	

An inorder traversal of this binary tree thus visits the nodes in the following order:

C E M O P T U

Note that the letters are in alphabetical order. This is because this binary tree has

the special property that *the values in the left subtree of each node are less than the value in that node, which in turn is less than all values in the right subtree.* A binary tree having this property is called a **binary search tree** (**BST**) because it can be searched using an algorithm that is much like the binary search algorithm for arrays.

To illustrate, consider again the binary tree given earlier:

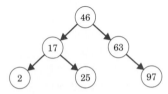

Suppose we wish to search this BST for 25. We begin at the root, and since 25 is less than the value 46 in this root, we know that the desired value is located to the left of the root; that is, it must be in the left subtree, whose root is 17:

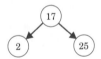

Now we continue the search by comparing 25 with the value in the root of this subtree. Since $25 > 17$, we know that the right subtree should be searched:

Examining the value in the root of this one-node subtree locates the value 25.

Similarly, to search for the value 55, we start at the root and compare 55 with its value 46:

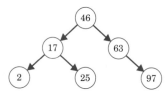

The result of that comparison leads us to search its right subtree:

Now, because $55 < 63$, if the desired value is in the tree, it will be in the left subtree. However, this left subtree is empty, allowing us to conclude that the value 55 is not present in the tree. We were thus able to determine that an element was not in the list by visiting two nodes, where a preorder traversal pattern would have required that five of the six nodes be visited.

By imposing an ordering on its values, the operations on a binary search tree that access a value can usually be performed more efficiently than the same operations on an (unordered) binary tree. In the next section, we examine how a binary search tree class can be implemented in C++.

Exercises

1. For each of the following lists of letters:

   (i) M, I, T, E, R   **(ii)** T, I, M, E, R
 (iii) R, E, M, I, T   **(iv)** C, O, R, N, F, L, A, K, E, S

   (a) Draw the binary search tree that is constructed when the letters are inserted in the order given.
   (b) Perform inorder, preorder, and postorder traversals of the tree, and show the sequence of letters that results in each case.

2. For the trees in Exercise 1, traverse each tree using the following orders:

   (a) VRL   **(b)** RVL   **(c)** RLV

3. For each of the following arithmetic expressions, draw a binary expression tree that represents the expression, and then use tree traversals to find the equivalent prefix and postfix (RPN) expressions:

(a) A + B + C / D
(b) (A + B) / C - D
(c) (A + B) * ((C + D) / (E + F))
(d) A - (B - (C - (D - E)))

4.

(a) Preorder traversal of a certain binary tree produced

    A D F G H K L P Q R W Z

and inorder traversal produced

    G F H K D L A W R Q P Z

Draw the binary tree.

(b) Postorder traversal of a certain binary tree produced

    F G H D A L P Q R Z W K

and inorder traversal gave the same result as in part (a). Draw the binary tree.

(c) Show by example that knowing the results of a preorder traversal and a postorder traversal does not uniquely determine the binary tree. That is, give an example of two different binary trees for which a preorder traversal of each gives the same result, as does a postorder traversal.

5. As noted in the text, every tree can be represented by a binary tree. This can be done by letting node *x* be a left child of node *y* in the binary tree if *x* is the leftmost child of *y* in the given tree and by letting *x* be the right child of *y* if *x* and *y* are siblings (have the same parent) in the original tree. For example, the tree

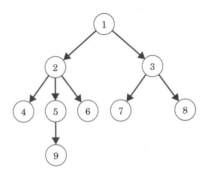

can be represented by the binary tree

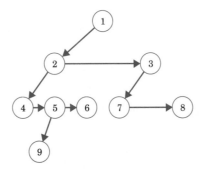

or, if it is drawn in the more customary manner,

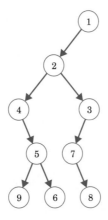

Represent each of the following by binary trees:

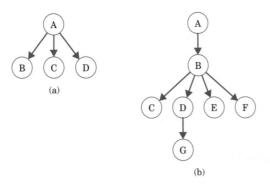

(a)

(b)

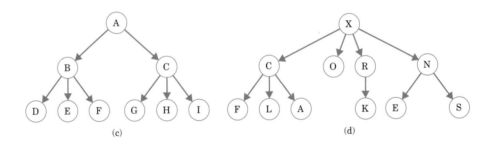

(c)   (d)

6. Complete the binary tree begun in this section for decoding messages in Morse code.

7. Design the **BinaryTree** member functions to perform inorder, preorder, and postorder traversals of a binary tree object using the **BinaryTree** declaration of Figure 17.2.

17.3   Implementing a Binary Search Tree Class

In this section, we examine how a binary search tree class can be implemented in C++. As usual, we examine separately the design of the class and the implementation of the operations on the class.

Designing the Class

Designing a class to represent binary search trees consists of two steps:

- Designing data members used to represent a binary search tree
- Selecting the operations appropriate for a binary search tree

Designing the Data Members.   We have already seen the data members for a binary tree (see Figure 17.2), which provide us with a model for our binary search tree class, as shown in Figure 17.3.

  FIGURE 17.3   The data members of a binary search tree class.

```
/* This file contains the declaration of class BST.

...
-----------------------------------------------------------*/

#ifndef BSTREE
#define BSTREE

typedef SomeType BinTreeElement;
```

FIGURE 17.3   The data members of a binary search tree class. (cont.)

```
class BST
{
protected:                  // allow derived classes to access members

  struct Node               // the nodes of the tree
    {
      BinTreeElement        //    the value of the node
        Data;
      Node
        *Left,              //    the left subtree of the node
        *Right;             //    the right subtree of the node

                            // ... Node member functions omitted ...

    };

  typedef Node *NodePtr;    // an easy-to-read pointer type

  NodePtr
    Root;                   // pointer to the root node of the BST

                            // ... BST member functions omitted ...
};

#endif
```

Note that the **Node** members **Left** and **Right** are declared as pointers to a **Node**. That is, in using the name **Node**, the members of a node are **declared recursively**. As we saw with the nodes in a linked list, an object that refers to itself in its declaration is called a **self-referencing structure**.

Selecting BST Operations. Since we are designing a **BST** class in which we have a nested structure called a **Node**, we can immediately identify the following operations:

- A class constructor(s) to initialize the data members of a **Node**
- A class constructor(s) to initialize the data member of a **BST**

From the data representation of the class, it is apparent that the **BST** class will use run-time memory allocation to create **Node** objects. This dynamic allocation implies that we will need the following operations:

- A copy constructor for a **BST**
- A copy constructor for a **Node**
- A destructor for a **Node**
- A destructor for a **BST**

There are also standard binary search tree operations, including

- Insert a value into the **BST**,
- Search the **BST** for a given value, and
- Delete a value from the **BST**,

as well as other useful operations such as assignment and I/O.

Designing the Operations. The key observation regarding the operations for the **BST** class is to recognize that we have two fundamentally different structures with which we must be concerned:

1. The **BST**, which contains a pointer to a **Node**
2. The **Node**, which contains pointers to other **Node** objects

That is, the data members of a **BST** do not define it recursively, but the data members of a **Node** define it recursively. The practical consequence of this is that the operations on a **Node** are conveniently implemented using recursion, but the operations on a **BST** are not. This implies that most of our operations will actually require two functions:

- A nonrecursive **BST** member function in the public section of the class
- A recursive **Node** member function called by the **BST** member function that actually performs (most of) the operation.

Implementing BST Operations

A Node Constructor. A constructor for class **Node** should provide a convenient way to initialize a **Node**. The key observation is that the memory for a **Node** will be dynamically allocated using the **new** operation, and so a **Node** constructor should allow a **Node** object to be initialized when its memory is allocated. Ideally, we would like the operation

```
new Node(DataValue, LeftPtrValue, RightPtrValue)
```

to initialize the new **Node** with the indicated values, whereas the operation

```
new Node(DataValue)
```

should initialize the **Data** member of the new **Node** with the supplied value and use default values (e.g., NULL) for the values of the **Left** and **Right** pointer members. Finally, the operation

```
new Node
```

should simply initialize the **Left** and **Right** pointer members of the **Node** to default values and leave the **Data** member undefined.

Since we cannot anticipate the type for which **BinTreeElement** might be a synonym, we are unable to provide a default value to initialize the **Data** member of a **Node**. This means that two **Node** class constructors are needed to accomplish these three objectives, as shown in Figure 17.4.

FIGURE 17.4 Node constructors.

```
/* ----- This function constructs a Node with default values.

   Precondition:  A Node has been declared (no arguments).
   Postcondition: The Node has been initialized with default values.
   ----------------------------------------------------------------*/

Node(void)
{
   Left = Right = 0;
}


/* ----- This function constructs a Node with supplied values.

   Precondition:  A Node has been declared with arguments.
   Receive:       Elem, a BinTreeElement value
                  LPtr and RPtr, two node addresses (default NULL)
   Postcondition: The Node has been initialized with the given
                  values.
   ----------------------------------------------------------------*/

Node(const BinTreeElement& Elem, Node *LPtr = 0, Node *RPtr = 0)
{
   Data = Elem;
   Left = LPtr;
   Right = RPtr;
}
```

Because of the relative simplicity of these constructors, we define them within the body of struct **Node**.

Given such constructors, the expression

```
new Node
```

uses the first constructor to construct a new **Node** whose pointer members are NULL and whose **Data** member is undefined. If **BinTreeElement** is a synonym for the type **double**, then the expression

```
new Node(3.5)
```

uses the second constructor to construct a new **Node** whose pointer members are NULL and whose **Data** member is initialized to 3.5. Similarly, the expression

```
new Node(5.0, SomePtr, AnotherPtr)
```

uses the second constructor to construct a new **Node** whose **Left** and **Right** members are initialized to *SomePtr* and *AnotherPtr*, respectively, and whose **Data** member is initialized to **5.0**.

A BST Constructor. In our implementation of class **BST**, we provide a single constructor that initializes the **BST** as an empty tree, as shown in Figure 17.5.

 FIGURE 17.5 A **BST** constructor.

```
/* ----- This function constructs a BST as an empty tree.

   Precondition:  A BST has been declared (no arguments).
   Postcondition: The BST has been initialized as an empty tree.
----------------------------------------------------------------*/

BST(void)
{
   Root = 0;
}
```

The simplicity of this constructor argues for its inclusion in the public section of class **BST**. Given such a constructor, the definition

```
BST
    MyTree;
```

will initialize the object **MyTree** as an empty **BST**, which we might visualize as:

More sophisticated constructors might be defined for a **BST** that would permit the construction of a nonempty binary search tree from a list of values. Such a constructor can be implemented using the ellipses mechanism (see Section 7.5) and is left as an exercise.

Inserting a Value into a BST. Once we can define **BST** objects, we want to be able to insert values into a **BST**. There are two cases to be considered:

- If the **BST** is empty (i.e., the value of its **Root** member is NULL), then a new **Node** must be constructed to hold the value being inserted.
- If the **BST** is not empty, then a root **Node** exists, and so the **BST** insertion function should pass the value to be inserted to a member function of that **Node**, which will recursively perform the insertion at the appropriate place in the tree.

The **Insert()** member of class **BST** simply distinguishes between these two cases, as shown in Figure 17.6.

FIGURE 17.6   Inserting a value into a BST.

```
/* This function inserts a BinTreeElement into a BST.

   Receive: Elem, the BinTreeElement being inserted
   Return:  The BST containing this function,
            with Elem inserted in the appropriate BST position
----------------------------------------------------------------*/

void BST::Insert(const BinTreeElement& Elem)
{
   if (Root == 0)              // is the BST empty?
      Root = new Node(Elem);   //    yes - create a root node
   else
      Root->Insert(Elem);      //    no - pass the buck to Node::Insert()
}
```

The function begins by checking whether a root node exists. If not, it creates a root node and initializes its **Data** member using the second class constructor function. Otherwise, it calls the recursive member function **Node::Insert()** of the root node, passing it the value to be inserted.

It is convenient to define the member functions of struct **Node** recursively, since a **Node** is defined recursively. The **Insert()** function in Figure 17.7 uses the following recursive binary-search–like algorithm to insert a value into a binary tree.

RECURSIVE ALGORITHM FOR INSERTING A VALUE INTO A NONEMPTY BST

```
/* This algorithm recursively inserts a value into a (sub)tree with a given Node
   as its root.

   Receive:  A value to be inserted into a BST
   Return:   The BST with the value inserted
------------------------------------------------------------------*/
```

If the value being inserted is less than the **Data** member of this **Node**:
    If the left subtree is empty:
      Make the left subtree a new **Node** whose **Data** member is the value being inserted.
    Else
      Recursively call the **Insert()** member of the root **Node** of the left subtree.
    End if.
Else if the value being inserted is greater than the **Data** member of this **Node**:
    If the right subtree is empty:
      Make the right subtree a new **Node** whose **Data** member is the value being inserted.
    Else
      Recursively call the **Insert()** member of the root **Node** of the right subtree.
    End if.

Else
    Print a warning message, since the value is already present in the binary search tree.
End if.

Because of the complexity of this algorithm we would store the definition of this function (and that of **BST::Insert()**) in the implementation file of **BST**.

FIGURE 17.7 Inserting a value into a **Node**.

```
/* This function inserts a BinTreeElement into a Node.

   Receive: Elem, the BinTreeElement being inserted
   Return:  The Node containing this function, with Elem
            inserted in the appropriate subtree position
-----------------------------------------------------------*/

void BST::Node::Insert(const BinTreeElement& Elem)
{
   if (Elem < Data)             // if Elem belongs in left subtree
      if (Left == 0)            //    if left subtree is empty
         Left = new Node(Elem); //       make Elem root of left subtree
      else                      //    else
         Left->Insert(Elem);    //       pass the buck to root of
                                //          left subtree
   else if (Elem > Data)        // if Elem belongs in right subtree
      if (Right == 0)           //    if right subtree is empty
         Right = new Node(Elem);//       make Elem root of right subtree
      else                      //    else
         Right->Insert(Elem);   //       pass the buck to root of
                                //          right subtree
   else                         // else, Elem already is in the BST
      cerr << "\n*** Insert: " << Elem
           << " is already in this tree!\n";
}
```

Note that because struct **Node** is nested within class **BST**, the full name of this function is

    BST::Node::Insert()

The name **Node** is not visible outside of the class unless it is qualified with the name **BST**—both **BST** and **Node** must be named when defining it.

    More important, note that a traversal is not needed to find the insertion point because in a **BST**, every node to the left of the root node has a value less than the value of the root node, and every node to the right of the root node has a value greater than the root node. This allows the function to apply a binary-search–like strategy, so that each recursive call eliminates from consideration approximately one-half of the nodes below its root. If the tree is balanced and contains n nodes, then approximately $\log_2(n)$ recursive calls will be performed to insert a value.

Building a BST from an Unordered Input List. Given an insertion function, an input function that reads a sequence of unordered values (from the keyboard or from a file) is easy to construct, using a standard input loop. Constructing definitions for **operator>>** to implement this algorithm for an **istream** and an **fstream** is left as an exercise.

It is important to note that the order in which items are inserted into a **BST** determines the shape of the tree. For example, inserting the letters **O, E, T, C, U, M, P** into a **BST** of characters in this order gives the nicely *balanced* tree

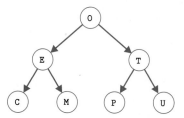

but inserting them in the order **C, O, M, P, U, T, E** yields the unbalanced tree

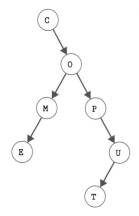

and inserting them in alphabetical order **C, E, M, O, P, T, U** causes the tree to degenerate into a linked list:

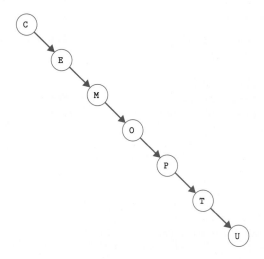

In such unbalanced **BST**s, the time to access a value in the **BST** increases (on average), because the **BST** degenerates into a (linear) linked list. Insertion algorithms that avoid constructing such unbalanced trees are beyond the level of this introductory text.[4]

Displaying a BST.   The function in Figure 17.8 displays the values in a **BST**, separated by spaces. It shows the definition of **operator<<**, which should be declared as a friend of class **BST**.

FIGURE 17.8   Displaying a **BST**.

```
/* This function displays a BST.

   Receive: An ostream and a BST
   Output:  The values of the BST onto the ostream
   Return:  The ostream
-------------------------------------------------------------*/

ostream& operator<<(ostream& Out, const BST& Tree)
{
    if (Tree.Root != 0)
       Out << *(Tree.Root);

    return Out;
}
```

The function simply checks that the **BST** is not empty and then invokes a definition of **operator<<** to display a **Node**, passing it the **ostream** and the node pointed to by the **Root** member of the **BST**. Note that in order to pass the root node to **operator<<**, it is necessary to dereference the member **Root**.

The implementation of **operator<<** for a **Node** is a recursive function that displays a node and its subtrees in left-to-right order (i.e., using the LVR pattern), as shown in Figure 17.9.

FIGURE 17.9   Displaying a **Node**.

```
/* This function recursively displays a Node (and its subtrees),
   using the inorder traversal pattern.

   Receive: An ostream and a Node
   Output:  The values from the left subtree, the Node, and its
            right subtree onto the ostream, in ascending order
   Return:  The ostream
-------------------------------------------------------------*/
ostream& operator<<(ostream& Out, const BST::Node& N)
{
    if (N.Left != 0)
       Out << *(N.Left);
```

---

[4] See, for example, Larry Nyhoff and Sanford Leestma, *Data Structures and Program Design in Pascal*, (New York: Macmillan, 1992), or Robert Kruse, *Data Structures and Program Design* (Englewood Cliffs, NJ: Prentice Hall, 1987).

FIGURE 17.9   Displaying a **Node**. (cont.)

```
    Out << N.Data << ' ';

    if (N.Right != 0)
       Out << *(N.Right);

    return Out;
}
```

This function begins by recursively displaying the nodes in the left subtree (if it is not empty). It then displays the **Data** member of the current node and, finally, recursively displays the nodes of the right subtree (if it is not empty). Since the **Data** member of each node in the left subtree is less than the **Data** member of this node, which is less than the **Data** member of each node in the right subtree, the result is a listing of the contents of the **BST** in ascending order, which is to be expected, because the inorder traversal pattern is being used to:

- Recursively display the left subtree.
- Display the **Data** member of the current node.
- Recursively display the right subtree.

Searching a BST for a Value.   Because of its special structure, a **BST** can be searched for a value far more quickly than a linked list can. As with other searching functions, the function to search a **BST** is a boolean function that returns true if and only if the value being sought is found. Like the **BST** insertion function, a **BST** search function is nonrecursive and must consider two cases:

1. If the **BST** is empty, then the value is not present (i.e., return false).
2. If the **BST** is not empty, then pass the value to a **Node** member function (of the node pointed to by **Root**) that will recursively search the binary search tree for the value.

The **BST** search function in Figure 17.10 simply distinguishes between these cases.

   FIGURE 17.10   Search for a value in a **BST**.

```
/* This function searches a BST for a BinTreeElement.

   Receive: Elem, the BinTreeElement being sought
   Return:  True, if Elem is in the BST containing this function,
            False, otherwise
   ------------------------------------------------------------------*/

Boolean BST::Search(const BinTreeElement& Elem) const
{
   if (Root == 0)                    // if the tree is empty
      return False;                  //    Elem is not in it
   else                              // otherwise
      return Root->Search(Elem);     //    have Node::Search() look
}
```

A **Node** is implemented recursively, and the member function
Node::Search() thus carries out a recursive search of a nonempty tree using a
binary-search-like strategy, as shown in Figure 17.11.

FIGURE 17.11   Searching a **Node** for a value.

```
/* This function recursively searches the Nodes of a BST for a
   BinTreeElement.

   Receive: Elem, the BinTreeElement being sought
   Return:  True if Elem is in the Node containing this function
            or in either of its subtrees,
            False, otherwise
   -----------------------------------------------------------------*/
Boolean BST::Node::Search(const BinTreeElement& Elem) const
{
   if (Elem == Data)                      // if this node contains Elem
      return True;                        //    success!

   else if (Elem < Data)                  // else if Elem belongs left
      if (Left == 0)                      //    if left subtree is empty
         return False;                    //        not in tree!
      else                                //    else
         return Left->Search(Elem);       //        search left subtree

   else                                   // else (Elem belongs right)
      if (Right == 0)                      //    if right subtree is empty
         return False;                    //        not in tree!
      else                                //    else
         return Right->Search(Elem);      //        search the right subtree
}
```

There are three cases for this function:

- The value is in the current node.
- The value belongs in the left subtree of the current node.
- The value belongs in the right subtree of the current node.

In the first case, the function can simply return true, since the value is present in the
tree. In each of the other two cases, there is the possibility that the subtree is empty,
in which case the function can simply return false, since the value is not in the tree.
Otherwise, these latter cases recursively search their respective subtrees.

As with insertion, no traversal is necessary to find the element being sought. If
the **BST** is balanced and contains n values, then approximately one-half of the
nodes in the tree are eliminated from consideration with each recursive call, so that
the search requires time proportional to $\log_2 n$.

Deleting a Value from a BST.   Deleting a value from a binary search tree is
somewhat more complicated than the insertion operation in several ways. One
difficulty is that the value to be deleted may not be in the tree. We therefore design
the function as a boolean function that returns true if it is successful and false if the
value to be deleted is not present.

A second complication stems from the fact that the storage of the **Node** that contains the value to be deleted must be reclaimed. The problem is that **delete**, the operation to deallocate memory, requires a pointer to the object being deallocated; the command

```
delete PtrName;
```

reclaims the storage pointed to by *PtrName*. This implies that deleting a value from a **BST** requires a pointer to the **Node** containing that value.

Another complicating factor is that the value to be deleted may not reside in a leaf node. To illustrate, again consider the binary search tree:

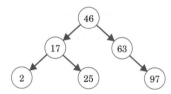

Suppose that we wish to delete the value 2, which is stored in a leaf node. Then clearly that node's storage should be reclaimed, and the value of the **Left** member of its parent node should be changed to the NULL address. However, the member functions of a node are unable to access the data members of its parent node, since a one-directional pointer allows a parent node access to a child node, but not vice versa.

One straightforward solution is to pass **Node::Delete()** a second argument, which is a reference to the **NodePtr** by which that **Node** was reached. If necessary, the **Node::Delete()** function can then change the value of the parameter corresponding to that argument and, in so doing, change the value of the argument.

Figure 17.12 presents an implementation of the **Delete()** function for class **BST**.

 FIGURE 17.12 Deleting a value from a **BST**.

```
/* This function deletes a BinTreeElement from a BST.

   Receive: Elem, the BinTreeElement being deleted
   Return:  The BST containing this function with Elem deleted
            True if and only if the operation is successful
   ------------------------------------------------------------*/

Boolean BST::Delete(const BinTreeElement& Elem)
{
   if (Root == 0)                       // is the BST empty?
      return False;                     //    value is not in the tree
   else
      return Root->Delete(Elem, Root);  //    have Node::Delete() do it
}
```

Note that since the root node might contain the value to be deleted, the call

```
Root->Delete(Elem, Root);
```

passes a reference to the pointer **Root** to the **Delete()** member of that **Node**—a pointer to itself. This allows the **Delete()** member of struct **Node** to change the value of **Root**, if necessary.

The **Delete()** member of struct **Node** then receives both the element being deleted and a reference to the **NodePtr** by which it was accessed. Figure 17.13 presents an implementation of **Delete()** whose form is similar to that of the other **Node** member functions.

 FIGURE 17.13   Deleting a value from a **Node**.

```
/* This function recursively deletes a value from the Nodes of a BST.

   Receive: Elem, the BinTreeElement being deleted
            AccessPtr, a (reference) to the pointer by which the Node
               containing this function was reached
   Return:  The BST containing this function, with the Node
               containing Elem deleted
            True if and only if the operation succeeds
------------------------------------------------------------------*/

Boolean BST::Node::Delete
                  (const BinTreeElement& Elem, BST::NodePtr& AccessPtr)
{
   if (Data == Elem)                       // if current node = Elem
   {
      DelNode(AccessPtr);                  //    delete that node
      return True;                         //    indicate success
   }

   else if (Elem < Data)                   // else if Elem belongs left
      if (Left == 0)                       //    if left subtree is empty
         return False;                     //       indicate failure
      else                                 //    else
         return Left->Delete(Elem, Left);  //      check left subtree

   else                                    // else (Elem belongs right)
      if (Right == 0)                      //    if right subtree is empty
         return False;                     //       indicate failure
      else                                 //    else
         return Right->Delete(Elem, Right);//       check right subtree
}
```

This definition is deceptively simple—it appears to be quite similar to those we have seen previously. It uses the VLR pattern to see if the **Data** member of a **Node** contains the value to be deleted. If so, it calls **DelNode()**, which uses **AccessPtr** to delete the node. Otherwise, it checks to see if the value being deleted belongs in the left subtree. If so and that subtree is empty, it returns false; otherwise, it processes the left subtree recursively. If the value being deleted does not belong in the left subtree and is not in the current node, then it must belong in the right subtree. If that subtree is empty, then the function returns false; otherwise, the right subtree is processed recursively.

The function is relatively simple because it calls function **DelNode()**, a private member function of class **BST** that does most of the work. There are three cases that **DelNode()** must handle.

1. The node being deleted is a leaf node:

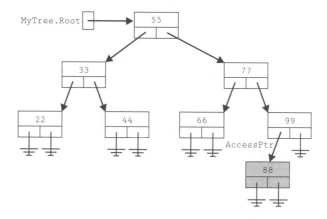

the function can simply reclaim its storage and set the pointer to that node to NULL:

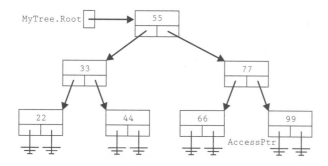

2. The node being deleted is not a leaf node and has only 1 (nonempty) subtree:

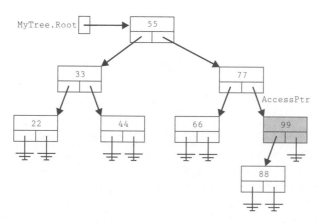

the function can simply save the address of the root of that subtree,

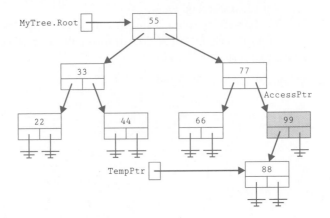

deallocate the node being deleted,

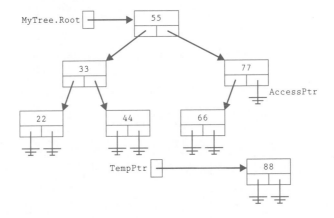

and reattach the subtree in place of the deleted node:

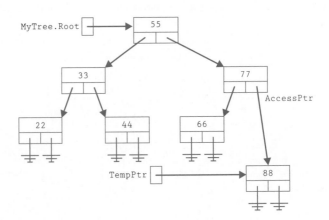

3. The node being deleted is not a leaf node and has 2 nonempty subtrees:

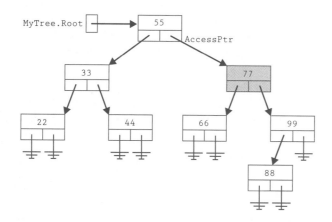

One approach is as follows: First, find the leftmost node in the right subtree.

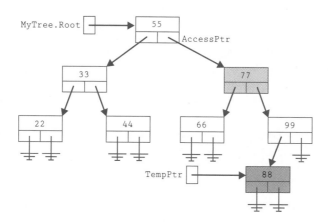

Save the value of the **Data** member of that node,

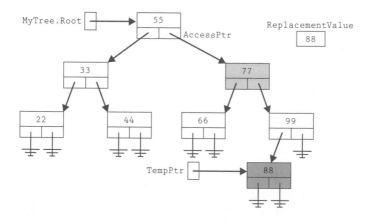

and then deallocate the storage for that node (instead of the node containing the value to be deleted):

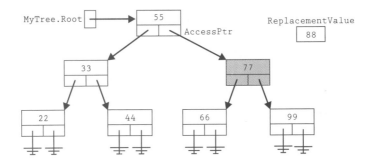

Now replace the value being deleted with the value saved from the deleted node:

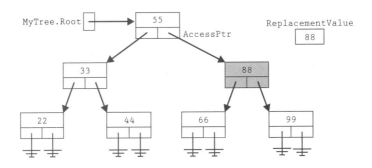

Figure 17.14 presents a definition of function **DelNode()**, which is implemented as a friend of class **BST**.

FIGURE 17.14   Deleting a particular **Node**.

```
/* This function deletes a Node from a binary search tree.

   Receive: AccessPtr, a pointer to the Node from its parent (if
              there is one)
   Return:  The BST of which this node is a part, but with this
              Node removed
----------------------------------------------------------------*/

void DelNode(BST::NodePtr& AccessPtr)
{
   BST::NodePtr
      TempPtr;

   if (AccessPtr != 0)                          // just in case...
      if ((AccessPtr->Left == 0) &&
         (AccessPtr->Right == 0))               // if it's a leaf
      {
         delete AccessPtr;                       //    delete the Node
         AccessPtr = 0;                          //    set the ptr to NULL
      }
```

FIGURE 17.14 Deleting a particular **Node**. (cont.)

```
        else if (AccessPtr->Left == 0)          // right subtree not empty
        {
           TempPtr = AccessPtr;                  //    save node address
           AccessPtr = AccessPtr->Right;         //    replace with right
           TempPtr->Right = 0;                   //    detach node
           delete TempPtr;                       //    delete node
        }
        else if (AccessPtr->Right == 0)         // left subtree not empty
        {
           TempPtr = AccessPtr;                  //    save node address
           AccessPtr = AccessPtr->Left;          //    replace with left
           TempPtr->Left = 0;                    //    detach node
           delete TempPtr;                       //    delete node
        }
        else                                     // both subtrees nonempty
           Access Ptr->Data =                    //    replace Data with
              LeftMostValue(AccessPtr->Right);// //       leftmost value in
}                                                //       the right subtree
```

To find the replacement value for a nonleaf node with two nonempty subtrees, `DelNode()` calls function `LeftMostValue()`, a recursive function that behaves as follows:

If this node is the leftmost node in the subtree, then   // Anchor
    a. Save the *Data* value of this node.
    b. Save a pointer to this node.
    c. Replace the pointer by which this node was accessed with the right
       subtree of this node.
    d. Detach the node and deallocate its memory.
    e. Return the (saved) *Data* value of this node.
Else   // Induction Step
    Return the result of recursively processing the left subtree of this node.

Figure 17.15 gives a definition of this algorithm as a **BST** member function.

FIGURE 17.15 Finding the replacement for an interior node.

```
/* This function finds the leftmost value in a given subtree,
   deletes the node containing that value, and returns the value.

   Receive: NPtr, the pointer by which this Node was accessed
   Return:  The value from the deleted Node
            The BST of which this node is the root, with its
               leftmost Node deleted
-----------------------------------------------------------------*/
```

FIGURE 17.15 Finding the replacement for an interior node. (cont.)

```
BinTreeElement LeftMostValue(BST::NodePtr& NPtr)
{
    if ((NPtr != 0) && (NPTr->Left == 0))// if this is leftmost node,
    {                                     // then it has no left subtree
        ListElement
            ReturnValue = NPtr->Data;     //    save its Data value
        BST::NodePtr
            TempPtr = NPtr;               //    save its address

        NPtr = NPtr->Right;               //    replace it with its
                                          //       right subtree
        TempPtr->Right = 0;               //    detach the node
        delete TempPtr;                   //    deallocate the node

        return ReturnValue;               //    return the saved value
    }
    else
        return LeftMostValue(NPtr->Left); //    move left & down
                                          //       recursively
}
```

To illustrate, suppose that a **BST** named **MyTree** is as follows:

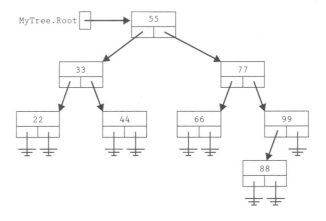

If the statement

        `MyTree.Delete(77);`

is executed, the **Delete()** function of class **BST** begins by checking whether **MyTree** is empty. Since it is not, the function calls the **Delete()** function of the root node, passing it the value to be deleted (**77**) and a pointer to itself. (For clarity, we have shaded the node in which execution currently resides.)

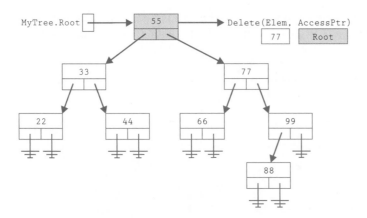

Since **Elem** is greater than the **Data** member of this **Node** (55) and the right subtree of this node is not empty, the **Delete()** member function of the right subtree's root **Node** is called recursively with the values **77** and **Right** passed as arguments:

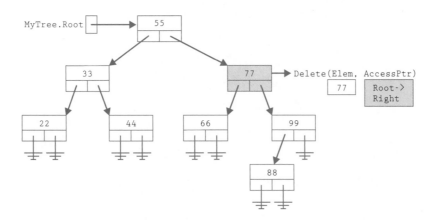

Here, **Elem** is equal to the **Data** member of the **Node**, so the function **DelNode()** is called, with the argument **AccessPtr** passed:

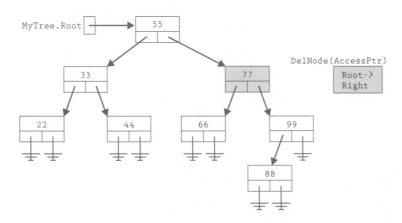

Since the **Node** pointed to by **AccessPtr** has two nonempty subtrees, the function **LeftMostValue()** is called, with the **Right** pointer in this **Node** as its argument:

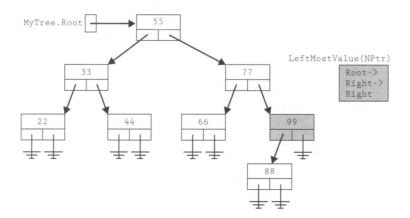

LeftMostValue() finds that the left subtree of this **Node** is not empty and so calls itself recursively, passing the **Left** member as an argument:

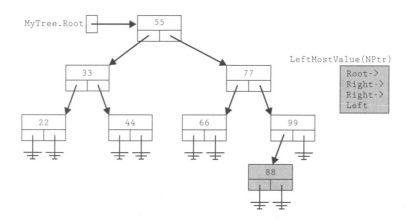

Here, **LeftMostValue()** finds that the left subtree is empty and so saves the **Data** member of this **Node**; it then deletes the **Node**:

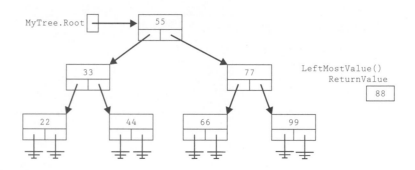

It then returns the value **88** to its caller (**LeftMostValue()**), which returns that value to its caller (**DelNode()**), which replaces the value of the **Data** member being deleted with the value returned by **LeftMostValue()**:

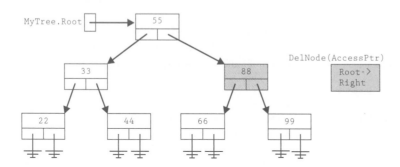

DelNode() then terminates, after which the **Delete()** function of struct **Node** terminates, after which the **Delete()** function of class **BST** terminates.

Making a Copy of a BST. Since class **BST** utilizes dynamic memory allocation, we must provide a copy constructor that will build a dynamic copy of a **BST** object when it is needed by the compiler. To distinguish between the two trees, we describe the **BST** being copied as the *original* and the copy being made as the *copy*.

As with the preceding operations, we implement this operation by building a nonrecursive **BST** copy constructor, which invokes a recursive **Node** copy constructor. The **BST** copy constructor has the usual two cases to consider:

- If the original is empty, then the copy's **Root** member is simply set to the NULL address;
- Otherwise, the **Node** class constructor is used to recursively copy the root node of the original and each of its subtrees.

Figure 17.16 shows our definition of this function, which we would place in the implementation file of class **BST**:

 FIGURE 17.16 A **BST** copy constructor.

```
/* This function makes a copy of a binary search tree.

    Precondition:  A copy of a BST is needed by the compiler.
    Receive:       OTree, reference to the original BST (being copied)
    Postcondition: The BST containing this function is a copy of OTree.
    --------------------------------------------------------------------*/
```

FIGURE 17.16 A **BST** copy constructor. (cont.)

```
BST::BST(const BST& OTree)
{
    if (OTree.Root == 0)                // if the tree is empty
        Root = 0;                       //    that's the easy case
    else                                // otherwise call the Node
        Root = new Node(*(OTree.Root)); //    copy constructor, and
}                                       // pass it the Root node
```

Note that when the **Node** copy constructor is invoked, it must be passed a **Node** to copy. Since **OTree.Root** is a pointer to a **Node** (as opposed to a **Node** itself), we must dereference that pointer, in order to pass the **Node** it points to. The copy constructor then receives a (const) reference parameter to a **Node**, and employs the following recursive logic:

- To copy the **Data** member of the original, an assignment statement is used.
- To copy the left subtree of the original: If that subtree is not empty, use the **Node** copy constructor to recursively copy the left subtree's root node. Otherwise, set the left subtree to the NULL address.
- To copy the right subtree of the original: If that subtree is not empty, use the **Node** copy constructor to recursively copy the right subtree's root node. Otherwise, set the right subtree to the NULL address.

Note that if the left or right subtrees are empty, the **Left** and **Right** members of the copy node must be explicitly set to NULL, in order to ensure that leaf nodes are properly configured. Figure 17.17 presents an implementation of this function:

FIGURE 17.17 A **Node** copy constructor.

```
/* This function recursively copies any binary subtree.

    Precondition:   A copy of a subtree is needed by the compiler.
    Receive:        ONode, a reference to the root of the subtree
                    being copied
    Postcondition:  The Node containing this function is a copy of
                    ONode, and the subtrees of this Node are
                    copies as well.
    -----------------------------------------------------------*/

BST::Node::Node(const Node& ONode)
{                                       // COPY THE DATA MEMBER
    Data = ONode.Data;
                                        // COPY THE LEFT SUBTREE:
    if (ONode.Left != 0)                // if it's not empty,
        Left = new Node(*(ONode.Left)); //    make a copy of it
    else                                // otherwise
        Left = 0;                       //    indicate emptiness
```

FIGURE 17.17   A **Node** copy constructor. (cont.)

```
                                    // COPY THE RIGHT SUBTREE:
   if (ONode.Right != 0)            // if it's not empty,
      Right = new Node(*(ONode.Right));//   make a copy of it
   else                             // otherwise
      Right = 0;                    //    indicate emptiness
}
```

Whenever the compiler needs a copy of a **BST** object, it will invoke the **BST** copy constructor. If the original **BST** is not empty, then the **BST** copy constructor will invoke the **Node** copy constructor to create a new node and pass it the root node of the original **BST**. This **Node** copy constructor then does the actual work of recursively copying the collection of **Node** objects that make up the tree.

Note that the traversal pattern used by the **Node** constructor is essentially a preorder (VLR) traversal: For a nonempty BST:

- The current node is "visited" (i.e., its **Data** member is copied);
- The left subtree of the original is copied (recursively, if it is not empty); and
- The right subtree of the original is copied (recursively, if it is not empty).

While any of the patterns could have been used, the VLR pattern seems the most readable.

Destroying a BST.   As noted previously, a **BST** uses memory allocated at run time, and so a destructor must be provided whereby this storage can be reclaimed. Our **BST** class destructor employs the following now-familiar logic:

- If the **BST** is empty, then there is no action to be taken.
- If the **BST** is not empty, then
   a. Invoke the **Node** destructor of the root node (which recursively tears down the subtrees of a node); and then
   b. Reset the members of the **BST** to indicate emptiness.

The "trick" is to remember the relationship between a destructor and the **delete** operation:

- If **delete** is used to destroy an object, then that object's destructor is invoked.
- Calling **delete** on a NULL pointer has no effect.

We can use these observations to encode the **BST** destructor quite simply (i.e., within class **BST**), as shown in Figure 17.18.

 FIGURE 17.18   A **BST** destructor.

```
/* This function tears down a BST, reclaiming its storage.

   Precondition:   The lifetime of the BST containing this function
                   is over.
   Postcondition: All of the dynamic storage allocated to this BST
                   has been reclaimed.
-------------------------------------------------------------------*/
```

FIGURE 17.18   A **BST** destructor. (cont.)

```
~BST(void)
{
   delete Root;      // invoke Root->~Node() indirectly
   Root = 0;         // reset as empty tree
}
```

The statement

```
      delete Root;
```

will have no effect if **Root** contains the NULL address; otherwise, the statement will invoke the **Node** destructor in the root node of the **BST**. We must thus write the **Node** destructor in such a way as to deallocate the memory of each of the node's subtrees.

Using the same insights that helped us write the **BST** destructor so simply, we can also encode the **Node** destructor quite simply (define it within class **Node**), as shown in Figure 17.19.

  FIGURE 17.19   A (recursive) **Node** destructor.

```
/* --- This function reclaims the storage of a Node's subtrees.

   Precondition:   The lifetime of the Node containing this function
                   is over.
   Postcondition: All of the dynamic storage allocated to the
                   subtrees of this Node has been reclaimed.
-----------------------------------------------------------------------*/

BST::Node:: ~ Node(void)
{
   delete Left;      // invoke Left->~Node() indirectly
   delete Right;     // do right subtree the same way
}
```

To see how this function solves our problem, suppose that the lifetime of the following tree named **MyTree** is over, so that the function **MyTree.~BST()** is invoked:

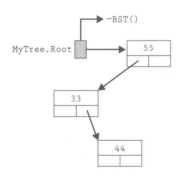

The **BST** destructor begins by calling

    `delete Root;`

which invokes `~Node()` in the node pointed to by **Root**:

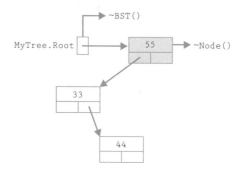

However, the first thing `~Node()` does is execute

    `delete Left;`

which invokes `~Node()` in the node pointed to by **Left**—an indirect recursion:

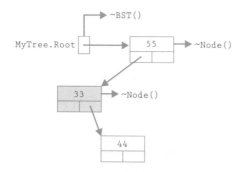

This destructor begins by executing the first statement

    `delete Left;`

but since **Left** contains the NULL address, this statement has no effect, and so execution proceeds to the second statement

    `delete Right;`

which invokes `~Node()` in the node pointed to by **Right**:

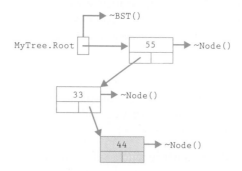

This function executes

```
delete Left;
delete Right;
```

and since both **Left** and **Right** contain the NULL address, nothing happens and **~Node()** terminates in that node (**44**). The storage for that node is then reclaimed and control returns to **~Node()** in its parent node (**33**):

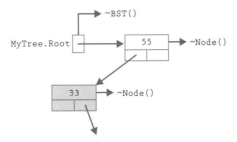

Since both of the statements in this instance of **~Node()** have been executed, this function call terminates, the storage of that node is reclaimed, and control returns to **~Node()** in its parent node (**55**):

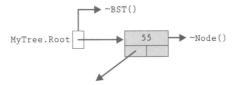

There, the first statement has just terminated, and so the second statement executes:

```
delete Right;
```

However, this statement has no effect because **Right** contains the NULL address. The function then terminates, the storage for this node (**55**) is reclaimed, and control returns to **~BST()**, which sets the **Root** member to the NULL address and terminates:

Note that the two destructors combine to destroy a **BST** in what is essentially a postorder (LRV) traversal: For each node in a nonempty **BST**:

- ■ **~Node()** uses **delete Left;** to recursively delete its left subtree;
- ■ **~Node()** uses **delete Right;** to recursively delete its right subtree;
- ■ The **delete** call by its parent node (or **~ BST()**) deallocates its storage.

Exercises

1. Write a recursive **BST** member function to count the leaves in a **BST**. (*Hint:* How is the number of leaves in the entire tree related to the number of leaves in the left and right subtrees of the root?)

2. Write a recursive **BST** member function to find the depth of a **BST**. The *depth* of

an empty tree is 0, and for a nonempty tree it is one more than the larger of the depths of the left and right subtrees of the root.

3. Write a recursive **BST** member function to find the level in a **BST** at which a given value is located. The root is at level 0, and its children are at level 1.

4. Repeat Exercise 3, but do not assume that the binary tree is a **BST**.

5. Write a nonrecursive version of the function **Node::Search()**.

6. Write a program to process a **BST** whose nodes contain characters. Allow the user to select from the following menu of options:

> **I** followed by a character: To insert that character into the **BST**
> **S** followed by a character: To search for that character in the **BST**
> **TI**: For inorder traversal of the **BST**
> **TP**: For preorder traversal of the **BST**
> **TR**: For postorder traversal of the **BST**
> **QU**: To quit

7. An alternative means of implementing a **BST** is using an array. We simply number each of the possible positions in the **BST** from top to bottom, numbering from left to right on each level, and then store an item in the ith position of the **BST** in the ith location of an array **B**.

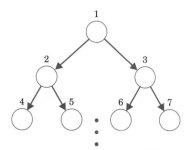

(a) Show what each element of array **B** would be for the **BST**s in Exercise 1.
(b) In general, why is this an inefficient way to store **BST**s? For what kinds of **BST**s is this a good storage structure to use?

8. Assume that a class **BST** is implemented using an array containing positive integers, as described in Exercise 7. Write the function **BST::Search()** for this implementation.

9. Read the next section, and then write a function **BST::TreeSort()** for a **BST** implemented using an array.

17.4   Using a Binary Search Tree for Sorting: Treesort

If we combine the operation of constructing a binary search tree with inorder traversal, we obtain a new scheme for sorting a list. We simply input the list of items, inserting each of them into a **BST** that is initially empty, and then use an inorder traversal to display them. The following algorithm uses this technique to sort a list stored in a file.

TREESORT ALGORITHM

/* This algorithm sorts an unordered list of elements using a binary search tree.

    Input: A list of items.
    Ouput: The sorted list.
_____*/

1. Construct an empty BST.
2. Input the first item.
3. While end-of-file has not been reached:
    a. Insert the item into the BST.
    b. Input the next item.
   End While.
4. Output the BST, using an inorder traversal.

Example: Sorting Student Records

The program in Figure 17.20 implements this algorithm and uses it to sort a file of student records.

FIGURE 17.20   Sorting a list of student records.

```
/* This program sorts a list of student records using class BST.

    Input (file):     A list of student records
    Output (screen): The list of student records, sorted so that
                     the last names are in alphabetical order
----------------------------------------------------------------*/
#include <iostream.h>
#include <fstream.h>
#include <stdlib.h>

#include "BST.h"                      // BinTreeElement = Student
#include "Student.h"

int main(void)
{
   BST
      BSTree;                         // an empty tree of students
   Student
      CurrentStudent;                 // container for a student
   fstream
      InF("student.dat", ios::in);    // stream to the input file
```

FIGURE 17.20   Sorting a list of student records. (cont.)

```
    if (InF.bad())                    // see if stream is ok
    {
       cerr << "\n*** Main: unable to open input file\n";
       exit (-1);
    }

    InF >> CurrentStudent;            // read the first student
    while (!InF.eof())                // While not eof:
    {
       BSTree.Insert(CurrentStudent);//   insert the student
       InF >> CurrentStudent;         //   read the next student
    }                                 // End while

    InF.close();                      // close the input file

    cout << BSTree;                   // view the students

    return 0;
}
```

Listing of input file `"student.dat"`:

```
777889999 Ben Dover
Junior     16.0  2.5

121212121 Carol Ina
Sophomore  16.0  3.51

333221111 Stan Dupp
Senior      8.0  3.75

666554444 Jose Canusee
Sophomore  16.0  3.25

999887777 Isabelle Ringing
Junior     16.0  3.8

111223333 Bill Board
Freshman   16.0  3.15

444556666 Ally Cat
Senior     16.0  3.125
```

FIGURE 17.20   Sorting a list of student records. (cont.)

Sample run:

```
111223333      Bill Board
   Freshman 16.0000   3.1500
666554444      Jose Canusee
 Sophomore 16.0000   3.2500
444556666      Ally Cat
     Senior 16.0000   3.1250
777889999      Ben Dover
     Junior 16.0000   2.5000
333221111      Stan Dupp
     Senior  8.0000   3.7500
121212121      Carol Ina
 Sophomore 16.0000   3.5100
999887777      Isabelle Ringing
     Junior 16.0000   3.8000
```

This program is remarkably simple: It opens a file and then executes an input loop that repeatedly reads a record and inserts that record into a binary search tree. For the sample run shown, a simplified version of the resulting tree (that shows only the student names) is as follows:

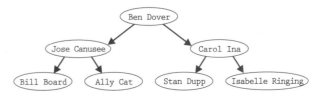

When execution leaves the loop, the binary search tree is displayed using an inorder traversal, and the records are listed in sorted order.

The treesort algorithm relies on the ordering a binary search tree imposes on a list of values stored in it. Although a linked list can also be designed as a structure that imposes an ordering on its values, inserting one of a sequence of random values into an ordered linked list takes time proportional to the number of values in the list (i.e., $O(n)$). As a result, the total time to sort a list of n items by inserting them into an ordered linked list is $O(n^2)$. By contrast, inserting a value into a binary search tree takes time proportional to the base-2 logarithm of the number of values in the tree (i.e., $O(\log_2 n)$). The total time to sort a list of n items by inserting them into a binary search tree is thus $O(n \cdot \log_2 n)$.

Programming Pointers

Most of the programming pointers that apply to the linked lists described in Chapter 16 also apply to trees, since trees are also linked structures.

Program Design

1. *When implementing an object using a class, keep the implementation details hidden by declaring them in a private or protected section of the class.* In class **BST**, the **Node** structure used to represent the tree's nodes is such a detail. By storing it as a protected member, derived classes can access it, but programs that use the class are prohibited from accessing (and thus becoming dependent on) the implementation details.

2. *When a class object's implementation uses another structure that is an implementation detail (i.e., is not generally reusable), declare the structure as a struct within the class.* By declaring **Node** as a struct within the protected section of class **BST**, casual users of class **BST** are prevented from accessing the members of a **Node** (see 1), but **BST** members can access those node members as necessary.

3. *When a class object's implementation uses another structure that is reusable, declare the structure as a class and store it in a separately compiled library.* This not only allows the class to use the structure, but also allows other classes to reuse your work, simply by using a **#include** directive to insert the library's header file and linking to the library's object file.

4. *When implementing an object that consists of structures that are allocated at run-time, make certain that constructors are provided that allow the data members of the run-time allocated structures to be initialized when such objects are created.* A great many initializing assignments in the implementation of the **BST** operations were avoided because of the **Node** constructor:

```
Node(const BinTreeElement& Elem,
     Node *LPtr = 0, Node *RPtr = 0)
{
    Data = Elem;
    Left = LPtr;
    Right = RPtr;
}
```

The execution of a statement of the form

```
NPtr = new Node(SomeValue);
```

uses this constructor to allocate space for a new **Node** object and initialize the **Data** members to *SomeValue* and the **Left** and **Right** members to the NULL address, all in one step.

5. *Always provide an output operation for an object to facilitate debugging.* The ability to ''dump'' the values in an object to the screen or to a file can be helpful in finding errors that may occur while implementing operations on the object. Once the object and its operations have been successfully implemented, the declaration of the output operation can be moved to the private section of the class (if such an operation is inappropriate for the object).

Potential Problems

1. *Take twice as much care when implementing binary trees, since their nodes contain two pointer members.* With two pointers to keep track of in every node instead of one, making logical errors is twice as easy. It is easy to write tree operations that compile correctly but that generate run-time errors. The easiest way to find such errors is to use a symbolic debugger and trace the execution of the program to find the statement that generates the error.

2. *Make certain that the pointer members of a class are initialized by its constructors.* Many errors can be avoided simply by ensuring that when an object is created, its pointer members are initialized by default to the NULL address.

3. *Always make certain that a tree is not empty before processing it.* The same holds true for subtrees. In most recursive tree-processing algorithms, the empty tree provides the anchor case for the recursion. As a result, checking whether a tree is empty makes it possible to avoid

   - Dereferencing a NULL pointer; and
   - Generating an infinite recursion.

4. *If an object contains pointer members, test its operations exhaustively.* It is quite easy for execution to miss the run-time and logical errors in sections of code that manipulate pointers, unless tests are performed that explicitly check those sections of code. Better yet, have others test your operations, since they will try to do things you might not have anticipated.

5. *In order to explicitly invoke a copy constructor, a class object must be passed to the call.* In the function definition

```
BST::BST(const BST& OTree)
{
   if (OTree.Root == 0)
      Root = 0;
    else
      Root = new Node(*(OTree.Root));
}
```

the call

```
Root->Node(*(OTree.Root));
```

invokes the *copy* constructor for a **Node**, since the constructor is being called with a **Node** as an argument. If the object is a run-time allocated object whose address is stored in a pointer, then that pointer must be dereferenced in order for the object to which it points to be passed.

6. *In order to explicitly invoke a destructor, a pointer to the object containing it is required.* For example, the destructor for class **BST** could have used the statement

```
Root->~Node();
```

to invoke the destructor in the **Node** pointed to by **Root**, which recursively deallocates the storage for each of its left and right subtrees. However, the same thing and more is accomplished by

```
delete Root;
```

that both invokes **~Node()** and then deallocates the **Node** pointed to by **Root**, once **~Node()** terminates.

Programming Projects

1. Write a program that uses a binary tree to decode messages in Morse code.

2. Write a *spell checker,* that is, a program that reads the words in a piece of text and looks up each in a *dictionary* to check its spelling. Use a BST to store this dictionary, reading the list of words from a file. While checking the spelling of words in a piece of text, the program should print a list of all words not found in the dictionary.

3. Write a program to construct a *text concordance,* which is an alphabetical listing of all the distinct words in a piece of text. The program should read a piece of text, construct a concordance that contains the distinct words that appear in the text and, for each word, the line (or page) number of its first occurrence, and then allow the user to search this concordance. Use an array of BSTs as a storage structure for the concordance.

4. Extend the program in Project 3 so that an ordered linked list of *all* occurrences of each word is used. When the concordance is searched for a particular word, the program should display the line (or page) numbers of all occurrences of this word.

5. For a certain company, the method by which the pay for each employee is computed depends on whether that employee is classified as an office employee, a factory worker, or a salesperson. Suppose that a file of employee records is maintained in which each record contains the following information for each employee:

> Name (20 characters).
> Social security number (integer).
> Age (integer).
> Number of dependents (integer).
> Employee code (character O, F, and S representing office, factory, and salesperson, respectively).
> Hourly rate if the employee is a factory worker.
> Annual salary if the employee is an office employee.
> A base pay (real) and a commission percentage (real) if the employee is a salesperson.

Write a menu-driven program that allows at least the following options to be selected by the user of the program:

GET: Get the records from the employee file and store them in a binary search tree, sorted so that the names are in alphabetical order.

INS: Insert a new employee's record into the BST.

UPD: Update the record of an employee already in the tree.

RET: Retrieve and display the record for a specified employee.

LIS: List the records (or perhaps selected items in the records) in order. This option should allow the following suboptions

ALL—to list for all employees.

OFF—to list for only office employees.

FAC—to list for only factory workers.

SAL—to list for only salespersons.

SAV: Copy the records from the BST into a permanent file.

DEL: Delete an employee's record from the BST.

The program should define a base class **Employee**, from which the classes **Office**, **Factory**, and **Sales** can be derived.

ASCII AND EBCDIC

ASCII and EBCDIC codes of characters

Decimal	Binary	Octal	Hexadecimal	ASCII	EBCDIC
0	00000000	000	0x0	NUL (Null)	NUL (Null)
1	00000001	001	0x1	SOH (Start of heading)	SOH (Start of heading)
2	00000010	002	0x2	STX (Start of text)	STX (Start of text)
3	00000011	003	0x3	ETX (End of text)	ETX (End of text)
4	00000100	004	0x4	EOT (End of transmission)	PF (Punch off)
5	00000101	005	0x5	ENQ (Enquiry)	HT (Horizontal tab)
6	00000110	006	0x6	ACK (Acknowledge)	LC (Lower case)
7	00000111	007	0x7	BEL (Ring bell)	DEL (Delete)
8	00001000	010	0x8	BS (Backspace)	
9	00001001	011	0x9	HT (Horizontal tab)	
10	00001010	012	0xA	LF (Line feed)	SMM (Repeat)
11	00001011	013	0xB	VT (Vertical tab)	VT (Vertical tab)
12	00001100	014	0xC	FF (Form feed)	FF (Form feed)
13	00001101	015	0xD	CR (Carriage return)	CR (Carriage return)
14	00001110	016	0xE	SO (Shift out)	SO (Shift out)
15	00001111	017	0xF	SI (Shift in)	SI (Shift in)
16	00010000	020	0x10	DLE (Data link escape)	DLE (Data link escape)
17	00010001	021	0x11	DC1 (Device control 1)	DC1 (Device control 1)
18	00010010	022	0x12	DC2 (Device control 2)	DC2 (Device control 2)
19	00010011	023	0x13	DC3 (Device control 3)	DC3 (Device control 3)
20	00010100	024	0x14	DC4 (Device control 4)	RES (Restore)
21	00010101	025	0x15	NAK (Negative ACK)	NL (New line)
22	00010110	026	0x16	SYN (Synchronous)	BS (Backspace)
23	00010111	027	0x17	ETB (EOT block)	IL (Idle)
24	00011000	030	0x18	CAN (Cancel)	CAN (Cancel)
25	00011001	031	0x19	EM (End of medium)	EM (End of medium)
26	00011010	032	0x1A	SUB (Substitute)	CC (Unit backspace)
27	00011011	033	0x1B	ESC (Escape)	
28	00011100	034	0x1C	FS (File separator)	IFS (Interchange file separator)
29	00011101	035	0x1D	GS (Group separator)	IGS (Interchange group separator)
30	00011110	036	0x1E	RS (Record separator)	IRS (Interchange record separator)
31	00011111	037	0x1F	US (Unit separator)	IUS (Interchange unit separator)
32	00100000	040	0x20	SP (Space)	DS (Digit select)
33	00100001	041	0x21	!	SOS (Start of significance)
34	00100010	042	0x22	"	FS (File separator)
35	00100011	043	0x23	#	

ASCII and EBCDIC codes of characters (cont.)

Decimal	Binary	Octal	Hexadecimal	ASCII	EBCDIC
36	00100100	044	0x24	$	BYP (Bypass)
37	00100101	045	0x25	%	LF (Line feed)
38	00100110	046	0x26	&	**ETB** (EOT block)
39	00100111	047	0x27	' (Single quote)	ESC (Escape)
40	00101000	050	0x28	(	
41	00101001	051	0x29	)	
42	00101010	052	0x2A	*	SM (Start message)
43	00101011	053	0x2B	+	
44	00101100	054	0x2C	, (Comma)	
45	00101101	055	0x2D	– (Hyphen)	ENQ (Enquiry)
46	00101110	056	0x2E	. (Period)	ACK (Acknowledge)
47	00101111	057	0x2F	/	**BEL** (Ring bell)
48	00110000	060	0x30	0	
49	00110001	061	0x31	1	
50	00110010	062	0x32	2	**SYN** (Synchronous)
51	00110011	063	0x33	3	
52	00110100	064	0x34	4	PN (Punch on)
53	00110101	065	0x35	5	RS (Record separator)
54	00110110	066	0x36	6	UC (Upper case)
55	00110111	067	0x37	7	EOT (End of transmission)
56	00111000	070	0x38	8	
57	00111001	071	0x39	9	
58	00111010	072	0x3A	:	
59	00111011	073	0x3B	;	
60	00111100	074	0x3C	<	DC4 (Device control 4)
61	00111101	075	0x3D	=	NAK (Negative ACK)
62	00111110	076	0x3E	>	
63	00111111	077	0x3F	?	SUB (Substitute)
64	01000000	100	0x40	@	SP (Space)
65	01000001	101	0x41	A	
66	01000010	102	0x42	B	
67	01000011	103	0x43	C	
68	01000100	104	0x44	D	
69	01000101	105	0x45	E	
70	01000110	106	0x46	F	
71	01000111	107	0x47	G	
72	01001000	110	0x48	H	
73	01001001	111	0x49	I	
74	01001010	112	0x4A	J	¢
75	01001011	113	0x4B	K	. (Period)
76	01001100	114	0x4C	L	<
77	01001101	115	0x4D	M	(
78	01001110	116	0x4E	N	+
79	01001111	117	0x4F	O		
80	01010000	120	0x50	P	&
81	01010001	121	0x51	Q	
82	01010010	122	0x52	R	
83	01010011	123	0x53	S	
84	01010100	124	0x54	T	
85	01010101	125	0x55	U	
86	01010110	126	0x56	V	
87	01010111	127	0x57	W	
88	01011000	130	0x58	X	
89	01011001	131	0x59	Y	

ASCII and EBCDIC codes of characters (cont.)

Decimal	Binary	Octal	Hexadecimal	ASCII	EBCDIC
90	01011010	132	0x5A	Z	!
91	01011011	133	0x5B	[	$
92	01011100	134	0x5C	\	*
93	01011101	135	0x5D	]	)
94	01011110	136	0x5E	^	;
95	01011111	137	0x5F	_ (Underscore)	¬ (Negation)
96	01100000	140	0x60	`	- (Hyphen)
97	01100001	141	0x61	a	/
98	01100010	142	0x62	b	
99	01100011	143	0x63	c	
100	01100100	144	0x64	d	
101	01100101	145	0x65	e	
102	01100110	146	0x66	f	
103	01100111	147	0x67	g	
104	01101000	150	0x68	h	
105	01101001	151	0x69	i	
106	01101010	152	0x6A	j	^
107	01101011	153	0x6B	k	, (Comma)
108	01101100	154	0x6C	l	%
109	01101101	155	0x6D	m	_ (Underscore)
110	01101110	156	0x6E	n	>
111	01101111	157	0x6F	o	?
112	01110000	160	0x70	p	
113	01110001	161	0x71	q	
114	01110010	162	0x72	r	
115	01110011	163	0x73	s	
116	01110100	164	0x74	t	
117	01110101	165	0x75	u	
118	01110110	166	0x76	v	
119	01110111	167	0x77	w	
120	01111000	170	0x78	x	
121	01111001	171	0x79	y	`
122	01111010	172	0x7A	z	:
123	01111011	173	0x7B	{	#
124	01111100	174	0x7C	|	@
125	01111101	175	0x7D	}	' (Single quote)
126	01111110	176	0x7E	~	=
127	01111111	177	0x7F	DEL	"
128	10000000	200	0x80		
129	10000001	201	0x81		a
130	10000010	202	0x82		b
131	10000011	203	0x83		c
132	10000100	204	0x84		d
133	10000101	205	0x85		e
134	10000110	206	0x86		f
135	10000111	207	0x87		g
136	10001000	210	0x88		h
137	10001001	211	0x89		i
.	.	.	.		.
.	.	.	.		.
.	.	.	.		.
145	10010001	221	0x91		j
146	10010010	222	0x92		k
147	10010011	223	0x93		l

ASCII and EBCDIC codes of characters (cont.)

Decimal	Binary	Octal	Hexadecimal	ASCII	EBCDIC
148	10010100	224	0x94		m
149	10010101	225	0x95		n
150	10010110	226	0x96		o
151	10010111	227	0x97		p
152	10011000	230	0x98		q
153	10011001	231	0x99		r
.	.	.	.		.
.	.	.	.		.
.	.	.	.		.
161	10100000	238	0xA0		~
162	10100010	242	0xA2		s
163	10100011	243	0xA3		t
164	10100100	244	0xA4		u
165	10100101	245	0xA5		v
166	10100110	246	0xA6		w
167	10100111	247	0xA7		x
168	10101000	250	0xA8		y
169	10101001	251	0xA9		z
.	.	.	.		.
.	.	.	.		.
.	.	.	.		.
177	10110001	261	0xB1		\
178	10110010	262	0xB2		{
179	10110011	263	0xB3		}
180	10110100	264	0xB4		[
181	10110101	265	0xB5		]
.	.	.	.		.
.	.	.	.		.
.	.	.	.		.
193	11000001	301	0xC1		A
194	11000010	302	0xC2		B
195	11000011	303	0xC3		C
196	11000100	304	0xC4		D
197	11000101	305	0xC5		E
198	11000110	306	0xC6		F
199	11000111	307	0xC7		G
200	11001000	310	0xC8		H
201	11001001	311	0xC9		I
.	.	.	.		.
.	.	.	.		.
.	.	.	.		.
209	11010001	321	0xD1		J
210	11010010	322	0xD2		K
211	11010011	323	0xD3		L
212	11010100	324	0xD4		M
213	11010101	325	0xD5		N
214	11010110	326	0xD6		O
215	11010111	327	0xD7		P
216	11011000	330	0xD8		Q
217	11011001	331	0xD9		R
.	.	.	.		.
.	.	.	.		.
.	.	.	.		.
226	11100010	342	0xE2		S
227	11100011	343	0xE3		T
228	11100100	344	0xE4		U

ASCII and EBCDIC codes of characters (cont.)

Decimal	Binary	Octal	Hexadecimal	ASCII	EBCDIC
229	11100101	345	0xE5		V
230	11100110	346	0xE6		W
231	11100111	347	0xE7		X
232	11101000	350	0xE8		Y
233	11101001	351	0xE9		Z
.	.	.	.		.
.	.	.	.		.
.	.	.	.		.
240	11110000	360	0xF0		0
241	11110001	361	0xF1		1
242	11110010	362	0xF2		2
243	11110011	363	0xF3		3
244	11110100	364	0xF4		4
245	11110101	365	0xF5		5
246	11110110	366	0xF6		6
247	11110111	367	0xF7		7
248	11111000	370	0xF8		8
249	11111001	371	0xF9		9
.	.	.	.		.
.	.	.	.		.
.	.	.	.		.
255	11111111	377	0xFF		

C++ RESERVED WORDS

The following table lists all the C++ keywords, together with a brief description of the context in which they usually appear.

Keyword	Contextual Description
asm	Used to declare that information is to be passed directly to the assembler
auto	Used to declare objects whose lifetime is the duration of control within their block
break	Used to terminate processing of a **switch** statement or loop
case	Used in a **switch** statement to specify a match for the statement's expression
catch	Used to specify the actions to be taken when an exception occurs (see **throw**, **try**)
char	Used to declare objects whose values are characters
class	Used to construct new types encapsulating data and operations (default **private**)
const	Used to declare objects whose values should not change during execution
continue	Used in a loop statement to transfer control to the beginning of the loop
default	Used in a **switch** statement to handle expression values not specified using **case**
delete	Used to deallocate memory allocated at run-time, returning it to the free store
do	Used to mark the beginning of a **do-while** statement, providing repetitive control
double	Used to declare objects whose values are (double precision) real numbers
else	Used in an **if** statement to mark the section to be executed if the condition is false
enum	Used to declare a type whose values are programmer-specified identifiers
extern	Used to declare objects whose definitions are external to the local block
float	Used to declare objects whose values are (single precision) real numbers
for	Used to mark the beginning of a **for** statement, providing repetitive control
friend	Used to declare **class** operations that are not member functions
goto	Used to transfer control to a label
if	Used to mark the beginning of an **if** statement, providing selective control
inline	Used to declare a function whose text is to be substituted for its call
int	Used to declare objects whose values are integer numbers
long	Used to declare 32-bit integer or extended double precision real numbers
new	Used to request memory allocation at run-time
operator	Used to overload an operator with a new declaration
private	Used to declare **class** members that are inaccessible from outside of the **class**
protected	Used to declare **class** members that are **private**, except to derived **class**es
public	Used to declare **class** members that can be accessed outside of the **class**
register	Used to declare objects whose values are to be kept in registers
return	Used to terminate a function, usually returning the value of some expression
short	Used to declare 16-bit integer numbers
signed	Used to declare an object in which the value's *sign* is stored in the high-order bit

Keyword	Contextual Description
sizeof	Used to find the size (in bytes) of an object or of the representation of a type
static	Used to declare objects whose lifetime is the duration of the program
struct	Used to construct new types encapsulating data and operations (default **public**)
switch	Used to mark the beginning of a switch statement, providing selective control
template	Used to declare type-independent **class**es or functions
this	Used within a **class** member to unambiguously access other members of the **class**
throw	Used to generate an exception (see **catch**, **try**)
try	Used to mark the beginning of a block containing exception handlers (see **catch**)
typedef	Used to declare a name as a synonym for an existing type
union	Used to declare a structure, such that different objects can have different members
unsigned	Used to declare an object in which the high-order bit is used for data (see **signed**)
virtual	Used to declare a base-**class** function, that will be defined by a derived **class**
void	Used to indicate the absence of any type (for a function or parameter list)
volatile	Used to declare objects whose values may be modified by means undetectable to the compiler (such as shared-memory objects of concurrent processes)
while	Used to mark the beginning of a **while** statement, as well as the end of a **do-while** statement, each of which provides repetitive control

C++ OPERATORS

The following table lists all the C++ operators and presents their precedence level (higher precedence operators are applied before lower precedence operators), associativity (in an expression containing operators of equal precedence, associativity determines which is applied first), whether they can be overloaded, their arity (number of operands), and a brief description.

Operator	Level	Associativity	Overloadable	Arity	Description
	17				
`::`		Right	No	Unary	Global scope
`::`		Left	No	Binary	Class scope
	16				
`.`		Left	No	Binary	Direct member selection
`->`		Left	Yes	Binary	Indirect member selection
`[]`		Left	Yes	Binary	Subscript (array index)
`()`		Left	Yes	N/A	Function call
`()`		Left	Yes	N/A	Type construction
	15				
`sizeof`		Right	No	Unary	Size (in bytes) of an object or type
`++`		Right	Yes	Unary	Increment
`--`		Right	Yes	Unary	Decrement
`~`		Right	Yes	Unary	Bitwise NOT
`!`		Right	Yes	Unary	Logical NOT
`+`		Right	Yes	Unary	Plus (sign)
`-`		Right	Yes	Unary	Minus (sign)
`*`		Right	Yes	Unary	Pointer dereferencing
`&`		Right	Yes	Unary	Get-address-of an object
`new`		Right	Yes	Unary	Memory allocation
`delete`		Right	Yes	Unary	Memory deallocation
`()`		Right	Yes	Binary	Type conversion (cast)
	14				
`.*`		Left	No	Binary	Direct member pointer selection
`->*`		Left	Yes	Binary	Indirect member pointer selection
	13				
`*`		Left	Yes	Binary	Multiplication
`/`		Left	Yes	Binary	Division
`%`		Left	Yes	Binary	Modulus (remainder)

Operator	Level	Associativity	Overloadable	Arity	Description
	12				
+		Left	Yes	Binary	Addition
-		Left	Yes	Binary	Subtraction
	11				
<<		Left	Yes	Binary	Bit-shift left
>>		Left	Yes	Binary	Bit-shift right
	10				
<		Left	Yes	Binary	Less-than
<=		Left	Yes	Binary	Less-than-or-equal
>		Left	Yes	Binary	Greater-than
>=		Left	Yes	Binary	Greater-than-or-equal
	9				
==		Left	Yes	Binary	Equality
!=		Left	Yes	Binary	Inequality
	8				
&		Left	Yes	Binary	Bitwise AND
	7				
^		Left	Yes	Binary	Bitwise XOR
	6				
|		Left	Yes	Binary	Bitwise OR
	5				
&&		Left	Yes	Binary	Logical AND
	4				
||		Left	Yes	Binary	Logical OR
	3				
? :		Left	No	Ternary	Conditional expression
	2				
=		Right	Yes	Binary	Assignment
+=		Right	Yes	Binary	Addition-assignment shortcut
-=		Right	Yes	Binary	Subtraction-assignment shortcut
*=		Right	Yes	Binary	Multiplication-assignment shortcut
/=		Right	Yes	Binary	Division-assignment shortcut
%=		Right	Yes	Binary	Modulus-assignment shortcut
&=		Right	Yes	Binary	Bitwise-AND-assignment shortcut
|=		Right	Yes	Binary	Bitwise-OR-assignment shortcut
^=		Right	Yes	Binary	Bitwise-XOR-assignment shortcut
<<=		Right	Yes	Binary	Bitshift-left-assignment shortcut
>>=		Right	Yes	Binary	Bitshift-right-assignment shortcut
	1				
,		Left	Yes	Binary	Expression separation

DATA FILES

This appendix contains sample data files that may prove useful with some of the exercises in the text: **InventoryFile**, **InventoryUpdate**, **LeastSquaresFile**, **StudentFile**, **StudentUpdate**, and **UserIdFile**. Descriptions of these files and sample listings follow. (On the disk that accompanies this text, these files are named **INVEN.DAT**, **INVUPDAT.DAT**, **LSQUARES.DAT**, **STUDENT.DAT**, **STUPDATE.DAT**, and **USER.DAT**, respectively.)

InventoryFile

Item number: an integer
Number currently in stock: an integer (in the range 0 to 999)
Unit price: a real value
Minimum inventory level: an integer (in the range 0 to 999)
Item name: a character string

File is sorted so that item numbers are in increasing order.

Sample InventoryFile

```
1011  20   54.95   15 Telephoto-Pocket-Camera
1012  12   24.95   15 Mini-Pocket-Camera
1021  20   49.95   10 Polaroid-1Step-Camera
1022  13  189.95   12 Sonar-1Step-Camera
1023  15   74.95    5 Pronto-Camera
1031   9  279.99   10 8MM-Zoom-Movie-Camera
1032  15  310.55   10 8MM-Sound/ZoomMovieCamera
1041  10  389.00   12 35MM-Minolta-SLR-XG-7-Camera
1042  11  349.95   12 35MM-Pentax-SLR-AE-1-Camera
1043  20  319.90   12 35MM-Canon-SLR-ME-Camera
1044  13  119.95   12 35MM-Hi-Matic-Camera
1045  20   89.99   12 35MM-Compact-Camera
```

Sample **InventoryFile** (cont.)

1511	7	129.95	5	Zoom-Movie-Projector
1512	9	239.99	5	Zoom-Sound-Projector
1521	10	219.99	5	Auto-Carousel-Projector
1522	4	114.95	5	Carousel-Slide-Projector
2011	4	14.95	5	Pocket-Strobe
2012	12	48.55	10	StrobeSX-10
2013	10	28.99	15	Electronic-Flash-SX-10
3011	13	32.99	15	Tele-Converter
3012	14	97.99	15	28MM-Wide-Angle-Lens
3013	13	87.95	15	135MM-Telephoto-Lens
3014	8	267.95	5	35-105MM-Zoom-Lens
3015	7	257.95	5	80-200MM-Zoom-Lens
3111	4	67.50	5	Heavy-Duty-Tripod
3112	10	19.95	5	Lightweight-Tripod
3511	10	159.99	5	35MM-Enlarger-Kit
4011	4	35.98	5	40x40-Deluxe-Screen
4012	10	44.98	5	50x50-Deluxe-Screen
5011	17	4.29	25	120-Slide-Tray
5012	33	2.95	25	100-Slide-Tray
5021	12	6.25	15	Slide-Viewer
5031	12	55.95	10	Movie-Editor
6011	10	59.95	5	Condenser-Microphone
6111	80	0.89	100	AA-Alkaline-Battery
7011	19	19.79	20	Gadget-Bag
8011	45	1.49	50	135-24-Color-Film
8021	60	0.99	50	110-12-Color-Film
8022	42	1.45	50	110-24-Color-Film
8023	37	0.59	25	110-12-B/W-Film
8024	43	0.95	25	110-24-B/W-Film
8031	44	0.89	50	126-12-Color-Film
8032	27	0.59	25	126-12-B/W-Film
8041	39	6.89	50	8MM-Film-Cassette
8042	25	11.89	20	16MM-Film-Cassette
9111	10	959.99	12	Combination-Camera-Kit

InventoryUpdate

Order number: three letters followed by four digits
Item number: an integer (same as those in **InventoryFile**)
Transaction code: a character (**S** = sold, **R** = returned)
Number of items sold or returned: an integer in the range 0 to 999

The file is sorted so that item numbers are in increasing order. (Some items in **InventoryFile** may not have update records; others may have more than one.)

Sample **InventoryUpdate**

CCI7543	MAP8102	UOX7714
1012 S 2	1031 S 13	1043 S 2
LTB3429	JRJ6335	ERZ2147
1012 S 7	1031 S 1	1043 S 7
DJS6762	UWR9386	MYW2540
1021 S 9	1032 S 3	1044 S 1
NQT1850	TJY1913	UKS3587
1022 S 1	1032 S 11	1045 S 2
WYP6425	YHA9464	AAN3759
1023 S 4	1041 S 5	1045 S 2
YOK2210	SYT7493	WZT4171
1023 R 2	1041 S 3	1045 S 12
QGM3144	FHJ1657	TYR9475
1023 S 1	1042 S 7	1511 S 1
NPQ8685	QJQ2215	FRQ4184
1031 S 5	1043 S 8	1511 S 1
TAV3604	SVC6511	VIZ6879
1512 S 2	3014 S 4	8011 S 16
DCW9363	XJQ9391	GXX9093
1522 S 1	3014 S 4	8011 S 19
EXN3964	ONO5251	HHO5605
1522 R 1	3111 S 3	8021 S 41
OIN5524	CXC7780	BOL2324
1522 S 1	3111 S 1	8021 S 49
EOJ8218	VGT8169	PAG9289
1522 S 1	3112 S 8	8023 S 15
YFK0683	IMK5861	MDF5557
2011 S 2	3511 S 2	8023 S 17
PPX4743	QHR1944	IQK3388
2012 S 4	3511 S 1	8024 S 12
DBR1709	ZPK6211	OTB1341
2013 S 4	4011 S 2	8024 S 28
JOM5408	VDZ2970	SVF5674
2013 S 3	4012 S 6	8031 S 24
PKN0671	BOJ9069	ZDP9484
2013 S 1	5011 S 6	8031 S 15
LBD8391	MNL7029	OSY8177
3011 S 9	5011 S 9	8032 S 15
DNL6326	MRG8703	GJQ0185
3012 S 9	5021 S 10	8032 S 8
BTP5396	DEM9289	VHW0189
3013 S 1	5021 S 1	8041 S 20
GFL4913	BXL1651	WEU9225
3013 S 8	5031 S 2	8041 S 6
EHQ7510	VAF8733	YJO3755
3013 S 7	6111 S 65	8041 S 8
QQL6472	UYI0368	
3013 S 5	7011 S 2	

LeastSquaresFile

This is a text file in which each line contains a pair of real numbers representing the *x* coordinate and the *y* coordinate of a point.

Sample **LeastSquaresFile**

2.18	1.06	5.44	8.25
7.46	12.04	1.21	-0.76
5.75	8.68	9.07	15.5
3.62	4.18	3.95	5.0
3.59	3.87	9.63	17.01
7.5	12.32	9.75	16.91
7.49	11.74	9.99	16.67
7.62	12.07	3.61	4.69
7.39	12.17	9.06	15.0
1.88	0.58	5.03	6.62
6.31	10.09	4.45	6.12
2.53	2.04	4.54	5.89
0.92	-1.02	1.48	0.3
0.82	-1.5	6.58	9.8
2.62	2.1	3.05	3.56
5.66	8.53	6.19	9.62
8.05	13.05	6.47	9.83
8.99	14.85	8.13	10.75
5.12	7.03	7.31	11.73
3.85	4.43	0.33	-1.93
6.08	9.21	5.12	7.41
1.42	0	5.23	7.73
2.58	2.38	7.14	11.02
5.99	9.42	1.27	-0.21
0.63	-1.63	2.51	1.59
9.98	17.25	5.26	7.86
5.63	8.58	4.74	6.19
8.94	15.27	2.1	2.12
7.34	11.48	5.27	7.73
6.55	9.92	2.85	2.63
4.89	7.07	1.99	1.09
9.59	15.82	8.91	15.03
1.81	0.45	2.19	1.21
0.99	-0.71	1.6	-0.05
4.82	6.91	8.93	15.12
9.68	16.24	3.19	3.56
1.21	-0.22	3.37	3.64
4.54	5.64		

StudentFile

This is a file of student records, each of which is organized as follows:

Student number: an integer
Student's name: two character strings (last, first) and a character (middle initial)
Hometown: two character strings of the form city, state
Phone number: a character string
Gender: a character (**M** or **F**)
Year: a 1-digit integer (**1**, **2**, **3**, **4**, or **5** for special)
Total credits earned to date: an integer
Cumulative GPA: a real value
Major: a character string

The file is arranged so that student numbers are in increasing order.

Sample **StudentFile**

```
10103 Johnson, James L
Waupun, Wisconsin
7345229
M 1 15 3.15
ENGR
10104 Andrews, Peter J
Grand_Rapids, Michigan
9493301
M 2 42 2.78
CPSC
10110 Peters, Andrew J
Lynden, Washington
3239550
M 5 63 2.05
ART
10113 VandenVander, Vanessa V
Fremont, Michigan
5509237
F 4 110 3.74
HIST
10126 Aristotle, Alice A
Chino, California
3330861
F 3 78 3.10
PHIL
10144 Lucky, Lucy L
Grandville, Michigan
7745424
F 5 66 2.29
HIST
```

```
10179 Euler, Lennie L
Three_Rivers, Michigan
6290017
M 1 15 3.83
MATH
10191 Nakamura, Toky O
Chicago, Illinois
4249665
F 1 12 1.95
SOCI
10226 Freud, Fred E
Lynden, Washington
8340115
M 1 15 1.85
PSYC
10272 Speareshake, William W
Grand_Rapids, Michigan
2410744
M 5 102 2.95
ENGL
10274 Tchaikovsky, Wolfgang A
Byron_Center, Michigan
8845115
M 3 79 2.75
MUSC
10284 Orange, Dutch V
Graafschaap, Michigan
3141660
M 2 42 2.98
ENGR
```

Sample **StudentFile** (cont.)

10297 Caesar, Julie S
Denver, Colorado
4470338
F 4 117 3.25
HIST
10298 Psycho, Prunella E
De_Motte, Indiana
5384609
F 4 120 2.99
PSYC
10301 Bull, Sitting U
Gallup, New_Mexico
6632997
M 1 14 2.95
EDUC
10302 Custer, General G
Badlands, South_Dakota
5552995
M 3 40 1.95
HIST
10303 Fahrenheit, Felicia O
Sheboygan, Wisconsin
5154997
F 2 40 3.85
CHEM
10304 Deutsch, Sprechen Z
Sparta, Michigan
8861201
F 5 14 3.05
GERM
10307 Mendelssohn, Mozart W
Peoria, Illinois
2410747
M 3 76 2.87
MUSC
10310 Augusta, Ada B
Lakewood, California
7172339
F 2 46 3.83
CPSC
10319 Gauss, Carl F
Yorktown, Pennsylvania
3385494
M 2 41 4.00
MATH
10323 Kronecker, Leo P
Traverse_City, Michigan
6763991
M 3 77 2.75
MATH

10330 Issacson, Jacob A
Silver_Springs, Maryland
4847932
M 5 25 2.99
RELI
10331 Issacson, Esau B
Silver_Springs, Maryland
4847932
M 5 25 2.98
RELI
10339 Dewey, Johanna A
Salt_Lake_City, Utah
6841129
F 2 41 3.83
EDUC
10348 Virus, Vera W
Saginaw, Michigan
6634401
F 4 115 3.25
CPSC
10355 Zylstra, Zelda A
Downs, Kansas
7514008
F 1 16 1.95
ENGL
10377 Porgy, Bess N
Columbus, Ohio
4841771
F 2 44 2.78
MUSI
10389 Newmann, Alfred E
Cheyenne, Wyoming
7712399
M 4 115 0.99
EDUC
10395 Medes, Archie L
Whitinsville, Maryland
9294401
M 3 80 3.10
ENGR
10406 Macdonald, Ronald B
Seattle, Washington
5582911
M 1 15 2.99
CPSC
10415 Aardvark, Anthony A
Grandville, Michigan
5325912
M 2 43 2.79
ENGR

Sample **StudentFile** (cont.)

10422 Gestalt, Gloria G
Wheaton, Illinois
6631212
F 2 42 2.48
PSYC
10431 GotoDijkstra, Edgar G
Cawker_City, Kansas
6349971
M 1 15 4.00
CPSC
10448 Rembrandt, Roberta E
Sioux_Center, Iowa
2408113
F 1 77 2.20
ART
10458 Shoemaker, Imelda M
Honolulu, Hawaii
9193001
F 1 15 3.15
POLS
10467 Marx, Karl Z
Hawthorne, New_Jersey
5513915
M 3 78 2.75
ECON
10470 Scrooge, Ebenezer T
Troy, Michigan
8134001
M 4 118 3.25
SOCI
10482 Nightingale, Florence K
Rochester, New_York
7175118
F 1 15 3.15
NURS
10490 Gazelle, Gwendolyn D
Chino, California
3132446
F 2 43 2.78
PE
10501 Pasteur, Louise A
Window_Rock, Arizona
4245170
F 1 16 3.10
BIOL
10519 Elba, Able M
Bozeman, Montana
8183226
M 3 77 3.40
SPEE

10511 Lewis, Clark N
New_Era, Michigan
6461125
M 4 114 3.37
GEOG
10515 Mouse, Michael E
Boise, Idaho
5132771
M 5 87 1.99
EDUC
10523 Pavlov, Bowser T
Farmington, Michigan
9421753
F 1 13 1.77
PSYCH
10530 Chicita, Juanita A
Oklahoma_City, Oklahoma
3714377
F 5 95 2.66
BIOL
10538 Busch, Arch E
St_Louis, Missouri
8354112
M 3 74 2.75
ENGR
10547 Fault, Paige D
Petoskey, Michigan
4543116
F 5 55 2.95
CPSC
10553 Santamaria, Nina P
Plymouth, Massachusetts
2351181
F 1 15 1.77
HIST
10560 Shyster, Samuel D
Everglades, Florida
4421885
M 1 13 1.95
SOCI
10582 Yewliss, Cal C
Rudyard, Michigan
3451220
M 376 2.99
MATH
10590 Atanasoff, Eniac C
Springfield, Illinois
6142449
F 1 14 1.88
CPSC

Sample **StudentFile** (cont.)

10597 Rockne, Newton K
New_York, New_York
4631744
M 4 116 1.98
PE
10610 Roosevelt, Rose Y
Spring_Lake, Michigan
9491221
F 5 135 2.95
POLS
10623 Xerxes, Art I
Cincinnati, Ohio
3701228
M 4 119 3.25
GREE
10629 Leibniz, Gottfried W
Boulder, Colorado
5140228
M 1 13 1.95
MATH
10633 Vespucci, Vera D
Ripon, California
4341883
F 5 89 2.29
GEOG
10648 Principal, Pamela P
Albany, New_York
7145513
F 1 14 1.75
EDUC
10652 Cicero, Marsha
Rapid_City, South_Dakota
3335910
F 3 77 2.87
LATI

10657 Weerd, Dewey L
Detroit, Michigan
4841962
M 4 115 2.99
PHIL
10663 Hochschule, Hortense C
Lincoln, Nebraska
7120111
F 5 100 2.70
EDUC
10668 Einstein, Alfred M
Newark, New_Jersey
3710225
M 2 41 2.78
ENGR
10675 Fibonacci, Leonard O
Nashville, Tennessee
4921107
M 4 115 3.25
MATH
10682 Angelo, Mike L
Austin, Texas
5132201
M 4 117 3.74
ART
10688 Pascal, Blaze R
Brooklyn, New_York
7412993
M 1 15 1.98
CPSC

StudentUpdate

This is a file of student grade records, each of which is organized as follows:

> Student number: an integer (same as those used in **StudentFile**)
> For each of five courses:
> > Course name: a seven-character string (e.g., **CPSC131**)
> > Letter grade: a two-character string (e.g., **A-**, **B+**, **C♭**)
> > Course credit: an integer

The file is sorted so that student numbers are in increasing order. There is one update record for each student in **StudentFile**.

Sample **StudentUpdate**

```
10103 ENGL176 C   4 EDUC268 B   4 EDUC330 B+ 3 PE281    C   3 ENGR317 D   4
10104 CPSC271 D+  4 ESCI208 D-  3 PHIL340 B+ 2 CPSC146 D+  4 ENGL432 D+  4
10110 ART 520 D   3 ESCI259 F   1 ENGL151 D+ 4 MUSC257 B   4 PSYC486 C   4
10113 HIST498 F   3 PE 317  C+  4 MUSC139 B- 3 PHIL165 D   3 GEOG222 C   3
10126 PHIL367 C-  4 EDUC420 C-  3 EDUC473 C  3 EDUC224 D-  3 GERM257 F   4
10144 HIST559 C+  3 MATH357 D   3 CPSC323 C- 2 PE246    D-  4 MUSC379 D+  4
10179 MATH169 C-  4 CHEM163 C+  4 MUSC436 A- 3 MATH366 D-  2 BIOL213 A-  4
10191 SOCI177 F   4 POLS106 A   4 EDUC495 A- 3 ENGR418 B+  2 ENGR355 A   4
10226 PSYC116 B   3 GERM323 B-  4 ART350  A  4 HIST269 B+  4 EDUC214 C+  3
10272 ENGL558 A-  4 EDUC169 D+  3 PSYC483 B+ 4 ENGR335 B+  2 BIOL228 B   4
10274 MUSC351 B   4 PSYC209 C-  4 ENGR400 F  1 ESCI392 A   4 SOCI394 B-  3
10284 ENGR292 D   4 PSYC172 C   4 EDUC140 B  4 MATH274 F   4 MUSC101 D+  4
10297 HIST464 F   1 HIST205 F   1 ENGR444 F  1 MATH269 F   1 EDUC163 F   1
10298 PSYC452 B   3 MATH170 C+  4 EDUC344 C- 2 GREE138 C-  2 SPEE303 A-  3
10301 EDUC197 A   4 PE372   B   3 ENGR218 D  4 MATH309 C   4 ESCI405 C-  4
10302 CHEM283 F   1 PE440   A   2 MATH399 A- 3 HIST455 C-  4 MATH387 C-  3
10303 HIST111 D-  3 ART151  C+  3 ENGL100 C- 3 PSYC151 D+  3 PE104    A-  1
10304 GERM526 C-  2 CHEM243 C   4 POLS331 B- 4 EDUC398 A   3 ENGR479 D+  4
10307 MUSC323 B+  3 MATH485 C   4 HIST232 B+ 4 EDUC180 A   3 ENGL130 B+  4
10310 CPSC264 B   2 POLS227 D+  3 ENGR467 D- 3 MATH494 D-  4 ART420  C+  4
10319 MATH276 B   2 ESCI434 A   3 HIST197 B- 4 GERM489 B-  2 ART137  C-  3
10323 MATH377 D-  4 EDUC210 D   4 MATH385 D- 4 ENGR433 C   2 HIST338 A-  4
10330 HIST546 C+  3 ESCI440 B+  3 GREE472 C+ 3 BIOL186 B   4 GEOG434 C+  2
10331 HIST546 C   3 ESCI440 B+  3 GREE472 C  3 BIOL186 B+  4 GEOG434 C+  2
10339 EDUC283 B   3 CPSC150 B   3 ENGR120 D  4 CPSC122 F   4 ART216  B   4
10348 CPSC411 C-  3 HIST480 C+  4 PSYC459 B  4 BIOL299 B+  4 ECON276 B+  3
10355 ENGL130 C-  3 CPSC282 C+  4 CPSC181 A- 4 CPSC146 C-  4 SOCI113 F   1
10377 SOCI213 D+  3 PSYC158 D   4 MUSC188 C  3 PSYC281 D-  4 ENGR339 B+  4
10389 EDUC414 D+  4 PSYC115 C-  2 PSYC152 D- 4 ART366  D-  3 ENGR366 F   4
10395 ENGR396 B   4 HIST102 F   3 ENGL111 A  4 PSYC210 D-  2 GREE128 A   4
10406 CPSC160 C+  4 CPSC233 C   1 LATI494 C+ 3 ENGL115 C-  3 MATH181 A   3
10415 ENGR287 C   4 EDUC166 B-  4 EDUC106 A- 3 PE190    F   3 MATH171 B-  3
10422 PSYC275 A-  4 MATH497 A   4 EDUC340 F  1 GERM403 C-  4 MATH245 D+  4
10431 CPSC187 D-  4 CPSC426 F   4 ENGR476 B- 4 BIOL148 B+  3 CPSC220 F   3
10448 ART171  D+  3 CPSC239 C-  3 SOCI499 B- 4 HIST113 D+  3 PSYC116 C   4
10458 POLS171 F   1 CPSC187 C+  4 CHEM150 B  2 PHIL438 D-  4 PHIL254 D   4
10467 ECON335 D-  3 ESCI471 B+  4 MATH457 C+ 3 MATH207 C   2 BIOL429 D   4
10470 MUSC415 C+  3 POLS177 C   3 CPSC480 A  4 PSYC437 B   3 SOCI276 D   4
10482 ENGL158 D-  4 EDUC475 B   3 HIST172 B- 2 PE316    F   4 ENGR294 A-  3
10490 PE239   F   4 ENGL348 F   3 LATI246 F  4 CPSC350 F   4 MATH114 F   1
10501 BIOL125 F   4 CPSC412 F   3 ESCI279 F  4 ENGR153 F   2 ART293  F   1
10519 SPEE386 B+  4 HIST479 C   4 PSYC249 B- 2 GREE204 B-  4 PE421    A   1
10511 ESCI416 B   3 MATH316 D-  4 MATH287 C  2 MATH499 A-  4 ESCI288 D   3
10515 EDUC563 D+  3 PHIL373 D-  3 ART318  B  4 HIST451 F   1 ART476  C+  3
10523 BIOL183 D-  2 HIST296 D+  4 HIST380 B+ 4 ENGR216 C   4 MATH412 B-  2
10530 ENGL559 F   1 EDUC457 D+  4 CPSC306 A  3 ENGR171 B+  1 CPSC380 A   4
10538 ENGR328 A-  4 ENGR336 C   3 EDUC418 D+ 3 PHIL437 B+  4 CPSC475 D   4
10547 CPSC537 A-  4 ART386  D   4 HIST292 D- 4 ENGR467 A-  4 PE464    B+  4
10553 HIST170 A-  4 SOCI496 D-  3 PHIL136 B+ 4 CPSC371 D-  4 CPSC160 A-  1
10560 SOCI153 D+  3 MATH438 D+  4 CPSC378 C  4 BIOL266 F   3 EDUC278 D+  3
```

Sample **StudentUpdate** (cont.)

10582	MATH388	A-	3	PE311	B	3	ECON143	D	4	MATH304	C+	3	PE428	C+	4
10590	CPSC134	B-	3	ESCI114	B+	3	CPSC492	C	4	ENGL121	C	4	ENGR403	A-	4
10597	PE423	A-	3	BIOL189	D+	3	PHIL122	D-	4	ENGL194	C-	4	SOCI113	D+	3
10610	ESCI594	C-	3	PHIL344	F	4	CPSC189	B+	2	ENGR411	D-	3	MATH241	A	4
10623	GREE412	B-	4	ENGL415	D-	3	ENGL234	D-	4	MATH275	F	1	SOCI124	B+	3
10629	MATH137	D	2	MATH481	F	3	ESCI445	F	1	MATH339	D	4	ART219	B+	4
10633	GEOG573	B	4	ENGL149	C+	4	EDUC113	B+	4	ENGR458	C-	2	HIST446	D+	4
10648	EDUC132	D+	4	MUSC103	D-	4	ENGL263	C	4	ENGL134	B+	4	ESCI392	A	3
10652	LATI363	F	3	BIOL425	F	1	CPSC267	C	4	EDUC127	C+	3	MATH338	B	4
10657	PHIL429	F	1	ART412	D-	4	MUSC473	B-	4	SOCI447	C-	4	MATH237	D+	2
10663	EDUC580	B-	4	ENGR351	B+	4	SOCI283	D	4	ART340	C	4	PSYC133	D+	3
10668	ENGR274	B+	4	SOCI438	C	1	PE327	C	4	BIOL158	A	4	EDUC457	A-	4
10675	MATH457	A	4	ENGR114	C	4	CPSC218	C	3	ESCI433	C-	3	PSYC243	C+	1
10682	ART483	D+	3	GERM432	C	3	ENGL103	B+	4	MUSC169	C-	3	SOCI381	C-	2
10688	CPSC182	F	1	HIST371	C+	4	PSYC408	F	1	MUSC214	B+	4	MATH151	C	3

UserIdFile

This is file of computer system user records, each of which is organized as follows:

Identification number: an integer
User's name: two strings of the form last name, first name
Password: a string
Resource limit (in dollars): an integer with up to four digits
Resources used to date: a real value

The file is arranged so that identification numbers are in increasing order.

Sample **UserIdFile**

```
10101 Miltgen, Joseph          10106 Pizzula, Norma
moe                            pizza
750 380.81                     350 223.95
10102 Small, Isaac             10107 VanderVan, Henry
large                          dutch
650 598.84                     750 168.59
10103 Snyder, Samuel           10108 Freeloader, Freddie
r2d2                           red
250 193.74                     450 76.61
10104 Edmundsen, Edmund        10109 Alexander, Alvin
abcde                          great
250 177.93                     650 405.04
10105 Braunschweiger, Christopher  10110 Mouse, Michael
brown                          ears
850 191.91                     50 42.57
```

Sample **UserIdFile** (cont.)

10111 Lukasewicz, Zzyzk
rpn
350 73.50
10112 Christmas, Mary
noel
850 33.28
10113 Adam, Joe
eve
750 327.53
10114 Nijhoff, Laran
kkid
550 382.03
10115 Liestma, Stan
saab
650 38.36
10116 Zwier, Apollos
PJ
350 249.48
10117 Jaeger, Tim
biker
250 246.73
10118 VanZwalenberg, Jorge
egypt
850 466.95
10119 Jester, Courtney
joker
450 281.16
10120 McDonald, Ronald
fries
250 35.00
10121 Nederlander, Benaut
dutch
550 28.82
10122 Haybailer, Homer
farm
850 37.32
10123 Spear, Bill
shake
450 337.01
10124 Romeo, Juliet
XOXOX
150 100.19
10125 Greek, Jimmy
wager
250 0.03
10126 Virus, Vera
worm
750 67.35
10127 Beech, Rocky
wreck
950 256.18

10128 Engel, Angel
wings
150 16.39
10129 Abner, Lil
daisy
950 89.57
10130 Tracy, Richard
crime
550 392.00
10131 McGee, Fibber
molly
750 332.12
10132 Bell, Alex
phone
850 337.43
20101 Cobb, Tyrus
bball
50 32.81
20102 George, Ruth
babe
350 269.93
20103 Descartes, Ronald
horse
250 109.34
0104 Euclid, Ian
greek
350 63.63
20105 Daniels, Ezekiel
lions
350 128.69
20106 Tarzan, Jane
apes
150 100.31
20107 Habbakuk, Jonah
whale
950 183.93
20108 Columbus, Chris
pinta
850 202.24
20109 Byrd, Dick
north
550 168.49
20110 Bunyan, Pauline
babe
550 333.47
20111 Chaucer, Jeff
poem
950 37.02
20112 Stotle, Ari
logic
750 337.74

Sample **UserIdFile** (cont.)

20113 Harrison, Ben
pres
550 262.97
20114 James, Jesse
guns
250 58.81
20115 Scott, Francine
flag
350 168.11
20116 Phillips, Phyllis
gas66
650 322.22
20117 Doll, Barbara
ken
350 26.34
20118 Finn, Huck
tom
350 22.86

20119 Sawyer, Tom
huck
950 460.30
20120 Newmann, Alfred
mad
450 116.00
20121 Simple, Simon
pie
550 486.05
20122 Schmidt, Messer
plane
250 35.31
20124 Luther, Calvin
ref
777 666.66
20125 Yale, Harvard
ivy
150 127.70

PROFESSIONAL ETHICS

In Chapter 1, we addressed the issue of professional ethics and presented the Canons of the ACM, the ethical statement of the Association for Computing Machinery. We now present the ethical statements of two other professional computing organizations: the Data Processing Management Association (DPMA) and the Institute of Electronic and Electrical Engineers (IEEE).

DPMA Code of Ethics

I acknowledge:

1. *That I have an obligation to management,* therefore, I shall promote the understanding of information processing methods and procedures to management using every resource at my command.

2. *That I have an obligation to my fellow members,* therefore I shall uphold the high ideals of DPMA as outlined in its Association Bylaws. Further, I shall cooperate with my fellow members and shall treat them with honesty and respect at all times.

3. *That I have an obligation to society* and will participate to the best of my ability in the dissemination of knowledge pertaining to the general development and understanding of information processing. Further, I shall not use knowledge of a confidential nature to further my personal interest, nor shall I violate the privacy and confidentiality of information entrusted to me or to which I may gain access.

4. *That I have an obligation to my employer* whose trust I hold, therefore I shall endeavor to discharge this obligation to the best of my ability, to guard my employer's interests, and to advise him or her wisely and honestly.

5. *That I have an obligation to my country,* therefore, in my personal business and social contacts, I shall uphold my nation and shall honor the chosen way of life of my fellow citizens.

I accept these obligations as a personal responsibility, and as a member of this Association. I shall actively discharge these obligations and I dedicate myself to that end.

IEEE Code of Ethics

Preamble: Engineers, scientists and technologists affect the quality of life for all people in our complex technological society. In the pursuit of their profession, therefore, it is vital that IEEE members conduct their work in an ethical manner so that they merit the confidence of colleagues, employers, clients and the public. This IEEE Code of Ethics represents such a standard of professional conduct for IEEE members in the discharge of their responsibilities to employees, to clients, to the community, and to their colleagues in this Institute and other professional societies.

Article I. *Members shall maintain high standards of diligence, creativity, and productivity and shall:*

a. Accept responsibility for their actions;
b. Be honest and realistic in stating claims or estimates from available data;
c. Undertake technological tasks and accept responsibility only if qualified by training or experience, or after full disclosure to their employers or clients of pertinent qualifications;
d. Maintain their professional skills at the level of the state of the art, and recognize the importance of current events in their work;
e. Advance the integrity and prestige of the profession by practicing in a dignified manner and for adequate compensation.

Article II. *Members shall, in their work:*

a. Treat fairly all colleagues and co-workers, regardless of race, religion, sex, age or national origin;

b. Report, publish and disseminate freely information to others, subject to legal and proprietary restraints;

c. Encourage colleagues and co-workers to act in accord with this Code and support them when they do so;

d. Seek, accept, and offer honest criticism of work, and properly credit the contributions of others;

e. Support and participate in the activities of their professional societies;

f. Assist colleagues and co-workers in their professional development.

Article III. *Members shall, in their relations with employers and clients:*

a. Act as faithful agents or trustees for their employers or clients in professional and business matters, provided such actions conform with other parts of this Code;

b. Keep information on business affairs or technical processes of an employer or client in confidence while employed, and later, until such information is properly released, provided that such actions conform with other parts of this Code;

c. Inform their employers, clients, professional societies or public agencies or private agencies of which they are members or to which they make presentations, of any circumstance that could lead to a conflict of interest;

d. Neither give nor accept, directly or indirectly, any gift payment or service of more than nominal value to or from those having business relationships with their employers or clients.

e. Assist and advise their employers or clients in anticipating the possible consequences, direct or indirect, immediate or remote, of the projects, work or plans of which they have knowledge.

Article IV. *Members shall, in fulfilling responsibility to community:*

a. Protect safety, health, and welfare of the public and speak out against abuses in these areas affecting the public interest;

b. Contribute professional advice, as appropriate, to civic, charitable, or other nonprofit organizations;

c. Seek to extend public knowledge and appreciation of the profession and its achievements.

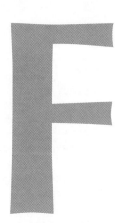

CLASSES STRINGS AND RANDOMINT

F.1. Class Strings

F.1. Class Strings

In Chapter 9, we provided a class **Strings** that could be used to conveniently manipulate character string data. This section of Appendix F presents the source code for class **Strings**.

Class **Strings** header file

```
/* This file presents the interface for the Strings class,
     a class that stores character strings using run-time
     allocated arrays, while providing convenient operations
     to manipulate them.

   Written by: Joel C. Adams, Spring, 1993, at Calvin College.
   ----------------------------------------------------------------*/

#ifndef STRINGS
#define STRINGS

#include <iostream.h>
#include <string.h>

class Strings
{
  char
    *String_;                        // container for starting
                                     //    address of the array
  int
    Length_;                         // the number of non-NUL
                                     //    chars in the array
```

Class **Strings** header file (cont.)

```
public:
    // *** Constructors, Destructor, and Converters.
    /*--- Constructor to build a Strings object from a char-string constant.

        Pre:      A Strings object has been declared,
                    to be initialized with a character string constant.
        Receive:  Str, the char-string constant.
        Post:     The Strings object has been constructed/initialized
                    appropriately to store the char-string constant.
    ------------------------------------------------------------------*/
    Strings(const char Str[] = 0);


    /*--- Constructor to make a distinct copy of a Strings object.

        Pre:      A copy of a Strings object is needed.
        Receive:  Str, the String to be copied.
        Post:     This Strings object has been constructed/initialized
                    as a copy of the original Strings object.
    ------------------------------------------------------------------*/
    Strings(const Strings& Str);


    /*--- Constructor to build a Strings object of a particular size.

        Pre:      A Strings object has been declared,
                    with an initialization character and
                    with a given length.
        Receive:  Ch, the initialization character;
                    Size, the length desired.
        Post:     This Strings object has been constructed/initialized
                    with its Length_ member set to Size, and
                    its String_ member pointing to an array of Size chars,
                    each element containing the value Ch.
    ------------------------------------------------------------------*/
    Strings(char Ch, unsigned Size = 1);


    /*--- Constructor to convert an int to a Strings object.

        Pre:      A Strings object has been declared
                    with an int as an argument.
        Receive:  IntVal, an int value.
        Post:     The object has been constructed and initialized
                    as the Strings object equivalent to IntVal.
    ------------------------------------------------------------------*/
    Strings(int IntVal);
```

Class **Strings** header file (cont.)

```
/*--- Constructor to convert a double to Strings object.

   Pre:     A Strings object has been declared,
               with a double as an argument.
   Receive: DoubleVal, a double value.
   Post:    The object has been constructed and initialized
               as the Strings object equivalent to DoubleVal.
----------------------------------------------------------------------*/
Strings(double DoubleVal);


/*--- Destructor to deallocate the memory of a Strings object.

   Pre:  A Strings object's lifetime is over.
   Post: The dynamic memory of that object has been reclaimed.
----------------------------------------------------------------------*/
~Strings(void);


/*--- This function converts a String of digits to a double value.

   Pre:    This Strings object contains a sequence of digits.
   Return: The double value equivalent to those digits;
               0.0 if the conversion cannot be performed.
----------------------------------------------------------------------*/
double Double(void);


/*--- This function converts a String of digits to a long value.

   Pre:    This Strings object contains a sequence of digits.
   Return: The long value equivalent to those digits;
               0 if the conversion cannot be performed.
----------------------------------------------------------------------*/
long Long(void);


/*--- This function converts a String of digits to an
         unsigned long value.

   Pre:    This Strings object contains a sequence of digits.
   Return: The unsigned long value equivalent to those digits.
----------------------------------------------------------------------*/
unsigned long Unsigned(void);


/*--- This function converts a Strings object to the equivalent char-
         string whenever such a conversion is needed.

   Return: The char-string component of this Strings object.
----------------------------------------------------------------------*/
operator const char*() const { return String_; }
```

Class **Strings** header file (cont.)

```
// *** Operations
/*--- Length returns the number of characters in a Strings object.

     Return: The number of characters in this object.
     ---------------------------------------------------------------*/
int Length(void) const { return Length_; }


/*--- Subscript: Retrieve the character with a given index.

     Receive: i, an index into this Strings object.
     Return:  The (reference of the) char at index i.
     ---------------------------------------------------------------*/
char& operator[] (unsigned i);
const char& operator[] (unsigned i) const


/*--- Assignment to a Strings object.

     Receive: Str, a (reference to a) Strings object.
     Return:  This Strings object as a copy of Str.
     ---------------------------------------------------------------*/
Strings& operator= (const Strings& Str);


/*--- Delete a portion of a Strings object.

     Receive: First, Last, two indices of this Strings object.
     Return:  This Strings object without the characters from First..Last
              True, if and only if the operation is successful.
     ---------------------------------------------------------------*/
int Delete(unsigned First, unsigned Last);


/*--- Insert one Strings object into another Strings object.

     Receive: Str, a Strings object; and
              Pos, an index within this Strings object.
     Return:  This Strings object with the characters of Str inserted
              starting at index Pos.
              True, if and only if the operation is successful.
     ---------------------------------------------------------------*/
int Insert(const Strings& Str, unsigned Pos);


/*--- Replace a part of a Strings object with another Strings object.

     Receive: First, Last, two indices of this Strings object;
              Str, a Strings object.
     Return:  This Strings object with its characters of First through
              Last replaced with those of Str.
              True, if and only if the operation is successful.
     ---------------------------------------------------------------*/
int Replace(unsigned First, unsigned Last, const Strings& Str);
```

Class **Strings** header file (cont.)

```
/*--- Find the position of a substring within a Strings object.

    Receive: Str, a Strings object.
    Return:  The index of the first occurrence of Str within this Strings
             object (-1 if it is not present).
 ---------------------------------------------------------------------*/
int Position(const Strings& Str) const;


/*--- Concatenate two Strings objects.

    Receive: S1 and S2, two Strings objects.
    Return:  The Strings object consisting of S1 followed by S2.
 ---------------------------------------------------------------------*/
friend Strings operator& (const Strings& S1, const Strings& S2);


/*--- Retrieve a substring of a Strings object.

    Receive: First, Last, two indices of this Strings object.
    Return:  The substring of this Strings object that begins at
             index First and ends at index Last.
 ---------------------------------------------------------------------*/
Strings operator() (unsigned First, unsigned Last);


//--- Relational operators for Strings objects
friend int operator== (const Strings& S1, const Strings& S2);
friend int operator!= (const Strings& S1, const Strings& S2);
friend int operator< (const Strings& S1, const Strings& S2);
friend int operator> (const Strings& S1, const Strings& S2);
friend int operator<= (const Strings& S1, const Strings& S2);
friend int operator>= (const Strings& S1, const Strings& S2);

// --- Relational operators for a String and a char-string
friend int operator== (const Strings& S1, const char* S2);
friend int operator!= (const Strings& S1, const char* S2);
friend int operator< (const Strings& S1, const char* S2);
friend int operator> (const Strings& S1, const char* S2);
friend int operator<= (const Strings& S1, const char* S2);
friend int operator>= (const Strings& S1, const char* S2);

//--- Relational operators for a char-string and a String
friend int operator== (const char* S1, const Strings& S2);
friend int operator!= (const char* S1, const Strings& S2);
friend int operator< (const char* S1, const Strings& S2);
friend int operator> (const char* S1, const Strings& S2);
friend int operator<= (const char* S1, const Strings& S2);
friend int operator>= (const char* S1, const Strings& S2);
```

Class **Strings** header file (cont.)

```
// *** I/O
friend ostream& operator<< (ostream& OutStream, const Strings& S);
friend istream& operator>> (istream& InStream, Strings& S);

// Bound on the number of chars that can be read ...
enum {MaxLength = 1024};

/*--- Operation to get a line of input from the keyboard or a file.

    Receive: InStream, the stream (i or f) being read from;
             MaxChars, a bound on the number of chars to be read
                         (default Strings::MaxLength);
             UntilChar, a char that halts the operation when it is read
                         (default newline).
    Return:  This Strings object, filled with either
             the next MaxChars characters from InStream, or
             all unread characters up to UntilChar in InStream,
             whichever is fewer.
---------------------------------------------------------------------*/
istream& GetLine(istream& InStream,
             unsigned MaxChars = Strings::MaxLength,
             char UntilChar = '\n');
};

#endif
```

The header file is, of course, named **Strings.h**, but as mentioned in Chapter 4, the name of the implementation file differs from one C++ environment to another. In the GNU environment (UNIX), we named our implementation file **Strings.C**; while in the Turbo C++ environment (DOS), we named it **STRINGS.CPP**; and in the Symantec C++ environment (MacOS), we named it **Strings.cpp**.

Class **Strings** implementation file

```
/* This file contains the definitions of the operations of class Strings.
   The declaration of class Strings can be found in Strings.h

   Written by: Joel C. Adams, Spring, 1993, at Calvin College.
---------------------------------------------------------------------*/

#include "Strings.h"                    // header for this file

#include <stdlib.h>                     // exit()
#include <assert.h>                     // assert()
```

Class **Strings** implementation file (cont.)

```
const char                                    // error/warning messages
   FirstPastLast[] = "\n*** 1st index exceeds 2cd index in call to ",
   LastTooBig[] = "\nw - 2cd index exceeds string length in call to ";


/*--- Constructor to build a Strings object from a char-string constant.

   Pre:     A Strings object has been declared,
               to be initialized with a character string constant.
   Receive: Str, the char-string constant.
   Post:    This Strings object has been constructed and initialized
               appropriately to store the char-string constant.
-------------------------------------------------------------------------*/

Strings::Strings(const char Str[])
{
  if (Str == 0)                          // if Str has default value
  {
     Length_ = 0;                        //    Length_ gets zero
     String_ = 0;                        //    String_ gets NULL
  }
  else                                   // else
  {
     Length_ = strlen(Str);              //    Length_ gets length of Str
     String_ = new char[Length_ + 1];    //    allocate array for String_
     assert(String_ != 0);               //    verify
     strcpy(String_, Str);               //    copy Str into the array
  }
}


/*--- Constructor to copy a Strings object.

   Pre:     A copy of a Strings object is needed.
   Receive: Str, the String to be copied.
   Post:    This Strings object has been constructed and initialized
               as a copy of the original Strings object.
-------------------------------------------------------------------------*/

Strings::Strings(const Strings& Str)
{
  Length_ = Str.Length_;                 // copy Length_ member of Str

  if (Str.String_ == 0)                  // if  Str is empty
     String_ = 0;                        //    make copy empty too
  else                                   // else
  {
     String_ = new char[Length_+1];      //    allocate new array
     assert(String_ != 0);               //    verify
     strcpy(String_, Str.String_);       //    copy Str into the array
  }
}
```

Class **Strings** implementation file (cont.)

```
/*--- Constructor to build Strings object of a particular size.

    Pre:     A Strings object has been declared,
                with an initialization character and
                with a given length.
    Receive: Ch, the initialization character;
                Size, the length desired.
    Post:    This Strings object has been constructed and initialized
                with its Length_ member set to Size, and
                its String_ member pointing to an array of Size chars,
                each element containing the value Ch.
------------------------------------------------------------------*/


Strings::Strings(char Ch, unsigned Size)
{
  Length_ = Size;                  // set Length_
  String_ = new char[Size+1];      // allocate new array
  assert(String_ != 0);            // verify
  for (int i = 0; i <= Size; i++)  // fill the array\'s elems
    String_[i] = Ch;               //    with Ch chars
  String_[Size] = '\0';            // tack on NUL terminator
}



/*--- Constructor to convert an int to Strings object.

    Pre:     A Strings object has been declared,
                with an int as an argument.
    Receive: IntVal, an int value.
    Post:    The object has been constructed and initialized
                as the Strings object equivalent to IntVal.
------------------------------------------------------------------*/


#include <stdio.h>                         // provides us with sprintf()

Strings::Strings(int IntVal)
{
  char
    A[80];                                 // char string to store value

  sprintf(A, "%i", IntVal);                // convert value to a string
  Length_ = strlen(A);                     // Length_ gets length of A
  String_ = new char[Length_ + 1];         // allocate array for String_
  assert(String_ != 0);                    // verify
  strcpy(String_, A);                      // copy A into the array
}
```

Class **Strings** implementation file (cont.)

```
/*--- Constructor to convert a double to Strings object.

   Pre:     A Strings object has been declared,
               with a double as an argument.
   Receive: DoubleVal, a double value.
   Post:    The object has been constructed and initialized
               as the Strings object equivalent to DoubleVal.
---------------------------------------------------------------------*/
Strings::Strings(double DoubleVal)
{
  char
    A[80];                              // char string to hold value

  sprintf(A, "%d", DoubleVal);         // convert value to a string
  Length_ = strlen(A);                 // Length_ gets length of A
  String_ = new char[Length_ + 1];     // allocate array for String_
  assert(String_ != 0);                // verify
  strcpy(String_, A);                  // copy A into the array
}
```

```
/*--- Destructor to deallocate the memory of a Strings object.

   Pre:  Control has left the scope of Strings object.
   Post: The dynamic memory of that object has been reclaimed.
---------------------------------------------------------------------*/
Strings:: ~ Strings(void)
{
  delete [] String_;        // deallocate array of this object
  String_ = 0;
  Length_ = 0;              // set its Length_ to zero.
}
```

```
/*--- This function converts a String of digits to a double value.

   Pre:     This Strings object contains a sequence of digits.
   Return:  The double value equivalent to those digits;
               0.0 if the conversion cannot be performed.
---------------------------------------------------------------------*/
double Strings::Double(void)
{
  return strtod(String_, NULL);
}
```

Class **Strings** implementation file (cont.)

```
/*--- This function converts a String of digits to a long value.

    Pre:    This Strings object contains a sequence of digits.
    Return: The long value equivalent to those digits;
            0 if the conversion cannot be performed.
------------------------------------------------------------------------*/

long Strings::Long(void)
{
  return strtol(String_, NULL, 0);
}



/*--- This function converts a String of digits to an unsigned value.

    Pre:    This Strings object contains a sequence of digits.
    Return: The unsigned value equivalent to those digits;
            0 if the conversion cannot be performed.
------------------------------------------------------------------------*/

unsigned long Strings::Unsigned(void)
{
  return strtoul(String_, NULL, 0);
}



/*--- Assignment to a Strings object.

    Receive: Str, a (reference to a) Strings object.
    Return: This Strings object as a copy of Str.
------------------------------------------------------------------------*/

Strings& Strings::operator= (const Strings& Str)
{
  if (String_ != Str.String_)              // if the two are different
  {
    Length_ = Str.Length_;                 //    copy Length_ member
    delete [] String_;                     //    deallocate the array

    if (Str.String_ == 0)                  //    if Str is empty
       String_ = 0;                        //       make this empty too
    else                                   //    else
    {
       String_ = new char[Str.Length_+1];  //       allocate a new array
       assert(String_ != 0);               //       verify
       strcpy(String_, Str.String_);       //       fill array using Str
    }
  }
  return *this;                            // return this object
}
```

```
/*--- Subscript: Retrieve the character with a given index.

    Receive: i, an index into this Strings object.
    Return:  The (reference of the) char at index i.
-------------------------------------------------------------------------*/

char& Strings::operator[] (unsigned i)
{
  if (i < Length_)
    return String_[i];
  else
  {
    cerr << "\n*** Attempted access past end of String in [].\n";
    exit (-1);
  }
}

const char& Strings::operator[] (unsigned i) const
{
  if (i < Length_)
    return String_[i];
  else
  {
    cerr << "\n*** Attempted access past end of String in [].\n";
    exit (-1);
  }
}


/*--- Delete a portion of a Strings object.

    Receive: First, Last, two indices of this Strings object.
    Return:  This Strings object without the characters from First..Last
             True, if and only if the operation is successful.
-------------------------------------------------------------------------*/

int Strings::Delete(unsigned First, unsigned Last)
{
  if (Last >= Length_)                       // if Last past end of string
  {
    cerr << LastTooBig << "Delete.\n";       //    issue warning message
    Last = Length_ - 1;                      //    build empty part part
  }

  if (First > Last)                          // if Last not <= First
  {
    cerr << FirstPastLast << "Delete.\n";    //    issue error message
    return 0;                                //       and terminate
  }
```

```
    Strings                                      // return value's
      LeftPart,                                  //   left and
      RightPart;                                 //   right substrings

    if (First == 0)                              // if start at first char
      LeftPart = "";                             //   Left is empty
    else                                         // otherwise
      LeftPart = (*this)(0, First-1);            //   Left is before First

    if (Last == Length_ - 1)                     // if end is at last char
      RightPart ="";                             //     Right is empty
    else                                         // otherwise
      RightPart = (*this)(Last+1, Length_ - 1);  //     Right is past Last

    (*this) = LeftPart & RightPart;              // concatenate Left and Right

    return 1;                                    // indicate success
}

/*--- Insert one Strings object into another Strings object.

    Receive: Str, a Strings object; and
             Pos, an index within this Strings object.
    Return:  This Strings object with the characters of Str inserted
             starting at index Pos.
             True, if and only if the operation is successful.
-----------------------------------------------------------------------*/

int Strings::Insert(const Strings& Str, unsigned Pos)
{
  const char
    PosTooBig[] = "\nInsert: insertion point past end of string !\n";

  if (Pos > Length_)                             // if Pos past end of string
  {
     cerr << PosTooBig;                          //     display warning msg
     Pos = Length_;                              //     set Pos to NULL char
  }

  Strings                                        // return value's
    LeftPart,                                    //     left substring
    RightPart;                                   //     and right substring

  if (Pos == 0)                                  // if inserting at beginning
    LeftPart = "";                               //     Left is empty
  else                                           // otherwise
    LeftPart = (*this)(0, Pos-1);                //     Left is before Pos

  if (Pos == Length_)                            // if inserting at end
    RightPart = "";                              //     Right is empty
  else                                           // otherwise
    RightPart = (*this)(Pos, Length_-1);         //     Right is after Pos
```

```
   (*this) = LeftPart & Str & RightPart;      // concatenate Left, Str, Right

   return 1;                                  // return success
}

/*--- Replace a substring of a Strings object with another Strings object.

   Receive: First, Last, two indices of this Strings object;
            Str, a Strings object.
   Return:  This Strings object with its characters of First through
               Last replaced with those of Str.
            True, if and only if the operation is successful.
---------------------------------------------------------------------*/

int Strings::Replace(unsigned First, unsigned Last, const Strings& Str)
{
   if (Last >= Length_)                       // if Last past end of string
   {
      cerr << LastTooBig << "Replace.\n";     //   display warning msg
      Last = Length_ - 1;                     //   and set Last to last char
   }

   if (Last < First)                          // if First not <= Last
   {
      cerr << FirstPastLast << "Replace.\n";  //   display error msg
      return 1;                               //   and terminate
   }

   Delete(First, Last);                       // remove the substring to
                                              //   be replaced
   Insert(Str, First);                        // insert the replacement
                                              //   at position First
   return 0;                                  // indicate success
}

/*--- Find the position of a substring within a Strings object.

   Receive: Str, a Strings object.
   Return:  The index of the first occurrence of Str within *this
               (-1 if it is not present).
---------------------------------------------------------------------*/

int Strings::Position(const Strings& Str) const
{
   for (int i = 0; i < Length_; i++)          // for each substring of *this:
      if (strncmp(String_ + i,                //   if the substring at offset i
                  Str.String_,                //     and the string in Str
                  Str.Length()                //       (not counting the NULL)
                 ) == 0)                       //     are equal
         return i;                            //       then return the location
   return -1;                                 // Str is not in *this
}
```

Class **Strings** implementation file (cont.)

```
/*--- Concatenate two String objects.

   Receive: S1 and S2, two Strings objects.
   Return:  The Strings object consisting of S1 followed by S2.
--------------------------------------------------------------------*/

Strings operator& (const Strings& S1, const Strings& S2)
{
   Strings
     S;                                    // return value

   if (S1.String_ == 0)                    // if S1 is empty
      S = S2;                              //    we'll return S2
   else if (S2.String_ == 0)              // else if S2 is empty
      S = S1;                             //    we'll return S1
   else                                    // else
   {
      S.Length_ = S1.Length_ + S2.Length_;  //    set Length_
      S.String_ = new char[S.Length_+1];    //    allocate new array
      assert(S.String_ != 0);               //    verify
      strcpy(S.String_, S1.String_);        //    copy S1 into array
      strcat(S.String_, S2.String_);        //    append S2 to array
   }

   return S;                               // return the result
}


/*--- Retrieve a substring of a Strings object.

   Receive: First, Last, two indices of this Strings object;
   Return:  The substring of this Strings object that begins at
            index First and ends at index Last.
--------------------------------------------------------------------*/

Strings Strings::operator() (unsigned First, unsigned Last)
{

   if (Last >= Length_)                    // if Last beyond end of String
   {
      cerr << LastTooBig << "Substring.\n"; //    issue warning message
      Last = Length_ - 1;                   //    and set Last to end
   }

   if (First > Last)                       // if First not <= Last
   {
      cerr << FirstPastLast                 //    display error message
           << "Substring.\n";               //       with function name
      exit (-1);                            //       and terminate
   }
```

Class **Strings** implementation file (cont.)

```
Strings
  S;                                     // return value

S.Length_ = Last - First + 1;          // set its Length_ member
S.String_ = new char[Length_ + 1];     // allocate a new array
assert(S.String_ != 0);                // verify

int
  j = First;                           // index of char to be copied
for (int i = 0; i < S.Length_; i++)    // copy array of *this into S:
{
    S.String_[i] = String_[j];         //    char-by-char
    j++;
}
S.String_[i] = '\0';                   // tack on string-terminator

return S;                              // return the result
}


/**** Relational Operators ********************************************

Each of these operations has a similar specification:

    Receive: S1 and S2, two Strings objects.
    Return: True, if S1 OP S2 is true, and False, otherwise.
-------------------------------------------------------------------*/

// --- Equality.
int operator== (const Strings& S1, const Strings& S2)
{
  if (S1.String_ == S2.String_)        // if strings are same
    return 1;                          //    True
  else if ((S1.String_ == 0) ||        // else if either empty
           (S2.String_ == 0))
    return 0;                          //    False
  else                                 // else use the C routine
    return (strcmp(S1.String_, S2.String_) == 0);
}


int operator== (const Strings& S1, const char* S2)
{
  if (S1.String_ == S2)                // if strings are the same
    return 1;                          //    True
  else if ((S1.String_ == 0) ||        // else if either empty
           (S2 == 0))
    return 0;                          //    False
  else                                 // else use the C routine
    return (strcmp(S1.String_, S2) == 0);
}
```

Class **Strings** implementation file (cont.)

```
int operator== (const char* S1, const Strings& S2)
{
  if (S1 == S2.String_)              // if strings are same
    return 1;                        //    True
  else if ((S1 == 0) ||             // else if either empty
           (S2.String_ == 0))
    return 0;                        //    False
  else                               // else use the C routine
    return (strcmp(S1, S2.String_) == 0);
}


// --- Inequality.
int operator!= (const Strings& S1, const Strings& S2)
{
    return ! (S1 == S2);             // negate == from above
}


int operator!= (const Strings& S1, const char* S2)
{
    return ! (S1 == S2);             // negate == from above
}


int operator!= (const char* S1, const Strings& S2)
{
    return ! (S1 == S2);             // negate == from above
}


// --- Less-than.
int operator< (const Strings& S1, const Strings& S2)
{
  if (S1.String_ == S2.String_)      // if strings are same
    return 0;                        //    False
  else if (S1.String_ == 0)          // else if S1 is empty
    return 1;                        //    True
  else if (S2.String_ == 0)          // else if S2 is empty
    return 0;                        //    False
  else                               // else use the C routine
    return (strcmp(S1.String_, S2.String_) < 0);
}


int operator< (const Strings& S1, const char* S2)
{
  if (S1.String_ == S2)              // if strings are same
    return 0;                        //    False
  else if (S1.String_ == 0)          // else if S1 is empty
    return 1;                        //    True
  else if (S2 == 0)                  // else if S2 is empty
    return 0;                        //    False
  else                               // else use the C routine
    return (strcmp(S1.String_, S2) < 0);
}
```

Class **Strings** implementation file (cont.)

```
int operator< (const char* S1, const Strings& S2)
{
  if (S1 == S2.String_)              // if strings are same
    return 0;                        //    False
  else if (S1 == 0)                  // else if S1 is empty
    return 1;                        //    True
  else if (S2.String_ == 0)          // else if S2 is empty
    return 0;                        //    False
  else                               // else use the C routine
    return (strcmp(S1, S2.String_) < 0);
}


// --- Greater-than.
int operator> (const Strings& S1, const Strings& S2)
{
  if (S1.String_ == S2.String_)      // if strings are same
    return 0;                        //    False
  else if (S1.String_ == 0)          // else if S1 is empty
    return 1;                        //    True
  else if (S2.String_ == 0)          // else if S2 is empty
    return 0;                        //    False
  else                               // else use the C routine
    return (strcmp(S1.String_, S2.String_) > 0);
}


int operator> (const Strings& S1, const char* S2)
{
  if (S1.String_ == S2)              // if strings are same
    return 0;                        //    False
  else if (S1.String_ == 0)          // else if S1 is empty
    return 1;                        //    True
  else if (S2. == 0)                 // else if S2 is empty
    return 0;                        //    False
  else                               // else use the C routine
    return (strcmp(S1.String_, S2) > 0);
}


int operator> (const char* S1, const Strings& S2)
{
  if (S1 == S2.String_)              // if strings are same
    return 0;                        //    False
  else if (S1 == 0)                  // else if S1 is empty
    return 1;                        //    True
  else if (S2.String_ == 0)          // else if S2 is empty
    return 0;                        //    False
  else                               // else use the C routine
    return (strcmp(S1, S2.String_) > 0);
}
```

Class **Strings** implementation file (cont.)

```
// --- Less-or-equal.
int operator<= (const Strings& S1, const Strings& S2)
{
  return !(S1 > S2);                 // negate > from above
}

int operator<= (const Strings& S1, const char* S2)
{
  return !(S1 > S2);                 // negate > from above
}

int operator<= (const char* S1, const Strings& S2)
{
  return !(S1 > S2);                 // negate > from above
}

//--- Greater-or-equal.
int operator>= (const Strings& S1, const Strings& S2)
{
  return !(S1 < S2);                 // negate < from above
}

int operator>= (const Strings& S1, const char* S2)
{
  return !(S1 < S2);                 // negate < from above
}

int operator>= (const char* S1, const Strings& S2)
{
  return !(S1 < S2);                 // negate < from above
}


//***** Input/Output ***************************************

/*--- Stream input.

   Receive: InStream, an istream object;
            Str, a Strings object.
   Input:   A line of (up to MaxLength) chars from InStream
   Return:  Str, filled with the input chars, and
            OutStream.
------------------------------------------------------------*/

istream& operator>> (istream& InStream, Strings& Str)
{
  char
    Buffer[Strings::MaxLength];              // temporary string storage

  InStream >> Buffer;                        // read in the string
```

Class **Strings** implementation file (cont.)

```
Str.Length_ = strlen(Buffer);                    // set Length_ member

delete [] Str.String_;                           // remove any prior array

Str.String_ = new char[Str.Length_+1];           // allocate new array
assert(Str.String_ != 0);                        // verify, and
strcpy(Str.String_, Buffer);                     // copy the buffer into it

return InStream;                                 // return the istream
}


/*--- Stream output.

   Receive: OutStream, an ostream object;
            Str, a Strings object.
   Output:  Str onto OutStream.
   Return:  OutStream.

Note: The same functions suffice for file I/O,
      since an fstream is-an istream and an fstream is-an ostream.
-----------------------------------------------------------------------*/

ostream& operator<< (ostream& OutStream, const Strings& Str)
{
  OutStream << Str.String_;                       // output the array

  return OutStream;                               // return the ostream
}


/*--- This Strings member acts like getline for an istream...

   Receive:   In, an istream,
              MaxChars, the maximum number of chars to be read, and
              UntilChar, a delimiter char to halt the operation.
   Input(In): Up to MaxChars characters, or until UntilChar is read,
                whichever comes first.
   Return:    The Strings object containing this function,
                filled with the input characters.
              In.

Note: The same function works for a file, as an fstream is-an istream.
-----------------------------------------------------------------------*/

istream& Strings::GetLine(istream& In, unsigned MaxChars, char UntilChar)
{
  char
    Buffer[MaxLength];                            // temporary string storage

  In.getline(Buffer,                              // read in the line
             (MaxLength < MaxChars) ? MaxLength : MaxChars,
             UntilChar);
```

Class **Strings** implementation file (cont.)

```
   Length_ = strlen(Buffer);                   // set Length_

   delete [] String_;                          // remove any prior array

   String_ = new char [Length_ + 1];           // allocate new array
   assert(String_ != 0);                       // verify, and
   strcpy(String_, Buffer);                    // copy the buffer into it

   return In;                                   // return the istream
}
```

F.2 Class RandomInt

In Chapter 7, we provided a class **RandomInt** that could be used to conveniently generate random numbers. This section of Appendix F presents the source code for class **RandomInt**.

Class **RandomInt** header file

```
/* This file presents the interface for the RandomInt class,
      a class that provides a RandomInt data type, as well as
      convenient operations on RandomInt objects.

   Written by: Joel C. Adams, Spring, 1993, at Calvin College.
   -----------------------------------------------------------*/

#ifndef RANDOMINT
#define RANDOMINT

#include <iostream.h>
#include <stdlib.h>

class RandomInt
{
   int
      LowerBound,            // the lower limit on random values
      UpperBound,            // the upper limit on random values
      RandomValue;           // the actual value chosen

   public:

   /*--- This is the class constructor for class RandomInt.

      Precondition:  A RandomInt object has been declared.
      Receive:       Low, the lower bound of the range of random values;
                     High, the upper bound of the range of random values.
      Postcondition: That object's members are initialized.
      -----------------------------------------------------------*/
```

Class **RandomInt** header file (cont.)

```
RandomInt(int Low = 0, int High = RAND_MAX);

/*--- This function converts a RandomInt to an integer,
        whenever its context is appropriate.

    Return: The RandomValue member of this object.
---------------------------------------------------------------*/

operator int() {return RandomValue;}

/*--- This function generates the next random number.

    Receive: Low, an optional lower bound on the range of random values;
             High, an optional upper bound on the range of random values
                (if Low and High are omitted, the constructed values are used).
    Return:  This object, its RandomValue member set to a random
             number from the range Low...High.
---------------------------------------------------------------*/

RandomInt Generate(int Low = 0, int High = 0);

/*--- This is the assignment operator for a RandomInt.

    Receive: A RandomInt object, RInt.
    Return:  This RandomInt object, its members identical to those
             of RInt.
---------------------------------------------------------------*/

RandomInt& operator=(const RandomInt& RInt);

/*--- This function performs the output operation for a RandomInt.

    Receive: An ostream and a RandomInt.
    Output:  The RandomInt onto the ostream.
    Return:  The ostream.
---------------------------------------------------------------*/

    friend ostream& operator<<(ostream& Out, const RandomInt& RInt);
};

#endif
```

The header file is, of course, named **RandomInt.h**, but as mentioned in Chapter 4, the name of the implementation file differs from one C++ environment to another. In the GNU environment (UNIX), we named our implementation file **RandomInt.C**; while in the Turbo C++ environment (DOS), we named it **RANDOMINT.CPP**; and in the Symantec C++ environment (MacOS), we named it **RandomInt.cpp**.

Class **RandomInt** implementation file

```
/* This file contains the definitions of the operations of class RandomInt.
   The declaration of class RandomInt can be found in RandomInt.h

   Written by: Joel C. Adams, Spring, 1993, at Calvin College.
   ----------------------------------------------------------------------*/

#include "RandomInt.h"

#include <time.h>

/*--- This is the class constructor for class RandomInt.

      Precondition:  A RandomInt object has been declared.
      Receive:       Low, the lower bound of the range of random values;
                     High, the upper bound of the range of random values.
      Postcondition: That object's members are initialized.
   ------------------------------------------------------------*/

RandomInt::RandomInt(int Low, int High)
{
   if (Low < 0)                          // check
   {
      cerr << "\n*** RandomInt: lower bound cannot "
           << "be negative (using zero).\n";
      LowerBound = 0;
   }
   else
      LowerBound = Low;

   if (High <= Low)
   {
      cerr << "\n*** RandomInt: upper bound must exceed "
           << "lower bound (using " << RAND_MAX << ").\n";
      UpperBound = RAND_MAX;
   }
   else
      UpperBound = High;

   long
      SeedVal = long(time(0));    // seed value

   srand(SeedVal);               // seed the generator

   RandomValue = LowerBound + rand() % (UpperBound - LowerBound + 1);
}
```

Class **RandomInt** implementation file (cont.)

```
/*--- This function generates the next random number.

   Receive: Low, an optional lower bound on the range of random values;
            High, an optional upper bound on the range of random values
               (if Low and High are omitted, the constructed values are used).
   Return:  This object, its RandomValue member set to a random
               number from the range Low...High.
   ---------------------------------------------------------------*/

RandomInt RandomInt::Generate(int Low, int High)
{
   if (Low || High)                      // new range specified
   {
      if (Low < 0)
      {
         cerr << "\n*** RandomInt: lower bound cannot "
              << "be negative (using zero).\n";
         LowerBound = 0;
      }
      else
         LowerBound = Low;

      if (High <= Low)
      {
         cerr << "\n*** RandomInt: upper bound must exceed "
              << "lower bound (using " << RAND_MAX << ").\n";
         UpperBound = RAND_MAX;
      }
      else
         UpperBound = High;
   }

   RandomValue = LowerBound + rand() % (UpperBound - LowerBound + 1);

   return *this;
}

/*--- This is the assignment operator for a RandomInt.

   Receive: a RandomInt object, RInt.
   Return:  This RandomInt object, its members identical to those
               of RInt.
   ---------------------------------------------------------------*/
```

Class **RandomInt** implementation file (cont.)

```
RandomInt& RandomInt::operator=(const RandomInt& RInt)
{
   LowerBound = RInt.LowerBound;
   UpperBound = RInt.UpperBound;

   RandomValue = RInt.RandomValue;

   return *this;
}

/*--- This function performs the output operation for a RandomInt.

   Receive: An ostream and a RandomInt.
   Output:  The RandomInt onto the ostream.
   Return:  The ostream.
------------------------------------------------------------------*/

ostream& operator<<(ostream& Out, const RandomInt& RInt)
{
   Out << RInt.RandomValue;

   return Out;
}
```

GRAPHICS

Section 14.5 (PART OF THE PICTURE: Computer Graphics) described how a graphics window can be thought of as a two-dimensional array of pixels. Using the Turbo C++ environment, we have constructed a class named **CartesianSystem** that provides an assortment of graphics capabilities. Section 14.5 illustrated its use with two programs, one that used the class to draw the graph of a function F(*x*), and one that used the class to draw the density plot of a function F(*x*, *y*).

As discussed in Section 14.5, graphics libraries are not standardized, so that a **CartesianSystem** class that is written for the Turbo environment is not directly portable to the Macintosh or UNIX environments (although class **CartesianSystem** can be converted to use the graphics libraries of either of these environments, instead of that of the Turbo environment). For the sake of clarity, we have marked each call to a Turbo graphics function with the comment:

    // GFX funct

and each use of a Turbo graphics constant with the comment

    // GFX const

Class **CartesianSystem** can be ported from one environment to another by replacing such calls with the equivalent graphics function in the new environment.

The class declaration is given in Figure G.1:

FIGURE G.1   Class **CartesianSystem**

```
/* This class models a Cartesian coordinate system.

   ... other documentation omitted ...
-------------------------------------------------------------------------*/


#include <graphics.h>                       // the Turbo graphics lib

#ifndef CARTSYS
#define CARTSYS

typedef double (*FunctionOfX)(double);
typedef double (*FunctionOfXandY)(double, double);

class CartesianSystem
{
  protected:

    // *** Constants *********************************************
    enum { NumColors = 7 };                 // density plot colors


    // *** Data Members (Set by Constructor) ********************
    long
        ColorArray[NumColors],              // array of the colors
        LastRow,                            // screen size variables
        LastCol,                            // (dependent on monitor)
        BottomMargin,                       // space for prompts
        xAxisRow,                           // useful values in
        yAxisCol;                           //   drawing the axes
    double
        xMin, xMax,                         // x-axis endpoints
        yMin, yMax,                         // y-axis endpoints
        zMin, zMax,                         // z-axis endpoints
        xDelta,                             // change per pixel
        yDelta,                             //   for x, y and z
        zDelta,
        xAxisIncrement,                     // useful values in
        yAxisIncrement;                     //   drawing the axes


            // *** PRIVATE UTILITY FUNCTIONS ***********

    long round(double RealVal)              // round off a double value
    {
        return long (RealVal + 0.5);
    }
```

FIGURE G.1   Class **CartesianSystem** (cont.)

```
long yToRow(double y)                    // map y-value to y-pixel
{
    return LastRow -                     // pixels run top to bottom
           BottomMargin -                // leave space for margin
           round( (y - yMin) / yDelta);  // scale into y-pixel range
}

long xToCol(double x)                    // map x-value to x-pixel
{
    return round( (x - xMin) / xDelta);  // scale into x-pixel range
}


public: // *** PUBLIC INTERFACE FUNCTIONS ***********

  /* --- Class Constructor-------------------------------------------

      Pre:     A CartesianSystem object has been declared.
      Receive: The extrema for the x, y, and z axes.
      Post:    The screen has been initialized to display
               a Cartesian system with the given extrema.
      ------------------------------------------------------------*/
  CartesianSystem(double xLo, double xHi,
                  double yLo, double yHi,
                  double zLo = 0, double zHi = 0);

  /* --- Class Destructor -------------------------------------------

      Pre:  A CartesianSystem object's lifetime is over.
      Post: The screen is returned to its previous status.
      ------------------------------------------------------------*/
  ~CartesianSystem(void) { closegraph(); }      // GFX funct

  /* --- DisplayMsg puts a message in the bottom margin.

      Receive: Msg, a character string to be displayed.
      Output:  Msg, within the CartesianSystem margin.
      ------------------------------------------------------------*/
  void DisplayMsg(char* Msg);

  /* --- AwaitUser pauses until the user presses <Enter>.

      Input: a single character.
      ------------------------------------------------------------*/
  void AwaitUser(void)
  {   char Ch; cin.get(Ch); }
```

FIGURE G.1 Class **CartesianSystem** (cont.)

```
/* --- DrawAxes displays labeled x and y axes ---------------------

     Output: Labeled x and y axes, appropriately scaled.
--------------------------------------------------------------------*/
void DrawAxes(void);

/* --- PlotPoint displays a single (x, y) point ------------------

     Receive: x and y, two double values.
     Output:  The pixel corresponding to (x, y) is "on".
--------------------------------------------------------------------*/
void PlotPoint(double x, double y,
               int Color = YELLOW)          // GFX const
     {putpixel(xToCol(x), yToRow(y), Color);}   // GFX funct

/* --- Graph displays the graph of a function F(x) -----------------

     Receive: F, a (pointer to a) function F(x).
     Output:  The CartesianSystem graph of F.
--------------------------------------------------------------------*/
void Graph(FunctionOfX F, int Color = YELLOW); // GFX const

/* DensityPlot displays a function F(x, y)'s density plot.

     Receive: F, a (pointer to a) function F(x, y).
     Output:  The CartesianSystem density plot of F,
              looking down the z-axis.
--------------------------------------------------------------------*/
void DensityPlot(FunctionOfXandY F);
};
#endif
```

The functions defined within class **CartesianSystem** contain two calls to Turbo graphics functions:

- The class destructor uses the function **closegraph()** to "turn off" graphics mode.
- The **PlotPoint()** function uses the function **putpixel()** to plot a particular (x, y) point.

The **CartesianSystem** class constructor must do all that is necessary to initialize the screen for graphics display, as well as initialize the various data members of the class. Figure G.2 presents the definition of the class constructor, minus its leading documentation:

FIGURE G.2 `CartesianSystem` class constructor

```
CartesianSystem::CartesianSystem(double xLo, double xHi,
                                 double yLo, double yHi,
                                 double zLo, double zHi)
{
    EnterGraphicsMode("C:\\TC\\BGI");    // set display for gfx

    xMin = xLo; xMax = xHi;              // initialize members
    yMin = yLo; yMax = yHi;
    zMin = zLo; zMax = zHi;

    LastRow = getmaxy();                 // GFX funct
    LastCol = getmaxx();                 // GFX funct
    BottomMargin = 15;

    xDelta = (xMax - xMin) / (LastCol+1-BottomMargin);
    yDelta = (yMax - yMin) / (LastRow+1-BottomMargin);
    zDelta = (zMax - zMin) / NumColors;

    xAxisIncrement = (xMax - xMin) / 12.0;
    yAxisIncrement = (yMax - yMin) / 10.0;
    xAxisRow = yToRow(0.0);
    yAxisCol = xToCol(0.0);

    ColorArray[0] = BROWN;               // GFX const
    ColorArray[1] = DARKGRAY;            // GFX const
    ColorArray[2] = BLUE;                // GFX const
    ColorArray[3] = CYAN;                // GFX const
    ColorArray[4] = LIGHTRED;            // GFX const
    ColorArray[5] = YELLOW;              // GFX const
    ColorArray[6] = WHITE;               // GFX const
}
```

The class constructor definition contains two calls to Turbo graphics functions:

- `getmaxx()` returns the index of the last (pixel) column on the screen; and
- `getmaxy()` returns the index of the last (pixel) row on the screen.

Note that *x* values map to *columns* and *y* values map to *rows*. A call to a drawing function such as `putpixel()`:

```
putpixel(x, y);
```

thus takes its arguments in (*column*, *row*) order; ordering them as (*row*, *column*) will result in a logical error.

In order for graphics functions to have any effect, the constructor must initialize the screen for graphics output. This is accomplished by the function `EnterGraphicsMode()`, whose definition is in Figure G.3:

 FIGURE G.3   Enabling Turbo graphics

```
#include <iostream.h>                        // cerr, <<
#include <stdlib.h>                          // exit()

void EnterGraphicsMode(char GraphicsPath[])
{
    int
        GraphDriver = DETECT;                // GFX const
    int
        GraphMode;
                                             // GFX function
    initgraph(&GraphDriver, &GraphMode, GraphicsPath);

    int
        GraphError = graphresult();          // GFX funct

    if (GraphError != grOk)                  // GFX const
    {
        cerr << "\nEnterGraphicsMode Error: "
             << grapherrormsg(GraphError)    // GFX funct
             << "\n\n";
        exit (-1);
    }
}
```

The function uses five names defined in Turbo graphics:

- `initgraph()`, a function that initializes the screen for graphics display;
- `DETECT`, a value that instructs `initgraph()` to sense the kind of monitor being used;
- `graphresult()`, a function that indicates the result of the preceding graphics operation;
- `grOk`, one of the constants returned by `graphresult()`; and
- `grapherrormsg()`, a function that given a `graphresult()` return-value, displays an informative error message.

Note that in Figure G.2, the call

```
EnterGraphicsMode("C:\\TC\\BGI");
```

is used to pass the path to the graphics library, which is in turn passed to `initgraph()`. *This path must be appropriate for your particular system,* and the double back slashes are needed, since that path is a character string (see Section 3.3).

The axes in a coordinate system provide a meaningful point of reference for whatever other values are displayed. We thus provide a **DrawAxes()** function that displays the axes appropriate for the particular **CartesianSystem** defined by the user of the class. Its definition is shown in Figure G.4:

FIGURE G.4   Drawing **CartesianSystem** axes

```
#include <stdio.h>                      // sprintf()

void CartesianSystem::DrawAxes(void)
{                                       // draw x-axis (GFX function)
    line(0, xAxisRow,                   //   starting at this point
        LastCol, xAxisRow);             //   and ending at this point
    line(yAxisCol, 0,                   // draw y-axis (GFX function)
        yAxisCol, LastRow-BottomMargin);

    char Buffer[12];                    // label axes
    const int Offset = 5;
    long PixelX, PixelY;


                                        // label y-axis
    settextstyle(                       // GFX funct
                SMALL_FONT,             // GFX const: the font
                HORIZ_DIR,              // GFX const: horizontal text
                3);                     // scaling factor
    settextjustify(                     // GFX funct: justification
                RIGHT_TEXT,             // GFX const: horizontal just.
                CENTER_TEXT);           // GFX const: vertical just.
                                        // draw the labels
    for (double y = yMax; y >= yMin; y -= yAxisIncrement)
    {
        if ((y > yAxisIncrement/2.0) ||         // avoid crowding
            (y < (-yAxisIncrement)/2.0))        //   the origin
        {
            PixelY = yToRow(y);
            line(yAxisCol-Offset, PixelY,       // GFX funct:
                yAxisCol+Offset, PixelY);       //   draw marker
            sprintf(Buffer, "%.3f", y);         // create label
            outtextxy(yAxisCol-Offset, PixelY,  // GFX funct: draw
                    Buffer);                    //   string in Buffer
        }
    }


                                        // label x-axis
    settextjustify(                     // GFX funct: justification
                CENTER_TEXT,            // GFX const: horizontal just.
                TOP_TEXT);              // GFX const: vertical just.
                                        // draw the labels as before
```

FIGURE G.4 Drawing **CartesianSystem** axes (cont.)

```
    for (double x = xMin; x <= xMax; x += xAxisIncrement)
    {
        if ((x > xAxisIncrement/2.0) ||           // avoid crowding
            (x < (-xAxisIncrement)/2.0))          //  the origin
        {
            PixelX = xToCol(x);
            line(PixelX, xAxisRow-Offset,         // GFX funct
                PixelX, xAxisRow+Offset);
            sprintf(Buffer, "%.3f", x);           // create label
            outtextxy(PixelX, xAxisRow+Offset,    // GFX funct
                    Buffer);
        }
    }
}
```

DrawAxes() is conceptually quite simple, but its implementation requires a number of graphics functions and constants. The details of these can be found in the documentation of **GRAPHICS.LIB**, or in the Turbo on-line help facility.

Once the axes are drawn, we are ready to graph a function. Figure G.5 presents the definition of function **Graph()**:

FIGURE G.5 Graphing a function

```
void CartesianSystem::Graph(FunctionOfX F, int Color)
{
    double
        x = xMin,                            // init x
        y;
    long
        PixelX,
        PixelY;

    DrawAxes();                              // draw axes

    for (PixelX = 0; PixelX <= LastCol; PixelX++) // for each x-pixel:
    {
        y = (*F)(x);                         // compute y-value
        if ((y >= yMin) && (y <= yMax))      // if it's viewable
        {
            PixelY = yToRow(y);              //   display it
            putpixel(PixelX, PixelY, Color); //   GFX funct
        }
        x += xDelta;                         // next x
    }
    DisplayMsg("Press <Enter> to continue..."); // prompt user
    AwaitUser();                             // await response
}
```

`Graph()` simply goes through each x-pixel and plots the appropriate y-value for that pixel. When graphing is completed, it displays a message in the bottom border using `DisplayMsg()`, whose definition of `DisplayMsg()` is given in Figure G.6:

FIGURE G.6   Displaying a message

```
void CartesianSystem::DisplayMsg(char* Msg)
{
    settextjustify(                   // GFX funct: justification
                CENTER_TEXT,          // GFX const: horizontal just.
                BOTTOM_TEXT);         // GFX const: vertical just.
    settextstyle(                     // GFX funct:
                DEFAULT_FONT,         // GFX const: the font
                HORIZ_DIR,            // GFX const: text orientation
                1);                   // scaling factor
    outtextxy(                        // GFX funct: draw text
                LastCol/2, LastRow,   // at this point
                Msg);}
```

Function `Graph()` then uses `AwaitUser()` to suspend execution until the user wants it to continue. The definition of `AwaitUser()` can be seen in Figure G.1.

The final member of class `CartesianSystem` is function `DensityPlot()`, whose definition is given in Figure G.7:

FIGURE G.7   Drawing a density plot

```
void CartesianSystem::DensityPlot(FunctionOfXandY F)
{
    long
        PixelX,
        PixelY,
        zColor;
    double
        x,
        y = yMin,
        z;
                                           // give user feedback
    DisplayMsg("When drawing is complete, press <Enter> to continue.");

                                           // for each row
    for (PixelY = 0; PixelY < LastRow-BottomMargin; PixelY++)
    {
        x = xMin;                          // for each column
        for (PixelX = 0; PixelX < LastCol; PixelX++)
        {
            z = (*F)(x, y);                // compute F(x,y)
```

FIGURE G.7 Drawing a density plot (cont.)

```
        if (z >= zMax)                // map z into a color
            zColor = NumColors-1;     // maximum color index
        else if (z <= zMin)
            zColor = 0;               // minimum color index
        else
            zColor = round( (z-zMin)/zDelta );

        putpixel(                     // GFX funct:
                PixelX, PixelY,       //   plot a pixel of the
                ColorArray[zColor]);  //   appropriate color

        x += xDelta;                  // next x
    }
    y += yDelta;                      // next y
  }

  DrawAxes();                         // draw axes when done
  AwaitUser();                        // await user response
}
```

Note that on a VGA monitor, **DensityPlot()** must separately plot each of the $640 \times 480 = 307,200$ pixels on the screen. It can thus be a fairly time-consuming function.

The preceding figures demonstrate the use of the **putpixel()**, **line()**, and **outtextxy()** functions that draw points, lines, and text, respectively. In addition to these functions, Turbo's **GRAPHICS.LIB** library provides the functions:

```
void circle(int PixelX, int PixelY, int Radius)
```

that can be used to draw a circle on the screen of radius *Radius* centered at (*PixelX, PixelY*); and

```
void rectangle(int UpperLeftCornerX, int UpperLeftCornerY,
               int LowerRightCornerX, int LowerRightCornerY);
```

that can be used to draw rectangles (boxes) on the screen; and the more general

```
void  drawpoly(int NumberOfVertices, int VertexArray[]);
```

that can be used to draw an arbitrary polygon, whose vertices' (x, y) coordinate pairs are stored in **PointArray**.

Each of these capabilities can be incorporated into class `CartesianSystem` by adding a member function that calls the appropriate function. For example, a `DrawBox()` function for class `CartesianSystem` can be defined as follows:

```
void DrawBox(int TopLeftX, int TopLeftY,
             int BottomRightX, int BottomRightY)
{
   rectangle(xToCol(TopLeftX), yToRow(TopLeftY),
             xToCol(BottomRightX), yToRow(BottomRightY));
}
```

These primitive graphics operations can then be used to construct more complicated graphics objects, such as bar graphs, pie charts, histograms, windows, menus, and so on.

There are many more capabilities provided by Turbo's graphics library (and those of the other environments). For more information, the interested reader is encouraged to explore the Turbo on-line help facility and/or the system documentation.

GAUSSIAN ELIMINATION

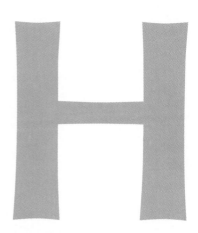

Section 11.4 (PART OF THE PICTURE: Numerical Methods) illustrated the method of Gaussian elimination for solving a system of linear equations. The following algorithm summarizes this method. To minimize the effect of roundoff error in the computations, it rearranges the rows to obtain as a pivot the element that is largest in absolute value. Note that if it is not possible to find a nonzero pivot element at some stage, then the linear system is said to be a singular system and does not have a unique solution.

GAUSSIAN ELIMINATION ALGORITHM

/* This algorithm solves the linear system $Ax = b$, using Gaussian elimination, where x is the $n \times 1$ vector of unknowns.

Input: An $n \times n$ coefficient matrix A and an $n \times 1$ constant vector b.

Return: The solution vector x, if one can be found.

Output: A message if the matrix is found to be singular.

——*/

1. a. Input A and b.
   b. Form the $n \times (n + 1)$ augmented matrix Aug by adjoining b to A:

$$Aug = [A \,\vert\, b]$$

2. For i ranging from 1 to n, do the following:
   a. Find the entry $Aug[k, i]$, $k = i, i + 1, \ldots, n$ that has the largest absolute value.
   b. Interchange row i and row k.
   c. If $Aug[i, i] = 0$, display a message that the linear system is singular and stop processing.
   d. For j ranging from $i + 1$ to n, do the following:

   Add $\dfrac{-Aug[j, i]}{Aug[i, i]}$ times the ith row of Aug to the jth row of Aug to eliminate $x[i]$ from the jth equation.

3. a. Set $x[n]$ equal to $\dfrac{Aug[n, n + 1]}{Aug[n, n]}$.

  b. For j ranging from $n-1$ to 1 in steps of -1, do the following:
    Substitute the values of $x[j + 1], \ldots, x[n]$ in the jth equation and
    solve for $x[j]$.

The function in Figure H.1 implements this algorithm for Gaussian elimination. Since each of the three steps of the algorithm are nontrivial, we have implemented them as the utility functions **ReadEquations()**, **Reduce()**, and **Solve()**.

 FIGURE H.1 Gaussian elimination

```
/* --- GaussElim performs the Gaussian elimination algorithm ----------

   Input:  The coefficients of a linear system and its constant vector.
   Return: The solution to the linear system.
   ------------------------------------------------------------------*/

#include <stdlib.h>

void ReadEquations(Matrix& AugMat);
int Reduce(Matrix& AugMat);
Matrix Solve(Matrix& AugMat);

Matrix GaussElim(void)
{
  Matrix                       // construct an empty matrix
     AugMat;

  ReadEquations(AugMat);       // fill it with coefficients and constants

  int
     Singular = Reduce(AugMat); // reduce to triangular form

  if (Singular)                // check for singularity
  {
     cerr << "\n*** GaussElim: Linear system is (nearly) singular!\n";
     exit (0);
  }

  Matrix
     SolVect = Solve(AugMat);   // solve from triangular form

  return SolVect;              // return solution
}
```

The definitions of functions `ReadEquations()`, `Reduce()`, and `Solve()` (as well as some other utility functions they utilize) are shown in Figure H.2:

FIGURE H.2 Gaussian elimination utility functions

```
/* --- ReadEquations inputs and builds the augmented matrix.

    Receive: AugMat, an (empty) matrix.
    Input:   The linear system coefficients, and constant values.
    Return:  AugMat, filled with the input values.
    -------------------------------------------------------------*/

void ReadEquations(Matrix& AugMat)
{
  int
    NumEquations;

  for (;;)                           // get matrix dimensions
  {
      cout << "\nPlease enter the number of equations in the system: ";
      cin >> NumEquations;
      if (NumEquations > 1)
        break;
      cerr << "\n*** At least two equations are needed ...\n";
  }
                                     // build a matrix of
  AugMat = Matrix(NumEquations,      // NumEquations rows &
                  NumEquations+1);   // NumEquations+1 columns

                                     // get the coefficients
  cout << "\nPlease enter the coefficient matrix row-by-row...\n";
  for (int r = 0; r < NumEquations; r++)
    for (int c = 0; c < NumEquations; c++)
      cin >> AugMat[r][c];
                                     // get the constants
  cout << "\nPlease enter the constant vector...\n";
  for (r = 0; r < NumEquations; r++)
    cin >> AugMat[r][NumEquations];
}

/* --- Abs performs the absolute value function on a double value --- */

double Abs(double Val)
{
  return (Val < 0) ? -(Val) : Val;
}
```

FIGURE H.2 Gaussian elimination utility functions (cont.)

```
/* --- Swap exchanges the values of two double variables ------------- */

void Swap(double& a, double& b)
{
  double
    t = a;

  a = b;
  b = t;
}

/* --- Reduce simplifies an augmented matrix into triangular form ------

    Receive: AugMat, and augmented matrix.
    Return:  If the linear system is non-singular:
                AugMat, reduced to a triangular matrix; and
                True.
             Else
                False.
------------------------------------------------------------------------*/

int Reduce(Matrix& AugMat)
{
  const double
    Epsilon = 1.0E-6;
  int
    Singular = 0,
    i = 0,
    j,
    k,
    n = AugMat.NumberOfRows(),
    PivotRow;
  double
    Mult,
    AbsPivot;

  while ((!Singular) && (i < n))
  {
    AbsPivot = Abs(AugMat[i][i]);
    PivotRow = i;

    for (k = i+1; k < n; k++)
      if (Abs(AugMat[k][i]) > AbsPivot)
      {
        AbsPivot = Abs(AugMat[k][i]);
        PivotRow = k;
      }

    Singular = AbsPivot < Epsilon;
```

FIGURE H.2   Gaussian elimination utility functions (cont.)

```
    if (!Singular)
    {
        if (i != PivotRow)
            for (j = 0; j <= n; j++)
                Swap(AugMat[i][j], AugMat[PivotRow][j]);

        for (j = i+1; j < n; j++)
        {
            Mult = -AugMat[j][i] / AugMat[i][i];
            for (k = i; k <= n; k++)
                AugMat[j][k] = AugMat[j][k] + Mult * AugMat[i][k];
        }
    }
    i++;
  }
  return Singular;
}


/* --- Solve determines the solution of the linear system -------------

    Receive: AugMat, an augmented matrix (reduced to triangular form).
    Return:  The solution vector to the linear system.
--------------------------------------------------------------------*/

Matrix Solve(Matrix& AugMat)
{
  Matrix
    SolVect(1, AugMat.NumberOfRows());
  int
    n = AugMat.NumberOfRows()-1;

  SolVect[0][n] = AugMat[n][n+1] / AugMat[n][n];

  for (int i = n-1; i >= 0; i--)
    {
      SolVect[0][i] = AugMat[i][n+1];

      for (int j = i+1; j <= n; j++)
        SolVect[0][i] -= AugMat[i][j] * SolVect[0][j];

      SolVect[0][i] /= AugMat[i][i];
    }

  return SolVect;
}
```

Note that because real numbers are not stored exactly, the statement implementing Step 2c checks if the absolute value of element [i][i] is less than some small positive number **Epsilon** rather than exactly 0.

Given function `GaussElim()`, we can construct a relatively simple driver program to solve an arbitrary system of linear equations. Figure H.3 presents such a driver program.

 FIGURE H.3   Gaussian elimination driver program

```
/* This program is a driver program for a Gaussian elimination function.

    Input:  A series of linear equation coefficients.
    Output: The solution of the linear equations.
-----------------------------------------------------------------------*/

#include <iostream.h>

#include "Matrix.h"

Matrix GaussElim(void);

int main(void)
{
   cout << "\nThis program solves a linear system"
        << " using Gaussian elimination.\n";

   Matrix
       SolutionVector = GaussElim();

   cout << endl << "The solution vector (x1, x2, ...)"
        << " for this system is:\n\n"
        << SolutionVector << "\n\n";

   return 0;
}
```

Sample runs

```
This program solves a linear system using Gaussian elimination.

Please enter the number of equations in the system: 3

Please enter the coefficient matrix row-by-row...
5 -1 -2
-1 5 -2
-2 -2 7

Please enter the constant vector...
11 0 0

The solution vector (x1, x2, ...) for this system is:

    2.84      1.01       1.10
```

FIGURE H.3   Gaussian elimination driver program (cont.)

```
This program solves a linear system using Gaussian elimination.

Please enter the number of equations in the system: 4

Please enter the coefficient matrix row-by-row...
4 4 -5 2
3 3 5 -1
2 1 -1 1
-1 1 -1 1

Please enter the constant vector...
7 9 4 1

The solution vector (x1, x2, ...) for this system is:

     1.00       1.00       1.00       2.00


This program solves a linear system using Gaussian elimination.

Please enter the number of equations in the system: 3

Please enter the coefficient matrix row-by-row...
1 1 1
2 3 4
3 4 5

Please enter the constant vector...
1 2 3

*** GaussElim: Linear system is (nearly) singular!
```

Given this implementation, it is easy to see that Gaussian elimination is essentially an operation on a special kind of matrix. It is accordingly quite easy to derive a new class **EquationSolver** from class **Matrix** (just as **Matrix** is derived from **Table**) and then implement **GaussElim()** as a public member function of this class (and the utility functions as private members). Doing so is left as an exercise for the reader.

TEMPLATES

Introduction

In Chapter 7, we saw that a library of `Swap()` functions could be written, with the header file:

```
/* This file presents the interface to library Swap,
     a collection of functions for exchanging the values of two variables.
 --------------------------------------------------------------------*/

                                          // exchange the values of:
void Swap(char& First, char& Second);           // chars
void Swap(short& First, short& Second);         // shorts
void Swap(int& First, int& Second);             // ints
void Swap(long& First, long& Second);           // longs
void Swap(float& First, float& Second);         // floats
void Swap(double& First, double& Second);       // doubles
void Swap(long double& First, long double& Second);// long doubles
```

and an implementation file, part of which might appear as follows:

```
. . .
#include "Swap.h"

void Swap(char & First, char & Second)
{
   char
      Temporary = First;

   First = Second;
   Second = Temporary;
}
```

```
void Swap(int& First, int& Second)
{
    int
        Temporary = First;

    First = Second;
    Second = Temporary;
}
```
. . .

This approach is inconvenient, because each of these functions uses exactly the same logic—the definition for a **double** version of **Swap()** will look exactly the same as that for the **char** version, except that its data objects will be of type **double** instead of type **char**. Moreover, if we wish to swap two values of some programmer-defined type (e.g., **Employee**), our library is useless, since it only defines the **Swap()** function for the C++ fundamental types.

Function Templates

Since each version of **Swap()** uses the same logic regardless of the type of its arguments, a superior approach would be to somehow define **Swap()** as a "generic" function, that is, a function that is independent of any particular type. This can be done in C++ using the *template* mechanism, as follows:

 FIGURE I.1   A swap template

```
#ifndef SWAP
#define SWAP

/* Swap exchanges the values of any two objects of the same type,
        for which the assignment operation is defined.

    Precondition:  First and Second are two objects of the same type.
    Postcondition: The values of First and Second have been exchanged.
-----------------------------------------------------------------*/

template <class Item>
void Swap(Item &First, Item &Second)
{
    Item
        Temporary = First;

    First = Second;
    Second = Temporary;
}

#endif
```

The **<class Item>** in this definition names **Item** as a **type-parameter**—that is, a parameter whose value will be supplied (by the compiler) by the type of the arguments when **Swap()** is called. This single function definition (stored in a header file **Swap.h**[1]) is then sufficient to exchange the values of any two data objects, provided the assignment operator is defined for their type. Consider the following simple driver program:

 FIGURE I.2   A driver program for **Swap**

```
#include <iostream.h>

#include "Swap.h"

int main(void)
{
    int
        Int1 = 11,
        Int2 = 22;
    double
        Double1 = 33,
        Double2 = 44;

    Swap(Int1, Int2);

    cout << endl << Int1 << ' ' << Int2 << endl;

    Swap(Double1, Double2);

    cout << endl << Double1 << ' ' << Double2 << endl;

    return 0;
}
```

Sample run

```
22  11

44  33
```

The template version of function **Swap()** thus allows us to exchange the values of **int** objects, **double** objects, and any other type of object for which the assignment operation is defined. A simplified[2] general form for a function template can be given as follows:

> **template <class *Item*> *FunctionDefinition***

---

[1] Unlike other functions, a template function does not have external linkage, and so its *complete definition* (as opposed to just its *declaration*) usually resides in a header file.

[2] Templates can also be defined with multiple type parameters or normal (nontype) parameters.

where *Item* is a type-parameter naming the ''generic'' type of value(s) on which the function operates, and *FunctionDefinition* is the definition of the function, using type *Item*.

Function templates provide a powerful mechanism whereby a family of functions (each of whose logic is exactly the same across its different versions) can be written using a single definition.

Class Templates

It should be evident that the same rationale for using templates of functions can be applied to classes. To illustrate, recall that in most of our implementations of class objects (**List**, **Table**, **LinkedList**, **Stack**, **Queue**, **BST**), we used the **typedef** mechanism to simplify the process of changing the type of value being stored within the object. The reason was that for some problems we might need to process a list of integer values, whereas in other problems we might need to process a list of character string values, and in other problems, a list of **Employee** values. By using the **typedef** mechanism to declare the name **ListElement** as an alias for whatever type of values we wanted to store in the list, and then building our **List** class by using the name **ListElement** throughout, our class achieved a sort of ''generic'' quality.

A preferable approach is to achieve this ''generic'' quality by declaring the class as a *class template,* in which a type-parameter provides the type of the data member, instead of using **typedef**. For example, to declare a ''generic'' **Stack** class, we might use the following template (shown with minimal documentation) (Figure I.3):

 FIGURE I.3   A stack template[3]

```
/* This file contains the declaration of a Stack class template.
...
---------------------------------------------------------------*/

#ifndef STACK
#define STACK

#include <iostream.h>
```

---

[3] This example compiles and links correctly in both the GNU and Turbo environments; however in the Symantec C++ environment, the declarations of **SNodePtr** generate errors such as the following:

```
File "Stack.h"; Line xxx
Error:   'Stack< char> ::SNodePtr' is not a variable
```

In member functions, removal of the **Stack< StackElem> ::** from those declarations solves the problem, but we are unable to find a solution to this problem for any friend function (such as **operator<<**).

The GNU environment was strangely inconsistent, usually permitting us to overload **operator<<** but generating a linking error whenever we tried to overload **operator>>** for a template class. The Turbo environment gave us no difficulties in either compiling or linking.

FIGURE I.3   A stack template (cont.)

```
template <class StackElem>         // a Stack of StackElem values
class Stack
{
   struct StackNode               // nodes to store & link StackElems
   }
      StackElem
         Element;                  // the node's data member
      StackNode
         *Next;                    // the node's link member

      StackNode(void)             // default class constructor
      {
         Next = 0;
      }

      StackNode(StackElem Elem,    // initialization class constructor
              StackNode *Nptr = 0)
      {
         Element = Elem;
         Next = Nptr;
      }

      ~StackNode() { delete Next; }

   };

   typedef StackNode *SNodePtr;    // pointer-type to a node

   SNodePtr
      Top;                         // the top node on the stack

 public:
   Stack(void) { Top = 0;}                      // constructor: empty stack

   ~Stack(void)                                 // deallocate a Stack
   {                                            //   using recursive
      delete Top;                               //   Top->~StackNode()
      Top = 0;                                  //   and reset Top
   }

   void Push(StackElem Elem)                    // push an element onto
   {                                            //   the stack using the
      Top = new StackNode(Elem, Top);           // StackNode constructor
   }
```

FIGURE I.3 A stack template (cont.)

```
    StackElem Pop();                          // remove top element

    int Empty(void) const {return Top == 0;}// is the stack empty?
    int Full(void const {return 0;}          // is the stack full?

    friend ostream& operator<<(ostream& Out,// display the stack
                            const Stack<StackElem>& S);
};

template<class StackElem>
StackElem Stack<StackElem>::Pop(void)        // remove top element
{
    StackElem
        Elem = Top->Element;                 // save return-value
    Stack<StackElem>::SNodePtr
        NodePtr = Top;                       // save ptr to top node

    Top = Top->Next;                         // update Top
    NodePtr->Next = 0;                       // detach old top node
    delete NodePtr;                          // deallocate it
    return Elem;                             // return its value
}

template <class StackElem>
ostream& operator<<(ostream& Out,            // interactive output
                const Stack<StackElem>& St)
{
    Stack<StackElem>::SNodePtr
        NodePtr = St.Top;                    // start at the top

    while (NodePtr != 0)                     // while not at bottom
    {
        Out << NodePtr->Element << endl;     //    display node's data
        NodePtr = NodePtr->Next;             //    move down 1 node
    }

    return Out;                              // allow chaining
}

#endif
```

In this declaration, the lines

```
    template <class StackElem>
    class Stack
```

stipulate that class **Stack** is a *parameterized* class—a class containing a type-parameter **StackElem**, whose value will be passed as an argument when a **Stack** object is defined. Each use of the class name (except for its constructor and destructor function names) should thus be parameterized. Note also that the general form of a class template is similar to that of a function template:

```
template <class Item> ClassDeclaration
```

and that each member or friend function of a class template must be defined as a function template.

When this single class declaration is stored in a header file (i.e., **Stack.h**), a program that inserts that file (using **#include**) can then construct a stack capable of storing any defined type. For example, the driver program below builds two stacks **CharStack** and **IntStack**:

FIGURE I.4   Driver program for **Stack**

```
/* This program tests the functionality of class template Stack.
...
----------------------------------------------------------------------*/

#include <iostream.h>

#include "Stack.h"

ostream& DisplayBinary(unsigned Num, ostream& Out = cout);

int main(void)
{
  cout << "\nEnter a string: ";         // PART I: characters

  char
    Ch;                                 // input container
  Stack<char>
    CharStack;                          // a Stack of char values

  for (;;)                              // loop:
    {
      cin.get(Ch);                      //    read a char into Ch
      if (Ch == '\n')                   //    if it was a newline
        break;                          //       we're done

      CharStack.Push(Ch);               //    push it onto the stack
    }                                   // end loop

  cout <<CharStack << "\n\n";           // display the stack

  cout << "Enter an integer: ";         // PART II: integers

  unsigned
    Number;                             // input container
  cin >> Number;                        // read a number into Number
```

FIGURE I.4   Driver program for **Stack** (cont.)

```
  cout << "\nThe binary representation of " << Number << " is ";
  DisplayBinary(Number) << "\n\n";      // display its binary
                                        // representation, using a stack
  return 0;
}

//--- Show the binary representation of an integer ------------------

ostream& DisplayBinary(unsigned Num, ostream& Out)
{
  Stack<int>
    IntStack;                           // build stack of integers

  while (Num != 0)                      // while Num not zero:
    {                                   //   integer-division Num/2,
     IntStack.Push(Num % 2);            //     push remainder on stack
     Num /= 2;                          //     replace Num with quotient
    }

  while (!IntStack.Empty())             // while Stack not empty:
    Out << IntStack.Pop();              //    pop the stack and display
                                        //       the popped value

  return Out;
}
```

Sample run

```
Enter a string: qwerty
y
t
r
e
w
q


Enter an integer: 17

The binary representation of 17 is 10001
```

Note that since **Stack** is a parameterized class, C++ requires that the type of value we wish to store in a **Stack** object be passed when we define that object. To illustrate, we write:

```
    Stack<char>
      CharStack;
```

to define a `Stack` that will contain character values, and write:

```
Stack<int>
  IntStack;
```

to define a `Stack` that will contain integer values. More generally, when an object is defined using a class template, the type of value to be stored in that object must be passed as an argument. This is done using the unusual notation:

```
ClassName < ValueType >
  ObjectName;
```

where *ClassName* is the name of the class template, *ObjectName* is the name of the class object being defined, and *ValueType* is the type of value to be stored in *ObjectName*. A definition of this sort is sometimes called an **instantiation** of the class template—the creation of an *instance* of the template.

Class templates provide a powerful capability by allowing the programmer to build "container" classes—classes whose operations are largely independent of the type of the values to be stored in the "container." List, stack, queue, and binary search tree classes are examples of classes that can be conveniently implemented using templates.

ANSWERS TO SELECTED EXERCISES

Section 1.4 (p. 32)

1. (a) Charles Babbage—English mathematician who combined the concepts of mechanized calculation and automatic control in the design of his "Analytical Engine"
   (c) John von Neumann—credited with the development of the stored program concept
   (e) Joseph Jacquard—inventor of a loom that was controlled by a "program" stored on punched cards
   (g) John Atanasoff—the first to develop a fully electronic computer in 1939
   (i) Robert Noyce—a pioneer in the development of transistors and a co-founder of the Intel Corporation
   (k) John Backus—developed FORTRAN, one of the first high-level languages to gain widespread acceptance
   (m) Dennis Ritchie—designed a language as a successor to B that he called C, the language in which most microcomputer applications have since been written

2. (a) ENIAC—Electronic numerical integrator and computer, the best known of the early electronic computers
   (c) Jacquard loom—early use of a "program" to control a mechanical device
   (e) Mark I—early electromechanical computer, built in the United States in 1944

4. (a) Stored program concept—the concept of storing a program in the memory of the computer rather than on some external media such as punched cards
   (c) C++—a successor of the programming language C, with object-oriented programming and other improvements to C
   (e) ALU—the part of the CPU that performs basic arithmetic and logical operations
   (g) Bit—a digit in the binary number system (0 or 1)

    (i) Word—a basic storage unit consisting of a machine-dependent number of bits (commonly 16 or 32) whose contents are directly accessible by means of its address

    (k) MS-DOS—Disk operating system, a popular operating system developed by Microsoft Corporation for use on many personal computers

    (m) Object program—a machine language program produced by a compiler

    (o) Machine language—a language used directly by a particular computer in all its calculations and processing

    (q) OOP—Object-oriented programming, a new approach to programming that became increasingly popular in the late 1970s

5. (a) Operating system—a program that allocates storage for programs and data, performs supervisory functions, and acts as an interface between the user and the machine.

    (c) Assembler—a program that translates assembly language programs into machine language programs.

6. (a) 9   **(c)** 64   **(e)** 1.5

7. (a) 83   **(c)** 4096   **(e)** 7.25

8. (a) 18   **(c)** 2748   **(e)** 8.75

9. (a) 1010011   **(c)** 1000000000000   **(e)** 111.01

10. (a) 10010   **(c)** 101010111100   **(e)** 1000.11

11. (a) 11   **(c)** 100   **(e)** 1.4

12. (a) 9   **(c)** 40   **(e)** 1.8

13. (a) (i) 11011_2 **(ii)** 33_8 **(iii)** $1B_{16}$
    (c) (i) 100111010_2 **(ii)** 472_8 **(iii)** $13A_{16}$

14. (a) (i) 0.1_2 **(ii)** 0.4_8 **(iii)** 0.8_{16}
    (c) (i) 0.101_2 **(ii)** 0.5_8 **(iii)** $0.A_{16}$

15. (a) (i) $0.0\overline{1001}_2$ **(ii)** $0.2\overline{3146}_8$ **(iii)** $0.4\overline{C}_{16}$
    (c) (i) $0.0\overline{0011}_2$ **(ii)** 0.03146_8 **(iii)** $0.0\overline{C}_{16}$

16. (a) 64   **(c)** -65 **(e)** -256

17. (a) 0000000011111111
    (c) 1111111100000001
    (e) 1100011010001001

19. (a) (i) 0110000000011111   **(ii)** Same as (i)
    (c) (i) 0100000000011100   **(ii)** Same as (i)
    (e) (i) 0110011001111001   **(ii)** Same as (i)

20. (a) (i)

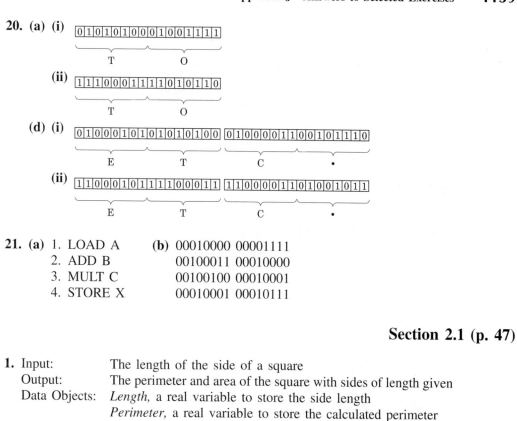

21. (a) 1. LOAD A   **(b)** 00010000 00001111
      2. ADD B   00100011 00010000
      3. MULT C   00100100 00010001
      4. STORE X   00010001 00010111

Section 2.1 (p. 47)

1. Input: The length of the side of a square
    Output: The perimeter and area of the square with sides of length given
    Data Objects: *Length*, a real variable to store the side length
                   Perimeter, a real variable to store the calculated perimeter
                   Area, a real variable to store the calculated area

---

Algorithm: 1. Enter *Length*.
             2. Calculate
                    Perimeter = 4 * *Length*.
                    Area = *Length* * *Length*
             3. Display *Perimeter* and *Length*.

5.
```
/* This program calculates the perimeter and the
   area of a square with sides of given length.

   Input (keyboard): The length of the side of a square
   Output (screen):  The perimeter and area of the square
   ------------------------------------------------------*/

#include <iostream.h>

int main(void)
{
    double
       Length;

    cout << "Please enter the length of a side of the square: ";
    cin >> Length;
```

```
double
    Perimeter = 4.0 * Length,
    Area = Length * Length;

cout << "\nPerimeter = " << Perimeter
     << "\nArea = " << Area << "\n\n";

return 0;
}
```

Section 2.6 (p. 69)

1.

Statement	A	B	X	Y	Z
1	?	?	0	5	25
2	?	?	0	5	25
2-a	1	?	1	20	25
2-b	1	?	1	20	25
2	1	?	1	20	25
2-a	2	?	2	5	25
2-b	4	15	2	5	20
2	4	15	2	5	20
2-a	3	15	3	15	20
2-b	9	0	3	15	15
2	9	0	3	15	15
2-a	4	0	4	0	15
2-b	16	10	4	0	10
2	16	10	4	0	10
2-a	5	10	5	10	10
2-b	25	−5	5	10	5
2	25	−5	5	10	5
3	25	−5	5	10	5

?=undefined

5. Input: A set of numbers
Output: The largest, the smallest, and the range of the numbers
Data Objects: *Number,* a real variable to store the last entered number
                Smallest, a real variable to keep track of the smallest number
                Largest, a real variable to keep track of the largest number

Algorithm: 1. Enter *Number.*
              2. Set *Smallest = Number* and *Largest = Number.*
              3. While *Number* is not the end-of-data flag, do the following:
                    a. If *Number < Smallest,* then
                            Set *Smallest = Number*
                       Else if *Number > Largest* then
                            Set *Largest = Number*
                       End If.
                    b. Enter *Number.*
                 End While.
              4. Display *Smallest, Largest,* and (*Largest − Smallest*).

9. Input: A positive number, a positive initial approximation to its square root

  Output: The square root of the number within a specified error allowance

  Data Objects: *Number,* a real variable to store the number

       Approx, a real variable to store the initial approximation

       NewApprox, a real variable to keep track of each successive approximation

       Allowance, a real constant to store the error allowance

---

Algorithm: 1. Enter *Allowance, Number,* and *Approx.*

      2. If *Number* ≤ 0 or *Approx* ≤ 0, then
        Display appropriate error message and quit.
       End If.

      3. Calculate $NewApprox = \dfrac{Approx + Number/Approx}{2}$

      4. While $|NewApprox - Approx| \geq Allowance,$ do the following
        a. Set *Approx = NewApprox.*

        b. Calculate $NewApprox = \dfrac{Approx + Number/Approx}{2}$

       End While.

      5. Display *NewApprox.*

Section 3.3 (p. 94)

1. (a) Legal

 (d) Legal

 (g) Identifiers cannot contain periods.

 (j) Identifiers cannot contain the slash symbol.

 (m) Legal

 (p) Identifiers cannot contain a space.

2. (a) Integer

 (d) Neither; single quotes not allowed around integers or reals.

 (g) Neither; the negation symbol must precede the number.

 (j) Neither; dollar signs are not allowed in numbers.

 (m) Neither; reals must start with a number, 1E3 would be a valid real constant.

 (p) Real

 (s) Real

3. (a) Legal

 (d) Legal

 (g) Legal

 (j) Legal

4. (a) `const double`
        `Rate = 1.25;`

   (c) `const int`
        `Year = 1776;`
       `const char`
        `Female = 'F',`
        `Blank = ' ';`

5. (a) `double`
        `Item,`
        `Number,`
        `Job;`

   (c) `double`
        `Mileage;`
       `unsigned int`
        `Cost,`
        `Distance;`

Section 3.4 (p. 102)

1. (a) 1
   (d) 0
   (g) 2
   (j) 2
   (m) 0
   (p) 18
   (s) 3
   (v) 4.0

2. (a) 8.0
   (d) 20.0
   (g) 6.25

3. (a) `10 + 5 * B - 4 * A * C`
   (e) `abs(A / (m + n))`

Section 3.5 (p. 114)

1. (a) Valid
   (d) Valid
   (g) Only a variable name can be on the left side of the equals.
   (j) Valid, but pointless
   (m) Valid

2. (a) 15.0
   (d) 6

(g) `'\004'`; valid, but not recommended because numbers should not be treated like characters

(j) `'\004'`; valid, but not recommended because numbers should not be treated like characters

(m) `50.0`; valid, but not recommended because characters should not be treated like numbers

(p) 3

3. (a) `Number += 77;`
   (d) `Number += Number % 10;`

4. (a) `Distance = Rate * Time;`
   (d) `Area = b * h / 2;`

5. (a) If $a = 2$, $b = 1$, $c = 2$, then the first value is 0 and the second value is 1. (Answers will vary.)

Section 3.6 (p. 128)

1. Note: Answers may vary slightly depending on the C++ compiler.

   (a) `436437438`
   (d) `Alpha =      -567.392`
       `Beta =        0`
       `Rho =     436`
            `-127.392`

   (g) Error: The string should be enclosed in double quotes, not single quotes.

2. Note: Answers may vary, depending on the C++ compiler.

   (a) `New balance =2.56e+03 Candy is     15      8.02`

3. Note: Answers may vary, depending on the C++ compiler.
   (a) `cout << setw(8) << R1 << "       " << C`
       `    << setw(5) << N1 << '\n'`
       `    << N2 << "PDQ" << R2 << '\n';`

4. (a) $A = 1$, $B = 2$, $C = 3$, $X = 4.0$, $Y = 5.5$, $Z = 6.6$
   (e) $A = 1$, $B = 2$, $C = 3$, $X = 4.0$, $Y = 5.5$, $Z = 6.6$

Section 3.8 (p. 136)

1. (a), (b), (c), (e), and (f) are valid things.

2. <thing> := <front>[<middle>] | <front> [<middle>] D <front>
   <front> := A | B | C
   <middle> := D | E

Section 4.2 (p. 159)

1. Here is function `PrintZero()`:

```
/*-----------------------------------------------
PrintZero displays a stick number for zero.

   Output: The stick figure for 0 (zero)
---------------------------------------------*/

void PrintZero(void)
{
    cout << " --- \n"
         << "|   |\n"
         << "|   |\n"
         << "|   |\n"
         << " --- \n";

}
```

5. Here is function `Wages()`:

```
/*----------------------------------------------------------
Wages calculates the wages earned given the number of
   hours worked and the hourly pay rate.

   Receive:  HoursWorked, the (double) number of hours worked
             PayRate, the (double) hourly pay rate
   Return:   The (double) amount of wages earned
---------------------------------------------------------*/

double Wages(double HoursWorked, double PayRate)
{
    return HoursWorked * PayRate;
}
```

Section 4.4 (p. 178)

1. Output produced by program:

```
6 5
12 18
```

4. (a)
```
/*----------------------------------------------------------------
SecondsToMinutes computes the number of minutes in a given number
   of seconds.

   Receive: Seconds, a (double) number of seconds
   Return:  The equivalent (double) number of minutes
---------------------------------------------------------------*

double SecondsToMinutes(double Seconds)
{
    return Seconds / 60.0;
}
```

Section 5.4 (p. 202)

1. (a)-(c)

a	b	a || !b	!(a && b)	!a || !b
0	0	1	1	1
0	1	0	1	1
1	0	1	1	1
1	1	1	0	0

2. (a) x > 3
   (d) (Alpha > 0) && (Beta > 0)
   (g) (a < 6) \|\| (a > 10)

3. (a) a && b && !c

Section 5.5 (p. 221)

1. (a) if (TaxCode == 'T')
          Price += TaxRate * Price;

3. (a) if ((Honors == 1) && (Awards == 1))
          GoodStudent = 1;
       else
          GoodStudent = 0;

4. (a) int IsLeapYear(int Year)
       {
          return !(Year % 4) && ((Year % 100) \|\| !(Year % 400));
       }

6. void DisplayIndex(int Index)
   {
      if (Index < 35)
        cout << "pleasant";
      else if (Index <= 60)
        cout << "unpleasant";
      else
        cout << "hazardous";
   }

Section 5.6 (p. 232)

```
2. void ShowCallLetters(int Station)
   {
       switch (Station)
       {
           case 2:  cout << "WCBS"; break;
           case 4:  cout << "WNBC"; break;
           case 5:  cout << "WNEW"; break;
           case 7:  cout << "WABC"; break;
           case 9:  cout << "WOR"; break;
           case 11: cout << "WPIX"; break;
           case 13: cout << "WNET"; break;
           default: cout << "N/A"; break;
       }
   }
```

Section 5.7 (p. 237)

1. This function returns the absolute value of the integer **Value**.

2. Hint: Examine the ASCII tables in Appendix A.

```
4. int SmallerOf(int Value1, int Value2)
   {
       return (Value1 < Value2) ? Value1 : Value2;
   }
```

Section 6.1 (p. 270)

```
1. (a) -2 squared = 4
       -1 squared = 1
        0 squared = 0
        1 squared = 1
        2 squared = 4
        3 squared = 9
   (c) 3
       0
       1
       2
       3
       4
```

5. ```
#include <iostream.h>
#include <iomanip.h>

int main(void)
{
   int
      row,
      col;

   cout << endl << "   ";

   for (col = 1; col <= 9; col++)
      cout << setw(3) << col;
   cout << endl;

   for (row = 1; row <= 9; row++)
   {
      cout << setw(3) << row;
      for (col = 1; col <= row; col++)
         cout << setw(3) << (row * col);
      cout << endl;
   }

   return 0;
}
```

## Section 6.2 (p. 285)

1. (a) 4
       5
       6

2. 0

## Section 6.3 (p. 298)

1. (a) 01
       1-1
       23

## Section 6.4 (p. 312)

1. (a) 000
       112
       228
       18
```

2. (a)

While loop		Do-while loop		Test-in-the-middle loop	
Number	Sum	Number	Sum	Number	Sum
0	0	0	0	0	0
1	1	1	1	1	1
2	3	2	3	2	3
3	6	3	6	3	6
4	10	4	10	4	10
5	15	5	15	5	15
				6	15

Section 6.5 (p. 318)

1. (a)
```
do
{
    cout << x << endl;
    x -= 0.5;
}
while (x > 0);
```

(d)
```
for (long x = 50; x > 0; x--)
    cout << (x * x * x) << endl;
```

(g)
```
for (double x = -2.0; x <= 2.0; x += 0.1)
    cout << '(' << x << ','
         << (x*x*x - 3*x + 1)
         << ')' << endl;
```

Section 6.8 (p. 345)

1.
```
#include <iostream.h>

long Factorial(long X);

main()
{
    cout << "\nThe first 10 partial sum approximations of e:\n\n";

    double
        E = 0;
    for (int i = 0; i < 10; i++)
    {
        E += (1.0 / Factorial(i));
        cout << E << endl;
    }

    return 0;
}
```

```
long Factorial(long X)
{
   long
      Product = 1;

   for (long i = 2; i <= X; i++)
      Product *= i;

   return Product;
}
```

Section 7.3 (p. 382)

1. **(a)** Valid
   (d) A character string (`"16"`) cannot be used as a **double**, nor should an integer constant (**13**) be used as an integer reference.
   (g) Valid (but not wise since **u**, being passed as a value parameter, cannot be changed by the function).
   (j) An expression (**p + q**) cannot be used as a reference to an integer.

7. ```
void Convert(double r, double t, double& x, double& y)
{
   x = r * cos(t);
   y = r * sin(t);
}
```

## Section 7.9 (p. 427)

1. **(a) (i)** 123      **(ii)** 1234567      **(iii)** a blank line (or an advance to a new line)

3. **(a)** (blank line)
   ```
   11
   12
   13
   13
   13
   14
   15
   14
   13
   14
   15
   15
   15
   16
   17
   ```
   ```

4. (a) Zero (Changing `return 0;` to `return 1;` will give n-factorial.)

(d) The sum of the digits of **n**

5. (d)
```
unsigned F(unsigned n)
{
    unsigned
        Answer = 0;

    while (n > 0)
    {
        Answer += n % 10;
        n /= 10;
    }
    return Answer;
}
```

10.
```
unsigned NumberOfDigits(unsigned n)
{
    if (n <= 9)
        return 1;
    else
        return NumberOfDigits(n / 10) + 1;
}
```

Section 8.2 (p. 464)

1. (a) Num1 = 1, Num2 = -2, Num3 = 3, Num4 = 4

2. (a)
```
fstream
    InStream;
InStream.open("InData", ios::in);
```

or

```
fstream
    InStream("InData", ios::in);
```

3. (a) N1 = 123, N2 = 78, N3 = -65
R1 = 45.6, R2 = -909.8, R3 = 32.1
C1 = X, C2 = 7, C3 = $, C4 = 4

4. (a) N1 = 54, N2 = 90, N3 = 1
R1 = 320.0, R2 = -6.78, R3 = ???
C1 = $, C2 = ???, C3 = ???

Section 8.5 (p. 494)

1. (a) IthinkthatIshallneverseeApoemlovelyasatree-JOYCEKILMER(1914)

Section 9.3 (p. 515)

```
1. #include <fstream.h>
   #include <stdlib.h>

   #include "Strings.h"

   int main(void)
   {
      Strings
         InputFileName;

      cout << "\nPlease enter the name of the input file: ";
      InputFileName.GetLine(cin);

      fstream
         InStream(InputFileName, ios::in);

      if (InStream.fail())
      {
         cerr << "\n*** Unable to open file '"
              << InputFileName << "'!\n";
         exit(-1);
      }

      Strings
         Line;
      unsigned
         LineCount = 0;

      while (!InStream.eof())
      {
         Line.GetLine(InStream);
         LineCount++;
      }

      cout << "\nThe number of lines in the file '"
           << InputFileName << "' is " << LineCount << ".\n";

      InStream.close();

      return 0;
   }
```

Section 9.4 (p. 533)

```
1. void ToLower(Strings& Str)
   {
      for (unsigned i = 0; i < Str.Length(); i++)
         if (isupper(Str[i]))
            Str[i] = tolower(Str[i]);
   }
```

Section 9.6 (p. 553)

2. **(a)** SXEOLF
   (c) HXWSOE
   (e) 0554 1486 2112

Section 10.1 (p. 578)

1. **(a)** enum MonthAbbrev {MonthUnderflow = -1,
                     Jan, Feb, Mar, Apr, May, Jun,
                     Jul, Aug, Sep, Oct, Nov, Dec,
                     NumberOfMonths,
                     MonthOverflow = 12};

   (b)
```
MonthAbbrev NumToMonth(unsigned Num)
{
    switch(Num)
    {
       case 1:  return Jan;
       case 2:  return Feb;
       case 3:  return Mar;
       case 4:  return Apr;
       case 5:  return May;
       case 6:  return Jun;
       case 7:  return Jul;
       case 8:  return Aug;
       case 9:  return Sep;
       case 10: return Oct;
       case 11: return Nov;
       case 12: return Dec;
    }
    return MonthOverflow;
}
```

Section 10.2 (p. 583)

1. **(b)**
```
ostream& operator<< (ostream& Out, RockKind Kind)
{
    const char
      ErrorMsg[] =
         "\n*** <<: invalid RockKind value received!\n";
    switch (Kind)
    {
       case Igneous:        Out << "Igneous";
                            break;
       case Metamorphic:    Out << "Metamorphic";
                            break;
       case Sedimentary:    Out << "Sedimentary";
                            break;
       default:
                            Out << ErrorMsg;
    }
    return Out;
}
```

2. (a)
```
istream& operator>> (istream& In, RockName& Rock)
{
    Strings
        Str;
    const char
        ErrorMsg[] =
            "\n*** >>: invalid RockName value received!\n";
    In >> Str;

    for (int i = 0; i < Str.Length(); i++)
        if (isupper(Str[i]))
            Str[i] = tolower(Str[i]);
    if (Str == "basalt")
        Rock = Basalt;
    else if (Str == "dolomite")
        Rock = Dolomite;
    else if (Str == "granite")
        Rock = Granite;
    else if (Str == "limestone")
        Rock = Limestone;
    else if (Str == "marble")
        Rock = Marble;
    else if (Str == "obsidian")
        Rock = Obsidian;
    else if (Str == "quartzite")
        Rock = Quartzite;
    else if (Str == "sandstone")
        Rock = Sandstone;
    else if (Str == "shale")
        Rock = Shale;
    else if (Str == "slate")
        Rock = Slate;
    else
    {
        Rock = NameError;
        cerr << ErrorMsg;
    }
    return In;
}
```

Section 11.1 (p. 621)

1. (c)
```
Temperature& operator+=(int Inc)
    { Degrees_ += Inc; }
```

3. (a)
```
class Card
{
    char
        Rank_,
        Suit_;
}
```

(c) class PhoneNumber
```
{
    int
        AreaCode_,
        LocalExchange_,
        Number_;
}
```

(e) class Point
```
{
    double
        X_,
        Y_;
}
```

Section 11.3 (p. 634)

1. Boolean operator<(const Student& Left, const Student& Right)
```
{
    return ( Left.LastName_ < Right.LastName_ ) ||
           ( Left.LastName_ == Right.LastName_ &&
             Left.FirstName_ < Right.FirstName_ );
}
```

```
Boolean operator>(const Student& Left, const Student& Right)
{
    return ( Left.LastName_ > Right.LastName_ ) ||
           ( Left.LastName_ == Right.LastName_ &&
             Left.FirstName_ > Right.FirstName_ );
}
```

Section 12.1 (p. 670)

1. (a)

	0	1	2	3	4	5	6	7	8	9
Number	0	0	1	1	2	2	3	3	4	4

(d)

	0	1	2	3	4	5	6	7	8	9
Number	1	2	4	8	16	32	64	128	256	512

2. (a)
```
int
    Array[6];
for (int i = 0; i < 6; i++)
    Array[i] = i;
```

3. (a) $b + 16$

Section 12.3 (p. 697)

```
2. void List::Delete(unsigned Loc)
   {
      if (Loc >= Length_)
      {
         cerr << "\n*** Delete: index " << Loc
              << " out of range!\n";
         exit (-1);
      }

      Length_--;

      for (unsigned i = Loc; i < Length_; i++)
         Array[i] = Array[i+1];
   }
```

Section 12.4 (p. 703)

1. (a)

i	0	1	2	3	4	5	6	7	
X[i]	10	50	80	30	60	20	70	40	← After pass 1
X[i]	10	20	80	30	60	50	70	40	← After pass 2
X[i]	10	20	30	80	60	50	70	40	← After pass 3
X[i]	10	20	30	40	60	50	70	80	← After pass 4

2. (a)

i	0	1	2	3	4	5	6	7	
X[i]	10	50	40	30	60	20	70	80	← After pass 1
X[i]	10	20	40	30	60	50	70	80	← After pass 2
X[i]	10	20	30	40	50	60	70	80	← After pass 3
X[i]	10	20	30	40	50	60	70	80	← After pass 4

5. (a)

(Sub)List Being Sorted	Low	High	Mid	Action
<u>5, 1, 6, 4, 3, 2</u>	0	5		Call **Quicksort()** with original list.
3, 1, 2, 4, |5|, 6			4	Split positions 5 in location 4.
<u>3, 1, 2, 4</u>, |5|, 6	0	3		Call **Quicksort()** with left sublist.
2, 1, |3|, 4, |5|, 6			2	**Split()** positions 3 in location 2.
<u>2, 1</u>, |3|, 4, |5|, 6	0	1		Call **Quicksort()** with left sublist.
1, |2|, 3, 4, |5|, 6			0	**Split()** positions 2 in location 1.
<u>1</u>, |2|, |3|, 4, |5|, 6	0	0		Call **Quicksort()** with left (one-element) sublist. **Low ≮ High**, so sublist is already sorted. Return to previous reference to **Quicksort()**.
|1|, |2|, |3|, 4, |5|, 6	0	1		Left sublist is now sorted.
|1|, |2|, =|3|, 4, |5|, 6	2	1		Call **Quicksort()** with right (empty) sublist. **Low ≮ High**, so sublist is already sorted. Return to previous reference to **Quicksort()**.
|1|, |2|, |3|, 4, |5|, 6	0	3		Right sublist has been sorted, so return to previous reference to **Quicksort()**.
|1, 2|, |3|, 4, |5|, 6	0	3	2	Left sublist is now sorted.
|1, 2|, |3|, <u>4</u>, |5|, 6	3	3		Call **Quicksort()** with right (one-element) sublist. **Low ≮ High**, so sublist is already sorted. Return to previous reference to **Quicksort**.
|1, 2|, |3|, |4|, |5|, 6	0	5		Right sublist has been sorted, so return to previous reference to **Quicksort()**.
|1, 2, 3, 4|, |5|, 6	0	5	4	Left sublist is now sorted.
|1, 2, 3, 4|, |5|, <u>6</u>	5	5		Call **Quicksort()** with right (one-element) sublist. **Low ≮ High**, so sublist is already sorted. Return to previous reference to **Quicksort()**.
|1, 2, 3, 4|, |5|, |6|	0	5	4	Right sublist is sorted, so return to previous reference to **Quicksort()**.
|1, 2, 3, 4, 5, 6|	0	5		Original reference to **Quicksort()** is complete, so entire list has been sorted.

Section 12.5 (p. 715)

1. (a) $O(n^3)$ **(c)** $O(n)$

3. (a) $O(n)$ **(c)** $O(n^3)$ **(e)** $O(n^3)$

Section 13.3 (p. 747)

1. (a)   {3, 5, 11}
   (d)   {1, 2, 4, 12}
   (g)   {6, 7, 8, 9}
   (j)   {2, 4, 6, 8}
   (m)   {1, 2, 3, 4, 5, 6, 7, 8, 9, 10, 11, 12}
   (p)   {}
   (s)   {3, 5, 11}
   (v)   {}

2. (a) Set
```
      SmallIntegers(9, 1, 2, 3, 4, 5, 6, 7, 8, 9);
```

   (d) Set
```
      Suit(13, 'A', '2', '3', '4', '5', '6', '7',
              '8', '9', 'T', 'J', 'Q', 'K');
```

3. (a) Set
```
      Evens,
      Odds;
   for (int i = 1; i < 100; i++)
      if (i % 2 == 0)
         Evens.Insert(i);
      else
         Odds.Insert(i) ;
```

   (d) Set
```
      Divisors;
   for (int i = 1; i <= Number; i++)
      if (Number % i == 0)
         Divisors.Insert(i);
```

   (g) Set
```
      FaceCards(3, 'J', 'Q', 'K'),
      NumberCards(10, 'A', '2', '3', '4', '5',
                      '6', '7', '8', '9', 'T');
```

4. (b)
```
Boolean Set::Insert(unsigned Elem)
{
  int
      Index = Elem / Set::BitsPerEntry;

  if (Index >= Set::ArrayLength)
  {
      cerr << "\n*** Insert: Set is too small to hold "
          << Elem << endl;
      return False;
  }

  int
      BitPosition = Elem % Set::BitsPerEntry;

  long
      Mask = 1;

  if (BitPosition > 0)
      Mask <<= BitPosition;

  Array[Index] |= Mask;

  return True;
}
```

7. (a) 1010101010101010101010101010101010

Section 13.4 (p. 756)

1. (b)

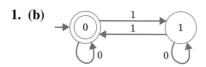

Section 14.1 (p. 773)

1. (a) 5000
   (d) 16

2. (a) $\begin{bmatrix} 0 & 1 & 2 \\ 1 & 2 & 3 \\ 2 & 3 & 4 \end{bmatrix}$

Section 14.4 (p. 816)

```
1. Matrix operator+(const Matrix& Mat1, const Matrix& Mat2)
   {
      if ( (Mat1.Columns_ != Mat2.Columns_) ||
           (Mat1.Rows_  != Mat2.Rows_) )
      {
         cerr << "\n*** Mat1+Mat2: Mat1 and Mat2 must "
              << "have the same dimensions!\n";
         exit (-1);
      }

      Matrix
         Mat3(Mat1.Rows_, Mat1.Columns_);

      for (int i = 0; i < Mat1.Rows_; i++)
         for (int j = 0; j < Mat1.Columns_; j++)
            Mat3.Grid[i][j] = Mat1.Grid[i][j] +
                              Mat2.Grid[i][j];
      return Mat3;
   }
```

Section 15.1 (p. 852)

```
6. typedef char *CharPointer;
```

Section 15.2 (p. 859)

```
1. (a) char
       *CharPtr = new char;

   (d) if (isupper(*CharPtr))
          *CharPtr = tolower(*CharPtr);

2. (a) cout << "\nPlease enter the number of values to be processed: ";
       cin >> N;

   (b) double
       *DoublePtr = new double [N];

   (e) delete [] DoublePtr;
```

Section 15.3 (p. 882)

2. (a)
```
void List::Delete(unsigned Loc)
{
    if (Loc >= Length_)
    {
        cerr << "\n*** Delete: index " << Loc
             << " out of range!\n";
        exit (-1);
    }

    ListElement
        *OldArray = Array;

    Length_--;

    if (Length_ == 0)
        Array = 0;
    else
    {
        Array = new ListElement [Length_];
        assert(Array != 0);

        for (unsigned i = 0; i < Loc; i++)
            Array[i] = OldArray[i];
        for (unsigned i = Loc; i < Length_; i++)
            Array[i] = OldArray[i+1];
    }

    delete [] OldArray;
}
```

Section 16.2 (p. 960)

1. (a) Nothing is wrong.
   (d) **new** must be used with a type as in **P1 = new int;**.

3. (a) 123456
   (d) **P3** is a pointer to an integer, not to a node.

4. (a)

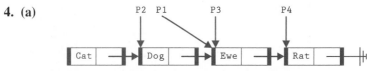

   (d) **P4->Next** is NULL and cannot be dereferenced.

Section 17.2 (p. 1019)

1. (a) (i)

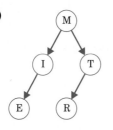

(b) (i) Inorder: EIMRT
Preorder: MIETR
Postorder: EIRTM

2. (a) (i) M T R I E
(m)(i) T R M I E
(c) (i) R T E I M

3. (a)

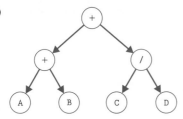

Prefix: + + A B / C D
Postfix: A B + C D / +

5. (a)

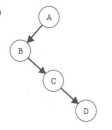

Section 17.3 (p. 1048)

7. (a) (i) B[0] ← 'M'
            B[1] ← 'I'
            B[2] ← 'T'
            B[3] ← 'E'
            B[4] ← ?
            B[5] ← 'R'
            B[6] ← ?
(All other array elements are undefined; also, ?= undefined.)

INDEX